STRATEGIC MANAGEMENT
TEXT AND CASES

FIFTH EDITION

JAMES M. HIGGINS
CRUMMER SCHOOL
ROLLINS COLLEGE

JULIAN W. VINCZE
CRUMMER SCHOOL
ROLLINS COLLEGE

THE DRYDEN PRESS

HARCOURT BRACE JOVANOVICH COLLEGE PUBLISHERS

FORT WORTH   PHILADELPHIA   SAN DIEGO   NEW YORK   ORLANDO   AUSTIN   SAN ANTONIO
TORONTO   MONTREAL   LONDON   SYDNEY   TOKYO

Editor in Chief	Robert A. Pawlik
Acquisitions Editor	Butch Gemin
Developmental Editor	Glenn E. Martin
Project Editor	Amy Schmidt
Production Manager	Jacqui Parker
Book Designer	Priscilla Mingus

Cover art Copyright © by Deborah Healy
Art program Tolbert and Michele Pitman/After Five Design

Address for Editorial Correspondence
The Dryden Press, 301 Commerce Street, Suite 3700, Fort Worth, TX 76102

Address for Orders
The Dryden Press, 6277 Sea Harbor Drive, Orlando, FL 32887
1-800-782-4479, or 1-800-433-0001 (in Florida)

ISBN: 0-03-054757-1

Library of Congress Catalogue Number: 92-81291

This book was printed on recycled paper made from
10% post-consumer waste and 40% pre-consumer waste.
The total recycled fibre content is 50% by fibre weight.

Printed in the United States of America

3 4 5 6 069 9 8 7 6 5 4 3 2 1

The Dryden Press
Harcourt Brace Jovanovich

To Susan

The Dryden Press Series in Management

Anthony, Perrewe, and Kacmar
Strategic Human Resource Management

Bartlett
Cases in Strategic Management for Business

Bedeian
Management
Third Edition

Bedeian and Zammuto
Organizations: Theory and Design

Boone and Kurtz
Contemporary Business
Seventh Edition

Bowman and Branchaw
Business Report Writing
Second Edition

Bracker, Montanari, and Morgan
Cases in Strategic Management

Calvasina and Barton
Chopstick Company: A Business Simulation

Czinkota, Rivoli, and Ronkainen
International Business
Second Edition

Daft
Management
Second Edition

Higgins and Vincze
Strategic Management: Text and Cases
Fifth Edition

Higgins and Vincze
Strategic Management Concepts

Hills
Compensation Decision Making

Hodgetts
Management: Theory, Process, and Practice

Hodgetts
Modern Human Relations at Work
Fifth Edition

Hodgetts and Kroeck
Personnel and Human Resource Management

Hodgetts and Kuratko
Effective Small Business Management
Third Edition

Hodgetts and Kuratko
Management
Third Edition

Holley and Jennings
The Labor Relations Process
Fourth Edition

Huseman, Lahiff, and Penrose
Business Communication: Strategies and Skills
Fourth Edition

Jauch, Coltrin, and Bedeian
The Managerial Experience: Cases, Exercises, and Readings
Fifth Edition

Kemper
Experiencing Strategic Management

Kuehl and Lambing
Small Business: Planning and Management
Second Edition

Kuratko and Hodgetts
Entrepreneurship: A Contemporary Approach
Second Edition

Luthans and Hodgetts
Business
Second Edition

McMullen and Long
Developing New Ventures: The Entrepreneurial Option

Matsuura
International Business: A New Era

Mauser
American Business: An Introduction
Sixth Edition

Montanari, Morgan, and Bracker
Strategic Management: A Choice Approach

Northcraft and Neale
Organizational Behavior: A Management Challenge

Penderghast
Entrepreneurial Simulation Program

Ryan, Eckert, and Ray
Small Business: An Entrepreneur's Plan

Sawaya and Giauque
Production and Operations Management

Sawyer
Business Policy and Strategic Management: Planning, Strategy, and Action

Schoderbek
Management
Second Edition

Schwartz
Introduction to Management: Principles, Practices, and Processes
Second Edition

Varner
Contemporary Business Report Writing
Second Edition

Vecchio
Organizational Behavior
Second Edition

Walton
Corporate Encounters: Law, Ethics, and the Business Environment

Wolford and Vanneman
Business Communication

Wolters and Holley
Labor Relations: An Experiential and Case Approach

Zikmund
Business Research Methods
Third Edition

The HBJ College Outline Series

Pierson
Introduction to Business Information Systems

Sigband
Business Communication

PREFACE

Business management today is far different than it was when the first edition of *Strategic Management* appeared in 1979. In 1979, the world was battling trends toward high inflation, and managers, for various reasons (including the continuing cold war), tended to think somewhat isolationally, rather than thinking globally about the world market. Today the global market concept, along with a united European economy, is at the forefront of modern strategic managers' minds. The first edition of *Strategic Management* also appeared before various scandals in business and financial circles—like those involving Ivan Boesky and Michael Milken—broke so thunderingly onto the scene. Ethics, consequently, is a subject that has taken on new meaning in the business community and is treated with great importance in this book.

Other changes have occurred in the business world in the 14 years since the appearance of the first edition. It has become a truly exciting arena in which managers, particularly strategic managers, have become champions of the businesses they represent. Applying an analytical eye to the strategic manager's function, we find that there are four models that emerge in twenty-first-century-management direction. The first of these is a metaparadigm that informs all of the others. It, therefore, pervades all the chapters of *Strategic Management.* In five steps, this model determines vision, missions, and goals; it establishes objectives; and it directs the formulation, implementation, and control of strategy. The other three models support this metaparadigm, helping strategic managers confront the challenges they face daily. Each model is examined carefully within this text.

OBJECTIVES OF THE TEXT

The text portion of *Strategic Management* is structured around the commonly recognized objectives of strategic management; that is, it develops the student's general perspective on management and on the role of the general manager/ strategist in a variety of domestic and global situations. It also integrates the functional business disciplines (marketing, finance, operations, human resources management, and information systems) with the strategic management process, illuminating the interdependence among them. Business environments and their multiple roles within society, especially with regard to external constraints, are critical elements in this dialogue.

One of the primary goals of the fifth edition is to enhance the student's analytical and research skills in a variety of decision-making settings. Stress is placed on teaching the student how to identify major issues in complex situations, how to prepare alternative solutions, and how to make decisions.

Another objective of this course is to acquaint the student with concepts in strategic management—the formulation of strategy content, its implementation and control, and the translation of these concepts into practice.

A very important objective is to foster understanding of the ethical issues involved in strategic management. With the advent of *glasnost* in the '80s and the new emphasis worldwide on honesty in business, ethics has become a major issue that needs to be examined in detail. We have provided many opportunities to address this subject in this edition, and coupled with an emphasis on cultural diversity, we feel the text will increase student awareness of moral and legal problems that face strategic managers and of the propriety of the decisions they make.

NEW FEATURES IN THE FIFTH EDITION

This fifth edition differs from its predecessors in several significant ways:

- Ten strategic management challenges are identified and introduced in Chapter 1. These challenges work together, under the metaparadigm discussed earlier, to provide a theme throughout the book. The challenges are identified when they appear in the text by chess-piece icons in the margins.

- Major efforts have been made to integrate global strategy throughout the text. The challenges facing Japanese and European firms frequently are discussed in addition to those faced by U.S.-based firms.

- The global chapter, Chapter 11, has been totally rewritten and substantially expanded. In-depth treatment is given to critical topics such as Porter's Dynamic Diamond Model of Global Competitiveness and the triad of key markets, including a discussion of Europe in 1992.

- A chapter on entrepreneurship and innovation strategy, Chapter 12, has been added to this edition because both are very important areas in the study of strategic management. Three-quarters-of-a-million entrepreneurial businesses are launched each year, providing jobs for workers and bolstering the economy. Innovation strategy is also important for the survival and prosperity of entrepreneurial businesses in the '90s.

- A new chapter, Chapter 3, has been added on internal environmental analysis that enables students to quickly review the key issues determining corporate strengths and weaknesses.

- The important issues of international strategy, cultural diversity, ethics, and quality have been highlighted and integrated throughout the text as boxed features. Among these are *Global Strategic Challenge* boxes showing how companies such as Harley-Davidson, when it decided to confront the Japanese market, compete in a world market. *Strategic Ethical Challenge* boxes discuss the ethical dilemmas of various firms such as those faced by American Express when its advertising practices were called into question; *Strategic Cultural Diversity Challenge* boxes discuss how companies such as DEC and Corning foster diversity and sharpen their competitive edge.

- Each chapter ends with a discussion of the Integrative Case, which illustrates how the key concepts introduced in the chapter apply to General Motors and the automobile industry as a whole. The Integrative Case on General Motors Corporation, discussed throughout Part 1, has been completely updated, along with the accompanying Industry Note focusing on the automobile industry in general, which follows Chapter 4.

- A series of videotapes is included for instructor use; these feature companies such as Caterpillar and McDonald's–Moscow discussed in the chapters and in several of the cases.

- A sample strategic planning document has been added. "Taisei Corporation Plans for the Year 2000," reprinted from the journal *Long Range Planning*, reviews nicely many of the major concepts of the text portion of the book as incorporated in a sample strategic plan and its documentation.

THE PLAN OF THE TEXT

The fifth edition of *Strategic Management* is divided into two major parts: text and cases. The following is a thumbnail sketch of material covered in each chapter.

Chapter 1—Introduces the strategic management process; identifies the four factors that determine an organization's objectives and strategy; identifies ten strategic management challenges that will shape strategy significantly in the 1990s; introduces the Integrative Case.

Chapter 2—Discusses organizational strategists and organizational purpose.

Chapter 3—Discusses the fourth major influential factor in strategy formulation: internal and external environments; discusses strategic information systems and forecasting.

Chapter 4—Continues the discussion on environments; features the Industry Note on the auto industry.

Chapter 5—Reviews the fundamentals of strategy formulation, concentrating on the steps employed and on the various techniques used for improving results.

Chapter 6—Reviews major business-level strategies and their content.

Chapter 7—Focuses on the major content of strategies and on the strategy formulation process in multiple-SBU firms.

Chapter 8—Continues the discussion of the strategic management process model, focusing on implementation and organizational structure.

Chapter 9—Concludes the discussion of implementation; reviews implementation systems, management style, and shared values or cultures.

Chapter 10—Completes the material on the strategic management process; reviews methods for carrying out evaluation and control.

Chapter 11—Presents global perspectives on strategy.

Chapter 12—Reviews the role of strategy in entrepreneurship; discusses innovation strategy.

Related comprehensive cases, grouped according to the primary components of the strategic management process model described in Chapter 1, are presented in Part 2 of the book.

ABOUT THE APPENDIXES

The appendixes for this book appear between Part 1 and Part 2. They are designed to increase the student's ability to analyze strategic situations.

Appendix 1, Sample Strategic Plan, lays out the plans of the Taisei Corporation of Tokyo. It affords the student an opportunity to see real-world applications of the concepts delineated in this textbook as Taisei Corporation formulates its strategy for the year 2000. Appendix 2 describes the case method and provides extensive guidance on how to prepare a case; it also contains a sample case analysis.

USING THE CASES

Virtually all of the 35 cases presented in this edition are current ones. This represents a major effort to bring today's issues to the forefront of case analysis. Many of these cases involve companies with which students will be familiar—Pier 1 Imports, Inc., Wal-Mart, American Greetings Corporation, John Deere & Company, Oryx, Carolco Pictures, Inc., Longs Drug, Nucor, Chaparral Steel Company, Goodyear Tire & Rubber Company, WordPerfect, Microsoft, NCNB, Honda, Toyota, McDonald's, and Club Med Inc. Three popular cases from the fourth edition, Perfumery on Park, Wall Drug, and Nucor, have been updated. The cases illustrate each major part of the strategic management process.

Part 2 of the book, in which the cases are presented, contains the following key features:

1. Major emphasis is placed on global/international cases. Nine cases focus on non-U.S.-owned firms, four of which pursue a global strategy. Three additional cases appear on U.S.-based firms that pursue a global strategy and four other cases involve global strategy issues in general.
2. Two cases focus on the emergence of Hungary as a capitalistic country from the Eastern European bloc, along with a note about the country itself.
3. A disk containing Lotus 1-2-3® spreadsheets for most cases also is available with this text.
4. Emphasis is placed on comprehensive and integrative cases that involve as many major components of the strategic management process as possible.
5. A concerted effort has been made to include cases that cover the full spectrum of organizational size. Ten cases deal specifically with small organizations.
6. The section on competitor analysis and strategy formulation has been revised to include the industry notes with their respective cases, rather than listing them as separate notes elsewhere.
7. The number of implementation cases has been increased to seven.
8. Three new cases deal with societal and ethical issues.

USING STRATEGIC MANAGEMENT

Strategic Management: Text and Cases is intended primarily for use in strategy/policy courses for fourth-year undergraduate students and for second-year MBA students. The book can be employed in conjunction with a variety of pedagogical approaches. It can be used alone in a strategic management course, or it can be used with an instructor's own cases or lectures, or with simulations or field exercises. It can also be used with analyses of reports on real-world organizations, such as those that appear in each issue of *Business Week* and in *The Wall Street Journal.*

The text may also be used by managers in management-development courses or by any individual manager as a means of "getting up to speed" in a given area. State-of-the-art implementation of strategic management is reviewed, with a focus on both research and new concepts in this rapidly expanding field.

ANCILLARIES

The ancillary materials that accompany this book form a more comprehensive package than those provided by any other strategy text.

1. The *Ancillary Resource Guide* explains in detail how to use all of the ancillary items.
2. The extensive two-part *Instructor's Manual* offers a unique and consistent format for analyzing cases. Part 1 contains chapter information and case analysis. Part 2 contains the financials, including common-size income statements, balance sheets, and ratio analyses. Part 2 also contains a video guide for the accompanying video tapes.
3. The extensive *Test Bank* provides true/false, multiple choice, and essay questions relating to the text. A computerized test bank is also available.
4. Videotaped segments cover companies discussed in the chapters and several of the cases. These segments include Caterpillar, Harley-Davidson, McDonald's–Moscow, and many more.
5. The *Instructor's Manual Enhancement Disk* accompanying the *Instructor's Manual* includes supplementary lecture materials for each chapter and additional transparency masters covering both chapters and cases.

ACKNOWLEDGMENTS

Many persons contributed to this book. First, we thank those who examined the previous edition, and those who reviewed the manuscript of this edition for areas that needed improvement:

Enoch Beraho, South Carolina State College
Michael Hergert, San Diego State University
Kay Hodge, Kearney State College
Daniel Jennings, Baylor University
Stephen Markell, Bloomsburg University
Michael Pitts, Virginia Commonwealth University
Howard Smith, University of New Mexico

Thanks go to the North American Case Research Association for their service in the development of cases and to the companies and managers examined in the cases for their cooperation. The scholars whose works are cited herein are to be commended for their efforts. Special thanks are offered to the dean of the Crummer School, Sam Certo, who provided a very supportive environment in which to work. We especially want to thank Susan Crabill, who input most of the manuscript and numerous ancillary materials, and who did so at an unbelievably high rate of productivity—and with a smile. In addition, we would like to thank the following reviewers of selected cases for this book:

Ari Ginsberg, New York University
Sal Kukalis, California State University at Long Beach
Cynthia A. Legnick-Hall, Wichita State University
Rhonda K. Reger, Arizona State University
James Thomas, Penn State University

Special thanks go to the authors who generously contributed cases to this edition:

Sexton Adams, University of North Texas
Nabil Ahmed, University of North Texas
Robert L. Anderson, College of Charleston
Tom Batley, University of Otago
Frank C. Barnes, University of North Carolina at Charlotte
Patricia Bishop, Portland State University
Gyula Bosnyak, Hungarian Rubber Company
Charles Boyd, Southwest Missouri State University
Colin Boyd, University of Saskatchewan
Steven N. Brenner, Portland State University
James Bresnahan, University of North Texas
James W. Camerius, Northern Michigan University
Gary J. Castrogiovanni, Louisiana State University
Dale Chamness, University of North Texas
James W. Clinton, University of Northern Colorado
David M. Currie, Crummer School, Rollins College
George W. Danforth, Louisiana State University
Bernard Deitzer, The University of Akron
Phil Fisher, University of Southern Indiana
Jim Frierson, University of Texas at Tyler
David Gentry, Crummer School, Rollins College
Lynda L. Goulet, University of Northern Iowa
Peter G. Goulet, University of Northern Iowa
Sue Greenfeld, California State University, San Bernardino
Adelaide Griffin, Texas Woman's University
Jacques Horovitz, Paris Chamber of Commerce and Industry
Fred Jacobson, University of Texas at Tyler
Robert Johnson, University of South Dakota
Karen Keniff, Texas Woman's University
Raymond M. Kinnunen, Northeastern University
Dan Kopp, Southwest Missouri State University

Alan G. Krigline, The University of Akron
Mark Kroll, University of Texas at Tyler
Stewart C. Malone, University of Virginia
Gregory Marchwinski, Crummer School, Rollins College
Robert N. McGrath, Louisiana State University
Jim McSorley, Crummer School, Rollins College
Mark Mitchell, University of North Texas
James F. Molloy, Jr., Northeastern University
Colleen Mullery, Portland State University
Thomas C. Peterson, The University of Akron
Jozsef Poor, International Management Center
Alan G. Robinson, University of Massachusetts at Amherst
George C. Rubenson, Salisbury State University
Dean M. Schroeder, Valparaiso University
John Seeger, Bentley College
Arthur Sharplin, McNeese State University
Madhav S. Shriram, DCM Shriram Industries, Ltd.
Lois Shufeldt, Southwest Missouri State University
F. Bruce Simmons III, The University of Akron
John W. Simmons, University of Texas at Tyler
James Taylor, University of South Dakota
S. Jill Thomas, Texas Woman's University
Catherine Tompkins, Texas Woman's University
Dan Twing, University of North Texas
Janos Vecesnyi, International Management Center
Robert P. Vichas, Florida Atlantic University
Wendy Vittori, Northeastern University
Connie Williams, Texas Woman's University
Joseph Wolfe, University of Tulsa

We would also like to thank Harold K. Wilson, at Southern Illinois State University at Carbondale, and Jeryl L. Nelson, at Wayne State College, for their reviews of the previous edition of the *Instructor's Manual*.

Butch Gemin at The Dryden Press provided us more support than we have ever before received from an acquisitions editor. We appreciate very much the special interest he took in the project. Special thanks are due to our project editor, Amy Schmidt, for without her this book would not have been completed on time or in such a satisfactory manner. She has a sense of humor that made working with her very easy. The developmental editor, Glenn E. Martin, helped us over the rough spots.

James M. Higgins
Julian W. Vincze
Roy E. Crummer Graduate School of Business,
Winter Park, Florida

August 1992

CONTENTS

PART ONE   TEXT

PART TWO   CASES

PART ONE

TEXT

STRATEGIC MANAGEMENT: THE CHALLENGES AHEAD

Of all the contrasts between the successful and the unsuccessful business, or between the corporate leader and its followers, the single most important differentiating factor is strategy.

J. Thomas Cannon
Author on Strategy

In an economy where the only certainty is uncertainty, the one sure source of lasting competitive advantage is knowledge.

Ikujiro Nonaka
Professor of Management
Hitotsubashi University, Tokyo

CHAPTER OBJECTIVES

By the time you complete this chapter, you should be able to:

1. Describe the strategic management process
2. Reproduce and discuss the hierarchies of purposes and strategies
3. Describe what strategists do
4. Discuss the various types of strategists
5. Describe the crafting of strategy and the role of intuition in strategy formulation
6. Discuss values, ethics, and social responsibility and how they affect strategy
7. Discuss the ten strategic management challenges for the 1990s
8. Describe the impact on strategy of the globalization of business
9. Discuss how strategic management is changing
10. Identify the strategic imperatives for the 1990s
11. Discuss strategic intent

BOEING—DOMINANT BUT VIGILANT

Boeing dominated the world's commercial aircraft industry with a 54-percent market share in 1990. A $91 billion backlog of orders ensures that its plants will be busy throughout most of the 1990s. Boeing is one of the few U.S. firms that still dominates a global heavy industry. In fact, Boeing is a major positive influence on the U.S. balance of trade with approximately 54 percent of its 1990 revenues of $27 billion coming from foreign sales. Boeing's Chairman, Frank A. Shrontz, isn't allowing the company to rest on its laurels, though. He looks for continuous improvement in sales, return on equity, product development, and manufacturing expertise. Furthermore, he is alert to the potentials of recession, increasing domestic and foreign competition, difficulties in finding experienced workers, and the complexities of selling in a global marketplace.

Much of Boeing's strategy has rested historically on its willingness to take risks. The 747 aircraft, when first launched in 1969, was a huge risk, one that almost bankrupted the company in a 1971 recession with its collapse of orders. Since then, however, the plane has proved to be the main supply of funds for the company as airlines all over the globe can't seem to get enough of them. From 1985 to mid-1990, 307 orders were placed for the latest version of the 747, the 747-400. This is especially impressive in light of the hefty price tag of $125 to $147 million per plane. Boeing pumps out five 747-400s and five 767s every month from its huge plant in Everett, Washington. (The plant is the world's biggest building with 63 acres under one roof.) The 747, however, is vulnerable to competition, and McDonnell Douglas is aiming right at the 747 with its MD-12.

Boeing has most recently bet the company on the development of its new 350-passenger airplane, the 777, which is targeted for airlines with long-distance routes. The 777 is, unfortunately for Boeing, a catchup effort to McDonnell Douglas Corporation's MD-11 and Europe's Airbus Industries' A330/340 family, which together have already received $30 billion in orders and can be delivered at least 2 years before the 777. The 777 will require $4 billion to launch, and Boeing only confirmed its first order in the fall of 1990. United Airlines had been the principal domestic target, but Airbus and McDonnell Douglas fought hard to win that contract, as well. United, playing the three competitors against each other, presented each with a list of 54 major demands, with numerous subdemands. Both Airbus and McDonnell Douglas are losing money, but Airbus, a combine from several European countries, is subsidized by its host governments. McDonnell Douglas is expected to survive with its airline business intact. Eventually Boeing won the contract, but had to provide United with several major financial and service incentives to do so.

In all of its contracts and sales efforts, Boeing stresses responsiveness to customer needs. It even redesigned the 777 to meet United's needs by developing folding wing tips so that the plane would fit existing gate sizes, but still have wings long enough to provide necessary fuel economy. It has carefully designed the aircraft to please customers, for example, by placing galleys where customers want them and adding other interior features easily, such as reading lights. One of Boeing's strategies has been to provide the level of technology in its aircraft that is necessary for safety and the stated needs of its customers. Airbus has stimulated much of the technological innovation in the industry. Boeing has chosen to follow this lead in many cases, as customers begin to ask for Airbus-type technological innovations. Yet Boeing remains dominant because of its quality and customer service.

One of Shrontz's overriding concerns is making sure that Boeing's 160,000 employees understand that success is fragile. Financial analysts, for example, suggest that a major recession, even a lengthy minor one, could cause existing orders to be withdrawn or delayed. Furthermore, Airbus and McDonnell Douglas are doing everything feasible to keep the 777 from succeeding by selling their own planes. Shrontz also seeks to make certain that a repeat of the firm's problems with implementation in 1988 and 1989 do not occur again. Boeing overcommitted itself with the 747-400. It had difficulty locating a sufficient number of skilled aircraft workers to meet schedules and to properly manufacture the product. It also overcommitted to accommodating customers' desires for features with the 747-400, and delivery schedules slid, infuriating some airlines. These problems had mostly been ironed out by 1990 with a tremendous investment in human resources, and through better product design on the 777 to simplify efforts to satisfy customers.

Flexibility and efficiency are considered to be essential parts of the Boeing success story. Boeing, for example, has adopted Japanese-style design–build teams for the 777. Members from marketing, engineering, manufacturing, finance, and customer service work jointly in teams to develop the plane. Also, the firm has prepared an extensive computer simulation that allows for "preassembly" by computer to work out manufacturing bugs in advance. Boeing has subcontracted some of its manufacturing, for example, to three Japanese firms in order to provide for better domestic flexibility.

As in any complex business, Boeing's strategy is complex. It requires care and attention to customers, to the actions of competitors, to developing new products, to merging the various functional areas of the firm in a consistent design effort, to insuring proper implementation, to quality control, to the use of technology, to learning the vagaries of the global marketplace, and so on. One must always be alert to existing opportunities and threats. The Japanese and Europeans, for example, are investing heavily in designing a quiet, environmentally sound supersonic transport aircraft. Boeing cannot afford to be left behind in that race by focusing exclusively on current successes or the 777.

Sources: Rick Wartzman, "Boeing Co. Is Girding for Dogfight over Market Share," *The Wall Street Journal*, January 14, 1992, p. B4; Willard C. Rappleye, Jr., "Last of the Titans," *Financial World*, August 20, 1991, pp. 16–17; Dori Jones Yang, "Will Boeing Build a Beheomoth to Defend Its Turf?" *Business Week*, August 19, 1991, pp. 28–29; James I. McKenna, "United Places Record Order for Up to 128 Transports," *Aviation Week and Space Technology*, October 22, 1990, pp. 20–21; Dori Jones Yang and Michael O'Neal, "How Boeing Does It," *Business Week*, July 9, 1990, pp. 46–50.

The strategic challenges that corporate strategists face in the 1990s are making this the most difficult decade ever for achieving effective strategic management. Frank A. Shrontz of Boeing is forging the kind of strategies that should result in high levels of organizational performance in this problematic period, but there are no guarantees. As Shrontz has realized, strategic management is becoming ever more necessary, and yet ever more difficult.[1] Strategists in all types of organizations are confronted with more strategic challenges than ever before. Ten key strategic challenges can be identified: changes in all aspects of business are accelerating, competition is increasing, business is globalizing, new technologies are revolutionizing competition, the work force is changing dramatically in terms of composition and expectations, significant resource shortages are developing, business functions in a newly forming knowledge-based society, unstable market and economic conditions create doubts as to suitable actions, all constituents are making increasing demands, and complexity is increasing in the strategic management environment.[2] Frank Shrontz at Boeing, and numerous other strategists in thousands of firms, have prepared and are preparing strategies for coping with these and other strategic challenges, but their tasks are complex and the consequences uncertain.

This chapter introduces the concepts of strategic management, organizational purpose, and organizational strategy, and reviews the processes of formulating, implementing, and controlling strategy. The types of strategists are discussed briefly, followed by the impacts on strategy of values, ethics, and social responsibility. The chapter concludes with an examination of the ten strategic management challenges for the 1990s, especially the globalization of business.

STRATEGIC MANAGEMENT

Strategic management is the process of managing the pursuit of the organization's mission while managing the relationship of the organization to its environment, especially with respect to its environmental **stakeholders,** the major constituents in its internal and external environments that are affected by its actions. Strategic management is concerned principally with the executive actions portrayed in the five-stage model of the strategic management process shown in Figure 1.1, and in the more detailed model of objectives determination and strategy formulation portrayed in Figure 1.2. The following paragraphs discuss the five stages of the process shown in Figure 1.1, along with organizational policy, an important factor in all five stages.

1. Formulation of Vision, Mission Statement, and Goals

An organization's **vision** is a general statement of its intended direction that evokes emotional feelings in organization members. The organization's **mission** is its purpose, its reason for being. A mission statement further defines the direction component of the vision. It should describe the organization's major areas of interest, the scope of

FIGURE 1.1 The Organization—A Strategic Management Process Model

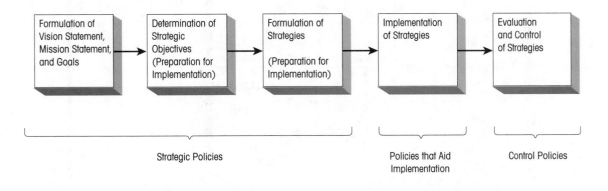

FIGURE 1.2 Objectives Determination and Strategy Formulation

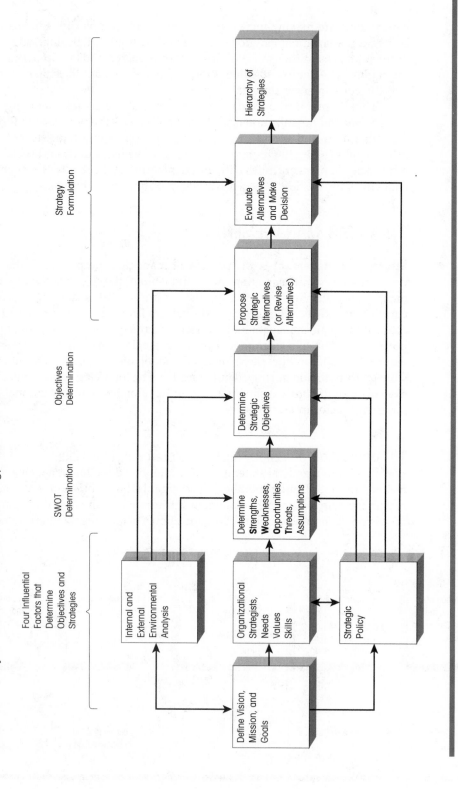

its intended actions, the basic market needs it intends to satisfy, and its primary values. **Strategic goals** are broad statements of organizational purpose established in the firm's key results areas. They further define the mission.

2. Determination of Strategic Objectives

Strategic objectives are more definitive statements of the criteria for goal accomplishment. The firm must determine the strategic objectives that will achieve its mission in its complex internal and external environments periodically, or as needed in view of environmental circumstances.

3. Strategy Formulation

Successful organizations engage in **strategy formulation,** generating alternative strategies and choosing from among them the one that will best achieve strategic objectives. **Strategies** are major, comprehensive, and usually long-term plans (although the typical time frame is shrinking) for accomplishing strategic goals and objectives, and hence fulfilling the organization's vision and mission. Strategies indicate the integrative and unifying pattern of decisions to achieve organizational purposes, resource allocations for achieving these purposes, and, at the business level, the firm's perception of a sustainable competitive advantage.[3] In setting strategic objectives and formulating strategy, organizational strategists examine information about the vision, mission, goals, policies, and internal and external environments. Strategy formulation is often referred to as **strategic planning.**

4. Strategy Implementation

Strategy implementation is the process of translating strategy into actions and results. Four primary issues are involved in implementation: structuring the organization, employing appropriate implementation systems, adopting the proper management style, and managing organizational culture (or shared values). Implementation is now recognized as critical to the success of strategic management, and, as shown in Figure 1.1, certain parts of the process begin with setting objectives and formulating strategy. The actions that prepare for implementation focus on building support for these strategies among organization members who will actually implement them, or who must support them in some other way to assure successful implementation.

5. Evaluation and Strategic Control

Strategic control is the process of determining whether strategy has accomplished its goals and objectives, or if it promises to do so, and acting to correct any problems. Strategists must assess the impacts of their strategies and respond appropriately.

6. Setting Organizational Policy

Organizational **policy** consists of broad guidelines established to help managers determine strategic goals and objectives and then formulate, implement, and control strategy.

In quite simple terms, the contents of this model address **three basic strategic questions** that are common to all strategic situations:

1. **Where are we now?**
2. **Where do we want to be?**
3. **How do we get there?**

To answer these three questions, that is, to complete the first three stages of the strategic management process, strategists must examine the organization's internal and external environments to determine organizational Strengths and Weaknesses (in its internal environment) and Opportunities and Threats (in its external environment). This gives the acronym **SWOT.** The organization then forecasts its future SWOT for the period for which it is setting objectives and formulating strategies. A firm's strategy aims at taking advantage of projected strengths and opportunities, while overcoming or reducing projected weaknesses and threats. Thus, strategies are based on these SWOT forecasts. A critical component of these strategies is the creation of value for customers by satisfying customer needs.[4]

AT BOEING

Frank Shrontz believes that his managers must continually improve and fine-tune strategy if Boeing is to survive and prosper. He has a vision, and has helped shape the company's mission. He has devised strategies to reach corporate objectives. He is especially concerned about the means to implement and control those strategies successfully. He remains flexible, recognizing the volatility of Boeing's strategic environment.

True strategic management takes time. It focuses on the long term, not on the short-term goals and objectives that many CEOs feel more comfortable pursuing and that investors often seek. In the short term, any firm with a strategic advantage can survive and even prosper, but in the longer run, only the organizations that practice sound strategic management will continue to flourish.

Fortunately, many organizations have begun to realize the importance of strategic management. These organizations are searching for the factors that combine to promote corporate excellence. As never before, research evidence is accumulating to define the proper content of strategy and the best processes to achieve that content.[5] We have learned that there is more to strategic management than just strategy. Hence, this book addresses not only the formulation of strategy, but its implementation and control, as well.

Figures 1.1 and 1.2 portray the elements of the process as sequential, but they do not always occur in sequence, nor are all parts of the process always fully undertaken. For example, many objectives are established without exhaustive internal and external analysis. Also, objectives may change after strategies have been formulated, and hence strategies will have to change. Even when objectives remain the same, the strategies to achieve them may be reformulated because of changing circumstances. Most firms, however, take the steps shown in these figures in sequence at least once a year as they engage in their annual planning processes.[6]

Note, however, that many corporations now begin implementation at the same time that they determine objectives or formulate strategy. It is especially important that implementation begin at these times to promote success in critical factors such as necessary changes in organizational structure or lower-level management commitment to the strategy. The references to implementation in these stages of Figure 1.1 refer to these types of preparation for full implementation.

The way these models are actually put into operation varies from organization to organization and, in some ways, from country to country.[7] The size of the organization may dictate, for example, whether highly formalized strategic planning is appropriate or not. Large organizations typically have formalized planning processes to develop written strategic objectives, plans, and policies. Xerox Corporation's highly formalized process for strategic planning and setting objectives coordinates all levels of the organization, telling every employee what he or she must do and how to do it for the coming year.[8] Small businesses have strategies, but often don't formalize them in writing; many don't even think them through, just taking actions that seem appropriate over time. Make no mistake, though—such a pattern of actions constitutes a strategy.

Although the specifics may vary, the strategic management process model contains the principal components of effective organization. Numerous research studies have indicated the importance of this strategic management approach and the processes depicted in Figures 1.1 and 1.2. Not all studies support this process, but most do, and most contrary findings can be attributed to methodological weaknesses in the strategic management process.[9] Strategic planning alone, however, does not ensure success. Implementation and control are critical. Furthermore, it is not sufficient for the firm to go through the motions of strategic planning once a year. Rather it must be an ongoing practice, always responding to and anticipating changing internal and external environmental factors.[10]

AT BOEING

After Frank Shrontz examined the external environment, he made changes in goals, objectives, and strategies. He followed the steps of the strategic management process, but not always in sequence. He was flexible, adapting to what he saw in a changing environment, but he also responded to his own values and to the company's SWOT (strengths, weaknesses, opportunities, threats). He created strategies to overcome weaknesses, for example, in the human resources area.

Leveraging Resources (Strategic Intent) versus Strategic Fit[11]

Strategy researchers Gary Hamel and C. K. Prahalad suggest that two distinct perspectives exist on how this basic model of strategic management should be implemented. (See Figure 1.1.) The strategic fit model appears to be more popular in western firms, while the leveraging resources model is more popular in Japan. The **strategic fit** model suggests that the firm adjust its strategy according to the fit between its strengths and weaknesses and the threats and opportunities in the external environment. Strategic fit suggests that ambitions be trimmed to match available resources. The **leveraging resources** approach suggests, however, that resources be leveraged to achieve seemingly unreachable goals, as embodied in the term *strategic intent.* The firm increases its strengths or looks for ways to use its strengths to overcome weaknesses and threats and to take advantage of opportunities. Strategic fit is a conservative interpretation of strategic management. Leveraging resources is an aggressive interpretation. **Strategic intent** encompasses not only unfettered ambition, but a management process that includes, "focusing the organization's attention on winning; motivating people by communicating the value of the target; leaving room for individual and team contributions; sustaining enthusiasm by providing new operational definitions as circumstances change; and using intent consistently to guide resource allocations."[12]

Examination of Japanese firms such as Komatsu, Toyota, Honda, and Canon suggests that under the strategic fit model they would never have become such powerful players in their respective industries. Rather, they would have been satisfied simply to be niche players, or perhaps even exit the scene. Their focus on intent made them powerful. Western firms, meanwhile, have seen their strategies lead them into decline following diminishing ambitions. They abandoned manufacturing televisions and most other consumer electronics products. They forfeited huge market shares in steel, automobiles, and textiles. Throughout this text, contrasts between these two perspectives will occasionally be drawn as a way of better demonstrating the requirements of successful strategy.

HIERARCHY OF PURPOSES AND STRATEGIES

Two ingredients of the strategic management process, a hierarchy of purposes and a hierarchy of strategies, are shown in Figure 1.3. The **hierarchy of purposes** presents the four types of organization purposes in a pyramid ranging from the least specific, vision, at the top to the most specific, objectives, at the bottom. Each of these types of purposes provides guidance that is relevant to each stage of the strategy formulation process, from broad conceptualization to definite strategy formulation in pursuit of specific objectives. These objectives also help the firm to guide implementation and control. Chapter 2 discusses organizational purpose.

Every organization's **hierarchy of strategies** has three components: corporate strategy, business strategy, and functional strategy.

1. **Corporate strategy** defines the organization's fields of endeavor—how it chooses the business or businesses in which to compete and how it plans to conduct itself fundamentally in that business or those businesses.

FIGURE 1.3 Hierarchies of Purposes and Strategies

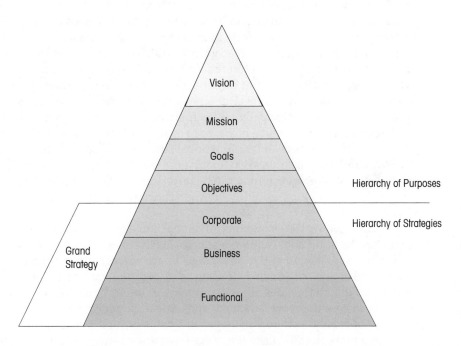

2. **Business strategy** indicates in very broad terms how a single business unit plans to compete against other firms in that same business.
3. **Functional strategy** consists of plans for achieving maximum resource utilization and efficiency in each economic and management function in support of corporate and business strategies.

Chapters 5, 6, and 7 discuss these levels of strategy in detail. The contents of these strategies vary principally with the mission, the strategists, and the type of organization.

Business organizations can be categorized in two primary groups. The first group includes organizations that sell a single product or a few products, largely in a single industry. This type of organization is known as a **strategic business unit (SBU).** Single-SBU firms include Delta Air Lines, individual McDonald's franchises, and most small accounting firms. The second group is made up of organizations that market their products in many industries through many SBUs. General Mills, Westinghouse, IBM, General Electric, Mitsubishi, Xerox, and Siemens are all multiple-SBU firms. A firm's membership in one of these two groups is important, because they have very different types of strategies.

The term *corporate strategy* generally refers to strategies for multiple-SBU organizations, while the term *business strategy* usually refers to the strategic actions of single-SBU organizations. Later, however, in Chapters 5, 6, and 7, we will indicate factors that clarify these general references.

When formulating strategy at the SBU, or business, level, the strategist is most concerned with developing a sustainable **strategic advantage** or **competitive advantage** over the competition by satisfying customer needs and creating value for the customer more effectively than competitors. This involves the choice of an appropriate grand strategy. The **grand strategy** combines strategic actions to define the driving force of the organization, that central character attribute that should specify all else. A firm might seek to grow through lower price or higher quality, for example. This level of strategy (sometimes referred to as the **master strategy**),[13] focuses principally on such elements of the corporate strategy as the decision to compete or find a niche, or to grow or stabilize (and how). Sometimes it focuses on the business and/or functional strategies, often singling out marketing, though some organizations may emphasize other areas, such as production and cost controls. Apple Computer has historically followed a grand strategy of innovation, while more recently Hewlett-Packard has focused on high quality at low cost.

Strategies in the economic functional areas of marketing, finance, operations/production, and human resource management are often critical to the achievement of a competitive advantage, as are strategies in the managerial areas, such as planning, organizing, leading, and controlling. The Strategic Challenge feature for this chapter describes a company, Delta Air Lines, whose grand strategy of careful growth is well-defined and whose supportive economic functional strategy of human resource management helps ensure its success.

In a multiple-SBU firm, the overall corporate strategy focuses on obtaining a strategic advantage over similar firms, usually conglomerates, by achieving a synergistic balance among all the SBUs and by pursuing the correct business strategy for each business unit. The techniques employed to achieve this balance are known as *portfolio management*. In addition, strategy at this level must examine the same fundamental issues as those that concern single-SBU organizations. A multiple-SBU firm must have a competitive strategy for competing against similar corporations, and it must have corporatewide functional strategies, if only to state policies. Typically, corporate headquarters informs major SBU divisions of overall organizational goals and of its perspective on the unit's objectives, plans, policies, and resource allocations. The SBUs are free to function within these guidelines. Previously, corporate headquarters had typically controlled most decisions in multiple-SBU firms. The current trend is to allow SBUs to function totally autonomously, almost as separate businesses. They may even have their own boards of directors.[14] In December 1991, for example, IBM announced that it was making its businesses autonomous and de-emphasizing the role of corporate headquarters, to provide guidance rather than direct control of decision making.[15]

ORGANIZATIONAL STRATEGISTS

In concept, **organizational strategists**—the people involved in general management—include the owners, the board of directors, the CEO, and the top corporate and SBU line and staff officers, including professional planners. Evidence suggests, however, that in reality an organization's strategic decision processes tend to be dominated by an entrepreneurial chief executive, a coalition of high-ranking

STRATEGIC CHALLENGE

HOW DELTA COMBINES SOUND GROWTH WITH GOOD PEOPLE MANAGEMENT

How do you compete in a fast-paced world? Ask Delta Air Lines. By the criterion of continued profit, Delta Air Lines is the most successful airline firm in the United States. It has even managed to recover from a slight profit problem that followed deregulation (although it is having some problems as a result of its recent acquisition of parts of Pan Am). There are many reasons for Delta's success. Its marketing strategies have included an advertising campaign focused around the theme, "Delta loves to fly and it shows." Delta emphasizes quality of service in these ads. Its former slogan, "Delta is ready when you are," emphasized the availability of flights, but even then, the airline stressed service. Delta still has a product—a flight—available when people need it most, but in the 1990s, it felt it had to stress its high levels of service to customers. Its planes run on time, its employees are courteous, and it strives to make the customer feel important. Behind its ability to succeed at providing service while achieving a profit are two critical factors: its growth strategy and its people strategy.

Delta has followed a careful growth strategy, adding routes here and there. It was slow to follow the acquisition trend of the 1980s, but finally did so by merging with Western Airlines in 1986. It did not move rapidly to expand globally, but gobbled up selected assets from ailing Pan Am in 1991. Chairman Ronald Allen observes, "We think it is a very conservative move. To have missed this opportunity would have been the risky course." For a total expense of about $1 billion, $726 million in cash, Delta received Pan Am's New York shuttle, dozens of routes to Europe from New York's Kennedy Airport, a hub in Frankfurt, Germany, and 45 airplanes. Some believe Delta paid too much for these assets, and in October 1991, it renegotiated its cash flow support contract with the remainder of Pan Am, since that firm was gobbling up much more cash than Delta had anticipated. Yet, most bet that the Pan Am acquisition will be sound.

Delta has carefully constructed a global growth strategy based on the acquisition of Pan Am assets and global alliances combined with its existing international route structure, for example, its Atlanta to London route. Delta has recently entered into alliances in both the Pacific Rim with Singapore Airlines and in Europe with Swissair in order to shore up its global operations. Analysts view these alliances as necessary for competing globally. Delta is preparing for the globalization of the airline industry, because if it doesn't, it won't be able to compete.

The second key factor in Delta's success has been its people strategy. Delta attempts to maintain a family feeling among members of its work force to encourage employee loyalty and productivity. Despite, or perhaps partially because of, the difficulties it has encountered, Delta's employees were so loyal to the firm that in 1983 they purchased a $30 million plane for the company to show their appreciation for the way it had treated them. Delta has an open door policy and holds informational meetings with employees every 6 weeks. These meetings are run by department heads who keep people informed on the company's financial picture, airplane purchases, new equipment, and other topics of interest. Delta has never laid off one of its 60,000 employees. These policies are a major reason the firm provides such outstanding service. Some wonder, however, if Delta can successfully turn around the morale of former Pan Am employees and make them part of the Delta family. Only time will tell.

Sources: Kenneth Labich, "Delta Aims for a Higher Altitude," *Fortune*, December 16, 1991, pp. 79–81; Bridget O'Brian, "Highest Flier: Delta, Despite Victory in Pan Am Bid, Faces Some Big Challenges," *The Wall Street Journal*, August 13, 1991, pp. A1, A11; Asra Q. Nomani and Laurie McGinley, "Going Global: Airlines of the World Scramble for Routes in Industry Shakeout," *The Wall Street Journal*, July 23, 1991, pp. A1, A8; Michael Westlake, "Aviation and Aerospace: The Mating of Planes," *Far Eastern Economic Review*, February 15, 1990, pp. 37–38; Bill Leonard, "Making the Message Clear: Delta's Head Believes that 99 Percent of Problems Can Be Solved by Understanding," *Personnel Administration*, November 1989, pp. 46–49; Carole A. Shifran, "Marketing Pacts, Equity Agreements Bring World's Airlines Closer Together," *Aviation Week & Space Technology*, December 18/December 25, 1989, pp. 67, 69.

corporate or SBU officers, professional strategic planners, or top-line executives. Top line executives, especially, are becoming more and more involved in the strategic process as intrapreneurship increases in U.S. corporations. The strategic decisions made by all of these strategists are affected by their needs, values, and skills. Inputs from corporate professional planners may substantially affect the decisions made by other strategists.

The principal function of the strategists is to determine objectives and formulate strategy after considering the firm's mission and goals, its strategic policies, and the information available about strengths, weaknesses, opportunities, and threats derived from analyses of its internal and external environments. How the major strategists go about their tasks may vary, however. These strategists are discussed in more detail in Chapter 2.

What Strategists Do—Crafting Strategy

While the model presented in this chapter suggests that strategists formulate strategy quite rationally and analytically, Henry Mintzberg's concept of crafting strategy offers another perspective. Mintzberg suggests that **crafting strategy** is a more appropriate idea than merely planning strategy and that strategists must learn to live with strategy. They must get involved with it, have a feel for it, learn how it changes over time, learn from these changes, and guide them. They must also know when not to change. They must respond to the discontinuities that might undermine the firm in the future. The word *crafting* suggests that strategists develop a feeling of intimacy and harmony with the strategic process; the firm's strengths, weaknesses, opportunities, and threats; and the other elements of strategic management.[16]

Mintzberg's observations are not meant to suggest that strategists abandon rational/analytical approaches to strategic management, but rather that they conduct these procedures within a craftsmanlike framework. Strategic management isn't something you do 2 weeks a year at the annual strategy meeting. Strategy formulation is an ongoing activity, if only in terms of fine-tuning.

Intuition and Strategy Formulation

As we enlarge on the concept that strategic management is not a totally rational/analytical process, it becomes extremely important to realize that strategy formulation not only can be and often is an intuitive process, but that it should be. In fact, strategists must consider so many variables, so many unknowns, that according to Henry Mintzberg, their decision processes often seem to defy rationality and must be based at least partly on intuition perhaps guided by rational analysis.[17] In fact, studies reveal that executives do frequently use intuition in strategic decisions.[18] Also, creativity is increasingly viewed as critical to successful strategy formulation.[19] In fact, strategy formulation has even been described as a "process of structured creativity."[20] A number of executives have described how intuition is used in their firms. For example, F. A. Maljers, then CEO of the Dutch firm Unilever, indicates that it has been critical in strategic decisions at that firm.[21]

Research has clearly revealed that making complex decisions such as those involved in strategy formulation involves a different kind of thinking process than the process of analytical problem solving. Rational approaches look for the linear path from A to B to C to D, and so on, but in very complex, unstructured situations (like strategic problems), A may lead to F, which is interconnected with both C and K, with K leading to both A and B, and so on. Some variables may even lack labels, and there is precious little time to make a major decision. Such situations call for **multidimensional thinking** in which the decision maker seems to somehow understand these complex interrelationships. This process is not well-understood, but it is clear that the better executives, as measured by the results of their decisions, do possess such an ability to go beyond linear thinking to multidimensional thinking.[22]

How Values, Skills, and Needs Influence Strategic Choices

Just as strategic managers' skills affect their strategic decisions, so do their personalities. Their needs, values, emotions, ethics, and feelings, their propensity to take risks, approaches to problem solving, and attitudes toward people and life, along with numerous other personality factors, influence the decisions they make. Of all these variables, the most frequently discussed behavioral determinant of organizational success or failure has been values.[23]

Values embody what the holder views as desirable. They reflect the history of experiences of an individual, group, organization, or society. While the perception processes trigger decision-making actions, values enter into perceptions. Thus, values play a critical role in decision making. Though managers may not consciously articulate their values as they make decisions, those values nonetheless greatly affect their decisions at the subconscious level.

How are values reflected in decisions? We can't be sure, but it seems likely that values enter into virtually every decision, and that more than one value is usually involved. For example, when L. M. Clymer resigned as president of Holiday Inns in protest of the directors' decision to establish a gambling casino, he may have been motivated by religious values.[24] When resort owners hire Peter Dye to design a golf course, they seem primarily to want his ability to create a course that is both aesthetically pleasing and economically successful.[25] Philip Friedman and Michael Keiser founded Recycled Paper Products, Inc. to help keep trees from being cut down to make greeting cards.[26] These decision makers were satisfying social or perhaps aesthetic values. Many more examples could be cited; all would reinforce the point that values underlie managerial decisions.

Shared values, often referred to as organizational *culture,* usually reflect the values of the organization's strategists. Shared values relate to key issues such as mission, vision, goals, objectives, and strategies, and how these strategies should be implemented. For example, the organization's structure, its management style, and the type of systems to be employed all reflect a set of values. Shared values also reflect "what's important around here," and "how we do things around here." The more the values that arise in connection with the issues to be decided are common to those articulated by strategy, the more likely a firm is to successfully achieve its mission. Understanding the role that shared values play in making strategy successful is important, and they are discussed in more detail in Chapter 8.

AT BOEING

Boeing values all of its stakeholders. It has established programs, for example, focusing on customers, employees, and society, and has established objectives to be satisfied relative to each of these. The set of values indicated in these objectives helps to guide Boeing's strategic actions.

Other managerial personality traits play important roles in strategic decisions, as well. A study by Danny Miller suggests that a top manager's trait such as conservatism or extremely arbitrary risk taking is a significant determinant of a firm's success or lack of it.[27] Miller found that unsuccessful firms did not employ environmental scanning, environmental analysis, or other analyses in strategy formulation as often as successful firms did. If, as Miller's study suggests, the human variable may be an important predictor of strategic success, then strategy may be contingent on this variable. Miller describes one bold and reckless entrepreneur who was so proactive that he took too many risks. Yet, as we all know, risk taking can pay off. For example, while Citicorp has taken its lumps in global business development (its United Kingdom Equities unit had to be shut down), its aggressive tendency allowed it to corner the market on auto loans in Spain, completely changing the Spanish approach to auto loans. It also introduced the 20-year home mortgage to Taiwan, bringing substantial financial gains.[28]

How Strategists' Ethics and Social Responsibility Perspectives Influence Strategic Choices

Ethics are the norms of a society, organization, profession, group, or individual. Ethical behaviors are behaviors that comply with these norms. Ethics often encompass more than the law. Many actions that are legal may be considered unethical. Many professors' codes of ethics, for example, prohibit certain consulting practices even though the law permits them. Ethics differ from morality in that ethics tend to be situational and defined by one of the five reference groups. Morality implies absolutes, often determined by religion. A person's or firm's code of ethics usually determines how socially responsible that person or a firm will be.[29] Ethics are becoming increasingly important as issues become cloudier, as such prominent individuals as Michael Milken (who was convicted of insider trading on Wall Street) break society's norms, and sometimes the law, as well. Donald P. Robin and Eric Reidenbach suggest that many ethical dilemmas could be avoided by more fully incorporating social impacts into the strategic and tactical planning process.[30]

Social responsibility is an elusive concept. To some it means making a profit. To others, it means accounting for the impact of organizational decisions on the organization's stakeholders. For still others, it suggests that social power begets social obligation. The latter perspective seems to be the most likely to influence strategy in the 1990s.[31] It is clear, however, that organizations may choose to do virtually nothing, to do only what is legal, to do what is ethical, or to go beyond that and perform above what might be expected.[32]

STRATEGIC MANAGEMENT CHALLENGES IN THE 1990s

The opening paragraph of this chapter identified ten **strategic management challenges for the 1990s.** If strategists are to be successful in this decade, they must cope with and/or take advantage of these challenges.[33] The following paragraphs discuss each of these in more detail.

1. Accelerating Rates of Change   Alvin Toffler, in his 1970 book *Future Shock,* predicted that as we approached the 21st century, all aspects of life, including organizational life, would encounter accelerating rates of change.[34] His predictions have come true. The collapse of the Soviet Union, a united Germany, laptop PCs as powerful as mainframes of 15 years ago, Japan's emerging dominance in biotechnology and mainframe computers, instant color copiers, the invasion of Kuwait and the resulting war with Iraq, the demands for increasing shareholder value, on and on come the changes. Furthermore, these changes are not only increasing at an accelerating rate, but also in the magnitude of their significance.[35]

Managers must not only embrace change and learn how to manage it, but they must also insure that all organization members join this effort.[36] This provides a tremendous challenge for the organization's strategists, given a clear historical preference in organizations for stability and status quo. Strategists must change their entire organizations so that they will, as Thomas J. Peters suggests, be able to "thrive on chaos."[37] The external and internal factors affecting organizations (and individuals) simply won't allow them to avoid incorporating change as part of organizational reality. "Change is the order of the day. Choose it or chase it. Adapt or die," proclaimed Theodore Levitt, then editor of the *Harvard Business Review.*[38]

2. Increasing Competition

The 1990s will be the most competitive decade of this century. More and more competitors are entering the marketplace, both domestically and globally. Strategists must formulate strategies to compete in markets that offer little hope of overall growth, and in which, therefore, market share becomes ever more critical. Modern business is a market share game.[39] Innovation in products, processes, marketing, and management determines life or death in times of increasing competition.

3. Globalization of Business

European economic integration in 1992, the probability of the Pacific Rim emerging as the world's most significant economy of the 21st century, and increased levels of foreign competition in most domestic economies dictate that the strategist must develop and maintain a global perspective on business. It just isn't enough to consider the domestic market as sufficient to support the firm's future. Foreign competitors will be entering markets everywhere in an effort to gain market share in the face of stagnant growth in their own domestic economies. Strategists must not fail to consider the global perspective when formulating strategy.

4. Technological Change

Most firms depend in some way on technology to attain the competitive advantage necessary to survive or prosper, whether it be product or process technology. Technology changes rapidly in virtually all industries, but technological discontinuity poses the major threat to firms. Firms must be prepared for competitors to develop new ways of competing, that is, technologies that leapfrog their own, giving their competitors strategic advantage and creating strategic discontinuities.

5. Changing Nature of the Work Force

The U.S. work force of the 1990s will differ ever more significantly from work forces of the past. Demographics, expectations, preparedness for work, and average age will all change rapidly. The traditional white-male dominated work force will give way to a world of cultural diversity.[40] This chapter's Strategic Cultural Diversity Challenge feature discusses how one firm copes with these issues. The percentages of women and minorities in the work force will continue the increases they have shown in the recent past.

A major increase in the number of foreign-born workers entering the U.S. work force is expected to compensate for the shortage of workers expected in the overall economy. Many think workers will expect higher rewards, and change their values toward seeking more meaningful work. Yet, worker skill levels are expected to decrease because of declines in overall education levels. Finally, the overall work force is expected to age, primarily due to the aging of the baby boomers.[41] The strategist's challenge is to survive and prosper in a world of strategic challenges with a work force that is predicted to be less productive, but ever more important to strategic success.[42]

6. Resource Shortages

It is increasingly apparent that supplies of several significant resources, principally energy, water, and human resources, will be

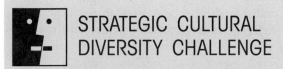

STRATEGIC CULTURAL DIVERSITY CHALLENGE

HOW DEC CELEBRATES DIVERSITY

Digital Equipment Corporation was one of the first companies to develop a cultural-diversity management program. Digital's program focuses on the concept of "celebrating diversity," that is, viewing diversity from its positive aspects rather than seeing it as something a company must do, but from which it won't benefit. Digital believes cultural diversity training can offer fresh insights into problem solving. Managers, consequently, receive rigorous training in different environments, both domestic and foreign. By focusing on the needs of other cultures and increasing their sensitivity to diverse lifestyles and people, managers are better equipped to deal with change and challenge on all fronts and are better equipped to compete.

insufficient in the 1990s in many areas of the globe, especially in the United States.[43] In addition, specific industries may find certain raw material resources in short supply. Strategists must cope with these resource shortages at a time when the firm is being asked to do more. A resource utilization/conservation strategy must be developed. Energy and water supplies will, in all likelihood, be controlled by federal, state, and local authorities where shortages affect the general welfare.

7. Transition from Industrial to Knowledge Society   Knowledge has become strategically powerful. Knowledge can establish strategic advantage; some say it is the only long-term, sustainable competitive advantage. For example, firms can compete based on their knowledge of a new process or their ability to create new products and services. Knowledge about customers may also give competitive advantage. For example, electronic data interfaces, which customers and suppliers share data bases, result in closer relationships that help lock out competitors. Strategists must learn to manage knowledge, not just as a routine SWOT input, but as a critical factor in success. Managing knowledge can lead to continuous innovation, a critical factor in strategic success.[44]

8. Unstable Market and Economic Conditions   U.S. firms will face unparalleled instability in market and economic conditions during the 1990s. For example, consider the savings and loan bailout program, which is expected to cost at least $500 billion,[45] at a time when federal budget deficits have reached significant proportions of the economy.[46] In addition, an extremely high U.S. trade deficit is fueled by several factors, including a lack of investment in research and development,[47] unfair Japanese trade practices,[48] oil imports, and past inability to compete globally on the basis of price or product differentiation factors such as quality. Consider, too, the effect of the baby boomers as a significant age wave in the population. It is easy to understand how and why firms have strategic difficulties in this decade. The strategist must successfully deal with the consequences of these variables.

9. Increasing Demands of Constituents

Constituent groups are making ever more vocal demands in the areas of the environment, employee health and safety, employee security during mergers and acquisitions, increasing shareholder value, high quality and service to customers (including those internal to the firm), equal employment opportunity, philanthropy, and ethical behavior in the 1990s. Strategists will need to formulate and reformulate strategies and policies for dealing with these concerns.

10. Complexity of the Strategic Management Environment

Rapid changes in the business environment are increasing its overall complexity. As the above list of nine items suggests, strategists must consider more and more variables. Simple environments exist in only a few industries today.

Change in the Nature of Strategic Management

As a consequence of the above challenges together with others, the strategic management process must change in order that the firm can survive and prosper. New ways of formulating strategy and new types of strategies must be developed. Strategic information systems must be refined to function well in highly unstable and complex environments. Competitor intelligence becomes critical. New forms of organization must evolve to accommodate the new strategies. More proactive strategies to influence environmental stakeholders, such as government, will be necessary. To cope with these challenges, companies will find that many new activities are necessary.[49]

1. They must prepare several scenarios of potential futures, and strategies for coping with the most probable scenarios.
2. They must prepare contingency strategies for the most volatile of situations when chosen strategies might be left behind if the situation changes.
3. They must formulate strategies for coping with strategic discontinuities, in which competitors leapfrog a firm's product or service capabilities.
4. They must remain extremely flexible, preparing for most eventualities.
5. They must focus on the customer, and what the firm can do best for that customer.
6. They must emphasize resource-based strategies, in which the firm builds upon its strengths, and works to mitigate its weaknesses.
7. They must recognize the importance of **strategic thinking,** that is, examining the forecasted situation and formulating strategies for that situation. The thinking through is what is important, not the actual strategies themselves. Why? Because the situation and strategies to face it will change. What's critical is awareness of what's important and what's not.[50]

8. They must focus on **strategic imperatives,** strategies that must be followed in the 1990s. Among these are innovation and quality. The success of any SBU's business strategy rests upon the firm's ability to do one or both of two things: to differentiate its products or services in the market from those of its competitors and/or to be a relative low cost provider.[51] To carry out these two strategies requires innovation, according to Michael Porter, the leading U.S. expert on strategy.[52] Other experts also attribute future success to innovation.[53] Furthermore, no product or service can succeed in the future without comparatively high levels of quality.[54] Other strategic imperatives include speed, flexibility, and continuous improvement. Chapter 5 discusses these and other strategic imperatives in more detail.

STRATEGY FORMULATION: A GLOBAL PERSPECTIVE

Of the ten strategic challenges, the one that may be most significant is the globalization of business. The world is fast becoming a global business community. Technology enables us to monitor events instantaneously in countries around the globe. Due to any number of circumstances, especially the desire to increase profits in the face of slowly growing or stagnant domestic markets, firms are entering foreign markets at a record pace. According to a 1989 survey conducted by the consulting firm of A. T. Kearney, Inc., 30 percent of U.S. manufacturers report that three of their top five competitors are foreign. Almost 45 percent project that three in five competitors will be foreign in 1992. An A. T. Kearney survey in 1984 found that only 5 percent of these same firms faced foreign firms among their top five competitors.[55]

AT BOEING

Even Boeing, although it controls 54 percent of its industry's market, is feeling intense global competition. Airbus, the European consortium, is taking market share, and before long the Japanese may enter the airplane manufacturing industry.

We know all too well the success stories of foreign firms (mostly Japanese firms) in U.S. markets such as textiles, steel, automobiles, consumer electronics, and more recently laptop computers and computer chips. With Europe 1992 moving ahead at a brisk pace, European firms are moving into U.S. and Canadian markets, as U.S. and Canadian firms move into Europe. The economies of the world are becoming interconnected to such a degree that what affects one affects another.

No fact brings this point home quite like this one: *Japan is now the dominant global financial force*, with vast amounts of wealth, accumulated, principally, through its favorable trade balance with the United States.[56] The evidence reveals that Japanese actions in the U.S. stock market caused the October 1987 crash, not program trading, as is commonly believed.[57] The United States is no longer the world's pre-eminent financial power. Grasp that concept. How did Japan become so powerful? It succeeded primarily through a sound strategy, as this chapter's Global Strategic Challenge suggests.

We live in a global market where firms from other countries may dominate. Strategic decisions, often for even the smallest of firms, must be made from a global perspective. Even if a U.S. firm chooses not to enter the markets of other nations, firms from foreign countries will be entering this country. U.S. firms must be prepared to compete with them. We are only now beginning to fully understand how to achieve global competitive advantage, and we've got to learn fast or face the prospect of a significantly lower standard of living.[58] Firms must formulate strategy with a **global perspective** or face the prospect of extinction.

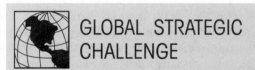

GLOBAL STRATEGIC CHALLENGE

JAPANESE MANAGEMENT AND THE STRATEGIC VIEW

Several factors have contributed to the enormous strides the Japanese have made economically in recent years. Careful examination of the evidence reveals that the following eight factors have contributed especially to this success:

1. Cooperation between government and business. Japan's government steers firms in the proper strategic direction, toward areas in which potential profits appear highest. Tax incentives, subsidies, import quotas and other trade barriers, and research and development funding are used to this end.
2. Cooperation between labor and business. The confrontation that characterizes the interaction of labor and business in the United States is largely absent in Japan.
3. Management style. Employee participation in decision making, recognition of employees' performance and human needs, and employee job security have clearly contributed to Japanese successes. U.S. managers typically give little consideration to these factors, but they are being given increasing emphasis by U.S. firms eager to become more competitive.
4. Management development and education. Japanese managers continually receive training on how to manage, especially with respect to interpersonal relationships. U.S. companies, in contrast, invest relatively little in such endeavors.
5. Strategic management. Japanese managers take the strategic view. Their marketing actions, production actions, and personnel actions reflect a concern for the long-run viability of the firm. They usually stress market share more than profits, for example, believing that, in the long run, market share will lead to profits. This attitude contrasts with U.S. management objectives, which often emphasize short-run results such as

annual profit. Because Japanese managers know their firms will be competitive in ten years and that they will still be employed by these firms, they are willing to sacrifice now for that future success. Japanese strategists focus on knowledge-based strategies, alliance-based strategies, productivity-based strategies, and a combination of strategies aimed at achieving market share.

6. Quality control. Statistical analysis is employed at every stage of the production or service process to measure the quality of inputs, to make certain that the process is operating as it should, and to measure the quality of outputs. A similar emphasis on statistics and quality control was suggested by an American consultant, W. Edwards Deming of Washington, D.C., a prophet not recognized until recently in his own land. The Japanese success story has, however, brought recognition to his work.

7. Kaizen. The Japanese pursue kaizen, or continuous improvement, in every aspect of their organizations. This adds tremendously to the ability to provide newer, better quality products and services at lower cost.

8. Political savvy. In the United States and increasingly in Europe, the Japanese have astutely manipulated the political environment, making some laws favor their interests, making sure that regulations don't hurt them, buying politicians and federal employees, and so on.

The first seven points can be derived from numerous resources. The last part of Point 5 is taken from: Norman P. Smothers, "Patterns of Japanese Strategy: Strategic Combination of Strategies," *Strategic Management Journal*, 1990, pp. 521–533. Point 8 is from Pat Choate, "Political Advantage: Japan's Campaign for America," *Harvard Business Review*, September–October 1990, pp. 87–103.

STRATEGIC MANAGER'S SUMMARY

1. Strategic management encompasses six critical stages:
   a. Mission and goal determination
   b. Strategic objective determination
   c. Strategy formulation
   d. Strategy implementation
   e. Evaluation and control
   f. Organizational policy formulation

2. A firm's purposes form a hierarchy, with vision at the top, followed by mission, goals, and objectives. The hierarchy of strategies includes corporate, business, and functional strategies, with grand strategies focusing on corporate, business, and/or functional areas.

3. Strategists determine internal strengths and weaknesses and match them against external opportunities and threats (SWOT) in determining strategic objectives and formulating strategies. In this work, organizational strategists consider mission and goals, policy, and internal and external environmental factors.

4. The various strategists include: the board of directors, the CEO, coalitions of top managers, top line managers, professional planners, owners, and others.
5. Strategists don't just formulate strategy, they craft it, creating it over time, making adjustments, living with it, developing a feel for it. Strategists often use intuition in formulating strategy, at least partly because the complexity of the strategic situation almost defies rational analysis.
6. Strategists' values, ethics, and social responsibility have a major impact on strategy.
7. The strategic management process and the functions of strategists are changing, principally because the strategic environment is changing. Ten challenges will dominate the strategist's environment in the 1990s.
8. Strategists must take a global perspective to formulate successful strategies.
9. Strategic management is changing in many ways, for example, from a focus on strategic fit to a focus on strategic intent, from a strictly analytical perspective to an analytical perspective that actively uses intuition, and from a static orientation to a dynamic orientation.
10. The strategic imperatives for the 1990s include: innovation, quality, speed, flexibility, and continuous improvement.
11. Strategic intent is an aggressive approach to strategic management, calling for the accomplishment of seemingly impossible goals based on leveraging resources.

KEY TERMS

business strategy
competitive advantage
corporate strategy
crafting strategy
ethics
functional strategy
global perspective
grand strategy
hierarchy of purposes
hierarchy of strategies
leveraging resources
master strategy
mission
multidimensional thinking
organizational strategists
policy
shared values
social responsibility
stakeholders

strategic advantage
strategic business unit (SBU)
strategic control
strategic fit
strategic goals
strategic imperatives
strategic intent
strategic management
strategic management challenges for the 1990s
strategic objectives
strategic planning
strategic thinking
strategies
strategy formulation
strategy implementation
SWOT
three basic strategic questions
values
vision

DISCUSSION QUESTIONS

1. What is the major concern of strategic management? How does strategic management differ from traditional approaches to strategy and policy?
2. Locate two recent issues of *Business Week* and examine the "Corporate Strategies" section of each. Explain how Figures 1.1 and 1.2 apply to the articles' discussions.
3. Apply the strategic management process model to a profit and a nonprofit organization with which you are familiar. What differences do you note? What similarities?
4. Now apply the objective-setting and strategy-formulation model to any organization on which you can gather the information necessary to complete it.
5. Explain the role of mission in the formulation of strategies.

STRATEGIC AUDIT QUESTIONS

At the end of this and subsequent chapters, a list of questions derived from the text material will appear. You may find these questions useful as you examine the cases presented in Part 2. Some of these questions will be answered in the Integrative Case section that follows each chapter. Not every question is answered, nor does every case provide sufficient information to answer all questions. These questions may also be used to analyze a real-life corporate situation in which you are involved.

1. Does the firm have a vision, mission, goals, objectives?
2. Does this organization follow the stages of the strategic management process?
   a. Mission and goal determination
   b. Strategic objective determination
   c. Strategy formulation
   d. Strategy implementation
   e. Strategic control
   f. Organizational policy formulation
3. To what degree does it succeed in following each step?
4. Does the organization pay strict attention to corporate, business, and functional strategies?
5. Who are the strategists in this organization? Are they fulfilling their roles properly?
6. How do their values, skills, and needs influence strategy formulation?
7. How do ethics and social responsibility influence strategy formulation?
8. Do they craft strategy?
9. Do they use intuition and multidimensional thinking?

10. Are they prepared or preparing for the ten strategic challenges? How good are their efforts?
11. Do they leverage resources and focus on strategic intent?
12. Are they using the strategic imperative strategies?

Endnotes

1. For a discussion of some of the problems of strategic management in complex and unstable environments, see the interview with Bell & Howell's chief strategist in "Strategists Confront Planning Challenges: An Interview with Bell & Howell's Ingeborg A. Marquardt," *Journal of Business Strategy*, May/June 1990, pp. 4–8.

2. James M. Higgins, *The Management Challenge* (New York: Macmillan, 1991), pp. 23–27, reviews ten challenges that will affect the practice of management at all levels. Seven of the ten challenges identified in *The Management Challenge* are discussed in this book as having strategic significance. Three additional strategic challenges have also been identified here.

3. These descriptors come principally from Arnoldo C. Hax, "Redefining the Concept of Strategy and the Strategy Formulation Process," *Planning Review*, May/June 1990, pp. 34–41.

4. Kenichi Ohmae, "Getting Back to Strategy," *Harvard Business Review*, November–December 1988, pp. 149–156.

5. "Strategy Content Research," special issue of *Strategic Management Journal*, edited by Cynthia Montgomery, Summer 1988; Anne S. Huff and Rhonda Kay Rezer, "A Review of Strategic Process Research," in *Yearly Review of Management of the Journal of Management*, edited by James G. Hunt and John D. Blair, Summer 1987, pp. 211–236; Liam Fahey and H. Kurt Christensen, "Evaluating the Research on Strategy Content," in *Yearly Review of Management of the Journal of Management*, edited by James G. Hunt and John D. Blair, Summer 1986, pp. 167–284.

6. For a description of the annual planning conference, see William B. Carper and Terry A. Bresnick, *Business Horizons*, September–October 1989, pp. 34–40.

7. For example, see Norman P. Smothers, "Patterns of Japanese Strategy: Strategic Combination of Strategies," *Strategic Management Journal*, November/December 1990, pp. 521–533; Robert Ackelsberg and William C. Harris, "How Danish Companies Plan," *Long Range Planning*, December 1989, pp. 111–116.

8. Author's review of Xerox's strategic plan for 1991.

9. Major relevant studies are reviewed in Deepak K. Sinha, "The Contribution of Formal Planning to Decisions," *Strategic Management Journal*, September/October 1990, pp. 479–492; David M. Reid, "Where Planning Fails in Practice," *Long Range Planning*, April 1990, pp. 85–93; Charles B. Shrader, Charles Mulford, and Virginia L. Blackburn, "Strategic and Operational Planning, Uncertainty, and Performance in Small Firms," *Journal of Small Business Management*, October 1989, pp. 45–60; John A. Pearce II, D. Keith Robbins, and Richard B. Robinson, Jr., "The Impact of Grand Strategy and Planning Formality on Financial Performance," *Strategic Management Journal*, March/April 1987, pp. 125–134; Gordon E. Greenley, "Does Strategic Planning Improve Company Performance?" *Long Range Planning* April (1986), pp. 101–109; L. C. Rhyne, "The Relationship of Strategic Planning to Financial Performance," *Strategic Management Journal*, September/October 1986, pp. 423–436; Jeffrey S. Bracker and John W. Pearson, "Planning and Financial Performance of Small, Mature Firms," *Strategic Management Journal*, November/December 1986, pp. 503–522; Charles B. Shrader, Lew Taylor, and Dan R. Dalton, "Strategic Planning and Organizational Performance: A Critical Appraisal," *Journal of Management*, Summer 1984, pp. 149–171.

10. For a critique of this strategic management process and its realization in the firm, see Henry Mintzberg, "The Design School: Reconsidering the Basic Premises of Strategic Management," *Strategic Management Journal*, March/April 1990, pp. 171–195.

11. Gary Hamel and C. K. Prahalad, "Strategic Intent," *Harvard Business Review*, May–June 1989, pp. 63–76.

12. Hamel and Prahalad, "Strategic Intent," pp. 64 and 65.

13. James A. Belohlav and Karen Giddens-Ering, "Selecting a Master Strategy," *Journal of Business Strategy*, Winter 1987, pp. 76–82.

14. Peter Drucker, "How to Be Competitive though Big," *The Wall Street Journal*, February 7, 1991, p. A12.

15. John W. Verity, Thane Peterson, Deidre Depke, and Evan I. Schwartz, "The New IBM," *Business Week*, December 16, 1991, pp. 112–118.

16. Henry Mintzberg, "Crafting Strategy," *Harvard Business Review*, July–August 1987, pp. 66–75.

17. Andrew Campbell, "Brief Case: Strategy and Intuition—A Conversation with Henry Mintzberg," *Strategic Management Journal*, January/February 1991, pp. 108–110; Henry Mintzberg, "Planning on the Left Side, Managing on the Right," *Harvard Business Review*, July–August 1976, pp. 49–58.

18. Weston Agor, "The Logic of Intuition: How Top Executives Make Important Decisions," *Organizational Dynamics*, Winter 1986, pp. 5–18.

19. For example, see Robert Lawrence Kuhn, "How Strategic Management Builds Company Value," *Journal of*

Business Strategy, November/December 1989, pp. 57–59.

20. Mary Jean Parson with Matthew J. Culligan, *Back to Basics: Planning* (New York: Facts on File, 1985), p. 8.

21. F. A. Maljers, "Strategic Planning and Intuition in Unilever," *Long Range Planning*, April 1990, pp. 63–68.

22. Dina Ingber, "Inside the Executive Mind," *Success*, January 1984, pp. 33–37; Daniel Coleman, "Successful Executives Rely on Own Kind of Intelligence," *New York Times*, July 13, 1984, pp. C1, C2. These articles report on the research of Dr. Siegfried Streufert of Pennsylvania State College of Medicine on the decision processes of executives.

23. For a partial discussion of the impact of values on strategy formulation, see Warren Keith Schilit, "What's the Logic of Strategy Planning?" *Management Review*, November 1988, pp. 41–43.

24. "Holiday Inns Sets Its First Hotel-Casino, Prompting Clymer to Resign as President," *The Wall Street Journal*, October 2, 1978, p. 16.

25. Peter Dye is known for his dramatic use of water and sand in combination with wood retainers. Among his courses are the Campo de Campo in the Dominican Republic; Amelia Island in Jacksonville, Florida; Oak Tee in Edmond, Oklahoma; and Harbor Town on Hilton Head Island, South Carolina.

26. S. Graham, "I Think that I Shall Never See a Greeting Card Lovely as a Tree," *The Wall Street Journal*, September 3, 1980, p. 29.

27. Danny Miller, "Towards a Contingency Theory of Strategy Formulation," *Academy of Management Proceedings*, 1975, pp. 64–66.

28. Robert Guenther and Richard E. Rustin, "Citicorp Lifts Reserves $1 Billion for Quarterly Loss, Picks President," *The Wall Street Journal*, January 17, 1990, p. A3; Robert Guenther, "Global Reach: Citicorp Strives to Be McDonald's and Coke of Consumer Banking," *The Wall Street Journal*, August 9, 1989, pp. A1, A6.

29. Adapted from Archie Carroll, "A Three-Dimensional Conceptual Model of Corporate Performance," *Academy of Management Review*, October 1979, pp. 499–500; and William C. Frederick, Keith Davis, and James E. Post, *Business and Society: Corporate Strategy, Public Policy, Ethics*, 6th ed. (New York: McGraw-Hill, 1988), p. 36.

30. Donald P. Robin and Eric Reidenbach, "Balancing Corporate Profits and Ethics: A Matrix Approach," *Business*, October/December 1990, pp. 11–15.

31. Milton Friedman is the chief proponent of the profit orientation. See Milton Friedman, *Capitalism and Freedom* (Chicago: University of Chicago Press, 1962), p. 133. The stakeholder perspective is described in R. Edward Freeman and David Reed, "Stockholders and Stakeholders: A New Perspective on Corporate Government," *California Management Review*, Spring 1983, pp. 88–106. The corporate power, corporate social responsibility (or obligation) perspective is

spelled out in Frederick et al., *Business and Society*, p. 36.

32. Carroll, "Model of Corporate Performance."

33. Higgins, *Management Challenge*. For another set of challenges, several of which encompass at least parts of these ten challenges, see Fred G. Steingraber, "Managing in the 1990s," *Business Horizons*, January/February 1990, pp. 50–61. For additional discussion of impending challenges, several of which overlap with those noted in the above materials, see Brian Dumaine, "What the Leaders of Tomorrow See," *Fortune*, July 1989, pp. 48–62; Thomas J. Peters, *Thriving on Chaos: Handbook of a Management Revolution* (New York: Knopf, 1987); John Naisbitt and Patricia Auberdene, *Megatrends 2000* (New York: William Morrow, 1990); and Ronald Henkoff, "How to Plan for 1995," *Fortune*, December 31, 1990, pp. 70–78.

34. Alvin Toffler, *Future Shock* (New York: Bantam, 1970), Chapter 1.

35. Michael Naylor, Executive Vice President for Strategic Planning for General Motors, speech to the Academy of Management, Chicago, August 12, 1986.

36. Steingraber, "Managing in the 1990s," p. 50.

37. Peters, *Thriving on Chaos*.

38. Theodore Levitt, Editorial in *Harvard Business Review*, January–February 1988, p. 4.

39. Steingraber, "Managing in the 1990s," p. 50.

40. For a discussion of the issues, see R. Roosevelt Thomas, Jr., "From Affirmative Action to Affirming Diversity," *Harvard Business Review*, March–April 1990, pp. 107–117.

41. For a review of the demographics, see "Needed: Human Capital," *Business Week*, September 19, 1988, pp. 102–103; William B. Johnston and Arnold H. Packer, *Workforce 2000: Work and Workers for the 21st Century* (Indianapolis: Hudson Institute, 1987).

42. "Needed: Human Capital."

43. For a discussion of European labor shortages, see Charles R. Day, Jr., "The West: In the Single Market, Imports Might Include Personnel," *Industry Week*, February 5, 1990, pp. 19–22.

44. Ikujiro Nonaka, "The Knowledge Creating Company," *Harvard Business Review*, November–December 1991, pp. 96–109.

45. Alan Farnham, "The S&L Felons," *Fortune*, November 5, 1990, pp. 90–100.

46. Edward H. Gramlich, "U.S. Federal Budget Deficits and Gramm-Rudman-Hollings," *American Economic Review*, May 1990, pp. 75–80.

47. Charles W. L. Hill, Michael A. Hitt, and Robert E. Hoskisson, "Declining U.S. Competitiveness: Reflections on a Crisis," *Academy of Management Executive*, January 1988, pp. 51–60.

48. Robert T. Green and Trina A. Larson, "Only Retaliation Will Open Up Japan," *Harvard Business Review*, November–December 1987, pp. 22–28.

49. Manuel Werner, "Planning for Uncertain Futures: Building Commitment through Scenario Planning,"

Business Horizons, May/June 1990, pp. 55–58; Henry H. Beam, "Strategic Discontinuities: When Being Good May Not Be Enough," *Business Horizons*, July/August 1990, pp. 10–14; Timo Santalainen and James M. Higgins, "Resource-Based Strategies," unpublished paper; David Ulrich and Margarethe F. Wiersema, "Gaining Strategic and Organizational Capability in a Turbulent Business Environment," *Academy of Management Executive*, May 1989, pp. 115–122.

50. Donald R. Schmincke, "Strategic Thinking: A Perspective for Success," *Management Review*, August 1990, pp. 16–19.

51. Adapted from Michael Porter, *Competitive Strategy* (New York: Free Press, 1980); and William K. Hall, "Survival Strategies in a Hostile Environment," *Harvard Business Review*, September–October 1980, pp. 73–86.

52. Porter, *Competitive Strategy*, pp. 177–178.

53. Also see Brian Dumaine, "Closing the Innovation Gap," *Fortune*, December 2, 1991, pp. 56–62; Tom Peters, "Get Innovative or Get Dead," *California Management Review*, Part I, Fall 1990, pp. 9–26, and Part II, Winter 1991, pp. 9–23.

54. "The Quality Imperative," special issue, *Business Week*, October 25, 1991.

55. Steingraber, "Managing in the 1990s," p. 50.

56. R. Taggart Murphy, "Power without Purpose: The Crisis of Japan's Global Financial Dominance," *Harvard Business Review*, March–April 1989, pp. 71–94.

57. Ibid.

58. Michael Porter, "The Competitive Advantage of Nations," *Harvard Business Review*, March–April 1990, pp. 73–93.

INTRODUCTION TO THE INTEGRATIVE CASE

To show how to apply the concepts of strategic management, each chapter features a brief analysis of an integrative case that discusses the concepts in that chapter in the context of their application or misapplication in the company discussed in the case. (The integrative case follows this brief introduction and will be discussed after all but the last of the chapters that follow.) Examining the integrative case chapter by chapter should prove to be helpful when you begin to study the cases in Part 2 of this book, and it will help you to understand the concepts presented in each chapter. Our concern is that you see a practical application of the concepts. While many examples are provided in the body of each chapter and in the Strategic Challenge features, your understanding of how all of the strategic concepts work together will be enhanced if you see how they affect one organization. Through this integrative case you will gain a consistent perspective on the formulation, implementation, and control of strategy.

We have chosen to concentrate on the General Motors Corporation in the integrative case for the following reasons:

1. It is probably the best-known firm in the world.
2. It is confronted with serious strategic problems.
3. It is a multiple-business firm with global operations, and these factors have significant effects on its strategies.
4. At the same time, GM has one primary business, manufacturing automobiles; since most of its business organizations are single-business enterprises, examination of GM enables you to understand the classic single-business organization while studying a multiple-business firm.
5. The decline of GM, Ford, and Chrysler has had serious impacts on the U.S. economy.

Now read the integrative case that follows for a general understanding of strategy with respect to the terms to which Chapter 1 has introduced you, including strategic management, vision, mission, goals, objectives, strategy, grand strategy, corporate strategy, business strategy, and functional strategy. Pick out examples of each as you go along. As later chapters refer back to this case in Integrative Case Analysis sections, you may want to reread this case or parts of it to make sure you fully understand how the various aspects of strategic management discussed in that chapter are applied or misapplied by General Motors. Use the strategic audit questions in each chapter as you examine the integrative case and later, as you examine other cases. Appendix 1 at the end of the text section of this book contains a detailed outline of how to use cases, how to prepare cases, and a sample case preparation. You should read Appendix 1 after you read the integrative case.

Following the integrative case you will find an example of how the integrative case will be handled in succeeding chapters in this chapter's Integrative Case Analysis. In addition to the integrative case, a note about the auto industry appears at the end of Chapter 4. This provides more information that will help you analyze General Motors' strategic position within its industry. This industry note will be analyzed to show you how to use the industry information that appears with cases in Part 2 of this book.

INTEGRATIVE CASE

THE STRATEGIC CHALLENGES FACING GENERAL MOTORS IN 1992

On April 6, 1992 General Motors' board of directors demoted President Lloyd E. Reuss and replaced him with John F. "Jack" Smith, Jr. William Hoglund was appointed chief financial officer replacing demoted Robert O'Connell, whose rosy forecasts angered the board when they failed to materialize. Historically, top executives in such circumstances at GM had received lateral moves rather than demotions. The board also relieved CEO and Chairman Robert C. Stempel as head of the board's executive committee. These actions signaled quite clearly to everyone that GM could no longer afford to do business as usual. "With the plant-closing announcements, we shook up the troops," observes Robert L. Dorn, chief engineer of GM's Cadillac division. Edward V. Regan, who as New York state's comptroller controls a large block of GM stock asserts, "With this, we shook up the generals."[1]

Stempel's basic strategy for turnaround was acceptable to the board, but his and Reuss' timetable to accomplish it was not. The board wanted action now, not next year, and Reuss had failed to turn around the troubled North American auto operation. When Stempel unveiled plans to reorganize General Motors on February 24, 1992, he indicated that it might take over a year to accomplish the task. Smith, after assuming the role of president, suggested he would have it completed by May 1, 1992—not 1993.[2] Stempel had been criticized by several board members for his go-slow approach. Now it was clear that he would be forced to act more quickly or lose the chance to act at all. It was also clear that Smith now wielded a big stick at GM. The board was counting on his turning around the North American operation as he had GM–Europe.

1991 had not been a good year for GM, nor for Stempel. General Motors had lost $4.5 billion in 1991, $3.0 billion on operations and a $1.5-billion one-time charge for restructuring. This amount was the single largest operating loss ever by any corporation, and it followed on the heels of an annual loss of $2 billion for 1990. (See Exhibits 1.1 and 1.2.)

GM's losses would have been even worse. Profits of $2.1 billion from auto sales overseas, principally in Europe, and profits of $2.5 billion from three electronics and finance subsidiaries had helped offset a $7.5-billion loss in North American auto operations, headed by Reuss. Stempel and GM's stockholders could take little consolation in the fact that Ford had lost $2.2 billion and Chrysler $785 million in 1991. The big three U.S. automakers had just suffered the most serious combined losses in a single year ever.

At a press conference February 24, 1992 Stempel had announced the most sweeping change in GM's organization structure in 8 years, much of which eliminated or revised the largely inefficient structural changes put into place in 1984 by Stempel's predecessor, Roger Smith. Stempel also identified 12 of the 21 plants GM had announced on December 18, 1991 it would close by 1995.[3]

The December 1991 decision had been agonizing, resulting from many hours of deliberation with corporate leaders and the board of directors. Closing these 21 plants followed shutdowns of 23 plants since 1987 and would result in unemployment for 74,000 employees.[4]

Despite the challenges facing GM, Stempel had believed the company could be turned around, at least partly because of actions he had taken since becoming chairman, and partly because of actions he would take in the near term and over longer periods, in order to restore General Motors to profitability and strategic viability. The road to recovery would not be an easy

EXHIBIT 1.1 General Motors Statement of Consolidated Income ($millions except per-share amounts)

	Years Ended December 31,		
	1991	**1990**	**1989**
Net Sales and Revenues			
Manufactured products	$105,025.9	$107,477.0	$109,610.3
Financial services	11,061.1	11,756.3	11,216.9
Computer systems services	3,666.3	2,787.5	2,384.6
Other income	3,302.7	2,684.3	3,720.1
Total net sales and revenues	123,056.0	124,705.1	126,931.9
Costs and Expenses			
Cost of sales and other operating charges, exclusive of items listed below	97,550.7	96,155.7	93,817.9
Selling, general, and administrative expenses	10,817.4	10,030.9	9,447.9
Interest expense	8,296.6	8,771.7	8,757.2
Depreciation of real estate, plants, and equipment	5,684.9	5,104.1	5,157.8
Amortization of special tools	1,819.5	1,805.8	1,441.8
Amortization of intangible assets	411.4	451.7	568.6
Other deductions	1,547.0	1,288.3	1,342.4
Special provision for scheduled plant closings and other restructurings	2,820.8	3,314.0	—
Total costs and expenses	128,948.3	126,922.2	120,533.6
Income (Loss) before Income Taxes	(5,892.3)	(2,217.1)	6,398.3
United States, foreign, and other income taxes (credit)	(900.3)	(231.4)	2,174.0
Income (Loss) before cumulative effect of accounting changes	(4,992.0)	(1,985.7)	4,224.3
Cumulative effect of accounting changes	539.2	—	—
Net income (loss)	(4,452.8)	(1,985.7)	4,224.3
Dividends and accumulation of redemption value on preferred and preference stocks	70.4	38.2	34.2
Earnings (loss) on common stocks	(4,523.2)	(2,023.9)	4,190.1
Earnings (Loss) Attributable to Common Stocks			
$1⅔ par value before cumulative effect of accounting changes	(5,384.6)	(2,378.3)	3,831.0
Cumulative effect of accounting changes	533.2	—	—
Net earnings (loss) attributable to $1⅔ par value	(4,851.4)	(2,378.3)	3,831.0
Class E before cumulative effect of accounting change	229.7	194.4	171.0
Cumulative effect of accounting change	(6.1)	—	—
Net earnings attributable to Class E	223.6	194.4	171.0
Class H before cumulative effect of accounting changes	92.5	160.0	188.1
Cumulative effect of accounting changes	12.1	—	—
Net earnings attributable to Class H	104.6	160.0	188.1
Average number of shares of common stocks outstanding (in millions)			
$1⅔ par value	614.6	601.5	604.3
Class E	195.3	187.1	189.1
Class H	73.7	88.1	95.7
Earnings (Loss) Per Share Attributable to Common Stocks			
$1⅔ par value before cumulative effect of accounting changes	($8.85)	($4.09)	$6.33
Cumulative effect of accounting changes	0.88	—	—
Net earnings (loss) attributable to $1⅔ par value	(7.97)	(4.09)	6.33
Class E before cumulative effect of accounting change	1.17	1.04	0.90
Cumulative effect of accounting change	(0.03)	—	—
Net earnings attributable to Class E	1.14	1.04	0.90
Class H before cumulative effect of accounting changes	1.26	1.82	1.94
Cumulative effect of accounting changes	0.13	—	—
Net earnings attributable to class H	1.39	1.82	1.94

Source: General Motors, *Annual Report*, 1991.

EXHIBIT 1.2 General Motors Consolidated Balance Sheet ($millions except per-share amounts)

	December 31,	
Assets	**1991**	**1990**
Cash and cash equivalents	$ 4,281.9	$ 3,688.5
Other marketable securities	5,910.5	4,132.9
Total cash and marketable securities	10,192.4	7,821.4
Finance receivables—net	81,373.8	90,116.2
Accounts and notes receivable (less allowances)	6,498.5	5,731.3
Inventories (less allowances)	10,066.0	9,331.3
Contracts in process (less advances and progress payments of $2,500.9 and $2,353.1)	2,283.1	2,348.8
Net equipment on operating leases (less accumulated depreciation of $3,246.6 and $2,692.6)	8,186.6	5,882.0
Prepaid expenses, deferred income taxes, and other deferred charges	11,212.5	4,721.6
Other investments and miscellaneous assets (less allowances)	7,505.7	7,252.5
Property		
Real estate, plants, and equipment—at cost	68,431.6	67,219.4
Less accumulated depreciation	40,025.4	38,280.8
Net real estate, plants, and equipment	28,406.2	28,938.6
Special tools—at cost (less amortization)	8,419.5	7,206.4
Total property	36,825.7	36,145.0
Intangible assets—at cost (less amortization)	10,181.2	10,886.4
Total assets	$184,325.5	$180,236.5
Liabilities and Stockholders' Equity		
Liabilities		
Accounts payable (principally trade)	$ 10,061.3	$ 8,824.4
Notes and loans payable	94,022.1	95,633.5
Unites States, foreign, and other income taxes—deferred and payable	4,491.2	3,959.6
Other liabilities	45,602.2	38,255.2
Deferred credits (including investment tax credits—$644.5 and $723.0)	1,531.5	1,410.1
Total liabilities	155,708.3	148,082.8
Stocks Subject to Repurchase	1,289.6	2,106.3
Stockholders' Equity		
Preferred stocks ($5.00 series, $153.0; $3.75 series, $81.4)	234.4	234.4
Preference stocks (E $0.10 series, $1.0; Series A Conversion, $1.8 in 1991; Series B $9\frac{1}{8}$% Depository Shares, $1.1 in 1991)	3.9	1.0
Common stocks		
$1\frac{2}{3}$ par value (issued, 620,967,021 and 605,592,356 shares)	1,034.9	1,009.3
Class E (issued, 103,833,719 and 100,220,967 shares)	10.4	10.0
Class H (issued, 37,691,027 and 34,450,398 shares)	3.8	3.5
Capital surplus (principally additional paid-in capital)	4,710.4	2,208.2
Net income retained for use in the business	21,525.2	27,148.6
Subtotal	27,523.0	30,615.0
Minimum pension liability adjustment	(936.8)	(1,004.7)
Accumulated foreign currency translation and other adjustments	741.4	437.1
Total stockholders' equity	27,327.6	30,047.4
Total liabilities and stockholders' equity	$184,325.5	$180,236.5

Source: General Motors, *Annual Report,* 1991.

one, however, and he saw no hope of government intervention to prevent what appeared to many to be the inevitable slide of the U.S. auto market into the hands of the Japanese.

With Harold A. Poling, chairman of Ford, and Lee Iacocca, chairman of Chrysler, Stempel had frequently visited Washington, D.C. during 1991 trying to garner support for voluntary restraint agreements to limit the market share of Japanese auto companies. These three CEOs and several other major business leaders had accompanied President Bush to Japan in January 1992. However, this visit had resulted in very little real progress toward Japanese cooperation in reducing its auto and auto parts sales in the United States and encouraging sales of U.S. autos and auto parts in Japan. Vague promises, soon discounted by Japanese officials, were the most visible results. Many saw these promises as just another Japanese tactic, with little chance that they would deliver on their promises. Bush had hoped to reduce the sizeable trade deficit between the two countries, and keep the United States from losing any more jobs to the Japanese, which, during an election-year recession, was obviously an important campaign issue. While a lot of Japan bashing and U.S. bashing had occurred after the trip, it was not clear if the trip's apparent failure would produce any U.S. government intervention.[5]

Stempel knew that he had a major series of tasks facing him, but he believed in his company, and in the strategies that he, his staff, and the board had formulated, and were still formulating. John Smith would also now play a major role in the process. In addition to restoring the firm to profitability, Stempel and Smith had to make certain that it would be well-positioned to cope with a number of strategic challenges that had been identified:

Internal Challenges[6]

1. A Chevrolet-Pontiac-Canada car division that was losing almost $5 billion a year, with little hope of profits before 1995
2. A reliance on GM Europe, and to some extent the Electronic Data Systems, Hughes Aircraft Company, and GMAC subsidiaries, for profit contributions
3. The most expensive cost structure of any major car seller in the United States (GM was an astounding 40 percent less efficient than Ford, for example.)
4. An inability to perform flexible manufacturing, that is, to produce more than one kind or model of car per plant
5. A negative image in the minds of many potential customers. A J. D. Power survey, for example, revealed that 42 percent of those surveyed would not even consider buying a General Motors automobile
6. A series of new products that had been less successful than hoped
7. The Saturn subsidiary that would be a drain on profits for several years at projected sales levels
8. A work force, including blue-collar, white-collar, and executive personnel, that had been demoralized by cutbacks, bonus eliminations, and uncertainty
9. A lack of accountability for performance among white-collar workers
10. Too many divisions and overlapping markets (Oldsmobile overlapped heavily with Buick, losing half of its market share, from 10.9 percent in 1980 to 5.2 percent in 1991.)
11. An extremely slow product-design process, even by Detroit's standards

External Challenges

1. A global recession of uncertain depth and duration
2. Intense competition in the North American market, especially from the Japanese automakers

(They had eight plants in the United States and more are on the way. Combined sales of Japanese cars accounted for 31 percent of the U.S. market in 1991.[7])

3. The Japanese government–business alliance that all but excluded most U.S. auto products from Japan
4. A U.S. president and Congress who were unwilling to impose trade barriers to oppose the slow, but sure Japanese progress toward domination of the U.S. auto market
5. Increased levels of competition in Europe, as unification in 1992 rapidly approached
6. A glut of nearly new rental cars being dumped on the market each year[8]
7. A union that balked at every concession and went on strike over work-rule changes aimed at making the company more efficient

Further, Stempel and Smith had to achieve results quickly. With Smith as president, swift action was more likely to be taken than when Reuss had been president.

HISTORY OF THE FIRM

In 1908 two events occurred that would profoundly affect the history of the automobile industry and perhaps even the world. Henry Ford announced the development of the Model T and William C. Durant formed General Motors Company, which would eventually become General Motors Corporation. Durant, while a creative genius, was not much of an administrator. He departed the firm in 1920 after two successful years in 1918 and 1919, leaving it in management disarray. During this period Alfred P. Sloan, who eventually would serve as chief executive officer of General Motors for 23 years and chairman from 1937 to 1956, became a prominent force in the organization. He suggested that a large organization cannot be run in the same way as a small one, instead advocating a new system of management for such an organization. In a 1921 report, Sloan recommended that GM adopt a decentralized form of management in which each of the car companies would be run independently, yet with the guidance of the overall corporation. In 1921, he sat on the committee that formulated the now-famous General Motors product policy that positioned cars in each of several overlapping price areas from the lowest to the highest. This strategy allowed individuals, as they progressed economically, to move up in General Motors cars from a Chevy to a Pontiac to an Olds to a Buick and finally to a Cadillac.[9]

In 1923, Pierre S. DuPont resigned as president of General Motors and Alfred P. Sloan succeeded him. During his early years in the presidency, Sloan encouraged the use of committees, developed financial controls, formulated policies, developed an effective incentive compensation plan, and generally changed the way in which major corporations were managed.

After Sloan stepped down in 1946, his influence remained for another quarter of a century, as most of the strategies, policies and procedures, organization structures, and programs he instituted remained in force. General Motors prospered to become the largest corporation (as measured by sales) in the world. At one time it held 60 percent of the domestic automobile market. Fearing U.S. government antitrust action, it created a complicated, interdependent plant and auto division structure, with plants producing parts and assemblies for more than one division. This made it virtually impossible to break up the company, but it also proved later to reduce efficiency and market response capabilities in the 1980s and 1990s. GM's world changed drastically in 1973, when the Arab nations embargoed their oil. To GM's credit, it acted quickly to reduce the sizes of its cars to meet the demand for fuel economy. These efforts to meet the challenges of a rapidly changing environment ultimately led to awareness of the need for a major change in the company's corporate strategy.[10]

Strategy for the 1980s

In 1979, Chairman Thomas A. Murphy and President Elliott M. Estes masterminded a strategy to prepare GM to realize its ambitions. In 1979 the company was selling almost half of the cars sold in the United States; it had $65 billion in sales and $3.5 billion in profits. Their strategic plan was based on the following assumptions:

1. Gasoline prices would continue to rise.
2. Fuel would continue to be scarce.
3. Therefore, consumers would be shopping for smaller cars.
4. High technology was the way to achieve the high levels of efficiency necessary to compete in the market they foresaw.[11]

This plan was to be carried out by Roger Smith, who became GM's tenth chairman on January 1, 1981. The plan's details were relatively straightforward:

1. Every factory would be redesigned to produce the new, smaller cars at an estimated cost of $40 billion, 14 times Ford Motor Company's pretax earnings at that time. (This redesign eventually cost $77 billion and was still not completed.)
2. State-of-the-art, high technology, fuel-saving, small, front-wheel-drive cars would be the firm's mainstay products.
3. Quality vehicles, the world's best, would be produced.
4. High technology would be employed throughout all manufacturing, research, and design areas.
5. High volume plus high technology would allow the firm to make cars more cheaply than anyone else.

Murphy and Estes based their plan on the belief that by exploiting their brute financial strength, they could squeeze their domestic competitors out of the market and stop the inroads of Japanese car producers by producing the cheapest cars. They felt they had the staying power to outlast their foreign competition, and they were certain they could outlast both Ford and Chrysler, which were experiencing serious financial difficulties. By the time Smith took over in 1981, General Motors appeared to be much stronger than either Ford or Chrysler, despite a loss of $762 million in 1980, the company's first loss since 1921. Chrysler was barely surviving on federal life support in the form of loan guarantees and Ford was in the middle of three straight years of losses, which eventually totaled $3.3 billion.

Smith believed, as Murphy and Estes had believed before him, that technology was the key to the future. To provide this technology, the company sought to diversify, not only to yield additional sources of revenue, but also to generate revenue unrelated to the cycles in the automobile industry that would even out cash flows. Primarily, though, the acquisitions were motivated by automobile strategy. General Motors wanted the technology not only for the automobile products themselves, but for the manufacturing processes, as well. Much of its acquisition strategy was aimed at improving robotics, machine vision, computer use, and related electronic technology designed to improve its manufacturing.

The two most important acquisitions were Electronic Data Systems (EDS) and Hughes Aircraft. EDS was absorbed into the GM structure more thoroughly than Hughes, which remained largely independent. Bickering between Smith and EDS founder and CEO Ross Perot led to a $743 million buyout of Perot's stock. Perot had been especially critical of Smith and GM's "fat."[12]

Smith not only embraced the strategy designed by Murphy and Estes, but went beyond it. Seeing technology as the key to the future of the automobile industry, Smith never made an acquisition that did not coincide with that vision.[13] He also recognized a need to learn from others. If the Japanese were such good managers, why not learn how they managed? He formed a joint venture with Toyota called New United Motor Manufacturing, Inc. (NUMMI) to build Chevy Novas in the company's plant in Fremont, California, which had been notorious for its poor performance. Worker relations there had typically been very difficult, but that situation turned around quickly. Within a matter of months after the adoption of the Japanese management style, the plant became GM's most efficient and it produced better-quality cars than any other plant in the GM system.[14]

Smith also determined that if the company was to be competitive at the low end of the market, it had to develop a new car with a new system based on the Japanese management model. This car was the Saturn. GM announced in 1983 that the project would be carried out in Tennessee.

Roger Smith's Reorganization

Smith also believed that this strategy would require downsizing and reorganizing the company. To him the company seemed to have become a bureaucracy in need of surgery. His initial downsizing efforts were less drastic than those of some other corporations, but later, much more substantial restructurings led to a much leaner and meaner look. From 1987 through 1990, the firm eliminated 23 plants and cut over 100,000 people from its North American car operations, including 40,000 middle managers and staff.[15]

Besides cutting people and positions, in 1984 Smith created two supergroups of car companies—Chevrolet-Pontiac-Canada (CPC) and Buick-Oldsmobile-Cadillac (BOC). This move was intended to improve accountability and to get R&D back to an improved market orientation. Both seem like good reasons and the strategy seemed appropriate, but mass confusion resulted as 200,000 reporting relationships were changed and relations built over 50 years fell apart overnight. These disruptions still plague the company. Also, because the work could not be parcelled out as effectively as planned, both groups ended up making cars for all five U.S. divisions. Ironically, each supergroup adopted its own structural style. BOC is highly decentralized. CPC is highly centralized. The complex arrangement at CPC has slowed designs and left the overall R&D function's market orientation problem largely unresolved.[16] The structure just prior to the February 1992 reorganization is shown later in Exhibit 1.4.

The Saturn Project[17]

A focus group participant summed up the challenge facing General Motors to regain customers by creating a new car, the Saturn. When he found out that the car they were discussing was not an import, but a new car from GM, he paused for a moment and said, "O.K., I'll give you guys one more chance." Richard G. LeFauve, president of Saturn Corporation, remembers that statement vividly. "That 'give you one more chance,' burned into my brain. This is really what it's all about."[18]

The Saturn project was conceived in 1982 and announced in 1983 as a revolution in automobile manufacturing. The Saturn plant, built in Spring Hill, Tennessee, was to be a completely computerized facility. Human labor was to be minimal. The announced $5-billion plant was seen as a way to eliminate the $2,000 to $2,500 cost gap between General Motors' cars and Japanese imports in 1983. Both insiders and outsiders viewed the Saturn project as the culmination of GM's attempts to integrate technology and computers, both in the car itself and in the manufacturing process.

GM broke ground for the complex on April 8, 1986, but did not roll out the first car until late summer 1990, more than two years after originally scheduled and eight years after conception. Part of the delay occurred because, as the project began to take shape, market changes triggered concern about its viability. Observers suggest that the introduction of the Hyundai and other very cheap imports may have rendered the Saturn concept obsolete. The Japanese cars against which Saturn was originally intended to compete were no longer the lowest-priced cars, but competed at the low end of the medium-priced range. Consequently, Saturn ended up being a compact car, not a subcompact as originally intended. Furthermore, the plant was downsized from the original capacity of 500,000 units per year to 240,000 units per year. Total project investment was also reduced from $5 billion to $3.5 billion.

Furthermore, experience with robots and other technology throughout GM, and experience with participative management, especially at the NUMMI plant, taught GM that better management offered a more likely route to improved productivity than better technology. Thus, while the plant uses the latest technology, it uses less of it than had been originally planned. While participative management had always been a part of the plant's management structure, additional participative management arrangements were added. Work teams were formed and a sense of teamwork was spread throughout the plant. This approach seemed to work despite the fact that the plant employs union employees working under a modified contract from phased-out plants around the United States.

Despite concerns about market positioning, aggressive pricing by Saturn executives has brought Saturn into direct competition against Hyundai and Japanese cars at the low end of the medium price range, which had recently been reduced in price. Analysts seem to believe that the Saturn may be able to make substantial inroads against these cars, especially because of Saturn's emphasis on providing quality equal to or better than the Japanese competition, something Hyundai has not done. It is too soon to tell if the Saturn will be a financial success, though it appears to have been a marketing success. Planned production levels will not pay off capital expenditures for plant and equipment ($2 billion) for many years, and some analysts believe that additional expansion may be necessary to pay off the huge investment, $1.5 billion, in research and development costs.

STEMPEL'S AND JOHN SMITH'S STRATEGIES FOR THE 1990s[19]

In some ways, Stempel's strategies repudiate those of Smith. Stempel's main thrust is going after market share by satisfying the customer. Smith seemed to be content to lose market share as long as he could keep profits high. Stempel has sought an open, participative culture. Smith was more authoritarian. Stempel has moved to make the firm more productive. Smith was slow to close plants. Stempel has reorganized, bringing many changes to Smith's 1984 reorganization. Stempel has moved to introduce more new models in 1992 than in any year in GM's history. Also, while Stempel was slow to get started, he has acted quickly once he has seen the need. These few sentences have captured the essence of his strategies: gain market share, improve products, cut costs, improve design, make the structure manageable, make the culture functional. The following pages examine these and related strategies in more detail. At the time of this writing, it is too soon to tell what Jack Smith's strategies will be. However, it is believed Smith will follow Stempel's plans but be much more demanding when it comes to timetables and manager expectations. One major

EXHIBIT 1.3 General Motors Statement of Consolidated Cash Flows ($millions)

	Years Ended December 31,		
	1991	**1990**	**1989**
Cash Flows from Operating Activities			
Income (Loss) before cumulative effect of accounting changes	($ 4,992.0)	($ 1,985.7)	$ 4,224.3
Adjustments to reconcile income (loss) before cumulative effect of accounting changes to net cash provided by operating activities			
Depreciation of real estate, plants, and equipment	3,762.5	3,699.2	3,680.3
Depreciation of equipment on operating leases	1,922.4	1,404.9	1,477.5
Amortization of special tools	1,819.5	1,805.8	1,441.8
Amortization of intangible assets	411.4	451.7	568.6
Amortization of discount and issuance costs on debt issues	194.4	291.7	263.2
Provision for financing losses	947.1	814.5	841.9
Special provision for scheduled plant closings and other restructurings	2,820.8	2,848.0	—
Provision for inventory allowances	40.1	92.2	177.1
Pension expense, net of cash contributions	1,167.7	364.9	810.4
Net gain on sale of GM New York building	(610.3)	—	—
Net gain on sale of partial interest in Isuzu Motors Limited and its affiliates	—	—	(133.5)
Change in other investments, miscellaneous assets, deferred credits, etc.	526.7	246.5	(354.0)
Change in other operating assets and liabilities			
Accounts receivable	(1,067.6)	(285.2)	(856.3)
Inventories	(310.4)	(1,431.8)	(184.5)
Prepaid expenses and other deferred charges	(1,432.5)	(516.5)	273.5
Deferred taxes and income taxes payable	(3,874.9)	(1,711.8)	678.2
Other liabilities*	3,390.4	1,701.9	700.4
Other	1,192.4	(1,008.7)	(603.1)
Net Cash Provided by Operating Activities	5,907.7	6,781.6	13,005.8
Cash Flows from Investing Activities			
Investment in companies, net of cash acquired	(779.1)	(906.9)	(121.3)
Expenditures for real estate, plants, and equipment	(4,343.4)	(4,432.5)	(4,577.3)
Expenditures for special tools	(2,956.8)	(3,155.5)	(2,927.8)
Proceeds from disposals of real estate, plants, and equipment	519.1	416.1	490.6
Proceeds from sale of GM New York building	254.9	—	—
Proceeds from sale/leaseback of capital assets	954.1	—	—
Proceeds from sale of trade receivable	349.3	—	—
Change in other investing assets			
Other marketable securities	(1,777.6)	455.0	(206.8)
Finance receivables—acquisitions	(108,268.4)	(104,609.8)	(100,688.9)
Finance receivables—liquidations (net)	112,643.1	102,429.0	94,957.7
Finance receivables—other	493.7	2,548.6	11.6
Proceeds from sales of finance receivables	2,926.9	1,056.1	—
Notes receivable	(48.8)	1.3	(50.5)
Operating leases—net	(4,227.0)	(2,155.8)	(1,603.5)
Net Cash Used in Investing Activities	(4,260.0)	(8,354.4)	(14,716.2)

EXHIBIT 1.3 Cont'd. General Motors Statement of Consolidated Cash Flows ($millions)

	Years Ended December 31,		
	1991	**1990**	**1989**
Cash Flows from Financing Activities			
Net increase (decrease) in short-term loans payable	(4,670.7)	(2,133.7)	844.7
Increase in long-term debt	15,830.4	14,406.5	14,422.1
Decrease in long-term debt	(12,665.1)	(10,355.8)	(10,235.3)
Redemption of Series H preference stocks	(225.1)	(207.2)	—
Redemption of Howard Hughes Medical Institute put options	(600.0)	—	—
Repurchases of common stocks	(10.4)	(362.3)	(1,655.1)
Proceeds from issuing common and preference stocks	2,506.6	375.7	173.2
Cash dividends paid to stockholders	(1,162.3)	(1,956.5)	(1,964.1)
Net Cash Provided by (Used in) Financing Activities	996.6	233.3	1,585.5
Effect of Exchange Rate Changes on Cash and Cash Equivalents	(57.7)	(130.8)	(50.0)
Net increase (decrease) in cash and cash equivalents	593.4	(1,936.9)	(174.9)
Cash and cash equivalents at beginning of the year	3.688.5	5,625.4	5,800.3
Cash and cash equivalents at end of the year	$ 4,281.9	$ 3,688.5	$ 5,625.4

Source: General Motors, *Annual Report*, 1991.

difference will likely be a willingness on the part of Smith to tackle bloated white-collar bureaucracy—something Stempel had been reluctant to do.

FINANCIAL CONDITION AND DOWNSIZING STRATEGY[20]

General Motors has historically had sufficient internal cash flow to finance virtually any acquisition or other project that it desired. (See Exhibit 1.3 for a recent cash flow analysis.) It paid out some $77 billion worldwide from 1979 to 1990 to finance its 1979 technology-based strategy. It spent $5 billion for Hughes Aircraft and $2.5 billion for EDS. (Ultimately it will pay another $2.5 billion for Hughes in a complicated stock buy-back scheme.) It paid H. Ross Perot $743 million for his silence about GM's weaknesses. It spent $3.5 billion on Saturn. The period 1987 to 1991, however, brought its vulnerability to light, especially its inability to tolerate sustained losses in its North American auto operation and to still retain sufficient cash flow for its projects. GM was forced to cut costs and downsize dramatically and to delay new models. In January 1992, its debt was downgraded by Moody's. Fortunately, the commercial paper issued by its GMAC unit still received a top rating.[21] GM was running lower on cash in 1991 than it had in many years.

From 1987 to 1990, the company cut $13 billion a year from its cost structure, much of it by closing auto plants and eliminating related jobs, and by eliminating some 40,000 white-collar jobs, axing 25 percent of its white-collar work force and saving $2 billion a year. GM scaled down its capital spending, cutting back on its technology strategy to the tune of $4 to $6 billion a year between 1987 and 1990. In fall 1990, it announced another 25-percent reduction in the white-collar work force scheduled to be completed by the end of 1993. This would cut 15,000 jobs in all, starting with 6,000 in 1991. In 1991, the company slashed its dividend by 47 percent, saving $800 million a year in cash for the estimated 5-year length of the cut. It further announced a cut in capital spending of $500 million a year (down to about $7 billion a year) for the period from 1991 to 1994. These slashes later became deeper. Suppliers were to be asked (politely required) to make cutbacks of $2 billion a year by 1993.

The December 18, 1991 Announcement of Plant Closings

Prompted by the board of directors to take decisive action, Stempel announced on December 18, 1991 that GM would be closing 21 more factories, cutting 74,000 more jobs, and slashing capital spending for the next 4 years. These closings, which included a projected elimination of 9,000 white-collar jobs, will bring GM's employment levels to 71,000 white-collar and 250,000 blue-collar employees, approximately half the size of these segments of the work force in 1985.

While critics welcome these cuts, they point out a down side. While previous plant closings have affected largely older, less efficient plants, these closings will shut down several plants that have been extensively updated as part of the $77-billion capital improvement program from 1979 to 1987. GM's announcement pitted some plants against others for survival. In its February 25, 1992 announcement of 12 specific plant closings, GM made it clear that it kept its Arlington, Texas plant open while closing its Ypsilanti, Michigan plant because workers at the Arlington plant had made concessions on work rates and other issues, making it a more financially viable plant. GM was clearly sending a message to the union with this action.[22]

ORGANIZATION STRUCTURE

Exhibit 1.4 shows GM's organization structure prior to April 6, and February 24, 1992 changes. As of April 6, 1992, GM had three major automobile divisions (the two supergroups plus Saturn) and several other divisions under President John Smith, an electronics division under Vice Chairman Robert J. Schultz that included Hughes and EDS, a financial division under Executive Vice President William Hoglund that included GMAC, a parts and defense components division under a yet-to-be-named executive vice president, an international division under a yet-to-be-named vice chairman and a support division under Executive Vice President F. Alan Smith. The company's structure is more streamlined than it was several years ago, yet it is still highly complex. Thousands of middle-management and staff positions have been eliminated, and many more will be eliminated in the future. Aside from the obvious wish to cut costs, the company aims to become more responsive to its markets, especially in the auto division. Still, the existing structure, as noted previously, has numerous problems that hinder design and market orientation.

The February 24, 1992 Reorganization

On February 24, 1992 Stempel announced a sweeping reorganization of the company. Consolidation of overlapping jobs in the various divisions will eliminate 9,000 jobs, including 10 percent of North American staff jobs. The three vehicle engineering and manufacturing groups created in the 1984 reorganization will disappear, to be replaced by a single unit responsible for their activities. Sales and marketing will be separated from manufacturing. However, GM will keep a unit to make engines and transmissions, and another to manufacture components. Consolidation will reduce staffs at the company's Technical Center from five divisions to three. The separate engineering staffs that perform current engineering and advanced engineering for different classes of vehicles will be consolidated, and will report to Mr. Reuss, instead of an executive in charge of nonautomotive units. Staff for functions such as planning, personnel, materials management, public relations, and other activities will also be merged. Finally, GM will merge its staffs for environmental activities and for research. To oversee this change in structure, GM has created a North American Strategy Board composed of President Smith and seven other executives.[23]

Critics like Eugene Jennings, business professor emeritus at Michigan State University's Broad School, feel that this restructuring is insufficient. "Anyone can lop off heads and close plants. The real trick is to organize and manage what you've got left so that it's an improvement. . . . I'm not confident GM even knows what kind of management system—policies and practices—it needs to regain competitiveness." These sentiments are echoed by consultant George Peterson of Auto Pacific Group. "I'm guessing it'll not be enough, and that once done, GM will still be too big."[24] It was this kind of reaction to Stempel's plan that helped usher in Smith as president.

CORPORATE STRATEGIC PLANNING

Ronald M. Pirtle is executive in charge of strategic planning for GM. In the past, GM's strategic planning system has been designed fundamentally to answer the following questions: Where are we now? Where do we want to be? How do we get there? The complexity of answering those questions is staggering in a firm that employed some 761,400 people worldwide in 1990 (365,100 in the United States alone, exclusive of GMAC, EDS, and Hughes) with sales of $124.7 billion across seven major divisions. Establishing a planning orientation in a company that before 1979 had no total corporate strategic plan has been almost overwhelming. To do this, the company annually trains thousands of managers in the strategic planning process, emphasizing its vision, mission, objectives, and strategies.

HUMAN RESOURCE STRATEGY

General Motors allows major business divisions to set their own human resource strategies, but corporate policy clearly intends to move them all toward leaner staffing profiles. Consolidation of personnel announced in February 1992 will likely increase corporate influence and reduce division influence.

The Auto Division's Human Resource Strategy

The central thrust of the auto division's human resource strategy appears to be to cut costs. It has cut white-collar labor everywhere and closed plants to eliminate blue-collar labor. Reduction of compensation expenses is a major goal. The results have been predictable. Cost pressures have declined, but morale has plummeted. Workers spend a lot of their workdays wondering who's next. It's difficult to increase productivity when workers are concerned about losing their jobs.

Under Stempel, however, General Motors' auto division has changed its approach to human resource strategy from that of Roger Smith. While it is still downsizing, a sense of fair play seems more common among employees at all levels than when Smith was chairman. Stempel has made a concerted effort to be equitable to all involved. For example, he virtually eliminated executive bonuses for 1990 at a time when many front-line employees were losing their jobs. He has focused

EXHIBIT 1.4 General Motors Organization Chart

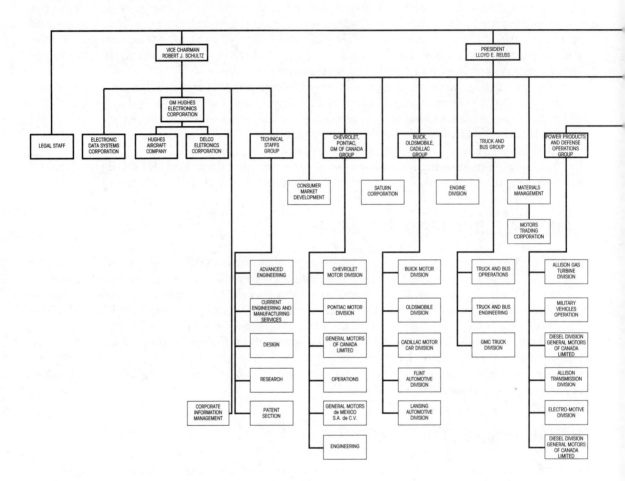

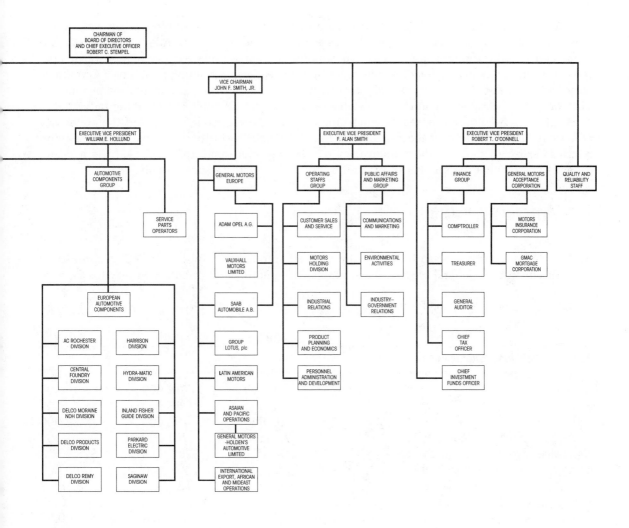

on improving the firm's relationship with the union, and with other employees, as well. Roger Smith, in contrast, alienated many employees with his actions. For example, he once extracted concessions from the union, and the next day announced increases in executive bonuses.[25] General Motors is improving management by offering extensive leadership training programs.[26] GM is also improving communications, and is, plant by plant, trying to introduce participative management.[27] The company's worldwide employment statistics are shown in Exhibit 1.5. Note the reduction in North American auto division employment for the three-year period shown, and the previously noted cuts of 74,000 jobs, including 9,000 white-collar jobs to further reduce 1991 levels. John Smith is expected to make the human resource strategy more performance-based. As a result, expectations are that the number of pink slips issued will increase substantially.

THE AUTOMOBILE DIVISION

Aggressive modernization and downsizing in the automobile division forced conglomerate diversification upon General Motors. It also resulted in a nonmarket-oriented strategy for the auto

EXHIBIT 1.5   Employment and Payrolls

	1991	1990	1989
Average Worldwide Employment			
GM (excluding units listed below)	578,400	595,100	608,800
GMAC	19,200	18,600	18,400
EDS	65,800	59,900	55,000
GMHE	92,900	93,600	98,900
Average number of employees	756,300	767,200	781,100
Worldwide Payrolls (in millions)	$29,641.1	$29,250.8	$28,684.3
Average U.S. hourly employment	258,700	278,600	299,800
U.S. hourly payrolls (in millions)	12,194.6	12,664.4	13,165.9
Average labor cost per hour worked—			
U.S. hourly	$ 34.60	$ 31.30	$ 29.50
North American employment at December 31 (including outside contract personnel, excluding saleable engineers and excluding GMAC, EDS, and GMHE)			
Salaried	91,600	96,400	99,900
Hourly	278,100	258,700	318,900
Total	369,700	355,100	418,800
Equal Employment Opportunity			
Minorities as percent of GM U.S. work force	21%	21%	21%
White-collar	15	15	15
Blue-collar	22	23	23
Women as percent of GM U.S. work force	19	19	19
White-collar	28	28	27
Blue-collar	16	16	16

Source: General Motors, *Annual Report*, 1991.

division as cost cutting became the focus instead of customer satisfaction. The automobile division is now attempting to pay more attention to the market and to the customer. Auto production still guides the overall corporate strategy because 90 percent of the company's sales revenue is derived from it, as Exhibit 1.6 indicates. Technological diversification efforts combined with improvements in the use of human resources are seen as a way to lower costs in order to compete in the marketplace.

1980s Business Strategy Problems

Several major assumptions upon which both corporate and auto-division business strategy for the 1980s were based turned out to be false. Gasoline prices did not continue to increase as much as expected, the oil shortage did not continue, and consumers, therefore, sought larger cars—not smaller ones. Furthermore, as GM has learned with NUMMI, its joint venture with Toyota, the proper use of human labor combined with automation is more efficient than total robotization. Its high-tech approach failed to produce the cost-savings that General Motors had sought.

Several problems resulted from the strategy based on these assumptions. In an effort to reduce costs, for example, the company followed a manufacturing strategy of designing similar components for all of its cars, so an Oldsmobile might have a Chevrolet engine. As a major consequence of this decision, all the cars began to look alike. The look-alike syndrome plagued various divisions of the auto company, but especially Cadillac and Oldsmobile, whose sales plummeted. As GM nets about $5,000 per unit on its more expensive cars, such a decline did not bode well for its total profits.[28]

Several additional major problems emerged with the decision to make smaller, more fuel-efficient cars. GM's decision to go to front-wheel drive required redesigning engines, transmissions, and suspensions. To cut more weight, the firm decided to drop the traditional method of welding car bodies and make unitized bodies instead. Since this required overhauling the entire assembly line, GM decided to rebuild virtually all of its factories, and a $77-billion program was under way. Once the first domino fell, others inevitably followed. Unfortunately for General Motors, its major strategic decisions have so far largely been unsuccessful.

General Motors' executives also failed, at least for a while, to recognize that their new technology functioned at the level that they had anticipated only when it was combined with the proper cost–benefit-driven use of human resources. A massive reorganization early in 1981 to centralize and another in 1984 to decentralize burdened the organization with tremendous costs and in time sapped company energy. GM executives became so preoccupied with carrying out the strategy that they failed to see that it wasn't as good as they thought it was. Plant closings and the elimination of white-collar jobs in 1987 and 1992 have further lowered company energy.

Another key was the structure of GM's manufacturing operation. The structure was designed less to improve manufacturing than to keep the federal government from breaking up a highly successful automobile division. In the 1960s when the structure was designed, GM thought it might drive all other competitors from the market. The bureaucracy reduced the efficiency of the highly successful decentralized operation started by Alfred P. Sloan, Jr. In the mid-1970s, the company also shifted the design and engineering functions to project centers in the belief that it could speed up the time between design and production and save money besides if the cars shared more components. In 1977 the distinctions between the cars began to blur, and this blurring became more pronounced as the 1979 strategy was implemented. More downsizing brought more common parts. These project centers—"corporations within the corporation" as some called them—became so powerful that they controlled virtually every aspect of the development of a new car line. The five car divisions themselves had become isolated from the marketplace. The key decisions were

EXHIBIT 1.6   General Motors Sales by Major Group, 1989–1991 ($millions)

1991	Automotive Products	Financing & Insurance Operations	Other Products	Total
Net Sales and Revenues				
Outside	$94,607.1	$11,115.8	$14,030.4	$119,753.3
Intersegment	220.9	9.2	3,373.4	—
Total	$94,828.0	$11,125.0	$17,403.8	$119,753.3[a]
Operating profit (loss)	(6,194.1)[b]	N/A[c]	1,020.1	(5,174.0)[c]
Identifiable assets at year-end	72,676.5	91,415.3	19,659.0	183,750.8
Depreciation and amortization	4,671.1	2,050.6	1,194.1	7,915.8
Capital expenditures	5,783.6	196.4	1,320.2	7,300.2
1990				
Net Sales and Revenues				
Outside	$96,905.7	$11,812.3	$13,302.8	$122,020.8
Intersegment	406.3	—	286.1	—
Total	$97,312.0	$11,812.3	$13,588.9	$122,020.8[a]
Operating profit (loss)	(3,445.5)[b]	N/A[c]	1,016.8	(2,428.7)[c]
Identifiable assets at year-end	69,264.0	92,965.7	18,101.7	180,331.4
Depreciation and amortization	4,595.5	1,501.6	1,264.5	7,361.6
Capital expenditures	6,057.6	146.3	1,384.1	7,588.0
1989				
Net Sales and Revenues				
Outside	$99,106.1	$11,254.0	$12,851.7	$123,211.8
Intersegment	334.8	—	3,014.7	—
Total	$99,440.9	$11,254.0	$15,866.4	$123,211.8[a]
Operating profit	5,131.1	N/A[c]	579.9	(5,711.0)[c]
Identifiable assets at year-end	64,598.0	89,851.8	16,782.2	171,232.0
Depreciation and amortization	4,206.2	1,583.5	1,378.5	7,168.2
Capital expenditures	6,287.6	127.2	1,090.3	7,505.1

[a]After elimination of intersegment transactions.
[b]Includes a special provision for scheduled plant closings and other restructurings of $2,820.8 million.
[c]Excludes Financing and Insurance Operations as they do not report Operating Profit.
Source: General Motors, *Annual Report*, 1991.

now made by centralized engineering and manufacturing staffs. GM was building cars first and looking for markets later.

Roger Smith responded to this situation by arranging the company into two car groups. This move seemed to help put the organization more in line with the market, but GM remained bureaucratic. It had 14 management layers, while Toyota had 5. Even recently announced cuts probably won't cut the layers to fewer than 8 or 9. Innovation is badly needed to get the cost of cars down and to provide exciting styles. Even GM's high-tech plants have suffered because of archaic management styles. GM's management style was not generally perceived by its employees as consistent with an attempt to reduce costs. An officer of UAW Local 599 commented, "GM is way overloaded with supervision and they won't listen to people on the floor."[29] Stempel has undertaken many measures to try to change GM's culture and improve its management style.

Positive Results of the Business Strategy

In sum, many of the results of the business strategy were disappointing. However, there were some very positive results. Defects dropped from 740 per hundred cars in 1980, to 168 per hundred in 1989. While trailing Ford's 149 per hundred and the Japanese car average of 129, this represented substantial gains. In fact, quality at Buick has risen so much that this division consistently places cars in the top ten in surveys, and Cadillac won the Malcolm Baldrige Award in 1990 and the Motor Trend Car of the Year Award for its 1992 Cadillac Seville STS.

Adjustments in the Business Strategy

During 1986 and 1987, it had become apparent that the technology-based grand strategy was not working. Many changes were made in the various strategies. The business strategy was altered to focus more on the marketplace. Cars were designed more with the consumer in mind, at the same time that cost cutting was occurring. Design-to-manufacture product design programs simplified designs and helped reduce costs. A 26-part strategy has been introduced to cut costs and improve profitability. Called a *framework for greatness,* it consists of a pyramid of 26 blocks, each representing a cost-cutting strategy described in a 100-word definition. Examples include an engineering study of how to use more common parts across several product lines without taking away uniqueness and reducing the number of car batteries across all divisions from 12 to 5.

These tasks are difficult because of the size of the company, its bureaucracy, and the redesigning that must be done. Still, some results are impressive. For example, the number of parts in a pickup truck has been cut by 46 percent.[30] In summary, Stempel has focused on increasing market share, improving quality, cutting costs, and using innovative designs.

New Product Lines[31]

Once the 1984 reorganization was complete, GM's new cars were to be designed in accord with market demands. For example, General Motors introduced two new lines of Chevrolets—Geo and Lumina. Geo did well, but Lumina did not. Lumina was simply out of date when it was introduced.

The Chevrolet Caprice received the dubious distinction symbolizing GM's crusade to dispel the company's reputation for boring styling. Although its square-shouldered, rear-drive design had long been a favorite of taxi drivers and police officers, a complete face-lift was in the offing. With its new, aggressively styled aerodynamic skin, however, GM found that it had once again missed the mark. Older drivers were simply not attracted to the spaceship looks of the new model, and its immense size repelled many young buyers who had grown accustomed to agile compact cars. The Buick Reatta was dropped and several Oldsmobile models generated declining sales. Several models of Buicks and Cadillacs did well, though.

General Motors' stylists have had successes, however, and they will break new ground in styling over the coming years. The 1992 Cadillac Eldorado has been given an imposing new look that reportedly is as grandiose as any of GM's luxury classics of the 1950s. A futuristic cab-forward look has been designed for the slow-selling Chevy Lumina and Pontiac Grand Prix for the 1993 and 1993½ model years. Some analysts believe this could catapult GM to the leading edge of automotive design. In fact, GM says that by 1994 all of its current (1991) models will have been replaced.

Further, on the not-too-distant horizon lies the Impact, General Motors' very viable entry into the world of electric automobiles.[32] Its more aerodynamic, aluminum body allows it to jump to 60 mph in 8 seconds and to reach around 100 mph. With environmental concerns looming very large, the Impact may produce just what its name implies.

A detailed study by the Electric Power Research Institute in Palo Alto, California sought to evaluate cars. This research group is funded by electric utilities, but it is widely viewed as objective. One comparison matches GM's Impact against gas vehicles, and according to Tim Yau, author of the study, the Impact makes a very strong showing.

Of course, no prototype is completely free from question. The Impact carries 32 ten-volt lead-acid batteries similar to those in gas-powered cars. GM engineers estimate that these batteries will have to be replaced every 2,000 miles at a cost of $1,500. Accounting for the price of electricity, the operating cost of the Impact amounts to about $80 a month, approximately twice that of a conventional automobile with gas at $1 per gallon. The batteries and low-friction tires will allow the Impact to travel about 120 miles on a six-hour charge from a 110-volt household outlet, yet this is still less than half of the range of conventional cars. Also, such lightweight material as aluminum adds greater expense. Until the 2,200-pound Impact is produced in great volume and component prices come down, the price will continue to remain very high.

Operation Strategies

Cut costs, integrate technology, improve the use of labor, differentiate the product, cut product lines—these are the focal points of General Motors' 1992 operation strategies. Technology was the watchword. In the course of its $77-billion modernization program, GM constructed six new assembly plants and modernized 12 others. It also emerged with a sizeable overcapacity, hence the plant closings.

The technology involved in manufacturing is so complex that an entire communication network had to be developed just to manage it. In 1984 GM started a five-step process to implement its Machine Automation Protocol (MAP) communication system. By 1990, most computer and control equipment at GM plants was on the MAP network. GM's desire for its computers to be able to talk to each other adds staggering complexity to this process. Each factory will be totally integrated. The design will allow equipment from different vendors to communicate appropriately, so long as vendors tailor their equipment to the needs of the MAP network.

No corporation of GM's size has ever before attempted such fundamental changes. The way cars are manufactured has a tremendous effect on productivity. Plants must be closed down as production technologies change. Workers must learn how to use the new technology. Each plant converted to make a new product must ride the learning curve. GM is the largest manufacturing company in the world, and its sheer immensity makes it difficult to turn around.

One laboratory in which it had hoped to learn was the Saturn plant, and it has learned, even though Saturn was late getting started. The company has already adapted much of the technology used there to other plants. Furthermore, the strategy of differentiating its cars, already begun, is being accelerated. The company is attempting to learn how to make changes late in the engineering process in order to meet market demands, and it is reducing the time of design.

ORGANIZATIONAL CULTURE

Roger Smith made a valiant effort to change the culture of General Motors' automobile division and of the corporation as a whole. Smith faced a daunting task in the attempt to integrate Hughes, EDS, and other acquisitions into the GM system and at the same time to improve the GM culture. He attempted to orient the company toward the long term; he gave managers permission to fail; he forced managers to make decisions by refusing to decide for them; he changed compensation and bonus plans; he changed reward and motivation systems; he changed the security-need satisfiers offered by the company; he reduced the number of white-collar workers by more than 25 percent; he attempted to reduce the number of levels of management; he issued culture cards to all managers stating the corporate mission so they would remember it when making decisions. All observations indicate, however, that he did not significantly change the fundamental shared values in the way necessary to turn the company's fortunes around.

As Roger Smith reflected back on what he tried to accomplish, he made one glaring observation.

> I sure wish I'd done a better job of communicating with GM people. I'd do that differently a second time around and make sure they understood and shared my vision for the company. Then they would have known why I was tearing the place up, taking out whole divisions, changing our whole production structure. If people understand the why, they'll work at it. Like I say, I never got the message across. There we were, all charging up the hill right on schedule, and I looked behind me and saw that many people were still at the bottom, trying to decide whether to come along."[33]

Robert C. Stempel is now left with that task, and he may have more of an impact than Smith for several reasons. First, he is a team player, while Smith was the whole show. The movie *Roger and Me* hurt Smith's attempts to change the culture since it hurt his credibility. Stempel is more employee oriented, and has worked to improve relations with employees, especially unionized employees. Stempel creates a sense of fair play, while Smith apparently played favorites. Finally, there is an urgency in the situation that may cause employees to rally around the company. John Smith adds a new dimension to the culture of the North American operation. Results will be obtained or else those responsible will depart.

GM'S GLOBAL STRATEGY

General Motors recognizes the existence of a global economy, a global automobile industry. GM's executives recognize that "the growth opportunities outside North America are going to surpass our experiences here in North America in the decades ahead."[34] General Motors has developed a multidomestic strategy that is evolving into a global strategy to compete in that environment. Europe accounts for 68 percent of GM's sales outside the United States and Canada, and 21 percent of GM's total sales, as Exhibit 1.7 indicates.[35] GM has wholly owned operations in 17 countries in Western Europe and in Hungary. These operations in cars and trucks had a 12.6 percent share of the European market in 1991.

The European operation has been especially important to GM since it has been highly profitable since 1986. Europe had been unprofitable, but new president John Smith helped oversee a very successful turnaround from 1986 to 1988. Plants were modernized, high quality was established as a major goal, and new models were introduced. In 1986, GM acquired Group Lotus,

EXHIBIT 1.7 Sales by Geographic Division, 1989–1990 ($millions)

1991	United States	Canada	Europe	Latin America	All Other	Total[a]
Net Sales and Revenues						
Outside (excluding GMAC)	$ 73,049.9	$ 6,542.7	$23,394.8	$4,174.3	$1,995.2	$109,156.9
GMAC and related operations	7,600.3	1,017.1	1,682.7	69.8	226.5	10,596.4
Other income	3,322.7	67.1	(49.6)	223.6	(261.1)	3,302.7
Subtotal outside	83,972.9	7,626.9	25,027.9	4,467.7	1,960.6	123,056.0
Interarea	11,284.7	10,659.5	336.7	1,713.5	195.2	—
Total	95,257.6	18,286.4	25,364.6	6,181.2	2,155.8	123,056.0
Net income (loss)	(7,087.3)[b]	578.7	1,762.9	457.5	(145.6)	(4,452.8)
Total assets	$143,209.2	11,626.6	24,547.6	$3,971.6	2,979.3	184,325.5
Net assets	$ 15,057.4	3,177.9	5,664.3	$2,278.4	7,152.2	$ 27,327.6
Average number of employees (in thousands)	491	36	128	87	14	756
1990						
Net Sales and Revenues						
Outside (excluding GMAC)	$ 76,459.3	$ 5,713.0	$22,146.8	$3,871.7	$2,606.5	$110,797.3
GMAC and related operations	8,236.9	1,085.2	1,538.1	87.1	276.2	11,223.5
Other income	2,271.1	25.6	237.4	87.9	62.3	2,684.3
Subtotal outside	86,967.3	6,823.8	23,922.3	4,046.7	2,945.0	124,705.1
Interarea	10,315.9	10,166.2	520.4	1,314.2	139.1	—
Total	$ 97,283.2	$16,990.0	$24,442.7	$5,360.9	$3,084.1	$124,705.1
Net income (loss)	($ 4,570.1)[b]	$ 169.3	$ 1,914.6	$ 244.8	$ 255.9	($ 1,985.7)
Total assets	$140,187.2	$12,549.9	$22,041.2	$3,488.7	$3,345.1	$180,236.5
Net assets	$ 18,867.6	$ 2,610.1	$ 5,294.2	$2,011.2	$1,341.4	$ 30,047.4
Average number of employees (in thousands)	508	37	127	82	13	767
1989						
Net Sales and Revenues						
Outside (excluding GMAC)	$ 81,650.7	$ 6,903.5	$17,850.3	$3,507.2	$2,621.5	$112,533.2
GMAC and related operations	8,405.3	883.1	1,080.5	87.8	221.9	10,678.6
Other income	3,107.6	34.8	414.1	120.3	43.3	3,720.1
Subtotal outside	93,163.6	7,821.4	19,344.9	3,715.3	2,886.7	126,931.9
Interarea	10,185.1	9,825.3	395.1	1,293.2	128.5	—
Total	$103,348.7	$17,646.7	$19,740.0	$5,008.5	$3,015.2	$126,931.9
Net income (loss)	$ 1,279.0	$ 288.5	$ 1,830.0	$ 488.4	$ 345.3	$ 4,224.3
Total assets	$137,083.0	$12,760.4	$17,665.6	$3,405.4	$3,410.5	$173,297.1
Net assets	$ 24,915.8	$ 2,652.8	$ 4,104.7	$2,171.3	$1,237.2	$ 34,982.5
Average number of employees (in thousands)	531	42	120	75	13	781

[a]After elimination of interarea transactions.
[b]Includes a special provision for plant closings and other restructurings of $1,777.1 million in 1991 and $2,087.8 million in 1990.
Source: General Motors, *Annual Report*, 1991.

the United Kingdom firm, largely for its engineering and design capabilities. In 1989, GM purchased 50 percent of SAAB, the Swedish auto firm, as part of its efforts to become more global. In 1989, it formed a joint venture with Isuzu to manufacture and market vehicles through GM's Australian subsidiary. GM has moved rapidly to develop dealer networks in Eastern Europe. Stempel is reportedly interested in strengthening ties to Toyota.

GM's global approach in its international operations may be seen in its global manufacturing and sales operations. While Europe is its major overseas operation, it has sold more cars in Australia than any other company. It has additional wholly owned operations in Australia, New Zealand, four countries in South America, Japan, Singapore, and Taiwan. In addition, it has associated companies (in which its ownership is less than 51 percent) in 15 countries. GM is in some way represented in all major countries except the Soviet Union and China, and will soon sell auto parts to the Soviet Union as the result of a contract agreement reached in 1990. To enhance its competitiveness in the global economy, GM invested $17 billion outside North America between 1980 and 1990.

GENERAL MOTORS' SOCIAL RESPONSIBILITY ACTIVITIES

General Motors has provided an annual accounting of its social responsibility performance since 1971. This action reflects its ongoing social concern. It has not, however, lost sight of its fundamental purpose, maximizing shareholder wealth. As Roger Smith noted, "Any consideration of a corporation's place in society, and of the citizenship obligations that it owes to that society, must begin with the understanding that profitability and competitiveness are the foundation of all of its social goals—that the corporation must do well before it can do good."[36]

General Motors has expressed concern for its social responsibility in the following areas: quality, its conduct of its international businesses, transportation safety, impact on the physical environment (the disposition of acid, for example), philanthropic activities, and programs for minorities and women. General Motors has made basic philosophical statements with respect to its operations in each of these areas. For example, the following principle guides its international business: "We will participate in all societies in which we do business as a responsible and ethical citizen dedicated to continuing social, economic, and environmental progress."[37] In 1986 following this guiding philosophy, GM sold its South African manufacturing operation to a group headed by local management. Exhibit 1.8 breaks down GM's U.S. employment for the purposes of equal employment opportunity analysis.

General Motors is making new headway with its commitment to be socially responsible. For example, DuPont Company unveiled a new air conditioner coolant in early 1991 that will replace ozone-depleting chlorofluorocarbons (CFCs). GM has become the first automobile manufacturer to announce that it will begin using the new coolant starting in the 1994 model-year cars. The use of the new coolant, called HFC-134a, will, however, require mixing a new lubricant with the refrigerant. The significance of this announcement comes from the fact that a new lubricant has not yet been found that is compatible with HFC-134a. GM will have to spend up to $1 billion over the next few years to convert cars to the new coolant, as estimated by DuPont officials. One GM spokesperson reported that the new coolant is also less efficient, but "we are confident that we'll solve the problems."[38]

REGAINING MARKET SHARE

Robert Stempel has made regaining market share a primary goal for GM. GM has managed its way to a steadily declining market share for the past 10 years. From 1980 to 1986, it lost 5 percentage

EXHIBIT 1.8   General Motors Equal Employment Opportunity Data

						Minority Employees				
Job Category	Year	Total Employ-ment	Total Women Employ-ment	Percent	Black	Asian or Pacific Islander	American Indian or Alaskan Native	Hispanic	Total Minorities Employ-ment	Percent
Officials and	1988	36,112	3,673	10.2%	3,426	195	148	514	4,283	11.9%
managers	1989	36,210	3,908	10.8	3,478	223	145	525	4,371	12.1
	1990	34,703	3,942	11.4	3,444	226	151	518	4,339	12.5
Professionals	1988	34,179	7,821	22.9	2,594	923	111	512	4,140	12.1
	1989	36,663	8,655	23.6	2,907	1,099	120	557	4,683	12.8
	1990	36,383	8,714	24.0	2,939	1,206	128	543	4,816	13.2
Technicians	1988	7,040	1,215	17.3	698	96	41	126	961	13.7
	1989	7,527	1,358	18.0	711	160	48	160	1,079	14.3
	1990	7,370	1,406	19.1	707	169	52	175	1,103	15.0
Sales workers	1988	2,109	331	15.7	207	20	11	42	280	13.3
	1989	2,125	355	16.7	219	23	12	43	297	14.0
	1990	2,071	353	17.1	223	26	8	47	304	14.7
Office and	1988	23,970	15,275	63.7	3,950	254	88	851	5,143	21.5
clerical	1989	22,679	14,522	64.0	3,719	263	83	863	4,928	21.7
	1990	20,835	13,427	64.4	3,468	252	82	829	4,631	22.2
Total white-	1988	103,410	28,315	27.4	10,875	1,488	399	2,045	14,807	14.3
collar employees	1989	105,204	28,798	27.4	11,034	1,768	408	2,148	15,358	14.6
	1990	101,362	27,842	27.5	10,781	1,879	421	2,112	15,193	15.0
Craftsmen	1988	81,029	1,934	2.4	6,181	145	238	1,277	7,841	9.7
(skilled)	1989	78,080	2,036	2.6	6,047	146	244	1,253	7,690	9.9
	1990	77,207	2,219	2.9	6,050	159	245	1,268	7,722	10.0
Operatives	1988	208,164	44,422	21.3	47,410	658	500	7,930	56,498	27.1
(semiskilled)	1989	196,063	41,392	21.1	44,667	622	456	7,279	53,024	27.0
	1990	190,702	40,316	21.1	43,146	631	459	7,020	51,256	26.9
Laborers	1988	27,317	4,770	17.5	6,013	76	51	774	6,914	25.3
	1989	24,618	4,155	16.8	5,492	75	54	718	6,339	25.8
	1990	24,237	4,119	17.0	5,387	69	51	655	6,162	25.4
Service workers	1988	10,767	1,598	14.8	2,651	18	26	309	3,004	27.9
	1989	10,246	1,504	14.7	2,496	14	29	275	2,814	27.5
	1990	9,456	1,438	15.2	2,317	16	30	250	2,613	27.6
Total blue-	1988	327,277	52,724	16.1	62,255	897	815	10,290	74,257	22.7
collar employees	1989	309,007	49,087	15.9	58,702	857	783	9,525	69,867	22.6
	1990	301,602	48,092	16.0	56,900	875	785	9,193	67,753	22.5
Grand totals	1988	430,687	81,039	18.8	73,130	2,385	1,214	12,335	89,064	20.7
	1989	414,211	77,885	18.8	69,736	2,625	1,191	11,673	85,225	20.6
	1990	402,964	75,934	18.8	67,681	2,754	1,206	11,305	82,946	20.6

Equal Employment: While total employment in 1990 was reduced from 1989, the overall work force representation of women and minorities remained basically constant.
Source: General Motors, *Public Interest Report*, 1991, p. 16.

points, to 41 percent from 46 percent. In the following 3 years GM's share of the market plunged another 6 points to just under 35 percent. In some quarters, its market share has even dropped below 32 percent.

While Roger Smith seemed to view market share as just another boardroom statistic, Stempel understood that it actually encompasses not only profits, but factories and jobs, as well. Almost all of the Japanese gains in the U.S. market during the 1980s came at GM's expense. During the 1980s, the Japanese gained 10 points in the market, Ford gained close to two points, to 22 percent, and Chrysler dropped nearly three points, to 10 percent. The decline in GM's market share is "absolutely horrifying," says John A. Casesa, automotive analyst at Wertheim Schroder & Company in New York. "What's happening now has long-term implications. GM's share erosion is a sign that the fundamental problems of the company haven't been fixed."[39]

GM executives are well-aware of the problems, including a reservoir of negative feelings from car buyers that received poor-quality cars in the early and mid-1980s. As mentioned, quality has greatly improved from an average of 740 defects per 100 cars in 1980 to 168 per 100 in 1989, but many of the newer GM cars are still failing to generate enthusiasm from consumers.

"Our market share was in the 40s, and now we're in the 30s," says Stempel. "Those are the facts. We've made those facts, and we've got to own up to them. We learned the hard way because we took our eye off the customer. We're not about to [do that] again. The customer is going to get exactly what he wants, and get it in a GM product."[40]

Robert C. Stempel is confident that General Motors is on an upswing. Stempel also believes GM will regain 40 percent of U.S. car sales by 1994 and make Saturn profitable by 1995.[41] John Smith aims to gain market share by cutting costs, cutting poor-selling models, creating new products, and improving quality.

Endnotes

1. James B. Treece, "The Board Revolt," *Business Week*, April 20, 1992, p. 31. This article discusses the board revolt in some detail as does Alex Taylor III, "The Road Ahead at General Motors," *Fortune*, May 4, 1992, pp. 94, 95.
2. James B. Treece, "Jack Smith is Already on a Tear at GM," *Business Week*, May 11, 1992, p. 37.
3. Paul Ingrassia and Joseph B. White, "GM Posts Record '91 Loss of $4.45 Billion and Identifies a Dozen Plants for Closing," *The Wall Street Journal*, February 25, 1992, pp. A3, A8.
4. Marty Baumann, "Hard Times, Choices at GM," *USA Today*, February 25, 1992, p. 1B; Ingrassia and White, "Record '91 Loss."
5. Zachary Schiller, "The Backlash Isn't Just against Japan," *Business Week*, February 10, 1992, p. 30; Micheline Maynard and Jessica Lee, "Japan Insults Workers; U.S. Fights Back," *USA Today*, February 4, 1992, p. 1A; Christopher J. Chipalto and Urban C. Lehner, "Miyazawa Calls U.S. Work Ethic Lacking," *The Wall Street Journal*, February 4, 1992, p. A11; James R. Healey, "Japan Backing off Trade Deals," *USA Today*, January 21, 1992, p. 1A; Jessica Lee and James R. Healey, "Trade: 'Much More' to Do," *USA Today*, January 10, 1992, p. 1A.

6. Compiled from several sources: Alex Taylor III, "Can GM Remodel Itself?" *Fortune*, January 13, 1992, pp. 26–34; James B. Treece, "War, Recession, Gas Hikes . . . GM's Turnaround Will Have to Wait," *Business Week*, February 4, 1991, pp. 94–96; Joseph B. White and Paul Ingrassia, "Smaller Giant: Huge GM Write-off Positions Auto Maker to Show New Growth," *The Wall Street Journal*, November 1, 1990, pp. A1, A11; Joseph B. White, "GM Slashes Dividend by 47%, Launches a Sweeping Program to Reduce Costs," *The Wall Street Journal*, February 4, 1991, p. A3; Alex Taylor III, "Can American Cars Come Back?" *Fortune*, February 26, 1990, pp. 62–65.
7. Joseph B. White, "Besieged Big Three Court Congress, but Their Joint Effort May be in Vain," *The Wall Street Journal*, April 29, 1991, p. A6.
8. Joseph B. White and Paul Ingrassia, "Traffic Jam: Auto Firms See Profits Undermined by a Glut of Former Rental Cars," *The Wall Street Journal*, December 11, 1990, pp. A1, A12.
9. Alfred P. Sloan, Jr., *My Years With General Motors* (New York: McFadden Books, 1965). Chapters 3 and 4.
10. William J. Hampton and James R. Norman, "General Motors: What Went Wrong," *Business Week*, March 16, 1987, pp. 102–110.

11. Hampton and Norman, "What Went Wrong", p. 103.
12. "Perot's War with GM Ends in $743 Million Goodbye," *U.S. News & World Report*, May 26, 1987, p. 18.
13. "GM Moves into a New Era," *Business Week*, July 16, 1984, pp. 48–54.
14. Hampton and Norman, "What Went Wrong?" p. 207.
15. Taylor, "Come Back?" p. 64; White and Ingrassia, "Smaller Giant," p. A11.
16. Alex Taylor III, "The Tasks Facing General Motors," *Fortune*, March 13, 1989, pp. 52–59.
17. Summarized from the following sources: Taylor, "GM Remodel"; Neal Templin and Joseph B. White, "GM's Saturn, in Early Orbit, Intrigues Buyers," *The Wall Street Journal*, October 25, 1990, pp. B1, B8; James B. White and Melinda Grenier Guiles, "Rough Launch: GM's Plan for Saturn, to Beat Small Imports, Trails Original Goals," *The Wall Street Journal*, July 9, 1990, pp. A1, A10; James B. Treece, "Here Comes GM's Saturn," *Business Week*, April 1990, pp. 56–62.
18. Treece, "Here Comes Saturn," p. 56.
19. "GM's Leaders Go on the Record—An Interview with *Fortune*," *Fortune*, March 9, 1992, pp. 50–60; Taylor, "GM Remodel"; Ingrassia and White, "Record '91 Loss"; Joseph B. White, "GM's Problems Have Overtaken Stempel's Go-Slow Approach," *The Wall Street Journal*, December 16, 1991, pp. B1, B5; Joseph B. White, "GM Sets off on a Market Share Drive," *The Wall Street Journal*, August 22, 1991, p. B1; Treece, "War, Recession, Gas Hikes."
20. The following descriptions are derived from a number of sources: *General Motors Annual Report, 1991*; White and Ingrassia, "Smaller Giant"; White, "GM Slashes Dividend"; Treece, "War, Recession, Gas Hikes."
21. Joseph B. White and Bradley A. Stertz, "GM's Debt Is Downgraded by Moody's; Big Three Chiefs Warn Japan on Trade Gap," *The Wall Street Journal*, January 8, 1992, p. A2.
22. Lawrence Ingrassia, "GM Plans to Close 21 More Factories, Cut 74,000 Jobs, Slash Capital Spending," *The Wall Street Journal*, December 19, 1991, p. A3; Ingrassia and White, "Record '91 Loss."
23. Ingrassia and White, "Record '91 Loss."
24. James R. Healey and Micheline Maynard, "Is Shakeup Enough for a Turnaround?" *USA Today*, February 25, 1992, p. 1B.
25. Paul Ingrassia and Joseph B. White, "Deft Steering: GM's New Boss Runs into Many Problems—but Little Opposition," *The Wall Street Journal*, February 8, 1991, pp. A1, A4.
26. Jack Falvey, "Before Spending $3 Million on Leadership, Read This," *The Wall Street Journal*, October 3, 1988, p. A26; Chris Lee, "Can Leadership Be Taught?" *Training*, July 1989, pp. 19–26.
27. M. M. Petty, James F. Cashman, Anson Seers, Robert L. Stevenson, Charles W. Barker, and Grady Cook, "Better Communications at General Motors," *Personnel Journal*, September 1989, pp. 40–49; Stewart L. Tubbs and Ruth A. Dischner, "From the Brink of Death," *Industry Week*, May 21, 1990, pp. 15–18; Jacob M. Schlesinger and Paul Ingrassia, "People Power: GM Woos Employees by Listening to Them, Talking of Its 'Team,'" *The Wall Street Journal*, January 12, 1989, pp. A1, A6.
28. Russell Mitchel, "GM's New Luxury Cars: Why They Are Not Selling," *Business Week*, January 19, 1987, p. 94.
29. Hampton and Norman, "What Went Wrong?" p. 106.
30. Joseph B. White and Bradley A. Stertz, "Crisis in Galvanizing Detroit's Big Three," *The Wall Street Journal*, May 2, 1991, pp. B1, B6; Treece, "War, Recession, Gas Hikes," p. 95.
31. Thanks to David Plitnik for researching this topic.
32. William J. Cook, "Jump-Start to the Future," *U.S. News & World Report*, April 30, 1990, p. 48; David Woodruff, "GM Drives the Electric Car Closer to Reality," *Business Week*, May 14, 1990, pp. 60–61.
33. Roger Smith, "The U.S. Must Do As GM Has Done," *Fortune*, February 13, 1989, pp. 70–73.
34. General Motors, *Public Interest Report*, 1987, p. 27.
35. Treece, "War, Recession, Gas Hikes," p. 95.
36. Ibid., p. 1.
37. General Motors, *Public Interest Report*, 1987, p. 19.
38. Amal Kumar Naj, "DuPont Unveils New Coolant: GM Will Switch," *The Wall Street Journal*, January 22, 1991, p. 1.
39. Paul Ingrassia and Joseph B. White, "Losing the Race: With Its Market Share Sliding, GM Scrambles to Avoid a Calamity," *The Wall Street Journal*, December 14, 1989, p. A1.
40. Ingrassia and White, "Losing the Race," A1.
41. Alex Taylor III, "The New Drive to Revive GM," *Fortune*, April 9, 1990, pp. 52–61.

INTEGRATIVE CASE ANALYSIS
CHAPTER 1

THE CHALLENGES FACING GENERAL MOTORS IN 1992

In these integrative case analysis sections, we seek to accomplish two objectives. First, we want to integrate the conceptual material from the text to the case. Second, we want to give you insight into how to analyze cases. We have integrated these objectives into an "Applications of Concepts" section. In this section we may provide samples of how you should proceed, and/or a list of the kind of questions you should be asking. In most chapters, what you do to apply the concepts to the case, you would also do for an independent case analysis. We have also added a second section that asks you to look at the effect of the ten strategic management challenges on the company and the related concepts.

Now that you have read the case and Chapter 1, let's see how the material from Chapter 1 relates to the case. This will help you achieve a better understanding of both the concepts from the chapter and how to analyze cases.

APPLICATIONS OF CONCEPTS TO THE CASE

In 1992 General Motors confronted a complex, changing environment that demanded a change in its corporate goals and strategies, especially for the auto division. Its strategic efforts in that division included, for example, actions to maintain market share by cutting prices. It also reduced the scope and size of the Saturn project. It has established major cost-reduction and reorganization goals as it positions itself for the industry situation that it sees in the future, principally characterized by overcapacity and increased competition. It has closed numerous plants and will close many more. Stempel, however, was not moving fast enough to suit the board—enter John Smith.

Strategic Management

Does General Motors practice strategic management? Yes, it does. It has actively engaged in a broad strategic course of action since 1979. More than most organizations, General Motors addresses the issues concerning each of its major stakeholders in formal policy statements, strategies, or corporate reports. For example, its social responsibility statement identifies key stakeholders and its responses to their interests.

Now let's review the focal points of the three major levels of strategy at General Motors.

Corporate Strategies   Its principal strategies at the overall corporate level for the whole company have included growth and stabilization through technological innovation and diversification. It has depended heavily on its three nonautomotive subsidiaries and on its European auto division for profits. The automobile division strategy has focused on retrenchment and stabilization through technological innovation. Historically GM has pursued a growth strategy, but it has more recently found its growth stymied by competition.

Business Strategy   At the business level, its auto division has emphasized brute force marketing, focused on quality, and attempted to match the prices of its competitors, and it is beginning to be more responsive to the market. It has launched new products, attempted to improve styling, and cut costs.

Functional Strategy   At the functional level, GM has worked hard to update its operational facilities and improve its management of human resources in order to be the most efficient and effective producer of low-cost, high-quality automobiles in the world. Its related information strategy has sought to provide managers across the entire corporation with the information they need to be able to adjust instantly to changing conditions. Some of its functional strategies have included reductions in both blue- and white-collar work forces. It has also worked hard to improve relations with the union. It will now focus on further reducing white- and blue-collar work forces and becoming more performance oriented.

Additional Case Analysis Questions

You might now ask yourself a series of questions:

> How do General Motors' strategies work to fulfill its mission? Are its goals consistent with that mission?
> Who are its strategists? How will recent changes in strategists likely affect strategy?
> What is strategic planning like at General Motors?
> What are some of the major concerns of the company with respect to strategic management?
> What is GM's grand strategy?
> How does it implement and control various strategies?
> Has Stempel crafted strategy, or relied totally on analysis?
> Does Stempel have a vision, a strategic intent?
> How might values have affected Roger Smith's strategies? Stempel's strategies? John Smith's?
> What probable scenarios will GM face in the next 10 years?
> How can strategic intent help GM overcome problems?

Once you have answered these questions, you will have a better understanding of the concepts discussed in the chapter.

STRATEGIC MANAGEMENT CHALLENGES

All of the ten strategic management challenges affect GM's strategic management process. For example, GM is experiencing accelerated rates of change in virtually all areas. For example, by the time it could complete development of the Saturn, the original intended market had disappeared and then reappeared again. The globalization of business has meant increased competition at home and in Europe.

How does each of the other ten strategic management challenges for the 1990s affect GM's strategic management?

ORGANIZATIONAL STRATEGISTS AND ORGANIZATIONAL PURPOSE

Undertaking the definition of a company mission is one of the most easily slighted tasks in the strategy management process. . . . But the critical role of the company mission as the basis of orchestrating managerial action is repeatedly demonstrated by failing firms whose short-run actions are ultimately found to be counterproductive to their long-run purpose.

John A. Pearce II
Author on Strategy

Objectives are needed in every area where performance and results directly and vitally affect the survival and prosperity of the firm.

Peter Drucker
Noted Author and Management Consultant

CHAPTER OBJECTIVES

By the time you complete this chapter, you should be able to:

1. Discuss the roles of the various strategists in strategy formulation
2. Describe how vision, mission, goals, and objectives relate to each other
3. Describe the roles of vision, mission, goals, and strategic objectives in the strategy formulation process
4. Determine whether a company's mission statement is sound
5. Identify typical goals and objectives of business organizations, describe some of these objectives in specific terms, and identify four components of sound objectives
6. Define MBORR and indicate how it is used in the strategic planning process
7. Define the term *policy*, describe the major strategic policies, and distinguish between these policies and vision, mission, goals, strategic objectives, and strategies

AT XEROX, IT'S ONCE MORE INTO THE BREACH

In the 1970s, Xerox Corporation was successful almost beyond belief. It had a virtual monopoly on the copier market. As it entered the 1980s, however, it found itself losing market share rapidly to less expensive and higher-quality Japanese machines. Only a major cost cutting program in manufacturing, a renewed focus on the customer's needs, and a total dedication to improving quality spearheaded by then-Chairman and CEO David T. Kearns, culminating in the firm's winning the U.S. Commerce Department's Malcolm Baldrige Award in 1989, enabled Xerox to stop the erosion and begin to regain market share. The firm changed its mission and diversified into financial services. Furthermore, internal strife among various corporate divisions had led to problems in launching new products.

In 1990, however, the firm still faced major Japanese competitors across all sizes of copying machines, resulting in small profit margins due to price competition. Furthermore, the firm continued to experience the flat revenues that had plagued it for most of the 1980s. Also, it found diversification into financial services to be riskier and much less profitable than it had anticipated following a $400-million writeoff in its real estate affiliate and a significant loss of profits in its Crum & Forster insurance subsidiary. Technology was also changing rapidly, not only in copying, but in other office systems as well, some of which, such as fax machines, were beginning to overlap traditional copier functions. Thus the firm's corporate strategy once again called for diversification into technology-related products and away from the lower profits of copying. Xerox had failed at several diversification efforts in office systems before, among them mainframe computers, word processors, computer peripherals, and workstations. This time, though, the firm intends to leapfrog its competitors into a field that is related to copiers, but goes beyond them—image processing.

President Paul A. Allaire, who became CEO on August 1, 1990 when Kearns retired, and former IBM staffer William C. Lowe, executive vice president for development, have directed the firm's development of an all new, all digital image processing machine. Xerox has developed a single box that does what formerly required separate image scanners, laser printers, copiers, and fax machines. Machines were successfully tested at various sites, and the first machine was sold in October 1990. This new product could play a major role in reshaping the way offices function because it can network with computers, converting paper documents to electronic bits of information and vice versa. Unfortunately for Xerox, the new machine won't contribute significantly to the company's bottom line for several years. Its $150,000 price limits its potential sales to 400 customers through 1992. Still, less expensive models are already on their way and could begin to contribute substantial profits before long. However, Japanese firms are already offering less expensive image processing machines for the copying function and cannot be far behind the Xerox effort. A weak economy in 1991 further delayed a substantial impact on the bottom line for Xerox and allowed competitors to gain time to imitate the new product.

Sources: Todd Vogel, "At Xerox, They're Shouting 'Once More into the Breach,'" *Business Week*, July 23, 1990, pp. 62–63; John T. Tanner, Jr., "Leadership through Quality," *Journal of Personal Selling & Sales Management*, Winter 1990, pp. 49–51; James R. Norman, "Xerox Rethinks Itself—and This Could Be the Last Time," *Business Week*, February 13, 1989, pp. 90–93.

Xerox has learned that strategy must be flexible. Today most organizations operate in extremely volatile environments and they must adapt and anticipate in order to remain viable. Strategists must continually analyze internal and external environments and fine-tune, or occasionally dramatically change, vision, mission, goals, objectives, strategies, and policies to respond. As Xerox has painfully learned, not all strategic actions are successful, but new strategies must be attempted or the business may be left behind its competition and its organizational purposes may be left unfulfilled. This chapter focuses on organizational purpose—vision, mission, goals, and strategic objectives together with strategic policy. The chapter reviews the objectives-determination process, discussing objectives as integrative mechanisms; management by objectives, results, and rewards (MBORR); the roles played by each of the four major types of organizational purpose in the formulation of strategy; and the role of policy in strategic management. Before the chapter discusses organizational purposes, however, it reviews the roles of the various strategists in strategy formulation. Figures 2.1 and 2.2 indicate the parts of the strategic process discussed in this chapter.

Several **strategists** may influence an organization's strategies: The board of directors, chief executive officers, coalitions of top managers, top line managers, professional planners, and others, such as middle managers. The degree to which each can influence strategy, and the processes by which they do vary, as the following paragraphs describe.

THE STRATEGISTS

Several **strategists** may influence an organization's strategies: The board of directors, chief executive officers, coalitions of top managers, top line managers, professional planners, and others, such as middle managers. The degree to which each can influence strategy, and the processes by which they do vary, as the following paragraphs describe.

The Board of Directors and Strategic Management[1]

Research reveals that few firms' **boards of directors** have historically performed many of the classic functions conceptualized for them, such as strategic decision making. While a board may passively approve the organization's objectives and strategies, normally it has very little impact on their formulation and does not scrutinize them in great detail. Furthermore, evidence indicates that most board members have been ill-prepared to make such decisions.[2] During the 1980s, however, the failure of boards of several major corporations to take appropriate actions, combined with lawsuits and proxy actions by disgruntled stockholders and citizens' groups, led many boards to become much more professional, diverse, and responsive.[3] Many boards have sought to increase their roles in making strategic decisions, monitoring executive performance and compensation, and ensuring sound budgeting and policies as you discovered in the GM case discussed after Chapter 1. The number of outside directors has increased significantly, and a trend toward professional board members has become apparent. While board

FIGURE 2.1   The Organization—A Strategic Management Process Model

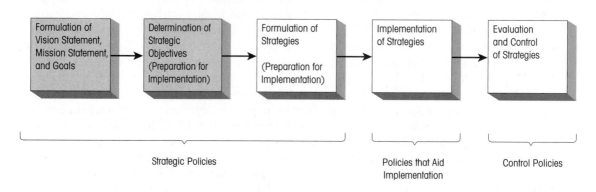

actions naturally vary from firm to firm, we can anticipate that boards will continue their efforts to participate more actively in organizations' strategic processes.[4] Many companies still resist such changes, though. For example, a survey of the Inc 500 companies revealed that 43 percent of them have no outside directors at all, which limits the sources of opinions contrary to those of internal management.[5]

One research study indicates that boards may be classified into four types according to combinations of high and low levels of CEO power and high and low levels of board power. Where CEO power is low and board power is low, a caretaker board exists. Where CEO power is high and board power low, a statutory board exists. Where the CEO power is low and board power high, a proactive board exists. Where both CEO and board powers are high, a participative board exists.[6,7]

In addition to their classic function of stockholder representation, boards can serve as important educational experiences for CEOs. Daniel E. Gill, CEO of Bausch & Lomb, Inc., believes CEOs should serve on two to five boards as outside members in order to learn how other firms approach problem solving.[8]

Chief Executive Officer As Strategist

The **CEO as strategist** clearly dominates strategy formulation in practically all smaller firms, in most medium-sized firms, and in many, if not most, large ones. The corporate strategies of multiple-SBU companies are determined by corporate CEOs or other strategists, with SBU CEOs or other strategists determining SBU strategies. CEOs who chart strategy may be either owner/entrepreneurs or professional managers who take risks and seek the power that comes with such positions and decisions.

Examine the businesses in your town or city. How many are run by a CEO or a family dominated by one person? Almost all businesses are headed by one person, aren't they? These managers form the backbone of the system of free enterprise, which rewards the investor, the innovator, and the risk taker.

FIGURE 2.2 Objectives Determination and Strategy Formulation

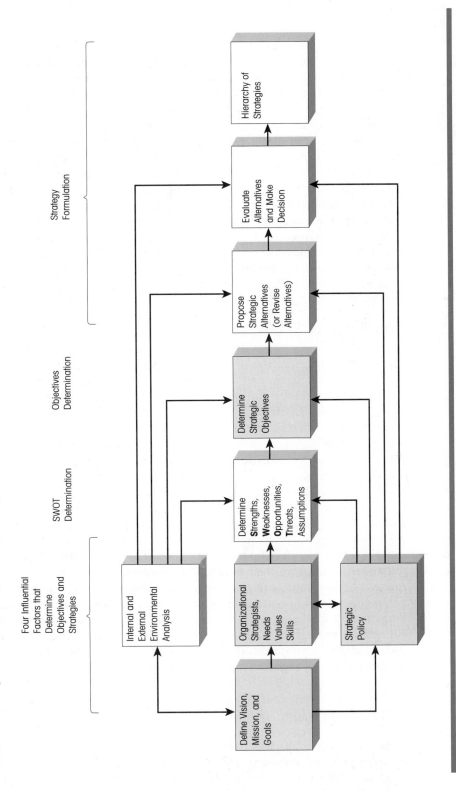

In recent years, substantial concern has been expressed that this entrepreneurial motivation is missing from large, dominant corporations. This concern appears to be well-founded. As a result, many U.S. firms find themselves at a disadvantage in the international arena, particularly in their efforts to compete with Japanese firms, which actively seek to succeed as organizations in the long run rather than concentrating on short-run performance. Consequently, many firms are now sponsoring entrepreneurship programs in which managers run divisions as if they were their own businesses, thus becoming **intrapreneurs.**[9]

Many U.S. firms recognize their error in overemphasizing the short term and seem to be responding to the challenge of international competition; others haven't yet achieved this insight. One key to success in competition is a policy of correlating the strategist's compensation with long-term successes, not with short-term successes such as those indicated by current profits and return on investment. Furthermore, the way in which CEOs influence strategy is also changing somewhat. Providing inspirational vision, managing culture, and transforming the organization have become part of the strategic management process.[10]

Coalitions As Strategists

The business organization, whether a single- or multiple-SBU firm, is a formal authority system composed of subsystems. Within these formal systems and subsystems, informal social systems develop. These informal relationships often play major roles in strategy formulation. Studies of the objectives-setting and strategy-formulation processes have revealed that one or more powerful, informal groups of top managers may emerge within the formal planning group. These informal groups, or **coalitions,** may establish an organization's objectives and strategies, depending on its formal leader's entrepreneurial characteristics and the ability of one or two coalitions to dominate the others.

Organizational objectives, strategies, and policies often emerge from bargaining among coalitions. Members of the dominant coalition negotiate strategic matters among themselves, with other powerful individuals, or with other coalitions that may develop inside or outside the organization. Because managers must seek to improve their subunits' performance in organizations with scarce resources, they must compete with other managers for resources. Unbridled competition would be detrimental to the firm, however, so managers engage in bargaining and trade-offs in strategy and policy matters. The result is often suboptimal strategy and failure to accomplish missions. While many of the ideas presented here oppose the traditional view of the all-powerful chief executive officer, significant empirical support substantiates these ideas.[11]

Top Line Managers As Strategists

Influenced by many factors (recessions and changing management philosophies, for example), organizations and their top managers have begun to realize the importance of involving the people who are closer to a problem or opportunity in its handling. These people are the ones who are most likely to have to implement strategic decisions. This has led to a change in management philosophy to encourage the delegation of decision making to the personnel closest to the situation.

This brings more and more **top line managers** into the strategic decision making process. Plant managers, for example, have much more input in strategic decisions than they did five years ago. Operations have assumed much greater strategic importance than they had in the 1970s and early 1980s. Furthermore, those who have responsibility for both profit and loss have become intrapreneurs, gaining control over their divisions and running them as their own businesses.[12]

Professional Planners As Strategists

When the duties associated with strategy formulation become too extensive for the CEO to handle alone, he or she normally delegates many of them to a planning committee of top managers or, in larger organizations, to a professional planning department. Such a professional planning unit usually collects and analyzes data and generates and evaluates alternatives. Such a unit might vary in size from two people—a planner and a secretary—to a staff of 50 or more in one of the largest corporations. The **professional planner** should manage and design the strategy-formulation system. The planner influences the top and lower levels of management in their planning efforts, providing information, establishing rules, and consulting on and integrating the various plans as submitted.

The planner in most firms is less an active planner than a coordinator and provider of information, a monitor, controller, and critic of subsystem plans and the overall planning process. From time to time, the professional planner may in fact decide future courses of action for the organization. The power to do so comes from knowledge and skill in strategy formulation and from control of the information needed to make strategic decisions. This role often leads to conflict with line managers.

The Future of the Professional Planner

While many firms have reduced their professional planners' roles in decision making, cut staffs, and more fully involved top line managers in their strategic-planning processes, the future holds the promise of an expanded role for such professionals. The evidence indicates that organizational environments are becoming more variable and more volatile with each passing year. Businesses' major environmental concerns—society, government, technology, competition, labor, the economy, suppliers, creditors, customers, industry, international events, and the availability of natural resources—are increasingly unpredictable. As a result, organizations may depend increasingly on professional strategists to track these changes.

Computer simulations of corporate strategies will become necessities because, as the environment becomes more turbulent, the need to ask what-if questions becomes more pressing. The time horizon of a firm's objectives and strategies may be compressed, but objectives and strategies must nonetheless be formulated. In fact, wise firms will develop numerous alternative contingency strategies to cope with numerous possible situations. Many firms currently generate multiple strategies, each designed to be employed under a certain set of circumstances. Such complex planning usually requires the help of a professional planning staff.

Other Strategists

Many tout middle management as a potentially important contributor to strategy, believing that their involvement leads to better strategy, and especially to better implementation. Limited research supports this view.[13] Additionally, persons outside the organization's chain of command, such as strategic management consultants and influential board members, can become active participants in strategic decision making. For example, institutional investors are demanding increasing influence over companies.[14]

Having discussed the various strategists, the chapter now begins the discussion of the purposes established by these strategists, beginning with vision.

VISION

It has been recognized that a strategist must have a vision of what the organization is to become to be successful.[15] A **vision** is a form of nonspecific guidance normally provided to an organization by its CEO. It describes where the company is going in the most general, conceptual terms, but it must also provide emotional direction.[16] Some suggest that it should also empower those it is intended to motivate.[17]

A vision results from more than foundationless dreaming. It results from the ability to pull together a number of divergent strands and identify the beginnings of underlying trends suggesting change in different parts of the business world.[18] The resurgence of Chrysler in the 1980s, Canon's development of the PC-10 and PC-20 personal copiers to sell for under $1,000, and the resurgence of Levi Strauss as a global competitor are all examples of companies whose CEOs' visions moved them to exceptional performance.[19]

Father Theodore Hesburgh, former president of Notre Dame University, commented, "The very essence of leadership is [that] you have to have a vision. It's got to be a vision you articulate clearly and forcefully on every occasion. You can't blow an uncertain trumpet."[20] Visions must be inspiring to be effective; they also must be clear and challenging. Most visions of business leaders and business organizations are aimed to develop the ability to compete in the marketplace.[21] The vision leads to the statement of mission. Figure 2.3 portrays the relationship of vision to the other types of organizational purposes.

AT **XEROX**

The changing vision at Xerox calls for the company to renew its pursuit of technological diversification, away from the low-profit core business of photocopying. The digital image processing machine is expected to revolutionize the marketplace.

FIGURE 2.3   Relationship of Vision to Organizational Purposes

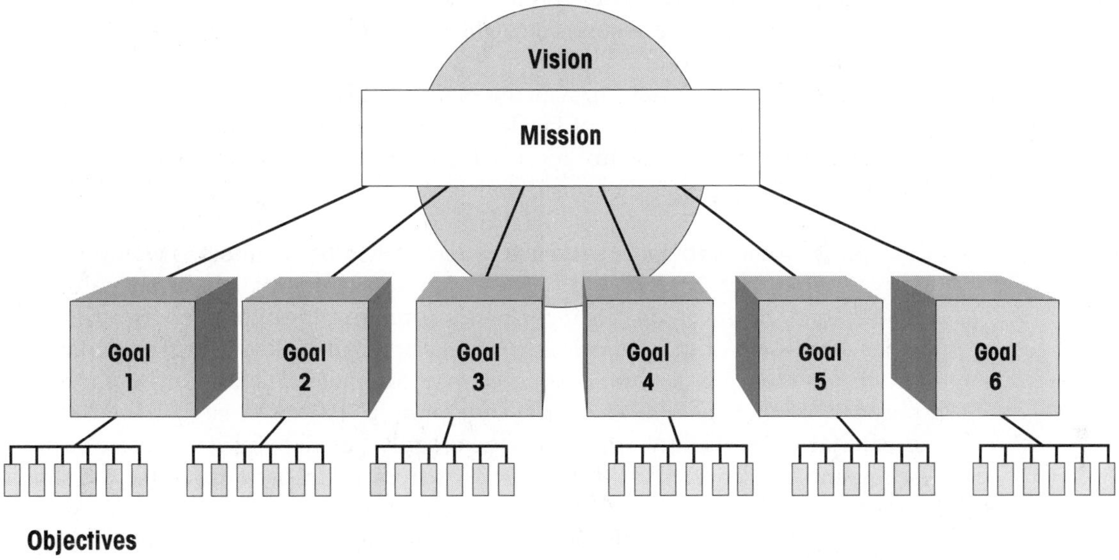

Source: Adapted from James M. Higgins, *The Management Challenge: An Introduction to Management* (New York: Macmillan, 1991), p. 145.

MISSION

Categorizing organizations in various ways is useful in efforts to understand and predict organizational strategy. Classification factors that might be expected to affect strategy include:

- The organization's size—small, medium, or large
- Its geographic scope—local, regional, national, multinational, or global
- The number and diversity of businesses within it—single-SBU or multiple-SBU organizations

Mission, however, exerts the most basic influence on strategy, so categorizing organizations by type of mission is very meaningful. Mission is the organization's reason for being, the primary consideration on which organizational goals, objectives, strategies, and policies are based.

The most obvious division of organizations by mission is to identify them as profit and nonprofit. More definitively, Peter M. Blau and W. Richard Scott have identified four major types of organizations according to the groups that receive the greatest benefit from their existence. This classification scheme is based essentially on mission. Its classifications are not mutually exclusive; an organization may be appropriately placed in more than one category. The **organizational categories** are:

1. The business concern or for-profit organization, which benefits its owners (and, it might be added, the employees and most others who transact business with it); for example, General Motors.
2. The mutual benefit association, which benefits the members themselves; for example, a union or a club
3. The service organization, which benefits its clients; for example, United Way or the U.S. Department of Health and Human Services
4. The commonweal organization, which benefits society in general; for example, the U.S. Department of Defense[22]

One would anticipate that such differences in basic missions would result in varying strategies, and they do. These simple statements of purpose alone are insufficient, however, to distinguish one organization's mission from another when both have the same primary beneficiary. All business organizations seek profit, for example, so profit alone cannot completely define an organization's purpose. Rather, as Philip Kotler and John A. Pearce II suggest, a **business organization's mission** is viewed as the broadly stated definition of basic business scope and operations that distinguishes it from other organizations of a similar type.[23]

The primary thrust of this mission statement is external, focuses on markets and customers, and typically specifies current fields of endeavor. Many mission statements include descriptions of additional basic concerns, covering such factors as product quality, location of facilities, important aspects of perceived strategic advantage, corporate philosophy, self-concept, and public image. Preliminary research by Pearce and Fred David suggests that the successful organization's mission statement is more comprehensive than that of the less successful firm, which tends to focus on simple product/market issues.[24] More recent research by David found nine components of mission statements: customers, products or services, locations, technology, concern for survival, philosophy, self-concept, concern for public image, and concern for employees.[25] As companies expand into the global marketplace, recognition of their global nature and a corresponding statement of global strategic philosophy, either in the mission statement or elsewhere, will be necessary.[26]

Obtaining profit by satisfying a societal need is the overriding purpose of every business organization. A mission statement simply further identifies how one business intends to achieve profit as opposed to how another, similar firm might do so. These statements must be carefully worded as they provide direction for goals, objectives, and strategy. The basic question they seek to answer is, What business are we in or do we want to be in? It is critical to organizational success that this question of business engagement be answered properly.

In 1975 W. T. Grant, a retail chain with almost $2 billion in sales and 1,000 stores, went bankrupt. One of the major underlying reasons for its collapse was its failure to answer this basic question. One W. T. Grant executive commented that the company could not make up its mind whether it wanted to be a full-service store like J. C. Penney and Sears or a discounter like Kmart. The company compromised between the two, and ended up standing for nothing. Consequently, it went bankrupt. While planning experts agree that mission statements are vital, research by Fred David found that only 41 percent of the firms he surveyed had drafted formal mission statements.[27]

Exhibit 2.1 contains two mission statements abstracted from these organizations' annual reports or statements of purpose. Note the differences in these statements, as well as their similarities and common components. As you can see, not all mission statements address each of the issues that are felt to be appropriate. Zale's statement is quite comprehensive. Ford's is not. Yet, Ford's separate statements on corporate philosophy address all the same major issues. The successful company must address these issues somewhere, in a statement of vision, mission, goals, philosophy, or policy. **Corporate philosophy** is a term that can describe a firm's statements of how it views itself, its operations, and its values. Some firms have a formal statement of such a philosophy, others include it in

EXHIBIT 2.1 Mission Statements

Zale Corporation

Our business is specialty retailing. Retailing is a people-oriented business. We recognize that our business existence and continued success are dependent upon how well we meet our responsibilities to several critically important groups of people.

Our first responsibility is to our customers. Without them we would have no reason for being. We strive to appeal to a broad spectrum of consumers, catering in a professional manner to their needs. Our concept of value to the customer includes a wide selection of quality merchandise, competitively priced and delivered with courtesy and professionalism.

Our ultimate responsibility is to our shareholders. Our goal is to earn an optimum return on invested capital through steady profit growth and prudent, aggressive asset management. The attainment of this financial goal, coupled with a record of sound management, represents our approcah toward influencing the value placed upon our common stock in the market.

We feel a deep, personal responsibility to our employees. As an equal opportunity employer, we seek to create and maintain an environment where every employee is provided the opportunity to develop to his or her maximum potential. We expect to reward employees commensurate with their contribution to the success of the company.

We are committed to honesty and integrity in all relationships with suppliers of goods and services. We are demanding but fair. We evaluate our suppliers on the basis of quality, price, and service.

We recognize community involvement as an important obligation and as a viable business objective. Support of worthwhile community projects in areas where we operate generally accrues to the health and well-being of the community. This makes the community a better place for our employees to live and a better place for us to operate.

We believe in the Free Enterprise System and in the American Democratic form of government under which this superior economic system has been permitted to flourish. We feel an incumbent responsibility to insure that our business operates at a reasonable profit. Profit provides opportunity for growth and job security. Therefore, we are dedicated to profitable growth—growth as a company and growth as individuals.

This mission statement spells out the creed by which we live.

Ford Motor Company

Ford Motor Company is the world's second-largest industrial corporation and the second-largest car and truck concern. Ford has two business groups: the automotive group and the financial services group. Ford's 367,000 employees serve customers in more than 200 countries and territories. Ford's other businesses include electronics, glass, plastics, castings, climate-control systems, service and replacement parts, vehicle leasing and rental, space technology, satellite communications, defense systems and land development.

Sources: Reprinted from "The Company Mission As a Strategy Tool," by John A. Pearce II, p. 16. By permission of the publisher. Copyright 1982 by *Sloan Management Review*. All rights reserved. "Ford Annual Report 1989," inside cover.

mission, goal, or policy statements. Others have statements of values that serve this function.

Mission statements change for a variety of reasons. The appearance of an opportunity or threat is a common reason. For example, Federal Express's founder, Frederick W. Smith, recognized that underlying changes in the way business was being conducted, moving from a domestic to a global perspective, would eventually affect Federal Express's profits. His vision was to make Federal Express a global leader in the package distribution industry. To do so, he had to change the company's mission from that of an essentially domestic firm to that of a global firm. This required the expansion of the company's operations. He chose to have the firm grow largely internally for expansion into Europe, but in the Pacific Rim he added to internal growth efforts by acquiring Flying Tiger Airlines, another airfreight firm, for $880 million in August 1989. He changed the mission in recognition of a change in world business conduct. This acquisition was truly strategic, and risky, since no profits are expected from overseas operations until 1993.[28] Sometimes changes in mission can lead to some bizarre results such as abandoning an original and long-time core business. For example, Singer no longer makes sewing machines, Greyhound no longer actually owns a bus line, and USX, formerly U.S. Steel, has considered selling off its steel-making units since its energy businesses are much more profitable.[29]

This chapter's Global Strategic Challenge feature discusses the changing mission of General Accident (GA), a global insurance company based in Scotland, and the firm's attempts to ensure that employees understand and are guided by this mission. GA's mission statement is somewhat more comprehensive than we have defined the term, reflecting the broader definition used in much of Europe, and to some extent in some U.S. firms' cultures and strategies.[30]

Vision, Mission, and Strategic Intent

These three concepts overlap somewhat, especially when the motivational aspect of vision and the philosophical component of mission correspond closely to strategic intent. However, the perspective of this book is that strategic intent reflects an aggressive stance on strategy that would not be part of the vision, mission, goals, and objectives of a firm pursuing a strategic fit approach to strategy.

AT XEROX

Due to global competition, principally from the Japanese, Xerox has chosen to change its mission to include a technologically new line of products—digital image processing. Xerox has tried such diversification before, but feels it has no choice but to try again.

GOALS

Goals further define a firm's mission in terms of several key results areas. Goals are less specific than objectives; objectives further define goals. Strategic goals help managers to think of what the firm ought to accomplish in general without getting bogged down in issues of measurement and timing.[31] Goals are sometimes almost

 GLOBAL STRATEGIC
CHALLENGE

GENERAL ACCIDENT OF SCOTLAND REVISES ITS MISSION TO HELP IT MEET THE DEMANDS OF A CHANGING ENVIRONMENT

In 1988 and 1989, General Accident Insurance Company (GA), a global insurance firm headquartered in Perth, Scotland, experienced its two years of highest profits. In 1990, it experienced its greatest loss ever, losing over $100 million. Top management, led by Walter Farnham, director, determined that losses were not caused by a one-time event, but rather by fundamental changes in the insurance industry and the firm's lack of an appropriate strategy for coping with these changes. Although the firm had been monitoring these changes, it had not been significantly affected by them until the global recession began in 1990, influencing firms in several areas, but especially in mortgage insurance where losses were substantial. In addition to the recession, the primary factors affecting most insurance firms around the globe, including GA, were increased competition, high levels of insurance losses, the consumer movement seeking to lower insurance rates, encroachment by banks on the insurers' markets, the U.S. junk bond debacle, increased regulatory controls, and an increasingly hostile legal environment.

Top management undertook an examination of the fundamental purposes of the firm, and its strategies, structure, systems, and organizational culture. Since customer service had become so critical to the industry, much of the investigation focused on how it affected each of these areas. In-depth interviews with employees revealed quite quickly that few of them knew the firm's vision and mission and that the importance of customer service had not become a part of the organizational culture. Many employees did not know what the term *strategy* meant, much less that the company's strategy was to differentiate itself from the competition by providing superior performance. The organization's performance measurement and reward systems, for example, were not directed at improving customer service. Finally, the organization's structure was extremely rigid in terms of coordinating rules and policies, and thus while the structure was flat, it nonetheless hindered independent initiatives to make customers happy.

A program of change was embarked upon by mid-1991, with the focus on changing the company's culture, that is, its shared values. At the center of this effort was a change in the firm's mission and strategies, and an effort to educate employees on this change. Systems and structure were changed accordingly in order to reinforce and enable the changes sought. Under the broad concept of mission (much broader than defined in this text), the firm sought to institute new goals, strategies, and systems, and have them become part of corporate values (culture).

Sources: Stephen E. Bailey, Robert C. Capobianco, and Karen H. Sparkman, "General Accident—A Case Analysis," unpublished working paper, Roy E. Crummer Graduate School of Business, Rollins College, December 2, 1991. Also see "British Insurers: Another Disaster," *The Economist*, September 7, 1991, pp. 83, 86.

philosophical representations of purpose. Exhibit 2.2 identifies goal areas defined by Hewlett-Packard.

Peter Drucker, noted management author and consultant, suggests a similar, but somewhat different set of **key results areas** for the organization from those seen in Exhibit 2.2. He suggests that an organization should have objectives in each of these goal areas:

1. Market standing—The firm should state the market share percentage it seeks.
2. Innovation—The firm should establish targets for new products and services (and, we would add, for new ways of performing other marketing functions), reduction of costs, financing, performance of operations, and management of human resources and information.
3. Productivity—The firm should set objectives for efficient use of resources.
4. Physical and financial resources—The firm should state how it intends to acquire and efficiently use these resources.
5. Profitability—It should establish targets for return to owners as measured by various indices.
6. Manager performance and development—It should define how well managers are expected to perform and how it will measure actual performance. Desired future performance levels should be ensured through development programs and targets.
7. Worker performance and attitude—Specific performance levels should be sought and actual performance measured. Attitude types and levels should also be sought.

AT XEROX

Two major goals that Xerox pursued in the 1980s were low cost and high quality. Related objectives throughout the firm were established. Xerox eventually won the Malcolm Baldrige Award for its quality efforts, and it won back customers, as well.

EXHIBIT 2.2   Hewlett-Packard's Strategic Goals

The following is a brief description of the Hewlett-Packard goals in 1989:

1. Profit: To achieve sufficient profit to finance our company growth and to provide the resources we need to achieve our other corporate objectives.
2. Customers: To provide products and services of the highest quality and the greatest possible value to our customers, thereby gaining and holding their respect and loyalty.
3. Fields of Interest: To participate in those fields of interest that build upon our technology and customer base, that offer opportunities for continuing growth, and that enable us to make a needed and profitable contribution.
4. Growth: To let growth be limited only by our profits and our ability to develop and produce innovative products that satisfy real customer needs.
5. Our People: To help people share in the company's success which they make possible; to provide employment security based on their performance; to ensure them a safe and pleasant work environment; to recognize individual achievements; and to help them gain a sense of satisfaction and accomplishment from their work.
6. Management: To foster initiative and creativity by allowing the individual great freedom of action in attaining well-defined objectives.
7. Citizenship: To honor our obligations to society by being an economic, intellectual, and social asset to each nation and each community in which we operate.

Source: "Hewlett-Packard Company, Inc., Corporate Objectives," 1989; confirmed in 1992 by Hewlett-Packard Officials.

8. Public responsibility—The firm should set objectives for the impact it will have on society.[32]

STRATEGIC OBJECTIVES

If the promises of the vision, mission, and goals statements are to be fulfilled, **strategic objectives**—the specific intended results of strategy—must be identified. Objectives are more specific than goals. Objectives steer the organization in the direction of these desires within the constraints of the SWOT of the firm within a strategic intent or strategic fit perspective. Without objectives, the organization is assured of eventual failure. Objectives depend on mission, goals, policy, strategists, internal and external analysis, and the resultant SWOT. They state where the firm wants to be in terms of actions to get there.

Sound Objectives and Their Components

The **components of sound objectives** consist of:

1. The attribute sought
2. An index for measuring progress toward the attribute
3. A target to be achieved or hurdle to be overcome
4. A time frame within which to achieve the target or overcome the hurdle[33]

Table 2.1 portrays the components of several typical objectives. Typical strategic business objectives answer concerns for the impacts of operations on both

TABLE 2.1 Some Typical Business Objectives

Possible Attributes	Possible Indices	Targets and Time Frame		
		Year 1	Year 2	Year 3
Growth	Dollar sales, unit sales	$100 million, 1.00 × units	$120 million, 1.10 × units	$140 million, 1.20 × units
Efficiency	Dollar profits, profits/sales	$10 million, 0.10	$12 million, 0.10	$15 million, 0.11
Utilization of resources	ROI, ROE	0.15, 0.25	0.15, 0.26	0.16, 0.27
Contributions to owners	Dividends per share, earnings per share	$1, $2	$1.10, $2.40	$1.30, $2.80
Contributions to customers	Price, quality, reliability	Equal to or better than competition	Equal to or better than competition	Equal to or better than competition
Contributions to employees	Wage rate, employment stability	$3.50/hour, <5% turnover	$3.75/hour, <4% turnover	$4.00/hour, <4% turnover
Contributions to society	Taxes paid, scholarships, awarded, etc.	$10 million, $100,000	$12 million, $120,000	$16 million, $120,000

Source: C. W. Hofer, "A Conceptual Scheme for Formulating a Total Business Strategy," no. BP-0040, Dover, Mass.: Case Teacher's Association, 1976, p. 2. Copyright 1976 by C. W. Hofer. Reproduced by permission.

the organization and the external environment. Table 2.1 shows that the fundamental internal concerns of the organization include the attributes of efficiency (profits, especially in relation to sales), growth (sales), utilization of resources (return on investment, or ROI), and contributions to owners (earnings per share) and to employees (wages, employee development). Externally, the organization must be concerned with contributions to customers (quality, price) and to society (taxes paid, corporate citizenship). Contributions to other major stakeholders—the individuals and groups on whom the actions of the organization have direct impacts—are also vital concerns. Nonbusiness organizations have similar objectives, but they don't state them in terms of profit.

If you don't know where you're going, any road will get you there, says the old saw. Without objectives, "there" is usually nowhere! First, you must decide where you are going, then you can decide what road to take. Objectives provide direction and motivation. The **objectives-setting process** also provides valuable communication within and among organizational subunits. Objectives make strategic goals more specific.

Peter Drucker's list of key results areas, shown earlier in this chapter, varies slightly from the factors noted in Table 2.1. His principal additions to the list in the table are market standing, innovation, management performance, and employee development and attitudes.[34] Most experts on strategy suggest similar, if slightly different, areas for goals and objectives setting. These types of objectives are widely recognized as the best, in practice.

Firms in every part of the globe are facing increasing competition. Even firms that have enjoyed virtual monopolies in their markets in the past find themselves needing to adapt to changing environments. Daimler-Benz, the maker of Mercedes-Benz automobiles, is also a conglomerate with businesses in aerospace, engine manufacturing, and consumer products. This prestigious firm finds itself in need of infusing high technology into its staid, conservative manufacturing processes. Edzard Reuter, head of Daimler-Benz, recognizes that global competition and changing technology demand changes in a firm that has become rather self-satisfied. He has insisted that every unit of the company innovate, from washing machines to jet fighters, and he has promoted high technology, for example, using microelectronics and new materials. Transforming Daimler-Benz will not be easy, since major German industrial firms are interlocked with major banks and government ministries through interlocking directorates and common shareholders. Furthermore, with conglomerate expansion a recent and sizeable undertaking, cultures of firms must be merged and synergies of technology transfer achieved.

To assist in achieving desired changes, Reuter has established goals and specific objectives for various areas of innovation, high-tech integration, and culture transformation. He has also set priorities for major revamping of firms, with Mercedes being the first to undergo dramatic transformation. He has established objectives and related timetables for rehabilitating the firm's diesel models, which have come under severe criticism by environmentalists, for revamping S-class models, and for moving rapidly into smart cars, which will feature electronic devices that enhance customer safety and comfort (for example, devices that enhance vision and warn of road hazards). Daimler-Benz has also sought to acquire new technology through alliances with firms such as Mitsubishi and United Technologies.[35]

The Objectives Established

Organizations establish many types of objectives. Unfortunately, some organizations set no specific objectives; some establish only a limited number; others establish objectives only in areas of operating performance.

Les Rue, reporting on a survey of 400 mostly large firms in several major industries, found that most firms have multiple, quantitative, written statements of objectives. He found that firms established objectives for earnings and sales more often than for returns, and that many organizations established objectives for capital growth, market share, and sales or earnings. Rue also examined financial analyses associated with established objectives and found that profit (as derived from income statements) was the primary concern, but that most firms were also concerned with balance-sheet and cash-flow analysis.[36]

When J. W. Dobbie examined 50 large California-based firms (all with over $100 million in annual sales), he found that they tended to express objectives according to the type of strategy they employed. His strategy classifications included personal (based on the aims of the chief executive), opportunity, geographic expansion, financial growth, and business (for planning or diversified firms). The types of objectives he examined included various return methods, growth in sales or earnings, and pro forma financial statements or resource control. Dobbie observed that managerial style and the position of the planning unit within the organization structure affected the types of objectives chosen. While Dobbie's sample size limits the applicability of his findings, his study at least suggests that increases in complexity of operations and experience in strategy formulation bring increases in the number of objectives and their diversity.[37]

Y. K. Shetty, in a study of 82 companies, found a wide range of corporate objectives, as Table 2.2 indicates. Most companies had 5 or 6; one company had only 1 objective, and another had 18. As Table 2.2 indicates, economic objectives dominated corporate concerns. Shetty found that objectives varied by industry. Social responsibility was the second most frequently cited objective of chemical and drug companies, for example, but the fifth most frequently cited objective of electrical and electronics firms. Shetty concluded that as organizations grow, their environments tend to become more turbulent, and as they become more responsive to stakeholders outside their immediate economic constituencies, their objectives change.[38]

In recent years, firms have stressed objectives related to increasing shareholder value. Alan J. Schneider, in a study of 118 firms with sales of over $1 billion, found an increasing emphasis on higher returns on assets.[39] This trend reflects the growing concern among investors for protection of their interests after the frantic takeover activity in the 1980s, most of which was sparked by weak shareholder values in target firms.

TABLE 2.2 Range of Corporate Goals for 82 Firms

Category	Number	Percent[a]
Profitability	73	89
Growth	67	82
Market share	54	66
Social responsibility	53	65
Employee welfare	51	62
Product quality and service	49	60
Research and development	44	54
Diversification	42	51
Efficiency	41	50
Financial stability	40	49
Resource conservation	32	39
Management development	29	35
Multinational enterprise	24	29
Consolidation	14	17
Miscellaneous other goals	15	18

[a]Adds to more than 100 percent because most companies have more than one goal.

Source: © 1979 by the Regents of the University of California. Reprinted from the *California Management Review*, Volume XXII, no. 2, p. 73, by permission of the Regents.

As these studies indicate, the objectives formulated by organizations to further their strategies are dominated by, but not limited to, economic concerns. Other types of objectives include employee development and social responsibility. While it is apparent that most business organizations today are concerned primarily with mission-based objectives, other issues are expected to become increasingly important as society continues to demand more of business.

Notably absent in studies to date is the innovation objective, which becomes ever more critical in a highly changeable and competitive environment. Thomas J. Peters and Robert H. Waterman, Jr. found early in their research that organizations with strictly financial goals and objectives were less successful financially than companies whose goals and objectives reflected broader concerns and values.[40] While no other research to date discusses similar relationships, the comments of Peters and Waterman are certainly worth noting, for they suggest that a philosophy of overall excellence may outperform one of strictly financial excellence. Intuitively, that philosophy seems sensible. In collaboration with Nancy Austin, Peters later reiterated this view, and together they added that all truly excellent companies are highly innovative.[41] This view has been substantiated recently by the research of Michael Porter on global competitiveness.[42]

Levels of Objectives

There are three major **levels of objectives** and planning within the organization: strategic, intermediate, and operational. The compression of planning time horizons often narrows these levels to two: strategic and operational. The objectives toward which strategic plans are directed should be specific at all levels. For example, a firm might set objectives of a 15-percent return on investment, a 20-percent penetration of the product market, a 1-percent increase in sales per year, and so forth. At the strategic planning stage, however, the plans need not be stated so specifically; in fact, such plans are usually broadly stated. As planning progresses through the next two stages, however, intermediate and operational plans set out more specifically how objectives will be achieved.

Intermediate plans translate strategy into more specific courses of action for major organization subsystems. Operational plans translate intermediate plans into very specific courses of action for lower-level subsystems, work groups, and individuals. Usually the planning process generates a series of increasingly complex and detailed subobjectives, subplans, subpolicies, and so forth, until responsibility for corporate objectives and actions is distributed to individual

AT XEROX

Xerox has established a series of profit objectives for its new digital image processing products. Due to pricing structures, these processors won't add much to the bottom line for several years.

workers. Again, as with most management terminology, firms use different definitions to describe the various levels of plans established to accomplish the firm's missions. One must allow for differences in terminology in examining strategy and in the practice of strategic management.

Organizational Objectives As Integration Mechanisms: MBORR

Management by objectives, results, and rewards (MBORR) is a management system that encompasses planning, control, motivation, communication, and the development of subordinates. Many programs of this kind have been identified by such names as management by objectives (MBO), management by results (MBR), and management by compensation (MBC), as well as MBORR. These techniques have probably been more frequently discussed than any other type of management practice in the last 30 years. Few people can agree on their specific contents, but most agree on four general dimensions:

1. Establishment of objectives
2. Employee participation in setting objectives and plans
3. Evaluation and control of performance
4. Rewards for results

The normal MBORR process involves the establishment of specific objectives by top management in all performance areas. These objectives are then communicated to the next lower level of management, which may or may not have participated in their development. At each level, objectives may then be distributed to the appropriate managers for their acceptance or rejection, or to generate alternative proposals that state the objectives lower-level managers want to or can achieve. A manager and his or her superior negotiate the subordinate's objectives. Once they agree, the process shifts to the next lower level of management and continues until the distribution of objectives reaches the supervisory level. The process usually stops there, as first-line managers ordinarily cannot properly utilize this technique.

Peter Drucker first introduced MBORR-type techniques to the public in 1954 as MBR, after observing the method's success at General Motors. Since that time, countless studies and reviews of the techniques' effectiveness and ineffectiveness have been reported, variations in methods suggested, and corrective actions for weaknesses proposed. George Odiorne popularized the concept as MBO. James Higgins has added the *RR* to emphasize the importance of measuring results and rewarding them.[43]

A few of the major findings regarding MBORR-style programs are listed below. Positive results include the following:

1. Performance is improved in both quantity and quality.
2. Communications and understanding are improved.
3. Job satisfaction is improved.

4. Individual growth is enhanced.
5. Roles are clarified.

Negative results include the following:

1. Managers may become more critical.
2. Managers may use MBORR objectives as whips.
3. The establishment of objectives entails all sorts of problems: scale-unit bias, objectives set too high or too low, worker refusal to accept objectives, inflexible objectives, and difficulty setting objectives in nonquantifiable areas.
4. The process may focus too closely on the short run.
5. The process seems to lose effectiveness over time.
6. Monetary rewards are sometimes inadequate to maintain performance.
7. The process often takes too much time.
8. It usually ignores group dynamics.
9. Individuals' physical and mental limitations may inhibit the process.
10. Goals established tend to become maximums, even when they could have been exceeded.

The negative results reported here far outnumber the positive effects, and at least 20 more could have been listed. Studies of MBORR's effectiveness in widely varying settings lead to inconsistent findings. More important, many investigators have reported that the technique's implementation, not the technique itself, is the problem. It appears that when an appropriate implementation procedure is followed and top management is involved and concerned, MBORR is effective. G. P. Latham and G. A. Yukl, in reviewing published and unpublished field research, have reported that whether or not MBORR-type programs were specifically used, setting objectives has led to superior performance.[44] In summary, without specific objectives, strategy eventually fails to elicit sufficient performance.[45]

One recent criticism of MBO-type systems is that they are too complex and too bureaucratic for the rapidly changing environments in which most organizations function today. MBO takes too long and requires too much paperwork to change objectives to reflect the demands of the changing environment. This criticism contradicts the experience of companies that use MBO systems that employ computer-based information systems. (Cultural adaptation to such systems, however, will require considerable effort for many companies.)

Two companies have made extremely successful use of computer-based MBORR systems: Barnett Banks, a southeastern regional bank headquartered in Jacksonville, Florida, and Cypress Semiconductor, headquartered in San Jose, California. Barnett is the nation's 23rd largest bank holding company, and Cypress has sales in excess of $200 million each year. Each of Barnett's 35 regional bank groups and its managers is evaluated every month according to a 36-page computer-generated report that rates their performance on numerous, previously agreed-upon objectives. Rewards are directly tied to performance on these criteria. The bank's entire culture focuses upon performance, as managed through the MBORR process.[46] At Cypress Semiconductor, the process is even more computerized, as the Strategic Challenge reveals.

Prioritizing Objectives

One of the most perplexing problems confronting the strategic manager is prioritizing objectives. Many objectives seem important, and in the hectic, day-to-day, crisis-management environment, it's easy to forget that the swamp still needs draining. Even during the cyclical or periodic planning process, the task of establishing priorities among objectives is not easy. Some objectives inevitably conflict with others. Among the objectives listed in Table 2.1, for example, one might expect conflicts between contributions to society, to employees, and perhaps to customers and returns to owners (in the short term, at least). Conflicts also often arise between corporate and business objectives, or between business and functional objectives. Some strategic and operational objectives almost always conflict.

STRATEGIC CHALLENGE

AT CYPRESS SEMICONDUCTORS, OBJECTIVES RULE

How do you make money in a business in which just about everybody else is losing money? How do you keep track of company, division, unit, work group, and individual performance in a rapidly changing, highly competitive, technological environment? One way is by using what has come to be known as turbo MBO. T. J. Rogers, founder and CEO of Cypress Semiconductor, swears by it. The process begins every Monday morning with project leaders sitting down with their staffs and assigning the jobs that need attention that week. Everyone's new objectives are put into the firm's minicomputer, which is linked to executives and managers via personal computers. Lotus 1-2-3 spreadsheets display objectives. On Tuesday, people prioritize individual objectives. On Wednesday, they review progress toward accomplishment of objectives. On Friday, they evaluate performance, and the cycle begins again.

Other features of the system assist T. J. Rogers and his managers. For example, the computer alerts the president when his executives are delinquent on 20 percent of their objectives. Rogers looks for trends in performance levels. At Cypress, no surprises is a way of life. Managers can analyze performance at all levels of the organization. Rogers believes that the system "forces each of us to face reality every day." He continues, "All of Cypress's 1,400 employees have goals [objectives], which in theory, makes them no different from employees at most other companies. What does make our people different is that every week they set their own goals, commit to achieving them by a specific date, enter them into a data base, and report whether or not they completed prior goals." Rewards are directly related to performance, as defined by the system.

Source: T. J. Rogers, "No Excuses Management," *Harvard Business Review*, July–August 1990, pp. 84–98; Steve Kaufman, "Going for the Goals," *Success*, January–February 1988, pp. 38–41.

The problem of prioritizing is further compounded by objectives' normal interdependence. Also, every organization has power centers that demand attention to their own objectives. Finally, one's personal objectives may conflict with organizational priorities. How, then, does the strategist determine which objectives are most important?

There are few proven decision rules for determining appropriate priorities. Managers may simply react to problems as they arise, establishing the resolution of the most current issue as the major priority. This tactic does not seem proper for a true strategic planner, but some managers use it. In fact, sometimes it's necessary to be flexible and recognize that a current issue has taken on critical and strategic importance and needs to take priority. Major decisions are made reactively, on the spur of the moment more often than one would like to think. Even though we would like strategists to initiate proactive action, many times they need to react to situations. Thus, general managers also respond to crises as they evolve. When AT&T attempted a takeover of NCR in 1990, for example, NCR's CEO had to react and launch an immediate defense of the company in an effort to attain the objective that dominated all others at the moment.[47]

A rational approach to prioritizing objectives is more desirable. Certainly the periodic strategic planning process gives participants the opportunity to evaluate and weigh alternative objectives and assign them priorities. The preponderance of evidence suggests that firms benefit from a participative approach involving the key managers affected, the strategists, in this case. Simple ranking, paired-comparisons ranking, nonparametric statistics, or any other generally recognized method of ranking objectives would seem to move the organization in the right direction, so long as the method chosen is supported by appropriate information and those who must implement the objectives take part in the process. Often several objectives will be viewed as equally important and all of them will be pursued simultaneously.[48]

ORGANIZATIONAL POLICY

The term *policy* here designates broad guidance to ensure the successful establishment of goals and objectives and the successful formulation, implementation, and control of strategy. Most policies have broad and major impacts on the organization, but some have more limited impacts and are designed to guide decisions through more specific constraints. Policies provide organization members, primarily managers, with a framework within which they can make decisions. Here are two examples of policies:

- Only products that promise at least a 15-percent return on investment (ROI) will be considered as additions to existing product lines.
- Only products the firm can manufacture with high quality will be chosen for inclusion in the product line.

Because of these policies, this firm's corporate, business, and product division managers will not select products that do not provide at least the stated rate of return and that do not have the potential for high quality. Because the managers do not have to determine the appropriate level of ROI or the level of product quality to seek, these policies save time and effort.

As with the term *strategy,* the meaning attached to the term *policy* varies widely. The student of strategic management should recognize this fact and should not allow semantic problems to interfere with organizational analysis. *Policy* is often employed to describe what is here defined as strategy, or the term may be used to describe very specific rules, such as smoking restrictions or retirement ages for top managers. Policy often is considered to be a component of strategy. In various contexts, strategies have a way of shading into policies, and vice versa.

No matter what we call them, however, an organization must have major plans of action in order to accomplish its mission. The organization must also have some form of broad guidance for formulating, implementing, and controlling these plans. These components of effective organizations are labeled here *strategy* and *policy,* respectively.

You will note that Figure 2.1 identified three major types of policies: strategic policies, policies that aid implementation, and control policies. Let us now examine the first of these in more detail. The second and third will be discussed in later chapters.

Organizational Policy at the Strategic Level

Strategies derive from the organization's mission and from the policies that guide its formulation. These policies, which are here called **strategic policies,** are usually created by the owners, the board of directors, the chief executive officer, top line and staff personnel, top SBU managers, or professional planners. Other organization members may, however, aid in their formulation. Some organizations refer to these policies as *basic assumptions* or *primary intents.* Regardless of their designations, certain guidelines must be available to the organization's strategists as they determine strategic goals and objectives and formulate strategy. In the business organization, these strategic policies normally relate to the following issues, though they vary in detail from firm to firm:

1. The return on investment desired, and other performance criteria
2. The scope of the strategy
3. The basic actions in which the organization may engage: competition, growth, diversification, and so on
4. The industries to be entered
5. The qualifications of products to be offered
6. The organization's culture and management philosophy
7. The geographic location of the basic actions
8. The role of the organization in the total society
9. The ethical behavior expected of organization members (See the Strategic Ethical Challenge feature in this chapter.)

On the basis of these policies and the organization's mission (the components of which sometimes overlap with strategic policies) along with internal and environmental information, the organization's strategists determine goals and

AT XEROX

If you further examined Xerox's policies for its new product line, you would expect to find policies related to several of the above nine areas, for example, the return on investment expected, the quality level desired, geographic target markets, and so on.

objectives and formulate strategies. After considering information related to internal and external environmental factors, the organization's strategists may periodically redefine the mission and/or the basic policies that guide the formulation of various strategies and their goals and objectives.

Conceptually, strategic policies differ from mission, goals, and objectives. In practice, however, the four are often intermingled, as Table 2.3 suggests. Policies are found at every level of the organization. At the highest level, strategic policies guide the formation of objectives and strategy. Lower-level policies should be

TABLE 2.3   Components of Mission, Goals, Objectives, and Strategic Policies

Mission	Goals[a]	Representative Objectives	Strategic Policies
Business(es)	Market share	20%	Return on investment
Target markets	Innovation	20% of profits must come from products less than 5 years old	Scope
Business scope			Basic actions
Corporate philosophy	Productivity	Gross profit margins of 32%	Industries
Geographic location	Physical and financial resources	0.01% waste of raw materials	Qualifications of products
Self-concept			Culture and philosophy
Public image	Profit	15% ROI	Geographic location
	Manager performance and development	20% of all managers in development programs	Role of organization in society
	Worker performance and attitude	75% of sales force to reach sales quotas	
	Public responsibility	To be an affirmative action employer	
	Customer service	100% product quality	

[a]Key results areas identified in Peter Drucker, *The Practice of Management* (New York: Harper & Bros., 1954), p. 62.

subordinate to those at higher levels of the strategy. Exhibit 2.3 shows the strategic policies of a highly successful firm, the Coca-Cola Company. Note that some of these policies are so specific that they constitute strategies.[49]

Once strategic policies are established, the organization literally lives or dies by them. Both implementation and control policies (discussed in later chapters) are based on the outcomes of the strategic policies. All three types of policies are critically important. As all actions will follow the guidance provided by policy, proper policy formulation is critical to the organization's success. Such firms as Martin-Marietta and Kmart have highly functional policies based on mission and information. Such policies allow firms to survive and prosper.

EXHIBIT 2.3   Coca-Cola's Strategic Policies

Our Challenge

In order to give my vision of our Company for 1990, I must first postulate what I visualize our mission to be during the 1980s. I see our challenge as continuing the growth in profits of our highly successful existing main businesses, and those we may choose to enter, at a rate substantially in excess of inflation, in order to give our shareholders an above average total return on their investment. The unique position of excellence that the trademark Coca-Cola has attained in the world will be protected and enhanced as a primary objective.

Our Business

I perceive us by the 1990s to continue to be or become the leading force in the soft drink industry in each of the countries in which it is economically feasible for us to be so. We shall continue to emphasize product quality worldwide, as well as market share improvement in growth markets. The products of our Foods Division will also continue to be the leading entries in those markets which they serve, particularly in the U.S. The Wine Spectrum will continue to be managed for significant growth with special attention paid to optimizing return on assets.[1]

In the U.S. we will also become a stronger factor in the packaged consumer goods business. I do not rule out providing appropriate services to this same consumer as well. It is most likely that we will be in industries in which we are not today. We will not, however, stray far from our major strengths: an impeccable and positive image with the consumer; a unique franchise system second to none; and the intimate knowledge of, and contacts with, local business conditions around the world.

In choosing new areas of business, each market we enter must have sufficient inherent real growth potential to make entry desirable. It is not our desire to battle continually for share in a stagnant market in these new areas of business. By and large, industrial markets are not our business.

Finally, we shall tirelessly investigate services that complement our product lines and that are compatible with our consumer image.

Our Consumers

Company management of all levels will be committed to serving to the best of its ability our Bottlers and our consumers, as well as the retail and wholesale distribution systems through which these consumers are reached. These are our primary targets. The world is our arena in which to win marketing victories as we must.

Our Shareholders

We shall, during the next decade, remain totally committed to our shareholders and to the protection and enhancement of their investment and confidence in our Company, its character and style, products and image.

Our "Bottom Line"

My financial vision is not complicated, but it will require courage and commitment to attain financial goals consistently and effect growth in real profits, most especially during uncertain and fast changing economic times.

Our strong balance sheet and financial position will be maintained so that the Company can withstand any economic windstorm, as well as enable us to take advantage of expansion opportunities which complement our existing business and that offer acceptable earnings growth and return on investment.

It is our desire to continue to pay ever-increasing dividends to our shareholders. This will be done as a result of rapidly increasing annual earnings while of necessity reducing our dividend pay-out ratio, in order to reinvest a greater percentage of our earnings to help sustain the growth rate which we must have. We shall consider divesting assets when they no longer generate acceptable returns and earnings growth. Increasing annual earnings per share and effecting increased return on equity are still the name of the game—but not to the extent that our longer term viability is threatened.

Our People

Finally, let me comment on this vision as it affects our "life style"—or business behavior—as a viable international business entity. (To) the courage and commitment that will be indispensable as we move through the 1980s . . . I wish to add integrity and fairness, and insist that the combination of these four ethics be permeated from top to bottom throughout our organization so that our behavior will produce leaders, good managers, and—most importantly—entrepreneurs. It is my desire that we take initiatives as opposed to being only reactive and that we encourage intelligent individual risk-taking.

As a true international company with a multi-cultural and multinational employee complement, we must foster the "international family" concept which has been a part of our tradition. All employees will have equal opportunities to grow, develop and advance within the Company. Their progress will depend only on their abilities, ambition and achievements.

Our Wisdom

When we arrive at the 1990s, my vision is to be able to say with confidence that all of us in our own way displayed:

■ The ability to see the long-term consequences of current actions;

■ The willingness to sacrifice, if necessary, short-term gains for longer-term benefits;

■ The sensitivity to anticipate and adapt to change—change in consumer life styles, change in consumer tastes and change in consumer needs;

■ The committment to manage our enterprise in such a way that we will always be considered a welcomed and important part of the business community in each and every country in which we do business; and

■ The capacity to control what is controllable and the wisdom not to bother with what is not.

---

[1] In Implementing our strategy, the sale of The Wine Spectrum to Joseph E. Seagram & Son, Inc., was completed in November 1983.
Source: Roberto C. Goizueta, Chairman, Board of Directors, and Chief Executive Officer, The Coca-Cola Company, in a 1983 update of a March 4, 1981, endorsement by the Board of Directors, "Strategies for the 1980s."

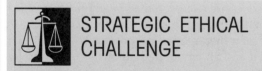

STRATEGIC ETHICAL CHALLENGE

CODES OF ETHICS

One of the major concerns of businesses today is that their employees behave in an ethical manner. The 1980s seemed to many to have been a decade of unethical behavior in many firms. Some firms, such as Drexel Burnham Lambert, which ultimately declared bankruptcy, suffered severely from the unethical and sometimes illegal acts of their employees. As a consequence, many firms have established codes of ethics, and in many cases, conducted training programs to help ensure employee compliance with these codes. Ethics codes, even those accompanied by training programs, are not enough, though. The organization must build a culture that demands ethical behavior. Such cultures do not happen overnight. They result from a complex series of interactions of attitudes, events, rewards, policies, education, and values. Furthermore, it is imperative that companies alert their employees to probable ethical dilemmas they may face, and how to cope with them. Finally, a firm needs to provide its employees with a series of practical approaches to cope with ethical problems. Even a checklist of questions to ask when problem solving is helpful.

Dana Corporation, the Toledo, Ohio manufacturer of automobile and industrial equipment components, lives by its credo, "The Philosophy and Policies of Dana." This document sets the tone for the organization's culture. Among the issues addressed are the importance of increasing shareholder value, the fact that people are the company's most important asset, and that employees should behave in an ethical fashion. The document, in fact, defines what is ethical and what is not, but it is the uses of thoughts conveyed in this document, and not the document itself, that make Dana an ethical company. This creates a culture that demands ethics.

Sources: Priscilla S. Rogers and John M. Swales, "We the People? An Analysis of the Dana Corporation Policies Document," *Journal of Business Communication*, Summer 1990, pp. 293–313; Michael R. Hyman, Robert Skipper, and Richard Tansey, "Ethical Codes Are Not Enough," *Business Horizons*, March/April 1990, pp. 15–22; Alan L. Otten, "Ethics on the Job: Companies Alert Employees to Potential Dilemmas," *The Wall Street Journal*, July 14, 1986, p. 23; Laura L. Nash, "Ethics without the Sermon," *Harvard Business Review*, November–December 1981, pp. 79–90

STRATEGIC MANAGER'S SUMMARY

1. Boards of directors have historically been passive approvers of top managements' strategies, but, recently they have become more active. The CEO is most often the dominant setter of strategy, and coalitions may also play important roles. Top line managers have begun to play more prominent roles in strategizing while the role of the professional planner seems to be waning.
2. Vision, mission, goals, and objectives are related in that, beginning with vision and ending with objectives, each term in the sequence further defines the previous term. Together they form a hierarchy of purposes.
3. Vision provides general direction and an emotionally motivating component to invoke commitment, as well as inspiring people to help the organization achieve its objectives. Mission defines the vision in terms of the business(es) in which the firm wants to compete, the target market(s), the geographic scope of operations, and important philosophical or operating conditions such as product quality or social responsibility. Goals further define mission in terms of generally desirable, philosophically based key results areas. Strategic objectives define goals in terms of specific results expected.
4. A company's mission statement is more sound if, in addition to the basic financial achievement issues, it focuses on broader issues.
5. Table 2.1 identifies typical business objectives and their components.
6. Management by objectives, results, and rewards (MBORR) is a management planning, control, and development process. It is a major way of distributing responsibility for strategic objectives and related actions for achieving strategy to all employees of the organization. It emphasizes evaluation of performance and relating rewards to this performance.
7. There are often overlaps in the ways that the terms *vision, mission, goals, strategic objectives, policies,* and *strategies* are used. Table 2.3 examines some of these for mission, goals, objectives, and policies.

KEY TERMS

boards of directors
business organization's mission
CEO as strategist
coalitions
components of sound objectives
corporate philosophy
goals
intrapreneurs
key results areas
levels of objectives

management by objectives, results, and
   rewards (MBORR)
objectives-setting process
organizational categories
professional planners
strategic objectives
strategic policies
strategists
top line managers
vision

DISCUSSION QUESTIONS

1. It has been suggested that a universal mission statement should be created, such as, "To improve the economic well-being and quality of life of all stakeholders."[50] Evaluate such a mission statement in terms of the definitions and criteria established in the chapter.
2. Why do organizations function better when they have objectives than when they don't?
3. What are the major processes in MBORR?
4. Describe, as best you can with the information from the opening vignette, how Xerox's vision, mission, goals, and objectives may have changed in the period from 1980 to 1990.
5. Discuss how each of the ten strategic management challenges identified in Chapter 1 might affect organizational vision, mission, goals, objectives, and policies.

STRATEGIC AUDIT QUESTIONS

1. Does the CEO provide this organization with a vision, or do others? How good is it?
2. Does this organization have a mission statement? If so, evaluate it, and assess its impact.
3. Does this organization have goals? How good are they?
4. Does this organization have strategic objectives?

5. Do they have all of the components of sound objectives?
    a. Attribute sought
    b. Index for measuring progress
    c. Target to be achieved or hurdle to be overcome
    d. Time frame for the target to be achieved or the hurdle overcome
6. Are objectives found in all key results areas? Strategic goals areas?
7. Does the organization have an integrated system for setting objectives and controlling and rewarding performance, such as MBORR? How good is it?
8. Are its objectives prioritized properly?
9. What are the strategic policies and philosophies of this firm? How good are they? What impact do they have on strategy?

Endnotes

1. For a theoretical discussion of the role of the board, see Shaker A. Zahra, "Increasing the Board's Involvement in Strategy," *Long Range Planning*, December 1990, pp. 109–117.

2. For a discussion of these problems in the health-care industry, see David Hunter and Merrilee Gerew, "Four Symptoms of a Troubled Board," *Trustee*, June 1990, pp. 12–13.

3. For example, see "Taking Charge: Corporate Directors Start to Flex Their Muscles," *Business Week*, July 3, 1989, pp. 66–74.

4. Idalene F. Kesner and Roy B. Johnson, "Crisis in the Boardroom: Fact & Fiction," *Academy of Management Executive*, February 1990, pp. 23–35; Judith H. Dobrzynski and Eric Schine, "Lockheed's Lesson: It's Open Season on Yes-Man Boards," *Business Week*, April 16, 1990, p. 25; Arch Patton and John C. Baker, "Why Won't Directors Rock the Boat?" *Harvard Business Review*, November–December 1987, pp. 10–18; Laurie Baum, "The Job Nobody Wants," *Business Week*, September 8, 1986, pp. 56–61.

5. "Board of Directors: Inside Job," *Inc*, October 1990, p. 151.

6. John A. Pearce II and Shaker A. Zahra, "The Relative Power of CEOs and Boards of Directors' Associations with Corporate Performance," *Strategic Management Journal*, February 1991, pp. 135–153.

7. Jack Young, "Pawns or Potentates: The Reality of America's Corporate Boards," *Academy of Management Review*, October 1990, pp. 85–87.

8. James Kristie, "The Chairman and the Board," *Directors & Boards*, Spring 1990, pp. 58–60.

9. "How Intrapreneuring Can Change the Face of North America," *Management World*, April 1983, p. 24.

10. For an analysis of how several executives perceive their roles to be changing, see Harry S. Jones III, Ronald E. Fry, and Suresh Srivasta, "The Office of the CEO: Understanding the Executive Experience," *Academy of Management Executive*, August 1990, pp. 36–47.

11. See, for example, James Bryan Quinn, *Strategies for Change: Logical Incrementalism* (Homewood, Ill.: Irwin, 1980); L. J. Bourgeois III and J. V. Singh, "Organizational Slack and Political Behavior among Top Management Teams," *Academy of Management Proceedings*, 1983, pp. 43–47; H. Mintzberg, D. Raisinghani, and A. Theoret, "The Structure of Unstructured Decision Processes," *Administrative Science Quarterly*, June 1976, p. 258.

12. Peter Drucker, "The Coming of the New Organization," *Harvard Business Review*, January–February, 1988, pp. 45–53; Gordon Pinchot III, *Intrapreneuring* (New York: Perennial Library/Harper & Row, 1985).

13. Benjamin B. Tregoe and Peter M. Tobia, "Why Involve Middle Managers in Strategy?" *Manage*, October 1990, pp. 30–33; Robert O. Metzger, "Middle Managers in the Middle of Planning," *Bankers Monthly*, July 1990, p. 68; Bill Wooldridge and Steven W. Floyd, "The Strategy Process, Middle Management Involvement, and Organizational Performance," *Strategic Management Journal*, March/April 1990, pp. 231–241.

14. Robert Norton, "Who Owns This Company, Anyhow?" *Fortune*, July 29, 1991, pp. 131–142.

15. For example, see Ellen Morris, "Vision and Strategy: A Focus for the Future," *Journal of Business Strategy*, Fall 1987, pp. 51–58; Thomas J. Peters, *Thriving on Chaos: Handbook for a Management Revolution* (New York: Knopf, 1987), pp. 398–408; Noel M. Tichy and Mary Anne DeVanna, *The Transformational Leader* (New York: Wiley, 1986), pp. viii, ix, Chapters 1 and 5; and Robert H. Waterman, Jr., *The Renewal Factor* (New York: Bantam, 1987), pp. 222–225.

16. Tichy and DeVanna, *Transformational Leader*, p. 130.

17. Donald R. Schmincke, "Strategic Thinking: A Perspective for Success," *Management Review*, August 1990, pp. 16–19.

18. Steve Shirley, "Corporate Strategy and Entrepreneurial Vision," *Long Range Planning*, December 1989, p. 107.

19. The Chrysler example is well-documented. For information on the other two examples, see Teruo Yamanouchi, "Breakthrough: The Development of the Canon Personal Copier," *Long Range Planning*, October 1989, pp. 11–21; and Tracy E. Benson, "Robert Haas' Vision Scores 20/20," *Industry Week*, April 2, 1990, pp. 19–23.

20. Peters, *Thriving on Chaos*, p. 399.

21. Peters, *Thriving on Chaos*, pp. 401–404.

22. Peter M. Blau and W. Richard Scott, *Formal Organizations* (New York: Chandler, 1962), pp. 250–253.

23. Philip Kotler, *Marketing Management: Analysis, Planning, Control*, 6th ed. (Englewood Cliffs, N.J.: Prentice-Hall, 1988), pp. 37–43; John A. Pearce II, "The Company Mission As a Strategic Tool," *Sloan Management Review*, Spring 1982, p. 15.

24. John A. Pearce II and Fred David, "Corporate Mission Statements: The Bottom Lines," *Academy of Management Executive*, May 1987, pp. 109–116.

25. Fred David, "How Companies Define Their Mission," *Long Range Planning*, February 1989, pp. 90–97.

26. John A. Pearce II and Kendall Roth, "Multinationalization of the Mission Statement," *Advanced Management Journal*, Summer 1988, pp. 39–44.

27. David, *How Companies Define*, p. 92. The sample base was 181 responding firms from the *Business Week* 1,000 list.

28. Alexandra Biesada, "Federal Express: Pride Goeth . . ." *Financial World*, September 4, 1990, pp. 38–41; Clemens P. Work, "The Flying-Package Trade Takes Off," *U.S. News & World Report*, October 2, 1989, pp. 47–50.

29. The first two examples are well-documented. For information on USX, see Thomas F. O'Boyle, "Raider Referendum: Icahn Forces the Issue at USX—Is It Time to Get Out of Steel?" *The Wall Street Journal*, March 9, 1990, pp. A1, A4.

30. Andrew Campbell and Sally Yung, "Brief Case: Mission, Vision, and Strategic Intent," *Long Range Planning*, August 1991, pp. 145–147; Andrew Campbell and Sally Yung, "Creating a Sense of Mission," *Long Range Planning*, August 1991, pp. 10–20.

31. Max D. Richards, *Setting Strategic Goals and Objectives*, 2d ed. (St. Paul, Minn.: West, 1986), p. 22.

32. Peter F. Drucker, *The Practice of Management* (New York: Harper & Row, 1954), pp. 65–83.

33. Charles Hofer and Dan Schendel, *Strategy Formulation: Analytical Concepts* (St. Paul, Minn.: West, 1978), pp. 21–22.

34. Drucker, *Practice of Management*, pp. 65–83.

35. John Templeman, "Daimler's Drive to Become a High-Tech Speedster," *Business Week*, February 12, 1990, pp. 55, 58; Charles Smith, "Two's Company: Mitsubishi and Benz Plan Wide Links," *Far Eastern Economic Review*, May 24, 1990, p. 67; and Stanley W. Kandebo, "GE Sues Daimler-Benz, MTU over United Technologies Pact," *Aviation Week & Space Technology*," April 16, 1990, pp. 19, 20.

36. L. W. Rue, "Tools and Techniques for Long Range Planning," *Long Range Planning*, October 1974, pp. 61–65.

37. J. W. Dobbie, "Guides to a Foundation for Strategic Planning in Large Firms," paper presented to the 34th Annual Meeting of the Academy of Management, Seattle, August 1974.

38. Y. K. Shetty, "New Look at Corporate Goals," *California Management Review*, Winter 1979, pp. 71–79.

39. Alan J. Schneider, "How Top Companies Create Shareholder Value," *Financial Executive*, May/June 1990, pp. 34–39.

40. Thomas J. Peters and Robert H. Waterman, Jr., *In Search of Excellence* (New York: Harper & Row, 1982), Chapter 1.

41. Thomas J. Peters and Nancy K. Austin, *A Passion for Excellence* (New York: Random House, 1985).

42. Michael Porter, *The Competitive Advantage of Nations* (New York: Free Press, 1990).

43. James M. Higgins, *Human Relations: Behavior at Work*, 2d ed. (New York: Random House, 1987), Chapter 11.

44. G. P. Latham and G. A. Yukl, "A Review of Research on the Application of Goal Setting in Organizations," *Academy of Management Journal*, December 1975, pp. 827–832.

45. For a discussion of how specific objectives at the line level increase performance, see Georg Kellinghusen and Klaus Wubbenhorst, "Strategic Control for Improved Performance," *Long Range Planning*, June 1990, pp. 30–40.

46. Thomas E. Ricks, "Branching Out: Attentive to Service, Barnett Banks Grows Fast, Keeps Profit Up," *The Wall Street Journal*, April 3, 1987, pp. 1, 27.

47. Peter Coy, "AT&T Bares Its Teeth," *Business Week*, December 17, 1990, pp. 24–26.

48. For a review of the objective-setting process, see Max Richards, *Setting Strategic Goals and Objectives* (St. Paul, Minn.: West, 1986).

49. In most of the early strategic management writings, most of which came from professors at the Harvard Business School, *strategy* was defined as that "set of major policies which defined what the organization wanted to be or become."

50. Stephen R. Covey, "Universal Mission Statement," *Executive Excellence*, March 1989, pp. 7–9.

INTEGRATIVE CASE ANALYSIS
CHAPTER 2

THE CHALLENGES FACING GENERAL MOTORS IN 1992

Now that you have read Chapter 2 and reviewed the GM case for related concepts, let's see how the chapter's concepts apply to GM.

APPLICATIONS OF CONCEPTS TO THE CASE

GM's Strategists   Stempel, John Smith, the board of directors, and Ronald M. Pirtle, executive in charge of strategic planning, along with top SBU managers are the primary strategists at GM. The board has shown an unusually strong interest in formulating strategy.

Vision   A vision does not seem to drive this company, although Stempel has better articulated his purposes and better motivated those in the organization to support his vision, than did Roger Smith. Stempel's vision seems to be to make the customer number one. John Smith's vision is unknown at this date.

Mission   Mission is the next stage in the strategic management process. Once mission and goals are formulated—or reformulated, more typically—strategic managers examine the internal and external environments and strategic policies to determine objectives and formulate strategies to reach those objectives. The mission of the organization has changed. It has gone from a single business to a multiple-SBU organization.

Strategic Intent   An all-encompassing strategic intent seems to be missing. GM is looking more to pursue strategic fit than to leverage its resources. John Smith may, however, change this.

Goals   The goals of the organization have changed, as well. Some of the goals for the automobile division include exceeding the expectations of its customers, returning the North American operation to profitability, increasing market share, and continuing to improve product quality. Cutting costs by cutting white-collar jobs is a major new goal.

Additional Case Analysis Issues

The mission of General Motors is printed on the card that Chairman Roger Smith issued to every manager: "to provide products and services of such quality that our customers will receive superior value while our employees and business partners will share in our success and our stockholders will receive a sustained superior return on their investment."

Is this a mission statement or a vision statement? If a mission statement, how good is it? How could it be improved? Given GM's vision and mission, what might some additional goals be?

The objectives of GM have changed, as well. What might some of the firm's objectives be for 1993 through 1995? How should they be stated?

How could this firm use a strategic intent? What might its strategic intent be?

STRATEGIC MANAGEMENT CHALLENGES

All of the ten challenges affect the organization's purposes. For example, GM has focused on technology as a way of gaining competitive advantage. (However, as you will learn from the Industry Note after Chapter 4, the Japanese are also focusing on this and may be doing a better job of gaining a strategic advantage in this way.) Thus, GM's goals and objectives have been strongly influenced by the desire to put the latest technology in its plants and cars.

How do the other strategic management challenges affect GM's organizational purposes?

CHAPTER 3

ENVIRONMENTAL ANALYSIS AND THE COMPANY PROFILE

It is only when one is pursued that one becomes swift.

Kahlil Gibran
Poet and Prophet

If U.S. business fails to make long-term commitments to R&D in favor of short-term profits, one can expect competitive advantages to be lost to the Japanese.

Vida Scarpello, William R. Boulton, Charles W. Hofer
Researchers on Research and Development Practices

CHAPTER OBJECTIVES

By the time you complete this chapter, you should be able to:

1. Describe the purpose of, and what is involved in, internal and external environmental analysis
2. Describe SWOT analysis, including its purposes and expected outcomes
3. Indicate how firms use best practices and benchmarking to improve their performance levels
4. Indicate the importance of strategic information systems
5. Discuss information as strategy
6. Relate the importance of the value chain to strategy formulation
7. Describe current and expected strategic issues for the 1990s in several business-level economic functional areas, including marketing, finance, operations, human resources, and research and development, and for several business-level management functional areas, including management capabilities, management systems, organization structure, and organizational culture
8. Discuss generally how firms can become more innovative in product development, process improvement, marketing, and management

MRS. FIELDS' COOKIES INFORMATION SYSTEM

Mrs. Fields' Cookies of Park City, Utah owns and operates some 500 retail cookie stores throughout the United States and has licensing agreements for sales in other countries. Mrs. Fields' has developed what many believe to be the most sophisticated information system in the food industry. This information system is the brainchild of Randy Fields, the husband of Mrs. Fields' Cookies founder, Debbi Fields. Both wanted to keep the organization with 500 stores functioning in a very personal way, as the company had functioned when it only had 10 or 15 stores. They also wanted extremely tight controls over the operations of the firm and the ability to provide decision guidance to store managers. Consequently, they developed a PC-based information system that provides instantaneous information on the operation of each store. Furthermore, each store is provided with expert system software that gives advice about store management. For example, the program provides information on just how many cookies to make, hour by hour. It also orders supplies, and provides information on hiring and advice on marketing. Through the use of voice mail and PC-based network mail, Debbi Fields can be in contact with store managers on almost a one-to-one basis. Several times a month she sends out personal messages to store managers providing creative tips for selling, new ways of motivating employees, and so on. Similarly, store managers can leave PC messages at the Park City headquarters and Debbi Fields can respond within 24 hours.

Unfortunately, much of what the Fields have done is internally focused. While this information system provides excellent control over day-to-day operations and excellent information on the operations of the organization for determination of strategic strengths and weaknesses, it fails to account sufficiently for external factors such as the actions of competitors. More important, in the past it has not incorporated some extremely important factors related to the external environment such as site location variables. At one time Mrs. Fields' Cookies had over 600 stores, but it had to close over 100 of these because of improper site location. These poorly chosen store locations had caused the firm to lose $15 million in 1988, its first loss in its history. To be truly efficient, an information system cannot focus singly on internal factors.

Despite its weaknesses, the information system is so well regarded that Mrs. Fields has been able to start an independent subsidiary to sell Mrs. Fields' Information Systems to other food industry members, such as grocery stores and other restaurant chains that need better control over internal operations.

Sources: Denise Pancari, Ann Senn, and Sue Smiley, "Are Retailers Sold on Expert Systems?" *Chief Information Officer Journal*, Winter 1991, pp. 10–14; Michael Fitzgerald, "Cooking with Expert Systems," *Computer World*, October 15, 1990, p. 45; Buck Brown, "How the Cookie Crumbled at Mrs. Fields," *The Wall Street Journal*, January 26, 1989, p. B1; and Tom Richman, "Mrs. Fields' Secret Ingredient," *Inc*, October 1987, pp. 65–72.

Mrs. Fields' Cookies made operational what many experts have been predicting for many years—an online, real-time information system that allows instant access to information on the operation of the organization at every level. This strategic information system was especially adept at internal environmental analysis, that is, analyzing those factors internal to the organization that relate to the successful implementation of its strategy. Among these would be marketing, operations, finance, and human resources. Furthermore, it enabled Debbi and Randy Fields to keep the organization's culture intact as the company grew.

Organizations today must develop such internal information systems, along with systems that focus on the external environment, if they are to succeed in the long term. An organization must be aware of its internal capabilities and its strengths and weaknesses, as Mrs. Fields' Cookies was, and it must recognize its external opportunities and threats, which, for some issues such as site selection, Mrs. Fields' did not. Living in this information age, firms can and must be constantly attuned to the changing world about them. Some information systems do more than just provide information. Some of them, such as Mrs. Fields', include **expert systems,** which provide decision guidance rather than just information.

This chapter examines the issues of internal and external environmental analysis, information systems (especially strategic information systems), and sources of information. The chapter then discusses in some detail the construction of an organizational profile. This section constructs the rationale for examining the organization profile to build a distinctive competency that leads to a competitive advantage. This chapter does not review introductory material for the functional areas covered, but rather discusses current and future requirements for strategies in each of the major economic functions, including marketing, finance, operations, human resources, and research and development, and in several management functions, as well. The critical work of developing and pursuing organizational innovation is also examined. Information defines all stages of strategic management—formulation, implementation, and control. However, the discussion in this chapter focuses on strategy formulation, as shown in Figures 3.1 and 3.2.

INTERNAL AND EXTERNAL ENVIRONMENTAL ANALYSIS

The world is constantly changing. Organizations must be able to adapt strategically to ever-changing internal and external environments in order to survive and prosper. Furthermore, the **rate of change** is accelerating and firms are confronted

FIGURE 3.1 The Organization—A Strategic Management Process Model

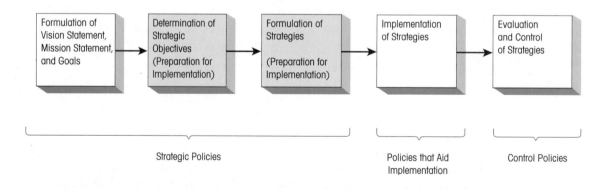

FIGURE 3.2 Objectives Determination and Strategy Formulation

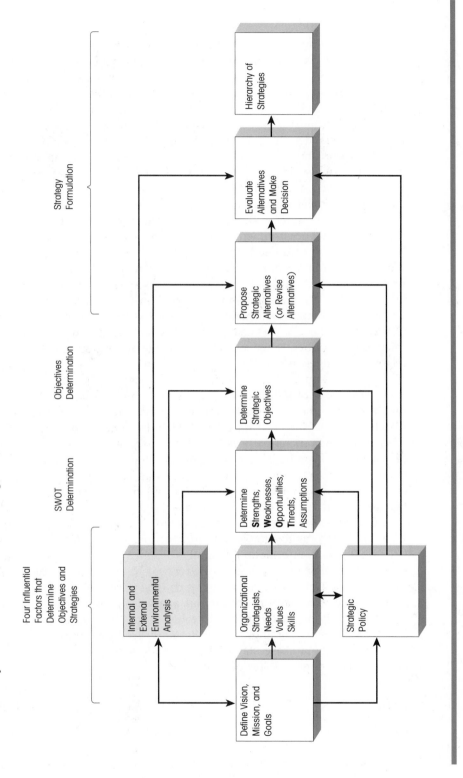

every day by future shock and others of the ten strategic challenges, which make their strategic management tasks more difficult. Compact discs, IBM's second generation of personal computers, gourmet frozen dinners, stealth aircraft, natural soda, and the short haircut all became prominent in the years from 1988 to 1991. In the same period we also saw the Dow Jones Industrial Average exceed 3,000 points after it had collapsed on October 19, 1987 and dropped more than 500 points, a federal debt of more than $4 trillion and continued massive foreign trade deficits, major changes in energy supplies from surplus to rationing, disillusionment with supply-side economics, a weakened dollar, tax reform, the fall of the Berlin Wall and unification of Germany, war with Iraq, and the collapse into near chaos of the Soviet Union.

These and numerous other developments remind us that business currently faces an external environment more changeable and more demanding than any it has previously encountered. The future holds little promise of greater stability. At the same time, internal organizational environments are also changing rapidly. Employees' education levels and expectations are rising while overall skill levels fall; computers are providing more information-processing capabilities; the mix of employees is changing; corporate emphasis is veering toward quality (and quality of life). As all these factors change, strategic (and operational) management of the internal environment must also change, while at the same time the organization adapts to changes in the external environment.

It can be argued that if a business is not growing, changing, meeting society's current needs, and preparing to meet its future needs, then it is declining. To the unaware, strengths too soon become weaknesses, opportunities too soon become threats. Just ask Harcourt Brace Jovanovich, Inc. Once a powerful publisher and diversified conglomerate, it was forced, due to excessive debt acquired in fending off takeovers, eventually to sell out to General Cinema Corporation.[1] Query a major airline about the impact of price wars on its profits.[2] Numerous other examples are readily found in the records of bankruptcy courts and in reports of management terminations and corporate takeovers.

Organizational strategists must make themselves aware of the changing world and the organization's internal situation, as well. The basis of successful strategic action is information. Chapters 1 and 2 have discussed mission, strategists, and strategic policy, three of the four major influences on the determination of strategic objectives and the formulation of strategy. Information obtained from **internal and external environmental analysis** is the fourth major factor. It is information about reality, not the reality itself, that causes firms to formulate strategies in one way or another. Furthermore, predicted future states of reality, or assumptions about these states, should guide strategy formulation rather than perceptions of current states of reality.

STRENGTHS, WEAKNESSES, OPPORTUNITIES, AND THREATS (SWOT)

The organization's strategists observe vision, mission, goals, strategic policies, and current and forecasted information about their environments, and then determine where they are. Based on these, they determine current and future organizational strengths, weaknesses, opportunities, and threats (SWOT), they decide where they want to be (determine strategic objectives) and how they plan to get there (formulate strategy). As mentioned in Chapter 1, firms may leverage resources in pursuit of strategic intent or they may seek strategic fit. Current and predicted SWOT must be identified at both the single-business and multiple-business levels if the organization is to be successful.[3] The process is complicated, and there are no simple solutions, as you will see in later chapters. Now that you understand the overall concept of SWOT, it is important to consider each element.

Strengths are positive internal abilities and situations of sufficient magnitude to enable the organization to gain a strategic advantage in its efforts to achieve its objectives. At the business level, strengths determine how the SBU can market its products competitively. There are five primary variables in marketing strategy: target market, product, promotion, price, and distribution. Effective strategies in these five areas are essential to success, but functional strategies, both economic and managerial, can also make important contributions to a successful marketing effort. In 1990, for example, Ford purchased Jaguar for $2.5 billion because it wanted access to the luxury segment of the car market, a product market segment in which it offered no product. (Ironically, attempting to overcome this weakness in the product line contributed to an even greater weakness in cash flow as car sales fell and the cost of making Jaguar competitive approached a total of $5 billion.)[4]

AT MRS. FIELDS'

Mrs. Fields' internal information system was definitely a strength. Yet because it was only internal, it had a glaring weakness. It didn't provide sufficient information on external factors, principally desirable site location characteristics.

In multiple-SBU firms strengths at the corporate level are defined most often in terms of the synergy and balance among the SBUs within the firm. **Synergy** is the degree to which SBUs reinforce each others' pursuit of objectives. An organization such as General Electric, for example, is considered to have very strong synergy among its SBUs. All are based essentially on technology and have more than adequate actual or potential profit margins. **Balance** refers to the relative cash requirements of the SBUs. The balance among GE's SBUs is also satisfactory; some are growing, some are stable, and some have strong cash flows that can support the total company's growth efforts.

Many firms today define strengths (and weaknesses) by **benchmarking,** that is, by comparing their own products and/or processes to those of the best firms. They seek to determine why these firms' products and/or processes are so excellent, and then to build strengths by emulating these firms' **best practices.**[5]

Such strategies are viewed as a valuable way of coping with environmental change and complexity. Organizational capability is becoming more and more a focal point for building a sustainable competitive advantage.[6] In the late 1980s and early 1990s many organizations, for example GE, sought to stockpile sufficient resources to seize opportunities and mitigate threats. They sought to eliminate weaknesses wherever possible. These firms used **resource-based strategies** to beat the competition.[7] They sought sufficient resource bases to pounce on opportunities and to mitigate threats.

Weaknesses are internal inabilities and negative situations that may result in or have resulted in the firm's failure to achieve its objectives. At the business level, marketing is the principal concern. Even such successful firms as Burger King have marketing weaknesses. In 1990 Burger King found itself very vulnerable to competition because its product line was dated and its advertising campaigns had failed to produce an image. Under new owner Grand Metropolitan (from the United Kingdom), the firm pumped an immediate $215 million into a focused advertising campaign designed to produce an image, and it introduced several new products.[8] At the corporate level in the multiple-SBU firm, weaknesses, like strengths, are primarily a function of synergy and balance. For example, AT&T initiated a $7.4-billion hostile takeover of NCR in order to shore up its weak computer division.[9] Weaknesses can be readily identified and corrected by benchmarking and pursuing best practices.

Opportunities are external factors and situations that will substantially assist the organization in its efforts to achieve or exceed its objectives. At the business level, they, too, are almost always expressed in terms of market potentials. The founders of Apple Computers saw a need for a personal computer at a low price. They created one and made a fortune. At the corporate-strategy level in multiple-SBU firms, opportunities usually involve acquisitions or mergers. The Coca-Cola Company acquired Columbia Pictures to become less dependent on soft drinks, especially on Coke, its single most important product, and to move into an often-profitable industry.

Michel M. Robert suggests that when companies prepare to react to perceived opportunities, they should ask themselves four critical questions in order to avoid grasping at false opportunities.

1. Does the opportunity violate the corporate purpose or mission?
2. Is the opportunity counter to the firm's current driving force or grand strategy?
3. Does the opportunity require the firm to learn a whole new field?
4. Does the opportunity meet the firm's financial requirements?

Answering these questions may keep a company from following the wrong path.[10]

Threats are external factors that may result in or have resulted in the firm's failure to achieve its objectives. Historically, the concept of threats has been limited to competitors, but more recently the focus has expanded to include government, unions, society, and other stakeholders. One of the major necessities for the 1990s is to view changes and all strategic challenges as opportunities. Viewing these as problems, or threats, risks creating a self-fulfilling prophecy of doom.

At the business-strategy level, an example of a threat would be a technological innovation introduced by a competitor. Within a few months of the introduction of the digital watch, time had begun to run out on the Bulova Watch Company's reign as a dominant force in the industry. Bulova still depended on pin-lever watches, and digital watches quickly captured its traditional markets. In another example, government can be a threat to business through safety and environmental legislation that may place extensive demands on an industry. A societal threat is seen in the successful campaigns of environmental groups to keep real estate developers from turning natural areas into suburbs in such states as Florida, California, Oregon, and the Carolinas.

At the corporate-strategy level, multiple-SBU firms often face the same threats as at the SBU level, plus additional threats involving acquisitions and mergers. Rival multiple-SBU firms may compete to acquire the same SBU. A threat may also take the form of an unfriendly takeover attempt. The Walt Disney Company, for example, was embroiled in an unfriendly takeover battle with "greenmailers" Saul Steinberg and Irwin Jacobs in 1983 and 1984. Though Disney thwarted the attempts, both CEO Ron Miller and Chairman of the Board Ray Watson were deposed as a consequence of the ultimate resolution of this takeover attempt.[11]

How Managers Define SWOT

Howard H. Stevenson studied 50 managers in six diverse business organizations to find out how they defined organizational strengths and weaknesses. He found that, while the steps for defining strengths and weaknesses were essentially the same, the specific factors examined and the criteria used to judge them varied, and many factors modified exact definitions. Strengths tended to be relatively well-known and based on historical data; weaknesses were less well-known, and often little relevant data about them were available. Further, managers' interpretation of data depended partly on their positions and responsibilities in their organizations, their personalities, and their perceived roles in the organizations.[12]

The implications of this study are important. Stevenson notes that in conducting an internal evaluation, managers should (1) view the evaluation as an aid to task accomplishment, (2) develop areas of examination tailored to the responsibility and authority of each manager, (3) make criteria explicit to provide a common framework, (4) understand the differences in uses of identified strengths and weaknesses, and (5) recognize the strategic importance of defining these attributes. Hiring an external consultant to conduct the evaluation may alleviate most of these problems.

When Omar A. El Sawy interviewed 37 executives of small- and medium-sized high-tech firms, he found that scanning of the external environment was an ongoing process characterized by at least three stages: initial detection, threshold attainment, and confirmation. To verify threats and opportunities, strengths and weaknesses, managers used various cues and, in a very important finding, high levels of intuitive input. In short, SWOT identification was less rational than we have conceptualized it here.[13]

Two research studies hardly justify discounting the rationality of all evaluations of strengths and weaknesses, threats and opportunities. These studies do, however, point out the need to be aware of the human variable in the strategic decision process. That process is extremely complex, much more so than the models that describe it usually depict. In fact, the human variable negates much of the rationality the firm desires and builds into the decision system through managerial techniques.[14] Again, the choice of approach to using SWOT remains leveraging resources or strategic fit.

INFORMATION

Information plays a primary role in two strategic areas—objective setting and strategy formulation. Information on the strengths and weaknesses of the organization in relation to external environmental opportunities and threats supports the firm's efforts to set objectives and formulate strategies. Information systems are critical to the implementation and control of strategies, as well, and control systems provide much of a firm's internal information.

Information systems point out many strengths, weaknesses, opportunities, and threats. Most will not require reformulation of strategy, but many cause changes in strategic objectives. Most threats are resolved and most opportunities seized at lower levels of planning, control, and implementation. Occasionally, strategic information systems may indicate the need to formulate or reformulate several strategies.

Strategic Information Systems

Strategic information systems (SISs) provide the informational inputs required in the strategic decision process. Any decision, and especially any strategic decision, can be only as good as the information on which it is based. An information system that provides accurate, timely, and relevant information to the strategic decision process is an important organizational resource, because executives can be virtually overwhelmed by information.

Organizations devise various structural arrangements to provide strategic information. In a larger organization, an elaborate management information system (MIS) may provide this information. **Scanning,** the process of searching the environment for relevant information, is critical to strategic success.[15] In a smaller organization, the CEO may scan the environment and assess his or her organization in an attempt to collect information to help determine where the organization is and where it ought to be. Numerous variations can be found between these two extremes. Personal computer data bases and other software have provided smaller organizations with scanning, analysis, and forecasting capabilities that only larger firms used to enjoy. In addition to providing strategic information, major functions of the MIS include communication of objectives and plans and providing information related to performance control.

Gathering information is not always easy, as this chapter's Strategic Challenge feature illustrates. Also, information doesn't always ensure success, especially when not enough or contradictory information is gathered. Strategic information systems can be either formal or informal. Both types play vital roles in strategy formulation. The formal SIS is a component of the formal MIS. SBU strategic planning requires special emphasis on demand forecasts for products and services, balanced against the capacity and capabilities to produce them. Ultimately these balances are reflected in the operating plan and the operating budget. The

STRATEGIC CHALLENGE

THE INTELLIGENCE FUNCTION

In the past few years competition has intensified. For many firms it has become global. Finding out what your competitor is doing isn't always easy, but it's a lot easier than most people think. Some ways of finding out about competitors include monitoring numerous data bases. These help identify competitors and what is being said about them, for example, in the news media. Patent literature also provides important information on competitor activity. Furthermore, companies like to talk about themselves, and if they don't, their employees do. This latter source of intelligence information is coming to be widely exploited. True, companies still analyze competitors' annual reports, advertisements, job-opening announcements, and other potential information sources, but there is apparently no substitute for listening to your competitors' current or former employees.

Managers use a variety of strategies to gather intelligence from competitors' employees: probing former employees of competitors in real or phony job interviews, picking the brains of competitors' employees at conferences and trade shows, and hiring competitors' former employees and then debriefing them. One of the most interesting ways is simply to sit in a popular restaurant or bar frequented by competitors' employees and listen. Any of Silicon Valley's popular night spots may provide the astute and educated listener with numerous bits of tactical and often strategic information. Accurate descriptions of several new products to be released are known to have been leaked several weeks to several months in advance of release. Other common secrets that have been uncovered in such after-hours spots are the existence of joint venture agreements, or the strengths and weaknesses of competitors, for example, customer relationships, circuit diagrams, and software capabilities. It pays, so it appears, to become an eavesdropper.

It's all quite legal, although rules have developed as to what's fair in this game. Many firms today have professional intelligence units. For example, at Corning, all employees from the janitor to the CEO, feed information to a centralized data base. The data are analyzed and sent to interested employees around the globe. Nutrasweet keeps personality profiles on key decision makers in rival firms. Helene Curtis's intelligence unit is run by a trio that includes a former Army intelligence officer. At Prime Computer, a manager of competitor intelligence and sales analysis for the computer vision unit collects product and process information on U.S. and foreign competitors.

Source: Michele Galen, "These Guys Aren't Spooks, They're Competitive Analysts," *Business Week*, October 14, 1991, p. 97; Jack B. Rochester, "Using Information Systems for Business and Competitor Intelligence," *I/S Analyzer*, May 1990, pp. 1–12; Marylee Ojala, "A Patently Obvious Source for Competitor Intelligence: The Patent Literature," *Database*, August 1989, pp. 43–49; Marylee Ojala, "Getting Ahead of the Competition," *Link Up*, January/February 1990, pp. 10–11, 14; Steven Flax, "How to Snoop on Your Competitors," *Fortune*, May 14, 1984, pp. 28–33; Erik Larson, "Many Top Secrets in the Silicon Valley Are Spilled at Tables," *The Wall Street Journal*, June 29, 1984, pp. 1, 26.

operating budget also details resource distribution actions and actual production commitments.

Most organizations plan strategy on an annual cycle. For such purposes they need routine data storage and reporting. Since strategic decision making may occasionally focus on crises, however, few predictable boundaries define the conceivable types of information that may be useful in efforts to meet the demands of various situations.

As Figure 3.3 indicates, a centralized, formal data bank stores the data necessary to generate both routine and nonroutine reports on internal and external environmental phenomena. Figure 3.3 shows reports of internal information on a functional basis, but it could be sorted on a divisional/functional or other basis, if necessary. Much of the firm's strategic information is available in reports that it already routinely generates, including financial statements, cost control reports, quality reports, inventory level reports, division performance reports, absenteeism and turnover reports, and the like.

One manifestation of the computerized information system is the corporate war room with comprehensive computer-linked visual data display systems. While firms have maintained such war rooms for many years, in the past they relied on hand-printed charts on limited subjects. Now any piece of corporate information can appear instantaneously on large television screens. A microcomputer functioning as a smart terminal further increases the capabilities of such systems, providing top line managers and staff with strategic information and sophisticated analysis and forecasting capacities. Leading-edge companies and firms with proven track records apparently monitor their environments continuously through their environmental analysis units.[16] Globalizing the SIS has become extremely important.[17]

Globalizing Competitor Intelligence

Japanese firms are, on the average, the most formidable competitors that U.S. firms face. Many firms in the rest of the Pacific Rim and Europe are also formidable competitors. To fully understand its competition in a global marketplace, a U.S. firm can't be satisfied merely to study its U.S. competitors. Rather, it must understand its competitors around the globe. Japanese firms have based much of their success on an extensive network of industrial intelligence gathering (some would say, industrial espionage). U.S. firms must seek extensive knowledge of their global competitors' strategies and internal operations to compete successfully against them. To do so, most U.S. firms have chosen to emulate their Japanese competitors' intelligence efforts. After all, the Japanese are experts at knowing the enemy.

How exactly do U.S. firms get to know the enemy? There are several appropriate actions. First, firms must follow all of the appropriate competitor analysis techniques discussed previously, and then expand these internationally. One problem is that the Japanese and many other global competitors do not provide information as openly as their U.S. competitors. Nonetheless, traditional sources offer much information, including annual reports, newspaper and journal articles, scientific studies, press releases, and so on.

FIGURE 3.3   Strategic Information Systems

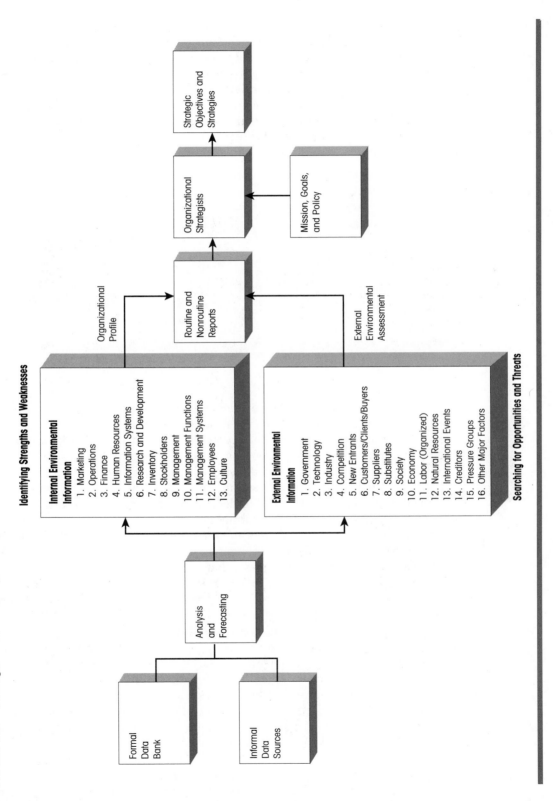

Motorola, for example, systematically follows scientific developments in Japan by participating in Japanese standards bodies, talking to trade associations, reviewing patents, and attending trade shows.[18] One can learn much from current and former employees. They can provide important information in any number of ways, for example, in job interviews. In addition, a number of firms are aggressively pursuing Japanese scientific talent by opening research laboratories in Japan, hiring leading Japanese scientists away from Japanese firms, and luring top Japanese science students with scholarships. Many top U.S. researchers are also learning about Japanese scientific efforts by becoming part of Japanese research teams.[19]

AT MRS. FIELDS'

Mrs. Fields' Cookies maintains constant contact with its stores. Day-to-day, hour-by-hour "battle plans" are drawn up for each store by the expert systems. So far, globalization of the system has not been necessary as the firm has used licensing agreements to expand globally, rather than opening its own stores.

Networking should not be overlooked. Personal contacts with individuals inside or outside the organization often produce significant information. Tips on federal legislation, for example, may prove extremely beneficial. Rumors about a competitor's strategy may, when investigated, give important indications of profitable strategic actions. The director of strategic planning for Phillips, the Dutch electronic giant, mentioned to one of the authors that things were happening so quickly that he had to depend on networking or his firm might be left behind.[20] Robert K. Mueller, former chairman of Arthur D. Little, Inc., has described several types of networks and their functions. He, too, feels that formal systems are too slow to track changing environments.[21]

The evidence strongly suggests that, while many see formal information systems as the critical elements, informal systems are consistently the bases for many top-management decisions. Research indicates that 40 to 80 percent of the information used by top managers comes from informal sources.[22]

Finally, remember: management must base its strategic decisions on forecasts, not simply on past history. Most people understand this necessity with respect to the external environment; the time horizon of information about the past often has already changed before it reaches top management. Strategists often overlook forecasting, however, when they are dealing with internal strengths and weaknesses. Even for decisions that must be made now, future as well as current strengths and weaknesses must be compared with future as well as current threats and opportunities in the strategic decision process.

Sources of Internal and External Environmental Information

As we suggested earlier, information related to the internal strengths and weaknesses of the organization should be available in the organization's MIS. This information may also be gathered through informal sources. Typically this type of information will be found in annual, quarterly, and monthly financial reports, cost analyses, capital budget statements, cost–benefit analyses, personnel reports on major human resource concerns, marketing reports on sales and related information, and so forth. One should encounter few problems in obtaining relevant internal information if the MIS is properly designed and implemented (a big *if*). Most systems, however, give only limited information on human resources and cultural matters. Organizations are only beginning to recognize the need for and applications of this type of information. While organizations usually collect data on absenteeism, tardiness, turnover, and so forth, they seldom measure organizational climate, satisfaction, leadership style, and the like, all of which are important ingredients in productivity.

The strategic purpose of obtaining information on internal strengths and weaknesses is to compare them with perceived external environmental threats and opportunities and to make decisions on the basis of these comparisons. F. J. Aguilar has described four modes of scanning the external environment for information about threats and opportunities.[23]

1. Undirected viewing—General exposure to information with no purpose other than exploration
2. Conditioned viewing—Directed exposure to, but not active searching for, specific kinds of data, assessing them as they are encountered
3. Informal search—Searching for specific information in a limited and relatively unstructured manner
4. Formal search—Active, deliberate, structured searching for specific information undertaken with a purpose in mind.

For an example of formal search techniques, Phillips Petroleum Company's highly sophisticated decision support system integrates environmental information with internal capabilities.[24] Many expert systems available on the market also integrate internal and external environmental information. Commander EIS from Comshare of Ann Arbor, Michigan, for example, provides executives such as those at the Bank of New England in Boston with performance information and assessments of external economic conditions.[25]

Most organizations use all four types of scanning, depending on the costs and benefits of each. These four approaches form a continuum from general exposure to information to active and deliberate searching for specific information. Every firm must remain alert to the general environment and to its own operations. Bits and pieces of information obtained in the course of this scanning will indicate changes in factors relevant to the formulation of strategy, triggering other, more directed types of scanning. A formal search is desirable any time specific information is needed for strategy formulation.[26]

Information on environmental factors can be obtained through various sources, such as *The Wall Street Journal* and other newspapers, *Fortune, Business Week, Harvard Business Review,* and other scholarly, popular, and trade journals. Any number of government, industry, news media, research, and reporting services provide additional information.

Information from various sources may vary in validity and reliability, as well as in accessibility and timeliness. Much of a firm's information comes from secondary sources, but it may gather primary data if it can afford the cost of research. While internal information sources may allow the organization to approach a real-time, on-line MIS, constraints on environmental sources make a real-time environmental MIS unlikely. The informal information system may be used more than the formal system. Information sharing among organizations is useful and has proved to be beneficial.

We've named some sources of information, described how to find them, and stated their purposes, but we have not yet examined exactly what types of information we seek. We'll do so later in the chapter. Perhaps a more important question is the ethics of obtaining information, as this chapter's Strategic Manager's Ethical Challenge feature suggests.

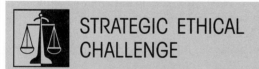

STRATEGIC ETHICAL CHALLENGE

THE ETHICS OF INTELLIGENCE GATHERING

More and more, firms are involved in systematic competitor analysis efforts, intelligence gathering, and even industrial espionage. Some have proposed that the CIA be used to gather intelligence for U.S. firms now that the cold war is over. The intensity level of intelligence gathering efforts is as high as the stakes—economic survival and prosperity. The temptation to take unethical actions to gather information is also high. Few, if any, firms, however, have addressed the ethics of competitor analysis in their codes of ethics. It's clear that firms need to address the issue of what is ethical and what is not in intelligence gathering.

For example, David P. Settle, competitive analysis manager for Convex Computer Corporation of Richardson, Texas was recently given a copy of a rival's sales presentation for a soon-to-be-announced product. A prospective customer had slipped the presentation to a Convex sales representative with whom the prospective customer had a long relationship. The sales rep in turn passed the presentation along to Settle. Because of the information contained in the presentation, Convex changed its pricing strategy, and is offering certain extras on its models. Was this action ethical?

Sources: Michele Galen, "These Guys Aren't Spooks, They're Competitive Analysts," *Business Week*, October 14, 1991, p. 97; Lynn Sharp Paine, "Corporate Policy and the Ethics of Competitor Intelligence Gathering," *Journal of Business Ethics*, June 1991, pp. 423–436; Amy Borrus, "Should the CIA Start Spying for Corporate America?" *Business Week*, October 14, 1991, pp. 96–100.

Information As Strategy

Michael Porter and Victor E. Miller suggest that information can give a firm a competitive advantage. Information can help a firm to cut costs and differentiate its products. Caesar's Palace in Las Vegas, for example, was able to cut its budget for complimentary services to high rollers by 20 percent by scientifically tracking these important customers on its computers. American Express has been able to differentiate its travel services from those of other companies by tracking costs and obtaining the lowest fares and rates for its customers, all on computer.

Porter and Miller suggest the following five steps for devising information strategy:

1. Assess intensity of information use
2. Determine the role of information technology in industry structure
3. Identify and rank the ways in which information technology might create competitive advantage
4. Investigate how information technology might spawn new businesses
5. Develop a plan for taking advantage of information technology[27]

One of the major strategic uses of information recently has been electronic data interchange (EDI), in which firms share data bases. This is especially common between customer and supplier. Such activities usually make the customer more dependent on the supplier.

United Technology Corporation's Pratt and Whitney jet engine subsidiary is an example of a firm that has designed its information system to serve a more traditional strategic function. Under Doug Lewis, vice president for management information systems, the MIS was redesigned as a strategic MIS that could provide the firm with information for strategic decisions.[28]

AT MRS. FIELDS'

Mrs. Fields' clearly uses information as strategy. It is especially important for operational/control strategy, but also for gaining a competitive edge through the use of expert systems.

SUSTAINABLE COMPETITIVE ADVANTAGE

Every organization must seek a strategic **sustainable competitive advantage,** an advantage over its competitors due to superior ability to transform inputs into products and services at a higher level of profit. Normally such an advantage comes from a lower cost structure, and/or an ability to differentiate the product or service to support a higher price and thus increase margins.[29] Determining this competitive advantage is one of the main purposes of constructing an organizational profile. By assessing strengths and weaknesses and comparing them to external opportunities and threats (specifically competitors in this situation), a firm can determine what its competitive advantage is or what it should be. Periodic re-examination of these factors is necessary as circumstances change, and the firm must re-evaluate its current efforts toward strategic advantage in light of other possible directions. Firms seek a long term, sustainable competitive advantage, but as competition intensifies, both domestically and globally, sustainable advantages are much harder to develop, especially those based on technology because technology is transferred so quickly between competitors, even across the globe.

Strategic Field Analysis and the Value Chain

Peter Lorange, Michael F. Scott Morton, and Sumantra Ghoshal suggest that strategists should examine the nature and extent of the synergies that exist or do not exist among the firm's internal components. These authors call the process of making such an examination **strategic field analysis.** The process involves two steps: first, one examines the company's value-added chain, and then one examines the potential synergies between the firm's products, markets, or businesses.[30]

Michael Porter defines the **value-added chain** as the various functions involved in the production of a product or service. Porter identifies five primary activities in any firm.[31]

1. Inbound logistics (raw materials)
2. Operations
3. Outbound logistics (finished goods)
4. Marketing and sales
5. Customer service

Porter also identifies four support activities:

1. Procurement
2. Technology development
3. Human resource management
4. Infrastructure, including planning, accounting, finance, legal, government affairs, and quality management

To achieve a competitive advantage, Porter suggests focusing on the value added by the firm in this value chain. For example, the firm that adds value through service may obtain a competitive advantage by focusing on this activity. Textile giant Milliken has been able to sustain this kind of competitive advantage over its foreign competitors, for example, by providing services such as just-in-time inventories packed in a truck in the order needed, starting from the rear end and moving toward the front. In this way, Milliken has provided customers such as Levi Strauss with service that few if any foreign competitors can match.[32] The important concept here is the value added by the firm. Focusing on this concept of competitive advantage will allow the firm to develop ways of adding value at one or more points in the value-added chain. As you can see, Porter includes virtually all functions of the organization in the value-added chain. Benchmarking costs can help improve value-chain analysis significantly.[33] The following sections are arranged according to the more traditional functional approach, but include the same components as Porter's primary and support categories.

Lorange, Morton, and Ghoshal further suggest that, besides adding value through each of the primary and support components, the firm may be able to develop synergies between its various products, markets, or businesses in doing so. They suggest that economies of scope exist in how products or businesses might share various activities.[34] For example, a brochure can be designed to advertise not just one product, but several. Similarly, the waste by-products of one product may serve as raw materials for another product the firm manufactures, creating synergy. As many chemical firms worked to reduce environmental waste, they found that they actually purchased materials that they had disposed of previously. Cost savings in such situations can be significant.

Typically, a corporation prepares two profiles: a profile for the company as it now exists and one as it will need to exist at some point in the future. Some firms pick 3 years in the future, others 5 or more years, as their target dates. As the profile extends out into the future, its specific contents are more difficult to predict realistically.

Each of the following sections describes only briefly a traditional overview of the economic functional area or management functional area under discussion. Since strategy is a capstone course taken during the senior undergraduate year or the second year of an MBA program, it is presumed that students are sufficiently familiar with the fundamental framework for each of these functional areas. Therefore, these discussions focus on the most recent thinking about the strategies that will be necessary in the next few years. Remember that these functions cannot be treated independently, but rather one must recognize that occurrences in each of the functions affect strategy and related activities in each of the other functions. It is especially critical to deal jointly with marketing, engineering/research and development, and operations considerations and to calculate the human resource impacts of all strategies.

MARKETING

Marketing strategies traditionally focus on the marketing mix—product, promotion, price, and distribution (three *P*s and a *D*) aimed at some target market.[35] The soundness of each of these strategies, singly and in conjunction with other functional strategies, must be determined.

Target Market

Much of the current and near-term future thinking has focused on determining the needs and wants of those in the target market (customers or clients), in order to suit the components of the marketing mix, especially the product or service requirements, to the customer. Corporations became extremely concerned with this issue of **closeness to the customer** when it was raised most prominently in the 1980s by

Thomas J. Peters and Robert H. Waterman, Jr. in *In Search of Excellence*.[36] Those who pay attention to their customers find their bottom lines enhanced.[37]

For example, Trinova, a Maumee, Ohio manufacturer of engine components, had been a loose confederation of three businesses with no clear mandate. Trinova asked itself and its customers what the customers would need in 15 years and what skills the company would have to develop in response. After thorough examination of customer needs based on lengthy discussions with customers, the corporation, led by CEO Darryl Allen, divested some subsidiaries and acquired others in an effort to develop the skills that its customers would need. For example, Trinova's Vickers division was a global leader in hydraulic components, pumps, and valves for airplanes. Research revealed that Vickers's customers were thinking about enhancing and replacing some of their hydraulic components with electromechanical and electronic parts. Vickers resolved to master those new technologies through acquisitions as well as its own research and development. These are actions it would never had taken if it had not talked to its customers.[38]

Another significant effect on the target market is the age wave of baby boomers moving through the U.S. population. This also includes a trough due to a dip in births that followed the baby-boom generation, and then a new wave as births increased when baby boomers themselves had children. These waves and troughs affect all sorts of industries from consumer products to housing.

Another influence on strategic decision making due to the target market is its changing income structure. Most experts agree that the economy is moving from domination by manufacturing to a situation where, by the year 2000, only 5 percent of U.S. jobs will involve manufacturing.[39] This restructures wages because higher-paying manufacturing jobs are being replaced by lower-paying service jobs. It also restructures the types of products and services that firms will need as we move toward the information society predicted by John Naisbitt.[40] For many firms, one of the major shifts in target market considerations will be toward global customers. Most firms must set strategy globally, including the identification of foreign target markets.

Product/Service and Product/Service Development

As discussed in Chapter 1, change is accelerating rapidly throughout all of society, especially as technology advances. Consequently, firms must develop the products or services needed by customers more quickly than they have in the past. Thus, the **speed strategy** has recently emerged as a major basis of competition to enhance the speed of new product development.[41] These strategies typically require the creation of **cross-functional development teams** bringing together personnel from marketing, manufacturing, product development and design, research and development, finance, and even, in some cases, human resources. Human resources are prominently involved in the service industries where, for all practical purposes, operations is essentially the same as human resource management. One of the major issues of the 1990s will be improving the quality of service products.[42]

One of the principal means of competing in the future is **kaizen,** meaning continuous improvement. Kaizen has long been a key strategy of Japanese firms. Kaizen is not limited to product enhancement, but encompasses organizational processes such as manufacturing, as well. For the Japanese, it is a philosophy of life.[43] Many U.S. firms have adopted kaizen as a guiding principal, but more must do so in the future if U.S. firms are to be competitive.[44]

Just as important as kaizen is understanding and undertaking the **leap-frog strategy**. It isn't sufficient merely to follow your competitors, especially global competitors such as the Japanese who have years of experience improving products. Rather, a firm must work to leapfrog the competition. As will be discussed in the section on research and development, it is often necessary to do something that competitors have not done in order to surpass them in the marketplace.

AT MRS. FIELDS'

Mrs. Fields' Cookies leapfrogged its competitors through the use of information systems, especially expert systems. These information systems also allowed for a management style that greatly assisted achievement of objectives that would not otherwise have been possible.

Promotion

One of the more important ways of promoting a product now and for the future is to build alliances with customers so that they become dependent upon the firm's products or services. For example, by becoming one of the few vendors that supplies Xerox with parts for its products, a firm could lock in Xerox to new products it develops.

Pricing

Pricing is becoming a very complex strategy. For example, in some cases, pricing is becoming intertwined with the financing of a product. For example, when United Airlines went to purchase new planes from Boeing, it sought favorable financing as part of the deal. In essence, Boeing reduced its price by providing financing at below-market rates.[45] A host of pricing strategies is evolving.

Distribution

In the 1990s, the distribution of many goods and services will change dramatically. Many services can be provided electronically as more and more companies, offices, work groups, workers, and consumers go online. Furthermore, these unique distribution systems help keep customers. For example, **electronic data interchange (EDI),** in which the customer and the provider share data bases, allows the provider to more securely bind the customer to its offerings because the customer becomes dependent upon the services provided through the particular distribution network. For example, McKesson Corporation of California, a wholesale drugstore supplier, prices customers' products automatically through its own computer system.[46] It also provides customers with labels for their products and inventory services. Such services make it difficult for firms to leave one service provider for another.

FINANCE

One of the major issues in analyzing an organization's strategic profile is its financial soundness and financial strategies. The firm must have appropriate strategies for raising funds and distributing funds, and for operating in an efficient and effective manner.

Financial Control—Ratio Analysis

One of the quickest ways to determine whether or not a firm is financially sound is to examine financial ratios. The following paragraphs define key financial ratios and provide examples of them. Two financial statements, the income statement and the balance sheet, generally are used for financial ratio analysis. These statements provide the figures used to calculate the four categories of financial ratios: liquidity, leverage, activity, and profitability ratios.

Liquidity Ratios
There are two critical liquidity ratios: the current and quick ratios. The current ratio measures the firm's ability to repay short-term debts and liabilities. It is found by dividing current assets by current liabilities. The result shows how many dollars of current assets the firm holds per dollar of current liabilities. A rule of thumb for manufacturing firms is to maintain a current ratio of at least 2 to 1 (assets to liabilities), but each firm must compare its position with the industry average. Service firms can operate with lower ratios because they have no inventories.

The quick ratio, or acid-test ratio, is the result of subtracting inventories from current assets and then dividing this figure by current liabilities [(CA − Inventories)/CL]. This ratio is sometimes seen as a more accurate indicator of liquidity than the current ratio, since a firm with large, obsolete inventories included in its current assets could be misrepresenting its ability to meet short-term obligations. The quick ratio is also expressed as asset dollars per liability dollar. It is generally believed that a quick ratio of 1 to 1 is typical.

Leverage Ratios
There are three critical leverage ratios: debt-to-total assets, times interest earned, and fixed charge coverage. The debt-to-total assets ratio equals total debt divided by total assets, expressed as a percentage. A ratio of 0.50 means that the firm's debt equals 50 percent of the value of its assets. Generally, a

lower percentage is better, since a high ratio could mean that the firm has little ability to withstand losses. A low ratio indicates that the firm has a buffer of funds available to creditors should it become insolvent, pleasing many analysts. Some, however, prefer higher ratios indicating a strong leveraging of other people's money. Some industries, especially capital-intensive ones, tend to be highly leveraged.

To find the times-interest-earned ratio, divide profit before taxes plus interest charges by interest charges. This figure gives an indication of how well the firm's income covers its interest payments. Net income before taxes is used because the firm's ability to pay interest is not a function of taxes payable. This ratio varies from industry to industry. A ratio of 6 times interest earned may be adequate in one industry and poor in another.

The fixed-charge-coverage ratio serves the same basic purpose as the times-interest-earned ratio. It shows how well the firm is able to meet its fixed costs. The ratio is the result of dividing income available for meeting fixed charges by the amount of the fixed charges. Again, there is no universal standard for this ratio; each firm should compare its position with those of others in its industry.

Activity Ratio   There are four critical activity ratios: inventory turnover, average collection period, fixed assets turnover, and total assets turnover. Dividing sales by inventory gives the inventory turnover, which indicates how many times per year the firm sells its inventory. A general average for U.S. companies is 9 times, but this figure can vary. More expensive items, such as autos, major appliances, and jewelry, normally have lower turnover rates than less expensive items.

The average collection period is the number of days, on the average, that the firm takes to collect payment on its credit sales. It is found by dividing receivables by sales per day. A good indicator of whether the collection period is adequate is the firm's own credit policy. An average collection period of 41 days is unsatisfactory for a firm with a 30-day collection policy, but adequate for a firm with a 60-day collection policy.

Like inventory turnover, fixed assets turnover measures how effectively the firm uses its resources and thus gives a measure of overall efficiency. This ratio is the result of dividing sales by fixed assets. The resulting turnover calculation is then compared with the industry average to find out if the firm is employing its fixed assets more or less efficiently than competitors.

Total assets turnover is found by dividing sales by total assets. It serves the same purpose and is evaluated in the same way as fixed assets turnover. This ratio will be smallest in capital-intensive industries.

Profitability Ratios   There are three critical profitability ratios: profit margin on sales, return on total assets, and return on net worth. Profit margin on sales is expressed as a percentage and calculated by dividing sales into net profits after taxes. The percentage shows how much of each dollar of sales the firm realizes as profit. The U.S. average profit margin is 5 percent, but this percentage varies by industry.

The return on total assets is a percentage determined by dividing net profit after taxes by total assets. Comparing this percentage with the industry average indicates the firm's earning power. It shows the rate of return the firm is getting per dollar invested in assets.

Return on net worth is the result of dividing net profit after taxes by net worth, also expressed as a percentage. Net worth is defined as total equity, so it indicates the return stockholders are receiving on their investments. This percentage, again, is compared with the industry average and evaluated by stockholders and other firms to determine the desirability of investing in the firm.

Ratios can be compared to the company's past ratios or to those of other firms. Figure 3.4 portrays typical ratios and comparisons to firm averages.

FIGURE 3.4 Summary of Financial Ratio Analysis

Ratio	Formula for Calculation	Calculation	Industry Average	Evaluation
Liquidity				
Current	$\dfrac{\text{Current assets}}{\text{Current liabilities}}$	$\dfrac{\$\ 700,000}{\$\ 300,000} = 2.3$ times	2.5 times	Satisfactory
Quick, or acid test	$\dfrac{\text{Current assets—inventory}}{\text{Current liabilities}}$	$\dfrac{\$\ 400,000}{\$\ 300,000} = 1.3$ times	1.0 times	Good
Leverage				
Debt to total assets	$\dfrac{\text{Total debt}}{\text{Total assets}}$	$\dfrac{\$1,000,000}{\$2,000,000} = 50$ percent	33 percent	Poor
Times interest earned	$\dfrac{\text{Profit before taxes plus interest charges}}{\text{Interest charges}}$	$\dfrac{\$\ 245,000}{\$\ 45,000} = 5.4$ times	8.0 times	Fair
Fixed charge coverage	$\dfrac{\text{Income available for meeting fixed charges}}{\text{Fixed charges}}$	$\dfrac{\$\ 273,000}{\$\ 73,000} = 3.7$ times	5.5 times	Poor
Activity				
Inventory turnover	$\dfrac{\text{Sales}}{\text{Inventory}}$	$\dfrac{\$3,000,000}{\$\ 300,000} = 10$ times	9 times	Satisfactory
Average collection period	$\dfrac{\text{Receivables}}{\text{Sales per day}}$	$\dfrac{\$\ 200,000}{\$\ 8,333} = 24$ days	20 days	Satisfactory
Fixed assets turnover	$\dfrac{\text{Sales}}{\text{Fixed assets}}$	$\dfrac{\$3,000,000}{\$1,300,000} = 2.3$ times	5.0 times	Poor
Total assets turnover	$\dfrac{\text{Sales}}{\text{Total assets}}$	$\dfrac{\$3,000,000}{\$2,000,000} = 1.5$ times	2 times	Poor
Profitability				
Profit margin on sales	$\dfrac{\text{Net profit after taxes}}{\text{Sales}}$	$\dfrac{\$\ 120,000}{\$3,000,000} = 4$ percent	5 percent	Poor
Return on total assets	$\dfrac{\text{Net profit after taxes}}{\text{Total assets}}$	$\dfrac{\$\ 120,000}{\$2,000,000} = 6.0$ percent	10 percent	Poor
Return on net worth	$\dfrac{\text{Net profit after taxes}}{\text{Net worth}}$	$\dfrac{\$\ 120,000}{\$1,000,000} = 12.0$ percent	15 percent	Poor

Additional Financial Controls

Another way of analyzing organizational income statements and balance sheets is through common-sized statements. A common-sized income statement shows all accounts as percentages of gross sales. On a common-sized balance sheet, all items are shown as percentages of total assets. The purpose behind common-sized balance sheets and income statements is to make comparisons of percentages over a period of years or with those of other companies. When percentages change significantly or are out of line with comparable percentages from the industry, the organization should be alert to a possible need to change certain financial strategies or other strategies in order to bring these percentages into line. Furthermore, firms set target percentages for such items as income and research and development costs and therefore may have to alter their strategies throughout all functional areas in order to achieve those targets.

AT MRS. FIELDS'

The firm's information system is used to control financial activity. Standard control measurements are used, but new ones are created for each store to allow hour-by-hour control.

Evolving Financial Strategies

The 1980s were the decade of the junk bond, the leveraged buyout, and the acquisition. In the 1990s, many corporations will have to face the consequences of junk-bond financing as well as huge amounts of debt undertaken in leveraged buyouts or acquisitions of other firms. In many cases, debt will have to be restructured and in others acquisitions or parts of organizations may have to be sold.[47] Cost reduction strategies will be necessary for such firms and the problem will be further compounded by low-cost competitors evolving throughout most industries, especially in global markets.

Firms will also have to cope with financing global operations and the requirements host country governments place on various types of financing. For example, many require financing through host country banks or other financial institutions.

OPERATIONS MANAGEMENT

Operations management is the planning, organizing, leading, and controlling of "all the activities of productive systems—those portions of organizations that transform inputs into products and services."[48] Operations units follow the basic input–transformation–output model.

Operations includes both manufacturing and service considerations. The manufacturing organization transforms inputs into physical outputs and products. A service organization transforms inputs into nonphysical outputs and services, which usually cannot be inventoried, and involve customer interaction. Most organizations really do both. There are very few pure service or pure manufacturing organizations.

Many of the operations gains to be made in the future will be made in the service industry. While operational manufacturing productivity has increased substantially in the 1980s, similar gains did not appear in the service industries.[49] Basic strategies and tactics for all aspects of operations should be assessed. The following paragraphs discuss additional operations strategies that will be important in the 1990s.

Manufacturing Operations

Manufacturing strategies support the organization's business strategy. Typically, manufacturing strategy is most concerned with supporting a low cost strategy but it may also support a differentiation strategy, for example, by providing high-quality or otherwise unique products. Global manufacturing for the 21st century will focus on speed, computer-integration, meeting the requirements of the European Economic Community as expressed in the International Organization For Standards (ISO) 9000, global networks of suppliers, and a perception of manufacturing as service.[50]

The cross-functional design and development teams mentioned earlier are extremely important to increasing the productivity of manufacturing operations. By coordinating efforts among the various functions, these teams can substantially reduce the time from product development to delivery. One of the major contributions such teams can make is the use of **robust design**, sometimes referred to as **design for manufacturing.** Such programs reduce the number of parts in a product significantly in order to make it easier and quicker to manufacture.[51] Such design also helps reduce the number of maintenance problems for the customer, which improves quality. Milliken, the $2-billion textile giant, uses such teams, often with customer members, to improve both manufacturability and customer satisfaction, as well.[52] In another example, Ford Motor Company has actively sought to reduce the number of options and components in all of its cars, which would save it several billion dollars a year in manufacturing and warranty costs.[53]

Focused factories will also be important. Some operations experts, but not all of them, believe that factories perform more efficiently and effectively if they are focused upon some particular product, process, or market niche.[54] For example, Outboard Marine, a manufacturer of outboard motors, has dedicated each of its factories to specific tasks in the manufacturing process. Its Spruce Pine, North Carolina plant, for example, casts engine blocks. Other plants add pistons, fuel systems, and other parts to the engine.[55] Conversely, marketing-oriented experts such as Thomas J. Peters believe that factories in the future will have to be more flexible and less focused with the capability of turning out products for what are known as *mass customized markets.*[56]

Flexible manufacturing systems will be critical in the future. The organization will need to adjust its manufacturing operations to provide a wide range of products rapidly using the same manufacturing systems. Allen Bradley Corporation employs flexible manufacturing to help it overcome its global competition, as discussed in this chapter's Global Strategic Challenge feature.

Computer-integrated manufacturing is one of the most important manufacturing concepts of the 1990s. **Computer-integrated manufacturing (CIM)** is a broad label applied to manufacturing using computers in both design and manufacturing. This has also been called *computer-aided design/computer-aided manufacturing* (CAD/CAM). Just-in-time inventory systems, flexible manufacturing, high levels of automation, and automatic storage and retrieval systems are all part of CIM.[57] Firms seeking to compete in a global marketplace must become computer-integrated manufacturers, or in all likelihood they will not survive the 1990s.

The whole philosophy of **kaizen**, or continuous improvement, will drive product design and service industry delivery, and manufacturing processes, as well. In manufacturing, kaizen is aimed mainly at improving quality. Kaizen is a strategic imperative for the 1990s. Companies that wish to compete on a global basis must produce quality levels at least equal to, and preferably superior to, those of their foreign competitors. This is an especially difficult task when one realizes

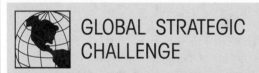

GLOBAL STRATEGIC CHALLENGE

ALLEN BRADLEY MANUFACTURES FLEXIBLY

Allen Bradley Corporation of Milwaukee, Wisconsin, a manufacturer of industrial controls, found itself losing market share to foreign competition, especially in its electrical motor control business. As a result it began using flexible manufacturing in combination with CIM, including computer-aided design/computer-aided manufacturing (CAD/CAM) systems. Allen Bradley chose to use flexible manufacturing and CIM after studying the possibilities of offshore manufacturing. This alternative costed out higher than keeping operations in the United States when all factors were considered.

Many consider Allen Bradley to have the most modern factory in the United States. The flexible manufacturing feature allows rapid change from manufacturing one type of product to another using the same equipment. The computer analyzes the various orders and materials requirements, and determines the schedule for each day. It then informs the totally robotized CIM assembly line what to produce, when and where to ship it, the materials to use, and the source of the materials. Bar coding allows the computer to keep track of the production process, as all input, output, and process areas are bar coded. The line is so sophisticated it can make different products of different sized lots, even down to a single unit, at assembly-line speeds.

Source: John S. DeMott, "American Scene: In Old Milwaukee, Tomorrow's Factory Today," *Time*, June 16, 1986, pp. 66–67; and Gene Bylinski, "Breakthrough in Automating the Assembly," *Fortune*, May 26, 1986, pp. 64–66.

the Japanese have been producing much higher quality products for substantially longer than their U.S. counterparts. Quality control is much more difficult in service than in manufacturing, yet it can mean the difference between success and failure. Kaizen can be applied in service operations, as well.

Firms must also develop and implement **productivity management programs** to achieve strategic success. Such programs improve productivity in an organized and totally committed fashion. For example, Westinghouse, through its corporate productivity center, continuously revises its manufacturing and service strategies to improve productivity. Its program has shown substantial success. For example, within 5 years of introducing a productivity management program into its Sumter, South Carolina plant, that plant's sales doubled, it filled orders faster, and it freed up 14 percent of its space for expansion although it had been operating at capacity. As part of the program, the company installed semiautomated machinery, formed quality circles, and retrained employees to teach them to perform more tasks in smaller work areas. The program also reorganized the work flow. The same plant and the same people with different productivity management skills improved productivity.[58]

Firms wishing to be successful in the 1990s must have **quality management programs** because high quality will be the minimal level acceptable in virtually every industry. Quality is a strategic imperative for the 1990s. Typically, a quality program involves hiring a consulting firm, training managers and operations workers in the objectives and practices of the program, implementing the program, and then controlling performance. Often such programs have at least some form of a quality circle. A **quality circle** is a group of people who typically meet on the company's time to discuss the resolution of quality problems within their work groups. Such circles are voluntary in nature and most organizations compensate employees for their efforts.[59] Over time such groups tend to lose their momentum because, unless the manufacturing process changes, they make the process so efficient that they run out of problems to solve. What typically happens then is the circles are disbanded for a period of time and re-initiated perhaps a year or two later.[60]

Expert Systems

Part of virtually all economic functions, but especially applicable to manufacturing and service operations, are expert systems in which the computer recommends solutions to problems, rather than just supplying information for solving those problems. These recommendations are based on the logic of experts in the field which is incorporated into the computer's software. United Airlines, for example, uses expert systems to reduce delays at its airport hubs.[61]

Service Operations[62]

Because of increasing domestic and global competition, one of the major strategic challenges service organizations face is improving their strategic and tactical operations. Management of service operations and human resource management are virtually synonymous. The ability to manage people is what makes service operations successful. In many cases, however, some of the same kinds of solutions suggested for manufacturing operations are applicable. For example, the use of technology is critical, especially expert systems and computer-integrated service operations (CIS as opposed to CIM). For example, Federal Express has developed expert systems and computer-assisted parcel control in order to speed delivery of parcels overnight to virtually anywhere in the United States and within 2 days to virtually anywhere in the world.[63]

But the central thrust of service operations is scheduling human resources, influencing their motivation and increasing their productivity in such a way as to improve the company's response to customer needs.

HUMAN RESOURCE MANAGEMENT

Managing human resources in the 1990s will be more difficult than ever. Labor is in short supply across most skill levels, but especially for jobs requiring the highest mathematical, technological, and engineering skills.[64] The issues involved are extremely complex. The United States appears to be heading toward a two-tiered labor system with highly skilled technological workers, managers, and professionals at one end of the spectrum and numerous lower-skilled, primarily service-oriented workers at the other. As we saw in Chapter 1, a major part of one of the ten strategic management challenges is increased worker expectations at all levels.

The style of management expected to be most effective in the future will probably be more participative than that currently employed by most organizations. Organizations must begin to develop programs to enculturate such styles of management. Regardless of what style is dominant or which mix of styles is used, an organization must develop a formal strategy for its organization structure, detailing how much decision-making authority individual employees and groups of employees will have.

Additionally, organizations must begin and/or continue to develop strategies for the traditional human resource management functions of attraction, selection, orientation, compensation, safety and health monitoring, motivation, separation, and assuring equal employment opportunity. The complexities of managing a work force in the 1990s and beyond, especially in issues such as the changing composition of the work force and anticipated increases in government regulation, make it imperative that organizations formulate strategies for coping with work force problems.

RESEARCH AND DEVELOPMENT

According to virtually every expert on strategy, innovation will be one of the major keys to success in the 1990s.[65] Corporate strategists also agree with this position. For example, John Naylor, former strategic planner for General Motors, and John Sculley, CEO of Apple Computers, both claim that innovation is the key to future success in their industries.[66] An **innovation** is a creative product, service, or process that has a significant impact on an industry, company, or society.[67] (The process by which an innovation is created is also referred to as *innovation*.)

An organization must deal with four types of innovation: product, process, marketing, and management innovation.[68] **Product innovation** results in new products and/or services, or enhancements to old products or services. A **process innovation** improves the processes in an organization, for example, operations, human resource management, or finance. **Marketing innovation** includes new approaches to the marketing functions of promotion, pricing, and distribution as well as those parts of the product function other than product development, for example, packaging. **Management innovation** improves the management of the organization. Empowerment is a management innovation, as is the use of executive information systems. Marketing and management innovation are specific types of process innovation.

Historically, firms in the United States have been extremely good at product innovation. They have developed many new products and services, and new technologies that have generated still more new products or services. Little attention has been paid to process innovation in the United States, but the Japanese have been extremely successful in such efforts. Cutting costs on their products and improving them slightly through kaizen has differentiated Japanese firms from their global competitors and given their products or services lower costs, as well. Finally, firms in the United States and more recently firms from other countries, especially Japan and Europe, have become extremely proficient at marketing innovation. The Japanese have been very good at management innovation.

In order to be innovative, it has become increasingly clear that an organization needs to establish a certain type of culture. It is not necessary that every subunit of the organization be innovative, but at least in most of the organization, innovation must be encouraged and rewarded, and procedures must exist to move creative ideas up through the organization hierarchy. Many firms need substantial creativity training. Firms such as Frito-Lay, Inc. have trained thousands of employees to be more creative.[69] Furthermore, firms must encourage risk taking, open communication, allowance for error, a participative climate, training in creative processes, and flexibility.[70]

Further, managers must learn to manage creative individuals. They must learn to encourage a different approach to doing the job throughout the organization, and especially in the process areas. Doing the job should come to include creating new ways to do a better job. This requires refocusing most managers' attitudes. Many Japanese organizations, for example, have replaced or enhanced their traditional quality circles with creativity circles. Creativity circles have essentially the same dynamics as quality circles except that they focus on creative process and product innovation rather than quality.[71]

The *S* Curve

"The *S* **curve** is a graph of the relationship between the effort [funds] put into improving a product or process and the results one gets back for that investment."[72] Figure 3.5 portrays an example of an *S* Curve. The *S* curve gets its name from its shape. Initially, as funds (effort) are put into a project, results come slowly.

FIGURE 3.5 The *S* Curve

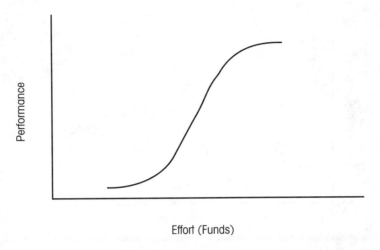

Source: Richard N. Foster, *Innovation: The Attacker's Advantage* (New York: Summit Books, 1986), p. 31. Copyright © 1986 by McKinsey & Co., Inc. Reprinted by permission of Summit, a division of Simon & Schuster.

Then suddenly, dramatic results follow. Eventually, increases in effort, even significant efforts, produce only limited results. This has several implications for research and development. For example, at what point does the firm stop investing in improvement and move on to new products?

From the viewpoint of strategic planning in the 1990s, additional concerns are raised. Typically a firm would like to have overlapping *S* curves so that its new product introductions would slowly, conveniently replace its older products. What happens, though, when a competitor's new product introduction leaves the firm's products behind in a leap-frog maneuver like the one shown in Figure 3.6? In some cases, the firm may very well go out of business as a result of strategic discontinuity. Innovation becomes the attacker's advantage. This happened when video rentals virtually eliminated the drive-in movie, jet engines replaced propeller aircraft, calculators replaced slide rules, and digital watches replaced pin lever watches. The *S* curve is affecting sales of some products significantly, as workstations replace PCs in many industrial applications, and antilock brakes replace standard systems in many cars. It will happen in the future as new products emerge to replace old ones.

The company that is attacked can respond. The Macintosh did not replace the IBM PC, although it has dampened its sales considerably. Defenders of old products can take several actions. They can add "sails"-features that enhance current products' capabilities until they have a chance to leapfrog the new competitor (as sailing ships did in order to increase their speed to match that of the steamships that invaded their markets). IBM stressed its name, image, quality, and power to counter the Macintosh. A company can use superior resources, as IBM did, to outsell even a superior product. It can develop hybrids of the old and new technology. IBM now has a mouse and software similar to those on the Macintosh. It can counter-attack at the weaknesses of the attacker's product. Macintosh had

FIGURE 3.6 Technological Discontinuity and the *S* Curve

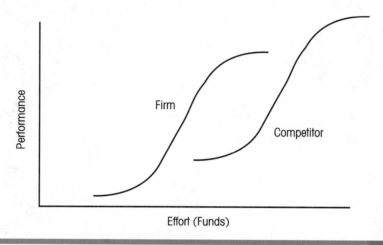

Source: Richard N. Foster, *Innovation: The Attacker's Advantage* (New York: Summit Books, 1986) p. 33. Copyright © 1986 by McKinsey & Co., Inc. Reprinted by permission of Summit, a division of Simon & Schuster.

several flaws, including a small screen and limited software, and it was perceived as cute, but not very useful for business, its main market. Aggressive price cutting may help a firm respond. IBM employed this strategy, as well. In addition, a firm can copy the new product, also as IBM did by adding features to its PC.[73]

Perhaps the best defense is to constantly attack yourself, changing the company as necessary to stay ahead of any attackers. The company must be able to attack and counterattack over and over in any given period of time.[74]

MANAGEMENT CAPABILITIES

Any organization depends upon its managers for success. Assessing management capabilities is never easy, but it will be ever more difficult in the future. In the 1990s, it is evident that strategists must cope with significant levels of change, formulate innovative strategies that enable the organization to be competitive, manage on a global basis, and, in general, formulate strategies to deal with all of the strategic challenges the organization will face. To do so, the strategist must be capable of intuitive, multidimensional thinking, as well as rational/analytical thinking.

All managers must manage knowledge. Knowledge must not only be gained, but shared throughout the organization. This ability to create and transfer knowledge will be the key to competitive success.[75]

The operational-level manager will be especially concerned with establishing a management style that will enable him or her to function with a much different work force. In fact, the entire managerial environment, both internal and external, will be much different and much more complex than it now is. Thus, the operational manager will face essentially the same types of problems that strategists do, but at another level. The operational manager handles strategy implementation, as opposed to strategy formulation. In assessing an organization's management profile, it is especially important to determine whether or not it is preparing its managers for the future. Is it engaging in sufficient management development?

ORGANIZATIONAL CULTURE

The management of organizational culture was an important aspect of strategic management in the 1980s. It will be even more important in the 1990s. Everything that strategists foresee for the 1990s indicates changes in organizational life. Thus, culture will have to be managed in such a way that it enables, rather than limits, the organization's ability to cope with change. Chapter 9 discusses the management of organizational culture in more detail.

ORGANIZATIONAL CAPABILITIES AND CORE COMPETENCIES

Since 1989, organizations have been actively struggling to compete in highly volatile environments. As discussed in Chapter 1, this has led to the development of resource-based strategies in which organizations attempt to build as many resource bases as is financially possible. These resource bases focus on core competency areas. **Core competencies** are the fruition of the collective learning of the organization. They are the combination of the individual technologies and production skills that underly a company's myriad product lines. These are skills and processes that the organization does sufficiently well that they provide competitive advantages, or they are other resources from which competitive advantages can be built.[76] More recently firms have begun to strategize in terms of organizational capabilities. **Organizational capabilities** are business processes that consistently provide the customer with superior value. Organizational capabilities go beyond resource bases in that resource bases imply stagnant but available resource stocks of all kinds. They go beyond core competencies in that these are defined as existing in various points in the value chain while organizational capabilities are more broadly based, encompassing the entire value chain.[77] As of June, 1992 capabilities strategies have only begun to be understood, but it is clear that a shift is occuring in the strategy paradigm towards viewing strategy as a set of processes. Thus, SWOT analysis takes on a whole new meaning, specifically here in terms of the determination of internal strengths. Such an analysis is now moving away from the condition of various functional activities to broader organizational processes.

STRATEGIC MANAGER'S SUMMARY

1. Organizations undertake internal and external environmental analysis to make certain that they remain aware of ever-changing external and internal

environments. The process involves extensive collection and analysis of substantial formal and informal data banks.

2. A SWOT analysis determines organizational strengths and weaknesses, relative to environmental opportunities and threats. Ultimately, this determination should lead to the establishment of a strategic, competitive advantage.

3. By comparing themselves to the best firms in the industry at particular skills through best practices analysis and benchmarking, firms can make giant strides toward becoming as good as their best competitors.

4. Strategic information systems are the lifeblood of strategic management. Without them, SWOT cannot be assessed, nor can objectives and strategies be satisfactorally determined and formulated.

5. Information may have strategic value because it provides competitive advantage. Information management may therefore be a strategy.

6. Strategy may be perceived as one way of creating value. To do this, strategists examine the value chain to determine the points at which the firm may add value in order to obtain a strategic, competitive advantage.

7. The chapter reviewed several strategies expected to be important in the 1990s for each of the major economic functions of the organization. It also discussed issues relevant to determining an organizational profile in the areas of management capabilities and organizational culture.

8. Improving innovation depends significantly upon creating an organizational culture that not only allows, but encourages and rewards, perhaps even demands, innovation.

KEY TERMS

balance
benchmarking
best practices
closeness to the customer
computer-integrated manufacturing (CIM)
core competencies
cross-functional development teams
design for manufacturing
electronic data interchange (EDI)
expert systems
flexible manufacturing systems
focused factories
innovation
internal and external environmental
   analysis
kaizen
leap-frog strategies
management innovation
marketing innovation
operations management

organizational capabilities
opportunities
process innovation
product innovation
productivity management programs
quality circles
quality management programs
rate of change
resource-based strategies
robust design
scanning
S curve
speed strategy
strategic field analysis
strategic information systems (SISs)
strengths
sustainable competitive advantage
synergy
threats
value-added chain
weaknesses

DISCUSSION QUESTIONS

1. Why is closeness to the customer a critical success factor for the 1990s?
2. Discuss why a cross-functional design team improves both the speed with which products reach the market and their quality.
3. Why is innovation such an important factor for strategic success in the 1990s?
4. Explain how kaizen works, and how it can be a philosophy of life.
5. Explain the S curve and related strategic discontinuity. How are leap-frog strategies critical to strategic success in times of strategic discontinuity?
6. Develop an organizational profile for an organization with which you are familiar.
7. Discuss the ethics of competitor intelligence when such information is gained through job interviews of competitors' former employees or through listening to idle chatter at restaurants and bars.
8. Indicate how the ten strategic management challenges would affect the requirements for a strategic information system.
9. Indicate what strengths the organization will need to possess in order to cope with the ten strategic management challenges.

STRATEGIC AUDIT QUESTIONS

1. Does the organization under consideration have an MIS or an SIS? How good are they? What can be done to make them better?
2. Does the organization develop an organizational profile? Does this organization know what its strengths and weaknesses are, and what they may be and should be in the future?
3. If you develop an organizational profile for the organization in question, what does it tell you about that company? What are its strengths and weaknesses? (Make sure you check for the basics as well as the strategies noted in this chapter. Also, due to space limitations, this chapter only reviewed functional considerations. Don't forget to examine overall corporate factors.) What should its profile look like in a few years? What strengths will it need? What weaknesses must it overcome?
4. Is the organization preparing for the next 5 to 10 years by developing strengths and reducing weaknesses?
5. Does this organization use information as strategy? If yes, how? If no, how could it?
6. How are the ten strategic challenges likely to affect this organization's profile in the next few years?

Endnotes

1. Susan G. Strother, "Buyout by General Cinema Puts HBJ Books in Order," *Orlando Sentinel*, January 25, 1991, p. A1.

2. Jennifer Lawrence, "Cost Spiral Could KO Some Airlines in '91," *Advertising Age*, November 5, 1990, p. SS1.

3. Michael A. Hitt and R. Duane Ireland, "Corporate Distinctive Competence, Strategy, Industry, and Performance," *Strategic Management Journal*, November/December 1985, pp. 273–293.

4. Paul Ingrassia and Neal Templin, "Cash Crunch: Hemorrhaging Money, Ford Cuts Spending and May Sell Assets," *The Wall Street Journal*, January 24, 1991, pp. A1, A6.

5. Thomas A. Stewart, "GE Keeps Those Ideas Coming," *Fortune*, August 12, 1991, pp. 41–49; Karen Bemowski, "The Benchmarking Bandwagon," *Quality Progress*, January 1991, pp. 19–24; Beverly Geber, "Benchmarking: Measuring Yourself against the Best," *Training*, November 1990, pp. 36–44.

6. David Ulrich and Dale Lake, "Organizational Capability: Creating Competitive Advantage," *Academy of Management Executive*, February 1991, pp. 77–92.

7. For a full review of the resource-based strategy issue, see "Special Theory Forum: The Resource Based Model of the Firm," *Journal of Management*, March 1991, pp. 97–212.

8. Ian Williams, "Burger Bun-Fight," *Business* (United Kingdom), May 1990, pp. 76–78.

9. Ellis Booker, "Retiring Exley Sees NCR/AT&T Synergy," *ComputerWorld*, September 30, 1991, p. 6.

10. Michel M. Robert, *Strategic Thinking: Charting the Course of Your Organization*, 2d ed. (Woburn, Mass.: Decision Process International, 1984).

11. John Taylor, "Project Fantasy: A Behind-the-Scenes Account of Disney's Desperate Battle against the Raiders," *Manhattan Magazine*, November 1984. Ray Watson remained as a member of the board, but was no longer chairman.

12. Howard H. Stevenson, "Defining Corporate Strengths and Weaknesses," *Sloan Management Review*, Spring 1976, pp. 51–66.

13. Omar A. El Sawy, "Undertaking the Process by Which Chief Executives Identify Strategic Threats and Opportunities," Academy of Management *Proceedings*, 1984, edited by John A. Pearce II and Richard B. Robinson, Jr., pp. 37–41.

14. It is not clear, for example, that large organizations actually ever perform SWOT analyses. They often just move on to internally focused external strategies.

15. Jordan D. Lewis, "Scanning for Opportunities," *Across the Board*, May 1990, pp. 52–57, provides description of how the process should occur. For a discussion of how it's done in the banking industry, see George Warfel, "Keeping Up with Technology," *Bank Management*, August 1990, pp. 28–32.

16. R. T. Lenz and Jack L. Engledow, "Environmental Analysis Units and Strategic Decision Making: A Field of Selected 'Leading-Edge' Corporations," *Strategic Management Journal*, January/February 1986, pp. 69–89.

17. Kate Berhand, "Competitive Intelligence: The Global Spyglass," *Business Marketing*, September 1990, pp. 52–56.

18. Mitch Betts, "Keeping an Eye on the East," *ComputerWorld*, April 29, 1991, pp. 97, 101.

19. Susan Moffat, "Picking Japan's Research Brains," *Fortune*, March 25, 1991, pp. 84–96.

20. One of the authors' discussion with the director.

21. Robert K. Mueller, *Corporate Networking* (New York: Free Press, 1986); see also J. Carlos Jarillo, "On Strategic Networks," *Strategic Management Journal*, January/February 1988, pp. 31–41, for a discussion of strategic networks.

22. J. A. Turner and H. C. Lucas, Jr., "Developing Strategic Information Systems," in *Handbook of Business Strategy*, edited by W. D. Guth (Boston: Warren, Gorham, and Lamont, 1985), p. 21.2; Marjorie A. Lyles and Ian I. Mitroff, "Organizational Problem Formulation: An Empirical Study," *Administrative Science Quarterly*, March 1980, pp. 102–119; P. Lorange, "The Planner's Dual Role—A Survey of U.S. Companies," *Long Range Planning*, March 1973, pp. 12–16; and R. N. Taylor, "Psychological Aspects of Planning," *Long Range Planning*, April 1976, pp. 66–74.

23. F. J. Aguilar, *Scanning the Business Environment* (New York: Macmillan, 1967).

24. "DSS at Phillips Gushes Strategic Information," *Data Management*, February 1986, pp. 20, 21, 28.

25. "Systems Review—Commander EIS: Providing Strategic Information to Bank Executives," *Banking Software Review*, Spring 1990, pp. 8, 11.

26. For a review of the relationship of forecasting to scanning, see Ronald D. Michman, "Why Forecast for the Long Term?" *Journal of Business Strategy*, September/October 1989, pp. 36–40.

27. Michael E. Porter and Victor E. Miller, "How Information Gives You Competitive Advantage," *Harvard Business Review*, July–August 1985, pp. 149–160.

28. Douglas Barney, "Seizing the Day at Pratt & Whitney," *ComputerWorld*, July 31, 1989, pp. 57–58.

29. Michael E. Porter, *Competitive Advantage* (New York: Free Press, 1985), Chapter 1.

30. Peter Lorange, Michael F. Scott Morton, and Sumantra Ghoshal, *Strategic Control* (St. Paul, Minn.: West, 1986), pp. 104–107.

31. Porter, *Competitive Advantage*, pp. 33–61.

32. Thomas J. Peters, "The Home-Team Advantage," *U.S. News & World Report*, March 31, 1986, p. 49.

33. Robert M. Fifer, "Cost Benchmarking Functions in the Value Chain," *Planning Review*, May/June 1989, pp. 18–27.

34. Lorange et al., *Strategic Control.*

35. Lewis T. Boone and David Kurtz, *Marketing Management*, 6th ed. (Fort Worth, Texas: Dryden Press, 1990).

36. Thomas J. Peters and Robert H. Waterman, Jr., *In Search of Excellence* (New York: Harper & Row, 1982).

37. Stephen Phillips and Amy Dunkin, "King Customer," *Business Week*, March 12, 1990, pp. 88–94.

38. Ronald Henkoff, "How to Plan for 1995," *Fortune*, December 31, 1990, pp. 78–79.

39. Thomas J. Peters, *Thriving on Chaos* (New York: Knopf, 1987).

40. John Naisbitt, *Megatrends* (New York: Warner Books, 1982).

41. William J. Spencer, "Research to Product: A Major U.S. Challenge," *California Management Review*, Winter 1990, pp. 45–53; Thomas M. Rohan, "World Class Manufacturing: In Search of Speed," *Industry Week*, September 3, 1990, pp. 78–83; Takla S. Perry, "Teamwork Plus Technology Cuts Development Time," *EEE Spectrums*, October 1990, pp. 61–67; Karen Bronikowski, "Speeding New Products to Market," *Journal of Business Strategy*, September/October 1990, pp. 34–37; Brian Dumaine, "How Managers Can Succeed through Speed," *Fortune*, February 13, 1987, pp. 54–59.

42. Robin L. Lawton, "Creating a Customer-Centered Culture in Service Industries," *Quality Progress*, September 1991, pp. 69–72.

43. Robert W. Goddard, "Kaizen!" *Manage*, May 1991, pp. 4–5, 21; Sheridan M. Tatsuno, "Hitting for Singles: The Japanese Are Demonstrating that You Don't Have to Hit a Home Run with Every Product to Stay ahead of the Market," *Across the Board*, April 1990, pp. 30–35; Annabeth L. Propot, "In Search of a New Process," *Quality Progress*, June 1989, pp. 43–47.

44. Masaaki Imai, "Kaizen Wave Circles the Globe," *Tokyo Business Today*, May 1990, pp. 44–48, discusses why some firms in the U.S. resist adopting the concept. Often it involves a lack of willingness on the part of top management.

45. James I. McKenna, "United Places Record Order for Up to 128 Transports," *Aviation Week and Space Technology*, October 22, 1990, pp. 20–21; Dori Jones Yang and Michael O'Neal, "How Boeing Does It," *Business Week*, July 9, 1990, pp. 46–50.

46. Jordan D. Lewis, "Using Alliances to Build Market Power," *Planning Review*, September/October 1990, pp. 49, 48; John G. Sifoms, "Mining for Gold in Your Information Systems," *Directors & Boards*, Summer 1989, pp. 21–25.

47. Fred R. Bleakley, "Bad Hangover: Many Firms Find Debt They Piled on in 1980s Is a Cruel Taskmaster," *The Wall Street Journal*, October 9, 1990, pp. A1, A15.

48. Norman Gaither, *Production and Operations Management: A Problem Solving and Decision Making Approach* (Hinsdale, Ill.: Dryden Press, 1987), p. 3.

49. Martha E. Mangelsdorf, "Making It," *Inc.*, October 1991, pp. 20–24.

50. Joel D. Goldbar, "The Shape of Twenty-First Century Global Manufacturing," *Business Strategy*, March/April 1991, pp. 37–41.

51. For a discussion, see John R. Dixon and Michael R. Duffey, "The Neglect of Engineering Design," *California Management Review*, Winter 1990, pp. 9–24; Otis Port, "How to Make It Right the First Time," *Business Week*, June 8, 1987, pp. 142–143.

52. Peters, "Home-Team Advantage," p. 49.

53. David Woodruff, "Manufacturing: Miles Traveled, More to Go," *Business Week*, October 25, 1991, pp. 70–73; Donald E. Peterson, "Ford Has a Lesson for America," *Industry Week*, February 15, 1990, p. 55.

54. Wickham Skinner, "The Focused Factory," *Harvard Business Review*, May–June 1974, p. 113.

55. Douglas R. Sease, "Getting Smart: How U.S. Companies Devise Ways to Meet the Challenge from Japan," *The Wall Street Journal*, September 16, 1986, pp. 1, 25.

56. Peters, *Thriving on Chaos*, pp. 16–44, 47–190, with a discussion of flexible manufacturing on pp. 161–163, 203. For a discussion of the principles of flexible manufacturing, see Robert H. Hayes and Steven C. Wheelwright, *Restoring Our Competitive Edge: Competing through Manufacturing* (New York: Wiley, 1984).

57. Frederick C. Weston, Jr., "Computer Integrated Manufacturing Systems: Fact or Fantasy," *Business Horizons*, July/August 1988, pp. 64–68.

58. Thomas A. Stewart, "Westinghouse Gets Respect At Last," *Fortune*, July 3, 1989, pp. 92–98; Vinoid K. Kapoor, "Just in Time and the Focus Factory: A Case History at Westinghouse," *Manufacturing Systems*, December 1989, pp. 47–49; and Gregory L. Marlows and David Griffiths, "How Westinghouse Is Revving Up after the Rebound," *Business Week*, March 28, 1988, pp. 46–52.

59. Frank Shipper, "Quality Circles Using Small Group Formation," *Training and Development Journal*, May 1983, p. 82; also see Edward E. Lawler III and Susan A. Mohrman, "Quality Circles after the Honeymoon," *Organizational Dynamics*, Spring 1987, pp. 42–54.

60. Robert Wood, Frank Hall, and Koya Azumi, "Evaluating Quality Circles: American Application," *California Management Review*, Fall 1983, p. 43.

61. Carole A. Shifrin, "Gate Assignment Expert System Reduces Delays at United Hub," *Aviation Week and Space Technology*, January 25, 1988, pp. 112–113.

62. For a review of strategic service management, see Risk Roscitt, "Strategic Service Management," *Journal of Business and Industrial Marketing*, Winter/Spring 1990, pp. 27–40.

63. Mary Kathleen Flynn, "Business Focus Is Key to Success," *Datamation*, July 15, 1987, p. 48; also see Blake Ives and Richard O. Mason, "Can Information Technology Revitalize Your Customer Service," *Academy of Management Executive*, November 1990, pp. 52–69.

64. William B. Johnston and Arnold H. Packer, *Workforce 2000: Work and Workers for the 21st Century* (Indianapolis: Hudson Institute, 1987).

65. For example, see Porter, *Competitive Advantage*; Peters,

Thriving on Chaos; Rosabeth Moss Kanter, *When Giants Learn to Dance* (New York: Simon & Schuster, 1989).

66. Michael Naylor, speech to the Academy of Management, August 13, 1986; John Sculley, speech to MacWorld, February 1988.

67. James M. Higgins, "Innovate or Evaporate," article in progress.

68. Michael E. Porter, *Competitive Strategy* (New York: Free Press, 1980), pp. 177–178, describes the first three. Ray Stata, "Organizational Learning—The Key to Management Innovation," *Sloan Management Review*, Spring 1989, pp. 63–74, describes the last.

69. Charlene Marner Solomon, "What an Idea: Creativity Training," *Personnel*, May 1990, pp. 64–71.

70. A number of sources could be cited. For example, see Charles O'Reilly, "Corporations, Culture, and Commitment: Motivation and Social Control in Organizations," *California Management Review*, Summer 1989, pp. 7–25.

71. Tatsuno M. Sheridan, "Creating Breakthroughs the Japanese Way," *R&D*, February 1990, pp. 136–142.

72. Richard Foster, *Innovation: The Attacker's Advantage* (New York: Summit Books, 1986), p. 31.

73. Ibid., pp. 185–220.

74. Ibid., pp. 221–240.

75. Ikujiro Nonaka, "The Knowledge Creating Company," *Harvard Business Review*, November–December 1991, pp. 96–109.

76. C. K. Prahalad and Gary Hamel, "The Core Competence of the Corporation," *Harvard Business Review*, May/June 1990, pp. 79–91.

77. George Stalk, Phillip Evans, and Lawrence E. Shulman, "Competing on Capabilities: The New Rules of Strategy," *Harvard Business Review*, March/April 1992, pp. 57–69.

INTEGRATIVE CASE ANALYSIS
CHAPTER 3

THE CHALLENGES FACING GENERAL MOTORS IN 1992

Now that you have read Chapter 3 and reviewed the GM case for related concepts, let's see how the chapter's concepts apply to GM.

APPLICATION OF CONCEPTS TO THE CASE

SWOT   GM's strategic actions from 1979 to 1989 were based on an internal environmental analysis of its strengths and weaknesses as well as an analysis of its external environment, including threats of foreign and domestic competition (see Exhibit 3.1). The firm's strategies recognized an opportunity to seize the entire market from Ford and Chrysler. Matching GM's strengths and weaknesses against its opportunities and threats (SWOT), strategists felt they had sufficient strengths, especially with respect to cash flow, to drive their competition from the marketplace. The world was changing, however, and GM's SWOT changed accordingly. The threats grew larger and stronger; GM's weaknesses were magnified. Top management was slow to recognize this change.

Exhibit 3.2 shows the four factors that determined the company's strategy in 1992—its most obvious strengths, weaknesses, opportunities, and threats. When we examine its SWOT and identify its strategists for these two time periods, we can see significant changes since 1979. Some of the strengths have become weaknesses and some new weaknesses have become apparent over these 13 years. While the company perceives technology to be a future strength, it may represent only an opportunity. GM's only major strength may be its diversification. Its evolving weakness in cash flow results from its costs (especially labor costs) and the quality and styling of its cars in relation to their domestic and foreign competition, which has restricted sales. In its auto division, obvious threats include Japanese competition, the rejuvenation of Ford and Chrysler, and European and Korean car makers. Opportunities exist for the use of technology and innovation.

GM's internal information system is described as extensive and in the process of becoming totally integrated. This may eventually lead to some type of strategic advantage.

EXHIBIT 3.1   GM's 1979 SWOT and Strategists

Strengths
Cash flow
Work force
Technology (future)
Weaknesses
Technology (present)

Opportunities
Condition of Ford and Chrysler
Capture market
Threats
Government regulations
Strategists
Thomas A. Murphy
Elliott M. Estes

EXHIBIT 3.2 GM's 1992 SWOT and Strategists

Strengths	**Opportunities**
Technology (perceived)	Diversification
European auto division	Pacific Rim
Electronics and finance subsidiaries	**Threats**
Weaknesses	Recession
Cash flow	Competition, especially Japanese
Market share	Government regulations
Morale	**Strategists**
Styling of cars	John Smith
Complexity of organization structure	Robert Stempel
North American auto operations	Ronald M. Pirtle
	Top staff members

GM seems not to add as much in the manufacturing portion of the value chain as do its Japanese competitors. For example, its inputs from suppliers are not as free of defects as inputs to Japanese firms, and GM products, on average, do not have the same high level of quality. Furthermore, as you will learn from the Industry Note at the end of Chapter 4, the Japanese are changing the definition of the value added by quality, and GM is not yet even competing in adding value according to the old definition.

Functional Strategies

Marketing GM is focusing on getting closer to the customer. The customer is now number one. It has changed pricing strategies to include discounts and rebates, it has changed product strategies by attempting to improve styling, and it has changed its advertising strategies.

Operations GM is attempting to sort out its manufacturing operations to state what plant should produce what car. In the past it has invested heavily in technology. It has also invested heavily in improving the work force and gaining their cooperation in its new strategies. It is not yet capable of significant flexible manufacturing. In its effort to be the most efficient producer of automobiles in the world, it has begun employing many Japanese manufacturing techniques such as just-in-time inventories.

Human Resources GM has worked to improve its relationship with the union, and Stempel has brought a sense of fair play to all relations with employees. It has sought to improve communications with employees, and utilized much more participative management than in the past. It has eliminated numerous jobs and plants in order to streamline operations, and it will eliminate many more.

Finance   GM gave up a stock buy-back plan due to lack of cash flow. It is implementing a major cost-cutting program in order to be more efficient, and also to generate sufficient operating cash flows.

GM has encountered strategic discontinuities. For example, the Japanese have leapfrogged GM with superior quality and, more recently, superior use of technology in the product itself. Many of GM's products are at the ends of their S curves, and GM will apparently be unable to market a number of new cars with superior designs before 1993. John Smith is eliminating older nonperforming product lines.

STRATEGIC MANAGEMENT CHALLENGES

GM's internal profile is significantly affected by several strategic challenges. For example, it has difficulty coping with rapid change, partly because it is so large and bureaucratic. It is improving its information systems, recognizing the transition to an information society. Also, it has a very culturally diverse work force.

How do the other challenges affect GM's organizational profile?

CHAPTER 4

EXTERNAL ENVIRONMENTAL ANALYSIS AND FORECASTING

Management's job is to see the company not as it is, but as it can become.

John W. Teets
Chairman, The Greyhound Corporation

New competitors, new technologies, and new lifestyles demand a new breed of American management.

John A. Young
President and CEO, Hewlett-Packard

CHAPTER OBJECTIVES

By the time you complete this chapter, you should be able to:

1. Describe key issues for each of the external factors to be considered in each of the three environments—general, competitive, and global
2. Discuss the reasons for gathering information for each of these factors
3. Perform an industry analysis and a competitor analysis for a firm
4. Discuss the roles of technology and innovation in strategy
5. Discuss the forecasting process and how it is used in the firm
6. Describe how SWOT is used to formulate strategy

APPLE COMPUTERS DOES BATTLE WITH ITS COMPETITION
THEN DECIDES, IF YOU CAN'T BEAT 'EM, JOIN 'EM

Perhaps as in no other industry, firms in the personal computer industry must have information about domestic and global competitors' actions to survive and prosper. They must know what is happening with technology, and if they really want to prosper, they should probably be on the leading edge of that technology. They must also be alert to changes in the economy, both domestic and global, and be able to predict with some accuracy the availability and prices of raw materials and subcomponent inputs. They must also respond to their social responsibilities for disposal of manufacturing wastes, equal employment opportunity, and employee safety and welfare. All of these factors and others require constant surveillance of the external environment.

Apple Computers, Inc. of San Jose, California constantly analyzes its external environment, reacts to it, and anticipates it. More important, the firm tries to create events within that environment to which others must react. Apple's business strategy has always been based on innovation (combined with low-cost production). Apple tries to live on the leading edge of technology, creating personal computers that other firms must catch up with. First it was the Apple II, then came the Apple III, the Lisa, and finally the Macintosh. Two of these products were not very successful, but the Apple II and Macintosh have been enormously successful. Now, Apple engineers are working feverishly on the Knowledge Navigator, the personal computer for the late 1990s. Undoubtedly, an early version will appear in the mid-1990s, before the impressive technological innovations predicted for the Navigator can be fully developed. Such features include voice recognition for commands, interaction with data bases by telecommunications, and all types of modeling capabilities.

Apple competes with IBM, Compaq, and a host of other companies. This competition is intense. With the advanced technology of the Macintosh (introduced in 1984), and with spirited prosecution of all clonemakers attempting to use the same technology, for 5 years Apple was able to charge premium prices and earn substantial margins. As IBM and other competitors began to offer similar features, however, Apple was forced in late 1990 to introduce new, lower-priced models. Response was immediate and positive from the consumer market. Apple and all other computer manufacturers, however, found 1991 to be a period of slow sales as the economy became mired in a recession.

Apple is concerned about various economic events looming in the 1990s. For example, capital is expected to be scarce, the Japanese are moving rapidly to try to dominate the mainframe computer market, the S&L bailout will probably dampen the economy, and energy will be in short supply. Apple must prepare strategies for coping with these and other factors in its external environment.

One of the strategies it settled on was a strategic alliance with IBM. In an agreement reached in the late summer of 1991, Apple and IBM will share technology and software. Apple will share its Macintosh software and IBM its workstation technology. Joint new products are planned. Earlier, in 1989, due to a shortage of engineers, Apple commissioned Sony to design and manufacture a new palm-top computer, which it released in 1991.

Source: Brenton R. Schlender, "Apple's Japanese Ally," *Fortune*, November 4, 1991, pp. 151–152; James Daly, "IBM, Apple Seal Promise-Laden Pact," *ComputerWorld*, October 7, 1991, pp. 1, 135; Deidre A. Depke, "IBM-Apple Could Be Fearsome," *Business Week*, October 7, 1991, pp. 28–30; Brenton R. Schlender, "Yet Another Strategy for Apple," *Fortune*, October 22, 1990, pp. 81–87; John Schwartz, "Apple's Third Revolution," *Newsweek*, October 22, 1990, p. 53; Barbara Buell, Jonathan B. Levine, and Neil Gross, "Apple: New Team, New Strategy," *Business Week*, October 15, 1990, pp. 86–96; Bart Ziegler, "Apple Preparing to Take on Macintosh Competition," *The Orlando Sentinel*, July 15, 1990, pp. D1, D5; John Sculley's speech at Macworld, February 1988.

Chapters 1 and 2 introduced the concept of SWOT; Chapter 3 presented the concepts of strategic information systems, strategic information, and the organizational profile. This chapter discusses in more detail the external factors that strategists analyze in their search for relevant strategic information. There are three external environments to be considered: the general environment, which includes factors such as government, technology and innovation, and the economy; the competitive environment, which focuses on industry and competitor analysis; and the global environment, which is concerned with general and competitive factors on a global basis, plus multinational and multicultural issues. Once data have been collected and analyzed, the resultant information forms the foundation for a forecast of the future. Forecasts of SWOT are the assumptions on which strategic objectives are determined and strategies formulated.

This chapter focuses on the areas highlighted in Figures 4.1 and 4.2. Apple Computers faces stiff competition and many strategic challenges in the 1990s, but it relies on its innovation and information to do battle with its competition and overcome or exploit these challenges. Its new products for the early and late 1990s should help it continue its sustained growth in sales and profits.

EXTERNAL FACTORS FOR ANALYSIS

Table 4.1 lists the **external factors** that will have a direct impact on opportunities and threats or provide inputs for defining internal strengths and weaknesses. Note how the ten strategic management challenges identified in Chapter 1, listed on the right in the table, coincide generally with these external factors. Virtually all are involved with accelerating rates of change, the first strategic challenge, and result in a more complex environment, the tenth strategic challenge. Furthermore, virtually all challenges result in the need for more innovative approaches to strategic management.

The primary purpose of seeking information about external factors is to assess the environment and determine its opportunities and threats, in order to

FIGURE 4.1 The Organization—A Strategic Management Process Model

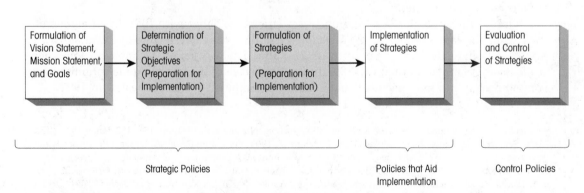

FIGURE 4.2 Objectives Determination and Strategy Formulation

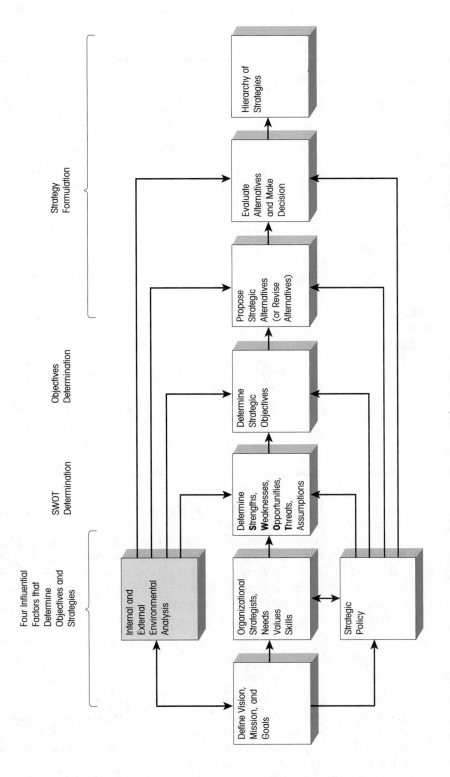

TABLE 4.1   External Environment and Strategic Challenges

External Environmental Factors	Relevant Strategic Challenges
The General Environment	
Government	9. Increasing constituent demands
Technology and innovation	4. Technological change
Society and social responsibility	9. Increasing constituent demands
Ethics	9. Increasing constituent demands
The Economy	8. Unstable market/economy
Organized labor	
Natural resources	6. Resource shortages
Other significant factors, such as accelerating change	1. Accelerating rates of change
The Competitive Environment	
Industry analysis	
Intensity of rivalry among existing firms	2. Increasing levels of competition
Threat of new entrants	3. Globalization of business
Threat of substitutes	
Power of buyers	
Power of suppliers	
Results of industry analysis	
Competitor analysis	2. Increasing levels of competition
The Global Environment	3. Globalization of business
	2. Increasing levels of competition
All of These Factors	1. Accelerating rates of change
	2. Increasing complexity

match these with the organization's strengths and weaknesses, as revealed in the organizational profile developed by internal analysis. The underlying assumption behind this matching process is that certain strategies and implementation activities should be undertaken in certain environments, but not in others.[1] As noted in Chapter 1, the firm must determine whether its strategic philosophy is based on strategic fit or strategic intent. However, strategic fit implies a reactive perspective, and strategic intent a proactive perspective in formulating strategic purposes and strategies after performing SWOT analysis.

GENERAL ENVIRONMENT

Factors in the **general environment** tend to affect business less frequently than day-to-day concerns. These are not direct competitive factors, although technology and the economy greatly affect most organizations' abilities to compete. The following paragraphs discuss each of the general environmental factors from Table 4.1 in more detail.

Government

During the 1960s and 1970s, government dominated the external business environment. Businesses probably spent as much time complying with government requirements as they did worrying about their competition. The 1980s brought relatively less government intervention, but evidence suggests that federal and state governments will probably become much more active in regulating business activity in the 1990s.[2] For example, federally legislated clean air requirements are already estimated to cost business $21 billion a year in this decade, which, of course, will be passed on to the consumer.[3] Thus, lobbying will be ever more necessary.[4] This is especially true because Japanese firms spend so much more money than U.S. firms lobbying the U.S. Congress and top regulators. Some feel that the Japanese control much of our federal government's conduct of trade relations, and they have great influence in many government agencies, winning important concessions.[5]

Table 4.2 presents a list of major federal laws in relevant areas. Some were passed recently; some have been on the books for some time, but have been enforced more stringently in recent years. As the table suggests, these laws have narrowed many of business's strategic alternatives in several major categories. These laws have also served to increase business's social responsibility.

For example, virtually all organizations of any size have had to make comprehensive changes in their personnel practices as a result of equal employment opportunity laws. Consumerism has resulted in numerous recalls of automobiles and other products by their manufacturers. Periodic energy problems, the impacts of which will probably be compounded by future laws, cause U.S. firms to establish energy strategies. For example, U.S. automakers have already redesigned their automobiles completely, making them lighter, smaller, and more fuel efficient.

Some U.S. organizations do campaign vigorously to change the constraints imposed by federal legislation and court actions. U.S. West, one of the seven Baby Bells, demanded further deregulation to allow it to move forward strategically.[6] Evidence clearly shows, however, that if U.S. firms expect to compete at home against the Japanese, they've got to try harder to improve government regulations. President Bush's trip to Japan in January 1992 did little to change Japanese business strategies, but it may have added to the power of automakers to sway Congress to enact protective legislation.

Federal legislation is not the only government constraint on business. A large number of federal regulatory agencies have been established for the purpose of observing and controlling business. In addition, state agencies control all public utilities, protect the environment and consumers, regulate practices in the construction industry, and oversee the licensing of various professionals. Similar agencies are active at the local level. All of these agencies, as well as a wide range of pressure groups from the NAACP to the Sierra Club, have significant impacts on strategy formulation in many businesses. As some of the cases presented in this book make clear, strategies often have to be revised to accommodate the demands of such organizations. The courts, especially the U.S. Supreme Court, may also greatly influence business activity through their interpretations of laws and regulations.

TABLE 4.2 Laws, Court Rulings, and Regulations that Affect Business

Environment
Federal Insecticide, Fungicide, and Rodenticide Act, 1947
Federal Water Pollution Control Act, 1956
Clean Air Act, 1963
Solid Wastes Disposal Act, 1965, as amended
Water Quality Act, 1965
Broad interpretation of the Refuse Act of 1899 by a federal court, 1966
Air Quality Act, 1967
National Environmental Policy Act, 1970
Noise Abatement and Control Act, 1970
Resource Conservation and Recovery Act, 1970
Clean Air Act amendments, 1970
Equal Employment Opportunity
Equal Pay Act, 1963, as amended in 1972
Title VII of the Civil Rights Act, 1964, as amended by the Equal Employment Opportunity Act, 1972
Presidential Executive Orders 11246, 11478, 11758, 1967–1975
Age Discrimination in Employment Act, 1967
Sections 500 and 503 of the Rehabilitation Act amendments, 1974
Veterans' Employment and Readjustment Act, 1972, as amended
Pregnancy Act, 1978
Americans with Disabilities Act, 1990
Civil Rights Act, 1991
Consumerism
Meat Inspection Act, 1906
Federal Food, Drug, and Cosmetics Act, 1938, as amended by presidential executive order creating the
    Office of Consumer Affairs, 1964
National Traffic and Motor Vehicle Safety Act, 1966, as amended
Fair Packaging and Labeling Act, 1966
Federal Cigarette Labeling and Advertising Act, 1967
Consumer Credit Protection Act, 1968
Toy Safety Act, 1969
Truth-in-Lending Act, 1969
Consumer Product Safety Act, 1972
Fair Credit Billing Act, 1974
Equal Credit Opportunity Act, 1974
Consumer Product Warranties Act, 1975
Consumer Goods Pricing Act, 1975
Repeal of Fair Trade Laws, 1977
Fair Debt Collection Practices Act, 1978
Energy
Federal Energy Administration Act, 1974
Energy Reorganization Act, 1974
Energy Supply and Environmental Coordination Act, 1974
Energy Policy and Conservation Act, 1975

TABLE 4.2 Cont'd.   Laws, Court Rulings, and Regulations that Affect Business

---

Economics
Chrysler Loan Guarantee Act, 1979
Revised Bankruptcy Act, 1980 (used to avoid major economic catastrophes by some firms)
Tax Act, 1981
Deregulation of airlines and trucking, 1979–1981
FCC allows AT&T to sell nonregulated services, 1979
Federal Reserve Bank permits banks to pay interest on checking accounts, 1980
Economic Recovery Act, 1981
Tax Acts, 1984, 1986, 1990
AT&T divests itself of local telephone companies, 1984
S&L bailout acts
Bank Regulation Act, 1991
Labor
Occupational Safety and Health Act, 1970
Employee Retirement Income Security Act, 1974
Other Laws
Interstate Commerce Act, 1887
Sherman Antitrust Act, 1890
Pure Food and Drug Act, 1906
Sixteenth Amendment (income tax), 1913
Clayton Act, 1914
Federal Trade Commission Act, 1914
Federal Communications Act, 1934
Wagner Act, 1935
Social Security Act, 1936
Robinson-Patman Act, 1936
Fair Labor Standards Act (Wage and Hour Act), 1938
Taft-Hartley Act, 1947
Antimerger Act, 1950
Automobile Information Disclosure Act, 1958
Landrum-Griffin Act, 1959

Because of these frequently changing constraints, business must continually monitor the environment and adapt to it or change it. Legal, ethical, and socially responsible political actions and lobbying are important strategic actions.

Technology and Innovation

Most businesses depend on some type of technology for a competitive advantage or for products to sell. The global way of life calls for consumption of more and more of the latest and greatest, and that requires technological advances. Since business is so dependent on technology, it must watch constantly for technological surprises from competitors. Technological discontinuities can be disastrous, both in product and process areas. Firms therefore need to systematically scan the technological environment.[7]

Few major industries in this country are immune to dependence on technology. Television sets, computers, calculators, airplanes, pacemakers, bioengineered plants, lasers, fax machines, and photocopy machines are just a few of the major industrial products that are based on technology. A major new technology may create an entire new industry, as occurred with the microcomputer and photocopier industries.

A business must first of all concern itself with new technology in its particular industry, that is, with the technological developments of its competitors. Rapid changes in the technological environment have required businesses to increase their efforts to forecast technology. This process involves many judgmental forecasting techniques. Technology forecasting is neither easy nor often very accurate. The management of strategic surprises is difficult at best. This is one reason that environmental scanning for weak signals of change is so critically important.

AT APPLE COMPUTERS

Apple developed a new technology with its Macintosh. This technology gave Apple a 5-year competitive advantage. Over time, however, competitors were able to duplicate its features, so Apple moved to short-run price strategies and more innovation for the long term.

In an important study of responses to technological threats, A. C. Cooper and his colleagues reported that traditional firms find it difficult to respond successfully to major technological innovations in their industries, especially during the maturity or saturation stages of the product life cycle. While their sample was small, virtually no well-established firm they studied successfully launched a counterthreat to a new technology introduced by a competitor.[8] This finding suggests that even when firms know about new technologies and respond to them, their response strategies may be ill-advised.

The product life cycle implies that introducing new technology gains a firm a distinct strategic advantage over those who lack the technology. If the new technology captures a considerable share of the market, the new technology still gives the competitor who introduced it an advantage over any other firm coming into the market for the new product. J. M. Utterback and M. J. Abernathy found that firms in early stages of growth tended to introduce more technological innovations than did very large and complex firms.[9] This finding suggests that as firms mature, they tend to stagnate. Richard Foster, in summarizing his lengthy tenure at McKinsey and Company, including a stint as a director, observes that virtually every successful company he has seen has been a product innovator.[10]

In sum, these studies suggest that technological innovation may be difficult to counteract for a firm in the mature stage of the product life cycle, though certainly numerous firms have prolonged their products' life cycles through technological innovation or adaptation. Available information also suggests that technology drives product innovation, and that new firms and new industries can spring from such innovation. Success itself may depend on it.

The Japanese have been quite successful in adapting to others' technology and underpricing international competitors through highly productive and innovative operations and other management strategies. Only a few U.S. and Canadian firms have been able to achieve the high levels of productivity that allow firms to follow on others' technological advances. The firm that does not keep pace with new developments is destined to decline. The Strategic Challenge feature reviews the efforts of one firm to stay ahead of its competitors.

Technology and Social Responsibility While technology plays an important role in business success, it also poses problems for many companies. Unexpected

STRATEGIC CHALLENGE

MILLIKEN BEATS ITS COMPETITION WITH INNOVATIVE IDEAS

Milliken is a $2-billion textile company with products ranging from carpets to facecloths. In the early 1980s the firm's managers realized that the world was changing rapidly and they had to change with it. They recognized that their competition, especially their foreign competitors, could beat their prices in many areas. They felt they had to offer superior service and new products to their customers, and they had to cut costs.

In one program, they developed a team consisting of representatives of their marketing and production departments together with their customers. With this team approach, they have developed several new techniques for improving the productivity and enhancing the product line of one customer, Levi Strauss. Milliken makes sure, for example, that the materials it trucks to Levi are loaded in the reverse of the order in which Levi will need them. The trucks serve as miniwarehouses. Furthermore, the materials are delivered on a just-in-time basis, that is, just as Levi needs them. This saves Levi the cost of carrying the materials in inventory.

Source: Thomas J. Peters, "The Home-Field Advantage," *U.S. News & World Report*, March 31, 1986, p. 49.

consequences of new technology can sometimes damage the physical environment. All organizations, not just business firms, must constantly assess the impacts of their technologies on the physical environment. In the disposal of nuclear wastes (both governmental and commercial), oil spills, DDT damage to the food chain, acid rain, and PCB contamination we can see a few of the problems that arise when technology gets out of control. Throughout the United States waste materials produced by the oil, chemical, and other industries have significantly polluted the environment. Health problems in affected areas have caused concern. People see cancer and other major diseases at rates much higher than normal and link these problems to pollution. This is also the case with automobile exhaust, waste water, and garbage. Industry strategy must, therefore, be responsive not just to the profit motive, but also to the greater needs of the society and the quality of life. This is not only a moral position; it is hard reality. Where business has failed to respond to these needs, it has often been forced by society and government to respond in a manner that has ultimately been more costly and less profitable. These problems are not limited to the United States. Europe, especially Eastern Europe, is extremely polluted, with health being adversely affected in many countries.[11]

Society and Social Responsibility[12]

Until the 1960s, business usually considered itself a closed system, with no significant transactions with outsiders. The demands placed on business by society, primarily through state and federal legislation in the 1960s and 1970s, however, convinced business that society did not hold the same view. People were concerned about the impact of business on their lives. Government responded to citizens' concerns and enacted numerous laws that affected the operation of business, as Table 4.2 makes clear.

The perceived role of business expanded to include much more than the mere production of goods and services. Jerry Anderson suggests that business must go beyond obeying the law. It must abide by moral and ethical standards, and participate in corporate philanthropic giving in order to be a socially responsible corporate citizen.[13] Business has learned that it must respond to the demands of stakeholders, especially groups that can bring significant pressure to bear. Table 4.3 indicates the key **social responsibility areas** in which business may be expected to respond.[14]

Business's responses can lead to a reduction in strategic alternatives. In many businesses, especially those subject to government regulation or pressure by well-organized groups, decisions are often made more by negotiation than by internal formulation. Many companies have abandoned strategies under pressure of interest groups, for example, numerous steel plants have been shut down because needed environmental protection equipment was too expensive. It should be noted that the demands of these external organizations are usually appropriate, given the greater requirements of the society. Some businesses' actions produce highly questionable overall benefit to society.

TABLE 4.3 Categories of Social Responsibility

Product Line
Internal standards for products
Average product life
Product performance
Packaging impacts
Marketing Practices
Sales practices
Credit practices against legal standards
Accuracy of advertising claims—specific government complaints
Consumer complaints about marketing practices
Provision of adequate consumer information
Fair pricing
Packaging
Employee Education and Training
Policy on leaves of absence
Dollars spent on training
Special training program results (systematic evaluations)
Plans for future programs
Career training and counseling
Failure rates
Personnel understanding
Corporate Philanthropy
Contribution performance
Selection criteria for contributions
Procedures for performance tracking of recipient institutions or groups
Programs to permit and encourage employee involvement in social projects
Extent of employee involvement in philanthropy decision making
Environmental Control
Measurable pollution
Violations of government (federal, state, local) standards
Cost estimates to correct current deficiencies
Extent to which various plants exceed current legal standards (e.g., particulate matter discharged)
Resources devoted to pollution control
Competitive company performance (e.g., capital expenditures)
Effort to monitor new standards as proposed
Programs to keep employees alert to spills and other pollution-related accidents
Procedures for evaluating environmental impact of new packages of products
External Relations
Community development
Support of minority and community enterprises
Investment practices
Government relations
Specific input to public policy through research and analysis
Participation and development of business/government programs
Political contributions
Disclosure of information (communications)

TABLE 4.3 Cont'd. Categories of Social Responsibility

Extent of public disclosure of performance by activity category
Measure of employee understanding of programs (relations/communications with stockholders, fund managers, major customers, etc.)
International relations
Comparisons of policy and performance with those of other countries and against local standards
Employee Relations, Benefits, and Satisfaction with Work
Comparison of wage and other policies with competition and/or national averages
Comparison of operating units on promotions, terminations, hires
Performance review system and procedures for communication with employees whose performance is below average
Promotion policy—equitable and understood
Transfer policy
Termination policy (e.g., how early is notice given?)
General work environment and conditions
Fringe benefits as percentage of salary at various salary levels
Evaluation of employee benefit preferences (questions can be posed as choices)
Evaluation of employee understanding of current fringe benefits
Union/industrial relations
Confidentiality and security of personnel data
Employment and Advancement of Minorities and Women
Current hiring policies in relation to requirements of affirmative action programs
Company versus local, industry, and national performance
Percent minorites and women employed in major facilities in relation to minority labor force available locally
Number of minorities and women in positions of high responsibility
Promotion performance of minorites and women
Specific hiring and job upgrading goals established for minorities and women
Programs to ease integration of minorities and women into company operations (e.g., awareness efforts)
Specialized career counseling for minorites and women
Special recruiting efforts for minorities and women
Opportunities for the physically handicapped
Employee Safety and Health
Work environment measures
Safety performance
Services provided (and cost of programs and human resources) for safety equipment, instruction, special safety programs
Comparisons of health and safety performance with competition and industry in general
Developments/innovations in health and safety
Employee health measures (e.g., sick days, examinations)
Food facilities

Source: By Terry W. McAdam. Adapted with permission from *Business and Society Review*, Summer 1973. Copyright © 1973, *Business and Society Review*.

Regardless of their moral value, however, these external forces act as constraints on business, and business must have strategies to cope with them. Businesses must continually explore their social responsibilities to determine their impacts on society and avoid surprises. A business needs to develop an operational approach to social performance.[15] One increasingly popular response to social concerns is developing not only an elaborate social policy process, but hiring a vice president of environmental policy to oversee it.[16]

One perspective that companies must keep in mind is that some social values create economic opportunities. The trend toward conserving energy, for example, is opening up markets for new products.[17] Still, it seems that no matter which way you turn, you may find yourself in error, as Perrier has discovered. It sought to be socially responsible, perhaps more than it needed to be, as this chapter's Strategic Ethical Challenge feature reveals.

Ethics

It is debatable whether a company can really teach anyone ethics. What it can do is teach someone how to think through an **ethical dilemma,** a situation that involves a conflict between the firm's economic performance and its social performance. In most situations, the ethical answer is obvious, but many present multiple alternatives with uncertain consequences that extend beyond the immediate decision. Personal implications for the manager making the decision are common, and available choices typically have mixed outcomes (positive and negative).[18]

The disconcerting reality about ethics is that the "ethical signpost does not always point in the same direction."[19] Information may indicate that opposite courses of action are equally appropriate. Furthermore, managers often have to make decisions for others in addition to resolving their own personal ethical dilemmas, weighing numerous variables. Business ethics practice is applied ethics. Managers have to come up with real answers in situations that are more complex than academic debates.

A corporate culture establishes its own ethical values. The tremendous pressure to perform in an organization often leads to compromises of personal principles. People tend to lose sight of their personal values because of the demands corporations place upon them. To avoid this, a corporation can and should establish a culture that requires ethical behavior. Companies can improve ethical performance in a variety of ways: codes of ethics, whistleblowing, ombudsmen, corporate ethics committees, task forces on ethics, and other inculturation programs.

How the Individual Manager Should Decide

Still, the issues are complex. Many variables often influence important decisions for managers. There are few guidelines, but academician Laura L. Nash has provided a list of 12 questions that managers should ask themselves when making a business decision to assure an ethical action:

1. Have you defined the problem correctly?
2. How would you define the problem if you stood on the other side of the fence?

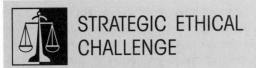

STRATEGIC ETHICAL CHALLENGE

PERRIER FINDS IT DIFFICULT TO RESTORE THE SPARKLE

In February 1990, Source Perrier S.A. of France voluntarily recalled over $200 million in Perrier sparkling water inventory from around the world because traces of benzene, a suspected carcinogen, had been found in some bottles. By mid-July 1990, Perrier was back on U.S. supermarket shelves, but at the end of 1990 its share of the imported bottled water market had shrunk from 44.8 percent to 20.7 percent, and the brand's sales volume had plunged 42 percent to $60 million. Evian, the bottled water product of BSN S.A., seized the number one position in imported bottled water, and a host of other competitors made major market share gains. It wasn't the fear of benzene that kept customers away from Perrier's "Nouvelle Production"; it was the realization that Perrier wasn't that much different from other bottled waters that consumers had tried while Perrier was off the shelves.

Being socially responsible can be a tricky ethical dilemma at times. Such was the case with Perrier's bottled water recall. It is not clear from test results that Perrier had to withdraw the product from distribution. The amount of benzene found was so small that it probably wouldn't have been carcinogenic. Fear of higher levels elsewhere in the production run, coupled with a desire to be totally ethical responsible, apparently led to the recall. As with any ethical dilemma, pros and cons could be found for either action or nonaction, but the real problem came not so much in the recall as in how the firm handled the new production.

The firm appeared disorganized and somewhat overconfident of its ability to continue to dominate a market it had always owned. It took far too long to return Perrier to grocers and restaurants alike. The firm promised to have the product back on the shelf by May, but it did not make it until mid-July. Consumers found that other bottled waters tasted just as good, and sparkled just as effervescently. The company's marketing strategy for reintroducing the product seemed nonfocused to many. Further, the company ran afoul of the Food and Drug Administration and had to remove the words "naturally sparkling" from the label. The Federal Commerce Commission took exception to other label claims. These issues have yet to be resolved, but Perrier promises they will be. Nonetheless, this negative publicity served only to keep customers away. In an effort to regain market share, Perrier lowered its prices. The bottle that had sold for $1.09 or $1.19 was selling for $.89 or $.99 in 1991. This has brought some gains in the grocery stores, but virtually none in the restaurants where many customers have moved to other suppliers. All of these factors have reduced the mystique that Perrier formerly enjoyed.

Source: Alix M. Freedman, "Perrier Finds Mystique Hard to Restore," *The Wall Street Journal*, December 12, 1990, pp. B1, B6; and Annetta Miller, "Perrier Loses Its Fizz," *Newsweek*, February 26, 1990, p. 57.

3. How did this situation occur in the first place?
4. To whom and to what do you give your loyalty as a person and as an employee?
5. What is your intention in making this decision?
6. How does this intention compare with the probable result?
7. Whom could your decision or action injure?
8. Can you discuss the problem with the affected parties before you make your decision?
9. Are you confident your decision will be as valid over a long period of time as it seems now?
10. Could you disclose your decision or action without qualm to your supervisor, CEO, board of directors, family, and society as a whole?
11. What is the symbolic potential of your action if understood? If misunderstood?
12. Under what conditions would you allow exceptions to your stand?[20]

The Economy

Significant changes in the economy often arise from the actions of the federal government, either through its fiscal policies or through the monetary policies of the Federal Reserve Board. Many argue that budget deficits caused by excessive spending on federal programs have been the main contributors to inflation in the past, that the monetary policies of the Federal Reserve have increased unemployment, and that a president's economic strategies, such as President Bush's hoped-for, but-failed deficit reductions, clearly move the economy in certain directions.[21] Whatever the specific causes, the results of federal action often have dictated the level and composition of business activity, the evidence suggests, not only in the United States, but around the globe, as well.[22] On the other hand, sometimes government efforts fail to stimulate the economy. For example, lowering interest rates did little to boost the economy in 1991 and the federal government was scrambling to find another way to improve the economy.[23]

The areas in which federal expenditures are heaviest have changed significantly over the years, producing a clear impact on the economy.[24] Direct benefit payments to individuals, which were relatively low 20 years ago, accounted for 49 percent of the federal budget in fiscal year 1991. Expenditures by the Department of Defense (DOD), which not too many years ago constituted almost 60 percent of the total federal budget, accounted for 26 percent of the 1991 budget.

Another major impact of federal spending in these two major areas—transfer payments and defense—is the manner in which these expenditures are funded. In 1991, slightly more than 14 percent of the federal budget covered debt service. It is no secret that the huge deficits in current federal budgets are a matter of major concern to all because of their impact on the long-term viability of the economy. At the very minimum, these deficits tend to raise interest rates and tighten the supply of money available for business expansion. The federal bailout of savings and loan associations will add to the national debt, and Operation Desert Storm and policing the peace also impose costs, further raising federal debt.[25]

Businesses must respond to these changes in how federal monies are spent. Many firms will be greatly affected by the amount spent on military hardware, and others will find opportunities in basic industries that benefit from the spending of transfer payments. All firms must also be prepared to respond to changing monetary conditions. Change is the name of the game.[26] If you're a defense contractor, for example, you know you need to be looking for diversification programs.[27] Finally, our economy is inextricably linked to those of other nations. Economies throughout the globe tend to move together.[28] With many U.S. firms dealing with overseas customers and/or suppliers, the states of foreign economies have major impacts in the United States.

Labor

Organized labor has made significant strides over the years in increasing wages and benefits for workers. It can be expected to continue its efforts to organize both blue-collar and white-collar workers, especially in the South. Organized labor has an extremely powerful influence on the national economy and on the supportive strategies and policies of the businesses that operate within that economy. Labor has historically had significant impacts on presidential as well as gubernatorial and mayoral races. This impact on government and the economy declined in the 1980s, but may again increase in the 1990s. Businesses must be attuned to that change.[29]

Changes in employees' attitudes also affect business. Recent changes are related primarily to the work ethic and the extent to which lower-level employees seek to help the organization's management make decisions, sometimes at strategic as well as operational levels. The evidence indicates that the work ethic is still reasonably strong, except perhaps among teenagers.[30] Emphasis seemed to shift in the 1970s from equality of opportunity to equality of reward regardless of effort, but the country now appears to be moving away from that approach. Workers at most levels of the organization have also begun to expect more personal satisfaction from their work and more participation in decision making.

The work force is becoming much more culturally diverse. The white-male-dominated work force will be no more. Women and ethnic and racial minorities will play major roles in the work force of the year 2000.[31] These and other factors make successful implementation of strategy difficult, because they make motivation more complex. Managers who must influence employee motivation are constrained by many conditions they cannot control. When a business must increase productivity to survive, it must pay close attention to the attitudes of workers and their different cultures.

Natural Resources

Energy is not the only scarce resource in the United States, but it was a critical one long before the Iraqis invaded Kuwait.[32] Government studies have revealed that several major metals and other primary manufacturing materials are in short supply. Living space in large cities, clean air and water, and areas of natural beauty are also scarce. Food is in extremely short supply for most of the world's population, and the earth's population is increasing rapidly further straining resources. This situation poses great problems for businesses and for governments.

The shortage of resources will be compounded as developing nations seek to emulate industrialized nations. The United States depends on many developing nations to provide scarce materials. Any country that has resources needed by the industrialized nations has a bargaining advantage.

While some metals and other needed materials may be stockpiled, stockpiling some resources—energy, for example—is rather difficult. While the United States has made some strides toward energy independence, this goal probably will not be reached until the late 1990s, if then.

While shortages of certain materials and water appear to be the key resource problems of the United States, an inadequate supply of food is the most critical problem for many other nations. The United States can produce a great deal of food, but its technology for this work is highly energy-dependent. It is clear that the nations of the world must come to grips with limits on the supply of materials and accept restrictions on the number of people who will live upon this planet if each individual in the world is to enjoy a desirable quality of life. As a result of these worldwide problems, businesses have faced expropriation, import or export quotas, higher prices, and demonstrations of political power by the developing nations that supply natural resources.

For an added complication, the needs for materials change and supplies diminish. Astute strategists observe such changes. More important, they anticipate them. If you are a top manager for Red Lobster, for example, you've got to be wondering where you are going to get your fish as many of the world's fishing grounds are all fished out. If you are a commercial fisherman, you may soon be out of business for the same reason.[33]

AT APPLE COMPUTERS

Managing scarce materials is no easy task. On the advice of staff, Apple CEO John Sculley invested in a large inventory of computer chips for the Macintosh in 1988. Prices were expected to double. However, they fell by half instead. Thus Apple's prices were far too high compared to competition. Prices had to be lowered. Apple's total estimated loss from this hedging was $80 million.

Demographics

Numerous other factors affect individual businesses; perhaps the most significant remaining factor is demographics. The most significant demographic changes that will affect businesses are increases in population, geographic shifts in population, and changes in the age composition of the population. The median age of the U.S. population has risen as the baby-boom generation has aged and the birth rate has fallen.[34] (The Strategic Challenge feature profiles the baby boomers.) Another critical emerging group consists of the couples designated by the acronym *DINKS* for double income, no kids. They have large amounts of discretionary income and businesses are actively seeking to serve them.[35]

Further, Americans are notorious for their propensity to move where the grass is greener. Many people who currently live in the North, Northeast, and Midwest are expected to move to the South and West in search of milder climates and expanding opportunities.

The most significant international demographic factor is the sheer increase in population, especially in the developing nations. In 1990 the world's population was about 5 billion. Some demographers estimate that the world population could nearly double by the year 2000, and most believe that it will certainly reach 7 billion by then. The consequences of this enormous population growth have not even begun to be fully imagined. Many feel that the thousands who were dying of starvation in 1990, for example, will turn into millions worldwide by the year 2000. One current negative impact on the United States has been an increase in the entrance of illegal aliens. On the other hand, the increasing population represents a huge potential market if the developing nations can achieve economic success. Businesses must continue surveillance of these critical population changes to take advantage of the opportunities they create and negate the threats they represent.

Among other demographic changes that are expected, more employment opportunities will be created in white-collar jobs than in blue-collar occupations. Incomes may rise, but it is difficult at this time to determine the impact of inflation on them. Another factor that compounds the problem is the short labor supply compared to demand, especially in highly skilled jobs.[36] Furthermore, the previously mentioned population shift toward the Southeast and West will produce shifts in market areas, as well as in the composition of the market. This will provide both growth opportunities and problems for the business community.

AT APPLE COMPUTERS

These changes in demographics generally bode well for Apple Computers. More people should mean more personal computer sales, as well as an increase in white-collar jobs.

COMPETITIVE ENVIRONMENT

Two principal concerns govern examination of the competitive environment: industry analysis and competitor analysis.

Michael Porter's Industry Analysis

In recent years, considerable interest has focused on what has come to be known as **industry analysis.** Michael E. Porter has shown that the intensity of rivalry among

STRATEGIC CHALLENGE

THE BABY BOOMERS

The baby boomers are the people who were born during the years from 1946 to 1962. Since the people at the leading edge of this group are now in their 40s and entering ages of peak consumption, the baby boomers will greatly influence the economy in the next 30 to 40 years. These 68 million people, nearly one-third of the U.S. population, are under close observation by marketers for the latest trends in their consumption patterns. They are also being closely watched by government, especially as they age and require increased government services, such as Social Security. They are also being closely observed by personnel managers for their impact on the work force.

As they enter their peak buying years, boomers buoy up, many industries including housing, furniture, appliances, automobiles, specialty foods, clothing, cosmetics, travel, financial services, and children's goods and services as the boomers themselves reproduce. Not all industries, however, have fared well under the boomers' consumption patterns. As they grew up, they left behind several markets that consequently dwindled, at least for a time—education, soft drinks, candies, and beer, for example. Now that the boomers have outgrown these products and their children do not yet constitute a comparable market, we see increasing numbers of older persons in most of these industries' advertisements as they try to prolong the lives of their products and reposition them in the market.

The baby boomers are also going to have a significant effect on the organizations in this country, and on U.S. politics, as well. Many of them have already arrived in positions of power in business and government and have substantially altered the strategies and policies of their organizations. Because they are better educated than their predecessors and have higher expectations, they demand more from organizations and their jobs, and these expectations are changing the way business and other organizations must be managed. Conflicts between old and new values within organizations and within the society will not always be easily resolved. Because industrial environments tend to be more highly structured than offices, blue-collar boomers have been called the most frustrated boomers of them all.

The yuppies (or young urban professionals) have come to symbolize the boomers, but in reality they constitute only about one-third of the group. Many other boomers are unskilled and poorly educated, and are likely to be drains on the economy in the future.

Sources: Joe Schwartz and Susan Krafft, "Managing Consumer Diversity: The 1991 American Demographics Conference," *American Demographics*, August 1991, pp. 22–29; Patricia Galazan, "The Age Wave," *Training and Development Journal*, February 1990, pp. 22–30; Regina Eisman, "The Boomers' Baby Market," *Incentive*, February 1990, pp. 39–41; B. Robey, "Baby Boomers in the Future," *Marketing Week*, July 6, 1987, p. 18; Geoffrey Colvin, "What the Baby-Boomers Will Buy Next," *Fortune*, October 15, 1984, pp. 85–90.

existing firms, the threat of new entrants, the power of customers/clients (buyers), the potential for substitutes, and the power of suppliers all combine to drive competition in a given industry. You can apply his model directly to most cases in Part 2 of this book.

Porter proposes that one determine the strategic profitability of an industry by examining five basic competitive forces, as depicted in Figure 4.3. Porter contends that "the collective strength of these forces determines the ultimate profit potential in the industry, where profit potential is measured in terms of long-run return on invested capital."[37]

According to Porter, a corporation must carefully monitor its environment to determine the impact of these five factors on the firm's potential for success.[38]

1. Threat of New Entrants   New entrants typically:

- Have substantial resources
- Pursue actions that increase industry capacity
- Attempt to increase their market shares

FIGURE 4.3   Forces Driving Industry Competition

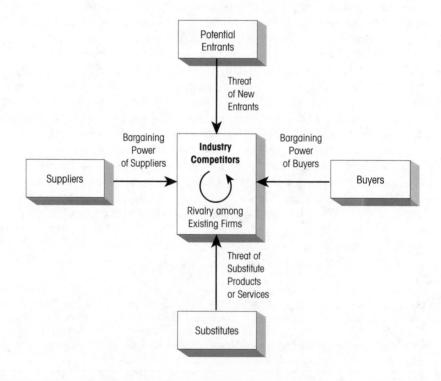

As a consequence,

- Prices often go down
- Incumbents' costs may become inflated
- Incumbents' profits may therefore go down

For these reasons, new entrants must be viewed as threats to incumbents.

Porter identifies eight major barriers to entry into an existing industry, which assist incumbents because they reduce the number of potential new entrants:

- Economies of scale, which require large startup investments
- Existing product differentiation, which leads to customer loyalty
- Capital requirements
- Costs to buyers of switching from the incumbent's product to the new entrant's product
- Access to distribution channels
- Cost disadvantages independent of scale
- Government policy
- Expected retaliation

2. Intensity of Rivalry among Existing Firms   Porter views rivalry as a process of move and countermove among existing, mutually dependent competitors employing such tactics as price competition, advertising, and new products. He sees intense rivalry as resulting from any number of critical industry factors, which can and do change, including:

- Numerous or equally balanced competitors
- Slow industry growth
- High fixed or storage costs
- Lack of differentiation or switching costs
- Enlargement of capacity in large increments
- Diverse competitors
- High strategic stakes
- High exit barriers

AT APPLE COMPUTERS

Apple Computers engages in intense rivalry with IBM, Compaq, and a host of other PC manufacturers. There are numerous competitors and only IBM is significantly larger than the others. The market in 1991 is somewhat stagnant, and Macintosh's capabilities have been duplicated by other machines.

Competition in the theme park industry, for example, is relatively equally balanced except for Disney's two parks. Consequently, all parks are adding more high-tech thrills and chills to lure customers. Ohio's Kings Island, for example, invested $4 million in its Vortex roller coaster, the first one with six upside down loops.[39]

3. Pressure from Substitute Products

"All firms in an industry are competing, in a broad sense, with industries producing substitute products."[40] These substitutes place a lid on prices on industry products. The key to identifying substitutes is to look for products that perform the same function as those produced by the established industry, even though they may not appear to be obvious substitutes. In particular, firms should pay attention to products whose price–performance trade-offs with the industry's products are improving. Higher industry profits increase the chance that substitutes will be sought.

The problem of substitution can be seen in the security guard industry. Electronic alarms are a strong substitute for human guards. They are cheaper and they are effective. Their advantage should increase as the costs of labor increase and the costs of electronic devices decline.

4. Bargaining Power of Buyers

Customers/clients (buyers) compete with the industry in the sense that they can force prices down, bargain for higher quality or more goods and services, or play one competitor against another. A particular buyer or group of buyers is powerful in the industry if:

- The buyer purchases a large portion of the seller's total sales
- The buyer's purchases from the industry are a significant portion of its cost of goods sold
- The buyer's purchases from the industry are standard or undifferentiated
- Switching costs are low
- The buyer earns low profits
- The buyer has the potential for backward integration
- The industry's product has little relevance to the quality of the buyer's product
- The buyer has full information

5. Bargaining Power of Suppliers

Suppliers can affect an industry through their ability to control prices and quality. The conditions that make suppliers powerful tend to mirror those that make buyers powerful. A supplier group is powerful if:

- It is dominated by a few companies and is more concentrated than the industry to which it sells
- Few substitutes for its products or services are available
- Its products are differentiated or switching costs are high
- It poses a threat of forward integration

Labor, by the way, is a supplier group. Porter suggests that 3 sources can be used to determine information about the 5 industry forces: industry observers, such as the press and unions; internal staff, such as the sales force and research and development personnel; and service organizations, such as trade associations and consultants.

Implications of Industry Analysis

After performing an analysis of the industry, firm strategists may assess whether or not it has long term profitability potential, and perhaps more important, whether or not the firm has sufficient potential profitability within the industry. The analysis also points the way toward the proper strategy for the firm. Additional information will be necessary, though. For example, the determination of whether or not the firm can achieve sufficient profits within the industry will require analysis of strengths and weaknesses and other threats and opportunities. Still, the industry analysis is a good beginning.

According to Porter, once the industry analysis has been completed, the firm must determine the appropriate strategy. He offers three strategic possibilities:

1. Positioning the firm to enhance its capabilities to provide the best defense against the existing array of competitive forces
2. Influencing the balance of forces through strategic moves, which will improve the firm's relative position
3. Anticipating shifts in the factors underlying the competitive forces and responding to them to exploit impending change by choosing a strategy appropriate to the new competitive balance before rivals recognize it.[41] The more specific details of these strategic possibilities are discussed in Chapter 6.

Competitor Analysis[42]

For business-level strategy formulation, competition is a critical concern. Any business must seek to know what its competitors are doing and what they are going to do and how these actions will affect the firm. These are the results expected from **competitor analysis.** William E. Rothschild, an integrative strategist for General Electric, suggested that the following key questions must be answered if a firm is to be successful:[43]

- Who are the competitors now and who will they be in the future?
- What are the key competitors' strategies, objectives, and goals?
- How important is a specific market to the competitors, and are they committed enough to continue to invest?
- What unique strengths do the competitors have?
- Do they have any weaknesses that make them vulnerable?
- What changes are likely in competitors' future strategies?
- What are the implications of competitors' strategies on the market, the industry, and one's own company?

As Rothschild suggests, these questions boil down to two: Who are they? and What are they up to?

Although these questions seem rather straightforward, answering them, according to Rothschild, is complicated by three problems:

1. Many managers are overconfident. They have won earlier battles and assume they'll win subsequent ones, becoming lax.
2. Many strategists do not know what they need to know or how to obtain information.
3. Many strategists are concerned that they may have to act unethically to obtain necessary information.

In response to problems 2 and 3, Rothschild assures strategists that the environment abounds with information. To help them find it, he provides a table indicating the information required and another giving sources of this information. These tables appear here as Tables 4.4 and 4.5.

Inputs from competitor analysis contribute to the identification of SWOT. Benchmarking and best practices are especially important. Without such inputs, management is operating like a ship captain without charts of local waters. At FMC Corporation, a giant conglomerate, competitor analysis is viewed as a way of confirming competitive advantages. FMC likes to determine how well competitors are satisfying customer needs.[44] Strategists must be careful to include their international competitors in such analyses.[45]

Numerous competitor analysis techniques exist. John Prescott and John Grant, for example, have identified 21 different techniques and rated each according to a complex series of criteria.[46] The most important aspect of selecting a technique is asking yourself what information you need and then choosing a way of getting that information.

Some firms' competitor intelligence units engage in corporate war games, launching strategic attacks with simulated products, services, etc., against the firm. The firm's strategists must respond. GE, Xerox, and ITT devote substantial resources to such endeavors.[47]

GLOBAL ENVIRONMENT

We live in a global economy, and there is no turning back.[48] Functioning in this highly competitive and interdependent global economy requires a new strategic management perspective.[49] European integration in 1992 will continue the world's ongoing redistribution of economic power. Japan, not the United States, is now the most financially powerful nation and Europe is making great strides.[50]

Additional major economic changes are occurring in Mexico, Brazil, the Middle East, Russia, China, and the newly united Germany. As part of these changes, many nations are undergoing internal social change in efforts to redistribute wealth. Consider events in the countries involved in the recent social and economic revolutions in Eastern Europe, for example. U.S. firms must have strategies for coping with such changes. The ability of U.S. businesses to trade with these countries is limited because trade with them is often reduced to barter, since their currencies have no value outside their own borders. Also, most of these countries lack infrastructures to support market economies. These factors restrict prospects for both potential consumers and sources of raw materials for U.S.

TABLE 4.4 Information Needed for Competitor Analysis

Conceptive Design	Physical Resources	Market	Finance	Management
Technical Resources	**Plant**	**Sales Force**	**Long-Term**	**Key People**
Concepts	Capacity	Skills	Debt/equity ratio	Objectives and priorities
Patents and copyrights	Size	Size	Cost of debt	Values
Technological sophistication	Location	Type	**Short-Term**	Reward systems
Technical integration	Age	Location	Line of credit	**Decision Making**
Human Resources	**Equipment**	**Distribution Network**	Type of debt	Location
Key people and skills	Automation	**Research**	Cost of debt	Type
Use of external	Maintenance	Skills	**Liquidity**	Speed
technical groups	Flexibility	Type	**Cash Flow**	**Planning**
Funding	**Processes**	**Service and Sales Policies**	Days of receivables	Type
Total	Uniqueness	Advertising	Inventory turnover	Emphasis
Percentage of sales	Flexibility	Skills	Accounting practices	Time span
Consistency over time	**Degree of Integration**	Type	**Human Resources**	**Staffing**
Internally generated	**Human Resources**	**Human Resources**	Key people and skills	Longevity and turnover
Government supplied	Key people and skills	Key people and skills	Turnover	Experience
	Work force	Turnover	**Systems**	Replacement policies
	Skills mix	**Funding**	Budgeting	**Organization**
	Unions	Total	Forecasting	Centralization
	Turnover	Consistency over time	Controlling	Functions
		Percentage of sales		Use of staff
		Reward systems		

Source: Reprinted by permission of the publisher. From *Management Review*, July 1979. © 1979. American Management Association, New York. All rights reserved.

TABLE 4.5 Sources of Information for Competitor Analysis

	Public	Trade/ Professionals	Government	Investors

What Competitors Say about Themselves	Advertising
	Promotional materials
	Press releases
	Speeches
	Books
	Articles
	Personnel changes
	Want ads
		Manuals
		Technical papers
		Licenses
		Patents
		Courses
		Seminars
			Security and Exchange
			  Commission reports
			Testimony at FTC
			  hearings
			Lawsuits
			Antitrust actions
				Annual meetings
				Annual reports
				Prospectuses
				Stock/bond issues

What Others Say about Them	Books
	Articles
	Case studies
	Consultants
	Newspaper reporters
	Environmental groups
	Consumer groups
	Unions
	Who's Who
	Recruiting firms
		Suppliers/
		  vendors
		Trade press
		Industry study
		Customers
		Subcontractors
			Lawsuits
			Antitrust actions
			State/federal
			  agencies
			National plans
			Government
			  programs
				Security analyst
				  reports
				Industry studies
				Credit reports

businesses in these areas. These countries are attempting, however, to become economically viable global trading partners.

Just becoming a global firm presents large difficulties. Typical problems encountered in doing business in foreign countries include cultural differences, different consumer needs, double taxation, fluctuating exchange rates, and tariff and trade barriers. Developing countries may also suffer from limited management talent and lack of infrastructure. Such difficulties have led many firms to reassess the need to operate in developing countries.

Yet the world is full of consumers. The problem is to find them and meet their needs. A business has only to find out what these consumers want to consume and whether it can supply the goods. Firms must learn how to compete on a global basis.[51]

MAKING USE OF INFORMATION: ANALYTICAL AND FORECASTING TECHNIQUES

Once strategic data have been accumulated, they must be transformed into information that will enable strategists to determine objectives, formulate strategies, and make appropriate choices among them. These decisions, while made in the present, relate to future events. Techniques designed specifically to provide inferences about the future are called **forecasting techniques.** Other methods, labeled **descriptive techniques,** provide information about current situations; decision makers can draw inferences about the future after examining the information provided by these techniques. Some familiar forecasting methods include regression, correlation, Delphi techniques, Box-Jenkins models, seasonal trend analysis, and expert opinion. Simulation, one of the most important forecasting techniques, is reviewed later in this section.

The role of forecasting in strategic management is to reduce uncertainty and support decision making. Strategic decision situations always involve some uncertainty. Ultimately, decision makers attempt to quantify any uncertainty that remains in a process referred to as *risk analysis.*

The problem of reducing uncertainty is compounded by increases in uncertainty as the environment becomes more volatile. Changes have more pronounced effects because of the time horizons of most long-range strategies. One or more years frequently elapse between the conception of a new product and its actual marketing, or between the decision to acquire or sell an SBU and the transaction. During this time the assumptions or premises on which the strategy was based may change significantly. Rapid change is compressing these time horizons.

Much uncertainty can be reduced, however, and the strategic manager should become familiar with techniques to do this. Put simply, forecasting is vital. While most planning models assume availability of forecasts, generating them is not an easy task. David M. Georgeoff and Robert G. Murdick have created an easy-to-use and readily available guide to choosing a forecasting model to reduce the complexity of the process.[52]

Simulation Modeling and Other Uses of the Computer

One of the most significant analytical/forecasting techniques is simulation modeling. Simulation allows the strategist to ask what-if questions like what if the price of a raw material rises 1 percent. What if the union negotiates a 10-percent increase in benefits? What if our firm raises prices by 5 percent? A valid simulation model of an organization's operations can provide accurate answers to such vital questions quickly.

Simulations are computerized models that aid management in decision making. Simulation models abstract reality, normally representing an organization's internal flows in logically arranged symbolic equations. These models are interactive, that is, they allow managers to exchange information with them. The normal procedure is to assume a change in one or more inputs to the system and view the resulting changes elsewhere in the system as portrayed by the model. Simulations have evolved over many years, but have been important only since 1970 when appropriate systems-oriented software packages were developed and time sharing became feasible. The more complex simulation models are so expensive that not every organization can afford one. For those that can, such models are becoming a necessity, not a luxury.

AT APPLE COMPUTERS

Apple purchased a Cray supercomputer in order to run simulations and do computer-aided design (CAD) for its Knowledge Navigator.

To date, complex simulations are available only for internal operations. Environmental simulations, with the exception of models of the national economy, are not widely available, but they are being developed. The complex simulations commence with exhaustive analysis of the actual interrelationships of the organization, its subsystems, and the subsystems' components. A typical simulation uses a modular approach: it develops a model for each major structural division, function, or subsystem, and combines them all at interface points into a total corporate model. The modules combine to give a total model, usually at the business or functional level. Eventually, a modular model accounts for every quantifiable internal resource, event, or flow.

Spreadsheet programs for microcomputers offer the smallest of firms the opportunity to ask what-if questions for some fairly complex issues.[53] Typically they analyze only major variables, but as memory capacities increase, spreadsheets will be able to handle more complex analyses. Lotus 1-2-3® and similar programs already have this capability, especially Commander® EIS (Executive Information System).

Evidence indicates that the number of business firms employing complex simulations is large and growing. They use many types of simulations, but few totally integrated corporate models exist; that is, only the rare firm has combined simulations of various aspects of its operations to develop a model of the total corporation. Firms employ models most frequently in the areas of financial analysis and planning and evaluation of policy alternatives. Virtually any firm can employ a spreadsheet package.

Scenario Forecasting   A **scenario** is a systematic description of a future possibility.[54] A number of scenarios can be forecasted for any variable or any combination. The forecast is usually based on the most likely scenario.

Scenario forecasting is a judgmental forecasting technique used when the future is very uncertain. Since the 1990s will present waves of strategic management challenges, for example, accelerating rates of change, increased competition, and globalization of business, scenario forecasting is likely to be used in more and more firms.[55] For example, in reviewing its 20 years of strategic planning experience, Southern California Edison found that unanticipated events had rendered accurate forecasting impossible. Thus, the firm's top managers decided to incorporate uncertainty into their planning process. They identified key variables, prepared a number of plausible scenarios for them, and prepared response strategies for each scenario. They believe that scenario planning has greatly enhanced their ability to meet future challenges.[56]

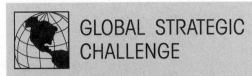

GLOBAL STRATEGIC CHALLENGE

ROYAL DUTCH/SHELL'S SCENARIO PLANNING

"Strategies are the product of the worldview. When the world changes, managers need to share some common view of the new world, otherwise decentralized strategic decisions will result in management anarchy. Scenarios express and communicate this common view shared and increase understanding of the new realities to all parts of the organization." So speaks Pierre Wack, retired head of the business environment division of Royal Dutch/Shell Group Planning Department. Along with Edwin Newman, he developed Shell's system of scenario planning.

The scenarios used by Royal Dutch/Shell are much more complex, much more detailed, and much more participatively determined than those many of us use in the United States. They aren't simply forecasts, but they do involve forecasting. Shell developed its scenario planning system in the early 1970s. It was so successful that the company was prepared for the 1973 oil crisis, and in 1981, when other oil companies were stockpiling their output, Shell managed to sell its oil before the glut forced prices to plunge.

Originally the scenarios had quite long time horizons, at one point as many as 15 years. Then Shell began to focus on 5 years for the long term and a 1-year short-term forecast. Eventually it turned to 3-year projections as the ability to make accurate forecasts over a longer period diminished. Shell perceived that as the tempo of world change increased, business-as-usual decisions would no longer be sufficient. Scenario forecasting with short-term horizons enabled the firm to be much better prepared for short-term strategic actions as well as for the long term. One major advantage of scenario forecasting is that it encourages top management to think strategically.

Sources: Christopher Knowlton, "Shell Gets Rich by Beating Risk," *Fortune*, August 26, 1991, pp. 79–82; Adrienne Lisenmeyer, "Shell's Crystal Ball," *Financial World*, April 16, 1991, pp. 58–63; Arie De Gues, presentation to the Strategic Management Society, Boston, October 15, 1987; Pierre Wack, "Scenarios: Shooting the Rapids," *Harvard Business Review*, November–December 1985, pp. 139–150; Pierre Wack, "Scenarios: Uncharted Waters Ahead," *Harvard Business Review*, September–October 1985, pp. 73–89.

One of the most impressive simulation programs, that of Royal Dutch/Shell, can model extremely complex scenarios. The Global Strategic Challenge feature examines the Royal Dutch/Shell scenario forecasting program in more detail.

In addition to simulation modeling, the computer serves other purposes in strategic management. It provides timely information at lower levels, which eventually should improve strategic decision making. It provides more common models for financial analysis, forecasting, descriptive statistical analysis, capital budgeting, and so on. It even helps train executives to ask the right questions when formulating strategies. The future seems to offer a mainframe tied to PC terminals, giving access to the strategic information system to affected personnel throughout the organization. Stand-alone micros will serve this function for smaller firms.

It is important to remember that the computer only aids strategists; it does not and cannot replace them. Strategists must rely on a certain amount of intuition to guide the science of strategic management. It is the ability to interpret and relate scientifically derived information and to make appropriate strategic decisions that separates the successful strategist from the unsuccessful one.

Microcomputers and Forecasting Ability

The microcomputer has brought information and its processing within reach of a much larger segment of the management population than ever before. Numerous software programs now give critical assistance to individuals and corporations in managing strategically. Spreadsheet analyses, for example, allow managers to forecast the impacts of selected changes in financial and operating performance, enabling even the smallest organizations and their managers to make more sophisticated, more rational decisions. Numerous manipulations of balance sheet, income statement, and cash flow statement data are also available. Many smaller organizations will now be able to develop such fundamental planning statements as budgets, which, while apparently simple, are time consuming to prepare, a problem that appropriate software packages solve easily. Similar advances have been made in word processing, ratio analysis, capital-needs forecasting, sales forecasting, and a host of other areas. Even some of the more sophisticated programs, such as those employing Box-Jenkins, IFPS, or Commander® EIS, are available for microcomputers. Even very complex econometric models of the U.S. economy have been adapted for personal computers.[57] The ability to crunch numbers better and faster does not guarantee improved decision making, but the improvement in both hardware and software does at least suggest that better decisions are possible.

Analytical Techniques: A Comment

Numerous forecasting techniques have been developed. Hundreds have been suggested for societal and technological forecasting, for example—far too many to discuss in this limited space. The important points to remember are these:

1. Numerous techniques are available, some better than others for a particular situation.
2. The use of more than one technique should improve forecasting.
3. The output of a technique is no better than its inputs and its assumptions.
4. Cost–benefit analysis should be performed to assess the value of expensive techniques.
5. All techniques should be evaluated.
6. Regardless of the amount of time and money invested, the environment is uncertain and change is increasing. Some forecasts will be wide of the mark. Flexibility must be maintained.

7. Somebody has to put all the pieces together and decide what the information means. That person is not always right.

STRATEGIC ASSUMPTIONS

We can forecast future growth rates, interest rates, GNP, demographics, consumer trends, and other key variables, but all such forecasts are based on assumptions about levels, attitudes, legislation, spending power, and the like. These assumptions can make or break a company. In 1990, virtually all personal computer manufacturers assumed that growth rates in consumption would continue at high levels. They didn't. The result was industry oversupply and overcapacity, price cutting, and reduced firm and industry profits.

Firms must analyze their strategic assumptions periodically, especially when formulating strategies in order to ensure that they remain valid. Monsanto controls its strategic assumptions through its Strategic Premises program in which it analyzes, condenses, prioritizes, and catalogues assumptions. They must then pass this three-question test:

1. What will we do if the worst occurs?
2. Do we accept the premise?
3. What preventive action can we take to make sure the premise holds?

Only a few very basic premises pass this test. These are communicated to the writers of strategic plans. Refinements in the program have led to increased accuracy of earnings forecasts and improved strategic planning.[58]

STRATEGIC MANAGER'S SUMMARY

1. The external factors to be considered include: (a) in the general environment, government, technology and innovation, society and social responsibility, the economy, organized labor, natural resources, and other significant factors such as demographics; (b) in the competitive environment, existing rivalry in the industry, new entrants, customers/clients, substitute products, and suppliers; and (c) in the global environment, international aspects of the other 2 environments.
2. External information is gathered to determine opportunities and threats.
3. Industry analysis requires careful consideration of new entrants, competitors, substitute products, buyers, and suppliers. Competitor analysis seeks to learn a competitor's strategies, strengths, and weaknesses.
4. Technological change, especially innovation, is a major threat, but can also be an important strategy. Research continues to show the importance of enhancing old products and developing new ones for long-term business survival.
5. Strategic forecasting involves a number of techniques and assumptions. It

often involves judgment. Scenario forecasting and simulations appear to be critical factors for the 1990s.

6. Strategic objectives are determined and strategies are formulated on the basis of forecasted SWOT: strengths, weaknesses, opportunities, and threats. Strategies are based on assumptions about SWOT and expected changes in SWOT.

KEY TERMS

competitor analysis
descriptive techniques
ethical dilemma
external factors
forecasting techniques
general environment

industry analysis
scenario
scenario forecasting
simulations
social responsibility areas

DISCUSSION QUESTIONS

1. Why is information critical to strategy formulation?
2. Discuss any organization and its strategic situation with regard to each component of external analysis.
3. Michael E. Porter proposes that the intensity of competition is the most critical element in the firm's environment. He then suggests five basic competitive factors that should be monitored. What are those five factors? Show how they apply to a particular organization.
4. What is the role of forecasting in strategy formulation?
5. What is scenario forecasting and why will it be so important in the 1990s?

STRATEGIC AUDIT QUESTIONS

1. What are the key strengths and weaknesses of each SBU in a particular firm in each of the following areas?

	Strengths	Weaknesses
Marketing		
Finance		
Operations		
Human resources		
Information management		
Research and development		
Facilities		

2. What are the implications for strategy of each of the following?
   a. Management values and capabilities
   b. Performance of management systems
   c. Stockholder orientations
   d. Employee perspectives
   e. Organizational culture
3. What opportunities and threats confront each SBU and the corporation as a whole in each of these areas?

	Opportunities	**Threats**
Government		
Technology		
Competition		
Industry		
New entrants		
Customers/clients		
Substitute products		
Suppliers		
Society		
Economy		
Labor (organized)		
Natural resources		
International events		
Pressure groups		
Creditors		
Others		

4. What opportunities and threats confront the corporation in each of the key areas identified by Porter?
   a. New entrants
   b. Existing rivalry among competitors
   c. Substitute products
   d. Buyers
   e. Suppliers
5. Supply information about these additional factors in competitor analysis.
   a. Who is the firm's competition now and who will it be in the future?
   b. What are the key competitors' strategies, objectives, and goals?
   c. How important is a specific market to the competitors, and are they committed enough to continue to invest?
   d. What unique strengths do the competitors have?
   e. Do they have any weaknesses that make them vulnerable?
   f. What changes are likely in the competitors' future strategies?
   g. What are the implications of competitors' strategies on the market, the industry, and the company?
6. Which forecasting techniques does the firm use? How effectively?
7. Does it use simulations? How appropriately?
8. On the basis of what assumptions was the firm's strategy formulated? How good were they? Are they still valid?

9. Should this firm be using scenario forecasting? How good is this forecasting, if the firm uses the technique?
10. How prepared is the firm for each of the ten strategic management challenges identified in Chapter 1?

Endnotes

1. Several studies suggest this concept. For example, see Michael W. Lawless and Linda K. Finch, "Choice and Determination: A Test of Hrebinak and Joyce's Framework on Strategy-Environment Fit," *Strategic Management Journal*, July/August 1989, pp. 351–365; Jeffrey G. Covin, "Strategic Management of Small Firms in Hostile and Benign Environments" *Strategic Management Journal*, January/February 1989, pp. 75–87.

2. Robert E. Norton, "Can Business Win in Washington," *Fortune*, December 3, 1990, pp. 75–84.

3. Barbara Rosewicz and Rose Gutfeld, "Breathing Easier, Clean-Air Legislation Will Cost Americans $21.5 Billion a Year," *The Wall Street Journal*, March 28, 1990, pp. A1, A16.

4. Norton, "Can Business Win."

5. Pat Choate, "Political Advantage: Japan's Campaign for America," *Harvard Business Review*, September–October 1990, pp. 87–103.

6. Johnnie L. Roberts, "Tough Operator, U.S. West, Demanding Further Deregulation; Sparks Much Criticism," *The Wall Street Journal*, September 24, 1987, pp. 1, 18.

7. Gerald S. Rosenfelder, "How to Stay at the Forefront of Technological Innovations," *Journal of Business Strategy*, May/June 1991, pp. 44–46.

8. A. C. Cooper et al., "Strategic Response to Technological Threats," Academy of Management, *Proceedings*, 1974.

9. J. M. Utterback and M. J. Abernathy, "The Test of a Conceptual Model Linking States in Firms' Process and Product Innovation," working paper no. 74-23, Harvard School of Business, 1974.

10. Richard Foster, *Innovation: The Attacker's Advantage* (New York: Summit Books, 1986).

11. Ronald A. Taylor, "Eastern Europe: The World's Greatest Polluter," *Europe*, October 1990, pp. 17–19; Ruth Hawk, "The 'Greening' of Europe," *Europe*, October 1990, pp. 6–8.

12. For a review of corporate social performance issues, see Donna J. Wood, "Corporate Social Performance Revisited," *Academy of Management Review*, November 1991, pp. 691–718; for several articles on the subject see "Creating the Great Society: To Whom Is the Corporation Responsible?" *Business Horizons*, special issue, July/August 1991.

13. Jerry W. Anderson, Jr., "Social Responsibility and the Corporation," *Business Horizons*, July/August 1986, pp. 22–27.

14. For a discussion of the strategic issues, see R. Edward Freeman and David L. Reed, "Stockholders and Stakeholders: A New Perspective in Corporate Governance," *California Management Review*, Spring 1983, pp. 88–106.

15. Edward W. Stead, Jean Garner Stead, and Edmund R. Gray, "Toward an Operational Model of Corporate Social Performance," *Advanced Management Journal*, Summer 1990, pp. 19–23.

16. Joann S. Lublin, "'Green' Executives Find Their Mission Isn't a Natural Part of Corporate Culture," *The Wall Street Journal*, March 5, 1991, p. B1, B8.

17. Robert Buderi and Emily T. Smith, "Conservation Power," *Business Week*, September 16, 1991, pp. 86–92.

18. LaRue Tone Hoerner, *The Ethics of Management* (Homewood, Ill.: Irwin, 1987), pp. 3–12.

19. Adrienne Cadbury, "Ethical Managers Make Their Own Rules," *Harvard Business Review*, September–October 1987, pp. 69–73.

20. Laura L. Nash, "Ethics without the Sermon," *Harvard Business Review*, November–December 1981, pp. 79–90.

21. Ann Reilly Dowd, "A Look into Bush's Budget Strategy," *Fortune*, September 24, 1990, pp. 57–58.

22. John Mueller, "The World's Real Money Supply," *The Wall Street Journal*, March 5, 1991, p. A16.

23. Alan Murray, "Finding a Tonic: As the Economy Sags, Washington Scrambles for Ways to Fix It," *The Wall Street Journal*, December 12, 1991, pp. A1, A4.

24. *The Budget of the United States Government, Fiscal Year 1991* (Washington, D.C.: Government Printing Office, 1990), p. A31.

25. For example, see Dean Foust, "How Deep Is the Hole?" *Business Week*, December 9, 1991, pp. 30–32.

26. For a discussion of projections of economic trends for the early 1990s by business strategists, see "Top Economic Trends of the 1990s," *Management Review*, January 1990, pp. 20–27.

27. John Barry, "The Coming Cutbacks in Military Money," *Newsweek*, March 18, 1991, pp. 42–43.

28. Christopher Farrell and Michael J. Mandel, "Global Chill," *Business Week*, December 16, 1991, pp. 26–28.

29. Art Hartman, "Organized Labor in the 1990s," *Manage-*

ment Quarterly, Summer 1990, pp. 9–12, reviews labor's decline, but gives reasons for cautious optimism for the 1990s. Also, see "America's Trade Unions: Return From the Dead," *The Economist*, February 10, 1990, pp. 66–67.

30. Michael Rozek, "Is the Work Ethic Dead?" *Incentive*, October 1990, pp. 65–68; James W. Sheehy, "New Work Ethic Is Frightening," *Personnel Journal*, June 1990, pp. 28–36.

31. "Needed: Human Capital," *Business Week*, September 19, 1988, pp. 102–103.

32. "Anything but Oil," *The Economist*, May 26, 1990, pp. 23–24; William H. Miller, "Energy Crunch Looming for the Nineties," *Industry Week*, August 7, 1989, pp. 32–36.

33. Lawrence Ingrassia, "Dead in the Water: Overfishing Threatens to Wipe Out Species and Crush Industry," *The Wall Street Journal*, August 16, 1991, pp. A1, A8.

34. Michael Maren, "Catch the Age Wave," *Success*, October 1991, pp. 54–56.

35. Martha Smilges, "Here Come the DINKS," *Time*, April 20, 1987, p. 75.

36. "Educational Mismatch: The Workplace Revolution," *The Wall Street Journal*, February 9, 1990, p. R7.

37. Michael E. Porter, *Competitive Strategy* (New York: Free Press, 1980), p. 3.

38. The material on Porter's model is from Porter, *Competitive Strategy*, pp. 3–33.

39. Nancy Jeffrey, "Joy Rides: Theme Parks Introduce More High-Tech Thrills and Chills," *The Wall Street Journal*, July 2, 1987, p. 21.

40. Porter, *Competitive Strategy*, p. 23.

41. Porter, *Competitive Strategy*, pp. 20–30.

42. For a review of competitor analysis efforts in three large firms, see Sumantra Ghoshal and D. Eleanor Westney, "Organizing Competitor Analysis Systems," *Strategic Management Journal*, January 1991, pp. 17–31.

43. W. E. Rothschild, "Competitor Analysis: The Missing Link in Strategy," *Management Review*, July 1979, pp. 22–39.

44. Stewart Early, "Issues and Alternatives: Key to FMC's Strategic Planning System," *Planning Review*, May/June 1990, p. 32.

45. Michael R. Czinkota, "International Information Needs for U.S. Competitiveness," *Business Horizons*, November/December 1991, pp. 86–91; Diane J. Garsombke, "International Competitor Analysis," *Planning Review*, May/June 1989, pp. 42–47.

46. John E. Prescott and John H. Grant, "A Manager's Guide for Evaluating Competitor Analysis Techniques," *Interfaces*, May/June 1988, pp. 10–22.

47. David J. Rogers, "Department of the Enemy," *Success*, July/August 1988, p. 18.

48. "Special Report: The Global Economy—Can You Compete," *Business Week*, December 17, 1990, pp. 60–95.

49. Richard M. Steers and Edwin L. Miller, "Management in the 1990s: The International Challenge," *Academy of Management Executive*, February 1988, pp. 21–23.

50. R. Taggart Murphy, "Power without Purpose: The Crisis of Japan's Financial Dominance," *Harvard Business Review*, March–April 1988, pp. 71–83.

51. Michael Porter, "How Nations Triumph," *Fortune*, March 12, 1990, pp. 94–95; George Rabstejnek, "Let's Go Back to the Basics of Global Strategy," *Journal of Business Strategy*, September/October 1989, pp. 32–35.

52. David M. Georgeoff and Robert G. Murdick, "Manager's Guide to Forecasting," *Harvard Business Review*, January–February 1986, pp. 110–120.

53. Jaclyn Fierman, "A Safe Way to Test Financial Fantasies," *Fortune*, April 28, 1985, p. 58; "How Personal Computers Are Changing the Forecasters' Jobs," *Business Week*, October 1, 1984, pp. 123–124.

54. C. L. Jain, "Scenario Forecasting," *Journal of Business Forecasting*, Fall 1986, p. 31.

55. Manuel Werner, "Planning for Uncertain Future: Building Commitment through Scenario Planning," *Business Horizons*, May/June 1990, pp. 55–58, contains an excellent discussion of the characteristics of an effective scenario planning system.

56. Fred Mobasheri, Lowell H. Orren, and Fereidoon P. Sjoshansi, "Scenario Planning at Southern California Edison," *Interfaces*, September/October 1989, pp. 31–44.

57. H. Igor Ansoff, "Competitive Strategy Analysis on the Personal Computer," *Journal of Business Strategy*, Winter 1986, pp. 28–36.

58. Margaret A. Stromp, "Questioning Assumptions: One Company's Answer to the Planner's Nemesis," *Planning Review*, September 1986, pp. 10–15.

 INDUSTRY NOTE

A GLOBAL PERSPECTIVE ON THE U.S. AUTOMOBILE INDUSTRY, FEBRUARY 1992

In February 1992 the U.S. automobile industry was characterized by sluggish sales caused mainly by a recession, intense global competition based especially on price and quality, technological change, severe overcapacity, shifting market segments, new entrants in various segments, increasingly sophisticated consumers, a blurring of cars' national origins, cost cutting, attempts by labor unions to protect jobs, international politics, and numerous market-related changes. GM, Ford, and Chrysler lost $4.5 billion, $2.2 billion, and $0.8 billion, respectively, for a combined total of $7.5 billion in losses, making 1991 the worst year in U.S. auto history.

U.S. automobile companies continued to face rising levels of competition from foreign firms, especially Japanese firms, both at home and in Europe. U.S. auto firms' combined share of the U.S. market is expected to continue to decline and that of Japanese firms is expected to continue to increase in this decade. In 1980, Japanese firms held 16.3 percent of the U.S. market. By 1990, their share had increased to 27.6 percent, and by 1991, to 31 percent. In 1991, the industry had U.S. sales of 12.3 million units, 8.2 million automobiles and 4.1 million light trucks, down 11.5 percent from 1990 for the lowest annual sales since 1983. Estimates varied, but from 40 to 50 percent of the new vehicles forecasted to be sold in the United States for the year 2000 were expected to be sold by Japanese firms if no actions were taken to stop U.S. firms' market share erosions.[1]

While the devaluation of the dollar in the late 1980s drove up the price of the average Japanese import, Japanese auto manufacturers still held a basic cost advantage on many cars. Furthermore, customers seemed to prefer the quality levels of Japanese cars to those of U.S. cars despite significant gains in U.S. car quality. U.S. consumers were willing to pay more to get that quality, often more than the difference in price might rationally justify. The triad of key global markets in the auto industry included North America, Europe, and Japan. Japan was virtually closed to foreign competition, despite promises to open markets.

INDUSTRY SEGMENTS

The industry recognizes four major segments based on price to the customer: low, medium, high, and luxury. The luxury category includes Cadillac's Allante, Nissan's Infiniti, Toyota's Lexus, and the high-priced models of Mercedes, BMW, and Jaguar. In addition, a whole new segment of extremely low-priced automobiles came to the U.S. market in 1986, such as Korea's Hyundai, introduced then at a base price of $4,995. GM, Ford, and Chrysler sold 1992 models at prices just slightly less than $7,000, matching the 1992 prices of import autos in that segment.

The market may also be perceived to be segmented by the nationalities of manufacturers. Some persons prefer American cars, for example; some prefer Japanese cars, and some prefer European cars. There is clear buyer loyalty to Japanese, German, English, and a few American cars because of their perceived superior quality or styling. Buyers demonstrate less loyalty to many U.S. cars, especially when their choices are based on perceived quality. Lee Iacocca calls the fascination with Japanese cars a cult, pointing out that U.S. citizens will pay more and report better quality for the Japanese version of equivalent cars built in the same U.S. factory by the same workers, with the only difference being the nameplates, for example, the Plymouth Laser versus the Mitsubishi

EXHIBIT 4.1   Percentages of Total U.S. Market Represented by Domestic
and Japanese Manufacturers, 1980–1991

	1980	1985	1989	1990	1991
Domestic Manufacturers					
General Motors	46.1%	41.8%	35.0%	35.4%	35.4%
Ford	16.5	18.8	22.2	20.8	19.9
Chrysler	7.4	10.3	10.4	9.2	8.5
All domestic manufacturers	73.3%	74.4%	67.6%	65.4%	63.8%
Japanese Manufacturers					
Toyota	6.5%	5.6%	6.9%	8.3%	9.0%
Nissan	5.8	5.3	5.2	4.9	5.0
Honda	4.2	5.0	8.0	9.1	9.8
Mazda	1.8	1.9	2.7	2.9	3.3
Mitsubishi	N.A.	N.A.	N.A.	1.7	2.1
Others (Including European Firms)	8.4	7.8	9.6	7.7	7.0
All foreign manufacturers	26.7%	25.6%	32.4%	34.6%	36.2%

N.A. = Not available.
Sources: "Auto Sales Data," *The Wall Street Journal*, January 8, 1981, p. 17, and January 8, 1987, p. 13; "U.S. Car and Light-Truck Sales, 12 Months—1990 vs. 1989," *Automotive News*, January 7, 1991, p. 33; Bradley E. Stertz and Jacqueline Mitchell, "Auto Makers Hobble into the New Year with Little Hope for a Robust Recovery," *The Wall Street Journal*, January 7, 1992, p. B1.

Eclipse. The same holds true for perceptions of the Dodge Stealth and the Mitsubishi 3000, which are identical sports cars built by the same workers in the same factory in Japan. Exhibits 4.1 and 4.2 indicate domestic and foreign auto sales in the United States for selected years from 1980 to 1991.

Blurring of National Lines

Cars' national identities are, however, becoming increasingly blurry. For example, the Stealth, Dodge's hot-selling sports car, is actually assembled in Japan and has a German engine. Similarly, the Mazda Navajo sport utility vehicle is assembled in a Ford plant in the United States. Several "American" cars are assembled in Canada. The Japanese have eight assembly plants in the United States and one in Canada. Many U.S.-assembled cars have significant Canadian, Japanese, and Mexican parts. Three Chrysler car models are assembled in Mexico. The Cadillac Allante is partly assembled in several countries. Only one car assembled in the United States is made entirely from U.S.-supplied parts, the Cadillac Brougham.[2]

TECHNOLOGICAL CHANGE

Technological change is affecting both manufacturing methods and product composition. General Motors has based much of its intended future strategy on improving its technological position in both manufacturing and end-product technologies. It is generally recognized as the U.S. leader in the auto industry's technological revolution, although it has not always been able to make its technology achieve its manufacturing and product objectives. Automation has been supplanted by robotization in many factories. This appears to correspond to a critical component of success in the

EXHIBIT 4.2   Unit Sales of Cars in the United States by Selected Manufacturers, 1980–1991

	1980	1986	1987	1989	1990	1991
General Motors						
Chevrolet/Geo Division	1,747,534	1,718,839	1,500,398	1,348,265	1,364,096	1,161,236
Pontiac Division	614,897	841,441	694,826	678,968	636,490	489,812
Oldsmobile Division	820,681	1,059,390	714,394	600,037	511,781	426,306
Buick Division	720,368	769,434	557,411	542,917	536,667	544,325
Cadillac Division	213,002	304,057	281,284	266,899	258,168	213,288
Saturn	—	—	—	—	—	74,493
All GM cars	4,116,482	4,693,161	3,748,313	3,437,086	3,308,983	2,909,460
Ford						
Ford Division	1,074,675	1,397,141	1,416,636	1,502,878	1,321,149	1,081,290
Lincoln-Mercury Division	400,557	683,681	614,918	674,988	622,454	554,580
All Ford cars	2,101,550	2,080,822	2,031,554	2,177,866	1,943,603	1,635,870
Chrysler						
Chrysler-Plymouth Division	393,557	783,530	647,217	502,286	438,499	318,576
Dodge Division	266,460	525,462	405,651	447,688	361,689	324,595
Eagle Division			43,517	69,719	60,646	59,347
All Chrysler cars	660,017	1,308,992	1,096,385	1,019,693	860,834	702,518
Toyota/Lexus	582,204	641,087	628,662	660,637	779,208	742,021
Honda/Accura	375,388	593,515	738,306	641,041	854,879	803,367
Nissan/Infiniti	516,890	546,151	529,154	499,336	453,756	412,852
Mazda	161,169	222,716	208,025	226,267	268,807	269,699
Mitsubishi	—	49,436	67,964	111,769	161,964	161,879
Subaru	142,968	183,242	175,864	136,112	108,547	105,052
Acura (Honda)	—	—	—	142,061	138,384	(with Honda)
Hyundai	—	168,882	263,610	183,261	137,448	117,630
Volkswagen/Audi	219,929	277,027	233,027	149,786	150,811	103,971
Volvo	56,827	113,261	106,539	102,580	89,940	67,697
Mercedes-Benz	47,904	99,314	89,518	75,714	76,966	58,868
BMW	34,520	96,759	87,839	64,881	62,794	53,343
AMC-Renault	116,797	77,005	—	—	—	—
Saab	—	47,414	45,105	31,576	26,397	26,103
Lexus (Toyota)	—	—	—	16,302	63,534	(with Toyota)
Infiniti (Nissan)	—	—	—	1,759	23,960	(with Nissan)
Jaguar	—	24,464	22,919	18,967	18,728	9,376
Porsche	—	30,471	23,632	9,476	9,139	4,388

Sources: "U.S. Car and Light-Truck Sales, 12 Months—1990 vs. 1989," *Automotive News*, January 7, 1991, p. 33; "Auto Sales Data," *The Wall Street Journal*, January 8, 1981, p. 17; and "Domestic Car Sales, December and Year-to-Date," *Automotive News*, January 13, 1992, p. 30.

future: the ability to employ robots to increase labor efficiency and effectiveness. Job redesign is at the heart of this strategy. General Motors' experience with NUMMI (for New United Motor Manufacturing, Inc.), its joint venture with Toyota, has demonstrated that the proper mix of robots and human labor in combination with Japanese-style management techniques is both more effective and more efficient than a totally robotized plant. Using the same work force with only moderate technological change, but with a major change in management styles, GM turned one of its worst plants into its most efficient. The Japanese management system apparently works with American workers.[3] Similarly, GM's experiences with its Saturn plant in Tennessee and with other plants have confirmed the validity of this approach.[4]

The automobile itself will continue to include more electronics in the future. If present trends continue, several hundred on-board computers of various sizes, functions, and descriptions will be included in the average car by the year 2000. In addition, car bodies are continually moving away from sheet steel and other types of metal toward plastics and aluminum. The downsizing and weight-reduction effort to meet federal gas mileage standards has led to abandonment of metal to a significant degree. Major changes will also occur in all sorts of operating technology as U.S. firms (GM principally) and Japanese firms move to develop electric cars, largely due to a California law requiring significant sales of these cars (1 million units) in California by the year 2003.[5]

One of the major strategies of Japanese firms is the use of high- and low-tech devices to improve their cars. *Miryokuteki hinshitsu*, as it is called in Japanese, means making the car reliable, fascinating, bewitching, and delightful. It is part of the effort to leapfrog American firms by redefining the concept of quality to go beyond statistical perfection.[6] The Lexus and the Mazda Miata are cars that exemplify this approach. Japanese cars, according to their advertisements, "just feel right." They look right, too, and the Lexus is full of dazzling technology.[7]

BARRIERS TO ENTRY AND TRANSPORTATION/DISTRIBUTION COSTS

The barriers to entry into the auto industry are surprisingly low. Korea's Hyundai went from no participation to become a major manufacturer of cars for the U.S. market in just a few years. Calculations of breakeven sales vary. The Japanese claim they can break even on annual sales of just 40,000 units.

Transportation and distribution costs are significant only for foreign competitors. Shipping a car from Japan or Europe adds $600 to $800 to the cost of each unit. This differential helps offset the lower production costs of Japanese manufacturers, but they have attempted to avoid this distribution cost and other barriers by opening plants in the United States. Over half of the cars in Japan's 31-percent market share in the United States in 1991 were manufactured in the United States by American labor in Japanese-owned plants.[8]

PRODUCT DIFFERENTIATION

Historically, the U.S. automobile buyer has been more concerned with style than any other factor. Price has always been important, of course, and quality was critical in the 1980s as well. Styles changed cyclically, typically every two years, until the late 1970s, but dramatic changes have become progressively fewer because the cost of making them drove prices higher. As North Americans began to seek low cost, higher quality cars that got better mileage, Japanese automobiles began to make a strong impact on the U.S. market. Style changes were less important as car and gas prices rose and the concern for quality increased. In the 1980s, however, gas prices dropped, the quality of American cars improved, the dollar lost substantial ground to the yen; as a result product style differentiation again became a critical factor. Both Ford's and Chrysler's product lines came to be clearly differentiated, but General Motors' cars still tended to look alike. Furthermore, GM's boxy styles were unappealing to many buyers.[9] In recent years, the Japanese have been abandoning their boxy look for sleekness, as have the Germans.

INDUSTRY CAPACITY

General Motors closed a total of 23 plants in the United States between 1987 and 1991 and is expected to close 21 more by 1995. Chrysler closed three plants during this same time frame and will close a small facility in Canada in 1993.[10] Yet estimates are that by 1995, automakers will be able to produce 14.3 million cars and trucks in the U.S. and Canada, but consumers will demand only 13.8 million—resulting in an overcapacity of 500,000 units. This overcapacity can be mostly attributed to increased Japanese investment in plants in the United States. In 1990, Japanese firms had a production capacity of 2.5 million units in the United States—about twice that of Chrysler. There are three such plants in Canada and eight in the United States, with more on the way.[11] Two of these eleven plants are 50-percent owned by U.S. firms. The other nine are wholly owned.

COMPETITORS AND THEIR STRATEGIES

There are 29 sizeable competitors (those with sales greater than 18,000 units) in the U.S. auto market. They use varying strategies, but the major firms attempt to position several models across different price segments of the market, following the traditional strategy of General Motors, Ford, and Chrysler. Even luxury cars, such as Mercedes and BMW, have several models ranging across several price classifications.

Domestic Competitors

Ford and Chrysler seem to emulate General Motors' full-line pricing strategies. Both have historically been more aggressive than GM in initiating such sales-incentive programs as rebates and low interest rates. In 1991, however, GM slashed prices and increased rebates in order to protect its market share.

Ford More than any other American manufacturer, Ford has identified quality as a strategy. Quality has been Ford's number 1 goal. Ford has also used exterior design as a major competitive weapon, winning awards for its innovative designs for Taurus, Sable, Thunderbird, Continental, and the Lincoln Town Car. It has the oldest models of any of the major U.S. players, though. It will introduce a host of new models in the next few years, but its main seller, Taurus, was only slightly restyled in 1992 and will stay the same for three more years, causing many to question that car's future in a style-conscious market. Largely by reducing the number of blue-collar and salaried employees, Ford cut $5 billion in annual costs from 1981 through 1986, and it will further reduce white-collar labor by 20 percent in the early 1990s.[12]

Ford bet its design future on a globally integrated design program. Donald E. Peterson, Ford's chairman until 1990, wanted Ford to become the world's first global car company. He wanted to design a new car in whatever "Ford Technical Center worldwide has the greatest expertise in that product" with the goal of completing each project once for all markets. Ford failed to implement this concept earlier with the Escort. It found that the car required substantial modification for each market. The Merkur, another global design, was a hit in Europe, but failed miserably in the United States. The strategy seems to have been abandoned, although it would have saved hundreds of millions of dollars on each car designed if it had succeeded. Ford is in the process of cutting design times to be competitive with the Japanese (allowing 3 years from concept to rollout) and it is cutting design bureaucracy to improve speed and reduce costs.[13]

Ford lost $1.08 billion in Europe in 1991, including $354 million on Jaguar, which it purchased in 1989. Estimates project that it will spend another $2.5 billion to make the firm competitive. Most analysts are critical of this purchase.[14] Part of Ford's strategy consists of foreign alliances. It owns 25 percent of Mazda, for example, and depends on Mazda for a substantial number of parts. It worked feverishly with Mazda to produce the new Escort for global markets.[15] Ford's alliance with Mazda has been one of the few major global alliance success stories.[16]

General Motors   GM has focused on technology and acquisition strategies. It has invested over $77 billion worldwide in new plant and equipment, robotizing many plants. It bought Electronic Data Systems (EDS) in 1984, Hughes Aircraft in 1985, and numerous other organizations to acquire needed manufacturing technologies and product components. Revenues from both EDS and Hughes have also helped offset auto industry cycles. GM moved in 1984 and again in 1992 to restructure itself to gain flexibility and cut costs dramatically. GM closed 23 plants from 1987 to 1991, and it will close 21 more by 1995. GM's current focus is on improving market share, quality, and design. It has suffered through a series of losing product designs. It is also engaged in a massive cost-cutting program.[17]

Chrysler   Chrysler has stressed quality and close relationships with suppliers. Most recently, it has emphasized cutting costs, reducing design times, and producing snazzy new designs.[18] Like its domestic competitors, Chrysler wants to reduce its breakeven point, which fell from 2.4 million units in 1979 to 1.2 million units in 1985, but rose to 1.9 million units in 1987. Chairman Iacocca took control and pushed the level back to 1.5 million in 1990, and it is continuing to fall. Chrysler, too, believes in strategic alliances. It owns 12 percent of Mitsubishi, but that relationship is a very rocky one, and may end soon. Unfortunately for Chrysler, it sells few cars in Europe and must depend on the highly competitive North American market. The bright spots for Chrysler include a dazzling new product line due in 1993 and 1994 led by the Viper sports car in 1992. It has developed a new design process based in its new $1-billion design center, and it has successfully cut costs.

Quality

All domestic auto manufacturers have learned that simpler is better. Fewer parts mean fewer potential problems in manufacturing and assembly. Many cars are now being redesigned to allow for simpler manufacturing processes in a practice known as *design for manufacturing* or *robust quality*. Genichi Taguchi, a Japanese qualilty expert, has championed this idea. Rather than tighten controls, he believes that a firm should design the product so that it can be built easily regardless of fluctuations or problems in product levels. Taguchi has devised a statistical method to eliminate many of the judgments necessary to find the right combination of parts for a product. His simulated design of the actual product allows engineers to go back and design a simpler product. Design and manufacturing will be more closely linked in the future. Taguchi's system is now available for computer-aided engineering systems.[19] Quality will probably not be a major differentiation factor in the U.S. market of the middle to late 1990s, although it will be important in Europe.

Diversification

General Motors has the most diverse conglomerate package of the Big Three U.S. manufacturers. GM's diversification efforts are technologically related to automobile manufacture or financing. Chrysler's diversification is now limited, since it divested Gulf Stream Aerospace Corporation in 1989. Chairman Lee Iacocca admits he erred in acquiring Gulf Stream because it took too much of top management's time away from the auto industry.[20] Chrysler purchased American Motors Corporation in spring 1987 largely to increase its capacity. It purchased three rental car companies in the late 1990s, presumably to give it an expanded, captive market for its cars.[21] Since December 1985, Ford has purchased Sperry Corporation's new home and farm equipment businesses and an 81-percent interest in the First Nationwide Financial Corporation, the holding company of the ninth largest U.S. savings and loan association. Ford also bid on Hughes, but felt the price was too high. (GM paid $5.5 billion for the firm.)[22] Ford later purchased Jaguar for $2.6 billion.

Cost Reduction

Chrysler has implemented a major cost-reduction effort, having squeezed $3 billion out of the cost structure between 1989 and 1991. Ford's cost-reduction effort is aimed at research and development as well as manufacturing and overhead. GM also has a major cost-cutting and restructuring program under way.

Far-East Competition

Everyone in the auto industry is afraid of the Japanese, and they should be. The Japanese sold 42 percent of the cars delivered in the United States in the first quarter of 1991 and 31 percent for the whole year.[23] Peter Slater, then international strategist for Ford, observed, "Toyota is our number 1 competitor. It is far more dangerous than General Motors. And if Honda keeps improving the way it has over the last ten years, we'll all be hard-pressed to keep up with it."[24] First, Japan entered the low end of the market, then it moved upscale. Recently the Japanese have moved into the luxury segment of the market with such entries as Nissan's Infiniti and Toyota's Lexus.

Historically, Japanese firms have competed on the basis not just of cost, but also of quality. On average, their cars do have fewer defects than American cars, but that gap is narrow and several U.S. cars have fewer defects than many Japanese models.[25] The significant decline in the value of the dollar and the resulting relative rise in the value of the yen spurred Japanese auto manufacturers to launch a massive cost-cutting program in the late 1980s, including freezes on wages, renegotiation of contracts with suppliers, the use of more common components, and outsourcing to Taiwan and Korea.

The Japanese strategy for competing in the United States has several parts:

1. They are redefining quality. As noted earlier, they are moving to a total quality approach involving not just statistical quality control, but an attitude defined by the term *miryokuteki hinshitsu,* in which quality includes reliability, fascination, bewitchment, and delight.[26]
2. As the U.S. firms' market shares fall, the Japanese have prepared for calls for import quotas by U.S. firms by building manufacturing plants in the United States.[27]
3. Their North American plants assemble components from their Japanese suppliers, for the most part. Local parts content is 38 percent for Japanese plants, but 88 percent for U.S. plants.[28]

4. They are not only building their cars in the United States, but designing them here, and thus Americanizing them, as well.[29]
5. The Japanese don't trade fairly. They keep U.S. cars and virtually all other foreign autos out of their markets.[30] President Bush's trip to Japan in January 1992 was expected to change very little of Japan's protectionist activity and, by all accounts, it had little impact.[31]
6. The Japanese seek joint ventures with U.S. firms where possible.
7. They lobby heavily in Washington and in state capitals.

Toyota   Toyota has a larger share of the Japanese market than any other Japanese manufacturer and ranks second in the U.S. market to Honda (see Exhibit 4.3). Nissan and Honda rank second and third, respectively, in Japan.[32] Toyota is the third largest car manufacturer in the world, behind GM and Ford. It employs effective cost-cutting measures, advanced manufacturing technologies, and joint ventures to further its position in the international market and is expected to pass Ford in 1993.

Kaizen, or continuous improvement, is Toyota's focal strategy. Iwas Isomina, director of personnel for Toyota, observes, "Our current success is the best reason to change things."[33] Toyota tends to be a more risk-averse company than Nissan or Honda, allowing its competitors to make innovations and then adopting those that prove successful. With a production facility in Britain, it is prepared for an assault on Europe. Toyota's success comes largely from its manufacturing process. Above all else, the goal is quality. Any worker can stop the assembly line to fix a problem. An interesting study of production operations at Nissan and Toyota by MIT's Michael Cusumano indicates that Toyota gained market share from Nissan because it focused its strategy on managing workers while Nissan, like GM, poured millions into computers and robots. Productivity per employee is higher for Toyota than for any other auto manufacturer.[34] Many feel Toyota is the best car manufacturer in the world. It is so successful that it holds $22 billion in cash, enough to buy both Ford and Chrysler at fall 1990 stock prices.[35]

Nissan   Nissan was battered by Toyota at home in the mid-1980s. Consequently, it went on a cost-cutting binge, but to no avail. Sales were still lackluster at home and in the United States. Its first loss in 1987 led to a major shakeup. Analysis showed that, both at home and in the United

EXHIBIT 4.3   Japanese Firms' Market Shares in Japan

	1990 Unit Sales*	Percentage Change from 1989
Toyota	1,756,621	8.7%
Nissan	986,352	7.3
Honda	394,908	1.1
Mazda	308,554	18.0
Mitsubishi	160,285	14.6

*First 10 months.
Source: Karen Lowry Miller and James B. Treece, "Honda's Nightmare: Maybe you Can't Go Home Again," *Business Week*, November 4, 1990, p. 36.

States, the company was perceived as selling look-alike econoboxes. Furthermore, U.S. consumers still had not figured out that Nissan was the old Datsun.

As a consequence, Nissan adopted a strategy focusing on advanced design. The strategy worked especially well in Japan where it began once again to contest with Toyota for market share. This strategy also worked well in the United States, where Nissan posted a slight gain in market share in 1989. In 1990, however, it lacked the capacity to continue to sell additional cars in both markets, so it opted to supply its home market first. To hike capacity, Nissan is spending $500 million to expand its Smyrna, Tennessee plant to double annual production to 450,000 vehicles in 1992; virtually all of the expansion is aimed at producing the hot-selling, redesigned Stanza. Another redesigned Stanza is due in 1992. It will be the first Nissan car totally designed and manufactured in the United States. Nissan has generally straddled the gap between a semi full-line producer and a niche player. Most of its recent successes have been niche products, but Stanza is aimed clearly against Toyota's major products. Nissan is positioned to expand in Europe, where its sales are growing, with a plant in Great Britain.[36]

Honda   Honda is the most Americanized of the Japanese companies, and the one whose fortunes are most clearly tied to the U.S. market. It even outsells Toyota in the United States. Because it was a postwar creation and has no ties to the industrial giants of Japan, and because its share of the Japanese market is small compared to those of Toyota and Nissan, Honda is viewed as a maverick in its own country. Honda has succeeded by building automobiles for niches in the market. It is well-known for its ability to hit important market trends with just the right product at the right time, as it did with the Civic, Prelude, Accord, and Acura. It is also known for its lack of organization structure, capitalizing on a fluid structure to meet the conditions of a rapidly changing marketplace. It is also known for innovation and willingness to take risks. Honda has been more willing than any other Japanese company to use American suppliers in its U.S.-manufactured products. It employs a global strategy that focuses on localizing products, profits, production, and management. Its research and development unit, Honda R&D, has historically played an important role in its success.[37]

Mazda   Mazda is determined to be a global competitor, and much of its global strategy rests on joint ventures with foreign firms, especially Ford, which owns 24 percent of the company. It also has relationships with Citroen of France and Suzuki of Japan. Because it is a small player in both Japan and the United States, it believes it needs alliances to be successful. It clearly does not have the cash or asset base to go head-to-head with the major players. President Norimasa Furuta believes that the future of auto companies lies not in head-to-head competition, but in cooperation. Mazda has relied principally on just a few car models to sustain its sales effort. It has changed the way cars are sold in Japan by importing the U.S. concept of showrooms, as opposed to the traditional Japanese sales agent, who is almost, but not quite, a door-to-door peddler. Mazda is now broadening its product line with a flexible manufacturing facility in Hiroshima that can turn out nine major product lines. Mazda has had success of late with some models, such as the Miata, but others have sold less well, especially in the all-important Japanese market.[38]

Mitsubishi   A major player in neither Japan nor the United States, Mitsubishi seems determined to advance in both markets. A major push is under way to gain U.S. market share with snazzier cars and a new dealer network. Two major new models include the 3000GT sports car and the Diamante luxury sedan. It has learned to operate in the U.S. market from its 50-percent ownership with cash-starved Chrysler of Diamond-Star Motors in Illinois. (Many say its share will soon rise to 75 percent.) This partnership has produced several cars, some sold under each or both partners' brand names. Mitsubishi has pushed hard at home, and in 1991 it was battling hard with both Honda and Mazda for the number three spot in market share in Japan. It has been moving from a role as a niche player to market a fuller line. It hopes to be seen as offering the latest in technology in its cars. It is moving rapidly to follow traditional Japanese entry strategies in a country—start small, learn the market, then drive for market share.[39]

Hyundai   This Korean manufacturer had tremendous success in entering the U.S. market in 1986 with the low-priced Excel, in 1987 establishing record sales for a new import with over 263,300 units sold. Since then, however, the firm has had major problems in the U.S. market. The introduction of an upscale model failed to produce hoped-for results, and the poor quality of the Excel has left it floundering in the face of Japanese and U.S. products with greater quality and similar prices. Its earlier advantage as a low-cost producer (with labor rates that were 25 percent of those of comparable Japanese and U.S. companies) has eroded with the blossoming of the Korean economy and the significantly increased value of the Korean currency.

European Competition in the U.S. Market

European automobile companies continue to play less and less active roles in the U.S. market. Mercedes-Benz, BMW, and Jaguar, who had long dominated the luxury segment of the market, found themselves losing substantial sales to the Infiniti and the Lexus in 1990 and 1991. U.S. luxury taxes on expensive cars and major promotional, price competition, and leasing campaigns by Lexus and Infiniti to remedy declines in sales have led these three European prestige-car makers to offer substantial discounts and aggressive leasing arrangements.[40] Mercedes and BMW each have several models, the cheapest of which fall at the top of the high-price segment, with the rest in the luxury price range. Both use quality and styling as key differentiation factors. Mercedes has suffered substantially as Infiniti and Lexus cut into its markets. Mercedes sold 99,000 units in 1986, but only 59,000 in 1991.[41]

Jaguar has only two basic models and has restructured its prices to enable them to better compete with the Japanese. Jaguar has long been thought of as offering good value for the money, but its quality is lower than that of its competition, and Ford is working hard to improve quality where it can. Ford will bring out several new Jaguar models, but not before the mid 1990s, investing $2.5 billion to modernize Jaguar and bring its research and development unit up to speed. Porsche has long dominated the expensive sports car segment of the market, focusing on the top end of that segment, having dropped its lowest-priced model in the late 1980s. This proved devastating to sales, especially in the United States.[42] Honda's Acura NSX sports car model, priced at $62,000, has generated extremely high demand in Europe and the United States, and future Japanese and U.S. sports models may pose other serious problems for Porsche. All four of these companies will benefit from declining values in their respective currencies, especially the German car makers, who have seen their currency drop significantly against the dollar since reunification.

The European Auto Market

Exhibit 4.4 indicates the 1990 market shares of the major players in the European market. Annual sales in 1990 were $156 billion, with 13 million units sold. The market may buy 15 million units by

EXHIBIT 4.4 European Market Share through the First Half of 1991

Volkswagen	16.7%
Fiat	13.3
GM	12.6
Japanese companies	12.3
Ford	12.1
Peugeot	11.3
Renault	9.9
Others	11.8

Source: John Templeman, "Lining Up for the World's Biggest Demolition Derby," *Business Week*, September 23, 1991, pp. 54–55.

1999, with Japan expected to get at least 16 percent of that market.[43] Historically, the market has been segmented by country. Several countries have what seem like national car companies, which are often owned by the government, Fiat in Italy, for example. Thus in France, Great Britain, Germany, Italy, and Sweden, each country segment has been dominated by that country's national car company or companies. (For all practical purposes, however, Great Britain no longer has a national car company.) Ford and GM have skirted this problem by offering models in several countries. Not every country has had a national company, and selling across borders has ranged from very little to a considerable amount, depending upon government policies.

Tariffs, quotas, government subsidies, and other barriers have been erected to protect national companies, or for other economic purposes such as to reduce trade deficits or support employment rates. Consequently, most European manufacturers are overstaffed and less than competitive on a global basis. Their quality levels do not approach those of their U.S. or Japanese counterparts, except for the German car companies. Ford's manufacturing and distribution are extremely well-integrated across the continent. GM outsold Ford for the first time in Europe in 1990 and did it again in 1991. Both have invested heavily in Europe in recent years and Ford has a $7-billion modernization program under way. Both Ford and GM have improved their quality significantly in recent years to be competitive with the Japanese.[44]

The integration of Europe in 1992 has brought a move to eliminate trade barriers. To understand their significance, consider that the Peugeot 205, which is manufactured in France, had pretax 1990 prices ranging from $10,241 in Britain to $8,536 in France, $7,858 in Belgium, and $5,831 in Denmark. It will probably be 1995 before these prices average out across Europe because of a special 10-year exemption granted automobile manufacturers by the EEC back in 1985. Still, price competition and other forms of competition were increasing in Europe as sales began to decline in 1990 for the first time in 5 years.[45] European auto firms are striving to improve productivity to prepare for the Japanese onslaught, but have faced stiff resistance from organized labor.[46]

The Japanese Threat   Countries with very stiff quotas have managed to protect their markets from the Japanese. For example, France imposes a 3-percent quota and Italy a 1-percent quota. Where there are no quotas or generous quotas, Japanese auto manufacturers dominate. For example, in Germany, Ireland, Greece, and Denmark, the Japanese have 30 percent or more of the markets.[47] There seems to be general agreement that the major European players want to keep the Japanese out of the continent as much as they can.

On the other hand, the Japanese have already made substantial investments in Europe, betting that if they manufacture in a European country, they will be able to import into the other European countries under likely EEC laws. The Japanese are lobbying heavily to protect their investments (projected to amount to $2.6 billion by the mid-1990s), but so are Fiat, Renault, and Peugeot. Nissan already has a plant in Great Britain, and by the mid-1990s Toyota, Nissan, and Honda will have the combined capacity to turn out 500,000 cars a year in Britain. Mitsubishi has a joint venture with Volvo to build cars in Holland.[48] The safest bet is that the Japanese will be given a higher overall quota for Europe, with all quotas removed by the year 1999.[49] The Japanese are following essentially the same strategy they did in the United States. They have started small, offering well-made, low-priced products. They have then begun to strive for market share. They have also introduced high-priced models that still under-price their European competition. This builds market share and profits. They are building plants in Europe to prevent damage from quotas.

The European market is plagued by overcapacity, much of it using antiquated plant and equipment. The market is extremely soft, having been fueled for some time by discounts and various other purchase incentives. Only the German market remains strong, making Volkswagen number one in all of Europe; and the economy continues to move forward, although not as rapidly as it did prior to reunification. The odds are that one or more of Europe's "big six" national firms will fold before 2000. Eastern Europe does not offer as much promise as earlier thought because it will take years to build the necessary infrastructure to support capitalistic economies, and hence put money into the hands of consumers to buy automobiles.

UNION CONTRACT NEGOTIATIONS

In 1990, GM signed a landmark agreement with the United Auto Workers Union. General Motors needed to improve productivity and reduce its relative labor costs. In exchange for increased productivity and the right to manage in accordance with modern labor–management practices, the union membership received income security for current employees, idled workers, and retirees. For example, in an unprecedented move, workers at plants to be closed will receive up to 3 years' pay.[50]

SUBSTITUTE PRODUCTS

Used-car prices have been rising substantially in recent years, reflecting the increase in the prices of new cars. Used cars of higher quality will be more readily available in the future as the quality of new cars improves. Mass transit provides a suitable substitute in many areas, but in the long term is not expected to reduce the size of the automobile market. Motorcycles are not a significant force in the U.S. marketplace. Used rental cars are a major substitute problem.

THE GLOBAL NATURE OF THE AUTOMOBILE INDUSTRY

It is becoming increasingly evident that, in the future, the successful firms in any marketplace will be global competitors. Firms can compete globally using either a global strategy or a multidomestic strategy. The Japanese are the most globally oriented of the automakers. Ford is the most globally oriented of the U.S. automakers. GM is more multidomestic.

In 1990 automakers around the world produced more than 46 million cars, trucks, and buses, often selling them halfway around the world. The most significant short-term profit potential is in Europe, with good long-term prospects in the Pacific Rim. The latter is almost totally the domain of the Japanese. While this note concentrates on the U.S. industry segment, the most potentially profitable segment of the global market—sales in other geographic segments—should not be overlooked.

Global competition hinges on tariffs, quotas, and other barriers as well as on technology, capacity, and the other concerns addressed earlier. Most governments, except those of a few nations such as the United States and Germany, protect their manufacturers. Global competition is also a matter of flexibility, which determines the ability to react to markets and to satisfy diverse groups of customers by adapting a basic model to their needs. Alliances also seem to be becoming critically important.

DISTRIBUTION

The number of domestic auto dealers has declined during 29 of the last 30 years. In addition, the structures of dealerships are changing as megadealers selling from 5 to 15 makes of cars are beginning to dominate city markets. Such a dealer may have as many as 30 locations. Sometimes the land a dealer's lots occupy is worth $100 million or more. So far, only about 1 percent of the 25,000 U.S. dealers fit the megadealer category, but they accounted for 25 percent of all vehicle sales in the United States in 1990. Among the pluses of the megadealers is their ability to reduce costs and improve distribution and service. Among the negatives is their independence: they won't necessarily sell the cars that Detroit wants them to sell and they may not sell certain models at all. They can choose the models they want to sell and may sell 10 or more different lines.

CONSUMERS

Individual buyers of automobiles have little or no power to affect the price of a car or the conditions under which they get it. While they are free to negotiate, the experience is often unpleasant, and most people don't seem to like buying automobiles. In recent years, however, buyers have become more sophisticated and perhaps somewhat jaded as they look for the low-interest loans and other price incentives that they know will come if they just wait long enough to buy.

ECONOMIC FACTORS

Worldwide demand for automobiles has been dropping and is expected to continue to drop in the near future, primarily due to the recession. Sales incentives to induce customers to buy 1990 models reduced the demand for 1991 models. Also, consumers are becoming much more knowledgeable; they have come to expect special packages, interest rates, and price breaks. The automobile companies must provide them. U.S. population growth in the next few years will be most rapid in the 35- to 57-year-old age bracket and in nonurban areas. People in this age group tend to have more disposable income than their juniors and seniors, and therefore demand for autos may increase, but only slightly. Disposable income and general economic conditions are continuing to have a major impact on automobile sales.

Prices are greatly affected by inflation; price increases typically reflect the rate of inflation and pay raises won by union members. Overall, the domestic companies' market share is expected to drop significantly in the next 10 years as foreign companies gain more market share. The low end of the market has been virtually abandoned by American manufacturers except for Saturn.

A long recession would have a major impact on American car manufacturers. It would challenge the staying power of Chrysler. It could also challenge such foreign competitors as Nissan and Honda, but Toyota would surely survive. A major recession would definitely also hurt the upscale markets of the European competitors. The economy is expected to remain stagnant in the near future.

As the U.S. population ages and the number of young people declines, styling changes may be necessary to accommodate changing tastes. The middle-class population base may be eroded, producing a devastating effect on the automobile industry, probably including a need for a massive reduction in relative costs. No major regulatory changes seem to be in store for the next few years, although proposals offered in December 1991 in Congress raised a chance of protectionist measures to limit Japanese firms' sales in the United States.[51]

Endnotes

1. "Automakers' Sales Worst Since 1983," *Orlando Sentinel*, January 7, 1992, p. C-1; Bradley A. Stertz and Jacqueline Mitchell, "Auto Makers Hobble into the New Year with Little Hope for a Robust Recovery," *The Wall Street Journal*, January 7, 1992, pp. B1, B6; Mary Ann Keller, "The Japanese Can Take 50% of the U.S. Car Market," *Fortune*, March 26, 1990, pp. 36, 37; Paul Ingrassia, "Losing Control: Auto Industry in U.S. Is Sliding Relentlessly into Japanese Hands," *The Wall Street Journal*, February 16, 1990, pp. A1, A5.

2. Julie Stacey, "No Domestic Is Truly All-American," *USA Today*, March 2, 1992, p. 3B.

3. William J. Hampton, "General Motors: What Went Wrong?" *Business Week*, March 16, 1987, p. 107.

4. David Woodruff, "At Saturn, What Workers Want Is Fewer Defects," *Business Week*, December 2, 1991, pp. 117–118; Gregory A. Patterson, "Building 'Em Better: Two GM Auto Plants Illustrate Major Role of Workers' Attitudes," *The Wall Street Journal*, August 29, 1991, pp. A1, A5.

5. David Woodruff, "GM: All Charged Up over the Electric Car," *Business Week*, October 21, 1991, pp. 106, 107.

6. David Woodruff, "A New Era for Auto Quality," *Business Week*, October 22, 1990, pp. 84–96.

7. For a discussion of some of the technological changes expected in the 1990s, see Bradley A. Stertz and Joseph B. White, "Driving into the Next Decade," *The Wall Street Journal*, July 12, 1989, p. B1.

8. Paul Ingrassia and Clay Chandler, "Slowing Down: Japan's Car Makers Now See Advantages in Restraining Growth," *The Wall Street Journal*, January 7, 1992, pp. A1, A6; James B. Treece, "Shaking Up Detroit," *Business Week*, August 14, 1989, pp. 74–79.

9. Annetta Miller, "GM Aims for the Fast Lane," *Newsweek*, October 22, 1990, pp. 50, 51.

10. Paul Ingrassia and Joseph B. White, "GM Posts Record '91 Loss of $4.45 Billion and Identifies a Dozen Plants for Closing," *The Wall Street Journal*, February 25, 1992, pp. A3, A8; Ingrassia, "Losing Control," p. A5; Joseph B. White and Paul Ingrassia, "Smaller Giant: Huge GM Write-Off Positions Auto Maker to Show New Growth," *The Wall Street Journal*, November 1, 1990, pp. A1, A11; Joseph B. White and Bradley A. Stertz, "Crisis Is Galvanizing Detroit's Big Three," *The Wall Street Journal*, May 2, 1991, pp. B1, B9.

11. Treece, "Shaking Up Detroit."

12. Alex Taylor III, "The Odd Eclipse of a Star CEO," *Fortune*, February 11, 1991, p. 96.

13. Ibid.; White and Stertz, "Crisis Is Galvanizing."

14. Robert L. Simison, "Jaguar Slowly Sheds Outmoded Habits," *The Wall Street Journal*, July 26, 1991, p. A6; Mark Maremont, "A Jaguar Buyer May Be in for a Long, Slow Drive," *Business Week*, November 13, 1989, pp. 48–49.

15. James B. Treece, "How Ford and Mazda Shared the Driver's Seat," *Business Week*, March 26, 1990, pp. 94–96.

16. James B. Treece and Karen Lowry Miller, "The Partners," *Business Week*, February 10, 1992, pp. 102–107.

17. Alex Taylor III, "Can GM Remodel Itself?" *Fortune*, January 13, 1992, pp. 26–34; White and Stertz, "Next Decade."

18. David Woodruff, "Chrysler May Actually Be Turning the Corner," *Business Week*, February 10, 1992, p. 32.

19. Otis Port, "How to Make It Right the First Time," *Business Week*, June 8, 1987, pp. 142–143.

20. Paul Ingrassia and Bradley A. Stertz, "Mea Culpa: With Chrysler Ailing, Lee Iacocca Concedes Mistakes in Managing," *The Wall Street Journal*, September 17, 1990, pp. A1, A7.

21. Gregory A. Patterson, "Chrysler to Acquire Dollar Rent a Car, Eyeing Broader Market in Rental Sector," *The Wall Street Journal*, June 27, 1990, p. A4.

22. James B. Treece, "Can Ford Stay on Top?" *Business Week*, September 28, 1987, pp. 78–86.

23. Joseph B. White, "Big Three Auto Executives Seek Help from Visiting Congressional Delegation," *The*

Wall Street Journal, April 19, 1991, p. A9.

24. Alex Taylor III, "Who's Ahead in the World Auto War?" *Fortune*, November 9, 1987, p. 86.

25. Woodruff, "A New Era," p. 90.

26. Stertz and White, "Next Decade"; Woodruff, "A New Era for Auto Quality."

27. Treece, "Shaking Up Detroit"; and Joseph B. White and Jacqueline Mitchell, "Detroit Rolls Out Old Ploy: Quotas," *The Wall Street Journal*, January 14, 1991, p. B1.

28. Stacey, "No Domestic Is American."

29. Alex Taylor III, "Japan's New U.S. Car Strategy," *Fortune*, September 10, 1990, pp. 67–80.

30. "Iacocca Talks on What Ails Detroit," *Fortune*, February 20, 1990, pp. 68–72.

31. Jessica Lee and James R. Healey, "Trade: 'Much More' to Do," *USA Today*, January 10, 12, 1992, p. 1A.

32. Alex Taylor III, "Why Toyota Keeps Getting Better, and Better, and Better," *Fortune*, November 19, 1990, p. 68.

33. Ibid., p. 66.

34. Ibid.

35. Ibid., p. 69.

36. Larry Armstong, "So Far, Nissan's Catch-Up Plan Hasn't Caught on," *Business Week*, September 17, 1990, pp. 59–66; Alex Taylor III, "Nissan's Bold Bid for Market Share," *Fortune*, January 1, 1990, pp. 99–101.

37. Krystal Miller, "Honda Motors Seeks to Reclaim Its Youth," *The Wall Street Journal*, October 2, 1991, p. A4; Steve Kicken, "Honda's Next Move," *Forbes*, December 24, 1990, pp. 146, 147; Hideo Sugiura, "How Honda Localizes Its Global Strategy," *Sloan Management Review*, Fall 1990, pp. 77–82; Stewart Toy, "The Americanization of Honda," *Business Week*, April 25, 1988, pp. 90–96.

38. Carla Rapoport, "Mazda's Bold New Global Strategy," *Fortune*, December 17, 1990, pp. 109–113; Treece, "Ford and Mazda Shared"; Patrick E. Cole, "Mazda Rolls out a Poor Man's Maserati," *Business Week*, June 26, 1989, p. 66.

39. Karen Lowry Miller and Larry Armstrong, "Mitsubishi Pulls out the Stops," *Business Week*, May 6, 1991, pp. 64–68; Cleveland Horton, "Mitsubishi Maps Solo Success," *Advertising Age*, July 2, 1990, pp. 3, 33.

40. Krystal Miller, "European Luxury Auto Makers Resort to Discounts in Drive to Jump Start Sales," *The Wall Street Journal*, April 29, 1991, pp. B1, B8.

41. Martha T. Moore, "Rivals Gain Ground with Lower Prices," *USA Today*, March 3, 1992.

42. Terence Roth, "Porsche Drives through Rough Market, Managing to Steer Away from Suitors," *Wall Street Journal*, September 20, 1991, p. B3.

43. John Templeman, "Lining Up for the World's Biggest Demolition Derby," *Business Week*, September 23, 1991, p. 55.

44. Shawn Tully, "Europe Hits the Brakes on 1992," *Fortune*, December 17, 1990, p. 137.

45. Ibid.; Richard A. Melcher, "The Nasty Pileup in Europe's Auto Industry," *Business Week*, September 17, 1990, pp. 48–49.

46. E. S. Browning, "Europe's Car Makers Struggle to Adopt Japan's Efficient Style, but Labor Balks," *The Wall Street Journal*, November 22, 1991, p. A8.

47. Tully, "Europe Hits the Brakes."

48. Jonathan Kapstein, "Mitsubishi Is Taking a Back Road into Europe," *Business Week*, November 19, 1990, p. 64.

49. James B. Treece, "Will Japan Do to Europe What It Did to Detroit?" *Business Week*, May 7, 1990, pp. 52–53.

50. Brian S. Moskal, "It's Back-Scratching Time in Detroit: UAW–GM Contract Fulfills Needs on Both Sides," *Industry Week*, October 15, 1990, pp. 72–73.

51. Micheline Maynard, "Democrats Aim Bill at Trade Deficit," *USA Today*, December 23, 1991, p. 5B.

INTEGRATIVE CASE ANALYSIS
CHAPTER 4

THE CHALLENGES FACING GENERAL MOTORS IN 1992

Now that you have read Chapter 4 and the Industry Note and reviewed the GM case for related concepts, let's see how the chapter's concepts apply to GM and its industry.

APPLICATIONS OF CONCEPTS TO THE CASE

Business Strategy—External Analysis

The fundamental concern of any single-business organization is beating its competition in the marketplace. The concern of a multiple-business organization is developing an appropriate corporate strategy to beat competitors in a variety of markets. Since the GM case focuses primarily on General Motors' major business, the manufacture and sale of automobiles, when you examine that case and when you do industry and competitor analyses for that company, you should focus primarily on that single business. The firm's other major and minor businesses could be analyzed in a similar fashion. You could, for example, do industry and competitor analyses for EDS, Hughes, GMAC, and some of the smaller companies that General Motors owns wholly or in part.

Global Environment

GM operates in a very competitive global environment. It has operations throughout the world, but its principal markets are in North America and Europe. The Japanese are formidable competitors in both markets. As business globalizes, GM must change. It must be more flexible, more responsive to customers. Its market share has plummeted due to increased global competition and its only major auto profits, those from its European markets, are threatened by the Japanese. President Bush's trip to Japan in January 1992 did little to change Japanese business strategies, but it did increase the likelihood of protective legislation for the U.S. auto industry.

General Environment

Technology and innovation drive the auto industry. GM has focused on a technology strategy, but the Japanese are beating it at its own game. GM recognizes innovation as critical, but its effort is lacking in comparison to competitors. GM is very concerned about its social responsibility and provides an annual report on its activities. The economy has a major impact on GM, for example, the 1991 recession sharply reduced sales. GM has made a substantial effort to improve relations with the UAW, giving it an outstanding benefit package in exchange for greater management control over operations. GM is using different raw materials to satisfy environmental and energy laws. Plastics and aluminum are slowly but surely replacing steel. Change is happening all around and throughout GM. In fact, GM's future rests on its efforts to cope with change and its ability to innovate.

Competitive Environment

There are two main components of concern in the competitive environment—industry and competitor analyses.

Porter's Analysis of the Auto Industry from GM's Perspective

Intensity of Current Competition

When we examine the Industry Note, it is clear that the high level of competition in the industry is based on a variety of factors. Cost, quality, styling, price, product line, and segmentation are all critical. General Motors pursued a strategy of employing high technology to get cost and quality in line, almost ignoring styling. Ford and Chrysler attempted to compete on the basis of cost and quality by better use of their employees through a variety of techniques. Toyota and Honda followed a strategy of lowering cost and improving quality by improving management methods, while Nissan, like General Motors, emphasized technology. Interestingly, both General Motors and Nissan failed to gain the competitive advantage at which their strategies were aimed. Toyota, Honda, Ford, and Chrysler fared better with their strategies. With the exception of Volkswagen, most European manufacturers compete at the high end of the market. They offer prestige, luxury, and engineering as key factors. Quality has always been the principal appeal of Mercedes, BMW, and Porsche. Quality will be a major issue in the resurgence of Jaguar.

Suppliers

Suppliers have a tremendous impact on General Motors. At the end of Chapter 3, we analyzed SWOT for GM since that chapter focused on that topic. You now should significantly extend your examination of strengths, weaknesses, opportunities, and threats as revealed in external environmental analysis. The Industry Note at the end of Chapter 4 provides you with considerable information on GM's external situation.

GM is working closer with its suppliers to improve quality and efficiency and reduce costs. It is requiring suppliers to cut back on prices, as well. Japanese auto manufacturers are noted for their ability to impose extremely rigid standards on their suppliers in terms of cost, quality, and time of delivery, so that they can use just-in-time manufacturing systems, which help to reduce cost and keep quality high.

Substitutes

For all practical purposes, there are no substitutes for automobiles, except in a few major cities such as New York, where subways carry millions of people a day, and in such cities as Miami and San Francisco, where public transportation carries a smaller, but still substantial percentage of the total traffic in a given day.

Buyers

The consumer is becoming more sophisticated and the automobile companies' distribution systems are contracting as a multitude of small dealers give way to a smaller number of megadealers. As buyers become more sophisticated, the product must improve to meet their demands. Firms that fail to consider customers' wants, as General Motors did in the past, will be in deep trouble.

New Entrants   In 1986 Hyundai entered the American car market, principally in the economy-car area, with its Excel model. A host of firms are entering the luxury-car market. Recent entrants include Cadillac, Nissan, and Toyota joining such stalwart favorites as Jaguar, BMW, Mercedes, and Porsche. Honda jumped into the upper end of the market, but not quite into the luxury field, with its Acura Legend. From a global perspective, the Japanese are entering Europe in force.

Other key factors that emerge in the Industry Note include concerns about the economy, union contract negotiations, and industry overcapacity.

Additional Case Analysis Considerations

Competitor Analysis   You should now choose whether to perform a competitor analysis. You should examine the strategies of all major competitors.

SWOT   At this point you should be able to identify the major strengths, weaknesses, opportunities, and threats facing General Motors in more detail than you did in Chapter 3. You have analyzed its strategy and its situation and you now have sufficient information about the industry to determine competitors' strategies and related factors. In the spaces below, create a profile of General Motors' strengths, weaknesses, opportunities, and threats in May 1991.

Strengths

1.
2.
3.
4.
5.
6.
7.
8.
9.
10.

Weaknesses

1.
2.
3.
4.
5.
6.
7.
8.
9.
10.

Opportunities

1.
2.
3.
4.
5.
6.
7.
8.
9.
10.

Threats

1.
2.
3.
4.
5.
6.
7.
8.
9.
10.

Some Questions to Ask Yourself

1. What impact did the assumptions GM strategists made have on the failure of GM's strategy?
2. How could GM have improved its forecasts?
3. How do you formulate strategy in a discontinuous environment?

STRATEGIC MANAGEMENT CHALLENGES

Virtually all of the strategic management challenges from Chapter 1 confront GM in its external environment. For example, GM is facing the potential of increased environmental regulation from the federal government. How do the other challenges affect GM?

CHAPTER 5

FUNDAMENTALS OF STRATEGY FORMULATION

I've been in this business 36 years, I've learned a lot and most of it doesn't apply anymore.

Charles E. Exley
CEO of NCR speaking of change
in the computer industry

The thing to do with the future is not to forecast it, but to create it. The objective of planning should be to design a desirable future and to invent ways to bring it about.

Russell Ackoff
Author and Consultant

CHAPTER OBJECTIVES

By the time you complete this chapter, you should be able to:

1. Define corporate, business, and functional strategies for the single business unit
2. List the basic action strategy choices a single business unit typically goes through, starting with finding a business
3. Describe how firms grow, discussing the types, areas, speed, and methods of growth
4. Indicate the ways in which firms may reduce investment
5. Describe each of the basic action strategies
6. Indicate the purposes of and give examples of pre-emptive strategies

CITICORP HAS LOTS OF DIFFERENT STRATEGIES

When John S. Reed became chairman of Citicorp in 1984, he immediately instilled a vision for the firm. It was to become a global consumer bank pursuing growth relentlessly. He set out to make that happen. He also established a strategy that dictated keeping the bank's portfolio of businesses diversified, partly so he could operate with minimal capital reserves, partly to keep the firm a major player, and partly because he inherited that broader strategy from the former chairman, Walter Wriston. Still, Reed's focus was clearly on the consumer side.

With $228 billion in assets, Citicorp was the largest U.S. banking company and the 11th largest in the world as of January 1991. Reed saw the global strategy as a very viable one. The Japanese, he noted, were not seeking to be global competitors. Rather, he felt that certain French and German banks were Citicorp's main competitors. When asked about how soon he expected visible progress toward his global strategy, Reed replied, "In terms of the institution as a whole, building the kind of global financial organization I would like to lead, we're dealing with a time horizon of 6 or 7 years. Short-term progress will show much sooner. We have lots of work to do—we're building a global business." Having revolutionized certain aspects of banking in countries as far apart as Spain and Taiwan, with 8 million households in 40 foreign countries already customers of Citibank, and with 16 million the target for 1994, Citibank certainly appears to be becoming a global bank.

Becoming a global bank hasn't been without its risks, however, or its costs. Reed inherited a troubled loan portfolio. High percentages of loans for real estate (15 percent), less developed countries (50 percent), and leveraged buyouts (18 percent) were nonperforming as of the third quarter of 1990. Reed had been so engrossed in building a global consumer bank that he had been unattentive to other segments of the bank's strategies. He was forced to turn his attention to those areas, as well. Furthermore, the Citicorp culture under Reed has shown an obliviousness to costs. The drive for global growth proceeded irrespective of costs. Now, Reed promises to cut $800 million from Citicorp's $10 billion in annual expenditures. Much of this will come from cutting personnel. Reed promises to cut employees from 92,000 to 84,000. Almost 4,000 have already been let go. Of the remainder, 1,850 will be from businesses that will be shut down or sold.

Reed has appointed individuals in each of the troubled loan areas to solve the nonperforming loan problems. New CEO Richard S. Braddock is expected to ride herd on costs. While Reed is a wholistic visionary, Braddock is very micro-oriented in his approach to management. He gets involved in details.

Reed has also been looking for a capital infusion. He has considered selling 20 percent of the firm's lucrative credit card business for a stake of $1 billion. He is said to be open to both a public stock offering or a sale to one individual. He might even consider selling stock in Citicorp itself.

Reed comments, "We're being criticized mainly on our real estate assets and on the capital front. Both criticisms are valid, and I take them to heart. One thing I hate is for people to dismiss criticism. That's a passport to suicide."

Sources: Carol J. Loomis, "Citicorp's World of Troubles," *Fortune*, January 14, 1991, pp. 90–99; David B. Hilder and Fred R. Bleakley, "Citicorp Reportedly Is Trying to Sell 20% of Credit-Card Unit for $1 Billion," *The Wall Street Journal*, February 20, 1991, p. A3; Noel Tichy and Ram Charan, "Citicorp Faces the World: An Interview with John Reed," *Harvard Business Review*, November–December 1990, pp. 135–144; Robert Guenther, "Global Reach: Citicorp Strives to Be McDonald's and Coke of Consumer Banking," *The Wall Street Journal*, August 9, 1989, pp. A1, A6.

John Reed and the other strategists at Citicorp continuously scan the firm's external and internal environments for signs that objectives and/or strategies must be changed. They practice strategic management in an often hostile and rapidly changing external environment. In recent years they have focused primarily on consumer banking, and they have had to change various strategies from time to time because of successes or failures in their strategic efforts. Through the changes, however, the vision and mission remain the same. Citicorp seeks to be a global consumer bank, but one with diversified businesses, as well.

When Reed recognizes that a strategy isn't working, he changes it. He won't stay with a strategy beyond its useful life. He realizes that strategies must be flexible, and managers must implement them flexibly. Reed has also learned that he must manage all aspects of Citicorp's strategies, not just the area in which he is most interested. John Reed is willing to roll the dice, to take risks, knowing that this may bring strategic failures. A major question is whether investors are willing to accept such failures as the price of success.

This chapter is concerned with the parts of the models shown in Figures 5.1 and 5.2. The chapter begins with a brief review of the history of business strategy, followed by an examination of the basic action strategies available to business as part of corporate strategy. Brief discussions of business strategies, grand strategies, pre-emptive strategies, and emerging strategies conclude the chapter.

STRATEGY

Once strategists have assessed and forecasted present and future SWOT, determined core competencies and strategic capabilities, and determined and prioritized strategic objectives, they proceed to formulate strategy. Strategies tell how the firm will get to where it wants to be.

The word *strategy* is derived from the Greek word for general, *strategos*. Until the 19th century, the term related strictly to the plans of action used by military forces in battle. More recently, it has taken on new meanings, now frequently

FIGURE 5.1   The Organization—A Strategic Management Process Model

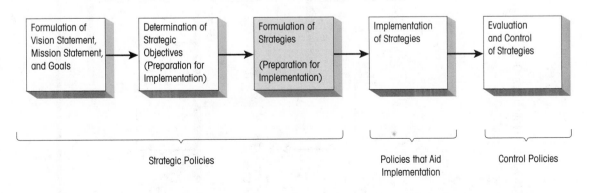

FIGURE 5.2 Objectives Determination and Strategy Formulation

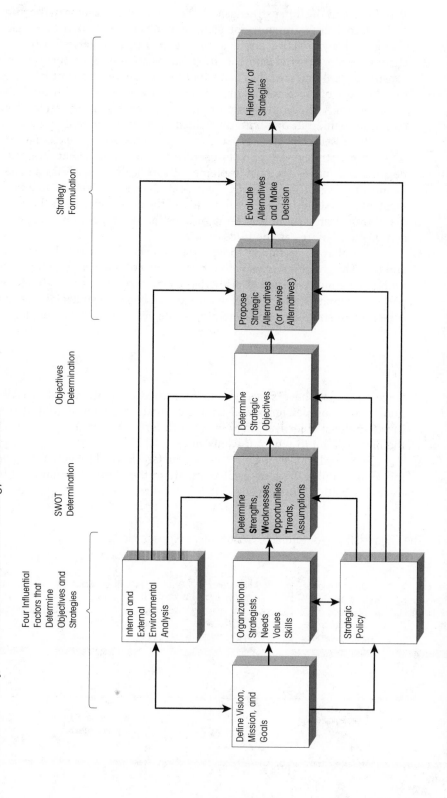

referring to the endeavors of organizations, primarily business organizations, to anticipate, respond to, and survive in their environments. As we mentioned in Chapter 1, *strategy* is defined differently in the various organizational contexts in which the term may be encountered; however, there is general agreement that a strategy is a major organizational plan of action to reach a major organizational objective.

Evolution of the Process

Strategy is formulated as part of the strategic management process. Strategic management evolved from the process of **long-range planning.**[1] Historically, most organizations concentrated their strategic efforts on the development of either of two primary strategies, or sometimes both in combination: a basic-action strategy, such as internal growth, conglomerate diversification, or retrenchment and/or a focal marketing strategy, such as low price. While almost every organization established this type of long-range plan or strategy, few formulated strategies in other critical areas of the organization.

That has all changed. As more and more organizations recognized that their strategic environments had become much too complex and unstable for such limited approaches, they began looking beyond customers, suppliers, and competitors to focus on virtually all key elements of both internal and external environments. For example, more firms, both single- and multiple-SBU organizations, incorporated social responsibility strategies into their hierarchies of strategies. Similarly, organizations formulated strategies for developing and maintaining beneficial organizational cultures.

As shown in Figure 5.3, comparing the degree of environmental complexity (from simple to complex) and environmental stability (from stable to dynamic) has led to four types of environments and four historical patterns of strategic management. This figure shows the influence of various key factors. In the 1960s, the economy grew naturally as it had since World War II and the Korean conflict. There was little competition and not much changed. Slowly, however, the environment became more dynamic and a little more complex, giving rise to a need for strategic management characterized by more scientific, quantitative, financially driven techniques. The term *strategic management* was applied in the 1970s to recognize the whole process of formulation, implementation, and control, rather than stopping at formulation. This term also recognized the increasing of complexity of the environment.

Under the influence of Michael Porter, a competitor-based approach evolved through much of the 1980s. Only near the end of the decade, when change and complexity threatened to become overwhelming, did the need for change-based strategic management become obvious. **Change-based strategic management** is concerned with managing in complex, turbulent environments. Characteristics of this type of strategic approach were noted at the end of Chapter 1.

Since 1970, strategic environments have become both more complex and more dynamic. The type of strategic management necessary in the 1990s is much different from what worked in the 1960s. In fact, many organizations did not even develop comprehensive strategic management processes until the late 1970s or

FIGURE 5.3 Four Types of Environments and Related Strategic Management Concepts

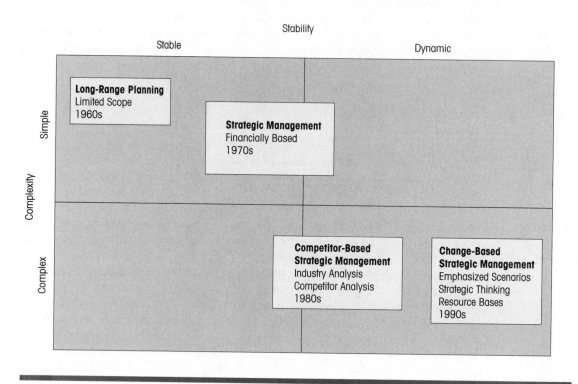

early 1980s. For example, GM drafted its first comprehensive corporate strategy in 1979, and the Walt Disney Company first did so in 1984.

Heublein's story is typical of a long-range planning approach based largely on the corporate and business components of strategy. In 1965, Heublein stated only three strategic objectives:

1. To make Smirnoff vodka the number 1 brand of liquor in the world
2. To continue sales growth of 10 percent a year through internal growth, acquisition, or both
3. To maintain a return on equity above 15 percent

The essence of its strategic plan of action to achieve these objectives involved the following elements:

1. Substantial advertising
2. Certain types of distribution
3. Careful selection of products and acquisitions with high cash flows (to fund the advertising)[2]

Heublein thus succinctly captured its perceived objectives and its methods of achieving those objectives. Note that Heublein did not embellish its strategy with any considerations that were not associated directly with its grand strategy. Competitive strategies have generated renewed interest as the works of Michael

Porter (which are discussed in Chapters 4 and 6) and others in the field have become widely known.

In contrast to the Heublein example, such firms as IBM, Toyota, GM, Siemens, and Xerox take broad approaches to strategy formulation. Their hierarchies of strategies cover all elements of corporate, business, and functional concerns. These **hierarchies of strategies** embody strategies for coping with the business-choice decision, competition, and efficient functional operations. They are also highly coordinated. (See Table 5.1.) These firms review all of their strategies annually as SBUs, and support functions (such as production facilities) establish annual objectives and plans. This process takes place within the framework of corporate policies established for strategy formulation, since some corporate strategy considerations, such as diversification and divestment, constrain business and functional strategies.

Whether or not a hierarchy of strategies is consciously determined or formally stated, every organization has one, if only by default in the sum of effects of actions taken. Many organizations can enjoy impressive successes in the short run without consciously formulating strategic objectives or plans to reach those objectives. It is exceedingly rare, however, for a firm to succeed in the long run without first determining what it wants to be (stating its vision, mission, goals, and objectives), and how it plans to realize those purposes (formulating strategy and policies).

Strategists must learn to manage complexity and change, as executives in the auto, banking, personal computer, and health-care industries, among others, have discovered. A major part of the strategic management process in the 1990s is strategic thinking. Strategists use strategic planning sessions to make sure that they have considered all pertinent issues. They formulate strategies to provide direction, recognizing that many required actions will change, often rapidly, in response to turbulent environments. The important part of strategy thus becomes the process itself, the action of thinking through the issues. This process is often employed in conjunction with scenario forecasting, as discussed in Chapter 4. As Lawrence G. Bossidy, then GE's vice chairman and director of strategic planning, acknowledged, "We find it impossible to forecast beyond three years any more."[3] GE uses strategic thinking to focus its strategic efforts.

Strategic thinking as an approach to strategy formulation becomes even more important when strategic discontinuities are considered. A **strategic discontinuity** occurs when gaps appear in the logical sequence of events in some strategic arena. For example, a competitor may discover a new technology that makes another firm's technology obsolete, making it impossible for that firm to proceed on its familiar path.[4] By constantly scanning the environment for signals of potentially discontinuous events, asking what-if questions, constructing scenarios, and thinking through the issues, firms can be better prepared strategically. Chapter 6 will discuss other strategies for coping with strategic discontinuity. Chapter 3 covered measures to counter technological discontinuities.

Levels of Strategy

Organizations have to formulate strategies at three major levels: corporate, business, and functional.[5] (See Table 5.1.) These levels of strategy may be described as follows:

TABLE 5.1   Hierarchy of Strategies, Primarily for a Single Business Unit

Corporate Strategy

Determines the business or businesses in which the firm will or should compete and how it will fundamentally conduct the business or businesses. (This is the focus of many grand strategies.) Corporate strategy answers these questions.

A. Does the organization have a strategic advantage or an innate interest in some business?
B. Does the company want to compete or find a niche?
C. Does the company seek to concentrate on one product or product line, or on multiple products or product lines?
D. Will the corporation be innovative or imitative?
E. Does the company want or need to grow, stabilize, reduce its investment, turn company fortunes around, or defend itself against a takeover?

Basic-action strategies available to single-SBU or multiple-SBU corporations (related to B through E above):

1. Competing or finding a niche
2. Concentration or multiple products
3. Strategic imperatives
   a. Innovation
   b. Quality
   c. Continuous improvement
   d. Flexibility
   e. Speed
4. Growth
   a. intensive, integrative, or diversified
   b. Regional, national, or international
   c. Internal, or by acquisition, merger, or joint venture
   d. Gradual or rapid
5. Stabilization
6. Investment reduction
   a. Retrenchment
   b. Divestment (for multiple-SBU firms only)
   c. Selected asset reduction
   d. Cost cutting
   e. Liquidation
   f. Selling out
   g. Profit extraction
7. Turnaround
8. Takeover defense
9. Combination

Business (SBU) Strategy

Answers the question, how do we compete in this business? (This is the focus of many grand strategies.)

A. Marketing
   1. Target market
   2. Product

TABLE 5.1 Cont'd.   Hierarchy of Strategies, Primarily for a Single Business Unit

    3. Promotion
    4. Distribution
    5. Price
B. Generic
    1. Differentiation
    2. Low cost
    3. Focus

Functional Strategy

Supports other strategies and answers the question, how do we obtain the most effective and efficient use of our resources? (This is the focus of a few grand strategies.)

A. Economic functional strategies
    1. Marketing (all aspects that are not the focus of business strategy)
    2. Operations—production or service generation
    3. Finance
    4. Personnel/human resource management
    5. Information systems
    6. Research and development, market research
    7. Other significant areas
B. Management functional strategies
    1. Planning
    2. Organizing (includes human resource management)
    3. Leading
    4. Controlling
    5. Problem solving
    6. Communicating
    7. Representing
    8. Integrating
    9. Management systems
    10. Organizational culture

- **Corporate strategy** is the process by which the firm identifies the business or businesses in which it should compete and indicates how it will conduct itself fundamentally in that business or those businesses.
- **Business strategy** describes how the organization will compete in a specific business.
- **Functional strategy** describes how the organization will support its business strategy, focusing on making the most effective and efficient use of resources.

CORPORATE STRATEGY

Corporate strategy focuses on two questions: In what business(es) will we or should we compete? How shall we fundamentally conduct that business/those businesses? The answer to the first question is derived directly from vision and mission. In the single-business-unit organization, this determines the owner's choice of business. It answers the first question, strategic advantage or innate interest, in Table 5.1 under Corporate Strategy. The multiple-business-unit organization must answer this question for each business and for all businesses considered together in an organized fashion. This usually involves some type of portfolio analysis.

A correct answer to this question is vitally important because being in the wrong business is usually fatal. Railroad firms, for example, decided at the turn of the century to stay out of the automobile industry, and later they opted out of the air travel industry. To their ultimate misfortune, they saw themselves as being in the railroad business, not the transportation business. Sears, on the other hand, has seen itself as a provider of consumer services, not just a retailer of durable goods. Partly because of improved consumer marketing in its core retail business and partly because of other actions that seemed appropriate from this perspective, Sears is financially viable while it might not have survived had it stuck to retailing only.[6] Figure 5.4 details the decisions required by corporate strategy. While this figure portrays strategic actions primarily from a single-SBU perspective, it also includes the multiple-SBU options that become available as firms begin to grow.

The **basic action strategies** identified in Figure 5.4 include finding a niche, head-on competition, concentration, multiple products, strategic imperatives, growth of several types, stabilization, investment reduction, turnaround, takeover defense, and an option to combine the above strategies. Because basic action strategies, most of which can become grand strategies, position a firm in an industry or across industries, the answer to the second question of how a firm fundamentally conducts itself is also critically important. A poorly positioned firm has little or no chance of long-term success. At one time, for example, Westinghouse had poorly positioned businesses in many industries, largely because of inferior productivity and quality. By creating a Productivity Center and changing business-unit cultures to make them more productivity and quality oriented, Westinghouse cut costs, penetrated more markets, divested nonproductive businesses or those that didn't fit with the others, and became much more profitable in its nonfinancial-service SBU.[7]

The answers to the two questions about the business(es) in which to compete and fundamental business conduct depend on the firm's answers to the four basic questions listed below. The first of these questions concerns what business or businesses the firm will enter. The second, and third, and fourth concern how the firm will engage in its business or businesses and what its other basic action strategies will be.

1. Does the organization have a strategic advantage or an innate interest in some business?
2. Does the company want to compete or to find a niche?
3. Will the company obey the strategic imperatives?

FIGURE 5.4 Basic Action Strategies

For Principally Single-SBU Organizations

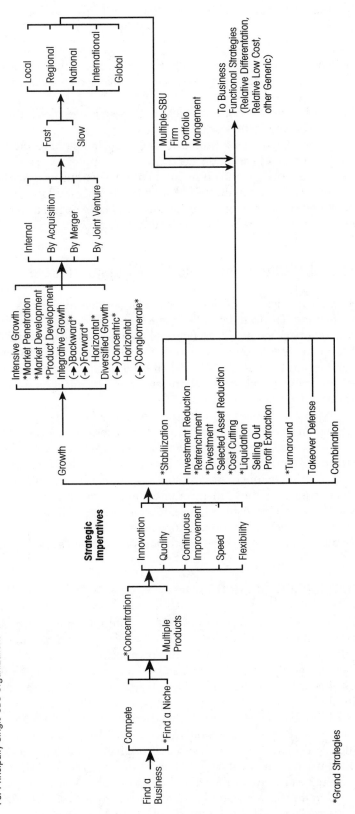

*Grand Strategies

(→)Multiple-SBU Strategies

4. Does the company want or need to grow, stabilize, reduce its investment, defend itself against a takeover attempt, or turn its fortunes around?

The specific ways a firm's answers to these questions affect its corporate strategy vary with many factors.

Clearly, whether a firm has a single business or is a multiple-SBU organization has a major bearing on the details of its strategies. The single-SBU organization is primarily caught up in competition—its business strategy—and is much less concerned than multiple-SBU firms with other available basic action strategies. Many firms engage in only one business and have no intention of leaving that field, but others are not bound by such restricted views.

Natural Strategic Advantage or Innate Interest

Many companies enter a field of endeavor because they perceive a need that no one is satisfying. The founder of Federal Express, Frederick W. Smith, saw the need for overnight package deliveries between major cities. He believed that a fleet of small jet airplanes could do what no other mail service could do. He was right. Other examples of natural strategic advantages include the sale of various forms of technology to developing nations and the gas-mileage advantage that Japanese cars have historically had over U.S. autos.

Many businesses, on the other hand, are formed simply to satisfy the owner or top manager's desire to be in a particular business, or, especially in the case of small businesses, because the founder's expertise focuses on the area. Many people start restaurants because they have always wanted to own one, and good mechanics often open service stations. Similarly, the top manager of a larger organization may move the firm into a new venture simply because of a personal desire to own a publishing house, foundry, or restaurant chain. The multiple-SBU firm must develop a rationale for choosing and managing businesses from the overall corporate perspective. Such portfolio strategies are the subject of Chapter 7.

Competition or Niche

Organizations, whether single-SBU or multiple-SBU, must decide whether to compete directly with others or to find a niche. Of course, all businesses compete with other businesses (or nonprofit organizations) in some way. The question is whether the firm chooses to compete head-on with other firms in the same business or to seek a niche, that is, a market that no other firm has chosen to enter directly.

Most businesses compete head-on with others. Historically, for example, Sears, J. C. Penney, and Montgomery Ward have completed directly with each other. Wal-Mart, on the other hand, originally sought to locate in small towns where it would have no competition. In recent years, however, it has chosen to compete head-on with Kmart and other discount stores.[8]

Another firm that employs a niche strategy is Eastern Connection. Would you trust a package that absolutely, positively had to be there overnight to a firm with

200 trucks and no airplanes. A lot of people do. Eastern Connection has found its niche by serving a very small geographic area very well. Eastern delivers by 9 a.m. for an average price of $11.64 versus Federal Express's $15.50, and Federal Express doesn't guarantee delivery until 10:30 a.m.[9] Nordstrom's (or Nordie's, as it is affectionately known to its customers) has found a unique niche for its market in apparel: it provides excellent service at high prices. Few among its clientele balk at paying more. In fact, Nordstrom's has been so successful in the northwestern United States that it has expanded to California and New Jersey.[10] More recently, even big firms are going after niches as their main markets mature. For example, between 1988 and 1991, IBM purchased equity stakes of over $500 million in niche players in order to gain access to smaller markets.[11]

Niches are not always secure, however; successful niche strategies tend to provoke competition, as the makers of the Mercedes luxury car line discovered. Mercedes demonstrated that there was a market for high-quality, high-priced cars; now it has 30 or so competitors for its market, including the Japanese automakers with the Lexus and Infiniti.[12] A niche can involve other disadvantages, too. Wendy's had the high-priced hamburger niche all to itself, but found that its high prices made it vulnerable to competitors selling chicken and seafood.

Concentration or Multiple Products/Businesses

A concentration strategy focuses the organization on one product or product line, in essentially one market, using primarily one type of technology.[13] It is by far the most frequently encountered grand strategy. Kentucky Fried Chicken's slogan says it only does one thing, and therefore it does it right.

There are obvious reasons for choosing a concentration strategy. First, an entrepreneur typically begins this way, entering a field that corresponds to a personal interest or an area of expertise. Second, this strategy involves less risk, at least in terms of resources, for a fledgling enterprise. In addition, the competition can more readily be identified and analyzed. Also, as the firm grows, the expertise required to manage it properly remains essentially the same. Such a firm's competitive advantage comes from employing a highly developed and focused marketing strategy. The details of this strategy vary, but most frequently include product quality and/or price, sensitivity to the demands of the customer or client, and some element of recognition in the marketplace.

A firm that used a concentration strategy would choose a basic action strategy from Figure 5.4, that would allow it to grow, but only through one product or service. Sometimes a firm diversifies only to find that it should have stayed with the one business or singular product or service in which it had developed expertise. Levi Strauss, for example, diversified, only to find that jeans were its most globally saleable product.[14] Other firms choose to stay with concentration strategies even after growing to enormous sizes. Michelin did this, for example, as this chapter's Global Strategic Challenge reveals.

This strategy has problems, as well. Concentration exposes the organization to the vagaries of the marketplace and the economy and to changes in technology. After all, people tire of products, as Izod found out when sales declined in the 1980s. Furthermore, growth reaches its peak once the market is saturated;

investment opportunities are fewer, and long-term profit potential declines as new entrants emerge in the industry. (Watch out, Mrs. Fields; here come The Original Cookie Company, Famous Amos, Chocolate Chip Factory, Cinnamon Sam's, and a host of others.) Such firms may choose to pursue the kinds of growth that result in multiple products in the next basic action strategy stage.[15]

Strategic Imperatives

In the 1990s survival depends on at least five **strategic imperatives,** or strategies that firms must follow: innovation, quality, continuous improvement, speed, and flexibility.

Innovation

Innovation is a vital grand strategy for numerous organizations. For example, for fiscal 1990, half of Hewlett-Packard's orders came from products that hadn't existed 2 years previously. Hewlett-Packard also has a major program of process innovation.[16] Other firms known for innovation include American Airlines, Apple Computers, Campbell Soup, Intel, 3M, GE, and Merck. As change accelerates and competition increases, innovation is becoming a strategic imperative. Recall from Chapter 3 that a firm can innovate based on product, process, marketing, or management techniques. The strategic choice at this point is whether or not to adopt a philosophy of innovation; it decides later to focus on product, process, marketing, and/or management innovation. Chapter 12 discusses a number of options for a firm to achieve an innovation strategy.

Quality[17]

Virtually every authority on strategy for the 1990s believes that high levels of quality will be necessary to compete. High quality will be part of table stakes for the game of business, and without it, firms' products or services simply won't be considered.

Continuous Improvement[18]

Continuous improvement, or kaizen, has been an important strategy for Japanese firms. Continuous improvement in products and processes allows them to beat their competitors by achieving both high differentiation and relatively low costs. North American and European firms have no choice but to follow.

Speed[19]

Allied very closely with the continuous improvement strategy is the speed strategy. The quicker the product or service can reach the market, the better the ability of the firm to gain market share. Smaller, more frequent changes, as required by continuous improvement, get the new product or service to market, or the new process implemented, more quickly.

Flexibility[20]

Vast changes in the internal and external environments mean that strategies must be flexible. Changes in strategy are inevitable, and incorporating an

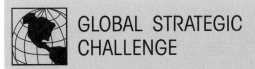

GLOBAL STRATEGIC CHALLENGE

MICHELIN DOES ONLY ONE THING, BUT IT DOES IT VERY WELL

The French firm, Michelin, makes only tires. A broad range of its tires are manufactured and sold in many countries. It is the ultimate example of the concentration strategy. It behaves as it always has; it secretly pursues only two objectives: long-term quality and market share. François Michelin runs the company with a tight fist. The company is extremely paternalistic, but punishes those who turn against it. The company is, as one former employee labeled it, "a paradox of sorts—a 19th century company that produces a 21st century product."

As a player in a global industry, however, Michelin has had to act strategically with 21st-century acumen. Michelin opted for global growth long before most of its competitors. It moved rapidly and extensively in the 1970s to become a global competitor. It also invested heavily in research and development, producing the first successful radial tire. While its research leadership has dimmed a bit, it is still recognized as producer of the highest-quality tire in the world. In 1990, however, it finds itself up against Japanese competitors, principally Bridgestone, with the purchase of Firestone, which has amassed the size to compete globally with Michelin and Goodyear.

The company pondered what strategic action to take to protect its interests. Diversification was a possibility, but the company opted instead to purchase Uniroyal-Goodrich, the American firm, for $1.5 billion. This made Michelin the largest player in the game with 20 percent of the market, compared to Goodyear's 17 percent and Bridgestone's 17 percent. The purchase is expected to pull earnings for the company down significantly for at least 2 years, but Monsieur François is not overly concerned. His obsession is with the long term, and the purchase was made with that in mind. He wants to be able to beat the Japanese at their own game of lowering prices to gain market share.

Source: E. S. Browning, "On a Roll: Long-Term Thinking and Paternalistic Ways Carry Michelin to Top," *The Wall Street Journal*, January 1, 1990, pp. A1, A8.

attitude of flexibility into their design helps forestall difficulties later in their implementation.

More Basic Action Strategies

Once the firm has decided whether to compete or find a niche, whether to concentrate on one product area or pursue multiple products, and whether to follow the strategic imperatives, the next major issues are whether to grow, stabilize, reduce investment, protect against a takeover, turn company fortunes around, or pursue a combination of these strategies. The answers to these questions form the crux of corporate strategy for single- and multiple-SBU firms. At the single-SBU level, these critical decisions depend on SWOT and a multitude of other factors. At the multiple-SBU level, these critical decisions depend on portfolio strategies.

Growth

Growth involves four primary considerations: the type of growth (intensive, integrative, or diversified growth), its geographic focus (on regional, national, or international markets), how it will take place (internally or externally through acquisitions, mergers, joint ventures, or other alliances), and how quickly it will take place.

Types of Growth   The choice of type of growth—intensive, integrative, or diversified—is critically important. **Intensive growth** is appropriate for the firm that has not fully exploited the existing opportunities in its current products and markets. There are three ways to achieve intensive growth: market penetration, market development, and product development.[21]

Market penetration efforts seek increased sales of present products through more aggressive marketing. Market penetration is characteristic of the mature industry with homogeneous products. Coca-Cola had operated in Great Britain for many years when, in 1986, it formed a joint venture with Cadbury-Schweppes to bottle Coca-Cola products there. The partners poured millions into plant construction and advertising to gain market share. In just two years, Coke's sales rose 55 percent.[22]

Market development involves taking existing products into new markets. When U.S.-based United Parcel Service expanded into 180 other countries, it took its product to new markets.[23] The market development strategy is especially important to firms whose products, while sound, have not reached all markets.

Product development consists of developing improved products for current markets. When you see Colgate toothpaste in a pump, you are witnessing this strategy in action. Product development is extremely important to firms with maturing products that need to extend their product life cycles. The Datsun 240Z became the 260Z, which became the 280Z, which became the 280ZX, which has become the 300ZX. Most recently, Nissan has "started with a clean page" to produce a whole different look for the 300ZX. Why? Because of competition in a maturing high-performance sports car industry.

The second type of growth, **integrative growth,** can move the firm in three directions: backward, forward, and horizontally.[24] This is generally, but not always, a multiple-SBU strategy. The organization that opts for **backward integration** attempts to acquire control over its suppliers.[25] When Birmingham Steel Corporation acquired scrap and iron ore suppliers, it was practicing backward integration.[26] A business typically follows this acquisition strategy for the purpose of reducing costs to make the firm's sales and distribution arrangements more cost-competitive or more responsive to its needs. This strategy is particularly important to the firm in a mature industry, where price becomes a major strategic weapon.

The firm that opts for **forward integration** attempts to acquire control of its distributors. When Kodak acquired American Photo, a major photo-finishing company, in 1987, it was ensuring an outlet for its photographic papers and chemicals.[27]

When a firm attempts to acquire its competition, it is practicing **horizontal integration.** Both Humana and Hospital Corporation of America, for instance, have acquired several hundred hospitals as they seek to dominate the health-care industry.[28] This is a single-SBU strategy.

The final major type of growth is **diversification,** in which firms seek businesses in other industries or, more narrowly, in other product lines. Diversification becomes an important alternative when an organization has all of its eggs in one basket and has the internal expertise and extra cash flow to expand into other areas. Diversification can smooth out corporate revenues from highly seasonal businesses. Bernard Arnault, the French business visionary, has built a huge business empire in Europe, including firms in luggage and leather goods (Louis Vuitton); retailing (Bon Marché, Celine, Givenchy, Christian Dior); clothing, accessories, and toiletries (Christian Dior, Givenchy); champagne (Moët & Chandon, Dom Perignon); cognac (Hennessy); and spirits (Johnnie Walker, Dewars, Gordon's, and Simi).[29] Diversification is also advisable when current businesses or products are in mature or declining stages of the product life cycle, ultimately threatening revenues. It may also be desirable when significant external opportunities are perceived. Diversification is predominantly a multiple-SBU strategy. Michael Porter's research indicates that most diversification strategies dissipate rather than increase returns to stockholders, because most acquisitions are quickly divested.[30]

There are three kinds of diversification: concentric, horizontal, and conglomerate diversification. With **concentric diversification,** the business seeks to add new products that are technologically related to its current products. Normally these products will be marketed to new customers. When Levi Strauss added women's clothing to its men's clothing line, it was practicing concentric diversification. When Josephine Rissich, a professional photographer who shows her work at regional art shows, reveals her new line of photo imprints at museums, she is practicing concentric diversification. This is normally a single-SBU strategy, but it may also be adopted by multiple-SBU organizations.

Horizontal diversification involves the development of new products aimed at current customers, but the new products are not technologically related to existing ones. Over the years, AMF has added pleasure boats, bicycles, skis, and other athletic equipment to its original offerings in order to provide new products for its current customers. This is usually a multiple-SBU strategy.

Conglomerate diversification involves both new products or businesses and new customers. The firm usually enters into conglomerate diversification to offset some deficiency, but it may also pursue this strategy to take advantage of a significant opportunity. Technically, of course, once a firm enters into more than one business, it ceases to be a single-business firm. Such organizations as RJR-Nabisco and GE are conglomerate companies. This is always a multiple-SBU strategy. Not all conglomerate diversification efforts prove beneficial. When

Chrysler acquired aerospace and defense firms, Lee Iacocca admits it diverted money and management attention from the crucial task of developing a new line of autos. Chrysler eventually sold those companies.[31]

Where to Grow   Most firms start by serving a particular geographic region. They may then mount national sales efforts, and even attempt to repeat domestic successes in foreign countries. Naturally, geographic growth is highly desirable because it increases total market size, but not all firms can be national or global. Hooter's, a prominent regional restaurant chain in the southeastern United States, has stated that it does not believe it should go national and attempt to compete with major chains.[32] It intends to grow, but only in the South or in areas where it feels it has a similar target market such as in Colorado. Most firms find, however, that geographic growth and success go hand-in-hand. What is imperative is that such growth not come too quickly. International growth, in particular, involves many difficulties. It is not simply an extension of domestic efforts, but requires an understanding of numerous, complex differences in culture, logistics, social standards, economics, and politics. One area of bright promise for U.S. firms in their competition with foreign firms lies in exporting services, an opportunity that Federal Express and UPS have seized with their overnight delivery services.[33]

AT CITICORP

Citicorp chose to become a global company. With 8 million customers in over 40 countries, it is rapidly becoming global.

How to Grow   The organization can grow in two basic ways: internally or externally by means of acquisitions, mergers, joint ventures or other strategic alliances, licensing, and other arrangements.[34] Internal growth offers many advantages, one of the most important of which is continuity of management style. This strategy also has its limitations. It takes much longer to expand and become more diverse through internal growth than through external growth. Nonetheless, many firms have grown to substantial size primarily through internal growth, including Coca-Cola Company, Radio Shack (Tandy), Anheuser Busch, and American Airlines. On the other hand, such firms as PepsiCo, TransAmerica, and Banc-One have grown externally, primarily through acquisition.

Coca-Cola looked more favorably on acquisitions in the early 1980s in an effort to become less dependent on the soft-drink industry. Its 1981 acquisition of Columbia Pictures was a major step toward that end. Banc One has been touted as the bank with the most skill at acquiring other banks and turning them around. It succeeds at this primarily by applying tight controls and culture management.[35] This chapter's Strategic Challenge discusses the Banc One strategy. One of the primary means of going global has been alliances, often in the form of mergers and

STRATEGIC CHALLENGE

BANC ONE CORPORATION— GROWTH THROUGH ACQUISITION

Banc One Corporation, headquartered in Columbus, Ohio, has grown by leaps and bounds in recent years. For years, its only market was Columbus, but then Banc One slowly, but surely, began to acquire other banks throughout Ohio, expanding into Indiana and Louisiana. Then in 1990, Banc One's expansion efforts exploded. It made three acquisitions, ranging from $463 to $45 million. Two of these acquisitions were in Texas; the other in Ohio. A year later, it expanded to Kentucky and Colorado, with three sizeable acquisitions ranging from $210 to $378 million. Then in early 1992, Banc One made five acquisitions, ranging from $81.4 million to $1.2 billion, moving into Arizona for the first time with the acquisition of Valley National Corporation, headquartered in Phoenix. It also consolidated its already strong position in Texas with its $782-million acquisition of Texas Bankshares of Dallas. Having tripled its asset base in less than three years, these latest acquisitions enabled Banc One to become the seventh-ranked bank in the U.S. with $72 billion in total assets.

Chairman John B. McCoy described the acquisitions as Banc One's continuing pattern of acquiring firms whose bottom lines it believed it could improve dramatically—with changes in management style, organizational culture and improved management control, especially with regard to loan policies. Banc One has improved acquired firms in the past, but some analysts fear that the two huge acquisitions in 1992 could stretch the banks's capabilities to enact such changes. Furthermore, Valley National is perceived by several analysts to have numerous, sizeable risky loans in its portfolio, a situation Banc One has always avoided in the past. However, McCoy downplays this issue, indicating the firm feels comfortable in its abilities to overcome problems. Banc One markets itself as the Wal-Mart or McDonald's of the banking industry, focusing on low risk portfolio choices, such as auto and home loans. Says Mr. McCoy, "We're Like McDonald's. If they open one hundred new restaurants, they're not going to have a problem. They know hamburgers."

The real question remains as to whether Banc One can sustain high profit levels while undergoing rapid growth. But McCoy, the architect of much of the bank's recent success, firmly believes his staff can make the acquisition of four large banks in under two years a very profitable strategy.

SOURCE: Gabriella Stern, "Banc One Corp. Continues to Expand Across the U.S.," *The Wall Street Journal*, April 15, 1992, p. B4.

joint ventures. Peat Marwick, the giant U.S. accounting firm, merged with Netherlands based KMG Main Hurdman to form KPMG in order to build a global presence.[36]

Typically, businesses begin as single-SBU firms, commonly with one product. As they grow, normally internally, they begin to look for new markets, new products, or new areas of supply, distribution, or competition. At this point growth often comes to depend on external sources of nourishment. Still, internal actions carry many firms for many years before external growth strategies become an issue.

Both acquisition and merger involve combining organizations; they differ mainly in the nature of the organization that emerges. When one firm acquires another, the acquiring firm retains its identity as the dominant firm and the other becomes subordinate to it. When RJR Industries acquired Nabisco Brands, for example, Nabisco's top management began to report to RJR's top management, though Nabisco managers later began to rise to the top of the combined organization. Typically, acquisitions have the goal of increasing diversification. When two firms merge, however, a new organizational entity is born. When Nabisco and Standard Brands had merged earlier, a new entity, Nabisco Brands, resulted. A new management structure was formed, with top managers of both organizations taking various positions in the new hierarchy.[37]

Joint ventures are temporary partnerships formed for one specific project. For example, when Alcoa and Japan's Kobe Steel combined to build a plant in Moka, Japan to produce aluminum cans for the Asian market, they did something that neither could have accomplished equally as well alone.[38] Similarly, when the U.S. firm Cypress Semiconductor formed a joint venture called Interconnect with a Soviet chip research and design firm, both firms prospered. The Soviets lacked the manufacturing expertise that Cypress provided. Similarly, the Soviets had some of the best chip designers in the world, which Cypress felt it lacked.[39] Historically, firms in Europe, South America, and Asia have made more use of joint ventures than firms in the United States and Canada, but in recent years U.S. and Canadian firms have turned increasingly to this mechanism.[40]

Speed of Growth   One of the greatest mistakes a firm can make is to grow beyond its capabilities. Such a mistake was one of the major causes of Ames Department Stores' bankruptcy. It takes time to develop the managers and management systems necessary to cope with the problems that accompany a large size, especially in rapid growth by acquisition (as Ames learned from acquiring Zayre). Further, Ames's high debt put it in a precarious position.[41]

A firm's problems vary with its stage of growth and with the type of growth it attempts. Organizations must manage their way through these problems before further growth is advisable.

AT CITICORP

Citicorp has used a combination of strategies to grow. It grew internally and through acquisition. Now, it is turning to cost cutting strategies, as well.

Stabilization

Some organizations are satisfied not to grow (or to grow very little) and to follow the **stabilization** strategy. Many owners of small businesses, such as restaurants, insurance agencies, and small manufacturing firms, are satisfied to make only limited profits and not to grow beyond a certain size. Understandably, the president of a large bank in a highly competitive metropolitan area told one of the authors that he would be quite happy just to maintain his 46-percent market share.

Stabilization provides an opportunity to catch one's breath between growth periods or during turnaround periods. As a long-term strategy, however, it leaves the organization vulnerable to aggressive competition.

Investment Reduction

A firm may choose to follow a program of **investment reduction** in which it simply reduces the amount of capital invested in the organization or in a specific SBU. This move may become necessary in financial difficulties or it may be an intentional program to remove assets from a successful business (a profit extraction) to create cash flow for other parts of the business or for distribution to owners. Investment may be reduced by several means.

Retrenchment is a major, across-the-board effort to reduce cash outflows, and where possible, through the sale of assets, for example, increase cash inflows. This reduces the scope and size of the business, lessens the firm's exposure to risk, allows the company to concentrate on what it does well in order to become more profitable, or simply promotes survival. Retrenchment is generally viewed as a temporary measure. One company forced to retrench substantially in order to survive was BankAmerica. It sold off major assets, cut expenses, and reduced the number of its branches significantly in order to survive.[42]

At the corporate level of multiple-SBU firms, **divestment**—selling or liquidating individual SBUs—is the primary means of retrenchment. Often firms acquire businesses that fail to provide sufficient ROI. When this occurs, firms are often divested. Occasionally, such a divestment generates a loss, but long-term losses that might result from failure to divest must be estimated and balanced against short-term losses from divestment.

At the single-SBU level, reduction of selected assets is the usual course taken to reduce investment. A firm may decide not to build a new plant, for example, thus limiting the number of markets it can serve. A firm may close existing plants, as Ford did in the mid-1980s and GM began to do a few years later. Another common form of asset reduction is the decision not to give pay raises. Cost cutting is often emphasized, as well; for example, a manufacturer may cut costs by moving corporate headquarters from its plush rental facility back into the plant. When Cummins Company encountered problems in its turnaround efforts in 1989, one of its first actions was to reduce expenses across the board.[43]

Liquidation and selling out represent the ultimate in investment reduction, since the amount of investment is reduced to zero. At the single-SBU level, these options signify the ultimate disaster, but the multiple-SBU firm can use cash from these processes to purchase other, more desirable SBUs.

Profit extraction is a strategy commonly followed by multiple-SBU firms for business subunits that are in profitable, usually mature industries in which growth is either not possible or not desirable for some reason. The firm can use the cash flow from reducing investment and extracting profits for the benefit of other SBUs. Typically the SBU that yields profits will be sold to another organization. It is also common for an entrepreneur to extract profits before selling a firm to an acquiring organization.

Takeover Defense

Several **takeover defense** strategies are available. In a very popular one, a firm can add a fair price provision to the corporate charter that requires that all stockholders receive the same price for their stock in the event of a takeover bid. This defense prevents anyone who attempts to acquire a controlling interest from offering progressively higher prices for outstanding shares. The charters of many firms also contain provisions that require overwhelming stockholder approval of takeovers (80 percent is a common figure). Other firms rely on stockholders with extremely substantial holdings to prevent takeover bids from succeeding. Still others attempt to buy back voting stock to increase their control or to stagger the terms of the directors, thus making it difficult for dissident stockholders to gain control of the board. Some companies attempt to issue new stock.

Many firms have relied on "poison pills", in which shareholders receive the right to purchase stock at discounted prices. The firms attempting the takeover are forced to deal with existing management for these shares, which become so exorbitantly expensive when offered externally that bidders quickly forget the idea. Other firms have employed what is known as "the PAC-Man defense", attempting to acquire the companies that are attempting to acquire them. Yet another tactic is to establish special voting requirements when certain levels of unfriendly stock purchases are reached.

Many firms defend themselves by closely guarding their cash positions, reinvesting quickly to avoid having tempting amounts of cash on hand; diversification is a sound way of using such cash. Some have added terms to their bond contracts allowing bondholders to demand principal repayment in the event of a hostile takeover. This "poison-put" provision makes a company less digestible. Many firms seek the help of third parties, offering to sell their stock to friendly individuals or companies known as *white knights*, who will in fact control the company. (This might be known as the lesser-of-two-evils defense.) Some assume heavy debt loads to seem less valuable. Others use ESOPs (Employee Stock Option Plans) to put stock in friendly hands. In an unusual defense, all top managers of Borden Inc. signed a contract to quit in the face of a hostile takeover.[44] Many experts provide advice on how to estimate a company's vulnerability and then prepare a defense.

In case their defenses fail, however, most management groups prepare "golden parachutes" for themselves to make sure that, in the event of a takeover, they will be handsomely compensated. Finally, the U.S. Supreme Court upheld an Indiana law prohibiting hostile takeovers. This ruling has resulted in an increase in the number and impact of such laws (over 30 states have adopted such statutes) leading to a decrease in hostile takeovers.[45] Many people wonder about the ethics of corporate raiders, as this chapter's Strategic Ethical Challenge feature reveals.

Turnarounds

Turnaround strategies are efforts to reverse company fortunes when the firm has suffered a period of poor sales, or revenues, or even losses.[46] A turnaround strategy usually involves some kind of investment reduction and an attempt to stabilize, followed by a growth strategy of some sort. Under CEO Kenneth A. Macke, Dayton Hudson has turned its earnings around substantially, partly through improving effectiveness, growth through its Target stores, focusing on its primary businesses, and divesting marginal businesses.[47] General Cinema has high hopes of turning around Harcourt Brace Jovanovich, for which it paid approximately $1.5

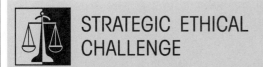

STRATEGIC ETHICAL CHALLENGE

ARE RAIDERS ETHICAL?

Do corporate raiders abide by generally accepted ethical codes of conduct? Many people think not. Raiders like to describe their motivations as weeding out bad management and increasing returns to investors. Few could argue with such lofty aims, but observers feel that more raiders are motivated by the money they can make by "doing deals."

The evidence suggests that both sides are correct. Many raiders do eliminate bad management and improve acquired companies' returns to shareholders. Others simply buy stock to elicit offers of greenmail, selling back stock holdings for sums significantly above market prices. Still other raiders do not turn out to be any better managers than those who preceded them.

Perhaps one of the least strategically ethical activities undertaken by raiders is acquiring stock in firms that have taken long-term perspectives, sacrificing short-term earnings, making them vulnerable to raiders. A firm such as Boeing, for example, has sufficient short-term earnings, but not great earnings, partly because it has invested so much in long-term development, especially research, but also employee training and other infrastructure development activities. It could be vulnerable to raiders.

It's apparent that raiders do perform some useful functions, but the ethics of their activities depend upon whose perspective you take. From the point of view of society, in general, both sides seem arguable, depending on circumstances.

Source: Edmund Faltermeyer, "The Deal Decade: Verdict on the '80s," *Fortune*, August 21, 1991, pp. 58–70; David Carey, "Can Raiders Run What They Raid?" *Fortune*, June 4, 1990, pp. 193–204. Charles M. Kittrell, "The Pirates of Profitability: When Takeovers Are Wrong," *Executive Speeches*, May 1988, pp. 28–32.

billion in late 1991.[48] Vasudevan Ramanujam suggests that contextual factors play an important role in the success of turnaround strategies. The firm may not succeed at turning itself around unless, for example, its industry's fortunes change.[49] Donald C. Hambrick and Steven Schecter suggest that, for certain types of firms, a successful turnaround is a function more of cost control than of marketing strategy.[50] In sum, we have some clues about tactics for a successful turnaround, but we still are uncertain about the proper strategies for specific situations. Some people who specialize in corporate turnarounds seem to be able to take a dog and turn it into a winner.[51]

Combinations

These strategies are not mutually exclusive. Firms at either the SBU or the corporate level normally employ combinations of the basic actions described above as they pursue their missions. When you examine Figure 5.3, you can see that several strategies can be used simultaneously.

BUSINESS STRATEGY

Once the organization has determined what business or businesses it wants to be in and how it will conduct each business, that is, once it has formulated its corporate strategy, then it must determine how it will compete within each business—its business strategy. We could also call this the *competitive strategy*, because a single business's major concern is to develop a strategic advantage that allows it to beat the competition in the marketplace. This strategy is discussed in considerable detail in Chapter 6.

FUNCTIONAL STRATEGY

Organizations perform certain functions that are critical to the success of all other strategies. These are its functional strategies. There are two major types of functional strategies. Economic functional strategies include those concerned with marketing, operations, finance, human resource management, research and development, and information, among other areas. Management functional strategies include those related to planning, organizing (including staffing), problem solving, communicating, management systems, and organizational culture. Functional strategies support corporate, business, and other functional strategies. These strategies, too, are discussed in more detail in Chapter 6.

GRAND STRATEGY

A number of authorities in strategic management have employed the term **grand strategy** or master strategy.[52] Although the various definitions have subtle differences, most call for the basic action strategies enumerated in this chapter. In a representative definition, John A. Pearce II describes grand strategy as "the comprehensive, general plan of major actions by which a firm intends to achieve its long-term objectives within its dynamic environment." Pearce identifies 12 major grand strategies: concentric diversification, conglomerate diversification, product development, market development, concentration on current activities, joint ventures, horizontal integration, vertical integration, innovation, retrenchment, liquidation, and divestiture.[53] Pearce suggests that these appear to be the 12 most commonly employed basic action strategies, and we would add that these strategies drive the remainder of the firm's strategies. Others, such as Charles Hofer and Dan Schendel, have identified generic (basic action) strategies that they suggest suit various stages of the product life cycle, depending on the firm's relative competitive position. Hofer and Schendel see six strategies: share-increasing, growth, profit, market concentration or asset reduction, turnaround, and liquidation or divestment.[54]

As the definition of grand strategy in Chapter 1 indicated, we believe that grand strategies include more than basic action strategies. They may include marketing or other economic functional strategies; for large conglomerates, they may include portfolio strategies. What constitutes that driving force of the organization, that characteristic to which all else must adhere, is the primary issue.

Michael Porter has developed three generic strategies: cost leadership, differentiation, and focus.[55] (These are discussed in more detail in Chapter 6.) These are marketing strategies. At the single-business level, the marketing strategy very often drives the organization. Our identification of grand strategies, as seen in Figure 5.3, does not differ significantly from Pearce's. The grand strategy focuses on the entire firm's goals, not just those of a single SBU, although each SBU may have its own grand strategy.[56]

Given this more inclusive perspective, the strategies identified above are but a few of the grand strategies currently under study in the field of strategic management. Chapter 6 examines several of those identified in studies of various firms and industries in various situations. In general, grand strategies drive the supportive efforts of the organization. RJR-Nabisco, for example, has chosen the path of conglomerate diversification. That single grand strategy drives all else that it does as a multiple-SBU company (though not necessarily what its individual strategic business units do).

This observation is not limited to anecdotal evidence. When Michael A. Hitt, R. Duane Ireland, and K. A. Palia examined relationships in 93 industrial firms, they found that any of seven economic functional areas (marketing, finance, etc.) may receive more attention than the others, depending on the type of basic action or grand strategy employed by the firm.[57]

Because of the large number of such strategies and their combinations, the limited research evidence to support theorists' contentions, and the infancy of the research, it seems best at this point simply to recognize their existence and the way in which they affect the remainder of the organization. Additional industry-specific, research-supported grand strategies, such as those discussed in Chapter 6, might also be viable in some situations. Beyond that, one must be quite careful not to place too much faith in unverified recommendations. An organization must, however, always choose among the basic action strategies and/or marketing strategies, settling on one as the central thrust of the grand strategy. Exactly which one is the appropriate choice for given circumstances is still unknown.

PRE-EMPTIVE STRATEGIES

Ian MacMillan has proposed that **pre-emptive strategies** are appropriate mechanisms by which to secure advantages over competitors. He defines a pre-emptive action as, "a major move by a focal business ahead of moves by its adversaries, which allows it to secure an advantageous position from which it is difficult to dislodge because of the advantages it has captured by being the first mover."[58] MacMillan offers an example of such a move in which a firm expands capacity ahead of industry demand, anticipating that it will increase its market share by discouraging competitors from expanding. Pre-emptive moves are based on the strategists' assumptions about the marketplace. If these assumptions are inaccurate, then the pre-emptive moves may leave strategists vulnerable. MacMillan details the characteristics of an ideal pre-emptive move:

- It should be possible to occupy a prime position rapidly at any advantageous point along the industry (value-added) chain.
- Once the move is made, it should be difficult for most adversaries to follow the firm and contest those positions.
- Existing conditions should slow the response rates of any competitors that can respond.
- It should be relatively easy for the pre-empting business to reverse its move if it wants to do so.

MacMillan identifies two basic classes of pre-emptive opportunities that a firm should seek:

- Opportunities that exploit a rival's weaknesses or lack of commitment
- Opportunities that exploit a rival's strengths or strong commitments

If a firm elects to exploit a rival's weaknesses, MacMillan suggests the following moves:

- Reshape the industry infrastructure, or the conditions necessary to ensure a smooth flow from raw materials to finished goods
- Occupy prime positions, either geographically or in control of key accounts, distributors, service organizations, suppliers, or government contracts
- Secure critical skills in all functional areas
- Pre-empt a psychological position—develop an appeal to the customer that is hard for competitors to overcome

If a firm elects to exploit a rival's strengths, MacMillan suggests the following tactics:

- Make moves that force the opponent to cannibalize current advantages in order to respond (an opponent is not likely to do this willingly)
- Damage the opponent's image, company tradition, or strategy
- Threaten the competitor's major investment, perhaps in its production capacity, distribution system, or supply system
- Force the competitor to antagonize a powerful third party (when a response to a pre-emptive move will upset a powerful third party, few competitors are likely to respond at all)

MacMillan suggests that major opportunities for pre-emptive strategies (largely single-SBU strategies) may be found in the areas shown in Table 5.2.

TABLE 5.2 Sources of Pre-emptive Opportunities

Supply Systems
1. Secure access to raw materials or components
2. Pre-empt production equipment
3. Dominate supply logistics

Product
1. Introduce new product lines
2. Develop a dominant design
3. Occupy a prime position
4. Secure accelerated approval from agencies
5. Secure product development and delivery skills
6. Expand the scope of the product

Production Systems
1. Secure proprietary processes
2. Expand capacity aggressively
3. Integrate vertically with key suppliers
4. Secure scarce and critical production skills

Customers
1. Target appropriate market segments
2. Build early brand awareness
3. Train customers in the skills required to use the product to best advantage
4. Capture key accounts

Distribution and Service Systems
1. Occupy prime locations
2. Secure preferential access to key distributors
3. Dominate distribution logistics
4. Secure access to superior service capabilities
5. Develop distributor skills

MacMillan's pre-emptive strategy approach seems intuitively sound. Much research evidence, in fact, suggests that actions of this sort (not necessarily those he specifically suggests) are generally quite effective. One must always keep in mind the SWOT involved in the situation.

EMERGENT STRATEGY

Henry Mintzberg cautions us to recognize that the strategy we pursue often differs from the strategy we intend. He suggests that the strategy we formulate is more properly called an *intended strategy;* the strategy we actually follow is "a pattern in a stream of decisions." Sometimes it is deliberate, sometimes it is not. His concept, as discussed further in Chapter 10, is that many intended strategies never are realized, and **emergent strategies** take their place. Intended strategies that are realized Mintzberg terms *deliberate.* When we analyze the success of strategies, we typically seek to measure performance related to deliberate, realized strategies. We must be alert, however, to the possibility that we may be measuring something that was not planned or that just happened along the way, a pattern of decisions that emerged over time.[59] Usually this is not a critical matter, but when we come to measure the performance of a specific unit or a specific manager, we should bear this distinction in mind, for overall corporate security may be at stake.

STRATEGIC MANAGER'S SUMMARY

1. The corporate strategy is concerned with how the firm determines the business or businesses in which it will engage and how it will fundamentally conduct the business or businesses as described by basic action strategies. The business strategy is concerned primarily with the way the firm will compete through marketing strategies, and occasionally other functional strategies. Finally, functional strategies focus on the ways in which economic functional strategies (such as marketing, production, finance, and human resource management) and management functional strategies (such as planning, organizing, leading, and controlling) support the business or other strategies. The chief concern of functional strategies is the effective and efficient use of resources.
2. A firm first selects a business, then determines whether to compete or find a niche. It then identifies whether it wants to be an innovator or an imitator, and determines whether to grow, stabilize, reduce investment, turn itself around, mount a takeover defense, or engage in some combination of these strategies.
3. An organization's growth may be intensive, integrative, or diversified. It may grow internally or externally, by acquisition, merger, joint venture, licensing, or other alliance arrangements. It may grow quickly or slowly. It may grow locally or expand to become a regional, national, or multinational firm.
4. Investment may be reduced by retrenchment, divestment, selected asset reduction, cost cutting, liquidation, selling out, or profit extraction.

5. Grand strategies include:

Finding a niche	Stabilization
Concentration	Retrenchment
Market development	Divestment
Product development	Selected asset reduction
Backward integration	Cost cutting
Forward integration	Liquidation
Horizontal integration	Turnaround
Concentric diversification	Innovation
Conglomerate diversification	Quality

6. Pre-emptive strategies enable firms to beat their competitors to the punch.

KEY TERMS

basic action strategies
business strategy
change-based strategic management
concentric diversification
conglomerate diversification
corporate strategy
diversification
divestment
emergent strategy
forward integration
functional strategy
grand strategy
growth
hierarchies of strategies
horizontal diversification
integrative growth

intensive growth
investment reduction
long-range planning
market development
market penetration
pre-emptive strategies
product development
retrenchment
stabilization
strategic discontinuity
strategic imperatives
takeover defense
turnaround

DISCUSSION QUESTIONS

1. Give examples of each of the major strategies discussed in this chapter, including corporate and business grand strategies.
2. Discuss as many strategic mistakes of well-known large firms as you can, and categorize each of these mistakes in terms of the strategies outlined in Table 5.3.
3. Explain each of the following takeover defenses: fair price provisions, golden parachutes, PAC-Man defenses, poison pills, lesser-of-two-evils, ESOPs, and top management control.

STRATEGIC AUDIT QUESTIONS

1. Does this organization know these critical things?
   a. Where it is
   b. Where it wants to be
   c. How to get there
2. Does it have a hierarchy of strategies, as in Table 5.1?
3. Has it properly used or considered using the following?
   a. Direct competition or finding a niche
   b. Concentration or multiple products
   c. Innovation or other strategic imperatives
   d. Growth (intensive, integrative, or diversified; regional, national, or international; internal or external, by acquisition, merger, joint venture, licensing, or other alliances; quickly or gradually)
   e. Stabilization
   f. Investment reduction (retrenchment, divestment (for multiple-SBU firms only), selected asset reduction, cost cutting, liquidation, selling out, profit extraction)
   g. Turnaround
   h. Takeover defense
   i. Combination
4. Has this firm given proper attention to corporate strategy?
5. Has it given proper attention to business strategy?
6. Has it given proper attention to functional strategy?
7. Does it have a grand strategy at the corporate and/or business level? What is it? How good is it?
8. Does this firm take advantage of pre-emptive strategies? How well? If not, could it do so?
9. Is it about to be pre-empted?

Endnotes

1. Bernard Taylor, "Corporate Planning for the 1990s: The New Frontier," *Long Range Planning*, December 1986, pp. 13–18.
2. G. A. Smith, Jr., C. Roland Christensen, and N. A. Berg, *Policy Formulation and Administration* (Homewood, Ill.: Irwin, 1968).
3. Lawrence G. Bossidy, address to the Strategic Management Society, Boston, October 13, 1987.
4. For a discussion of strategic discontinuities, see Henry H. Beam, "Strategic Discontinuities: When Being Good May Not Be Good Enough," *Business Horizons*, July/August 1990, pp. 10–14. Our definition is broader than that used in this article, but the author gives good examples of discontinuities. For a discussion of

technological discontinuities, see Richard N. Foster, *Innovation: The Attacker's Advantage* (New York: Summit Books, 1986).
5. C. W. Hofer and D. E. Schendel, eds., *Strategic Management: A New View of Business Policy and Planning* (Boston: Little, Brown, 1979), pp. 11–14. The main difference between the way Hofer and Schendel use these terms and the way we use them is that they include marketing among functional strategies alone, whereas we include it among business strategies, as well.
6. Kevin Kelly, "At Sears, The More Things Change . . .," *Business Week*, November 12, 1990, pp. 66–68.
7. Thomas A. Stewart, "Westinghouse Gets Respect at

Last," *Fortune*, July 3, 1989, pp. 92–98; Gregory L. Marlows and David Griffiths, "How Westinghouse Is Revving Up after the Rebound," *Business Week*, March 28, 1988, pp. 46–52.

8. John Huey, "America's Most Successful Merchant," *Fortune*, September 23, 1991, pp. 46–59; Bill Saporita, "Is Wal-Mart Unstoppable?" *Fortune*, May 6, 1991, pp. 50–59; "Explosive Decade," *Financial World*, April 4–17, 1984, p. 72.

9. Suzanne Alexander, "Small Firm's Single-Coast Strategy Delivers the Goods," *The Wall Street Journal*, March 6, 1991, p. B2.

10. Dori Jones Yang and Laura Zinn, "Will the 'Nordstrom Way' Travel Well?" *Business Week*, September 3, 1990, pp. 82–83; Nancy K. Austin, "A Hell of a Store," *Success*, April 1987, p. 10; P. A. Bellew, "Nordstrom Strategy of Coddling Shoppers Facing Challenge in California Expansion," *The Wall Street Journal*, May 10, 1984, p. 37.

11. Laurence Hooper, "Big Blue Cultivates New Markets by Thinking Small," *The Wall Street Journal*, February 27, 1991, p. B2.

12. Jack A. Seamonds and Micheline Maynard, "Detroit Takes on Porsche and Jaguar," *U.S. News & World Report*, June 2, 1986, pp. 49–50.

13. John A. Pearce II and James W. Haney, "Concentrated Growth Strategies," *Academy of Management Review*, January 1990, pp. 61–67.

14. Marcia Shaw, "For Levi's, A Flattering Fit Overseas," *Business Week*, November 5, 1990, pp. 76–77.

15. For a discussion see John A. Pearce II and Harvey W. James, "Concentrated Growth Strategies," *Academy of Management Executive*, February 1990, pp. 61–68.

16. John Young, "Investing in Innovation," *Executive Excellence*, August 1991, p. 20.

17. Edward de Bono, "Quality Is No Longer Enough," *Journal for Quality & Participation*, September 1991, pp. 34–39; Laura B. Forder, "Quality: American, Japanese, and Soviet Perspectives," *Academy of Management Executive*, November 1991, pp. 63–74.

18. Nicholas R. Aquino, "Constant Improvement: A Strategic Imperative," *Business & Economic Review*, July–September 1991, pp. 18–21; John W. Moran, Jr., "Leading the Organization to Perfection through Daily Management," *National Productivity Review*, Summer 1991, pp. 369–378.

19. William J. Spencer, "Research to Product: A Major U.S. Challenge," *California Management Review*, Winter 1990, pp. 45–53; Thomas M. Rohan, "World Class Manufacturing: In Search of Speed," *Industry Week*, September 3, 1990, pp. 78–83; Brian Dumaine, "How Managers Can Succeed through Speed," *Fortune*, February 13, 1987, pp. 54–59.

20. For an example of how critical this can be to survival, see Laura Zinn, "The New Stars of Retailing," *Business Week*, December 16, 1991, pp. 120–122. This article shows how firms that continued to be inflexible in strategy went out of business, while those that prospered were willing to change the way they retailed.

21. Philip Kotler, *Marketing Management*, 5th ed. (Englewood Cliffs, N.J.: Prentice-Hall, 1984), pp. 57–58.

22. Gary Hector, "Yes, You *Can* Manage Long Term," *Fortune*, November 21, 1988, pp. 64–76.

23. Todd Vogel, "Can UPS Deliver the Goods in a New World?" *Business Week*, June 4, 1990, pp. 80–82.

24. For a review of success factors in vertical integration, see Sayan Chatterjee, "Gains in Vertical Acquisitions and Market Power: Theory and Evidence," *Academy of Management Journal*, June 1991, pp. 436–448. For a review of theory, see Kathryn Rudie Harrigan, "Formulating Vertical Integration Strategies," *Academy of Management Review* 9, no. 4 (1984), pp. 638–652.

25. G. C. J. M. Vos, "A Production Allocation Approach for International Manufacturing Strategy," *International Journal of Operations & Production Management*, no. 3, 1991, pp. 125–134.

26. George J. McManus, "On Your Mark, Get Set, Grow!" *Iron Age*, May 1991, pp. 14–19.

27. Clare Ansberry, "Kodak Acquires Atlanta-Based Photofinisher," *The Wall Street Journal*, September 3, 1987, p. 4.

28. "Health Care," *Standard & Poor's Industry Survey*, April 16, 1987, pp. H26–H30; Richard Koenig, "Guarded Condition: Hospital Chains Curb Ambition in the Wake of Setback at Humana," *The Wall Street Journal*, October 9, 1987, pp. 1, 20.

29. Stewart Tog, "Meet Monsieur Luxury," *Business Week*, July 30, 1990, pp. 48–52.

30. Michael E. Porter, "From Competitive Advantage to Corporate Strategy," *Harvard Business Review*, May–June 1987, pp. 43–60.

31. Paul Ingrassia and Bradley A. Stertz, "Mea Culpa: With Chrysler Ailing, Lee Iacocca Concedes Mistakes in Managing," *The Wall Street Journal*, September 17, 1990, pp. A1, A8.

32. James Hagy, "How Big Can Hooter's Get?" *Florida Trend*, September 1987, pp. 80–88.

33. Chuck Hawkins, "Is Federal Express an Innocent Abroad?" *Business Week*, April 2, 1990, p. 34; Vogel, "Can UPS Deliver."

34. For a discussion of these hybrid organizations, see Bryan Boris and David P. Jemison, "Hybrid Arrangements as Strategic Alliances: Theoretical Issues in Organizational Combination," *Academy of Management Review*, April 1989, pp. 234–249; also, see Rosabeth Moss Kanter, "Becoming PALs: Pooling, Allying, and Linking across Companies," *Academy of Management Executive*, August 1989, pp. 183–193.

35. Rahul Jacob, "Banking's Best Acquirers," *Fortune*, July 29, 1991, p. 106.

36. Lee Berton, "Bottom Line: Peat Experience Shows Why Accountants Are Rushing to Merge," *The Wall Street Journal*, July 17, 1989, pp. A1, A7.

37. Betsy Morris, "New Ballgame: RJR Nabisco's Jolted by

Big Chief Who Arrived through a Takeover," *The Wall Street Journal*, January 20, 1987, pp. 1, 31.

38. John Ambrosia, "Aluminum Firms' Foreign Affairs Paying off," *Iron Age*, October 1991, pp. 26–30.

39. Rich Thomas, "From Russia with Chips," *Newsweek*, August 6, 1990, p. 48.

40. For a review of the joint venture process and a discussion of which situations suit it best, see Kathryn Rudie Harrigan, "Joint Ventures and Competitive Strategy," *Strategic Management Journal*, January/February 1988, pp. 141–158.

41. Todd Vogel, "'They Took Their Shot at Being a Giant' —and Missed," *Business Week*, May 7, 1990, pp. 39, 40.

42. A. W. Clausen, "Strategic Issues in Managing Change: The Turnaround of BankAmerica Corporation," *California Management Review*, Winter 1990, pp. 98–105.

43. Robert L. Rose, "Cummins Company Hits Roadblocks in Turnaround Drive," *The Wall Street Journal*, September 25, 1989, p. A7.

44. Christopher Farrell, "First It Was Poison Pills—Now It's People Pills," *Business Week*, January 16, 1989, pp. 33–34.

45. Tim Smart, "More States Are Telling Raiders: Not Here, You Don't," *Business Week*, February 13, 1989, p. 28; Michael W. Miller and Laurie P. Cohen, "Corporate Raiders Predict Harder Times," *The Wall Street Journal*, April 23, 1987, p. 6.

46. For a recent review, see Richard C. Hoffman, "Strategies for Corporate Turnaround: What Do We Know about Them?" *Journal of General Management*, Spring 1989, pp. 46–66.

47. Russell Mitchell, "From Punching Bag to Retailing Black Belt," *Business Week*, November 20, 1989, pp. 62–66.

48. Gary Putka, "General Cinema Hopes to Hit the Books," *The Wall Street Journal*, November 5, 1991, pp. A4.

49. V. Ramanujam, "An Empirical Examination of Contextual Influences in Corporate Turnaround," paper presented to the Academy of Management, Boston, August 1984.

50. D. C. Hambrick and S. Schecter, "Turnaround Strategies for Mature Industrial Product Business Units," *Academy of Management Journal*, June 1983, pp. 231–248.

51. Brian Dumaine, "The New Turnaround Champs," *Fortune*, July 16, 1990, pp. 36–44; Gregory L. Miles and Matt Rothman, "The Green Berets of Corporate Management," *Business Week*, September 21, 1987, pp. 110–113.

52. Karen Giddens-Ening, "Selecting a Master Strategy," *Journal of Business Strategy*, Winter 1987, pp. 76–82.

53. J. A. Pearce II, "Selecting among Alternative Grand Strategies," *California Management Review*, Spring 1982, pp. 23–31.

54. Hofer and Schendel, *Strategy Formulation*, pp. 104, 162–177.

55. Michael E. Porter, *Competitive Strategy* (New York: Free Press, 1980), Chaps. 1 and 2.

56. Michael A. Hitt and R. Duane Ireland, "Corporate Distinctive Competence, Strategy, Industry, and Performance," *Strategic Management Journal*, July/August 1985, pp. 273–293.

57. M. A. Hitt, R. D. Ireland, and K. A. Palia, "Industrial Firms' Grand Strategy and Functional Importance: Moderating Effects of Technology and Uncertainty," *Academy of Management Journal* 25, no. 2 (1982), pp. 265–298.

58. For the following material, we are indebted to Ian C. MacMillan, "Preemptive Strategies," *Journal of Business Strategy*, Fall 1983, pp. 16–19.

59. Henry Mintzberg, "Patterns in Strategy Formulation," *Management Science*, 1978, p. 945.

INTEGRATIVE CASE ANALYSIS
CHAPTER 5

THE CHALLENGES FACING GENERAL MOTORS IN 1992

Now that you have read Chapter 5 and reviewed the GM case and the Industry Note for related concepts, let's see how the chapter's concepts apply to GM.

APPLICATIONS OF CONCEPTS TO THE CASE

General Motors (where MBORR originated) has established a series of goals for itself. Among them are exceeding customer expectations and improving quality, market share, and North American profitability. Related objectives were established, including reducing costs by closing several plants and cutting 25 percent of the white-collar work force by 1993. Numerous other goals and strategic objectives were established.

The company subsequently established a series of strategies to achieve both its short-term objectives and its long-term goals. The company is engaged in a primary business—the automobile business. It is not a niche player; it is a full-line competitor. Until recently it concentrated on essentially one group of products in essentially one SBU, but now it is becoming a more serious multiple-business organization. It has pursued strategies of growth through market penetration, market development, diversification, conglomerate diversification, and vertical and horizontal integration over the years, but most recently it has entered into periods of stabilization and even asset reduction as it has gone through major cost-cutting efforts, plant closings, and consolidations.

It has not yet begun to think of itself as a multiple-SBU firm. It still focuses its attention on the auto business and doesn't really practice portfolio management. Most of its acquisitions have been intended to bolster the technological competence of its automobile business, but they could hold promise for the future growth of the company. GM seems to be following a grand strategy of low costs, high quality, and improved style through innovation (especially technological innovation) and human resource management. This strategy has yet to pay off or to be fully realized.

Additional Case Analysis Questions

1. How can GM increase innovation in the company?
2. How could GM use pre-emptive strategies against the Japanese and other competitors?

STRATEGIC MANAGEMENT CHALLENGES

GM has been confronted with virtually every strategic management challenge identified in Chapter 1: accelerating change, increased competition, globalization, technology, changing nature of the work force, resource shortages, transition to an information society, unstable economic and market conditions, increasing demands of constituents, and a complex strategic management environment. How has GM taken strategic action to solve related problems and/or take advantage of related opportunities?

CHAPTER 6

BUSINESS STRATEGY: STRATEGY AT THE SBU LEVEL

Of course it is important to take the competition into account, but in making strategy, that should not come first. It cannot come first. First comes painstaking attention to the needs of customers. . . . First comes the willingness to rethink, fundamentally, what products are and what they do.

Kenichi Ohmae
Senior Partner, McKinsey & Company, Tokyo

Marketing is so basic that it cannot be considered a separate function. It is the business seen from the final result, that is, from the customer's point of view.

Peter Drucker
Noted Management Author and Consultant

CHAPTER OBJECTIVES

By the time you complete this chapter, you should be able to:

1. Describe the contingency approach to strategy formulation and enumerate its strengths and weaknesses
2. Define the generic approach to strategy
3. Describe and be able to use Porter's model of competitiveness
4. Describe and be able to use Hall's model of competitiveness
5. Describe the PIMS concept of strategy formulation
6. Discuss the role of functional strategies in supporting competitive efforts

THE OLIVE GARDEN

Red Lobster Restaurants, one of the two principal chains in the company's restaurant division, produced 20 percent of General Mills' profits in 1986. In 1982 General Mills' restaurant division recognized that it needed both to modernize its Red Lobster chain, which accounted for significant portions of its corporate profits, and to expand the division's offerings in order to grow, to take advantage of changing consumer tastes, and to compensate for the effects of the aging of Red Lobster. Almost simultaneously, it began to develop a restaurant based on an Italian theme, The Olive Garden, and purchased Darryl's, a fern-bar restaurant chain headquartered in North Carolina; The Good Earth, a California-based health-food restaurant; and Casa Gallardo, a small Mexican-food restaurant chain. Of these four expansion efforts, the home-grown variety proved to be the best. The Olive Garden was a not-too-Italian Italian restaurant. While much of its menu was based on Italian cuisine, the company made limited use of garlic, and relied heavily on market research to tell it what consumers liked about existing and potential products. Its first restaurant was in operation almost 3 years before the company, after many menu variations, began to feel comfortable with the menu, the service, the restaurant design, and other features of the potential chain.

Joe Lee, then president of the restaurant division, recognized the potential for growth that The Olive Garden chain offered. In 1985 he authorized the establishment of seven more Olive Gardens. All of the new restaurants immediately fared well, turning profits of $300,000 on sales of about $2.5 million. By August 1990 the chain had grown to 200 units across the country and had strategic plans for approximately 250 more in the future.

Consistent with its experience with Red Lobster, General Mills' restaurant division sought to provide customers with a perception of good value for the money. At the same time the company sought to provide an innovative theme restaurant based on the country's largest ethnic preference as indicated by market research—Italian food. Authentic Italian food was too strongly flavored for many customers, however, so the company turned to more bland and diversified offerings, such as teriyaki chicken. The Olive Garden bypassed conventional advertising in favor of a localized approach that included community events. The restaurant targeted white-collar workers who tend to eat out frequently. Average dinner entree prices at the restaurants ran from $8 to $10. Research and surveys told the firm what customers wanted.

The Olive Garden treated a restaurant as a manufacturing facility, applying quality controls and value analysis in all segments of the process from the making of fresh pasta daily, until the time it was served. This helped the firm give high value to the customer at lower cost. The restaurant chain also trained its employees to provide high levels of service to customers as part of adding value.

Sources: John Harris, "Dinnerhouse Technology," *Forbes*, July 8, 1991, pp. 98–99; Karen McNeil and William Hale, "The Service Slide: the New Imperative: Service as a Product," *Restaurant Business*, March 20, 1991, pp. 121–136; Tom Johnson, David Farhas, Michael DeLuca, Howard Reill, "The X Factor Is Alive and Well," *Restaurant Hospitality*, August 1990, pp. 127–139; Gail Fenta, "Inside Sauces," *Restaurant Hospitality*, November 1988, pp. 108–110; Robert Johnson, "Costly Creation: General Mills Risks Millions Starting Chain of Italian Restaurants," *The Wall Street Journal*, September 21, 1987, pp. 1, 13; authors' discussion with top executives of Red Lobster.

General Mills' restaurant division is a strategic business unit. It engages in a single line of business—restaurant sales to consumers—in two principal markets, seafood and Italian cuisine. Most business organizations engage in only one line of business. Think of your local auto dealer, doctor's office, or flower shop; a wholly owned national restaurant chain, such as McDonald's; a subsidiary of a major conglomerate, such as the Sylvania division; or a retail grocery organization such as Kroger, Safeway, A&P, Publix, or Albertson's. All are organizations with essentially one line of business. The business strategies of such organizations are the subject of this chapter.

The principal concern of most single-business organizations is establishing a **competitive strategic advantage,** a distinctive competency, by which it can beat the competition in the marketplace.[1] At the business level, the organization's strategic focus is primarily on basic action strategies in conjunction with its marketing strategy. Supportive functional strategies are critical to the firm's grand strategy, and indeed may be the focus of its grand strategy. The primary thrust of business strategy is determining and satisfying customer needs and creating value for customers in order to be competitive. This often means very fundamentally rethinking what its products are, and it may mean dramatically changing the business system that designs, builds or delivers, and markets the products or services of the firm.[2]

General Mills' restaurant division has sought to offer food of good value and, in its Red Lobster and Olive Garden divisions, it has been an innovator in the marketplace. The Olive Garden concept continues the division's focus on the customer, refined after many years of hard work at Red Lobster.

This chapter reviews major contingency and generic approaches to the formulation of business strategies. Also, since the stage of the product life cycle has special importance to the development of successful business and supportive functional strategies, its impacts on strategy formulation are noted, as well. Figures 6.1 and 6.2 indicate the portions of the strategic process that are examined in this chapter.

FIGURE 6.1   The Organization—A Strategic Management Process Model

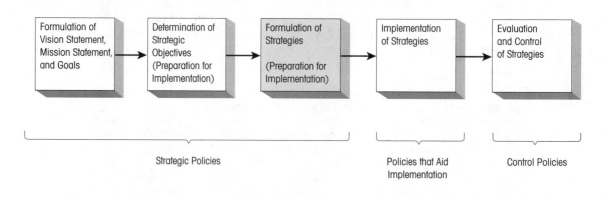

FIGURE 6.2 Objectives Determination and Strategy Formulation

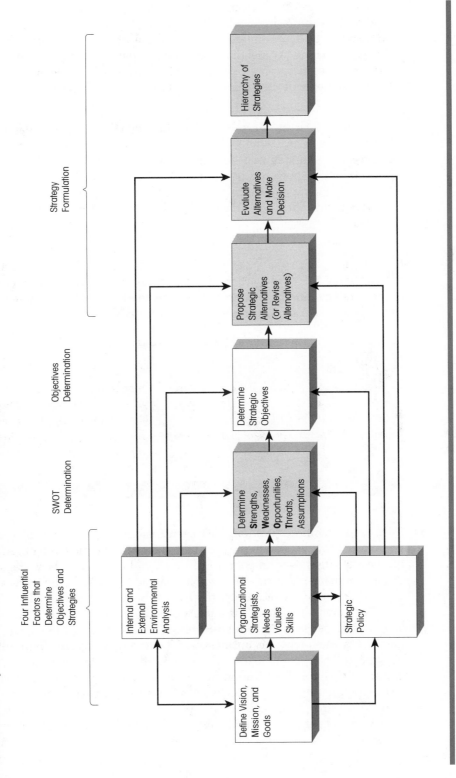

As we noted in Chapters 1 and 5, the corporate and business strategies of single business units are highly interdependent and intertwined, but they remain different. They address different issues. While this chapter focuses on business strategy, from time to time, the business unit must re-examine the central question that determines its corporate strategy: What business are we in or should we be in? The answer depends on the answers to four more questions:

1. Is there some business in which the organization has a natural strategic advantage or an innate interest?
2. Does the company want to compete or to find a niche?
3. Will the firm obey strategic imperatives?
4. Does the company want or need to concentrate, grow, stabilize, engage in investment reduction, defend against a takeover, or turn company fortunes around?

Several basic strategic options are available, as revealed previously in Figure 5.4 and Table 5.1. These basic action strategies will lead to the formulation of the grand strategy. At the business level, the marketing strategy often drives the organization. Obviously it does at General Mills.

AT THE OLIVE GARDEN

General Mills' Olive Garden restaurants benefit from the firm's natural strategic advantage—experience with Red Lobster. The company competes with other restaurants, but in a sense is niching, since it focuses on Italian food. The firm is innovative in many ways, and it seeks rapid growth.

Even after these questions have been answered, the single-business organization must always be alert to the possibility of redefining the business. After all, any business changes over time, or at least it should change, as its strategic variables change. In many industries these variables tend to change at an increasing rate. It also must continually reconsider the basic actions in which it engages.

For example, Domino's is a pizza company, right? It is, after all, the second largest pizza seller in the United States. When Thomas S. Monaghan, Domino's owner was asked what his business was, however, he replied, "Basically we are a delivery company, and it just so happens that people want us to bring them pizza."[3] This type of realization can open many new product horizons to a firm; just as importantly, this perspective has helped Monaghan to understand that his competitive strength lies primarily in providing a service, the real, central focus of Domino's competitive effort. His firm adds value to pizza by delivering it.

BUSINESS STRATEGY OF THE SINGLE-BUSINESS ENTERPRISE

The business strategy addresses the issue of how the firm will compete in one business or in a particular segment of a product market. The objective of a business strategy is to obtain a competitive strategic advantage over the competition.[4] This is accomplished essentially by doing something that's different from what other firms do (or at least by convincing people it is different) or by doing what it does more cheaply than other firms do it, or by developing some combination of the two.[5] Either of these alternatives will be accomplished by implementing basic action strategies (as discussed in Chapter 5) in combination with a sound marketing strategy based on the fundamental marketing mix of target market, product, promotion, distribution, and price. These actions create value for customers by satisfying their needs. Satisfying customer needs is the core of the market driven firm, the firm of the future.[6] To be successful, the business strategy must integrate the various functional strategies that support its competitive effort. For example, a low-cost/low-price strategy cannot be accomplished without sound manufacturing and human resource strategies. Figure 6.3 shows the relationships among the various strategies in the single-SBU firm.

Beating the competition can easily become an obsession in an organization. Perhaps it should, as long as customers' needs are being satisfied to create value for them. This obsession is subject to another proviso, however: the competition should be conducted ethically. It isn't always, as this chapter's Strategic Ethical Challenge feature reveals.

CONTINGENCY APPROACH TO BUSINESS-LEVEL STRATEGY FORMULATION

How does a firm know what strategy to use? One way, the contingency approach, suggests that a given set of circumstances make a certain strategy the best. The contingency approach is concerned with grand strategies—basic action, marketing, and other functional strategies that drive an organization. Though the theory behind this idea is currently in the formative stage, related research is increasing. The approach has been applied largely to profit-oriented organizations so far, but it may be more extensively applied to nonprofit organizations in the future.

The science of the contingency approach to strategic management has not yet attained the degree of sophistication necessary to indicate the exact strategy that should be followed in every situation. Far from it. However, research and theory have pointed toward a set of environmental and organizational variables that have significant impacts on the content of strategy, at least with regard to a single product line or to multiple products in a single business area. Furthermore, appropriate strategies have been identified for some specific situations, most of them also for single product lines.

FIGURE 6.3 Relationships among Strategies in Single-SBU Firms

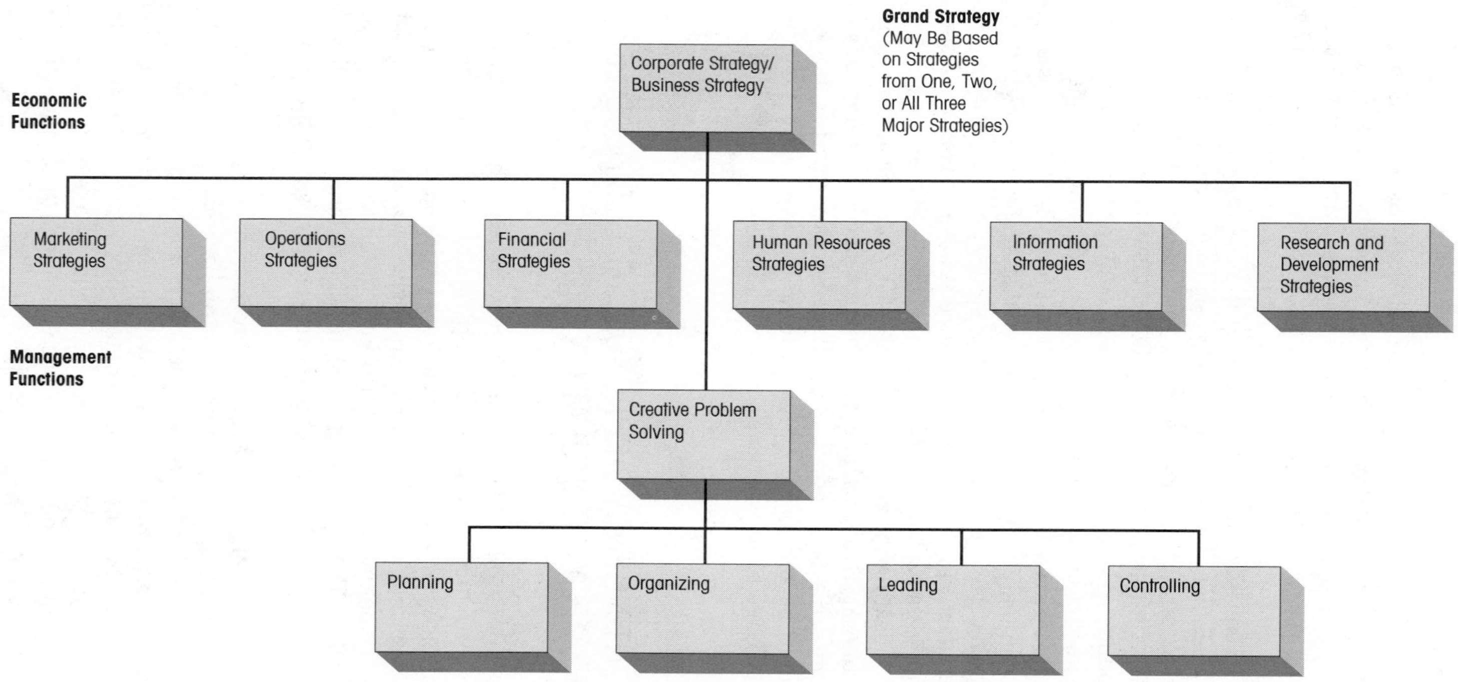

Economic Functions

| Marketing Strategies | Operations Strategies | Financial Strategies | Corporate Strategy/ Business Strategy | Human Resources Strategies | Information Strategies | Research and Development Strategies |

Grand Strategy (May Be Based on Strategies from One, Two, or All Three Major Strategies)

Management Functions

| Planning | Organizing | Creative Problem Solving | Leading | Controlling |

Strategic Contingency Variables: Factors to Be Considered When One Product or Business Is Involved

After reviewing the relevant research and theories, Charles W. Hofer concluded that the most important single variable in the determination of strategy is the life cycle stage of the product for which the strategy is being formulated.[7] After examining numerous research studies he identified several factors that strategic managers should take into account in formulating strategy in each of the product life cycle stages, including buyer needs, buyer concentration, type of product, rate of technological change, market share, market segmentation, and elasticity of demand, among others. Each of these might raise issues of several subfactors or characteristics, and over time more factors will be added to this list.

This points to a major problem. One of the largest barriers to the formulation of a viable contingency theory is the large number of variables to be considered. Hofer suggests that more than 50 major market-related variables could affect strategy, and he admits that circumstances, such as management techniques and social responsibility, may add others. Nevertheless, the variables Hofer has identified generate some 18 quadrillion combinations of circumstances to consider. A truly inclusive contingency theory would require formulation of an almost

STRATEGIC ETHICAL CHALLENGE

WHAT ARE THE LIMITS OF ACTIONS TO BE USED IN DEFEATING A COMPETITOR?

As part of its corporate diversification effort, American Express acquired Edmond Safra's Geneva-based Trade Development Bank (TDB) in 1983. Within a year and a half, it was evident that Mr. Safra was not going to fit into the culture at American Express. His personality was almost the direct opposite of what American Express's culture stood for. In December 1984, Mr. Safra resigned as chairman of the TDB-American Express banking operation, and agreed not to attempt to re-enter banking until 1988. Mr. Safra and the company parted ways, but not amicably.

As part of the deal, American Express had agreed to sell Mr. Safra certain assets, including his old corporate headquarters in Geneva. Several problems surfaced, including the price Mr. Safra should pay for his old headquarters. For example, it soon became evident to American Express upper management that Mr. Safra was hiring away key personnel to staff his 1988 banking re-entry. An important computer tape on the banking industry disappeared from American Express offices. Robert Smith, the banker who replaced Mr. Safra as chairman, became obsessed with stopping his efforts, even hiring detectives to follow employees suspected of preparing to leave the firm (presumably with insider knowledge of key strategies). Eventually, American Express filed suit to block Mr. Safra's return to banking, but he received a license from Swiss authorities and the suit was dropped.

That seemed like the end of the adventure, and it should have been, but it wasn't. Shortly thereafter, Mr. Safra began to find himself the subject of numerous newspaper articles throughout the world, all designed to smear his public image. These articles linked him with organized crime figures, the Iran-Contra Affair, and cocaine smugglers. Mr. Safra's top aides launched an investigation, retaining well-known attorneys and private investigators. Eventually, after numerous dead ends, the search led to American Express. A faxed document that supported one of the newspaper articles' authenticity had the tell-tale American Express document identification on it. This led investigators, after thousands of hours of diligent work, to be able to provide Mr. Safra with sufficient evidence to prepare a case against American Express that resulted in an out-of-court settlement of $8 million, $4 million to Mr. Safra, and $4 million to four charities of his choosing, in July 1989. Furthermore, American Express made a public apology for the actions of its employees. Mr. Safra's life has probably been changed forever, as his image has been tarnished and reprints of the original articles continue to appear.

American Express denies an intentional strategy of character assassination. Rather, executives explain the events as resulting from a case of unfortunate overzealousness by two company employees. No evidence exists to suggest an intentional smear campaign, nor that Jim Robinson, American Express chairman and CEO, ever knew of the campaign. Robinson's closest aid, Harry L. Freeman, was in charge of the two employees who arranged for the stories to appear in newspapers and magazines. Since Robinson had delegated to Freeman a great deal of authority to handle "special projects," he may well have known nothing of these events. Freeman also denies knowledge of any illegal activity on the part of his employees. Although there is no evidence to implicate Freeman in a plot against Mr. Safra, an organized plot did exist to harm the character of Mr. Safra, and it was carried out by American Express employees. Freeman retired shortly after American Express settled with Mr. Safra.

Source: Bryan Burrough, "The Vendetta: How American Express Orchestrated a Smear of Rival Edmond Safra," *The Wall Street Journal*, September 24, 1990, pp. A1, A8, A9.

infinite number of **contingency strategies.** Approaching the task from the vantage point of the life cycle stage, as Hofer has done, allows the number of situations to be reduced substantially. Even so, the number of possible situations is so great that the best use of contingency theory probably lies in identifying the major factors that should be considered and combining them with hypothesized strategies such as those shown in Table 6.1. Identifying strategies that work within particular contexts will be discussed later in the chapter.[8]

Directional Policy Matrix

One contingency business-strategy technique, developed by Royal Dutch/Shell and used primarily in Europe, employs a nine-cell **directional policy matrix** as a means of determining product investment strategies within a particular industry. The matrix approach is quite commonly used to evaluate resource allocations among multiple businesses within the same firm, as Chapter 7 describes, but it can also can be used to formulate product investment strategies within a particular industry. One of the axes of the matrix in Figure 6.4 measures the prospects for market sector profitability, while the other shows the company's competitive position. Each of these two critical dimensions is evaluated at one of three levels of desirability. The prospects for market sector profitability may be unattractive, average, and attractive; the company's competitive position is either weak, average, or strong. The combinations of these three levels of the two dimensions yields situations in which eight strategies become advisable. (Phased withdrawal appears twice on the matrix.)

A firm that used this matrix would compare its prospects for sector profitability with its competitive position and then choose the strategy indicated by the intersection of the determined levels on each dimension. The resultant eight strategies include:

1. Disinvestment: This product is losing money with its long-term average performance and should be eliminated from the product line.
2. Phased withdrawal: Slowly, but surely the business should eliminate this product from the product line. It may be earning money, but only a marginal amount, and not enough to justify its investment.
3. Cash generation: This product or service has no long-term future, and probably it is in the late-maturity stage of the product life cycle. No further investment should be contemplated.

FIGURE 6.4   Directional Policy Matrix

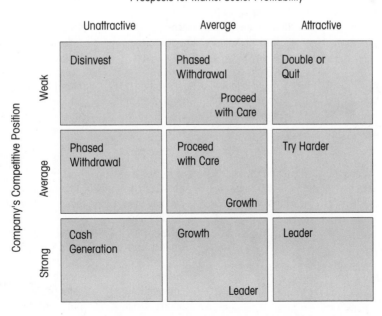

Source: Adapted from D. E. Hussey, ''Portfolio Analysis: Practical Experience with the Directional Policy Matrix,'' *Long Range Planning*, Vol. II (August 1978), p. 3. Reprinted by permission.

TABLE 6.1 Harold Fox's Suggested Business Strategies over the Product Life Cycle

	Functional Focus	R&D	Production	Marketing	Physical Distribution
Precommercial- ization	Coordination or R&D and other functions	Reliability tests Release blueprints	Production design Process planning Purchasing department lines up vendors and subcontractors	Test marketing Detailed marketing plan	Plan shipping schedules, mixed carloads Rent warehouse space, trucks
Introduction	Engineering: debugging in R&D production and field	Technical corrections (engineering changes)	Subcontracting Centralize pilot plans; test various processes; develop standards	Induce trial; fill pipelines; sales agents or commissioned salespeople; publicity	Plan a logistics system
Growth	Production	Start successor product	Centralize production Phase out subcontractors Expedite vendors' output; Long runs	Channel commitment Brand emphasis Salaried sales force Reduce price if necessary	Expedite deliveries Shift to owned facilities
Maturity	Marketing and logistics	Develop minor variants Reduce costs through value analysis Originate major adaptations to start new cycle	Many short runs Decentralize Import parts, low-priced models Routinization Cost reduction	Short-term promotions Salaried salespeople Cooperative advertising Forward integration Routine marketing research; panels, audits	Reduce costs and raise customer service level Control finished goods inventory
Decline	Finance	Withdraw all R&D from initial version	Revert to subcontracting; simplify production line Careful inventory control; buy foreign or competitive goods; stock spare parts	Revert to commission basis; withdraw most promotional support Raise price Selective distribution Careful phaseout, considering entire channel	Reduce inventory and services

Source: Reprinted by permission from Georgia State University Press, ''Operational View of a Product Life Cycle,'' exhibit from ''A Framework for Functional Coordination,'' by Harold W. Fox, November/December 1973, pp. 10–11. Copyright 1973 by the College of Business Administration, Georgia State University, Atlanta.

Personnel	Finance	Management Accounting	Other	Customers	Competition
Recruit for new activities Negotiate operational changes with unions	LC plan for cash flows profits, investments, subsidiaries	Payout planning; full costs/revenues Determine optimum lengths of LC stages through present-value method	Final legal clearances (regulatory hurdles patents) Appoint LC coordinator	Panels and other test respondents	Neglects opportunity or is working on similar idea
Staff and train middle management Stock options for executives	Accounting deficit; high net cash outflow Authorize large production facilities	Help develop production and distribution standards Prepare sales aids like sales management portfolio		Innovators and some early adopters	(Monopoly) Disparagement of innovation Legal and extralegal interference
Add suitable personnel for plant Many grievances Heavy overtime	Very high profits, net cash outflow still rising Sell equities	Short-term analyses based on return per scarce resource		Early adopters and early majority	(Oligopoly) A few imitate, improve, or cut prices
Transfers, advancements; incentives for efficiency, safety, and so on Suggestion system	Declining profit rate, but increasing net cash inflow	Analyze differential costs/revenue Spearhead cost reduction, value analysis, and efficiency drives	Pressure for resale price maintenance Price cuts bring price wars; possible price collusion	Early adopters, early and late majority, some laggards; first discontinued by late majority	(Monopoly competition) First shakeout; still many rivals
Find new slots, encourage early retirement	Administer system, retrenchment Sell unneeded equipment Export the machinery	Analyze escapable costs Pinpoint remaining outlays	Accurate sales forecast very important	Mainly laggards	(Oligopoly) After second shakeout, only few rivals

4. Proceed with care: Two average levels on the two critical dimensions suggest possible cautious future investment.
5. Growth: When the company is strong and the industry is moderately attractive, the firm should continue to support growth in its product or service. The business's position should allow the product or service to finance itself.
6. Double or quit: If the firm is weak in an attractive industry, it should either invest heavily in the product or service or withdraw from the marketplace.
7. Try harder: If the firm finds itself an average performer in an attractive industry, it should increase investment or withdraw from the marketplace.
8. Lead: A business should attempt to maintain a leadership position in an attractive market by investing, even diverting funds from other sources, if necessary, because earnings will be above average.[9]

This matrix seems to offer some very prudent, logical advice. As with any concept of strategic management, however, there are further factors to consider. Are only two sets of variables relevant? What is the specific life cycle of the product, and what is its impact? Do the two dimensions have more than three levels of desirability? Are the recommended strategies the most satisfactory? Does this model make assumptions that do not hold in every situation? Is it always best to be the leader, or can one make substantial profits as a follower?

This model is only one approach to the determination of a business-level strategy. Because of its sound conceptual foundation, it has been adapted for related, but different purposes, such as setting priorities on various industries for support for export promotion.[10] Some firms may find it to be useful in some circumstances. It should be regarded not as a universal guide, but as a starting place for further investigation.

An additional consideration should affect the search for an appropriate strategy. The generic theory of grand strategy formulation, which has often been considered part of the contingency theory, identifies some common behaviors among more successful firms in most, if not all, circumstances. Let us consider some of the postulates of this theory of business strategy formulation.

GENERIC THEORY OF STRATEGY FORMULATION

In the past few years, several studies have demonstrated by regression analysis and other analytical techniques that successful firms engage in definite patterns of behavior in order to increase return on investment. While this research has uncovered some surprises and some contradictions, most of its findings have identified factors that promote success. These theories of strategy formulation suggest that certain strategies are almost always appropriate, regardless of the situation. Hence, they are referred to as **generic strategies.** The best-known of these have been researched by Michael Porter.

Porter's Competitive Strategies

As discussed in Chapter 3, Michael Porter suggests that firms can take three basic approaches to setting strategy after completing industry and SWOT analysis:

1. Position the firm to enhance its capabilities to provide the best defense against the existing array of competitive forces
2. Influence the balance of forces through strategic moves as a way to improve the firm's relative position
3. Anticipate shifts in the factors underlying the forces and respond to the shifts to exploit change by choosing a strategy that is appropriate to the new competitive balance before rivals recognize it[11]

Within the philosophical framework established by these three approaches, Porter has suggested three major generic business-level strategies that may help a firm outperform other corporations engaged in similar activities: overall cost leadership, differentiation, and a focus strategy. These generic strategies allow a firm to cope with the five competitive forces that Porter identifies in his competitor analysis, as discussed in Chapter 3. They give the firm a way to add value and achieve a competitive advantage.

Cost Leadership   **Cost leadership** "requires aggressive construction of efficient-scale facilities, vigorous pursuit of cost reductions from experience, tight cost and overhead control, avoidance of marginal customer accounts, and cost minimization in areas like R&D, service, sales force, advertising, and so on. Low cost relative to competitors becomes the theme running through the entire strategy; though quality, service, and other areas cannot be ignored."[12] In fact, it's likely that high quality and good service will help achieve lower costs. This has generally been the experience at Stanley Works, Monroe Auto Equipment, Compaq Computer, and Rubbermaid.[13] The firm that has the lowest costs, or at least relatively low costs, will still have satisfactory returns even after it has met the costs of competition. Its competitors will not be able to match its levels of return.

Note, this is cost leadership, not price leadership. The difference between the two is margin. Ideally, a firm seeks to produce at relatively low cost and to sell at relatively high prices, thus yielding substantial margins. Wholesale cost cutting to achieve low-cost leadership, or at least to be cost competitive, does not appear to work as a single method for achieving low cost. Work must also be redesigned. In a process known as **right sizing,** firms not only cut their employment levels, but redesign work, changing how they manufacture or provide service, how they market, and how they manage.[14] Process mapping, in which work flows are systematically analyzed and streamlined, is also critical.[15]

Differentiation   **Differentiation** involves the development of a product or service that is perceived as unique in the industry. High levels of differentiation allow a firm to maintain sizeable profit margins because customers' brand loyalty reduces their sensitivity to price. Entry barriers arise from customer loyalty, as fewer substitutes can really replace such products as compared to competitors' undifferentiated products. While quality was a major differentiating factor in the 1980s, it will become a minimal cost of entry in the 1990s, making other differentiating factors necessary, for example, the ability to create and dominate whole new product markets, or to create high levels of service.[16] Gateway 2000 Inc. of South Dakota is a low-cost producer of IBM PC clones, which it sells by phone.

All of its strategic efforts, from its location in South Dakota, where labor is cheap and no state corporate taxes are imposed, to its supplier choices, its nimble but effective advertising campaign, and its control of overhead, are aimed at being the least-cost competitor (and in this case also the least-priced competitor by $200).[17]

FOCUS   A **focus strategy** consists of serving a particular target market very well, be it a specific buyer group or a segment of the industry product line. The strategy makes the underlying assumption that focusing its efforts allows the firm to provide better service or a better product more efficiently. The consequences of this strategy will be either lower cost or differentiation. In fact, as shown in Figure 6.5, Porter identifies focus as having two components—focused low cost and focused differentiation according to the scope of the target market. When the scope is narrow, the strategy is said to be focused.

For example, in 1991 Rubbermaid introduced an environmentally sound lunch box aimed at school kids who either wanted to protect the environment or were no longer allowed to have disposable containers of milk or juice at their schools. The green box, as it's known, has all plastic parts, eliminating the need for plastic wrap, paper cartons, and so on. All the rage among school children, it took less than a year to develop from concept to first sale. This is focused differentiation.[18]

Successful implementation of these three strategies requires differing skills, resources, and other organizational requirements. Porter's perspectives on these requirements are seen in Table 6.2.

FIGURE 6.5   Three Generic Strategies

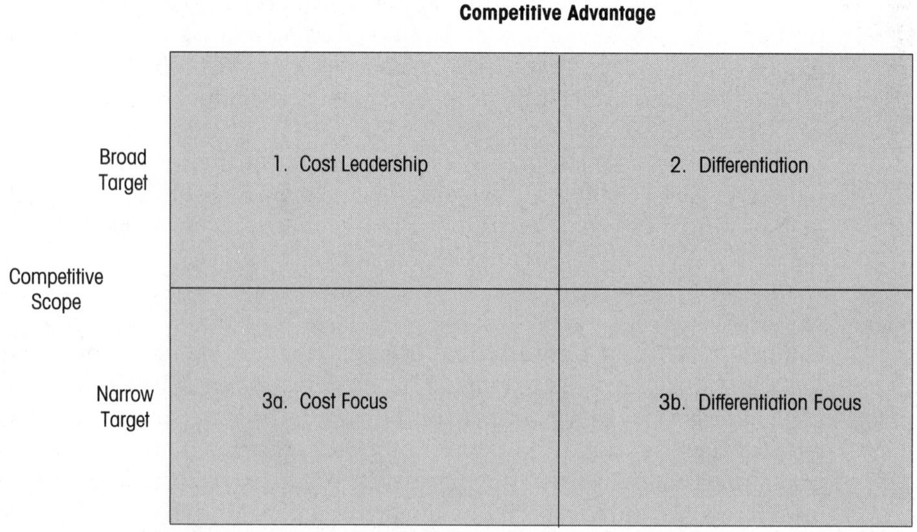

TABLE 6.2   Requirements for Generic Competitive Strategies

Generic Strategy	Commonly Required Skills and Resources	Common Organizational Requirements
Overall cost leadership	Sustained capital investment and access to capital Process engineering skills Intense supervision of labor Products designed for ease in manufacture Low-cost distribution system	Tight cost control Frequent, detailed control reports Structured organization and responsibilities Incentives based on meeting strict quantitative targets
Differentiation	Strong marketing abilities Product engineering Creative flair Strong capability in basic research Corporate reputation for quality or technological leadership Long tradition in the industry or unique combination of skills drawn from other businesses Strong cooperation from channels	Strong coordination among functions in R&D, product development, and marketing Subjective measurement and incentives instead of quantitative measures Amenities to attract highly skilled labor, scientists, or creative people
Focus	Combination of the above policies directed at the particular strategic target	Combination of the above policies directed at the regular strategic target

Source: Reprinted with permission of The Free Press, a Division of Macmillan, Inc. from *COMPETITIVE STRATEGY: Techniques for Analyzing Industries and Competitors* by Michael E. Porter, pp. 40–41. Copyright © 1980 by The Free Press.

Porter's generic strategies suggest first of all that these actions are appropriate to most situations, but in light of contingencies revealed by assessing industry characteristics and other factors. (Porter's industry analysis method was reviewed in Chapter 5.) Still, generic approaches overlook many complexities of particular situations. Analysis by Alan Murray suggests that each strategy will work only in certain environments.[19] On the other hand, Porter's strategies are conceptually and intuitively sound. A study by Roderick E. White lends support to Porter's cost and differentiation strategies. White examined 69 business units and found, not surprisingly, that firms with both cost and price advantages had the highest ROIs. The highest sales growth was achieved by those businesses that employed pure differentiation strategies. White also found that these strategies were positively correlated with organization performance when environmental factors were taken into account.[20]

Additional research by Gregory G. Dess and Peter S. Davis also supports the view that firms that use Porter's generic strategies perform better than other firms in the same industry that do not follow such strategies.[21] Recent research in France has shown that differentiation is a very successful strategy in stalemate industries.[22] Not all research, however, supports these findings. Some analysts question whether any generic strategy can cover all the contingencies of the strategic process.[23]

Value Added   The term **value added** describes the change a firm makes and thereby adds value to a product or service by some step in the manufacturing or service-generation process (activity chain), proceeding from raw materials to final product or service at its delivery point. The term comes from microeconomics, but Michael Porter has popularized it in the strategic management literature primarily because he views successful strategy as focusing on adding value at every point possible in the value chain. Thus, a firm can review each stage of the manufacturing or service-generation process for ways of reducing costs or providing meaningful differentiation. The significant point of the value-added concept is that one can add value at each step of the activity chain, by breaking the process down into its stages and uncovering ways of adding value at each stage.

The relative least-cost strategy concentrates on reducing costs in the value-added activity chain of the manufacturing or service-generation process. The major ways a cost advantage may be achieved by changing the **activity chain** include:[24]

1. Changing the product to eliminate all frills and extras (offer only a very basic, no-frills product or service)
2. Changing the production process to make it more efficient
3. Automating some high-cost/labor-intensive activity
4. Finding cheaper raw materials
5. Changing advertising and promotional activities common in the industry
6. Changing channels of distribution to sell through one's own sales force instead of through dealers or distributors
7. Relocating facilities closer to suppliers and/or customers in order to cut transportation costs
8. Practicing forward or backward vertical integration to eliminate other firms' profit margins
9. Focus on some particular segment of the market, eliminating the need to do something for everybody

Differentiation and Cost Position: *The* Generic Strategies

Porter suggests that the two dominant generic strategies of differentiation and least cost are virtually mutually exclusive. A firm that tries to combine them will be "stuck in the middle" between strategies and will thus be ineffective.[25] Alan Murray and Charles W. L. Hill, who have carefully studied these strategies, suggest that just the opposite is true. They believe the strategies can frequently be interdependent, and that they often should be.[26]

The perspective that more than one generic strategy can be pursued at a given moment is supported by research on 64 firms across eight domestic industries by William K. Hall of the University of Michigan. Hall's research revealed that for all practical purposes, there are only two generic strategies, and that combinations of them are successful. First, any company may (and most must) differentiate its product from all others in order to be successful. Second, the company must establish a cost position that is appropriate to its ability to differentiate its product.[27] The ideal combination of high differentiation and low cost is almost unbeatable in the marketplace, but a highly differentiated product that creates strong demand can succeed despite relatively high cost. Similarly, a very low-cost product with little differentiation will still be competitive.

Figure 6.6 shows the potential profit position that results from combinations of product differentiation and low-cost operation. Hill's research led directly to the formulation of this model. As Figure 6.6 indicates, the organization that has a highly differentiated product has a power alley in the market. So does the firm that produces a product at considerably lower cost than other firms in the industry. A firm that has double access to the power alley through both differentiation and low cost is in the Garden of Eden, a situation in which it is almost impossible to lose competitively. Conversely, high costs and poor differentiation land a firm in Death Valley.

Other possibilities exist. For example, when Apple Computers first introduced its Apple II, it had a highly differentiated product at a high cost and a high price. Since it had no competitors, Apple could charge virtually anything it wanted for the product early in the product life cycle. Later, as it moved to the Macintosh, it had a very low-cost product in relation to the market, but a highly differentiated

FIGURE 6.6   Hall's Competitiveness Model

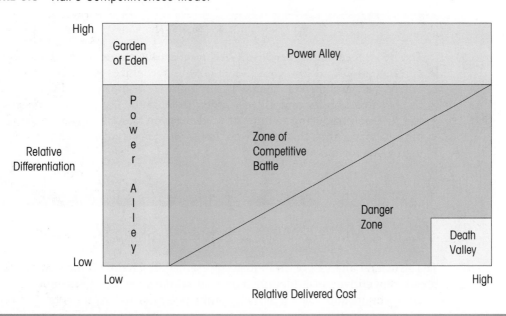

product, so it was virtually in the Garden of Eden. Apple chose not to pass on all of its savings from its low-cost strategy to consumers, instead increasing its profits by keeping prices relatively high, supported by high differentiation. Similarly, Caterpillar, the heavy-equipment manufacturer, had differentiated its product based on quality, but had high costs. Komatsu entered its heavy-equipment niche with a high quality product at low cost, throwing Caterpillar into a dramatic upheaval as it carried out a strategy to become a low-cost competitor. It also sought to improve its already high level of quality differentiation. These efforts proved successful in winning back market share, as the chapter's Global Strategic Challenge feature reveals.

Under the assumption that all additional generic grand strategies are based on the principle of differentiation, **Hall's competitiveness model** quickly and readily explains the strategic options available to a company. His research on this model has been substantiated by Peter Wright, Mark Kroll, Ben Kechia, and Charles Pringle. In researching 47 firms in the hand-tool industry, they found that firms that combined a low-cost strategy with a differentiation strategy outperformed those firms that competed mainly with one strategy or the other.[28] The work of Murray and Hill cited earlier suggests this model, as well.[29] Finally, Ray Stata, CEO of Analog Devices, Inc., of Boston, observes that in the early 1980s his firm followed either low-cost or differentiation strategies, but found that only when it pursued both did it achieve maximum profit potential.[30] Thus, we now know that both strategies can be pursued simultaneously, and they probably should be. Least cost must always follow differentiation as competitors duplicate product or service features in maturing industries.[31] Finally, both Porter and Hall assume competition. Niching is another possibility, as noted previously.[32]

AT THE OLIVE GARDEN

The Red Lobster and The Olive Garden reflect the combined strategies of differentiation and low cost. General Mills recognizes that it must first differentiate and then, at later stages in the product life cycle, lower costs. In both Red Lobster and Olive Garden restaurants, the firm's emphasis was first on introducing an innovative idea *and* on making sure, even in the introductory stages, that costs were low, that the customer perceived very high value for money spent.

Structural Analysis within Industries—Strategic Groups

The structural analysis of an industry presented in Chapter 5 focused on the five broad competitive forces identified by Michael Porter, which determine the nature of competition and the underlying profit potential in an industry.[33] However, within any industry, more in-depth analysis may be desirable. This was discussed in Chapter 4 as part of competitor analysis, on the work of learning about

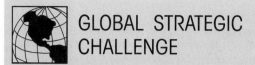

GLOBAL STRATEGIC CHALLENGE

CATERPILLAR FOCUSES ON THE FUTURE

Prior to 1982, Caterpillar Inc. had experienced 50 consecutive years of profits, with annual returns on owner's equity as high as 27 percent. For decades, this Peoria, Illinois-based earth moving equipment manufacturer had seemed almost invincible. Then, as chairman and CEO George Schaefer recalled, "almost overnight the whole world changed for us." Construction markets around the world collapsed. Commodity prices plunged, killing the demand for the mining, logging, and pipe-laying equipment the company produced. As the dollar rose in value, Japanese firms, especially Komatsu, aggressively attacked its markets. In addition, Caterpillar's unionized work force went on strike for 7 months. Caterpillar reported profits of $579 million in 1981, but losses for the next 3 years totaling $953 million.

Caterpillar already had the highest-quality product on the market, but it was being undercut by lower-priced competitors. It undertook major cost-cutting efforts, laying off 40 percent of its work force, 33,000 people. It redesigned work, increased automation, adopted just-in-time inventory practices, installed computerized production processes, changed plant layouts, and invested heavily in improved equipment for manufacturing. The results were significantly lower costs, allowing Caterpillar to regain market share against Komatsu. When the dollar fell, it did not raise its prices, as did U.S. auto manufacturers, enabling it to retain its market share. It also sought new markets and went after niches that it had largely ignored before. Part of the success of Caterpillar has been Schaefer's efforts to improve the use of people. Labor relations have improved significantly and participative management has been used to take advantage of worker expertise. Record profits of $616 million resulted in 1988.

Caterpillar is not resting on its laurels, though. It has formulated a global strategy that has resulted in significant inroads in the European market, with great expectations for profits as Europe 1992 construction momentum continues. It is moving to flexible manufacturing for several of its products. It has simplified product design to make manufacturing less expensive and to produce higher-quality products. It has improved its materials handling systems, worked closely with suppliers and distributors, and improved its information systems to give it a strategic advantage, not only in manufacturing, but in competitor intelligence and analysis. It is now the lowest-cost and highest-quality producer, and it seems well-positioned for the 1990s, in the United States as well as around the globe. In the United States, for example, it will benefit greatly from the need to enhance infrastructure and the effort to clean up the environment.

Sources: Neil S. Novich, "Leading Edge Distribution Strategies," *Journal of Business Strategy*, November/December 1990, pp. 48–53; Thomas N. Cochran, "Cat Fancier," *Barron's*, July 9, 1990, p. 30; Jeremy Main, "Manufacturing the Right Way," *Fortune*, May 21, 1990, pp. 54–64; Barbara Dutton, "Cat Climbs High with FMS," *Manufacturing Systems*, November 1989, pp. 16–22; Ronald Henkoff, "This Cat Is Acting Like a Tiger," *Fortune*, December 19, 1988, pp. 70–76; and "Going for the Lion's Share," *Business Week*, July 18, 1988, pp. 70–71.

competitors' resources, goals, objectives, strategies, skills, SWOT, and so on. The subject arises in several chapters in discussions of opportunities and threats. In addition, Michael Porter suggests that a firm must attach special importance to determining each competitor's strategy according to what he labels *strategic dimensions.* (These are essentially the same as what we have called *basic action strategies,* but also include generic strategies and relationships with major constituents such as a parent company or government.) Determining competitors' strategies allows one to map the firms into strategic groups. A **strategic group** is, "the group of firms in an industry following the same or a similar strategy along the strategic dimensions."[34] Typically, an industry accommodates a small number of strategic groups. One group might follow low-price, low-quality strategies. Another group might have medium prices, but offer high quality. Another group might offer high quality at high prices. A fourth group might keep prices low, and still offer high levels of quality.[35]

The basic belief is that, by analyzing which group a firm belongs to, several important strategic issues can be explored and related strategic decisions can be made. Most fundamentally, by looking at firms' membership in strategic groups, one understands competition in the industry and what opportunities remain to compete within the industry. Furthermore, different groups typically have different performance levels, based on return on investment and profit, for example, so firms may choose to change groups to raise profit levels. To do so, they must change strategy by altering strategic dimensions. Different groups face different levels of mobility barriers, different levels of bargaining power from suppliers and buyers, and different threats from substitutes and new entrants. Furthermore, each strategic group differs in intensity of rivalry among firms. Porter suggests that formulating competitive strategy can be viewed as choosing a strategic group in which to compete. Strengths and weaknesses would be compared against those of firms in the group.

Porter goes on to identify opportunities and risks according to strategic group analysis.[36] A strategic opportunity facing a firm would include:

1. Creating a new strategic group
2. Shifting to a more favorably situated group
3. Strengthening the structural position of the existing group or the firm's position in that group
4. Shifting to a new group and strengthening that group's structural position

Risks facing a firm are identified as follows:

1. Potential of other firms entering one's strategic group
2. Risks of factors reducing the mobility barriers of a firm's strategic group, lowering its power with customers or suppliers, eroding its position relative to substitute products, or exposing it to greater rivalry
3. Risks that accompany investments designed to improve the firm's position by increasing mobility barriers
4. Risks of attempting to overcome mobility barriers into more desirable strategic groups or entirely new groups

The first two risks, Porter suggests, are threats to the firm's existing position, or risks of inaction, whereas the latter two are risks of pursuing opportunities.

Strategic Group Mapping As an Analytical Tool

In using group mapping, it is best to begin with a simple matrix of two dimensions, perhaps placing low cost on one dimension and quality on the other. One could evaluate degrees of each of these dimensions from low to high. One could then plot firms in groups to determine their strategies and analysis could then lead to strategic decisions. Once this method has been practiced, then more complicated matrices could be created. It would be very useful to practice this strategic group analysis with some of the cases presented in Part 2 of this text.

The research related to strategic groups has been substantial for such a complex and recent development in strategic management. Generally speaking, the concept of strategic groups is not only appealing intuitively and conceptually, but it is also empirically demonstrable.[37] Differences in strategic group performance have appeared in some studies, but not in others.[38] The stability of the environment has been shown to be an important factor in examining strategic groups (for example, critical strategic dimensions change with time[39]) and a number of applications have been pursued.[40] In summary, however, the concept clearly seems valid, but, like all strategic management techniques, is no panacea. The strategist should consider strategic group analysis as part of the strategy formulation process, but rely on integrative skills, often employing intuition, once this and other analyses are completed.

The Miles and Snow Typology

Raymond E. Miles and Charles C. Snow have identified three strategic stances firms take to cope with varying degrees of environmental complexity, from solid stability to extreme instability: those of the defender, the analyzer, and the prospector. Defenders, who basically seek to defend narrow market positions, do best in stable environments. Prospectors continually seek new product and market opportunities, and therefore do best in changing environments. Analyzers follow a middle strategy and seem to proper best in moderately stable environments. A fourth type, the reactor, essentially relies on unplanned reactions to environmental conditions.[41] Since one of strategic management's ten challenges for the 1990s is an increasingly complex environment, these typologies offer a cue as to which strategy might be the better choice. The prospector seems likely to be the best of the three options for most firms.[42] WordPerfect Corporation of Orem, Utah is a good example of a prospector. It continually seeks new products for new markets, trying to meet new customer needs, for example, by moving boldly with computer graphics in 1989, and into a Windows® environment in 1991.

The Miles and Snow typology has been examined by several research studies for both its validity and its ability to predict performance. Generally, the concept of the four types has been supported.[43] Firms have been shown to change strategic type, generally toward the prospector, as their environments have grown more turbulent.[44] The reactor has been shown to be the least strategically successful of the four types.[45]

ADDITIONAL GENERIC STRATEGIES

Several strategies have been recommended for firms in specific situations.

Strategies for Firms Competing in Stagnant Industries

Richard G. Hamermesh and Steven B. Silk suggest that successful firms in stagnant industries do three things:[46]

1. **They identify, create, and exploit growth segments in their industries.** Despite a decline in the number of motion picture theaters over a 20-year period, General Cinema recognized that the shopping center segment was growing. It moved into this market in full force, successfully avoiding the pitfalls of a stagnant industry.
2. **They emphasize product quality and product improvement.** Despite stagnation in the coffee industry, General Foods' innovative freeze-dried coffee has proved to be a big money maker. Perhaps one of the best firms at this strategy is Gillette, which somehow manages to improve either its blades or its razors every 3 to 5 years.
3. **They systematically and consistently improve the efficiency of their production and distribution systems.** The Japanese auto, camera, and steel industries epitomize this approach.

Strategies for Dominant Firms

Philip Kotler suggests the following strategies for dominant firms:[47]

1. **Keep the offensive.** Keep pushing for increased market share. Don't give competitors a chance to strengthen themselves. Be efficient and innovative; don't be content. IBM does this well.
2. **Use a fortification strategy.** Introduce individual brands to compete with your own successful brands, keeping the competition from entering the market. Philip Morris has been adept at this strategy. As an alternative, you can protect your product's technology or patents. Coca-Cola has done this well; only three people at any one time know Coke's formula.
3. **Use a confrontation strategy.** Be prepared to beat the competition in advertising and in price. Ward off all price challenges of smaller firms by meeting or beating their prices. General Motors has done these things for years.
4. **Use a maintenance strategy.** Set objectives for the firm's market position and

then maintain investment accordingly, using excess cash flows to support growth businesses.

Strategies for Firms in Declining Industries

Kathryn Rudie Harrigan suggests that firms in declining industries most frequently have the following alternatives:[48]

1. **Early exit.** We might call this getting out while the getting is good.
2. **Milking the investment.** Remove all possible cash flows.
3. **Shrinking selectively.** Choose the available remaining markets and advance into them strongly.
4. **Employing holding patterns.** Hold your own.
5. **Increasing investments.** Increase investment only where this creates a long-term advantage.

Strategies for Firms with Low Market Share

Richard B. Hamermesh, M. Jack Anderson, Jr., and J. Elizabeth Harris have found that firms that succeed with low market share have four common characteristics: "they carefully segment their markets, they use research and development funds efficiently, they think small, and their chief executives' influence is pervasive."[49]

1. **Market segmentation.** They segment their markets because they can serve only a limited number. They segment not just by products and customers, but "by level of customer service, stage of production, price performance characteristics, credit arrangements, location of plants, characteristics of manufacturing equipment, channels of distribution and financial policies."[50]
2. **Efficient R&D.** They channel their research into the areas that will be most beneficial for them because they usually cannot match their larger competitors' R&D budgets.
3. **Think small.** They limit their growth and they diversify cautiously.
4. **Ubiquitous chief executives.** They are strong-willed and involved in almost all aspects of the company. This might change, however, as employees demand more say in their companies' fortunes.

A number of other strategies have been suggested for firms in specific situations. Among these are contingency strategies for service firms, strategies for attacking industry leaders, underdog strategies, endgame strategies, and strategies for pursuing intensive growth.[51]

These and numerous other strategy suggestions have been based on the successes of a limited number of firms. This is not to discount their validity, but only to remind you that, because of the sizes of the samples on which the recommendations are based, these strategies cannot be considered firm rules for action.

Strategic Recommendations According to Strength and Product Life Cycle Stage

As you have seen in Harold Fox's model in Table 6.1, and as you have no doubt learned in your studies of marketing, certain strategies suit certain stages of the product or industry life cycle. A review of the research confirms that firms do indeed follow different strategies at different stages of the product life cycle, and that such a course of action is appropriate.[52] Strategies may also vary by industry. A generic model developed by Peter Patel and Michael Younger, seen in Table 6.3, shows strategies that take into account the **product life cycle** and the relative strength of the company.[53] Strategies must also consider the business cycle.[54]

Product/firm/industry life cycles affect strategy in another way as firms face different dominant problems in each growth stage. Robert K. Kazanjian found this to be true, at least for some stages, in a study of 105 firms. However, some problems remained dominant across all stages. This suggests that both stage and problem type and strength should be considered when formulating strategy.[55] Based on what we know about contingency theory, this interpretation certainly seems reasonable.

The whole concept of speed strategies discussed in Chapter 3 and earlier in this chapter focuses on reducing the time it takes to get to the product life cycle stage of introduction. Research clearly shows that products that reach the market

TABLE 6.3 Strategic Guidelines As a Function of Industry Maturity and Competitive Position

	Embryonic	Growing	Mature	Aging
Dominant	All-out push for share	Hold position	Hold position	Hold position
	Hold position	Hold share	Grow with industry	
Strong	Attempt to improve position	Attempt to improve position	Hold position	Hold position or harvest
	All-out push for share	Push for share	Grow with industry	
Favorable	Selective or all-out push for share	Attempt to improve position	Custodial or maintenance	Harvest
	Selectively attempt to improve position	Selective push for share	Find niche and attempt to protect	Phased withdrawal
Tenable	Selectively push for position	Find niche and protect it	Find niche and hang on or phased withdrawal	Phased withdrawal or abandon
Weak	Up or out	Turnaround or abandon	Turnaround or phased withdrawal	Abandon

Source: Reprinted by permission from *Long Range Planning*, April 1978, Peter Patel and Michael Younger, "A Frame of Reference for Strategy Development." Copyright 1978 Pergamon Press Ltd., Oxford, England.

ahead of their competition are more profitable.[56] It is also increasingly apparent that long product life cycles are relics of the past. Product life cycles are getting shorter and shorter.[57] This is a major reason that firms are attempting to exploit products' service life cycles.[58]

Generic Theories: A Commentary

You have been exposed to a number of generic strategy formulation theories. Considered in total, they may seem somewhat bewildering. Indeed, they overlap and even contradict one another. They typically do not build on one another, although we have noted relationships among Porter's and Hall's efforts. We present the various strategies to provide you with a feel for the alternatives and with some ideas for your own strategy formulation efforts as you do case analysis. You may wish to investigate some details of individual strategies if you encounter companies in the situations for which they are recommended.

DESCRIPTIVE CHARACTERISTICS APPROACH TO STRATEGY FORMULATION

One way to investigate the reasons for a firm's success may be called the *descriptive characteristics approach*. A number of authors have attempted to determine the characteristics of successful firms, but none has received as much overwhelming acceptance as Thomas J. Peters and Robert H. Waterman, Jr.

In Search of Excellence

In their book *In Search of Excellence*, Peters and Waterman identify eight characteristics that their research reveals to be common to the best-run companies.[59] These **excellence characteristics** are business management practices that seem to account for the successful companies' performance. During a 2-year period, Peters and Waterman examined, through interviews, questionnaires, and secondary sources of information, the characteristics of 36 of the most successful large, single-industry firms in the United States. They narrowed their original sample of some 75 firms on the basis of various performance criteria, or of representativeness in the cases of 13 European firms. The eight common characteristics they found are highlighted in Exhibit 6.1. Though the book is not without its critics,[60] many company presidents swear by it, encouraging, and often requiring, their executives to read it.

Daniel T. Carroll provides a critical profile of the methodological and conceptual problems in Peters and Waterman's book. Carroll explains that their sample is small and is not truly representative of American business. Perhaps most telling, the sample does not contain a group of unsuccessful companies for comparison, giving no guarantee that unsuccessful companies do not share these same eight characteristics. Peters and Waterman fail to give a detailed description of how they identified these characteristics or how they analyzed the firms.

EXHIBIT 6.1 Excellence Characteristics Identified in *In Search of Excellence*

1. **A bias for action**—for getting on with it. Even though these companies may be analytical in their approach to decision making, they are not paralyzed by that fact (as so many others seem to be). In many of these companies the standard operating procedure is "Do it, fix it, try it." Says a Digital Equipment Corporation senior exccutive, for example, "When we've got a big problem here, we grab ten senior guys and stick them in a room for a week. They come up with an answer *and* implement it."

2. **Close to the customer.** These companies learn from the people they serve. They provide unparalleled quality, service, and reliability—things that work and last. They succeed in differentiating—à la Frito-Lay (tortilla chips), Maytag (washers), or Tupperware—the most commodity-like products. Many of the innovative companies got their best product ideas from customers. That comes from listening, intently and regularly.

3. **Autonomy and entrepreneurship.** The innovative companies foster many leaders and many innovators throughout the organization. They are a hive of what we've come to call champions; 3M has been described as "so intent on innovation that its essential atmosphere seems not like that of a large corporation but rather a loose network of laboratories and cubbyholes populated by feverish inventors and dauntless entrepreneurs who let their imaginations fly in all directions."

4. **Productivity through people.** The excellent companies treat the rank and file as the root source of quality and productivity gain. They do not foster we/they labor attitudes or regard capital investment as the fundamental source of efficiency improvement. Texas Instruments' chairman, Mark Shepherd, talks about it in terms of every worker being "seen as a source of ideas, not just acting as a pair of hands"; each of his more than 9,000 People Involvement Program, or PIP, teams (TI's quality circles) does contribute to the company's sparkling productivity record.

5. **Hands on, value-driven.** Thomas Watson, Jr., said that "the basic philosophy of an organization has far more to do with its achievements than do technological or economic resources, organizational structure, innovation and timing." Watson and Hewlett-Packard's William Hewlett are legendary for walking the plant floors.

6. **Stick to the knitting.** Robert W. Johnson, former Johnson & Johnson chairman, put it this way: "Never acquire a business you don't know how to run." Or as Edward G. Harness, past chief executive at Procter & Gamble, said, "This company has never left its base. We seek to be anything but a conglomerate."

7. **Simple form, lean staff.** The underlying structural forms and systems in the excellent companies are elegantly simple. Top-level staffs are lean; it is not uncommon to find a corporate staff of fewer than 100 people running multibillion-dollar enterprises.

8. **Simultaneous loose/tight controls.** The excellent companies are both centralized and decentralized. For the most part, they have pushed autonomy down to the shop floor or product development team. On the other hand, they are fanatic centralists around the few core values they hold dear.

Source: *In Search of Excellence: Lessons from America's Best-Run Companies*, by Thomas J. Peters and Robert H. Waterman, Jr. Copyright 1982 by Thomas J. Peters and Robert H. Waterman, Jr. Reprinted by permission of Harper Collins, Publishers.

Depending heavily on secondary data, they focus primarily on management practices and fail to examine carefully the impacts of other factors on success, considering neither technology nor market share or competitors' actions, for example. Finally, Carroll charges that Peters and Waterman's arguments are unfortunately biased and unsystematic.[61]

Interestingly, five additional studies reported similar results. Michael A. Hitt and R. Duane Ireland found reason to doubt whether Peters and Waterman's excellent companies were all that excellent when compared by a broader array of performance criteria.[62] Kenneth E. Aupperle, William Acar, and David E. Booth compared the excellent firms to the 1,000 firms reported in *Forbes* for its annual survey. The upper quartile of these firms consistently outperformed the excellent firms on return on assets, return on equity, market valuation, and sales growth.[63] Vasudevan Ramanujam and N. Venkatraman compared 41 of the excellent companies to a randomly selected group of 41 firms from the Fortune 1,000. They did not find the excellent companies among the highest performers, and the randomly selected firms seemed to have many of the same characteristics.[64] Similar studies by Michelle Chapman and by Richard Kolodny, Martin Lawrence, and Arabinda Ghosh also show that the excellent companies didn't all remain excellent performers and that other companies often outperform them.[65]

On balance, *In Search of Excellence* must be considered a major contribution to management thought, one that is perhaps intuitively sound, but limited in critical ways in its research design. Its findings are suspect and its comments on the need for improvement in the rational model, though perhaps well-founded, are not sufficiently supported by hard evidence. (Hard evidence may, of course, be more difficult to come by than rationally and empirically oriented researchers care to admit.) As a consequence of these complaints and similar ones made by other critics, Peters and Waterman's eight characteristics should be regarded with caution. Furthermore, the ten strategic management challenges identified in Chapter 1 may cause some of these characteristics to wax or wane in importance in the future.

An example of an excellent company is Florida's Barnett Banks. As this chapter's Strategic Challenge feature indicates, Barnett meets each of Peters and Waterman's eight criteria. As you read the feature, ask yourself, how this firm meets the criteria from Exhibit 6.1.

In a later book, *A Passion for Excellence*, Peters and Nancy K. Austin suggest that only two things really distinguish excellent companies: they are customer-oriented and they are innovative. Peters and Austin also emphasize the importance of a system they call **management by wandering around (MBWA),** a very participative, loose/tight leadership style.[66] Barnett's customer orientation and its management style could fairly be described as management by wandering around, and such programs as Senior Partners clearly mark it as innovative, hence it meets the new criteria established by Peters and Austin, as well.

Ironically, in his more recent book, *Thriving on Chaos*, Peters implies that excellence is principally a function of the ability and willingness to adapt to change. Set characteristics such as he and Waterman described appear to be losing value. Peters seems to have come to believe that innovation, a one of five prescriptions for chaos, is a key, if not *the* key, for functioning in chaos.[67]

PIMS and Related Studies

Profit Impact of Market Strategies, or PIMS, was a project organized in 1972 by the Market Science Institute, a nonprofit research organization affiliated with the

STRATEGIC CHALLENGE

BARNETT BANKS GROW BY PROVIDING SERVICE

Barnett Banks' share of Florida bank deposits grew from 8.2 percent in 1976 to 20.2 percent in 1986. Its assets grew from slightly over $2 billion to $20 billion in the same period. It expanded rapidly, from 75 offices in 1977 to 457, grouped into 35 regional divisions, in early 1987. Many of these new banks were acquisitions.

Much of Barnett's success depends on innovation. Barnett was the first U.S. bank to buy a healthy savings and loan and the first Florida bank to buy an out-of-state bank. It claims to be the first bank in the United States to offer stock directly to depositors; it was one of the first banks to form a political action committee. It didn't lend much money abroad, as most other major banks did. It was an early user of sophisticated electronics. It was one of the first banks to heavily target the older, senior citizens market. It was an early user of sophisticated credit analysis expert systems.

Despite its extensive innovation, much of its success is attributed to the service it provides. Barnett, the nation's 28th largest bank holding company, perceives itself as a retailer of services, comments Steven Hansell, Barnett's chief financial officer. Barnett tries the mom-and-pop approach as opposed to its lower-cost, supermarket-style competitors, but so far (to borrow a favorite Barnett phrase), it works.

Barnett's culture rewards risk-taking and results. It is an informal bank with few squabbles about turf. Seniority and social connections count for little. It is highly market-oriented, advertises heavily, and seeks customers aggressively. Barnett caters to the senior market, for example, with its Senior Partners program, which accumulated $3.9 billion in deposits in 4 years, an amount equal to the assets of a sizeable bank. Barnett segmented even this market into many tiny niches. The services provided by its branches in such affluent areas as Naples, Florida differ from those offered in less affluent areas. Individual bank managers are given unusual freedom of operation for the industry. One manager is reported to have won over a major client simply by striking through a line that offended the client in a loan form. Each branch manager feels that he or she is managing his or her own business. Barnett wants to compete on some basis other than price whenever possible. One customer notes, "What I like is if you have a problem, they know your name."

But autonomy does not mean lack of control. Every month hundreds of top managers receive 36-page reports analyzing the operations of the banks in the 35 divisions according to 23 measures. Each bank president's efforts are compared not only with his own goals, but with the performance and goals of others. Barnett is banking on the future; it had 600 branches in 1990, thus securing the state for itself. Branches take approximately 5 years to become profitable, so currently 77 percent of Barnett's profits come from the one-third of its offices that are more than 10 years old. Expectations are high, although some observers, such as Charles Wick, Southeast Bank's chairman, say that Barnett's high operating cost will make it uncompetitive. Barnett's people retort that they serve the customer, and that if what they offer is what the customer wants, they will survive and prosper.

Source: Danette Niedospial and Clinton R. Swift, "Image & Telecommunications," *Bank Management*, November 1990, pp. 60–64; Michael P. Sullivan, "Seniors—Today's Hottest Market," *United States Banker*, June 1990, pp. 16–20; Vanessa Bush, "Why Are Banks Buying Savings Institutions?" *Savings Institutions*, April 1990, pp. 30–36; Alan Redding, "New Technologies Support Credit Analysis at Barnett Banks, Canadian Imperial," *Bank Administration*, December 1989, pp. 48–52; Thomas E. Ricks, "Branching Out: Attentive to Service Barnett Grows Fast, Keeps Profit Up," *The Wall Street Journal*, April 3, 1987, pp. 1, 27.

Harvard Business School. This project was a strategic information-sharing experience among 57 major North American corporations. It had two initial phases: in the first, only 36 corporations supplied information on some 350 businesses; in the second, 57 companies provided information on 620 businesses. Later more firms were added.

The original intent of the program was to determine the impact of market strategy on profit. In addition, the project sought a bias on which to estimate ROI for organizations in varying situations. If such a basis could be determined, it could help an organization to select businesses in which to diversify, projects in which to invest, projects to divest, and projects with which, in general, to balance its investment portfolio. Information related to 37 major variables in these corporations was regressed against their ROIs to determine which of these variables was the most explanatory. Some of the more significant contributory variables, according to PIMS, included the following:[68]

1. **Market share**—the ratio of dollar sales in a given time period to total sales by all competitors in the same market (The importance of market share to profitability has been generally, but not always, supported by other research.[69])
2. **Product (service) quality**—the quality of each participating company's offerings appraised on several bases
3. **Marketing expenditures**—total cost of sales force, advertising, sales promotion, market research, and marketing administration
4. **R&D expenditures**—total cost of research and development in process improvement
5. **Investment intensity**—ratio of total investment to sales (high investment has a negative impact on sales)
6. **Corporate diversity**—ratios that affect the number of industrial categories in which most corporations operate
7. **Other company factors**—The primary concern here is organizational size.

Additional studies across a wide variety of industries have provided general support for the original **PIMS factors.**[70] As with any research, however, these findings are limited in their applicability until additional supporting research is reported. The correlation/regression techniques used in the PIMS project do not truly explain relationships, but rather indicate their statistical strength. Further, some of the variables identified apply more to some situations than others. These *universal truths,* as the PIMS factors have sometimes been called, do not apply equally to all industries or to all firms in an industry, given such variables as market conditions, the economy, and market position. Recent research shows market share and profit to be strongly related only in some situations.[71] Indeed, we have already noted strategies recommended for firms in various market positions, and we shall be examining others. It is possible that the PIMS findings would not hold in time periods other than the one of the study (although later studies have supported the PIMS findings). Further, the PIMS study very probably suffers from statistical methodological problems, multicollinearity, to be specific. Also, PIMS assumes only one performance objective.[72] Other variables can be cited that either were not examined by the PIMS researchers or did not prove to be sufficiently explanatory in this particular study.

Nevertheless, this project has shown some common ROI indicators for large, multifaceted corporations in varying industries and in differing situations. Choice of a strategy is still at least in part a function of industry. Additional research should isolate behaviors that succeed in certain industries and in groups of firms within those industries. For example, two studies indicate that the five industry analysis factors defined by Michael Porter may have a bearing on the market share a firm commands.[73] Finally, it is very difficult to implement the knowledge gained from such research. Knowing that market share, for example, is a critical factor is one thing; gaining it is another.

FUNCTIONAL SUPPORTIVE STRATEGIES AS FOCAL POINTS OF THE GRAND STRATEGY

Functional strategies are designed to support the competitive efforts of business strategies. There are two types of functional strategies:

1. Economic functional strategies define the firm's functions as an economic entity. They focus on marketing and the functions that support it, and on such functions as finance, operations, human resource management, information systems, and research and development. These functions are the focus of many generic strategies.
2. Management functional strategies focus on the management functions of planning, organizing (including staffing), leading, controlling, decision making, communicating, representing, and integrating.

Marketing is the first consideration in the business strategy because it is basic to the SBU's central focus—competition. The other support functions are grouped with it because they promote the competitive effort of the business strategy.

It is important to think of the management functions as integrated with rather than separate from the economic functions. As the **managerial matrix** shown in Figure 6.7 indicates, the management functions cross the boundaries of all functions of the organization. Thus marketing, finance, operations, human resources, and the like must all be managed; marketing planning is necessary, as are financial organizing, leading of operations, and human resource control.

FIGURE 6.7   Managerial Matrix

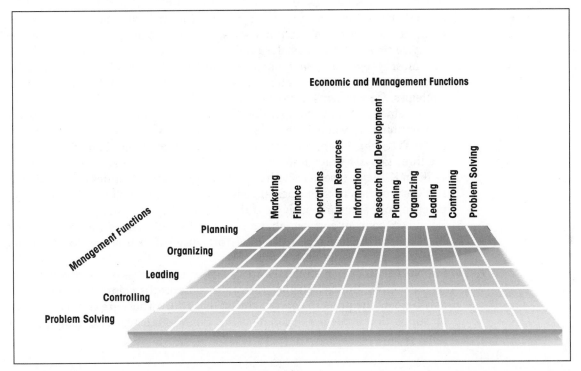

Source: Reprinted with permission of Macmillan Publishing Company from *The Management Challenge* by James M. Higgins. Copyright © 1991 by Macmillan Publishing Company.

Similarly, the management functions must be managed—planning, organizing, leading, and controlling must be planned, organized, led, and controlled.

In examining the roles of functional strategies, this text will not describe each function in detail. The key components of such strategies are the subjects of other courses, and Chapter 3 discussed strategies for the 1990s in these areas. Furthermore, Table 6.1 reviewed some of the principal strategies for these functions over the product life cycle.

STRATEGIC MANAGER'S SUMMARY

1. The contingency approach to strategy formulation involves the identification of strategic variables and their impacts on what strategies should be formulated, given various conditions of those variables. The approach is conceptually appropriate, but difficult to put into practice because of the numerous variables involved. It does offer the opportunity to improve strategy formulation by relating strategy to the factors that influence it, but because of its complexity, models are most often overly simplified.

2. Several generic strategies offer sound alternatives to the contingency approach. These strategies, based partly on research and partly on experience, suggest that some strategies are appropriate in most situations or in certain kinds of situations. Most contingency and generic strategies are based on the life cycle stage of the particular product or service.

3. The most recognized generic strategy model is that of Michael Porter, who identifies focus, differentiation, and cost leadership as the key generic strategies. He views five factors as defining the industry situation: intensity of rivalry among current competition, buyer power, supplier power, threat of new entrants, and substitutes. Based on these factors, strategic group analysis, and SWOT, plus its approaches to strategy, the firm would then choose one of the three generic strategies.

4. William K. Hall's research, with support from others, identifies differentiation and cost position as the principal generic strategies. He believes that firms can practice both simultaneously, and the research supports that contention.

5. The PIMS concept suggests that a series of factors/actions can be identified that lead to high levels of profit performance. Market share, for example, correlates very highly with profit.

6. Supportive functional strategies are critical to the success of the organization. In a few firms, these strategies do not just support the competitive effort, but may become the primary components of that effort. There are two major types of supportive strategies: economic functional strategies and management functional strategies.

KEY TERMS

activity chain
competitive strategic advantage
contingency strategies
cost leadership
differentiation
directional policy matrix
excellence characteristics
focus strategy
functional strategies
generic strategies

Hall's competitiveness model
management by wandering around
  (MBWA)
managerial matrix
PIMS factors
Porter's generic strategies
product life cycle
right sizing
strategic group
value-added

DISCUSSION QUESTIONS

1. Table 6.1 identifies appropriate business strategies over the product life cycle. Refer to this table as you discuss the types of actions IBM might take over the life of its personal computer series.

2. Examine the directional policy matrix represented in Figure 6.4. One of the strategies, phased withdrawal, appears twice. Why?

3. Peters and Waterman, in their book *In Search of Excellence*, identified eight characteristics that they believe to be common to the best-run companies. What are these eight characteristics? Are they still recognized as primary in today's business environment? Evaluate a company in accordance with these criteria.

4. Peters and Nancy K. Austin re-emphasized closeness to the customer, added innovation, and stressed the importance of leadership, especially MBWA (management by wandering around), in *A Passion for Excellence*. Discuss these factors and their implications for future strategies.

5. What was the original intent of the PIMS project? How has its focus changed over the years since 1972?

6. What are the three generic strategies proposed by Michael Porter? What are the two proposed by William Hall? Describe Hall's competitiveness model. Use it to illustrate some company's strategy.

7. Provide examples illustrating the importance of both economic and management functional support strategies. Can you name firms where these strategies are the focus of the grand strategy?

8. Peters and Waterman have said that "the excellent companies live their commitment to people." Analyze a firm, such as Hewlett-Packard, which owes its success in large part to its implementation of this concept. Why does the concept work? If it is so successful, why don't more firms employ people orientations?

STRATEGIC AUDIT QUESTIONS

1. Does this company know what business or businesses it's in? Is it in the right business or businesses?

2. Could this firm use strategies such as those recommended by Harold Fox (in Table 6.1)?

3. Position the products of each of its businesses on the directional policy matrix (Figure 6.4). What does this exercise tell you about the firm's strategy? What do you recommend?

4. Is each of this company's businesses using one of Porter's focus, differentiation, or cost leadership strategies? None of them? What strategy do you recommend it adopt?

5. Position the firm's businesses on Hall's competitiveness model (Figure 6.5). Where do you locate it? What do you recommend?

6. Would any of the additional generic strategies be appropriate to this company?

7. Could the firm make better use of its knowledge of its industry's life cycle status, as by using the Patel and Younger model (Table 6.3)? How?

8. Is this an excellent company as measured by the criteria proposed by Peters, Waterman, and Austin?

9. How does the organization stack up against the PIMS findings? How high is its market share, for example?

10. How well do each of the management functional strategies support the corporate and business strategies?
Economic functions:

- Marketing
- Finance
- Operations

- Human resources
- Management information system
- R&D

Management functions:

- Planning
- Organizing
- Leading

- Controlling
- Communicating
- Problem solving

Endnotes

1. Michael A. Hitt and R. Duane Ireland, "Corporate Distinctive Competency, Strategy, Industry, and Performance," *Strategic Management Journal*, July/September 1985, pp. 273–293.

2. Kenichi Ohmae, "Getting Back to Strategy," *Harvard Business Review*, November–December 1988, p. 149.

3. Bradley A. Stertz, "Domino's Beefs Up Menu to Keep Pace with Rivals," *The Wall Street Journal*, April 21, 1989, pp. B1, B4.

4. Joseph Bower's opening remarks at the Strategic Management Society conference, Boston, October 14, 1987.

5. Based on William K. Hall, "Survival Strategies in a Hostile Environment," *Harvard Business Review*, September/October 1980, pp. 73–86; Michael E. Porter, *Competitive Strategy* (New York: Free Press, 1980).

6. Regis McKenna, "Marketing Is Everything," *Harvard Business Review*, January–February 1991, pp. 65–79.

7. C. W. Hofer, "Towards a Contingency Theory of Business Strategy," *Academy of Management Journal*, December 1975, pp. 784–810.

8. Ari Ginsburg and N. Venkatranan, "Contingency Perspectives of Organizational Strategy: A Critical Review of the Empirical Research," *Academy of Management Review*, Fall 1985, pp. 421–434.

9. D. E. Hussey, "Portfolio Analysis: Practical Experience with the Directional Policy Matrix," *Long Range Planning*, August 1978, pp. 1–9.

10. I. Ayal, A. Peer, and J. Zif, "Selecting Industries for Export Growth—A Directional Policy Matrix Approach," *Journal of Macromarketing*, Spring 1987, pp. 22–33.

11. The list is a close paraphrase of one in Porter, *Competitive Strategy*, pp. 29–30.

12. Ibid.

13. Erik Calonius, "Smart Moves by Quality Champs," in *The New American Century*, special issue of *Fortune*, Spring/Summer 1991, pp. 24–28.

14. Max Messner, "Right-Sizing Reshapes Staffing Strategies," *Human Resource Magazine*, October 1991, pp. 60–62; Ronald Henkoff, "Cost Cutting: How to Do It Right," *Fortune*, April 9, 1990, p. 40.

15. Thomas A. Stewart, "GE Keeps Those Ideas Coming," *Fortune*, August 12, 1991, pp. 40–49.

16. Gary Hamel and C. K. Prahalad, "Corporate Imagination and Expeditionary Marketing," *Harvard Business Review*, July–August 1991, pp. 81–91; Eric Rolfe Greenberg, "Customer Service: The Key to Competitiveness," *Management Review*, December 1990, pp. 29–31; Barry Farber and Joyce Wycoff, "Customer Service: Evolution and Revolution," *Sales & Marketing Management*, May 1991, pp. 44–51.

17. Andrew Kupfer, "The Champ of Cheap Clones," *Fortune*, September 23, 1991, pp. 115–120.

18. Zachary Schuller, "At Rubbermaid, Little Things Mean a Lot," *Business Week*, November 11, 1991, p. 126.

19. Alan I. Murray, "A Contingency View of Porter's 'Generic Strategies,'" *Academy of Management Review*, July 1988, pp. 390–400.

20. R. E. White, "Generic Business Strategies, Organizational Context, and Performance: An Empirical Investigation," *Strategic Management Journal*, July/August 1986, pp. 217–231.

21. G. G. Dess and P. S. Davis, "Porter's (1980) Generic Strategies as Determinants of Strategic Group Membership and Organizational Performance," *Academy of Management Journal*, September 1984.

22. R. Calori and J. M. Ardisson, "Differentiation Strategies in 'Stalemate' Industries," *Strategic Management Journal*, May/June 1988, pp. 255–269.

23. C. Y. Woo and K. O. Cool, "Generic Competitive

Strategies: Performance and Functional Strategy Complements," paper presented to the Strategic Management Society, Paris, October 1983.

24. Michael E. Porter, *Competitive Advantage* (New York: Free Press, 1985) pp. 97–115.

25. Ibid., p. 17.

26. Murray, "Contingency View"; Charles W. L. Hill, "Differentiation versus Low Cost or Differentiation and Low Cost: A Contingency Framework," *Academy of Management Review*, July 1988, pp. 401–412.

27. Hall, "Survival Strategies."

28. Peter Wright, Mark Kroll, Ben Kechia, and Charles Pringle, "Strategic Portfolio, Market Share and Performance," *Industrial Management*, May/June 1990, pp. 23–28.

29. Murray and Hill, "Contingency View," pp. 401–412.

30. Ray Stata, "Organizational Learning: The Key to Management Innovation," *Sloan Management Review*, Spring 1989, pp. 63–74.

31. William E. Fulmer and Jack Goodwin, "Differentiation: Begin with the Consumer," *Business Horizons*, September/October 1988, pp. 55–56.

32. Peter Wright, "The Strategic Options of Least-Cost, Differentiation, and Niche," *Business Horizons*, March/April 1986, pp. 21–26.

33. Porter, *Competitive Strategy*.

34. Ibid., p. 129. The strategic dimensions, or basic action strategies, that Porter identifies include specialization, brand identification, push versus pull, channel selection, product quality, technological leadership, vertical integration, cost position, service, price policy, leverage, relationship with parent company, and relationship with homes and host government.

35. Ibid., p. 131 (abbreviated and adapted).

36. Ibid., pp. 150, 151.

37. Pam Lewis and Howard Thomas, "The Linkage between Strategy, Strategic Groups, and Performance in the U.K. Retail Grocery Industry," *Strategic Management Journal*, September 1990, pp. 385–397.

38. Michael W. Lawless, Donald D. Bergh, and William D. Wilsted, "Performance Variations among Strategic Group Members: An Examination of Individual Firm Capability," *Journal of Management*, December 1989, pp. 649–661; Karel O. Cool and Dan Schendel, "Strategic Group Formation and Performance: The Case of the U.S. Pharmaceutical Industry, 1963–1982," *Management Science*, vol. 33, no. 9, pp. 1–24.

39. Briance Mascarenhas, "Strategic Group Dynamics," *Academy of Management Journal*, June 1989, pp. 333–352; Avi Fiegenbaum, D. Sudharshan, and Howard Thomas, "The Concept of Strategic Time Periods in Strategic Group Research," *Managerial & Decision Economics*, June 1987, pp. 139–148.

40. For example, see Raphael Amit, Ian Domowitz, and Chaim Fershtman, "Thinking One Step Ahead: The Use of Conjectures in Competitor Analysis," *Strategic Management Journal*, October 1988, pp. 431–442.

41. Raymond E. Miles and Charles C. Snow, *Organizational Strategy, Structure, and Process* (New York: McGraw-Hill, 1978).

42. For a discussion of the prospective importance to health care in the 1990s, see Stephen M. Shortell, "Diversification Strategy Benefits Innovative Leader," *Modern Healthcare*, March 12, 1980, p. 38.

43. For example, see Shaker A. Zahra and John A. Pearce II, "Research Evidence on the Miles-Snow Typology," *Journal of Management*, December 1990, pp. 751–768; Stephen M. Shortell and Edward J. Zajac, "Perceptual and Archival Measures of Miles and Snow's Strategic Types: A Comprehensive Assessment of Reliability and Validity," *Academy of Management Journal*, December 1990, pp. 817–832; Ken G. Smith, James P. Gutherie, and Ming-Jer Chen, "Strategy, Size and Performance," *Organizational Studies*, no. 1, 1989, pp. 63–81; and Nobuaki Namiki, "Miles and Snow's Typology of Strategy, Perceived Environmental Uncertainty, and Organizational Performance," *Akron Business & Economic Review*, Summer 1989, pp. 72–88.

44. Gregory O. Ginn, "Strategic Change in Hospitals: An Examination of the Response of the Acute Care Hospital to the Turbulent Environment of the 1980s," *Health Services Research*, October 1990, pp. 565–591.

45. Jeffrey S. Conant, Michael P. Mokwa, and Rajan P. Varadarajan, "Strategic Types, Distinctive Marketing Competencies and Organizational Performance: A Multiple Measures-Based Study," *Strategic Management Journal*, September 1990, pp. 365–383.

46. R. G. Hamermesh and S. B. Silk, "How to Compete in Stagnant Industries," *Harvard Business Review*, September–October 1979, pp. 161–168.

47. Philip Kotler, *Marketing Management*, 7th ed. (Englewood Cliffs, N.J.: Prentice-Hall, 1990), pp. 273–281 (condensed in 5th edition to three strategies; we prefer the prior separation).

48. K. R. Harrigan, "Strategy Formulation in Declining Industries," *Academy of Management Review*, October 1980, pp. 599–604.

49. Richard B. Hamermesh, M. Jack Anderson, Jr., and J. E. Harris, "Strategies for Low Market Share Businesses," *Harvard Business Review*, May–June, 1978, p. 98. Following material taken from pp. 95–102.

50. Ibid.

51. Lee Moonkyu, "Contingency Approach to Strategies for Service Firms," *Journal of Business Research*, (1989), No. 4, pp. 293–301; Michael E. Porter, "How to Attack the Industry Leader," *Fortune*, April 29, 1985, pp. 153–166; Kathryn Rudie Harrigan, "Guerrilla Strategies for Underdog Competitors," *Planning Review*, November 1986, pp. 4–6; Kathryn Rudie Harrigan, "Strategic Planning for Endgame," *Long Range Planning*, 1982, no. 6, pp. 45–48; P. Varadarajan, "Intensive Growth Strategies," *Atlanta Economic Review*, November/December 1978, pp. 4–11.

52. Brian Fahey and H. Kurt Christenson, "Evaluating the

Research on Strategy Content," in *Yearly Review of Management of the Journal of Management*, edited by James G. Hunt and John D. Blair, Summer 1986, pp. 175–176.

53. Peter Patel and Michael Younger, "A Frame of Reference for Strategy Development," *Long Range Planning*, April 1978, pp. 6–12.

54. Briance Mascarenhas and David A. Aaker, "Strategy over the Business Cycle," *Strategic Management Journal*, May/June 1989, pp. 199–210.

55. Robert K. Kazanjian, "Relation of Dominant Problems to Stages of Growth in Technology-Based New Ventures," *Academy of Management Journal*, June 1988, pp. 257–299.

56. "Information Systems that Speed Product Delivery," *I/S Analyzer*, June 1990, pp. 1–12, reports on a McKinsey & Company study.

57. Marvin L. Patterson, "Accelerating Innovation, a Dip into the Mime Pool," *National Productivity Review*, Autumn 1990, pp. 409–418;

58. George W. Potts, "Exploit Your Product's Service Life Cycle," *Harvard Business Review*, September–October 1988, pp. 32–36.

59. Thomas J. Peters and Robert H. Waterman, Jr., *In Search of Excellence* (New York: Harper & Row, 1982).

60. S. Benner, "Peter's Principles: Secrets of Growth," *Inc*, July 1983, pp. 34–38.

61. Daniel T. Carroll, "A Disappointing Search for Excellence," *Harvard Business Review*, November–December 1983, pp. 78–88.

62. Michael A. Hitt and R. Duane Ireland, "Peters and Waterman Revisited: The Unended Quest for Excellence," *Academy of Management Executive*, February 1988, pp. 91–98.

63. Kenneth E. Aupperle, William Acar, and David E. Booth, "An Empirical Critique of *In Search of Excellence*: How Excellent Are the Excellent Companies?" *Journal of Management*, Winter 1986, pp. 499–512.

64. Vasudevan Ramanujam and N. Venkatraman, "Excellence, Planning and Performance," *Interfaces*, May/June 1988, pp. 23–31.

65. Michelle Chapman, "*In Search of Excellence*: The Investors Viewpoint," *Financial Analysts Journal*, May/June 1987, pp. 54–63; and Richard Kolodny, Martin Lawrence, and Arabinda Ghosh, "*In Search of Excellence* . . . For Whom?" *Journal of Portfolio Management*, Spring 1989, pp. 56–60.

66. Thomas J. Peters and Nancy J. Austin, *A Passion for Excellence* (New York: Random House, 1985).

67. Thomas J. Peters, *Thriving on Chaos: Handbook for a Management Revolution* (New York: Knopf, 1987), pp. 1, 2, 38.

68. S. Schoeffler, "Profit Impact on Marketing Strategy," internal memorandum, Marketing Research Institute, November 1972; S. Schoeffler, R. D. Buzzell, and D. F. Heany, "The Impact of Strategic Planning on Profit Performance," *Harvard Business Review*, March–April 1974, pp. 137–145.

69. William L. Shanklin, "Market Share Is Not Destiny," *Journal of Consumer Marketing*, Fall 1988, pp. 5–15; Dimitris Bourantas and Yiorgos Mardes, *Long Range Planning*, October 1987, pp. 102–108.

70. K. J. Hatten, "Strategic Models in the Brewing Industry," Ph.D. dissertation, Purdue University, 1974; "Strategy, Profits, and Beer," paper presented at the Academy of Management, New Orleans, August 1975; W. E. Fruhan, Jr., "Pyrrhic Victories and Fights for Market Share," *Harvard Business Review*, September–October 1972, pp. 100–107; C. R. Anderson and P. T. Paine, "PIMS—A Reexamination," *Academy of Management Review*, July 1978, pp. 602–612; M. Lubatkin and M. Pitts, "PIMS: Fact or Folklore?" *Journal of Business Strategy*, Winter 1983, pp. 38–43; for a review and critique, see Fahey and Christenson, "Evaluating the Research"; Robert D. Buzzell and Bradley Gale, *PIMS Principles* (New York: Free Press, 1987).

71. John F. Prescott, Ajay K. Kohli, and N. Venkatraman, "The Market Share–Profitability Relationship: An Empirical Assessment of Major Assertions and Contradictions," *Strategic Management Journal*, July/August 1986, pp. 377–394.

72. T. Taylor, "PIMS through a Different Looking Glass," *Planning Review*, March 1978; M. Porter, "Market Structure, Strategy Formulation and Firm Profitability: The Theory of Strategic Groups and Mobility Barriers," in J. Cady, ed., *Marketing and the Public Interest* (Cambridge, Mass.: Market Science Institute, 1978); Anderson and Paine, "PIMS—A Reexamination"; Lubatkin and Pitts, "PIMS: Fact or Folklore?"; Vasudevan Ramanujam and N. Vankatraman, "An Inventory and Critique of Strategy Research Using the PIMS Database," *Academy of Management Review*, January 1984, pp. 138–151.

73. William Boulding and Richard Staelin, "Environment, Market Share, and Market Power," *Management Science*, October 1990, pp. 1,160–1,177; P. R. Cowley, "Market Structure and Business Performance: An Evolution of Buyer/Seller Power in the PIMS Database," *Strategic Management Journal*, May/June 1988, pp. 271–278.

INTEGRATIVE CASE ANALYSIS
CHAPTER 6

THE CHALLENGES FACING GENERAL MOTORS IN 1992

Now that you have read Chapter 6 and reviewed the GM case for related concepts, let's see how the chapter's concepts apply to GM.

APPLICATIONS OF CONCEPTS TO THE CASE

In Search of Excellence

1. **A bias for action.**   GM seems to be able to make decisions almost as quickly as Ford and Chrysler, but because its hierarchy has several more layers of management than Toyota's, for example, it can't make decisions as quickly as its Japanese competitors.
2. **Closeness to the customer.**   Until relatively recently, General Motors appeared to design cars in a vacuum, depending on sales promotion rather than design to sell its products. It designed the car and then attempted to find a market for it. Though it has tried to get closer to the customer, some of its designs have still faltered.
3. **Autonomy and entrepreneurship.**   The company's restructurings in 1982 and 1984 tended to remove entrepreneurship from the automobile divisions and distanced them further from the marketplace, as well. Centralized design functions caused many of the cars to look alike even though they were intended for different market segments. Additional, less extensive restructurings have helped. The 1992 restructurings are no guarantees for success.
4. **Productivity through people.**   General Motors is working very hard to improve its productivity, but it still has the highest costs of the Big Three. Much of its cost problem has to do with its union contract, the number of layers in its management structure, its overhead, and its vertical integration.
5. **Hands on, value-driven.**   General Motors does not seem to be guided by a vision of strategic intent at this moment, but Stempel's focus on the customer may be just what the company needs. John Smith's bottom-line orientation will change values.
6. **Stick to the knitting.**   General Motors' efforts to diversify technologically, partly for the purpose of leveling its cash flows, moves it to some degree away from the automobile industry. Furthermore, the problems of integrating high technology into the automobile manufacturing process and into the automobiles themselves have proved much more difficult than General Motors anticipated. Interestingly, its diversification efforts plus its European markets are providing profits.
7. **Simple form, lean staff.**   Again, General Motors has too many layers of management and too much white-collar overhead, but it is working hard to reduce these.
8. **Simultaneous loose/tight controls.**   Until recently GM was the very model of a decentralized firm at the corporate level, but at the shop level its operations were tightly controlled from the top. GM is now attempting to reorganize its top management into units that will be more responsive to the market. It has introduced quality circles to the shop floor and given more responsibility to lower-level managers. This system has made its plant in Fremont, California its most efficient and quality-conscious.

If we consider one more characteristic identified in Peters and Austin's *A Passion for Excellence*—innovation—we find that General Motors' product design has not been particularly innovative in comparison with Ford's and Chrysler's, nor those of the Japanese. Several of its products are still called dull and monotonous, but several new ones are exciting. The firm has indeed been innovative in the use of technology, but the results have not yet been gratifying. Its additional investment of $77 billion in technology has not enabled it to produce one additional automobile per hour or to produce cars more cheaply than its Japanese, Korean, or even U.S. competitors.

This exercise reveals that General Motors has many strategic problems and cannot be judged an excellent company.

PIMS

When we look at the PIMS variables, we find that GM's market share is the largest in the industry, and that obviously helps its profit situation, except that the North American operation is so cost-laden, that it loses money on many product lines. GM's product quality is not as high as Ford's or Chrysler's. Its marketing expenditures are extremely high. Its R&D expenditures are high, but if you examine other company factors, you'll find that all of its costs are extremely high. Hence, even though it has a large market share and is spending a great deal of money on marketing, the quality and cost issues hurt it in competition with other firms in the industry. The worst news is that the Japanese are gaining ground fast in market share.

Porter's Competitive Strategy and Hall's Competitiveness Model

Overall, General Motors doesn't seem to be following Porter's strategies. It certainly is not a cost leader, although it wants to be; it has not been able to differentiate its products; it has not served a particular target market segment very well, so it is not using the focus strategy, either. However, Cadillac and Buick have succeeded at low cost and differentiation. Certain models of Pontiac, Oldsmobile, and even Chevrolet have also been very successful.

Positioning General Motors in Hall's competitiveness model, its products overall have a relatively high delivered cost and relatively low differentiation. The firm is not yet in Death Valley, but it is certainly approaching the Danger Zone. Marketing muscle is probably all that is saving GM. It is still selling millions of cars, but its market share has eroded rapidly and significantly, and unless it improves its relative position in regard to differentiation and delivery cost, its future is not bright. To more effectively use the model, you should position various products, i.e., individual car models, on it.

Product Life Cycle

General Motors is a dominant firm at a mature stage of its industry's life cycle. When we look at Table 6.1, it becomes clear that General Motors had struggled to hold its position in the market, but it had failed to do so.

As GM's market share declines, profits decline in relation to sales, and it closes plants and lays off employees. GM's strategies appear not to be the best it could have chosen. All of the models by which we examined General Motors (*In Search of Excellence* characteristics, Porter's and Hall's models, the PIMS model, the product life cycle model, and the functional strategies perspective) indicate that General Motors has strategic difficulties. GM's losses reveal these problems.

Additional Questions You Might Ask Yourself

1. Are any of the additional generic strategies applicable? For example, for a dominant firm, what would Philip Kotler suggest that GM should have done?
2. How has GM used functional strategies to support its business strategy?

STRATEGIC MANAGEMENT CHALLENGES

How have the ten challenges affected GM's ability to effectively enact, or perform well on, the various models from the chapter?

CHAPTER 7

CORPORATE STRATEGY IN MULTIPLE-SBU FIRMS

The corporate strategies of most companies have dissipated instead of created shareholder value.

Michael E. Porter
Author on Strategy

Far from consensus emerging, radically different management approaches are strenuously advocated in different successful [multiple-SBU] companies.

Michael Goold and Andrew Campbell
Researchers of Strategy

CHAPTER OBJECTIVES

By the time you complete this chapter, you should be able to:

1. Describe the tasks of strategists in multiple-SBU organizations
2. Describe corporate strategy in multiple-SBU firms
3. Describe the Boston Consulting Group's business matrix
4. Describe General Electric's stoplight strategy/business screen
5. Describe the product/market/industry evolution portfolio matrix
6. Describe the Arthur D. Little portfolio-planning matrix
7. Indicate what factors determine industry attractiveness and competitive position
8. Describe what happens when a gap separates corporate performance and objectives
9. Describe the pitfalls in the portfolio approach
10. Describe the differing perspectives of corporate and SBU strategists
11. Discuss the current issues in multiple-SBU management

THE WALT DISNEY COMPANY

The Walt Disney Company identifies seven strategic business units:

1. Walt Disney Attractions—Walt Disney World in Florida (Magic Kingdom, EPCOT, Disney-MGM Studios Theme Park, hotels and numerous recreation facilities), Disneyland in California, and revenues from Tokyo Disneyland
2. Walt Disney Studios—motion pictures, network television, syndication, the Disney Channel, home video, and TV station KCAL-TV in Southern California
3. Disney Consumer Products—Disney specialty retailing in various parts of the globe
4. Disney Imagineering—the imagination and engineering arm of the firm, whose primary function is to design the theme parks and attractions from idea to final construction
5. Euro Disneyland—Magic Kingdom and Disney-MGM Studios Theme Park near Paris, France
6. Disney Development Company—real estate development in Florida, Europe, and Southern California
7. Hollywood Records—recorded music across a number of styles

The key factor in Disney's selection of its strategic business units is the synergy they generate. Everything is not only related to everything else, but all units can somehow be advertised by the others. For example, movies can be advertised at the theme parks and on TV. The theme parks depend on movies for their characters. Disney Development can sell its alternative vacation residences (timeshare units) to theme park customers. Furthermore, the skills learned in the attractions division can be used in Euro Disneyland. Imagineering can contribute to all of the other units. (Imagineering is considered an SBU because it is a profit center, capable of selling its services to anyone its chooses.)

Disney has not bought and sold a large number of firms, but rather chooses to develop most of its SBUs internally. It has however, purchased Arvida Realty in 1984, as part of a strategy to overcome an unfriendly takeover. Later, this unit was divested and Disney Development took its place. As part of this same strategy to prevent an unfriendly takeover, Disney came close to purchasing Gibson Greeting Cards, but chose not to do so. Disney does acquire smaller firms that fit into its SBUs. For example, in 1988 it acquired KCAL-TV and a direct-mail marketer of children's consumer goods.

Sources: The Walt Disney Company, *Annual Report*, 1991, Burbank, California, November 25, 1991; and discussions with Disney managers in Fall 1991.

The Walt Disney Company is one of the most successfully managed portfolios of businesses in the world. The company has stockpiled sufficient resources to seize opportunities as they become available, but it has historically recognized the risks in repeatedly buying and selling companies as many other multiple-SBU firms do. Rather, it looks for an overriding strategic synergy, culture, and management style in its SBUs to help meet its strategic challenges in the 1990s. On the other hand, Disney has from time to time considered acquisitions of various firms in related industries, and it has bought and sold one or two companies.

This chapter identifies the ways in which a multiple-SBU organization can combine the strategic efforts of its various component businesses to achieve its overall objectives. The strategy of multiple-SBU organizations, often called *corporate strategy*, focuses primarily on portfolio management techniques in combination with limited policy guidance, to solve three basic problems:

1. What businesses should the firm be in?
2. How can existing businesses be managed most efficiently and effectively?
3. How can the overall firm be managed synergistically?

The 1980s was a hectic period of mergers and acquisitions leading to numerous multiple-SBU firms. The trend toward multiple-SBU will probably not end soon, so we must learn to manage these organizations better.[1]

In the conglomerate or other multiple-SBU firm, the general belief today is that each SBU should operate as an independent company with only limited guidance from above. Historically, corporate headquarters have often exercised strong control, but as the need to become more competitive has increased, SBUs are generally believed to need autonomy.[2] Yet, Disney's experiences show that central guidance of a very specific type, related to management style and culture, for example, can be extremely beneficial. GE has also found this to be true.[3] There must be a proper balance, but it is clear that in most firms, the roles of corporate headquarters are diminishing.

The principal tasks facing a multiple-SBU firm's strategists are:

1. To establish strategic objectives and strategies relevant to a multiple-SBU firm
2. To determine whether current businesses are helping to achieve those objectives and implement those strategies, and then to determine appropriate actions to take in regard to those businesses
3. To provide support to, and policies for, SBUs as they strive to achieve their objectives and carry out their strategies
4. To accomplish the previous steps efficiently, which usually means with minimal corporate-level staff

The establishment of strategic objectives was discussed in Chapter 2. This chapter reviews the processes involved in completing steps 2, 3, and 4 above, focusing primarily on portfolio management techniques. This chapter also discusses policies, functional support, and decentralization as key elements in the successful strategic management of multiple-SBU firms. The relevance of portfolio strategies in today's environment is then discussed. This chapter also comments briefly on the differences between the perspectives of corporate and divisional strategists. Finally, emerging issues in managing multiple-SBU firms are reviewed.

Figures 7.1 and 7.2 indicate the portions of the major strategic processes that are examined in this chapter. Figure 7.3 illustrates the relationships among the various types of strategies in a multiple-SBU firm.

CORPORATE STRATEGY FOR MULTIPLE-SBU FIRMS

Corporate strategy for multiple-SBU firms primarily involves the management of a portfolio of businesses, deciding on acquisitions and divestitures, and making

FIGURE 7.1   The Organization—A Strategic Management Process Model

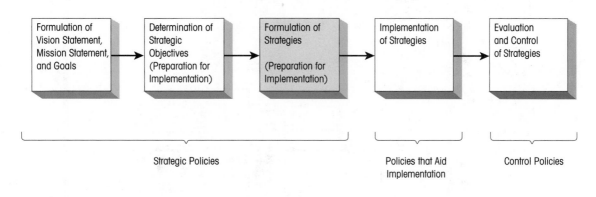

Formulation of Vision Statement, Mission Statement, and Goals → Determination of Strategic Objectives (Preparation for Implementation) → Formulation of Strategies (Preparation for Implementation) → Implementation of Strategies → Evaluation and Control of Strategies

Strategic Policies ⎵ Policies that Aid Implementation ⎵ Control Policies

investment decisions relative to industry attractiveness and competitive position in the industry. Corporate headquarters also provides certain functional services and guidance, and defines policies for areas that are common to the firm's SBUs, typically finance, personnel, and strategic planning. Corporate headquarters often provides advice on business and functional strategies, as well. In addition, multiple-SBU corporate strategy may involve other corporate strategies, such as restructuring, transferring skills, sharing activities, forming alliances, and managing culture. Still, the primary concern of most multiple-SBU firms' headquarters remains the corporate strategy of portfolio management.

Like an investment counselor who supervises an individual's investment portfolio, a strategist for a multiple-SBU firm seeks synergy and balance in the organization's portfolio of businesses. The same issues that are basic to any strategic situation must be addressed:

1. **Where are we now?**
2. **Where do we want to be?**
3. **How do we get there?**

PORTFOLIO MANAGEMENT TECHNIQUES

The portfolio matrix is only one of several portfolio management techniques used by multiple-SBU firms, but probably the most vital one. **Portfolio management techniques** essentially involve plotting two or three factors against each other on a grid or cube in order to arrive at some appropriate strategy. Several major types of portfolio matrices have been advocated, the most important of which are the business portfolio matrix of the Boston Consulting Group (BCG), the General Electric business screen, and the product/market/industry evolution portfolio matrix. Their applicability depends on the circumstances in which they are used.[4] The BCG matrix has largely been superseded by more sophisticated techniques that examine variables that are now considered more important. A GE-style matrix

FIGURE 7.2 Objectives Determination and Strategy Formulation

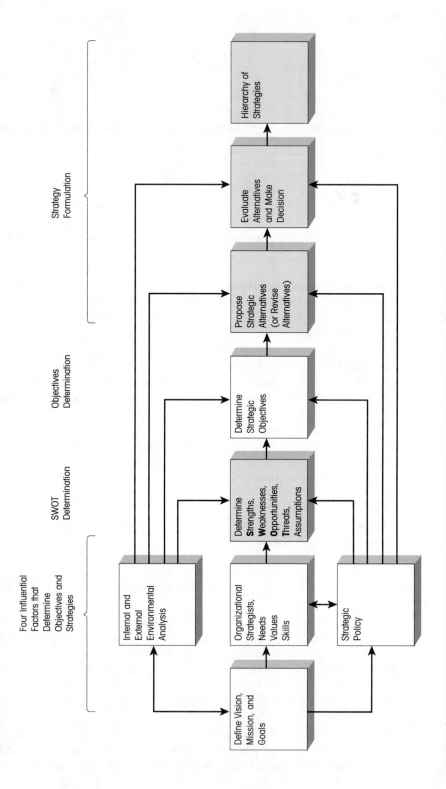

FIGURE 7.3   Relationships among Strategies in Multiple-SBU Firms

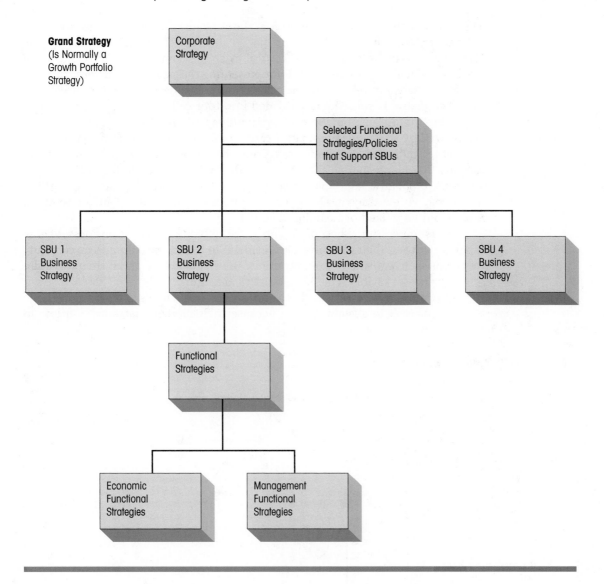

can help make sense of diverse products and market segments. The product/market/industry evolution matrix should be used for limited ranges of products and market segments.[5] Understanding how these grids function will enhance your insight into why they are used.

These grids should be combined with other strategic management techniques. For example, Royal Dutch/Shell acquires firms to add to its existing portfolio based on scenario forecasting.[6]

BCG Business Matrix

The **BCG matrix** is shown in Figure 7.4. The strategist plots the business's relative competitive position (as expressed by market share) on the horizontal axis and the growth rate of its industry on the vertical axis. The company is represented as a circle on the matrix, with its diameter representing the size of the business (usually in terms of sales) in relation to the sizes of other businesses in the portfolio.

The matrix is subsequently divided into four cells according to the relative desirability of four combinations of competitive and growth positions, which are symbolized by stars, question marks, cash cows, and dogs. The firm's position on the matrix indicates the strategic actions that it should employ. This matrix assumes that a large market share in a growth market leads to profitability, but that an effort to obtain a large market share in a slowly growing market requires too much cash. A few firms in slowly growing markets may warrant investment; the rest should be milked of cash and divested.

Stars represent the best profit and growth potentials. These businesses show rapid growth and their cash flow permits them to be self-sustaining. The company that owns such a business should continue full steam ahead, and it should acquire other businesses of this type, if their prices are right.

Question marks usually have the poorest cash flows. They require large amounts of cash to sustain growth because their market shares are too low to

FIGURE 7.4   BCG Business Matrix

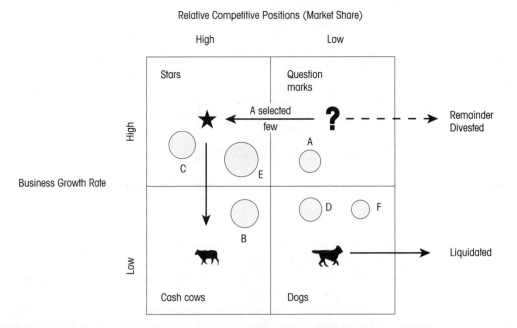

Source: Adapted from Barry Hedley, ''Strategy and the Business Portfolio,'' *Long Range Planning*, February 1977, p. 10. Reprinted by permission of Pergamon Press Ltd., Oxford, England.

generate the necessary cash from operations. As their symbol indicates, their progress must be monitored closely. The organization that owns such a business naturally hopes it will grow into a star; if it does not, it should be divested. If a firm believes a question mark business it does not already own may grow into a star, acquisition at the right price is desirable.

Cash cows have low growth and high market share. Their large market shares bring large cash flows. Their limited growth prospects require little investment, so they can be milked of cash to support other businesses, especially new enterprises or question marks. If market share declines and cash flow consequently subsides, they may be divested, or the firm may choose to invest in them once again. The firm must be careful, however, to keep them from becoming dogs. Cash cows seldom become available for acquisition, but any opportunity to acquire one at a good price should be seized.

Dogs are not desirable investments. They require large cash flows, but have poor competitive positions and therefore either yield no profit or, at best, marginal profits. The owning firm should divest these units, as GE did with its dogs during the early 1980s. Normally dogs are not suitable targets for acquisition, although some investors have done well turning dogs around.[7]

AT DISNEY

Disney acquired Arvida Development Corporation, which it later divested in favor of starting its own SBU, Disney Development Corporation. An acquisition of Gibson Greeting Cards had been considered as a way of helping stave off takeover attempts in 1984. Acquisitions of airlines, hotel chains, cruise ship lines, Seaworld, and other firms have been considered, but rejected for various reasons, not the least of which is a focus on the vision of the finest in family entertainment. Disney's theme parks have generally been cash cows, suggesting development of the SBUs. Recent actions have turned them into stars, however.

The BCG matrix was an important development in multiple-SBU strategic planning because it measured three key factors in such organizations' strategic successes: cash flow, market share, and industry growth. It can be modified to analyze any number of variables. For example, in modified form, it has been used to analyze political risk.[8] Like most single management systems, however, the matrix oversimplifies many critical factors. In the real world, there are many gradations between high and low positions on any dimension, and growth rate is only one aspect of a business's attractiveness, just as market share is only one aspect of its competitive position.[9] Furthermore, certain underlying assumptions are no longer true and in some markets were not true even when this model was formulated. For example, high market share in very competitive, low-margin industries doesn't necessarily lead to sufficient cash to support other SBUs. The GE business screen forces strategists to consider additional variables.

GE Business Screen

The General Electric Company pioneered the development of an advanced portfolio matrix to determine which SBUs or major products it wished to retain in its portfolio, which it wished to delete, and how it wanted to treat those it retained. With minor adjustments in the criteria employed, this matrix can also be used to evaluate potential acquisitions, mergers, and new product developments. Most of the weaknesses inherent in the BCG matrix are eliminated in the **GE business screen** (Figures 7.5 and 7.6).[10] General Electric's matrix employs composite measures of both business strength and industry attractiveness and uses three gradations of each. These measures are essential additions.

The GE Strategic Business Planning Grid, or **GE stoplight strategy,** as it is known, consists of nine cells and three colors to indicate the strategies appropriate for various businesses. The locations of SBUs or products on the grid reflect an evaluation of the attractiveness of their industries and the firm's strengths in those businesses, rated as either high, medium, or low. The stoplight strategy gets its name from the green, yellow, and red color coding employed to indicate the desirability of various categories of businesses or products. Firms in the green (G) cells justify investment and growth strategies. SBUs in the red (R) cells no longer deserve investment and may become cash cows and/or be divested. Those in the yellow (Y) cells are monitored for change in either industry attractiveness or business strength. A large SBU may have products that fall into all three categories, so evaluation can be tricky.

FIGURE 7.5 General Electric's Stoplight Strategy for Planning

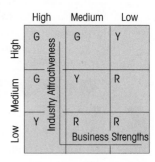

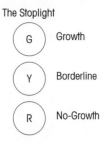

FIGURE 7.6   Alternative Related Strategies for GE Business Screen

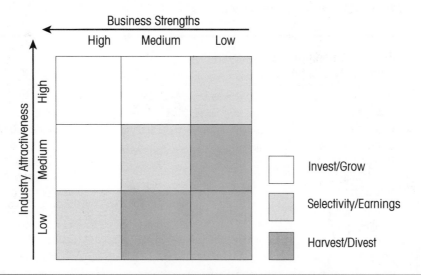

A future perspective must always be maintained in this analysis. In addition to current conditions of competitive position and industry attractiveness, future conditions must be considered, as well. For example, Banc One, a large regional bank headquartered in Columbus, Ohio with interests in Indiana, Texas, Arizona and California believes that it can improve an acquired firm's financial performance as well as its culture, and factors these beliefs into its decision process.[11]

In Figure 7.5, stoplight grid A indicates a moderately strong organization in a highly attractive industry. The evaluations intersect in a green box, suggesting an **invest-and-grow strategy.** Stoplight matrix B portrays a business in the red zone: its business strength is low and so is the attractiveness of its industry. As a result, investment will be reduced or stopped altogether, and any available cash will be siphoned off before the business is divested. Stoplight grid C shows a firm with high business strengths in an unattractive industry. Consequently, the firm lands in a yellow cell of the matrix and will be monitored for progress. Those firms that provide worthwhile potential earnings will follow strategies of investment and growth; those that do not will be divested.

One intriguing point about the grid is that it allows the firm to use one system to compare apples and oranges. With some 650 product groupings aligned in five major SBU groups, GE needs just such a system. Perhaps more important, the grid allows GE to evaluate such factors as social responsibility and employee loyalty as well as such quantitative factors as return on investment, market share, and cash flow. Each SBU or major product is evaluated during the annual planning review, almost always producing a consensus. Final strategic decisions are made by the corporate policy committee, which consists of several members of top management. The criteria shown in Table 7.1, which guide the annual review, are typical

TABLE 7.1 Assessment Criteria

Business Strength/ Competitive Position	Industry Attractiveness
Size	Size
Growth	Market growth, pricing
Share	Market diversity
Position	Competitive structure
Profitability	Industry profitability
Margin	Technical role
Technology position	Social factors
Image	Environmental factors
Pollution	Legal factors
People	Human factors

of those used by most multiple-SBU organizations. Note that the factors considered include not only competitive and supportive factors, such as sales, profits, and losses, but also factors that are more difficult to quantify, such as technology position, social responsibility, and employee needs.

Like the BCG matrix, GE uses the screen primarily to manage its current or prospective businesses, with special emphasis on balancing the investment portfolio. The grid helps GE determine the type of strategy it should employ on the basis of the factors shown in Figure 7.5. Figure 7.6 shows the related strategies. For a current or potential business judged to be in a green sector of the matrix, as mentioned, an invest-and-grow strategy will be followed. This is clearly the strategy Sony follows for its entertainment division, as this chapter's Global Strategic Challenge feature reveals. The yellow sectors of the matrix suggest a **selectivity/earnings strategy.** The red sectors call for a **harvest/divest strategy.** The matrix can be used to re-evaluate investments as environments change; the strategists simply consider different criteria and weigh them differently. The matrix seems to work best in less turbulent environments, so strategies in turbulent environments must be carefully considered.[12]

Large organizations have commonly used this matrix technique to select business projects and products. The 50-odd organizations engaged in the PIMS (Profit Impact of Marketing Strategy) project, for example, have employed this type of matrix for several years to analyze their market shares and select products. McKinsey & Company has employed a similar nine-cell business assessment array matrix in its strategic consulting practice.

Product/Market/Industry Evolution Portfolio Matrix

One of the major criticisms of nine-cell matrices is that they do not give sufficient importance to information on market growth. The product/market/industry

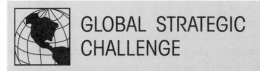

GLOBAL STRATEGIC CHALLENGE

SONY MOVES TO BECOME THE WORLD'S ENTERTAINMENT SOURCE

"Let me entertain you" could very well be Sony's corporate slogan. The Japanese manufacturer, already the world's leading maker of electronic gadgets, gobbled up CBS Records, Inc. (now Sony Media Entertainment) in 1988 for $2 billion, and Columbia Pictures Entertainment Inc. for $3.4 billion in 1989. The latter purchase included two film studios, a television unit, and the Loews theater chain. In February 1991, Michael (Mickey) P. Schulhof, head of Sony Corporation's entertainment operations, announced the creation of an electronic-publishing arm to sell electronic games and multimedia software capable of delivering sound, images, and text on a computer. Sony sees hardware-software combinations as necessary to dominate either market in the future.

Schulhof oversees this five-SBU entertainment division, recently incorporated under an umbrella firm as Sony Software Corporation, which, for the year ending in March 1991, will gross approximately 20 percent of Sony's $27 billion worldwide. Schulhof, a noted rational thinker and former technical analyst for Sony, will be required to make intuitive judgements about people's entertainment preferences. He has already formulated the business strategy for Sony Electronic Publishing, the Sony arm that will oversee the push into electronic publishing and multimedia software. His plan is to produce a hardware-software combination that will be cheaper than anything currently on the market. Much of Sony's interest in acquiring hardware-software combinations results from the Betamax fiasco. Sony introduced that technology in 1975 as the first videocassette recorder. Because rivals united behind another format, VHS, however, Sony sold few machines. Now with its own movie software from the video enterprises, it can help assure that its hardware gets used. Sony learned the lesson that you often can't sell hardware without the proper software.

Schulhof indicates that he'll rely heavily on Columbia Chairmen Peter Guber and Jon Peters to run the film and television companies, and much of the music unit will have a similar arrangement, as well. Similarly, SVS, the video distribution unit, and Digital Audio Disc Corporation, which handles compact discs, are treated autonomously. Thus, he is taking two different approaches to the three SBUs. He is delegating power to four units—Columbia, Sony Music Entertainment, SVS, and Digital Audio, but overseeing Sony Electronic Publishing. This goes along with his presidency of that division, an office he holds in addition to being the vice chairman/president in charge of all five SBUs.

The road won't be easy for Schulhof or for Sony. Columbia has not been one of the major players in Hollywood since *Ghostbusters*, and a few more bombs like the $45-million *Hudson Hawk* could keep it from being any kind of player at all. Nonetheless, Sony is shelling out millions to well-known stars such as Julia Roberts, Dustin Hoffman, Robin Williams, and Warren Beatty in an effort to build its box office. The electronic publishing arm will take several months, if not years, to launch in a market that has historically been less than excited about such offerings. While some synergies exist, especially between music and movies, it's not clear just how much additional synergy can be generated among the five divisions.

Sources: Andrea Rothman, "Media Colossus," *Business Week*, March 25, 1991, pp. 64–74; also, see Nancy J. Perry, "Will Sony Make It in Hollywood?" *Fortune*, September 1991, pp. 158–166.

matrix attempts to overcome this deficiency. As Figure 7.7 indicates, the strategist who uses a **product/market/industry evolution portfolio matrix** plots the firm's competitive position against the life cycle stages of the product, market, and industry. Various businesses are shown as pie slices (indicating market share) of circles (indicating total industry size).[13] It is generally believed that conglomerate and other multiple-SBU organizations should seek to operate businesses in all stages of their industry and product life cycles, the largest and most profitable firms being in the maturity or late growth stages. This concept is, of course, similar to the classic marketing strategy of offering products in various stages of the product life cycle within an industry. Arthur D. Little, Inc., has modified the product/market/industry evolution matrix (Figure 7.8) to incorporate recommended strategies. (Note that the axes have been rotated in this version.) The strategies of the **ADL portfolio-planning matrix** are essentially the same as those of the GE business screen (Figure 7.6).

It is probably best to use all three matrices in the assessment process. They all require similar information, and the sophistication of the results is greatly enhanced when all are used. While the underlying concepts of the matrices appear to allow for substantial precision, the actual mechanics of their use often involve

FIGURE 7.7 Product/Market/Industry Evolution Portfolio Matrix

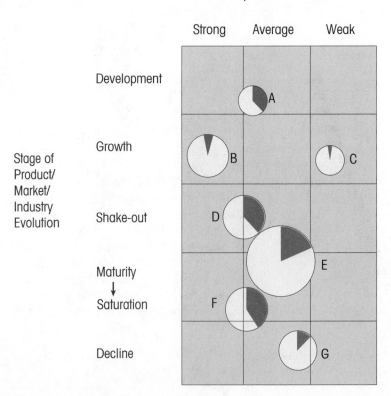

FIGURE 7.8   ADL Portfolio-Planning Matrix

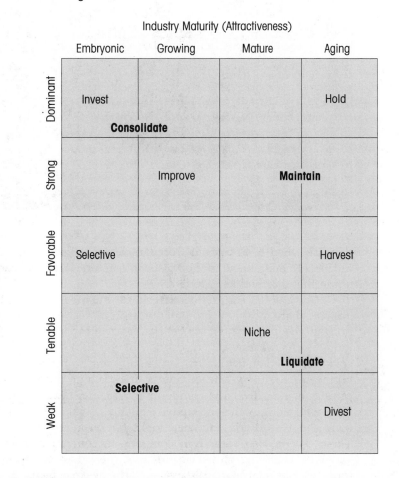

considerable subjective estimation. Furthermore, the matrices provide only one approach, albeit an important one.

Assessment Process

Like the business and corporate strategies of single-business organizations, the corporate strategy of a multiple-SBU firm focuses on SWOT. Assessment of competitive position (GE's business strength) requires a thorough analysis of business strengths and weaknesses. Assessment of industry attractiveness requires a thorough analysis of opportunities and threats. The matrices merely organize these factors. Using the GE business screen as an example, we will now examine how a business's position is determined. Note that the information called for by the matrix addresses the questions of both where we are and where we want to be.

The process begins with statements of criteria for both business strengths (competitive position) and industry attractiveness. The development of these criteria is, of course, a complex and highly subjective process, although research (such as the PIMS project) and experience can help. Sometimes a firm looks for a long time before it finds an acquisition candidate that meets its criteria. This was

AT DISNEY

In 1983 and early 1984, Chairman of the Board Ray Watson performed an assessment of the various Disney SBUs. He apparently concluded that the movie business was not a good one for Disney. Speculation that Watson might sell off the movie business led Roy Disney, Jr. to begin a successful plot to remove Watson and CEO Ron Miller, because he believed that Disney movies were a vital part of the company.

Source: John Taylor, *Storming the Magic Kingdom* (New York: Knopf, 1987); John Taylor, "Project Fantasy: A Behind-the-Scenes Account of Disney's Desperate Battle against the Raiders," *Manhattan*, November 1984.

the case when L. S. Starrett Company acquired Herald Engineering Equipment Ltd., a U.K. manufacturer of optical comparators. It took 6 years for Starrett to find a firm that matched its criteria.[14]

As we noted earlier, the **criteria for business strengths** often include size, growth, share, position, profitability, margin, technology position, image, pollution, and people. The criteria believed to determine success vary from industry to industry. As we saw our discussion of the PIMS findings in Chapter 6, some common criteria, such as market share, seem to influence success in almost all businesses. Industry **attractiveness criteria** may include size, market growth, pricing, market diversity, competitive structure, industry profitability, and technical role, along with social, environmental, legal, and human factors. The company chooses criteria and then looks for businesses that score well on them. These criteria also vary from company to company, depending on numerous variables, including propensity for risk, the values of top management, and so forth. Various quantitative assessment schemes may be used. Estimation of values is frequent.

Gap Analysis

Corporations often find gaps between an SBU's performance and corporatewide objectives. **Gap analysis** assesses the current contributions from businesses or potential future contributions to the organization's achievement of its strategic objectives. The various business matrices are good indicators of what businesses are contributing and may be expected to contribute. Matrices also recommend a contingency strategy for each business.

The most desirable portfolio of businesses obviously contains no money losers. Certainly it is advisable to have no more than one or two SBUs awaiting divestment. Meanwhile, the organization's largest and most profitable businesses should be growing in sales or profits. This is an ideal, but infrequently obtainable, profile. Also, a firm may prefer a different type of portfolio, such as one that emphasizes long-term growth over current profit.

Hofer and Schendel have identified six possible actions that firms may take if current businesses are not contributing sufficiently to achievement of organization objectives, or are expected to contribute little in the future:[15]

1. Change the investment strategies of some or all of the SBUs and change the resource allocations among them
2. Change the business strategies of one or more SBUs
3. Add some new SBUs to the corporate portfolio
4. Delete some existing SBUs from the corporate portfolio
5. Change the way the organization relates to external environmental stakeholders—suppliers, consumers, government, and so on (this move involves political strategies)
6. Change strategic objectives

Closing the Gap   The choice of action among these six possibilities is not based strictly on portfolio matrix results. These results are part of a broader group of considerations, including the mix of businesses in the current portfolio, recent portfolio management actions, the ability to integrate new firms into the portfolio, the corporate cash position, major potential environmental threats and opportunities, current policies on the allocation of resources, the values of top managers (especially their propensity to take risks), corporate objectives, and the current strategies of the SBUs themselves.

In selecting the businesses in which the organization will engage, strategists look for synergy and balance among existing and future businesses. **Synergy,** you may recall, is the degree to which SBUs reinforce each others' pursuit of objectives. The strategists may consider whether the units' managerial skills are transferable, whether they employ similar technologies, whether they share something such as a market, whether their distribution systems are compatible, and so forth. Synergy is often elusive. When Central Life Insurance Company acquired Inter-State Assurance through a merger, it sought to satisfy its goal of expanding its product line and distribution channels. However, Central Life didn't find the synergies it had envisioned. Therefore, it sold Inter-State to Caring International, a subsidiary of Irish Life.[16] This chapter's Strategic Challenge feature reveals some of the intricacies involved in the search for synergy at Tenneco.

Balance is the degree to which business cash flows support one another. Firms in growth markets, for example, usually require more cash infusions than firms in older, more mature industries. The profits from the latter can help support the former. Similarly, a firm with strong summer revenues, such as a soft-drink firm, can balanced income from a firm with stronger winter revenues, such as a restaurant chain, to provide the total corporation with strong year-round cash flows.

When necessary, prospective businesses can be plotted on a matrix to help identify suitable investments. Forecasts of major changes in both competitive and noncompetitive environments require special attention. These factors might include projected political events, expected changes in major economic factors (GNP, interest rates, wage controls, and so forth), and citizens' responses to particular investments (in chemicals or energy, for example). Such influences must be monitored for their potential impacts on the desirability of certain businesses as

STRATEGIC CHALLENGE

IN SEARCH OF SYNERGY AT TENNECO

After Michael Walsh accepted the board's invitation to become Chairman of Tenneco in August 1991, he immediately lived up to his reputation as a tough cost cutter. He announced a $2 billion restructuring plan, cut dividends by 50 percent, and eliminated 8000 jobs. But his major work lay ahead of him. Walsh had to find the right mix of companies for Tenneco's portfolio. The company's earnings had been erratic over the past decade, and the board wanted the trend changed. They also wanted to turn a profit, something that had been elusive during the recent recession.

Previously as CEO of Union Pacific, where he had garnered the reputation of a cost cutter and successful reshaper of company fortunes, Walsh had managed only one major business. He looked forward to the challenge of managing a diversified conglomerate such as Tenneco. One of his major concerns was choosing which businesses to retain and which to sell. He hinted that he might follow the lead provided by Jack Welch of GE in applying criteria to the existing portfolio. Walsh recognized, however, that he still was stuck with one major loser in the portfolio. He had to turn it around, although the prospects looked bleak, yet he couldn't afford to sell it. Consequently, other firms in Tenneco's portfolio would have to bear the brunt of saving money in order to carry the loser for some time.

Sources: Brian Bremner, "Tough Times, Tough Bosses," *Business Week*, November 25, 1991, pp. 174–179; Nora E. Field, an interview with Michael Walsh, "Success Depends On Leadership," *Fortune*, November 18, 1991, pp. 153–154.

members of the portfolio. Table 7.2 lists some of the major external factors that should be considered. These must be evaluated from an international and/or global perspective when firms' operations are multinational in scope.

Part of this balance issue is the ability to transfer skills and share various activities between companies. A company that has a particularly strong management culture, for example, may be able to energize another company's weaker culture. Similarly, organizations may share distribution systems, proprietary software, and so on. Corporate staff integration committees, or task forces may be called on to effect such a transfer of skills. It is extremely important for senior management to get involved in both transferring and sharing activities. The executive who assumes that such activities will take place in the natural course of events is usually doomed to disappointment.[17]

Pitfalls in the Portfolio Approach

From the mid-1970s through the early 1980s, portfolio analysis was a major concept in strategic planning. It became very popular quite rapidly as major U.S.

TABLE 7.2 Some Strategically Significant Broad Environmental Variables

Economic Conditions	Demographic Trends	Technological Changes	Social and Cultural Trends	Political and Legal Factors
GNP trends	Growth rate of population	Total federal spending for R&D	Lifestyle changes	Antitrust regulations
Interest rates	Age distribution of population	Total industry spending for R&D	Career expectations	Environmental protection laws
Money supply			Consumer activism	
Inflation rates			Rate of family formation	Tax laws
Unemployment levels	Regional shifts in population	Focus of technological effort		Special incentives
Wage/price controls	Life expectancies	Patent protection		Foreign trade regulations
	Birth rates			
Devaluation/ revaluation				Attitudes toward foreign companies
Energy availability				

industries avidly pursued mergers and acquisition, to which the portfolio techniques were well-suited. As firms gained experience with these techniques, however, doubts began to arise as to their effectiveness. Nonetheless, they are still widely used. Malcolm B. Coate has identified several major **pitfalls in the portfolio approach:**[18]

1. The portfolio approach is based on assumptions that must be examined in each particular situation:
   a. Each firm is divisible into independent business units. (Coate questions the ease of distinguishing these units in the real world.)
   b. The dominant firm earns the highest profits in each market. (Coate suggests that this assumption is not necessarily sound. Other research cited elsewhere in this book supports his objection.)
   c. An industry's attractiveness depends on its life cycle stage. (This assumption tends to ignore differences in capital requirements among industries.)
   d. Investment funds are limited, and they must be allocated among all businesses in the organization. (This assumption tends to ignore the long-term perspective; funds may be more available in the long term than they are in the short run.)
2. The portfolio models tend to overlook additional considerations that should be incorporated in an optimal investment-planning model.
   a. The funds invested in various SBUs should be allocated in such a way as to equate marginal rates of return.
   b. It is possible that firms engaged in tacit collusion may do better by ignoring

the strategies recommended by these techniques and reducing investment as they exploit market power.

c. The liquidation value of the SBU is a better measure of its value than the more commonly used cost basis. This makes liquidation a much more acceptable strategy.

d. Portfolio models give very little quantitative attention to risk.

Coate then identifies pitfalls in the application of portfolio models:

1. The actual process of defining business units is quite complex, more akin to an art than a science.

2. Use of the portfolio matrix involves considerably more time and attention than the concept suggests. It requires a large number of value judgments about some very uncertain numbers, and measurements are often vague. Detailed information on each unit is vital to the success of the portfolio approach.

3. The validity of the strategies recommended by the model is questionable. If some of the model's assumptions are ill-founded, strategies based on them may not be sound. The availability of resources, financial, human, and others, always affects the ability of any business to implement strategy.

Other researchers have identified other problems associated with portfolio techniques. When Philippe Haspeslagh surveyed the *Fortune* 1,000, he found wide variations in the 345 respondents' use of these approaches, their rate of successful stabilization, and the degree to which individual SBUs adhered to recommended strategies. Respondents perceived these approaches to be useful primarily in generating better strategies through more selective allocation of resources and in encouraging more differentiated management of specific SBUs.

He points out, however, that the user of these strategies must face some complex realities when the time comes to implement them. His respondents reported problems categorizing businesses. A large conglomerate may have 100 to 500 businesses, and no one can be expected to comprehend all the issues involved in that many units simultaneously. Therefore, SBUs are typically grouped into categories for purposes of analysis. This practice causes all sorts of difficulties in the implementation of strategies because the businesses in a category are not, after all, identical, but they are directed to follow a single strategy. Haspeslagh implies that the distribution or redistribution of power is accompanied by behavioral adjustment, and the most frequent behavioral response may well be resistance. He also found that, while portfolio techniques should be used to allocate all resources, most firms focused on capital investment.[19]

Haspeslagh does not discuss in depth additional implementation problems related to such factors as motivation, budgets, leadership, and communication. Walter Kiechel III has indicated just how critical these aspects of implementation can be. Together with other authors, Kiechel observes that strategic planning can carry the organization only so far. Ultimately, the strategies derived from the strategic management process have to be implemented.[20] Their implementation requires the proper structures and support systems, an appropriate leadership style, and a receptive culture. In short, the process leaves many questions to answer. These difficulties with implementation will gain more meaning as you read Chapters 8 and 9.

Is Portfolio Management Still Viable?

After examining the strategic performance of 33 major companies managed by the portfolio technique, including Beatrice, Du Pont, GE, IBM, ITT, Raytheon, Rockwell, Sara Lee, 3M, and Westinghouse, Michael Porter concluded that portfolio management was woefully inadequate to the task of formulating corporate strategy. The sheer magnitude of the task of managing strategy for a corporation with hundreds of businesses defeats the best efforts of corporate strategists. "In most countries, the days when portfolio management was a valid concept of corporate strategy are past."[21]

After examining several facets of corporate strategic success, Porter concludes that the rate at which a firm divests its businesses is the critical measure of the contribution of corporate strategy to its success. Retaining businesses, he reasons, must indicate a long-term successful portfolio strategy. During the period of study, the companies he surveyed entered an average of 80 new industries and 27 new fields. Just over 70 percent of the new entries were acquisitions, 22 percent were startups, and 8 percent were joint ventures. Porter then reveals what he calls a "sobering picture": on the average, these 33 corporations' divestment rate was a startling 74 percent.

Some have suggested that portfolio management, as typically practiced through a decentralized SBU structure with corporate control of resource allocation, is not only detrimental to the earnings of each SBU, but is preventing many U.S. firms from being globally competitive. Charles W. L. Hill, Michael A. Hitt, and Robert E. Hoskisson, after examining substantial evidence, suggest that U.S. strategists are risk averse and are oriented toward the short term. These perspectives in turn have led to a substantial reduction in research and development, which has stifled innovation and, hence, long-term competitiveness in the global arena. These researchers cite several causes for these events, one of which is the typical M-form multiple-SBU firm, or multidivisional firm, in which SBUs are given substantial control over their operations along with short-term profit objectives and centralized resource allocations. The result is managers who don't invest in the future.[22]

One solution for this problem is to structure organizational reward systems to induce executives to focus on long-term results and investment for the future, otherwise a real dilemma exists for the strategist. Does he or she pursue short-term profit to satisfy stakeholders, or long-term profits, which are probably better for stockholders? This chapter's Strategic Ethical Challenge feature discusses this problem.

Additional Corporate Strategies

Several additional multiple-SBU strategies have been identified. For example, Michael Porter points to three corporate strategies other than portfolio management that he believes must be considered:

- Restructuring—significantly altering marketing, finance, operations, and human resource functions of the units acquired and their managers (restructuring is discussed in more detail in Chapter 8)

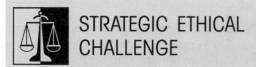

STRATEGIC ETHICAL CHALLENGE

SHORT-TERM OR LONG-TERM PROFITS?

One of the most difficult issues for top executives to resolve is balancing the long-term and short-term objectives of the firm. This becomes a double bind for subsidiary managers in multiple-SBU firms. Stock market investors react to short-term profits, and not, generally, to long-term actions taken to increase profits. Many, if not most, firms encourage short-term performance through their performance reward systems. Furthermore, the crisis orientation of many firms means a totally short-term focus. Yet the long-term viability of the firm is in danger if long-term investments are not made, many of which reduce short-term profits.

Career advancement for manager's often depends upon making a strong showing of financial performance in a smaller firm before moving on to a bigger firm, or on up the pyramid in the parent corporation. To do this, some managers may sacrifice the long-term profitability of their subsidiaries. For example, by limiting investment in plant and equipment, and in human resources development, costs in the short term can be cut and profits increased. But in the long term, such investments must be made. But in innovative firms such as Georgia Pacific, Avon Products, and Becton Dickinson compensation packages are designed to encourage a long-term future.

Source: Geoffrey Colvin, "How to Pay the CEO Right," *Fortune*, March 6, 1992, pp. 60–69.

- Transferring skills—applying the skills acquired in one business unit to the activities of another unit
- Sharing activities—coordinating SBUs' mutual use of such functions as distribution channels in order to gain competitive advantage[23]

Thus Porter offers four alternatives for corporate strategy. In our opinion, however, each of the last three depends in some way on the first—portfolio management. Restructuring adjusts the structures of firms in the portfolio and/or the size of headquarters staff. Skills are transferred and activities are shared between units within a portfolio. Certainly Porter is right when he says that these techniques should be considered. Nonetheless, in the next few years, the concept of portfolio management as we have described it is likely to retain its force, though the forms it takes in practice may vary.

In addition to those additional corporate strategies identified by Porter, two additional strategies are becoming increasingly important: forming strategic alliances, and managing culture. The formation of alliances for specific SBUs by corporate headquarters has become an increasingly important part of corporate strategy.[24] For example, one of the most popular strategies for achieving global competitiveness is to form alliances with selected competitors in order to compete more effectively with remaining competitors. Some firms, such as General Electric, maintain numerous alliances in many countries and industries. In the auto industry, for example, General Motors has joint ventures with Toyota, Ford is allied with Mazda, and Chrysler with Mitsubishi.

Other firms, such as Apple Computers, are just beginning to explore alliances. In fact, we could find no more dramatic example of the trend toward alliances than that announced in June 1991 between Apple and arch-rival IBM. Under CEO John Sculley's direction, Apple had become a sort of Blue Buster, with employees zealously attempting to oust Big Blue as the dominant PC manufacturer. By late 1990, however, Sculley was willing to consider any possibility. One option was the first major pricing strategy change in Apple history with the introduction of new, low-priced Macintosh models. The most dramatic option he explored, however, was an alliance with IBM.

Exploratory talks began in early 1991. Eventually the parties agreed that Apple would receive workstation hardware from IBM, and IBM would receive advanced, user-friendly software technology from Apple. Furthermore, they agreed to develop software and redesign hardware jointly to make their machines much more compatible than they had been in the past. Much of the impetus to pursue this alliance came from both firms' desire to be more globally competitive, especially against Japanese manufacturers.[25]

Another important strategy is managing culture. By actively changing and controlling values, beliefs, norms, and "the way in which things are done around here," organizations can mold more competitive cultures. Chapter 9 discusses this issue in more detail using General Electric as a primary example. While it is mostly an issue of implementation, culture management can be a viable strategy for a corporation.

Multiple-Point Competition

For a tiny number of large conglomerates, the central strategic question is how to compete with the other large conglomerates. We raise this issue primarily to alert you to its existence. *Very few* strategists are involved in such concerns, but their endeavors do control significant corporate resources. Hofer and Schendel, among others, have provided guidance to people involved in this **multiple-point competition,** suggesting strategies for responding to competitors and for initiating competition.[26]

DIFFERENCES IN PERSPECTIVE: BUSINESS VERSUS CORPORATE STRATEGISTS

Large business organizations usually define divisions based on numerous businesses (SBUs) or products. Normally these divisions develop their own objectives and plans, choosing among new products, new marketing strategies, and new research and development projects for investment. Many, if not most, need the approval of top corporate management, though. To the business division, these plans constitute strategy, but to the corporation they are intermediate forms of planning. Strategic perspective at the division level differs significantly from that at the corporate level. The most obvious difference is that the division must respond to corporate objectives and policies, including resource allocations, while the corporate top management establishes those objectives and policies. Furthermore, corporate-level strategy emphasizes portfolio techniques, while division-level strategy emphasizes the business strategy of marketing.

The corporate general manager acts primarily as an overseer, setting objectives and policies and allocating resources. The role of the business unit general manager usually involves great responsibility with less than commensurate authority. The divisional general manager must translate objectives into actions and actions into results. He or she must satisfy superiors, compete and cooperate with peers, and lead subordinates, usually the managers of the unit's functional, product, or geographical divisions.

The division manager operates in a highly political environment. He or she is, in fact, stuck in the middle. The position of division manager is usually filled by a former functional specialist, and many people have found this transition too dramatic, the new viewpoint too different, or the political pitfalls too numerous. One such SBU general manager, despite a spectacular turnaround of a real loser in a stagnant industry, was bypassed for promotion because he had already made too many suggestions to the corporate CEO about how to turn around the sluggish parent. He was consoled with a 30-percent raise, however.[27]

Peter Lorange suggests that, because the differences between **division and corporate strategists' perspectives** are too little appreciated, divisional strategies tend to be more conservative than the total corporate portfolio warrants. A very large organization can average out potential losses from a risky venture, but divisional managers tend to believe they cannot accept a product that appears risky because their performance is measured against return and their compensation is based on performance. The result is often the forfeiture of opportunities for considerable gain. Lorange has proposed that the business strategy matrix, with its industry attractiveness and competitive strength axes, be made three-dimensional to allow firms to assess the attractiveness of business-level investment opportunities in the context of the overall corporate portfolio (adding a consolidation attractiveness axis).[28]

TRENDS IN MANAGING MULTIPLE-SBU CORPORATE STRATEGY

In addition to broadening multiple-SBU corporate strategy to incorporate restructuring, transferring skills, sharing activities, forming alliances, and managing culture, several trends in corporate strategy management are emerging.

More Autonomous SBUs, Smaller Corporate Staffs

First, corporate strategists are trying to learn how to better manage portfolios of businesses to make them more competitive. Much of this interest in better management is motivated by studies that suggest that had SBUs remained independent, they probably would have been more profitable, on average, sold higher percentages of the total goods sold in their industries, and employed more workers.[29] Interest in improving management is also spurred on by the recognition that management must change to cope with the strategic challenges of the 1990s. Improving management almost always means increasing the autonomy given individual businesses, letting them manage on their own. It also almost always means reducing corporate staff, and keeping this staff as lean as possible.[30] Numerous firms have attempted this right sizing, searching for strategic competitiveness, including General Motors, United Technologies, and, more recently, RJR Nabisco, for example. According to Michael Porter, to justify acquisitions or retaining firms in the portfolio, parent firms must be able to provide skills and bring assets to bear on problems that make subsidiaries better off than they would have been without the parent.[31]

AT DISNEY

Eisner and Wells have decentralized much of the decision making in the firm. They have tried to establish as many profit centers within each SBU as possible, hoping to improve efficiency of operation.

Some firms have actually recognized the need for such leanness from their inception. No firm better epitomizes this approach than Nucor Corporation, the nation's fifth-largest steel manufacturer. With six major SBUs and 5,600 employees, its corporate staff numbers under 30. Nucor has always maintained a lean corporate staff and granted field managers tremendous authority. High levels of employee participation and profit sharing have also added to its success. Nucor has been the only U.S. steel manufacturer to compete successfully on both cost and quality with foreign manufacturers for the past two decades. Its niche in specialty steel provided it an early advantage. Now it has moved into more competitive rolled steel, but is still coming out on top of its competition.[32]

Providing Improved Services to SBUs

The recognition that the corporate headquarters should grant more autonomy to SBUs was accompanied by the recognition that it should also quit taxing SBUs with bureaucratic requirements. At RJR-Nabisco, for example, new CEO Louis Gerstner did away with the lengthy "rainbow reports" required by his predecessors. In these monthly reports, named for their red, blue, and green covers, SBUs reviewed every event of the month. Gerstner observed that if he was doing his job, he would know what was happening in the divisions.[33] At Hercules Inc., senior financial managers have been assigned as liaisons to business units to help improve relations and speed problem solving.[34]

Restructuring Debt

Many acquisitions in the merger mania during the 1980s were financed with extremely risky and costly junk bond and/or leveraged buyout arrangements. Strategists of firms involved in such arrangements will spend a lot of time figuring out how to restructure this debt and equity to alleviate costly interest and make the firms more profitable.[35]

Providing the Right Kinds of Motivation

Numerous studies and conceptual analyses strongly suggest that linking the pay of CEOs and other executives to short-term performance criteria such as return on investment is a major problem in much of U.S. business, especially in multiple-SBU firms. Pay should strike a proper balance between both short- and long-term performance measure. Linking pay to strategy is critical.[36]

A firm following an invest-and-grow strategy, for example, might want an entrepreneurial leader. A strategy to harvest and divest might call for someone very solid and experienced. An organization following a strategy of selectivity of earnings might be willing to allocate a higher percentage of its bonuses or merit pay on the basis of expected future performance than an organization that was following a harvest strategy. Both firms would base a considerably lower percentage of pay on future performance than would one that pursued a strategy of investment and growth. Conversely, current financial performance would probably be much more important to a firm committed to a harvest strategy or a strategy of selectivity of earnings than it would be to a firm determined to invest and grow. The experiences of George E. Hall, former director of strategic planning for SCM, bear out such observations. SCM modified its rewards to fit each of four general situations among its 27 businesses. "Headquarters must specify what a particular business unit is expected to do in a given period and must hold out rewards for accomplishing those objectives."[37] Similarly, IBM has both short-term and long-term components in its executive compensation plan.[38]

RELATIONSHIPS BETWEEN SINGLE-BUSINESS AND MULTIPLE-SBU FIRM STRATEGIES

Many people use the term *corporate strategy* to generically describe multiple-SBU strategy, while its generally accepted definition also applies to corporate strategies at the single business unit level. This often creates confusion as to exactly how single- and multiple-SBU firm strategies relate. As shown in Figure 7.9, corporate, business, and functional strategies guide both single- and multiple-SBU firms. The following paragraphs discuss how these strategies interrelate.

Corporate Strategy

Corporate strategy, for both single- and multiple-business firms describes how the firm determines the business or businesses in which to compete, and how it will

FIGURE 7.9 Relationship between Single-Business and Multiple-Business Strategies

	Single Business	Multiple Businesses

Corporate	Find a business
	Compete or find a niche
	Concentration or multiple products
	Innovation
	
	Growth-all nine types
	Stabilization
	Investment reduction
	Turnaround
	Takeover defense
	Combination
	
	Internal, acquistion, merger, joint
	   venture, other alliances
	Fast – slow
	Local, regional, national,
	   multinational, global
		Portfolio management
		Restructuring
		Transferring skills
		Sharing activities
		Forming alliances
		Management of culture

Business	Generic strategies
	   Cost
	   Differentiation
	   Focus
	   Others, e.g. PIMS
	Contingency strategies
	Marketing mix strategies
	Preemptive strategies
	Occasionally other functional
	   strategies, management of culture
		Multiple point competition
		   strategies

Functional	Economic functions
	   Marketing
	   Finance
	   Operations
	   Human resourses
	   Information
	Management functions, creative
	   problem solving in:
	   Planning
	   Organizing
	   Leading
	   Controlling
		Economic functions (often only
		   guidance policies)
		   Marketing
		   Finance
		   Operations
		   Human resource
		   Information
		Management functions, creative
		   problem solving in:
		   Planning
		   Organizing
		   Leading
		   Controlling

fundamentally conduct that business or those businesses. For the single-SBU firm or the division of a multiple-SBU firm, this means finding a business or evaluating whether or not to remain in the business, deciding whether to compete head-on or find a niche, concentrating on one or multiple products, determining the firm's strategic imperatives, for example, innovation strategy, and then making decisions about basic action strategies of growth, stabilization, investment reduction, turnaround, takeover defense, or some combination. Subsequently, the firm must determine whether to pursue growth or stabilization internally or externally through acquisition, mergers, joint ventures, or other alliances; quickly or slowly; and locally, regionally, nationally, multinationally, or globally.

For the multiple-SBU firm, corporate strategy becomes primarily an issue of portfolio management. It involves deciding the criteria for business selection and then setting a strategy for each business depending upon how it meets the various criteria established by several different portfolio management techniques, normally some type of matrix approach. More recently, broader perspectives on how the firm will fundamentally conduct itself have led to the recognition of additional corporate strategies including restructuring, transferring skills, sharing activities, forming alliances, and managing organizational culture. Restructuring was a major issue in the 1980s and will continue to dominate discussion in the 1990s. Forming alliances and managing culture will be focal points for multiple-SBU firms in the 1990s.

Business Strategy

Business strategy expresses how the organization will compete. The single-SBU firm competes essentially through relative differentiation and/or relative low-cost strategies. Both differentiation and low-cost strategies affect efforts in a particular target market, hence the focus strategy relies on applying differentiation or low cost to a particular market. As William K. Hall's research has indicated, one can pursue both relative differentiation and relative low cost in varying degrees simultaneously and this is appropriate.[39]

Multiple-SBU firms compete through multiple-point competition. The few firms that compete in several industries may choose to build competitive portfolios and then employ related business strategies. They may also choose not to actually compete, but simply to make the portfolio perform its best without seeking out other firms with similar portfolios to compete against. For example, GE has the number one or number two firm in every industry in which it competes. More recently, multiple-SBU corporate strategies have become increasingly important as a means of improving SBU competition. Multiple-SBU firms must provide sufficient value to their SBUs or these units might very well face disadvantages against single-SBU firms or similar firms of another multiple-SBU firm.

Functional Strategies

Functional strategies are concerned with the effective and efficient use of resources in support of corporate and business strategies. Functional strategies are especially important for the single-SBU firm. Occasionally they may even become means of competing, and hence business strategies in their own right.

At the multiple-SBU level, there is a continuum of degree to which functional strategies and policies become important determinants of overall corporate success. Virtually all theorists agree that the corporation should set the tone for its SBU divisions, but the level of detail is not clear. Some firms, such as TRW, have very strong influences over many facets of subsidiary operations. Others, such as GE, manage only certain issues such as culture and management style. Others, such as Disney, allow divisions wide latitude within their industries, yet seek synergy in marketing opportunities. Most often, corporate staff oversees finance more closely than any other function.

STRATEGIC MANAGER'S SUMMARY

1. The principal tasks of strategists in the multiple-SBU firm are to establish strategic objectives, determine the extent to which current and future businesses are helping or can help achieve those objectives, examine what remains to be accomplished, determine strategies to achieve those objectives, establish support functions and policies to achieve those objectives, and accomplish all this with a minimum of staff.

2. These activities are guided by portfolio management techniques. In addition to portfolio management, other important corporate strategies for multiple SBUs include restructuring, transferring skills, sharing activities, forming alliances, and managing culture.

3. The Boston Consulting Group (BCG) matrix is a mechanism for relating two key factors—business or industry attractiveness and the firm's competitiveness within that industry—to help identify businesses to enter and businesses in which to remain. The BCG model has given way to other, more sophisticated matrices.

4. The General Electric business screen has proved to be even more useful than the BCG matrix, because it incorporates more specific considerations.

5. A third matrix, the product/market/industry evolution portfolio matrix, allows strategists to consider additional critical variables related to the product life cycle.

6. The ADL portfolio-planning matrix combines features of the GE business screen and the product/market/industry evolution portfolio matrix.

7. A variety of criteria may be used to help the strategist assess both industry attractiveness and competitive position. For industry attractiveness, a few of the factors include size, growth, pricing, market diversity, competitive structure, and industry profitability. For competitive position a few of the factors include market share, SBU growth rate, breadth of product line, sales distribution effectiveness, product quality, and research and development advantage.

8. Sometimes a gap appears between an SBU's performance and corporate objectives. As a result, corporate strategists may be required to adjust investment strategies or business strategies, add or delete SBUs from the portfolio, change enterprise strategies, or change strategic objectives.

9. Both the concept and the implementation of portfolio management suffer from limitations, including faulty assumptions.

10. The corporate strategist and the business-level executive tend to have different perspectives. Division managers are usually oriented toward either a function or a product. The corporate executive must be a generalist. It is often difficult for the specialist to make the transition to generalist. Corporate reward programs must be tailored to the specific situation of the SBU.

11. Current issues in multiple-SBU management include increased SBU autonomy, improved provision of services to SBUs, restructuring debt, and executive compensation.

KEY TERMS

ADL portfolio-planning matrix
attractiveness criteria
balance
BCG matrix
cash cows
criteria for business strengths
division and corporate strategists'
    perspectives
dogs
gap analysis
GE business screen
GE stoplight strategy

harvest/divest strategy
invest-and-grow strategy
multiple-point competition
pitfalls in the portfolio approach
portfolio management techniques
product/market/industry evolution
    portfolio matrix
question marks
selectivity/earnings strategy
stars
synergy

DISCUSSION QUESTIONS

1. Select a conglomerate and describe its major SBUs in terms of the BCG matrix, the GE business screen, the product/market/industry evolution portfolio matrix, and the ADL portfolio-planning matrix.

2. Describe how the processes of setting objectives and formulating strategy differ at the SBU and corporate levels.

3. If you were describing the differences between the BCG matrix and the GE business screen to a person who was unfamiliar with them, what distinguishing elements would you highlight?

4. Provided you have successfully answered question 3, how would you now explain the differences between the GE business screen and the product/market/industry evolution matrix to the same person? The differences between the product/market/industry evolution matrix and the ADL portfolio-planning matrix?

5. Discuss the problems that limit both the concept and the implementation of portfolio approaches.

6. Where are we headed with multiple-SBU corporate strategy?

STRATEGIC AUDIT QUESTIONS

1. Does this organization have a corporate portfolio strategy? What is it? How good is it? What changes need to be made in it, if any?
2. Evaluate its businesses in accordance with the BCG matrix. What results do you find? What strategies do you recommend?
3. Evaluate its businesses in accordance with the GE business screen. What results to you find? What strategies do you recommend?
4. Evaluate its businesses in accordance with the product/market/industry evolution portfolio matrix. What results do you find? What strategies do you recommend?
5. Evaluate its businesses in accordance with the ADL portfolio-planning matrix. What results do you find? What strategies do you recommend?
6. Do you find balance and synergy among the company's businesses?
7. Can skills be transferred between the company's businesses? How well?
8. Does restructuring offer any advantages to the company?
9. Can activities be shared among its businesses?
10. Are the proper alliances being formed?
11. Is this organization pursuing multiple-point competition? Adequately?
12. Do you find any problems arising from differences between the perspectives of corporate and business strategists? If so, how would you solve them?
13. Is the focus on the long term and on innovation?
14. Is it properly managing SBU culture, management style, etc.?

Endnotes

1. Brian Bremner, "The Age of Consolidation," *Business Week*, October 14, 1991, pp. 86–94.
2. Peter F. Drucker, "How to Be Competitive though Big," *The Wall Street Journal*, February 7, 1991, p. A14.
3. Thomas A. Stewart, "GE Keeps Those Ideas Coming," *Fortune*, August 12, 1991, pp. 41–49.
4. For discussions, see R. A. Proctor and J. S. Hassard, "Towards a New Model of Portfolio Analysis," *Management Decisions*, no. 3 (1990) pp. 14–17; Y. Wind and V. Mahajan, "Designing Product and Business Portfolios," *Harvard Business Review*, January–February 1981, pp. 155–165; Malcolm B. Coate, "Pitfalls in Portfolio Planning," *Long Range Planning*, June 1983, pp. 47–56.
5. "The Future Catches Up with a Strategic Planner," *Business Week*, June 23, 1983, p. 62.
6. "Royal Dutch Shell: According to Plan," *The Economist*, July 22, 1989, pp. 62–63.
7. Bruce Hedley, "Strategy and the 'Business Portfolio,'" *Long Range Planning*, February 1977, pp. 9–15.
8. Charles R. Kennedy, Jr., "Political Risk Management: A Portfolio Planning Model," *Business Horizons*, November/December 1988, pp. 26–33.
9. Charles W. Hofer and Dan Schendel, *Strategy Formulation: Analytical Concepts* (St. Paul, Minn.: West, 1978), pp. 31–32.
10. Not all, however. For example, environmental factors are not sufficiently accounted for, according to Proctor and Hassard, "New Model."
11. Bernard Reimann, "More Highlights of the Planning Forum's International Conference," *Planning Review*, September/October 1990, p. 341, citing Rosabeth Moss Kanter's comments at the conference.
12. Proctor and Hassard, "New Model," pp. 14–17.
13. Charles W. Hofer, "Conceptual Constructs for Formulating Corporate and Business Strategies," no. 9-378-754, Intercollegiate Case Clearing House, 1977.
14. Charles H. Morrow, "How Suppliers Make Acquisitions Work," *Industrial Distribution*, May 15, 1991, p. 103.
15. Hofer and Schendel, *Strategy Formulation*, Chapter 2.
16. Roger K. Brooks, "Divestiture Seen as New Phenomenon in Insurance Industry Corporate Patterns; Divesting Non-Core Businesses," *International Insurance Monitor*, August/September 1989, pp. 13–15.
17. Michael E. Porter, "From Competitive Advantage to

Corporate Strategy," *Harvard Business Review*, May–June 1987, pp. 53–56.

18. Coate, "Pitfalls in Planning."

19. P. Haspeslagh, "A Survey of U.S. Companies Shows How Effective Portfolio Planning Could Be but Often Isn't," *Harvard Business Review*, January–February 1982, pp. 58–73.

20. Walter Kiechel III, "Corporate Strategists under Fire," *Fortune*, December 27, 1982, pp. 35–39. Kiechel's sentiments are supported by H. K. Christensen, A. C. Cooper, and C. A. DeKluyver, "The Dog Business: A Reexamination," *Business Horizons*, November/December 1982, pp. 12–18.

21. Porter, "From Competitive Advantage," p. 51.

22. Charles W. L. Hill, Michael A. Hitt, and Robert E. Hoskisson, "Declining U.S. Competitiveness: Reflections on a Crisis," *Academy of Management Executive*, February 1988, pp. 51–60.

23. Porter, "From Competitive Advantage," p. 51.

24. Rosabeth Moss Kanter, "Becoming PALs: Pooling, Allying, and Linking across Companies," *Academy of Management Executive*, August 1989, pp. 183–193.

25. Robert D. Hof and Deidre A. Depke, "An Alliance Made in PC Heaven," *Business Week*, June 24, 1991, pp. 40, 42.

26. Hofer and Schendel, *Strategy Formulation*, Chapter 7. See also A. Karnani and B. Wernerfelt, "Multiple Point Competition," Academy of Management, *Proceedings*, August 1983, pp. 27–31.

27. Personal interview with author.

28. Peter Lorange, "Divisional Planning: Setting Effective Direction," *Sloan Management Review*, Fall 1975, pp. 77–91.

29. Kenneth M. Davidson, "Why Acquisitions May Not Be the Best Route to Innovation," *Journal of Business Strategy*, May/June 1991, pp. 50–52.

30. Drucker, "Competitive though Big," p. A14.

31. Michael Goold and Andrew Campbell, "Brief Case: From Corporate Strategy to Parenting Advantage," *Long Range Planning*, February 1991, pp. 115–117.

32. Terence P. Pare, "The Big Threat to Big Steel's Future," *Fortune*, July 15, 1991, pp. 106–109; George J. McManus, "Hot Strip Mills Bridge Generation Gap," *Iron Age*, June 1991, pp. 30–33; Thomas M. Rohan, "Maverick Remakes Old-Line Steel," *Industry Week*, January 21, 1991, pp. 26–30.

33. George Anders, "Back to Biscuits: Old Flamboyance Is out as Louis Gerstner Remakes RJR-Nabisco," *The Wall Street Journal*, March 21, 1991, pp. A1, A6.

34. Arden B. Engebretsen, "How Key Is Finance to Corporate Strategy?" *Financial Executive*, July/August 1990, pp. 50–54.

35. For a representative discussion, although more favorable to LBOs than the text paragraph, see Edmund Faltermayer, "The Deal Decade: Verdict on the '80s," *Fortune*, August 26, 1991, pp. 58–70.

36. Bernard C. Reimann, "Shareholder Value and Executive Compensation," *Planning Review*, May/June 1991, pp. 41–48; John A. Bryne, "The Flap over Executive Pay," *Business Week*, May 6, 1991, pp. 90–112; Patricia M. Dechow and Richard G. Sloan, "Executive Incentives and the Horizon Problem: an Empirical Investigation," *Journal of Accounting & Economics*, March 1991, pp. 51–89; Anthony H. Hampson, "Tying CEO Pay to Performance: Compensation Committees Must Do Better," *Business Quarterly*, Spring 1991, pp. 18–21; "Long-Term Incentives Gaining Popularity," *Employee Benefit Plan Review*, April 1991, pp. 56–58.

37. George E. Hall, "Reflections on Running a Diversified Company," *Harvard Business Review*, January–February 1987, pp. 88–89.

38. Donald H. Edman, "Compensation for the 1990s: A Look at IBM," *Compensation and Benefits Review*, November/December 1990, pp. 32–39.

39. William K. Hall, "Survival Strategies in a Hostile Environment," *Harvard Business Review*, September–October 1980, pp. 73–86.

INTEGRATIVE CASE ANALYSIS
CHAPTER 7

THE CHALLENGES FACING GENERAL MOTORS IN 1992

General Motors' diversification efforts can be evaluated by each of the portfolio management techniques reviewed in this chapter. We haven't enough information on many of the smaller acquisitions and strategic business units to determine how to plot them, but we can analyze the automobile business itself, which still accounts for 80 percent of General Motors' sales.

The automobile division would have a low position on the "business growth rate" axis of the BCG matrix, but General Motors would have a relatively high position. The auto division has been a cash cow. Some of the cash was used to acquire EDS, Hughes, and some additional firms, but most of it ($77 billion) went for new technology for the auto division whence it came as GM strove to position itself in its major business for the 1990s and beyond.

If we used the General Electric stoplight strategy or business screen, we would be tempted to evaluate GM's automobile division as having medium industry attractiveness and medium business strength, for a strategy of selectivity and earnings; or we could rate it as high-high, for a strategy of investment and growth, depending on if we assume that in the future GM can overcome its current weaknesses and can mitigate its threats in its external environment. To overcome its weaknesses, GM is restructuring, cutting costs, improving quality, and revamping product lines. General Motors perceived itself to be in an invest-and-grow situation in 1979, and certainly it was. While this perception may have been correct in 1979, and it may still have been correct even as late as 1987, GM's auto business was destined to operate in a less attractive industry and the company's strength was waning. So while GM may have earned high ratings on the GE matrix in 1979, it earns medium ratings in 1992. EDS, Hughes, GM's European Auto Division, and GMAC would all be in invest-and-grow areas of the matrix.

If we used the product/market/industry evolution portfolio matrix, many of GM's new product/business developments would be in the growth or shake-out stages, while the auto industry is in maturity and saturation. The EDS electronics business may be in the maturity/ saturation stage. Hughes is certainly in maturity and saturation. GM's biggest cash flows are coming from mature products and industries. These industry life cycles can go on for many, many years, however. The way to handle that situation is to make sure that the products, not just the firms in the industry, are new. One of John Smith's first actions as new president was to analyze which product lines should have been dropped. GM has many, with new models coming on line to replace older ones.

If we use the ADL portfolio-planning matrix, we find that General Motors' automobile competitive position is still dominant, or at least strong, in an aging or mature industry, so holding and maintaining are the key strategies to be followed there. This is what General Motors is currently attempting to do.

As far as synergy is concerned, some of GM's people wondered who acquired whom in the $2.5 billion transaction with Electronic Data Systems. This acquisition has demonstrated that the culture of the parent organization does not always dominate that of the acquired firm. EDS employees came on like gangbusters. Austerity was in, spending lavishly was out. GM has essentially adopted much of the EDS frugality philosophy throughout the rest of the company. Other EDS policies and cultural phenomena may wear off as well. It is clear, however, that the technology that General Motors thought it was purchasing has not yet been of any significant value in the production of automobiles or in the products themselves.

The Hughes acquisition seemed to make similar sense. Hughes is electronics, automobiles are coming to incorporate increasing amounts of electronics, so why not buy a large electronics company? But Hughes's electronics have not been very transferable. Will its skills be sharable? So far General Motors has found it more difficult to transfer technology than it thought it would be.

CHAPTER 8

IMPLEMENTATION THROUGH MANAGEMENT OF STRUCTURE

Over the past 20 years, strategic thinking has far outdistanced organizational capabilities.

Christopher A. Bartlett and Sumantra Ghoshal
Researchers on Strategy

If you were to ask a CEO in the year 2000 to . . . draw the organization chart of his company, what he'd sketch would bear little resemblance to . . . the flattened pyramid of today. Spinning around the straight lines [of the basic chart] will be a . . . pattern of constantly changing teams, task forces, partnerships, and other structures.

Brian Dumaine
Senior Writer for *Fortune*

CHAPTER OBJECTIVES

By the time you complete this chapter, you should be able to:

1. Define implementation and describe the role of structure in the implementation process
2. List the major components of organizational structure
3. Describe the shapes of the four principal organizational structures and explain why they assume those shapes
4. Identify the five major types of pyramidal organizational structures, and be able to identify both project and matrix structures
5. Describe the effects on structure of each of the seven determinants of structure
6. Briefly explain why an organization's structure must change as the organization grows, and discuss those changes
7. Describe the types of structures that seem to be best suited to simple, steady-state environments and to complex and changing environments; indicate which structural type will be most necessary in the future and why
8. Identify current trends in organizational structure

HEWLETT-PACKARD REORGANIZES
TO COPE WITH ITS STRATEGIC CHALLENGES

Hewlett-Packard has always been admired as one of America's best-managed corporations. The HP Way has always meant innovation and responsiveness to customer needs, but a 1984 decision to place its disparate computer operations under a single organizational umbrella almost spelled disaster for this intrapreneurially oriented corporate giant. This restructuring decision was made in order to help set common standards among the then-separate HP computer product lines and thus be more responsive to market requirements. The decision to set common standards proved to be sound, but a common organization structure proved to be almost fatal to corporate innovation.

As part of the decision to have a common management structure, committees were established to improve coordination and communication. The few that were initiated in 1984 quickly mushroomed into an immense bureaucracy. In 1990, Bob Frankenberg, the HP General Manager, had no fewer than 38 committees reporting to him. It's a wonder that he had time to do anything but meet with the committees.

Virtually every new product decision had to go through these committees and they took forever to act. "The result was gridlock." New product introductions were continually delayed. Nine committees with over 100 total members took 7 months just to agree on a name for a new software package.

Another part of the 1984 restructuring decision grouped all sales staff under a single head who reported to the HP executive committee rather than to the product managers who used these services. Under this structure, people below the executive level made few decisions. Even minuscule decisions came to the attention of CEO John Young. For example, to establish a sales rebate program, a group manager needed eight signatures, including those of two executive vice presidents.

In a related structural matter, HP failed to control costs, especially overhead costs. It spent 52.4 percent of 1990 revenues to sell and service equipment compared to 49.9 percent in the previous year.

The consequences of HP's structural problems were substantial, although not immediately obvious. By 1990, however, HP had lost significant market share in critical markets, new orders had fallen, already thin profits suffered from a bloated work force, earnings fell in several successive quarters, HP stock fell to low levels not recently experienced, and employee morale hit a new low.

A New Structure

CEO John Young became increasingly aware of serious corporate structural problems. He made minor adjustments in the structure in 1988 attempting to get at the problem, but in the early spring of 1990, he realized that things had gotten out of hand. A manager reported to him that the most important product that HP was to develop over the next several years, a high-powered workstation codenamed Snakes, had reportedly fallen behind schedule by 1 year. The manager blamed the bureaucracy. The always-calm Young was furious. "I nearly came unglued that day," Young admits. Something had to be done.

He sought the counsel of cofounder, chairman, and still largest shareholder David Packard, 78. The two didn't have to look very far for a model to follow. The company's most successful product division, the LaserJet printer division, was allowed to exist outside the main HP structure. Under the direction of executive vice president Richard A. Hackborn, it had met new product deadlines, made significant improvements, and retained a market share of 60 percent in a market that Apple, IBM, and a host of Japanese firms had entered. In a bold move, Young removed all of the engineers working on Snakes and placed them under a single manager, Dennis Georg, and gave him almost dictatorial powers. Other product development projects were then similarly structured.

Committees were all but abolished; Bob Frankenberg only has three reporting to him now. The computer division was divided into two structures based on the way the machines were sold. The sales division was broken into several parts, each reporting to the product group it served. Excessive layers of management were eliminated. The results were just short of spectacular. Bob Frankenberg exclaims, "The results were incredible. We are doing more business and getting product out quicker with fewer people." The Snakes project was completed on time and the machine wowed the industry. It was three times faster than those of several competitors and quickly captured significant market share. Another product launched in the spring of 1991, the 95LX palm-top PC with built-in Lotus 1-2-3 spreadsheets, was so tremendously successful that an additional production line had to be built.

The HP turnaround has had its human costs, however. Over 3,000 people were let go in a process known as *excessing*. HP doesn't lay people off, it excesses them. Those excessed have 3 months to find another job in HP or they are let go. As one marketing staffer noted, "Now there's just dread of the E-word."

Sources: Stephen Kreider Yoder, "Quick Change: A 1990 Reorganization at Hewlett-Packard Already Is Paying off," *The Wall Street Journal*, July 22, 1991, p. A1; Barbara Buell and Robert D. Hob, "Hewlett-Packard Rethinks Itself," *Business Week*, April 1, 1991, pp. 76–78.

Hewlett-Packard (HP) has always relied on innovation and customer responsiveness as strategies, but its organization structure very nearly sabotaged those strategies in the late 1980s and 1990. Only when HP CEO John Young drastically reorganized the firm did it begin to successfully implement its strategies. What happened at HP clearly conveys the importance of matching organization structure to the needs of implementing strategy. If structure is not designed to carry out strategy, then strategy may very well fail.

HP is not the only firm with structural problems. IBM suffers from similar, and perhaps even worse structural roadblocks to successful strategy implementation. Many, including HP CEO John Young, feel a bloated bureaucracy lies at the heart of IBM's problems. Facing the stiffest competition of its life, however, IBM has reorganized and is continuing to do so, eliminating some 4,000 positions in 1991. Yet its bureaucracy remained and growth and profits were at best flat for most IBM divisions.[1] Thus, IBM decided to eliminate 20,000 more positions in 1992.[2] At another firm, NV Philips, the electronics giant headquartered in the Netherlands, thousands of white-collar workers had to be laid off in order to make the firm sufficiently lean to compete in the post-1992 European economy.[3] Finally, even at highly successful Toyota, jobs are being redesigned, work flows changed, information systems reconstructed, and new global operations initiated to make

the fiercest automaker of them all even leaner and meaner in this age of global competition.[4]

This chapter begins the examination of **implementation**—the means by which strategy is translated into accomplishment. Formulating strategy is difficult, but successfully implementing strategy is an even more complex task.[5] The most elegantly conceived, precisely articulated strategy is virtually worthless unless it is implemented successfully. Far too many firms and managers forget this vital component of the strategic management process.

Implementation may be approached in a variety of ways; most authorities, however, point to four factors as the key ingredients in successful implementation: an organization structure that fits the strategy, appropriate systems to implement the strategy, an appropriate management style, and an appropriate system of shared values (organizational culture).[6] These four factors are not independent; rather they are interdependent, and events occurring simultaneously in each of these areas may affect the others. Similarly, change in strategy may simultaneously affect one or all four factors. Figure 8.1 identifies the component of the strategic management process model discussed in this chapter. Figure 8.2 identifies the component of implementation discussed in this chapter, organization structure.

All of the ten strategic challenges noted in Chapter 1 will in some way cause changes in organization structures in the 1990s. Accelerating rates of change, increasing competition, especially global competition, and changing technology will dramatically alter structures in most organizations. For many firms, such as IBM, this will mean eliminating jobs to cut away at bureaucracy. Many firms have already completed the easy restructurings, eliminating numerous jobs. The task now is to redesign the work itself and to better manage the relationships between the various operations within the firm.[7]

ORGANIZATION AND IMPLEMENTATION

Once it has formulated strategy, the organization must develop a structure that will permit it to carry out that strategy, as shown in Figure 8.2. The structuring process

FIGURE 8.1 The Organization—A Strategic Management Process Model

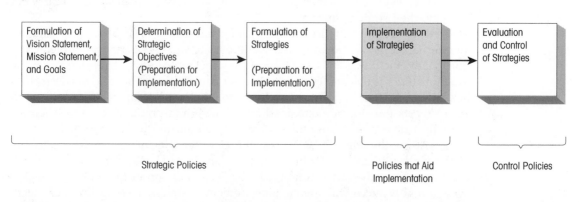

FIGURE 8.2   Implementation

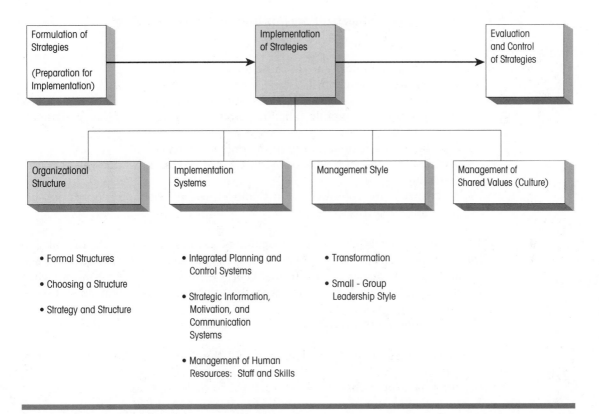

involves two steps. (1) The tasks required to achieve objectives and enact plans are determined and grouped into jobs, which are then combined into work groups and departments. (2) The authority to perform these tasks is delegated. This structuring process has a significant effect on the organization's ability to accomplish its mission, for two principal reasons:

1. The organization's structure defines the specific actions to be taken to implement strategy.
2. The organization's structure establishes the degree of autonomy each individual, work group, department, or division has in carrying out the activities designed to implement strategy.

Organization structure and implementation are highly interdependent. A manager's ability to lead, for example, depends in large part on the degree of authority he or she commands. Because most organizations are ongoing concerns, most firms already have structures of some sort; such a firm's structuring task requires assuring that the structure supports the proper implementation of the strategy. Sometimes this requires fine-tuning, sometimes it requires a major overhaul of existing structure as occurred at Hewlett-Packard.

ORGANIZATION STRUCTURE CONCEPTS

The principal **components of organization structure** are these:

1. Jobs
2. Delegation of authority to do those jobs
3. Manager's span of control
4. Departmentation, or grouping jobs into departments on the basis of task specialty, time, economic function, product, customer, project, geographic area, or SBU division
5. Number of levels of authority in the organization
6. Amount of authority delegated organizationwide (centralization versus decentralization)
7. Mechanisms for coordination, including rules, policies, procedures, job descriptions, objectives

The organization's overall structure is a combination of its formal and informal structures. Most people think of the organization structure as boxes and connecting lines depicted on a formal chart. To realistically envision the actual relationships portrayed there, however, the informal organization must also be considered.

The informal organization consists of all that is not formal, primarily:

1. Personalities of the individuals who fill the roles prescribed by the formal structure
2. Informal groups that develop within the formal structure

While the influences of individuals and groups on structure are not neglected in our discussion, our primary concern here is formal structure. Also, in our ever-changing world, the organization's place in networks with other organizations must be viewed as part of structure. When a purchasing department has an electronic data interchange link with suppliers, or when cross-functional product development teams include customers, structural arrangements have been created.

FORMAL STRUCTURES

A firm may have any of four **basic organization structures:** the pyramid, the matrix, the team, and the alliance or joint venture (see Figure 8.3). Each has its own characteristic distribution of authority. The pyramid is the most common form of structure.

Pyramidal Forms of Structure

The pyramidal form, the primary structure in most organizations, is the product of classical organization theory. It is common among both single- and multiple-SBU firms. The addition of staff positions throughout the pyramid does not change its basic shape. Normally the team and matrix forms appear within pyramidal

FIGURE 8.3 Shapes of Organization Structures

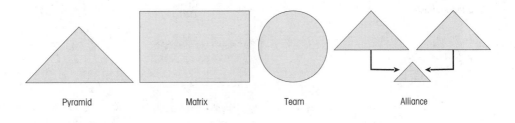

Pyramid   Matrix   Team   Alliance

structures rather than defining a firm's entire structure. Alliances and joint venture structures usually connect organizations structured with pyramidal forms.

Figure 8.4 indicates the major variations on the pyramidal form in a very basic format, since you should already be familiar with these concepts. The **simple structure** is normally found in the small organization in the early stages of its existence, or in later stages if it does not grow. The **economic functional structure** is usually the next step, adopted as an organization grows. The **product structure** is adopted when the firm reaches a certain size and two or more products come to make significant contributions to the achievement of its objectives. One of the major issues in a growing firm is when to switch from a functional structure to a product structure.

Once enough product lines in a specific industry or target market area become sufficiently large, the organization normally proceeds to develop some form of **SBU structure,** like the one in Figure 8.5. This is often referred to as the **M-form structure.** The **geographic structure** is becoming more important as firms operate more globally. In this structure, a geographic region, for example, Europe, North America, and the Pacific Rim (see Figure 8.4), or East, South, Midwest, and West (see Figure 8.5) form the basis for defining departments. The geographic structure normally supplements a functional, product, or SBU/M-form structure. Within any of these five pyramidal forms, jobs may be further organized into departments on the basis of their relations to each other and on the basis of relations to clients or customers, task specialization, or time (day shift, night shift). A very large, complex organization, like the one pictured in Figure 8.5 and like General Motors, may be departmentalized and structured in all of these ways.

The exact shape of an organization's pyramid is a function primarily of the spans of control and related delegation of authority within the organization. A flat pyramid indicates large spans of control and considerable delegation of authority. A tall, slim pyramid indicates small spans of control and little delegation of authority. Shapes can be deceiving, though. Actual delegation may far exceed or fall far short of what the shape indicates. Delegation is also a matter of interpersonal relationships, rather than simply lines on an organization chart.

Still, the shape of the pyramid is important in today's complex and ever-changing external environment. The evidence clearly indicates that more flexible organizations are more likely to adapt successfully to changeable environments. Flatter pyramids are generally believed to indicate more flexible organizations. This is a major reason that NV Philips of Europe is moving to restructure to flatten its pyramid, as this chapter's Global Strategic Challenge suggests.

FIGURE 8.4 Types of Pyramids

I. Simple Structure

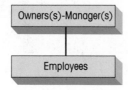

II. Economic Functional Structure

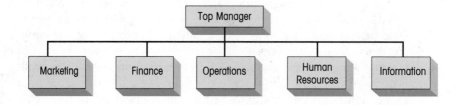

III. Product Structure

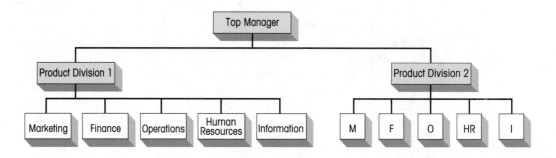

IV. Geographic Structure

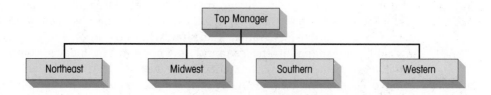

FIGURE 8.5 Typical Multidivisional Organization

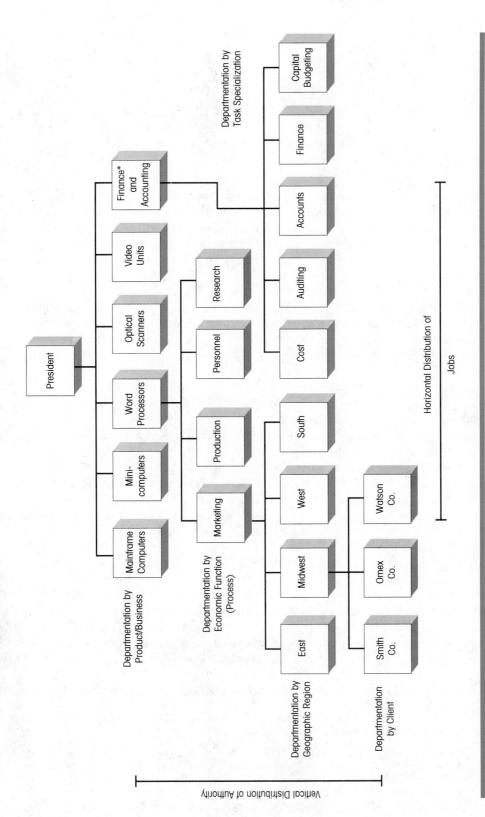

Normally this particular staff job is centralized; that is, operating divisions do not usually have their own finance departments. Source: James M. Higgins, *Human Relations: Behavior at Work*, 2d ed., p. 167. Copyright © 1987, Random House, Inc.

GLOBAL STRATEGIC CHALLENGE

PHILIPS RESTRUCTURES TO REMAIN COMPETITIVE

Philips Electronics NV, the European electronics giant, terminated 10,000 employees in 1989. It will lay off another 45,000 before the end of 1992, bringing the total it has eliminated to 55,000, one-fifth of its work force. Many of these employees will be white-collar managers and staff, and the result will be devastating for Philips' headquarters city of Eindhoven, where many of these white-collar workers are employed. The primary reason for such layoffs was to regain competitiveness.

Europe's industrial giants have long been bloated with bureaucracy, but since Europe has been largely a series of closed country markets, inefficient organization structures didn't matter. Governments encouraged such bureaucracies in order to keep people employed. Competition from other European firms in the newly opened markets within each country, from U.S. firms, and most especially from Japanese firms, means that European firms must now become more efficient.

Another more imminent reason for Philips to lay off employees was its substantial financial loss of $2.4 billion in 1990. (A significant part of the loss was advance writeoffs of expected costs of cutting 45,000 more employees.) Former cash cows were not doing well, and the firm was suffering with a computer operation that suffered heavy losses in Europe. The firm has accelerated its layoff program as a result.

Layoffs are expensive for Philips. The first round of 10,000 employees laid off, almost all Europeans, cost Philips $700 million. European employees must be paid 15 months' pay for severance, with some managers receiving as much as 3 years' pay. To avoid these costs, Philips diverted several thousand layoffs to the United States, where it had 40,000 employees and where layoffs cost relatively little. On the other hand, slashing the work force by 55,000 people will save Philips at least $1.2 billion annually.

In addition to those in the United States, other corporate layoffs were not randomly distributed throughout the company, but rather involved closing numerous very carefully selected factories and support divisions. In further restructuring actions, the company sold the beleaguered computer division to Digital Equipment Corporation for $300 to $350 million. Digital welcomed the acquisition as a way of penetrating the European market, while Philips welcomed the divestiture as a way of ridding itself of a product division that was losing substantial amounts of money despite major corporate investment. Philips, meanwhile, plans to focus on PCs.

Since all of these restructuring efforts, the company has begun doing much more with a lot fewer people.

Sources: Jonathan B. Levine, "Philips' Big Gamble," *Business Week*, August 5, 1991, pp. 34–36; Geoffrey Foster, "Hanging on the Fate of Philips," *Management Today*, June 1991, p. 31; Jonathan Kapstein, "A Chilling New Era for Philips—and Europe," *Business Week*, November 12, 1990, pp. 58, 59; Jonathan Kapstein, "European High Tech is Sinking Mighty Low," *Business Week*, September 17, 1990, p. 52.

Matrix Form of Structure

The **matrix structure,** seen in some detail in Figure 8.6a, involves simultaneous authority over line or staff employees by both a project or product manager and a functional manager. Matrix organizations are common among aerospace firms, such as Lockheed and Martin Marietta, which must assign functional specialists to projects or products for limited time periods. Matrix management is also appropriate to firms that assign functional specialists to continuing organizational subunits, but want to maintain control by both subunit and functional managers. A loan officer in a branch of a large bank might be in such a position, for instance.

AT HEWLETT-PACKARD

Hewlett-Packard abandoned its committee structure and replaced it with project development groups, each headed by a powerful manager in a simple structure. These groups are part of the traditional pyramid and in effect help make the structure work much like a matrix.

Many organizations adopt the matrix structure to overcome the problems presented by diversity of either projects or products. A strict project form of management structure (Figure 8.6b) differs from the matrix form in that the project structure is principally a temporary pyramid, with line and staff personnel assigned to projects for limited periods of time. Employees are usually hired only for the duration of the project. The construction industry is the only major user of the project structure. Aerospace firms abandoned it in favor of the matrix in order to provide employment security for employees and to ensure a steady supply of employees. Employees of an organization with a matrix structure move from project to project, so no one loses a job at the completion of a project (as long as future projects are forthcoming).

Unfortunately, the employee always has two bosses in a matrix structure, one in charge of the function, and one overseeing the project. In a large matrix organization, an individual could have five or six bosses in any given year. This can lead to confusion about objectives, job requirements, and performance, unless the functional and project managers coordinate their efforts extremely well.

Team Forms of Structure

The **team management** concept emphasizes sharing authority among team members (hence the circle in Figure 8.3 to indicate equally distributed authority). The term *team* implies an attitude as much as a structure. The actual distribution of authority depends on numerous factors, but the essence of team management is participation in decision making, sharing authority between leader/manager and

FIGURE 8.6a The Matrix Organization

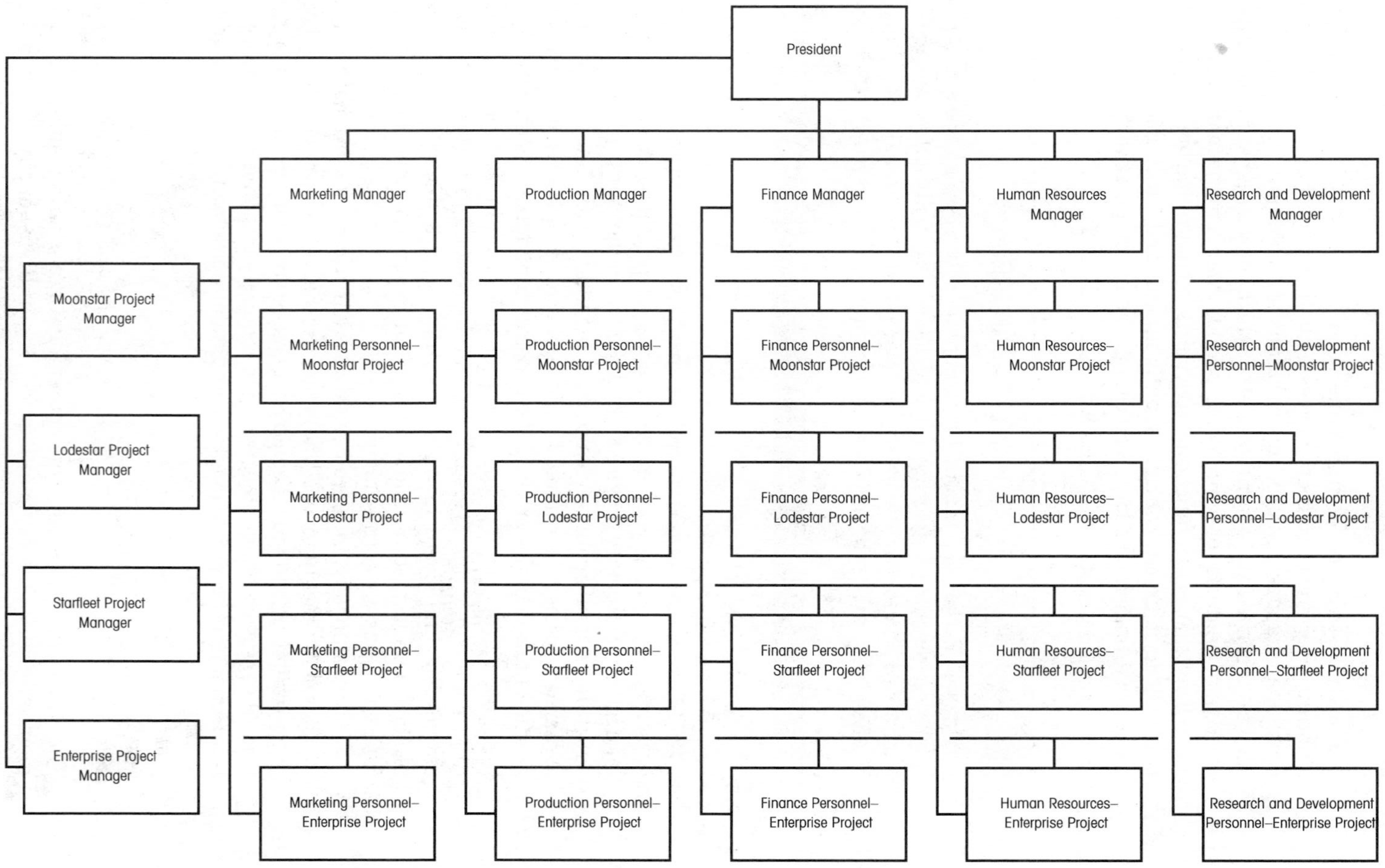

FIGURE 8.6b   Project Structure

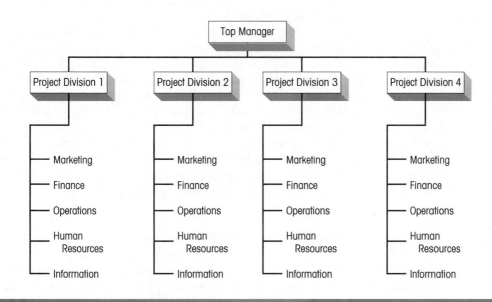

followers/subordinates in an effort to increase both productivity and employee satisfaction. Each work group could be viewed as a team as long as the attitudes of its members favor participation. Normally, however, special training is necessary to fully develop a true team. Teams usually function within a pyramid or matrix, and occasionally in an alliance, as well.[8]

More and more organizations are adopting one type of team approach or another in an effort to achieve their objectives. In addition to the traditional team management approach, in which work groups are reformed as teams, organizations are making substantial use of task teams, project teams, cross-functional teams, and customer/supplier teams. The **task team** is a temporary team that comes together to accomplish a specific task, such as redesigning company compensation packages. The **project team** is a temporary team that comes together to accomplish a specific project. It is similar to a task team, except that projects are usually larger in scope than tasks, and they usually take longer to accomplish. The terms are often used interchangeably.

The **cross-functional team** is a task or project team that includes members from various economic functions of the organization, such as marketing, research and development, and manufacturing, in order to gain the insight these functions can provide on a common problem. Cross-functional teams have become very common in product development projects in order to cut the time from design to finished product, and to make the design more easily manufactured and the whole process more efficient. Such teams have been used by Square D Company's Chatsworth, California plant to improve manufacturing of resistance welding controls, and they help provide total satisfaction to customers such as Chrysler Corporation.[9] Chrysler also uses cross-functional teams in the development of new vehicle platforms to improve quality and manufacturability.[10] **Customer/supplier**

teams may be task, project, or cross-functional teams that include customers and/or suppliers in order to better meet customer needs, and/or to articulate what the company needs from suppliers.

Thus, teams are becoming a major trend in organization structures. The ten strategic challenges imply the need for teams. For example, Beech Aircraft faced a collapsing market and significant global competition; it restructured its sales and top management around the team concept. This restructuring helped Beech become more competitive internationally, and helped improve efficiency, as well. Similarly, Northern Telecom Canada Ltd. saw its Morrisville, North Carolina repair facility sales increase 26 percent and profits increase 46 percent from 1988 to 1990 after it introduced teams in 1988.[11] Finally, Apple Computers uses teams extensively, constantly forming and reforming them. Apple has developed an internal software program called Spider that allows a team manager to access employee records to search for needed skills, availability, experience, and so on.[12]

Alliance/Joint Venture Structure

Yet another structural form remains to be considered—the strategic alliance. A **strategic alliance** involves any close association of corporations to achieve common objectives. The most common form of strategic alliance is the joint venture. A **joint venture** is basically a partnership between two distinct organizations for a limited purpose. Joint ventures are formed to exploit the strengths of one partner to mitigate the weaknesses of the other. Thus they can accomplish a task together that neither could manage alone. A firm's need to resolve capital or cash-flow problems may lead it to seek a joint venture agreement with a cash-rich organization. The need to enhance technology, research and development, and management skills may also bring two firms together.

Quite often a smaller, technologically innovative firm will combine with a larger, cash-rich, marketing-oriented firm to market a particular product, often for a specified period of time. The rewards from such ventures can be great, and the joint venture is an increasingly popular form of organization structure. Even such giants as IBM and Sears have recently entered into joint ventures.[13] Such an alliance is especially useful in developing global competitiveness.[14]

STRATEGY AND STRUCTURE

Strategists must design and implement an appropriate structure to carry out strategy. As strategy consultants Ian MacMillan and Patricia Jones have noted, "The challenge is not to design organizational structures that are perfect, but to design structures that are better than those of competitors."[15] Benchmarking and best practices comparisons may help a firm determine what structural designs or changes to existing structures are necessary.

While organization charts make structures appear stagnant, structure is fluid by nature, and this fluidity will be intentional in the well-managed organization of the 1990s. Due to the ten strategic challenges confronting firms in the next few years, especially change, increasing competition, global competition, and rapidly changing technology, firms will continually revise strategy and the structure to implement it. Furthermore, these external variables have a direct effect on the organization's structure, because certain structures seem to support various strategies more effectively than others, given certain types of environments.

Structures to carry out strategies must be determined for both single- and multiple-business organizations, including those for the SBU divisions of a multiple-business organization. Strategists must make several choices concerning structure:

1. What should the basic overall structure be for the organization?
2. Should the organization be organic or mechanistic?
3. Should the organization be centralized or decentralized?
4. What are the cost implications of structure design? How do we best rightsize?
5. What new or special structural devices are necessary to make the structure work?

Basic Overall Structure for the Organization

Strategists have choices among the structure types identified earlier: pyramid, matrix, team, and alliance/joint venture. For all practical purposes, most organizations are structured as pyramids, with matrix, team, and alliance/joint venture components somehow worked into or around the pyramidal framework. For the pyramid, the primary issue is the choice of first and second level structural forms beneath the CEO/COO.

Within the pyramidal forms, including simple, economic functional, product, strategic business unit or M-form, and geographic organizations (plus client, time, and task subdivisions), several possible combinations make the structuring process more complex. The following pyramidal combinations commonly appear, especially in the first two levels of structure, once the organization outgrows its simple structure: economic functional/task specialization; economic functional/product; economic functional/client; product (group)/product; product/economic functional; product/client; geographic/client; client/economic functional; client/product; SBU/product; SBU/functional; SBU/geographic; geographic/SBU.[16] The joint venture or other form of alliance is an increasingly common means of globalizing a firm.

First-Level Choices   All choices depend on the ability of structure to carry out strategy. Pragmatically speaking, however, as noted earlier, much of the decision about the first level of structure depends on size, as resulting from growth. The typical progression as a firm grows is from simple to economic functional, to product, to SBU, to geographic (or global) structures.

Second-Level Choices   The choice at the second level is a matter of judging which second level structural type best accomplishes the strategy in conjunction with the first level. Often, this depends on product/market/industry characteristics and how the customer may best be served.

Mechanistic or Organic Organizations

Organization researchers have identified two classifications of organizations according to general adaptability to their external environments: mechanistic organizations, which are not very adaptable, and organic organizations, which are.[17]

Mechanistic organizations are characterized by highly and rigidly defined tasks, hierarchical control structures based on rigid authority and impersonal relationships, limited distribution of information, vertical communication (principally from the top down), decisions from above, and demands of loyalty to organization and management. Importance and prestige depend upon organization membership.

Organic organizations are essentially the opposite of mechanistic organizations. They are characterized by interdependent tasks, stress on tasks' relationships with organizational objectives, continual adjustment and redefinition of tasks, network structures of authority and control, and community interest. Knowledge for decision making is seen as spread throughout the organization rather than being concentrated in the leader. Communication flows vertically and horizontally in both directions. Commitment to organization purposes is more highly valued than loyalty. Importance and prestige are attached to factors outside the organization.

The most commonly depicted structural scenario for the next 10 years calls for flexible, adaptive, organic organizations capable of responding to the tremendous change expected in customer needs, competitor strategies, technology, labor market conditions, and so on. Inflexible, mechanistic organizations are generally not regarded as suitable to the type of environment that most organizations will face. However, mechanistic organizations will still be appropriate to firms operating in the few stable environments that will remain.[18]

Organic organizations have flat pyramids, very limited corporate staff, and usually high decentralization. Most future organizations will have complex, user-friendly management information systems to help firms manage and coordinate their structures. Mechanistic firms have tall pyramids and large staffs, and are usually centralized. Recognizing that it needed to be more organic and less mechanistic, IBM began by downsizing by 20,000 employees in 1992. Downsizing raises certain ethical issues for a company like IBM as this chapter's Strategic Ethical Challenge feature describes.

Centralization versus Decentralization

Centralization means that most significant organization decisions are made by the managers at the top of the organization. **Decentralization** means that authority is distributed down the hierarchy so that managers at various levels can participate in important decisions, at least those relevant to their particular departments or divisions. Centralization and decentralization are the ends of a continuum, with many degrees of delegation resting between the two extremes. The general belief is that decentralization is advisable in a complex external environment that affects

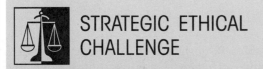

STRATEGIC ETHICAL CHALLENGE

HOW TO RESTRUCTURE AT IBM

Competition, especially global competition, advances in technology, declining profit margins, customer dissatisfaction with responsiveness, and several related factors led IBM to eliminate 4,000 jobs in 1991, and to announce that another 20,000 (some predict 25,000) cuts would come in 1992. One-third of these cuts would come from the firm's European operation, and two-thirds from the U.S. operation, with 11,000 expected to come from the U.S. marketing operation. The reduction of 20,000 personnel was accompanied by a reorganization of the firm, with headquarters providing guidance only as requested and the various businesses becoming autonomous, at least in theory. From a high of 407,000 employees in 1986, down to 350,000 in December 1991, by the end of 1992 IBM would shrink to only 325,000 employees. Analysts all agree that the reorganization and cutbacks were necessary, and some say not enough.

The question facing IBM's top management, as well as all other employees, was how to achieve these cutbacks without reneging on the no-layoff policy that had been sacred at IBM since its inception. In addition, management also somehow had to identify those it wished to entice to leave the firm, and offer the proper incentives to do so. The no-layoff policy had played an integral role in motivating people who felt they had a job for life, and therefore (most observers believed) were very loyal to IBM and very motivated to help the firm.

Top management's primary solution for cutting the work force was to seek voluntary reductions in force, offering very attractive early retirement or termination packages to those who would leave the firm. IBM also encouraged its managers to fire people for failure to perform, something that had not been stressed in the past. A ranking system was developed to facilitate these performance-related terminations. All IBM workers are now evaluated on a scale of 1 to 5. Those getting 4 or 5 ratings are in jeopardy if firing becomes necessary to reach the work force reduction goals. During the week that the cutbacks were announced, IBM demoted George H. Conrades, marketing head of its struggling U.S. unit. Many employees believe this was done to send the message that no job is safe.

Employee reactions to these strategies are mixed. "I feel betrayed. If IBM isn't growing, is it the fault of the employees, or of the senior management?" questioned a White Plains, New York worker. Similarly, "We are all panicked. Everybody thinks they're going to be out of a job," said a programmer in IBM's Austin, Texas operation. Another employee commented, "It's fine to weed out people, but they should have done it years ago." In contrast, research staffers generally share the belief that now products may get to market much faster than they had with a bloated sales bureaucracy. Critics note, however, that severance packages have been getting slimmer and slimmer and that voluntary actions will not be enough to reach the 20,000 to 25,000 cutback level. If IBM does resort to layoffs, some would question the action as unethically reneging on a company promise.

Sources: John W. Verity, Thane Peterson, Deidre Depke, and Evan I. Schwartz, "The New IBM," *Business Week*, December 16, 1991, pp. 112–118; Paul B. Carroll, "IBM Announces Details of Plan to Break Its Business into More Autonomous Pieces," *The Wall Street Journal*, December 12, 1991, p. B3; Paul B. Carroll, "IBM Plans $3 Billion Charge and about 20,000 Job Cuts," *The Wall Street Journal*, November 27, 1991, p. A3; Paul B. Carroll, "IBM Is Likely in 1992 to Trim 20,000 Positions, *The Wall Street Journal*, November 20, 1991, p. A3.

strategic decisions in several major ways. If, however, the external environment is simple and presents a limited number of major factors for consideration, then centralization is acceptable.[19]

Other factors also intervene. Extremely large organizations tend to be more decentralized than smaller ones, apparently in an effort to speed decisions and to give authority to decide to those nearest the decision issues, and presumably the most knowledgeable about them.[20] This certainly seems advisable, for example, for SBUs and geographically dispersed units. Furthermore, to the extent that environmental instability increases uncertainty, decentralization is recommended.[21] Similar to the movement from a preponderance of stable external environments to a preponderance of unstable ones, the most common scenario for the next 10 years forecasts more complex environments to replace simple ones, even in the most mundane of industries. Hence, decentralization would seem to be preferred over centralization in the future, and organic characteristics will be preferred over mechanistic ones.

For example, in 1991 Paul H. O'Neill, CEO of Aluminum Company of America, split the firm into smaller, more autonomous units. This restructuring was aimed at orienting the firm more toward performance and customers.[22] Such moves indicate an understanding of the more complex and changeable environment ALCOA has faced, resulting in lower earnings in 1989 and 1990.

Right Sizing: The Implications of Cost for Structural Design

While our underlying premise is that strategy dictates structure, much of the preceding discussion has focused on the external environment and its impact on structure. From the strategic perspective, however, if the firm is pursuing any effort to reduce costs, it must deal with certain structural repercussions. For example, if a single-SBU firm is pursuing a relative low-cost strategy, it must cut costs in a number of ways to succeed. One way is to reduce labor costs by cutting positions. Similarly, the multiple-SBU firm frequently mandates cost-reduction strategies in its SBUs for the same reason; such a firm may also reduce costs at the corporate level in order to reduce the overhead burden it distributes to its SBUs. In this way, most organizations have significantly reduced their corporate personnel staffs, pushing decisions on issues such as compensation packages down to subsidiaries.[23] Such actions are also intended to make SBUs more cost competitive.

Put simply, increasing competition, especially global competition, has forced organizations to continually flatten their pyramids, eliminating layers of management and other white-collar employees, as well as decreasing the numbers of blue-collar positions. These are strategic structural decisions aimed at supporting relative low-cost business strategies. Another result of this is wider spans of control in most instances. These changes imply more decentralization and more organic organizations. Combined with the trend toward the team approach, and with the impacts of other factors, these changes will transform the manager's job from boss to facilitator and coach.[24] A major implication of downsizing is poor morale and reduced motivation. Management must attend to these issues to make downsizing effective.[25]

New and/or Special Structural Devices

A number of new and/or special structural devices are being devised to make an organization's structure better support strategy, and to overcome the strategic challenges of the 1990s. We have mentioned several of these devices already, for example, teams and joint ventures. Others include linkages through networking and electronic data interchange, empowerment, and substitutes for hierarchy, primarily computer technology.

Linkages/Networks

To reduce the impacts of domestic and global competition, changing customer needs, and technological change on the firm's competitive position, firms are moving to develop special **linkages** in which they make their customers, and in many cases their suppliers, quasicomponents of their organizations' structures. The resulting **networks** are dramatically changing how firms do business. At their least intense level, such actions involve constant customer and supplier surveillance through active discussion groups. At the next level, cross-corporate teams may develop, for example, for product development or improving supply quality. At the next level, the firms may share data bases through electronic data interchange (EDI) systems. Firms may even pool assets to solve joint problems.[26] Milliken and Company, the $2-billion textile conglomerate, shares data bases and participates in cross-corporate problem-solving teams with Levi Strauss, largely to shut out Pacific Rim competitors who cannot provide such services.[27]

Empowerment

Empowerment can be a strategy for improving productivity, or a structural strategy on its own. **Empowerment** means giving substantial authority to subordinates to make decisions. Philosophically it goes beyond delegation. It implies a different way of managing than has characterized most U.S.-based organizations. It is a very extreme form of decentralization that many predict will become the norm in the coming years.[28]

AT HEWLETT-PACKARD

In an interesting twist on the empowerment concept, HP bestowed tremendous power on directors of research projects and product development units. This was a reaction to the overwhelming bureaucracy of the committees.

Substitutes for Hierarchy

Traditional **substitutes for hierarchy** have included rules and regulations, policies, planning and control systems like higher-level objectives, and more recently self-managed work teams, as discussed previously. The principal new substitute will be the computer. The computer has served in this capacity, but never has it been capable of quite the degree of control it can now achieve. Earlier in Chapter 2 we described the use of the computer at Cypress Semiconductor as an example of just such an all-powerful control mechanism. Cypress's CEO can review the weekly performance of all 1,500 employees in just over 4 hours, using a sophisticated computer program that matches weekly employee performance against weekly employee objectives.[29] Such programs reduce the need for managers in an organization, and this is just the beginning of a trend toward computerized substitutes for hierarchy.[30]

Unique Structural Units
It will be increasingly necessary to develop unique units within the organization to help carry out strategy. For example, Digital Equipment Corporation, the world's second-largest computer maker, has formed a special marketing organization called the Industry Marketing Group. This unit has three subunits, each focused on a particular industry. Each of these units has two principal objectives: (1) to provide an external, industry-oriented customer view-point within DEC, and (2) to communicate to customers that DEC understands their needs.[31]

Another interesting structural possibility is the creation of a sort of shell company that manages the efforts of other companies that perform the traditional economic functions of marketing, operations, finance, and information. This requires only a few people to coordinate these other companies' work.[32] Large Japanese companies already practice this sort of structuring, shoving work down on their suppliers.

Causes of Current Trends in Organization Structure

Five factors have brought about major changes in firms' approaches to structure, and all are visible in the current trends in organizational restructuring.[33] First, as more firms have followed cost competition strategies, they have begun to cut staff and middle-management positions. The lean-and-mean look became a popular objective as firms trimmed employees to save money.

Second, management philosophy regarding structure began to change. Spurred on by such books as *In Search of Excellence*, many top managers began to believe that running lean was better structurally regardless of the condition of the economy. Financial success, in fact, began to be seen as a consequence of that approach, making layers of staff and middle management decreasingly desirable. (The available evidence suggests that this approach is, indeed, financially beneficial.)[34] Not all restructurings work, however.[35]

Disenchantment with the current process and results of strategic planning, especially with the role of professional strategists, is a third cause of firms' changing perspective on structure. Influenced by the proponents of intrapreneurship, the top managers of many firms began to practice decentralization, making line management more responsible for strategic decision making and implementation.

The personal computer and related software have also changed the view of structure, enabling almost anyone with access to information to engage in strategic planning. This innovation further reduces the need for middle-management and professional advisory personnel. Note that the options include not only increased decentralization, but also increased centralization because it gives better control of the availability of information. The computer will even process information, a function that middle management and staff used to perform.

Finally, a fifth cause of changing attitudes toward structure developed from the continued concern of employees for the quality of work life, spurring an increase in workers' participation in decision making. Most of this restructuring seems to be taking place in manufacturing. We see less activity in service industries to improve productivity, although improvements are coming in health care, information handling, and food services, among other fields.

One of the major changes in attitudes about structure is a symbolic change designed primarily to indicate a cultural change in the organization and in its relationships with its constituents, mainly customers. An increasing number of organization charts are showing the customer at the top of the chart. The first well-known application of this perspective was at Scandinavian Airline Systems when Jan Carlzon began his well-documented, successful efforts to turn the company around. The implication for all employees at SAS and at other firms that use this technique, is that the customer is the boss and that succeeding levels of employees and managers are employed to help those above best serve the customer. Other firms such as AM International and Nordstrom, the Seattle-based up-scale clothier, have adapted similar charts. Nordstrom's chart is shown in Figure 8.7. Such charts reflect a change in corporate focus.

Developing a Structure

The determinants of structure have been examined extensively in both the normative and empirical literature. It is evident that no single factor determines structure. Rather, multiple, often interdependent factors influence the structures adopted by organizations. The primary determinants appear to vary from situation to situation. Available information points to the following seven factors as the most important **determinants of structure** in most situations.[36] As these factors and related research should be familiar, we shall review them here only briefly.

1. Size (Growth)   The size of an organization is a major determinant of its structure. As mentioned, organizations normally adopt simple, functional, product, and SBU structures in sequence as they grow. For example, as Apple Computers grew in the early 1980s, it went from a simple to a functional to a product structure, and then back to a functional organization as it tried to come to grips with product versus functional issues.[37] Later, it moved to a global geographic structure in recognition of the changing global competitive environment.[38]

Size is becoming a more important determinant of strategic success than ever before. Many consultants and CEOs now believe that organization units should be made up of 500-person (or smaller) divisions, each with its own strategic identity.[39]

FIGURE 8.7   Nordstrom's Organization Chart

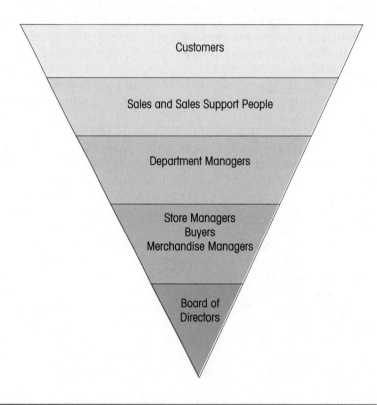

Source: ''Organization Chart of the Month,'' *Inc*, April 1991, p. 14. Reprinted by permission of *Inc*. Magazine. Copyright 1991 by Goldhirsh Group Inc., 38 Commercial Wharf, Boston, Mass. 02110.

Performance is easier to measure for such units, groups, and individuals than in larger organizations. Also, employees have an intrapreneurial stake in the firm and share a sense of ownership, and overhead remains low. Hewlett-Packard has always followed this approach, although its basic units are somewhat larger. Cypress Semiconductors, the most successful firm in that business as measured by consistency of profits and profit margins, relies on units of 200 people or fewer.[40]

Limited research does show that smaller organizational units are more efficient than larger ones.[41] On the other hand, large size is necessary in certain industries to amass the resources necessary to continue new product development. Boeing, for example, probably could not compete in the aircraft manufacturing industry, where several billion dollars may be necessary to launch a new product, if it weren't huge.[42] The trick is managing the large organization effectively and efficiently.

2. Technology   The types and complexity of the technology employed to accomplish an organization's tasks have been shown to be significantly related to its structure, especially in operations. It's obvious that jobs will be redefined when

manufacturing operations become highly automated. At the same time, this flattens the hierarchy, sometimes to an extreme.

Technological complexity is an issue not only at lower levels of the organization, but at its upper reaches, as well. The complex tasks facing top management often require structural solutions. Computers are having a substantial impact on structure everywhere, permitting increases in either centralization or decentralization, depending on management's philosophy. Executive information systems (EISs) and other decision support systems such as Comshare's Commander™ EIS provide executives with the ability to coordinate and control more functions than they could previously. For example, executives at The New England, a mutual life insurance company, use such a system for performance comparisons of general agents throughout the United States, and for other analyses.[43] Managers at the Bank of New England in Boston and Home Federal Savings & Loan in San Diego use Commander™ extensively to monitor bank operations and make critical decisions.[44]

3. Environment
Several environmental factors seem to influence structure, but the amount of change appears to be the most important of these, although competitors' structures are often emulated. Decentralized organizations respond more quickly than centralized firms to environmental flux, so a decentralized structure is preferable in a changing environment. A centralized structure fares well in a stable environment. Strategic information systems are allowing centralized firms greater flexibility in changing environments. As the environments of most firms become increasingly changeable, we will continue to see restructuring to flatten hierarchies.[45]

This environment–structure interface becomes extremely difficult to manage for the multinational firm that has subsidiaries in several different external environments.[46] As competitors flatten hierarchies, eliminate staff, and use special structural devices such as cross-functional teams to become responsive and/or cut costs, other firms follow their lead.

4. Top-Management Philosophy
Top management may intentionally choose to structure the organization in a certain manner for reasons related to technology, size, environment, or other factors. In an effort to develop their managers' decision-making abilities, for example, some firms want large spans of control. Many others, seeking to cut costs, are eliminating middle-management positions. One such firm, Kodak, is highlighted in this chapter's Strategic Challenge feature.

5. Geographic Considerations
As organizations expand geographically, either within one country or into two or more countries, some tasks obviously must be reallocated. Decentralization of decision making does not necessarily follow geographic decentralization, though it may. Geographic decentralization does, however, require new divisions of labor. Martin Marietta, for example, has four SBU divisions, one of them an international division. The research evidence suggests that multinational firms do not have the same structure in subsidiaries in different countries, instead adapting structures to environmental circumstances.[47]

STRATEGIC CHALLENGE

EASTMAN KODAK STRUGGLES TO RETAIN ITS STRATEGIC ADVANTAGES

Eastman Kodak had long dominated its markets, but Japanese competition made serious inroads in the late 1970s and early 1980s. In 1982 Kodak's chairman, Walter A. Fallon, observed, "It's time to make this elephant dance." The elephant was Kodak, but a program to revitalize the company did not begin in earnest until 1984 as Kodak began to use small, intrapreneurial business units under new CEO Colby H. Chandler.

The use of these intrapreneurial units was an important move. Kodak recognized that its marketplace was highly competitive. Historically, the chairman of the company had been responsible for even very minor decisions, but no longer. With the exception of decisions on major capital investments, intrapreneurial division managers determine their own courses of action. Thus the company's divisions were able to respond more quickly to changes in their external environments. As is often the case, the external environment precipitated this change in the top management's views on the best way to organize the company. It further sought to promote creativity in the company by instituting an innovation division.

This effort was not enough. Kodak cut a total of 25,000 people from a work force of about 146,000 in 1986 and 1987. One of Chandler's major additional challenges was to change the organizational culture at Kodak to make it more competitive, more market driven. Chandler began by changing compensation to link with performance, and by setting examples of how to delegate decisions. Another restructuring came in 1989, as 1,500 additional employees were let go. This restructuring continued the types of changes made earlier. Meanwhile, in 1988, Kodak acquired Sterling Drug with about 20,000 employees. A few hundred positions were eliminated at that time. In early 1992, Kodak's employment stood at 135,000. Only minor restructurings were necessary from 1989 to early 1992, except for the firm's money-losing office equipment unit, which was restructured and given a new management team in late 1991. Earlier efforts have helped revitalize the once-lumbering giant. New products, markets, and processes have all been developed.

Source: Authors' discussion with public relations department, January 1992; Joan E. Rigdon, "Kodak Plans to Restructure Corporate-Wide," *The Wall Street Journal*, November 11, 1991, p. A4; Jim Rosenberg, "No Ax at Atex," *Editor & Publisher*, August 31, 1991, p. 26; Peter Pae, "Kodak to Again Restructure Operations," *The Wall Street Journal*, August 18, 1989, p. B2; Clare Ansberry, "Uphill Battle: Eastman-Kodak Company Has Begun Struggle to Regain Lost Edge," *The Wall Street Journal*, April 2, 1987, pp. 1, 20; Leslie Helm, "Why Kodak Is Starting to Cook Again," *Business Week*, February 23, 1987, pp. 134–138.

6. Informal Organization   The people who fill positions in an organization may demand a particular type of formal structure. Professionals, like engineers, accountants, or scientists may not tolerate mechanistic, formalized, authoritarian work situations.

7. Strategy   A. D. Chandler was the first writer to explore the relationship between strategy and structure.[48] His examination of the histories of General Motors, Du Pont, Standard Oil of New Jersey, and Sears, Roebuck showed him clearly that their decentralized, multidivisional structures resulted largely from trial-and-error attempts to adapt to environmental conditions. He saw outside market opportunity as the variable that most affects structure, because **structure follows strategy.**

While he shared the view that size contributes to variations in structure, he observed that the complexity of the tasks required of top management also accounts for a significant amount of variation in organization structure. It seems reasonable to suppose that what an organization wishes to become and the means it chooses to realize that vision and to manage its interactions with the environment must to a great extent decide most of the other structural determinants, as well—technology, size, environment, and geographic dispersion. Structure, by definition and in practice, follows strategy.

It has been observed that **strategy follows structure,** as well. Indeed, some structures prohibit some strategies. Centralized bureaucracies, for example, find it difficult to be responsive to their customers.[49] Vijay Gooindarajan has shown conceptually that the strategies identified by Porter and by Miles and Snow, discussed in Chapter 5, must be varied to adapt to the structure of the firm.[50] Many firms experience difficulty carrying out a new strategy unless they first change their structures. This chapter's second Strategic Challenge feature reviews the efforts of Harley-Davidson to turn around its company fortunes. Much of its turn around was based on changing its structure and its culture.

The seven determinants of structure are not mutually exclusive. In fact, their interdependence has made scientific analysis difficult, though not impossible. Clearly, strategy and top management's philosophy are the primary determinants. Once these commitments are made, however, the other factors influence the eventual structural pattern. Only in recent years, as multivariate techniques have been developed, has the relative importance of these factors been clearly understood. It has become apparent that the importance to be assigned to each factor depends on the situation.

To structure an organization to meet the demands of the situation is not an easy task. There are few authoritative guidelines, and research is only now beginning to identify the factors that distinguish effective from ineffective organizations. It has often been assumed that a given environment or technology called for a certain structure. So far, however, empirical evidence does not support this assumption. Rather, many factors contribute to the selection of a strategy and hence to the organization's structure, and the eventual compatibility of the two is by no means assured.

Strategy and Structure, Size and Growth

Given the findings of research and the nature of the strategy formulation process, the organization's primary concern with structure becomes the task of matching strategy to structure and structure to size and environment. Philosophy must also be considered. Size is invariably a direct result of growth. The importance of growth as a factor in the determination of structure is obvious, since most

 STRATEGIC
CHALLENGE

HARLEY-DAVIDSON CHANGES STRUCTURE TO SURVIVE

In 1983, President Vaughn Beals of Harley-Davidson could envision a scenario in which his company would not exist in just a few years. Harley-Davidson had downsized significantly since its heyday of the 1960s, a downsizing forced by the influx of inexpensive, high-quality Japanese motorcycles that had devoured its market in the 1970s. Manufacturing for the U.S. motorcycle market—a market Harley-Davidson once held virtually unto itself—had moved across the Pacific. Between 1960 and 1987 Harley's market share dropped to a low of five percent.

To meet the Japanese challenge, Harley decided that the best strategy would be to create a niche in the big bike category. But even that effort began to fail as the firm sold only 26,000 bikes in 1985 compared to 50,000 in 1979, the result of Japanese manufacturers "dumping" their bikes in the United States in order to gain market share. Finally, in 1983, the United States passed a law prohibiting the importation of large motorcycles for five years.

Beals recognized that his firm had to change in order to survive. Their inefficient plants, outmoded technology, unmotivated work force, and low product quality all had to be changed if the company were to survive. Beals decided that to save Harley-Davidson, he had to imitate his Japanese competitors. Accordingly, he took his whole top management team to Japan to visit motorcycle factories and learn how to compete. One of the major factors of success they learned from the Japanese was the importance of employee participation. As a consequence, Harley redesigned its entire organization structure to focus on small work groups; vertical hierarchy was abolished. The small work group gave employees a sense of identity, and because they were allowed to make decisions, they provided the company with their expertise.

Employees participated in making changes in the manufacturing process as well. New technology was acquired, the factory was modernized, and the organization's culture changed to emphasize quality, the customer, and employee empowerment. In return for employee contributions, the company provided guarantees of employee security. The results were nothing short of spectacular. By 1989, the company had captured 50 percent of the super heavyweight market.

Source: "How Harley Beat Back the Japanese," *Fortune*, September 25, 1989, pp. 155–164; Rod Willis, "Harley-Davidson Comes Roaring Back," *Management Review*, March 1986, pp. 20–27.

organizations, especially businesses, tend to grow and to follow growth strategies. Growth has, of course, been researched at length, and several theories of resultant structural relationships have emerged. When we examine these theories and the related research, we find several common problem areas in the relationships among growth, size, and structure.[51]

In its most rudimentary form, a firm begins as an individual entrepreneur with an idea. After starting a business, the entrepreneur soon realizes that one person cannot perform all of the tasks involved in production or service creation. Hence the first structural problem arises. To solve it, the entrepreneur must institute a division of labor and hire people to perform some of the business's functions. Often he or she must seek professional managerial assistance.

Soon, however, a second structural problem arises. The entrepreneurial leader often does not delegate any authority to the functional personnel. They are not allowed to manage; they have no autonomy. At this juncture, either the leader or the recently hired professional management must delegate some authority. As the firm continues to expand, the amount of authority delegated usually increases.

Continued growth makes geographic expansion desirable, creating the third structural problem. If the expansion occurs entirely within one country, geographic decentralization (division of labor) follows, with the possibility of increased decentralization of decision making close behind. If the firm expands into other countries, then its actions follow a somewhat different pattern.

The fourth structural problem (or third, if the firm has not expanded geographically) then arises: the organization may decide to offer additional product lines or services, but the tasks involved may become too numerous and complex for one leader to manage effectively. As a result, a decision-decentralized product, project, or SBU division structure normally emerges, though sophisticated information systems may allow for centralization.

Thus arises a fifth problem associated with all acts of decentralization: control. When authority is delegated, results must be ensured. An effort to ensure results through formalization may cause the organization to become mechanistic and maladaptive. Eventually the organization must develop a means of control by specific objectives, ceding the division or functional manager's authority to proceed within policy guidelines toward those objectives. Some other approach, such as team management or a matrix organization, may be added to the structure, depending on such factors as environmental complexity. Various forms of departmentalization also become necessary as the organization grows.

STRATEGIC MANAGER'S SUMMARY

1. Implementation is the means by which strategy becomes action. Structure, along with systems, management style, and shared values are the main ingredients of the implementation process.
2. The major components of organization structure include jobs, authority, span of control, departmentalization, number of levels in the hierarchy, amount of authority delegated, and coordination.
3. Organizations have a choice among four basic structures: the pyramid, matrix, team, and alliance/joint venture. Their shapes are a triangle, a square, a circle, and an altered triangle. They assume those shapes because of the way they distribute authority.
4. The five major types of pyramidal organizations are simple, functional, product, SBU/M-form, and geographic.

5. Organization structure has seven major determinants, whose importance varies with the situation: size, technology, environment, top management philosophy, geographic considerations, informal organizations, and strategy.
6. The organization's structure must change as it grows to meet the challenges of the various situations.
7. The organic structure is best suited to changeable, complex environments; the mechanistic structure suits stable, simple environments. Organic structures will dominate the future.
8. Current trends include downsizing/rightsizing, movement to organic structures, linkages, empowerment, substitutes for hierarchy, and unique structural units.

KEY TERMS

basic organization structures
centralization
components of organization structure
cross-functional team
customer/supplier team
decentralization
determinants of structure
economic functional structure
empowerment
geographic structure
implementation
joint venture
linkages

matrix structure
mechanistic organization
networks
organic organization
product structure
project team
simple structure
SBU or M-form structure
strategic alliance
strategy follows structure
structure follows strategy
substitutes for hierarchy
task team
team management

DISCUSSION QUESTIONS

1. Describe a situation in which each of the seven determinants of organization structure plays the major role in determining structure.
2. What did Chandler mean when he said that structure follows strategy? Why does strategy sometimes follow structure?
3. How are size (growth) and structure related?
4. By the end of 1991, had Hewlett-Packard resolved satisfactorily the problems of reorganization noted in the opening vignette?

STRATEGIC AUDIT QUESTIONS

1. What problems are evident in the structure of the organization? How would you solve those problems?
2. Does the organization's structure follow strategy, or vice versa? What are the implications of your answer?
3. Is this organization too centralized or too decentralized? What actions are required?
4. Could this organization use more team management? Quality circles?
5. Does it need to change basic macrostructures?
6. How do each of the following affect the overall structure of the company?
   a. Size/growth
   b. Technology
   c. Environment
   d. Top-management philosophy
   e. Geographic considerations
   f. Informal organization
   g. Strategy
7. How could the organization's strategy be improved in regard to each of the seven factors listed in question 6?
8. What restructurings are occurring? Why? What needs to be restructured?
9. Should the structure be more organic?
10. Are EISs being used? Properly? Effects on structure?
11. Is the firm making use of the latest structuring techniques and processes?

Endnotes

1. Carol J. Loomis, "Can John Akers Save IBM?" *Fortune*, July 15, 1991, pp. 40–56; John A. Byrne, Deidre A. Depke, and John W. Verity, "IBM: As Markets and Technology Change, Can Big Blue Remake Its Culture?" *Business Week*, June 17, 1991, pp. 25–32; Joel Dreyfuss, "Reinventing IBM," *Fortune*, August 14, 1989, pp. 30–39.
2. Paul B. Carroll, "IBM Plans $3 Billion Charge and about 20,000 Job Cuts," *The Wall Street Journal*, November 27, 1991, p. A3.
3. Jonathan Kapstein, "A Chilling New Era for Philips—and Europe," *Business Week*, November 12, 1990, pp. 58, 59.
4. Alex Taylor III, "Why Toyota Keeps Getting Better and Better and Better," *Fortune*, November 19, 1990, pp. 66–79; Kathryn Groven and Bradley A. Stertz, "Gaining Speed: Toyota Is Gearing Up to Expand Output Extending Global Reach," *The Wall Street Journal*, July 20, 1990, pp. A1, A8.
5. For a discussion see Lawrence G. Hrebiniak, "Implementing Strategy," *Chief Executive*, April 1990, pp. 74–77.
6. For a related discussion, see Jay R. Galbraith and Robert K. Kazanjian, *Strategy Implementation: Structure, Systems, and Process* (St. Paul, Minn.: West, 1986), p. 2. While these authors do not use the same terms as we do, they discuss the same basic issues. See also Richard Daft, *Management* (Hinsdale, Ill.: Dryden Press, 1988), Chapter 4. Daft adds technology as a key factor in implementation. Also see Hrebiniak, "Implementing Strategy."
7. Jewell G. Westerman and William A. Sherden, "Moving beyond Lean and Mean," *Journal of Business Strategy*, September/October 1991, pp. 12–16.

8. For example of the latter, see George D. Rodgers, "Strategic Planning and Sales Teams," *Journal of Business & Industrial Marketing*, Fall 1990, pp. 65–70.

9. Floyd R. Leslie, "Where Customer Satisfaction Begins," *Quality*, October 1991, pp. 46–47.

10. Gary S. Vasilash, "Teams Are Working Harder at Chrysler," *Production*, October 1991, pp. 51, 52.

11. Anna Versteeg, "Self-Directed Work Teams Yield Long-Term Benefits," *Journal of Business Strategy*, November/December 1990, pp. 9–12.

12. Brian Dumaine, "The Bureaucracy Busters," *Fortune*, June 17, 1991, pp. 45, 46.

13. Bill Saporito, "Are IBM and Sears Crazy or Canny?" *Fortune*, September 28, 1987, pp. 74–80.

14. Joel Bleeke and David Ernst, "The Way to Win in Cross-Border Alliances," *Harvard Business Review*, November–December 1991, p. 127.

15. Ian C. MacMillan and Patricia E. Jones, "Designing Organizations to Compete," *Journal of Business Strategy*, Spring 1984, p. 11.

16. Adapted from MacMillan and Jones, "Designing Organizations." The last four structures in this list are our additions.

17. As described by Richard M. Steers, *Organizational Effectiveness: A Behavioral View* (Santa Monica, Calif.: Goodyear, 1977), p. 90. Adapted from Tom Burns and George M. Stalker, *The Management of Innovation* (London: Tavistock, 1961), pp. 119–122.

18. Various research studies have examined this structure/environment relationship over the years. The first major effort was Burns and Stalker, *Management of Innovation*. Virtually all such studies since have verified their findings as described here. A recent study confirming their findings in small firms is Jeffrey G. Govin and Dennis P. Slevin, "Strategic Management of Small Firms in Hostile and Benign Environments," *Strategic Management Journal*, January/February 1989, pp. 75–87. One study suggests that the relationships between environment and structure are related to the chosen strategy; see Danny Miller, "The Structural and Environmental Correlates of Business Strategy," *Strategic Management Journal*, January/February 1987, pp. 55–76.

19. For example, see Henry Mintzberg, *Structure in Fives: Designing Effective Organizations* (Englewood Cliffs, N.J.: Prentice-Hall, 1983), pp. 142–146; and Robert Duncan, "What Is the Right Organization Structure? Decision Tree Analysis Provides the Answer," *Organizational Dynamics*, Winter 1979, pp. 60–65.

20. Jerald Hage and Michael Aiken, "Relationship of Centralization to Other Structural Properties," *Administrative Science Quarterly*, no. 12, 1967, pp. 72–91.

21. Duncan, "Right Structure."

22. Dana Milbank, "Alcoa Chairman Plans to Begin Reorganization," *The Wall Street Journal*, August 9, 1991, pp. A3.

23. Huey Burkett, "The Impact of Decentralization on the Design and Management of Benefit and Compensation Programs," *Benefits & Compensation International*, September 1988, pp. 3–6.

24. For a discussion of these and other structural changes see James M. Higgins, "2001: A Management Odyssey," unpublished working paper.

25. Harold P. Weinstein and Michael S. Leibman, "Corporate Scale Down—What Comes Next?" *Human Resources Magazine*, August 1991, pp. 33–37.

26. Rosabeth Moss Kanter, "Becoming PALS: Pooling, Allying, and Linking across Companies," *Harvard Business Review*, July/August 1989, pp. 183–193, contains a discussion of several of these actions, as well as joint ventures. Also see Thomas J. Peters, "Restoring American Competitiveness: Looking for New Models of Organizations," *Executive*, May 1988, pp. 103–109.

27. "An Electronic Pipeline Is Changing the Way America Does Business," *Business Week*, August 3, 1987, p. 8.

28. Clay Carr, "Managing Self-Managed Workers," *Training & Development*, September 1991, pp. 36–42; Wayne C. Shannon, "Empowerment: The Catchword of the '90s," *Quality Progress*, July 1991, pp. 62–63; Howard E. Hyden, "Winning Organizations," *Executive Excellence*, July 1991, p. 20.

29. Dumaine, "Bureaucracy Busters."

30. Edward E. Lawler, "Substitutes for Hierarchy," *Incentive*, March 1989, pp. 39–45.

31. Dan T. Dunn and Claude A. Thomas, "High Tech Organizes for the Future," *Journal of Personal Selling & Sales Management*, Spring 1990, pp. 43–55.

32. Discussed by Thomas J. Peters during a presentation to the Strategic Management Society, Toronto, October 24, 1991.

33. Peter G. W. Keen, "Redesigning the Organization through Information Technology," *Planning Review*, May/June 1991, pp. 4–9; David O. Heenan, "The Right Way to Downsize," *Journal of Business Strategy*, September/October 1991, pp. 4–7; Gary L. Neilson, "Restructure for Excellence: The Secret in Downsizing," *Management Review*, February 1990, pp. 44–47; "Shifting Strategies: Surge in Restructuring Is Profoundly Altering Much of U.S. Industry," *The Wall Street Journal*, August 12, 1985, pp. 1, 12–13.

34. Myron Magnet, "Restructuring Really Works," *Fortune*, March 2, 1987, pp. 37–46.

35. Norman F. Whitely, Jr., "Where Restructurings Fail," *Across the Board*, September 1991, pp. 13–14.

36. Galbraith and Kazanjian, *Strategy Implementation*, reviews the current research on structures.

37. "Apple Computer's Counterattack against IBM," *Business Week*, January 16, 1984, pp. 78–81.

38. Maria Shao and Geoff Lewis, "Apple Turns from Revolution to Evolution," *Business Week*, January 28, 1989, p. 90.

39. For example, see Thomas J. Peters, "Doubting Thomas," *Inc*, April 1989, p. 92; and Steve Kaufman, "Going for the Goals," *Success*, January/February 1988, pp.

38–41; "Is Your Company Too Big?" *Business Week*, March 27, 1989, pp. 84–94.

40. Kaufman, "Going for Goals."

41. Phoebe M. Carillo and Richard E. Kopelman, "Organization Structure and Productivity," *Group & Organizational Studies*, March 1991, pp. 44–59.

42. Walter Guzzardi, "Big Can Still Be Beautiful," *Fortune*, April 25, 1988, pp. 50–64.

43. Jagannath Dubashi, "Systems Users: Drawing in Data," *Financial World*, March 19, 1991, pp. 54–55.

44. "Systems Review: Commander EIS—Providing Strategic Information to Bank Executives," *Banking Software Review*, Spring 1990, pp. 8, 11.

45. For a philosophical discussion, see Thomas J. Peters, *Thriving on Chaos: Handbook for a Management Revolution* (New York: Alfred A. Knopf, 1987), pp. 3–35, 355–367; Peter F. Drucker, "The Coming Age of the New Organization," *Harvard Business Review*, January–February 1988, pp. 45–53; for a review of the research, see Richard L. Daft, *Organization Theory and Design*, 2d ed. (St. Paul, Minn.: West, 1986), 47–90.

46. For a discussion of this issue in multinational management, see Philip M. Rosenzweig and Jitendra V. Singh, "Organizational Environments and the Multinational Enterprise," *Academy of Management Review*, April 1991, pp. 340–361.

47. Sumantra Ghoshal, "Internal Differentiation within Multinational Corporations," *Strategic Management Journal*, July/August 1989, pp. 323–337.

48. Alfred D. Chandler, *Strategy and Structure* (Cambridge, Mass.: MIT Press, 1962). D. J. Hall and M. A. Saias, "Strategy Follows Structure," *Strategic Management Journal*, April/June 1980, pp. 149–165.

49. Hall and Saias, "Strategy Follows Structure."

50. Vijay Gooindarajan, "Decentralization, Strategy, and Effectiveness of Strategic Business Units in Multibusiness Organizations," *Academy of Management Review*, Winter 1986, pp. 844–856.

51. Robert R. Blake, W. E. Avis, and Jane S. Mouton, *Corporate Darwinism* (Houston: Gulf, 1966); N. C. Churchill and V. L. Lewis, "The Five Stages of Small Business Growth," *Harvard Business Review*, May–June 1983, pp. 30–50; Larry E. Greiner, "Evolution and Revolution as Organizations Grow," *Harvard Business Review*, July–August 1972, pp. 37–46; John R. Montanari, "Operationalizing Strategic Choice," paper presented to the Academy of Management, Kissimmee, Florida, August 1977; R. P. Rumelt, *Strategy, Structure, and Economic Performance of the Fortune "500"* (Cambridge, Mass.: Division of Research, Harvard Graduate School of Business, 1974); M. Salter, "Stages of Corporate Development," *Journal of Business Policy*, Autumn 1970; B. R. Scott, "The Industrial State: Old Myths and New Realities," *Harvard Business Review*, March–April 1973, pp. 133–149, and *Stages in Corporate Development: Part II* (Cambridge, Mass.: Harvard Graduate School of Business, 1971); D. H. Thain, "Stages in Corporate Development," *Business Quarterly*, Winter 1969, pp. 32–45.

INTEGRATIVE CASE ANALYSIS CHAPTER 8

THE CHALLENGES FACING GENERAL MOTORS IN 1992

From the 1920s to the 1960s, General Motors' decentralized automobile divisions were models of independent management. They were close to the market; they made decisions. The division system was so effective that at one time General Motors could claim over 60 percent of the American automobile market. During the 1970s, however, the system became overburdened by complex manufacturing and engineering systems designed to keep the firm from being broken apart by antitrust actions. When the five automobile divisions were restructured into two large divisions in 1984, the organization moved further away from the customer.

Apparently Chairman Roger Smith was convinced that technology was going to drive the automobile business in the future and he wanted technology to drive the structure of the company. Technology drove not only its structure, but its product development, as well. In a move to cut costs, common parts were developed, and they caused the cars to look so much alike that customers shunned them. Several changes in engineering and market research served to distance the car companies even further from the marketplace. Recent attempts to restructure the organization, significant downsizing by Smith and later by Stempel, have proved helpful, but numerous problems still exist. Manufacturing still overlaps boundaries among several car companies, making dedicated manufacturing, a must to compete, *still* impossible. John Smith is expected to alter that situation dramatically.

When we examine the seven determinants of structure, we can make the following observations:

1. *Size.* General Motors has a strategic business unit (M-form) structure. The automobile strategic business unit is a complex structure involving two relatively decentralized groups (or perhaps two and one-half, with Cadillac somewhat split off). An overlay of engineering, market research, and manufacturing has blurred the effects of decentralization. A bureaucratic mess results, except at Cadillac. Saturn is treated as a separate company.
2. *Technology.* Technology clearly determines the structure of each of GM's automobile plants and certain of the facilities of EDS, Hughes, and other subsidiaries, with the exception of NUMMI, Cadillac, and Saturn. Their jobs are designed in groups, and feature significant delegation of authority. (The structuring of jobs is also technology of a sort.)
3. *Environment.* With its recent restructurings, GM appears to have made a more concerted effort to structure itself in relation to its external environment, but it has a long way to go. It must cut several more layers to be as market responsive as Japanese firms.
4. *Top-management philosophy.* The NUMMI structure is one reflection of top management preference or philosophy; so, unfortunately, are the structures of its other divisions, devised with an eye to technology and other factors that had preoccupied GM's executives. Stempel and John Smith are trying to change that. General Motors' decision in December 1991 to downsize and eliminate thousands of white-collar and blue-collar jobs is consistent with the current trends in organization structure we have noted. Here, too, we see management philosophy in action, as well as the influence of competitor's structures. As antitrust laws no longer threaten the firm, it must shed outdated structures.
5. *Geographic considerations.* General Motors has numerous subdivisions throughout the United States and is active in Europe, South America, and Asia. Its structure reflects these geographic subdivisions.

6. *Informal organization.*   As in all other organizations, coalitions, personal relationships, and personal values are affecting developments at General Motors. Low morale is hurting productivity. More downsizing will drive morale even lower.

7. *Strategy.*   Structure is supposed to follow strategy. The trouble at GM was that the structures already in place had to be altered to prepare for the new strategies, and General Motors simply has not been able to do the job properly as yet. The restructuring it devised to prevent a possible government breakup of the company, together with splitting off design from the auto divisions, left it unprepared for the challenges of the 1980s and 1990s. It was too bureaucratic and unresponsive to the external environment to be successful. It faces an uphill battle to regain market share—a major objective of Stempel. One of the major ways GM has moved to improve its product development time is by restructuring.

Most of our comments have been directed toward macroorganizational structures, but microstructures, too, are greatly affected by such factors as technology, the environment, and management preference or philosophy. Certainly strategy, insofar as it concerns job redesign and the technological imperative of this company, has changed the structures of thousands of jobs. The Cadillac division has been especially effective in these efforts. As management moves forward with job redesign, quality circles, team management, and other efforts to improve productivity, individual jobholders will increasingly feel their effects.

CHAPTER 9

IMPLEMENTATION THROUGH MANAGEMENT OF SYSTEMS, STYLE, AND SHARED VALUES (CULTURE)

The proof is in the execution.

Robert H. Waterman, Jr.
Author and Consultant

Real live businessmen have learned that the big challenge isn't concocting strategy but making it work.

Walter Kiechel III
Senior Writer, *Fortune*

CHAPTER OBJECTIVES

By the time you complete this chapter, you should be able to:

1. Define and describe the key implementation systems
2. Discuss the impact of the management of human resources on implementation
3. Indicate the roles of transformational and work group leadership in strategy implementation
4. Discuss shared values (culture) and how they affect implementation of strategy
5. Indicate how organizational learning can be a competitive advantage
6. Describe the impact of cultural diversity on implementation and discuss ways in which cultural diversity can be managed to the firm's advantage
7. Describe how you would use the McKinsey seven Ss framework
8. Describe why a strategist who succeeds in one situation may be unsuccessful in a situation of a different sort

GENERAL ELECTRIC: MANAGING CULTURE FOR STRATEGIC SUCCESS

After taking over as CEO in 1981, Jack Welch completely transformed General Electric. By 1989 he had squeezed 350 product lines and business units into 13 major businesses, each first or second in its industry. He had sold $9 billion in assets, mostly companies that didn't fit his aggressive criteria for retention in the GE portfolio, and spent $18 billion acquiring firms that did fit. He collapsed GE's management structure and reduced 29 pay levels to five broad bands. He eliminated 100,000 positions, many through selling firms, but many also from reducing staff. Welch practices resource-based strategy. He has accumulated sufficient resources that he can pounce on any opportunity that is available to the firm.

The results have been impressive. GE's 298,000 employees were paid $13 billion in 1990, more than the personal incomes of all of the residents of Alaska, Montana, North Dakota, South Dakota, or Wyoming. GE grossed $58.4 billion, an amount greater than the GNPs of most countries. Its sales growth of $3.8 billion exceeded the total sales of all but 126 of the Fortune 500. The firm makes everything from 65-cent light bulbs to 400,000-pound locomotives to billion-dollar power plants. It owns more commercial aircraft than American Airlines, manages more credit cards than American Express, and one out of every five couch potatoes tunes in to its TV network, NBC. GE's stock has a total market value of $65 billion, up from $12 billion in 1981 and second among U.S. corporations only to Exxon in 1991.

Having succeeded in assembling the firms that he wanted, Welch began to recognize by 1988 that the future was going to call for a different kind of management and a different corporate culture than he saw at GE. He recognized that the firm's entire culture had to focus on speed, flexibility, and the ability to cope with change. At the center of this change would be a new type of manager. Welch believed that the manager's roles was changing from a focus on planning, organizing, implementing, and measuring to a focus on new activities such as counseling groups, providing resources for them, and helping employees think for themselves.

To accomplish these ends, GE has pioneered a number of new techniques. For example, it has created process champions, employees at any level of the organization whose function is to get ideas moving and to get the best ideas to the top so action can be taken. The real core of the cultural change effort involves three management techniques: work-outs, best practices, and process mapping. All foster employee involvement, and all are aimed at increasing productivity by raising levels of innovation, the essential ingredient for remaining competitive in the 1990s, according to Welch.

Work-outs are forums for employees to tackle problems. A work-unit manager kicks off the 3-day session by defining objectives and stating problems for the 40 to 100 employees that attend the session to solve. He or she then departs and returns 2 days later. Employees make recommendations, to which managers can react in only three ways—approve them, say no, or support a team to do a further examination of the problem by a specific date. Most managers end up giving the go ahead to most recommendations. The sessions are grueling, but have helped raised productivity, improve morale, and increase the flow of ideas.

In its **best practices** project, GE studies a number of extremely productive firms to learn what they do well, then it emulates their best efforts. As opposed to past functional-area studies comparing similar operations at other firms, the research also focuses on overall management. GE has learned one very important lesson. It was measuring the wrong things. Business development manager George Zippel observes, ''We should have focused more on how things got done than on what got done.'' The primary offshoot of the research is a change in managing processes throughout the company. This too has resulted in major productivity gains. Best practices is a form of benchmarking oneself against the best at some skill.

Finally, GE implemented **process mapping** throughout the company. This technique requires a detailed flowchart showing every step in any manufacturing or service process. Employees then figure out ways of eliminating steps, shortening steps, and so on. Process management has added tremendously to productivity. For example, jet engines are now manufactured twice as quickly as they once were.

What Welch has done and is doing is to apply an overall management approach and redesign of organizational culture to a conglomerate multiple-SBU firm. This is unusual; subsidiaries tend to stand alone. Where such approaches have been utilized, they usually have worked only to add overhead without much effect on profits. The approach and the results are different, however, at GE. Culture management has paid off.

Source: Thomas A. Stewart, "GE Keeps Those Ideas Coming," *Fortune*, August 12, 1991, pp. 41–49.

Jack Welch is typical of the leader needed to make companies succeed in the 1990s and into the 21st century. He transformed his organization from what it was into what it needed to be. He changed GE's strategy, and orchestrated the successful implementation of that strategy. He made things happen. Now he faces new strategic challenges virtually covering the range of all ten identified in Chapter 1. As a result, new strategies have emerged to reach GE's strategic intent. New implementation efforts then became necessary, but Welch has gone beyond the typical implementation process. He is revolutionizing organizational implementation processes. What GE is doing will set the example for many, if not most, North American firms.

Implementation is the process of translating strategic plans into results. It is the summation of activities in which people marshall and use various resources to accomplish the objectives of a strategy. Figure 9.1 identifies the implementation component of the strategic management process model. In conjunction with the

FIGURE 9.1 The Organization—A Strategic Management Process Model

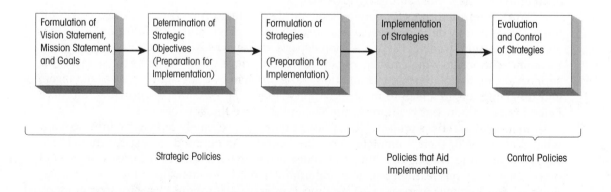

FIGURE 9.2 Implementation

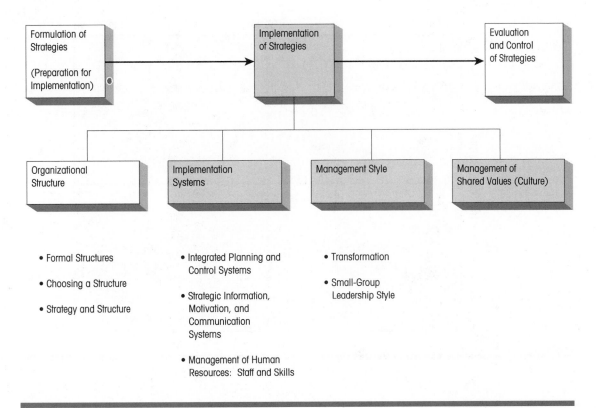

management of structure (discussed in Chapter 8), three other key elements are necessary to implement strategy successfully. As Figure 9.2 indicates, management systems must be adequate to the task, management style must be appropriate, and values must be shared within the organization. Successful implementation requires a certain synergy and consistency among these four elements—structure, systems, style, and shared values.[1] Jack Welch has dramatically altered all four of these elements of implementation is his efforts to make GE strategically successful.

Figure 9.3 indicates just how vital the relationship between strategy and implementation can be. An organization with a sound strategy that it implements effectively has the best of all possible conditions. It is accomplishing its mission, and it will eventually accomplish its strategic intent. Jack Welch's strategy was sound and has been successfully implemented. An organization with a sound strategy that it does not implement effectively is not likely to be successful. Hewlett-Packard was in just such a situation with its product development strategy, as discussed in Chapter 7. Research suggests that few firms manage to secure full commitments and energy levels for their strategies, and these strategies therefore fail.[2]

An unsound, but well-implemented strategy does not help the organization to accomplish its mission. General Motors had a strategy that no longer fit its environment in the mid-1980s, but it kept on implementing the strategy, anyway.

FIGURE 9.3 Relationships between Effective and Ineffective Strategy and Implementation

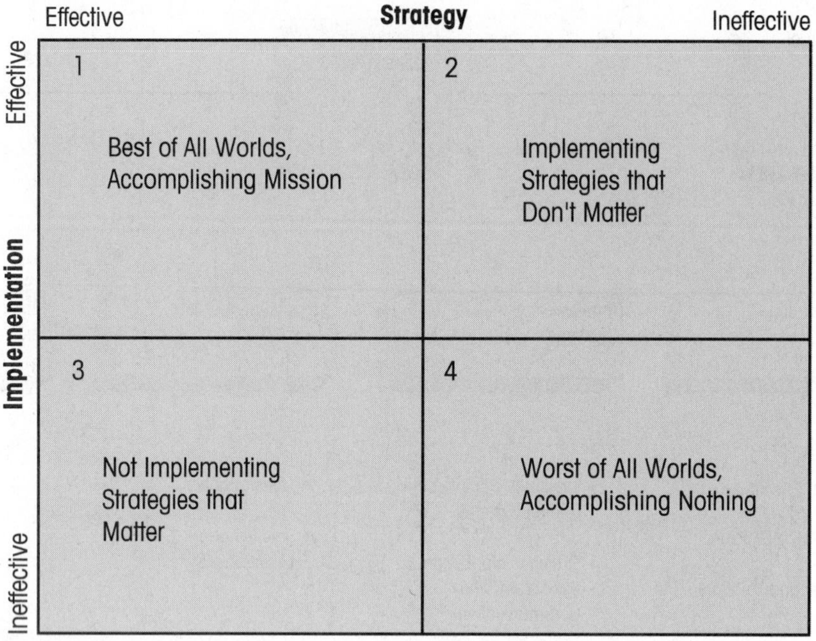

Strategy

	Effective	Ineffective
Effective	**1** Best of All Worlds, Accomplishing Mission	**2** Implementing Strategies that Don't Matter
Ineffective	**3** Not Implementing Strategies that Matter	**4** Worst of All Worlds, Accomplishing Nothing

(Implementation is labeled along the vertical axis; Strategy along the horizontal axis.)

An unsound strategy that is implemented badly is not likely to accomplish anything. Goodyear Tire & Rubber Company decided to become a conglomerate rather than focusing on what it knew. This was probably an unsound move, but then, to make matters worse, it purchased an oil pipeline firm just as oil prices dropped, making this acquisition a $1.7-billion white elephant. The pipeline is now empty most of the time.[3]

Only one of the four situations in Figure 9.3 is satisfactory. All things being equal, this gives the organization a 75-percent chance of not implementing a sound strategy. To be successful, strategy and its implementation must work together.[4]

IMPLEMENTATION SYSTEMS

Integrated planning and control systems, strategic information systems, appropriate motivation and communication systems, and relevant human resource management systems must be established to ensure that the firm's staff has the appropriate skills and uses them to its best advantage. These **implementation systems** function to ensure that all of the firm's activities, from decision making to physical labor, harmonize with its strategy.

Objectives, plans, and policies are vital to this end. Most organizations set out their implementation schemes in detail first in intermediate objectives, plans, and programs, then in operational objectives and plans, including, finally, the activities expected of individuals and work groups. Operational plans are especially important to successful implementation because they spell out the actions to be taken by first-line employees. One of the major operational plans is the budget, which is a financial plan. It guides expenditures of funds during the year in pursuit of the firm's mission. Once resources—human, financial, and capital—are committed to the tasks detailed in the operational plan, these resources must be properly managed.

Integrated Planning and Control Systems

Integrated planning and control start with formulation of strategies and they influence the formulation of all plans derived from a strategy. Successful implementation requires stipulation of precise objectives for strategies and for the intermediate and operational plans derived from them. Objectives are established by means of an MBORR system of some sort, as discussed in Chapter 2. Precise objectives, by clarifying role prescriptions, lead to at least three desired results:

1. They ensure that executives, other managers, and first-line employees know what the firm expects of them.
2. They provide built-in standards against which to measure performance.
3. They ensure that each action taken contributes to achieving the organization's mission.

Unfortunately, few firms coordinate their strategic and operational objectives as thoroughly as necessary.[5]

Intermediate Planning   In the **intermediate planning** phase, the broad outlines of strategy take substantial form in what are often referred to as *programs*. **Programs** define the activities involved in a single-use plan. They normally involve sizeable amounts of organizational resources. The large, diversified organization devises a program for each of its SBUs or product divisions. The business or product division itself, or the firm that makes a single product or a few products, formulates such plans for its various functions (marketing, production, finance, personnel). Some firms attempt to skip the intermediate phase and move directly from strategy to operations, but the results are seldom satisfactory, especially in larger firms. Strategies are so broad and operating actions so specific that additional intermediate planning is required for a smooth transition. Yet as the need for speeding strategic responses increases, planning at the intermediate stages becomes more difficult.

Intermediate plans vary greatly in scope, time horizon, comprehensiveness, and degree of detail. Normally, several successive intermediate plans are required to translate strategy into operations. However, accelerating change is forcing firms to reduce the details involved to increase the flexibility of intermediate plans and generally streamline them.

Let us examine a product substrategy as an example. A global firm needs an intermediate plan to translate its production strategy into requirements for operations in various countries. It needs another intermediate plan to allocate objectives and prescribe actions to plants within specific countries. It needs yet another intermediate plan to allocate objectives and prescribe actions to departments within each plant. Finally, operational planning allocates objectives and assigns tasks to individuals. At each of these levels, the firm generates coordinated policies to guide managers' decisions. These all must be linked to global strategy.[6]

Operational Planning   **Operational planning** is a key component of implementation. An operational plan normally covers a period of 1 year, although the period varies among organizations. Many organizations label these 1-year operating plans *profit plans.* Profit plans translate intermediate plans into definite, result-producing actions. Descriptions of these actions and their objectives normally are referred to as *procedures, rules,* or *job descriptions.* These operational plans give substance to strategy. Profit plans have more detailed objectives and more specific activity requirements than any other plans. They specify the exact resources needed and the precise manner in which workers will obtain and use those resources. Operational planning involves the middle and lower levels of management.

Operational plans have historically emphasized automatic decision-making rules, procedures, and integrative activities, but these plans are coming to require more autonomous decisions in firms such as GE. Operational plans adjust production, marketing, and financial capacity to the levels of operation. They aim to increase the efficiency of operating activities and to specify short-term operations in detail. In short, operational planning focuses on the specific ways and means by which the firm will accomplish strategic objectives.

AT GE

Among GE's problems was its failure to properly manage processes—and day-to-day operations. It learned how to do this. It learned that operational planning could not be skimped on, and that creativity alone was not enough; it also had to run the business from day to day. GE learned that everyday operations could be improved significantly by allowing participation in process planning and other operational decisions by front-line managers and their subordinates.

Budgets   The most common specific operational planning and control system is the budget. The **budget** is usually considered a financial operating plan. It translates plans of action, usually operating plans, into dollar commitments. The budget tells the organization whether an operating plan produces an acceptable bottom-line figure (anticipated profit). It is also the primary means by which a firm commits funds.

Normally a firm has two major budgets: an operating budget and a financial budget. The operating budget, which combines various functional budgets, begins with a revenue forecast. For a business such as The Free Press publishing company, this is the net sales forecast; for a government such as the state of Indiana, it is the estimated tax receipts (modified by the forecast of monetary manipulations for the federal government); for a nonprofit, private-sector organization such as United Way, it may be a forecast of contributions. Matching estimated expenditures against anticipated revenues in the budgeting process fleshes out role expectations. Most budgets make some provisions for unforeseen variations in performance expectations. The financial budget shows the operational budget's effect on the financial health of the firm. It is composed of various cash and capital budgets. These budgets, in turn, are used to develop pro forma financial statements. Figure 9.4 details the relationships of the major types of budgets.

Interestingly, Japanese firms use 6-month budget cycles. They believe this forces their managers to revise short-term plans more frequently and thus improves control and planning. Japanese firms do this in recognition that environments change and that short-term plans need to change more often than once a year.[7]

Strategic Information Systems (SISs) and Motivation and Communication Systems

The SIS is a critical systems component that assists top management in managing strategy formulation, implementation, and control. Strategic decisions can only be as good as the information on which they are based. Chapter 3 discussed SISs in some detail, and Chapter 10 discusses their effect on control.

Motivation and communication systems are also critical to the success of strategy. Principally, strategists use vision, compensation, and other forms of influence to motivate subordinates. To spread this influence, communications systems today include a variety of media from video newsletters to group meetings to computer networks. Management uses such systems to inform and elicit commitment to strategic intent. These systems are discussed in introductory management and organizational behavior courses, so they need no elaboration here other than to note that U.S. top-management compensation systems have often been criticized for their emphasis on the short run. Many firms are now changing their compensation systems to build in risk-taking and longer-term orientations.[8]

Management of Human Resources

Many motivation and communication activities are managed through the personnel or **human resource management (HRM) function,** which plays a much larger role in most organizations than it has in the past. Due to strategic challenges such as the changing nature of the work force (especially cultural diversity and the shortage of skilled labor) and global competition, the management of human

FIGURE 9.4   The Budget

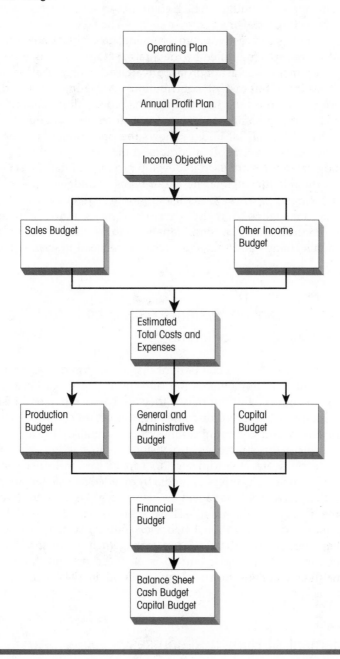

resources will be even more important in the future. Recognizing this, firms such as TRW Inc. are seeking to become preferred employers, offering superior benefits and employee-friendly work environments.[9]

The HRM or Personnel Department   The human resource department is charged with carrying out two primary sets of duties. The first series focuses on the placement of employees:

- *Personnel planning.*   Determining the jobs necessary to carry out the organization's mission, and then determining the number of people needed to fill those jobs, the capabilities they must have, and where and when they will be needed (This function is especially important in times of rapid change, restructuring, and strategic flexibility. Firms are moving to shorter HRM planning cycles to match shorter strategic planning cycles.)[10]
- *Recruiting and attracting.*   Obtaining a pool of applicants for the jobs to be filled (This function is especially important in a time of worker shortages in certain skills.)
- *Selecting.*   Choosing from among the applicants those best-suited to perform the jobs (This becomes critical when many in the recruitment pool have fewer skills than the firm needs.)
- *Training and development.*   Preparing prospective employees to perform the jobs (This will be critical in the next decade as new employees will be lacking vital skills. Many firms find the work place so complex that they must develop training programs to indoctrinate new employees to the basic expectations of their jobs. Atlanta Gas Light Company, for example, runs a voluntary 8-week program to teach basic job-site information, work-related vocabulary, and computer skills to its staff. A number of firms have even found it necessary to train employees in very basic reading and writing skills. Aetna Life & Casualty Company in Hartford, Connecticut, for example, has trained over 1,000 entry-level employees in these basic skills in recent years. This need is expected to increase dramatically in the future.[11]

The second series of personnel practices comes into play once the employee has been placed in the job:

- *Orienting.*   Integrating the individual into the work unit
- *Training and development.*   Providing ongoing training to employees as they gain experience and seek advancement (As the firm attempts to implement new strategies, it must develop new employee skills. For example, IBM Canada has formed partnerships with various educational institutions to try to keep its work force up to date on technological and other changes.)[12]

- *Providing compensation, benefits, motivation.*   Motivating employees, most often through compensation and benefit systems, but increasingly through other programs as well, such as workshops to improve management skills
- *Ensuring employees' health and safety.*   Monitoring and improving the work environment and securing insurance coverage for employees
- *Managing union relations.*   Supervising negotiations and day-to-day relations with unionized employees and their representatives

- *Assuring equal employment opportunities.* Establishing policies, procedures, and rules to govern the organization's fulfillment of its EEO objectives
- *Evaluating and controlling.* Establishing and administering performance-appraisal and disciplinary systems (This function covers promotions, terminations, and transfers, for example.)
- *Managing change.* Preparing employees for changes in the work environment and ensuring smooth transitions to new work systems (This function will grow even more important as the firm confronts accelerating rates of change.)
- *Improving productivity.* Administering job redesign, introduction of technological measures, kaizen, and other means to increase productivity
- *Improving organizational communication.* Administering employee-assistance programs, listening posts, company newspapers and magazines, bulletin boards, television broadcasts, video newsletters, discussion groups, meetings, and the like

The purpose of all of these human resource management functions is to ensure that organizational behavior accords with strategic objectives. To be effective, the organization must have an appropriate staff with appropriate skills. The organization's systems for managing organizational behavior are to a great extent designed and controlled by this department.

The human resource department, in conjunction with strategists' and other managers' managerial styles, determines to a great extent the nature of the organization's culture. When you examine the functions of a human resource manager, such as operating the motivation/compensation system, managing change, and managing productivity, you can see that this person has a tremendous influence on organizational culture, and we know that culture has a tremendous influence on the formulation, implementation, and control of strategy.[13]

MANAGEMENT STYLE/TRANSFORMATIONAL LEADERSHIP

Once the organization is committed to a course of action, it needs leadership to ensure successful implementation. **Leadership** is the process of influencing individual and group motivation. Leaders may choose among many kinds of leadership behaviors. The more or less consistent pattern of these choices and resulting actions is known as **leadership style** or **management style.** Two leadership/management styles affect implementation. The first is transformational leadership. The second is work group leadership/management style.

Transformational Leadership[14]

Transformational leadership refers to the set of behaviors in which managers engage to transform their organizations from what they are into what they need to be. Normally, top managers, principally CEOs, are seen to transform organizations. Lee Iacocca of Chrysler is probably the best-known transformational leader, but others, such as Jack Welch of GE and Alain Gomez of France's Thomson

Group, have successfully transformed their organizations to make them more competitive. Alain Gomez is featured in this chapter's Global Strategic Challenge feature.

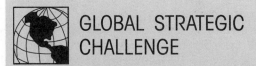

GLOBAL STRATEGIC CHALLENGE

ALAIN GOMEZ TRANSFORMS FRANCE'S THOMSON GROUP

Alain Gomez, a 52-year-old former French paratrooper and left-wing radical during France's turbulent 1960s, has transformed France's Thomson CSF, from a bankrupt company into a globally powerful firm strong in defense and consumer electronics. Upon becoming CEO in 1982, Gomez immediately began to cut costs by reducing staff, selling off losing businesses and those that didn't fit in with his strategy of pursuing businesses in which Thomson could be a dominant force. He introduced consistent management systems, restructured, replaced older managers with younger ones under 40 (breaking with French tradition), and changed the corporate culture to improve both effectiveness and efficiency. Gomez is a very numbers-oriented manager with a keen memory, often grilling subordinates about meetings several months before. This, too, is somewhat unique in France, where managers have more traditionally managed by intuition alone. Yet, Gomez uses his intuition as well. Representative of his actions to change the staid and lethargic state-owned firm into a competitive one was the move of its corporate headquarters from an elegant nineteenth-century building on the fashionable Boulevard Haussmann to a modern, but comparably drab, office tower at the suburban complex La Défense.

Gomez is viewed at home, and occasionally abroad, as somewhat of a maverick. One of the main criticisms of his management style is his sharp tongue. In a country where verbal *politesse* has been refined to an art, he aims for the jugular vein with reckless abandon. He has axed nonperforming units and executives without the usual face-saving niceties. "I didn't have to shake them out of the trees," he comments. "Most of them were already senile and fell out on their own." Such actions and commentary have made him many enemies both in government and among former business associates. In a state-owned firm, playing politics and not offending the public are expected. "I don't make political decisions," he claims notwithstanding. Gomez has also made enemies of the company's union employees, cutting the labor force during profitable times, another break with French tradition.

Yet, the CEO has returned the firm to profitability and saved it from bankruptcy. He has inspired employees to new levels of productivity and raised innovation within the firm to its highest levels ever. And he has positioned the firm for the long term. For example, early on Gomez recognized a decline in future defense spending and began to reduce the labor force in that division, even in the profitable years. In a move that then looked very inappropriate, he swapped one of Thomson's divisions and cash for General Electric's RCA television division, seeking to move the firm to number one in worldwide consumer electronics. Though hurt by the 1990-1991 recession in the United States, the long-term move looks solid for Thomson.

Though successful, Gomez faces unparalleled challenges in keeping Thomson profitable in the long term. Defense is vulnerable to reduced defense expenditures, especially in the Middle East, where much of Thomson's sales have occurred. Perhaps more tellingly, consumer electronics must complete in Europe and in the United States with Japanese firms that have come to dominate global consumer electronics. (Note that Japan essentially locks out foreign firms through various market-control mechanisms in order to keep them from competing in Japan's consumer electronics and most other markets.) Gomez and Thomson are betting the company's future on the firm's ability to capture the European HDTV (high-definition TV) market. Gomez, who must face his triannual review in 1992 (as mandated by French law for top managers of state-owned firms), is betting that 1991 will be profitable, he will be returned to another three-year term and thus realize his HDTV goal.

The HDTV strategy was based on the belief that only by competing with the Japanese could Thomson hope to survive. Indeed, most observers believe that Gomez is betting the company on this roll of the dice. He is betting that not only can Thomson catch the Japanese, but pass them. Gomez offers, "The Japanese have a high regard for their own capacity, and rightly so. They are unbelievable managers. They have great companies, and their technology is superb. But that does not mean that other companies in other countries cannot catch up." Gomez's efforts to move Thomson to the forefront of technology have been aided greatly by the French government's desire to keep the Japanese out of France to the extent possible. As a result, the French government will fund a third of Thomson's $1.8 billion in expected HDTV research and development, and another $1.2 billion in fresh capital has been promised.

Sources: Jonathan B. Levine, "The Heat on Alain Gomez," *Business Week*, March 11, 1991, pp. 66–67; Janice McCormick and Nan Stone, "From National Champion to Global Competitor: An Interview with Alain Gomez," *Harvard Business Review*, May/June, 1990, pp. 127–135; Thane Petersen, "Alain Gomez, France's High-Tech Warrior," *Business Week*, May 15, 1989, p. 106; Deborah Wise, "Thomson's French Revolution," *Business*, June 1989, pp. 48–56; "Thomson: Battling On," *The Economist*, July 15, 1989, pp. 64–66.

Transformational leadership appears to involve three key sets of activities. The first is creating a vision, the second is mobilizing commitment to that vision, and the third is institutionalizing change throughout the organization.[15] It is easy to understand how fulfilling strategic intent (or vision) requires a transformational leader, especially to elicit commitment to the intent. The evidence indicates that employee commitment clearly depends at least partially on top management's actions.[16]

How the leader gains commitment to strategic intent varies, but it often requires charisma. Financial motivation systems, especially for top managers, may be critical.[17] Participative management, team management, total quality management, restructuring, process mapping, work-outs, best practices, culture management, organizational development, and other programs may help the manager to bring about organizational transformation. Not all strategic leadership is transformational in nature.[18] However, as the strategic challenges change life in the 1990s, we feel that transformational leadership will become more clearly the primary influence on operations, as organizations will have to change to meet these challenges.

AT GE

Jack Welch has articulated two visions of what GE should be. First, he placed huge demands upon employees and called for the firm to meet seemingly unobtainable goals. The second time around, his strategic intent lay in becoming a world-class competitor in all industries by increasing productivity through innovation. He changed his firm's management style and organizational culture to achieve these ends.

Work Group Leadership/Management Style[19]

After the firm establishes operational plans, it must ensure that resources are appropriately used. If human resources fulfill their roles effectively and efficiently, then the remaining resources will be effectively and efficiently managed, as well. An exhaustive treatment of small-group leadership and management style is beyond the scope of this text, but a brief review to relate its importance to strategy will be helpful. Lower-level managers and work group leaders, those primarily responsible for this phase of implementation, must also plan, organize, control, communicate, and solve problems.

The situational approach to leadership proposes that managers identify the major factors in each situation and adjust their leadership techniques to match those factors. The difficulty lies in identifying the most critical factors. Some critical factors that affect the manager's choice of a leadership style are subordinates' needs and personalities, the nature of the subordinates' work groups, the types of tasks the subordinates perform, and the organization's culture, structure, and climate. Managers must make leadership choices in at least five areas:

1. *Task.* How much should I emphasize goals, objectives, the job, performance levels?
2. *Relationships.* How much do I do to build strong social relationships with subordinates? How much do I do to satisfy their social needs?
3. *Rewards.* How much should I and can I reward behavior?
4. *Attitude.* What attitude do I convey with this person or group? Positive or negative?
5. *Participation.* To what extent do I let this person or group participate in decision making?

Preferences in organizational leadership style are defined by top management. Often described in policy, they eventually become a part of culture. These leadership choices allow managers to influence individual motivation. While this section has focused on the front-line manager, top and middle managers must also practice sound work group management for the managers who report to them.

MANAGEMENT OF SHARED VALUES: CORPORATE CULTURE

An organization's **culture** is the pattern of behaviors and values that separates one organization from a similar organization operating within the same society and industry. Organizations are attempting to improve their management of corporate culture (shared values) because this often increases strategic success.[20] A company that successfully manages culture first establishes a set of beliefs or values and then elicits its employees' commitment to them.[21]

Often, a company adopts one dominant value. At IBM, it's customer service. Ford believes "Quality is Job 1." Chrysler values "becoming the best there is because what else is there?" More than one value has to be shared, however, and often organizations share many. In Chapter 2 we reviewed the corporate goals that guide Hewlett-Packard. These are shared values, as is HP's now famous practice of management by wandering around, in which managers act as coaches, helping employees make decisions. Similarly, Coca-Cola's objectives and policies, noted in Chapter 2, set the tone for its employees' actions.

Though these values may not be articulated, they are usually understood. If they are neither articulated nor understood, they are, in fact, not shared. Many managers have wanted to change their firms' values, but found they could not be budged. In such a situation, changing the firm's strategic direction becomes impossible. Hewlett-Packard has had this experience. As we saw in Chapter 8, HP could not provide its customers with new products in a timely fashion because its highly bureaucratic product/market structure got in the way of strategic success. HP had to manage its structure together with the associated culture. This chapter's Strategic Challenge feature reviews how one firm successfully implemented strategy by managing organizational culture.

Numerous obstacles impede the management of culture, not the least of which is the difficulty of defining it. A working definition that everyone can accept is elusive; the definition presented above combines elements of the more common definitions. Depending on which definition is used (which depends on the book or consultant that guides the company), the corporation will emphasize one aspect of culture management or another. Maintaining the desired corporate culture is another major problem, especially when both the internal and external environments are changing. Furthermore, once firms have established values among current employees, they must develop these values in new employees. This usually requires a major socialization program.[22] The diversity of new work force entrants as compared to the traditional white-male–dominated work force makes efforts to develop a common culture even more difficult in the near future, as the later discussion on cultural diversity will reveal. Managing culture is much like shooting at a moving target; it requires constant re-aiming.

Another factor that complicates culture management is the need for it to complement strategy, parts of which often change. The description of Hewlett-Packard in Chapter 8, for example, demonstrates that a strong culture of the wrong

STRATEGIC CHALLENGE

IMPLEMENTATION AT LAKEWAY RESORTS

Lakeway Resort and Conference Center had flourished in its early years, but by 1987 it had begun to show signs of aging. Nestled in the Texas hill country along Lake Travis just 18 miles west of Austin, Texas, the resort offered a number of amenities, but not all that the newer resorts offered. With its age and significant competition aimed at a 90 percent Texan clientele, Lakeway's owners felt it was time to sell rather than to invest more money in the property. Andy Dolce, an entrepreneur and resort developer, on the other hand, saw the property as a way of anchoring his strategic plan to own five world-class resorts and conference centers spread geographically around the United States. He saw Lakeway as an opportunity to create the first world-class resort in Texas. Accordingly, the Dolce Company invested $15 million in the hotel, adding 125 country-villa styled rooms to the existing 138 rooms. The firm added a dining room, game room, and fitness facilities. A spa and $800,000 meeting room were also added. Three 18-hole golf courses were made available to guests staying on the property, as were 3 swimming pools, 32 tennis courts, horseback riding, sailboats, and other recreational amenities.

   Andy Dolce and the Dolce management team felt the several million dollars worth of improvements they made had been absolutely necessary. But beyond that, significant changes in attitudes had to be made as well. Andy saw employee commitment and motivation as critical to any organization's success, but especially a service organization such as Lakeway. The human resources strategy was viewed as critical to overall strategic success, and the differentiation factor had to come somehow from providing superior service. Andy and his top management team, including Larwrence Barbir, general manager, and Eva Medford, director of human resources, set out to design such a strategy. They worked hard to provide special programs of motivation, reward, recognition, and employee participation. They worked hard to develop a central theme that would help focus employee behavior on providing superior service. The team also designed a culture management program based on the theme of "aggressive hospitality" and encouraged their 250 employees to provide superior service by making it an ingrained part of their behavior. The results have been nothing short of spectacular. By changing the culture as well as the facilities, the Dolce management group turned Lakeway into a world-class resort.

Source: Richard L. Daft, "Lakeway Resort and Conference Center," *Management*, 2d ed. (Fort Worth: Dryden Press, 1991), pp. 365–367; "Lakeway Resort and Conference Center," video to accompany this text, Dryden Press.

kind can prevent, at least in the short term, the satisfactory implementation of a new strategy. The evidence is clear that a strong set of shared values is essential, employees must be committed to management's values, and these values must complement all else that happens in the firm. However, culture must be flexible enough to change over time.

> ### AT GE
>
> It is much more difficult to share values among the many businesses in a conglomerate such as GE than in a single-industry firm such as McDonald's. Some people argue that shared values are needed only at the business level of multiple-SBU firms, not at the corporate level; GE does not agree.

Organizational Learning and Organizational Culture

Organizations learn just as individuals do. **Organizational learning,** or the ability of an organization to benefit from its experiences or those of other firms, is critical to successful strategic management. It requires that top management teams change their shared mental models of their company, their markets, their competitors, and other critical internal and external environmental factors. Arie P. de Geus, former head of strategic planning for Royal Dutch/Shell, currently with the London School of Business, views strategic planning as a learning experience, and organizational learning as a competitive advantage. Corporate strategic planning is learning because such planning leads the organization to discover its future. Organizational learning becomes a competitive advantage when the firm learns how to cope faster than its competitors do. Arie de Geus believes that this rapid learning may well be the only sustainable competitive advantage.[23]

Organizational learning affects organizational culture because changes in top management's mental models must be reflected in those of the rest of the organization. Cultural change will naturally follow. Furthermore, institutionalizing learning depends on an organizational culture that values learning. Ray Stata, chairman of Boston-based Analog Devices, Inc., reports that changing the culture of his organization to emphasize the importance of organizational learning has made Analog a much more competitive corporation. Stata was introduced to organizational learning by Arie de Geus during an MIT-sponsored executive management-style redefinition project. Stata views organizational learning as the principal source of management innovation. He believes that without innovative management, a company is doomed to lose its competitive edge. Organizational learning helped Analog improve product quality, focus corporate strategy on new directions, and modify corporate information systems to make them more functional. The organization's culture had to be changed twice: once to institutionalize organizational learning and again to incorporate the desired quality ethic, to implement the new strategy, and to develop the new information system.

CULTURAL DIVERSITY AND THE MANAGEMENT OF CULTURE

As discussed in Chapter 1, organizations are becoming much more culturally diverse. **Cultural diversity** means that people of different races, sexes, ages,

national origins, and capacities are bringing different cultural perspectives to the workplace. Women of all races and male racial minorities will make up 85 percent of the net new entrants into the work force in the 1990s.[24] White males have historically dominated the work force and the management structure, but this will change dramatically. Recognizing this, organizations must make special efforts to ensure that their cultures not only accept cultural diversity, but promote it. DEC, IBM, Avon, Procter & Gamble, Pillsbury, Ortho, U.S. West and numerous other firms maintain active cultural diversity programs, training managers and other personnel to tolerate, and even celebrate, the differences in people, and how to manage a culturally diverse work force. Such programs attempt to alter organizational culture by changing underlying values about people of varying races, sexes, ages, physical and mental capacities, and national origins.[25]

Cultural diversity programs promote the philosophy that cultural diversity is a reality and that an employer not only must learn to live with it, but should turn it into a strategic advantage.[26] A number of arguments have been offered in support of this position. Managing in a multinational environment can benefit from the additional insight into diverse national cultures that comes with diverse ethnic backgrounds. Also, diverse cultural perspectives should increase the level of creativity in the organization and improve problem solving. Increased fluidity caused by diversity should lead to greater flexibility in the organization, which is vital in coping with rapidly changing environments. Further, soundly managed cultural diversity programs will cost less than poorly managed programs, and the best-managed programs will attract the best talent among women, minorities, and culturally diverse groups, in general. A review of the available research supports these views, although the amount of this research is limited.[27] Thus, it appears that successfully managing cultural diversity may result in a strategic advantage not only conceptually, but pragmatically.

Cultural diversity and equal employment opportunity/affirmative action are closely related issues.[28] The Civil Rights Act of 1991 places employers at considerably greater financial risk than previous civil rights laws did. The financial penalties for discrimination have been raised substantially from twice the amount of compensation lost due to the discriminatory act to a sliding scale from $50,000 for employers with 15 to 100 employees to $300,000 for employers with more than 500 employees.[29] Sexual harassment became an especially thorny issue for employers as a consequence of Clarence Thomas's Supreme Court confirmation hearings.[30] Since women made up 45 percent of the work force in 1990, and that percentage is expected to increase to 47 percent by the year 2000, employers must develop programs to cope with this and other, related work force problems.[31] This chapter's Strategic Cultural Diversity Challenge feature reveals how Corning manages cultural diversity.

Globalization, Cultural Diversity, and Managing Organizational Culture

A seldom-considered, but important aspect of cultural diversity arises with the globalization of business. As firms around the globe increasingly operate in contact with foreign cultures, the concerns of managing cultural diversity naturally extend

STRATEGIC CULTURAL DIVERSITY CHALLENGE

HOW CORNING AFFIRMS CULTURAL DIVERSITY AS PART OF ITS STRATEGY FOR THE 1990s

When Jamie Houghton assumed the role of CEO of Corning, Inc., the upstate New York manufacturer, he brought the vision necessary to turn the very profitable firm into one that could compete in the 1990s. When he took over the reins of the corporation from his older brother (the Houghtons own 15 percent of the company's stock), 70 percent of the firm's revenues came from slow-growth businesses in which Corning held low-to-moderate market shares. Profits had declined in these businesses for three straight years. From 1983 to 1989, Houghton divested some $500 million in companies that had limited futures, and acquired some $500 million in companies in industries with substantial growth opportunities. He followed many of the strategies critical for improving competitiveness—cutting costs, increasing employee participation in operational decisions, and making high levels of quality imperative to all product lines. He also formed 19 global strategic alliances in areas important to the firm and encouraged the organized management of technological knowledge, using a centralized research center to communicate information to the divisions and within and among the divisions.

But two of Houghton's more visionary actions were to promote diversity within the company and to improve the community. Corning, for example, acquires and reconstructs commercial properties, and then locates tenants, some of whom are minority owners. It also works to attract new business, and it built the local Hilton hotel, museum, and city library.

Corning's cultural diversity program is a standout in corporate America. As with quality, Houghton turned cultural diversity into a personal crusade. Late in 1987, the CEO established two companywide teams headed by top executives. All managers and salaried employees attended seminars to increase sensitivity and support for women and black co-workers. A network of mentors was established to help women and blacks with their career efforts. One of the teams studied factors in upstate New York that might make minorities feel uncomfortable. Corning sought to increase minority employment throughout all firms in the area, and even convinced the local cable operator to carry the Black Entertainment Television channel. The results have been very positive, with a substantial number of blacks and women reaching management ranks and with attrition rates down over 50 percent in 1991 from 1987 levels. Asians and Hispanics are targeted next.

Source: Keith H. Hammonds, "Corning's Class Act: How Jamie Houghton Reinvented the Company," *Business Week*, May 13, 1991, pp. 68–76.

to include managing workers with distinctly different national origins and national cultural perspectives. These concerns might be conceptually broadened to become a general concern for successfully conducting business in foreign countries. The importance of successfully managing this strategic challenge will only increase as time passes.

U.S. managers have often been criticized for culturally insensitivity when working in foreign countries and/or with persons from other nations, but they are hardly alone in their reputed ineptness. The Japanese, for example, have a history of racial and sexual discrimination in those countries where they do business, including the United States. Anyone who is not a Japanese male seems to suffer from discrimination in most Japanese firms. Such a person simply doesn't get promoted. Few women or nonwhites even get hired.[32]

For another example, when the French firm Hachette S.A. acquired the U.S. magazine empire Diamandis Communications, publisher of *Woman's Day*, *Stereo Review*, *Road & Track*, and *Popular Photography*, among others, immediate problems arose in a clash of egos between former owner Peter Diamandis, who stayed on as chairman, and Hachette's representatives, most notably Daniel Filipacchi. Diamandis couldn't cope with the new authority over him and apparently began mocking the French, fighting them at every turn. The French didn't like the way Diamandis did business. They thought he was too bureaucratic (by which they actually seemed to mean too participative), and not instinctive enough for them. Eventually, Diamandis and two of his top vice presidents left in a huff.[33]

Cultural Diversity and Mergers and Acquisitions

The Hachette/Diamandis example just discussed also demonstrates another common cultural diversity problem. How do you combine the cultures of two organizations that have merged, or absorb that of an acquired firm into the parent? In some cases you don't merge the cultures; you may choose to keep them separate. Quite often, problems associated with merging the cultures offset synergies that other characteristics might have brought.[34] GM experienced this with its acquisition of Electronic Data Systems, for example. To make such cultural mergers work, plans for change must be carefully formulated, implemented, and controlled.

A NOTE ON IMPLEMENTATION POLICIES

Just as the organization establishes policies to guide the formulation of strategy, it must also establish policies to guide its implementation. The nature of implementation policies varies with the level of the organization. Top managers deal largely with the management functions of staffing, leading, and motivating. By the time these policies reach the operational level of the organization, they may spell out procedures to be followed in numbing detail: how employees are recruited and selected, how employees will be developed, how managers will treat employees, what reward systems will be employed, how managers will treat employees, what reward systems will be employed, how employees may progress in careers within the organization, how groups should work together, what control measures will be used, how and when and where tasks will be performed, how budgets will be prepared, how performance will be evaluated, and more.

AN IMPORTANT PERSPECTIVE ON STRATEGY AND IMPLEMENTATION: McKINSEY'S SEVEN Ss FRAMEWORK

Consulting firm McKinsey & Company has developed a model known as the seven elements of strategic fit, or the seven Ss. The **seven Ss framework** is seen in Figure 9.5. The seven Ss—strategy, structure, systems, style, staff, skills, and shared values—are defined briefly in Table 9.1. In its underlying concept, the model assumes that all seven of these variables must fit with one another to successfully implement strategy; that is, successful strategy implementation depends on a proper culture, and only if all seven Ss are working in coordination will such a culture exist.[35] A number of McKinsey's clients have adopted this framework to model their efforts to implement strategy.

Conceptually, the framework is appealing. It incorporates the major elements discussed in this chapter, including structure, management systems, management style, and the creation of shared values. Thus the seven Ss generally agree with much of the strategic management literature regarding the keys to successful implementation.[36] Using this framework to analyze firms often proves very beneficial.

APPROACHES TO IMPLEMENTATION

The classic model of strategic management, seen in Figure 9.1, states that strategy is formulated, implemented, and controlled in that order and in a very segmented

FIGURE 9.5   McKinsey's Seven Ss

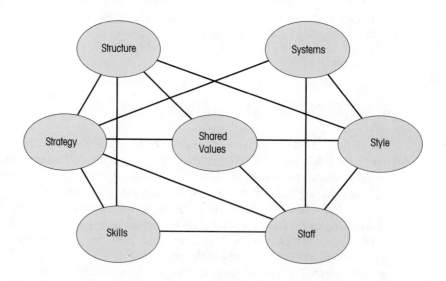

TABLE 9.1 Summary of the Seven *S*s

1. *Strategy.* A coherent set of actions aimed at gaining a sustainable advantage over competition, improving position vis-à-vis customers or allocating resources
2. *Structure.* The organization chart and accompanying baggage that show who reports to whom and how tasks are both divided and integrated
3. *Systems.* The processes and flows that show how an organization gets things done from day to day (information systems, capital budgeting systems, manufacturing processes, quality control systems, performance measurement systems)
4. *Style.* Tangible evidence of what management considers important by the way it collectively spends time and attention and uses symbolic behavior (what managers say is less important than the way they behave)
5. *Staff.* The people in the organization (here it is very useful to think not about individual personalities, but about corporate demographics)
6. *Shared values (or superordinate goals).* The values that go beyond, but might well include, simple goal statements in determining corporate destiny (to fit the concept, these values must be shared by most people in an organization)
7. *Skills.* A derivative of the rest (Skills are those capabilities that are possessed by an organization as a whole as opposed to the people in it. The concept of corporate skill as something different from the skills of the people in it seems difficult for many people to grasp, yet some organizations that hire only the best and the brightest cannot get seemingly simple things done, while others perform extraordinary feats with ordinary people.)

manner. As Chapter 1 suggested, however, strategy proceeds incrementally, and the political realities of most organizations demand that many strategists and nonstrategists alike accept a strategy before it can be implemented. Consequently, strategy formulation includes the first steps of implementation, or it should. The standards for exercising control are evolving and being defined at the same time. The smart strategist gains support for his or her strategy during formulation. Often, this involves encouraging participation in formulation from those who would be involved in implementation.

Paul C. Nutt examined 91 strategic change situations and identified four principal types of implementation processes: implementation by intervention, by participation, by persuasion, and by edict. Managers who adapted the tactic of intervention monitored the entire change process, preparing people for change, offering new definitions of acceptable performance, unfreezing previous behavior, and refreezing new behavior. Managers who chose participative processes encouraged stakeholders to help determine essential changes. Strategists who relied on persuasion attempted to sell the change to subordinates. Strategists who ruled by edict directed the change process. Nutt found that intervention had a 100-percent success rate, but he observed it in only 20 percent of the cases he examined.

TABLE 9.2 General Management Requirements for Various Strategic Situations

Situation	Major Job Thrusts	Characteristics of Ideal Candidate
Startup	Creating vision of business Establishing core technical and marketing expertise Building management team	Vision of finished business Hands-on orientation—a ''doer'' In-depth knowledge in critical technical areas Organizing ability Staffing skills Team-building capabilities High energy level and stamina Personal magnetism; charisma Broad knowledge of all key functions
Turnaround	Rapid, accurate problem diagnosis Fixing short-term and, ultimately, long-term problems	Take-charge orientation; strong leader Strong analytical and diagnostic skills, especially financial Excellent business strategist High energy level Risk taker Handles pressure well Good crisis management skills Good negotiator
Extract Profit/ Rationalize Existing Business	Efficiency Stability Succession Sense of signs of change	Technically knowledgeable: knows the business'' Sensitive to changes Anticipates problems Strong administrative skills Oriented to systems Strong relationship orientation Recognizes need for management succession and development Oriented to getting out the most—efficiency over growth
Dynamic Growth in Existing Business	Increasing market share in key sectors Managing rapid change Building long-term health toward clear vision of the future	Excellent strategic and financial planning skills Clear vision of the future Ability to balance priorities, e.g., stability versus growth Organizational and team-building skills Good crisis management skills Moderately high risk taker High energy level Excellent staffing skills
Redeployment of Efforts in Existing Business	Establishing effectiveness in limited business sphere Managing change Supporting the dispossessed	Good politician/manager of change Highly persuasive, high interpersonal influence Moderate risk taker Highly supportive, sensitive to people Excellent systems thinker, understands how complex systems work Good organizing and executive staffing skills

---

TABLE 9.2 Cont'd.   General Management Requirements for Various Strategic Situations

---

Situation	Major Job Thrusts	Characteristics of Ideal Candidate
Liquidation/ Divestiture of Poorly Performing Business	Cutting losses Making tough decisions Making best deal possible	Callous, tough-minded, determined—willing to be the bad guy Highly analytical of costs/benefits—does not easily accept current ways of doing things Risk taker Low glory seeking, willing to do dirty, unglamorous jobs Wants to be respected, not necessarily liked
New Acquisitions	Integration Establishing sources of information and control	Analytical ability Relationship-building skills Interpersonal influence Good communication skills Personal magnetism, some basis to establish instant credibility

---

Source: Adapted from Marc Gerstein and Heather Gerstein, "Strategic Selection: Matching Executives to Business Conditions," *Sloan Management Review*, 24, No. 2 (Winter 1983): 37, by permission of the publisher. Copyright © 1983 by Sloan Management Review Association.

Persuasion and participation tactics had 75-percent success rates; persuasion was used in 42 percent of the cases, participation in 17 percent. Implementation by edict, found in 23 percent of cases, had a success rate of only 43 percent.[37]

The strategist should anticipate the reactions of the individuals who must implement the strategy. They will be interpreting it, making inferences about how useful it will be, and identifying possible problems with it.[38] The strategist should have a plan for overcoming these potential obstacles. In choosing a model for implementation, such as those suggested by Nutt, strategists should consider how well each approach may help overcome potential problems.

MATCHING STRATEGISTS TO STRATEGY

Many authors have proposed that the strategist's skills as an implementer must match the strategy of the firm.[39] Chase Manhattan Bank, Texas Instruments, Corning Glass, and General Electric are among the companies that select top managers with management styles that fit the firms' strategic requirements.[40] The universal manager seems not to exist. Some people are certainly more skillful managers than others and some are adept at transferring those skills from situation to situation. An understanding of the industry and the firm's situation seems to be a prerequisite to successful strategic decisions, however. Some managers may be able to adapt their management styles to varying situations, but the evidence suggests that not many do.[41]

Thus it becomes important that organizations match managers' abilities to various strategic circumstances. Most of the literature keys strategist/strategy matches to stages of the product life cycle or related grand strategies. Table 9.2 summarizes representative scenarios. While the supporting research is at best preliminary, enough information is available to suggest that strategists should indeed be matched to strategies, or that strategists must adapt their management styles to their situations.

STRATEGIC MANAGER'S SUMMARY

1. Successful implementation of strategy requires these four systems: integrated planning and control systems, strategic information systems, systems of motivation and communication, and human resource management systems. The success of these systems depends on management style and shared values.
2. The management of human resources will be especially critical in the 1990s to meet the challenges of a changing work force, especially cultural diversity and a shortage of skilled labor, and to compete in a global marketplace.
3. Transformational leadership sets the vision for the firm, elicits commitment to that vision, and institutionalizes change. Work group leadership focuses on influencing individual motivation, achieving effectiveness, and efficiently using resources in implementing strategy.
4. Every organization has a set of shared values (a culture) that distinguishes it from similar organizations. These shared values must match strategy for successful implementation.
5. Organizational learning becomes a competitive advantage when an organization learns faster than its competitors, allowing it to do things its competitors cannot.
6. Cultural diversity complicates implementation in some ways because it is harder to achieve a common organizational culture. Yet, it can also contribute to competitive capabilities, primarily through offering diverse inputs in problem solving.
7. The McKinsey seven Ss provide a way of assuring a chance for successful implementation of strategy, or for determining reasons for failure. All seven elements should complement one another.
8. Strategists should match strategy. A mismatch of talents with the needs of the situation may result in trouble otherwise.

KEY TERMS

best practices
budget

leadership style
management style

cultural diversity
culture (shared values)
human resource management function
implementation systems
integrated planning and control
intermediate planning
leadership

operational planning
organizational learning
process mapping
programs
seven Ss framework
transformational leadership
work-outs

DISCUSSION QUESTIONS

1. In what way is structure related to implementation?
2. Why are systems so important to successful implementation? Discuss the importance to successful implementation of organizational motivation and control systems, human resource management systems, and planning and control systems.
3. Why are both transformational and work group leadership styles so critical to successful implementation?
4. Why are shared values (culture) so important to successful implementation?
5. Discuss the implications of cultural diversity for strategy and for changing organizational culture.
6. Use the seven Ss framework to describe a well-known company you have researched or about which you have sufficient knowledge.
7. What criteria does Table 9.2 suggest for matching the manager with the strategy?

STRATEGIC AUDIT QUESTIONS

1. Evaluate the relationships between the strategy of the firm and its implementation in view of Figure 9.3.
2. Evaluate the firm in regard to each of the following:
    A. Implementation systems
        i. Integrated planning and control systems
            a. Intermediate planning programs
            b. Operational planning
            c. Budgets
        ii. Strategic information systems
        iii. Motivation and communication systems
        iv. Management of human resources
    B. Management style
    C. Management of shared values
3. Does this firm have a cultural diversity program? How good is it?

4. How well are the seven *S*s coordinated in this company?
5. Are the firm's strategists well-matched to its strategy?
6. Would another style of strategy implementation be more effective? In what way?

Endnotes

1. Lawrence G. Hrebiniak, "Implementing Strategy," *Chief Executive*, April 1990, pp. 74–77; Jorge De Vasconcellos e Sa, "How to Implement a Strategy," *Business*, April/June 1990, pp. 23–32; Richard Reed and M. Ronald Buckley, "Strategy in Action—Techniques for Implementing Strategy," *Long Range Planning*, June 1988, pp. 67–74.

2. David M. Reid, "Operationalizing Strategic Planning," *Strategic Management Journal*, November/December 1989, pp. 553–567.

3. Zachary Schiller, "Hefty Sell-offs May Help Fix Goodyear's Flat," *Business Week*, April 15, 1991, p. 35.

4. Michael M. Robert, "The Critical Weakness," *Success*, January/February 1987, p. 16.

5. Michael Goold and John J. Quinn, "The Paradox of Strategic Controls," *Strategic Management Journal*, January/February 1990, pp. 43–57.

6. For a discussion of relating manufacturing strategy to global strategy, see Jeffrey G. Miller and Warren Hayship, "Implementing Manufacturing Strategic Planning," *Planning Review*, July/August 1989, pp. 22–27, 48.

7. John E. Rehfeld, "What Working for a Japanese Company Taught Me," *Harvard Business Review*, November–December 1990, pp. 167–176.

8. For example, see James M. Higgins, *The Management Challenge: An Introduction to Management* (New York: Macmillan, 1991), Chapters 13 and 16.

9. Chris W. Chen, "Becoming a 'Preferred Employer' for the 1990s," *Personnel*, July 1990, p. 48.

10. James W. Walker, "Human Resource Planning: 1990s Style," *Human Resource Planning*, vol. 13 no. 4 (1990), pp. 229–240.

11. Amanda Bennett, "Company School: As Pool of Skilled Help Tightens, Firms Move to Broaden Their Role," *The Wall Street Journal*, May 1989, pp. A1, A4; Stuart Feldman, "School Days: Businesses Hit the Books," *Personnel*, August 1991, pp. 3–4.

12. Anita K. Ross, "IBM Canada's Involvement in Education," *Canadian Business Review*, Autumn 1990, pp. 21–23.

13. Paul Shrivastava, "Integrating Strategy Formulation with Organizational Culture," *Journal of Business Strategy*, Winter 1985, pp. 103–111.

14. For a representative discussion, see Bruce J. Avolio, David A. Waldman, and Francis J. Yammarino, "Leading in the 1990s: The Four Ts of Transformational Leadership," *Journal of European Industrial Training*, vol. 15, no. 4 (1991), pp. 9–16.

15. Noel M. Tichy and David M. Ulrich, "The Leadership Challenge: A Call for Transformational Leadership," *Sloan Management Review*, Fall 1984, pp. 59–68.

16. Brian P. Niehoff, Cathy A. Enz, and Richard A. Grover, "The Impact of Top Management Actions on Employee Attitudes and Perceptions," *Group & Organizational Studies*, September 1990, pp. 337–352.

17. David R. Balkin and Luis R. Gomez-Mejia, "Matching Compensation and Organizational Strategies," *Strategic Management Journal*, January/February 1990, pp. 153–169.

18. For a review of strategic leadership research based largely on the events of the 1980s, see Dan Schendel, editor, Derek Channon, co-editor, Donald Hambrick, guest editor, "Strategic Leaders and Leadership," special issue of *Strategic Management Journal*, Summer 1989; for another perspective on the behavior of executive leaders, see Mansour Javidan, "Leading a High-Commitment, High-Performance Organization," *Long Range Planning*, April 1991, pp. 28–36.

19. This section is taken from Higgins, *Management Challenge*, pp. 518–524.

20. Brian Dumaine, "Creating a New Company Culture," *Fortune*, January 15, 1990, pp. 127–131.

21. For a review of the impacts of organizational culture, common norms found in organization culture, innovative cultures, and how to manage culture, see Charles O'Reilly, "Corporations, Culture, and Commitment: Motivation and Social Control in Organizations," *California Management Review*, Summer 1989, pp. 9–25.

22. Richard T. Pascale, "Fitting New Employees into the Company Culture," *Fortune*, May 20, 1984, pp. 28–42.

23. Arie de Geus, "Planning As Learning," *Harvard Business Review*, March–April 1988, pp. 70–74.

24. "Needed: Human Capital," *Business Week*, September 19, 1988, pp. 102–103.

25. R. Roosevelt Thomas, Jr., "From Affirmative Action to Affirming Diversity," *Harvard Business Review*, March–April 1990, pp. 107–127; Marcus Mabry, "Past Tokenism," *Newsweek*, May 14, 1990.

26. Thomas, "From Affirmative Action"; Marilyn Loden and Judy B. Rosener, *Workforce America: Managing Employee Diversity as a Vital Resource* (Homewood, Ill.: Business One Irwin, 1991); and Taylor H. Cox and Stacy Blake, "Managing Cultural Diversity:

Implications for Organizational Competitiveness, *The Executive*, August 1991, pp. 45–55.

27. Cox and Blake, "Managing Diversity."

28. Thomas, "From Affirmative Action."

29. Amy Saltzman and Ted Gest, "Your New Civil Rights," *U.S. News & World Report*, November 18, 1991, pp. 93–95.

30. Joann S. Lublin, "Thomas Battle Spotlights Harassment," *The Wall Street Journal*, October 9, 1991, pp. B1, B5.

31. William B. Johnston and Arnold H. Packer, *Workforce 2000: Work and Workers for the 21st Century* (Indianapolis, Ind.: Hudson Institute, 1987), p. 85; Lublin, "Thomas Battle."

32. John Hoerr and Leah Nathans Spiro, "Culture Shock at Home: Working for a Foreign Boss," *Business Week*, December 17, 1990, pp. 80–84; Wade Lambert, "Sumitomo Sets Accord on Job Bias Lawsuit," *The Wall Street Journal*, November 8, 1990, p. B1; Michele Galen and Leah J. Nathans, "White People, Black People, Not Wanted Here," *Business Week*, July 10, 1989, p. 31; and Edward Boyer, "Are Japanese Managers Biased against Americans?" *Fortune*, September 1, 1986, pp. 72–75.

33. Patrick M. Reilly, "Mal de Mariage: Egos, Cultures Clash When French Firm Buys U.S. Magazines," *The Wall Street Journal*, February 15, 1991, pp. A1, A6.

34. Kenneth M. Davidson, "Innovation and Corporate Mergers," *Journal of Business Strategy*, January/February 1991, pp. 42–44.

35. Robert H. Waterman, Jr., "The Seven Elements of Strategic Fit," *Journal of Business Strategy*, Winter 1982, pp. 69–73; see also Robert H. Waterman, Jr., Thomas J. Peters, and Julien R. Phillips, "Structure Is Not Organization," *Business Horizons*, June 1980, pp. 14–26.

36. Jay Galbraith and Robert K. Kazanjian, *Strategy Implementation: Structure, Systems, and Process* (St. Paul, Minn.: West, 1986).

37. Paul C. Nutt, "Tactics of Implementation," *Academy of Management Journal*, June 1986, pp. 230–261.

38. Les S. Sproull and Kay Ramsey Hofmeister, "Thinking about Implementation," *Journal of Management*, Spring 1986, pp. 43–60.

39. Andrew D. Szilagyi, Jr. and David M. Schweiger, "Matching Managers to Strategies: A Review and Suggested Framework," *Academy of Management Review*, Winter 1984, pp. 626–637; J. G. Wissema, H. W. Van der Pol, and H. M. Messer, "Strategic Management Archetypes," *Strategic Management Journal*, January/March 1980, pp. 37–47; M. Gerstein and H. Reisman, "Strategic Selection: Matching Executives to Business Conditions," *Sloan Management Review*, Winter 1983, pp. 33–49; A. K. Gupta, "Contingency Linkages between Strategy and General Management Characteristics: A Conceptual Examination," *Academy of Management Review*, July 1984, pp. 399–412.

40. "Wanted: A Manager to Fit Each Strategy," *Business Week*, February 25, 1980, pp. 166–173.

41. Szilagyi and Schweiger, "Matching Managers."

INTEGRATIVE CASE ANALYSIS
CHAPTER 9

THE CHALLENGES FACING GENERAL MOTORS IN 1992

General Motors conceived of a strategy based on technology. Its diversification efforts were directed largely at gaining access to the technology it perceived to be necessary to give it a competitive advantage or distinctive competency. In its zeal it cut costs, it redesigned its products to incorporate many parts common to all of them, giving no thought to the wants of the customers it expected to buy them. GM all too successfully implemented an apparently inappropriate strategy. When Robert Stempel took over from Roger Smith, he had to totally rework the seven Ss at GM.

Strategy

The company became so enmeshed in implementing the strategy it initiated in 1979 that even 6 years later it still failed to notice that the strategy wasn't working. Strategists did, however, at last become aware of problems. They could not overlook the fact that NUMMI, their joint venture with Toyota, had produced a plant that was more efficient than another that employed mostly robots. The key to effective performance clearly lay not in technology alone, but in the appropriate combination of technological and human skills.

Interestingly, Roger Smith had been chosen for his ability to manage a firm that was in a steady state or growing slowly. Instead, he found himself required to turn the company's fortunes around as its market share plummeted from 48 percent in 1979 to 36 percent in 1987. The characteristics that stood Smith in good stead in earlier years seemed not to fit the revised strategies that GM was forced to adopt. Smith admits he didn't do a good job of communicating the new strategy and culture. Now John Smith has been chosen to turn around company fortunes.

Roger Smith's new strategy was not much different from the old strategy, except to be more market oriented and to increase employee participation. He focused mainly on downsizing and trying to make the structure more productive. Cadillac and Buick, and to some extent Oldsmobile, prospered by separation from the rest of the firm, but Chevy and Pontiac suffered by being grouped together.

When we examine General Motors' 1992 situation from the perspective of the seven Ss, we see that Robert Stempel has not altered the long-term strategy that much, but he has changed the primary objective from profit to market share. This, in turn, requires a whole new cultural attitude. GM's long-term strategy now apparently calls for reducing its costs less by infusions of capital, as it had done earlier, than by the proper use of human workers in conjunction with appropriate levels of technology, the system that proved so effective in the NUMMI plant. More autonomy is being sought for the various auto companies, but Stempel still has not conquered the antiquated structure, which makes it impossible to dedicate a manufacturing plant to just one nameplate. Quality control systems have been established in an effort to achieve the quality necessary to compete in the marketplace. GM had used Philip Crosby and Associates as quality consultants, and it more recently hired W. Edwards Deming, the world's most respected authority on quality.

Structure

GM has done a tremendous amount of restructuring to cut costs, speed decision making, eliminate layers of management, and unnecessary jobs, close plants, and reduce overcapacity in manufacturing. It is making an increasing effort to differentiate its products from one another. Unfortunately, early sales of new Chevrolet products have been disappointing. Several new models of Cadillacs, Buicks and Pontiacs have been successful. Though strategy reportedly leads to structure, General Motors' strategy has not yet brought the structural changes that are necessary for success. GM's design and marketing efforts for the Chevy and Pontiac division are still too far removed from the customer. Oldsmobile has not quite found its market yet, either. Centralized design hurts everyone but Cadillac, which has its own design group, which produced the award winning SST. At GM, structure is still driving strategy. John Smith has been chosen to change that.

Systems

GM is installing new compensation systems and new types of individual and group control systems, such as quality circles and job enrichment. The new compensation systems have not been well-received. GM's new information systems are impressive, at least conceptually.

Style

GM's management style now appears to be more participative than before, but at the same time it is somewhat aggressive, so employees tend to find it less than congenial. Also, style varies dramatically from plant to plant. It's very participative in some places, but not in others. Stempel is much more open than Roger Smith and allows for discourse, something Smith would not do. GM has always had a very strong task orientation. The rewards offered to upper-level managers seem to have been reduced, and relationships at that level are strained. When an organization cuts back, it can expect morale to be low, and GM is no exception. Stempel does not appear to be a transformational leader. John Smith is expected to be a transformational leader with a very demanding management style.

Staff

GM has been reducing its staff. How large a staff it will need in the future no one knows. The firm must take care not to eliminate positions that it will need in the months to come, as Chrysler is reputed to have done in the mid-1970s. GM announced another major restructuring and downsizing in December 1991.

Skills

General Motors' strategy, structure, systems, style, and staff do not seem to work together sufficiently well to produce the synergistic set of skills that propels a company into the front ranks of competitors in its industry. Cadillac and Buick seem to have competitive skills. GM Europe also does well.

Shared Values

Among the new values that are now shared at General Motors are quality, cost-consciousness, harder work, and lower rewards. The firm professes a customer orientation, though it does not seem to have altered its structure. The firm is also committed to high technology, innovation, and strategic planning.

The Bottom Line on the Seven Ss

The bottom line is that GM lost $4.5 billion in 1991. Its seven Ss aren't working together. It is a dinosaur in need of vast change. Stempel is trying to bring that change as is John Smith.

CHAPTER 10

EVALUATION AND CONTROL OF STRATEGY

If it ain't broke, fix it anyway.

Tom Peters
Author and Consultant on Strategy

Control's managerial role has often been mistakenly considered to be synonymous with financial control.

Giovanni Giglioni and Arthur G. Bederan
Researchers on Control Practices

CHAPTER OBJECTIVES

By the time you complete this chapter, you should be able to:

1. Describe the meaning of strategic control, management control, and operational control
2. Describe why strategic control is important and discuss how it is changing
3. Indicate the uses and the pros and cons of return on investment as a strategic control mechanism
4. Discuss how quality functions as a control mechanism
5. Discuss the advantages to strategic management of typical financial controls
6. Indicate the value of the social audit to strategic control
7. Discuss the possible dysfunctional consequences of control systems
8. Discuss the various measurements for an organization's strategic management and operational performance
9. Discuss growing concerns in strategic control

CYPRESS SEMICONDUCTORS: THE SYSTEM IS THE SOLUTION

Chapter 2 on establishing strategic purpose contained a Strategic Challenge feature on Cypress Semiconductors, the only Silicon Valley semiconductor manufacturer to make money each year from 1983 to 1990. It's only fitting that this chapter on control also feature Cypress, since planning and control are inextricably linked. A niche player, Cypress uses information technology to facilitate the establishment of objectives for each and every employee on a weekly basis, and for longer periods of time if major projects are involved. Employees typically enter their objectives for 4- to 6-week periods and for each week. Progress toward these is reviewed on Wednesday and again on Friday by T. J. Rogers, Cypress's CEO. Cypress's "killer software" goals-tracking system allows Rogers to scan the performance of all divisions and all 1,400 employees in just about 4 hours. It is this linking of planning and control through information technology that makes Cypress a leader in moving control from a periodic activity to a virtually continuous one.

Few, if any, other U.S. firms so directly and frequently link strategic and operational planning objectives and related control measurements. Some say the system is unwieldy, too time consuming, and would be unmanageable in a larger firm, but Rogers attributes much of the firm's success to this and other management information systems. In what might be called management by software, Rogers and other top managers continuously guide the firm's substantial sales growth (40 percent per year since its inception in 1983), significant profits, and competitiveness superior to other U.S. chipmakers. The killer software includes programs to check the status of every manufacturing lot every 3 hours, checking how long it has been in process and calling for certain automatic actions if managerial initiatives aren't taken to change trigger conditions. This has facilitated significant improvements in inventory control, purchasing, and marketing. Customer on-time delivery has improved from 65 to 90 percent, as an example. Similar programs exist for managing credit. If, after 6 months, the account of a customer whose credit has been cancelled is not reviewed, credit is automatically restored. "The finance groups are deathly afraid of that one," says Rick Foresman, director of strategic systems and administration.

Another part of Cypress's competitive edge comes from its huge investment in R&D, amounting to some 25 percent of sales in 1990. Rogers believes that managers, professional staff, and other employees have more time to innovate if they don't have to do so many routine tasks by hand, so he uses the computer to accomplish much routine management work and other tasks. The firm is organized around entrepreneurial divisions, which are given high levels of autonomy, but are still controlled by the goals-tracking system.

Sources: Richard Brandt, "The Bad Boy of Silicon Valley," *Business Week*, December 9, 1991, pp. 64–70; Stephen J. Govoni, "The Systems Are the Solution at Cypress," *Electronic Business*, October 7, 1991, pp. 154, 156; Charles Procter, "Top 100 R&D Spenders: Dog Days for R&D," *Electronic Business*, August 5, 1991, pp. 44–47; T. J. Rogers, "No Excuses Management," *Harvard Business Review*, July–August 1990, pp. 84–98; Kathleen Melymuka, "Controlled Fusion," *CIO*, August 1990, pp. 57–59.

The whole concept of control, especially strategic control, is changing in North America and Europe for a number of reasons. For example, firms from these regions must compete with Japanese firms. Because of their higher emphasis on product and process quality, the Japanese engage in strategic control more frequently than do most of their global counterparts, so there is no choice but to change and keep up. Further changing the practice of control is the Japanese concept of kaizen or continuous improvement, which is now being adopted by many North American and European firms; this concept requires continuous control efforts to be successful. Fortunately, sophisticated computer software enables more frequent and more accurate control, thus facilitating this transition.

In order to improve control, especially strategic control, new mechanisms and new philosophies are being implemented, for example, regarding management accounting and how to make it more strategically relevant.[1] Firms are totally redesigning their control systems and redefining how they measure performance.[2] Cypress points the way to the future of organizational control. For example, Cypress Semiconductor's use of computer performance tracking for its three weekly progress-review sessions may very well be typical in 10 years, rather than atypical, as it is now.

There are three primary forms of **organizational control:** strategic control, management control, and operational control. **Strategic control,** the process of evaluating strategy, is practiced just after strategy is formulated, while it is being implemented, and after it is implemented.[3] The organization's strategists evaluate strategy once it has been formulated to ascertain whether it is appropriate to the mission, and during and after implementation to determine if it will accomplish or is accomplishing its objectives. Cypress Semiconductor's killer software systems are aimed at both objectives. While virtually everyone agrees that strategic control is necessary, very few firms have actually integrated strategic control systems into their strategic management processes.[4] One of those that has is Cypress.

Management control is the process of ensuring that major subsystems' progress toward strategic objectives is satisfactory. For example, is Division A's ROI performance acceptable? Is the production department meeting its quality control objectives? Cypress's goal-tracking system provides management control. **Operational control** is the process of ascertaining whether the role behaviors (performance) of individuals and work groups satisfy their job descriptions. (Is a particular salesperson reaching his or her sales quota?) Cypress's goal-tracking system summarizes operational activities, yet retains the detail.

Like the phases of planning, the forms of control are not clearly separable. In some organizations, one form of control may be almost indistinguishable from another. Devices used in one form of control may also be employed in another. Such management control devices as ROI, for example, may be used to measure the performance not only of organizational components, but of the total organization, as well. Cypress's goal-tracking system works on all three levels. While most operational and many management control systems may incorporate automatic correction activities, evaluating strategy requires executive judgment.

This chapter is concerned with those parts of the strategic management process model indicated in Figure 10.1. This chapter first reviews the process of

FIGURE 10.1 The Organization—A Strategic Management Process Model

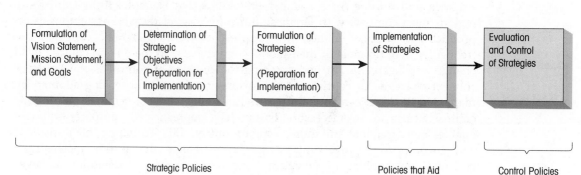

control and how it applies to strategy. Next, the chapter discusses the three types of control—strategic, management, and operational control—in more detail. It then reviews various measures of performance and discusses several types of audits and their contributions to control. The chapter finishes with a discussion of other aspects of control.

CONTROL AND STRATEGY

Control may be depicted as a six-step feedback model:

1. *Establish standards of performance.* Standards are specific measures against which actual performance will be judged. As more detailed expressions of strategic objectives, they form the bases of job descriptions. Establishing standards of organizational subcomponents is the first step in management control, and establishing them for individuals is the first step in operational control. Too many strategic control measures are established without integrating them with management and operational controls.[5]

2. *State acceptable tolerances.* The standard is a single point on a continuum of possible behaviors, but it is not always necessary to perform exactly to that point. Normally, deviation from standards will be tolerated within limits.

3. *Measure actual performance.* Measurement involves identifying role behavior of either the total organization, groups, or individuals. Measurement techniques vary from situation to situation. Though they are often imprecise, they are indispensable. The way you measure your managers' performances will have a major impact on their behavior.[6]

4. *Compare standards and performance.* While comparing performance with standards may appear to be a simple task, it is anything but simple to measure quality of performance. Quality often cannot be quantified.

5. *Act.* When performance is satisfactory, that is, congruent with standards, no action is necessary. When it is not, however, corrective action must be taken.

6. *Take preventive action.*   As William Greenwood has observed, it is not enough simply to correct problems: one must act to ensure that the same problems do not occur again.[7] For example, the focus of creative problem solving efforts in total management (TQM) and of kaizen is to ensure that problems do not occur.[8]

This model, like most control systems, focuses on results (outputs). Often the consequence of such a feedback control system is continued unsatisfactory performance until the malfunction is discovered. This is a major reason that organizations are moving toward **continuous control,** checking results at least weekly and often daily. In some organizations control occurs simultaneously with the event.[9] Another technique for reducing the problems associated with feedback control systems is feedforward control. First suggested by Harold Koontz and Robert W. Bradspies, **feedforward control** focuses on inputs to the system and attempts to anticipate potential problems with outputs.[10] (See Figure 10.2.) This has been another focal point for Japanese control systems, culminating in programs such as TQM.

Feedforward control has wide applicability. For example, the feedforward principle underlies the concept of simulation modeling. What-if questions are, after all, examinations of hypothesized inputs to project their effects on system outputs. Performance can be simulated in any number of hypothetical situations to test for changes in basic assumptions. In fact, any situation with identifiable inputs that can be modeled can and should use feedforward control techniques.

Strategic control systems perform at least three critical functions: coordinating all the units within the firm (in conjunction with management and operational control systems), motivating unit managers, and indicating when and how to intervene if strategy goes awry.[11] Additional purposes include evaluating the underlying validity of the business, evaluating strategists' abilities, broadening the perspectives of all participants, and providing a forum for evaluating the mettle of strategists.[12]

Experience and research have revealed that any number of variables may cause performance to deviate from strategy. The assumptions under which strategy was formulated may change, or someone may fail to follow strategy, plans, and policies. As deviations from either assumptions or guidelines lead to unsatisfactory results, the successful strategy must have some means of control.

FIGURE 10.2   The Organization As a Processing System

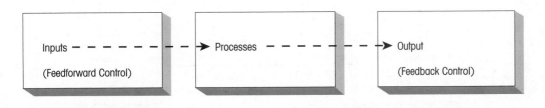

Inputs – – – – – – – → Processes – – – – – – – → Output
(Feedforward Control)   (Feedback Control)

What is controlled varies from level to level in the organization. The organization's strategists are responsible for strategic control, as are the stockholders through the board of directors.[13] Management control is a function primarily of top management, especially the CEO, while operational control is primarily a concern of lower-level managers. Traditionally, strategic control and management control have focused on broader perspectives than detail-oriented operational control. Note, however, that modern strategic information systems allow top managers to review the details of operations if they must. While much of our discussion deals with formal control systems, informal control systems may suffice in smaller organizations.

As we have suggested, strategic, management, and operational controls are not always clearly distinguishable. In general, however, strategic control is practiced principally at the corporate level, management control primarily at the business level, and operational control primarily at the functional level (see Figure 10.3). The figure suggests the important idea that these planning and control efforts should be linked horizontally to the relevant coprocesses, and vertically through objectives and standards to the other components of the respective processes—planning or control. What is evolving is an approach to control that

FIGURE 10.3 Relationship between Strategy and Control

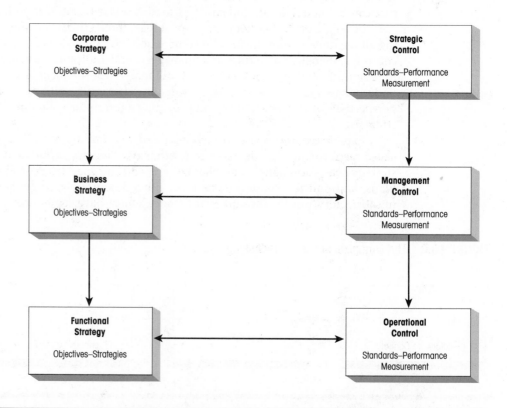

tightly integrates operational control and strategic control. The condition of the firm must be questioned at all levels, always, is the thinking of many.[14]

What is controlled strategically in multiple-SBU firms varies from what is controlled in single-SBU firms. In the multiple-SBU firm, business-unit performance is the primary issue.[15] In the single-SBU firm, both business-unit performance and functional-subunit performance must be controlled. However, the principles involved are virtually identical.

STRATEGIC CONTROL: EVALUATION OF CORPORATE STRATEGY AND BUSINESS STRATEGY

Once strategy has been formulated, it should be evaluated. Several criteria for strategic control have been suggested. The best-known set of criteria, developed by Seymour Tilles, can be summarized as follows:

1. Is the strategy internally consistent? Is it consistent with the organization's mission? Are its components consistent with each other?
2. Is it consistent with the environment (constituents' demands, competition, economy, product/industry life cycle, suppliers, customers)?
3. Is it consistent with internal resources?
4. Does it impose an appropriate amount of risk?
5. Does it have a proper time horizon?
6. Is it workable? Can it be implemented?[16] (The McKinsey seven S approach discussed in Chapter 9, is applicable here.)

E. P. Learned and his colleagues, building on the Tilles model, add the following questions:

7. Is the strategy identifiable? Has it been clearly and consistently stated and are people aware of it?
8. Is it appropriate to the personal values and aspirations of key managers?
9. Does it constitute a clear stimulus to organizational effort and commitment?
10. Is it socially responsible?
11. Do markets and market segments give early indications of responsiveness to the strategy?[17]

John Argenti adds four questions of his own:

12. Does the strategy rely on firm weaknesses or do anything to reduce weakness?
13. Does it exploit major opportunities?
14. Does it avoid, reduce, or mitigate the major threats? If not, does the firm have adequate contingency plans?[18]

Finally, Georg Schreyogg and Horst Steinman add:

15. Are the premises on which the firm based its strategy and implementation plans still valid?[19]

Intuitively, these questions seem sound. More important, they relate directly to the strategic management process model seen in Figure 1.1. In fact, these questions comprise a checklist that can be used to determine if the firm has properly followed strategic management process model. All these questions can be raised as the strategy progresses through its various stages, including implementation. They help define progress and changes and support establishment of specific standards of performance based on strategic objectives and subsequent component objectives. Milestones are important tools for this step-by-step strategic control.

Milestones are performance standards for various stages in the implementation of strategy. They may mark stages of project completion, market penetration, or other aspects of performance that concern management. By establishing these milestones, the organization does not have to wait until the completion of a strategy's implementation to determine whether or not the strategy will work.[20]

Once strategy is implemented, measurements will be taken to determine if the objectives have been reached. With variations from firm to firm, the tolerances established in Step 2 of the model are primarily judgmental. They tell how much deviation from the standard management can tolerate. Corrective and preventative actions may require changes in strategy.[21]

MANAGEMENT CONTROL: CONTROLLING BUSINESS STRATEGY AND OTHER MAJOR SUBUNIT STRATEGIES

Management control becomes a distinct concern in a decentralized organization structure. Management control functions within the framework established by the strategy to evaluate achievement of the objectives of the various substrategies and intermediate plans that make up the hierarchy of strategies. Normally these objectives (or standards) are established for major subsystems of the organization, such as SBUs, projects, products, functions, and responsibility centers, with allowable tolerances that vary from organization to organization. Typical management control measures include budgets and ROI, income, cost, product quality, and efficiency measures. These control measures are essentially summations of operational control measures. Corrective or preventive action may involve either very minor or very major changes in the strategy. When control measures indicate that performance is poor, top-management strategists may be replaced.

OPERATIONAL CONTROL

Operational control systems are designed to ensure that day-to-day actions are consistent with established plans and objectives. Operational control is concerned with the performance of individuals and groups in comparison with the roles prescribed for them by organizational plans. Such control systems normally are concerned with the past, except in feedforward systems. Focusing on events in a recent period, operational control systems are derived from the requirements of the management control system. Specific standards for performance are derived from the objectives of operating plans, which are based on intermediate plans, which in turn are based on strategy. Individual and group performance data are compared with objectives and corrective or preventative actions are taken when performance does not meet standards. Such actions may include training, motivation, leadership, discipline, or termination.

BENCHMARKING AND BEST PRACTICES[22]

As mentioned in Chapter 9, benchmarking and best practices evaluations are becoming common activities in U.S. firms. **Benchmarking** and **best practices** are essentially synonyms for control-based competitor analysis techniques that compare a firm's products (or services) and processes (including management) with those of the firms that set the highest standards for those products and/or processes   in the world. Learning how these high levels of performance were achieved allows the firm to seek to equal or surpass these best practices. Xerox pioneered benchmarking in the United States and General Electric initiated best practices. As control devices, these techniques use external standards (other firms' performance levels) as opposed to internal standards, typically corporate objectives. Such analyses fit neatly with programs of continuous improvement and innovation.

One of the major problems in benchmarking is finding competitors who will willingly cooperate to share information on their best practices. Some firms, therefore, use internal divisions as benchmarks. In addition, firms often seek information for benchmarks on the best practices of anyone in any industry, at a particular function rather than limiting themselves to competitors' practices. The U.S. government has encouraged these techniques by making benchmarking an important criterion in presenting the Malcolm Baldrige Award for quality.

TOTAL QUALITY MANAGEMENT

Total quality management (TQM) is the name for the effort to manage all aspects of the organization's input–transformation–output processes to control their impacts on quality. TQM commits the entire organization to improving quality. TQM is widely perceived as a major strategic weapon.[23] In fact, it has become so important to global competitiveness that we consider it to be a basic prerequisite for all firms and a strategic imperative for the 1990s. Failure to achieve relative high quality as perceived by the customer will simply prevent a firm from competing. Customer-perceived relative high quality has helped Japanese firms to dominate the consumer electronics and automobile industries in the U.S. marketplace for several years, for example. U.S. firms have made outstanding strides in improving quality in many industries, including in the auto industry, making them much more globally competitive.

One of the pioneers of total quality management was William Edwards Deming. Deming and Joseph M. Juran are widely credited with having taught the Japanese how to improve their quality to make them world-class competitors.[24] As

U.S., Canadian, and European firms have suffered competitively as a result, they have hired Deming, Juran, Zero-Defects creator Philip Crosby, and other quality consultants to help them achieve high quality.

Most firms implement the TQM concept by envisioning every user of firm output a customer. Subsequently, stages in the production process have internal customers who need to be satisfied if external customers are ultimately to be well satisfied. TQM normally tries to involve both customers and suppliers in an all-encompassing effort to achieve sound product/service development and customer satisfaction. Japanese firms now intend to leapfrog U.S. and European firms, which are just now adopting TQM, by aiming for zero defects.[25]

MEASURES OF STRATEGIC AND MANAGEMENT PERFORMANCE

Step 3 of the control process requires that the firm measure the results of strategy implementation. Most firms define identical strategic and management control techniques to follow the implementation of strategy. In fact, other than differentiating by organization level, strategic and management control may be one and the same thing.[26] The most common **measures of strategic and management performance** among U.S. firms are strategic plans, long-range plans, budgets, performance appraisals, policies and procedures, and statistical reports, including analyses of financial statements, profit measures, financial ratios like return on investment, and several additional factors.[27] These items may be inspected during routine reporting cycles, as part of consulting efforts, or as part of an internal or external audit. The objective of all of these endeavors is financial control. Financial control requires information on revenues, costs, profits, and funds flows for responsibility centers and the organization as a whole.

Financial control reports are changing in order to better provide strategic information upon which to make decisions. Accounting information based on typical U.S. cost-accounting procedures has proved insufficient to support strategic decisions and such programs as just-in-time inventory and TQM.[28] To remedy this lack of information, firms are moving to activity-based accounting and cost-drivers, trying to identify actual components of a product's cost, as opposed to using traditional overhead allocation systems based on more general factors.[29]

Thus, additional financial measures are being created to better support strategic decisions. Al Pipkin of Coors Brewing Company has called for the establishment of strategic accounting techniques to provide such information.[30] Such approaches are heavily influenced by Japanese management accounting (JMA) processes, which are used to influence decisions, not just to provide information. Whereas western management accounting tends to view reality as fixed and given, JMA views it as flexible and amorphous. The Japanese also interpret accounting to support strategy in a way that few western firms do, as this chapter's Strategic Challenge feature suggests.[31]

Firms are also examining their performance measures, recognizing that many of their current financial tools may be obsolete.[32] Firms are moving toward cross-functionally designed performance measures and accounting systems.[33] At Hewlett-Packard, for example, the manufacturing and accounting functions jointly

STRATEGIC CHALLENGE

HOW ACCOUNTING PROVIDES JAPANESE FIRMS WITH A STRATEGIC ADVANTAGE

Toshiro Hiromoto of Hitotsubashi University in Tokyo believes that Japanese management accounting practices give Japanese firms a source of competitive advantage. Japanese management accounting systems are designed to influence as much as to inform. These systems are also designed around market-driven strategies. For example, managers at Hitachi express an opinion shared by most managers in other Japanese firms that it is more important that the overhead allocation system and other aspects of management accounting motivate employees to work in harmony with the company's long-term goals than it is to pinpoint production costs. Japanese managers want their accounting systems to help create a competitive future, not quantify the performance of their organizations at present.

As an example of how accounting might be used strategically to motivate, Japanese firms don't set product costs according to the current states of their manufacturing capabilities, but rather according to what they want that state to be in order for the product to be cost competitive. Japanese management accounting is integrated with strategy and subservient to it, not independent, as in most western firms. Japanese management accounting systems are designed for strategic purposes. Western managers often use systems designed to keep track of costs for other purposes, such as calculating income taxes, as cost bases for strategic decisions.

Source: Toshiro Hiromoto, "Another Hidden Edge—Japanese Management Accounting," *Harvard Business Review*, July–August 1988, p. 23.

designed a cost accounting system that measured manufacturing costs much more accurately than the previous system had.[34]

Still, financial control is only part of the total strategic or management control process, because much nonfinancial activity affects financial performance. In recognition of this fact, many firms employ measures of strategic and managerial performance that are more comprehensive than those found on traditional financial statements. They focus on labor efficiency and productivity (which are especially important when firms compete internationally), quantity and quality of production, such human resource variables as personnel satisfaction, information from management by objectives systems, social performance measures (found by social audits), cost–benefit analysis results, operational audits of structural units, distribution cost and efficiency, network planning models, Gantt charts, market share data, inventory information, management audit results, model results, and so forth. Such perspectives become critical to future performance levels since many firms are coming to perceive these nonfinancial measures as more important than financial measures.[35]

When financial measures stress short-run results, as they often have in the past, they obviously induce managers to give more thought to looking good in the short run than to the long-term results that should claim their attention. A notable exception is SCM Corporation, which seeks a balance between long-range and short-range objectives, and emphasizes personnel development, as well.[36]

Return on Investment (ROI)

Wide coverage of the positive aspects of a decentralized structure have made it a popular organization design goal. As we saw earlier, however, a decentralized firm must control its subsystems. Such firms use two primary types of control systems to exert financial control over these units: those that control projects and those that control responsibility centers. Five responsibility centers can be identified:

1. *Standard cost centers* are those for which standard costs can be computed. Standard cost multiplied by number of units yields a measure of output.
2. *Revenue centers* are those for which revenues can be determined.
3. *Discretionary expense centers* are organizational units, normally staff units, whose outputs are not commonly measured in financial terms.
4. *Profit centers* are subsystems for which both costs and revenues can be measured, and to which responsibilities for the difference—profits—have been assigned.
5. *Investment centers* are profit centers for which the assets employed in obtaining profit are identified. (These are SBUs or major project divisions.)[37]

ROI (net income divided by total assets) is the performance measure most frequently used to evaluate the investment center. As we suggested when we discussed top-management motivation in Chapter 8, ROI is a critical issue in large organizations, for an inappropriate division control system that reduces executives' motivation can, and usually does, reduce profits. Indeed, while ROI analysis has several advantages, it also has several limitations.

Among the advantages of ROI analysis:

1. ROI is a single comprehensive figure influenced by everything that happens in the firm.
2. It measures how well the division manager uses the assets of the company to generate profits. It is also a good way the check on the accuracy of proposals for capital investment.
3. It is a common denominator that facilitates comparisons among many entities.
4. It provides an incentive to use existing assets efficiently.
5. It provides an incentive to acquire new assets only when they would increase returns.

Among the limitations of ROI analysis:

1. ROI is very sensitive to depreciation policy. Variations in depreciation write-offs among divisions affect it. Accelerated depreciation techniques reduce ROI, conflicting with discounted cash-flow analysis in capital budgeting.

2. ROI is sensitive to book value. Older plants with more depreciated assets and lower initial costs have relatively lower investment bases than newer plants, especially when considering the effect of inflation on the costs of newer plants and on replacement costs. This boosts the ROIs of older plants. A firm may defer investment in assets or dispose of them in order to increase ROI.

3. In many firms that measure performance by ROI, one division sells to another. As a result, transfer prices must be computed, and the expenses incurred affect profit. Since, in theory, the transfer price should reflect the transaction's impact on the firm's total profit, the managers of some investment centers are bound to suffer. Equitable transfer prices are difficult to determine.

4. If one division operates in an industry with favorable conditions and another in a depressed industry, ROI for the first will automatically look better than that for the other.

5. The time span of control for ROI is short, while the performance of division managers should be measured over the long run. The time span over which to evaluate top managers' is the length of time required for their performance to realize results.

6. The business cycle strongly affects ROI, often despite managerial performance.

Despite these criticisms, ROI is likely to continue as the leading index of management performance, if for no reason other than its simplicity. It must be supplemented by other decision information, though.

AT CYPRESS

Cypress's killer software is designed to help overcome the weaknesses of reliance on financial measures. Its performance measures help management to control performance across a wide variety of activities.

ROI is an important tool to control both the total organization and its subsystems. As we have noted, it is the most widely used measure of operating efficiency. While ROI represents net income as a percentage of total assets, it is a function of many variables, especially profit margin on sales and asset turnover. Figure 10.4 shows the factors that contribute to these two figures.

Management Audits, Strategic Audits, and Quality Audits

One of the major questions confronting organizations today is how to evaluate the performance of the top-management team. Several factors must be considered here:

1. Did top managers state a clear, compelling vision and establish viable goals and objectives? (Consider strategic intent here.)

FIGURE 10.4   Financial Analysis Based on ROI

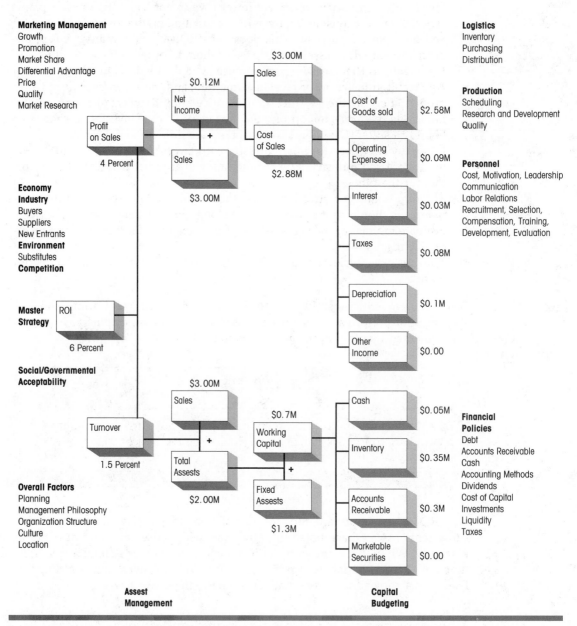

Source: Adapted from Ray Bressler, unpublished working paper. Reprinted with permission.

2. Did top managers achieve the objectives they established?
3. How good were their strategies to achieve objectives?
4. What factors beyond the control of top managers affected their performance?
5. How well have top managers anticipated and responded to these factors?
6. Have they proactively managed the future?

These questions set operational control criteria for top management, but strategy is the issue at hand.

Several systems have been devised to measure top managers' performance. One of the best, the **management audit,** examines all facets of organizational activity. The American Institute of Management (AIM) pioneered the management audit.[38] A typical management audit consists of 200 to 300 questions designed to test organizational performance. Completed questionnaires are analyzed by a team of auditors. Additional information comes from interviews with organizational managers, analyses of reports, and third-party sources. At the end of the audit process, the auditors may assign a point value to the organization in each of the audit categories, or they may reach a consensus on firm performance in some other way. Such audits have been widely used by many large corporations and by smaller firms, as well. These audits can be adapted to organizations with missions other than profit.

Management audits may follow a format that parallels the hierarchy of strategies (refer back to Table 5.1). Such an analysis is divided into three major parts: evaluation of corporate, business, and functional strategies. This approach recognizes product divisions, but examines strategy on the basis of functional activities within divisions. This appendix should be a key part of your analyses of companies and their situations. The strategic audit questions you have reviewed at the end of this text's chapters are the basis for such an audit.

The management audit technique has often predicted corporate performance successfully, but such audits have also predicted success for some companies that failed miserably. Probably the most important reason for such failures is drastic changes in the environment. Emerging strategic issues must always be monitored for surprises. Second, the technique assigns ratings rather arbitrarily. Few audits have developed specific point values for responses to individual questions. In fact, strict values would probably not be feasible. Auditors often disagree on their ratings of the firms.

Despite their weaknesses, management audits serve an important function. The bottom line may indicate problems, but only an audit of other areas can uncover the causes of those problems. A management audit is effective primarily because it looks beyond financial information and systematically appraises the performance of the organization and its management at all levels. Several authors have provided brief checklists of key issues that should concern firms including, for example, strategic focus, organization structure and culture, performance management, technology, product development and delivery, and quality and customer satisfaction.[39]

A **strategic audit** goes one step beyond the management audit and examines the organization's external environment. This allows for a full SWOT analysis. Strategic audit questions focus on the firm's relation to its external environment as well as on its internal functioning. The strategic audit is becoming an increasingly accepted technique in the formulation, evaluation, and control of strategy. The strategic audit questions at the end of each chapter of this book are typical of those you might find in a formal strategic audit.[40]

Because quality has become an important global competitiveness issue, top managers face increasingly thorough examination of their ability to achieve high product/service quality throughout the corporation. This is often determined by a quality audit. The **quality audit** is a thorough examination of the organization from the quality perspective. Perhaps the best known of such audits in the United States is that necessary to apply for the Malcolm Baldrige Award, which is given annually to the one or two best applicants in the areas of manufacturing, service, and small business. The Baldrige Award has been especially important in helping transform U.S. businesses to make them more globally competitive.[41] High levels of quality often reflect efforts in benchmarking and employee participation in quality improvement. This was certainly the case when Xerox won the award.[42] This chapter's Global Strategic Challenge feature discusses the quality effort at Xerox.

The many who do not win the Baldrige Award gain simply from applying. Completing the lengthy questionnaire requires a thorough self-examination, which leads to significant quality improvement in most cases.[43] For example, San Antonio-based USAA, a leading U.S. insurance firm, has failed to win the award in two previous attempts; as a runner-up, however, it feels it has improved the quality of all aspects of its operations, but especially customer service, in its attempt to win.[44]

The quality issue has long been important in Japan, which for many years has awarded the Deming and Juran Awards, more recently joined by the Crosby Award, named, ironically (and respectively), for U.S. quality-management consulting firms headed by William Edwards Deming, Joseph M. Juran, and Philip Crosby. European firms have increased their concerns for quality substantially in recent years as the 1992 initiative approached.[45]

Social Audits and Stakeholder Audits

Critics of business have called for social audits of corporations. A **social audit** is any device that attempts to evaluate an organization's social performance in areas such as environmental protection, equal employment opportunity, consumer satisfaction, government relationships, energy use, employee job satisfaction, and employee health and safety.

The aim of the social audit is to determine the impact of the firm on its stakeholders. While in some social areas, performance standards are readily definable, requirements and performance in many of these areas are extremely difficult to quantify. Also, parties frequently disagree as to exactly what a business ought to accomplish in these areas. Each group seems to have its own set of criteria, and obviously no business can respond to all of them. Nevertheless, many corporations have audited their activities in several areas of social responsibility. An expansion of the social audit concept leads to the **stakeholder audit** of performance from the viewpoints of all who are significantly affected by the organization's actions.[46]

Shareholder Value: Value-Based Strategic Management

Accounting measures rely on historical data. Rules govern the valuation of corporate assets on the basis of historical cost. There is evidence that the profit

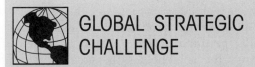

GLOBAL STRATEGIC CHALLENGE

XEROX COMPETES GLOBALLY ON THE BASIS OF QUALITY

Xerox Corporation was the dominant firm in the photocopying industry until the mid-1970s, when Japanese firms entered the low end of the market with less expensive products and higher levels of quality than Xerox offered. By 1980, it had become obvious that, in order to survive, Xerox had to evolve rapidly into a world-class organization and compete effectively on a global basis. Xerox began with SWOT analysis, including a study of the best practices of its competitors. In 1981, the company instituted a formal benchmarking program, adopting the best practices of its competitors, a technique it pioneered in the United States. It learned quickly that it took too long to develop new products, that these products cost too much, and that they didn't fully satisfy customer needs.

Xerox reacted by embracing kaizen, or continuous improvement. It cut costs to the bone and increased quality significantly, winning it the label of American Samurai for its Japanese-style results. It closed inefficient plants and modernized others. Xerox's Leadership through Quality program has become a way of life for all of its employees and for its suppliers' 30,000 employees. The program has two dominant philosophies: employees work as teams, and quality starts at the top of the chain of command. Then-CEO David T. Kearns claims that in 1990 the program reduced the firm's defective parts rate to 350 parts per million. Customer satisfaction has increased almost 40 percent and complaints have dropped almost 60 percent. But this was not enough. The 1991 strategic plan called for even more improvement, setting extremely challenging quality goals for everyone in the company. Strategic intent is at work at Xerox.

After a decade of hard work, Xerox won the Malcolm Baldrige Award for quality in 1989. It has met its Japanese competitors head-on in the copying business and stopped their erosion of its market share. Its latest advertising campaign guarantees 3 years of perfect service from its machines or they are repaired or replaced free, no questions asked. New products are being developed faster, and Xerox is now staking its future on a line of digital copying products using a new type of technology in an attempt to leapfrog its Japanese competitors.

Sources: Mohan Kharbanda, "Back from the Brink," *CMA Magazine*, July/August 1991, pp. 9–14; Kate Evans-Correia, "Quality 1991—Buying Quality: How Xerox Made Its Comeback," *Purchasing*, January 17, 1991, pp. 134–145; Beverly Geber, "Benchmarking: Measuring Yourself against the Best," *Training*, November 1990, pp. 36–44; "Xerox Unlocks Future with Training, Teamwork," *Purchasing World*, April 1990, p. 34; "Xerox Rethinks Itself and This Could Be the Last Time," *Business Week*, February 13, 1989, pp. 90–93.

made by a conglomerate may actually be lower than the combined profits that its individual companies would make if they were operated independently. Investors make investments on the basis of potential cash flows and risks. Considering these factors, we are not surprised that corporate raiders want to sell off corporate assets after a takeover. Stockholders want to see their interests protected, their cash flows increased, and their risks reduced. Following this trend, Bernie Reiman suggests that strategic decisions, such as SBU portfolio choices, should be based on **shareholder value**, that which brings the shareholder the greatest return.[47] Shareholder value analysis is especially useful if rigorous strategy analysis accompanies it.[48]

Ethics Audits

One of the most important audits that any firm can perform is the **ethics audit.** Such an audit examines how well managers have resolved ethical dilemmas in a recent period. Generally speaking, ethical audits examine managerial decision-making situations in terms of their complexity: ethical and legal, ethical but illegal, unethical but legal, and unethical and illegal.[49]

GROWING CONCERNS IN STRATEGIC CONTROL

Several additional factors should be considered with respect to strategic control. Among them are control policies, the role of information in the control process, integrated planning and control systems, the dysfunctional consequences of control systems, controlling the strategists, and organizational learning.

Control Policies

Just as organizations establish strategy and implementation policies, they must also establish policies to guide control. Control policies naturally evolve from the objectives and standards established for performance. The organization must indicate to its managers and other employees what specific objectives are, how performance will be measured, what comparisons will be made, and how differences between expectations and performance will be handled.

The organization needs policies establishing measurements for total performance, intermediate-level performance, and work-group and individual performance. The primary concern is to define the performance to be measured and the techniques for its measurement sufficiently explicitly that this will motivate employees to perform.

Information in the Control Process

A decision can be only as good as the information on which it is based. Both feedforward and feedback systems of strategic, management, and operational control permit comparisons and adjustments as information is received. Lack of information, as is common in management-by-exception control systems, can also

TABLE 10.1   Information Requirements by Type of Control

Characteristics of Information	Operational Control	Management Control	Strategic Control
Source	Largely internal	Internal, partly environmental	Internal and environmental
Scope	Well-defined, narrow	Moderately broad	Broad
Level of aggregation	Detailed	Aggregated	Aggregated
Time horizon	Historical	Historical	Future and historical
Frequency of use	Very frequent, continuous	Periodic	Occasional, but with increasing frequency

Source: Reprinted from ''A Framework for Management Information Systems,'' by G. Anthony Garry and Michael S. S. Morton, *Sloan Management Review*, Fall 1971, p. 59, by permission of the publisher. © 1971 by the Sloan Management Review Association. All rights reserved.

be significant. The information requirements for strategic control, management control, and operational control vary in scope, level of aggregation, time horizon, and frequency of use, as Table 10.1 indicates. The mass of information generated for operational control must be meaningfully reduced for reports to top management.

AT CYPRESS

Cypress Semiconductors has developed a sophisticated information system to keep its strategies working and to receive advance warning if they should falter. Unfortunately, most organizations lack a system as sophisticated as this for tracking strategic results.

Integrated Planning and Control Systems

Chapter 9 stressed the importance to planning of integrated planning and control: objectives, achievement of which is regularly evaluated, provide direction and motivation. Since objectives are anticipated results, they provide standards against which to measure performance. Management by objectives, results, and rewards (MBORR) and similar systems, budgets, and other planning and control systems can and should be employed to ensure successful mission accomplishment. Effective implementation requires careful control. Continuous improvement and monitoring are important characteristics of the new style.

Dysfunctional Consequences of Control Systems — The Need for Commitment

Control systems are sometimes formulated without considering the human beings whom they will control. The behavioral results in such a case are often dysfunctional. Divisional managers may intentionally neglect to invest in needed new plant and equipment, for example, in order to reduce total assets and thus improve their ROI figures. They may short-sightedly refuse to spend money to develop personnel to increase ROI by increasing net profit.

Budgets have also been shown to have undesirable consequences. In fact, managers and their subordinates may resent the pressures associated with budgets so deeply that inefficiency may result. Pressure from staff agencies to provide data for budget preparation may lead to conflicts between staff and line personnel. Such dysfunctional consequences of control systems may be found in even the best-managed firms. Organizations must recognize that individuals can find ways to beat control systems and they will work hard to get around unsound systems.

A sound approach to overcoming such dysfunctional consequences, and one in increasing use in organizations, is to induce employees to commit themselves strongly to their jobs and to the organization. Based largely on participative management and self-management, including self-control, the commitment approach makes employees eager to perform at high levels.[50] This approach has long been the cornerstone of Japanese management.

Controlling the Strategists

In Chapter 1, we noted that most boards of directors historically haven't asserted themselves in their relationship with top corporate management. But as more and more firms face disgruntled stockholders and the potential for stockholder lawsuits, more and more boards are taking action to control the behavior of corporate strategists. For example, General Motors' board of directors ousted Lloyd E. Reuss as president and COO in April 1992 and replaced him with John F. Smith, Jr. They also relieved chairman and CEO Robert Stempel from his duties as head of the board's executive committee. The board's outside members simply got tired of the red ink, and Stempel's slow-moving actions to alleviate it. They felt Reuss was not doing a proper job, so they replaced him with Smith, who had, four years earlier, completed a major turnaround of GM's European operations.[51]

Another major issue of control with regard to strategists has been their level of compensation. CEO pay is a much discussed issue in the United States. Stockholders and other stakeholders are asking whether or not executives should be compensated as much as some are. When annual pay plus stock options are totaled, a few executives will make tens of millions of dollars. Many make several million dollars. For example, in 1991 Leon Hirsch, chairman and CEO of U.S. Surgical was compensated with $114 million, Roberto Goizueta, chairman and CEO of Coca-Cola, $82.5 million, and Anthony O'Reilly, chairman and CEO of H.J. Heinz, $71.5 million. These megabuck rewards are greeted with outcrys in good times, but especially amid the layoffs of the recession of 1990–1992. Many are calling for a formula to determine CEO total compensation; for example, 20, 30, or 40 times the earnings of the average firm employee.[52] But in an ironic twist of corporate ethics, some firms, recognizing the potential for public concern over their CEO's compensation, attempted to hide the amount rather than address the issue. One such firm was Coca-Cola, as discussed in this chapter's Strategic Ethical Challenge feature.

Control As Organizational Learning

Earlier, in Chapter 9, we related Arie de Gues's observation that organizational learning might be the only sustainable competitive advantage. Since planning and control are so inextricably linked, it is only natural then that control be perceived as involving organizational learning. The standard control model as shown in most management texts depicts control as involving four steps: (1) establishing objectives; (2) measuring performance; (3) comparing performance against standards;

STRATEGIC ETHICAL CHALLENGE

COCA-COLA, SHOULD YOU HIDE YOUR CEO'S TRUE COMPENSATION?

Fortune magazine writer Geoffrey Colvin suggests that Coca-Cola is a leading contender for the Compensation Obfuscation Award of 1991. He notes that Coca-Cola artfully buried its reward of a one-million-share stock option to its CEO, Roberto Goizueta, in the fine print in its annual report. Quoting the report and its discussion of executive compensation: "Of the named executive officers, only Mr. Goizueta received an award in 1991. Mr. Goizueta received one million shares from the 1989 Restricted Stock Award Plan, which does not provide for reimbursement for taxes."

Colvin suggests that this prose violates SEC rule 240.14(a)-5(a), which requires that corporations report such rewards in figures. Since Goizueta's options were recently worth over $80 million, this is an amount most stockholders would like to know about. Coke officials indicate that they feel they have complied with SEC regulations with the above prose.

Goizueta has been an outstanding CEO, and some feel he justly deserves a major reward, having raised Coke stock's market value by 1,400 percent during his ten years as CEO. The questions being asked, however, are: Should he earn $80 million, even if averaged over several years, and did Coke properly, and in an upfront way, inform stockholders of his compensation?

Source: Geoffrey Colvin, "CEO Pay: How Coke Buried $80 Million," *Fortune*, May 4, 1992, p. 13.

and (4) taking action to correct any problems found and to prevent them from occurring again. The assumption of the model is that organizations learn something between steps three and four. New strategies clearly, then, depend on organizational learning.[53] This means that knowledge management must become an important part of strategic control.[54]

WHAT SHOULD BE MEASURED?

Having just stated that results are what counts, we may appropriately ask whether results are indeed all that should be considered when one evaluates the success of a strategy. Are other factors just as important as results? If so, what are they?

We believe that results-oriented systems are fundamental to organizational success. However, results do not always tell the whole story. This is a major reason that management audits typically incorporate questions on process and that strategic audits include questions on external environmental factors. Moreover, it is the reason that firms such as GE have employed process mapping and similar methods for examining processes and how they produce results. In fact, results could even exceed objectives if processes were scrutinized in more firms. Processes won't be examined in most companies, though, as long as results are sufficient to meet established standards.

STRATEGIC MANAGER'S SUMMARY

1. Strategic control is concerned with the appropriateness of strategy to the mission. Such control is ongoing. Management and operational control systems are extensions of the strategy—that is, once the strategy has been more specifically defined and implemented, the firm must ascertain whether the planned results or objectives have been achieved at within the organization as a whole and its major components (via management control) and among groups and individuals (via operational control).
2. Control techniques ensure that the organization accomplishes its missions. Strategic control is changing in that it is becoming more continous and is concerned with more than just financial results.
3. The pros of ROI include the fact that it is a comprehensive figure; the cons include the possibility of it leading to short-term orientation by managers. ROI allows companies and divisions to be compared.
4. Quality serves as a control mechanism because it defines acceptable performance critera at various points in the organization and at all points for TQM.
5. Typical financial controls give a quick and generally accurate look at the health and performance of the organization.
6. The value of the social audit in strategic control is ensuring the satisfaction of key stakeholders and ensuring that the firm is a good corporate citizen.
7. Some of the dyfunctional consequences of control strategies include "beating the system," lack of motivation, lowered performance, and short-sighted strategies on the part of managers and employees.
8. The management audit is an audit of essentially all areas of an organization's performance, not just those of a financial nature. The strategic audit expands

the management audit to include a more in-depth look at the environment in which the company operates. Ethics audits examine the ethics practices of the firm. Benchmarking and best practices uncover the best firms in the industry, what they do and why they do it. Total Quality Management (TQM) is a mind-set or philosophy aimed at improving quality at every point in the organization.

9. Growing concerns about strategic control include establishing control policies, the role of information in control, integrating planning and control systems, controlling strategists, organizational learning, and concern about that which should be measured.

KEY TERMS

benchmarking
best practices
continuous control
ethics audit
feedforward control
management audit
management control
measures of strategic and management
   performance
milestones
operational control
organizational control

quality audit
ROI
shareholder value
social audit
stakeholder audit
strategic audit
strategic control
total quality management (TQM)

DISCUSSION QUESTIONS

1. What is controlled by each of the three types of control? Why are three different types of control necessary?
2. Describe each of the strategic and management control measures discussed in this chapter. Why is each necessary?
3. How is control changing, and why?
4. What are the six steps of the feedback model?
5. What is feedforward control?
6. What three aspects of an organization should a management audit examine?
7. How would you explain a social audit to someone who was unfamiliar with the term?
8. What is the role of information in control?
9. How can the dysfunctional consequences of control be overcome?

STRATEGIC AUDIT QUESTIONS

1. Is the company properly controlling its strategy? If not, what actions should it take to improve strategic control?

2. Evaluate the company's strategy by answering the following questions:
   a. Is the strategy internally consistent? Is it consistent with the organization's mission and are its components consistent with each other?
   b. Is it consistent with the environment (constituents' demands, competition, the economy, product/industry life cycle, suppliers, customers)?
   c. Is it consistent with internal resources?
   d. Does it impose an appropriate amount of risk?
   e. Does it have a proper time horizon?
   f. Is it workable? Can it be implemented? (The McKinsey seven S approach, discussed in Chapter 8, is applicable here.)
   g. Is it identifiable? Has it been clearly and consistently stated and are people aware of it?
   h. Is it appropriate to the personal values and aspirations of key managers?
   i. Does it constitute a clear stimulus to organization effort and commitment?
   j. Is it socially responsible?
   k. Do markets and market segments give early indications of responsiveness to the strategy?
   l. Does the strategy rely on firm weaknesses or do anything to reduce weakness?
   m. Does it exploit major opportunities?
   n. Does it avoid, reduce, or mitigate major threats? If not, does the firm have adequate contingency plans?
   o. Are the premises that underlie the strategy and plans for its implementation still valid?
3. Perform ratio analysis on the firm, covering 3 to 5 years. What results do you find? What actions do you recommend?
4. Prepare common-sized income statements and balance sheets for this firm, covering 3 to 5 years. What results do you find? What actions do you recommend?
5. How strong is this firm's ROI? What steps do you recommend?
6. Using the model in Figure 10.4, analyze the firm's need for a change in strategy.
7. What would a social audit be likely to reveal about this firm?
8. Does this firm give evidence of any dysfunctional consequences of control?
9. Is this firm following an emergent strategy or an intended strategy?
10. How good are the firm's control systems?
    a. Strategic control
    b. Management control
    c. Operational control
11. Is the firm achieving the proper quality?
12. Is the firm approaching control in a continuous way, with a strategic orientation, for example, in its cost accounting system?

Endnotes

1. Lianabel Oliver, "Accountants as Business Partners," *Management Accounting*, June 1991, pp. 40–42.

2. Robert G. Eccles, "The Performance Measurement Manifesto," *Harvard Business Review*, January–February 1991, pp. 131–137.

3. For a review of recent strategic control literature, see Michael Goold and John J. Quinn, "The Paradox of Strategic Controls," *Strategic Management Journal*, January 1990, pp. 43–57; see also Peter Lorange, Michael F. Scott Morton, and Sumantra Ghoshal, *Strategic Control* (St. Paul, Minn.: West, 1986).

4. Goold and Quinn, "Paradox of Controls," p. 43.

5. For a discussion, see Michael M. Grady, "Performance Measurement: Implementing Strategy," *Management Accounting*, June 1991, pp. 49–53.

6. John Dearden, "Measuring Profit Center Managers," *Harvard Business Review*, September–October 1987, pp. 84–88.

7. See the following works by William T. Greenwood: *Business Policy: A Management and Audit Approach* (New York: Macmillan, 1967); *Decision Theory and Information Systems* (Cincinnati: SouthWestern Publishing, 1965); and *Management and Organizational Behavioral Theories* (Cincinnati: SouthWestern Publishing, 1965.)

8. Albert M. Koller, Jr., "TQM: Understanding the Basics of 'Total Quality Management'," *Manage*, May 1991, pp. 15, 27–28; Brian Burke and David Scalfano, "Toward Continuous Improvement," *Training*, January 1990, pp. 75–79.

9. For example, see Georg Kellinghusen and Klaus Wubbenhorst, "Strategic Control for Improved Performance," *Long Range Planning*, June 1990, pp. 30–40; and Georg Schreyogg and Horst Steinmann, "Strategic Control: A New Perspective," *Academy of Management Review*, January 1987, pp. 91–103.

10. W. Harold Koontz and Robert W. Bradspies, "Managing through Feedforward Control," *Business Horizons*, June 1972, pp. 25–36.

11. Goold and Quinn, "Paradox of Controls," p. 44.

12. Ram Charan, "How to Strengthen Your Strategy Review Process," *The Journal of Business Strategy*, Winter 1982, pp. 51–52.

13. Adrian Davies, "Strategic Planning for the Board," *Long Range Planning*, April 1991, pp. 94–100.

14. For example, see Richard Tanner Pascale, *Managing on the Edge* (New York: Simon and Schuster, 1990).

15. Michael Goold, "Strategic Control in the Decentralized Firm," *Sloan Management Review*, Winter 1991, pp. 69–81.

16. Seymour Tilles, "How to Evaluate Corporate Strategy," *Harvard Business Review*, July–August 1963, pp. 111–121.

17. Edward P. Learned et al., *Business Policy: Text and Cases* (Homewood, Ill.: Irwin, 1969), pp. 22–25.

18. John Argenti, *Systematic Corporate Planning* (New York: Wiley, 1974), pp. 266–267.

19. Schreyogg and Steinmann, "Strategic Control."

20. Davies, "Planning for Board."

21. For the history of the development of strategic control at General Electric Company PLC, see Stephen Bungay and Michael Goold, "Creating a Strategic Control System," *Long Range Planning*, June 1991, pp. 32–39.

22. Thomas A. Stewart, "GE Keeps Those Ideas Coming," *Fortune*, August 12, 1991, pp. 41–49; "First Find Your Bench," *The Economist*, May 11, 1991, p. 72; Regina Eisman, "Why It Pays to Lose the Baldrige Competition," *Incentive*, April 1991, pp. 33–43, 98; Karen Bemowski, "The Benchmarking Bandwagon," *Quality Progress*, January 1991, pp. 19–24; Beverly Geber, "Benchmarking: Measuring Yourself against the Best," *Training*, November 1990, pp. 36–44;

23. J. M. Juran, "Strategies for World-Class Quality," *Quality Progress*, March 1991, pp. 81–85.

24. For example, see "The Leading Light of Quality," *U.S. News & World Report*, November 28, 1988, pp. 53–56; Myron Tribus, "Deming's Way," *Mechanical Engineering*, January 1988, pp. 26–30.

25. Peter Drucker, "Japan: New Strategies for a New Reality," *The Wall Street Journal*, October 2, 1991, p. 12.

26. Ralph E. Drtina, Helen Deresky, and Theodore T. Herbert, "Toward Designing Strategic Control Systems for Strategic Management," paper presented to the Eastern Academy of Management, 1988.

27. Richard L. Daft and Norman B. Macintosh, "The Nature and Use of Formal Control Systems for Management Control and Strategy Implementation," *Journal of Management 10*, no. 1 (1984), pp. 43–66.

28. Gerald H. Ross, "Revolution in Management Control," *Management Accounting*, November 1990, pp. 23–27.

29. Robin Cooper and Robert S. Kaplan, "Measure Costs Right: Make the Right Decisions," *Harvard Business Review*, September–October 1988, pp. 96–103; Frank Collins and Michael L. Werner, "Improving Performance with Cost Drivers," *Journal of Accountancy*, June 1990, pp. 131–134.

30. Oliver, "Accountants as Partners."

31. Jusuf Hariman, "Influencing Rather Than Informing: Japanese Management Accounting," *Management Accounting*, March 1990, pp. 44–46.

32. Eccles, "Measurement Manifesto"; and Daniel P. Keegan, Robert G. Eiler, and Charles R. Jones, "Are Your Performance Measures Obsolete?" *Management Accounting*, June 1989, pp. 45–50.

33. Michael W. Grady, "Performance Measurement: Implementing Strategy," *Management Accounting*, June 1991, pp. 49–53.

34. Debbie Berlant, Reese Browning, and George Foster, "How Hewlett-Packard Gets Numbers It Can Trust,"

Harvard Business Review, January–February 1990, pp. 178–183.

35. Eccles, "Measurement Manifesto."

36. George E. Hall, "Reflections on Running a Diversified Company," *Harvard Business Review*, January–February 1987, pp. 84–92.

37. Robert N. Anthony, John Dearden, and Richard F. Vancil, *Management Control Systems* (Homewood, Ill.: Irwin, 1972), pp. 200–203.

38. Jackson Martindell, *The Appraisal of Management* (New York: Harper, 1962).

39. For an example, see Robert O. Knorr, "A Corporate Self-Assessment Checklist," *The Journal of Business Strategy*, September/October 1990, pp. 61–62.

40. For an overview, see A. J. Prager and M. B. Shea, "The Strategic Audit," in *The Strategic Management Handbook*, edited by K. J. Alpert (New York: McGraw-Hill, 1983).

41. David A. Garvin, "How the Baldrige Award Really Works," *Harvard Business Review*, November–December 1991, pp. 80–95.

42. "Leadership through Quality," *Transportation & Distribution*, May 1991, p. 14.

43. Eisman, "Lose the Baldrige."

44. Heather C. Waldron, "The Quality Revolution: 'Do the Right Thing'," *Limra's Marketfacts*, July/August 1991, pp. 33–39.

45. For example, see Brooks Tigner, "Crusading for Quality," *International Management*, July/August 1989, pp. 34–36.

46. R. E. Freeman, *Strategic Management: A Stakeholder Approach* (Boston: Pitman, 1984).

47. Bernard C. Reiman, *Managing for Value* (Oxford, Oh.: Planning Forum, 1987).

48. George S. Day and Liam Fahey, "Putting Strategy into Shareholder Value Analysis," *Harvard Business Review*, March–April 1990, pp. 156–167.

49. Judy C. Nixon, Carolyn Wiley, and Judy West, "Beyond Survival: Ethics for Industrial Managers," *Industrial Management*, May/June 1991, pp. 15–18.

50. Richard E. Walton, "From Control to Commitment in the Work Place," *Harvard Business Review*, March–April 1985, pp. 77–85.

51. James B. Treece, "The Board Revolt," *Business Week*, April 20, 1992, pp. 30–35.

52. Kevin Maney and Michelle Osborn, "Megabucks Amid Layoffs Stoke Outrage," *USA Today*, March 27, 1992, p. B1.

53. Robert Simons, "Strategic Orientation and Top Management Attention to Control Systems," *Strategic Management Journal*, January 1991, pp. 49–62.

54. Ikujiro Nonaka, "The Knowledge Creating Company," *Harvard Business Review*, November/December 1991, pp. 96–104; Thomas A. Stewart, "Brainpower," *Fortune*, June 3, 1991, pp. 44–57.

INTEGRATIVE CASE ANALYSIS
CHAPTER 10

THE CHALLENGES FACING GENERAL MOTORS IN 1992

General Motors failed to monitor its strategy in relation to changing environmental conditions. The SWOT it forecast failed to materialize, and the firm had numerous warning signals by 1985. It should then have reoriented its investment strategy from technology toward human resources. It should have seen the need for styling changes. It got too caught up in implementing Smith's vision to recognize that something was amiss. People who did see this apparently were afraid to rock the boat, so GM floundered, requiring massive restructurings in 1987, 1988, 1991, and 1992.

From 1989 to 1991, GM's profits declined substantially and then became losses. An early strategic audit would have revealed market problems that could not be uncovered by financial analysis. Record profits in 1988 might actually have been seen to portend the strategic problems that later became all too apparent: lack of differentiation, excessive costs, lack of responsiveness to the market, and living off cash from the European auto operation and nonautomotive SBUs.

A company such as GM uses all of the standard control measures, especially financial controls. While GM was concerned about strategy, however, it was not attuned to changes in its environment. It ought to have been forecasting strategic scenarios and monitoring the environment for signals of change. GM was engaging in strategic planning when it would have done better to practice strategic thinking. It should have been lobbying more in Washington, D.C., to forestall Japanese lobbying efforts.

Stempel brought a breath of fresh air to GM. He recognized the need to increase market share. As a result of programs begun under Roger Smith's tenure, Cadillac won the Malcolm Baldrige Award in 1990.

Changes in control procedures have been instituted. Control is now more continuous. Information systems are being integrated. Employee participation is being sought to improve quality in broader segments of the company. Yet, in some cases, problems remain, even at Saturn. As 1991 drew to a close, GM found it necessary to restructure for the fourth time since 1987, announcing additional plant closings and layoffs in an attempt to eliminate unprofitable lines, cut layers of management, and become more responsive while it cut costs. It is likely John Smith, the firm's new president, will focus on increasing control of costs and quality.

CHAPTER 11

GLOBAL STRATEGY

Clearly, Japan has replaced the United States as the world's financial leader.

R. Taggart Murphy
Chase Manhattan Asia Limited

The new global competitors approach strategy from a perspective that is fundamentally different from that which underpins western management thought.

Gary Hamel and C. K. Prahalad
Authors, Consultants, and Researchers

CHAPTER OBJECTIVES

By the time you complete this chapter, you should be able to:

1. Describe what globalization of business means and give some examples
2. Describe Porter's competitive-advantage-of-nations model and use it to evaluate a country such as the United States
3. Identify the triad of key markets and enumerate important factors about each
4. Discuss the Japanese as competitors
5. Review the strengths of the four Asian tigers
6. Describe Europe in 1992 and its impact on North American and Japanese firms
7. Discuss the implications of East/West integration
8. Describe global strategy and how managers should manage in a global environment, identifying varying impacts of economic, political/legal, social/cultural, and technological forces
9. Identify the various stages of strategic activities in a global business
10. Describe typical macro-organization structures for global corporations
11. Describe the problems involved in implementing global strategy
12. Discuss controlling global strategy

MOTOROLA: A SUCCESSFUL GLOBAL COMPETITOR

Few companies can compete head-on with Japanese firms anywhere on the globe, and only a handful can compete with them in Japan. Motorola is one of those companies. It has been successful against Japanese companies in many ways by imitating them. It invests heavily in research and development, insists on supreme quality, and provides zealous service to its customers. At a time when European firms such as Philips and SGS-Thomson are forging ahead to take advantage of Europe 1992, Motorola is still increasing its European market share in chips and telecommunications. It has been leapfrogging the industry with new products thanks to its heavy investment in research and development, for example, the Micro Tac cellular phone, a "Star Trekky" unit that slips into a coat pocket and is a third lighter than the next lightest portable phone from a Japanese competitor. Another product, the first wristwatch pager, also resulted from extensive research and development and team design. Both products seem to have scooped the world by several months. As a result of these and other actions, Motorola is now the number one chip maker in the United States, number four in the world, and on the rise in Japan thanks largely to its strategic alliance with Toshiba. It has become the number three supplier of chips in Southeast Asia. It has developed a whole new breed of chips, digital signal processing (DSP) chips, which are special-purpose microprocessors tailored to handle images, sounds, and similar streams of information. Motorola's real strengths lie in the cellular phone market, where it captured at least 50 percent of the revenues of over $10 billion in 1990 with profits of $500 million.

This success has not come easily. What is surprising is that it has come so quickly. As late as 1986, Motorola was on the ropes, beaten back by Japanese competitors, but Chairman of the Board Robert W. Galvin, son of the firm's original founder and owner of 6 percent of the company's stock, determined along with CEO George Fisher that Motorola would battle Japan, Inc. in as many markets as it could and beat them at their own game. The firm has three critical objectives. The first is Six Sigma Quality, statistical jargon for near-perfect manufacturing at a rate of just 3.4 defects per million products. The second is to continue to improve already high levels of customer satisfaction. Canon, Inc. was so impressed with the company's desire to please that it chose a Motorola microprocessor as the heart of its hot-selling EOS 35-mm camera. The third point of its strategy is its investment in long-term research and development. Japanese firms really do not have to react to stock market investors because stocks are so tightly held there, so they are able to invest long term without much hassle. Motorola stock trades on the New York Stock Exchange and consequently the firm has had to figure out ways to get higher returns on its money and to get capital to work much faster.

Another important part of Motorola's strategy is to increase employees' awareness of corporate goals and make them better managers and employees. All 105,000 employees have been trained in corporate goals. Some courses explore global competitiveness and risk taking, others hone practical skills in statistics and ways of reducing product cycle times. This type of commitment from employees is expensive. In 1989 the company spent $60 million on employee education. Another key factor is improving commitment to company goals; approximately 3 percent of Motorola's total pay was spent on bonuses pegged to improving quality. Finally, Motorola works to improve team orientation of people within the various divisions. Motorola uses cross-functional teams to speed products to market faster. The company does not overlook the important political side either. Much of Galvin's time is spent lobbying in Washington, Tokyo, or other cities where politics play an important role in breaking down foreign countries' trade barriers.

Sources: Lois Therrien, "The Rival Japan Respects," *Business Week*, November 13, 1989, pp. 108–118; Amy Borrus, "Carving Out a Place in the Pacific Century," *Business Week*, November 11, 1991, pp. 64–68.

Probably no other global competitor could more clearly demonstrate the significance of strategic intent and vision than Motorola. Badly bludgeoned by Japanese firms and forced to withdraw from several markets because of these firms' superiority, Motorola formed a vision of long-term product development and cost improvement and made it pay off. It motivated its employees to fulfill its strategic intents, and this has made it a successful global competitor, even competing with the Japanese in their home market by forging an alliance with Toshiba.

The world is changing so rapidly, especially in interdependent and economic aspects, that many firms find it difficult to adapt. For example, since 1989 the Iron Curtain has fallen as, one-by-one, eastern European countries have asserted their independence from the Soviet Union and have overthrown their governments. In December 1991, the Soviet Union followed its policies of perestroika and glasnost by dissolving itself to become the Commonwealth of Independent States, at least partly because of its failure to build infrastructure quickly enough to support the trend toward capitalism. Gorbachev is out; Yeltsin is in.[1]

Germany has been reunited. China went through a counterrevolution that culminated in the massacre at Tiananmen Square. In 1992 the single most important economic event since the formation of OPEC was to be completed when the 12 nations of the European Economic Community continued their movement toward totally free trade, including the elimination of all barriers and setting common standards for products. Mexico's new president has taken strong action to improve business conditions, and Canada, Mexico, and the United States have moved to create a free trade zone.[2] Korea, Taiwan, Singapore, and Hong Kong have become such formidable competitors that many people see the 21st century as the century of the Pacific Rim. Japan has slowly admitted a few foreign competitors and has reduced some trade barriers, yet it remains a closed country by most accounts. The Iraqi war devastated, for a short period of time, several industries, among them travel and oil. A recession struck most industrialized countries throughout the globe.

All of these events took place from 1989 through 1991 and all have presented opportunities and threats to business organizations throughout the globe. For example, European organizations may well benefit greatly from integration in 1992, which gives them the largest of the three major domestic markets—Japan, North America, and Europe. Similarly, U.S. and European firms are expected to benefit significantly from the rebuilding of Kuwait after the Iraqi war.

These are but a few of the events changing global strategic management. There are several indicators of just how global business has become. Over 80 percent of Coca-Cola Company's 1989 profits came from its foreign subsidiaries; Coke made more profit in Japan than in the United States.[3] For years the Japanese have been successfully penetrating U.S. markets in automobiles, electronics, steel, and other manufactured goods. Thousands of Americans daily purchase shoes made by Reebok, a British company that manufactures in Korea. The British annually purchase thousands of automobiles from Ford, an American company, that have been assembled in England with parts manufactured in 13 different European countries. Finally, many U.S. firms have moved manufacturing facilities to Mexico in search of cheap labor.

The world of business has changed and there is no going back. Global competition is the name of the game. Firms must formulate and successfully implement and control global strategies in order to survive and prosper in the 1990s and the 21st century.

This globalization of business has given rise to a need to formulate global strategy, and has made significant impact on the practice of strategic management. This chapter addresses the key issues of how strategic management is changing and will have to change to adapt to this changing situation. This chapter reviews the globalization of business, the requirements of global competition, the triad of key global markets, strategy management in a global environment, various entry strategies, and the risks involved in global competition.

THE GLOBALIZATION OF BUSINESS

A brave new world of almost borderless trade is evolving. Hybrid companies and products lacking clear nationalities are emerging. Joint ventures, mergers, acquisitions, and other forms of alliances will characterize the future business world. For example, Ford Motor Company's compact car, the Probe, was designed in Detroit, engineered in Hiroshima by equity partner Mazda, and assembled in Michigan. Similarly, Mitsubishi and Chrysler have jointly produced identical versions of two cars, the Mitsubishi Eclipse/Plymouth Laser and the Mitsubishi 3000GT/Dodge Stealth. Hewlett-Packard and Canada's Northern Telecom pooled their know-how to tap the enormous new market for corporate information systems. A leather processing subsidiary of Tata, the Indian conglomerate, is teaming up with France-based TFR to compete with Italian marketers of upscale leather goods. Caterpillar and Mitsubishi are teaming up to make giant earth movers.[4]

Thomas J. Peters and John Naisbitt have both identified the trend toward global business as one of the ten key changes of the present and the near future.[5] Naisbitt sees a change from national to global business. Peters sees United States firms getting serious about being global competitors. He thinks that U.S. firms won't just take products designed and manufactured in the United States and sell them abroad, but rather will create new markets and new products abroad, and will run finance and manufacturing operations there. He feels it is especially important for CEOs to have international experience and learn languages of other countries. *The Wall Street Journal*'s description of the CEO of the next century clearly includes experience abroad as an important characteristic, and this may very well be someone from abroad.[6]

Changes in Global Business—The Global Perspective

A fundamental change is occurring in the nature of business. Many firms are moving beyond accepting the possibility of international opportunities and threats to a point where they recognize that global considerations must be part of their overall game plans. Most small- and medium-sized firms won't actively pursue global strategies in the sense of integrated strategic efforts in several countries, but they must view their businesses from a global perspective. They must learn to **think global.** They must recognize that global competitors will enter their marketplaces as part of global strategies, and that global opportunities and even global threats must influence formulation of strategy.

Yet, based on the success of firms such as Sony, firms must also **think local.** Chairman Akio Morita of Sony explains Sony Corporation's policy of **global localization** as a combination of local management styles and marketing with an overall global corporate philosophy.[7]

AT MOTOROLA

Motorola was vulnerable to Japanese competition. While it had not truly thought globally before, once Japanese competition entered and dominated its markets, it had to learn to compete globally.

The fundamentals of the game are also changing, however. In a key change, non-U.S. firms are gaining more relative power in the global economy. Nine of the world's ten largest banks in 1990 were Japanese, as shown in Table 11.1. In 1980, only one of the world's ten largest banks was Japanese.[8] Whether measured by deposits or assets, only one U.S. bank, Citicorp, made the top 25 in 1990. Japanese-owned banks supplied more than 20 percent of all credit granted in the state of California in 1988.[9] Further, as shown in Table 11.2, in 1989, 9 of the world's 25 largest industrial companies were American, 11 were European, 4 were Japanese, and 1 was Korean. Fourteen were American and 11 were European in 1980; none of the 25 largest industrial companies were Japanese, and none were Korean.[10]

The United States ran foreign trade deficits of $100 billion a year or greater for seven consecutive years from 1984 to 1990.[11] Much of this deficit came from trade with Japan and other Pacific Rim countries, and with OPEC countries. These deficits have made Japanese banks and private investors in OPEC nations rich and powerful. These deficits also give the Japanese still more ability to affect the world's capital markets. Correlated with this, the United States went from the world's largest lending nation in 1980 with a surplus of $106 billion to the world's largest debtor nation in less than 10 years with a debt of $368 billion in 1987.[12] This gives Japanese banks great power to influence American firms' debt structures and capability to expand because they hold much of that debt.[13]

Firms from member nations of the European Economic Community in 1992 have a home market of 320 million people. U.S. firms' home market numbers 243 million, and Japanese firms have a home market of 120 million people. For the first time in history, European firms have a domestic consumer base large enough to enable them to be true global competitors. In addition, the international debt crisis seems to be affecting American banks more than any others. U.S. banks hold nearly $50 billion in potentially bad foreign loans.[14]

It is becoming clear that the U.S. leadership role in the world, especially in the world of business, is being challenged.[15] Yet, for all its difficulties, it is likely to retain its overall global leadership based on its strengths, principally its consumer base and its military power. With the world changing so rapidly, however, and with the role of military power changing so rapidly, it is difficult to predict the global situation in a few years.[16]

PORTER'S COMPETITIVE ADVANTAGE OF NATIONS

Michael Porter, strategic consultant, author, and researcher, has thoroughly analyzed the nature of global competition. He suggests that whether or not a firm will be competitive globally depends on the four key factors identified in Figure 11.1: factor conditions; demand conditions; related and supporting industries; and company strategy, structure, and rivalry. These constitute **Porter's dynamic diamond**.

Factor conditions determine a nation's abilities to turn the basics, for example, natural resources, education, and infrastructure, into a specialized advantage. **Demand conditions** depend on the number and sophistication of domestic customers for the industry's product or service. **Related and supporting industries,** or the company a company keeps, include suppliers and competitors in supportive industries. Finally, **company strategy, structure, and rivalry** complete Porter's dynamic diamond.[17] (Rivalry reflects the conditions governing a nation's businesses, especially competition.)

Porter's work suggests that fierce domestic competition is one of the most significant factors in being competitive globally. Furthermore, the notion that a simple resource or special advantage can make you competitive globally just does not hold. The more points of the diamond that are positive for a firm, the better the firm's chances and the more likely that it will have a sustainable competitive advantage. Porter suggests, for example, that Japanese firms are more likely than United States firms to have sustainable competitive advantages for several reasons. They face intense domestic competition and U.S. firms don't. The Japanese education system is superior. Japanese firms have strong supportive industries. Finally, there is strong consumer demand for many products in Japan. It is clear that U.S. firms face an uphill battle in world competition based on brain power.[18]

Porter also identifies chance and government as two factors that influence a firm's success. Chance is outside a firm's influence, but government is not. Again, Japanese firms have generally closer ties to government than do U.S. firms. Furthermore, they lobby at home and abroad, especially in the United States, much more, and much more effectively, than do U.S. firms, as this chapter's Strategic Ethical Challenge feature suggests.[19]

TRIAD OF KEY MARKETS

Kenichi Ohmae, senior partner in Tokyo for the consulting firm McKinsey & Company, has identified a triad of key global business markets: Japan, Europe, and

TABLE 11.1   World's 25 Largest Banks, December 31, 1990

			Assets	Deposits		Loans
			$Millions	$Millions	Rank	$Millions
1	Dai-Ichi Kangyo Bank	Japan	$435,718.4	$317,149.2	1	$227,998.8
2	Sumitomo Bank	Japan	407,105.5	290,411.6	2	201,882.6
3	Fuji Bank	Japan	403,725.3	280,739.7	4	209,124.0
4	Mitsubishi Bank	Japan	392,208.9	280,905.1	3	205,773.1
5	Sanwa Bank	Japan	387,452.2	278,049.5	5	200,747.5
6	Crédit Agricole	France	304,706.1	220,212.6	9	237,576.7
7	Banque Nationale de Paris	France	291,394.6	245,616.2	6	227,742.0
8	Crédit Lyonnais	France	286,859.8	222,905.7	8	218,110.8
9	Industrial Bank of Japan	Japan	285,158.8	214,892.9	10	155,818.2
10	Deutsche Bank	Germany	267,308.1	239,750.7	7	214,968.4
11	Barclays Bank	Britain	260,129.6	213,654.7	11	208,862.3
12	Tokai Bank	Japan	246,017.3	180,378.4	15	131,265.0
13	National Westminister Bank	Britain	233,541.3	205,061.3	13	202,558.1
14	ABN Amro Holding	Netherlands	232,831.9	211,240.4	12	133,381.3
15	Bank of Tokyo	Japan	228,443.0	154,084.9	22	110,476.8
16	Mitsubishi Trust & Banking	Japan	226,291.2	193,741.5	14	97,120.2
17	Norinchukin Bank	Japan	224,034.7	177,656.7	16	95,345.5
18	Mitsui Bank	Japan	221,297.5	159,083.3	21	127,302.1
19	Société Générale	France	219,622.9	163,889.8	19	153,023.1
20	Citicorp	United States	216,986.0	142,452.0	26	151,857.0
21	Long-Term Credit Bank of Japan	Japan	201,674.3	151,574.2	23	122,491.7
22	Sumitomo Trust & Banking	Japan	194,407.3	172,370.5	18	83,866.4
23	Dresdner Bank	Germany	189,222.0	172,781.6	17	149,114.5
24	Compagnie Financière de Paribas	France	185,279.2	123,856.3	35	122,896.1
25	Mitsui Trust & Banking	Japan	185,004.2	160,417.4	20	104,884.4

Source: "The 100 Largest Commercial Banking Companies," *Fortune*, August 26, 1991, p. 174. Reprinted by permission from *Fortune* © 1991 (1990). The Time Inc. Magazine Company. All rights reserved.

North America.[20] Any global corporate player must be able to compete in each of those markets. The following sections examine each of the major legs of the triad.

Japan

Using a western analogy, the Japanese economy has proven to be a phoenix, rising from the ashes of World War II to unparalleled heights. The following paragraphs

Loans	Profits		Stock-holders' Equity		Employees	
Rank	$Millions	Rank	$ Millions	Rank	Number	Rank
2	$1,012.2	7	$11,828.0	4	18,466	50
10	1,287.1	2	12,936.6	2	16,479	55
6	1,075.6	5	11,414.7	6	15,377	60
8	995.7	9	10,491.3	10	14,026	62
11	1,134.5	3	11,088.9	8	13,604	64
1	862.5	11	12,777.9	3	74,451	8
3	296.8	55	6,730.4	21	59,772	12
4	680.8	18	10,246.1	11	68,486	10
12	592.5	24	8,196.3	15	5,067	89
5	633.9	22	10,904.9	9	68,552	9
7	1,051.4	6	11,773.5	5	116,500	3
19	349.0	51	6,535.5	22	11,754	69
9	662.2	20	11,393.6	7	112,600	4
18	727.4	14	8,530.5	14	59,634	13
27	550.2	29	5,868.9	28	17,081	52
36	477.1	37	4,751.5	42	6,513	81
37	245.4	60	1,266.3	91	3,094	95
20	502.6	34	5,502.2	32	10,565	72
13	491.8	36	5,474.1	33	45,776	17
14	458.0	39	9,730.0	13	95,000	5
23	428.2	42	6,493.2	23	3,593	94
42	492.6	35	4,984.5	39	7,089	79
15	559.0	28	6,859.1	18	42,217	20
22	467.0	38	6,055.9	27	26,900	34
30	377.3	46	3,820.2	52	6,354	84

discuss what makes the Japanese so successful, and then review some of the changes affecting their potential for continued success.

What Makes Japanese Firms Successful The official view of the Keidanren, the powerful federation of Japanese businesses, is that Japanese success results from a complex interaction of macro and micro variables involving government, capital, labor, and technology, as shown in Table 11.3. Note how

TABLE 11.2 World's 25 Biggest Industrial Corporations, December 31, 1990

		Sales		Profits
		$Millions	Percent Change from 1989	$Millions
1 General Motors	United States	$125,126.0	(1.5)	$(1,985.7)
2 Royal Dutch/Shell Group	Britain/Netherlands	107,203.5	25.3	6,442.1
3 Exxon	United States	105,885.0	22.2	5,010.0
4 Ford Motor	United States	98,274.7	1.4	860.1
5 International Business Machines	United States	69,018.0	8.8	6,020.0
6 Toyota Motor	Japan	64,516.1	6.7	2,993.3
7 Iri	Italy	61,433.0	25.2	926.5
8 British Petroleum	Britian	59,540.5	20.3	3,013.1
9 Mobil	United States	58,770.0	15.3	1,929.0
10 General Electric	United States	58,414.0	5.7	4,303.0
11 Daimler-Benz	Germany	54,259.2	33.6	1,041.6
12 Hitachi	Japan	50,685.8	(0.4)	1,476.9
13 Fiat	Italy	47,751.6	30.0	1,346.4
14 Samsung	South Korea	45,042.0	28.0	N.A.
15 Philip Morris	United States	44,323.0	13.4	3,540.0
16 Volkswagen	Germany	43,710.2	25.8	651.6
17 Matsushita Electric Industrial	Japan	43,516.1	1.0	1,649.1
18 Eni	Italy	41,761.9	54.0	1,696.9
19 Texaco	United States	41,235.0	27.2	1,450.0
20 Nissan Motor	Japan	40,217.1	11.5	808.2
21 Unilever	Britain/Netherlands	39,971.5	13.3	1,636.8
22 E. I. du Pont de Nemours	United States	39,839.0	13.2	2,310.0
23 Chevron	United States	39,262.0	33.3	2,157.0
24 Siemens	Germany	39,227.6	20.1	913.0
25 Nestlé	Switzerland	33,359.0	13.6	1,634.5

Source: "The World's Biggest Industrial Corporations," *Fortune*, July 29, 1991, p. 245. Reprinted by permission from *Fortune* © 1991 (1990). The Time Inc. Magazine Company. All rights reserved.

these items, and others to be mentioned shortly, fit into Porter's diamond model. Items 3 and 4 in the table, macro and micro labor factors, are essentially the same factors that William G. Ouchi identified in his research on the relationship of Japanese management practice to success.[21] In addition, factors such as a highly educated work force, favorable government policy, and a high savings rate are

Profits		Assets		Stock-holders' Equity		Employees	
Rank	Percent Change from 1989	$Millions	Rank	$Millions	Rank	Number	Rank
485	(147.0)	$180,236.5	1	$30,047.4	5	761,400	1
1	(0.6)	106,349.1	4	53,716.4	1	137,000	37
3	42.7	87,707.0	5	33,055.0	4	104,000	62
58	(77.6)	173,662.7	2	23,238.1	7	370,400	6
2	60.2	87,568.0	6	42,832.0	2	373,816	4
7	13.8	55,340.3	10	27,803.5	6	96,849	67
53	(21.3)	N.A.	—	N.A.	—	419,500	2
6	(13.9)	59,199.2	9	21,215.4	9	116,750	49
13	6.6	41,665.0	20	17,072.0	11	67,300	102
4	9.2	153,884.0	3	21,680.0	8	298,000	10
46	(70.9)	44,982.6	17	11,531.1	21	376,785	3
28	2.1	49,455.6	12	16,226.3	13	290,811	11
34	(44.2)	66,026.6	7	14,757.4	16	303,238	9
—	—	N.A.	—	N.A.	—	N.A.	—
5	20.2	46,569.0	14	11,947.0	20	168,000	24
78	24.5	41,892.3	19	9,027.6	31	268,744	13
21	(0.9)	49,747.9	11	20,282.0	10	198,299	18
19	50.7	60,466.5	8	13,076.7	18	130,745	41
29	(39.9)	25,975.0	39	9,385.0	28	39,199	185
64	(9.2)	36,402.4	25	11,235.7	22	129,546	42
22	(5.4)	24,806.3	42	5,561.8	66	304,000	8
9	(6.9)	38,128.0	23	16,418.0	12	143,961	33
10	759.4	35,089.0	26	14,836.0	15	54,208	135
55	16.0	41,142.7	21	10,704.1	23	373,000	5
23	10.9	27,859.0	35	9,924.8	26	199,021	17

important. A survey of Japanese business executives indicates that most believe that cultural factors are the predominant cause of Japanese business success.[22]

In the highly competitive Japanese economy, the individual corporation attempts to establish a "winner's competitive cycle"[23] which begins with growth. Japanese companies believe they must grow faster than their competitors; they

FIGURE 11.1 Porter's Dynamic Diamond

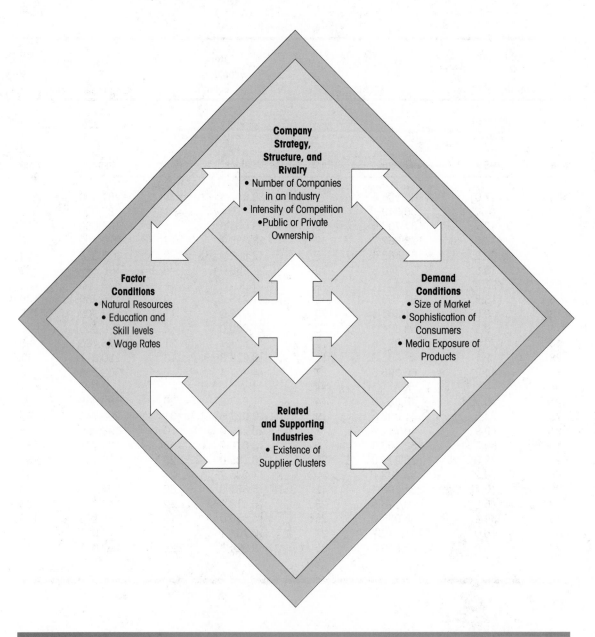

Source: Michael Porter, *The Competitive Advantage of Nations* (New York: Free Press, 1990).

must increase their market share to keep volume of business growing faster than that of competitors. This in turn depends on a higher rate of investment, which can take many forms, including price cutting, capacity expansion, advertising, and product development. The individual Japanese firm carries out this strategy within

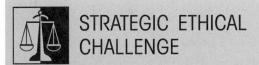

STRATEGIC ETHICAL CHALLENGE

JAPAN'S CAMPAIGN FOR AMERICA

According to Pat Choate, the Japanese run an ongoing political campaign in the United States just as if Japan were a third political party. They apparently spend more than $100 million each year to hire over 1,000 Washington, D.C., lobbyists, powerful lawyers, former high-ranking government officials, government public relations specialists, political advisers, and even former presidents. They spend another $300 million each year building a nationwide grassroots political network to influence government decisions and public opinion. They spend this $400 million a year to advance their own economic interests, influence U.S. trade policy, and win market share for Japanese firms in targeted U.S. industries.

None of this is illegal, nor is it imaginary. The Japanese political campaign is a *serious* threat to U.S. businesses in the United States and globally. It is clear that the Japanese have failed consistently to live up to promises such as voluntary import restraints, at the same time lobbying for U.S. public opinion to support their efforts to gain economic advantage within our boundaries. Through propaganda, Japan has been able to defend itself against American criticism of its own protectionist economic policy, which virtually bars many American products from importation to Japan.

It uses six very simple excuses for its protectionist actions and repeats them in countless variations in various media. These six excuses are:

1. Japan creates jobs for Americans.
2. Japan's critics are racist.
3. It's America's fault.
4. Globalization is unavoidable.
5. Japan is unique.
6. Japan is changing.

Each of these six excuses has some element of half truth, but when examined in detail, either statistically or in terms of Japan's own internal policies compared to U.S. policies, it becomes quite clear that these six excuses are part of a propaganda campaign and are not true. They are at best half-truths.

Lobbying and seeking political influence (down to the grassroots level) are two parts of a five-part strategy for gaining economic advantage in the United States. The other parts include intelligence gathering, dispensing propaganda, and influencing U.S. education and classroom instruction.

Japan is not only influencing American political decisions, but those in Europe, as well, especially directives for Europe 1992. For example, in Fall 1988, Cores, a Japanese consulting firm that specializes in foreign marketing, prepared a blueprint for lobbying, politicking, and propagandizing in Europe with a goal of influencing the EEC's 1992 efforts to directly benefit Japan. "Japanese companies were advised to: join every local industry association they could; hire lobbyists and public relations personnel in each of the EEC's 12 nations; establish an intelligence-gathering network in each country; spread their facilities across the EEC; hire European lawyers and hire experts who could monitor local development; invite as a figurehead chairman for Japan's European operations . . . someone who would be willing to open doors and lay the groundwork for the systematic lobbying of national officials and politicians."

This essentially duplicates the strategy they have employed in the United States. They are now attempting to use it in Europe, as well. It is quite clear that the Japanese understand the rules of the game. The major question is this: while it is legal, is it ethical? Politicking, lobbying political influence, and intelligence gathering are major Japanese business tactics. While U.S. firms may not be used to competing in such a way, the Japanese are competing in the U.S. according to their own value systems.

Sources: Pat Choate, "Political Advantage: Japan's Campaign for America," *Harvard Business Review*, September–October 1990, pp. 87–103. Please note that critics of Choate's material accuse him of telling his own half-truths, but Choate's documentation is substantial. Also see Robert T. Green and Tina Larsen, "Only Retaliation Will Open Up Japan," *Harvard Business Review*, November–December 1987, pp. 22–28.

the framework suggested above. Failure to do this leads ultimately to failure in the Japanese system, as it would in most capitalist economies.

AT MOTOROLA

The Japanese, their skills honed by fierce competition at home, entered Motorola's markets and successfully dominated several of them. Recognizing that it had been thrust into global markets, Motorola took the necessary actions to become competitive.

U.S. analysts also attribute Japan's success to protecting its markets from U.S. and other foreign firms. It is clear from an analysis of Japanese business/government relations that a few (10 to 20) very powerful men run Japan, and that political favors control many business opportunities. The Japanese are also lax on societal control of and play by different rules, and a powerful organized crime element there often significantly influences government and business decisions.[24] As mentioned, some U.S. analysts see Japan's success as a result of lobbying and financially influencing U.S. and state government decisions that might affect Japanese businesses in the United States.[25]

The Japanese are building a new economic power base across Asia and the Pacific. They are moving rapidly ahead in Thailand, the Philippines, Indonesia, Malaysia, and China and are beginning to work to develop ties in Taiwan, Korea, Singapore, and Hong Kong. It seems certain that Japan will replace the United States as the most powerful economic influence in Asia.[26] Furthermore, the limited reduction in the trade deficit of the United States makes it likely that Japan's financial strength relative to other nations will continue to grow. Finally, the Japanese are already beginning to move to dominate key technologies for the 21st century, including super conductivity, biotechnology, and microelectronics, and they are taking great pains to improve their research capability.[27]

TABLE 11.3 Factors that Contribute to the Success of the Japanese Economy

---

1. Macro Capital Factors
   - high savings rate
   - effective industrial financing through the banking system
   - industrial grouping, such as the large trading companies
   - government industrial policy
2. Micro Capital Factors
   - modern management: ownership and management are separated
   - middle and long-term gains, emphasizing the long-term view
   - capital investment by individual corporations
   - fund raising made easy through excellent access to sources
3. Macro Labor Factors
   - high education levels of the work force
   - flexible labor supply moving from declining to growth industries
   - good labor–management cooperation: only 32 percent of workers are unionized
   - wages reflect productivity
4. Micro Labor Factors
   - employment system characterized by three elements: (1) lifetime employment, (2) promotion system based on seniority, to which wages are tied, and (3) incentives for training employees
   - deciding by consensus, popularly called ``bottom-up management''
   - labor transfers within the company: given employment security, employees are most willing to move
5. Macro Technology Factors
   - aggressively importing overseas technology, and integrating and improving that technology
   - development of production technology
   - effective research and development that, while low, is helped by the government's implementation of policy
6. Micro Technology Factors
   - TQC—total quality control system
   - workers' suggestions
   - parts availability through small business
   - highly competitive technologically; i.e., keeping abreast of and using new technology

---

Source: Adapted from Masaya Miyoshi, Managing Director, Keidanren, Tokyo, as printed in Norman Coates, ``Determinants of Japan's Business Success: Some Japanese Executives' Views,'' *Academy of Management Executive*, January 1988, p. 70.

Asia's Four Tigers South Korea, Taiwan, Hong Kong, and Singapore, especially South Korea and Taiwan, have reaped the rewards of their hard work, competitive spirit, and free enterprise economies with increasing prosperity. Unfortunately for the United States, these four tigers also have accounted for a significant percent of our annual trade deficit in recent years. Despite increasing American pressure, the four tigers have resisted attempts to remove import barriers. Taiwan is the least resistant and has a buy-American policy that seems to be working. For example, Japanese companies are not being allowed to bid on Taipei's new subway. Hong Kong and Singapore have pegged their currencies to the American dollar, assuring continuing deficits with those countries. Finally, South Korea has balked at opening its borders to U.S. firms and is not offering much hope for compromise.[28] Furthermore, in 1999 Hong Kong will revert to Chinese rule, probably causing substantial disruption.

Europe 1992 and East-West Economic Integration

Europe is the second leg of the triad of markets, and potentially the most economically significant, depending on the outcome of the 1992 market integration and the potential for stronger East-West ties which began to grow in 1989.

Europe 1992

The benefits of the 1992 integrated market joining firms in the EEC will extend to much of the rest of Europe, as well. Firms in non-EEC Scandinavian countries, for example Skopbank in Finland, are planning strategies to ensure their preparedness.[29] This integration of markets for the first time gives European firms the ability to compete globally from a domestic market that is large enough to test a product and then go global with it. This will reduce, but not totally eliminate, the need for specialized products for various regions of Europe. It will make commerce and industry much easier to conduct. EEC countries are shown in Figure 11.2.

The problem in achieving a true common market hasn't been tariffs, which were abolished years ago. Rather the integration will eliminate numerous local regulations that encumber virtually every facet of business, especially the standardization of products across national borders. For example, before 1992 Europe had no common standards for auto emissions, radio wavelengths, mobile telephones, or capitalization rules for banks. Insurance companies were even prohibited from selling policies in more than one country.[30] Currency-exchange problems and cultural bias have also been barriers.

One critical action has already been taken. Numerous forms required from truckers when crossing borders have been replaced. Trucks would sit for hours at the Mont Blanc tunnel between France and Italy, for example, while customs agents checked exhaustive documents averaging 35 pages. These were replaced in 1988 by a two-page form later to be abandoned altogether. Shipping information will be supplied to governments on computer disks.

Cor van der Klugt, president of Philips Gloeilampenfabrieken, Europe's largest consumer electronics company, observes, "What Europe is doing is gigantic. The drive for economic unity is the most important thing that will happen for the next 50 years."[31]

What Is Likely to Happen[32]

There will be obvious changes in European firms' strategies because requirements for success in this new environment will be quite different from the strategies necessary for the current environment. Marketing will be a very important skill, and skilled marketers may be able to seize the opportunities created in advance of their competitors. European firms will have to think about the entire EEC and global markets. Cost structures will change tremendously and there will be widespread efforts to cut costs. Larger and smaller

FIGURE 11.2 Nations of the EEC

firms will probably be able to compete better than those stuck in the middle. Differentiation strategies will be employed by most firms.[33]

Furthermore, it is evident that some countries will obtain advantages due to certain factors such as lower wage rates. Spain, Greece, Portugal, southern France, and southern Italy are especially likely to benefit in this way. Eastern European countries are also expected to benefit from low wage rates, even though not yet part of the EEC.

The responses to 1992 will vary by country. For example, the newly united Germany is expected to become a veritable economic juggernaut, although it may take several years.[34] France has been highly receptive to the 1992 concept, Britain and Denmark less so. The cultural problems associated with European integration will be far greater than those experienced in the United States. It is highly likely that one currency may evolve. There will certainly be a period of consolidation of banks resulting in a significant shift of power among European banks.[35] Unemployment and other social problems may result. Power will shift to Brussels (the home of the EEC headquarters) from the nations' capitals.

Many believe that North American and Japanese firms may be locked out of this new market, but firms from both countries are trying to position themselves for the new order.[36] At best the rules of the game will change significantly. Firms such as Philips, KLM, KPMG (Klynvold, Peat, Marwick, Gourdeler), Avery International, Ford Motor Company, General Motors, General Electric, and Mazda, among hundreds of others have formulated strategies for 1992. Clearly, however, several industries, including car making, air transport, and agriculture, aren't going to change very much. They may even become more hostile and protectionist to outsiders.[37]

More than 250 directives covering economic and legal issues related to the establishment of the common market have been proposed, and over 80 percent were passed by mid-1991. Though several critical issues remain, it now seems apparent that these directives will also pass.[38] Europe is facing a severe recession, though, caused partly by firms getting lean and mean for 1992. This may hinder the 1992 initiative.[39]

AT MOTOROLA

Motorola stands to benefit from Europe 1992 because of its favorable product line. Europe has strong competitors, but Motorola has the new-product advantage and higher-quality products, as well.

Potential East-West Integration   In 1989 a series of changes in political and economic structures began in eastern Europe that may eclipse the economic significance of Europe 1992. It is not clear at this writing (June 1992) what these impacts will be, but it is clear that they will be significant. In the immediate future Poland, Czechoslovakia, Hungary, and what was East Germany seem the most likely candidates to benefit from looser economic and political constraints, but all nations in eastern Europe probably will eventually benefit from these changes.

The reunification of Germany may even have slowed progress toward 1992, but progress toward completing the unification initiative is ongoing.

North America

The principal economic powers of North America are the United States and Canada. Under its president Carlos Salinas de Gortari, Mexico is striving, however, to become more actively involved in North American trade and the global economy. Presidents Salinas and Bush are moving toward a free-trade agreement, speeding the process.[40] The United States and Canada signed a free-trade pact that took effect on January 1, 1989. It called for abolishing all tariffs over the following 10 years. This has significantly affected some firms, such as Harley-Davidson, which saw the Canadian price on one cycle model drop by an average of $1,250 per bike when the law went into effect. Many hope that this trade pact will increase the number of big deals between firms of the two countries and enable them to become more sizeable for competition in Europe and Asia.[41] The United States, Canada, and Mexico also are likely to establish a free-trade zone.

Declining U.S. Competitiveness   Perhaps the most significant threat to the U.S. and Canadian leg of the triad is its declining global competitiveness. The United States has found itself with a global competitive disadvantage in both manufacturing and service industries for a number of reasons, including the transition from a manufacturing economy to a service economy, declining investment in heavy manufacturing, declining quality, disadvantageous wage rates and benefit structures, technology transfer from the United States to foreign competitors, and a short-term perspective on the returns expected from an organization, which drives ROI-based financial controls and strategic portfolio management concepts inspiring buying and selling of businesses.[42] Factors cited more recently include diversification strategies and subsequent decentralized organizational structures, and evolutionary changes in the nature of the capital market.[43]

The principal consequence of several of these forces has been the reduction of investment in long-term product/market development. Innovation has been short-changed due to both the short-term perspective and the shortage of funds for investment in organizations that are oriented toward the long term. In fact, some have argued very strongly that U.S. competitiveness has declined principally because of declining innovation.[44] To survive and remain competitive internationally, firms have had to change how they think. A perfect example is ABB Asea Brown Boveri, as this chapter's Strategic Global Challenge feature reveals.

Potential for Other Global Change

Under Boris Yeltsin, the former Soviet Union, now the Commonwealth of Independent States, is attempting to improve the well-being of the populace. The possibility exists for an economic change even greater than those already seen in the Soviet Union and China, despite China's retreat from democracy in the summer of 1989, with both moving toward capitalism. In 1992, however, the

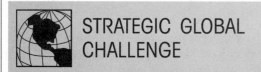

STRATEGIC GLOBAL CHALLENGE

THE LOGIC OF GLOBAL BUSINESS— ABB ASEA BROWN BOVERI

ABB Asea Brown Boveri emerged from the 1987 merger between Asea, a flagship of Swedish industry, and Brown Boveri, a major Swiss firm. The creation of ABB and the subsequent rationalization, including layoffs, plant closing, and product exchanges between countries, is a model of what will happen to much of European industry in the next few years. In early 1991, ABB had annual revenues of $25 billion and employed 240,000 people around the world. Europe accounted for approximately 60 percent of its total revenues. This business was split equally between European Community countries and the non-EC Scandinavian trading block. Germany was ABB's largest national market and accounted for 15 percent of its total revenue. It had annual revenues of $7 billion in North America with 40,000 employees. It also had 10,000 employees in India and South America.

Percy Barnevik, 49, president and CEO of ABB Asea Brown Boveri, is a corporate pioneer. He has moved rapidly and aggressively to construct a globally competitive firm in the electrical systems and equipment market. The perspective of the truly global firm is described by Barnevik as follows:

> ABB is a company with no geographic center, no national ax to grind. We are a federation of national companies with a global coordination center. Are we a Swiss company? Our headquarters is in Zurich, but only 100 professionals work at headquarters and we will not increase that number. Are we a Swedish company? I am the CEO and I was born and educated in Sweden. But our headquarters is not in Sweden, and only two of the eight members of our Board of Directors are Swedes. Perhaps we are an American company. We report our financial results in U.S. dollars and English is ABB's official language. We conduct all high level meetings in English. My point is that ABB is none of those things—and all of those things. We are not homeless, we are a company with many homes.

ABB and its CEO show an understanding of the perspective necessary to compete on a global basis. The company uses a sort of matrix organization structure with 1,100 local company presidents reporting to two bosses, the business area leader, who is usually located outside the country, and the president of the national company of which the local company is a subsidiary. Barnevik admits that ABB needs more global managers, but he cautions that you need relatively few, perhaps 500 out of 15,000 managers, to make the system work well. He notes: "If you are selling in Germany, you better be German." The point is you must tailor products sold and the marketing process itself to local markets. But he points out that you do need a core group of global managers at the top. However, he notes, "Global managers don't passively accept it when someone says 'You can't do that in Italy or Spain because . . .' or 'You can't do that in Japan because of the ministry of finance.' They sort through the debris of cultural excuses and find opportunities to innovate." They make things happen that benefit the company.

Source: William Taylor, "The Logic of Global Business: An Interview with ABB's Percy Barnevik," *Harvard Business Review*, March–April 1991, pp. 91–105.

CIS is suffering severe economic problems, including food shortages. Another political revolution is still possible. Building the infrastructure necessary for a capitalist economy and changing behaviors learned over most of a century have proved more difficult than anyone could have anticipated. Potentially, however, two of the world's largest markets may open up for European, Japanese, and American competitors alike.[45] Further, not just in eastern Europe, privatization (selling public corporations to private owners) is leading to major changes in business all over the globe.[46]

STRATEGIC MANAGEMENT AND THE GLOBAL ENVIRONMENT

Strategic management has been significantly affected by the globalization of business. Firms must learn to function strategically at several different levels: domestically, multidomestically, and globally. The following paragraphs discuss global strategy in light of four primary external environmental factors, focusing especially on strategy formulation.

Global Strategy

Global corporations follow a true **global strategy**. They operate with totally integrated operations, finance, marketing, and human resource functions across numerous borders, subsidizing a drive for market share in one country with the profits from those activities in other countries.[47]

Global strategic management is the performance of strategic management activities on a truly global basis. Global strategic management embodies the concepts of both global and multidomestic strategies, as well as simply thinking globally. Historically, firms such as AT&T, Apple Computers, and Federal Express have been multidomestic corporations. Rather than designing a product for a global market, they have taken a product that worked in the United States and sold it in another country. They have operated without highly coordinated international manufacturing/service, marketing, finance, and human resource operations. More recently, they have begun to follow global strategies.

Firms such as Ford Motor Company, Unilever, Mazda, Matsushita Electric Company, Sony, and General Electric are global companies. They produce products for global markets. However, even within these large corporations, for example, General Electric's major divisions may still operate essentially multidomestically. Both global and multidomestic companies are multinational corporations. A **multinational corporation (MNC)** is simply a firm that has significant operations in more than one country.[48]

AT MOTOROLA

Motorola is a global company following an integrated global strategy. For example, its other efforts are helping it penetrate the Japanese market.

Stages of Development

Most organizations don't become multinational or global overnight. Rather, they typically start as domestic organizations and move through a series of stages, reaching multidomestic, and sometimes global stages of multinationalization. Neil H. Jacoby and Christopher M. Korth have both identified a series of stages through which organizations pass on their way to becoming multinational.[49] Table 11.4 integrates Jacoby's materials into Korth's model of these stages and adds a fifth stage reflecting the concept of global competition. In examining Table 11.4, realize that not all organizations reach either the fourth or fifth stages, and some may reach them and subsequently withdraw. When Renault sold American Motors Corporation to Chrysler in 1987, it retreated to a multidomestic strategy from a global one.

One of the major changes in moving from stage 1 to stage 5 is that products designed for the domestic market are first sold overseas. In later stages, manufacturing and financing may occur in foreign countries. In the fifth stage, the organization becomes totally global, designing products for more than one national market and coordinating manufacturing, finance, human resources, and information management to manage the global competitive situation. This five-stage evolutionary process has been shown to be typical of U.S. firms.[50]

The global firm differs substantially from the multidomestic corporation. The **multidomestic corporations** operate across borders and in several different countries, but treat each country as a separate market, developing products for each market. The firm may have foreign manufacturing operations, sales organizations, alliances, and so on, but it does not think in global terms. It does not attack and counterattack in a totally integrated way, but rather it tends to operate as if each country's operations were independent of others. Hence, the multidomestic firm formulates a strategy for each country rather than an integrated global strategy.[51] Some industries are global industries, others are multidomestic.[52]

The following paragraphs examine strategic management in multinational environments, discussing how the four environmental forces differ there and how they might affect the formulation, implementation, and cost of strategy.

Four External Environmental Factors and the Global Environment

Four external environmental forces affecting organizations and their strategic management can be identified: economic/competitive, political/legal, social/cultural, and technological forces. Each of these forces reacts significantly to changes from domestic to multinational operations, and each influences corporate strategies in changing ways.

Economic/Competitive Factors
Organizations that operate multinationally will face a myriad of different economic and competitive environmental factors. They will face different monetary systems; they will operate in countries at different stages of economic development; they may even confront different

TABLE 11.4 Five Degrees of Internationalization

	Stage 1: First-Degree Internationalization	Stage 2: Second-Degree Internationalization	Stage 3: Third-Degree Internationalization	Stage 4: Fourth-Degree Internationalization	Stage 5: Fifth-Degree Internationalization
Nature of contact with foreign markets	Indirect, passive	Direct, active	Direct, active	Direct, active	Direct, active
Focus of international operations	Domestic	Domestic	Domestic and international	Domestic and international	International
Orientation of company	Domestic	Domestic	Primarily domestic	Multinational/ Multidomestic (domestic operations viewed as part of the whole)	Global (with domestic modifications)
Type of international activity	Foreign trade of goods and services	Foreign trade of goods and services	Foreign trade, foreign assistance contracts, foreign direct investment	Foreign trade, foreign assistance contracts, foreign direct investment	Foreign trade, foreign assistance contracts, foreign direct investment
Organizational structure	Traditional domestic	International department	International division	Global structure	Global structure

Source: Adapted from Christopher M. Korth, *International Business: Environment of Management*, 2d ed. (Englewood Cliffs, N.J.: Prentice-Hall, 1985), p. 7. Adapted by permission of Prentice-Hall.

economic systems such as the moderate form of socialism in Great Britain, the new capitalistic socialism in Hungary, a form of communism in China, a capitalist/socialist hybrid in France, or almost pure government-guided capitalism in Japan. There will be fierce global competitors, powerful or weak customers and suppliers, new entrants, and increasing numbers of substitutes. The demographics of nations will vary, with worker shortages in some countries and in some skills, and surpluses in others.[53]

Political/Legal Factors

Similarly, the multinational corporation faces widely varying political/legal systems. Many European governments take active roles in business, frequently changing monetary and fiscal policies and taxation rules, as well as offering various incentives for plant location or industry development. Similarly, the Japanese government provides research and development funds, steers its country's firms toward selected industries, and generally nurtures close ties to its multinationals. In Europe prior to 1992, organizations were faced with at least 12 different sets of laws, controls, and policies, a situation that will continue to some extent after 1992. Throughout the world, property rights differ, as do laws governing the operation of business. Very few countries practice truly free trade, and import and export controls are common.

R. Hall Mason notes that host countries, that is, countries that host operations of multinational corporations, often restrict the actions of MNCs. Some of the more important limits include requiring shared ownership with the host country or with its nationals, reserving certain management and technical jobs for local people, profit and fee ceilings, guidelines for contract renegotiations, limits on external debt capital, requirements for development of the host country's personnel and export markets, and a preference for technology-based industries over extractive industries (those that take raw materials from the country).[54]

Social/Cultural Factors

Multinational corporations must learn to operate in a widely varying context of culture and language. Educational systems, for example, differ widely from country to country. Stefan Robock and Kenneth Simmonds identify at least four distinct ways cultures differ:[55] assumptions and attitudes; personal beliefs, aspirations, and motivations; interpersonal relations; and social structures. To see the effect of assumptions and attitudes, consider that U.S. and Canadian management systems have been greatly influenced by those societies' shared belief in self-determination. In many other countries, beliefs are commonly much more fatalistic, assuming that human beings really cannot control their own futures. Other problems may arise, for example, with respect to time. Being "on time" is very important in most western societies, but is of little importance in China. In fact, being late is more common there than being on time.

Personal beliefs, aspirations, and motivations differ amazingly. The need to achieve is much less significant outside western/capitalist/Protestant countries, for example, in India or Peru. Underlying beliefs about authority affect how management functions. In Japan, teamwork is more highly valued than in the United States or Europe, although both are moving toward more teamwork in managing.

The status of women in the workplace varies throughout the world. In the Middle East they are second-class citizens. In Europe, degrees of acceptance of women in organizations vary. Scandinavian countries accept them wholeheartedly, while Spain tends to be much more resistant to integrating women into the managerial and professional work forces. In the United States women are integral to the work force at all levels. In Japan they play almost no role in the organization, although with the passage of an equal employment opportunity law in 1987, women are slowly beginning to be accepted in management and professional positions.

Finally, social structure, including social status and interclass mobility, play important roles in other cultures. Britain still has a very strong class structure, whereas Canada and the United States do not. The Japanese focus much of their energy on a group-oriented, patriarchal organization structure. In many communist countries, the social structure is divided into the members of the communist party and all others. In summary, social/cultural factors can have very significant impacts on management. Managers must operate with sensitivity to the nuances of each individual country. Underlying all of this, of course, are social and cultural barriers to communication.

Technological Factors   Within the global triad of markets, technology is easily transported and is losing value as a source of sustainable competitive advantage. Organizations must be prepared to reformulate products and services quickly, improving upon product and service technologies in order to maintain competitive advantages. In the future the Japanese and Europeans may lead the world toward new technology in a bid to overcome U.S. and Canadian technological advantages. In the developing countries, multinationals will find different levels of technology and will have to function within constraints they impose or bring in advanced technology.

Specific Impacts of Environmental Factors on Strategic Management

Differences will be found in the four sets of external environmental factors, and in the internal environmental factors that correspond to them, for example, personalities of individuals or organizational cultures. These differences may cause differences in vision, mission, goals, and objectives. The degree to which strategic planning is acceptable in a society could be affected greatly as a result. A nation's culture might affect strategy formulation in some countries, whereas in others only the CEO would determine strategy. In others, such as Japan, the organization might be highly participative, with several levels of management actively involved in strategy formulation. Whether or not a firm competes in a multidomestic industry or global industry has a significant impact on how strategies must be formulated. For example, in global industries, subsidiaries must be linked tightly, especially in their coordination of the economic functions of marketing, operations, service, purchasing, and R&D.[56]

The organization must carefully consider the nature of its global competitive advantage in tailoring a global product to each country's market.

SBU Strategies

The fundamentals of SBU strategy are applied internationally much as they are domestically, but the specific methods of application and the factors on which they are based are again significantly modified by multinational operations. Each of the five major components of the marketing mix is affected in some way by the international situation. For example, target markets are often much more difficult to identify, especially in terms of purchasing capabilities, because of varying demographic and socioeconomic factors. Simon Majaro identifies numerous potential problems with respect to the other components: product, promotion, price, and distribution.[57] He emphasizes the impacts of environment, competition, institutions, and the legal system on the components of the marketing mix.

The product itself and its aesthetic design, branding, and packaging are strongly affected by special needs for sizes, dimensions, and standards; available support resources; attitudes of local consumers toward colors, shapes, and appearances; local tastes and traditions; the product's name and how well it can be pronounced, recalled, and understood; legal constraints on the name; the availability of desired packaging materials; laws affecting the use of the product; safety rules; pollution rules; trademark design registration requirements; constraints on shapes; and labeling requirements for packages. Kellogg's, for example, had to convince millions of people in other countries that cereal was a proper breakfast food; most of them had never before eaten cereals in such a form. Its successful efforts now bring in 30 percent of its revenues from foreign markets.[58]

Among the factors related to promotion we find language, literacy, and readership; attitudes toward advertising, sales personnel, and sales promotions; influence patterns; demographics; symbolism; situational aspects of media, including availability; legislative bans on certain advertising; sales promotion or personal selling practices; and laws limiting expenditures on marketing.

Majaro suggests that many local market factors must be considered in pricing, among them whether social and cultural taboos affect the amount of money consumers can spend on a product; whether it is customary to overprice in anticipation of haggling; whether some local institutions must approve the price; and whether the host country's laws constrain price changes, limit margins, or require the price to be printed on the product or package.

Distribution is affected by the availability of roads and other transportation channels; customers' buying habits; whether products are distributed by local agents or the company's sales force; whether distribution channels are controlled by the government; the extent of red tape that restricts beginning and ongoing distribution; and whether the host country has special rules governing packaging, safety, size, materials, or other factors.

These are lengthy lists, but critical ones. Firms that do not take these factors into account suffer from their failure. When a U.S. auto manufacturer exported a sporty model to a Spanish-speaking country, it found that the car's name, which suggested novelty and brilliance in the English-speaking world, meant "doesn't go" in Spanish. Another U.S. firm failed to sell its razor blades in the host country's drugstores and supermarkets, but discovered at last that people in that country were accustomed to buying their razor blades in hardware stores. A fried-chicken firm, having scored an instant success in Japan, anticipated equal success when it introduced its "finger-lickin' good" chicken in Hong Kong; it was not aware that Chinese customers expected to be provided with moist towels after they were served foods to be eaten with the fingers. Finally, one U.S. manufacturer attempted to sell its gelatin dessert in a country where only 3 percent of the population owned refrigerators.

Financial strategies must, of course, be formulated with some concern for currency exchange rates. Most U.S. MNCs sought to manufacture overseas when the U.S. dollar gained strength in the mid-1980s, but this strategy backfired when the dollar faltered in the late 1980s. Japan's MNCs, conversely, began to outsource production as the yen rose in value.[59] Production strategies must cope with numerous logistical problems resulting from differing and often inadequate transportation systems, limited numbers of suppliers, and largely unskilled work forces. McDonald's, for example, grows its own potatoes in 18 countries that cannot supply potatoes that meet its quality requirements.[60] Personnel strategies must cope with laws and local customs that regulate work and authority. In much of Europe, for example, little work gets done in the summer months, when workers take their holidays—vacations that range from four to eight weeks. Other external factors may influence personnel matters. In Northern Ireland, for example, a work force segregated along religious lines is a cultural necessity, and plants have sometimes been firebombed in religion-related labor disputes.

Still, Europe is changing along with the rest of the world. There, too, firms are eliminating excess workers in efforts to remain competitive. The need for efficiency to compete globally has been recognized.[61]

There is no reason to believe that generic and contingency theories of strategy formulation similar to those employed in the United States could not be adopted in other countries. For example, Timo Santalainen and Risto Tainio studied 80 of the largest banks in Finland (some of which operated multinationally) in order to isolate factors that distinguished high performers from low performers. Of ten factors (and an indeterminate number of processes and mechanisms) studied, they found the following three to be most important: labor force and effort, attributes of top executives, and leadership orientation and management-development endeavors.[62] In another study, however, Tainio and Santalainen seriously question the universal validity of the opinion that American organizational models generate controllable and beneficial changes in other cultural settings.[63] The amount of reported research on this subject has been limited.

The specifics of management functions also differ in other countries. Managers often find themselves confronted with differing expectations for their motivation and leadership styles. First-line employees participate in decision making much more actively in much of Europe and Japan than they do in the United States and Canada. Yet in the Middle East, Central and South America, and most of the rest of the world, the manager's word is law and is seldom disputed. Long-range planning is revered in Japan, where it is viewed as critical to the success of the organization, but it is not much practiced in China. Motivation techniques vary primarily with needs levels, and people outside major industrialized countries tend to need things that are much lower in the hierarchy of needs than people in industrialized nations, who often seek high-level need satisfiers in their jobs. Control strategies are especially important in the multinational enterprise because of the multitude of factors already noted, especially geographic distance and, in many cases, familiarity of a host-country manager with the multinational's operation. Communication habits, decision-making skills and habits, and a host of other functional strategy factors vary, as well. The multinational organization must be extremely adaptive to survive and prosper.

Other Strategic Issues

Strategies for multinationals will focus on issues such as the extent to which and how to enter into or expand within a country or countries; the choice of whether to compete multidomestically or globally; how to proceed through the various stages of growth toward global competition, as shown in Table 11.4; and how to be an effective global competitor.

Donald A. Ball and Wendell H. McCulloch, Jr. suggest that the various reasons for going international are either aggressive or defensive.[64]

Aggressive Reasons	Defensive Reasons
1. Seek new markets	1. Protect home markets
2. Yield higher profits/cut costs	2. Protect other markets
3. Obtain additional products for other markets	3. Guarantee raw-material supply
4. Satisfy top management's desire to expand	4. Acquire technology
	5. Diversify geographically
	6. Obtain bases for new operations

How to Progress through the Stages Toward Global Strategy Table 11.4 clearly shows the various stages through which an organization may pass on its path to global strategy. Two important decisions are when to take such actions and upon what basis to take them.

Domestic, Multidomestic, or Global Not all products or services travel well. In an increasingly homogeneous international environment, however, more and more products are being accepted from one country to another. Organizations typically move to overseas locations for the reasons outlined by Ball and McCulloch. The decision to operate multidomestically or globally depends on a large number of variables, principally size and the changing nature of the industry. Most authorities believe, for example, that companies competing in the automobile industry must be able to compete globally.[65] Ford's belief in the need to be global led it to totally revise its strategy to build a platform (underbody) for a world car.[66] In other industries, however, such as fast food, it may be possible to sell an existing domestic product globally without altering or creating a world product. This has certainly been the case with McDonald's hamburger chain. While outlets obtain raw materials and manufacture the product in various countries, McDonald's really has not had to tailor the product to other countries in most cases.[67]

Choices of How to Enter the Country   Most firms enter a new market first on a marketing or manufacturing basis. From a marketing perspective, firms may choose to import or export, to license, to set up direct investment or to enter joint ventures.

Exporting and importing are usually the first international actions that organizations take. Exporting means making it here and selling it there, while importing means purchasing it there and bringing it back here. Firms can import and export either products or services. Mazda, Honda, and Toyota all export cars to the United States, where the same cars are viewed as Japanese imports. Similarly the United States exports management consulting services to many countries.

For a number of reasons, including transportation costs, government regulation, or home-country production costs, a company may decide to license its product for manufacture or delivery in a foreign country. In licensing, one company allows another to use its technology, patent, trademark, brand name, copyright, or some other asset or form of expertise, usually in return for a royalty.[68] For example, Mrs. Fields' agreed to license both its cookies and La Petite Boulangerie operations in the EEC to a French company, Paris-based Midial S.A., for $10 million, which included a 1-percent interest in the firm.[69]

Joint ventures involve two or more firms in joint equity ownership of some operation. The joint venture is becoming an increasingly popular form of cooperation between organizations. It provides a quick way for firms to enter another country. For example, the $580-million joint venture between General Electric and Britain's General Electric company allows each access to the other's home markets.[70] One drawback of such an alliance is that the technologically superior firm may give up some of its know-how to the other firm. Similar drawbacks may threaten other competitive advantages, for example, manufacturing processes.[71] In two studies, Kenichi Ohmae, and Howard V. Perlmutter and David A. Heenan argue that global alliances are both vital to global competition. Global companies incur and must defray immense fixed costs to compete globally. Ohmae argues that you need partners. Ohmae provides criteria for successful alliances, as do Perlmutter and Heenan.[72] Table 11.5 shows how complex relationships can be for single firm.

AT MOTOROLA

Motorola found that entering Japan was made much easier by forming an alliance with Toshiba than if it had attempted to enter by itself.

Finally, a firm can make a direct investment in two ways, by venture capital or purchasing assets. Europe 1992 has made mergers, acquisitions, joint ventures, and other forms of alliances extremely important means of entry into the EEC community.

TABLE 11.5 Corning's Global Ties

BICC (Britain)—Optical fibers
Ciba-Geigy (Switzerland)—Medical diagnostic equipment and materials
Compagnie Financière des Fibres Optiques (France)—Optical fibers
Siemens (Germany)—Optical fibers, cables
Societa Italiana Vetro (Italy), Indosuez (France), Finimi (Belgium)—Specialty glass products
Asahi Glass (Japan)—Glass for TV picture tubes, cookware
Beijing Electronic Glass Engineering Technology (China)—School for TV picture tube glass
   manufacturing
NGK Insulators (Japan)—Ceramics for catalytic converters
Samsung Group (South Korea)—Glass for TV picture tubes
Australian Consolidated Industries (Australia)—Cookware
Metal Manufacturers, Amalgamated Wireless Australasia (Australia)—Optic fibers

Source: Louis Kraar, "Your Rivals Can Be Your Allies," *Fortune*, March 28, 1989, p. 68.

What Countries to Enter Analysts must examine many major factors to determine which countries to enter. In recent years the political risk has been especially closely examined.[73] All four of the forces must be assessed: economic, political/legal, social/cultural, and technological.

How to Be an Effective Global Competitor W. Chan Kim and R. A. Mauburgne suggest that organizations must take several actions in order to be effective global competitors.[74] First, they must identify their competition, and, second, they must establish a global market presence. An MNC should view as potential competitors those companies that operate in related business segments either abroad or on the MNC's home turf, and those companies that operate in the same business segment, but in different geographic regions. Perhaps the most important action to establish a market presence is to invade the competitor's profit sanctuaries. By doing so the firm can limit the market shares and thus the cash flows available to competitors. Also, it will be in a better position to launch offensives against competitors if it has more places from which to launch them. It could also more easily identify strategic intents and gain inside information on new technology and product offerings in its competitors' backyards. It can more readily copy a new product offering or pre-empt a foreign company's opportunities in other geographic markets. Finally, it can lower its costs by increasing its economies of scale.

The MNC, to be a global competitor, must decide whether to initiate direct or indirect global competition. To do so it must look at various entry barriers, the potential for competitors' retaliation, and the sales volume of its overall market.

AT MOTOROLA

Motorola used its successful joint venture with Toshiba to begin penetration of the Japanese home market sanctuary. While its market share in Japan is not as great as in other countries, nonetheless this joint venture has allowed it to do what few other companies have been able to do. It may be able to compete more effectively elsewhere on the globe because of the information it gathers about Japanese intentions for new technologies and strategies.

James F. Bolt[75] identifies other factors that appear to be critical to competing successfully globally, including managers that are comfortable in the world arena, an integrated and innovative global strategy that makes it very difficult and costly for other companies to compete, an understanding that technological innovation is no longer confined to the United States, establishment of systems for tapping technology and innovation abroad, an organization structure (typically decentralized) that is well thought out,[76] a system that keeps managers informed of political changes abroad and applications for their business, an international management team, and a view of the world as a truly global market, not a series of domestic markets.[77] Finally, a successful global manager must truly understand the vagaries of each market. Strategy isn't about beating the competition, it's about serving customers' real needs.[78]

Michael Porter offers a final thought on how to be an effective global competitor: "Companies achieve competitive advantage through acts of innovation. They approach innovation in its broadest sense, including both new technologies and new ways of doing things."[79] It is easy to see how innovation derives from the four key components of Porter's dynamic diamond, as discussed earlier. When Federal Express decided to become a global firm, its entries into the Pacific Rim and European markets were heralded as innovative strategies. But going global is never easy and Federal Express probably underestimated the enormity of the task and the strength of the competition, as this chapter's Global Strategic Challenge reveals.

Sophisticated buyers and intense competition can pressure companies to innovate faster, either for new products or for lower costs. Note, however, the interdependencies of the four factors. The demands of sophisticated buyers may not result in increased innovation unless the human resources of the organization are creative enough to innovate. Porter argues that "innovating to overcome local disadvantages is better than outsourcing; developing domestic suppliers is better than relying on foreign ones."[80]

GLOBAL STRATEGIC CHALLENGE

FEDERAL EXPRESS: A HISTORY OF INNOVATION— WILL IT SUCCEED WITH GLOBAL INNOVATION?

The history of Federal Express is full of innovation. Frederick Smith, Federal Express founder and CEO, began the firm with the belief that his new idea of overnight delivery would work, even if others, including potential lenders, did not. He was right and skeptics were wrong. The rest, as they say, is history, as Federal Express created a whole new industry. Not all of Smith's ideas have been winners, as is true of most innovative individuals and firms. For example, Smith's "Zap Mail," which had Federal Express deliver faxes from its machines to customer offices, was a total flop. The Zap Mail strategy had not anticipated the advent of cheap fax machines that allowed virtually anyone, anywhere, to receive faxes.

Still, Smith has fostered an organizational culture aimed at continuing innovation, most of which has been successful. For example, Federal Express is highly regarded for its innovative use of computers, communications technology, and information systems to track packages from receipt to delivery. They have also been innovative in management development programs, opting for the unorthodox "wilderness experience" to help teach leadership. Smith himself has pioneered certain management practices, including his spending every Tuesday responding to employee complaints. Federal Express also has been at the forefront in the use of video technology to keep employees informed. Risk taking is encouraged, and innovation rewarded.

Smith's latest major innovation was to take the firm global, largely through the purchase of Tiger International, Inc., an air-freight firm, which gave the firm Pacific Rim capabilities, and through the pursuit of an internally generated European operation. But Federal Express has suffered major setbacks in its European operation. Citing the lack of speed in creating a borderless Europe and an inability to make its hub-and-spoke system work, Federal Express took a $254-million one-time charge for restructuring its European operation in 1992. In effect, it got out of the package delivery business intra-Europe and intra-UK, selling its assets to two former competitors in those regions. It now relies on those firms to perform its intracontinental deliveries. These actions eliminated two-thirds of its overseas losses. Having invested almost $2.5 billion in overseas operations since 1985, Federal Express has yet to see a profit from them. Many point to heavy competition from European-based DHL and U.S.-based United Parcel Service, and to a sagging economy, as additional reasons for Federal Express's financial woes.

Sources: Daniel Pearl, "Federal Express Pins Hopes on New Strategy in Europe," *The Wall Street Journal*, March 18, 1992, p. B4; Daniel Pearl, "Federal Express Plans to Trim Assets in Europe," *The Wall Street Journal*, March 17, 1992, p. A3; "Mr. Smith Goes Global," *Business Week*, February 13, 1989, pp. 66–72; Mary Kathleen Flynn, "Business Focus Is Key to Success," *Datamation*, July 13, 1987, p. 48; "Broadcast News Incorporated," *Newsweek*, January 4, 1988, pp. 34, 35; William H. Wagel, "An Unorthodox Approach to Leadership Development," *Personnel*, July 1986, pp. 4–6.

PROBLEMS UNIQUE TO MULTINATIONAL CORPORATIONS

Organizations doing business overseas face several situations that domestic organizations do not: political instability, terrorism, host government conflicts, monetary transactions, and human rights issues.

Political Instability

When doing business in developing nations, political instability can be a major problem. Governments rise and fall rather quickly in many developing nations because of their own economic instability and interference by outside political forces. Organizations obviously prefer licensing, joint venture, or exporting arrangements rather than investing heavily in countries where political risk is high. However, in many cases, the potential return from such an investment is so high that the political risk must be taken. Table 11.6 indicates several sources of political risk, some of the groups that become involved, and their effects on the international business operation.

TABLE 11.6   Political Risk of Investment in Foreign Countries

Sources of Political Risk	Groups through which Political Risk Can Be Generated	Political Risk Effects: Types of Influences on International Business Operations
Competing political philosophies (nationalism, socialism, communism)	Government in power and its operating agencies	Confiscation: Loss of assets without compensation
Social unrest and disorder	Nonparliamentary opposition groups (e.g., anarchist or guerrilla movements working from within or outside of country)	Expropriation with compensation: Loss of freedom to operate
Vested interests of local business groups	Nonorganized common interest groups: students, workers, peasants, minorities, and so forth	Operational restrictions: Market shares, product characteristics, employment policies, locally shared ownership, and so forth
Recent and impending political independence	Foreign governments or intergovernmental agencies such as the European Economic Community	Loss of transfer freedom: financial (for example, dividends, interest payments), goods, personnel, or ownership rights
Armed conflicts and internal rebellions for political power	Foreign governments willing to enter into armed conflict or to support internal rebellion	Breaches or unilateral revisions in contracts and agreements
New international alliances		Discrimination, such as taxes, compulsory subcontracting
		Damage to property or personnel from riots, insurrections, revolutions, and wars

Source: Stefan H. Robock and Kenneth Simmonds, *International Business and Multinational Enterprise*, 3d ed. (Homewood, Ill.: Irwin, 1983). Reprinted by permission.

Terrorism

For multinational corporate personnel operating overseas, especially in developing countries but also in parts of Europe, terrorism, kidnapping, and extortion are major threats. Furthermore, the physical plants of many companies are often targets for terrorists. Many firms are investing heavily in security fencing and guard forces, and body guards are often in demand for Americans and other foreigners.

Host Government Conflicts

Host country governments, as discussed earlier, often place restrictions on multinational corporations operating within their borders. In any country, organizations can take steps to reduce the potential for conflict.

Monetary Transactions

The values of currencies fluctuate tremendously. In the early 1980s the United States dollar was very strong, and United States firms that made money in overseas operations lost it again when translating the foreign currency gains back into American dollars. By contrast, in the late 1980s, American firms were reaping substantial benefits from the devaluation of the dollar because translation multiplied their overseas income. It is almost impossible to accurately account for currency translation in long-term strategic planning because of the wild fluctuations.

Human Rights

In developing countries, and even in some developed countries, human rights are often neglected or at least not given the same respect as they are in the United States and Canada. In recent years, South Africa has been the major human rights trouble spot on the globe. Many American companies have been caught up in an ethical dilemma of whether to remain in South Africa. Many of them employed principally blacks who would be unemployed or treated less well by new employers if they were to leave. Yet by staying, these companies seemed to support the apartheid policies of the government. For all practical purposes, to withdraw would mean they would never be able to return to South Africa's sizeable market, and they would take major losses on their capital investments. Still, many American companies have been under pressure from groups in the United States to pull out of South Africa. Pressures have been applied by stockholders, principally social responsibility investment funds, universities, the federal government (to some extent), and various antiapartheid groups. Many firms have chosen to withdraw or reduce their involvement in South Africa in order to reduce the negative publicity associated with remaining there. Fortunately, however, in 1991 and 1992, the South African government took several major steps aimed at ending apartheid.

Firms must develop strategies for coping with such complex situations. There are guiding principles for some of these situations, but in many cases organizations are left to attempt to determine appropriate, ethical courses of action, balancing many complex variables. South Africa is not the only country in which human rights have been violated. In much of the Eastern bloc, Tibet, China, many countries in South and Central America, and some Pacific Rim nations, people suffer significant violations of human rights. Businesses typically have tried to avoid involvement in internal issues such as human rights, but in many cases, such as in South Africa, they have been forced to become involved. What is ethically and economically correct?

STRATEGIC MANAGER'S SUMMARY

1. Globalization of business means that organizations are creating common, but tailored products for a number of markets in a number of different countries.
2. Porter describes global competitive advantage as coming from four sources: factor conditions, demand conditions, related and supporting industries, and company strategy, structure, and rivalry. Luck and government must also be considered.
3. The triad of key markets are North America, Europe, and Japan. The more important characteristics for each include: *Population*—EEC, 320 million; United States, 243 million; Japan, 120 million. *Gross national product*—United States, $4.4 billion; Japan, $1.6 billion; EEC, $3.8 billion; *relative financial power*; *balance of trade*.
4. The Japanese seek to grow faster than their competitors, and to increase their market share so that their volume of business will increase at a rate greater than their competitors. Increased volume means decreased costs and therefore more profitability and financial strength, and the whole cycle begins again.
5. The four Asian tigers' principal strengths are their cheap labor rates and their ability to quickly adapt foreign technology for their own purposes.
6. In 1992 the European Economic Community becomes one true common market with essentially all major barriers to free trade eliminated. North American firms may be frozen out of that market. The more likely scenario is that it will be more difficult for them to enter so they should have begun entering that market before 1992 by arranging for mergers, alliances, acquisitions, or joint ventures, or by exploring other ways in which to do business in Europe.
7. The potential of East-West integration and other changes occurring in eastern Europe, may even surpass the effects of Europe 1992. They will greatly affect 1992, especially because German reunification preceded it.
8. It is clear that managers must change the way they manage in different environments although, as the world becomes more globalized, each country will become more like the others. Both the economic functions and management functions are modified by differences in economic, political/legal, social/cultural, and technological forces.
9. Companies may export or license, they may move to become multidomestic, and, finally, they may become totally global companies.

10. Global organizations have, in one way or another, essentially the same organization structures as others, but you will seldom see functional or client-based structures. Most typically, global organizations begin with multi-product structures and eventually have divisional structures either by country or major region, depending on a number of variables.

11. Some of the unique issues in managing in multinational situations include political instability, human rights, terrorism, host country conflicts, and currency fluctuations.

12. Controlling global strategy requires the development of sophisticated information and control systems.

KEY TERMS

company strategy, structure, rivalry
  (Porter model)
demand conditions (Porter model)
factor conditions (Porter model)
global corporations
global localization
global strategy

multidomestic corporations
multinational corporations (MNCs)
related and supporting industries (Porter
  model)
Porter's dynamic diamond
think global
think local

DISCUSSION QUESTIONS

1. Describe how strategic management is becoming more complex because of the globalization of business.

2. Describe the major changes occurring in the globalization of business in the 1990s. Indicate their impact on the functions of management.

3. Based on Porter's dynamic diamond, what must U.S. firms do to overcome their difficult competitive situations? How will Europe 1992 help European global firms be better competitors?

4. Enumerate the reasons that Japanese firms have been so successful in global competition.

5. Why are joint ventures and acquisitions so popular for becoming competitive globally, in Europe especially?

STRATEGIC AUDIT QUESTIONS

1. Does the firm understand global competition? Does it have a global strategy? How good is it? Does it have a multidomestic strategy? How good is it? Does it think globally?

2. Does the firm adjust to the varying economic, legal, political, social, and cultural environments in which it does business? Does it account for technological variations in the countries in which it does business?

3. Does it have a currency exchange management program? How effective is it?

4. How well does it encourage government to support its competition with other firms that are protected by their governments, both locally and in foreign countries?

5. Does it adjust the strategic management process to different situations?

6. Does it have a global strategic information system with both formal and informal aspects? How effective is it?

7. How is it adjusted to the hierarchy of strategy of each situation?

8. Does it adjust implementation to each situation?

Endnotes

1. For example, see "Now, the Birth of a Nation," *U.S. News & World Report*, December 23, 1991, pp. 34–40.

2. For example, see "North American Free Trade Agreement," *HRM Magazine*, December 1991, pp. 85–86; Stephen B. Shepard, "President Salinas: 'My People Are in a Hurry,'" *Business Week*, August 12, 1991, pp. 34–36.

3. Michael J. McCarthy, "The Real Thing: As a Global Marketer, Coke Excels by Being Tough and Consistent," *The Wall Street Journal*, December 19, 1989, pp. A1, A6.

4. "Business without Borders," *U.S. News & World Report*, June 20, 1988, p. 48.

5. Thomas J. Peters, *Thriving on Chaos: Handbook for a Management Revolution* (New York: Knopf, 1987); and John Naisbitt, *Megatrends* (New York: Warner, 1982).

6. Amanda Bennett, "Going Global: The Chief Executive in the Year 2000 Will Be Experienced Abroad," *The Wall Street Journal*, February 27, 1989, pp. A1, A9.

7. "Thinking Ahead: Radically Redefined Global Competition in the 1990s," *Price Waterhouse Review*, vol. 34, no. 1 (1990), pp. 6–25.

8. "The Fortune Directory of the 50 Largest Commercial-Banking Companies Outside the United States," *Fortune*, August 10, 1981, p. 220; "The 50 Largest Commercial Banking Companies," *Fortune*, July 31, 1981, p. 117.

9. R. Taggart Murphy, "Power without Purpose: The Crisis of Japan's Global Financial Dominance," *Harvard Business Review*, March–April 1989, pp. 71–94. This article describes the tremendous financial influence of the Japanese in the world.

10. "The Foreign 500," *Fortune* August 10, 1981, p. 206; "The Largest U.S. Industrial Corporations," *Fortune*, May 4, 1981, p. 324.

11. "Will We Ever Close the Trade Gap?" *Business Week*, February 27, 1989, pp. 86–92.

12. "Fitting into a Global Economy," *U.S. News & World Report*, December 26, 1988, p. 80.

13. Murphy, "Power without Purpose."

14. Peter Truell, "Third World Debt Proposal Should Benefit Some Banks," *The Wall Street Journal*, March 16, 1989, p. A9; Charles F. McCoy and Peter Truell, "Lending Imbroglio: Worries Deepen Again on Third World Debt as Brazil Stops Paying," *The Wall Street Journal*, March 3, 1987, pp. 1, 24.

15. Karen Elliott House, "The 90s & Beyond: As Power Is Disbursed among Nations the Need for Leadership Grows," *The Wall Street Journal*, February 21, 1989, pp. A1, A10.

16. Karen Elliott House, "The 90s & Beyond: for All Its Difficulties, the U.S. Stands to Retain Its Global Leadership," *The Wall Street Journal*, January 23, 1989, pp. A1, A8; plus the events in eastern Europe in November 1989, the opening of the Berlin Wall, political and economic reforms in virtually all of Eastern Europe.

17. Michael Porter, "Why Nations Triumph," *Fortune*, March 12, 1990, pp. 94–95; excerpted from Michael Porter, *The Competitive Advantage of Nations* (New York: Macmillan, 1990).

18. Thomas A. Stewart, "Brainpower," *Fortune*, June 3, 1991, pp. 44–60.

19. For a critical review, see "Flaws in Porter's Competitive Diamond?" *Planning Review*, September/October 1990, pp. 28–32; separate reviews by Robert J. Allio and Milton Leontiades.

20. Kenichi Ohmae, *Triad Power* (New York: Free Press, 1985).

21. William G. Ouchi, *Theory Z: How American Business Can Meet the Japanese Challenge* (Reading, Mass.: Addison-Wesley, 1981).

22. Norman Coates, "Determinants of Japan's Business Success: Some Japanese Executives' Views," *Academy of Management Executive*, January 1988, pp. 69–72.

23. James C. Abegglen and George Stalk, Jr., "The Japanese Corporation as Competitor," *California Management Review*, Spring 1986, pp. 9–27.

24. Robert Neff, Ted Holden, and Karen Lowry Miller, "Hidden Japan," *Business Week*, August 26, 1991, pp. 34–58; Robert Neff, "Japan's Small, Smoke-Filled Room," *Business Week*, August 26, 1991, pp. 42–44; Karen Lowry Miller, "Good Fellas, Japanese-Style: Well-Connected and 20% Legit," *Business Week*, August 26, 1991, p. 44.

25. Pat Choate, "Political Advantage: Japan's Campaign for America," *Harvard Business Review*, September/October 1990, pp. 87–103.

26. "Japan Builds a New Power Base," *Business Week*, April 10, 1989, pp. 42–45.

27. "Battle for the Future," *Time*, January 16, 1989, pp. 42, 43.

28. "Can Asia's Four Tigers Be Tamed?" *Business Week*, February 15, 1988, pp. 46–50.

29. James M. Higgins and Timo Santalainen, "Strategies for Europe 1992," *Business Horizons*, July/August 1989, pp. 54–58.

30. Shawn Tully, "Europe Gets Ready for 1992," *Fortune*, February 1988, p. 81.

31. Tully, "Europe Gets Ready," pp. 81, 83.

32. For a review of expected events, see Higgins and Santalainen, "Strategies for 1992."

33. Lammert deVries, senior consultant for Klynvold, Peat, Marwick, Gourdeler (KPMG), presentation to the Strategic Management Society, Amsterdam, the Netherlands, October 19, 1988.

34. John Templeman, "Germany Takes Charge," *Business Week*, February 17, 1992, pp. 50–58; Herbert Henzler, "Managing the Merger: A Strategy for the New Germany," *Harvard Business Review*, January/February 1992, pp. 24–29.

35. Greg Forman, "Future Shock: Banks Face Shakeout as Europe Prepares for Unified Market," *The Wall Street Journal*, April 4, 1988, pp. A1, A18; "The Money Men Can't Wait for the Starting Gun," *Business Week*, December 12, 1988, pp. 72–73.

36. For example, see Achin A. Stoehr, "Japanese Positioning for Post-1992 Europe," *Planning Review*, July/August 1991, pp. 16–24; Alan M. Rugman and Alan Verbeke, "Europe 1992 and Competitive Strategies for North American Firms," *Business Horizons*, November/December 1991, pp. 76–81.

37. Shawn Tully, "Europe Hits the Brakes on 1992," *Fortune*, December 17, 1990, pp. 133–140.

38. Steven Tupper, presentation to the Strategic Management Society, Amsterdam, Netherlands, October 19, 1988.

39. Craig Forman, "Europe Crossroads: As EC Leaders Gather, The Program for 1992 Is Facing Big Problems," *The Wall Street Journal*, December 6, 1991, pp. A1, A10.

40. Shepard, "President Salinas;" William T. Holstein, David Woodruff, Amy Borrus, "Mexico: A New Economic Era," *Business Week*, October 12, 1990, pp. 102–113.

41. "Crossing the Line from Talk to Action," *Business Week*, January 9, 1989, pp. 54–55.

42. Robert H. Hayes and William J. Abernathy, "Managing Our Way to Economic Decline," *Harvard Business Review*, July–August 1980, pp. 67–77.

43. Charles W. L. Hill, Michael A. Hitt, and Robert E. Hoskisson, "Declining U.S. Competitiveness: Reflections on a Crisis," *The Academy of Management Executive*, February (1988), pp. 51–60. For a broad review of causes, see Abbas J. Ali and Abdulbrahman Al-Asli, "Expatriate and Saudi Managers' Perceptions of Japanese and U.S. Competitiveness: A Survey," *Business Horizons*, November/December 1991, p. 37.

44. Hill, et al., "Declining Competitiveness," p. 53.

45. "Is the Soviet Union Next?" *U.S. News & World Report*, January 15, 1990, pp. 31–38; also see "The Deal of the Decade May Get Done in Moscow," *Business Week*, February 27, 1989, pp. 54–55. This article details an agreement by which U.S. companies and the Soviets are nearing a significant breakthrough in East-West joint ventures.

46. William Glasgell, "The Global Rush to Privatize," *Business Week*, October 21, 1991, pp. 49–55.

47. Gary Hamel and C. K. Prahalad, "Do You Really Have a Global Strategy," *Harvard Business Review*, July/August 1985, pp. 139–148.

48. Stefan H. Robock and Kenneth Simmonds, *International Business and Multi-National Enterprises* (Homewood, Ill.: Irwin, 1973), p. 7.

49. Christopher M. Korth, *International Business, Environment of Management*, 2d ed. (Englewood Cliffs, N.J.: Prentice-Hall, 1985), p. 7; and Neil H. Jacoby, "The Multinational Corporation," *The Center Magazine*, May 1970, pp. 37–55.

50. *The Wall Street Journal*, April 25, 1988, p. 26.

51. Hamel and Prahalad, "Do You Have"; Porter, *Competitive Advantage*, pp. 139–148.

52. Michael E. Porter, "Changing Patterns of International Competition," *California Management Review*, Winter 1986, pp. 9–40.

53. William B. Johnston, "Global Work Force 2000: The New Labor Market," *Harvard Business Review*, March–April 1991, pp. 115–127.

54. R. Hall Mason, "Conflicts between Host Countries and a Multi-National Enterprise," *California Management Review*, Fall 1974, pp. 5–14.

55. Robock and Simmonds, *International Business*, pp. 243–249.

56. Porter, "Changing Patterns."

57. Simon Majaro, *International Marketing*, rev. ed. (London, Boston: Allyn & Bacon, 1982), pp. 88, 111, 178.

58. Kenneth Labich, "America's International Winners," *Fortune*, April 14, 1986, pp. 34–46.

59. Bernard Wyochci, Jr., "Changing Tactics: Battling a High Yen, Many Japanese Firms Shift Work Overseas,"

The Wall Street Journal, February 27, 1987, pp. 1, 10.

60. Labich, "International Winners."

61. Mark M. Nelson and Stephen D. Moore, "Europe's Industries Take on a Leaner Look," *The Wall Street Journal*, March 9, 1987, p. 26.

62. Timo Santalainen and Risto Tainio, "Factors and Mechanisms Affecting Business Performance of Banks," working paper F-39, Helsinki School of Economics, October 1982.

63. Risto Tainio and Timo Santalainen, "Some Evidence for the Cultural Relativity of Organizational Development Programs," *Journal of Applied Behavior Science* 20, no. 2 (1984), pp. 93–111.

64. Donald A. Ball and Wendell H. McCulloch, Jr., *International Business: Introduction and Essentials*, 2d ed. (Plano, Tex.: Business Publications, 1985), pp. 39–48.

65. Alex Taylor III, "Who's Ahead in the World Auto War," *Fortune*, November 9, 1987, pp. 74–88.

66. James B. Treece, "Can Ford Stay on Top?" *Business Week*, September 28, 1987, pp. 78–86.

67. Labich, "International Winners."

68. John D. Daniels and Lee H. Redebaugh, *International Business*, 4th ed. (Reading, Mass.: Addison-Wesley, 1986), pp. 508–516.

69. Buck Brown, "How the Cookie Crumbled at Mrs. Fields," *The Wall Street Journal*, January 26, 1989, p. B1.

70. For a discussion of joint ventures, see Kathryn Harrigan, *Strategies for Joint Ventures* (Lexington, Mass.: Lexington Books, 1985).

71. James R. Norman, "Why GE Took a European Bride," *Business Week*, January 30, 1989, p. 52.

72. Kenichi Ohmae, "The Global Logic of Strategic Allian-ces," *Harvard Business Review*, March–April 1989, pp. 143–154; Howard Perlmutter and David Heenan, "Co-operate to Compete Globally," *Harvard Business Review*, March–April 1986, pp. 136–152. Perlmutter and Heenan designate these alliances as global strategic partnerships (GSPs).

73. For a lengthy discussion of factors involved in making this choice, see Derek F. Channon with Michael Jalland, *Multinational Strategic Planning* (New York: Amacom, 1978), pp. 193–194.

74. W. Chan Kim and R. A. Mauburgne, "Becoming an Effective Global Competitor," *Journal of Business Strategy*, January/February 1988, pp. 33–37.

75. James F. Bolt, "Global Competitors: Self Criteria for Success," *Business Horizons*, January/February 1988, pp. 34–41.

76. Kenichi Ohmae, "Planning for a Global Harvest," *Harvard Business Review*, July–August 1989, pp. 136–145.

77. Kenichi Ohmae, "Managing in the Borderless World," *Harvard Business Review*, May–June 1989, pp. 152–161.

78. Kenichi Ohmae, "Getting Back to Strategy," *Harvard Business Review*, November–December 1988, p. 149.

79. Michael Porter, "The Competitive Advantage of Nations," *Harvard Business Review*, March–April 1990, p. 74.

80. "Pull out Parade," *Time*, November 3, 1986, pp. 32–34; "All Roads Lead out of South Africa," *Business Week*, November 3, 1986, pp. 24–25; "Fighting Apartheid, American Style," *U.S. News & World Report*, October 22, 1986, p. 45–46.

INTEGRATIVE CASE ANALYSIS
CHAPTER 11

THE CHALLENGES FACING GENERAL MOTORS IN 1992

General Motors has either manufacturing and/or marketing operations in all major countries of the world. However, it does not appear to think globally with respect to these operations, and it does not follow a true global strategy. Rather, it has followed a multidomestic strategy developing specific products for different foreign markets. If GM were thinking globally and pursuing a true global strategy, it would be entering the home markets of its major foreign competitors, attempting to hurt their profits. And it would be using the cash flow from successful markets, and the knowledge gained in these markets, to penetrate others. But GM is not pursuing Japanese firms' home turf to any degree. Thus, it leaves itself totally vulnerable to Japanese inroads into its markets. Make no mistake about it, most of Japan's gains in the United States have come at the expense of GM, not Ford and Chrysler.

The U.S. auto industry is a good case study for the use of Porter's dynamic diamond model of the competitive advantage of nations when compared with the Japanese auto industry. For example, Porter notes that there is intense rivalry in Japan, and less in the United States, giving Japanese firms an advantage when competing in the United States. On the other hand, U.S. market size is greater, potentially favoring U.S. firms. The tables turn, however, when customer sophistication is considered. Furthermore, Japanese auto firms have historically had much better supporting industries than U.S. auto firms, although U.S. firms are now emulating Japan's support group relationships. Finally, when factor conditions are considered, the United States often is worse off with regard to worker skill levels and wage rates, but better off with respect to natural resources.

GM has fortified its European operation and found significant success there. In fact, the European operation is one of the few GM units making money. It hasn't always been that way. Just a few years ago, it lost money. GM's European operation was turned around by John Smith. However, long term, GM's operations in Europe are potentially threatened by a growing Japanese presence. Japan already dominates several markets there, for example, holding 30 percent of the German market.

ENTREPRENEURIAL AND SMALL BUSINESS STRATEGY AND INNOVATION

The reasonable man adapts himself to the world: The unreasonable one persists in trying to adapt the world to himself, therefore, all progress depends on the unreasonable man.

George Bernard Shaw

The entrepreneurs sustain the world. In their careers there is little of optimizing calculation, nothing of delicate balance in markets. They overthrow establishments rather than establish equilibria. They are the heroes of economic life.

George Gilder
The Spirit of Enterprise

CHAPTER OBJECTIVES

By the time you complete this chapter, you should be able to:

1. Define entrepreneurship and distinguish it from small business management
2. Discuss several reasons why entrepreneurship is so interesting at this time in the United States, Canada, and the rest of the world
3. Discuss the stages-of-growth model and how growth affects entrepreneurship and small business management
4. Discuss the differences in strategic management in an entrepreneurship from that in a larger firm
5. Describe the choices available in pursuing innovation as a strategy

SAM WALTON—ENTREPRENEUR, STRATEGIST

Perhaps no one better exemplified the entrepreneur who made the transition to professional manager and strategist than did Sam M. Walton, founder of Wal-Mart, Sam's Wholesale Clubs, and Hypermart USA stores before his death in 1992. Sam was the son of a Depression-era mortgage banker. He graduated in 1940 from the University of Missouri with a degree in economics and went to work immediately for J. C. Penney as a trainee, but quickly the entrepreneurial spirit struck him. He opened his first Ben Franklin discount store in Newport, Arkansas in 1945. At just about the same time his brother, Bud, opened a second Ben Franklin store in rural Missouri. By the late 1950s Sam and his brother had opened 16 Ben Franklin stores and they were the largest Ben Franklin franchisees in the country. They located most of their stores in rural areas where there was no competition. Sam discovered that larger stores would do well in these rural areas. He took his idea to Ben Franklin management, but they were not responsive; they did not want to lower their profit margins. In 1962 he opened his first Wal-Mart store in Rogers, Arkansas, not far from the company's current main office in Bentenville, Arkansas. His stores offered low prices with comparatively high levels of service.

As of January 31, 1990 Walton's empire had grown to 1,402 Wal-Mart stores, 123 Sam's Wholesale Clubs, and 3 Hypermart USA stores across 29 states. Sales in excess of $32.6 billion for fiscal year 1990 generated profits of $1.3 billion. This allowed Wal-Mart to pass Sears and Kmart and become the number one retailer in the United States.

Sam had a vision of strategic intent and he made it work. What is so unique is that he kept the entrepreneurial spirit alive in the corporation while growing it to colossal size. His management style is well-known. He was particularly demanding while at the same time highly relationship-oriented. Until the number of stores became so great that the task became impossible, he could name all the store managers and many of their employees. Also, until recently when the number of stores became so large, he would visit each store at least once every year. He was well-known for his antics such as jumping on top of the board room table during Saturday morning management meetings and shouting "Who's number one!" to which all present responded, "Wal-Mart . . . Wal-Mart . . . Wal-Mart." He and his staff were meticulous about details and concerned about product and service quality. Their huge volume enabled the firm to be both price competitive and the low-cost leader in most lines of goods, yet insistence on service enabled it to differentiate itself from competitors.

At first Sam Walton focused on rural America, but as the strength of the company grew, he began to compete with Kmart, Sears, Penney's, and other large players head-on in larger cities. He made the leap from entrepreneur to professional manager. His company employs advanced information systems, including electronic data interchange with suppliers, highly sophisticated distribution networks, and intense performance evaluation and control systems. Human resources have been one of Wal-Mart's major competitive advantages for the past several years. The company invests heavily in training programs for its clerks, managers, and executives. Wal-Mart's policy is to treat people with dignity, respect, and responsiveness at all levels. Wal-Mart tries to provide an environment in which people can grow, not only through training, but through job responsibility. It has one of the best benefit packages in the industry, including a cafeteria-style benefit offering. Profit sharing has been a major incentive program to help motivate employees to do their best. Sam Walton himself invigorated the company with inspiration.

The consequence of all this for Sam Walton personally was that he was the richest man in America. His stock was valued at over $7 billion, but it didn't change him. He still drove the same old, battered pickup truck that he had driven for years and he still dressed like the good old country boy that he was.

Sources: Van Johnston and Herff Moore, "Pride Drives Wal-Mart to Service Excellence," *HRM Magazine*, October 1991, pp. 76–82; John Huey, "America's Most Successful Merchant," *Fortune*, September 23, 1991, pp. 46–59; Bill Saporitos, "Is Wal-Mart Unstoppable?" *Fortune*, May 6, 1991, pp. 50–59.

Sam Walton of Wal-Mart, Ken Olson of DEC, Steven Jobs and Stephen Wozniak of Apple Computers, Mary Kay Ash of Mary Kay Cosmetics, Ray Kroc of McDonald's, An Wang of Wang Laboratories, Debbi and Randy Fields of Mrs. Fields' Cookies, H. Ross Perot of Electronic Data Systems, Akio Morita of Sony, and hundreds of thousands of others share a very important characteristic—they are or were successful entrepreneurs. Recently there has been a significant increase in interest in entrepreneurship. Many people think that entrepreneurship makes America great. Much of this reverence for the phenomenon comes as a consequence of the realization that small, entrepreneurial firms have contributed very significantly to the well-being of the national economy, especially in the 10-year period from 1977 to 1987. In fact, most of the jobs created in that 10-year period came not from major corporations, but from startup operations and small businesses. From 1977 to 1987, 17 million new jobs were created in small businesses compared to a net loss of 3.1 million jobs among the Fortune 500 companies.[1] New corporations formed per year reached 700,000 for the first time in 1986.[2] Small businesses did experience a slowdown in 1990, as the recession began to affect this market segment.[3]

David Birch of MIT's Program of Neighborhood and Regional Change suggests that, while the impact of entrepreneurship on the national economy is very significant, it can have an even greater regional impact. In California, for example, 70 percent of the state's employment results from small-scale entrepreneurs.[4] In another example, many entrepreneurs emerged from the declining rustbelt, those areas of the Northeast and Midwest where heavy industry failed. What was unique about the situation in the rustbelt in the middle to late 1980s was that entrepreneurship resulted from massive layoffs as industrial firms collapsed one after another. Furthermore, many of these entrepreneurs were blue-collar workers.[5]

This chapter explores strategic management in entrepreneurships and small businesses, as well as the strategy of innovation, which is inextricably intertwined with entrepreneurship, but it is also necessary to the traditional larger corporation seeking to be competitive. The chapter begins by defining these terms, and distinguishing between them. Strategically managing the small business/entrepreneurship is then discussed, with an emphasis on the practical problems of formulating strategy. Global strategies for entrepreneurships and small businesses are reviewed. Ways of preserving entrepreneurship in large corporations are reviewed. A discussion of the innovation strategy and the choices available to those choosing an innovation strategy concludes the chapter.

DEFINITIONS OF *ENTREPRENEUR*[6]

Identifying exactly what entrepreneurship is has been a difficult task. Historically, entrepreneurship has been conceptualized partially as an economic function. In the early 18th century, Richard Cantillon observed that an entrepreneur was one who bore the risk of buying and selling.[7] Economists Adam Smith and Jean Baptiste Say suggested that an entrepreneur was someone who brought together the factors of production.[8] Austrian economist Joseph Schumpeter (1883–1950) later added innovation and exploiting opportunity as actions of the entrepreneur.[9] Some have suggested that the creation of new enterprises is entrepreneurship.[10] More recently, however, Howard H. Stevenson and William H. Sahlman point out that entrepreneurs can be identified who do not purchase or sell, who do not bring together the factors of production, who are not innovators but followers, who do not create businesses but manage the work of others.[11]

Today, entrepreneurship is recognized to be as much an attitude as a role practiced in small and large organizations.[12] Stevenson and Jose Carlos Jarillo-Mossi's broad definition, on which we will expand, defines an **entrepreneur** as "a person who perceives opportunity; finds the pursuit of opportunity desirable in the context of his [or her] life situation; and believes that success is possible."[13] It is also clear that an entrepreneur is one who initiates change.

Note that approach to problem solving is the key difference between entrepreneurs and others. Entrepreneurs look for opportunities. They are risk takers. They do not merely solve problems, they do not just react to problems, they look for opportunities. This view of the opportunity orientation of entrepreneurship was noted in 1964 by Peter Drucker, who indicated that "Resources, to produce results, must be allocated to opportunities, rather than to problems. . . . [M]aximization of opportunities is a meaningful, indeed a precise definition of the entrepreneurial job."[14] Later, in 1974, Drucker repeated this theme, writing, "an entrepreneur . . . has to redirect resources from areas of low or diminishing results to areas of high or increasing results. He or she has to slough off yesterday and to render obsolete what already exists and is already known. He [or she] has to create tomorrow."[15]

Entrepreneurship is also about change. Entrepreneurs initiate change.[16] They may initiate changes in all aspects of organizational functions, including marketing, finance, operations, human resources, and information. Drucker later combined his views of the opportunistic nature of entrepreneurs with this aspect of change, concluding, "the entrepreneur always searches for change, responds to it, and exploits it as an opportunity."[17] Fred Smith, founder of Federal Express, was just such an entrepreneur. He saw an opportunity and seized it, changing package delivery.

AT WAL-MART

By any definition, Sam Walton was an entrepreneur. He initiated change. He seized opportunities. He exploited change as opportunity.

In seeking to understand entrepreneurship, others have searched to identify the personal characteristics of entrepreneurs. Several commonly accepted characteristics include the need for achievement, the need for control, an intuitive orientation, and a risk-taking propensity. Other commonly discussed, but not universally accepted factors include childhood deprivation, minority group membership, and early adolescent economic experiences.[18]

Many people claim that entrepreneurs and entrepreneurships are one of the major ways in which U.S. firms are able to compete with foreign firms, principally through innovation.[19] Not all agree, however. George Gilder suggests that entrepreneurs often sell out to foreign competitors, posing problems for the economy by giving away our technology.[20] He also points out that only larger firms have the staying power necessary to compete in many industries, thus reducing the importance of entrepreneurships. Nonetheless, most would agree that entrepreneurs enable the United States to compete more successfully internationally because they have introduced literally hundreds of thousands of new products. It is clear that they are helping to create an export boom, and that reduces the U.S. trade deficit.[21]

There definitely is something exciting about being an entrepreneur. It offers several psychological payoffs: a chance to be your own boss, initiate change, do it your way, take advantage of opportunities, be at the forefront of change. There are also disadvantages: long hours, hard work, risk. Most small businesses end in failure.[22]

A review of several studies by John A. Hornaday states several common **characteristics of entrepreneurs:**[23] self-confidence, energy and diligence, ability to take calculated risks, creativity, flexibility, positive response to challenges, leadership, the ability to get along with people, responsiveness to suggestions, knowledge of market, perseverance and determination, resourcefulness, the need to achieve, initiative, independence, foresight, profit orientation, perceptiveness, optimism, and versatility of knowledge, especially as related to technology. A recent research study shows that attitude is a better predictor of entrepreneurship than personality or demographics.[24]

ENTREPRENEURSHIP AND SMALL BUSINESS MANAGEMENT[25]

Distinguishing between a small business and an entrepreneurship is relatively easy. The term **small business** describes a business according to its size, while entrepreneurship describes an attitude or behavioral process that may be found in a small, medium, or large business. Entrepreneurs run many small businesses, but not all of them, perhaps not even most of them. Many small businesses are run by people who do not have entrepreneurial leanings and do not engage in the entrepreneurial process. Furthermore, entrepreneurs may be found in larger businesses, as well. The most frequently cited definition of small business is that provided by the U.S. Small Business Administration (SBA).

How the U.S. Small Business Administration Defines *Small Business*

To qualify for a loan from the U.S. Small Business Administration, a small business must have three principal characteristics:[26]

1. It cannot dominate its industry.
2. It must have less than $10 million in annual sales.
3. It must have fewer than 1,000 employees.

There are some additional qualifications:

1. It must be independently owned and operated.
2. If in manufacturing, it should employ no more than 250 employees or be relatively small compared to other firms in a specific industry. In certain industries, 1,500 employees is considered small.
3. If in wholesaling, it should have annual sales no greater than $9.5 to $22 million, depending on the industry.
4. If in retailing or service, its annual sales should not exceed $2 to $8 million, depending on the industry.
5. If in general construction, its annual receipts cannot exceed $9.5 million for the three most recently completed fiscal years. In special trade construction, its annual receipts cannot exceed $1 to $2 million for the same time frame, depending on the industry.
6. If in agriculture, its annual receipts cannot be greater than $1 million.

The SBA uses these characteristics as guidelines. They are not hard and fast rules.

Numerous other definitions of what constitutes a small business may be found. For example, many consider a small business to be one that is family-owned, owned and operated by a small group of investors, a franchise, operating locally, employing fewer than 100 people, and so forth. Regardless of the criteria chosen, it is clear that the number of small businesses far exceeds the number of large businesses. As shown in Table 12.1, more than 99 percent of this country's 14 million businesses are small. These 14 million businesses include farms, franchises, and professional organizations.

STRATEGICALLY MANAGING THE ENTREPRENEURSHIP/SMALL BUSINESS

As organizations grow, they pass through a series of stages. The first stage might be called growth through creation.[27]

Getting Started

Even in this startup stage, it is critical to develop a (strategic) business plan, although many companies don't do this unless forced to by potential creditors. A business plan typically contains specific objectives and plans to reach those objectives across the major economic functions of the organization. Special attention is paid to target markets, product development, pricing, distribution, and promotion strategies, and the ability of the organization to finance marketing and operations.

TABLE 12.1 Small Businesses Classified by Size

Percentage of Business	Number of Employees
88.9%	Fewer than 10
94.7	Fewer than 20
99.2	Fewer than 100
99.9	Fewer than 500

Source: "The State of Small Business: A Report to the President," U.S. Government Printing Office, Washington, D.C., 1985. (Based on a population of 14 million business firms.)

A business plan includes at least the following information.[28]

1. An overview of the business that helps define the organization's vision, mission, goals, strategies, and functional parts
2. A specific set of objectives against which performance may be measured, both for the organization and employees

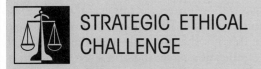

STRATEGIC ETHICAL CHALLENGE

WHEN YOU WANT THE BUSINESS SO BADLY . . .

Tom, president of a small but growing management consulting firm, offered the following commentary on ethics. "It's a real struggle out there, and sometimes you want the business so badly, that you will do just about anything to get it. A few years ago, I became friends with a person of some influence in an organization. A couple of years after we started playing golf on a twice monthly basis, a consulting contract came up for bid at his firm. He told me about it, and I submitted a bid. A week or so went by, and I got a call from him. He indicated that it was between my firm (just me and my secretary at that time) and a larger firm. He wanted to know if I wanted to see a copy of the competitor's proposal. I said sure without thinking. You know, you have a wife and two kids, house payments, car payments, and all that. But while that envelope containing the competitor's proposal was in the mail, I realized I couldn't look at that material ethically. I had gotten so caught up in winning the contract, it just hadn't occurred to me. I called my friend and told him that I would mail the package back to him unopened, and I did. To make a long story short, I didn't get the contract. His boss decided on the lower bidder, which was the other firm. I might not have gotten the contract even if I had looked at the other proposal, but we'll never know. But either way, you can't cheat and feel good about yourself. At least, I can't."

3. A plan by which capital may be raised (Most banks, for example, require a detailed business plan before they will loan money on a new enterprise or an ongoing smaller one. Pro forma income statements, balance sheets, and cash flow statements will be necessary.)
4. An operational plan, a materials purchasing plan, and related operations information
5. A research and development plan
6. A plan by which personnel may be recruited and managed
7. A risk analysis

About 85 percent of all new businesses will fail within 10 years of their startup, so planning to avoid such failure is critical.[29] Businesses fail for many reasons besides poor planning, for example, a lack of capital. Failing to set objectives and develop strategies and budgets, however, can only lead to failure for most. Strategic planning should continue after the business is launched. Usually it doesn't, at least not until the firm reaches a substantial size.

Crisis of Leadership

The growth-through-creation stage is often followed by a crisis of leadership. In this crisis, the entrepreneur or small business manager arrives at a point at which he or she can no longer run the business properly. The entrepreneur either needs to become a professional manager or hire others to manage the business. He or she may also need to structure the organization on an economic functional basis, dividing job tasks among several different people. The entrepreneur can no longer do it alone. Research makes it clear, though, that the style and intentions of the entrepreneur will remain, and will significantly affect the firm's future. Some can never let go.[30] Making the transition from hip-pocket management to more professional management is never easy; for some it is impossible.

At this point planning usually becomes more formal. The professional manager or professionalized entrepreneur begins to routinely set strategy. Most such efforts at first plod through the formal models of planning discussed throughout this book. Several software packages for PCs are available to lead the business through the steps. Some of the more complex PC simulation models allow small business people to think in terms of the impact of the external environment on business success.[31] This kind of strategic thinking is very helpful. Performing a SWOT analysis of the firm, for example, enables the entrepreneur/small business manager to prepare better strategic and operating plans. The budget enables managers to predict potential cash shortages and take necessary offsetting actions.

AT WAL-MART

Sam Walton was able to make the transition to more formalized planning. Wal-Mart employs many state-of-the-art management systems.

Now that simulation models such as Lotus 1-2-3, and several more complex ones are available for personal computers, virtually any small business can calculate pro forma financial statements (income statement, balance sheet, and cash flow statement) which should help management understand the internal operations of the organization. Just as with any major organization, the entrepreneur/small business manager must provide in-depth answers to three questions:

1. Where are we now?
2. Where do we want to be?
3. How do we get there?

Mature Firms

Most entrepreneurial firms and small businesses that survive and prosper will grow. As organizations grow, they typically change their structures, from functional to product to strategic business unit, for example. As pointed out in Chapters 8 and 9, one of the major factors in making organizations more efficient today is structuring to delegate more authority to lower level positions, eliminating as many middle-level management and staff positions as possible. These actions make the organization more efficient, and also more responsive to the external environment. A typical entrepreneur has high needs for achievement and power.[32] It is often difficult for them to delegate, especially to front-line employees. Unfortunately, many entrepreneurs and small business owners are unable to make this transition to delegation, and thus their organizations fail. As organizations grow, the processes by which strategies are derived change, as do the bases of strategies, for example from function to product to SBU. Keeping the organization's vim and vigor as it matures requires special effort.[33]

STRATEGIC CONCEPTS AND THE ENTREPRENEUR/SMALL BUSINESS MANAGER

Many people say that small businesses and entrepreneurships really shouldn't bother with formal strategic planning, but that perspective overlooks the contribution of strategic planning. Each of the concepts introduced in Chapter 1 and later in this text is extremely relevant to the entrepreneurship and small business. It may be, however, that the entrepreneurial or small business CEO thinks through the process rather than formally writing out all of the statements. The following paragraphs discuss how each of the major concepts presented in this book might be viewed from the perspective of an entrepreneur or small business CEO.

Vision and Strategic Intent

Entrepreneurs and small business CEOs often have much more vision and strategic focus and intent than do CEOs of large, monolithic organizations. In fact, according to John Case, the companies that make up the *Inc.* magazine list 500 of the fastest-growing small, private, U.S. companies seem to think about creating markets rather than serving them. More often than not, they seem to set out to do something that no one else is doing.[34] Entrepreneurs are invigorated by their vision for their companies and they invigorate and enliven those around them.

Perhaps even more than vision, however, their strategic intents of creating new markets or new products or services carry their companies forward. It is their single-minded pursuit of achieving the impossible that makes them successful.

AT WAL-MART

Sam Walton was unable to convince Ben Franklin Stores that his approach to discount retailing was appropriate. He therefore started his own company and the rest is history. Wal-Mart is now the largest retailer in the United States, dwarfing Ben Franklin.

Mission Statement

Most entrepreneurs and small business CEOs carry around in their heads ideas of the businesses they want to be in and the scopes of those businesses, the natures of their target markets, and the basic philosophies by which they will run their companies. Many entrepreneurs leave companies with whose philosophies they have disagreed to establish their own firms. Many leave because they are unable to carry out a vision that they have, so they seek to establish their own firms.

Strategic Goals

Many entrepreneurs and small business CEOs have in mind specific goals for their companies. They want to grow, they want to dominate a market, they want to niche, they want to create a new market, they want to provide the best in service or quality. Frequently they don't write these goals down, though; they simply carry them around in their heads and they convey them to others verbally. These goals may not be codified in written statements until the company is several months, or even several years, old.

Strategic Objectives

If there is one characteristic weakness of entrepreneurs and small business CEOs, it is their typical failure to set strategic objectives. They sort of have in mind what they want to do, but they don't always quantify it, nor do they set time frames for their objectives. In our consulting work with numerous companies of various sizes, many of them entrepreneurships and small businesses, we have always stressed the need to establish specific objectives to point a company in a very specific direction and to motivate performance within the company. Our experience is that, if the company does not have specific objectives to motivate employees, they do only what they can rather than what they should.

Strategies

Entrepreneurs such as Steven Jobs and Stephen Wozniak, who founded Apple Computers, have in mind strategies. They know generally what they want to accomplish. They find niches, they build products, and they move forward as rapidly as possible. Typically, however, until venture capitalists or other potential creditors ask them to identify their strategic business plans, they don't formalize them. Even if it isn't written down, such a firm has a strategy.

Entry Strategies

Research by Patricia McDougall and Richard B. Robinson, Jr. reveals that when firms are getting started, they follow one of eight strategic archetypes:[35]

1. Aggressive growth via commodity-type products sold in numerous markets with small customer orders
2. Aggressive growth via price-competitive new products to large customers
3. Aggressive growth via narrow, specialty products priced competitively to a few large buyers
4. Controlled growth via a broad product range to many markets with extensive backward integration
5. Controlled growth via premium-priced products sold directly to consumers
6. Limited growth in small niches via superior products and high levels of customer service
7. Average growth via steady development of new channels, brand/name identification, and heavy promotion
8. Limited growth via infrequently purchased products to numerous markets with some forward integration

PRESERVING ENTREPRENEURSHIP

As entrepreneurs and small business managers learn how to manage, they often lose their entrepreneurial orientations. Howard H. Stevenson and Jose Carlos Jarrillo-Mossi suggest several actions to keep an organization entrepreneurial.[36] The entrepreneur or small business manager must increase the perception of opportunity, build the desire to pursue opportunity, and make people believe that they can succeed.

They further indicate that, as companies grow, they must answer certain questions for themselves in entrepreneurial terms.

1. What is the appropriate concept of control?
2. How does one emphasize the individual sense of responsibility over authority?
3. What kind of failures is the company willing to accept?

AT WAL-MART

Whether through the strength of his character or through delegation and incentives, Sam Walton retained the entrepreneurial spirit at Wal-Mart.

TRENDS IN ENTREPRENEURSHIP

In addition to increases in interest in the process, several trends are identifiable in entrepreneurship:

1. There are an increasing number of campus capitalists and educational efforts to increase entrepreneurship.[37]
2. More and more kids are working in family businesses.[38]
3. More and more managers are leaving large corporations to start their own businesses.[39,40]
4. There are an increasing number of female entrepreneurs in what has historically been mostly an all-male activity.[41]
5. The level of international entrepreneurship is increasing.
6. Large organizations are attempting to put more entrepreneurship into their operations.

Two of these trends have special significance for strategy; international entrepreneurship and keeping entrepreneurship alive in major corporations.

International Entrepreneurship

All over the world, but especially in Europe and the Pacific Rim, entrepreneurship is gaining popularity. In the United States entrepreneurs are helping to overcome a large international trade deficit.[42] Recognizing America's success in creating jobs from entrepreneurship, many in France are going into business as the government is getting out of business.[43] For the first time in history, in 1989 more venture capital was invested in Europe than in the United States. France has been a veritable hotbed of innovation, especially in 1990 and 1991.[44] This is true in Great Britain, as well.[45] Even in Japan, where entrepreneurship has been discouraged by the loss of face incurred by leaving a company, entrepreneurship is increasing significantly.[46] In eastern Europe, a whole generation of entrepreneurs is emerging.[47] Finally, even in the communist People's Republic of China, entrepreneurship and capitalism were rising with the encouragement of the government prior to the 1989 crackdown on freedom.[48]

Intrapreneurship—Major Corporations Seek Entrepreneurship

An **intrapreneur** is a company employee who is allowed to act like an entrepreneur within the company rather than striking out on his or her own. Companies subsidize and encourage intrapreneurs to develop and implement their ideas. Gordon Pinchot developed the concept of intrapreneurship after realizing the frustration and discontent shared by many managers and employees in large organizations. Pinchot comments that "the problem is that organizations hire people for their intelligence and imagination and then tell them what to imagine." Pinchot continues, "Entrepreneurs are people driven by a need to see their visions become real; intrapreneurs share that need. Intrapreneurs are people with entrepreneurial personalities. Intrapreneurs, like entrepreneurs, are always self-starting and both cannot be primarily motivated by money. Instead they are motivated by visions. To them, money is just a way of keeping score."[49]

Intrapreneurs are best rewarded by the organization in programs that tie results to compensation, much as an entrepreneur would be financially rewarded for his or her success by the marketplace. 3M has been especially good at fostering intrapreneurship in this way.

Companies buy books such as *In Search of Excellence* and *Intrapreneuring* for their managers because they want them to emulate the successes detailed in these books.[50] Recognizing that success depends on innovation and seizing opportunity, more and more major corporations are attempting to incorporate entrepreneurship into their cultures. This attempt at encouraging intrapreneurship in large companies, could not come at a better time for major U.S. corporations, as they see many of their best employees leaving to become entrepreneurs. Large organizations may discover that these entrepreneurs will develop many new products that often compete directly with their former employers. How do firms go about fostering intrapreneurship? The Strategic Challenge feature for this chapter tells how Signode Industries achieves this end.

IBM's personal computer was developed using the intrapreneurial approach. IBM established a separate division located in Fort Lauderdale, Florida, far away from the Armonk, New York headquarters and all other major IBM divisions. This unique division was allowed to act as an independent subsidiary. Largely because of this independence, the PC was developed as quickly as it was and became a major market success. Pinchot continues, "Perhaps most importantly intrapreneurship makes corporations highly responsive and top management will be able to turn the corporation on a dime to respond to changes in the market."[51] United Airlines, IBM, 3M, Texas Instruments, Northwestern Bell, and Eastman Kodak all have extensive intrapreneurship programs.[52]

Entrepreneurship and Restructuring   The concept of restructuring discussed in Chapter 8 is aimed at increasing the independence of strategic business unit managers or new product managers, enabling them to act as if they were entrepreneurs. As intrapreneurs, corporate employees are allowed to take risks, solicit funds for their projects, and turn creations and inventions into innovations.

In *Thriving on Chaos*, Thomas J. Peters argues that most organizations face futures of constantly accelerating rates of change, with each change being more significant than the previous one.[53] This has been echoed by a number of authorities, including Alvin Toffler in *Future Shock*,[54] and Michael Naylor, executive in charge of strategic planning at General Motors.[55] Peters argues that these increasingly rapid changes and their increasing magnitude force organizations to restructure into smaller units in order to be responsive to the changing demands of

STRATEGIC CHALLENGE

HOW SIGNODE FOSTERS INTRAPRENEURS

Signode Industries, Inc. is a privately held corporation formed by a leveraged buyout. Based in Glenview, Illinois, it employs about 6,000 people worldwide, sells its products in more than 100 countries, and has annual sales of nearly $750 million. It is the leading manufacturer of steel and plastic strapping systems for use in packaging and handling systems. Other businesses include construction products, fastening tools, and bar coding systems. Signode wanted to foster intrapreneurship. As a big company, it sought ways to create new products and act like a small, entrepreneurial company. How did it go about it?

Signode developed a nine-step process that has made it successful in developing new ventures, all revolving around venture teams.

1. Define company strengths and weaknesses.
2. Define likes and dislikes.
3. Select the venture topic.
4. Form the venture team. Pick your best people. The profiles for venture team members at Signode include characteristics such as being a doer, a decision maker, a risk taker, a "big picture" thinker, able to work in an unstructured environment, creative, open minded, skilled at interpersonal relations, able to communicate, skilled in general business, tolerant of the creative thinking process and failure, good at problem solving.
5. Launch the team. Signode gives its people at least 6 months to prepare a proposal.
6. Send the team to the marketplace. The team should talk to potential customers, suppliers, and competitors. Most of Signode's teams conduct over 2,000 interviews per project. Researching the marketplace often leads the team to the best idea.
7. Funnel the ideas. The idea-development process starts with many ideas and ends with a few—a funneling process. Signode focuses on selecting the best, rather than eliminating the worst. Ideas are combined, changed, modified, and eliminated.
8. Present to management. The team presents a preliminary business plan to top management, addressing issues such as competitive advantage and cash flow. Signode's usual hurdle rate for ventures is a 15-percent ROI after taxes.
9. Launch the venture. When a new venture is launched, the business is usually formed around several core members of the team who become its directors. Signode uses a very ambitious incentive plan to encourage and reward performance.

Signode's adventure teams have proven so profitable that it expected 25 percent of its 1990 profits to be derived from new ventures created in the previous 3 years.

Source: Robert J. Schaffhauser, "How a Mature Firm Fosters Intrapreneurs," *Planning Review*, March 1986, pp. 6–11.

the marketplace. Responsiveness usually requires innovation. A new type of organizational culture is required to succeed economically in the future.

Honda is often used as a model of organizations in the future. It has, for example, been able to reduce the amount of time it takes from design to production of an automobile to 1 year, while the typical American firm takes 7 years.[56] Peters sees pursuing fast-paced innovation as one of the five key steps for surviving in this chaotic environment, and an organizationwide intrapreneurial orientation is one way to achieve innovation.[57]

GLOBALIZATION OF BUSINESS AND U.S. ENTREPRENEURSHIP

The globalization of business would seem to favor entrepreneurs with their flexibility and their ability to react quickly to changing environmental circumstances. Entrepreneurship has increased all around the globe, as discussed previously. U.S. entrepreneurs are often perceived as disadvantaged when competing globally because of their lack of global orientations and their normal lack of second-language capabilities, but this is not necessarily the case. U.S. entrepreneurs often have technological edges over their competitors. They often also have better achievement orientations, causing them to work harder to win contracts or sell lines of products or services. In some countries, such as Japan, entrepreneurship may even be generally discouraged for citizens, which can help open markets for U.S. entrepreneurs. This chapter's Global Strategic Challenge feature highlights the successful efforts of one entrepreneur to penetrate the Japanese marketplace.

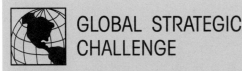

GLOBAL STRATEGIC CHALLENGE

COGNEX WINS IN JAPAN

CEO and founder Bob Shillman describes his company's success as a matter of combining intense preparation, perseverance, attention to detail, and negotiating skills with sensitivity to others' needs, punctuality, and an emphasis on quality. Shillman's firm, Cognex Corporation, is a small U.S. electronics company headquartered in Needham, Massachusetts. The firm manufactures advanced machine vision systems. It landed three major contracts with Japanese firms during 1988 and 1989 due to the above noted factors. Shillman notes that the firm made a number of changes in order to fit with the Japanese culture, both at home and in Japan. For example, it shortened its response times to customers, tightened its delivery schedules, and adapted its corporate style to accommodate its Japanese visitors.

Source: John Kerr, *Electronic Business*, November 13, 1989, pp. 72–73.

U.S. small businesses have the same three basic options for competing globally that larger firms have: exporting only, investing in foreign countries to establish wholly owned ventures, or forming alliances with foreign firms.[58] Sensitivity to culture is extremely important, regardless of which option is chosen. The third option is a good way to help overcome this problem. An alliance is also a good strategy for meeting local-content regulations, an expected Europe 1992 regulation. Still, many choose the easier export-only strategy, or the more complicated wholly owned strategy. Mike Strem, CEO of Strem Chemicals, is pleased that he opened two subsidiaries in Europe. He notes that it was a lot of work, but that subsidiaries generate more profits than joint ventures.[59]

ENTREPRENEURSHIP AND INNOVATION

In both large organizations and small entrepreneurships, innovation depends almost exclusively on entrepreneurial activity for its existence. By definition, an **innovation** is an application of something creative that has a significant impact on an organization, an industry, or a society.[60] The process of innovation is one of change. Entrepreneurs, not bureaucrats, promulgate change.[61] Not surprisingly, two recent studies of innovation suggest that it is more likely to occur in smaller companies than in larger ones.[62] On the other hand, several large firms such as 3M, Hewlett-Packard, Johnson & Johnson, Merck, Dow Corning, and others have mastered innovation, largely by adopting structures and cultures that resemble those in small entrepreneurships.[63] Since most of the strategic challenges for the 1990s require innovative responses, it would appear that entrepreneurship will have the advantage over larger firms.

THE INNOVATION STRATEGY[64]

Firms have many **choices** with respect to their **innovation strategies:** to innovate or imitate, to pursue research and development or search and development, to focus on product or process innovation, to invest in the old or the new, to use big bang or continuous innovation, to be market or technology driven, to commit selected divisions or the total organization, and to do basic research or applied research. Finally, in today's environment, firms have no choice but to pursue speed strategies.

Innovate or Imitate

The initial choice is whether to innovate or imitate. Imitation of products or services essentially leads to financial suicide if no process innovations are forthcoming. If the choice is to pursue product imitation together with process innovation leading to a relative low-cost position, then imitation is a viable strategy. This has long been the thrust of Japanese firms' innovation strategies. They buy, borrow, or steal U.S. and other country's firm's technologies or product and service ideas, then produce or provide them more cheaply based on process innovation. If the choice is product innovation with a steady-state process, it is clear that product innovation alone does not sustain competitive advantage. Ultimately, if innovation is the choice, both product and process innovations must occur in a coordinated fashion, as discussed earlier in the chapter, to obtain a sustainable competitive advantage.

R&D or S&D

The second choice is how to innovate. For product innovations, the issue is one of internal R&D versus what Marion Laboratories (purchased in 1991 by Merrell Dow Pharmaceuticals) labeled S&D, for search and development.[65] S&D normally leads to the acquisition of firms for their products or services, to joint ventures, or to licensing other firms' products or services. Major Japanese firms have followed acquisition strategies in recent years to feed a voracious appetite for research and technology in the United States and elsewhere. They have also invested heavily in startup companies, joint ventures, licensing arrangements, and U.S. research laboratories.[66] Of all of the U.S. high technology firms that changed hands in recent years, two-thirds were bought by the Japanese.[67]

The major question in R&D-based firms is how much to spend as a percentage of sales. The U.S. industrial average was about 2.0 percent in 1991, trailing Japan's 2.9 percent.[68] The average varies widely by firm. In 1990 highly successful Cypress Semiconductors, for example, spent 24.7 percent, and ethical drug manufacturer Merck spent 11.2 percent.[69] Unfortunately, U.S. firms' research and development investments for product innovation as a percentage of sales has dropped in real terms in recent years for several reasons. These include the short-term focus of performance measurements and the negative impacts of mergers and acquisitions, LBOs, and shortages of capital. As the economy turned downward in 1991, R&D investment took another major hit, dropping in real terms to cause the greatest slowdown since the 1970s.[70]

Product or Process Innovation[71]

North American firms are just beginning to fully appreciate the necessity for process research and development. Product research and development funding has long been understood to contribute to competitive advantage, and firms' reports of research investments focus on product R&D. Process R&D investment has received little attention, though. As has been clearly demonstrated in earlier sections of this chapter, however, both forms of research are necessary. Sufficient funding must be allocated to process R&D.

Managing process R&D is complicated by the nebulousness of the concept. Process creativity is a function of the efforts of individual employees, work groups, and managers improving their everyday efforts. How do you account for that? Product R&D funds, although sometimes difficult to justify in terms of concrete benefits, are at least identifiable in the budget. Process R&D depends on such varied activities as training and development, empowerment, decentralization, and so on.

Invest in the Old or the New

The important action is to create both new products (services) and processes. Richard N. Foster, senior partner in global consulting firm McKinsey & Company, believes that innovation is the attacker's advantage. His many years of experience as a consultant have taught him that successful firms, in the long run, "recognize that they must be close to ruthless in cannibalizing their current products and processes just when they are most lucrative, and begin the search again, over and over."[72]

Foster observes that product and process technology follows an *S*-curve relationship between effort (investment) and performance, as shown earlier in Figure 3.5. In the beginning, at the bottom of the curve, the firm must make a relatively large investment before seeing technological progress. Later breakthroughs produce substantial technological progress for relatively small investments in the middle of the curve. Eventually, though, the cost of achieving more progress rises once again, but produces only limited progress. At the top of the curve, firms must choose when to stop investing in new, improved versions of old products, and to create new products or processes. It is here that they must choose to invest in the old or the new.

The firm faces more problems besides scant progress at the top of the curve. Other curves represent newer technologies that displace the old technologies on which the firm has bet its products and processes. These innovations pose major problems in today's fast-changing world. As shown in Figure 3.6, firms may face technological discontinuities, that is, gaps between their technology (upon which they base their products and/or processes) and those of competitors. Such gaps existed when steamships replaced sailing ships, when the ballpoint pen replaced the fountain pen, and when PCs began to replace minicomputers for many functions. Technological discontinuity also exists between Japanese and North American and European manufacturing processes in many industries, and between Japanese and North American and European management styles in many firms. In both cases, the Japanese have replaced old technologies (broadly interpreted) with new ones that have left their competition in the dust. Certain strategies allow a firm to extend the life of an old technology, for example, by adding more sails to sailing ships to make them faster and thus more competitive with steamships, but inevitably, and often quickly, the new technology will supplant the old technology.[73] One study of U.S. and Japanese firms suggests that U.S. firms too often invest in research in the latter stages of the *S* curve, while Japanese firms are quick to move on incrementally or continuously to new products and processes.[74]

Big Bang or Continuous Improvement

U.S., Canadian, and European firms have generally followed strategies aimed at producing the big bang, the major new innovation around which products and processes can be established periodically, say every 3 or 4 years. This strategy has left U.S., Canadian, and European firms vulnerable to Japanese firms, which continuously improve existing products, their own or those of others, and combine these continuous improvements in products with continuous improvements in processes. Because they are constantly improving products and processes, the Japanese do not have to make the quantum leap in products and processes that their competitors do. They can bring new products to market faster, which is a tremendous advantage in a time of accelerating change in markets and economies, and among competitors.[75]

In Japan, as soon as the product is launched, the firm begins developing its replacement.[76] Ironically, like statistical quality control (which is so fundamental to Japan's success), continuous improvement programs were introduced into Japan by U.S. consulting firms after World War II.[77] The future for most firms includes a strategy of continuous improvement.[78]

Market or Technology Driven

Every U.S. business student in the past 20 years has read in an introduction to marketing text that new products begin with the customer, but many organizations have failed to pay much attention to that dictum. General Motors, for example, made the cars that fit its high-technology, low-cost strategy, regardless of whether the customer wanted them or not, believing that mass marketing could sell them. That strategy proved incorrect.[79] Ford Motor Company, on the other hand, surveyed thousands of consumers, and incorporated the 400 most-desired features in its highly successful Taurus and Sable models.[80]

Tom Peters and Robert H. Waterman, Jr., *In Search of Excellence* co-authors, tell us that getting close to the customer is critical to success.[81] While that may have seemed obvious, their words came as revelations to many. Fortunately, many firms have sought to do just that, for example, by including customers as part of product and process design teams.

Experience tells us, however, that being close to the customer is not enough. Numerous hot-selling products become important to consumers who did not even know that they wanted the products before they came to market. For example, research tells us that 11 of the hottest-selling 12 commercial breakthrough products from 1965 to 1985 were invented without market research; customers were convinced of their need for these products through advertising. Sony's Walkman is a classic example.[82] Later, TVman and Discman proved similar successes.

As *Fortune* magazine writer Brian Dumaine notes after examining the innovation situation in the United States and Japan, "An essential part of a creative culture is teaching people to lead the consumer, not follow him." Sony's Data Discman was developed after a Sony executive reasoned that executives would like to be able to carry large amounts of data around with them. Robert Hall, senior vice president of GVO, a Palo Alto, California industrial design firm, states that what is necessary is what he calls "needs analysis." Hall says, "To invent products out of thin air, you don't ask people what they want—after all, who would have told you 10 years ago that they needed a CD player? You ask them what problems they have when they get up in the morning."[83]

The solution seems to be to consider both market and technology. The Japanese approach of bringing the product to market in "small starts" and performing market research on the real target market with a real product, as opposed to a questionnaire about a proposed product, enables them to combine both approaches.[84]

Selected or Total Commitment

Firms can choose to depend on the R&D unit for all innovation, or on R&D together with operations, or they can involve the entire company in improving products and processes. By now, the choice should be obvious. In most industries, the firm that obtains a sustainable competitive advantage will be the one that involves everyone in improving products and/or processes. For example, in a year's time, employees at Toyota submitted 860,000 suggestions for improvement. Some 94 percent of these ideas were implemented. In Japan, about 66 percent of employees regularly submit suggestions, compared to only 8 percent of U.S. workers.[85] Similarly, at the Cadillac Division of General Motors, employees redesign work, make suggestions, solve problems in teams, and help in new product design. As a result, Cadillac has brought out highly successful new models and achieved substantial profitability, something that the rest of GM cannot seem to do.

Basic Research or Applied Research

U.S. firms have always believed in basic research. This Ph.D. Syndrome glorifies research for its own sake. Something useful may flow from knowledge, but it isn't necessary. In Japan, the culture works against basic research, although in the late 1980s this began to change as Japan sought to improve its basic research output. Japanese culture encourages applied research. The Japanese always think in terms of how to use what they have learned or acquired. They focus on applications. This is a major reason for their economic success.[86] Research by strategic consultant and author Michael E. Porter found that generic technology rarely improves competitiveness.[87]

Peter Drucker, noted consultant and author on management and, more recently, on innovation, found on a recent trip to Japan that Japanese firms are reorganizing their R&D efforts so that teams of engineers, scientists, marketers, and manufacturers work simultaneously on three levels of innovation. At the lowest level they seek incremental improvements of existing products. At the intermediate level they try for significant jumps in product design and capabilities, like Sony's jump from the micro tape recorder to the Walkman. At the highest level, the teams seek totally new, major leaps in product design and capability. This is basic research. "The idea is to produce three new products to replace each present product, with the same investment of time and money—with one of the three then becoming the new market leader and producing the innovator's profit."[88]

Speed Strategies

Speed of product and process development has become a major issue in competitive strategy, especially in industries characterized by rapid technological change. The Japanese are especially adept at rushing out instant imitations in a process known as *product covering*. They are also excellent at *product churning*, rushing new products to market without market research. They let the first production run tell them what they should do to improve the product. According to a McKinsey & Company study, Japanese firms develop new products in one-third to one-half the time and for one-tenth to one-quarter the cost of their U.S. counterparts.[89] Improved speed of product development is enhanced by cross-functional design teams.

STRATEGIC MANAGER'S SUMMARY

1. An entrepreneur is someone who perceives and pursues an opportunity, who believes that success is possible, and who initiates change. His or her business is an entrepreneurship, whatever resources it controls. A small business is defined by its financial or other operating characteristics and not by the process by which it is run. Some small businesses are entrepreneurial and others are not.

2. There are several reasons that entrepreneurship is critical at this point in American and Canadian history: Most new jobs in the last 10 years have been created by small businesses. Small businesses have higher returns on investment than larger businesses, and they tend to be more innovative than larger businesses. Finally, there is a certain mystique and psychological satisfaction in being an entrepreneur or running your own small business.

3. As organizations grow, they must formalize planning. Even in the beginning, a business plan should be developed. One of the key responsibilities of an entrepreneur as the organization grows is to learn how to manage, how to plan. As organizations grow, preserving entrepreneurship is critical. To retain the entrepreneurial spirit, organizations must increase the perception of opportunity, build the desire to pursue opportunity, and make people believe that they can succeed.

4. Organizations face more chaotic environments than ever before. Restructuring to encourage intrapreneuring is perceived by many experts as absolutely mandatory to future success for large organizations. Competitiveness and innovation have both been increased by such entrepreneurial (and intrapreneurial) arrangements.

5. The choices available in a strategy based on innovation include innovate or imitate, R&D or S&D, product or process innovation, investing in new or old, big bang or continuous improvement, market or technology driven, selected or total commitment, basic research or applied research, and speed.

KEY TERMS

characteristics of entrepreneurs
entrepreneur
innovation

innovation strategy choices
intrapreneur
small business

DISCUSSION QUESTIONS

1. Discuss why you would or would not want to be an entrepreneur.
2. Indicate why you think you might be an entrepreneur, or not.
3. Describe the major reasons that entrepreneurship is important in America's recent economic history.
4. Review the topics of entrepreneurship and intrapreneurship and their relationships to competitiveness and innovation.
5. Discuss two current trends in entrepreneurship.

STRATEGIC AUDIT QUESTIONS

1. Does this firm practice strategic management? How well?
2. Has this firm identified each of the major elements of strategic management—vision/strategic intent, mission, goals, objectives, strategies, implementation, and control?
3. Has this firm formalized the process? Should it?
4. How good is its strategic business plan?
5. How good is the firm's innovation strategy?
6. Has it made good innovation strategy choices?

Endnotes

1. David L. Birch, "The Hidden Economy," *The Wall Street Journal*, June 10, 1988, special "Small Business" section, p. R23.
2. Ibid.
3. Udayan Gupta and Jeffrey A. Tannenbaum, "Small-Business Hiring, a Locomotive for the Economy of the '80s, Is Slowing," *The Wall Street Journal*, March 16, 1990, pp. B1, B2.
4. Birch, "Hidden Economy."
5. Bill Richards, "Starting Up: Blue-Collar Worker Laborers Laid Off in Rustbelt Try to Run Own Firms," *The Wall Street Journal*, September 8, 1986, p. 1.
6. For recent reviews of relevant perspectives and research, see J. Barton Cunningham and Jos Lischeran, "Defining Entrepreneurship," *Journal of Small Business Management*, January 1991, pp. 45–61; Murray B. Low and Ian C. MacMillan, "Entrepreneurship: Past Research and Future Challenges," *Journal of Management*, June 1988, pp. 139–161.
7. For a review of Cantillon's theory, see Joseph A. Schumpeter, *History of Economic Analysis* (New York: Oxford University Press, 1954), pp. 215–223.
8. Robert C. Ronstadt, *Entrepreneurship: Text, Cases, and Notes* (Dover, Mass.: Lord Publishing, 1984), p. 8.
9. Joseph A. Schumpeter, *The Theory of Economic Development* (Cambridge, Mass.: Harvard University Press, 1934).
10. Low and MacMillan, "Entrepreneurship: Past," p. 141.
11. Howard H. Stevenson and William A. Sahlman, "Entrepreneurship: A Process Not a Person," working paper, Division of Research, Harvard Graduate Business School, 1987, pp. 15–17.
12. Ronstadt, *Entrepreneurship*, pp. 21–22; Stevenson and Sahlman, "Entrepreneurship: Process."
13. Howard H. Stevenson and Jose Carlos Jarrillo-Mossi, "Preserving Entrepreneurship as Companies Grow," *Journal of Business Strategy*, Summer 1986, p. 12.
14. Peter F. Drucker, *Managing for Results* (New York: Harper & Row, 1964), p. 5.
15. Peter F. Drucker, *Management: Tasks, Responsibilities, Practices* (New York: Harper & Row, 1974), p. 45.
16. Paul H. Wilken, *Entrepreneurship: A Comparative and Historical Study* (Norwood, N.J.: Ablex Publishing, 1979), p. 60.
17. Peter F. Drucker, *Innovation and Entrepreneurship* (New York: Harper & Row, 1986), p. 28.
18. Stevenson and Sahlman, "Entrepreneurship: Process," pp. 15–17.

19. Birch, "Hidden Economy."

20. George Gilder, "The Revitalization of Everything: The Law of the Microcosm," *Harvard Business Review*, March–April 1988, pp. 49–61; also see "Big vs. Small," *Time*, September 5, 1988, pp. 48, 49.

21. "The Long Arm of Small Business," *Business Week*, February 29, 1988, pp. 62–66.

22. For a discussion of successful entrepreneurship, see Jenny C. McCune, "The Entrepreneurial Revolution," *Success*, November 1991, pp. 7–10, 62–63, 70–71, 74–75. This article interviews entrepreneurial thinkers for their perspectives.

23. John A. Hornaday, "Research about Living Entrepreneurs" in *Encyclopedia of Entrepreneurship*, edited by Calvin A. Kent, Donald L. Sexton, and Karl H. Vesper (Englewood Cliffs, N.J.: Prentice-Hall, 1982), p. 28. For a discussion of one franchisor's perceptions of the perfect franchisee, see Richard Poe, "Take the Franchisee Test: Seven Traits of the Perfect Franchisee," *Success*, October 1990, pp. 62–66. For a recent review of studies on entrepreneurial characteristics, see Ari Ginsberg and Ann Buckholtz, "Are Entrepreneurs a Breed Apart? A Look at the Evidence," *Journal of General Management*, Winter 1989, pp. 32–40.

24. Peter B. Robinson, David V. Stimpson, Jonathan C. Huefner, and Keith H. Hunt, "An Attitude Approach to the Prediction of Entrepreneurship," *Entrepreneurship: Theory & Practice*, Summer 1991, pp. 19–31.

25. For a discussion of the relationship of these two topics, see Max Wortman, Jr., "A Unified Framework, Research Typologies, and Research Prospectuses for the Interface between Entrepreneurship and Small Business," in *The Art and Science of Entrepreneurship*, edited by Donald L. Saxton and Raymond M. Smilor (Cambridge, Mass.: Ballinger, 1986), pp. 273–332.

26. "The State of Small Business: A Report to the President," Washington D.C., U.S. Government Printing Office, 1985.

27. The descriptions of the first two stages here take their terminology from Larry Greiner, "Evolution and Revolution as Organizations Grow," *Harvard Business Review*, July–August 1972, pp. 37–46.

28. For a brief discussion, see Donald F. Kuratko and Arnold Cirtin, "Developing a Business Plan for Your Clients," *National Public Accountant*, January 1990, pp. 24–27; for a lengthier discussion, see Richard L. Leza and Jose F. Pacencia, *Develop Your Business Plan* (Grants Pass, Ore.: Oasis Press, 1988).

29. "Matters of Fact," *Inc.*, April 1985, p. 32.

30. Barbara Bird, "Implementing Entrepreneurial Ideas: The Case for Intention," *Academy of Management Review*, July (1988), pp. 442–453.

31. Tarek S. Amer and Craig E. Bain, "Making Small Business Planning Easier: Microcomputers Facilitate the Process," *Journal of Accountancy*, July 1990, pp. 53–60.

32. David C. McClelland, *The Achieving Society* (Princeton, N.J.: VanNostrand, 1961); J. W. Atkinson, *An Introduction to Motivation* (New York: American Book, 1964).

33. Joshua Hyatt, "Mapping the Entrepreneurial Mind," *Inc.*, August 1991, pp. 26–31.

34. John Case, "The *Inc.* 500: The Marketmakers," *Inc.*, December 1990, pp. 54–58.

35. Patricia McDougall and Richard B. Robinson, Jr., "New Venture Strategies: An Empirical Identification of Eight 'Archetypes' of Competitive Strategies for Entry," *Strategic Management Journal* 11, no. 6 (1990), pp. 447–467.

36. Stevenson and Jarillo-Mossi, "Preserving Entrepreneurship."

37. Peter Robinson and Max Haynes, "Entrepreneurship Education in America's Major Universities," *Entrepreneurship: Theory & Practice*, Spring 1991, pp. 41–52; Suzanne Alexander, "Student Entrepreneurs Find Road to Riches on Campus," *The Wall Street Journal*, June 23, 1989, pp. B1, B2; Martha Mangelsdorf, "Hotline," *Inc.*, June 1989, p. 20; William Tucker, "Campus Capitalists," *Success*, October 1985, pp. 42–49.

38. Richard I. Osborne, "Second-Generation Entrepreneurs: Passing the Batton in the Privately Held Company," *Management Decision*, Vol. 29, Issue no. 1 (1991), pp. 42–46; Irene Pave, "A Lot of Enterprises Staying in the Family These Days," *Business Week*, July 1, 1985, pp. 62–63.

39. Kenneth Labich, "Breaking Away to Go on Your Own," *Fortune*, December 17, 1990, pp. 40–56.

40. "How Sweet It Is to Be out from under Beatrice's Thumb," *Business Week*, May 9, 1986, pp. 98, 99.

41. Lisa I. Fried, "A New Breed of Entrepreneur— Women," *Management Review*, December 1989, pp. 18–25; Tom Richman, "The Hottest Entrepreneur in America," *Inc.*, February 1987, p. 54; Steven P. Galante, "Composition of Delegates Reveals Rise of Women in Small Business," *The Wall Street Journal*, August 8, 1986, p. 25.

42. Christopher Knowlton, "The New Export Entrepreneur," *Fortune*, June 6, 1988, pp. 87–102.

43. "America's Hottest New Export," *U.S. News & World Report*, July 27, 1987, pp. 39–41; "France Gets Set for a Capitalist Comeback," *Business Week*, March 31, 1986, pp. 42–43.

44. Edward O. Wells, "The French Connection," *Inc.*, November 1991, pp. 96–110.

45. Jay Finnegan, "Britain's New Generation of Company Builders," *Inc.*, November 1988, pp. 93–100; Victoria Schofield, "Leading the Charge: Britain's Hottest Young Businessman," *Success*, January/February 1989, p. 8.

46. "Hottest Export," p. 41.

47. Paul Hofdeimz, "New Light in Eastern Europe," *Fortune*, Summer 1991, pp. 34–42.

48. "China's Reformers Say: Let a Thousand Businesses Begin," *Business Week*, April 11, 1988, pp. 70–71; "China: New Revolution," *U.S. News & World Report*, September 8, 1986, pp. 26–32.

49. Gordon Pinchot, *Intrapreneuring* (New York: Harper & Row, 1985).

50. Thomas J. Peters and Robert H. Waterman, Jr., *In Search of Excellence* (New York: Harper & Row, 1982); Pinchot, *Intrapreneuring*.

51. "How Intrapreneuring Can Change the Face of North America," *Management World*, April 1983, p. 24.

52. Richard J. Ferris, "Capturing Corporate Creativity," *United*, January 1987, p. 7; John Naisbitt, "Helping Companies Hatch Offspring," *Success*, May 1987, p. 14; Colby H. Chandler, "Eastman Kodak Opens Windows of Opportunity," *Journal of Business Strategy*, Summer 1986, pp. 5–8.

53. Thomas J. Peters, *Thriving on Chaos: Handbook for a Management Revolution* (New York: Knopf, 1987), Chapter 1.

54. Alvin Toffler, *Future Shock* (New York: Bantam, 1970).

55. Michael Naylor, "General Motors: A 21st Century Corporation," presentation to the Academy of Management, August 14, 1986, Chicago.

56. Richard T. Pascale, "Perspective of Strategy: The Real Story behind Honda's Success," *California Management Review*, Spring 1984, pp. 47–72.

57. Peters, *Thriving on Chaos*, Chapters 1 and 5, section 3, pp. 191–280.

58. Keramat Poorsoltan, "Stay Home, Plunge, or Take the Middle Path: A Global Strategy for Small Business," *Advanced Management Journal*, Winter 1990, pp. 42–47.

59. Donna Brown, "Strategies for Europe's New Market," *Small Business Reports*, January 1991, pp. 36–42.

60. The traditional view holds that an innovation is simply the application of an invention. See, for example, Edward B. Roberts, "Managing Innovation," *Research Technology Management*, January/February 1988, pp. 1–19; and Jay R. Galbraith, "Designing the Innovative Organization," *Organizational Dynamics*, Winter 1982, pp. 5–15. I have added the requirement of significance.

61. For a discussion of this issue, see Rosabeth Moss Kanter, *The Change Masters* (New York: Touchstone, 1983).

62. David Birch, *Job Creation Process* (Cambridge, Mass.: MIT Press, 1978); and Karl H. Vesper, *Entrepreneurship and National Policy* (Chicago: Heller Institute, 1983).

63. "Masters of Innovation," *Business Week*, April 10, 1989, pp. 58–63. This observation is based on the descriptions of characteristics of these firms contained in the article.

64. Taken almost verbatim from James M. Higgins, "Innovation Strategy: Alternatives and Imperatives," unpublished working paper.

65. Marilyn L. Taylor and Kenneth Beck, "Marion Laboratories, Inc.," in James M. Higgins and Julian W. Vincze, *Strategic Management: Text and Cases*, 4th ed. (Hinsdale, Ill.: Dryden Press, 1989), p. 522.

66. Barbara Buell, "Japan: A Shopping Spree in the U.S.," *Business Week*, June 15, 1990, pp. 86–87; Otis Port, "The Global Race: Why the U.S. Is Losing Its Lead," *Business Week*, June 15, 1990, pp. 32–39.

67. Carla Rapoport, "Why Japan Keeps on Winning,"

Fortune, July 15, 1991, p. 76.

68. Frederick Shaw Myers, "Japan Pushes the 'R' in R&D," *Chemical Engineering*, February 1990, pp. 30–33; Bruce C. P. Rayner, "The Rising Price of Technological Leadership," *Electronic Business*, March 18, 1991, pp. 52–56; Fumiaki Kitamura, "Japan's R&D Budget Second Largest in World," *Business Japan*, November 1990, pp. 35–47.

69. Robert Buderi, "The Brakes Go on in R&D," *Business Week*, July 1, 1991, Table, p. 26; and Merck Corporation, *Annual Report*, 1990.

70. Buderi, "Brakes on R&D."

71. For a discussion of these issues, including relative amounts spent on the two types of R&D, see Ralph E. Gomory, "From the 'Ladder of Science' to the Product Development Cycle," *Harvard Business Review*, November–December 1989, pp. 99–105.

72. Richard N. Foster, *Innovation: The Attacker's Advantage* (New York: Summit Books, 1986), p. 21.

73. Ibid., Chapters 6 and 8.

74. Michael K. Badawy, "Technology and Strategic Advantage: Managing Corporate Technology Transfer in the USA and Japan," *International Journal of Technology Management*, 1991, pp. 205–215.

75. Michael Czinkota and Masaaki Kotabe, "Product Development the Japanese Way," *Journal of Business Strategy*, November/December 1990, pp. 31–36.

76. Peter Drucker, "Japan: New Strategies for a New Reality," *The Wall Street Journal*, October 2, 1991, p. 12.

77. Dean M. Schroeder and Alan G. Robinson, "America's Most Successful Export to Japan: Continuous Improvement Programs," *Sloan Management Review*, Spring 1991, pp. 67–81.

78. Roy Amara, "New Directions for Innovation," *Futures*, March 1990, pp. 142–152.

79. For a discussion, see James M. Higgins and Julian Vincze, "The Challenges Facing General Motors in 1987," in *Strategic Management: Text and Cases*, 4th ed. (Hinsdale, Ill.: Dryden Press, 1989), pp. 19–47.

80. James B. Treece, "Can Ford Stay on Top?" *Business Week*, September 28, 1987, pp. 78–86.

81. Peters and Waterman, *In Search of Excellence*, p. 14.

82. P. Ranganath Nayok and John M. Ketteringham, *Breakthroughs* (New York: Rawson Associates, distributed by Scribner, 1986)

83. Briane Dumaine, "Closing the Innovation Gap," *Fortune*, December 2, 1991, p. 58.

84. Peters, *Thriving on Chaos*, pp. 195–208; "What Makes Yoshio Invent?" *The Economist*, January 12, 1991, p. 61.

85. Rolf C. Smith, Jr. and Raymond A. Slesinski, "Continuous Innovation," *Executive Excellence*, May 1991, pp. 13, 14.

86. Edwin Mansfield, "Technological Creativity: Japan and the United States," *Business Horizons*, March/April 1989, pp. 48–53.

87. Otis Port, "The Global Race: Why the U.S. Is Losing Its Lead," *Business Week*, June 15, 1990, pp. 32–39.

88. Dumaine, "Innovation Gap."

89. "Yoshio Invent."

INTEGRATIVE CASE ANALYSIS
CHAPTER 12

THE CHALLENGES FACING GENERAL MOTORS IN 1992

General Motors needs to strive for improved intrapreneurship among its divisions and its managers in order to prevent bureaucracy from stifling its internal competitive forces. GM's top managers also recognize that innovation is critical to their future and consequently based the company's entire strategy on seeking both product and process innovation. But despite the $77 billion management invested in new technology, it was never implemented particularly well within the work force, and poor union relationships hampered efforts to achieve greater process innovation. Additionally, GM has been slow to encourage innovation elsewhere in the company. They have followed both research and development and S&D options, not always obtaining as much from their acquisitions, for example, of Hughes and EDS, as they would have liked. They have tended to continue to produce old products such as the Camaro for too long, and they have not invested enough capital in new products.

Adhering to the big bang strategy, General Motors has left itself vulnerable to the continuous improvement strategies of their Japanese competitors, who have paid close attention to consumer demands. Largely technology driven in the past, GM itself is now attempting to focus more on the market.

SAMPLE STRATEGIC PLAN

Throughout this text numerous examples have been provided describing how firms actually apply various concepts presented. This has been accomplished through the use of the General Motors case discussed in each chapter, boxed features, and in–text examples. The following reading offers you the opportunity to view how one firm uses many of the major concepts from this text in an integrated way, just as occurred with the General Motors examples, but all at once rather than chapter by chapter. This allows for reinforcement and for new understanding of how the concepts fit together.

The Taisei Corporation is Japan's third largest construction corporation. Its strategists have formulated a comprehensive strategic plan for the year 2000. Taisei has followed the basic strategic management model introduced in this text and incorporated many of the other models discussed in this text. The article begins by reviewing some of the changes in the construction industry in Japan. The Taisei organization structure is then discussed as background on the business and its leaders. The changing nature of the company's strategic planning process also is reviewed, allowing you to see that in Japan, as well as in the United States, Canada, and Europe, strategic management has evolved. Considerable time is spent discussing the future as Taisei's strategists see it in the context of vision. A SWOT analysis is presented. Parts of industry analysis and competitor analysis are discussed. With strategic issues identified, strategies are formulated. The BCG matrix is used to examine the company's portfolio of businesses. The company's five–year plan and its formulation are presented. Then implementation and what it encompasses are focused upon. It's important in the latter part of the reading to examine how their strategy is integrated between levels of the company, as well as to recognize the role of professional planners, the role of information, and how implementation is facilitated.

The reading discusses the more formal, analytical parts of the strategic management process. What you will miss are some of the behavioral aspects, and how intuition and strategic intent have been used and will be used to make sure that strategic goals are achieved.

TAISEI CORPORATION PLANS FOR THE YEAR 2000

The escalating competition in the construction industry in Japan has necessitated reorganization within the industry and Taisei Corporation has prepared a long-range planning system framed around a vision of the business in the year 2000. Strategies were considered and a companywide 5-year plan drafted. The strategy implementation was through division 5-year plans in conjunction with a management plan structure. The effects of the long-range plan are discussed and the problems in promoting the strategy.

The author of this appendix is Hisao Okuzumi, manager of the Corporate Planning Department at Taisei Corporation in Tokyo. Reprinted by permission of *Long Range Planning*, 1990, vol. 23, no. 1. pp. 53–65.

1. THE JAPANESE CONSTRUCTION INDUSTRY: ESCALATING COMPETITION

The Japanese construction market accounts for between 15 and 20 percent of the nation's gross national product. Due to increased domestic demand, construction investment in 1988 amounted to ¥67tn, equivalent to 18 percent of the GNP. This massive market is currently supplied by approximately 510,000 construction companies who employ more than 5 million workers. With annual sales of over ¥1tn, Taisei Corporation ranks as one of the leading companies in the Japanese construction industry, although it accounts for only 2.3 percent of investment in this sector. Japan's current business conditions are characterized by escalating competition, which has led to pressure for the industry's reorganization, especially now, as the construction industry nears full maturity.

2. TAISEI CORPORATION ORGANIZATION CHART

The outline of Taisei Corporation is shown in Figure 1. The head office is comprised of functional departments, while the branches and business divisions assume the role of profit centers. Within the head office, the Business Planning and Administration Division, Subsidiaries and Affiliates Division, and Technology Division act as the strategy group. The Marketing and Sales Division, Urban and Regional Development Division, Engineering Division, and Design and Proposal Division function within the Integrated Marketing and Sales Group. The Building Construction Division, Civil Engineering Division, Safety Administration and Machinery Division, and International Division provide support and guidance for the profit centers. In this way, through cooperation between the function-focused head office and business-focused branches and business headquarters, the promotion of management strategy and other objectives is handled primarily through project teams, with the various functional organizations providing significant cooperation in advancing these efforts.

3. CHANGES IN THE TAISEI LONG-RANGE PLANNING SYSTEM

Prior to 1980, Taisei Corporation planning was implemented through a short-term approach, with the emphasis placed on financial goals.

The company's first 5-year management plan, which aimed at corporate structure reform, was launched in 1981. [See Figure 2.] Under this plan, a system was introduced in which top management provided policy guidelines, with the various divisions working from this base to plan and implement their own independent strategies. This method failed to generate innovative strategy, and because it was updated every year, revisions of the goals made it difficult to evaluate the performance of individual departments.

FIGURE 1 Taisei Corporation Profile (1988)

Established	1873
Product Mix	Construction and Civil Engineering Housing Development Consulting Construction Machinery and Materials Land, Marine, and Air Transportation Building Maintenance and Management Facility Ownership and Management Information Processing Financial Services
Sales	1,270 Billion Yen
Current Profit	42 Billion Yen
Employees	11,400
Operational Units	12
Affiliated Companies	72

After considering the results of the first 5-year plan, the second 5-year plan was drafted in 1985. This second plan clarified the Taisei long-term management vision, and allotted strategic issues to the various organizational functions, which were given responsibility for coordinating the companywide strategy. Revisions were to be made every 3 years.

The third 5-year plan was introduced while the second plan was still in force, but due to radical market changes it was revised in 1989. [See Figure 3.]

The distinguishing characteristics of the current 5-year management plan are:

1. Expression of the company's future strategy, clarifying the direction of the 5-year management plan, and drafting a "Year 2000 Corporate Vision"
2. Setting out the contents of the 5-year management plan through the various strategic business units. Each of the individual unit plans is supported by the management resource strategy, which also serves to clarify each unit's objectives.

FIGURE 2 Taisei Corporation Organization Chart (1989)

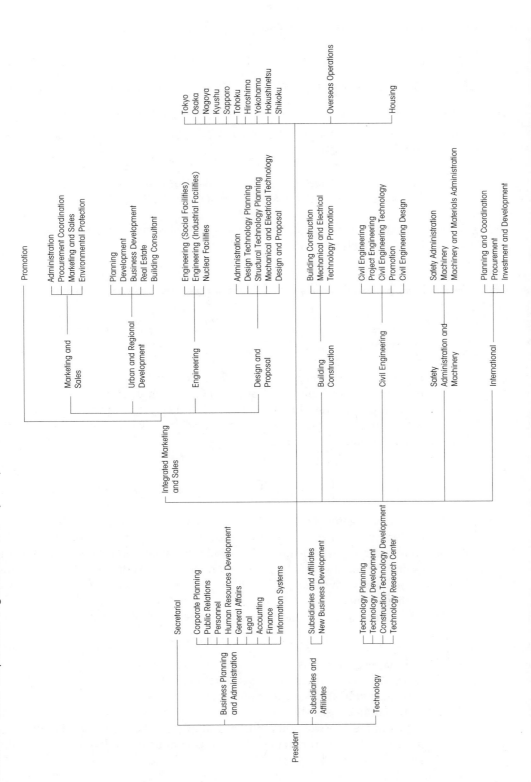

FIGURE 3 Strategy Management Change in Stages

Before 1980	Short- to Medium-Term Plan, Focused on Numerical Goals and Performance
1981 – 1985	Clarification of Management Ideology, Strategy Development in All Divisions, Too Comprehensive
1986 –1988	Expression of Management Vision, Companywide Strategy Coordination. Clear Assignment to Departments Responsible for Implementation
1989 and After	Formulation of Year 2000 Corporate Image, Establishment of Strategic Business Divisions, Project Emphasis

3. Clarifying the corporate strategic issues, defining the approaches for the issues, and assigning the implementation procedures to the management divisions as projects
4. Specifying the strategy planning and administration format to realize the optimum strategy implementation plans at each division
5. Encouraging the development of special strategic issues (other than designated issues) by individual divisions, thereby heightening the sense of participation in management planning.

4. VISION OF TAISEI CORPORATION IN THE YEAR 2000

The Taisei management vision has been expressed as: "An international corporate group, focused on the construction industry and the pursuit of all areas with potential to strengthen the group." To embody this vision in more concrete form, the Business Planning and Administration Division has drawn up "The Optimum Stance of Taisei in the Year 2000." This report specifically focuses on the discovery of "strategic issues."

The process of formulating the parameters of this corporate stance is based on:

1. International relations and economic forecasts
2. Domestic environment and economic forecasts
3. Domestic industrial structure and industrial relations
4. National lifestyle and values
5. Status of the construction industry and other materials. A simulation projecting the Taisei environment in 2000 was conducted, utilizing both optimistic and pessimistic values.

Next, a scenario was prepared to define the corporate mission within the social environment of the Year 2000, the type of business fields in which the company should advance, and the optimum management resources and corporate climate at that time. The top management was then asked to choose from the various alternatives presented, from which a final plan was drawn up.

The "Optimum Stance of Taisei in Year 2000" may be summarized as follows:

1. Strength in the construction industry together with expansion into peripheral industries, and attaining a business scale characterized by an annual turnover of ¥2tn and operating profits of ¥250bn
2. Positive advances as a social developer both at home and abroad, while functioning in a knowledge-intensive industry, with a focus on engineering and the capability to generate high added value
3. Development of personnel with a broad range of expertise, who work together to create an innovative and active corporate climate in which entrepreneurial spirit may be manifested
4. Group integration, to heighten overall strength
5. Expanded profit returns to stockholders and employees

5. DISCOVERING STRATEGIES

The companywide 5-year plan based on the "Year 2000 Corporate Image" functions as a bible for the strategies which should be promoted on a company-wide basis. Therefore, a broad range of analysis must be used as the foundation for selecting the optimum strategic issues. Figure 4 illustrates the process extending through the strategy proposal, as well as the principal methods of analysis.

FIGURE 4   Discovering Strategic Issues

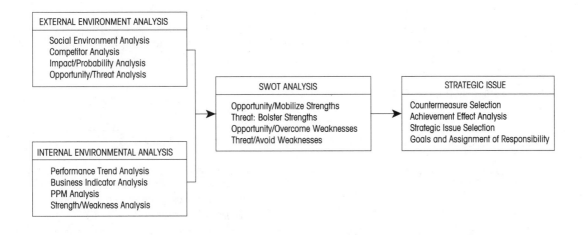

1. Forecasting the External Environment

The goal here is to abstract the primary factors of social trends prone to occur in the near future, and forecast the impact of these social trends on industrial trends. Also included is the use of brainstorming and other methods utilized to analyse the impact that social trends will have on the company's business. [See Figure 5.]

After this, the trends and management policies of competing companies are researched, in order to forecast trends with a high degree of impact on Taisei management. The company's current status and policies are compared to the primary trends of competitors, with analysis conducted to determine if these trends constitute opportunities or threats. These opportunities and threats are then prioritized according to their impact on the company. [See Figure 6.]

The impact factors on the company from the social environment and the impact factors abstracted from the competitive analysis are categorized as being either opportunities or threats. Next, brainstorming and other means are used to study the probability that such elements will occur, with this probability then positioned on a graph as shown in Figure 7. Importance is placed on intensive study of whether these factors constitute opportunities or threats to the company, as well as the interpretation of the occurrence rate. The factors positioned on the upper and lower right side of this graph are regarded as areas important to the company, and serve as a data source in determining the direction of the 5-year management plan.

2. Recognizing the Company's Abilities

Taisei business performance trends are categorized by field, region, and product, with a portfolio approach used to analyze growth and profitability in each sector. Portfolio analysis uses the market growth rate and share ratio with competing companies to determine the company's position in the industry (Figure 8). Comparisons are also run through combining the mutual growth and profitability of in-house business. It is important to gain a clear understanding of which fields are strong and which are problematic.

Along with analysis of the company's positioning, it is important to conduct an extensive range of efficiency analysis to recognize the company's strengths. In

FIGURE 5   Forecasting the External Environment

SOCIAL TRENDS	INDUSTRIAL STRUCTURE	TAISEI BUSINESS
Globalization	Increase of Foreign Investments	Response to Globalization Business Linked with Superior Companies Building Facilities for International Exchange Establishing Intellectual Property Rights

FIGURE 6 Competitive Analysis

Competitive Trends	Taisei Trends	Importance
Company A Entrance into Housing and Land Development	Accumulation of Land Development Know-How	◎
Company B Introduction of Flex Time	Trial Stage at Technical Research Center	○

addition to increasing production and earning efficiency, the changes in the profit and loss and balance sheet indexes are graphed to clearly grasp any trends. It is important to compare the results of this analysis with competing companies, in order to recognize the company's strengths and weaknesses. [See Figure 9.]

The company's strengths and weaknesses abstracted from the positioning and potential analysis are then analyzed to find the underlying causes. It is important to obtain an accurate grasp of whether the underlying causes of the company's strengths and weakness lie in people, commodities, money, technology, information, or other management resources, or, in the organization, system, or other operational areas. [See Figure 10.]

3. Discovering Strategic Issues

The opportunities and threats to the company obtained from the external environment analysis and the real causes of the company's strengths and

FIGURE 7 Impact Analysis

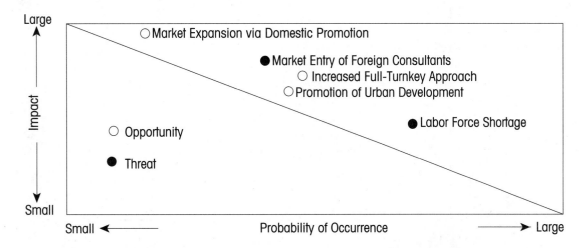

FIGURE 8 Portfolio Analysis

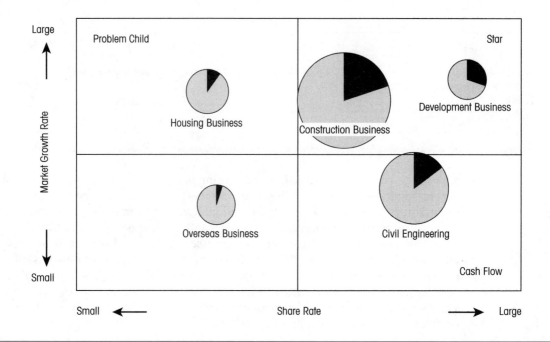

FIGURE 9 Trends of Sales and Profits per Employee

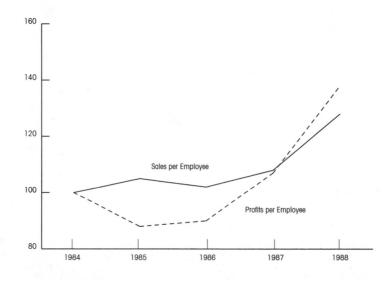

FIGURE 10   Strength/Weakness Analysis

	Management Resources	Organizational System
Strengths	High Social Credibility Large Assets	Highly Functional Departments Excellent Training Systems
Weaknesses	Incomplete Software Technology Management Capabilities of Affiliated Companies	Inadequate Organizational Teamwork Incomplete Long-Term Recruiting Plan

weaknesses abstracted from the internal environment analysis are arranged on a cross chart (Figure 11). Following this, the proper countermeasures for Taisei are studied [see Figure 12] from the perspectives of:

1. Mobilizing strengths to take advantage of opportunity
2. Overcoming weaknesses to seize opportunity
3. Bolstering strengths to withstand threat
4. Avoiding weaknesses in case of threat. Arrangement is performed through the KJ method and other approaches. (The KJ method is a problem arrangement method developed by Jiro Kawakita. The approach is characterized by the use

FIGURE 11   SWOT Analysis

Expanded Domestic Demand Industrial Reorganization Urbanization		Diversifying Construction Demand Market Entry by Overseas Companies Increased Construction Labor Costs	
	Opportunity	Threat	
	Strengths	Weaknesses	
Excellent Performance in All Construction Fields Extensive Technology Outstanding Problem-Solving Skills		Emphasis on Short-Term Profit Promotion of In-House Development Mutual Cooperation within Group	

FIGURE 12 Countermeasure Selection

	Opportunity	Threat
Strength	Metropolitan Zone Market Share Expansion	Full Manifestation of Organization's Strengths
Weakness	Expanding Joint Ventures with Other Industries	Enhancement of Discriminating Technology Enhancement of Marketing Function

of group discussions as the base for reaching solutions.) These analyses become the strategic issue proposals for the 5-year management plan.

4. Determining Strategic Issues

Each of the strategic issue proposals abstracted from the cross chart analysis is analyzed both for effects at the time of achievement and potential for achievement, with each issue then positioned on the graph. As a result of these studies, the strategic issues which are positioned at the upper right of the screen will constitute the areas which must be developed as the 5-year management plan. [See Figure 13.]

FIGURE 13 Effect and Possibility Analysis

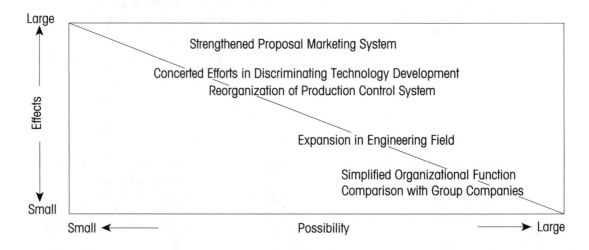

5. Strategic Issue Systemization

The strategic issues selected from the effect and possibility analysis are strategies which should be promoted by the company. The strategies selected are regrouped, further subdivided, and systemized by business domain and goal using the objective → goal sequence. Then the goals are set, and the divisions responsible for each strategy are determined. [See Figure 14.] The strategy system chart which has been prepared is studied again, followed by final coordination of the strategy development balance, the soundness of the goals, and the appropriateness of the implementation division, with the strategies then determined.

6. Setting Performance Goals

The setting of performance goals involves analysis of past performance figures, future market forecasts, and effects of the strategies selected. At this stage, a companywide profit and loss and balance sheet simulation is conducted, with an appropriate ratio established for each strategic business unit. The performance goals do not use real figures, but rather rates—such as growth rate, profit rate, productivity, and other fiscal year growth rates. This is to avoid excessive involvement in numerical targets and volume.

7. Drafting a Companywide 5-Year Plan

Based on the results of the various types of analysis and studies performed, the Corporate Planning Department plays the focal role in drawing up a medium-term management plan to serve as the companywide 5-year plan. [See Figure 15.]
      The plan consists of the following elements:

1. The Year 2000 Corporate Vision as a long-term vision
2. The president's management policy on the improvement of the principal Taisei sectors, expanding the business domain, strengthening the management resource structure, the companywide management scenario and the strategy system chart

FIGURE 14   Strategic Issue Analysis

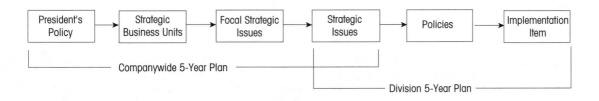

FIGURE 15 Companywide 5-Year Plan

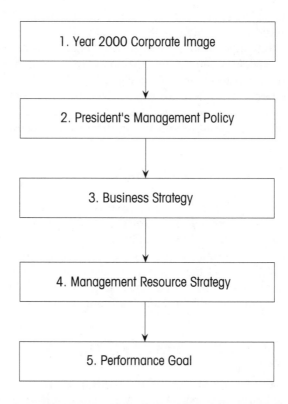

3. The basic scenario, performance targets, strategic systems, and issues for each strategic business unit
4. Management resource strengthening strategy to promote business strategy
5. Companywide performance goals

The strategic business units are comprised of the six fields of civil engineering, construction, housing, development, international business, and new business. The planning of the management resource strategy is carried out by the staff organization. Each strategic issue is assigned to divisions. A large number of project issues are planned for interorganization cooperation through project teams.

The major strategies are as follows:

1. In Taisei's principal sector, the goal is to enhance nonprice competitiveness through the strengthening of the commercialization proposal function. Under this method, first in the civil engineering sector the BOT (building operation and transfer) method will be developed to expand the market. Next, in the

construction sector the main strategies will consist of product development promotion for the purpose of commercialization proposals and the introduction of TASCOM (Taisei Systematic Controlling Method for Building Construction) to innovate the production control system.

2. Regarding expansion of the business realm, the company's development business will be aggressively developed in the areas of housing, international, and new business divisions, with a strategy focused on the creation of synergistic effects between the various divisions.

3. Regarding the strengthening of Taisei's management resources, the main strategies are to innovate the personnel systems in order to activate Taisei employees, and heighten the company's corporate image. These focal strategic issues are broken down into strategic issues, with implementation carried out by project teams and functional divisions.

7. STRATEGY IMPLEMENTATION THROUGH DIVISION 5-YEAR PLANS

The division 5-year plans are proposed on the basis of the strategic issues designated to the various divisions in the companywide 5-year plan, as well as the specific strategic issues developed by each division. [See Figure 16.] These plans correspond to the implementation plan for the companywide 5-year plan, and generally consist of:

1. The division chief's management policy, as expressed in the division's management policy (and based on the companywide 5-year plan)

2. The implementation plan for the designated strategic issues and division strategic issues

3. The implementation plan which breaks down the promotion of strategic issues

FIGURE 16   Division 5-Year Plan

into fiscal-year plans. These division 5-year plans are edited both by division and by business strategy according to the specific strategic issues, in order to maintain a balance in the promotion of the companywide strategy.

Division strategy plans are developed for each strategic issue, from policy formulation through fiscal-year implementation. The goal → means form is used, adopting a system in which the implementation item is developed within the business operations (Figure 14). All strategic issues, policies and implementation items are clarified in terms of the "4 Ws and 1 H" (what, where, who, when, and how), with care taken to ensure that the strategic administration loop of plan → do → check → action is carried out clearly.

The division 5-year plans are drawn up by the 14 divisions and 10 operation units, and it is vital for the strategies proposed by each division to maintain uniform content. To ensure this, the division chief policy, strategy plan, and implementation plan formats are standardized, to prevent discrepancies in the various division strategies. In addition, each strategic issue is given a strategic business unit code, to facilitate more effective consolidation. As a point of reference, the strategy planning sheet format is presented in Figure 17.

8. PROMOTION OF THE MANAGEMENT PLAN

1. The Role of the Corporate Planning Department

Promotion and following of the management plan are the duty of the Corporate Planning Department. This department must coordinate each division and help them achieve their goals. The Corporate Planning Department consists of the following four sections [see Figure 18]:

1. The Planning and Research Section, which analyzes the internal and external environments, and researches and analyzes the impact factors on the company's management
2. The Project Teams, which promote and help implement the medium-term plans, as well as working to improve organizational function and other aspects of Taisei management resources
3. The Auditing Section, which conducts business inspections of the company and its affiliates, analyzing management problems
4. The MTG Section Department, which mobilizes Quality Control methods to provide guidance for problem-solving skills in daily operations

As noted above, the Corporate Planning Department functions to coordinate and promote all aspects of management planning, and is comprised of 30 staff members who are fully acquainted with all business and functional divisions.

2. Autonomous Administration of Division Strategy

As noted above, the division 5-year plans are comprised of the division chief management policies, strategy plans for each strategic issue, and the fiscal-year

FIGURE 17 Strategy Planning Sheet

Category	Key Strategies		Fiscal-Year Goals	
	Strategic Issues		Final Goals	
Policy Name	Category	Achievement Goal	Implementation Manager	Process Plan
Follow-Up				

FIGURE 18 Organization of Corporate Planning Department

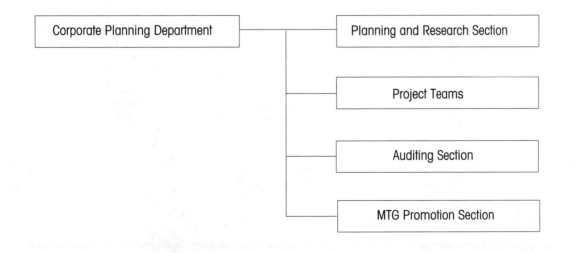

implementation plans, with each of these plans administered at the working level. For the fiscal-year implementation plans, the policy implementation manager (department manager) conducts regular inspections four times a year, checking on the progress of the plan and issuing directions and orders to the manager in charge of implementation (section manager). For the strategic plans, the division managers call for implementation managers (department managers) twice a year, to inspect the progress of strategic issues promotion and give directions and orders. The Corporate Planning Department joins the biannual division chief inspections, thus being kept informed of the strategy promotion status of each division. In other words, a system is adopted in which top-down planning is applied to the 5-year management plan, while administration is bottom-up in structure. This planning model is presented in Figure 19.

3. Top Management Administers Companywide Strategy

The Corporate Planning Department checks on the progress of the division strategies and projects, to verify their conformity as business strategies, to see whether the links between the divisions are being managed smoothly, and whether the original goals are attained. The evaluation results are channelled back to the divisions in question, and are also used as reference for the president's inspection.

For the companywide strategy, the president inspects all of the divisions once a year, and receives strategy progress reports from the various division managers. The president then issues directions and orders, indicating items considered important in terms of the business strategy. The Corporate Planning Department

FIGURE 19 Strategic Promotion Loop

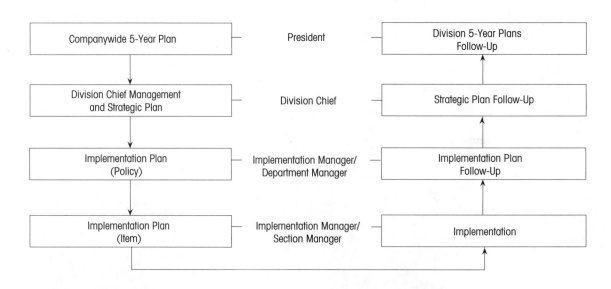

also joins the president's inspection, to verify that the president's specific directions and orders are reflected in the next fiscal year's division strategy plans.

9. MANAGEMENT PLAN STRUCTURE

The items contained in the Taisei Corporation 5-year management plan described above are shown in Figure 20.

1. Management Philosophy

An ideology expressing the corporate mission of Taisei Corporation [has been stated:] "Pooling the essence of knowledge and technology, to build an affluent environment through the pursuit of top-flight quality."

2. Management Vision

The proper future stance of Taisei Corporation [is] "An international corporate group, focused on the construction industry and pursuing all areas with potential."

FIGURE 20   Management Plan Framework

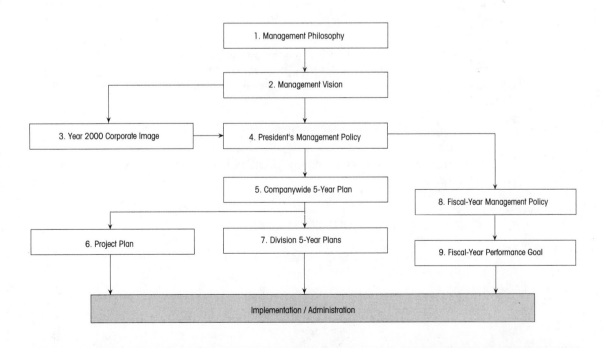

3. Year 2000 Corporate Image

A manifestation of the company's management vision clearly defines the social mission, business scale, management resources and other aspects of Taisei Corporation *vis-à-vis* Year 2000.

4. President's Management Policy

The president's 5-year management policy targets the management vision— "Strengthening the Principal Sector," "Expanding the Business Domain," and "Strengthening Management Resources."

5. Companywide 5-Year Plan

A strategy plan (document) shows how to implement the president's policy, determining the product-market and management resource strategies, and clarifying the strategy promotion role of each division.

6. Project Plan

One of the components of the companywide 5-year plan, this requires the cooperation of many departments.

7. Division 5-Year Plans

The implementation plans for the companywide 5-year plan are comprised of the "Division Chief Management Plan," "Strategy Plan," and "Fiscal Year Implementation Plan."

8. Fiscal Year Management Policy

The president's fiscal year management policy is based on the companywide 5-year plan.

9. Fiscal Year Performance Goal

The performance goal for each fiscal year is based on the president's fiscal year management policy.

10. EFFECTS OF LONG-RANGE PLANNING

Launched in 1980, the first 5-year management plan changed the corporate culture. It also attempted to introduce cost reduction. However, the company gradually turned toward an emphasis on sales, and experienced lower earnings. This situation was tackled by drafting the second 5-year management plan, which placed its focus on corporate structure. Under this plan, both sales and profit goals were achieved in 3 years. The third 5-year plan aims at further reform in corporate structure. Current efforts strive for the development of a new strategy. [See Figure 21.]

The effects of strategic planning are broadly categorized into two types: those which can be evaluated quantitatively, and those which can be evaluated qualitatively. In advancing structural change in a company, it is vital to achieve proper evaluation of the qualitative effects. The qualitative evaluations of the second 5-year management plan launched in 1985 are:

1. Clarification of the roles and necessary functions of each organization
2. The enhancement of a companywide strategic mentality and strategic skills
3. A shift from hardware technology to software technology, with improvements in latent earning power. In short, the foundation was established from which to launch the transition to a knowledge-intensive industry advocated by the third 5-year management plan.

11. PROBLEMS IN STRATEGY PROMOTION

Nevertheless, in the promotion of strategic management it is rare to have all factors go as planned. Several problems have emerged at Taisei. These problem areas are as follows:

1. Difficulties in maintaining conformity in business strategy promotion, due to the lack of linkage between the strategic business units and the organization format

FIGURE 21   Step 1   Profit Performance; Progressive Performance Index Trend

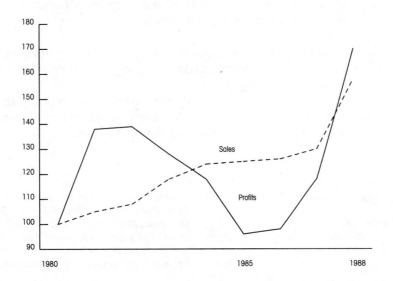

2. Difficulties in setting proper evaluation standards for qualitative targets
3. Lack of effective fusion between strategic issue promotion and everyday operations
4. Lack of a companywide system for evaluating the degree of strategic effect attainment
5. Lack of smooth resource allotment in strategy promotion. These problems tend to occur in every company, because companies are apt to restrict innovative activity. To change such culture, it is necessary to compile success stories.

12. EMBARKING ON A NEW CHALLENGE

Finally, we will examine the distinguishing features of Taisei management planning, and the strategy promotion direction to be adopted from now on. The features of the management plan are:

1. Clarification of corporate volition and dreams for the future which embody the long-term plan. This gives direction to medium-term 5-year management plans.
2. Medium-term plans set for 5 years, and updated every 3 years
3. Clarification of strategic issues and goals, which are assigned to divisions
4. Broad-scale adoption of project teams, in order to strengthen the ties between divisions
5. Establishing the strategy planning format, eliminating discrepancy at the division strategy level
6. In addition to corporate strategies assigned to each division, individual divisions may also develop their own peculiar strategies. This heightens the sense of participation in strategy management.
7. Strategy implementation is formulated as a system which enables development within the realm of daily business activity. Of importance, rather, is the implementation, revision, and improvement of the planning system.

The third 5-year management plan launched in 1988 projects the transition of Taisei toward a knowledge-intensive industry, characterized by its generation of high value-added quantities.

On the threshold of the 115th anniversary of its foundation, Taisei has embarked upon yet another challenge. The ultimate goal of this undertaking is to become a premier global company in the near future.

REFERENCES

Igor H. Ansoff, *Strategic Management*, Macmillan Press (1978).

Tom Peters, *Thriving on Chaos*, Excel (1987).

Michael E. Porter, *Competitive Strategy*, The Free Press (1980).

W. Warner Burke, *Organization Development*, Little, Brown (1982).

T. Kono, *Shoki Keiei Keikaku no Jitsurei (New Cases in Long Range Planning)*, Dobunkan, Tokyo (1978).

M. Iinuma, *Keiei Senryaku Guide (Management Strategy Planning Guide)*, Japan Management Association, Tokyo (1985).

S. Inoue, *Keiei no Susumekata (How to Advance Management Strategy)*, Japan Management Association, Tokyo (1985).

INTRODUCTION TO THE CASE METHOD

We learn best by doing.

Anonymous

In view of the diverse objectives of courses on strategic management and business policy, the specific contents of such courses may vary substantially. This book approaches these subjects primarily through text and cases. A case is a description of an organizational situation. Strategic management cases are usually lengthy and comprehensive.

The case method is a Socratic teaching method designed to help you apply what you have learned from the text materials to actual situations. Most cases focus on some core problem or problems. As a student you are asked to identify those problems and to solve them. The solution may call for you to take advantage of strategic opportunities. Sometimes you will simply be asked to analyze what a firm did correctly, not what its problems were.

Cases are usually written by professors or students, or by people involved in the organizational situation. Cases almost always involve real situations. Occasionally the identity of the organization involved is disguised, but normally you will know the identity of the company. Thus you will be able to obtain additional information about the organization if you wish or if your instructor asks you to.

Cases are often accompanied by industry notes. There are several such notes in this book appearing as part of several cases. Your instructor may choose to share them with you. As you approach any case, you should obtain as much information on the company's industry as you need to understand the situation described in the case.

OBJECTIVES

The case method's objectives are:

1. To add realism to the classroom; to enable students to apply what they have learned
2. To help students to integrate knowledge of the functional areas and to employ principles of strategic management
3. To improve students' decision-making ability, primarily through practice in making decisions
4. To help students see how actions are related and what they mean in a practical as well as a theoretical sense
5. To encourage students to be assertive through participation in class, through defense of their ideas, through the need to "seize the floor" in order to participate
6. To improve students' communication skills

APPROACHES

Case analyses may be oral, written, or both. They may be structured or unstructured. Students may be asked to take the role of the CEO, a consultant, or some other person involved in the situation. Normally the CEO's role is preferred because it forces the student to be responsible for the implementation of chosen alternatives.

TYPES OF ORGANIZATIONS ENCOUNTERED

Cases cover organizations of various sizes, missions (profit and nonprofit), and geographic market penetration (local, national, multinational, and global). The problems encountered by all of these organizations are similar yet distinct.

CASE PROBLEMS ENCOUNTERED

Most of the problems encountered in the cases in this book involve the formulation and control of strategy. Some require lengthy analysis of competition. Some involve implementation, through issues of either structure or systems, style or culture. A few cases involve social responsibility and ethical issues.

Group versus Individual Analysis

Students can engage in preclass and class analysis of a case in either of two ways—in a group or individually. The group method is used when the course is designed to teach people to work in teams and when it is feasible for people to meet in groups. The work load should be distributed fairly, but in all groups some people do their fair share and some do not. Appropriate peer-group evaluation should be carried out. Students should resist pressures to conform and be assertive in group meetings. Before the group meets, each student should go individually through the steps of analysis outlined in the following section. When the individual method is used, the student prepares all work by himself or herself.

PREPARING A CASE: A SUGGESTED COURSE OF ACTION

1. Read the case; become familiar with the situation. If possible, put the case aside for awhile.
2. Reread the case.
   a. Summarize pertinent information. Use the analysis forms provided later in this appendix. Use the strategic audit questions at the end of each chapter. Use what you have learned in other courses.
   b. Identify vision, mission, goals, objectives, strategists, current strategies, SWOT: strengths, weaknesses, opportunities, threats.

    c. Pay special attention to information in exhibits, take notes, perform analyses: ratios, financial statements, forecasts, pro forma financial statements.

    d. Answer any questions your professor has provided.

3. Establish a decision framework.

    a. What are the major problems?

    b. How do you know?

    c. What are the decision constraints?

    d. What are your strategic assumptions?

4. Try to get a comprehensive view of the problem. Do you have the strategic picture in mind? Do you see the interrelationships of the key variables? If not, mull over what you do know until you obtain an overall perspective.

5. Search for and delineate alternatives. When strategies must be formulated, follow the strategic management process discussed in the text. Match strengths and weaknesses against opportunities and threats. Be sure to use applicable materials from the text—the various product and business matrices, the Porter and Hall models, Fox's product life cycle model, Figure 5.4 for basic strategic options, and the rest.

6. Choose the appropriate alternatives. Match your choices against vision, mission, goals, objectives, SWOT. The evaluation process is largely rational, but partly intuitive. Once you have finished your analyses, your intuition must function to help you put the complex pieces together.

7. Set priorities for your solutions.

8. Be prepared to implement your decisions. You should know how to obtain support for your choices, and you should, if your professor desires, budget for your intended actions.

9. Review the McKinsey seven Ss framework and other materials in Chapter 9.

CLASS PARTICIPATION

The effectiveness of the case method depends in large part on students' comments in class. Unlike a lecture class, the case method requires the student to assume responsibility for learning, and for the learning of others. Sharing ideas, challenging comments, acknowledging issues, and defending positions are important parts of the classroom experience in the case method. In the classroom you should:

1. Participate often and intelligently. Much of your classroom grade will be based on your participation. An A average on other work can become a B or a C (or worse) for the course if you don't participate appropriately.

2. Substantiate your positions with facts.

3. Don't participate just to participate. Contribute. You will soon learn that your professor and your classmates can tell the difference.

4. Recognize that others will have thought of issues, analyzed facts, and come to conclusions that you have not.

5. Be prepared to seize the floor. As part of the case method experience, you must be assertive. You must be heard. If not, your classroom participation grade will suffer significantly.

6. Recognize that your instructor is going to disagree with you, sometimes simply

to see if you can defend your position. Furthermore, your classmates are often going to disagree with you to enhance their own situations. You must be prepared to defend your ideas.

7. Be willing to take risks. If you make a mistake, you make a mistake, but if you don't try, you'll never get anywhere.
8. Avoid the use of weak words, such as "I feel," "It appears," "It tends to." Be assertive. Use such words as "It is" and "The analyses reveal that . . ."
9. Be prepared to change your mind during the discussion of the case. Others may have presented analyses that suggest you missed something. Revising your opinion won't help your written report grade, as presumably you will already have turned in your written report. But be flexible enough to change your mind in your oral communications if you see you were wrong, because it will help your class participation grade to do so.
10. Try to maintain a general manager's orientation to what is going on in the classroom. Think of the way you should respond to the positions of others if you were the CEO of this organization, and react accordingly.

WRITTEN CASE REPORTS

Every instructor has specific requirements for written case reports, so the following guidelines must of course be modified to meet the needs of your particular professor. Normally your professor will expect you to follow the traditional problem-solving stages in your report: environmental analysis, problem recognition, problem identification, strategic assumptions or premises, generation of alternatives, choice, implementation, and control. SWOT analyses and financial analyses are important components of several of these stages.

1. Make certain that you have thoroughly analyzed the situation before you begin.
2. Take an overall perspective after analysis.
3. Outline your paper, then fill in that outline.
4. Be sure to use plenty of appropriate headings and subheadings in your report.
5. Be specific in the alternatives you recommend.
6. Make sure your recommendations are well-defended by your analyses.
7. Indicate your strategic assumptions.
8. Indicate how you would implement your strategies.
9. Use forecasts, graphics, and data to substantiate your views.
10. Use appropriate report-writing formats as prescribed by your professor.

ADDITIONAL PERSPECTIVES

As you engage in case analysis, the following additional issues may arise.

Degree of Difficulty

Sometimes the point of the case will be obvious. At other times it will be necessary to read, reread, and reanalyze the case in order to identify the major problem or opportunity. Many cases contain problems of technique that are not the major problems, only symptoms of a major problem.

Viewpoint

One factor to be considered is the viewpoint of the student. Should he or she envision himself or herself as a consultant or as a member of the organization? The ease with which solutions may be implemented is related to the choice of viewpoint.

Results

Most of the time your predicted results will be attainable, but in some situations, no matter what the decision, the results may be ineffective. Many factors, especially external environmental factors, are completely beyond the control of the organization. In such situations, the best decisions may be those that allow an organization to minimize its losses.

Strength of Analyses

Most students will not uncover all the factors that eventually will be revealed in the classroom discussions. This constitutes one of the most important learning factors gained from use of the case method—the realization that there is always something the individual will overlook. This is very much like real life.

Perspective

For both the student and the instructor, the case method is a difficult process. In traditional classroom learning situations, students have been assigned the roles of listeners and nonparticipants. To be effective, the case method requires that students think, act, and participate. In order for students to receive good grades, they must achieve these more active levels of learning as opposed to being merely receptive and passive members of a lecturer's audience. The role of a strategic manager, too, demands this kind of behavior.

Case Bias

One must be aware of the inherent bias in a case. The case is related as it is perceived by someone else, the casewriter. The reader of a case does not have the benefit of knowing how the information was obtained or what factors the individual considered in writing the case. What is presented as fact may not be as clear-cut as it seems. How facts are presented, which facts are included, and which facts are left out are critical factors. Occasionally facts may be distorted, especially facts related to statements about the personalities of individuals. Often, individuals' personalities are the key problems in a case; yet the reader can never be sure that the statements about these personalities are exactly accurate.

Answers

There are no right answers in a case situation. Some answers, however, are better than others. The only true test of the decision is in its implementation, and unfortunately, the case method does not allow for implementation of decisions. The right answer, then, is unknown. Only the better answer can be determined. Students whose decisions are based on insufficient analysis usually come up with worse answers and correspondingly worse grades. It is the facts on which decisions are based that are important; several acceptable solutions may be derived from them.

CASE ANALYSES GUIDELINE FORMS

Forms that can help you analyze cases appear on the following pages.

SAMPLE CASE AND CASE ANALYSIS

The following case on Holiday Inns is followed by a case analysis that is typical of the kind a student may be expected to prepare. This analysis is based on the case author's instructor's note, modified to fit the case study outline that we use. You will note that this case analysis is presented predominantly in outline form. Your instructor may wish you to verbalize more. The case on Holiday Inns, though shorter than the cases you will normally encounter, permits you to view a satisfactory demonstration of expectations without getting bogged down in a multitude of details.

Each case may be used for a variety of purposes—to begin to learn what strategy is all about, for example, or, once you are very familiar with strategy, to make a full analysis of a situation. Thus an instructor may skip some of the first parts of the analysis we show you and ask you to begin with a SWOT analysis, or perhaps ask you only to indicate solutions and give your reasons for them. Furthermore, there are two primary types of written analysis. The first is represented by our example—a detailed paper on the case. The second is a one- or two-page outline of key issues and solutions, often requested of every person or every group each time the class meets as a control device to ensure that everyone has read the case. Such outlines are often graded on a random basis. Remember, therefore, that the sample is just that, something to give you an approximate idea of what to expect.

Case Analysis Worksheet

Organizational Mission

Organizational Goals	**Your Assessment[a]**	**Related Objectives**	**Your Assessment[a]**
_____	_____	_____	_____
_____	_____	_____	_____
_____	_____	_____	_____
_____	_____	_____	_____
_____	_____	_____	_____
_____	_____	_____	_____
_____	_____	_____	_____
_____	_____	_____	_____

Strategists		**Needs, Values, Skills**	
_____	_____	_____	_____
_____	_____	_____	_____
_____	_____	_____	_____
_____	_____	_____	_____

Current Strategies	**Your Assessment[a]**
Grand _____	_____
Corporate _____	_____
Strategic imperatives _____	_____
Business _____	_____
Functional _____	_____
Marketing _____	_____
Finance _____	_____
Operations _____	_____
Human resources _____	_____
Information _____	_____
Management _____	_____

Key Factors in the External Environment	**Your Assessment[a]**
Economic (general) _____	_____
Technological _____	_____
Social _____	_____
Political/legal _____	_____
Competitive environment	
Competitors _____	_____
Substitutes _____	_____
Buyers/suppliers _____	_____
New entrants _____	_____
Customers _____	

[a]From 1 (very poor) to 10 (very good).

Case Analysis Worksheet Cont'd.

SWOT Analysis	Your Assessment[a]
Organizational strengths	
General _____	_____
Marketing _____	_____
Finance _____	_____
Operations _____	_____
Human resources _____	_____
Information _____	_____
Management _____	_____
McKinsey's Seven *Ss* _____	_____
Organizational weaknesses	
General _____	_____
Marketing _____	_____
Finance _____	_____
Operations _____	_____
Human resources _____	_____
Information _____	_____
Management _____	_____
McKinsey's Seven *Ss* _____	_____
Organizational opportunities	
Economic (general) _____	_____
Competitive situation _____	_____
Organizational threats	
Economic (general) _____	_____
Competitive situation _____	_____
Technological _____	_____
Social _____	_____
Legal/political _____	_____

Financial Worksheet

1. Information obtained from ratio analysis
   1.
   2.
   3.
2. Information obtained from common-sized financial statements
   1.
   2.
   3.
3. Information obtained from review of key financial strategies and policies
   1.
   2.
   3.

[a]From 1 (very poor) to 10 (very good).

4. Anticipated economic situation and other assumptions
   1.
   2.
   3.
5. Information obtained from forecasts, 5-year trend or other
   1.
   2.
   3.

Models
Models applicable to analysis of this case.
1.
2.
3.
4.

Problem Solving

Problem Identification
What are the major problems? _____

_____

How do you know? _____

_____

Strategic Assumptions
What assumptions must you make at this point about the future in order to solve this problem?

_____

_____

Generation of Alternatives
List each major alternative course of action and its positive and negative aspects.

Alternatives	**Positives**	**Negatives**
Corporate		
(including strategic imperatives)		
1.		
2.		
Business		
1.		
2.		
3.		
Functional		
1.		
2.		
3.		
4.		
5.		
6.		
Grand Strategy		
1.		
2.		

Case Analysis Worksheet Cont'd.

Your Final Choices

1.
2.
3.

Why?

1.
2.
3.

Implementing Your Final Choices

Please answer the following questions with regard to each of your final strategies:

1. Who will implement them? Do you have their support?
2. How much will they cost? Do you have the funds?
3. When will they be implemented?
4. What must be done to ensure that all types of resources are available to carry out your choices?
5. Are the Seven Ss satisfactory in this situation?

HOLIDAY INNS, INC., 1984

ARTHUR SHARPLIN

Holiday Inns, Inc. (HI), headquartered in Memphis, Tennessee, is the world's largest hospitality company, with interests in hotels, casino gaming, and restaurants, having sold its Delta Steamships subsidiary in 1982. For the first half of 1983, 64.6 percent of operating income came from hotels, 32.9 percent from gaming, and 1 percent from restaurants. First-half net income and sales were at respective annual rates of $123 million and $1.5 billion. More detailed financial information is provided in Exhibits 1 and 2.

The Holiday Inn hotel system includes 1,744 hotels with 312,302 rooms in 53 countries on five continents and produces an estimated $4 billion in annual revenues. Licensed, or franchised, hotels account for 86 percent of total Holiday Inn hotels, 81 percent of total rooms, and 6 percent of HI sales. Franchisees pay $300 a room initially plus a royalty of 4 percent of gross room revenues and a fee for marketing and reservation services of 2 percent of gross room revenues. The company's reservation system is the largest in the hotel industry.

In 1982, less than 3 percent of Holiday Inn customers dropped in without room reservations, down from 95 percent in the fifties. In 1981, the company started to deemphasize highway locations. Virtually all new Holiday Inn hotels are placed near airports, industrial parks, and similar sites.

Business travelers account for about 60 percent of Holiday Inn room nights occupied. The company is launching two new hotel chains aimed at the upscale business traveler. The first, Crowne Plaza hotels, offers fine dining, complimentary morning newspapers, continental breakfasts, 24-hour maid service, bellmen, and free HBO movies. Rates are $15 to $20 higher than the average rate of $44 at existing company-owned Holiday Inns. Crowne Plaza hotels are now located in Rockville (Maryland), San Francisco, Miami, and Dallas. Four more will open in Stamford (Connecticut), Houston, and New Orleans by year-end. The second new chain, Embassy Suite hotels, is targeted primarily at the business traveler near the upper end of the lodging market who stays three or four days instead of the usual two, and will pay for specialized service. Each suite will offer a separate living room with a wet bar and the option of one or two bedrooms. The company plans to have six all-suite hotels in varying stages of development in 1984.

In December 1983, the company announced plans to develop a new budget hotel chain, called Hampton Inn hotels, to include 300 company-owned and

The research assistance of Connie Shum is gratefully acknowledged. This case portrays neither the effective nor the ineffective handling of an administrative situation. Rather, it is to be used as a basis for classroom discussion.

EXHIBIT 1   Holiday Inns, Inc., and Consolidated Subsidiaries Statements of Income (in thousands, except per share)

	Three Quarters Ended		Fiscal Year Ended	
	September 30, 1983	October 1, 1982	December 31, 1982	January 1, 1982 Restated
Revenues				
Hotel	$ 667,644	$ 651,740	$ 840,698	$ 853,645
Gaming	449,239	360,608	472,792	388,148
Restaurant	71,016	70,865	100,584	96,366
Other	4,183	7,624	11,224	13,616
Total revenues	$1,192,082	$1,090,837	$1,425,298	$1,351,775
Operating income				
Hotel	143,552	132,280	150,205	170,944
Gaming	98,576	63,647	74,595	56,291
Restaurant	3,486	2,714	5,029	6,547
Other	2,741	3,424	4,999	10,826
Total operating income	248,355	202,065	234,828	244,608
Corporate expense	(22,058)	(17,860)	(24,487)	(25,736)
Interest, net of interest capitalized	(31,725)	(38,738)	(50,965)	(65,540)
Foreign currency translation gain (loss)	—	—	—	1,889
Income from continuing operations before income taxes	194,572	145,467	159,376	155,221
Provision for income taxes	85,612	58,187	62,157	56,515
Income from continuing operations	108,960	87,280	97,219	98,706
Discontinued operations				
Income from operations, net of income taxes	—	(22,100)	4,671	38,652
Loss on disposition, plus income taxes payable of $5,505	—	—	(25,910)	—
Net income	$ 108,960	$ 65,180	$ 75,980	$ 137,358
Income (loss) per common and common equivalent share				
Continuing operations	$ 2.86	$ 2.23	$ 2.50	$ 2.68
Discontinued operations	—	(.58)	(.56)	.98
Total income (loss)	$ 2.86	$ 1.65	$ 1.94	$ 3.66
Average common and common equivalent shares outstanding	38,055	38,305	38,216	39,449

franchised units within five years. The first will open in Memphis, Tennessee, in 1984. Room rates at these hotels will average about $30. They will feature rooms for smokers and nonsmokers, free television and movies, local telephone calls, continental breakfasts, and arrangements for children under 18 to stay free with their parents.

The Holiday Inn hotel group spent $60.1 million in 1982 to upgrade and renovate company-owned hotels. Old franchises were eliminated at the rate of about one a week, as minimum operating standards were raised. So drastic was the

EXHIBIT 2 Holiday Inns, Inc., and Consolidated Subsidiaries Balance Sheets
(in thousands, except share amounts)

	December 31, 1982	January 1, 1982 Restated
Assets		
Current assets		
Cash	$ 49,945	$ 39,655
Temporary cash investments, at cost	32,544	20,181
Receivables, including notes receivable of $12,618 and $31,927,		
less allowance for doubtful accounts of $18,925 and $15,080	73,008	91,782
Supplies, at lower of average cost or market	21,871	23,424
Deferred income tax benefits	13,510	11,190
Prepayments and other current assets	18,101	9,775
Total current assets	208,979	196,007
Investments in unconsolidated affiliates, at equity	108,480	46,535
Notes receivable due after one year and other investments	44,186	49,214
Property and equipment, at cost		
Land, buildings, improvements, and equipment	1,635,310	1,496,491
Accumulated depreciation and amortization	(367,434)	(313,947)
Subtotal	1,267,876	1,182,544
Excess of cost over net assets of business acquired, amortized evenly over		
40 years	54,314	55,787
Deferred charges and other assets	24,172	31,275
Net assets of discontinued operations	—	111,297
Total assets	$1,708,007	$1,672,659
Liabilities and Shareholders' Equity		
Current liabilities		
Accounts payable	$ 77,867	$ 66,375
Long-term debt due within one year	31,267	30,478
Accrued expenses	123,283	133,256
Total current liabilities	232,417	230,109
Long-term debt due after one year	436,356	581,465
Deferred credits and other long-term liabilities	33,938	34,851
Deferred income taxes	62,334	53,857
Shareholders' equity		
Capital stock		
Special stock, authorized—5,000,000 shares; series A—		
$1.125 par value; issued—491,541 and 576,410 shares;		
convertible into 1.5 shares of common stock	553	648
Common stock, $1.50 par value; authorized—60,000,000		
shares; issued—40,218,350 and 32,909,606 shares	60,327	49,364
Capital surplus	294,517	161,188
Retained earnings	671,609	626,310
Cumulative foreign currency transaction adjustments	(3,804)	—
Capital stock in treasury, at cost; 3,036,081 and 2,439,500 common shares		
and 72,192 series A shares	(78,660)	(63,170)
Restricted stock	(1,580)	(1,963)
Total shareholders' equity	942,962	772,377
Total liabilities and shareholders' equity	$1,708,007	$1,672,659

pruning that, even with 569 new hotels in the past eight years, there has been a net gain of only 45 in the number of Holiday Inns. At the end of 1982, there were 48 Holiday Inn hotels under construction worldwide. The Holiday Inn sign is being replaced with a new rectangular one bearing the chain's name topped with an orange and yellow starburst on a green background.

In March 1983, Roy E. Winegardner, Chairman, and Michael D. Rose, President and Chief Executive Officer, briefed stockholders on Holiday Inn's preparations for the future. Some excerpts from their comments follow.

With the disposition of our steamship subsidiary, Holiday Inns, Inc., is now strategically focused on the hospitality industry. We also introduced a new sign and logo for our Holiday Inn hotel system, better reflecting the range of property types and level of product quality that will characterize the Holiday Inn hotel system in the decades ahead. Recognizing the increasing segmentation of the lodging market, we also began construction on two new hotel products. We also embarked on an aggressive expansion plan for our core Holiday Inn hotel brand. This represents the most aggressive company hotel development effort in recent years, and reflects our continuing belief in the long-term strength of the lodging market and of our Holiday Inn brand within the large moderate-priced segment of that market.

Our company has prospered with the growth of Atlantic City, as our Harrah's Marina facility there has proven to be the most profitable hotel/casino in that market on a pre-tax, pre-interest basis. We entered into a joint venture to build a new 600-room hotel and 60,000-square-foot casino on the Boardwalk. We believe this should contribute to Harrah's ability to achieve the same brand leadership position in Atlantic City that it now enjoys in northern Nevada.

As a result of [a competitive] pricing strategy, operating margins suffered in our hotel business. However, this approach enabled us to maintain occupancy levels despite the fact that occupancies declined throughout the rest of the hotel industry. At Perkins Restaurants, Inc., our restaurant subsidiary, this pricing strategy paid off, contributing to substantially higher customer count and improved unit profitability. We also made the decision to dispose of a number of restaurants and hotels which were not performing to our financial standards.

In addition to strengthening our market position, we also strengthened our balance sheet. The company's 9⅝-percent convertible subordinated debentures were called for redemption on March 2, 1982. The result was conversion to $143 million of additional equity, which provides the basis for significant new debt capacity to fund our future expansion. Consistent with our stated intention to reduce floating rate debt, we issued $75 million in fixed-rate, 10-year notes in August. In 1982 we commissioned an update of an independent study of the appreciated value of the company's tangible assets and certain contract rights. This study indicated that the net market value of these assets approximated $2.5 billion. [This] appraisal reflects the value of the company's franchise and management contract income streams as well as the appreciation of our real estate assets. [We have] also made substantial progress in improving the productivity of our most important resource, our people. We undertook a thorough review of staffing levels and programs to assure that we were bringing sufficient resources to bear on those things that matter the most, and not expending time or money on those efforts that yield more limited returns. As a result, we have eliminated significant overhead costs and focused our attention more clearly on those things that are most critical to our success in the future. We *deliberately increased our expenditures on training and development. We believe that, in our businesses, people represent the greatest opportunity for competitive advantage.*

As we look ahead, the economic picture remains clouded. We cannot accurately predict the impact of the unprecedented massive Federal budget deficits on our economy. We remain confident in our ability to manage our businesses effectively under both good and difficult economic conditions.

SAMPLE CASE ANALYSIS—HOLIDAY INNS, INC., 1984[1]

BRIEF SUMMARY OF THE CASE

Holiday Inns (HI), with headquarters in Memphis, Tennessee, is the largest hospitality company in the world. Its interests are in hotels, casino gaming, and restaurants; it sold its Delta Steamships subsidiary in 1982. The hotel SBU accounted for about 60 percent of sales and profit in 1982, and gaming (Harrah's Casinos) for almost all the rest. Franchised hotels represent 81 percent of total rooms, but only 6 percent of revenues. Less than 3 percent of customers drop in without room reservations, down from 95 percent in the 1950s. HI has begun to deemphasize highway locations and move toward airports and industrial parks. HI's customers are mostly business travelers.

In 1984, HI is in the process of launching three new hotel chains—Crowne Plaza Hotels for upscale business travelers, Embassy Suite Hotels for business travelers who stay 3 or 4 days, and Hampton Inn Hotels, aimed at the low end of the market. Also the traditional HI hotels are being upgraded and renovated. The company's casino business is prospering. The 1981 to 1983 recession was met with competitive pricing, so sales were sustained, and HI replaced some debt with equity on its balance sheet and looks ahead to a cloudy economic picture, particularly in light of massive federal budget deficits in 1981 to 1983.

ISSUES

1. Advantages and disadvantages of diversification into related product or service segments
2. Market segmentation within a line of business
3. Changing retail unit location policy with changing market conditions
4. Market maturity and niche encroachment
5. Book values versus market values for strategic decision making

I. MISSION

Although HI's mission is not detailed in the case, HI desires to be the premier firm in the lodging industry. The comments by Winegardner and Rose in the case highlight current strategic thinking at HI.

II. STRENGTHS, WEAKNESSES, OPPORTUNITIES, THREATS

Strengths

Finance/Accounting Factors (for ratios, see below)
1. Good financial situation with limited use of leverage (debt ratio 0.39)
2. Size ($1.5 billion in sales)

Marketing/Distribution Factors
1. Name and image well-established
2. Largest reservation system in lodging industry

Production/Operations Factors
1. Growth largely through franchising plus operating leverage (The ratio of fixed to total costs is reasonably low.)
2. Rapid expansion through franchising possible
3. Geographic diversity; 1,744 hotels in 53 countries

Corporate Factors
1. Perceived competence of HI's management
2. Consistency of purpose and clarity of strategic plans (as noted by Winegardner and Rose)
3. Lodging revenues at 64 percent balanced by 31.8 percent from gaming, which is highly profitable, represent a well-balanced multiple-SBU organization
4. Heavy use of franchising has insulated HI somewhat from downturns in sales (HI has responsibility for little of the fixed costs)

Weaknesses

Finance/Accounting Factors
1. The current and quick ratios are so low as to be shocking until one realizes that because HI's casinos and hotels handle large volumes of cash and credit card receivables (nearly $3 million daily), these ratios do not have their usual significance.

Marketing/Distribution Factors
1. HI's image has suffered lately because of an aging and now somewhat poorly located fleet of franchises.
2. Few of HI's clients (less than 5 percent) stop without reservations.

Production/Operations Factors

1. Many locations are aging and in need of updating, which is a slow and costly process.
2. Many locations are near highways, in locations that now are suboptimum.

Corporate Factors

1. HI's star SBU is gaming, which is subject to government fiat. Although these operations are now highly profitable, they still must be viewed as risky.
2. Many of the older franchised locations do not fit in with HI's desired market position.

Opportunities

1. The richest opportunity for expansion is in gaming.
2. HI also has opportunities in continuation of its reconcentration and segmentation activities within the lodging industry.
3. Additional expansion opportunities utilizing HI's management competence outside of current operating areas also exist.

Threats

1. Declining occupancy rates in the lodging industry (71 percent in 1979, 65 percent in 1983)
2. Economic uncertainty, maybe leading to recession, which depresses business and pleasure travel
3. Overbuilding in lodging industry
4. Intense competition, new entrants

III. COMPETITOR ANALYSIS[2]

Industry Success Factors—Hotels

1. Effective reservation system
2. Physical locations chosen for lodging sites, dependent on:
   a. Type of lodging (airport, roadside, resort, etc.)
   b. Physical amenities
   c. Types of customers targeted
   d. Proximity to other desirable amenities/services
3. Actual facilities/amenities included at sites
4. Friendliness and efficiency of staff
5. Pricing policies
6. Aggressive marketing

Intensity of Existing Competition

The lodging industry has clearly moved into the mature stage of its development, and although this period may last for a considerable number of years, it is apparent that the industry is segmenting at a rapid pace. Competition is intense.

The traditional segmentation basis of price, service, and location has evolved into four fairly autonomous subdivisions: budget, mid-priced, upscale, and all-suite. The major players in this segmentation movement are noted in Exhibit 3. Several aspects of the four largest competitors in the integrated-hotels category are detailed in Exhibit 4.

In addition to competitive movements into multiple segments of the lodging industry itself, two other movements are evident: restaurant diversification and casino or gaming diversification.

Competitors' Strategies   Your professor may have you research each of the competitors' strategies.

New Entrants   In recent years, new entrants into Holiday Inns' principal markets have forced the company into diversification. Holiday Inns is itself a new entrant in the budget, upscale, and all-suite markets. New entrants can be expected in all segments.

Buyers   Buyers have little power over the market.

Suppliers   Labor costs must be cut. This requirement may lead to such innovative actions as redesigning rooms to enable a maintenance worker to clean more rooms per day.

Substitutes   Substitutes for Holiday Inns are competitors in the other price segments. There really are no substitutes for motel rooms.

EXHIBIT 3   Competitors' Entries in Four Market Segments

Organization	Budget	Mid-Priced	Upscale	All-Suite
Holiday Inns	Hampton Court	Holiday Inn	Crowne Plaza	Embassy Suites
Quality Inns	Comfort Inn	Quality Inn	Quality Royale	Quality Choice Suites
Ramada		Ramada Inn/Hotel	Ramada Renaissance	
Marriott		Marriott Courtyard	Marriott	Marriott Suites
Travelodge		Travelodge	Viscount	
Howard Johnson		Howard Johnson Motor Lodge	Howard Johnson Hotels	

EXHIBIT 4 Competitors in Integrated Hotels, 1983 (dollar amounts in thousands except earnings per share)

	Number of Properties	Number of Rooms	Occupancy Rate (percent)	Revenues	Net Income	Earnings per Share	Return on Equity (percent)	Main Businesses
Hilton Hotels Corp.		88,684	60.0%	$ 682,928	$112,637	$4.20	18.7%	Hotels and casinos (international)
Holiday Inns, Inc.	1,707	310,337	70.2	1,585,080	124,399	3.28	12.5	Hotels, restaurants, and casinos (international)
Marriott Corp.	131	55,000	69.5[a]	3,036,703	115,245	4.15	20.0	Hotels, contract food services, and restaurants (international)
Ramada Inns, Inc.	593	93,592	63.0	573,831	12,597	0.38	5.2	Hotels and casinos (international)

[a]Estimated.

IV. FINANCIAL ANALYSIS

Holiday Inns has strengthened its balance sheet by calling its convertible debentures and decreased its degree of financial risk by shifting from floating-rate to fixed-rate debt. In general, as the financial data shown in Exhibits 5 through 7 indicate, HI is financially sound.

V. MODEL ANALYSIS

Your professor may ask you to use selected models described in the text. You could, for example, use each of the following:

1. Hall's competitiveness model to indicate HI's competitive situation
2. The GE matrix to evaluate HI's major divisions (Outside research would be necessary.)
3. Fox's product life cycle model to indicate selected functional strategies for various businesses
4. The directional policy matrix to evaluate each of HI's hotel/motel product entries

Several other models could be used, as well.

EXHIBIT 5   Holiday Inns, Inc., Financial Ratios, 1981 and 1982

Ratios	1981	1982
Current	0.852	0.899
Quick	0.659	0.454
Collection period	24.443	20.811
Long-term debt/total capital funds	0.429	0.316
Long-term debt/stockholders' equity	0.753	0.463
Total debt/total assets	0.485	0.392
Operating income/total assets	0.146	0.137
Operating income/sales	0.181	0.165
Earnings before income tax/sales	0.162	0.148
Return on investment	0.082	0.044

VI. STRATEGIC CHOICE

Having previously been involved in unrelated diversification (it once had a steamship subsidiary), Holiday Inns appears to have decided to reconcentrate, practicing only concentric diversification, from the hotel industry to restaurants and gaming. For good reason, conglomerate diversification has been in disrepute recently. Holiday Inns' managers correctly concluded that their success in the hotel business is not necessarily transferrable to any business they might enter. By seeing themselves as a hospitality company, they are able to focus on business areas that require similar kinds of expertise.

EXHIBIT 6   Holiday Inns, Inc., Selected Common-Sized Items from Income Statements, 1981 and 1982 (in thousands of dollars)[a]

	1981		1982	
	Amount	Percent	Amount	Percent
Revenue	$1,351,775	100.0%	$1,425,298	100.0%
Operating income	244,608	18.1	234,828	16.5
Corporate expense	(25,736)	1.9	(24,487)	1.7
Interest	(65,540)	4.9	(50,965)	3.6
Provision for income tax	56,515	4.2	68,157	4.4
Income from continuing operations	98,706	7.3	97,219	6.8
Income from discontinued operations	38,652	2.9	4,671	0.3
Net income	137,358	10.2	75,980	5.3
Net working capital	(34,102)	0.3	(23,438)	0.2

[a]You should use common-sized income statements and balance sheets for your analysis.

EXHIBIT 7   Holiday Inns, Inc., Sales and Operating Income, by Business Segment, 1981 and 1982 (in thousands of dollars)

	1981		1982	
	Amount	**Percent**	**Amount**	**Percent**
Sales				
Hotels	$ 853,645	63.2%	$ 840,698	59.0%
Gaming	388,148	28.7	472,792	33.1
Restaurants	96,366	7.1	100,584	7.1
Other	13,616	1.0	11,224	0.8
Total	$1,351,775	100.0%	$1,425,298	100.0%
Operating Income				
Hotels	$ 170,944	69.9%	$ 150,205	64.0%
Gaming	56,291	23.0	74,595	31.8
Restaurants	6,547	2.1	5,029	2.1
Other	10,826	4.4	4,999	2.1
Total	$ 244,608	100.0%	$ 234,828	100.0%

RECOMMENDATIONS

The lodging industry is clearly in the mature stage of its life cycle—a stage that is very likely to last a long time. During periods such as the early 1980s, when already mature markets see depressed sales, the evidences of maturity become even more pronounced. Competitors encroach upon the market niches of others, price competition becomes prevalent, promotional efforts tend to be aimed at artificial product differentiation, cost pressures require strenuous efforts to improve efficiency, and major participants try to diversify into other businesses. All of these things have occurred in the hotel industry. HI at first tried to diversify away from hotels, but when the continuous recession and the distractions of managing those other businesses threatened the traditional dominance of Holiday Inns in its core business, the company decided to reconcentrate and to lead the industry in the segmentation that was already occurring.

Holiday Inns has chosen to segment the market primarily according to class of customer. For the upscale business traveler, HI will offer suite accommodations when the traveler wishes to stay several days and first-class standard accommodations at Crowne Plaza when the stay is two days or less. This is a logical approach to segmentation, especially since that is the direction in which the hotel market is moving in any case. While a number of hotel chains have tried to compete under different names in several of the identifiable market segments, Holiday Inns is the first to attempt to encompass the entire range, omitting only the very low-end accommodations, such as those provided by Motel 6, and those at the very high end, served by the Ritz and other world-class hotels. Holiday Inns may have spread itself just a little thin by attempting to do all of this at once, but the financial strength and management competence of the company suggest that the strategy is appropriate. It is recommended that HI continue to expand in gaming and also to update and, where necessary, weed out its franchised locations. Finally, HI should be alert to the potential for acquiring other, smaller quality motel/hotel chains. Additional research will also indicate the need to prepare a takeover defense.

IMPLEMENTATION ISSUES

Your professor may ask you to indicate more specifically how you would go about implementing the strategies you have recommended. For example, if you suggested, as we did, that HI should search for hotel chains to purchase, you might actually research some and perhaps draw up a purchase proposal. You may be asked to budget for various strategies. You may also be asked to use the McKinsey seven Ss model and indicate how the other six Ss would have to be changed to match your strategy. A number of options are available. Because this case is short and has limited information, we have not provided a detailed implementation write-up, but you may be asked to do so.

ADDITIONAL COMMENTS

We chose a short case with very broad and rather obvious issues, and managed to generate an eight-page report. For longer cases involving more complex issues, the amount of analysis will be significantly greater and so will the size of the report if you follow the above format. That is why professors often ask only for recommendations and supporting analysis, or some other portion of the format used above. In more complex cases, you might be asked to provide several different financial forecasts, a breakeven analysis, merger plans, new organization structures, and the like.

Finally, remember that this is only a sample intended to give you some understanding of what is required. Every professor has his or her own requirements. Some want heavy financial analysis, others focus more on marketing or human resource issues.

Endnotes

1. Adapted from casewriter's note.
2. Based principally on industry analysis.

PART TWO

CASES

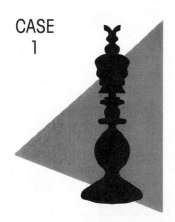

CASE 1

PERFUMERY ON PARK, 1991

DAVID M. CURRIE

In January 1991, Anna Currie wonders what strategy she should adopt for Perfumery on Park, Inc. Recent changes in the retail environment presented several opportunities that had not existed only a year earlier. Many of these opportunities were not likely to be available in the future, so it was important that they be taken advantage of while they existed. In a sense, the turmoil in the department store and discount store industries had altered the framework of competition among all retailers.

At the same time, Anna was very conscious of maintaining the strengths Perfumery on Park had developed through the years—product selection, knowledge of the fragrance industry, variety of fragrances, contacts with suppliers, and quality of service. Any result of strategic planning would be rejected if it jeopardized or did not build upon those strengths.

Anna also wondered what effects the predicted recession would have on the Perfumery's previously unblemished record of sales increases. The last recession in the United States occurred three years before Perfumery on Park was opened, so Anna had no experience on which to rely. The United States recently had initiated the war against Iraq, whose president, Saddam Hussein, had promised terrorist acts against his opponents. Would the combination of recessionary spending and fear of terrorism discourage people from visiting Central Florida and lead to a decrease in revenues at Perfumery on Park?

HISTORY
Market Niche

Perfumery on Park, Inc. was established in Winter Park, Florida in May 1984 by Anna and David Currie. Steady increases in sales led to the first profit in 1988, and profits increased in 1990 (Exhibits 1, 2, and 3). The number of employees had risen to five by 1990 from the original two in 1984. Anna was responsible for all aspects of the boutique's operations, including ordering, personnel, finance, and marketing. David worked at the shop only intermittently, although he maintained accounting records.

Winter Park is an affluent community adjacent to Orlando, the tourist center of Florida and the world. Winter Park's main street, Park Avenue, was bordered on one side by Central Park and on the other by numerous small boutiques and

EXHIBIT 1   Perfumery on Park, Inc. Income Statement, 1988–1990 ($000)

	1990	1989	1988
Sales	$405	$364	$281
Cost of goods sold	241	204	160
Gross margin	$163	$160	$121
Wages	43	27	20
Rent	12	10	10
Advertising	7	17	2
Supplies	12	12	9
Travel	17	3	3
Credit card charges	9	10	7
Shipping	5	5	3
Other expenses	24	37	26
Interest	24	39	36
Total expenses	$151	$162	$116
Net income	$ 12	($ 2)	$ 5

EXHIBIT 2   Perfumery on Park, Inc. Balance Sheet, 1988–1990 ($000)

	1990[a]	1989	1988
Assets			
Cash	$ 2	$ 10	$ 2
Inventory	104	102	80
Miscellaneous	0	65	65
Net fixed assets	156	49	49
Total assets	$262	$226	$196
Liabilities and Equity			
Accounts payable	$ 3	$ 14	$ 3
Sales tax payable	7	7	5
Payroll tax pay	2	2	2
Short-term loan	34	34	12
Long-term loan	260	143	167
Total liabilities	$306	$199	$189
Equity	−44	27	7
Total liabilities and equity	$262	$226	$196

[a]Reflects reclassification of second mortgage as loan to business and adjustments due to dissolution of subsidiary, Perfumery on the Avenue, Inc.

EXHIBIT 3 Perfumery on Park, Inc. Number of Transactions and Average Sale per Transaction, 1988–1990 ($000)

	1990	1989	1988
Number of transactions	8,220	8,050	7,081
Total revenue	$404,600	$363,800	$280,500
Average sale	$49.22	$45.20	$39.62

specialty shops. The ambience of the town was comparable to that of Carmel, California, Palm Beach, Florida, or the Hamptons of Long Island.

Perfumery on Park had carved a market niche by specializing in classic fragrances and fragrances from smaller houses or less famous designers. Personnel at department stores in the central Florida area referred customers to the Perfumery, and in return the staff of the Perfumery referred to department stores customers who requested fragrances from heavily advertised, national launches. The Perfumery's variety of fragrances was considered unsurpassed by United States standards, where most fragrance marketing was through department stores. Of more than 400 fragrances on the international market in 1990, Perfumery on Park carried almost 200. Because most department stores carried perhaps 15 to 20 fragrances that tended to be in fashion at the time, there existed a niche for a shop that specialized in traditional and hard-to-find fragrances.

The success at carving a niche in the competitive fragrance market caused a steady growth in sales at rates that exceeded growth in the fragrance industry generally. Over the past six years the perfume market had grown at a rate of 4 to 5 percent annually in real terms; sales at Perfumery on Park had grown at a rate of 10 to 12 percent. Price increases had averaged 5 percent per year since 1984 because of inflation in the United States and the decline in value of the dollar relative to the French franc.

Emphasis on Service

Anna's strong belief in service to customers affected many aspects. An important aspect was maintenance of inventory in a fragrance once the decision was made to carry it. The number of fragrance launches in the United States averaged more than 30 each year, so there was a constant turnover of fragrances as they experienced their life cycles. Once Anna decided to carry a fragrance, the fragrance was maintained in stock until it was no longer manufactured. Maintaining a fragrance also meant stocking whatever stock keeping units (SKUs) were available: perfumes, eaux de toilette, and body products such as dusting powder, lotion, and bath gel. The decision to carry a fragrance thus implied a significant investment in inventory.

Frequently, the U.S. distributor of a fragrance changed, resulting in the product's unavailability for a period of months. Locating the new distributor required considerable effort, but it was important to obtain that information if needs of the clients were to be met. If the Perfumery did not have an item in stock and no American distributor could be found, the item was special-ordered from France. As a courtesy to her customers, Anna special-ordered other fragrances for which an established U.S. market did not exist.

Great care was taken in educating the staff about all aspects of the fragrance industry—ingredients, manufacturers and couturiers, procedures for applying fragrances, and availability of new and classic fragrances. The staff was expected to know about all the fragrances carried at the Perfumery, whereas the staff at a department store typically specialized in the lines of one designer or manufacturer such as Christian Dior or Yves Saint-Laurent. The Perfumery received referrals from throughout the United States from customers trying to locate a fragrance they had worn for years but that no longer was carried in their local markets.

Aspects of merchandising played a key role in satisfying customers. Gift wrapping was complimentary, samples were provided as a means of testing alternative fragrances, and shopping bags were decorated with ribbons. Customers who visited the shop more than once were greeted by name, although the usual joke was that the staff recognized customers by fragrance rather than by name. Whenever possible, a file was maintained for the customer or spouse so the current fragrance favorite would be known to whoever was shopping for that individual.

CHANGES IN THE FRAGRANCE INDUSTRY
Turmoil in Department Stores

Sales through boutiques such as Perfumery on Park accounted for more than 90 percent of the sales of perfumes in France, but in the United States the usual channel of distribution was through department stores, which accounted for more than 98 percent of domestic sales. The domestic department store industry was in turmoil in 1990. The two major department store chains, Allied and Federated, had been purchased during the 1980s by Robert Campeau, a Canadian developer. Campeau had leveraged the purchase to such an extent that he was unable to service the debt, forcing him to file for protection for the Allied and Federated chains under U.S. bankruptcy statutes in January 1990. Included in the bankruptcy was the store considered the bellwether of perfume retailers in America, Bloomingdale's. Campeau's financial difficulties continued into 1990. According to an article in *Women's Wear Daily*, Federated stores reported a loss of $17.7 million in May 1990; Allied's loss for the same period was $9.2 million.

In Central Florida, most of the Perfumery on Park's major competitors were members of the Allied or Federated chains. Jordan Marsh, Burdine's, and Maas Bros. experienced the effects of Campeau's cash flow problems—constant discounting in an effort to move merchandise to generate cash, product shortages as ordering was curtailed to conserve cash, and customer dissatisfaction with untrained personnel at understaffed stores.

The turmoil was not limited to Allied and Federated stores, moreover. Some of the major names in U.S. retailing—B. Altman, Bonwit-Teller, and R. H. Macy—failed or experienced difficulty during the period. It was widely thought that consolidation would take place in the department store industry nationally, although it was not certain which stores would survive. Two surviving national chains had recently acquired local stores: Maison-Blanche acquired Robinson's, and Dillard's acquired Ivey's, which had been at the Winter Park Mall for almost 30 years.

Emergence of Perfume Boutiques

Although Perfumery on Park was the only perfume boutique in the Central Florida area, it was typical of a national trend toward specialty retailing. Two chains had opened several perfume or cosmetic boutiques in south Florida malls, and a German-based chain, Perfumery Douglas, was beginning to penetrate the U.S. market through New York and Washington.

As at the Perfumery, these boutiques offered a wider variety of fragrances and cosmetics than were available at most department stores. They did not account for a significant portion of industry sales as of 1990, but many industry experts predicted they would be the wave of the future. It was uncertain how much inroad these boutiques would make into the department stores' 98-percent share of the market for fragrances and cosmetics in the United States.

Diverters

Rights to sell French fragrances in the United States are purchased by a company that is authorized as the sole agent in the United States. In most cases the agent in turn sells fragrances through authorized retail outlets such as department stores or specialty shops such as Perfumery on Park.

Occasionally, a discount store such as Kmart or Service Merchandise will obtain a fragrance that it sells at a discount from the authorized distributor's suggested retail price. There also are firms that specialize in wholesaling selected fragrances at prices lower than those suggested by the authorized distributor. These products sold outside the purview of the authorized distributor are called *diverted* (or *gray market*) *goods,* and the source of supply for diverters is the subject of conjecture.

In most cases, diverters offer only a limited variety of products—100 ml. eau de toilette sprays, for example—rather than the complete line. The product is available intermittently, but may be in large quantities when it is available. The products frequently are old, resulting from distributor closeouts or repackaging.

Although authorized distributors and retailers might view these gray market goods as prohibited by the distribution contract and hence illegal, the Supreme Court of the United States upheld the right of discounters to obtain and sell diverted goods in 1988 in a suit involving Kmart, Inc.

Approaches by Sales Representatives

Because of the turmoil in department stores and the apparent increasing acceptance of specialty boutiques in general or Perfumery on Park in particular, Anna had been approached by sales representatives of several companies that previously had refused to sell to her. Although some companies apparently maintained their policy of distributing only through department stores, that number was fewer after Christmas 1989 than it was before. Many sales reps complained that department stores had reduced Christmas purchases, which meant a decrease in commission income to the sales reps. This observation was reinforced by the emergence of the local Belk's, a department store that previously had carried few major fragrances because many companies thought of Belk's as a less prestigious outlet.

Anna did not want to pass up the opportunity to carry other prestigious lines, so she began to invest in them throughout 1990. Due to her policy of carrying complete lines, the addition of these new fragrances meant increased investment in inventory. Anna felt this was worthwhile because she viewed this as a chance to penetrate markets that might not be penetrated under other circumstances.

STRATEGIC OPPORTUNITIES

In January 1991 Anna Currie is considering several alternative strategies for Perfumery on Park. She already had responded to one opportunity by expanding the selection of fragrances in response to invitations from sales representatives. Other strategies suggested alternative means of growth for the Perfumery. Because of the Curries' limited financial resources and the modest profits already generated by Perfumery on Park, any strategy was constrained by lack of financing. In fact, it was possible that any of the strategies under consideration were irrelevant so long as funding was not available.

Mail Order Sales

Anna had experimented with mail order sales over the past three or four years. She prepared a catalog listing the shop's fragrances according to a system prepared by Haarman und Reimer, a German chemical firm. The catalog was distributed to customers who visited the shop and was mailed to visitors who had filled out registration forms. She also received unsolicited requests for catalogs from throughout the United States.

The first catalog was printed on glossy, heavyweight paper and featured pictures of perfume bottles for most of the fragrances. Because that catalog was so expensive to produce, a new catalog was prepared when supplies of the original ran out. The second catalog was printed on comparable paper but did not contain pictures of fragrances. Despite the savings, the current catalog cost approximately $1.50 per copy to produce. The only way to reduce the cost per copy was to print the catalog on lower-quality paper, which Anna thought would decrease the image she was trying to convey.

Catalog sales were attractive because they provided an opportunity to increase sales without adding to the current size of the shop. Depending on the volume of sales obtained, it would be possible to receive orders, package products, and mail shipments with the existing staff. Of course, if the response to mail orders was overwhelming, it would be necessary not only to add additional staff, but to increase the level of inventory and shift mail operations to an alternative location.

Until she had some experience with mass mailings, Anna would not know whether she needed to address those issues.

Growth of the catalog industry had been a nationwide phenomenon during the 1980s, but by 1990 there was evidence that the market had become saturated. By 1984, for example, more than 6,500 catalog marketers sent approximately 8.5 billion catalogs to American households. The proportion of consumers who purchased at least one item through a catalog had stabilized since 1984 at about 50 percent.

National studies have shown that developing a catalog operation from concept to breakeven requires approximately $1.5 million over five years. At least 100,000 catalogs must be mailed in the first year for a nationwide effort. Response rates vary from 1 percent in the first year to the 6 percent necessary for breakeven in the fifth year, provided the catalog has a unique concept. Through time the mailing list is refined by emphasizing those customers who are repeat purchasers. The industry average is $90 per order. Customers could be targeted by income level, geographic area, age, or other demographic characteristics.

Anna thought the shop's typical customer earned an above-average income, was female and well-educated, and worked in an executive or professional capacity. Florida was the state most frequently represented in the shop's registration forms, but Georgia, North Carolina, and Ohio were listed numerous times. Anna thought it was possible to reduce the cost of introduction somewhat because she would not add to the staff at the shop, but that savings was likely to be offset by the catalog's higher cost of production.

Expand the Existing Shop

For several years Anna had considered expanding the existing shop, either by acquiring the space adjacent to the Perfumery or by moving into a larger location along Park Avenue. She would use the additional space to expand the variety of products and to build an office at which she could work. Besides carrying additional fragrances, Anna wanted to expand the lines of cosmetics she carried. Cosmetics represented repeat business that would reduce somewhat the seasonal and cyclical fluctuations in sales.

Expanding the shop would entail two major costs: the cost of acquiring the space from the current leaseholder and the cost of remodeling the space and installing new fixtures. She discussed the possibility of acquiring the adjacent space from its leaseholder, who asked $10,000 for approximately 300 square feet; that would bring the size of the Perfumery to 600 square feet. A larger space of approximately 1,000 square feet owned by the same landlord was vacant a few doors down the street. If she acquired that space she would not have to buy out an existing lease, but she would have to move the contents from the existing location. Installing new fixtures at either location would cost about $50,000 and she would have to invest $30,000 in additional inventory.

Anna also considered opening a treatment center to provide facials and body toning, but that line of business would subject her to state regulation that she did not encounter as a retailer. If she expanded into treatment she would have to purchase specialized equipment and hire qualified staff, both of which were outside Anna's expertise in fragrances and cosmetics. She had not yet investigated the treatment center alternative to the point of developing cost estimates or market studies.

Clouding the issue of expansion was the question of whether Park Avenue was the appropriate location for expansion to take place. Parking was more constrained than at a regional mall, which limited exposure and access. Although the ambience of Park Avenue was still attractive, national chain stores such as Benetton, Banana Republic, and The Limited recently had replaced many of the locally owned shops, giving the street the image of an outdoor mall. Many retailers worried that there was nothing special to differentiate Park Avenue from a typical mall.

Add More Stores

If perfume boutiques were increasing in importance as channels of distribution, it might be better to expand the number of locations than to increase the size of the existing location. Central Florida had several regional malls and numerous shopping areas oriented to the many tourists that visited attractions such as Disney World, Sea World, and Universal Studios. The opportunity for profit was much greater at these locations because of the increased exposure, but Anna had learned that profit was not the only consideration in operating additional stores.

For four years Anna had owned another perfume boutique in Naples, Florida, a five-hour drive from Winter Park. The second shop involved monthly visits to Naples to monitor the performance of the shop, problems in dealing with employees and the manager, and trauma when the shop was robbed one weekend before Christmas. Closing the shop was an expensive lesson, but it relieved much strain from being a long-distance manager. Anna was not anxious to duplicate that experience.

Opening other shops locally might not require extensive travel, but it would involve other, more subtle issues. For example, Perfumery on Park was open Monday through Saturday at hours Anna could set; opening at a mall would require being open every day at hours determined by mall management. Anna could decorate Perfumery on Park any way she wanted; in a mall she would be restricted by their guidelines and would have to participate in their promotions. Finding a manager and employees for another store would increase the proportion of time Anna spent on personnel issues. Anna wondered whether it was worthwhile growing a business if it meant less time doing the things she enjoyed.

It was impossible to predict sales at a mall location, but Anna thought they would be triple the level in Winter Park. Expenses also would increase: rent and mall fees would be 8 percent of sales, salaries could be as much as $100,000 depending on the number of employees, and expenses other than cost of merchandise could be up to 15 percent of sales. She would plan on cost of merchandise at 50 percent of sales. Up-front costs to furnish the space and provide a beginning inventory would be about $100,000.

Develop Her Own Fragrance

Almost since she opened Perfumery on Park, Anna was fascinated by the idea of creating her own fragrance. The fascination was heightened by the success of Giorgio, which had risen from a fragrance at a boutique on Rodeo Drive in Beverly Hills, California, to a major national launch during the mid-1980s. Anna thought a private fragrance would promote an identity with the shop as well as lead to a source of additional revenues. She had contacted representatives from a major fragrance manufacturer, who were more than anxious to help her by creating a fragrance to her specifications.

Just as there was evidence about saturation in the catalog market, there was evidence about saturation in the fragrance market. New launches in the United States numbered more than 30 per year over the past several years, creating confusion in the industry. Besides traditional sources of new fragrances—perfume houses and designers—new fragrances were introduced under the names of actors, actresses, singers, dancers, and other celebrities. Almost all of these introductions had short life cycles, although sales could be very high during the peak periods. Launching these fragrances nationally was very expensive; trade journals reported that Calvin Klein spent more than $17 million in advertising to launch Obsession.

Although it was not necessary to undergo a national launch just to have a private fragrance, creating her own fragrance would not be costless. Selecting the right fragrance would require time and patience during negotiations with the manufacturer, who had an incentive to minimize the time spent on development. Once the fragrance was selected, it would have to be purchased in bulk quantities that seemed far in excess of what Anna could expect to sell. The real costs of producing a fragrance would be packaging, which included the bottle and box, and distribution if the fragrance was sold at locations other than Perfumery on Park. Bottles were available in standard designs from glass manufacturers, but few of these designs were distinctive. Box designing and printing was a job for professionals, with whom Anna had little contact. Anna knew that commissions paid to sales reps amounted to perhaps 30 percent of the wholesale price of the product.

Anna had not pursued the alternative of producing her own fragrance beyond the point of trying several samples from the manufacturer, but she was ready to proceed with her investigation. Two events gave her conflicting impressions about the chance for success. A sales rep from one of the major companies had developed her own fragrance two years earlier and it appeared to be successful. It had been carried at the Perfumery and at several department stores in the area. However, when Anna attempted to reorder following the Christmas season the product was no longer available, indicating that the launch ultimately had failed. On the other hand, a visitor to the shop recently indicated that he was retired from the business of fragrance manufacturing, but maintained enough contacts in the business that he could help Anna reduce the costs of manufacturing and packaging. Of course, Anna had not proceeded far enough to consider how or whether she would market a fragrance beyond the shop.

THE DECISION

Faced with these alternatives, Anna wanted to decide on an appropriate strategy for Perfumery on Park. She was very interested in spending more time on long-range planning and devoting less time to the day-to-day operation of the boutique. Business had increased to the point that she could hire others to operate the business, but she wanted to make sure the boutique continued to expand.

It seemed to her that whatever strategy she chose would involve additional financing. The Curries had invested as much of their own money as they could and looked forward to the time after the bank loan was retired so they could draw more from the boutique. Of course, if the recession caused drastic decreases in sales, strategic planning might be irrelevant.

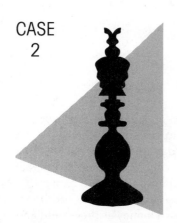

CASE 2

PEGGYDALE LEATHERCRAFT, BALCLUTHA, NEW ZEALAND

ROBERT ANDERSON & TOM BATLEY

When Bill, a paraplegic confined to a wheelchair, and Peggy Jones moved in 1974 to their new house just south of Balclutha, New Zealand, Bill's friends built him a small workshop so he could continue creating leather goods. Little did Bill and Peggy realize then that less than 15 years later that small workshop would have blossomed into a million-dollar business selling leather goods, sheepskins, and souvenirs to tourists and local people. (One New Zealand dollar equals $0.60 USD.) Tourists are the mainstay of Peggydale's business, so fluctuations in the New Zealand tourism industry are reflected in the company's bottom line. The years 1988 and 1989 were not good tourist seasons, and Peggydale's revenues declined in those years. Bill and Peggy are trying to devise ways of making their business less dependent on tourism.

BILL JONES: FROM LABORER TO PARAPLEGIC TO ENTREPRENEUR

William Jones was born in Invercargill, New Zealand, March 31, 1927. After school, Bill joined the army and was sent to Italy during World War II. He rose to the rank of sergeant with 10 Platoon, B Company, the 5th Reinforcements. When Bill returned to New Zealand, he left the army, married Peggy, and took a job in the Kaitangata coal mines near Balclutha, where he might have spent his working life except for a crippling accident in 1951. It was January 31, 1951 when a broken beam in the ceiling of the mine caught his shoulder and threw him back on a stack of boxes. Bill was permanently paralyzed from the waist down and was left with little except his own resources and those of his wife, Peg.

An article in the local paper, the *Southland Times*, recounted Bill's army service and ended with the following words of encouragement for his future:

> When the fall occurred in the mine it pinned him down and broke his spine. It is not hard to believe that only his unconquerable spirit prevented him from succumbing to his injuries. But he is still in hospital and he is still smiling. His

Case written by Robert L. Anderson, College of Charleston, and Tom Batley, University of Otago.

future, his livelihood, is uncertain. But no one who knows Jonesy can doubt for a moment that he will not triumph over every blow that life can deal him. It was plain in Italy, it is crystal clear here, now in New Zealand.

The accolades and expressions of sympathy lifted Bill's spirits, but they could not shorten his lengthy period of rehabilitation in the Dunedin Hospital.

Bill's rehabilitation was aided by another patient who taught him leatherworking. Recounting his experience, Bill recalled:

> Twenty-six years ago I couldn't darn a sock. After my accident I was in Ward 5 at Dunedin Hospital. A man there had been transferred from Waipiata—he'd been there some years—for surgery on a collapsed lung.
>
> He was a crackerjack at saddleworking. There he was, strung up in a plaster cast, blocks and tackles everywhere, doing bits of work on his bed. When I started taking notice, I'd have them push my bed down to his cubicle. I'd watch him and talk to him for half a day at a time. Occasionally I'd get a loan of his gear.
>
> When I got home I bought myself a set of tools and started getting leather from "Disabled Soldiers." It was a while before I could get it from tanneries so I worked through "Disabled Soldiers"—Rehabilitation League as it is now. They used to let me have my pick of what they could offer, at cost.

Bill learned a skill which occupied his idle hours and aided his rehabilitation, but he was still without an occupation.

After more than two years and a week-long Supreme Court case, Bill received compensation from the mining company for his accident. Bill and Peggy decided to use the money to buy a small farm, even though neither knew anything about farming. The Joneses continued to live in Kaitangata while a married couple ran the farm on a day-to-day basis. Eventually, the married couple was replaced by a single man, and the Joneses moved onto their property (named Peggydale, after Peggy Jones, whose maiden name was Dale).

Since Bill was confined to a wheelchair, Peggy was responsible for most of the farm chores, which she referred to as "jolly hard work," adding that "One year I raised 200 calves by bucket." It was a family joke that each Christmas Bill's gift to Peggy was a new pair of gumboots, an overall, and a mallet. Peggy noted that, "looking back, I don't think I could have done anything without Bill. He's always ahead of everyone and is a perfectionist too. Talk about women's lib . . . I'd be useless if I was left to my own devices." While Peggy was doing most of the farm work, Bill was not simply idling away the hours.

When the Joneses moved from the city to their farm, two friends and their son Mervyn built Bill a workshop on the end of the farm shed. Bill used a life insurance policy as collateral for a loan to buy his first sewing machine. Bill observed that, "we had it paid off in a year—three or four hundred dollars. It would cost a couple of thousand to replace." To enable Bill to work with both hands free, a friend made a forehead accelerator for the machine from the hydraulic clutch of a car. Bill's increasing skill with leather soon became the basis of their current business.

THE NEW BUSINESS

Soon after Bill acquired his new machine, his daughter Ailsa, who was in her third year of high school, wanted him to make her a handbag. "The first ones we tried looked pretty terrible, but it was a family affair, and we all chipped in ideas. After a few attempts, we got the job right, and we were off on a new line. We've never looked back since." Bill continued making leather goods for his friends and neighbors, who showed them to their friends who also wanted to purchase Bill's handicrafts. It was not long before the Joneses were earning more money from leather goods than from the farm.

In 1974 Bill and Peggy decided to sell the farm and buy property where they could build a house and a small workshop. The Joneses used the proceeds from the sale of their farm to purchase 25 acres of land, where they built a house designed especially for Bill. Since the land, three kilometers south of Balclutha, was designated as farm land, the Joneses needed a special permit so Bill could build a workshop on his property. The Joneses were granted a cottage-industry permit which would only allow them to have a small shop on their land. The permit did not allow for any type of retail or wholesale business on the property.

Once Bill had made enough leather handbags, moccasins, and other small articles, he and Peggy would load up their car and visit various retailers in the area who bought their goods for resale to both tourists and locals. The Joneses always returned from their trips with an empty car, convincing them that they should bypass the middlemen and establish their own retail business. The Joneses began the tedious and frustrating process of convincing Balclutha officials to change their cottage-industry permit to a tourist-industry permit. Tenacity paid off, and their property was approved for a tourist-industry permit.

Bill and Peggy enclosed the space between their house and the workshop, added toilets and display fixtures, and were soon in the retail business with their new company, Peggydale Leathercraft. Almost immediately tourists and locals began to visit Peggydale, the locals mainly to buy Bill's leather goods and the tourists to use the toilets and purchase goods. Business increased so quickly that Bill could not manufacture leather items fast enough to satisfy demand. The Joneses decided to add other merchandise which they purchased from about a dozen wholesalers and several travelers (traveling sales representatives).

The expanded product line and clean toilets attracted an increasing number of customers to Peggydale, especially the tour buses heading to Te Anau and Queenstown (see Exhibit 1). When one or more buses pulled into Peggydale, there was a mad dash for the toilet, and the lines that developed often spilled out the front door. At the suggestion of several bus drivers, the Joneses decided to build a tea kiosk, which would serve light meals, and to increase the number of toilets.

OPERATIONS
Location

Peggydale is located on State Highway 1 just south of the town of Balclutha. The town itself has a population of approximately 5,000 people, most of whom are involved in farming. The town is large enough to provide the needed employees

EXHIBIT 1 Map of New Zealand

for Peggydale's retail and restaurant business. The local people continue to patronize Peggydale; however, the townspeople alone could not keep the Joneses' business growing. Fortunately, the location of the business takes advantage of the South Island's domestic and international tourist trade. Tourists traveling by car or tour bus usually go from Christchurch or Dunedin to the popular resort cities of Te Anau and Queenstown, and many of those using State Highway 1 stop for a meal and some shopping at Peggydale.

Tourists are the mainstay of Peggydale's business; in fact, Bill estimates that tourists account for approximately 75 percent of his revenue. Unfortunately, the tourist business appears to be somewhat cyclical. The New Zealand Tourist and Publicity Department (NZTP) reports that the number of foreign tourists visiting New Zealand rose from 596,995 in 1985 to 855,492 in 1988, with Japanese, West German, and British visitors accounting for much of the increase (see Exhibit 2). The amount of money spent per day per tourist increased from $84 in 1986/87 to $97 in 1987/88; however, some of the tourists, notably the Japanese, who are visiting New Zealand in greater numbers, are not spending as much as they did previously.

Bill and Peggy are primarily interested in international and domestic tourists who travel and spend money in the provinces of Otago and Southland because those are the people who visit Peggydale. In 1988, domestic and international

EXHIBIT 2 Overseas Visitor Arrivals by Main Markets, Year Ended March (base: all visitor arrivals)

	1985	1986	1987	1988	Percentage Change 1987 to 1988
Australia	265,579	291,044	272,214	293,560	7.8%
United States	102,672	133,908	163,390	175,621	7.5
Japan	47,060	52,204	66,404	79,928	20.4
United Kingdom	41,254	45,534	53,146	66,749	25.6
Canada	23,816	32,157	34,550	34,501	−0.1
West Germany	10,135	10,956	13,182	18,705	41.9
Singapore	7,632	8,448	15,329	14,989	−2.2
Other	98,847	114,822	144,994	171,439	18.2
Total	596,995	689,073	763,209	855,492	12.1

Source: NZTP New Zealand Visitor Statistics 1987–1988 (Total Visitors).

Comparison of Overseas Visitor Expenditure, Year Ended March (base: 15 years and over)

	Total Travel Expenditure ($millions)		Mean Expenditure		Percentage Change
	1986/87	1987/88	Per Person 1986/87	Per Day 1987/88	
Australia	$ 339	$ 373	$ 73	$ 83	13.7%
United States	337	386	148	165	11.5
Japan	187	299	280	261	−6.8
United Kingdom	105	148	43	55	27.9
Canada	62	58	89	62	−30.3
West Germany	28	45	64	76	18.8
Singapore	25	24	162	85	−47.5
Other	229	278	54	68	25.9
Total	$1,309	$1,612	$ 84	$ 97	15.5

Source: NZTP New Zealand International Visitors Survey 1986/87 and 1987/88.

EXHIBIT 2 Cont'd. Overseas Visitor Arrivals by Main Markets (all age groups, year ended March 1988)

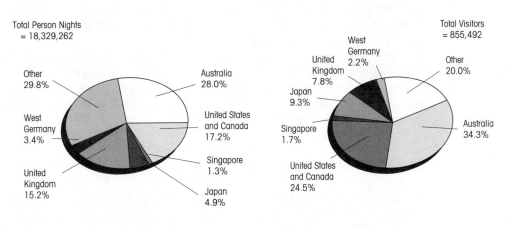

Source: NZTP New Zealand Visitor Statistics 1987/88 (Total Visitors).

Forecasts of Overseas Visitor Arrivals Comparing 1988 and 1993 (Year Ended March)

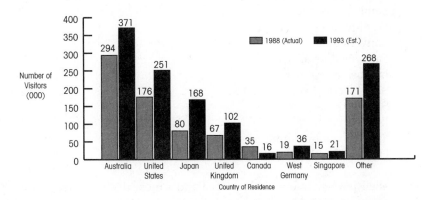

Source: NZTP New Zealand International Visitor Arrival Statistics 1988–1993.

tourists spent $416.3 million in Otago and Southland, and the NZTP predicts that that figure should increase steadily over the next few years. If the department's projections are incorrect, the Joneses can expect to see their sales remain stable or even decline.

Facilities

The small workshop and retail space used by the Joneses in 1975 have been enlarged five different times and now measure approximately 5,300 square feet. Bill's original workshop was enlarged to facilitate a growing manufacturing business. The retail space is attached to the Joneses' house, which allows Bill to get around quite easily. However, the proximity of the buildings does have some disadvantages. Tourists are often not aware that part of the space is a private residence, and they tend to walk through the house looking for things to buy. Fortunately, this does not happen too often.

The other building in the complex is the tea kiosk, which seats 120 people. Bill is convinced that this building, with its clean toilets and piped-in music, is a major reason people stop at Peggydale. Bill and Peggy know that people also stop at Peggydale because of easy parking for buses and cars, fresh food, the deer farm on the grounds, and the wholesome meals.

Retailing

The shop, or retail business, which generates approximately 85 percent of total revenue, is the heart of Peggydale's business. The product line, which is quite extensive, includes the following items:

> Lambskin rugs
> Sheepskins
> Hand-knitted sweaters
> Lamb suede suits
> Wool mattress overlays
> Souvenirs
> Paua shell jewelry
> Lambskin seat covers
> Short wool sheepskin slippers
> Sheepskin jackets
> Leather clothing
> Sundry wool clothing
> Handcrafted leather goods

Paua shell jewelry is one of New Zealand's most distinctive souvenirs. Paua, or abalone, is harvested, polished, and then made into jewelry, ash trays, and other usable or decorative objects.

Most of the items sold are purchased from various wholesalers; however, some leather and sheepskin products are still manufactured at Peggydale. The manufactured items (moccasins, sheepskin products, and leather goods) account for approximately 20 percent of gross sales. Most of these items are sold at Peggydale, but some are also sold to wholesalers.

All of the merchandise is attractively displayed, and there are no signs of any type of security devices. The leather coats, some costing as much as $750, have no chains through the sleeves or other kinds of alarm devices attached to them. The Joneses have experienced very little shoplifting; however, they did install an alarm system in the shop after thieves broke in and stole $46,000 worth of leather coats.

Bill and Peggy continue to manage Peggydale; however, most of the day-to-day operations are handled by their son Mervyn and his wife Alison. The younger Joneses are responsible for purchasing the majority of the items sold at

Peggydale, and Mervyn also does most of the paperwork. Bill and Peggy, both semiretired, are pleased that Mervyn has taken to the business and plans to make it his career.

Food Service

The tea kiosk, with sales of nearly $200,000 in 1988, continues to attract tourists and locals alike. The menu includes tea, coffee, cold beverages (nonalcoholic only), sandwiches, snacks, and baked goods. It is the baked goods, made daily on the premises, which are the tea kiosk's main attraction. In addition to food, the tea kiosk also sells some sheepskin items and souvenirs, just in case some tourists don't visit the shop.

Personnel

Because business is seasonal, May to August being the slowest time, Peggydale employs more people than are usually needed at one time. A roster system is used which allows all employees to work some hours every week, but very few are considered full-time workers. There are 23 employees, all female, on the roster for the tea kiosk and 8 on the shop's roster. There are four unions representing the employees; however, they create very few problems for the Joneses. Turnover is quite high because most of the employees work at Peggydale two or three years while they are in school and leave for other jobs when they graduate.

Exporting

Peggydale has been exporting in a small way since the business was founded. Many tourists who purchase items at the Peggydale shop have them shipped to their homes. When the packages are prepared for mailing, Bill inserts a four-page catalog and other promotional material to remind the customer of additional items they might wish to purchase. On many occasions tourists who have visited Peggydale write or call Bill or Peggy to purchase more merchandise for themselves or their friends. The Joneses could expand this export business if they were willing to become involved with the complexities and intricacies of international trade.

There is a market for hand-crafted items in other parts of the world, as Bill and Peggy discovered in 1981. That year, the Abilympics, an international ability and skill contest for disabled people, was held in Tokyo. Although Bill did not attend the Abilympics, he did send a variety of his leather and deer handbags, wallets, purses, and key rings for exhibition. The national president of the Paraplegic and Physically Disabled Federation, Dr. N. R. Jefferson, who traveled with the disabled team from New Zealand, said, "great interest was shown in Mr. Jones's entry." Several Japanese dignitaries were presented with Bill's leather goods that they had admired. The Joneses received a few orders for leather goods from Japanese companies, but the orders were not repeated, and no effort was made to establish formal links with those Japanese companies.

Marketing

The most effective advertising for Peggydale is what Bill calls the "bush telegraph" or word-of-mouth advertising. The Joneses know that the consistency of their clean facilities, good food, and quality merchandise keep tour bus drivers coming back to Peggydale with their passengers. Unlike some tourist businesses, the Joneses do not pay the drivers or give them commissions on tourist purchases to keep them coming back. Since word-of-mouth advertising is important, the Joneses have developed a philosophy that there is repeat business in the tourist industry. Tourists may only visit New Zealand once, but they tell relatives, friends, and associates what they liked and disliked. If those people visit New Zealand, they may make a point of stopping at Peggydale. Even though the bush telegraph seems to be quite productive, the Joneses do have more formal ways of advertising.

Bill and Peggy paid to have Peggydale included in a videotape which is run constantly at the tourist information office in Dunedin, and they have brochures which they provide to car rental agencies, hotels, motels, and restaurants. Radio advertising was tried, but proved to be quite ineffective, so the Joneses rely mainly on print advertising which appears primarily in local newspapers. The form of advertising that might be most successful, billboards and road signs, is not permitted by local government. The Joneses are allowed one small highway sign about one kilometer from Peggydale. Since the Joneses are not sure which form of advertising is the most productive, they have retained a consultant to analyze all aspects of their advertising campaign.

Finances

Peggydale has been profitable since its founding, and the Joneses have financed most growth with internally generated funds. In some instances they have had to borrow money from the Bank of New Zealand, but their debt has never been oppressive. The income (trading) statements (see Exhibit 3) reflect the decrease in sales from 1987 to 1989, which was due to the decrease in tourism. Even though sales declined, prudent inventory purchasing caused net income (trading proceeds) for 1988 to exceed 1987 by approximately $22,000; however, net income decreased by nearly $72,000 in 1989. The balance sheet contains an entry, livestock revaluation income, which needs explanation (see Exhibit 4). The Joneses keep a herd of deer and a few sheep on Peggydale's 25 acres to amuse tourists and to sell for meat and hides. This entry shows profit or loss from sales.

EXPANSION

In 1987, the Joneses noticed some subtle changes in the tourist business. People were taking shorter vacations and wanted to reach their destination as quickly as possible; therefore, fewer buses were calling at Peggydale. Also a number of buses and independent travelers were taking a more northerly route to Queenstown, completely bypassing Peggydale. In order to sell to those tourists who missed Peggydale, Mervyn began looking for a site on the other route to Queenstown

EXHIBIT 3   Trading Statements—Peggydale Leathercraft

Year Ending March 31, 1989

	This Year	Last Year
Income		
Sales	$778,128	$1,048,375
Net Sales	$778,128	$1,048,375
Less cost of sales		
Opening stock	361,420	203,155
Purchases	349,257	727,838
	710,677	930,993
Closing stock	295,260	361,420
	415,417	569,573
Gross proceeds	$362,711	$ 478,802
Less direct expenses		
Commission and discounts	12,733	22,720
Electricity	6,844	5,944
Packaging	—	3,067
Cartage	320	1,393
Wages	126,027	156,965
	145,924	190,089
Trading proceeds transferred	$216,787	$ 288,713

Year Ending March 31, 1988

	This Year	Last Year
Income		
Sales	$1,048,375	$1,259,000
Less sales tax	—	2,092
Net Sales	$1,048,375	$1,256,908
Less cost of sales		
Opening stock	203,155	176,974
Purchases	727,838	820,106
	930,993	997,080
Closing stock	361,420	203,155
	569,573	793,925
Gross proceeds	$ 478,802	$ 462,983
Less direct expenses		
Printing and stationery	13,468	21,528
Commission and discounts	22,720	9,868
Electricity	5,944	10,887
Packaging	3,067	5,128
Wages	156,965	$ 149,159
	$ 202,164	196,570
Trading proceeds transferred	$ 276,638	$ 266,413

EXHIBIT 4   Peggydale Leathercraft

Balance Sheet as of March 31, 1989

	This Year	Last Year
Partners' capital accounts		
Mr. W. H. Jones	$135,109	$135,109
Mrs. P. Y. Jones	135,108	135,108
Mr. M. R. Jones	180,145	180,145
Mrs. A. E. Jones	90,073	90,073
	$540,435	$540,435
Partners' current accounts		
Mr. W. H. Jones	$ 8,582	$ (328)
Mrs. P. Y. Jones	37,179	25,332
Mr. M. R. Jones	(16,486)	(45,884)
Mrs. A. E. Jones	22,602	15,241
	51,877	(5,639)
Livestock revaluation income	109	164
	51,986	(5,475)
Total proprietors' equity	$592,421	$534,960
Represented by:		
Fixed assets		
Land and buildings	$496,679	$504,031
Furniture and fittings	11,305	14,133
Plant and Machinery	24,449	27,811
Motor vehicles	45,437	51,906
	$577,870	$597,881
Less term liabilities		
Mortgage N.Z. Permanent Building Society	$325,624	$325,624
Term Loan Bank of New Zealand	4,641	8,971
	330,265	334,595
	$247,605	$263,286

where he could locate a second shop. While he was evaluating several sites, Mervyn ran into an old friend, Max Guthrie, who indicated that he was looking for a business to start.

After some discussion, it was decided that Max and his wife Kristin would form an equal partnership with the Joneses and start a business selling items similar to those sold at Peggydale, in Arrowtown. Arrowtown is only 18 kilometers from Queenstown and is itself a tourist destination. The major attraction is the buildings and shops that have been restored to reflect Arrowtown's gold mining past. Town officials note that, "Arrowtown is an ideal central point for the Southern Lakes tourist area with the bright lights of Queenstown only 15 minutes away. Arrowtown itself has many attractions to offer with an array of shops and services, eating houses, hotels and accommodations, craft outlets, and historical points of interest."

EXHIBIT 4 Cont'd. Peggydale Leathercraft

Balance Sheet as of March 31, 1988

	This Year	Last Year
Partners' capital accounts		
Mr. W. H. Jones	$135,109	$135,109
Mrs. P. Y. Jones	135,108	135,108
Mr. M. R. Jones	180,145	180,145
Mrs. A. E. Jones	90,073	90,073
	$540,435	$540,435
Partners' current accounts		
Mr. W. H. Jones	$ (329)	$ (5,895)
Mrs. P. Y. Jones	25,332	(1,994)
Mr. M. R. Jones	(45,883)	(41,438)
Mrs. A. E. Jones	15,240	15,040
	(5,640)	(34,287)
Livestock revaluation income	164	218
	(5,476)	(34,069)
Total proprietors' equity	$534,959	$506,366
Represented by:		
Fixed assets		
Land and buildings	$504,031	$511,383
Furniture and fittings	14,133	17,665
Plant and machinery	27,811	31,715
Motor vehicles	51,906	59,993
	$597,881	$620,756
Less term liabilities		
Mortgage N.Z. Permanent Building Society	$325,624	$219,333
Term Loan Bank of New Zealand	8,971	16,301
	334,595	235,634
	$263,286	$385,122

The new business, the Golden Fleece, is in a leased building about half the size of the Peggydale shop and is already producing revenue in excess of $600,000 (see Exhibit 5). It can be seen from the balance sheet that the partners did not incur much bank debt to start their new business (see Exhibit 6). While the Golden Fleece is only in its third year of operations, it appears that the business will be quite successful for both the Guthries and the Joneses.

PROBLEMS

Peggydale and the Golden Fleece are currently quite profitable, but there are at least two trends which concern the Joneses and the Guthries. The first is the general slowing of the New Zealand economy. Since deregulation, privatization,

EXHIBIT 5 Golden Fleece

Revenue Account for Year Ending March 31, 1989

	This Year	Last Year
Income		
Sales	644,220	509,751
	$644,220	$509,751
Less cost of sales		
Opening stock	200,112	170,153
Purchases	450,246	417,059
Commission	716	—
	651,074	587,212
Closing stock	200,112	200,112
	450,962	387,100
Gross trading proceeds	$193,258	$122,651
Less		
Direct costs		
Wages	30,598	20,952
Cartage	9,621	11,229
Repairs and maintenance	8,155	5,381
Electricity	3,966	2,161
	$ 52,340	$ 39,723
Administration expenses		
General expenses	2,802	4,276
Advertising and stationery	7,206	2,494
Telephone and tolls	4,051	2,668
Bank charges	9,922	—
Accountancy fees	3,896	2,579
	$ 27,877	$ 12,017
Fixed charges		
Accident compensation	386	—
Rates	—	739
Insurance	1,956	5,851
Interest bank overdraft	1,972	4,537
Rent	49,996	37,746
	$ 54,310	$ 48,873
	$134,527	$100,613

and restructuring began in the early 1980s, there has been a general downturn in the economy. Inflation is decreasing, but unemployment is high (about 11 percent), and the government is cutting spending in all areas. Reacting to this downturn, many New Zealanders are also spending less money, especially for nonessentials. If this trend continues, sales at both Peggydale and the Golden Fleece could decrease.

EXHIBIT 6 Golden Fleece

Balance Sheet as of March 31, 1989

	This Year	Last Year
Partners' current accounts		
Peggydale Partnership	$ 80,513	$ 82,312
M.C. and K.F. Guthrie	61,125	85,789
	$141,638	$163,101
Total proprietors' equity	$141,638	$168,101
Represented by:		
Fixed assets		
Lessees' improvements	$ 11,044	$ 12,425
Furniture and fittings	16,748	19,872
Plant and machinery	3,212	3,568
	$ 31,004	$ 35,865
Current assets		
Stock on hand	200,112	200,112
Goods and services tax refund	6,013	6,097
	$206,130	$206,209
Less current liabilities		
A.N.Z. Banking Group	$ 21,540	$ 12,031
Accounts payable	70,673	61,227
Goods and services discrepancy account	3,074	713
Goods and services tax under/over	208	—
	$ 95,495	$ 73,971
Working capital	$110,635	$132,238
Net assets equal to proprietors' equity	$141,639	$168,103

The other trend, a decrease in international tourist spending, is of more concern to the Joneses and Guthries than is the slowing economy. To maximize profits, the Joneses and Guthries need to be able to anticipate their inventory needs and purchase accordingly. Not being able to forecast tourist visits makes it difficult to determine inventory needs. Compounding the problem is the changing mix of international tourists visiting New Zealand. According to Mervyn, tourists from different countries do not necessarily have similar tastes. For example, items that appeal to Japanese may be of no interest to Americans, and items bought by Singaporeans may be ignored by West Germans.

The Joneses and Guthries know that they can do little about the slowing economy, and they cannot do much about the tourist business. However, if their businesses are to continue to prosper, the Joneses and Guthries need to devise ways to keep Peggydale and the Golden Fleece growing.

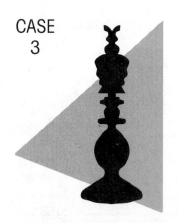

CROWLEY INN:
UN BON PLACE POUR RESTER

ARTHUR SHARPLIN

Crowley, Louisiana, hometown of colorful Louisiana governor Edwin "Fast Eddie" Edwards, is in the heart of Cajun country 60 miles west of Baton Rouge. Crowley Inn, with 59 rooms, a restaurant, and a bar, is at the intersection of Louisiana Highway 13, the main north–south route through Crowley, and Interstate Highway 10. Also at that intersection are a Texaco and an Exxon station, a Kentucky Fried Chicken store, and a Burger King restaurant. But many townspeople took special interest in the inn. Mayor Bob Istre said, "Crowley Inn is the first business you see, the only one out there that calls itself 'Crowley' anything." Inn manager Shirley Miller explained, "*C'est pour du monde de la village au Crowley.*" [It is for the people of the village of Crowley.]

The inn was completed in 1973. The owner defaulted on his $800,000 loan in 1986, resulting in seizure by the lender, a savings and loan company. The S&L was taken over by the Resolution Trust Corporation (RTC) in 1990. Then, on May 21, 1991, the RTC sold the inn to Art and Kathy Sharplin, of Lake Charles, 45 miles west of Crowley. Art taught business at McNeese State University in Lake Charles.

They formed Crowley Motel, Inc. (CMI) to hold the property and assigned Art's associate, Debbie King, to manage the investment with the help of an on-site manager. The RTC's manager, Pam Potts, soon quit without notice. Debbie promoted Shirley Miller, who was daytime front-desk clerk, to manager.

The bar, called Martin's Tavern, had been rented to Burnell Martin, a local barber, and CMI assumed that lease, which was to expire at the end of 1992. The tavern had become a popular night spot for Crowleyites, frequented by the mayor, the sheriff, and other leading citizens, as well as by rice farmers, crawfishers, and oilfield hands. A true Cajun, Martin had talked of setting up an off-track betting parlor and then arranged to get two of Louisiana's first video poker machines, which were to be legal beginning in June 1992.

In February 1992 famous Cajun chef Roy Lyons agreed to lease the restaurant for two years, naming it Chef Roy's Cafe Acadie. Debbie breathed a sigh of relief. She remarked, "The restaurant has been one big headache. It required more employees than the motel, took most of our management time, ate us alive with repairs, and lost money every month." Art had helped his brother build and

---

Arthur Sharplin, Professor of Management, McNeese State University, has donated case proceeds to the North American Case Research Association (NACRA).

operate several other motels years earlier and knew motel restaurants typically lose money.

The Sharplins had intended to sell the inn after fixing it up, and that remained a possibility. But Art had asked Debbie and Shirley to assume a 10-year holding period in management decisions. So they were looking for ways to improve motel operations and to implement a marketing plan. And the idea of getting a national franchise, such as Best Western or Red Carpet, was only temporarily on hold.

FACILITIES

The physical plant had presented quite a challenge to Debbie, who said she knew "less than nothing" about running a motel, let alone fixing one. Most rooms were distinctly substandard—sagging and stained bedding, broken furniture, 20-year-old TVs and room air conditioners, ceilings despackled and discolored by leaks, faded curtains hanging loose at one end, plumbing fixtures pitted and coated with white scum, washroom counters spotted with cigarette burns, mice holes in walls, and tacky traps behind credenzas, each holding a grizzly menagerie of dehydrated bugs and roaches. It all seemed even worse in the dim hue cast by the cheap, old incandescent lamps with their yellowed and tattered shades.

Outside, water seeped through cracked pavement from a broken underground pipe, nurturing a patch of green slime. The clack, clack, clack of the sewer plant blower gave notice of imminent failure in that vital system. From the sewer plant, it was possible to see into the small equipment room, where an aging water heater had piled clumps of damp rust on the floor. And to see past the dumpster, overflowing with customer and trespasser refuse, to where a pothole in the truck parking area had grown to become a muddy pond.

The lobby building was little better. Art discovered the air conditioning system heated and cooled the void above the hung ceilings, in addition to the usable space, and one of the two main condenser units had been inoperative for months. Someone had poured tar on leaks in the roof overhang and the black goo hung in stringy drops from the pegboard soffit and the shrubs beneath. In the restaurant kitchen, only one of the overhead exhaust systems worked; an oven door was tied shut with a stocking; cold air leaked from the walk-in freezer through a cocked door; and a long-disabled deep fryer held its last charge of grease, stale and mantled with scorched meal.

But the inn had originally been well-built, and it was still attractive. The guest room building was made of concrete blocks and steel-reinforced slabs, with front and back walls of grooved wood paneling over pine studs. Piping was copper and cast iron, not plastic. One wall in each room was latex enameled and the others had vinyl wall covering, torn and unglued in a few places, but of good quality. The lobby building, of brick veneer, was shrouded with 90-year-old live oaks and much younger pines, giving a sense of homeyness and comfort. The neat grey and blue decor, though not striking, added a subdued welcomeness.

From May 1991 to February 1992, Crowley Inn's cash flow was applied to upgrading the property. Art and Kathy bought 60 rooms of used furniture, drapes, lamps, and bedspreads from the refurbishment contractor for a Holiday Inn in Beaumont, Texas. Debbie purchased 60 each of new RCA TVs with remote controls, GE clock radios, and chrome clothes racks with hangers. She also got new shower rods and curtains, bed linens, pillows, and a full complement of new beds and foundations. Kathy modified and helped install the drapes, advised on aesthetics, and livened the lobby with greenery and art work.

Shirley arranged for several local men to help as needed, unemployed artisans she could hire for minimum wage. As each shipment would arrive, they would come in to take out the old and install the new. They did much more—sanding the cigarette burns off the washroom counters, painting, stopping mice holes, patching concrete, and so on. An air conditioning contractor replaced or repaired over 20 room air conditioners, renovated the lobby building heating, ventilating, and air conditioning system, and worked long hours on the restaurant coolers and freezers. A roofer replaced the leaky third of the motel roof and put proper patches on that of the lobby building. Total cost of the renovations: about $130,000.

Two prospective franchisors were asked to inspect the property. Best Western identified about $120,000 in needed improvements—more modern room lights and furniture, new carpeting, covering the concrete block walls with vinyl, and so on—but seemed anxious to do the deal. Red Carpet Inns was ready to franchise immediately, suggesting only minor changes. Debbie concluded the inn was then essentially up to standard for low-end franchises, such as Day's Inns, Comfort Inns, Scottish Inns, and Red Carpet, but not for lower mid-range ones, like Best Western and Quality Inns. Bubbly front-desk clerk Josie Forrestier put it differently: "Crowley Inn used to be just a dump. Now, it is *un bon place pour rester* [a good place to stay]."

PERSONNEL AND ORGANIZATION

When Pam Potts resigned, the motel employed six housekeepers plus a supervisor, a maintenance man, and five front-desk clerks, all at minimum wage. There was no written job description. The RTC had balked at paying overtime and it had become standard practice to show eight-hour shifts on time cards, although employees often worked more or less. A housekeeper explained, "Pam gives us more than we can do. So we have to punch out and then go back and finish the work."[1] In fact, most time cards for that period show handwritten checkout times, with no indication of who had made the entries. This was allegedly done because Pam could not keep the time clock working properly.

However much time the housekeepers actually spent, the rooms stayed dirty. Two large dogs, or maybe camels, had been left alone in 112. Pale spots in the soiled mauve carpet marked where they had done their "business" and the fetor gushed out to greet new guests. One such guest, a nurse from Florida, chose another room. She later wrote Mayor Istre,

I am writing to express my concern re the deplorable condition of the Crowley Inn. The mattresses and springs in our room would probably have been rejected by the worst flophouse in the country. The mattresses had a permanent swag, not to mention, sir, a urine stain about 36 inches in length. The tub has mildew all around the caulking. The drapes and spreads haven't seen a laundry in years, it appears. The carpet has stains. The pillows also are stained, not to mention lumpy. Neither mattresses nor pillows have protective covers that can be wiped down between customers. The swimming pool looked cloudy and green our entire stay, and though the desk clerk assured us it was okay, we declined.

No housekeeper, not even the head one, had worked at any other motel. Each was left to decide the best way to clean rooms. And there was no regular inspection by any manager. During that period, two or three people a night refused to stay after seeing their rooms.

Had the wounded nurse seen more rooms than two, she might have suffered even greater dissonance. In one room, toilet paper came off the bottom of the roll; in another, off the top. Here was a bed with a small, flowered pillow and a large, white one; next door, an identical set. In room 124 a double bedspread was stretched to half cover a king-sized bed, while a king-sized spread in 122 fell in clumps around a double bed. In this room, five tiny bars of soap; in that one, none at all. There were waste baskets of various sizes—one, two, or none per guest room, pint freezer boxes for ice buckets, shower curtains loose from hanger rings, a stiff bath cloth behind a commode, another hung on a shower curtain rod, and a KFC box with dehydrated chicken parts peeping from under a bed. And the furniture, old, cheap, and stained though it was, need not have been so misdistributed. Chair counts ranged from four to none. An orange sled chair was paired with a puce overstuffed one. Chairs with no tables; tables with no chairs.

Wallace Mayer, the maintenance man, was assumed responsible for cleaning the parking areas, mowing the lawn, taking waste to the dumpster, making bank deposits, moving heavy items, adding chlorine to the sewer plant, maintaining the swimming pool, and fixing anything which broke. At 67 years old, but physically strong and unfailingly good-natured, Wallace went about his tasks with consistency, if not speed. A motel begets refuse, and housekeepers often stacked bulging bags of it in the vending machine areas until Wallace could take them to the dumpster, 50 feet away. It was just as well; the bags hid the grey-matted residue next to the machines and the cans and candy wrappers cast behind them by long-forgotten guests. Wallace kept the lawn and shrubs trimmed, but dairy cups and flattened cans were often left for another day. Six-packs of defeated soldiers could sometimes be seen standing at the parking lot curb in mute, noontime tribute to Bacchus, whom Cajuns place just above Zeus.

The province of neither housekeeping nor maintenance, room windows and screens suffered from evasion. Rain splatter had formed rivulets on the dusty panes and layers of ancient cobwebs gave the half screens a fuzzy translucence.

As the renovation progressed, Debbie and Shirley began frequent, though sporadic, inspections. Art decreed, "No employee walks past a piece of trash. Nobody!" Cards saying "It was my pleasure to clean your room" were given to housekeepers to sign and leave on credenzas. Debbie obtained videos on proper bed making and room cleaning. She asked the head housekeeper to train her charges and to inspect all guest rooms daily. Of the six housekeepers, only Sandra Guillotte adapted—and survived. The head housekeeper soon decided she, too, could not meet Shirley's and Debbie's escalating demands. The new one, Carol Hoffpauir, promised she could. In February 1992 Shirley told of the improvement:

> We're getting compliments. We used to be afraid to ask if a guest enjoyed their stay. But today, at least five people commented on how nice the rooms were. Carol checks every room every day, and I do twice a week. We set a new record last week, a whole week without a complaint. The housekeepers still miss things—a bath cloth, or something left in a drawer—but they are doing so much better.

Art asked Shirley, "Why are the housekeepers doing better?" "Because we keep demanding more," she replied, "If we didn't demand it, they wouldn't do it." Carol Hoffpauir agreed, adding,

> I write them up every day, which rooms they clean and what they do wrong. We talk, and they can all read my notes on the clipboard, which I leave on the desk. If they do good, I tell them and I tell Shirley.
>
> I wish I could find five workers who take pride in cleaning the way I do. Two of the girls do, but the others seem to just tolerate it. I can hire and fire; I just have to tell Shirley my reasons. But I would rather just get them out of their old routine.

Art asked, "Doesn't the improved situation here inspire them?" "I reckon so," Carol replied, "But you have to tell them when they mess up." Debbie added, "We know that new surroundings don't motivate."

Exhibit 1 shows the organization and employees at the end of February 1992. The desk clerks and Wallace were paid $5 an hour; the housekeepers, minimum wage; Shirley, $300 a week; and Carol, $200. Art had instituted paid one-week vacations, but there was no company medical insurance and no retirement plan. Shirley talked about her job:

> I have a little problem supervising these people. You see, going from housekeeper, to the front desk, to being a manager—I was one of them; I can't come out and fuss at them. It was really hard at first. I called them together and told them it was business for eight hours. After that, we can go have a beer together. I told them, "I don't demand respect—don't call me 'Ma'am' or screen my calls. But when I say I want this done, I want it done. I don't want to stay on your butt." They are not kids. And I'm not running an old folks home, or a community center.
>
> Everybody is from Crowley or Church Point, all Cajun. They take things very lightly. They are all struggling. But they leave their problems at home, unless they get too big. Sometimes, you just need to talk. I listen. I cried when I had to fire Joanne (the former head housekeeper). She's happier though, drinking and trying to get unemployment. Marie works in the restaurant after she finishes here, because she needs the money. Her mother is sick—over 90 percent stoppage in her heart. I could go on and on. This is a second home, for all of us.

EXHIBIT 1   Crowley Inn Organization and Employees

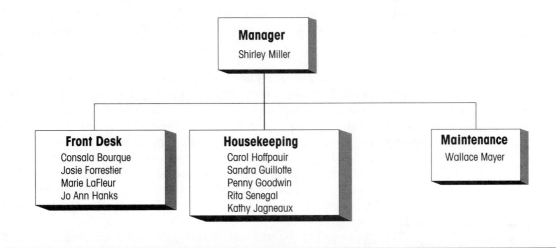

Mr. Wallace is part of the furniture. He has been here six, seven, maybe eight years. He does not want 40 hours—says it will cut his Social Security. Takes off Friday noon. He is good; you just have to point it out. He loves his job, and we all depend on him. We took a poll the other day on what Mr. Wallace enjoys most; we think he likes blowing off the parking lot best.

You get to know the customers. We talk; give them a little Cajun flavor: "Oh, you're from Texas. Well, we went to San Antonio last year . . . blah, blah, blah." It makes them come back. The truck drivers and oilfield hands holler at us when they come in the door. Whether we use the right English they don't care. It's like being a bartender. Our regular guests will just about tell you their life story. You even get to know the ones who come here for a couple of hours. They trust us; park their girlfriend right here in front. Some men leave women behind here. The other day, one stood on the interstate an hour with her thumb up, until somebody stopped.

Cajuns may seem a little stand-offish at first. Not at the front desk; this is *our* territory, and we feel secure. The girls always have a smile and gab for a guest. But at other places you're afraid to say the wrong thing. I was in Wisconsin with Byron [Shirley's son, a priest] last year and I told someone, "Catch me a Coke." They kidded me about it. Byron took me aside and said, "Mom, you don't *catch* a Coke; you just get one." He used to bring his priest friends home. I would beg him, "Byron, don't bring these educated people here." But, once I got to know them I get the biggest kick when they come. And I can't get them out of the house. We shouldn't be ashamed of our language, anyway. Listen to Governor Edwards: "Dis, dat, and dem." And he's a lawyer, definitely an educated man.

Jo Ann and Josie were at the front desk, just outside Shirley's office, and stepped to the door to listen. Jo Ann said, "All the improvements make us proud and we want to do better—makes me smile more. We bring a problem to Shirley and it gets taken care of, immediately. If it is a big one, Shirley gets on the phone with Debbie and it gets solved." Josie added, "It's exciting. Every day, I look forward to coming to work." Jo Ann's shift was over, and she excused herself. Josie continued,

> Customers like to hear us talk. They can't get over how friendly we are. Some say they expected to see a mean type of people. They think Cajuns are ignorant, uneducated, barefooted people with web toes. We are different. But we're Americans—Texas is over here and Mississippi is over there. I tell customers everybody around here is friendly. I make people feel welcome. I want them to feel they are getting their money's worth. I want them to know I am their friend and to think of this as a home away from home. I say, "It's a quiet little place," except on Saturday night, when the band gets too loud and some of the people are—what's a nice way of putting it?—highly intoxicated.
>
> The other night, a guy had invited two girls to his room and the second one showed up early. They were fighting and screaming, disturbing the other guests. So I called the sheriff. The one in the room reached right over the deputy and, "Pow!" laid the other one out. The deputy brought her up here in handcuffs and threw her in the car.
>
> The inn is like my home, too. When Kenny and the Jokers (a Lafayette, Louisiana band) play in the bar, I come about an hour early to hear them. And my kids (17, 15, 14, and 13 years old) love to come here, sometimes to go swimming. There is nowhere else to do that. We eat in the restaurant sometimes. When I worked in housekeeping, I would come by sometimes just to visit. I always try to be here 30 minutes early, and I usually hang around that long after my shift.

During the annual rodeo and the monthly horse show, the inn's regular guests merged with equestrians from sprite barrel racers to wrinkled Marlboro men. Drowsy tourists' senses were jostled by the too-metallic jangle of spurs on concrete stairs and the too-earthy aroma of a dozen horse trailers. Wide-brimmed hats were worn everywhere—at restaurant tables, on the crowded dance floor in the tavern, even in the bathroom. One inebriated October cowboy thought his bed a dance floor, until it collapsed. Another, dispirited by lost love, conjectured to aim at his head but blew just his palm away, spraying scraps of flesh and bone into a new mattress. And a famous Cajun musician, held hostage during drug withdrawal by two burly friends, broke a table and ripped a chrome fixture from the wall.

Mostly, though, Crowley Inn was, as Josie said, a quiet little place, a place where Texaco could house visiting executives and straying locals could enjoy secret liaisons. It seemed so much a part of the employees' and townspeoples' lives that Art wondered if he and Kathy had title in fee so simple as they had supposed.[2]

Ninety-two-year-old retired Catholic priest Msgr. Jules O. Daigle of nearby Welsh, Louisiana would agree with Shirley that Cajuns should not be ashamed of the way they talk. He insisted that Cajun was a true language, saying, "To call Cajun bad French is to call French and Italian bad Latin." Father Daigle fought for years to preserve the Cajun language and culture. In the preface to his Cajun language dictionary, he wrote,

> Historically, the Cajuns are the descendants of the French people who colonized the general area of ancient Acadia, now known as Nova Scotia, beginning in 1604. . . . In 1755, the British began a cruel, systematic program of deportation of our ancestors. . . . Penniless, ill-clad and, worst of all, being both French and Catholics, nothing but scorn and hatred awaited them in the colonies. . . . After serving their indenture to the British colonists, some of them made their way back to Acadia or to Canada. Others found refuge in the French islands of Martinique, Guadaloupe, St. Domingue, etc. In the meanwhile, many of the Acadians who had evaded capture by the British sought refuge in the forests among the friendly Indians of the north. Of all the Acadians deported by the British, a considerable number were brought to England as prisoners: eventually, most of these found their way into France. . . . It was from all the above groups that many of the Acadians came to Louisiana, beginning in the early 1760s. Free at last, they had to begin a totally new and different kind of life, in a strange land. . . . The Acadians had to invent a new vocabulary, find new types of foods, develop a new cuisine and a whole new way of life. Thus was born the Cajun language and Cajun culture. . . .
>
> To some, a Cajun is a crude, ignorant, backward person who speaks little or no English. . . . His principal interest in life is boozing, eating and having a good time. To be sure, there are such Cajuns, but they are an infinitesimal minority and are in no way characteristic of the Cajun people.[3]

Father Daigle went on to write that the Cajuns are our bishops, judges, lawyers, contractors, college professors, beauticians, bricklayers, farmers, teachers, and so forth. He concluded, "Yes, and sure enough some of them are lazy, ignorant bums and drunks: all in about the same proportion as the rest of the American population."

MARKETING

Art and Kathy had initially been inclined to seek a franchise—Best Western was the leading candidate, Quality Inns a close second—but the urge ebbed and flowed. Debbie and Shirley also expressed ambivalence about franchising, but were both excited about promotion and other aspects of marketing.

Crowley Best Western?

Most motels are franchised. Franchisors typically provide a reservation system, advice on pricing, national advertising, a franchisee directory showing locations and amenities, quality control standards, yearly inspections, training, informational services, design help, and an approved-supplier catalog. Best Western's 1992 charge for all this was about $350 per room initially plus a similar amount annually. Other franchisors get a certain percentage of room revenue. For example, Red Carpet quoted 4.5 percent for Crowley Inn, with no initial fee. Holiday Inns was collecting as much as seven percent then.

Art believed Crowley Inn could qualify for a Best Western franchise within six months by making the following expenditures (in additional to the annual fee):

Initial franchise fee	$ 21,000
Best Western signs	12,000
Reservation and accounting system	15,000
Required renovations	96,000
Total	$144,000

Debbie, Shirley, and Art reached consensus that this would allow hiking average daily rate (ADR) by $4 or increasing average occupancy by 15 percent, or some combination of the two. Art concluded, "Assuming 64-percent occupancy, which I think is about the industry average, the added revenue would be $56,000 a year, a good return on $144,000."

Debbie objected,

> Well, 68 percent has been about our average. Even that should jump this year with or without a franchise. We have really improved this property since last summer, when we ran 76 percent. Besides, some of the renovations Best Western requires won't improve customer service—things like covering the concrete-block wall with vinyl and replacing the two-by-four ceiling tiles in the baths and lobby with two-by-two squares. I'll bet we could do the worthwhile renovations, which would cost maybe $60,000, and raise ADR by $3, without a franchise.

"What about Red Carpet?" asked Art, "We can have their sign up in a month."

"I don't think they add a thing," replied Debbie. Shirley nodded concurrence.

Art said, "Okay, but you know there has been talk of a Day's Inn just 7 miles away, in Rayne. If we were Best Western, no one would dare do that."

After a few more minutes of discussion, they all agreed to defer the decision on franchising for at least 6 months. "We haven't taken a cent out of this thing," said Art, "And I would like for you to produce some cash before we reinvest any more big chunks."

The Marketing Plan

Art asked Debbie to help prepare a marketing plan. "What should be our main objective?" she asked. "What's wrong with 'maximize shareholder wealth'?" he replied. A few days later Debbie brought Art her rough draft. The final version is presented in Exhibit 2.

EXHIBIT 2 Marketing Plan

Mission

The mission of Crowley Inn is to maximize return on invested capital by providing quality lodging and related services delivered by competent and enthusiastic employees operating a clean, well-maintained facility—at prices fully reflecting the quality of service.

Marketing Objective

The objective of the marketing plan is to maximize motel revenue while keeping expenses low. Revenue targets for 1992 are:

Room revenue ($33 ADR; 72 percent occupancy)	$512,000
Telephone revenue (1991 rate + 10%)	24,453

Target Market

Our current guests are mostly blue-collar persons on business travel, about 20 percent from Louisiana and the rest from all regions of the country. About 45 percent pay with cash or check, 36 percent use credit cards, and 19 percent have us bill a third party. Here is data taken from 247 folios completed in February 1992:[a]

Purpose of Travel		Home Address		Payment	
Work crew	48	Louisiana	52	Employer	47
Truck driver	38	Northeast	27	Credit card	89
Local	15	Southeast	17	Cash	111
Tourist	10	Northwest	13		
Business	38	Southwest	21		
Military	2	Foreign	11		
Cannot tell	96	Cannot tell	106		

With average occupancy of 41 rooms, we serve a tiny percentage of those who pass our door. Daily traffic counts near the inn during 1990 were as follows:[b]

I-10 east of Crowley (both directions)	29,530
I-10 west of Crowley (both directions)	26,600
Hwy 13 north of I-10 (both directions)	7,570
Hwy 13 south of I-10 (both directions)	18,430

Visitors to families and businesses in Crowley (1990 population 14,038) and surrounding Acadia Parish (1990 population 55,882) may also be new customers. The Cajun tradition of fais-dodo and family togetherness in general pull many who leave the area back to it frequently.[c]

In addition to our present customer base, described above, we will seek to attract and serve more upscale guests, including (1) white-collar business travelers, (2) tourists, (3) sojourners in the local area.

Product

Our main product is a room-night, which includes the elements listed below.

1. An attractive, comfortable, secure room—well-supplied, clean, and with all amenities in good order
2. Attractive, functional vending machines

EXHIBIT 2 Cont'd. Marketing Plan

3. Attractive, clean, neat grounds and paved areas
4. Easy access to good food, drink, and entertainment
5. Daily servicing of rooms by attractive, well-dressed personnel to exceed standards set by Best Western or comparable franchisors
6. Guest services provided by enthusiastic, competent, attractive, articulate, well-dressed personnel who reflect the local culture

A room-night is more perishable than a bruised tomato. We accept delivery of 59 room-nights every day, and unsold ones spoil sometime around midnight.

Shirley and Debbie plan to enhance the value and salability of room-nights in 1992 by:

1. Aggressive training and supervision of housekeepers
2. Aggressive training of front-desk clerks, including role-playing of common types of guest contacts
3. Inspections of all rooms daily by the Head Housekeeper
4. Aggressive training and supervision of the maintenance person
5. Inspection of all rooms and facilities at least weekly by Shirley, and at least monthly by Debbie
6. Setting up control systems to assure creative compliance with vital policies
7. Upgrading of the work team through training, supervision, and/or replacement of employees

Price

Current prices at Crowley Inn are shown below. Pricing of room-nights is done by front-desk clerks, who have a list of approved commercial customers.

1.	Basic room-night	$31.00 ($29 commercial)
2.	Each guest above one/room	$4.00/night
3.	Local telephone calls	$0.50
4.	Long-distance calls	AT&T rates plus 40 percent
5.	Facsimile transmissions	$2.00/page
6.	Rollaway bed or crib	$5.00/night

Members of the American Association of Retired Persons and others over 65 are eligible for commercial rates. ADR has been about $32.50 since a $2 per room-night price increase in July 1991. Two factors tend to pull ADR down. First, few customers are charged the $4 per extra guest. In fact, only about 1 in 20 (based on a check of February 1991 folios) completes the ''No. of persons in room'' blocks on the folio. Second, front-desk clerks give commercial rates to most who ask for a discount. Shirley says pricing policies are clear, and understood by all front-desk clerks, but they do not follow policies well.

Shirley and Debbie plan to:

1. Review pricing policies and change them or enforce them
2. Set up control systems to identify and correct improper pricing practices

EXHIBIT 2 Cont'd.   Marketing Plan

3. Insure that telephone billing equipment and practices are correct
4. Price room-nights at no less than the double-occupancy rate during special events, when the inn normally fills up
5. Price room-nights at no less than the double-occupancy rate whenever as many as 40 rooms are reserved
6. Review pricing frequently and quickly implement justified changes, as when occupancy moves reliably above 75 percent

Promotion

Crowley Inn relies primarily on billboards for advertising. For eastbound traffic there are two signs, on the left 16 miles out and on the right 4 miles out. For westbound traffic, signs are on the left at 13 miles and on the right at 7. The signs carry the slogan, ''Comfort you can afford,'' and have a large inset saying, ''24 hr. Grill.'' They are yellow and white on a black background.

Debbie is developing an image involving a slogan, a logo, and sign designs. A consultant is helping. The new slogan is ''Comfortable, caring, and Cajun.'' This is intended to suggest comfortable lodging supplied by caring personnel with a Cajun flair. The logo is a large *C* containing a rice design, used alone or in spelling ''Crowley Inn.''

Debbie plans to rent two additional billboards on I-10, one each direction, and have all billboards repainted. Chef Roy agreed to pay a fifth of the cost, and a fifth of the sign space will be devoted to advertising Cafe Acadie. A ''board'' across the bottom of each sign will announce special features such as HBO-Showtime, Martin's Tavern, and live entertainment. Each billboard costs about $400 to repaint and about $400 per month.

She also plans to place two signs along Highway 13 a few miles on either side of the inn. Each of these is expected to cost about $300 to paint and $200 per month.

Debbie just purchased space on electronic bulletin boards at the Tourist Information Centers at the east and west I-10 entry points to Louisiana. Users will dial a two-digit code which will connect them to the front desk at the inn.

Crowley Inn will join the Louisiana Travel Promotion Association (LTPA). LTPA publishes the *Louisiana Tour Guide* annually and helps members with advertising, printing, and the like.

Though the inn is right beside I-10, an informal survey suggests many people pass without noticing it. So Kathy and Shirley plan to have the guest-room doors painted a noticeable color, such as burgundy, and to use bright colors elsewhere to make the inn more conspicuous.

Shirley and Debbie plan to start making sales calls on present and prospective direct-bill customers and sending them direct-mail advertisements from time to time. They also are seeking ways to entice tour groups to the inn.

Place

Crowley Inn is 16 miles east of its nearest competitor, a TraveLodge in Jennings. The Jennings Holiday Inn is 3 miles further west. East of Crowley, the larger town of Lafayette has a Holiday Inn, a La Quinta Inn, a Motel 6, and several other motels and hotels.

Crowley is home to the Louisiana Rice Festival and nearby towns sponsor festivals celebrating crawfish, frogs, ducks, and other animals and plants. During the days

EXHIBIT 2 Cont'd. Marketing Plan

surrounding each festival, the inn normally is booked solid. The inn also fills up during the monthly horse show in Crowley, and during the annual rodeo.

Crowley is the seat of Acadia Parish (county) and Art suggested that this makes it the "Capital of Acadiana." (Cajun country is often called Acadiana.) A famous Cajun restaurant, Belizaires', is half a mile south of the Crowley Inn, and its signs attract many visitors. Debbie and Shirley plan to feature the "Capital of Acadiana" theme in ads and signs and to encourage the Crowley Chamber of Commerce to do so. Mayor Istre thought this was a good idea.

---

[a]Folios are the forms guests fill out upon check-in. Marie LaFleur, who knows most regular inn guests, sorted the folios by purpose of travel. The local category, she said, mainly involved romantic liaisons.
[b]Provided by the Louisiana Department of Transportation.
[c]Fais-dodo is a country dance, usually involving staying overnight. Cajun families tend to be close-knit and children usually come along to a fais-dodo, bedding down on quilts when they get sleepy.

Debbie and Shirley were in essential agreement about each element of the marketing plan. During the last week of February 1992 they met to discuss both the process and the time frame for implementing it.

FINANCE

Art and Kathy paid $475,000 for the inn. They advanced another $21,000 then and more later for working capital. CMI gave the Sharplins demand notes earning 10 percent interest for all but $1,000 of their investment, and issued common stock for that. Exhibits 3 and 4 provide financial reports for CMI.

The Bank Loan

After buying Crowley Inn, Art and Kathy applied for a $380,000 loan from Evangeline Bank in Crowley to partly reimburse themselves and to fund improvements. The bank offered a half percent under bank prime (then 10.5 percent) for a seven-year loan with 15-year amortization. But the bank's attorney delayed approving the title, noting that the inn sign and the sewer plant encroached over the adjacent property and ten guest rooms had been built over an existing servitude. Art knew this when he bought the inn and thought it a small matter, since the problem had existed without complaint for 20 years. However, he suggested the loan amount be cut to $200,000 in view of the title problems.

The bank continued to delay closing and after a few weeks Art and Kathy resolved not to bother with the loan. Art explained,

> We might be happier taking $8,000 or $10,000 a month in interest, principal, and fees than we would getting, say $380,000 at once. I never have believed this "optimum debt ratio" stuff anyway. Of course, having the inn financed might make it easier to sell. But we will cross that bridge if we come to it.

Besides, Art acknowledged, there was no certainty they could get the loan anyway.

EXHIBIT 3   Income Statements

	May–December 1991	January 1992
Revenue		
Room revenue[a]	$272,011	$48,770
Telephone revenue	7,351	1,334
Restaurant revenue[b]	136,977	18,085
Rental income[c]	5,400	1,120
Miscellaneous revenue	9,218	637
Total revenue	$430,957	$69,946
Expenses		
Food purchases	$ 45,994	$ 5,857
Telephone	11,789	1,224
Salaries and wages	128,029	16,101
Payroll taxes	14,478	3,085
Operating supplies	11,147	2,376
Office supplies	4,209	127
Taxes, licenses, and fees	6,755	1,709
Credit card fees	1,348	715
Professional fees	14,529	1,520
Travel and entertainment	1,199	0
Advertising	12,223	4,984
Repairs and maintenance	14,707	7,447
Miscellaneous	1,358	440
Utilities	36,285	6,655
Cable television	1,307	148
Insurance	15,293	2,002
Interest	31,487	6,344
Depreciation	23,100	3,300
Total expenses	$375,237	$64,034
Income before taxes	$ 55,720	$ 5,912
Income taxes (at 22 percent)	12,258	1,301
Net income	$ 43,462	$ 4,611

[a]Monthly room revenue for May 21, 1991 through December 1991 was as follows: May, $16,648; June, $36,941; July, $46,720; August, $48,303; September, $38,240; October, $40,221; November, $38,738; and December, $23,364.

[b]The restaurant was leased beginning February 1, 1992 for $2,300 a month, including utilities (estimated at $600 a month). Up to that point, it had accounted for about 60 percent of salaries and wages, food purchases, and shares of several other expense items.

[c]This includes $900 a month for the bar. The remainder is for rental of the banquet room.

Cost Structure

The motel business typically involves high fixed costs, partly because of the capital required. For example, Holiday Inns claimed its cost for a new motel averaged $65,000 per room. Art's brother Jerry said a new 60-room Best Western would cost about $22,000 a room, including land.

EXHIBIT 4 Balance Sheets

	May 21, 1991	December 31, 1991	January 31, 1992
Assets			
Cash	$ 7,745	$ 12,007	$ 9,389
Accounts receivable		17,274	12,277
Land	40,000	40,000	40,000
Improvements	358,728	438,963	441,963
Furniture and fixtures	75,647	132,269	133,069
Accumulated depreciation		(23,100)	(26,400)
Security deposits	11,930	11,930	11,930
Total assets	$494,050	$629,344	$622,228
Liabilities			
Note payable, A and K Sharplin	$493,051	$570,969	$555,700
Accrued and withheld tax		13,913	17,455
Total liabilities	$493,051	$584,882	$573,155
Equity			
Common stock	$ 1,000	$ 1,000	$ 1,000
Retained earnings		43,462	48,073
Total equity	$ 1,000	$ 44,462	$ 49,073
Total claims	$494,051	$629,344	$622,228

The problem was not severe for CMI. Its debt was held by its owners, and interest charges had been accrued rather than paid. But Art directed Shirley to pay interest out, along with half the cash flow (which would be treated as payment of principal), beginning in April 1992.

Debbie calculated the variable cost per room-night at Crowley Inn as follows:

Housekeeping labor	$3.21
Supplies	2.61
Laundry	0.80
Avoidable utilities and telephone	1.70
Total	$8.32

Debbie had been keeping close tabs on room cleaning costs, supplies, and other variable items. After studying CMI's cost structure, she decided to concentrate more on marketing. Debbie explained,

At a $32.50 ADR, each extra room-night produces $24.18 for fixed costs and profit. That's $725 per month, about $8,700 a year, almost enough to pay for two billboards on I-10. If we raise prices rather than let occupancy rise, the result may be even better. At 72-percent occupancy, we sell about 1,275 room-nights a month. So anything that lets us raise rates by $1 produces $15,000 a year.

To Art's chagrin, Shirley also became less tight-fisted. On February 21, 1992, Debbie called from Crowley to say she was excited about all the nice improvements

Shirley was making. "The oak trees have been pruned and fertilized, she got someone to edge the lawn, and there is new paint all around," said Debbie. Later that day, Kathy told Art she had learned that Shirley wanted to paint the entire motel and lobby building.

Possible Sale of the Inn

In February 1992 Art was approached by two prospective buyers, Mahesh Patel, who owned an Econo-Lodge motel in Huntsville, Texas, and Fred Gossen, Jr., a businessman from Rayne, Louisiana, seven miles east of Crowley. The Patel name was familiar to Art. It was the surname used by thousands of emigres from western India, many of whom invested in low-end motels and convenience stores in the United States. In fact, Art believed that Patels owned half the economy motels in Louisiana and adjoining states.

Art convinced Kathy they should offer to sell the inn real estate, chattels, and leases to Gossen for $800,000, with $200,000 down and seller financing of the remainder at 12 percent for seven years, with 180-month amortization. They made a similar offer to Patel, but at $900,000 with $250,000 down and a five-year balloon.

Kathy had changed her mind by the next day. "Why don't we take out, say, $10,000 a month for a couple of years," she said, "We can probably still sell the motel for $800,000."

Art called Debbie to meet them at his campus office. "If we refuse an $800,000 offer," he began, "it is as if we just bought the inn for that amount." Debbie and Kathy agreed.

"Assuming Kathy is right," Art continued, "what discount rate should we use to settle the question?"

After a moment's thought, Debbie said, "This is effectively an equity investment in an entrepreneurial business. So I would suggest something like 40 percent."

"But can't we treat the project as a normally financed one; that is, say, $600,000 in 12-percent debt and $200,000 in equity?" Art asked, "If you stick with your 40 percent for equity, that gives a discount rate of 19 percent."

Kathy interjected, "I don't understand this discount rate stuff, Art. But if we get $200,000 in cash, we will have to put it in the Merrill Lynch account at about 5 percent. That's a far cry from 19."

"Instead of doing that, we could pay off the 11 percent debt on the Pepsi building [a building Art and Kathy owned in Pineville, Louisiana]," said Art.

After a few minutes' more discussion, Art promised to fax a note to Gossen withdrawing the offer. "What about Patel?" asked Kathy. "That offer is not in writing," replied Art, "Besides, there is zero chance a Patel is going to accept without negotiating. And when he makes the first counter, the law deems my offer withdrawn. Besides, real estate deals have to be in writing to be enforceable."

"By the way," Debbie asked, "why did you quote $100,000 higher to Patel?"

"Three reasons: I think Fred will treat our people better, I would not be as confident of getting paid, and a broker is involved on that deal," answered Art.

The next day, Art asked Shirley, "What do you think about the sale idea?"

She replied, "It's your decision, but $800,000 is a lot of money." Art knew Shirley hoped he would not sell. She had often said she loved her job; a sale would put it at risk.

He asked, "Do you know that if I put $800,000 in the bank at 6 percent it would only draw $4,000 a month?"

"Is that all?" exclaimed Shirley, "Debbie and I can get you a lot more than that without selling."

Art stopped by to see Chef Roy and get his input about a possible sale. Roy said, "I personally hope you keep the motel. But I can't advise you to turn down a profitable deal."

When Art saw Burnell Martin, Burnell volunteered, "I hear you are thinking about selling. Art, keep this place. It's a gold mine."

Endnotes

1. The industry standard for room cleaning time is about half an hour per room, including laundering. Of course, expensive hotels allow more, inexpensive ones less.

2. In legal jargon, fee simple title means absolute title.

3. Jules O. Daigle, *A Dictionary of the Cajun Language* (Ann Arbor, Mich.: Edwards Brothers, 1984), pp. viii–x.

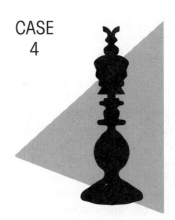

CASE
4

AKRON ZOOLOGICAL PARK, 1991

F. BRUCE SIMMONS III

As custodians of our wildlife heritage and animal preservation efforts, zoos remain an important educational and recreational resource. This case serves to illustrate the efforts made by the local zoo community in response to changes in consumer preferences, general price levels, governmental priorities, and international ownership of the rubber industry. The zoo's history, mission, relationship to its area competitors, administration, organization, and financial status are presented. The zoo has lowered its per-visitor operating costs and increased its annual attendance. It has embarked on a building program and engages in strategic planning. As a recognition of its achievements as an outstanding micro zoo, it has recently been awarded accreditation by the American Association of Zoological Parks and Aquariums.

BACKGROUND

Zoos are perceived as custodians of our cultural wildlife heritage and educators of the skills of conservation. Acting alone, zoos can collectively maintain about 1,500 species of rare and endangered birds and animals. This represents less than one-half of one percent of the species that are expected to become extinct during the next 10 years. Zoos are strategically placed to inform and to educate the public. More people annually visit zoos than enter all U.S. national parks. Collectively, more people attend North American zoological facilities and programs than the combined number of persons who attend professional football, basketball, baseball, and hockey games. Zoos have remained a strong attraction for the people of the United States.

Collectively, during 1990, member institutions of the American Association of Zoological Parks and Aquariums had 102,187,739 visitors; over $711 million in operating budgets; $408,072,905 in combined capital improvements; 3,681,570 support organization members; over 24,267 acres in parklands; and more than

This case was prepared as a basis for class discussion rather than to illustrate either effective or ineffective administrative practices. The cooperation and assistance of the Akron Zoological Park is acknowledged and appreciated. All rights are reserved to the author. © 1992.

842,000 specimens from among 36,746 species of mammals, birds, reptiles, amphibians, fish, and invertebrates.

Zoological parks, aquariums, and botanical gardens come in all sizes. For example, the largest institution had 4.3 million visitors and an annual operating budget of $50 million. The smallest institution had 3,000 visitors. Another had a $96,325 budget. Approximately 38 percent of AAZPA member institutions had annual operating budgets of less than $1 million. However, 17 percent had budgets in excess of $6 million. The association, at its annual 1989 meeting, awarded membership to the Akron Zoological Park. This recognition established that the zoo is one of the best 160 institutions in the Western Hemisphere.

During the late 1970s in Akron, changes in consumer preferences for radial automobile tires, the internationalization of the rubber industry, the economic ravages of rapidly increasing general price levels, and changes in governmental priorities almost resulted in the permanent closing of the Akron Children's Zoo. Sagging attendance and a low level of family memberships did not help matters. Faced with the uncertain prospect of continuing its zoo operations, the City of Akron sought to reduce or eliminate its financial commitment. As a response, the Akron Zoological Park was organized as an eleemosynary corporation under Section 501(c)3 of the Internal Revenue Code. The Board of Trustees contracted with the city to operate the zoo.

During the 1980s, the major employers in the Akron area were buffeted by the winds of change. For example, Firestone was purchased by Bridgestone, General Tire changed its name and sold off its broadcasting affiliates and its tire operations, Michelin acquired the combined Uniroyal-Goodrich company, and Goodyear had to sell several of its divisions to fend off an attempted takeover. In the 1980s and 1990s many area corporations are pursuing the strategies of delayering, destaffing, and operating under the just-in-time manufacturing philosophy.

Although the zoo made it through these turbulent and difficult times, its president and CEO remains mindful that yesterday's achievements do not guarantee tomorrow's survival. Under the guidance of this CEO, the zoo expanded its operations and facilities, increased its annual attendance, and received AAZPA accreditation. In order to keep the zoo open and financially solvent, the CEO believes she needs to develop more animal exhibits, restroom facilities, parking spaces, and community outreach programs. Yet, she must balance the costs of this approach with the flows of operating revenues. The zoo CEO is currently searching for a course of action to follow. What would you recommend? If you advise adding employees, exhibits, or events, how would you obtain the funds to build, operate, and employ them?

HISTORY

Residents of Akron, like people in many other cities, created their zoo by donating animals to their city. Earlier this century, two brown bears were given to the city of Akron. The city fathers constructed an appropriate facility in a neighborhood park. Subsequently, other individuals established a Museum of Natural History near the Perkins Park bears. In 1953 both facilities were combined to create the Akron

Children's Zoo. By the late 1970s the city's ability and willingness to satisfactorily husband its animals was questioned. The future of the zoo as a community resource and its continuing operation were in grave danger. In response to this turmoil, the trustees of the Akron Zoologcal Park contracted with the city to manage and operate the zoo.

While contemplating the future direction of the zoo, and mindful of severe financial constraints, the zoo's trustees decided to restrict their animal husbandry to North, South, and Central American birds, animals, and reptiles. The old Mother Goose exhibits were eliminated. They were replaced by more natural and native animal environments. These animal exhibits contain the zoo's collection of 183 specimens, which represent 66 different species of birds, reptiles, and animals.

During the past seven years, the zoo has expanded its operations. Although it continues to follow the western hemisphere exhibits policy, the zoo opened an animal clinic, renovated its "petting zoo" barnyard, and constructed a gift shop, an alpaca exhibit, a concessions area, a reptile building, and a North American River Otter exhibit. New maintenance facilities and educational display areas were built. Also, the zoo has completed phase one of its educational signs installation.

PURPOSE

The mission of the Akron Zoological Park is to manage its resources for the recreation and education of the people of Akron and surrounding communities and to promote the conservation of wildlife. To be successful, the Akron Zoological Park must maintain its image as a quality place where its visitors desire to spend their time. They seek to keep their animal exhibits clean and neat so that they are easy for all to see and enjoy. Flowers and plants abound. As resources become available for construction and continuing operations, they add new exhibits and new activities. For example, their attendance increased from 63,034 people in 1986 to its record of 133,762 people in 1988. As a unique institution, the Akron Zoological Park presents a balanced program of education, recreation, conservation, and scientific activities.

OPERATING SEASON

Due to its northern climate, the zoo conducts its open season from mid-April until mid-October. Except for Halloween and the winter holidays, the zoo is closed for the winter months. It reopens for one week during Halloween. For the month of December, it is decked out in 150,000 yuletide lights. Its operating season is shorter than many of its local competitors.

Also, it is totally dependent on the largess of nature. For the 1990 year, the Akron area experienced its wettest weather in its recorded history. More than 57 inches of rain and snow were received. New Orleans; San Juan, Puerto Rico; Miami, Florida; and Mobile, Alabama, are among the lush locales that generally have this type of wet weather. This 1990 weather far exceeded the Spring 1989 record precipitation. Additionally, in the month of December 1989 local records for the coldest temperature on this date, the lowest windchill factors, and the most snow were broken. Due to this record extreme cold and snow, several evenings of the Holiday Lights were cancelled. Attendance at this event in 1988 was over 48,000 patrons. In December 1989, the Holiday Lights attendance did not exceed 21,000 people. Weather influences zoo admissions.

The variations in weather also affect crop yields and the prices of fresh animal foods. A drought in 1988 and too much rain in 1989 and 1990 impacted the costs of feeding the animals. Weather can cause variations in the cost of animal feed.

In less extreme climatic circumstances, the zoo may be able to achieve its target attendance goal. Although its surrounding community suffered a declining population level, from 524,472 people in 1980 to 514,990 people in 1990, the zoo seeks to attract an annual attendance equal to 40 percent of its community. This goal may be too ambitious. The target audience for any zoological park tends to be young children and their parents. The Akron Zoo's community contains a high percentage (approximately two fifths) of senior citizens. As indicated in Exhibit 1, since the zoo has become better known as an innovative community resource, the annual attendance has doubled.

MEMBERSHIP

Membership in the Akron Zoological Park is available to all. Becoming a zoo member means one has unlimited, no-charge admission to the zoo grounds during the operating season plus reciprocal admission at over 130 other zoological parks, aquariums, and botanical gardens. Members receive a quarterly newsletter and invitations to members-only events. There exist differing types of memberships. They include family, grandparents, donor, patron, zookeeper, safari leader, and director's club. Each type of membership reflects different levels of financial support for zoo activities. As indicated in Exhibit 2, during the past several years the number of memberships have increased. As the variety and number of activities have increased, membership and attendance have more than doubled.

EXHIBIT 1 Annual Attendance

| Year | Total | Admission Fee | | |
		Adult	Child	Group
1991	125,363	$3.00	$2.00	$1.00
1990	126,853	3.00	2.00	1.50
1989	108,363	2.50	1.50	1.00
1988	133,762	2.50	1.50	1.00
1987	95,504	2.00	1.00	0.50
1986	63,034	1.50	0.75	0.50
1985	63,853	1.50	0.75	0.50
1984	61,417	1.50	0.75	0.50
1983	53,353	1.50	0.75	0.50

Source: Akron Zoological Park.

EXHIBIT 2 Annual Memberships

Year	Total
1991	1,825
1990	1,365
1989	1,100
1988	1,158
1987	1,200
1986	1,036
1985	1,295
1984	986
1983	492
1982	437
1981	312

Source: Akron Zoological Park.

Providing good customer service to the zoo's clientele pays dividends. Part of customer service is providing exciting events at the zoo. As indicated in Exhibit 3, during 1991 the zoo promoted several newsworthy and special events. These events serve to attract community media recognition. In return, this community attention increases annual memberships.

EDZOOCATORS

This unpaid volunteer group began in 1970s. These volunteers have no responsibility for the direct operations of the zoo. In 1983 the zoo created the position of education curator. One aspect of this position is to coordinate this group's educational activities. As volunteers, members of this group are trained to provide on-site and off-grounds educational programs using the zoo's birds, reptiles, and animals. They provide guided tours of the zoo grounds, give presentations at local schools, provide a speakers' bureau, and appear on radio and television programs. They also receive free admission to the zoo grounds.

OUTREACH PROGRAMS

In order to take the zoo's services to those who are not able to visit the zoo's location, two zoomobile programs exist. The fur, feathers, and scales and the rain forest offerings provide the opportunity for people to learn about the zoo's conservation mission and its animals in a personal way. These individuals are taught to respect the animal and to preserve its dignity. For a nominal fee, plus gas mileage if located outside the city, the zoo's educational services are available for citizens' groups, day care centers, schools, and other community organizations. If you are not able to travel to the zoo, it can come to you. If you can visit the grounds, the zoo offers a summer day zoocamp program and the opportunity for your child to celebrate a zoorific birthday party. Also, the zoo established a highly popular and well-known teen volunteer program. Young adults between the ages of 14 and 18 are trained and permitted to handle the animals while working one or two days per week at the zoo.

ADVERTISING

Akron and Summit County is situated just south of Cleveland, Ohio, a major metropolitan area. It has television stations that are affiliated with all four major networks. It has three independent and one public broadcasting station. By contrast, Akron has one affiliate, one independent, and one public broadcasting station. Since many people view Cleveland television broadcasts, the local residents are generally more conversant about Cleveland's events than they are about Akron's.

To gain media exposure in this market, the zoo must create media events. It must develop exciting activities that pass the threshold as newsworthy. Unlike the Cleveland MetroParks Zoo, the Akron Zoo does not possess access to sufficient funds so as to permit it to advertise on commercial television. Budgetary pressures just do not permit advertising expenditures. The zoo remains totally dependent on public service announcements, the zoo's public television series, and press coverage of the activities at the zoo.

PROMOTIONAL PROGRAMS

The zoo creates newsworthy activities and conducts several promotions. For example, in the spring when the animals give birth to their young, the zoo conducts a contest to name the new arrivals. In order to create the opportunity for members of the community to learn first-hand about the animals within the zoo's collection, the zoo sponsors an annual expedition. In the past, these expeditions have taken participants to the Amazon of Peru, the forests of Belize, the sea turtles and rain forests of Costa Rica, and the Galapagos Islands of Ecuador. In July 1992 the zoo offers its members the opportunity to travel to Kenya. The local press has been quite supportive in reporting these globetrotting activities. In Exhibit 3 the scheduled 1991 events are listed. These events have served to generate media attention. Many activities are but a few years old. They are a strong reason that zoo attendance increased.

SAFETY

In the event of an animal escape, zoo employees have a written procedure to follow for the recapture of the animal. As a good citizen, the zoo management, through its risk management and safety audit program, aims to ensure a safe environment for the visitor, employee, and the animals that inhabit the zoo. The zoo management

EXHIBIT 3 Special Events in 1991

Activity	Month
Snow Bowl	January
Spring Fling	April
Earth Day Observance	April
Super Saturday and Keep Akron Beautiful	April
Mother's Day	May
Little Spot Day	May
Sunday Sundae: Zoobilation	June
Reptile Day	July
Costa Rica Trip	July
Nocturnal Golf Classic	July
The Rhino Walk with Michael Werikhe	August
Recycle with Ohio Zoos	August
Members' Night	September
Boo at the Zoo	October
Annual Bird Seed Sale	October
Downtown Yule Display	November
Holiday Lights Celebration	December

Source: Akron Zoological Park.

remains committed to improving the quality of its exhibits and the habitats of their animals.

For example, in conformance with AAZPA's Code of Professional Ethics mandatory standards, exhibit animals are marked with identifying numbers. This animal marking system facilitates the proper care and security of the animal, bird, or reptile. Animal acquisition and disposal, breeding cooperation, and research for the health and preservation of endangered species is coordinated with other zoos. Cooperative research with colleges and universities is performed within written policy guidelines. As part of its strong commitment to customer service, the personnel of the zoo constantly strive to adhere to high standards of safety and professional conduct.

ADMINISTRATION

The president and CEO of the zoo is Patricia Simmons. She believes that her main function is to ensure the fiscal and conservational integrity of the zoo. She strives to maintain and improve the zoo's excellent customer service. A zoo employee for seven years, her contributions have resulted in increases in her operational authority and various promotions. She possesses a diverse background. Her training and education are in fishery administration, fund-raising, fine arts, and management. She possesses a graduate degree in arts management. A community organization, Leadership Akron, honored her contributions by enrolling her in its 1989 class. On April 17, 1989 the trustees adopted the business corporation structure of governance and elected Mrs. Simmons as the president and CEO. Mrs. Simmons holds a seat and a vote on the Board of Trustees and is a member of the Executive Committee.

The Board of Trustees oversees the policies of the zoo and sets the guidelines for memberships, and promotional activities. The board sees that all financial statements are audited by independent public accountants. Each trustee is elected to serve a three year term. There are currently 24 trustees. The executive committee consists of the president and CEO plus the five elected trustee officers and the chairs of three standing board committees. The officers, who are elected annually and have a limit on the number of years in office, are the chairman of the board, two vice chairmen, a secretary, and a treasurer. The three standing committees are planning and finance, promotion and sales, and animal care and education. The board has quarterly and annual meetings.

ORGANIZATION

The director of zoo operations, Mr. Pat Barnhardt, is provided via a grant with the city of Akron. He supervises the animal curator and keeping staff as well as the maintenance and security crews. When his father was the Akron Park's superintendent, he learned first-hand, as a volunteer, about the daily aspects of zoo operations.

The employees of the zoo are nonunion and non-civil service. As depicted in Exhibit 4, there exist 20 full time zoo employees. The education curator is responsible for the informational activities and coordinates the efforts of the volunteer groups. The public relations person seeks to obtain recognition for zoo events in the local media. The business manager supervises the accounting procedures and the daily commercial operations.

It is the zoo's policy that hiring, promotion, and employee transfer are based strictly on individual merit without favoritism or discrimination. A strong antinepotism policy is in place. For example, should an applicant for employment be under the direct supervision or within the same department as a relative, the zoo will not hire the relative of the employee.

OTHER AREA NONPROFIT INSTITUTIONS

With greater competition for private gifts and grants, the decline in the availability of donations due to changes in federal taxation law, and weather-related gate receipts from clientele patronage, the zoo must consider the actions of its competitors. The Akron Zoological Park must successfully compete for resources within its community. Four other museums currently exist. They are the Historical Society, Hale Farm and Village, the Art Museum, and Stan Hywet Hall and Gardens. A brief description of each institution is provided in Exhibit 5. The most recent addition to the local museums is the National Inventors' Hall of Fame. Its organizers have announced an intention to raise $40 million from the community

EXHIBIT 4   Administrative Structure

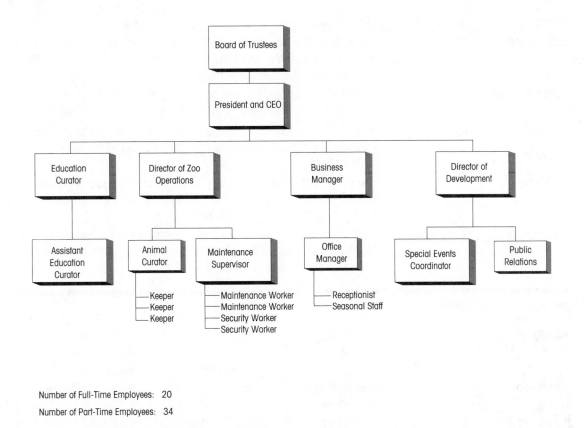

Number of Full-Time Employees: 20
Number of Part-Time Employees: 34

Source: Akron Zoological Park.

to construct a physical facility. Funds that are raised for this endeavor will necessarily not be available for other community institutions. When coupled with local universities' fund-raising activities, the competition for the community's resources and their allocation will be very intense.

A survey of current admission prices and operating statistics is given in Exhibit 6. The other institutions charge higher fees and have different sources of funding. For example, the historical society receives its funding from the county government. The zoo's admission pricing policy serves to keep it sensitive to other area attractions.

FINANCIAL STATUS

The zoo's ability to survive remains a function of its gate receipts, memberships, creative special events, donations, and its many volunteers. Nearly 75 percent of all operating funds are generated from zoo events and activities. During four of the past five years, excluding the grant contracted for with the city, the zoo received an

EXHIBIT 5 Brief Description of Competitors

Institution	Description
Historical Society	Consists of the General Simon Perkins Mansion and the abolitionist John Brown's home. Mansion, built in 1837, is 15 rooms of 19th-century items. Located near the zoo.
National Invention Center	Hall of Fame for holders of U.S. patents. Soliciting funds from community to construct a permanent site.
Hale Farm and Village	A living history museum, with authentic renovated buildings with costumed guides, that depicts rural life in mid-19th-century northeastern Ohio.
Art Museum	The major exhibition of modern art between New York state and Chicago. It houses the E. C. Shaw collection and contains the finest art from 1850 to the present.
Stan Hywet Hall and Gardens	An English country manor with 65 rooms that once was a self-sufficient estate of 3,000 acres. It is decorated with treasures collected from around the world.

Source: Akron Summit Visitors and Convention Bureau.

EXHIBIT 6 Summit County Museums' 1990 Operating Statistics

Institution	Operating Budget	Visitors 1990	Visitors 1989	Open Hours	Membership
Historical Society	$ 228,000	12,000	10,000	1,432	1,200
Zoological Park	594,759	126,853	108,363	1,467	1,365
National Invention Center	700,000	5,000	15,000	160	5,000
Hale Farm and Village	850,500	80,000	77,000	1,357	1,200
Art Museum	1,000,000	52,000	52,000	2,345	1,300
Stan Hywet Hall and Gardens	1,383,000	61,000	109,126	2,100	2,500

Survey of Competitors' Pricing and 1991 Admission Fees

Institution	Admission Fee Adult	Admission Fee Child	Group
Historical Society	$ 3.00	$ 2.00	$ 1.00
Zoological Park	3.00	2.00	1.50
National Invention Center		Not yet open	
Hale Farm and Village	6.50	4.00	None
Art Museum		No charge	
Stan Hywet Hall and Gardens	6.00	3.00	None
Cleveland Zoo	3.50	1.50	1.75
Sea World—Aurora	18.50	14.50	15.50

Source: Telephone survey.

average of $124,000 in donative grants. During the same period, membership sales increased by a net 144 percent; ticket and merchandise sales increased by more than 78 percent.

Financing its activities remains an important consideration to zoo management. The zoo has looked into alternate sources of financing. They have explored the feasibility of placing before the voters a property tax levy to sustain zoo operations. Also, they have discussed with the other area nonprofit organizations the possibility of a joint tax levy. These other institutions receive funding from other sources and believe that they must not join with the zoo in a joint effort as their access to these other funds would be placed in serious jeopardy. The zoo has been left alone in its struggle for fiscal integrity. Recently, a committee of the regional chamber of commerce (ARDB) studied the financial feasibility of merging the zoo with the county MetroPark system. Since executive management desires to reduce the uncertainty and to secure a more reliable source of operating revenues,

EXHIBIT 7 Akron Zoological Park Combined Balance Sheet as of December 31, 1990

	Unrestricted Fund	Restricted Fund	Plant Fund	Total
Assets				
Cash	$197,055	$109,363	$105,145	$ 411,563
Inventories	26,498	0	0	26,498
Accounts receivable	2,776	0	17,892	2,776
Other assets	1,000	0	0	1,000
Total current assets	$227,329	$109,363	$105,145	$ 441,837
Buildings and equipment	$ 0	$ 0	$936,251	$ 936,251
Less accumulated depreciation	0	0	308,371	308,371
Total fixed assets	$ 0	$ 0	$627,880	$ 627,880
Total assets	$227,329	$109,363	$733,025	$1,069,717
Liabilities and Equities				
Accounts payable	$ 35,674	$ 0	$ 1,695	$ 37,369
Accrued payroll	4,242	0	0	4,242
Accrued payroll taxes	7,686	0	0	7,686
Accrued bonus	20,000	0	0	20,000
Deferred membership	15,155	0	0	15,155
Deferred income	9,403	0	0	9,403
Deferred restricted contributions	0	109,363	103,450	212,813
Total liabilities	$ 92,160	$109,363	$105,145	$ 306,668
Fund Equities				
Fund balance	$ 89,875	$ 0	$627,880	$ 717,755
Board restricted	45,294	0	0	45,294
Total fund equities	$135,169	$ 0	$627,880	$ 763,049
Total liabilities and fund equities	$227,329	$109,363	$733,025	$1,069,717

Source: Akron Zoological Park.

they supplied whatever information the committee requested. At this time, the committee report has not been made public.

Audited financial statements are provided in Exhibits 7 through 12. Since nonprofit accounting is somewhat different from conventional business accounting practices, a brief description of the accounts is necessary. The unrestricted fund accounts for all revenues and expenditures which are not accounted for in other funds. The unrestricted expenditures for each calendar year are financed principally by admissions, donations, memberships, concessions, and a grant from the city of Akron. The restricted fund accounts for all grants and other revenue which are designated for specific uses by their benefactors. The plant fund accounts for all the acquisition and deletion of building and equipment plus related depreciation. Land is leased from the city of Akron for nominal consideration. Depreciation is straight line over an applicable 5- to 20-year period. Buildings typically represent approximately 80 percent of the amount. Deferred membership income is recognized at the time of receipt, but is amortized to operations over the one year

EXHIBIT 8   Akron Zoological Park Combined Balance Sheet as of December 31, 1989

	Unrestricted Fund	Restricted Fund	Plant Fund	Total
Assets				
Cash	$138,303	$1,938	$160,739	$300,980
Inventories	26,203	0	0	26,203
Accounts receivable	4,213	0	17,892	22,105
Other assets	824	0	0	824
Total current assets	$169,543	$1,938	$178,631	$350,112
Buildings and equipment	$ 0	$ 0	$843,142	$843,142
Less accumulated depreciation	0	0	250,167	250,167
Total fixed assets	$ 0	$ 0	$592,975	$592,975
Total assets	$169,543	$1,938	$771,606	$943,087
Liabilities and Equities				
Accounts payable	$ 25,828	$ 0	$ 36,745	$ 62,573
Accrued payroll	2,808	0	0	2,808
Accrued payroll taxes	6,745	0	0	6,745
Deferred membership	14,055	0	0	14,055
Deferred income	8,779	0	0	8,779
Deferred restricted contributions	0	1,938	141,886	143,824
Total liabilities	$ 58,215	$1,938	$178,631	$238,784
Fund Equities				
Fund balance	$ 54,686	$ 0	$592,975	$647,661
Board restricted	56,642	0	0	56,642
Total fund equities	$111,328	$ 0	$592,975	$704,303
Total liabilities and fund equities	$169,543	$1,938	$771,606	$943,087

EXHIBIT 9 Akron Zoological Park Combined Balance Sheet as of December 31, 1988

	Unrestricted Fund	Restricted Fund	Plant Fund	Total
Assets				
Cash	$197,519	$4,514	$113,480	$315,513
Inventories	9,088	0	0	9,088
Accounts receivable	4,166	0	12,920	17,086
Other assets	824	0	0	824
Total current assets	$211,597	$4,514	$126,400	$342,511
Buildings and equipment	$ 0	$ 0	$734,724	$734,724
Less accumulated depreciation	0	0	198,941	198,941
Total fixed assets	$ 0	$ 0	$535,783	$535,783
Total assets	$211,597	$4,514	$662,183	$878,294
Liabilities and Equities				
Accounts payable	$ 22,571	$ 0	$ 12,920	$ 35,491
Accrued payroll	2,202	0	0	2,202
Accrued payroll taxes	5,981	0	0	5,981
Deferred membership	17,082	0	0	17,082
Deferred income	10,668	0	0	10,668
Deferred restricted contributions	0	4,514	113,480	117,994
Total liabilities	$ 58,504	$4,514	$126,400	$189,418
Fund Equities				
Fund balance	$ 55,573	$ 0	$535,783	$591,356
Board restricted	97,520	0	0	97,520
Total fund equities	$153,093	$ 0	$535,783	$688,876
Total liabilities and fund equities	$211,597	$4,514	$662,183	$878,294

Source: Akron Zoological Park.

membership period. Deferred restricted contributions are recognized at the time of receipt and are recorded in operations when the expenditure for the specific purpose is made. Inventories are stated at the lower of FIFO cost or market. Contributed utilities and benefits are provided by the city of Akron. The city supplies the utilities to the zoo and provides the salary and benefits of one city worker.

Along with the skyrocketing increases in veterinary and trash disposal costs, the rapid escalation in health and liability insurance also are a major concern. The availability of health care insurance is not guaranteed. Few insurance companies are interested in writing a policy for an employer with but 20 employees. The few who are interested want to select only a few employees and leave the others without insurance. Should the zoo have one employee who is deemed to be a high risk by the issuing company, there may be no insurance available for any employee. The dilemma remains how to obtain health insurance for all employees at an affordable rate.

EXHIBIT 10 Akron Zoological Park Combined Balance Sheet as of December 31, 1987

	Unrestricted Fund	Restricted Fund	Plant Fund	Total
Assets				
Cash	$70,657	$6,021	$119,728	$196,406
Inventories	4,611	0	0	4,611
Accounts receivable	2,330	0	0	2,330
Other assets	824	0	0	824
Total current assets	$78,422	$6,021	$119,728	$204,171
Buildings and equipment	$ 0	$ 0	$661,947	$661,947
Less accumulated depreciation	0	0	154,098	154,098
Total fixed assets	$ 0	$ 0	$507,849	$507,849
Total assets	$78,422	$6,021	$627,577	$712,020
Liabilities and Equities				
Accounts payable	$19,766	$ 0	$ 3,677	$ 23,443
Accrued payroll	1,325	0	0	1,325
Accrued payroll taxes	5,286	0	0	5,286
Deferred membership	5,229	0	0	5,229
Deferred income	4,840	0	0	4,840
Deferred restricted contributions	0	6,021	116,051	122,072
Total liabilities	$36,446	$6,021	$119,728	$162,195
Fund Equities				
Fund balance	$19,455	$ 0	$507,849	$527,304
Board restricted	22,521	0	0	22,521
Total fund equities	$41,976	$ 0	$507,849	$549,825
Total liabilities and fund equities	$78,422	$6,021	$627,577	$712,020

Source: Akron Zoological Park.

As the costs of fringe benefits increase, the salary level available for employee cannot rise. This places the dedicated zoo employee at a distinct financial disadvantage relative to an employee at the city of Akron. The city of Akron wages are among the highest for municipal employees in the state of Ohio. By contrast, the basic wage rate at the zoo is the legally prescribed minimum wage. Recent increases in the federal minimum wage have significantly raised annual wage costs. One-half of the employees received a pay raise from the enactment of this recent legislation. Without corresponding increases in revenue, the zoo could become a victim of this legislation.

Although it possesses federal nonprofit status, the zoo must seek to ensure that its sources of income equal or exceed its operating and physical plant costs. Its continued existence and its promotion of wildlife conservation remain totally dependent on its ability to generate revenues and to reduce its expenses.

EXHIBIT 11 Akron Zoological Park Combined Balance Sheet as of December 31, 1986

	Unrestricted Fund	Restricted Fund	Plant Fund	Total
Assets				
Cash	$64,654	$12,171	$242,892	$319,717
Inventories	6,242	0	0	6,242
Accounts receivable	4,247	1,000	0	5,247
Due from unrestricted fund	0	7,718	0	7,718
Other assets	824	0	0	824
Total current assets	$75,967	$20,889	$242,892	$339,748
Buildings and equipment	$ 0	$ 0	$416,996	$416,996
Less accumulated depreciation	0	0	119,602	119,602
Total fixed assets	$ 0	$ 0	$297,394	$297,394
Total assets	$78,422	$20,889	$540,286	$637,142
Liabilities and Equities				
Accounts payable	$ 2,351	$11,579	$ 0	$ 13,930
Accrued payroll	1,910	0	0	1,910
Accrued payroll taxes	4,549	0	0	4,549
Deferred membership	3,915	0	0	3,915
Deferred income	0	0	0	0
Deferred restricted contributions	7,718	9,310	242,892	259,920
Total liabilities	$20,443	$20,889	$242,892	$284,224
Fund Equities				
Fund balance	$20,524	$ 0	$297,394	$317,918
Board restricted	35,000	0	0	35,000
Total fund equities	$55,524	$ 0	$297,394	$352,918
Total liabilities and fund equities	$75,967	$20,889	$540,286	$637,142

Source: Akron Zoological Park.

ADMISSIONS POLICY

The park is open to all persons who follow the general admission rules. These rules are printed on the visitor's brochure. All visitors must wear shirts and shoes. No alcoholic beverages are permitted. The zoo reserves the right to remove visitors who prove to be unruly, harass the animals, feed the animals, enter into the exhibit areas, or litter the park.

MASTER PLAN

The zoo is located in Perkins Park. The shade trees serve to keep the grounds relatively free from the harsh effects of the sun. The zoo consists of 25 acres and

EXHIBIT 12 Akron Zoological Park Statement of Support, Revenue, Expenses, and Changes in Fund Balances for the Years Ended December 31, 1990, 1989, 1988, 1987, and 1986

	Operating Funds				
Support and Revenue	**1990**	**1989**	**1988**	**1987**	**1986**
City of Akron grant	$180,000	$180,000	$175,000	$165,000	$160,000
City services in kind	58,597	55,367	51,160	49,722	50,398
Donations	152,289	155,143	227,102	311,263	201,842
Admissions	167,307	109,523	113,840	71,725	47,297
Concessions	76,788	55,177	54,419	41,054	42,297
Memberships	38,800	27,247	24,666	15,891	26,502
Interest	32,112	22,291	15,634	13,768	13,901
Total revenue	$705,893	$604,748	$661,821	$668,423	$542,857
Expenses					
Program					
Animal collections	$133,819	$127,410	$113,037	$113,897	$118,789
Buildings and grounds	233,121	189,763	169,870	161,605	141,914
Cost of concessions	13,489	14,267	14,434	13,888	26,336
Education	26,510	28,509	22,699	25,169	23,277
Strategic planning	0	3,838	0	0	0
Total expenses	$406,939	$363,787	$320,040	$314,559	$310,316
Supporting					
Administration	$228,391	$206,217	$175,426	$131,327	$ 95,629
Promotion	8,277	15,795	23,903	23,130	17,534
Legal and accounting	3,540	3,522	3,401	2,500	26,073
Total supporting	$240,208	$225,534	$202,730	$156,957	$139,236
Total expenditures	$647,147	$589,427	$522,770	$471,516	$449,552
Excess of Support and Revenue over Expenses	$ 58,746	$ 15,427	$139,051	$196,907	$ 93,305
Operating fund balance: beginning of year	$704,303	$688,876	$549,825	$352,918	$259,613
Operating fund balance: end of year	$763,049	$704,303	$688,876	$549,825	$352,918

Source: Akron Zoological Park. Auditors: Deloitte & Touche.

stretches across two plateaus. Between the upper and lower levels, there is a comparatively steep natural incline. This incline runs throughout the middle of the zoo. Nationally, zoos are responding to rapid changes in accreditation requirements. Since the Akron Zoo is now an accredited institution, it too must change. The terrain hinders the access to the grounds for the handicapped and disabled. Also, to improve zoo access, a higher quality of washroom facilities is necessary.

To continue to provide great customer service, the zoo will also need to expand its parking area. On days of special events when the crowds number 3,000 people or more, the parking space is inadequate. The zoo does have some space

EXHIBIT 13   Visitor Survey
Primary Competitors, December 1989

Other Attractions Visited in 1989	Percent
Cleveland Zoo	51.8%
Sea World	45.2
Stan Hywet Hall and Gardens	41.2
Hale Farm and Village	32.2
Geauga Lake Park Amusements	31.2

Reasons Not to Attend, December 1989

Multiple Reasons Given	Percent
Do not like zoos	16.3%
Transportation problems	6.1
Not personally able	16.7
Lack of time	27.2
No interest	13.6
Kids are grown	12.2
Unsafe urban neighborhood	2.4
New to area	1.7
Unable to supply an answer	12.0

Preferred New Projects, December 1989

New Projects	Response Ranking
Build exhibits for children	First (tie)
Bring back the bears	Second
Addition of small cats to collection	Third
More monkeys	Fourth
Addition of a railroad	First (tie)

Source: The University of Akron Survey Research Center Project Report.

within its fenced perimeter in which it can expand parking. However, the zoo is in Perkins Park. By expanding into this park, the zoo could double its size. Yet this presents a dilemma. To expand and to construct new exhibits will increase admissions, but it will require increases in both capital and operating funds. Without additional parking and concession areas, the zoo will not be able to increase its gate receipts. Further, extra exhibits can mean that customers will remain longer in the zoo and are likely to purchase more concessions and souvenirs. Continued pursuit of its educational and recreational objectives can become a financial burden. Failure to follow its expansion strategy is risking organizational decline and acceptance of the uncertainty of present financing. Zoo executive management will not accept a secondary community status.

SURVEY REPORT ON THE ZOO

The zoo contracted with the local university to conduct a study of zoo clientele. Telephone surveys were made the last week of September 1989. Interviewers received 757 usable responses. In general, those people who patronize zoos have a positive overall evaluation of the facility. They favorably rate its cleanliness, safety, convenience, and animal displays. Approximately one-half of the respondents avail themselves the opportunity to use the Akron Zoo. The zoo satisfies the current customer in terms of features and facilities.

However, nearly two-fifths of the people interviewed report never going to a zoo. The results of this survey are reviewed in Exhibit 13. The basic reasons given for not attending a zoo are a "dislike of zoos," "no time for a visit," "lacking in transportation," "the children are grown," and simply, "I do not have an answer."

When asked about the zoo, many people responded that it is too small. Seventy five percent of its patrons and two-thirds of the general public expressed concern at the relative smallness of the facility. The respondents offered suggestions for five additional facilities they would like the zoo to construct. These requests include "more exhibits for the children with visitor involvement," "a railroad," "bring back the black bears," and to "add more small cats and monkeys".

To better understand the needs of its customers, the survey asked whether the respondents visited any other attractions in the area during 1989. The responses indicated that the zoo's clientele attended five other area institutions. These were the Cleveland Zoo, Sea World, Stan Hywet Hall and Gardens, Hale Farm and Village, and Geauga Lake Park Amusements. Three-fifths who attend the Akron Zoological Park also visit these competing facilities.

Zoos, aquariums, and botanical gardens are evolving away from their origins in the museum community. They are caretakers of life in an age of extinction. They focus on life and its diversity. The employees and board members are concerned with the zoo's future viability, prosperity, and perspective. What recommendations would you make to enable the zoo to continue its operations?

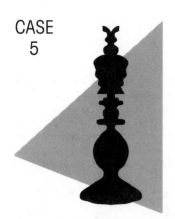

CASE
5

CSEPEL MACHINE TOOL COMPANY

JOSEPH WOLFE &
JOZSEF POOR

From many appearances, 1989 seemed to have been a good year for the Csepel Machine Tool Company. More importantly it had been part of a tumultuous, yet basically successful decade. Since 1985 sales had increased an average of 7.5 percent a year and the company had successfully weathered the financial crisis which had hindered its managerial freedom in the early 1980s. More recently management had been able to lessen the firm's dependency on domestic sales, doubly important because of Hungary's stagnant economy, and it had increased its vital hard currency sales 23 percent in just one year. Moreover, it appeared the firm's strategy of customizing its products as much as possible to suit the unique needs of various customer groups, especially those in the People's Republic of China, was a viable way to operate in an industry which had been only marginally profitable in other advanced industrial countries.

Something, however, was seriously wrong as numerous fears and misgivings were held in various quarters within Csepel. Profits were falling and the company's sales had been erratic for the past four years. Yet, after allowing for Hungary's double-digit inflation, many felt sales revenues were actually falling. Accordingly, top management was forecasting that 1990 revenues would range from 2.05 billion to 2.19 billion forints and profits would run between −55.6 million and 66.6 million forints for the three alternative pro forma income statements developed by top management in Exhibit 1. Various managers questioned whether Csepel should continue pursuing its customizing strategy, with its attendant high manufacturing costs and operations within a market easily accessed by superior Japanese machine tool technology, without instituting strict cost controls and modernizing the company's aging product line. As the decade of the 1990s began, Csepel's top management faced a number of thorny issues and problems and a clear course of action did not seem to be in existence.

This case, written by Joseph Wolfe, Professor of Management at the University of Tulsa, does not describe either correct or incorrect managerial actions or decisions but instead is intended to facilitate an understanding of the organizational and strategic management issues involved. The authors gratefully acknowledge the use of materials and consulting reports created by Maria Raboczki Bordané, Éva Tihanyi, Andras Farkas, and Anna Jakab Baané.

EXHIBIT 1 Csepel Machine Tool Company 1990 Pro Forma Income Statements under Three Scenarios (in millions of forints)

	A	B	C
Revenues			
Domestic	407.0	430.0	450.0
Exports			
CMEA ruble market	648.0	231.4	130.0
Hard currency	993.2	1,428.0	1,610.0
Total	2,048.2	2,089.4	2,190.0
Manufacturing Cost			
Direct	1,124.1	1,145.2	1,182.6
Overhead	900.0	900.0	900.0
Total	2,024.1	2,045.2	2,082.6
Other Income			
U.S.-dollar support	0.0	0.0	32.2
Ruble export	− 86.3	− 30.0	− 13.0
Profit before taxes	− 55.6	34.2	66.6
Less taxes	0.0	17.1	33.3
Profit after taxes	− 55.6	17.1	33.3

Source: Company internal forecast.

MACHINE TOOLS AND THE MACHINE TOOL INDUSTRY

The basic principle of using rotary motion to smooth, sharpen, or otherwise machine surfaces has been linked to the bow and arrow. The bow lathe and its near relative, the pole lathe, did not produce a steady, continuous motion, but the basic principle of rotary cutting to smooth, bore, or drill hard materials had been discovered. Progress in the technology's development was relatively slow as the wheel-driven lathe, which provided continuous rotation by either hand or foot, was not invented until the 14th century. Although the French were cutting screw-threads by the late 1500s, the lathe's efficiency and accuracy was not increased until Henry Maudslay invented the slide rest in 1794. Due to England's Industrial Revolution, machine tools of ever-increasing accuracy were soon required. Maudslay's screw-cutting lathe of 1800 and Eli Whitney's development of the capstan lathe did much to improve the speed and accuracy of this popular device.

While the lathe is still today's most widely used machine tool, other tools mill, drill, bore, plane, cut, and shape steel and castings into their final form. The demand for these tools is highly dependent on the amount of metal working activity conducted in both heavy and light industry. Perhaps the machine tool industry's largest customers are the automobile manufacturers and their parts and subassembly suppliers, followed by the aircraft industry and all others who finish, grind, or stamp metal. Accordingly the demand for machine tools (lagged by sometimes over a year for the manufacture of today's more-sophisticated machinery) is quite high in Western Europe and Japan and among Japanese automobile manufacturers regardless of the location of their plants. Alternatively the demand for these tools in Detroit and the Big Three's plants scattered throughout the United States, Canada, and Mexico has been relatively low during the past decade. In the near term, industry experts believe the American automobile industry will defer its purchases of the larger, more sophisticated flexible manufacturing systems due to the losses incurred by both Ford and General Motors in 1989 and the plant closings transpiring at Chrysler Motors as it tries to reverse its sagging fortunes.

Composite statistics for the American machine tool industry for the past seven years are presented in Exhibit 2. Sales growth has been less than GNP growth in the United States and net profit margins have only been 2.03 percent of sales during that period. A number of firms have restructured themselves such as Cross & Trecker, Acme-Cleveland, and Cincinnati Milacron, while others have attempted diversifications out of the industry. Certain Japanese machine tool manufacturers, such as Yamazaki Mazak Corporation, Okuma Machinery Inc., and Toyoda Machinery USA are very bullish about the industry's prospects. Yamazaki Mazak plans to enter a variety of world markets with innovative, cost-cutting machine tool stations which enhance end-user value by justifying their purchase as an investment in efficiency and higher end-product quality. Okuma, Toyoda, and other Japanese manufacturers are broadening the product lines being exported to the United States to include grinders and screw machines, which are machine tool categories not included in the industry's 1986 voluntary restraint agreements. Exhibit 3 outlines the nature of the machine tool industry's technology and the degree its technology has been diffused in most technologically advanced nations. Exhibit 4 presents data on the dollar value of worldwide production of machine tools by selected capitalist and socialist countries.

THE CSEPEL MACHINE TOOL COMPANY

Today's Csepel Machine Tool Company is an outgrowth of what was once the Manfred Weiss manufacturing complex. Although it began operations in 1882 as a can manufacturer, the firm began manufacturing military ordnance in 1889 and shortly thereafter an iron and steel plant was built. The Manfred Weiss Company

EXHIBIT 2 American Machine Tool Industry Performance

Measure	1985	1986	1987	1988	1989	1990	1993
Sales ($billions)	$ 3.2	$ 3.3	$ 3.4	$ 3.7	$ 4.0	$ 4.3	$ 5.6
Operating margin	8.5%	9.3%	9.2%	9.6%	9.5%	9.0%	12.0%
Net profits ($millions)	$28.8	$80.9	−$31.3	$76.4	$105.0	$185.0	$300.0
Net profit margin	0.9%	2.5%	− 0.9%	2.1%	2.6%	4.3%	5.4%

Notes: Results for 1989 and 1990 are estimates; performance figures for 1993 are mean estimates of the years 1992 to 1994.
Source: T. Brophy, "Machine Tool Industry," *Value Line Investment Survey*, November 17, 1989, p. 1,336.

EXHIBIT 3 Two Decades of Technological Progress in the Machine
Tool/Production Engineering Industry

By the early 1980s extensive software had been developed which fully automated and optimized all steps in the manufacture of a component. These programs select the machining sequence, selection of machine tools, clamping, selection of the operations sequence, tool selection, choose the optimum cutting conditions, and numerically control the entire machining operation. Programs and machines of this type were in wide use in many industries.

By the mid-1980s fully self-optimizing adaptive control of machine tools had been developed, and on-line process identification and on-line optimization was in general use in manufacturing plants. Work preparation in the form of machine loading and scheduling is being accomplished by computers in over 75.0 percent of all American factories.

In the 1990s standardized computer software systems will be commercially available. About 70.0 percent of industry will be using group technology in its manufacturing processes. The machine industry's traditional lathes, boring mills, and broaching machines are being rapidly replaced by plastic machinery, flexible manufacturing machinery, and advanced composite machinery to reflect the new materials which are being introduced as replacements for iron and steel.

Source: Adapted from M. E. Merchant, ``Delphi-Type Forecast of the Future of Production Engineering,'' *CIRP Annals* 20, no. 3 (1971), p. 213; and *U.S. Manufacturing Competitiveness—Profiles in Competitive Success* (Chicago: A. T. Kearney, 1989), p. 10.

began bicycle and automobile production in 1925 and airplane engine production was added to its industrial empire in 1927. Its machine tool business began in 1929 as an in-house supplier of its own needs, but one year later the firm began to sell its tools to outside firms in both Hungary and abroad. Over the years it developed a solid reputation by offering a series of innovative, high-precision products.

After supplying the Axis war effort in the 1940s, temporarily as in the guise of the Hermann Göring Werke after the forced withdrawal of the Jewish-born Weiss family, the firm was nationalized in 1946. Upon becoming state-owned the company became known as the Csepel Iron and Metalworking Trust, so named for its location on Csepel Island in the Danube River south of Budapest. Various Soviet industrial organization concepts were quickly introduced over the years. Rather than continuing the Taylorism which had been used by Manfred Weiss since its introduction in the 1930s by consultants from the German Method Time Measurement Association (RETA), a planning orientation comprised of a series of three- and five-year national plans was strictly applied. Workers were encouraged to over-fill the individual plans which were created for them, shops were given greater autonomy through the addition of staff support, and a new management level was added to monitor the company's conformity to the centralized plan.

The state government assumed control of the company's import/export effort through its Ministry of Commerce and its research and development function was removed to be housed within the Institution for Mechanical Industry Research in Budapest. From its nationalization in 1946 until 1968 the company quadrupled its number of shops while adding 112,800 square feet of factory space and a new office building to its manufacturing complex. Since that period Exhibit 5

EXHIBIT 4   World Production of Machine Tools (selected years in $millions)

Country	1975	1980	1984	1985
United States	$ 2,451.7	$ 4,812.3	$ 2,423.2	$ 2,575.0
West Germany	2,403.6	4,707.6	2,803.7	3,123.1
Japan	1,060.6	3,826.1	4,473.3	5,269.7
Italy	873.1	1,728.1	996.0	1,056.4
Great Britain	728.3	1,395.8	674.9	722.9
Switzerland	535.9	994.1	759.2	956.7
France	678.6	957.9	465.5	468.5
Total	$ 8,731.8	$18,421.9	$12,595.8	$14,172.3
Soviet Union	$ 1,984.4	$ 3,065.0	$ 2,776.4	$ 3,015.0
East Germany	585.2	891.5	789.1	789.3
Rumania	106.0	590.0	353.0	324.1
Czechoslovakia	305.4	331.5	325.2	334.4
Poland	422.8	605.0	120.7	97.3
Yugoslavia	65.0	231.8	225.9	238.6
Hungary	50.0	421.3	198.1	160.0
Bulgaria	25.5	43.0	192.5	192.5
Total	$ 3,544.3	$ 6,179.1	$ 4,980.9	$ 5,151.2
World total	$12,276.1	$24,601.0	$17,576.7	$19,323.5

Source: Cited by Istvan Nemeth, ``Machine Tools Export for the Hard Currency Market,'' unpublished dissertation, University of Economics, Budapest, 1987.

demonstrates that the company's general product mix has become more diversified after a heavy period of concentration in drilling and milling machines in the 1960s.

In late 1983 the company reorganized itself into an independent, state-owned company called the Machine Tools Factory of the Csepel Works. Its debut was inauspicious as the new entity was burdened by nearly 700 million forints worth of debt and delinquent accounts receivables of 500 million. The company's resulting low working capital forced it to abandon its ambitious modernization program and to find new sources of cash in an effort to stabilize operations. A manufacturing building was sold in 1986 and, more importantly, the company obtained equity financing by transforming itself into a publicly held shareholders' corporation. In this regard, Csepel became a pioneer within the Hungarian economy and this action became a model for others to emulate. The company split itself into two stock corporations in October 1988; the larger of the two was capitalized at 860 million forints and became known as the Csepel Machine Tool Company, while the smaller one, called the Csepel Fixture and Tool Corporation, was capitalized at 160 million forints. In making this division, the Csepel Machine Tool Company retained its original interests in manufacturing and providing parts for its lathes, machining centers, and drilling and milling machines, while the Csepel Fixture and Tool Corporation currently manufactures small fixtures, tools, and parts. Within the Hungarian economy itself, Csepel is only one of three

EXHIBIT 5   Production by General Machine Tool Groups

Product	1946	1960	1970	1980	1989
Drilling machines	110	500	700	500	172
Milling machines (including NC and CNC)	100	660	295	100	67
Lathe machines (including NC and CNC)	n.a.[a]	n.a.	40	240	93
Grinding and other high-precision machines	n.a.	1	29	160	36

[a]Product was not manufactured at this time.

Source: *90 Years of the Csepel Iron and Metal Company* (Budapest: Csepel Iron and Metal Company, 1982).

manufacturers available. As shown in Exhibit 6, the company is much smaller than the SZIM Machine Tools Company while DIGEP (Deutsche Industrieanlagen GmbH) has a minor claim to the market.

Although the Csepel Machine Tool Corporation has been able to retrench and stabilize its operations, Exhibit 7 shows the firm's profits peaked in 1987 while sales have continued their upward climb to about 2.6 billion forints in 1989. Over the next three to four years Csepel expects to boost its sales to over 3.5 billion while simultaneously changing its sales composition to that displayed in Exhibit 8. The 700 million new forint sales in parts contracts are planned as joint ventures with western companies. This has been planned as a revival of the once-flourishing business the firm had with the West in the 1970s. A large slump in demand in the early 1980s had caused this market to diminish significantly. Exhibit 9 displays the source of Csepel's sales by general market areas for 1985 through 1989.

Products and New Product Development

The Csepel Machine Tool Corporation produces the finished products listed in Exhibit 10. Its current product line consists of five basic types of equipment—radial drilling machines, computer numerically controlled (CNC) machining centers, CNC lathes, precision equipment, and special-purpose machinery. The radial drilling machines come in three different sizes with a moveable column and varying operating lever lengths. Ten years ago these units had annual sales of about 1,000 per year. Csepel's CNC machining centers consist of four different

EXHIBIT 6   Major Hungarian Machine Tool Manufacturers in 1987

Company	Employees	Revenue (million forints)	Fixed Assets (million forints)
Csepel Machine Tool Company	2,500	2,500.0	1,800.0
SZIM Machine Tool Company	15,000	10,000.0	2,590.0
DIGEP Mechanical Factory	3,000	300.0	910.0

Source: Istvan Nemeth, ''Machine Tools Export for the Hard Currency Market,'' unpublished dissertation, University of Economics, Budapest, 1987, p. 27.

models. The first is the Yasda model which comes in three different sizes whose design was purchased in 1979 from the Yasda Company. The next model, the MK-500, was created by Csepel itself and is a small machining center. The third set of models is the "M" family, consisting of the model numbers MVI-6-11 and MVI-10-11. These models come in both horizontal and vertical versions.

EXHIBIT 7 Csepel Machine Tool Company Sales and Profits, 1985–1989

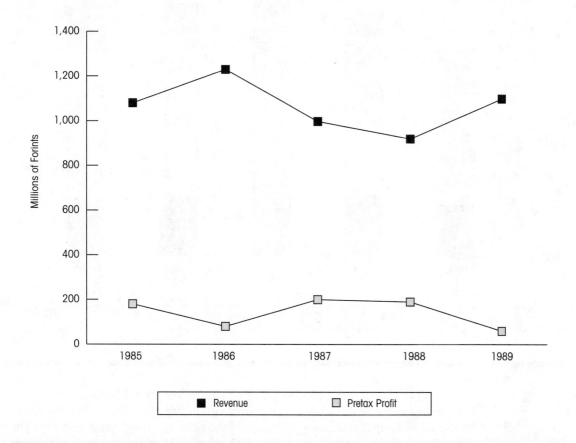

EXHIBIT 8 Planned Sales Compositions, 1988 versus 1993 (billions of forints)

Product or Service	1988	1993
Finished products	2.38	2.63
Services	0.08	0.00
Tools	0.05	0.00
Parts production	0.00	0.70
Other	0.00	0.18
Total	2.50	3.50

Source: Consultant's report and company interviews.

EXHIBIT 9 Csepel Sources of Sales, 1985–1989 (millions of forints)

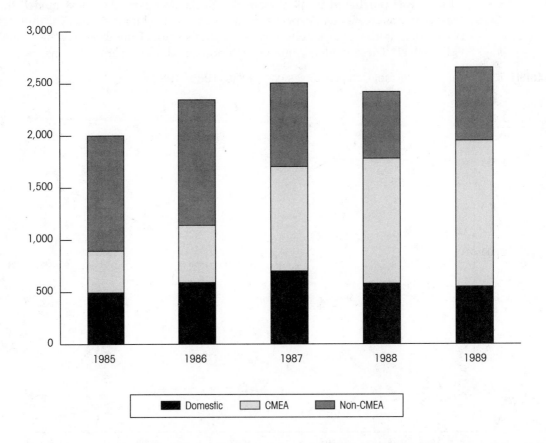

Csepel makes four different kinds of lathes. The first is a tailor-made shaft and pulley lathe made under a licensing agreement with Heid. The next was designed by Csepel and meets the needs of the precision instrument industry. The third model in this group is the TCFM-100, which is used for training purposes as well as being able to produce both revolution solids and box-shaped parts.

The company's next set of products is a high-precision gear-cutting system which comes with a twist-drill attachment and programmable logic control, and the UP-1, which is a small precision lathe. The last two products, the PTC-71-180 and SMC-71-180, are special-purpose systems currently being exported solely to the Soviet Union.

In commenting on the number of Csepel products in the late stages of their life cycles as well as the general lack of new products coming on-stream, Levente Godri, the Central Plant's Chief Designer, explained,

> We don't have enough engineers in the first place and those we do have get too involved in daily operations—so much so they don't have any time to do new product development. We could hire some good people from the

EXHIBIT 10 Csepel 1989 Product Mix and Product Prices by Geographic Market

Machine Type	Model Number	Product Price (thousands of forints)			Annual Production	Life Cycle Position	Competitive Strength
		Hungarian	U.S. Dollar	CMEA Countries			
Radial drilling machines	RF-50	747.7	577.5	577.9	200 for entire group	All very late	All are weak
	RFh-75	1,449.4	1,116.4	909.6			
	RFh-100	2,015.7	2,056.1	1,558.2			
CNC machining centers	Yasda	n.a.[a]	23,951.4	n.a.	30 to 40	Early	Average
	MK-500	11,683.4	9,460.0	12,072.9	35 to 55	Early	Average
	MVI6	10,903.6	n.a.	n.a.	10 to 15	Relatively late	Weak
	MVI10	11,989.6	13,294.9	n.a.	6 to 8	Relatively early	Average
CNC lathes	SDNC 610 1000	8,951.5	10,581.9	6,566.2	35 to 50	Relatively early	Strong
	SDNC 610 1500	n.a.	4,742.4	8,464.1	35 to 50	Relatively early	Strong
	RS-100	5,516.3	9,258.8	n.a.	15 to 25	Very early	Average
	TCFM-100	1,616.2	n.a.	2,047.2	25 to 30	Very early	Strong
High-precision systems	FKP-326-10	7,315.5	10,851.5	7,259.4	35 to 40	Mature	Weak
	UP-1	15,726.0	n.a.	n.a.	5 to 10	Very early	Strong
Special-purpose systems	PTC-71-180	n.a.	n.a.	4,431.7	10 to 15	Mature	Weak
	SMC-71-180	n.a.	n.a.	5,539.8	10 to 15	Mature	Weak

[a]Product not available in this market.

Source: Company internal records and consultant's estimates.

Technical University in Budapest and they could staff a new R&D department but I don't know if that would really solve our problem.

I see two ways to get more new products for us. We could use a project manager approach. We could pick out two to three projects to be pursued for the next year and we'd select project leaders who could hire personnel from those that are available within the company. These leaders would stay in charge of the project as long as they stayed within the budget. Another way would be to set up an independent engineering bureau to operate on its own or jointly with another firm.

Whatever we're doing we have to do a better job than we're doing now. Unfortunately our bonus system is based on the on-time delivery of machines so our R&D people spend time in the shop helping to get orders delivered instead of spending time developing new products.

The company's Research and Development expenditures for the past five years in addition to its planned budget for 1990, are presented in Exhibit 11.

As if to underscore Godri's observations about being saddled with plant production problems, the leader of the NC Assembly and Machining Shop interrupted the conversation by telephone demanding that an engineer be sent immediately to the production unit to make a substitute part in the Maintenance Department to replace a part which had not been delivered by a supplier. This call was made even though each shop has an on-duty technical assistant to handle these minor crises. Levente later explained these problems could be completely avoided if substitute parts could be identified and used, but Csepel's part numbering system does not disclose or cross-reference part substitutions.

In addition to producing machines for its finished goods inventory, Csepel willingly works to special customer specifications. As shown in Exhibit 12, the proportion of these special orders varies by product type. Overall, the firm has little trouble obtaining equipment orders as it attempts to satisfy each customer's unique requirements. It has also obtained a reputation for quality products and low prices.

Factories and Manufacturing Operations

The company manufactures its machine tools and parts in two factories. The Central Plant, which also houses its executive offices, is in Budapest, while its second plant is in Nyirbator, a countryside city of about 30,000 inhabitants in the

EXHIBIT 11   Csepel R&D Expenditures (millions of forints)

1985	1986	1987	1988	1989	1990[a]
37.4	27.1	81.2	55.7	18.7	15.0

[a]Planned.
Source: Company records.

EXHIBIT 12 Proportions of Special Order Work by Product Line

Product Line	Proportion
Radial drilling machines	2 to 3%
CNC machining centers	30 to 50
CNC lathes	20 to 40
High-precision systems	
FKP-326-10	5 to 10
UP-1	100
Special-purpose systems	100

Source: Consultant's report.

northeastern section of Hungary's Great Plain. Because of the high degree of specialization existing within the company, neither plant can make an entire machine tool. While the Nyirbator facility features a better plant layout because it is relatively new, outside experts generally agree Csepel's factories leave much to be desired. About 15 percent of its production equipment is zero to 10 years old, another 37 percent is 11 to 20 years old, and almost half is over 20 years of age. Overall the firm has only 24 numerically controlled machines of its own and about 59 percent of its equipment has been depreciated to scrap value. It is believed that an investment of $4.7 to $6.0 million would be needed to modernize Csepel's production equipment while an additional $12.0 million would be needed to introduce extensions to its current product lines and to acquire and introduce advanced production control and information systems. Exhibit 13 displays a repair status summary of the company's equipment.

Despite using technology which is frequently 20 to 25 years old, the technological gap has often been bridged by engineering know-how and exceptionally skilled and dedicated workers. In recent years, however, the Central Plant has begun to lose both its highly qualified and cross-trained senior factory technicians, as well as its younger trainees to local private-sector machine shops and small factories. This is due to their superior working conditions and freedom from forced overtime work near the end of the business year. Ironically they often work with old equipment sold to the private-sector machine shop by Csepel itself. Because of the lack of alternative employment opportunities in the Nyirbator area, a similar loss of blue-collar workers has not occurred at that facility.

EXHIBIT 13 Production Equipment State of Repair

Repair State	Proportion of Equipment
Good	46.3%
Average	48.0
Poor	5.7

Source: Consulting report.

Central Plant Operations

Due to the nature of the products being manufactured and the availability of various types of equipment, the manufacturing process in the Central Plant, as shown in Exhibit 14, is more complex than that found at Nyirbator. The Central Plant's formal organization, which also includes the firm's headquarters personnel, is also more elaborate. See Exhibit 15 for Csepel's Budapest Central Plant organization chart.

EXHIBIT 14 Central Plant Manufacturing Sequence

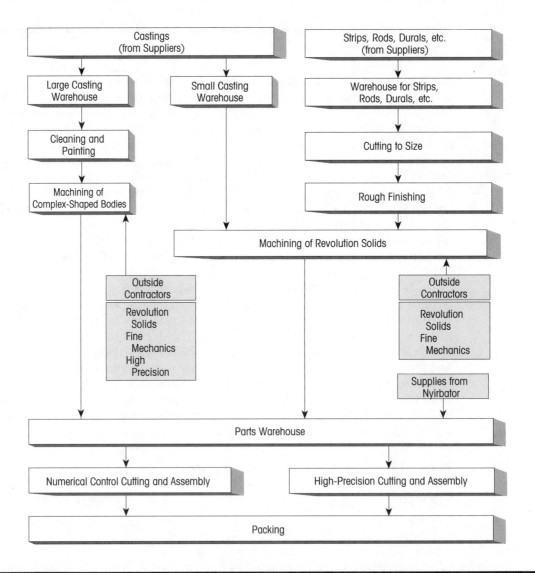

Note: About 5 percent of the company's 24,000 parts and subassemblies are manufactured in the Central Plant. The plant handles parts requiring extreme accuracy and/or state-of-the-art technology. Its layout is not very rational, although efforts are being made to create a more orderly plant configuration.

EXHIBIT 15 Organization Chart for Csepel Machine Tool Company

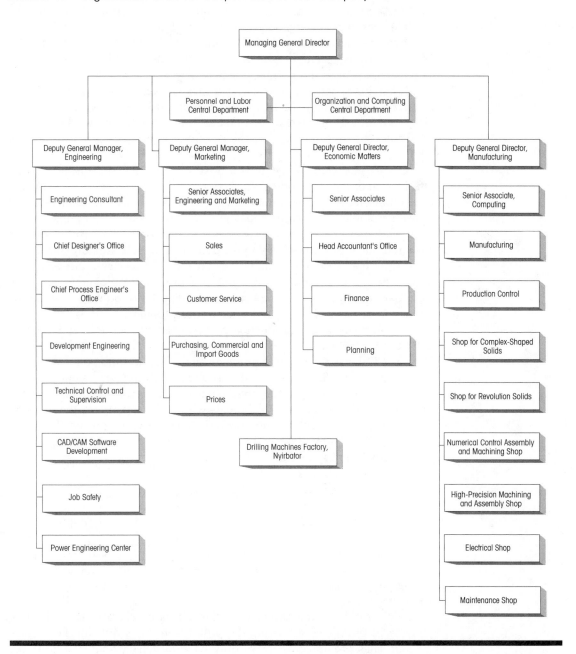

A conversation with Arpad Koknya, Deputy General Director in charge of the Central Plant's manufacturing operations, revealed both the complexity of the production control process and certain problems that have not been resolved.

Every quarter for each month and each shop my department produces a production plan. We also do this for Nyirbator. On the basis of this plan our department assembles a portfolio of shop cards, raw materials requisitions, and time and labor charges by order number. If everything is allright the portfolio goes to the Production Department. That department then launches a new shop order. When the shop manager gets the portfolios he assigns them to various foremen who have the workers get the tools and raw materials bill. That's the normal process.

When his assignment is completed each worker signs off on the bill. But we have a stupid quality control system that works well for simple, small things, but for complicated subassemblies like ours it doesn't work so well. It can really cause big problems if the assembly is produced in a number of steps.

Our quality control system is a mixture of worker self-inspection and staff department quality control inspection. Under worker self-inspection the worker himself says whether the work is good or not while the quality control department looks at the entire subassembly when it's been completed. Many of our workers sign off that their work is up to standard, but it isn't—and we don't find out about it until it shows up in the final subassembly. Or what's worse, after it's been delivered and we have to field service it ourselves. We should really punish these guys, but the present employment situation doesn't allow us to do this. We also have a quantitative bonus system in the production of parts and this also adds to our problems.

Another part of our production problem also has something to do with parts. Each month our department sets up a so-called parts shortage list (PSL). The PSL has a list of final products on the left side and on the right side the number of missing parts for that product with the part's identification number. This list is a key input into the parts manufacturing operation. They have a production schedule which deals with making parts for the PSL and parts for things currently being assembled. Those items on the PSL get a higher priority. Unfortunately because of a bad, six-plus one-digit code system, which looks like this,

our computer system can't handle it so a lot of parts searches kick out out-of-stock messages even though they're really in stock. Too often we're making parts we don't need and their higher priority slows up our regular production runs.

The creation of our production plan for assembly operations isn't so complicated but it's coordinating the production that's difficult. Because of how our sales orders come in we only have to deliver about 20 units per month in the first part of the year but about 60 to 100 units a month in the last part. Because we have a limited number of assembly workers they get very overworked by the end of the year—sometimes our best workers get sick from stress. But life isn't so easy for management either. These swings in production cause headaches for everybody. If the sales department could just forecast sales better we'd have fewer problems down the line.

EXHIBIT 16   Csepel Machine Tool Company Inventory Levels (thousands of forints)

Inventory Type	1985	1986	1987	1988	1989
Purchased stocks and raw materials	450.6	678.6	610.9	551.8	777.5
Goods in process	185.5	139.8	171.6	192.3	216.5
Finished goods	15.5	17.4	31.8	36.3	10.0
Total	651.7	635.2	814.3	780.4	1,017.4

Source: Internal company records.

Exhibit 16 presents data on the various inventory levels carried by Csepel within various stages of production.

Nyirbator Plant Operations

The Nyirbator plant was originally created to manufacture parts for all Csepel products, as well as serving as part of the Hungarian government's plan to bring industrial economic development to the country's rural areas. Accordingly the original labor supply was drawn from unskilled agricultural workers who had to be intensively trained in company-run technical training programs. Over the years Csepel has been a strong supporter of the city's technical school, which has now become the firm's major source of skilled labor. In 1989 the plant employed about 740 people and it generated sales of 649.1 million forints.

Currently the plant has moved from producing only parts to that of a manufacturer of both parts and the company's basic drilling machines. See Exhibits 17 and 18 for presentations of Nyirbator's production system and organization chart. Although the plant is more modern in its layout, various Nyirbator managers feel that constraints placed on them by headquarters rob them of their chances to be more profitable. The drilling machine plant's director of economic matters, Janos Fazekas, expressed it in the following manner.

> First of all our plant has to manufacture Csepel's low-profit items. As bad as that is many times we get urgent orders by fax from the Central Plant which forces us to shut down our machines to supply them. We argue about these things all the time.
>
> We want to be more independent and to have more power in these discussions with Production Control and Planning. These departments consider us to be their slaves and don't consider our specific bottleneck problems and they continue to bother us with their special orders which overuse our special machines.
>
> Also headquarters' sales operations are very slow in processing domestic orders. We could do a faster job on these sales if we could set up our own sales department.

Nyirbator's engineering director, Istvan Szatmari, also thinks the plant should have more freedom, if only to develop a line of more profitable products for the facility.

EXHIBIT 17   Nyirbator Manufacturing Sequence

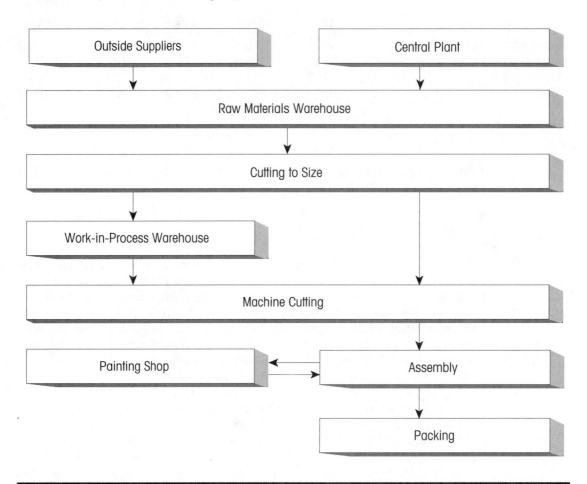

Notes: Almost 90 percent of Csepel's parts and subassemblies are manufactured in this factory. The process technology is simpler compared to that used in the Central Plant. Nyirbator's products are easier to assemble than those produced in the Central Plant, but their unit value is significantly lower. Except for high-precision parts, the plant is self-sufficient.

In recent years we've brought in new engineers for new product development, but all their time is spent in operations. They want to design new tools but can't. We're also in conflict with the Central Plant's R&D operations because they won't give us the freedom to operate on our own.

As much as Nyirbator's management feels shackled, they have occasionally taken advantage of the poor telephone communications between their two cities and the lack of tight internal auditing controls existing at headquarters. By falsely listing desired equipment as production parts, they have been able to purchase non-authorized office equipment at times. In one instance it was a prized Xerox machine.

EXHIBIT 18   Organization Chart for Nyirbator Factory

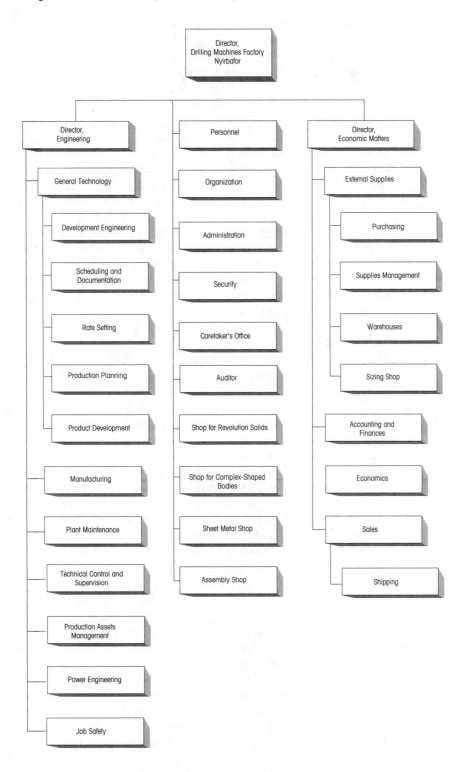

Headquarters Operations

Csepel's headquarters is staffed predominantly by people who have been promoted from within and they all have graduated from production operations after many years of service. The one exception is Istvan Rakoczy, the head of the company's computer services. Top management's pace and style appear to be dictated by that practiced by Gabor Hajnoczy, Csepel's managing general director. Two or three mornings a week beginning just after the shift opens, he tours the Central Plant's shops with Arpad Koknya. These rounds, which are conducted both here and occasionally at Nyirbator, can last up to three hours and can occur more often, should problems be plaguing a particular production run. Hajnoczy is very familiar with plant operations and its workers, and he knows many employees on a personal and first-name basis. Should he see something that appears to be wrong he will immediately order a change in either the production method or the order's schedule.

Later in the day, while holding a two-hour discussion in Gabor Hajnoczy's office, he was interrupted many times by short telephone calls from plant personnel and brief conferences with his secretary. He also had to sign a number of technical orders as well as a request for computer supplies. Several very lengthy telephone calls dealt with decisions about where pieces of shop equipment should be placed for a shop-floor layout change that was underway.

Although some appreciate top management's intimate working knowledge of plant operations and its accessibility, others see it as "always having someone breathing down our necks" or showing too much concern for production and the bonuses attached to on-time production deliveries. The head of the Central Plant's sales department, Gabor Nagy, commented that

> Top management's manufacturing bias is the company's major problem —it keeps us from being flexible. This company doesn't have its own selling rights because it must trade through Technoimpex. This was allright at one time because Technoimpex had traditionally been machine-tools oriented. Now Technoimpex wants to buy and sell a whole range of products so it doesn't represent us as well as it once did—their representatives can't emphasize us like they did before because they have so many other companies to represent and they really don't want to emphasize our machine tools any longer. To cover ourselves on this we now have service representatives, who can also help us with our sales, in such places as Rumania, West Germany, and the United States. Where we don't have our own people we use Austria's Intertrade which specializes in steel and machine tools.

The general manager's plant tours not only disturb many production workers, they also appear to interfere with the operations of other company functions. As an example, Nagy observed that,

> Sometimes our General Manager gets orders on his own when he's out in the field . . . and when he comes back he simply gives these orders directly to the production department. This is bad for us in Sales because we can't tell how effective we've been. We don't know if we got the order because of him

or because we had been developing the same customer over the past few months. By doing things this way we can't tell why the sale was ever made.

LOOKING TO THE FUTURE

For the head of the organization and computing department, 1990 and beyond were going to be exciting years. Istvan was proud to say,

> I've recently convinced top management they should buy the MAS-MCS (**M**anagement **A**ccounting **S**ystem-**M**anagement **C**ontrol **S**ystem) integrated software package from the British software firm Hoykens. It's being introduced at the Hungarian firms VIDETON, BHG, and SZIM and it's a system that can manage the MIS problems for a company our size—production planning, all the paperwork controls, operations scheduling, and operations finance.
>
> We bought a used IBM 4361 from a German firm late last year and 70 workstations, as well as some in Nyirbator, are being installed right now. It's the first time we've tried to implement a real integrated management system. It'll cost the company nearly 100 million forints but it should be completed in 1991. If this implementation is successful I'd like to make the department into a separate money-making operation. This would allow us to serve Csepel, keep our own people busy, and help them earn more money.

For Peter Toth, general manager of economic matters, the future was a bit more cloudy. As for Csepel's current situation, he noted the order book was very low in general and even more so for domestic clients. Overall prices were rising, the government was cutting its support for CMEA exports, and optimal production lot sizes have not been established. His suggestions for improving 1990 company performance entailed the following:

> Dismiss 15 percent of all personnel or about 200 employees
> Raise the salaries of all remaining personnel by 20 percent
> Reduce costs in general, including the stock level of various finished goods
> Investigate opportunities for new ruble exports
> Maintain the company's traditionally good relations with its creditors
> Accelerate the rate at which products are delivered to customers
> Find a joint venture partner

APPENDIX A   Csepel Machine Tool Company Balance Sheets (unaudited; millions of forints)

	1988	1989
Assets		
Current assets		
Cash	1,139	3,230
Bank account	32,646	16,276
Additional accounts	13,896	−32,949
Bonds	0	0
Domestic buyer	203,731	192,807
Foreign buyer	666,332	978,162
Total current assets	917,744	1,157,526
Employee fund	657	0
State budget fund	0	2,882
Total	870,720	1,173,851
Inventories		
Goods in process	192,216	216,533
Finished goods	36,315	23,362
Total	229,687	239,895
Raw material	428,644	678,293
Purchased stocks	123,201	99,229
Total inventories	551,845	777,522
Total	781,532	1,017,417
Contingency fund	0	0
Other active accounts	257,231	45,158
Temporary account	0	0
Total	257,231	45,158
Shares held	6,000	228,000
Assets held	0	0
Foreign investments	6,000	228,000
Fixed plant and equipment	928,097	1,091,681
Less depreciation	735,634	786,716
Plant additions	22,559	82,249
Net book value	215,022	387,214
Total assets	2,177,030	2,838,030

APPENDIX A Cont'd.   Csepel Machine Tool Company Balance Sheets (unaudited; millions of forints)

	1988	**1989**
Liabilities		
Accounts payable	0	840,399
Domestic deliverer	812,413	188,014
Foreign deliverer	89,070	221,510
Investment deliverer	24,962	12,935
Factoring	30,000	113,810
Creditors	308	36,144
Salaries payable	10,511	17,933
Social security payable	21,747	34,077
Prepaid taxes	−125,762	−33,389
Other accounts	200,270	262,972
Total	1,063,519	1,694,405
Paid-in capital	835,000	835,000
Retained earnings	−99	323,344
Total	834,901	1,158,344
Income tax liability	−35,910	−53,613
Profit account	−3,716	−22,428
Profit	318,236	61,489
Total liabilities	2,177,030	2,838,197

APPENDIX B   Hungarian Economic Deflators by Activity Segment

Market	1985	1986	1987	1988	1989[a]
Domestic[b]	100.0	104.4	112.1	111.2	117.4
CMEA[c]	100.0	107.2	110.1	110.1	110.0
Non-CMEA[d]	100.0	116.5	137.3	157.5	177.0

[a]Preliminary estimate by the Central Statistical Office.
[b]Domestic Sales Price Indices—Machine Tool and Machine Equipment Industry, *1988 Statistical Yearbook for Industry* (Budapest: Central Statistical Office, 1988), p. 134.
[c]Sales in CMEA Relations—Machine Tool and Machine Equipment Industry, *1988 Statistical Yearbook for Industry* (Budapest: Central Statistical Office, 1988), p. 130.
[d]Non-CMEA Foreign Trade Sales Price Indices—Machine Tool and Machine Equipment Industry, *1988 Statistical Yearbook for Industry* (Budapest: Central Statistical Office, 1988), p. 132.

APPENDIX C Csepel Machine Tool Company Income Statements (unaudited; thousands of forints)

	1985	1986	1987	1988	1989
Revenues					
Domestic	484.7	605.8	814.2	567.0	542.5
Exports					
CMEA ruble market	352.8	466.4	694.7	981.4	1,058.9
Hard currency	1,151.0	1,263.6	982.2	898.1	1,016.9
Total	1,988.6	2,335.8	2,491.1	2,446.5	2,618.3
Direct manufacturing cost	1,044.4	1,173.7	1,277.8	1,294.7	1,385.8
Operating profit	944.2	1,162.2	1,213.3	1,151.8	1,232.5
Overhead cost					
Factory overhead	351.2	478.0	478.4	282.0	352.6
Administrative overhead	325.5	293.8	299.2	505.8	689.8
R&D expense	37.3	27.1	81.2	55.7	18.7
Customer service	11.3	16.2	12.5	22.1	17.0
Land rent	4.0	3.7	0.0	0.0	0.0
Miscellaneous	53.4	64.9	70.4	97.1	8.1
Total	782.7	883.7	941.7	962.7	1,086.2
Additional expenses	156.3	129.8	107.4	62.9	137.2
Other income					
Export support	123.0	16.0	60.7	0.0	0.0
Ministry support	2.1	35.7	79.1	129.2	35.1
R&D subsidy	5.0	0.0	51.2	35.7	5.9
Vendor penalties	6.1	2.4	2.4	0.0	3.4
Other	2.5	5.7	3.0	0.0	8.3
Total	138.7	59.8	196.4	164.9	52.7
Profit before taxes	143.9	208.4	360.6	291.1	61.8
Taxes	109.6	133.1	151.4	49.3	.3
Profit after taxes	34.1	75.3	209.2	241.8	61.5

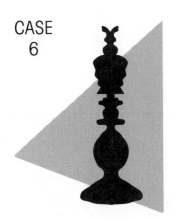

CASE
6

A Socioeconomic Note on Hungary in 1990

JOSEPH WOLFE &
JOZSEF POOR

Although a Soviet satellite for over 40 years, Hungary has always strongly identified with the West. Either through two disastrous world war alliances with Germany; the exportation of its filmmakers, musicians, mathematicians, and scientists to the United States; or the stocking of the Budapest Museum of Fine Arts with a rich collection of imported masterworks from the Flemish, Dutch, Spanish, Italian, and German schools, Hungary has always stood at the crossroads between the East and the West. Although economic progress had been made in the 1970s, declining real wages and rapid inflation in the 1980s caused some Hungarians to possess a deep and resentful understanding that their small, yet pivotal country was falling behind both economically and socially. To those living in the Great Plain, or in such provincial towns as Békés, Szigetvàr, or Pàpa, or to Budapesters walking the fashionable Vàci utca with its shops displaying increasingly inaccessible merchandise, it was painfully obvious that more aggressive economic reforms would have to be implemented. The current economic structure did not put as much food on the table, produce an adequate supply of living quarters, or deliver modern health care to all.

As shown in Exhibits 1 and 2, Hungary's economy in the 1980s demonstrated little real growth while experiencing rapid inflation in 1983 to 1984 and 1986 to 1989. Worker and employee real wages, after showing a modest improvement in 1986, continued their downward spiral and fell 8.3 percent from 1981, while those working in the agricultural cooperatives saw their real wages fall by 10.5 percent. On television programs beamed from Austria or West Germany, or from England via satellite, Hungarians saw a lifestyle that was increasingly not their own. They saw the common man driving better cars than their 20-year old Fiats/Ladas, while living their lives with much greater exuberance. In their desire to possess at least a semblance of the West's abundance, they worked more hours and took on extra jobs. Unfortunately the array and quality of the products available to them was inferior to those available to Westerners. Hungarians eagerly discounted their forints for black-market American dollars, West German marks, or Austrian schillings for shopping trips to Vienna or small Austrian villages near their border. The budget-minded Hungarian shopped at Vienna's Mariahilfer Strasse while comparatively affluent Hungarians forsook their own upscale stores for the Kärntner

The authors express their appreciation to Janos Vecsenyi for commentary provided on earlier drafts of this Socioeconomic Note and to Adrienne Simon for basic research support.

571

EXHIBIT 1 Gross Domestic Product

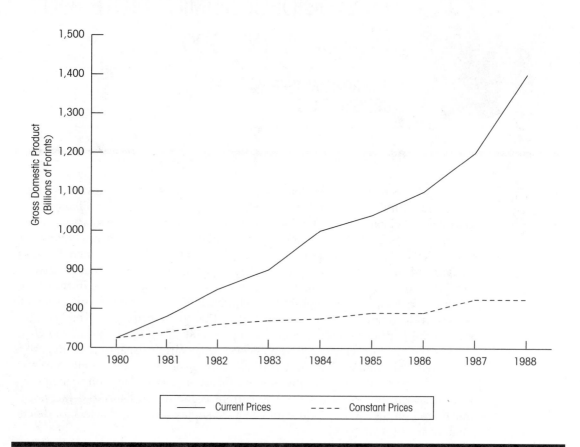

With those words the prime minister expressed both the hopes for and the barriers
to what has been Hungary's continuing and accelerating use of market-based
economic pressures and private enterprise incentives to revive its flagging
economy.

Strasse. By the end of the 1980s, government spending had caused its foreign debt
to total more than $19 billion and the service on that debt was becoming
oppressive.

Recognizing the grave economic problems facing his nation, Prime Minister
Miklos Nemeth stated, upon submitting his newest economic package to the
Hungarian Parliament's May 1989 session,

> we must place the enlivening of enterprise in the center of our economic
> strategy. Let us become the country of hundreds of thousands of small and
> medium enterprises. However, this necessitates the final elimination of
> several ideological taboos which came into being in the 1950s and have
> petrified since then into cliches.

With those words the prime minister expressed both the hopes for and the barriers
to what has been Hungary's continuing and accelerating use of market-based
economic pressures and private enterprise incentives to revive its flagging
economy.

EXHIBIT 2   Real Wages of Workers and Employees

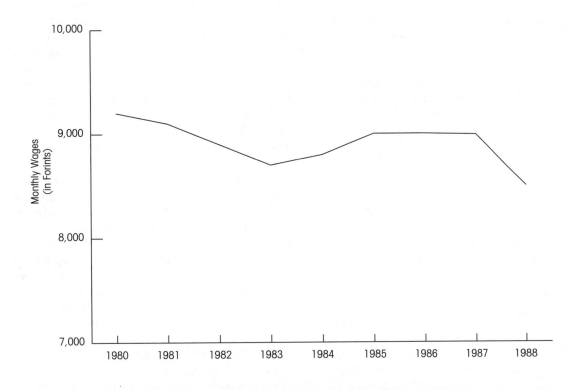

This note has been prepared to familiarize the reader with the unique and turbulent economic and social setting confronting the Hungarian manager of the early 1990s. The note will first briefly review the role of a society's economic system with elaboration of the varieties of economic systems employed by Soviet-bloc nations. The note then reviews legislation and rulings that have been created by Hungary's parliament as it attempts to make the nation more accessible to various Western capitalist interests and to obtain a greater degree of vigor and creativity from its managers and workers. The note then concludes with a review of the capital stock and human resources available to Hungary's enterprises as they attempt to compete with well-entrenched Western and Pacific Basin firms in sophisticated and highly developed markets.

PURE ECONOMIC SYSTEMS AND PRAGMATIC SOCIALISM

If the role of an economic system is to coordinate the interchange between those who have something to offer in return for something individuals or entities want, two pure or ideal economic types exist as the means for accomplishing this coordination—bureaucratic coordination, which is a vertical, hierarchically empowered relationship, and market coordination, which is a horizontal, economically equal relationship. While these are pure types, neither socialism, which is the closest embodiment of bureaucratic coordination, or American-style capitalism, which is the closest personification of market coordination as an economic system, are perfectly applied in the real world. American capitalism and its free enterprise system operate with numerous public and private controls over the behavior of its industries and economic entities. Trade unions, professional associations, lobbying groups, and trade associations operate in the private sector to alter the supply and demand structures with those they serve. Both federal, state, and local governments often act to either protect numerous companies or groups from the cruel vicissitudes of the marketplace, or to coerce them into actions which hurt at least their short-term economic interests.

Socialism also does not exist in a pure form, but instead exists in at least three variants.

The traditional Soviet-style brand of socialism was designed to be a pure command, bureaucratically controlled system. Attempts to practice this variation were made in the pre-World War II Soviet Union and this variant was initially cast on all nations coming within the Soviet sphere during the Cold War. In today's world it is being employed in Vietnam, North Korea, and Cuba. Socialism's second variety is a self-determined, or worker self-management, system. As introduced in Yugoslavia in the mid-1950s, it entailed giving workers distributive control over the profits of their enterprises. In that instance, however, the workers used this freedom to raise their wages, thus forcing the nation into rapid inflation while simultaneously lowering Yugoslavia's capital stock through the depletion of its physical plant. Socialism's third variant, such as that which was introduced in Hungary in 1968 and is currently practiced in Poland and Czechoslovakia, is a market-driven planning system. This hybrid system entails the indirect control of the economy's general direction through bureaucratic control of the investment priorities assigned its various sectors while simultaneously using internal and external market pressures to both force greater efficiency from its institutions and to benefit from the rationing aspects of freely floating prices.

THE WAVERING PATH TO HUNGARY'S MARKET-DRIVEN PLANNING SYSTEM

Although the Soviet Union felt Hungary was strongly within its grasp in the 1950s, Hungary's October 1956 revolution highlighted the low degree of popular support existing for the Communist Party. After quelling the revolution with troops, Russia subsequently took the tack of minimizing some of the Stalinist system's austere economics while demanding strict political obedience from the nation's citizens. Within this framework of reform or liberalism in the economic sphere and strict conformity in the political sphere, Janos Kadar guided Hungary's economic life from 1956 to 1988 with Karoly Grosz coming to head the government from May 1988. In June 1989 an interim government headed by Miklos Nemeth came to power. This government's role is to lead the country from its current market-driven socialist system to one that is politically pluralistic and completely market-driven.

The New Economic Mechanism (NEM) instituted in January 1968 has been central to Kadar's reforms, as well as serving as his formula for accelerating Hungary's economic growth. The reforms sought to make the economy more efficient by combining elements of a planned economy with elements of a free-market economy. Profit maximization was to be the ultimate goal of all state-owned enterprises. The Central Planning Office, and its ubiquitous intermediate planning agencies, were to be reduced in both their size and scope. The government maintained economic control, however, through such indirect measures as prices, credit, subsidies, and tax rate adjustments as well as in setting Hungary's macroeconomic goals. The NEM also allowed limited forms of private enterprise in the retail sector while encouraging the formation of agricultural cooperatives operating with little government regulation. The economy accordingly became divided into five disparately sized sectors:

1. State-owned enterprises and operations
2. Agricultural cooperatives
3. Nonagricultural cooperatives
4. Formal private sector
5. Informal private sector

Conceptually, the NEM was an enlightened program for it recognized the natural conflict that exists between employers and employees, and producers and consumers, and that consumption and investment are not always in harmony. Unfortunately, the NEM's mechanisms were not allowed to flower because of events in nearby Czechoslovakia. That country's prime minister and father of its own economic plans announced reforms in January 1968 which were too drastic for the Soviet Union's tastes. The Warsaw Pact nations' occupation of Czechoslovakia in August 1968 signaled antireform elements in Hungary to launch a counteroffensive against the spirit of NEM. Although the reform program was never formally withdrawn, the NEM's market elements were quickly curtailed and centralized control over prices was re-established.

The oil shock of 1973, which sent violent tremors throughout the Western nations, produced somewhat the same results in Hungary. Assuming the crisis would be short-lived, the authorities took on Western credits to finance their policies. Unfortunately, although Hungary's industrial sector was not operating badly, it was just not productive enough to ensure sustainable growth. By 1980 gross domestic product (GDP) and investment had stopped growing while consumption continued to grow at about 10 percent annually. Rather than investing in industries which would generate competitive foreign trade, Hungary's authorities had pumped money into its declining steel, coal, and heavy engineering sectors, as well as into heavy construction and chemicals—all areas where Hungary was not especially competitive. Faced with the problem of a foreign debt in excess of $10 billion at the beginning of the last decade, Hungary's efforts for the past 10 years have been to make its domestic industries more efficient, help its companies become more competitive in international markets, and to make its economy more attractive to foreign investors.

One of the government's major attempts at streamlining the country's state-run businesses resides in its Bankruptcy Law, which went into effect on September 1, 1986. The law requires all companies to publish their operating results and to make their books available for public inspection. Money-losing operations are expected to declare bankruptcy and a State Rehabilitation Office was created to both minimize entrepreneurial losses and the effects of short-term unemployment on workers displaced due to a company's bankruptcy or actions taken to improve its efficiency. Unemployment benefits lasting up to one year in length are now paid in a country where previous doctrine stated workers were never idle.

In an effort to provide Hungary with a modern and efficient banking system, three new commercial banks were created in early 1987. In total five banks (the Hungarian Credit Bank, the Commercial and Credit Bank, the Hungarian Foreign Trade Bank, the Budapest Bank, and the General Banking and Trust Company) now compete for business and issue shares to raise capital for companies and cooperatives. The Hungarian National Bank technically became the central bank of issue while retaining its (1) monopoly over foreign exchange, (2) exclusive right to borrow from foreign sources, and (3) control over gold and foreign exchange reserves. In addition to the National Bank and the five commercial banks, over 20 specialized financial institutions (including at least three foreign banks) now operate in Hungary. Certain banks, such as the General Bank of Venture Financing, Interinvest, and Innofinance, respectively specialize in providing financial services promoting profit-oriented ventures, foreign trade, and innovation. Three other banks helpful in bringing foreign investment into Hungary are the Central European International Bank, Citibank Budapest, and the United Credit Bank. Exhibit 3 lists the major types of financial institutions in Hungary while Exhibit 4 ranks Hungary's 11 largest financial institutions.

Perhaps the most sweeping demonstration of Hungary's desire to move toward a more open economic society can be found in its Foreign Investments Act XXIV of 1988. Enacted by the National Assembly to further encourage the direct presence of foreign capital, it ensures that foreign investors (1) are free from adverse discrimination, (2) will be compensated in their original currency should nationalization or expropriation of their investment occur, (3) can own up to 100 percent of the Hungarian firm in which they have invested, and (4) can transfer abroad their dividends and up to 50 percent of their wages. Additionally, certain "outstandingly important" foreign investment activities are given a 100 percent tax exemption. In Spring 1990 those activities were:

1. Electronics and electronization: the development and manufacture of active, passive, and electromechanical components; computer peripherals; electronic

EXHIBIT 3 Number and Types of Hungarian Financial Institutions

Financial Institutions	Number	Total Asset Valuation
Central bank	1	10.0 billion HUF[a] ($200 million)
Commercial banks	12	51.9 billion HUF ($780 million)
Specialized financial institutions	11	9.7 billion HUF ($160 million)
Joint-venture banks	8	10.2 billion HUF ($170 million)
Hungarian banks abroad	2	2.0 billion HUF ($30 million)
Insurance institutions	6	8.0 billion HUF ($130 million)

[a]Indicates Hungarian forints.

EXHIBIT 4 Hungary's Largest Financial Institutions

Financial Institution	Initial Year	Total Asset Valuation
Hungarian Credit Bank	1987	14.0 billion HUF ($230 million)
Commercial and Credit Bank	1987	10.6 billion HUF ($176 million)
Hungarian National Bank	1924	10.0 billion HUF ($151 million)
Budapest Bank	1986	6.4 billion HUF ($106 million)
Hungarian Foreign Trade Bank	1950	6.0 billion HUF ($100 million)
Industrial Development Bank	1984	3.2 billion HUF ($53 million)
Hungarian Insurance Company	1986	3.0 billion HUF ($50 million)
Allami Bistosito Insurance Company	1949	3.0 billion HUF ($50 million)
Cooperative Savings Bank	1989	3.0 billion HUF ($50 million)
General Savings Bank	1985	2.2 billion HUF ($36 million)
Hungarian Postal Savings Bank	1988	2.2 billion HUF ($36 million)

telecommunication main and subexchanges; robotics; CAD; and consumer electronics appliances

2. Automobile production and automobile components
3. Machine tool production
4. The manufacture of agricultural, food-processing, and forestry machinery and equipment
5. Engineering industry components such as castings, forgings, and pressings; general use components and subassemblies such as high-grade fittings, valves, and hydraulic and pneumatic elements; advance-state coupling elements; tools and devices; and technical ceramics
6. Packaging techniques
7. Manufacture of pharmaceuticals, plant protective agents, and intermediates
8. Production of articles which will generate hard currencies or decrease imports against convertible currencies
9. Development of the domestic protein-base
10. Production of propagating or breeding materials
11. Energy-saving or waste-saving materials or devices
12. Telecommunication services
13. Tourism in the guise of medical and thermal (steam bath) convalescent tourism, the construction and operation of medium-priced hotels, and reconstruction of historical castles and mansions
14. Biotechnology

Exhibit 5 reviews both the number and the pace at which the Hungarian government has enacted laws and incentives designed to make its economy more productive and to be more attractive to foreign investors.

In addition to governmental actions, other activities have been undertaken. In 1985 the Hungarian Chamber of Commerce, along with its six regional commissions, was entrusted with the mediation, conciliation, and representation

EXHIBIT 5   Summary of Market and Free Enterprise-Oriented Legislation

1. New Economic Mechanism, implemented January 1968: Central planning infrastructure to be reduced in size and scope; formation of agricultural cooperatives encouraged; private enterprise encouraged in the retail sector; managers of state-owned enterprises encouraged to create their own business strategies
2. Stock and bond market, created and implemented 1982 and revised August 1987
3. Act on the Prohibition of Unfair Economic Activity, implemented January 1985: Goods cannot be held or withdrawn from the market to raise prices; consumers cannot be misled regarding the quality or use of goods; collusion or price fixing is not allowed
4. Bankruptcy Law, implemented September 1986: Spells out the rules governing the bankruptcy of a firm including the payment of unemployment benefits to those displaced; law encourages the closure of money-losing enterprises
5. Two-Tiered Banking System, implemented January 1987 and July 1987: Created three new joint stock commercial banks; Hungarian National Bank continues to act as the nation's central bank and retains its monopoly over foreign exchange
6. Tax Reform, implemented January 1988: Created three new tax systems: A general (business) turnover tax, a personal income tax, and a venture tax
7. Foreign Investment Law, implemented January 1989: Protects the foreign investor against nationaliza-tion or expropriation of investment; generous tax benefits given to certain ``outstandingly important'' businesses; 100 percent of all dividends and 50 percent of wages can be transferred out of the country in the investment's original currency; foreigners can establish firms in customs-free zones
8. Corporation Law, implemented January 1989: Created six different types of enterprise ownership methods including the limited liability company and the joint stock company; all citizens can form joint companies and economic associations at will
9. Wage Regulation Law, implemented January 1989: Wage increases incurred by the firm are deducted from the firm's taxable income; the firm's effective taxes would be about 50 percent; firms can pay employees a bonus and/or a dividend after paying its government taxes; minimum wage for 1989 was set at 4,000 forints per month; the monthly minimum wage for 1990 was set at 4,800 forints
10. Business Transformation Law: Before a company transforms its ownership or ownership form, it must draw up a balance sheet of its assets. The company must publish the announcement of its transformation decision for two consecutive days in an officially recognized newspaper within fifteen days of that decision. The published declaration must include the company's balance sheet and information about the transformation
11. New Accounting System Law, implemented January 1989: All firms must employ commonly accepted accounting and bookkeeping practices. Firms with annual sales of less than 25 million forints per year can use single-entry bookkeeping. Firms with sales of more than 25 million, but less than 250 million forints must use at least simplified double-entry bookkeeping, while those with sales above 250 million must use double-entry bookkeeping. The basic principles of the bookkeeping methods and the contents of the balance sheet and cost and income statement accounts are kept on file in the National Economic Book of Accounts.
12. Unemployment Law, implemented January 1989: Unemployment benefits are available to all workers based on a schedule of the average of their prior 18-month wages. The schedule is as follows for different causes of unemployment:

Termination Condition	First 180 Days	Remaining Days
Terminated by company	70 percent of base	60 percent of base
Worker formally resigns	65 percent of base	55 percent of base
Worker resigns without notice	60 percent of base	50 percent of base

of Hungary in the promotion of international economic relations. Reciprocal trade sections have been established with 25 countries and permanent foreign representatives are housed in Moscow, Lyons, Dublin, New Delhi, and Shanghai. The most recent additions to the Hungarian Chamber of Commerce's offerings and activities include Venture Counseling, the Design Center, the Uniform Commodity Code Bureau, and the Joint Venture Club. The foreign private sector has also participated through the establishment of offices in Budapest of such consulting firms as Arthur Young Associates and Price Waterhouse. One financial magazine's views of the comparative business climates existing in the Eastern bloc countries can be found in Exhibit 6.

THE PROGRESS OF INDUSTRIAL RESTRUCTURING

Since the mid-1970s, Hungarian industry has demonstrated relatively low overall growth. Both mining and construction, after growing in the late 1970s, have exhibited decline while manufacturing, chemicals, and machinery and equipment have continued to expand relatively rapidly. Metallurgy and light industry have expanded slowly so the net result of the Hungarian government's reforms still leaves the economy with a structural imbalance in favor of heavy industry—many of which are in the mature or declining stages of their industrial life cycles. Certain

EXHIBIT 6   Comparative Business Climate Assessments in Early 1990

Bulgaria   The surprise package. Bulgarians ousted their dictator with little ado and have a flourishing Green movement.

Czechoslovakia   Difficult to call this one yet. Czechs are highly skilled and innovative, the infrastructure is relatively good, and basic services work well. Ventures with large Western companies are already under way, but no framework exists for native entrepreneurs.

East Germany   The safest bet in the East. West German cash is flowing, the people are skilled, and some modern infrastructure is in place. Provided the people don't go overboard politically, it is of definite interest.

Hungary   The most congenial, if not the most profitable. Small companies are flourishing, privatization is under way, and a multiparty system exists. Budapest is the liveliest city in the East, but the rural areas are backward and very poor.

Poland   The switch to multiparty democracy is complete. Cash flows from the United States and Germany are increasing. Poles are natural merchants, but they have no infrastructure. Rising expectations and an environmental crisis mean this one is still a toss-up.

Romania   Anyone's guess. The dictator is dead, but will a free system develop successfully? Not for the fainthearted, but it may be an opportunity for those with traditional links.

Soviet Union   Joint ventures are surging, major companies including the Big Blue, IBM, are moving in. But will the Communist party give up its leading role? Political and social instability looming.

Source: "The Economic Pulse Rate," *Austria Business & Economy*, vol. 2, no. 3 (January 1990), p. 9.

growth-industry bright spots nonetheless are in existence. Small computer manufacturing has increased more than five-fold to 12,592 units in 1987 and the manufacture of transistors has shown an average annual increase of 16.6 percent per year from 1985 to 1987. The production of integrated circuits, however, has fallen 3.5 percent over the same period.

Given the Hungarian government's desire to restructure its economic base via indirect controls, what degree of progress has been made? Under the Brezhnev doctrine, medium- and small-sized factories were consolidated into monopolistic units for easier operating control and planning coordination. Although these consolidations were politically efficient, they were not economically sound. By the end of 1979, the Central Committee of the Hungarian Socialist Workers' Party (HSWP) decided rationalizing state-run monopolies was incorrect and these firms should be divided into smaller, independent companies. Enterprise managers have been given more decentralized responsibility in setting production goals, product mixes, and marketing efforts, and during 1985 and 1986 many companies set up elected councils to facilitate the move to decentralized management. Csepel, one of Hungary's largest industrial trusts, was ultimately divided into 13 autonomous companies ranging from a bicycle joint venture to an education and development company.

While a modest amount of progress has been made in breaking up the high degrees of concentration shown in Hungary's industries in Exhibit 7, the process has been slow and has met with much resistance. The large firms have successfully lobbied for extra funds and tax breaks, thus allowing themselves to survive in their original inefficient states. Additionally they argue that downsizing creates diseconomies independent of size, the loss of marketing skills, the need to duplicate staff work, and the loss of scale economies in plant operations. Progress *has* been made in moving its economic structure more toward private enterprise, although the absolute levels are still quite insignificant. As shown in Exhibit 8 the percentage of all active wage earners in the private sector increased from 3.4 percent in 1980 to 6.1 percent in 1988 while the percentage of those working in state-run organizations has fallen .7 percent. This may indicate that growth in new employment has been in the private sector.

Contrary to official pronouncements, Hungary's government is still investing in its state enterprises, although investment in the private sector has increased by

EXHIBIT 7 Comparative Size Distribution of Manufacturing Firms

Employees by Firm Size	Hungary	Capitalist Sample[a]
1–100	14%	35%
101–500	26	33
501–1,000	19	13
More than 1,000	41	19
Average per firm	186	80

[a]Austria, Belgium, France, Italy, Japan, and Sweden for various years in the 1970s.
Source: Cited by J. Kornai, ''The Hungarian Reform Process: Visions, Hopes, and Reality,'' *Journal of Economic Literature*, vol. 24, (December 1986), p. 1,699.

EXHIBIT 8   Proportion of Active Workers by Sector (selected years)

Sectors	1980	1985	1987	1988
State	71.1%	70.0%	70.8%	70.4%
Cooperative	25.5	25.3	23.8	23.5
Private	3.4	4.7	5.4	6.1
Total	100.0%	100.0%	100.0%	100.0%

Source: *Statistical Yearbook* (Budapest: Hungarian Central Statistical Office, various years).

20.9 percent in real terms from 1980 to 1987 while simultaneously real investment in the socialist sector fell by 9.7 percent. Despite the increase in private sector investment, the majority of it is actually in new home construction although it has been claimed that 30 percent of the growth that exists in Hungary's national income emanates from this sector. For the 1990s the government has pledged to reverse its investment policy to emphasize light industry and the nation's infrastructure. As shown in Exhibits 9 and 10, however, the record for the late-1980s was not dramatic, although the changes from 1987 to 1988 were impressive in the area of communications. The proportional investment in transport and communications increased 8.4 percent although the annual average increase in this area has been only 1.5 percent per year since 1982. The absolute average annual forint increase in transport and communications investment has been a substantial 12.9 percent per year from 1985 to 1988.

INCENTIVES FOR INCREASED INTERNATIONAL COMPETITIVENESS

While Hungary has historically played a political and cultural role which belies its size, the country possesses few innate physical economic gifts. As a market, it ranks sixth out of the seven European Soviet-bloc nations and its only abundant

EXHIBIT 9   Proportion of Socialist Sector Investment by Branch

Socialist Sector	1985	1986	1987	1988
Industry	39.6%	39.5%	34.6%	34.2%
Construction	1.3	1.3	1.4	1.3
Agriculture and forestry	13.9	13.9	15.4	12.8
Transport and communications	13.3	14.2	14.3	15.5
Trade	5.2	4.4	4.4	4.5
Water	7.3	8.8	8.6	9.2
Other	19.7	19.4	21.3	22.5
Total	100.0%	100.0%	100.0%	100.0%

Source: Derived from data in *Statistical Pocket Book of Hungary 1988* (Budapest: Statistical Publishing House, 1989), p. 103.

EXHIBIT 10 Socialist Sector Investment by Branch (billions of current forints)

Socialist Sector	1985	1986	1987	1988
Industry	76.9	75.6	84.3	79.2
Construction	2.5	2.7	3.4	3.1
Agriculture and forestry	27.0	28.8	37.5	29.7
Transport and communications	25.8	29.5	34.8	35.8
Trade	10.1	9.1	10.7	10.5
Water	14.3	18.3	20.9	21.3
Other	37.7	43.6	51.9	51.7
Total	194.3	207.6	243.5	231.3

Source: *Statistical Yearbook* (Budapest: Hungarian Central Statistical Office, various years); and *Statistical Pocket Book of Hungary 1988* (Budapest: Statistical Publishing House, 1989), p. 103.

natural resource is bauxite. Accordingly, Hungary has traditionally relied on trade as its means for acquiring basic materials, economic wealth, and well-being. Other than the mining of its bauxite, the country has depleted its other natural resources of exportable value. Its last iron ore mine at Rudabanya was closed in early 1986 and the government's original plan to invest heavily in its coal industry has been abandoned. Several unprofitable pits were closed in 1989. Accordingly, more than half its total energy needs are imported, with major amounts of natural gas being obtained from the Soviet Union via a complex system of pipelines. In an effort to become energy independent and to be able to export energy, Hungary has four 440 megawatt pressurized nuclear reactors in operation near Paks. Two new 1,000 megawatt pressurized water reactors, also in Paks, are under construction but this construction has been delayed because of financial problems.

Hungary's merchandise exports and imports are almost equally divided between Soviet-bloc countries and the West. The Soviet Union (27.6 percent of total 1988 exports and 25.0 percent of imports) is Hungary's most important trading partner, followed far behind by West Germany, Austria, East Germany, Czechoslovakia, and Poland, respectively. Hungary's main exports are agricultural products (21.3 percent of all 1988 exports), machinery, and semifinished goods while its major imports are fuels (14.0 percent of all 1988 imports), semifinished products, and machinery.

Unfortunately for its well-being as a trader nation, Hungary has been bound to some large degree to the dictates and fortunes of the Council for Mutual Economic Assistance (CMEA, or Comecon in the Western press). Its current members are the Soviet Union, Bulgaria, Czechoslovakia, East Germany, Hungary, Poland, Romania, Mongolia, Cuba, and Vietnam. Founded in January, 1949 and claimed by many to have been created by Josef Stalin as his country's response to the Marshall Plan for Western European reconstruction, its ostensible aim was to accelerate economic development by encouraging specialization and cooperation between its members. Although it has basically failed in the mission of economic development, a degree of specialization has occurred—Bulgaria is the leading producer of forklift trucks, Czechoslovakia is the CMEA's leading producer of trams and nuclear power plant components, East Germany's Robotron has become the leading producer of electric typewriters and small and medium-sized computers, and Hungary is the leading producer of the Ikarus bus.

Regrettably these products, which have been relatively successful for CMEA consumption, are not competitive in world markets. Certain seeds of discord, however, *are* beginning to emerge within CMEA member nations. At CMEA's January 1990 meeting in Bulgaria, members discussed but did not decide that CMEA has to be reformed through the use of the American dollar for intercountry trade payments over the ruble (which is inconvertible) and to diminish the amount of planned and coordinated trading between themselves. Czechoslovakia even expressed the desire to leave CMEA if major reforms along the lines discussed were not enacted. Should this ultimately occur, it is highly likely that Hungary and Poland would soon follow. Because of Hungary's large trade surplus with CMEA countries Hungary has ordered strong export controls over activities with them. It is believed that these controls will ultimately result in very high Hungarian unemployment of approximately 500,000 workers, mostly in the bus and electronics industry.

While most CMEA countries have continued to trade between themselves despite the long-term disadvantages for doing so, Hungary has been an innovator in its dealings with the West. As part of its reform process, during 1985 to 1987 the country granted foreign trading rights to an increasing number of individual firms. Foreign trade is now a basic right of any firm, whether it is a state firm, a cooperative, or a private firm.

Hungary has also been the fastest-moving country in obtaining joint ventures. Although only the third nation to do so dating back to 1972, Hungary quickly made up lost time by having over 200 joint ventures in operation as of February 1990. The country has been relatively successful in attracting joint ventures because it does not reserve leading posts in the ventures for its own citizens and various tax allowances and duty concessions. Despite this progress, the absolute value of these ventures is a comparatively low $300 million. In 1988 Spain received $7.2 billion in joint venture money while Turkey received $3 billion.

INDUSTRIAL INFRASTRUCTURE AND HUMAN CAPITAL

It has already been seen that Hungary has done much to improve the conditions within which business can be conducted. Its banking system and the creation of a capital market facilitates the acquisition and flow of funds between different parties. It has also been seen that the Hungarian government has increased both the proportional and absolute amounts it has spent on improving the nation's transportation and communications systems. From 1985 to 1988 the budget increased 38.6 percent in billions of forints which is twice the rate of increase in the country's overall budget. Very few dirt roads still exist in Hungary and the length of its pipeline network and the tonnage it has transported have almost tripled since 1970.

For the foreign visitor, however, Hungary's telephone system appears to be one of its largest stumbling blocks. While possessing such quaint features as dialing an "A" for tuning stringed instruments, wake-up calls for early risers, and

Hungarian bedtime stories, it is extremely overburdened, despite the recent additions made to its system. Although by CMEA standards Hungary possesses more per capita telephones than either Poland or the Soviet Union, the country's 152 telephones per 1,000 persons is vastly inferior to the rates found in other nearby countries such as Austria (492), Greece (356), and West Germany (621). More important, however, is the quality of transmissions afforded. Many calls are misconnected, transmissions are often disconnected, and fidelity is poor. Most exchanges outside Budapest are manual and are often not staffed for long periods. A major investment program with World Bank assistance amounting to $70 million has recently begun. The World Bank is also supporting the installation of a cellular telephone system in cooperation with U.S. West and the Ericson Company. From 1987 to 1988 alone the number of kilometers of telephone and telegraph lines increased 8.3 percent and the admission capacity of Hungary's central telephone exchanges increased 6.2 percent. Despite these improvements in the availability of telephone service, the number of dwellings waiting for a telephone still stands at about half a million. Some families have been on the waiting list so long one member of parliament joked that placement on the list should be a right of inheritance.

Just as a nation's stock of capital and its infrastructure are important factors in assessing its ability to develop economically, consideration should be given to the nature and condition of its human resources. Hungary has a total population of about 10.6 million which has been falling over the past number of years. A large portion is concentrated in Budapest (2.2 million) with about 39.2 percent of its remaining population residing in other urban areas. The remaining 41.1 percent live in the countryside. As shown in Exhibit 11, this population decline has been long-term in nature despite the government's attempts to increase the birth rate through liberal maternity leave benefits, employer-reimbursed child care centers at the work place, tax relief for those with three or more children, and generous prenatal and obstetrical allowances. The size of the potential labor force also shows a negative trend. The absolute size of the working-age population has fallen since 1981 although its population proportion has risen slightly since 1986. The economically active portion of the population has fallen 3.4 percent since 1981.

Although the size of Hungary's work force has been falling over the years, it has been noted its population is very consumption oriented compared to other socialist countries. Most families have television sets, of which about 30 percent of them receive in color. Automobiles, although of varying ages and qualities, are becoming very common. By early 1988 Hungary had approximately 1.8 million private automobiles or 49 cars per 100 households.

EXHIBIT 11 Total Population for Selected Years (as of January 1)

Population	1985	1986	1987	1988	1989
Total (000)	10,657	10,640	10,621	10,604	10,590
Percentage change	—	−0.16%	−0.18%	−0.16%	−0.13%

Sources: *Statistical Yearbook, 1987* (Budapest: Hungarian Central Statistical Office, 1987), p. 40; and *Statistical Pocket Book of Hungary 1988* (Budapest: Statistical Publishing House, 1989), p. 9.

EXHIBIT 12 Work Hours Required for Selected Consumer Goods (1985)

Consumer Good	U.K.	West Germany	Hungary
Automatic washing machine	80	83	404
Automatic dryer	43	72	433
Color television set	—	88	927
Personal computer (Commodore 64)	33	—	1,053
VCR	159	125	2,133

Source: *Heti Vilaggazdasg*, vol. 431 (September 5, 1987), p. 51.

As seen in Exhibit 12, the average worker has to work many hours to obtain the goods so passionately desired. This has often been done by holding down more than one job at a time.[1] Because most factories operate only single eight-hour shifts beginning at 6 a.m., workers can moonlight in the afternoons and evenings. Western observers have remarked that many Hungarian workers are excessively tired from working their multiple jobs or, alternatively, are not totally dedicated to their major employers. Exhibit 13 presents data on the official hours of work completed by workers in a sample of various nations.

A large number of workers also operate in the "black economy" as either workers or customers, although more and more of these unofficial activities are being legalized by the government. Over the years, two basic economies have come into operation. The *first economy* is composed of government agencies, officially registered nonprofit institutions, state-owned firms, and cooperatives. The *second economy* is composed of (1) the *formal* private sector, comprised of officially licensed, petty capitalist operations which cannot employ more than seven individuals, excluding family members of the owner, and (2) the *informal* private sector, which is made up of all private activities pursued outside the formal private sector and all income that does not originate from parties in the first economy or the formal private sector. While difficult to measure the rate of participation in the second economy in all likelihood it is consuming more and

EXHIBIT 13 Hours of Work per Worker (1986)

Country	Hours
Hungary (per month)	144.7
South Korea (per week)	54.7
Poland (per month)	151.0
United States (per week)	40.7
Japan (per week)	46.0
Austria (per month)	142.1
Spain (per week)	38.6

Source: *1987 Yearbook of Labor Statistics* (Geneva: International Labor Office, 1987), pp. 675–678.

more of the citizenry's time. Many pensioners engage in full-time or half-time activities. Others moonlight in evenings, weekends, during paid vacations, while on sick leave paid for by the national health service, or during regular paid working hours at a first job.

While Hungarians have shown a historical preference for high income and high consumption over greater amounts of leisure, there are indications they have begun to work themselves to the point of psychological and physical exhaustion. The life expectancy for the average Hungarian male has declined from 67 years to 63 years of age in just the past eight years, and the suicide, alcoholism, and drug abuse rates are increasing. Hungary's second highest use of hospital bed space in 1987 was devoted to psychiatric cases while mental disorders and neuroses were the second highest reason for lost work days. The country also possesses the world's highest suicide rate (45 per 100,000 in 1987) although the reporting of suicide as a cause of death does not possess the same moral strictures they do in many other countries. In 1960 suicides accounted for 2.5 percent of all Hungarian deaths while they have consistently accounted for 3.3 percent of all deaths in most recent years. The estimated number of alcoholics in the population has jumped from 224,000 in 1980 to approximately 489,000 in 1987 while those being treated for alcoholism have increased 50.7 percent over the same time period. In total, this number of individuals constitutes about 5.5 percent of the over 15 year old population.

In addition to the vigor and health of its labor force, a nation's education level is important because of the high technological advance rates demonstrated in many growth industries. Schooling in Hungary is compulsory for those between the ages of 6 and 16 and about 95.3 percent of all students finish eight grades of education by the age of 16. The country supports 58 universities and colleges, and in 1984 7.9 percent of the adult population possessed a university education. Despite these education levels and the array of degrees and majors shown in Exhibit 14, Hungary suffers from a shortage of skilled labor. A near-term solution does not appear to be on the horizon as the proportion of the country's budget allocated to education has fallen 7 percent from 1985 to 1987. The Hungarian government, however, has recently legislated that private schools on all levels can be created through the use of both domestic and foreign capital. For comparative purposes, the expenditures on public education as a percent of GDP are presented for various nations in Exhibit 15.

One method for increasing the effective size of Hungary's labor force would be the retraining and movement of underutilized workers from inefficient, highly subsidized, low-growth industries. Only a modest degree of worker redeployment from money-losing factories has occurred, however, because the 1986 Bankruptcy Law has not been vigorously enforced. A recent Hungarian government review estimates that about 60 of its largest companies must either declare bankruptcy or remove sizeable work force redundancies. Accordingly it was approximated that 1 million individuals or 20 percent of the labor force is underemployed in certain subsidized operations while other, more promising employers operate with underqualified workers or short shifts. Although the Hungarian worker's basic right to full employment has been protected by the labor unions, temporary unemployment is now tolerated and unemployment benefits are paid to those put out of work due to bankruptcy or plant cost-cutting efficiency measures.

EXHIBIT 14   Degrees Obtained in High School and College (1988)

Major	Students	Percent
High School Graduates		
Industrial (technical) studies	20,087	48.2%
Agriculture	3,002	7.2
Economics	7,877	18.9
Commerce	2,419	5.8
Catering	1,435	3.4
Transportation	635	1.5
Postal service	833	2.0
Sanitation	3,646	8.8
Kindergarten teaching	1,201	2.9
Fine arts	498	1.2
Total	41,633	100.0%
College Graduates		
Engineering	5,561	23.5%
Agriculture	1,284	5.4
Economics	2,576	10.9
Medicine	1,109	4.7
Pharmaceutical studies	196	.8
Veterinary school	106	.4
Arts and philosophy	1,247	5.3
Law and public administration	1,113	4.7
Natural sciences	1,025	4.3
Teaching	8,432	35.6
Fine arts	550	2.3
Other	506	2.1
Total	23,705	100.0%

Source: *Statistical Pocket Book of Hungary, 1988* (Budapest: Statistical Publishing House, 1989), pp. 72, 74.

EXHIBIT 15   Public Expenditures on Education as a Percentage of GDP (1986)

Country	Percent of GDP
Hungary	4.8%
South Korea	3.8
Poland	4.6
United States	7.8
Japan	3.9
Austria	5.0
Spain	2.3

Source: *1985/1986 Statistical Yearbook* (New York: United Nations, 1988).

In addition to attempts at restructuring its economic base and increasing the level of competitiveness both inside the country and from the outside, Hungary's government has radically changed the conditions under which managers may operate their enterprises. In the previous system, the leading state-owned firm executives were appointed by a superior authority and successful managers were promoted by either moving up within the present organization or by transferring from another firm or state-controlled agency. There was no real executive job or labor market and career advancement depended largely on pleasing those at the bureaucracy's apex. Understandably, then, one of the manager's main objectives was simply to satisfy the bureaucracy and guard against making glaring mistakes.

Defensive, career-saving tactics were also used by the savvy manager. In a command economy situation with tight planning by the Central Planning Board, managers often hid their companies' true production capabilities to obtain lenient output goals given either eventually occurring problems with supplies, worker performance levels, or plant breakdowns. The manager's motivation was merely to meet the plan, or at best to exceed it slightly, but not by too much lest the new output level be incorporated into next year's plan. Accordingly output restriction was the common practice. Additionally, managers performed only to the measures that were applied. If output (and, accordingly, their rewards) were measured in raw units, a large number of units would be produced but with a sacrifice in product quality, cost reductions, and/or the proper maintenance of machinery and buildings if necessary. If output were measured in aggregate value the astute manager would produce goods containing large amounts of expensive material. If the output were measured in weight or square footage, such as rubber sheeting, the manager would produce sheeting which was either very heavy or very thin.

Since the reforms of the Company Council Law (1984), top managers in most state-owned firms are no longer appointed by higher authority. They are now directly or indirectly elected by the firm's employees. The determination of the firm's output levels and its product mix has also been decentralized. Since 1968 most factor costs are no longer administered, although they are still not completely determined in the marketplace. For many goods, strict cost-plus rules prevail, while in other cases a competitive pricing principle is mandatory where the profit margins for domestically sold products must not exceed their margins when sold in the export market. Laws against unfair profits or prices exist and the interpretation of what is a "fair" or "unfair" profit or price, however, can be arbitrary or subject to varying interpretations.

The firm's autonomy regarding its technological choices or investment alternatives has also increased substantially. A considerable fraction of a firm's profits can be retained for investment purposes. Nonetheless, central power is still very strong as most major investment projects attempted by firms require additional funds from either the network of state-controlled banks or from the government's operating budget. Only about one-fifth of the state sector's investment is financed exclusively from company retained earnings, so the role of centralized authority is substantial.

This is, however, a vast improvement over the past state of affairs. Previously the centralized allocation of investment monies was not guided by a profitability criterion, but was instead handled in a compensatory fashion. Those with excess funds (profits) had them taxed away for use in money-losing organizations. In one study of Hungarian investment decisions, no correlation was found between a firm's pretax or posttax profits and later year investment activities. Accordingly profit expectations have not been a factor in past investment decisions, although they should begin to be an important future consideration.

The expectation of profits has always been a major force in capitalist countries. Accordingly, the Hungarian government's official pronouncements now state that the size of a firm's profits will be the main determinant of its effectiveness. To put teeth into that pronouncement, managerial bonuses and employee profit sharing plans have been instituted. In the past, however, money-losing firms have either been given temporary or permanent subsidies, tax breaks, or bailout credits. Pricing authorities have often helped the unhealthy firm by increasing its administered prices or by allowing deviations from various interventionist price rules. In this regard the manager of a state-owned firm is not without influence concerning the procurement of central power indulgences. The firms they command are often either monopolies or oligopolies, and therefore alternative output sources are not immediately available. These firms were created by the state, which therefore has a vested interest in seeing them succeed. Thus the managers cannot be held completely accountable for their results because of the many prior interventions that have hampered their ability to rationalize company operations.

As important as the inducements for change instituted by the Hungarian government are, another very intangible but real aspect governing a manager's responsiveness to an environmentally originated opportunity has not been fathomed: That is the spirit of entrepreneurship. From an entrepreneurial perspective, most of Hungary's enterprises are governed by managers who have not been trained at meeting the rigors of the marketplace. These managers have traditionally conducted business in closed, production-oriented systems usually operating in marketplaces where a seller's market usually prevailed. The products they offered were either manufactured and distributed to captive nations within the CMEA or to captive domestic consumers with few choices and a low ability to express demand. Given irregularity in the delivery of raw materials and intermediate goods

EXHIBIT 16 Composition of Manufacturer's Inventories by Selected Countries

Country (Years)	Ratio of Input Inventories to Output Inventories[a]	
	Lowest	**Highest**
United Kingdom (1972–1977)	1.20	1.56
Austria (1975–1976)	1.04	1.07
Canada (1960–1975)	1.06	1.40
Hungary (1974–1977)	5.72	6.38
Hungary (1978–1984)	4.90	5.25

[a]Input inventory covers stocks of purchased materials and semifinished goods, and output inventory consists of finished goods.
Source: J. Kornai, "The Hungarian Reform Process: Visions, Hopes, and Reality," *Journal of Economic Literature*, vol. 24 (December 1986), p. 1,719.

and an almost guaranteed purchase of the manufactured product regardless of its quality, Hungary's managers have been trained to engage in uneconomic inventory hoarding. As shown in Exhibit 16, which details comparisons in input inventories to output inventories for various countries, in situations where a seller's market exists, the intelligent manager hoards inputs while the output is easily sold. Accordingly the ratio of input inventories to output inventories is relatively high. In an economy where a buyer's market exists, the reverse tends to be true.

In attempting to sell their products to the West, Hungarian managers will have to reorient their thinking about the marketplace's role and they will have to design and manufacture products which have eye appeal, utilitarian value, and technical competence. Unfortunately, as has been noted by Bela Belassa, only about 4 percent of Hungary's products are new, so its managers have not had much experience with rolling out new products. Hungary has never been a major force in international markets and its trading position has deteriorated even more in recent years. In 1973 Hungary's share of total world exports was 0.8 percent while in 1985 it was 0.4 percent. Moreover, Hungary's managers must now compete against the West's advancing technology with physical plants, which are becoming older, as shown in Exhibit 17. As stated by the Hungarian Chamber of Commerce, "the overwhelming majority of the machines used in industry are obsolete, and the proportion of machines and equipment to be written off is very high [23 percent]. Worst of all, the trend is increasing."

Based on partial evidence, Hungary's managers feel they will have a difficult time competing, with at least their American counterparts, although the differences between their managerial styles and orientations may be more imagined than real. In one study by Janice Jones and Lester Neidell, a sample of Hungarian managers with Hungarian/American joint venture experience felt Hungarian managers were less efficient, more authoritarian, less profit oriented, and less timely than the American managers they dealt with. They felt they were at parity in the areas of business experience and attention to detail. This may be an inferiority complex, however, because a comparable group of American managers rated Hungarian managers equal to themselves at least in the area of efficiency.

EXHIBIT 17   Average Age of State-Industry Factory Machinery (1982 versus 1987)

Industry	1982	1987	Change
Mining	7.3	7.4	+0.1
Electric energy	12.3	10.1	−2.2
Metallurgy	12.6	15.0	+2.4
Engineering	9.0	11.2	+2.2
Building material	10.4	11.9	+1.5
Chemical	9.0	10.4	+1.4
Light industry	10.8	12.0	+1.2
Food	8.1	9.3	+1.2

Source: *Statistical Yearbook, 1987* (Budapest: Hungarian Central Statistical Office, 1987), p. 164.

Moreover, other managers, such as those from West Germany, have commented that Hungarian joint venture partners are very responsive, hard working, are willing to learn, and possess an ownership mentality.

THE SPECTER OF COUNTERREFORM

In the last analysis, the opportunities presented to Hungary's organizational decision makers have been accomplished through the will of the country's central planners. In this regard managerial actions are still controlled, although now in a less direct fashion. Additionally, the amount of latitude afforded managerial discretion is a joint function of the pressures for liberalism felt by Hungary's parliament and the leeway they feel can be expressed within the crumbling Soviet bloc. Accordingly, Hungary's continuing movement toward a market-based economy depends upon the success of Mikhail Gorbachev's attempts at *glasnost* and *perestroika* and the use of Hungary and Poland as laboratories for structural economic reform without political reform. Following Lenin's maxim that progress is two steps forward and one step backward, each of Hungary's previous market-oriented moves has eventually been followed by backward steps. The country's present managerial group is extremely aware of this process and this awareness may dampen their desire to aggressively push for reform within their own companies. This hesitancy, plus mankind's basic resistance to change even when the change has real long-term benefits, may do much to frustrate Hungary's quest for greater economic development through a restructured, internationally oriented, market-based economy.

Just as pure capitalism or a completely free enterprise system does not exist, Hungary's reforms are an attempt to diminish the bureaucracy's role and to increase the role of the market. As pointed out by Hungarian economist Janos Kornai, however, Hungary has moved from a system of direct bureaucratic control to one of indirect bureaucratic control. While improvements have been made to allow its economic system to be more marketplace responsive, a great deal of intervention still occurs, and it is believed by some these interventions will continue to hamper Hungary's ability to become a true market economy.

Endnotes

1. In 1990 it was estimated the average worker's monthly earnings would be 9,104 Forints per month or about 109,250 Forints a year. While the government has set respective minimum subsistence and social minimum income levels for a city-living married couple with two children at about 3,700 and 4,300 Forints per month, the prices for commonly used items vary greatly in their relative costs. Using American sizes a pound of butter costs about 235.35 Forints, a gallon of milk 71.25 Forints, a dozen eggs 49.20 Forints, and a gallon of regular gasoline 103.12 Forints. Using the early-1990 exchange rate of 64 Forints to one U.S. dollar butter would be $3.68 a pound, milk and gasoline $1.11 and $1.61 a gallon, and eggs $.77 a dozen.

REFERENCES

"Act XXIV of 1988 on the Investments of Foreigners in Hungary." *Hungaropress Economic Information* (Budapest: Hungarian Chamber of Commerce, February 1989).

Ash, T. G. "The Empire in Decay." *The New York Review.* September 29, 1988, pp. 53–60.

Belassa, B. "The New Growth Path in Hungary." In *The Hungarian Economy in the 1980s.* Edited by J. C. Brada and I. Dobozi. Greenwich, Conn.: JAI Press, 1988.

Berend, I. T., and G. Ranki. *Hungary: A Century of Economic Development.* New York: Barnes and Noble, 1974.

International Financial Statistics. Washington, D.C.: International Monetary Fund, 1989.

Investors' Guide to Hungary 1989. Budapest: Foreign Investment Promotion Service, Hungarian Chamber of Commerce, 1990.

Jones, J., and L. Neidell. "American Joint Ventures in Hungary." Working paper, College of Business Administration, University of Tulsa, October, 1989.

Kelly, S. M. "Country Note on Hungary." Charlottesville, Va.: Darden Graduate School of Business Administration, University of Virginia, 1989.

Kerpel, E., and D. G. Young. *Hungary to 1993: Risks and Rewards of Reform.* Intelligence Unit Economic Prospects Series, Report No. 1153. London: Economist Intelligence Unit, 1988.

Kornai, J. "The Hungarian Reform Process: Visions, Hopes, and Reality." *Journal of Economic Literature* 24 (December 1986), pp. 1687–1737.

"A Minisztertanàcs 84/1988. (XII.15) MT Rendelete az Anyagi Érdekeltségi Rendszer Egyes Kérdéseirôl." *Magyar Kôzlôny* 11, no. 62 (December 1988), pp. 1,361–1,364.

"A Minisztertanàcs 114/1988. (XII.31) MT Rendelete a Munkanélkûli Segélyrôl." *Magyar Kôzlôny* 11, no. 69 (December 1988), pp. 1,731–1,733.

"1989.évi XIII. Tôrvény a Gazdàlkod. Szervezetek és a Gazdasàgi Tàrsasàgok Atalakulàsàr.1." *Magyar Kôzlôny* 12, no. 38 (June 1989), p. 665.

"A Pénzûgyminiszter 52/1988. (XII.24) PM Rendelete a Kônyvvitel Rendjérôl." *Magyar Kôzlôny* 11, no. 66 (December 1988), pp. 1,522–1,525.

Statistical Yearbook. Budapest: Hungarian Central Statistical Office, 1987.

Statistical Pocket Book of Hungary 1988. Budapest: Statistical Publishing House, 1989.

1985/1986 Statistical Yearbook. New York: United Nations, 1988.

1987 Yearbook of Labor Statistics. Geneva: International Labor Office, 1987.

APPENDIX A   Selected Economic Data on Hungary, 1980–1988
(all data in billions of forints unless otherwise noted)

Domestic Production	1980	1981	1982	1983	1984	1985	1986	1987	1988
Current GDP	721.0	779.5	847.8	896.3	1,008.5	1,033.7	1,088.8	1,226.4	1,406.0
Real GDP	721.0	741.7	762.8	768.3	788.8	786.7	798.8	831.6	832.3
Real per-capita GDP (in thousand forints)	67.3	69.3	71.2	71.9	73.9	73.9	75.2	78.2	78.3
GDP deflator (1980=100)	100.0	105.1	111.2	116.7	124.1	131.4	136.3	147.9	168.9
Official exchange rate (forints per U.S. dollar)	35.6	34.4	39.6	45.2	51.2	47.3	45.8	47.0	50.4
External Trade									
Exports	281.8	308.2	321.8	360.7	402.0	436.2	431.6	464.4	504.1
Imports	297.4	316.4	315.0	343.6	371.1	414.8	447.0	470.3	472.5
Trade balance	−14.4	−8.2	+6.8	+17.1	+30.9	+21.4	−15.4	−5.9	+31.6
Total reserves less gold[a]	2,090	1,652	1,154	1,564	2,109	3,119	3,062	2,272	1,867

[a]All data in millions of U.S. dollars.

Sources: Compiled from data presented in S. M. Kelly, "Country Note on Hungary" (Charlottesville, Va.: Darden Graduate School of Business Administration, University of Virginia, 1989), pp. 8–9; *Statistical Pocket Book of Hungary 1988* (Budapest: Statistical Publishing House, 1989), pp. 97, 185, and 214; *International Financial Statistics* (Washington, D.C.: International Monetary Fund, 1989), p. 401.

APPENDIX A Cont'd. Selected Economic Data on Hungary, 1980–1988
(all data in billions of forints unless otherwise noted)

External Trade	1980	1981	1982	1983	1984	1985	1986	1987	1988
Gold valuation	468	381	146	346	466	640	751	525	510
Foreign debt	10,314	10,024	8,989	9,617	10,096	13,012	12,636	18,957	19,000
Total debt service	1,417	1,611	1,786	2,050	2,736	2,097	3,769	3,228	2,800
Debt service ratio	29.1%	33.0%	36.6%	42.3%	55.1%	69.1%	91.2%	64.4%	n.a.

APPENDIX B Projected 1989–1990 Change in National Product
and Real Per-Capita Income for Selected Warsaw Pact Countries

Country	National Product	Real Income
Hungary	3.2%	2.1%
Czechoslovakia	3.5	2.3
Bulgaria[a]	6.2	4.0
Soviet Union	4.2	2.8

[a]1989 rather than 1990 data.
Source: "The Race for Survival," *Austria Business & Economy* 2, no. 3 (January 1990), pp. 53–54.

APPENDIX C Projected 1990 Per-Capita Gross Domestic Product
for Selected Countries in U.S. Dollars

Country	Per-Capita GDP
Hungary	$ 2,458
West Germany	19,560
United States	19,536
Austria	16,703
Italy	14,420
Great Britain	14,232

Source: "The Economic Pulse Rate," *Austria Business & Economy*, vol. 2, no. 3 (January 1990), p. 22.

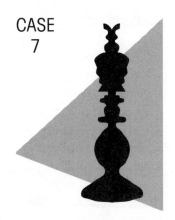

CASE 7

SIMONS LUMBER COMPANY, 1990

STEWART C. MALONE

Try as he might, Bob Simons couldn't get his yard foreman's comment out of his head. "You know, it's funny that the problems here at the lumber company started just after your father died." While the foreman intended no malice, the comment rankled Simons for several reasons. First, the slowdown in business that started in early 1989 had nothing to do with who sat in the president's chair. With mortgage rates moving up and the residential market overbuilt, the six-year building boom in the Northeast was coming to an end. Second, Simons' father had retired from the company over 15 years ago, and while he remained the majority stockholder and retained office space at the firm, he hadn't been active in the business. The younger Simons had run the business for the past 15 years and those had been the most profitable in the company's history.

It was true that last year he had misjudged the market when raw material prices started rising rapidly. Simons thought the run-up was temporary and hesitated in raising his prices. The new prices would be above $1 per board foot, and Simons believed that demand would drop off dramatically when he went above this price level. Belatedly, Simons did raise prices, but not before his miscalculation had severely hurt the firm's profit margins.

As traffic again slowed to a stop on the Beltway, Simons recollected it was about three years ago that he had decided the firm needed a major change in direction. While profits were still very good, it seemed that the firm wasn't aggressive enough. The salespeople were content to take orders rather than selling and the company hadn't picked up a new product line in at least four years (and the established products were very mature). Even the furniture in the office looked old and dingy. Simons recognized that part of the problem was that he was no longer at the company on a full-time basis, having started another venture two years before. While he had received some criticism from his father for not devoting his full attention to the company, Simons had felt he had enough managerial talent to run this small firm on less than 40 hours per week. He had known that he needed to expand the product line and to hire one or two more good people.

He smiled ruefully as the traffic began to move again. He believed he had done the right things, but now halfway through 1990, it looked as though his operating losses were already over the $100,000 mark. For someone who had prided himself on never having lost money in 15 years in a very cyclical industry, Bob Simons didn't think he was going to like 1990.

THE WHOLESALE LUMBER INDUSTRY

Wholesale lumber companies provide the linking pin between the lumber producer and retailer or end user of the lumber. These wholesale companies are generally small, family owned businesses, although the past 20 years have seen the rise of larger national or regional wholesalers. Even the larger wholesalers tend to be privately owned, and currently only one lumber wholesaler's stock is traded publicly.

There are at least two dimensions on which lumber wholesalers may differ. The first dimension is the breadth of product line handled. Full-line wholesalers carry the entire spectrum of lumber and building products. Studs, plywood, and dimension lumber for building are major product lines for these firms. These products are often regarded as commodities and the profit margin per unit may be extremely small, but the market for these products is large and they tend to sell in large blocks. Given the financial resources and exposure in this type of business, full-line wholesalers tend to be larger than average in size. As opposed to the full-line wholesaler, the specialty wholesaler has an extremely narrow product line, often only one or two products. Specialty wholesalers are generally found where there is a high degree of product or market knowledge required. Sales volumes are usually smaller for a specialty wholesaler, but markups are generally higher.

A second dimension that distinguishes wholesalers is their inventories. Direct shippers are wholesalers that seldom take physical possession of the products they sell. Their function is to obtain an order from a customer, place it with a mill for production, and the mill then ships it directly to the wholesaler's customer. A distribution yard wholesaler, however, maintains a physical inventory of the product line in the geographic market where business is conducted. Because the financial risk and requirements of maintaining a physical inventory, profit margins are generally considerably higher for a distribution yard wholesaler. Some wholesalers (primarily distribution yards) add additional value to their products by remanufacturing, or altering the size, shape, finish, etc., of certain products.

It is much easier to enter the wholesale business as a direct shipper than a distribution yard because the requirements for entry are limited to mill and customer contacts, as well as a credit line for working capital. Many wholesale lumber businesses are started by sales representatives leaving established firms to start their own direct-shipper companies. Often if the new venture is successful, the new wholesaler will then add distribution yard facilities to his company.

In actual practice, the distinctions between direct shippers and distribution yards should be considered a continuum since many companies may have both direct and distribution yard sales. The 1982 Census of the Wholesale Trade showed 1,317 lumber wholesalers without a yard (direct shippers) and 1,950 wholesalers with a yard (distribution yards).

Inasmuch as lumber is an undifferentiated product, suppliers in this industry compete heavily on price and service (product expertise, advantageous delivery schedules, etc.). Those products which are regarded as commodities, such as 2 × 4s, plywood, etc., are exceedingly price-sensitive, and most customers have little loyalty to a particular manufacturer or wholesaler. Specialty items are somewhat more differentiated, and a customer may be dependent on a wholesaler for highly technical information. Brand or supplier loyalty is somewhat greater in this class of product.

The major market for lumber in the United States is the housing industry, and the wholesale lumber industry shares many characteristics with it. First, housing demand is highly interest-rate sensitive. Generally when mortgage rates increase, the demand for new housing falls. Thus given the swings in interest rates, both the housing and lumber markets are highly cyclical. The industry suffered through a deep recession in 1980 to 1982, but a long-term prosperity started in 1983 and continued into 1988. However, business conditions quite often vary by geographic region, and the years 1984 to 1987 saw extremely favorable conditions in the northeastern United States, while much of the Texas and southwestern markets were very soft.

While demand for lumber may be cyclical, there have been certain changes in the industry in the past 10 years that have affected competition. With energy costs increasing through the 1970s and freight carriers deregulated in the 1980s, the cost of transportation became a significant portion of the lumber cost. Many wholesalers, especially those dealing in price-sensitive commodity items, found it necessary to add traffic managers to their staffs in order to remain competitive. Increased transportation costs also led wholesalers to focus on species of lumber that were geographically closer to the consuming market. In the last 20 years, the amount of lumber from the Pacific Northwest that shipped to markets East of the Rockies declined dramatically, while southern pine and eastern Canadian woods increased their market share in the eastern half of the United States.

COMPANY HISTORY

In 1894 Robert Simons joined with partner Bernard Taylor to open a lumber yard in downtown Baltimore. After 15 years of operation, Simons bought out Taylor to establish Robert Simons & Sons. The company followed a typical growth path for a lumberyard, that is, serving a wider and larger range of customers. Individual consumers, building contractors, and, later, industrial accounts were sought. As the company entered the 1920s, its customer base was centered around the building contractor and industrial trade.

This period of prosperity led to profitable years at the company, but Simons' son, who was now president, followed the same conservative financial methods as his father. Thus, the Great Depression was a serious, but not catastrophic event for the company. By World War II, the company entered its fastest growth period supplying material for the war effort. Its largest single customer was the federal government, with large contractors and shipbuilders making up the balance. As the war ended, the nation's attention turned to home building. The pent-up demand during the Depression and the war years produced a huge surge in building, and, by this time, the company had evolved into a large, full-line retailer carrying the inventory of plywood, studs, roofing materials, etc., as well as a wholesale supplier of timbers to other retail lumber companies within a 50-mile radius.

As the 1950s ended, the third Simons to manage the company was facing increasing competitive pressure from much larger retail lumber companies. Sales volume was at a record high for the company, but profits were down due to margins eroding under competitive price cutting. Since Simons was well-known and respected by the lumber retailers (he had just completed a three-year term as president of their national trade association), he decided to eliminate the high-volume, high-exposure retail business and concentrate on wholesaling, or supplying the needs of his former competitors. A year after the switch was made, annual sales had dropped 70 percent with profits down 10 percent.

The business continued basically unchanged through the 1960s until 1969 when the fourth Simons joined the company as a salesman. The difference between the two generations was apparent by the approach each took to the company. The elder Simons focused on sales and customer relations, even though many of the sales were not very profitable. The younger Simons concentrated on smaller, high-profit segments of the market. Profits, not total sales, were the emphasis of the young Simons. At that time, the company's customer base was approximately 40 percent retail yards and 60 percent large contractors and industrials.

Throughout the early 1970s, the company focused on developing the higher-margin retail lumber customer and de-emphasizing the contractor business, where sales were always subject to competitive bidding. The geographic trading area was expanded to a 200-mile radius of Baltimore. Products were added that were more architectural and less industrial in nature.

PERSONNEL

In 1986 there were 18 employees at Simons Lumber, 5 working in the office and 13 at the distribution yard 10 miles away. Robert Simons usually was at the office only one or two days each week. The remainder of the time, the office was supervised by Martha Herbert, an employee who started as a secretary some five years before. Martha's predecessor, Bev Tyler, had also started as a secretary, but through her sales expertise and energy, she was promoted to vice president of the firm. Unfortunately for Simons, Bev's husband was transferred to Denver in 1985, and as the most experienced employee, Martha was made office manager. Although she had nowhere near the same sales aptitude possessed by Bev, Martha was quiet, courteous, and efficient. She handled telephone sales and administrative matters, and kept Robert Simons advised on purchasing needs.

Ann Simons, Bob's 39-year-old sister, joined the office staff in 1985. Ann had married her high-school sweetheart within two years of graduating from junior college and had spent the past 15 years taking care of her family. She had just gone through a painful divorce, and was trying to make her way back into the work force. She had been offered the job by her father, who wanted to help her financially and also looked forward to still having one of his children around now that Bob was no longer at the company full time.

While Ann officially started as a secretary/bookkeeper/telephone order-taker, the elder Simons had intimated to her that she could probably run the business after a few years of experience. Although he expressed his reservations very quietly, Bob Simons did not share his father's optimism about Ann's immediate potential. While she possessed excellent interpersonal skills, she had no business training or education. For her part, Ann was attracted not only by the salary that her brother had collected, but also the career opportunity and the continuation of the family firm. The office staff was rounded out by a secretary and a clerk.

Overall, Simons judged his office staff to be competent, if not inspired—that was until the night in October when he received a call at home from Martha, who announced she was quitting. "I just can't work with Ann," she said. "She acts like she owns the company already, and she spends most of the time on the phone talking to her husband on his new car telephone. I've been here six years, and Bev was made vice president in less time than that. I just won't put up with this treatment."

Martha retracted her resignation when Bob Simons said he would look into the matter, but he soon discovered the problem was bigger than he imagined. First, the competition between Ann and Martha was becoming ugly, as Ann expected to ultimately lead the firm because she was a family member, while Martha expected to be vice president because she was doing the same job as her predecessor did, although not as well, in Simon's judgment. Second, the other employees were slowly being drawn into the dispute by listening to the complaints of each of the women. Finally, the problem was being exacerbated by the elder Simons, who clearly favored his daughter over Martha. "Let her quit," said the elder Simons. "Ann is much better with our customers than that sourpuss Martha, anyway."

"Dad, it's doubtful that we can afford to lose Martha right now. Ann just doesn't know enough yet to do Martha's work, and I'm not so sure that Martha doesn't have legitimate gripes in some areas. Ann does spend too much time on personal calls, and quite often, you let her leave early so she can do some personal errands. I'm not really criticizing Ann because this is the first real job she has ever had. She doesn't know what's expected, but she can't be treated like some sort of princess without causing problems with everyone else."

The elder Simons mumbled something about what's the use of having a family business if you can't favor family members, but essentially dumped the problem in Bob's lap while also suggesting that a good brother would support his sister. The conflict between Ann and Martha receded for a few months, but Bob realized that the situation was very unstable. It seemed the harder he tried to treat both Martha and Ann fairly, the more he felt he was being painted as the villain. It wasn't long before his mother would interject into their weekly phone conversations, "I just had a long talk with Ann and she is miserable at the lumber company. I think you should fire that Martha."

Aside from the conflict between Martha and Ann, there was one other development in the personnel at Simons Lumber. The company's outside sales efforts had been neglected over the past three years. He recruited Chris Haney, a young man who had just graduated with a marketing degree from a leading university. Bob Simons had known Haney for several years and had felt the young man possessed a high degree of potential. Haney was attracted by the informality of working in a smaller company as well as what he thought was the upside financial potential.

Simons did have some reservations, however. First, he was hiring a young person straight out of school, and he had heard that the job turnover rate of this group was very high. While General Motors might be able to employ a young person for two years only to watch them leave for graduate school, Simons Lumber could not. Since his company had little experience in hiring and training people fresh from college, Simons worried about how he could keep Haney sufficiently challenged and motivated. With his limited time in the office, it was clear that Bob couldn't do all the training necessary.

Second, there existed the question of interjecting another outside party into the Ann–Martha dispute. Bringing in another ambitious person could trigger a real mess, both in the family and in the business. Martha, although not a family member, felt she had a claim on the vice presidency of the company, while Ann believed her family position justified her eventual promotion to CEO. There was no doubt in Simon's mind that Haney possessed a level of skill and commitment that was far superior to both Ann and Martha.

Although Martha wanted a promotion, Simons didn't believe she possessed either the interpersonal skills or some of the more advanced financial skills that the position required. Likewise, Simons sensed that while his sister could be a valuable addition to the company, she wasn't strongly committed to a career in the lumber business. His suggestions that she take a few business courses at night were met with benign neglect. Neither Ann nor Martha seemed too willing to make any sacrifices, in terms of inconvenience or extra effort, to advance the company. Simons thought that this attitude might have been caused by the relative ease with which the company had made money in the past few years, but he knew those days were over and he doubted that either Ann or Martha would be a good choice for the rough days ahead. He hired Haney.

LVL EXPANSION

Simons knew that even for a specialty wholesaler, his firm's product lines were too narrow. The timber business was essentially static, and the laminated beams and decking products were becoming mature. A new product was essential for the future of the company, and customers were starting to inquire about a product called laminated veneer lumber (LVL). In 1987, LVL had been in the marketplace for at least a decade, but was only beginning to gain widespread acceptance.

The product was essentially thin sheets of veneer that had been glued together to form lumber of almost any size. LVL had a number of advantages over solid-sawn or traditional lumber. Because it was stronger, it could carry more weight or span longer distances than traditional lumber. It was also more uniform, especially in moisture content, so it would shrink less and be less likely to cause squeaky floors when used for floor joists. Finally, since LVL came out of the gluing machine in one continuous stream, it could be cut to whatever length was desired. The length of solid-sawn lumber was determined by the length of the log, and thus certain desirable lengths, such as 16 feet, commanded a price premium.

Because LVL was an engineered product and often required technical assistance, Simons was convinced that his firm's expertise in laminated beams could be transferred to LVL. He arranged a meeting with the manufacturer's representative in the area, John Larue, and soon found out that the manufacturer had other ideas about distributing the product. Essentially, the manufacturer wanted the product stocked by every retail yard in the country, and the manufacturer would sell the retailer at the same price he sold a wholesaler. While there was one other wholesaler in Simons' trading area selling LVL, that wholesaler was selling the bulk of the product directly to contractors, thus bypassing the retailer.

While the manufacturer may have wanted widespread distribution, most retail lumber yards had not started stocking LVL in 1987. An inventory of the product took up a substantial amount of room and handling LVL was fairly labor intensive. As the meeting progressed, Simons' enthusiasm for the product dimmed. Not only would he buy at the same price as his customer could, but the markups on the product were only about 15 percent, compared with 25 to 30 percent markup on a similar product. Cutting waste reduced those margins even further. (If a customer wanted two pieces 23 feet long and the distributor stocked 48 foot lengths, a distributor would often not be able to bill the extra 2 feet in order to stay competitive on price.) However, the product had potential for being a high turnover product, and it required little additional investment outside of the $80,000 required for the startup inventory. Simons figured he could always dump the inventory at close to cost so his downside risk would be low. He ordered two cars and was in the LVL business.

THE SPOTTED OWL

In an industry characterized by big trees, big machines, and big investments, it was hard to believe that the most critical environmental issue involved a two pound bird, the northern spotted owl. The habitat of the spotted owl was the old-growth Douglas Fir forests of the Pacific Northwest, which, along with the southeast portion of the United States, was one of the two major sources of commercial lumber. The Northwest differed from the Southeast, however, in forestry management since the southern forests were primarily privately owned, whereas most of the land in the Northwest was owned by the federal government and was managed by the U.S. Forest Service. Each year, the Forest Service auctioned lumber cutting rights on its managed land and these government auctions were an important source of raw material for lumber producers, especially smaller firms which did not own their own timberland.

During the late 1980s several environmental groups sued the U.S. Forest Service, alleging that current government forestry management practices threatened the survival of the owl. On June 22, 1990, the U.S. Fish and Wildlife Service listed the northern spotted owl as a threatened species under the Endangered Species Act. It was expected that the legally required government plan would remove almost 50 percent of the available forest land from potential harvest.

The debate over the spotted owl sparked bitter acrimony. At the core of the debate were the relative rights of the environment versus the economic impact on tens of thousands of people whose livelihoods depended on the forests. Lumber industry sources predicted that limiting the timber harvest would destroy 30,000 lumbering jobs in the affected region and add $3,000 to the cost of the average new home. The pejorative that the industry uses for the environmental groups was "preservationists," and they claimed that the environmental groups were merely using a cute little owl as an emotional symbol to accomplish their real objective: the complete prohibition of lumbering in the old-growth forests. Such a position, claimed the industry, ignored the substantial amount of forests that had already been set aside in wilderness areas and national parks.

While it was clear to Simons that the spotted owl issue would be decided at a much higher level than he could influence, it also seemed to him that there would be clear winners and losers. Producers dependent on western forests would see their raw material costs rise, and southern producers would gain an advantage. The large forest-products producers with their own forest lands would be in good shape while many smaller mills, whose access to the raw materials would be curtailed, would be forced to close. Finally, those products manufactured from prime, old-growth logs would become far more expensive, while products (such as LVL) produced from less desirable logs would gain market share. Since 60 percent of Simons' sales came from timbers produced from western old-growth Douglas Fir manufactured by small- to medium-sized mills, future prospects didn't look too bright for Simons Lumber.

RECENT DEVELOPMENTS AT SIMONS LUMBER

The marketplace's initial reaction to Simons' LVL introduction was encouraging. Simons' marketing approach emphasized excellent service, and promised that orders would be ready for pick-up within 24 hours of the time the order was placed. After three months of inventorying the product, Bob analyzed the sales records and found that while about 60 retailers were repeat LVL customers, two large retailers accounted for almost 65 percent of total LVL sales. These two accounts appreciated Simons' fast service, but within six months decided to purchase LVL directly from the manufacturer and stock it in their own yards. As one explained, "Your service is great and your prices are fair, Bob, but we are selling so much of this stuff that we must have our own inventory at our fingertips." With his two biggest customers gone (except for fill-in orders), Simons' inventory took almost six months to bleed down to a minimum level, and Simons intended to get out of this product.

In late 1989, LVL sales rep John Larue met with Bob Simons to see if he wanted to up his investment in LVL. The rep had formerly worked very closely with Simons' competitor, Johnson Lumber, and it now turned out that Johnson had dropped John's product line in favor of one of the new LVL manufacturers. John had built the LVL business in this trading area and was not ready to concede all of this business to Johnson and the new manufacturer. When Bob related how his biggest users were buying directly from John's company as well as other wholesalers, John had his answer ready.

"Look, Bob, last year Johnson sold about $6 million of LVL and about $2.5 million of that was to retailers who either didn't stock the product or who were stocked out at a given time. Even a 20-percent market share would be a pretty substantial amount of business for you."

"Does that mean that you will still be selling directly to retailers at the same price that you're selling us?" asked Bob.

"We have to, Bob. Not only has Johnson been distributing for a new manufacturer, but at least three additional manufacturers are entering this market. Now all of them will be selling direct to the retailer, or even the contractor, but I've heard rumors that at least five more national wholesalers that have locations here will be stocking LVL within the next six months. You are going to have to get in now with a big investment if you want to be a player in LVL six months from now. I know it's tough trying to sell a retailer when you purchase the product for the same price they do, but we have an offer that should make it easier. If you are willing to maintain an LVL inventory worth at least $150,000, we will allow you a six percent discount on all your purchases. That should make you much more competitive, Bob!''

"Is this discount only for wholesalers, John, or does any company with a big inventory get this? If the master distributor discount is available to anyone, I'd have to say you're just cutting your price, now that you finally have a little competition,'' smiled Bob.

"The only requirement for the master distributor discount is the appropriate inventory level, but I still think you can make some good money with this product, Bob.''

The meeting ended with Simons promising Larue he would give the matter serious consideration. There was no doubt that LVL was growing rapidly in popularity and that it was a natural substitute for some of Simon's current products, but its very popularity was also its vulnerability. LVL had almost bypassed specialty product status and moved immediately to a commodity. One of Simons' best retail accounts, an original LVL customer who put in its own inventory, told Bob recently that they just lost a big job because their price was 0.75 percent too high, and that was without a wholesaler in the distribution chain.

Another factor that worried Bob was the number of national wholesalers entering the local market. Not only did these companies have superior marketing power, which would make it difficult for Simons to gain an equal market share, but they also had vastly greater purchasing power. If anyone was going to get a discount on LVL, chances were Simons wasn't going to be first in line. A final concern was inventory. At least two of the national wholesalers had multiple yards within 100 miles of Baltimore. Their ability to exchange inventory would mean that Simons would need to carry a larger than normal inventory to compete, and it was obvious that any player in the LVL market would need the 6 percent master distributor discount if their prices were to be competitive. That meant carrying $150,000 in LVL.

Simons thought back to an industry seminar he had attended about inventory management where the concept of "turn and earn" had been presented. The instructor had said that looking at profit margins or inventory turns individually was not the correct way to approach product line decisions. Instead, one should calculate the number of annual inventory turnovers and multiply this result by the average profit margin in the product. Thus, a product that turned six times a year with an average profit margin of 15 percent would have a turn-and-earn index of 90. (The higher the resulting product, the better.) Simons had always heard that 120 was the minimum acceptable turn-and-earn for a specialty wholesaler, but he wasn't sure how much faith he should put in that number. The one thing he was sure of was that he had to do some number crunching soon, because John Larue was correct in stating that it was either time to get into the LVL market or stay out forever. In fact, mused Simons, it might already be too late.

REMANUFACTURING

While the LVL decision was important to the future of the company, Bob Simons was considering an even more fundamental change in the firm's product line, and, ironically, it represented a complete reversal in his thinking from just two years ago. The firm's largest-selling product, timbers for exposed beams, was a low-growth market. The timber segment, while having good margins, required an enormous amount of labor and investment to produce. Fifteen years ago, Simons had started distributing laminated beams, an engineered product that was often used as a timber substitute.

The laminated market had grown rapidly, and even with three local competitors, each company had been able to achieve average markups in the 30 to 40 percent range. Now four new competitors had entered the marketplace and at least one of them was selling based on a 15 percent markup. Bob Simons knew he wasn't making any money on laminated beams at these prices and expected no one else was either. Whereas a few years ago, he considered timber to be declining product and laminated beams to be a high-profit growth market, the ease of entry into the laminated beam business had caused him to rethink his product strategy. The timber business may be small, but his company was one of the few in it.

Over the years, Simons Lumber had been proud of its ability to fill any timber specification, regardless of length or size, and the firm's customers had become used to being able to buy one 4 × 6–40 [timber 4 inches thick by 6 inches wide and 40 feet in length] if that was what the job required. While Simons margins on this type of order were 50 percent or higher, the lower volume over the past three years made them less feasible in the future. As Bob explained, "On an order like a 4 × 6–40, we send two men down the yard on a $60,000 forklift to pick up a 8 × 12–40, bring it back to the mill where six men are required to mill it through two $150,000 machines, and then we put the finished piece in the shipment area, and return the unused piece to the inventory and hope we can sell it later. Basically, we are handling about 1,200 board feet of lumber, yet we are only billing out 80 board feet. Because we are pretty much a job-shop type of operation, we can't automate this process and no matter what our margins are on an order this small, it makes no economic sense anymore."

The fundamental change Simons was considering involved reducing the timber inventory from 16 lengths in 12 sizes down to 8 lengths in six smaller sizes. Furthermore, instead of buying rough-sawn timbers from a steadily dwindling number of suppliers, the company would buy surfaced lumber and then put a rough-sawn finish on the orders specifying it. In terms of inventory investment, the average dollar investment would be reduced by 60 percent and with less space required, the lumber yard could be located on a two-acre site rather than the current six-acre location. The total real estate investment would remain the same since the new location would possess covered warehouse space. Keeping the lumber under roof, instead of out in the weather as now done, would reduce inventory spoilage and improve the quality of the product.

Bob believed that the elimination of most remanufacturing and the reduction of the inventory would also reduce the yard labor costs by approximately 65 percent. While he estimated that timber sales would probably decline by as much as 15 percent, as some orders would now be unfillable, he also realized the consequences might be even more dramatic. For the past 30 years, large inventories and remanufacturing capabilities had been two of Simons Lumber's distinctive competencies and it was possible that his customers might be alienated by the new policy. "Giving up what worked in the past is very difficult," said Bob, "but this new policy could extend the profitability of the timber business for another 10 to 15 years. I think it is our only reasonable course of action for that segment of the business."

DIRECT SHIPPING AS A GROWTH ALTERNATIVE

Within a few days of the senior Simons' funeral, there occurred another event that directly impacted the lumber company. It was a discussion with one of Mr. Simons' old industry friends, Claude Fisher. Claude had stopped by the office to pay his respects to Bob, when the discussion turned to Claude's dissatisfaction with his current employer. Claude's background was in distributing southern pine and domestic hardwoods as a direct shipper, an area Simons had no expertise in. Bob and Claude tentatively talked about Claude joining Simons Lumber, and Claude seemed more than a little interested. The accounts that Claude would bring with him would more than pay his salary costs, and his joining would not only give Simons expertise with new products and suppliers, but Claude's presence would also add to the management depth at the company. The sticky issue was that Claude wanted some equity participation in the venture, and Bob did not want Simons Lumber stock held by nonfamily members.

As he pulled into the driveway of his home, Simons mentally reviewed the issues that he needed to focus on. First, he needed to resolve the conflict between Ann and Martha. He felt sure it was only a matter of time before this issue blew up again, and he wanted to be ready this time. Second was the decision on the possible LVL re-entry. Third, he needed to start analyzing the remanufacturing issue. It would take six to nine months to reduce his current inventory and find a suitable new location. Fourth, he needed to get back to Claude about joining forces.

The final issue was one that everyone in the company and the family had considered, but not discussed very much, and that was closing the whole business. While the company probably wouldn't sell for much above adjusted book value, in his lower moments, Simons occasionally thought that it may be time for the family to pick up the winnings it had made over three generations and walk away from the table. There were just so many major decisions that had to be made, and, realistically, Simons Lumber didn't have a surplus of talented managers that could help Bob with these decisions. While Bob had a list of rational reasons why this wasn't the time to consider selling, for every logical reason against selling Simons could enumerate, he also knew that the emotional reason was just as compelling. Like vultures, both acquaintances and strangers had been contacting him about his future plans for the business since his father's death, hoping to buy the business for a fraction of its value. He wanted to show them that Simons Lumber wasn't ready for the vultures yet.

APPENDIX A Simons Lumber Company Income Statement

	1989	1988	1987	1986
Sales				
Timber sales	$2,184,890	$2,562,143	$2,894,220	$2,013,160
Laminated beam sales	393,883	1,096,283	1,157,473	702,728
Decking sales	250,060	326,750	458,135	189,143
LVL sales	59,058	214,195	147,418	0
Total sales	$2,887,890	$4,199,370	$4,657,245	$2,905,030
Cost of Goods Sold				
Beginning inventory	$ 696,928	$ 805,343	$ 570,900	$ 635,328
Purchases	1,856,318	2,800,865	2,985,993	1,650,603
Goods available for sale	$2,553,245	$3,606,208	$3,556,893	$2,285,930
Less: ending inventory	603,848	696,928	805,343	570,900
Net cost of goods sold	$1,949,398	$2,909,280	$2,751,550	$1,715,030
Gross Profit	$ 938,493	$1,290,090	$1,905,695	$1,190,000
Yard Expenses				
Yard salaries	$ 291,603	$ 253,730	$ 282,983	$ 196,733
Yard payroll taxes	32,076	27,910	31,128	21,641
Group health insurance	41,380	30,388	25,768	23,125
Delivery expense	16,000	21,113	21,910	10,153
Electricity	18,528	23,428	21,483	14,413
Maintenance and repair	12,033	18,168	21,245	7,190
Gasoline and oil	15,600	16,085	20,705	16,588
Yard depreciation	9,460	9,460	9,495	8,500
Real estate taxes	12,780	12,380	11,933	11,908
Total yard expenses	$ 449,459	$ 412,660	$ 446,648	$ 310,248
Office Expenses				
Office salaries	$ 425,888	$ 464,100	$ 515,100	$ 340,575
Office payroll taxes	42,589	46,410	51,510	29,058
Group health insurance	23,083	17,363	14,693	10,000
Dues and subscriptions	8,315	10,880	6,343	4,755
Advertising	12,458	4,160	3,305	245
Telephone	26,125	33,188	36,475	20,803
Professional expenses	35,950	18,425	40,570	24,623
Office supplies	48,260	55,273	59,190	18,158
Contributions	0	10,000	13,555	0
Office rent	47,438	31,810	25,753	16,213
Insurance	67,268	75,883	75,533	42,785
Office depreciation	12,680	8,663	15,500	6,000
Other taxes	9,565	11,860	19,698	10,798
Total office expenses	$ 759,616	$ 788,013	$ 877,223	$ 524,010
Other Income				
Interest income	103,115	89,755	100,843	51,208
Life insurance proceeds	215,578	0	0	0
Net Income	$ 48,110	$ 179,172	$ 682,667	$ 406,949

APPENDIX B   Simons Lumber Company Balance Sheet

	1989	1988	1987	1986
Assets				
Cash	$ 424,228	$ 387,020	$ 447,815	$ 496,358
Marketable securities	1,364,500	625,000	750,000	750,000
Accounts receivable	80,278	193,418	245,298	242,348
Inventory	603,848	696,928	805,343	570,900
Notes receivable, officer	133,283	139,253	219,415	149,240
Prepaid taxes	9,793	2,763	4,443	0
Cash surrender value—Life insurance	137,045	659,143	621,185	563,618
Total current assets	$2,752,973	$2,703,523	$3,093,498	$2,772,463
Land	112,500	112,500	112,500	112,500
Buildings	108,775	108,775	108,775	108,775
Machinery and equipment	229,130	229,130	229,130	218,268
Office furniture and fixtures	157,453	132,930	132,930	94,390
Less: accumulated depreciation	(454,728)	(441,410)	(428,325)	(392,823)
	153,130	141,925	155,010	141,110
Total assets	$2,906,103	$2,845,448	$3,248,508	$2,913,573
Liabilities				
Accounts payable	$ 91,753	$ 18,365	$ 181,633	$ 72,093
Accrued expenses	73,650	55,725	79,940	26,443
Accrued salaries	4,988	17,125	39,500	37,498
Accrued profit sharing plan	0	30,000	56,250	40,000
Accrued corporate taxes	48,483	49,078	46,363	35,560
Total current liabilities	$ 218,873	$ 170,293	$ 403,685	$ 211,593
Long-term liabilities	0	0	0	0
Equity				
Common stock	244,500	244,500	244,500	244,500
Retained earnings	2,050,535	2,050,535	2,050,535	2,050,535
Accumulated adjustments	392,195	380,120	549,788	406,945
Total liabilities and equity	$2,906,103	$2,845,448	$3,248,508	$2,913,573

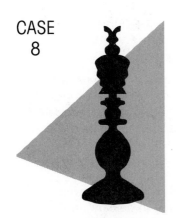

Wyndham Baking Company: Building a Cookie Company through Acquisitions

George C. Rubenson

BACKGROUND

"But why do you want to leave General Foods (GF) at all? As the General Manager of GF's new specialty cheese division, you've certainly done well. I'm sure there are still several nice promotions ahead for you. It seems like bailing out now to try and start a venture company is a very risky move."

Wyman Harris, tanned and fit at 44, gave the wheel of his beautiful new Bristol 38'8" a slight tug to starboard to get a better bite on the wind. It was a warm May afternoon and the wind on Long Island sound had picked up nicely. He thought for a few minutes about his old friend's question. At the time of his graduation from the Air Force Academy in 1963, his only thoughts were of a military career. When, as a young 1st lieutenant with less than five years' service, he was chosen for a plum assignment at the Pentagon, he had been convinced that his future was unlimited. But, after one year in Washington, it had become apparent that few nonflying officers ever became generals and, if they did, making it took years. He wanted to progress faster.

So, in 1969, when GF offered him a management trainee position at its White Plains, New York headquarters, he jumped at the chance. The 16 years since he left the Air Force had certainly been good. He had been on the fast track since the first day, holding numerous manufacturing positions at GF plants in New York, California, and Delaware. Management had twice brought him back to GF headquarters in White Plains. The first time he learned about corporate marketing as product manager for Jell-o puddings and was picked to attend Harvard Business School's Program for Management Development. Now, he was in charge of a major new specialty cheese division that he had created through the careful crafting of several domestic and foreign acquisitions. Integrating them was fun and he had several more possible acquisitions in mind.

But when the headhunter contacted him about a new food company that was being organized in Texas, it picqued his curiosity. Opportunities in a food giant like GF to operate in an entrepreneurial manner were few. Developing the cheese division was probably his only chance. If he stayed, what would the next 20 years hold? All of the exciting business unit positions were behind him. In the future he could expect vice president, group vice president, and executive vice president positions. In each, he would have less freedom, less authority, and less real control. After all, vice presidents didn't really operate anything and, as he knew from his own experience, SBU executives always tried to deal directly with the CEO when they could—not the vice-presidents. In the long run, if he was very fortunate, there might be one shot at the top job. But the chances seemed slim.

To Harris, the personal risk seemed small. He had built an impeccable record with GF. Experienced operations managers were always in demand in the food industry. Together with his corporate marketing experience and the acquisitions he had managed, it seemed clear that other excellent opportunities would always be available if this one soured.

COMPANY BEGINNINGS

In July 1985 Harris joined with Ian Wilson (formerly a vice chairman of Coca-Cola) and Ray Chung (formerly CFO of Colgate's Kendall unit) to build a new food company through acquisitions. Their basic philosophy was that a well-capitalized, professionally managed food company could offer existing smaller, proven, and well-managed food companies with additional opportunities for growth by providing capital, managerial expertise, and marketing resources. The first steps were to rent office space in Houston, Texas and give the new firm a name— Wyndham Foods, Inc.

The three executives were the perfect team to develop a new company through acquisitions. With his British background and many years of experience in Coca-Cola's international business, Wilson had contacts all over the world. Harris was the consummate judge of how well a company was operating and had first-hand experience in pulling together acquisition deals. Chung was the financial wizard who could uncover the smallest glitch in the balance sheet of an acquisition candidate.

During the latter half of 1985 the trio raised $35 million in equity commitments from institutional investors such as Mason Best (a Texas-based merchant bank), General Electric Pension Fund, Mutual of New York, and First Chicago, as well as from prominent families such as the Rockefellers and Crowns. Based on these commitments, four banks, led by Toronto-Dominion, agreed to serve as senior lenders, providing an additional $85-million line of credit. With this $120 million as a war chest, they set out to identify and purchase a group of core companies.

In January 1986, Wyndham made its first acquisition, Roush Bakery Products, a Cedar Rapids, Iowa company that makes bakery mixes for sale to wholesale bakers. These bakers sell their products using Roush trademarks such as Country Hearth, a brand name that sells more than 1 billion loaves a year. The second purchase in February was a New Orleans company called Zatarain's, which produces Cajun/creole foods such as crab boil, fish fry, various rice mixes, creole mustard, and other prepared foods. In March Wyndham acquired Shamitoff, a California company that manufactures frozen novelties.

Later that year, four baking companies were acquired. They included Plantation Baking Company of Chicago, the leading producer of packaged brownies; Jackson Cookie Company of Little Rock, Arkansas; Bishop Baking Company of Cleveland, Tennessee; and Greg's Cookies of Birmingham, Alabama. By the end of 1986, Wyndham could claim annual revenues of about $100 million.

In early 1987 the stock market soared and Wyndham's investors became convinced that the fledgling company could be sold quickly at a high premium. Thus, with First Boston acting as the investment banker, the company was placed on the market. Numerous investment groups bid for the company and an agreement was made to sell the firm for about $170 million. Unfortunately, the stock market crash on October 19, 1987 killed the deal before it was finalized.

BECOMING A FORCE IN THE COOKIE BUSINESS

Since market conditions for selling the firm were unfavorable in late 1987 and early 1988, management turned its attention to building the business. A review of the companies in Wyndham's portfolio revealed considerable diversity. For example, while the four baking companies fit nicely into one group, they had little in common with Roush, Zatarain's, or Shamitoff. Thus, in order to develop better focus, management decided to divest Zatarain's and Shamitoff and form a separate operating company within Wyndham Foods that could build the cookie business—*a strategic refocusing.*

As a step toward becoming a major force in the cookie business, in May 1988 Wyndham Foods set up a new company, Wyndham Baking Company, Inc., to operate the four baking companies and to purchase Murray Bakery Products, Inc. (formerly the cookie business of Beatrice Companies and the leading baker of Girl Scout cookies) of Augusta, Georgia for $170 million. This required a restructuring of the company's finances. Briefly, this entailed (1) repaying the original bank debt, (2) raising an additional $7 million in equity from the original investors, (3) establishing $127 million in senior bank debt with a group of banks led by Toronto-Dominion Bank, (4) providing for a $35-million revolving loan to be used for working capital, and (5) issuing $100 million in subordinated notes (commonly known as junk bonds) in a public offering.

As an important aside, while leveraged acquisitions and the junk bonds that make them possible have recently received considerable negative publicity, it is important to understand that, when used judiciously, such financing can permit the structuring of corporate building programs that work well with an acceptable level of risk. Regarding the Wyndham offering, Paine Webber, the investment banker for the Murray Cookie acquisition, called Wyndham Baking Company the best deal they have ever done. *Investment Age* named it the deal of the year. Characteristics of the business that were seen as positive included (1) it's a business that is fairly recession resistant, (2) it has stable cash flows, (3) good growth can be forecast with considerable confidence, (4) capital requirements are fairly low, and (5) there is little likelihood of technological obsolesence.

OPERATING THE COMPANY

Exhibit 1 depicts the group of regional competitors within Wyndham Baking Company's portfolio as of September 1988. Most of these companies are not new.

EXHIBIT 1 Locations of Regional Wyndham Baking Company Competitors

Products are distributed nationally under a number of brand names, which have attained strong regional maket shares.

Operating Locations

Birmingham, Alabama	Augusta, Georgia	Louisville, Kentucky	Charlotte, North Carolina
Little Rock, Arkansas	Marietta, Oklahoma	Lake Bluff, Illinois	Cleveland, Tennessee
		Cleveland, Ohio	

Their typical incorporation dates range in the 1930s and 1940s. But with the exception of Murray, most were relatively small ($10 to $40 million in revenues) and had limited resources compared to the giants of the industry such as Nabisco, Keebler, Sunshine, and Pepperidge Farm. The plan was to make them more competitive through (1) infusion of capital where needed, (2) improved management on a selective basis, and (3) intentional synergy whenever possible.

Strategy and Objectives

Wyndham's strategy has been to integrate and consolidate its operations and build upon its position as the leading supplier of popular-priced cookies in the United

States. In June 1988 the company established four objectives: (1) strengthen its market position in the popular-priced cookie market by coordinating the marketing functions of its cookie business, (2) increase sales and profitability by selectively increasing prices and by expanding the line of products it sells through its distribution channels, (3) increase profitability by combining similar operations and thereby reduce associated costs, and (4) increase sales productivity and generate cash by selling direct sales delivery (DSD) route franchises to independent operators.

Industry and Market Niche

Wyndham Baking Company is now the third largest cookie company in the United States and is the leading supplier to the popular-priced segment of the $3.7-billion domestic cookie market. Typical competitors include Interbake, Consolidated Biscuit, Mrs. Allison's Cookies, Ripon Foods, Delicious, and Mama's. Competition is fragmented and regionally focused with many companies producing under private labels for sale to grocery stores. The industry appears to be consolidating. Efficiencies gained by combining and adding to food distribution systems and the high costs of building brand names have spurred many mergers and acquisitions in the food industry. Following is a sampling of recent mergers within the industry:

Brand/Company	Acquired by	Date
Keebler	United Biscuit Holdings	1974
Mama's	Generale Biscuit	1981
Grandma's	PepsiCo/Frito Lay	1982
Midwest	Lance	1984
Nabisco	RJR	1986
Murray	Wyndham Baking	1988
Sunshine Biscuits, Inc.	G. F. Industries	1988

The popular-priced segment is characterized by products that are targeted at budget-conscious consumers and sell at retail prices that are significantly below those of the nationally advertised premium brands. For example, Wyndham's cookies sell for $.99 to $1.39 for a 16-ounce package while premium brands such as Nabisco or Keebler sell for $1.99 to $2.89 for a 16-ounce package.

Product Development

In the past year, Wyndham has launched three new products. First was Frookies. Frookies is a good-for-you cookie made with fruit juice instead of sugar. Frookie cookies are high in fiber, low in fat, and low in calories, and are aimed at the consumer interested in healthy eating. The second launch was Goldi's Honey Bears. This product is similar to Nabisco's Teddy Grahams, which was last year's most successful new product introduction. Finally, Wyndham introduced a line of Country Hearth cookies that are positioned as good-for-you, healthy cookies that are high in fiber, have no cholesterol, and are made without tropical oils. More Country Hearth cookie items are planned.

Marketing

Wyndham can provide lower-priced cookies with ingredients that are comparable to premium cookies because it does no media advertising. Instead, Wyndham depends on (1) the strength of its distribution system to get the products into the marketplace, (2) the presence of the products in the stores to get the initial trial (e.g., items such as Frito Lay chips and Tasty Kakes are often displayed prominently near the checkout), and (3) high quality at a budget price to generate the repeat business necessary to make the products successful.

Distribution

Distribution is an example of the synergies obtained. Currently, Wyndham has four separate methods of distribution: (1) vending distribution (Plantation began as a vending distributor and remains exceptionally strong), (2) broker sales (cookies are sold to supermarket chains through their warehouses), (3) Girl Scout distribution (some 2 million Girl Scouts deliver door to door), and (4) direct store delivery (DSD) using 700 trucks. When Wyndham Baking Company was formed, there were three overlapping direct store delivery systems. Now, all of the companies within Wyndham Baking share one DSD distribution system.

Additionally, the DSD route distributors have been turned into independent businessmen through the franchising of routes. In effect, Wyndham Baking Company sold the rights to distribute certain brands in specified territories to some 600 route drivers, who are now independent businessmen. They purchase cookies outright from Wyndham, which generates cash. Early statistics indicate that these new entrepreneurs are obtaining about a 10 percent volume increase over comparable company-owned distributors.

Employees

As of December 31, 1989, Wyndham had approximately 2,700 employees, approximately 1,200 of whom were members of the International Brotherhood of Teamsters Union; the Bakery and Confectionery Workers Union; the Bakery Drivers Union; or the Retail, Wholesale, and Department Store Union. The renewal of the company's contract with the Teamsters covering 700 employees at its Louisville, Kentucky facility was ratified in August 1988 for a three-year period. The number of employees at the company's facilities is generally stable, with the exception of seasonal Girl Scout cookie production. Management believes the company enjoys good relations with its employees.

Manufacturing Facilities

The company operates eight manufacturing facilities that are located primarily in the southeastern United States. Six are owned by the company and two are leased. The company also operates six distribution facilities and, as part of the direct delivery system, leases several miniwarehouses. Additional warehouse space is rented during the peak of the Girl Scout cookie season. The company operates a fleet of 80 tractors and 200 trailers, and uses additional contract and common carriers when needed.

MANAGEMENT

Wyndham Baking has never intended to provide operating management for the acquired companies. Instead, acquisition prospects are carefully analyzed for the quality of in-place management and considerable effort is expended to keep in-place managers on board. In fact, virtually all of the senior management people were still on board that were with the companies when they were acquired. For example, Plantation Baking Company was founded and owned by two brothers who had been running the company for 37 years. They simply considered selling the firm to Wyndham Baking and keeping their jobs to be a clever way to handle estate planning. According to Harris, "they now have a lot of money in the bank from selling the business and still run it like it was their own."

An organization chart is included as Exhibit 2. Biographical information regarding key officers and directors of Wyndham Baking Company are as follows.

The Officers (all are directors):

Ian R. Wilson (58). Mr. Wilson has been chairman and CEO of Wyndham Foods since its inception in 1985. He also holds the position of chairman and CEO of Wyndham Baking Company. Wilson has served as president and CEO of Castle and Cooke, Inc., a food and real estate concern, from January 1983 to December 1984. Before joining Castle and Cooke, Wilson spent 25 years with the Coca-Cola Company, most recently as a vice chairman. Wilson serves as a director on the boards of Astrop Advisory Corporation, Wilson Bottling Corporation, Plexus, Inc., and the OTC-100 Fund.

Wyman C. Harris (49). Mr. Harris served as executive vice president and COO of Wyndham Foods since its inception in 1985. Upon the formation of Wyndham Baking Company, he relinquished his positions with Wyndham Foods in order to assume the role of president, COO, and director of the new corporation. Prior to joining Wyndham Foods, Mr. Harris was employed by General Foods Company for 16 years, where he most recently led the development and execution of the company's specialty cheese division. In that capacity, Mr. Harris acquired several companies and served as their chairman and president. Other positions held at General Foods included operations manager of the Birds Eye Division, plant manager of General Foods' largest food plant, and product manager of Jell-o puddings. Mr. Harris received a bachelor of science from the U.S. Air Force Academy in 1963 and a Master of Science in Industrial Engineering from Purdue University in 1965. He attended the Harvard Business School Program for Management Development (PMD).

Ray Chung (40). Mr. Chung has served as vice president, chief financial officer, treasurer, and director of Wyndham Foods since its inception in 1985. He

EXHIBIT 2 Organization Chart

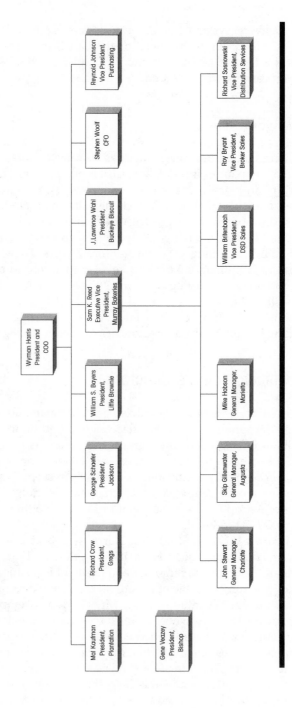

holds the same positions within Wyndham Baking Company. Prior to joining Wyndham, Mr. Chung served as vice president—finance of the Kendall Company, a health care supply company, from May 1984 to September 1985, and as vice president of Riviana Foods, Inc., from May 1981 to May 1984.

William G. Bayers (51). Mr. Bayers has been employed by Murray since 1963. In February 1985 he was appointed executive vice president of the company and holds the same position within Wyndham Baking. Bayers manages the company's Girl Scout operations and is general manager of the company's Louisville, Kentucky, bakery.

James J. Cairns, Jr. (52). Mr. Cairns joined Murray as executive vice president in February 1985 and continues to hold that position within Wyndham Baking. From 1973 to 1984 he served as vice president of finance and administration of Arnold Bakeries, Inc. and Orowheat Foods Company. From August 1984 to February 1985 Mr. Cairns was a private consultant.

Sam K. Reed (40). Mr. Reed joined Murray in 1986 and was appointed executive vice president and general manager of the company's Augusta, Georgia bakery in 1987, positions he continues to hold within Wyndham Baking. From 1984 to 1986, he was general manager of Quaker Oats' rice cake operations. Reed was employed by Orowheat Foods Company in various senior management positions from 1974 to 1984, including as general manager of the Hawaii operation and as regional vice president in charge of operations in northern California and the Pacific Northwest.

Outside directors include the following:

James S. Crown (35). Mr. Crown is general partner, Henry Crown and Company.

Donald E. Nickleson (55). Mr. Nickleson is president, Paine Webber Group, Inc.

Andrew H. Tisch (38). Mr. Tisch is president, Bulova Corporation.

Julie A. Wrigley (40). Ms. Wrigley is attorney-at-law and manager of Wrigley Estates.

FINANCIAL RESULTS

Exhibit 3 presents a pro forma statement of operations for 1987, the year that Wyndham Baking Company was formed. Included are data for (1) the cookie group of Wyndham Foods (shown as Old Wyndham), (2) Murray Bakery Products, Inc., (3) adjustments expected as a result of the acquisition, and (4) the proposed consolidated Wyndham Baking Company. As can be seen, while both companies are profitable prior to the acquisition, the projected operating costs, loan interest, and other expenses that result from combining the companies result in an expected one-time loss of almost $10 million. However, for Wyndham Baking Company, the important question for the future (as is true for any leveraged buyout) is whether it can develop the cash flows needed to meet operating costs and future loan payments without selling any pieces of the company.

Exhibit 4 presents summary financial data for 1987 and 1988 on a pro forma basis for the merged companies and actual data for 1989. Also included are

EXHIBIT 3   Pro Forma Consolidated Statement of Operations,
Year Ended December 31, 1987 (unaudited)

	Wyndham Baking Company, Inc. (Old Wyndham)	Murray Bakery Products, Inc. Pro Forma	Adjustments	Pro Forma Consolidated
Net sales	$64,697,000	$202,242,000		$266,939,000
Cost of goods sold	(43,448,000)	$136,749,000)	$ 343,000	(179,854,000)
Gross profit	$21,249,000	$ 65,493,000	$ 343,000	$ 87,085,000
Selling, distribution, and administrative expenses	(11,802,000)	(50,809,000)	(60,000)	(62,671,000)
Amortization of intangibles	(1,807,000)	(1,397,000)	(3,107,000)	(6,311,000)
Operating income	$ 7,640,000	$ 13,287,000	$ (2,824,000)	$ 18,103,000
Other income (expenses)				
Interest expense	(5,268,000)	(5,497,000)	(17,686,000)	(28,451,000)
Interest income	108,000	254,000		362,000
Other	30,000	74,000		104,000
Income (loss) before income taxes	$ 2,510,000	$ 8,118,000	$(20,510,000)	$ (9,882,000)
Provision for income taxes	(2,042,000)	(4,184,000)	6,226,000	—
Net income (loss)	$ 468,000	$ 3,934,000	$(14,284,000)	$ (9,882,000)
Ratio of earnings to fixed charges	1.5			(K)

projections for 1990 to 1993. From an operating point of view, it appears that financial aspects of the merger were well thought-out. For 1989 (1) revenues are growing at a rate of about 6 percent, (2) cash flow is steadily improving, (3) return on sales (before interest, taxes, and amortization of good will) is 11.9 percent, and (4) the firm's current ratio stands at 1.8, indicating a good level of liquidity.

However, for 1989 Wyndham Baking's leveraging (total debt/total assets) stands at .91. While this is certainly high enough to warrant close attention, it is not unusually high for a leveraged acquisition and Wyndham projects a reasonable plan for retiring it. Still, if we assume the figures for interest service on debt for 1989 (which are not available) are similar to those in the 1987 statement of operations shown in Exhibit 3 ($28.5 million), the 1989 profits (EBITA) would shrink from $35 million to $6.5 million (still before taxes and amortization of goodwill), or about 2 percent of sales. [See Exhibit 5.]

Nevertheless, management was quite pleased. In a speech, Harris noted that, compared to 1988: (1) 1989 sales were up 10 percent, (2) profits were up 40 percent, and (3) management had begun the process of paying down the debt. Additionally, $5 million in capital expenditures are planned for 1990, mostly for capacity expansion and cost reduction projects. Six hundred new computers will go on the DSD trucks so that each driver will be able to automatically make the

EXHIBIT 4   Wyndham Baking Company, Inc. Summary Financial Data
for Fiscal Years Ending December 31 ($millions)

	Historical			Projected		
	1987[a]	**1988**[b]	**1989**	**1990**	**1991**	**1992**
Income Statement						
Net sales	$266.9	$278.7	$295.0	$326.4	$350.0	$375.0
Gross profit	87.1	88.7	94.4	109.3	117.1	126.0
EBITA[c]	25.5	27.5	35.0	44.1	48.4	53.2
Funds Statement						
Operating cash flow[d]	$ 25.2	$ 28.6	$ 40.8	$ 49.1	$ 48.8	$ 53.4
Depreciation	4.3	4.7	4.6	4.8	5.0	5.2
Amortization	6.3	6.0	5.4	5.6	5.8	6.0
Capital expenditures	4.6	3.6	4.0	4.2	4.6	5.0
Balance Sheet						
Current assets	$ 10.9	$ 65.2	$ 69.3	$ 72.7	$ 76.7	$ 80.6
Property, plant, and equipment, net	13.1	53.9	53.3	52.7	52.3	52.1
Total assets	73.3	300.0	292.2	284.0	280.9	277.7
Current liabilities[e]	6.0	59.3	61.6	65.1	68.1	71.0
Long-term debt[f]	50.3	211.9	203.5	188.2	175.6	159.0
Net worth	16.4	30.4	28.8	32.4	38.9	49.4
Key Statistics						
Gross margin	32.6%	31.8%	32.0%	33.5%	33.5%	33.6%
Operating margin	9.1	9.9	11.9	13.5	13.8	14.2

[a]Operating figures for 1987 are pro forma for the acquisition of Murray; 1987 balance sheet figures do not reflect the Murray acquisition.
[b]Results for 1988 are pro forma for the acquisition of Murray.
[c]Earnings before interest, taxes, amortization of goodwill, and holding company charge. Holding company charge approximates $1 million annually and covers rent for San Francisco offices of holding company and chairman's salary, both of which would not be included in acquisition.
[d]Operating cash flow is defined as EBITA + Depreciation − Capital Expenditures + Route Sale Proceeds.
[e]Excludes current portion of long-term debt.
[f]Includes all funded debt, capitalized leases, and $5 million permanent component of revolver.

order and print out the invoice on the spot, improving inventory control and further reducing labor requirements.

FUTURE OUTLOOK

As of April 1990, Wyndham Baking was back on the market. Management believes the company should bring about $330 million. Numerous inquiries had been made by investor groups interested in making a bid for the company. Unfortunately, the price for which the firm can be sold may be negatively affected for several reasons: (1) the merger/buyout fever of the 1980s appears to be cooling and there are fewer

EXHIBIT 5 Historical and Projected Operating Results ($millions)

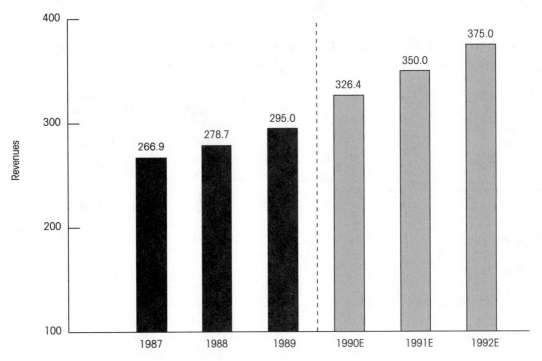

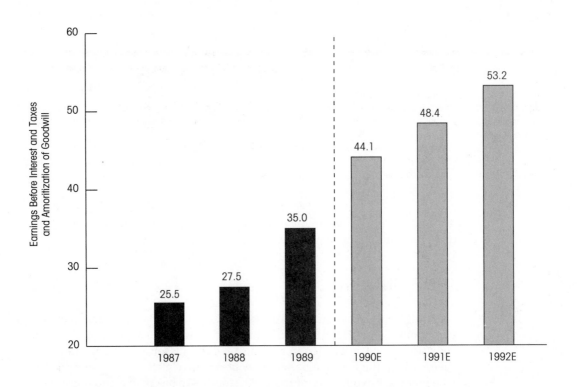

bidders than there would have been, (2) the junk bond market has been seriously damaged by a lack of investor confidence as a result of the apparent excesses of various investment companies, and (3) the economy has cooled off and investment money in general is harder to come by.

Since Wyndham Baking was originally organized as an alternative investment strategy for investors seeking higher-than-average return on investors' funds, holding the company too long can be a potential problem. For one thing, the quicker the company is sold, the greater the likelihood that the real and promised improvements and other synergies will be seen as increased value, resulting in high bids. Additionally, as time passes, the depressing effect of the heavy interest payments on profitability may tend to erode the firm's image and, as the company continues to grow, it will be harder to produce further improvements that will keep the company's value, and thus the investors' money, growing at a higher-than-average rate.

As the warm spring sun stretched across his desk in what had once been Murray Bakery Products' main offices in Augusta, Harris contemplated the options that were available. While the investors were clearly eager to sell Wyndham, it would make no sense to accept a fire-sale price. The firm was well-structured and consisted of excellent units. Cash flow was strong, profits were improving, and the company was well-positioned to produce excellent future results. One possibility that hadn't been fully explored was seeking a foreign buyer. But, if that didn't work out, a strategic plan for operating the firm would clearly be needed.

EPILOGUE

On August 2, 1990, Wyndham Baking Company, Inc., was sold. As part of the deal, Harris was given a contract to remain as CEO for 4½ years. In their early discussions with Harris, it was clear that the new owners wanted to continue to build the company. What should Harris recommend to them? Should Wyndham continue to concentrate on cookies? If it does, should it focus on developing its current holdings? Is it in a position to seek out other promising acquisitions? Can it compete successfully as a single-product company against the giants of the bakery industry such as Nabisco and General Foods? Would a careful program of diversification significantly improve the company's potential?

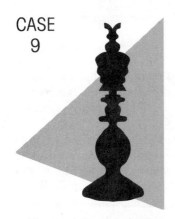

CASE
9

PIER 1 IMPORTS, INC.

MARK KROLL, JIM FRIERSON & FRED JACOBSON

INTRODUCTION

Clark Johnson moves uneasily in his seat on the airplane. Down below, patches of greens and browns extend into the never-ending horizon. A string made of silver and blue appears to divide the fields underneath. "It has to be the Mississippi," his mind wanders for a few seconds from his thoughts about the company, as the airplane continues its course toward the Dallas/Fort Worth Airport. The papers and charts on the table bring his thoughts back to the future of the firm.

Clark is chairman of the board and chief executive officer (CEO) for Pier 1 Imports, and he has just met with several investment bankers considering the possibility of issuing new stock to help finance an aggressive expansion program now under consideration. Pier 1 operates approximately 500 stores as of mid-1989, and plans to reach a corporate goal of 1,000 by the year 2000. The company imports almost all of its goods from overseas, primarily from the Pacific Rim countries, with about 23 percent coming from China.

In recent years, the company has enjoyed above-average sales growth. This sales growth, coupled with what many believe is excellent corporate management, has resulted in a strong financial position.

As the 1990s begin, the company faces a number of important issues. The recent upheaval in China has depressed the market price of Pier 1's publicly traded stock. Another important issue is whether the company has the necessary means to develop its distribution system and its managerial staff to handle the proposed 1,000-store operation.

Also, Pier 1's target market is another concern. The company has done extensive marketing research and identified its customer base. Consequently, Pier 1's product lines were modified to fit its customers' needs. Would this target market change?

Profits are above average for the industry. The company is doing well. "The time to make a move is now," he thought. A sudden deceleration was felt. The "Fasten Your Seat Belt" sign came on. Finally, the aircraft began its approach into the Dallas/Fort Worth area.

This case was prepared under the Department of Management and Marketing, University of Texas at Tyler.

IMPORTANT FACTS ABOUT PIER 1
Location

At first glance Fort Worth, Texas may seem an unlikely place to headquarter North America's leading specialty retailer of decorative home furnishings. After all, most people would imagine that a worldwide importer of unique merchandise would locate perhaps in New York City, not Fort Worth. The company occupies six floors in the prestigious Bass Towers in the City Center Two complex located in downtown Fort Worth.

Pier 1 operates approximately 500 retail stores in 37 states and three Canadian provinces and franchises approximately 50 retail stores in 26 states. The stores are located near large shopping malls. They lease or own eight major distribution centers. Most of these centers have recently been upgraded to handle the increasing volume.

Size—Sales Employees

In 1989 sales totaled approximately $414.6 million. The company employs over 7,500 people: 500 full-time employees at the home office, 4,400 part-time employees in its retail stores and distribution centers, and approximately 2,600 full-time sales employees. A typical Pier 1 store contains about 1,000 square feet and carries between 12,000 and 14,000 different items. About 8,000 of these products, called stock keeping units (SKUs), are offered on a continuous basis. The remainder are seasonal or opportunistic buys.

Product

Pier 1 offers four major types of merchandise: decorative home furnishings (approximately 37 percent), wicker and rattan furniture (approximately 20 percent), housewares and kitchen goods (approximately 12 percent), and specialty clothing and seasonal items (approximately 20 percent).

Decorative home furnishings are imported from approximately 40 countries and include furniture made from pine, beech, rubber wood, and selected hardwoods. This category also includes brass items, lamps, window covering, bedspreads, pillows, vases, and numerous other decorative items, most of which are handcrafted from natural materials.

Wicker and rattan furniture, primarily used in dens, sun rooms, and casual dining areas, is obtained from Taiwan, Hong Kong, China, the Philippines, and Indonesia. These goods are handcrafted from natural fibers including rattan, buri, and willow, and have either natural or painted finishes.

Housewares and kitchen goods include fine items, ceramics, dinnerware, and other functional and decorative products. They are brought from India, the Far East, and Europe.

Clothing items are shipped from India, Greece, and Indonesia. They are primarily women's specialty clothing made from cotton and other natural fibers.

Of the merchandise Pier 1 imports, approximately 22.7 percent comes from China, 17.9 percent comes from India, 18.5 percent comes from Taiwan, and another 15.1 percent comes from Hong Kong, Japan, Thailand, and the Philippines. The remaining 25.8 percent is not only imported from various Asian, European, Central American, South American, and African countries, but also obtained from U.S. manufacturers, wholesalers, and importers.

Target Market

The customer base has evolved from the flower children of the 1960s to the baby boomers of the 1980s. Pier 1 implemented an extensive marketing research operation after changing from its in-house advertising department to the Richards Group, a premier Dallas advertising agency. This agency began a series of focus group interviews followed by a random sample of 8,150 regular customers (Edmondson, 1986). Today, Pier 1 has a 1,500 member advisory board that answers four questionnaires a year.

These surveys show that over 50 percent of Pier 1's customers are college graduates, and another 30 percent have some college education. The average household of the Pier 1 customer base earns over $38,000 a year. Approximately 88 percent of Pier 1 customers are women, 65 percent of whom are between the ages of 25 and 44 (*Chain Store Age Executive*, 1986). This group should continue to be a very desirable customer base.

AN AMERICAN SUCCESS STORY
The Beginning

Pier 1 began as a rattan furniture wholesaler that opened as a single Cost Plus store to liquidate excess inventory. In 1962 Charles Tandy, a Fort Worth businessman and founder of Radio Shack stores, obtained the rights to open and operate stores under the Cost Plus name. In 1965, the name was changed to Pier 1 Imports when the business had grown to 16 locations. In early 1966 Tandy sold Pier 1 to a group of 30 investors led by Luther Henderson, now a member of the board of directors. By 1969 when the company went public, the chain consisted of 42 stores. In 1970 Pier 1 began trading on the American Stock Exchange, and in 1977 moved to the New York Stock Exchange. By this time, Pier 1 had 123 stores with a sales growth of 100 percent in four years.

In the 1960s, Pier 1 served a very specific customer group. This was the era of the flower children, and Pier 1 provided their incense, sandals, and love beads. The personnel of Pier 1 reflected their clients' fashions: long hair and casual attire.

In 1973, worldwide inflation coupled with deregulated exchange rates radically increased the cost of foreign-made goods. To further complicate matters, the retail chains began to stock many of the goods that were previously only offered by Pier 1. In the mid-1970s Pier 1 mounted several reorganization campaigns to enhance its performance capabilities. By 1977 the firm had grown to 280 stores, and in 1979 one store in Detroit achieved, for the first time in the history of the company, $1 million in sales. That same year Pier 1 merged with Cousins Mortgage and Equity Investments, creating a company with three subsidiaries. In 1983 Intermark, a California-based holding company located in La Jolla, purchased a controlling interest in Pier 1. By 1985 the current management team headed by Clark Johnson was formed and the other subsidiaries were sold. Since that time, sales have grown from $173.5 million to $414.6 million in 1989, which represents a 23-percent annual growth rate (see following table).

Net Sales ($millions)

1984	1985	1986	1987	1988	1989
$147.3	$173.5	$203.9	$262.3	$327.2	$414.6

Source: Pier 1 Annual Report 1989.

While expanding the number of stores from 300 to 500, Johnson and his team also closed unproductive stores and kept sales per square foot of store space constant. The firm has also not had to sacrifice gross profit margins in order to generate sales. Gross profits have continued to average better than 50 percent throughout the firm's period of rapid growth. Consequently, last year's net profit margin of 5.2 percent was slightly above the industry average.

PRESENT SITUATION

Pier 1 is confronted with numerous issues which keep reminding management of the inevitable interrelationship between the company's strengths and weaknesses and the environment. Furthermore, the international nature of the business exposes the company to a wide array of opportunities and threats. Following is a description of those external and internal factors that have a bearing on the firm.

External Factors

The external environment presents a number of opportunities and threats in both the domestic and international arenas. Internationally, the European Economic Community (EEC) will form a new common market in 1992. Many U.S. firms are establishing operations in the European market now because of the anticipated restrictions on entering it after 1992. This market, comprised of 320 million people, will be the largest integrated market in the world. Pier 1 expertise in international trade and import would be a significant strength if Pier 1 decides to pursue that market.

A number of countries with which Pier 1 deals are heavily indebted. The urge to acquire hard currencies to pay their debts has led to establishing incentive plans to promote exports. This is the case for many Asian and South American countries. For example, Colombia, after experiencing decreases in its export receipts, has developed aggressive export promotion policies (Business Latin America, 1986), particularly of nontraditional products. Some of these nontraditional products fit the Pier 1 product profile. Therefore, such countries may offer an opportunity for Pier 1.

Because China provides approximately 23 percent of Pier 1's products, political stability of this country is critical to Pier 1. Recent actions taken by the Chinese government to stop a democratic movement may affect the business environment in which the company has operated for the last 12 years. Although the United States government has not formally restricted trade with China, the possibility still exists with respect to future Chinese governmental actions. However, of the percentage that is imported from China, "more than 90 percent of these items can be purchased from other countries where Pier 1 already does business" (Drexel Burnham Lambert, 1989).

Another important supplier of goods to Pier 1 is Hong Kong, which is scheduled to be returned to China by Great Britain in 1997. Under the current agreement, China will allow Hong Kong to retain much of its political and economic autonomy for a period of 50 years.

As an importer of all of its products, Pier 1 is affected by the Omnibus Trade and Competitiveness Act. Among the many provisions of this law, "Super 301" targeting countries that systematically use unfair trade practices is seen as one of the most important. The effects of this legislation could be restrictions of the goods imported and sold by Pier 1.

The company competes for consumers' discretionary dollars with other specialty retailers offering similar lines of merchandise such as department stores (J. C. Penney, Dillard's, Sears) and discount stores (Wal-Mart, Target, Kmart). For example, analysts describe the Sears factor, which refers to Sears' new lower-price strategy as a potential threat. If Sears can attract new customers, incremental sales will be taken away from other stores.

World Bazaar is the only specialty retailer similar to Pier 1. This competitor operates a small chain of stores in the southeast United States. There is also a significant number of single-store entrepreneurs offering a product line similar to that of Pier 1.

Additionally, Pier 1 competes with import wholesalers and other major retailers in the acquisition of merchandise abroad. Unlike the retailers of domestically produced merchandise, Pier 1's retail operation is subject to risks associated with its imported products. Some of these risks include:

1. Need to order merchandise from four to twelve months in advance of delivery and to pay for such merchandise at such time by letter of credit
2. Dock strikes
3. Fluctuations in currency values and exchange rates
4. Restrictions on the convertibility of the dollar and other currencies, and duties
5. Taxes and other charges on imports
6. Import quota systems and restrictions generally placed on foreign trade

Internal Factors

There are a number of internal issues confronting Pier 1, including financial position, management and personnel, marketing and advertising, and distribution. Pier 1 enters the 1990s as a strongly capitalized and financially sound firm. The 1989 fiscal year ended with net earnings from operation of $21.9 million, up 36 percent from net earnings a year earlier of $16.1 million. Earnings per share were 70 cents, up 34.6 percent from 52 cents from the prior years. Also reported were record total sales of $414.6 million, which represented a 26.7-percent increase from a year earlier. These results leave the company with an attractive return on equity (ROE) of 20.6 percent (Pier 1 Annual Report, 1989). However, adding another 500 stores in 10 years will require tremendous financial resources.

Pier 1 directors and top management are an experienced group of team players who have collectively guided the affairs of the company to its present financial position. They have been responsible not only for successfully guiding it to its present position, but also for establishing the future direction of the company. Here too, however, the question has been asked whether the team can manage 1,000 stores as successfully as it has 500.

The board of directors is guided by Clark A. Johnson, who serves as chairman and chief executive officer. [See Exhibit 1.] He previously served as president of the company and is largely credited with the company's recent success. Under his leadership, the company sold its unprofitable subsidiaries and increased sales. In addition, under Johnson's leadership, the company's goal of a 500-store chain was accomplished.

The vice chairman of the board of directors is Charles R. Scott. He is president and CEO of Intermark, Inc., a diversified operating/holding company and Pier 1's largest shareholder. Another director who also plays an important role

EXHIBIT 1 Organizational Chart

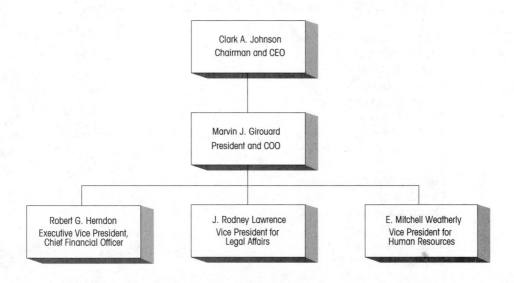

in the company's management is Marvin Girouard. He is the company's current president and chief operating officer. Formally, the vice president of merchandising, Girouard's efforts helped change the image and style of the stores. In addition, he is responsible for the plan to upgrade the stores' product line to include more collectibles and household items. In his present position, he directs the day-to-day operations of the corporation and is responsible for the company's financial performance. Luther Henderson is founding chairman of the company. He has been with the company since 1966 and served as president of the company between December 1979 and September 1983. Lawrence P. Klamon has been a director of the company since March 1983, and was vice president during 1982 and 1983. Presently, he is president and CEO of Fuqua Industries, and also serves as director of Advanced Telecommunication Corporation. Sally F. McKenzie has been a director of the company since November 1985. She has served as civic leader on a local, regional, and national basis for over five years. Thomas N. Warner has been a director and chairman of the executive committee of Intermark since 1975.

Pier 1's board of directors is backed up by the rest of the executive management team. This team includes, in addition to Clark Johnson and Marvin Girouard, Thomas A. Christopher, executive vice president and former vice president of operations. He has been with the company since 1980. Robert G. Herndon is the chief financial and administrative officer for the company, a position he has held since 1985. He is largely responsible for the provision of capital, as well as maintaining appropriate relationships with banks and other financial institutions. E. Mitchell Weatherly, vice president of human resources, tends to the needs of Pier 1's employees. This management group works closely with the board of directors and is responsible for implementing and controlling the strategic plans developed jointly by the board and management.

Successive years of increasing sales and earnings have demonstrated management's ability to guide Pier 1. Exhibit 2 presents the board of directors'

EXHIBIT 2 Board of Directors' Stock Ownership

Shares of Common Stock Held

Clark A. Johnson	489,138
Charles R. Scott	47,912
Marvin J. Girouard	244,907
Luther A. Henderson	122,246
Lawrence P. Klamon	48,544
Sally F. McKenzie	23,941
Thomas N. Warner	58,023

Executive Cash Compensation

Clark L. Johnson	$810,000
Marvin J. Girouard	412,250
Thomas A. Christopher	348,000
Robert G. Herndon	331,500
E. Mitchell Weatherly	135,725

Source: Pier 1 Proxy Statement for Annual Meeting of Shareholders, May 18, 1989, pp. 3, 5.

common stock holdings and management compensation. It is worth noting that Charles Scott, a member of the board, is also CEO of Intermark, Pier 1's controlling shareholder, which means controlling interest in Pier 1 is represented on the board.

Shortly after joining the firm, Johnson and the Richards Group adopted an intense marketing research program. This effort resulted in a clearly defined customer profile and suggested new methods of reaching them. These methods include enhancing the current advertising efforts and adding new media. Pier 1 adopted a slicker advertisement copy to reach their more affluent customers and incorporated magazine and television ads to supplement their weekly print advertising (Fischer, 1988). "The company anticipates that television advertising will create double-digit increases over and above the increases normally seen during that period" (Montgomery Securities, 1989). Pier 1 has tried television advertising before (1975 to 1977), but now feels there is a large enough store base in metropolitan markets to be cost effective. "The company has increased its advertising effectiveness through improved creative execution and media placement and thus has been able to reduce the advertising-to-sales ratio, without reducing the impact of its advertising" (Montgomery Securities, 1989).

In order to maintain the orderly flow of merchandise, Pier 1 relies on its modern distribution centers. These centers are strategically located by region and provide the traditional functions of receiving, sorting, storing, and delivering (Transportation and Distribution, 1988). The distribution centers are a critical element in the continued success of Pier 1 as it attempts to expand to 1,000 store-objective by the year 2000. Pier 1 has four leased and four owned distribution centers. (Exhibit 3 describes their locations and sizes.)

Typically, buyers for Pier 1 are people promoted from the retail store operation who know their clients' wants and needs. Buyers are led by Marvin Girouard in their worldwide search for products. This intensive search has taken Girouard over 33 times to China since his first visit in 1977 (Fischer, 1988). This group combs the world to import products suitable for their clientele.

The products are shipped by air and sea from over 60 countries. Some products, such as clothing, are exclusively shipped by air to take advantage of their

EXHIBIT 3 Distribution Centers

Location	Facility Size (approximate square feet)
Rancho Cucamonga, California	419,010[a]
Fort Worth, Texas	104,000[b]
Fort Worth, Texas	459,868[a]
Chicago, Illinois	297,552[a]
Chicago, Illinois	102,000[b]
Savannah, Georgia	393,216[a]
Montreal, Quebec, Canada	104,000[b]
Baltimore, Maryland	252,358[b]

[a]Owned.
[b]Leased.
Source: Pier 1 10K report, 1989, p. 14.

inherent, lightweight characteristics, which minimizes inventory by getting the product to market sooner and meeting seasonal demands.

The major points of entry into the United States are Rancho Cucamonga, California; Savannah, Georgia; and Fort Worth, Texas. Subsequently, these imported and domestic purchases are delivered to the distribution centers, unpacked, and made available for shipment to the various stores in the center's regions. The merchandise is then distributed to the retail stores by company-owned trucks and contract carriers (approximately half and half). Because of the long shipping times involved, a high inventory level is required at these distribution centers.

STRATEGIC ISSUES

As Clark Johnson continues his reflection on the future of Pier 1, he concludes there are two sources of strategic issues confronting the firm: the ambitious expansion program and the securing of product sources from foreign markets. Following is a brief description of these issues as Johnson sees them.

Expansion Program

The goal of doubling its size in the next 10 years will require extensive development of Pier 1's distribution, data processing, and sales management as well as developing the capital to accomplish these goals. Currently, Pier 1 enjoys strong same-store sales and an experienced, successful marketing team. The strategic issues result from the growth process itself and requires the development of the appropriate management systems. Despite Pier 1's success, competitors entering this unique and profitable marketplace cannot be ignored. Pier 1 has the ability to enter the market with such penetration that it can discourage competitors, but not completely. However, the expertise that the company has gained in international procurement is not only hard to develop, but can only be achieved through experience. However, even with no new competition, good store locations will be harder and harder to identify.

Product Sources

The other strategic issue deals with the securing of quality products on a dependable basis at an acceptable price. The lack of control over foreign events leaves the company vulnerable to face disruptions in product availability. The significant amount of products imported from China may require the establishment of some alternative product sources if the Chinese or United States government, for whatever reason, restrict trade. Also, if the expansion of distribution outlets is successful, the volume of purchases may exceed some suppliers' capacities.

APPENDIX A Pier 1 Imports, Inc. Financial Highlights ($millions, except per-share amounts)

	1989	Change	1988	Change	1987
For the year					
Net sales	$414.6	26.7%	$327.2	24.7%	$262.3
Gross margin	217.5	27.6	170.5	25.4	136.0
Operating expenses	175.6	26.2	139.1	25.2	111.1
Income before income taxes	31.9	37.5	23.2	8.9	21.3
Net income	21.9	36.0	16.1	34.2	12.0
Earnings per share of common stock	$0.70	34.6%	$0.52	26.8%	$0.41
Return on average equity	20.6%	9.6%	18.8%	(3.6)%	19.5%
At year end					
Common shares and equivalents outstanding (millions)	30.7	—	30.6	5.5%	29.0[a]
Number of employees	7,306	12.5%	6,493	44.3	4,500
Number of stores	450	13.6	396	13.1	350
Retail square feet (millions)	3.1	14.8	2.7	17.4	2.3

[a]Adjusted for stock split.
Source: 1989 Pier 1 Imports Annual Report, p. 1.

APPENDIX B Pier 1 Imports, Inc. Consolidated Statement of Operations ($000, except per-share amounts)

	Years Ended in February		
	1989	1988	1987
Net Sales	$414,646	$327,226	$262,297
Costs and expenses			
Cost of goods sold	$197,138	$156,753	$126,297
Selling, general, and administrative expenses	162,994	130,235	104,762
Depreciation and amortization	11,452	8,826	6,299
Interest expense, net	10,022	8,194	3,662
Credit card costs, net	1,120	—	—
	$382,726	$304,008	$241,020
Income before income taxes	$ 31,920	$ 23,218	$ 21,277
Provision for income taxes	(10,070)	(7,143)	(9,307)
Net income	$ 21,850	$ 16,075	$ 11,970
Cumulative dividends on preferred stock	250	250	—
Net income available to common stockholders	$ 21,600	$ 15,825	$ 11,970
Per common share	$ 0.70	$ 0.52	$ 0.41

APPENDIX C Pier 1 Imports, Inc. Financial Summary[a] ($millions, except per-share amounts)

	5-Year Compound Annual Growth Rate	Years Ended in February					
		1989	1988	1987	1986	1985	1984
Earnings							
Net sales	23.0%	$414.6	$327.2	$262.3	$203.9	$173.5	$147.3
Gross margin	24.5	217.5	170.5	136.0	101.0	82.8	72.6
Selling, general, and administrative expenses	24.0	163.0	130.3	104.8	78.3	65.8	55.7
Depreciation	30.0	11.5	8.8	6.3	3.9	3.1	3.1
Interest, net	28.1	10.0	8.2	3.6	3.6	3.0	2.9
Credit card costs, net		1.1	—	—	—	—	—
Earnings before income taxes	24.0	31.9	23.2	21.3	15.2	10.9	10.9
Earnings for common shareholders	35.1	21.6	15.8	12.0	8.6	5.9	4.8
Common share results (adjusted for stock splits)							
Net earnings	28.5	$ 0.70	$ 0.52	$ 0.41	$ 0.34	$ 0.25	$ 0.20
Cash dividends declared		0.09	0.06	0.02	0.01	—	—
Shareholders' equity	25.1	3.77	3.08	2.57	1.90	1.42	1.23
Weighted average number of shares outstanding (millions)	5.2	30.7	30.6	29.0	25.5	24.2	23.8
Other financial data							
Working capital	24.9	$117.2	$ 87.2	$ 96.8	$ 43.4	$ 38.6	$ 38.5
Current ratio		2.9	2.3	3.3	2.4	3.5	4.4
Total assets	34.8	299.9	257.9	218.3	106.6	76.5	67.4
Long-term debt	35.2	121.3	96.5	101.5	26.7	26.7	26.9
Shareholders' equity	31.6	115.8	94.1	74.4	48.5	34.3	29.3
Tax rate		31.5%	30.8	43.7	43.2	46.0	51.2
Return on common shareholders' average equity		20.6	18.8	19.5	20.8	18.6	22.5
Return on average total assets		7.7	6.6	7.4	9.4	8.2	7.8
Pre-tax return on sales		7.7	7.1	8.1	7.5	6.3	7.4

[a]This financial summary is prepared on the basis of continuing operations after the distribution of the common shares of two subsidiaries to shareholders in December 1985, and before the tax benefits of operating loss carryforwards fully utilized in fiscal 1986.

APPENDIX D Pier 1 Imports, Inc. Consolidated Statement of Cash Flows ($000)

	Years Ended in February		
	1989	**1988**	**1987**
Cash flow from operating activities			
Net income	$ 21,850	$ 16,075	$ 11,970
Adjustments to reconcile to net cash provided by operating activities			
Depreciation, amortization, deferred taxes, and other	$ 12,687	$ 8,309	$ 8,709
Increase in inventories	(26,698)	(20,954)	(21,069)
Increase in accounts receivable and other current assets	(12,125)	(2,472)	(2,137)
Change in other assets, net	150	(2,651)	(12)
Change in accounts payable and accrued expenses	12,362	6,607	8,410
Net cash provided by operating activities	$ 8,226	$ 4,914	$ 5,871
Cash utilized in investing activities			
Capital expenditures	$(48,146)	$(48,647)	$(22,119)
Proceeds from disposition of property, plant, and equipment	4,330	4,009	2,317
Investments in securities	19,507	3,794	(39,189)
Net cash used in investing activities	$(24,309)	$(40,844)	$(58,991)
Cash flow from financing activities			
Proceeds from sales of convertible debentures	—	—	$ 49,266
Proceeds from sales of capital stock and treasure stock	$ 2,971	$ 8,648	14,628
Cash dividends	(2,970)	(2,021)	(557)
Proceeds from issuance of long-term debt, net of repayments and costs	18,593	(1,202)	21,783
Net borrowings (payments) under line of credit agreements	(6,604)	17,499	(8,000)
Purchase of treasury stock	(637)	(3,323)	(552)
Restricted cash for distribution center construction, net of receivables for reimbursable construction costs	255	16,890	(25,000)
Net cash provided by financing activities	$ 11,608	$ 36,491	$ 51,568
Change in cash and cash equivalents	$ (4,475)	$ 561	$ (1,552)
Cash and cash equivalents at beginning of year	8,219	7,658	9,210
Cash and cash equivalents at end of year	$ 3,744	$ 8,219	$ 7,658

APPENDIX E Summary of Results of Operations ($millions, except percentages and numbers of stores)

	1989		1988		1987	
	Amount	Percent[a]	Amount	Percent[a]	Amount	Percent[a]
Net sales	$414.6	26.7%	$327.2	24.7%	$262.3	28.6%
Gross profit	$217.5	52.5	$170.5	52.1	$136.0	51.8
Selling, general, and administrative expenses	163.0	39.3	130.3	39.8	104.8	39.9
Depreciation and amortization	11.5	2.8	8.8	2.7	6.3	2.4
Interest expense, net	10.0	2.4	8.2	2.5	3.6	1.4
Credit card costs, net	1.1	0.3	—	—	—	—
Income before income taxes	$ 31.9	7.7	$ 23.2	7.1	$ 21.3	8.1
Provision for income taxes	10.0	31.5	7.1	30.8	9.3	43.7
Net income	$ 21.9	5.3	$ 16.1	4.9	$ 12.0	4.6
Cumulative dividends on preferred stock	0.3	0.1	0.3	0.1	—	—
Income available to common stockholders	$ 21.6	5.2	$ 15.8	4.8	$ 12.0	4.6
Number of stores at end of period	450		396		350	
Sales gain for same stores		7.8%		12.1%		11.4%

[a]The percentages related to net sales represent the percentage increases in sales compared with previous years' net sales. The percentages related to provision for income tax are expressed as percentages of income before tax. All other percentages are calculated as percentages of sales.

APPENDIX F Pier 1 Imports, Inc. Consolidated Balance Sheet ($000)

	Years Ended February	
	1989	1988
Assets		
Current assets		
Cash	$ 3,744	$ 8,219
Marketable securities	15,888	32,956
Accounts receivable, net	20,832	2,208
Inventories	130,224	103,526
Other current assets	7,714	6,358
Total current assets	$178,402	$153,267
Property and equipment		
Buildings	38,400	23,202
Equipment, furniture, and fixtures	53,946	40,598
Leasehold interests and improvements	39,647	27,513
Construction in progress	1,175	2,977
	$133,168	$ 94,290
Less accumulated depreciation and amortization	30,679	22,857
	$102,489	$ 71,433
Land	8,963	7,681
	$111,452	$ 79,114
Other assets—restricted cash ($8,100,000 in 1988) and other	10,052	25,550
	$299,906	$257,931

APPENDIX F Cont'd. Pier 1 Imports, Inc. Consolidated Balance Sheet ($000)

	Years Ended February	
	1989	**1988**
Liabilities and Stockholders' Equity		
Current liabilities		
Notes payable and current portion of long-term debt	$ 16,267	$ 33,480
Accounts payable and accrued liabilities	44,951	32,589
Total current liabilities	$ 61,218	$ 66,069
Long-term debt	121,313	96,530
Deferred income taxes	1,605	1,191
Stockholders' equity		
Formula rate preferred stock, $1.00 par, 10 votes per share, 5,000,000 shares authorized, 1,500,000 outstanding	1,500	1,500
Common stock, $1.00 par, 100,000,000 shares authorized, 30,399,000 outstanding	30,399	30,399
Paid-in capital	43,475	43,336
Retained earnings	40,895	22,015
Cumulative translation adjustments	568	153
Less 117,000 and 431,000 common shares in treasury, at cost, respectively	(1,067)	(3,262)
	$115,770	$ 94,141
Commitments and contingent liabilities	—	—
	$299,906	$257,931

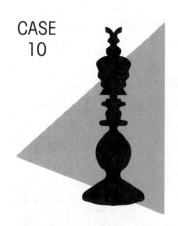

CASE
10

WAL-MART STORES, INC.: STRATEGIES FOR MARKET DOMINANCE

JAMES W. CAMERIUS

It's dusk in the foothills of the Ozark mountains in north central Arkansas. A battered, red 1980 Ford pickup minus two hubcaps with a hunting dog named Buck seated inside the cab, is headed down the rural road for some coffee and conversation with friends at Fred's Hickory Inn in Bentonville. Inside the truck, driving, is one of the most successful retailing entrepreneurs in modern history who continues to be down-to-earth and old fashioned in his views of the past, the present, and the future. "I didn't sit down one day and decide that I was going to put a bunch of discount stores in small towns and set a goal to have a billion-dollar company some day," Sam Walton says. "I started out with one store and it did well, so it was a challenge to see if I could do well with a few more. We're still going and we'll keep going as long as we're successful." From these humble beginnings, Wal-Mart has emerged as a modern retail success story.

AN EMERGING ORGANIZATION

Wal-Mart Stores, Inc., in 1991, with corporate offices at Bentonville, Arkansas, had completed its 28th consecutive year of growth in both sales and earning records. The firm operated stores under a variety of names and retail formats including Wal-Mart stores, which existed as discount department stores; Sam's Wholesale Clubs, which were wholesale/retail membership warehouses; and Hypermart*USA, which were combination grocery and general merchandise stores in excess of 200,000 square feet. It operated Wal-Mart Super Centers, scaled down versions of hypermarts; Dot Discount Drugstores, a super discount drug chain; and Bud's off-price outlet stores. In sales volume, it was not only the nation's largest discount department store chain, but had recently surpassed Sears, Roebuck & Company as the largest retail organization in the United States.

THE SAM WALTON SPIRIT

Much of the initial and continuing success of Wal-Mart was attributed to the entrepreneurial spirit of its founder and chairman of the board, Samuel Moore

Walton. Sam Walton, or "Mr. Sam" as some referred to him, traced his down-to earth, old-fashioned, home-spun, evangelical ways to growing up in rural Oklahoma, Missouri, and Arkansas. Although he was remarkably blasé about his roots, some suggested that it was a simple belief in hard work and ambition that had "unlocked countless doors and showered upon him, his customers, and his employees . . . , the fruits of . . . years of labor in building [this] highly successful company." "Our goal has always been in our business to be the very best," he said in an interview, "and, along with that, we believe that in order to do that, you've got to make a good situation and put the interests of your associates first. If we really do that consistently, they in turn will cause . . . our business to be successful, which is what we've talked about and espoused and practiced." "The reason for our success," Sam Walton said, "is our people and the way that they're treated and the way they feel about their company." Many have suggested it is this people-first philosophy which guided the company through the challenges and setbacks of its early years, and allowed the company to maintain its consistent record of growth and expansion in later years.

There was little about Walton's background that reflected his amazing success. He was born in Kingfisher, Oklahoma on March 29, 1918 to Thomas and Nancy Walton. Thomas Walton was a banker at the time and later entered the farm mortgage business and moved to Missouri. Sam Walton, growing up in rural Missouri in the depths of the Great Depression, discovered early that he "had a fair amount of ambition and enjoyed working," he suggested in a company interview. He completed high school at Columbia, Missouri and received a Bachelor of Arts degree in economics from the University of Missouri in 1940. "I really had no idea what I would be," he said, adding as an afterthought, "at one point in time, I thought I wanted to become president of the United States."

A unique, enthusiastic, and positive individual, Sam Walton was called "just your basic home-spun billionaire" by *Business Week* magazine. One source suggested that: "Mr. Sam is a life-long small-town resident who didn't change much as he got richer than his neighbors." Walton drove an old Ford pickup truck, would grab a bite to eat at Fred's Hickory Inn in Bentonville, and, as a matter of practice, would get his hair cut at the local barbershop. He had tremendous energy, enjoyed bird hunting with his dogs, and flew a corporate plane. When the company was much smaller, he could boast that he personally visited every Wal-Mart store at least once a year. A store visit usually included Walton leading Wal-Mart cheers that began, "Give me a *W*, give me an *A* . . ." To many employees, he had the air of a fiery Baptist preacher. Paul R. Carter, a Wal-Mart executive vice president, said, "Mr. Walton has a calling." He became the richest man in America, and by 1991 had created a personal fortune for his family in excess of $21 billion.

For all that Walton's success has been widely chronicled, its magnitude is hard to comprehend. Sam Walton was selected by the investment publication *Financial World* in 1989 as the CEO of the Decade. He had honorary degrees from the University of the Ozarks, the University of Arkansas, and the University of Missouri. He also received many of the most distinguished professional awards of the industry, like Man of the Year, Discounter of the Year, and Chief Executive Officer of the Year, and was the second retailer to be inducted into the Discounting Hall of Fame. He was recipient of the Horatio Alger Award in 1984 and acknowledged by *Discount Stores News* as Retailer of the Decade in December 1989. "Walton does a remarkable job of instilling near-religious fervor in his people," says analyst Robert Buchanan of A. G. Edwards. "I think that speaks to the heart of his success." In late 1989 Sam Walton was diagnosed to have multiple myeloma, or cancer of the bone marrow. He planned to remain active in the firm as Chairman of the board of directors.

THE MARKETING CONCEPT
Genesis of an Idea

Sam Walton started his retail career in 1940 as a management trainee with the J. C. Penney Company in Des Moines, Iowa. He was impressed with the Penney method of doing business and later modeled the Wal-Mart chain on "The Penney Idea" as reviewed in Exhibit 1. The Penney Company had found strength in calling employees *associates* rather than *clerks.* Founded in Kemerer, Wyoming in 1902, Penney stores were to locate on the main streets of small towns and cities.

Following service in the U.S. Army during World War II, he acquired a Ben Franklin variety store franchise in Newport, Arkansas, which he operated successfully until losing the lease in 1950. He opened another store under the name of Walton's 5 & 10 in Bentonville, Arkansas the following year. By 1962, he was operating a chain of 15 stores.

The early retail stores owned by Sam Walton in Newport and Bentonville, Arkansas, and later in other small towns in adjoining southern states, were variety store operations. They were relatively small operations of 6,000 square feet, were located on "main street," and displayed merchandise on plain wooden tables and counters. Operated under the Ben Franklin name and supplied by Butler Brothers of Chicago and St. Louis, they were characterized by a limited price line, low gross margins, high merchandise turnover and concentration on return on investment.

EXHIBIT 1   The Penney Idea (1913)

1. To serve the public, as nearly as we can, to its complete satisfaction
2. To expect for the service we render a fair remuneration and not all the profit the traffic will bear
3. To do all in our power to pack the customer's dollar full of value, quality, and satisfaction
4. To continue to train ourselves and our associates so that the service we give will be more and more intelligently performed
5. To improve constantly the human factor in our business
6. To reward men and women in our organization through participation in what the business produces
7. To test our every policy, method, and act in this wise: "Does it square with what is right and just?"

The firm, operating under the Walton 5 & 10 name, was the largest Ben Franklin franchisee in the country in 1962. The variety stores were phased out by 1976 to allow the company to concentrate on the growth of Wal-Mart Stores.

Foundations of Growth

The original Wal-Mart discount concept was not a unique idea. Sam Walton became convinced in the late 1950s that discounting would transform retailing. He traveled extensively in New England, the cradle of off-pricing. "He visited just about every discounter in the United States," suggested William F. Kenney, the retired president of the now-defunct Kings Department Stores. He tried to interest Butler Brothers executives in Chicago, in the discount store concept. The first Kmart, as a "conveniently located one-stop shopping unit where customers could buy a wide variety of quality merchandise at discount prices" had opened in 1962 in Garden City, Michigan. His theory was to operate a discount store in a small community and in that setting he would offer name-brand merchandise at low prices and would add friendly service. Butler Brothers executives rejected the idea. The first Wal-Mart Discount City opened in late 1962 in Rogers, Arkansas.

Wal-Mart stores would sell nationally advertised, well-known, brand merchandise at low prices in austere surroundings. As corporate policy, they would cheerfully give refunds, credits, and rain checks. Management conceived the firm as a "discount department store chain offering a wide variety of general merchandise to the customer." Early emphasis was placed upon opportunistic purchases of merchandise from whatever sources were available. Heavy emphasis was placed upon health and beauty aids (H&BA) in the product line and "stacking it high" in a manner of merchandise presentation. By the end of 1979, there were 276 Wal-Mart stores located in 11 states.

The firm developed an aggressive expansion strategy as it grew from its first, 16,000-square-foot discount store in Rogers. New stores were located primarily in towns of 5,000 to 25,000 population. The stores' sizes ranged from 30,000 to 60,000 square feet with 45,000 being the average. The firm also expanded by locating stores in contiguous areas, town by town, state by state. When its discount operations came to dominate a market area, it moved to an adjoining area. While other retailers built warehouses to serve existing outlets, Wal-Mart built the distribution center first and then spotted stores all around it, pooling advertising and distribution overhead. Most stores were less than a six-hour drive from one of the company's warehouses. The first major distribution center, a 390,000 square-foot facility, opened in Searcy, Arkansas outside Bentonville in 1978.

National Perspectives

At the beginning of 1991, the firm had 1,573 Wal-Mart stores in 35 states with expansion planned for adjacent states. Wal-Mart became the largest retailer and the largest discount department store by continuing to follow the unique place strategy of first locating discount stores in small-town America and later in suburban markets.

As a national discount department store chain, Wal-Mart Stores, Inc. offered a wide variety of general merchandise to the customer. The stores were designed to offer one-stop shopping in 36 departments, which included family apparel, health and beauty aids, household needs, electronics, toys, fabric and crafts, automotive supplies, lawn and patio, jewelry, and shoes. In addition, at certain store locations, a pharmacy, automotive supply and service center, garden center, or snack bar were also operated. The firm operated its stores with an "everyday low price" as opposed to putting heavy emphasis on special promotions, which called for multiple newspaper advertising circulars. Stores were expected to "provide the customer with a clean, pleasant, and friendly shopping experience."

Although Wal-Mart carried much the same merchandise, offered similar prices, and operated stores which looked much like the competition, there were many differences. In the typical Wal-Mart store, employees wore blue vests to identify themselves, aisles were wide, apparel departments were carpeted in warm colors, a store employee followed customers to their cars to pick up their shopping carts, and the customer was welcomed at the door by a "people greeter" who gave directions and struck up conversations. In some cases, merchandise was bagged in brown paper sacks rather than plastic bags because customers seemed to prefer them. A simple Wal-Mart logo in white letters on a brown background on the front of the store served to identify the firm. In consumer studies it was determined that the chain was particularly adept at striking the delicate balance needed to convince customers its prices were low without making people feel that its stores were too cheap. In many ways, competitors like Kmart sought to emulate Wal-Mart by introducing people greeters, by upgrading interiors, by developing new logos and signage, and by introducing new inventory response systems. In 1989 sales per square foot of retail space at Wal-Mart were $227. Kmart, in contrast, sold only $139 per square foot worth of goods annually.

A "Satisfaction Guaranteed" refund and exchange policy was introduced to allow customers to be confident of Wal-Mart's merchandise and quality. Technological advancements like scanner cash registers, hand-held computers for ordering of merchandise, and computer linkages of stores with the general office and distribution centers improved communications and merchandise replenishment. Each store was encouraged to initiate programs which would make it an integral part of the community in which it operated. Associates were encouraged to "maintain the highest standards of honesty, morality, and business ethics in dealing with the public."

THE EXTERNAL ENVIRONMENT

Industry analysts had labeled the 1980s as an era of economic uncertainty for retailers. Some firms faced difficulty upon merger or acquisition. After acquiring United States-based Allied Department Stores in 1986 and Federated Department Stores in 1988, Canadian developer Robert Campeau was declared bankrupt with over $6 billion in debt. Several divisions and units of the organization, upon re-evaluation, were either sold or closed. The flagship downtown Atlanta store of Rich's, a division of Federated, was closed after completing a multimillion dollar remodeling program. Specific merchandise programs in divisions like Bloomingdale's were re-evaluated to lower inventory and to raise cash. The notion of servicing existing debt became a significant factor in the success or failure of a retailing organization in the later half of the decade. Selected acquisitions of U.S. retailers by foreign firms over the past decade are reviewed in Exhibit 2.

Other retailers experienced changes in ownership. The British B.A.T. Industries PLC sold the Chicago-based Marshall Field department store division to the Dayton Hudson Corporation. L. J. Hooker Corporation, the U.S. arm of Australia's Hooker Corporation, sold its Bonwit Teller and Sakowitz stores; it liquidated its B. Altman chain after fruitless sale efforts. The R. H. Macy Company saddled itself with $4.5 billion in debt as a result of acquiring Bullock's and I. Magnin specialty department stores. Chicago-based Carson, Pirie, Scott & Company was sold to P. A. Bergner & Company, operator of the Milwaukee Boston Store and Bergner Department Stores. Bergner declared a Chapter 11 bankruptcy in 1991.

Many retail enterprises confronted heavy competitive pressure by lowering prices or changing merchandise strategies. Sears, Roebuck & Company, in an effort to reverse sagging sales and less than defensible earnings, unsuccessfully introduced a new policy of "everyday low pricing" (ELP) in 1989. It later introduced name-brand items such as Whirlpool alongside its traditional private label merchandise like Kenmore and introduced the store-within-a-store concept to feature the name-brand goods. Montgomery Ward, and to a lesser extent Kmart and Ames Department Stores, followed similar strategies. The J. C. Penney Company, despite repositioning itself as a more upscale retailer, felt an impending recession and concerns about the Persian Gulf War had combined to erode consumer confidence. "As a result," the company noted in its 1990 Annual Report, "sales and profits within the industry were more negatively impacted than at any time since the last major recession of 1980–82."

The discount department store industry by the early 1990s had changed in a number of ways and was thought to have reached maturity by many analysts. Several formerly successful firms like E. J. Korvette, W. T. Grant, Atlantic Mills,

EXHIBIT 2   Selected Acquisitions of U.S. Retailers by Foreign Firms, 1980–1990

U.S. Retailer	Foreign Acquirer	Country of Acquirer
Allied Stores (General Merchandise)	Campeau	Canada
Alterman Foods (Supermarkets)	Delhaize-Le Leon	Belgium
Bonwit Teller (General Merchandise)	Hooker Corporation	Australia
Brooks Brothers (Apparel)	Marks & Spencer	Great Britain
Federated Department Stores (Diversified)	Campeau	Canada
Great Atlantic & Pacific (Supermarkets)	Tengelmann	West Germany
Herman's (Sporting Goods)	Dee Corporation	Great Britain
International House of Pancakes (Restaurants)	Wienerwald	Switzerland
Talbots (Apparel)	JUSCO Ltd.	Japan
Zale (Jewelry)	PS Associates	Netherlands

Source: Barry Berman and Joel R. Evans, *Retail Management: A Strategic Approach*, 4th ed. (New York: Macmillan, 1989).

Arlans, Federals, Zayre, Heck's, and Ames had declared bankruptcy and as a result either liquidated or reorganized. Regional firms like Target Stores and Shopko Stores began carrying more fashionable merchandise in more attractive facilities and shifted their emphasis to more national markets. Specialty retailers such as Toys R Us, Pier 1 Imports, and Oshmans were making big inroads in toys, home furnishings, and sporting goods. The superstores of drug and food chains were rapidly discounting increasing amounts of general merchandise. Some firms like May Department Stores Company with Caldor and Venture and the F. W. Woolworth Company with Woolco had withdrawn from the field by either selling their discount divisions or closing them down entirely.

Several new retail formats had emerged in the marketplace to challenge the traditional discount department store format. The superstore, a 100,000- to 300,000-square-foot operation, combined a large supermarket with a discount general-merchandise store. Originally a European retailing concept, these outlets were known as "malls without walls." Kmart's Super Kmart, American Fare, and Wal-Mart's Super Center Store and Hypermart were examples of this trend toward large operations. Warehouse retailing, which involved some combination of warehouse and showroom facilities, used warehouse principles to reduce operating expenses and thereby offer discount prices as a primary customer appeal. Home Depot combined the traditional hardware store and lumber yard with a self-service home improvement center to become the largest home center operator in the nation.

Some retailers responded to changes in the marketplace by selling goods at price levels 20 to 60 percent below regular retail prices. These off-price operations appeared as two general types: (1) factory outlet stores like Burlington Coat Factory Warehouse, Bass Shoes, and Manhattan's Brand Name Fashion Outlet; and (2) independents like Loehmann's, T. J. Maxx, Marshall's, and Clothestime, which bought seconds, overages, closeouts, or leftover goods from manufacturers and other retailers. Other retailers chose to dominate a product classification. Some super specialists like Sock Appeal, Little Piggie Ltd., and Sock Market, offered a single, narrowly defined classification of merchandise with an extensive assortment of brands, colors, and sizes. Other niche specialists like Kids Mart, a division of F. W. Woolworth, and McKids, a division of Sears, targeted an identified market with carefully selected merchandise and appropriately designed stores. Some retailers like Silk Greenhouse (silk plants and flowers), Office Club (office supplies and equipment), and Toys R Us (toys) were called "category killers" because they had achieved merchandise dominance in their respective product categories. Firms like The Limited, Victoria's Secret, and The Banana Republic became minidepartment specialists by showcasing new lines and accessories alongside traditional merchandise lines.

Wal-Mart became the nation's largest retailer and discount department store chain in sales volume in 1991. Kmart Corporation, now the industry's second largest retailer and discount department store chain with over 2,300 stores and $32 billion in sales in 1990, was perceived by many industry analysts and consumers in several independent studies as a laggard, even though it had been the industry sales leader for a number of years. In the same studies, Wal-Mart was perceived as the industry leader even though according to the *The Wall Street Journal* "they carry much the same merchandise, offer prices that are pennies apart and operate stores

EXHIBIT 3 Competitive Sales and Store Comparison, 1980–1990

	Kmart		Wal-Mart[a]	
Year	Sales ($000)	Stores	Sales ($000)	Stores
1990	$32,070,000	2,350	$32,601,594	1,573
1989	29,533,000	2,361	25,810,656	1,402
1988	27,301,000	2,307	20,649,001	1,259
1987	25,627,000	2,273	15,959,255	1,114
1986	23,035,000	2,342	11,909,076	980
1985	22,035,000	2,332	8,451,489	859
1984	20,762,000	2,173	6,400,861	745
1983	18,597,000	2,160	4,666,909	642
1982	16,772,166	2,117	3,376,252	551
1981	16,527,012	2,055	2,444,997	491
1980	14,204,381	1,772	1,643,199	330

[a]Wal-Mart fiscal year ends January 31. Figures are assigned to previous year.

that look almost exactly alike." "Even their names are similar," noted the newspaper. The original Kmart concept of a "conveniently located, one stop shopping unit where customers could buy a wide variety of quality merchandise at discount prices," had lost its competitive edge in a changing market. As one analyst noted in an industry newsletter, "They had done so well for the past 20 years without paying attention to market changes. Now they have to." Wal-Mart and Kmart sales growth over the past 10 years is reviewed in Exhibit 3. A competitive analysis is shown of four major retail firms in Exhibit 4.

Some retailers, like Kmart, had initially focused on appealing to professional, middle-class consumers who lived in suburban areas and who were likely to be price sensitive. Other firms, like Target, which had adopted the discount concept

EXHIBIT 4 Industry Competitive Analysis, 1991

	Wal-Mart	Sears, Roebuck	Kmart	J. C. Penney
Sales ($000)	$32,601,584	$55,972,000	$32,070.000	$17,410,000
Net income ($000)	1,291,024	902,000	756,000	577,000
Net income per share	$1.14	$2.63	$3.78	$4.33
Dividends per share	$0.14	$2.00	$1.72	$2.64
Number of stores[a]	1,724	1,765	4,180	3,889
Percentage sales change	26.0%	1.2%	0.6%	2.1%

[a]Wal-Mart and subsidiaries: Wal-Mart Stores—1,573, Sam's Wholesale Club–148, Hypermart*USA–3; Sears, Roebuck & Company: department stores–863, Paint and hardware stores–98, catalog outlet stores–101, Western Auto–504, Eye Care Centers of America–94, Business Systems Centers–65, Pinstripes Petites–40; Kmart Corporation: general merchandise–2,350, specialty retail stores–1,830, PACE Membership Warehouses, Builders Square, Payless Drug Stores, Waldenbooks, The Sports Authority; J. C. Penney Company, Inc.: metropolitan market stores–697, geographic market stores–615, catalog units–2090, drugstores–487.

early, attempted to go generally after an upscale consumer who had an annual household income of $25,000 to $44,000. Fleet Farm and Menard's served the rural consumer, while firms like Chicago's Goldblatt's Department Stores returned to their immigrant heritage to serve blacks and Hispanics in the inner city.

In rural communities Wal-Mart success often came at the expense of established local merchants and units of regional discount store chains. Hardware stores, family department stores, building supply outlets, and stores featuring fabrics, sporting goods, and shoes were among the first to either close or relocate elsewhere. Regional discount retailers in the Sunbelt states like Rose's, Howard's, T.G.&Y. and Duckwall-ALCO, who once enjoyed solid sales and earnings, were forced to reposition themselves by renovating stores, opening bigger and more modern units, remerchandising assortments, and offering lower prices. In many cases, stores like Coast-to-Coast, Pamida, and Ben Franklin closed upon a Wal-Mart announcement to build in a specific community. "Just the word that Wal-Mart was coming made some stores close up," indicated a local newspaper editor.

CORPORATE STRATEGIES

The corporate and marketing strategies that emerged at Wal-Mart to challenge a turbulent and volatile external environment were based upon a set of two main objectives which had guided the firm through its growth years in the decade of the 1980s. In the first objective the customer was featured; "customers would be provided what they want, when they want it, all at a value." In the second objective, the team spirit was emphasized, "treating each other as we would hope to be treated, acknowledging our total dependency on our Associate-partners to sustain our success." The approach included aggressive plans for new store openings; expansion to additional states; upgrading, relocation, refurbishing, and remodeling existing stores; and opening new distribution centers. The plan was to not have a single operating unit that had not been updated in the past 7 years. In the 1991 annual report to stockholders, the 1990s were considered: "A new era for Wal-Mart; an era in which we plan to grow to a truly nationwide retailer, and should we continue to perform, our sales and earnings will also grow beyond where most could have envisioned at the dawn of the 80s."

In the decade of the 1980s, Wal-Mart developed a number of new retail formats. The first Sam's Wholesale Club opened in Oklahoma City, Oklahoma in 1983. The wholesale club was an idea which had been developed by other firms earlier, but which found its greatest success and growth in acceptability at Wal-Mart. Sam's Wholesale Clubs featured a vast array of product categories with limited selection of brand and model, a cash-and-carry business with limited hours, large (100,000-square-foot) bare-bones facilities, rock-bottom wholesale prices, and minimal promotion. The limited membership plan permitted whole-sale members, who bought memberships, and others, who usually paid a percentage above the ticket price of the merchandise. At the beginning of 1991, there were 148 Sam's Wholesale Clubs open in 28 states. Effective February 2, 1991, Sam's Clubs merged the 28 units of The Wholesale Club, Inc. of Indianapolis, Indiana into the organization.

The first Hypermart*USA, a 222,000-square-foot superstore which combined a discount store with a large grocery store, a food court of restaurants, and other service businesses such as banks or video tape rental stores, opened in 1988 in the Dallas suburb of Garland. A scaled-down version of Hypermart*USA called the Wal-Mart Super Center was similar in merchandise offerings, but with about half the square footage of hypermarts. These expanded store concepts also included convenience stores and gasoline distribution outlets to "enhance shopping convenience." The company proceeded slowly with these plans and later suspended its plans for building any more hypermarts in favor of the Super Center concept.

The McLane Company, Inc., a provider of retail and grocery distribution services for retail stores, was acquired in 1991. In October 1991 management announced that it was starting a chain of stores called Bud's which would sell damaged, outdated, and overstocked goods at discounts even deeper than regular Wal-Mart stores.

Several programs were launched to highlight popular social causes. The Buy American program was a Wal-Mart retail program initiated in 1985. The theme was "Bring It Home to the USA" and its purpose was to communicate Wal-Mart's support for American manufacturing. In the program, the firm directed substantial influence to encourage manufacturers to produce goods in the United States rather than import them from other countries. Vendors were attracted into the program by encouraging manufacturers to initiate the process by contacting the company directly with proposals to sell goods which were made in the United States. Buyers also targeted specific import items in their assortments on a state-by-state basis to encourage domestic manufacturing. According to Haim Dabah, president of Gitano Group, Inc., a maker of fashion discount clothing which imported 95 percent of its clothing and now makes about 20 percent of its products here, "Wal-Mart let it be known loud and clear that if you're going to grow with them, you sure better have some products made in the U.S.A." Farris Fashion, Inc. (flannel shirts), Roadmaster Corporation (exercise bicycles), Flanders Industries, Inc. (lawn chairs), and Magic Chef (microwave ovens) were examples of vendors that chose to participate in the program.

From the Wal-Mart standpoint, the "Buy American" program centered around value—producing and selling quality merchandise at a competitive price. The promotion included television advertisements featuring factory workers, a soaring American eagle, and the slogan, "We buy American whenever we can, so you can too." Prominent in-store signage and store circulars were also included. One store poster read, "Success Stories—These items formerly imported, are now being purchased by Wal-Mart in the U.S.A."

Wal-Mart was one of the first retailers to embrace the concept of green marketing. The program offered shoppers the option of purchasing products that were better for the environment in three respects: manufacturing, use, and disposal. It was introduced through full-page advertisements in *The Wall Street Journal* and *USA Today*. In-store signage identified those products which were environmentally safe. As Wal-Mart executives saw it, "customers are concerned about the quality of land, air, and water, and would like the opportunity to do something positive." To initiate the program, 7,000 vendors were notified that Wal-Mart had a corporate concern for the environment and asked for their support in a variety of ways. Wal-Mart television advertising showed children on swings, fields of grain blowing in the wind, and roses. Green and white store signs, printed on recycled paper, marked products or packaging that had been developed or redesigned to be more environmentally sound.

Wal-Mart had become the channel commander in the distribution of many brand-name items. As the nation's largest retailer, and in many geographic areas the dominant distributor, it exerted considerable influence in negotiation for the best price, delivery terms, promotion allowances, and continuity of supply. Many of these benefits could be passed on to consumers in the form of quality name-brand items available at lower than competitive prices. As a matter of corporate policy, management often insisted on doing business only with a producer's top sales executives rather than going through a manufacturer's representative. Wal-Mart had been accused of threatening to buy from other producers if firms refused to sell directly to it. In the ensuing power struggle, Wal-Mart executives refused to talk about the controversial policy or admit that it existed. As a representative of an industry association representing a group of sales agencies representatives suggested, "In the Southwest, Wal-Mart's the only show in town." An industry analyst added, "They're extremely aggressive. Their approach has always been to give the customer the benefit of a corporate saving. That builds up customer loyalty and market share."

Another key factor in the mix was an inventory control system that was recognized as the most sophisticated in retailing. A high-speed computer system linked virtually all the stores to headquarters and the company's distributions centers. It electronically logged every item sold at the checkout counter, automatically kept the warehouses informed of merchandise to be ordered, and directed the flow of goods to the stores and even to the proper shelves. Most important for management, it helped detect sales trends quickly and speeded up market reaction time substantially.

DECISION MAKING IN A MARKET-ORIENTED FIRM

One principle that distinguished Wal-Mart was the unusual depth of employee involvement in company affairs. Corporate strategies put emphasis on human resource management. Employees of Wal-Mart became "associates," a name borrowed from Sam Walton's early association with the J. C. Penney Company. Input was encouraged at meetings at the store and corporate level. The firm hired employees locally, provided training programs, and through a "Letter to the President" program, management encouraged employees to ask questions, and make words like *we, us,* and *our* a part of the corporate language. A number of special award programs recognized individual, department, and division achievement. Stock ownership and profit-sharing programs were introduced as part of a partnership concept.

The corporate culture was recognized by the editors of the trade publication *Mass Market Retailers* when it recognized all 275,000 associates collectively as the 1989 Mass Market Retailers of the Year. "The Wal-Mart associate," the editors noted, "in this decade that term has come to symbolize all that is right with the American worker, particularly in the retailing environment and most particularly at Wal-Mart." The store-within-a-store concept, as a Wal-Mart corporate policy, trained individuals to be merchants by being responsible for the performance of their own departments as if they were running their own businesses. Seminars and training programs afforded them opportunities to grow within the company. "People development, not just a good 'program' for any growing company but a must to secure our future," is how Suzanne Allford, vice president of the Wal-Mart People Division, explained the firm's decentralized approach to retail management development.

"The Wal-Mart Way" was a phrase that was used by management to summarize the firm's unconventional approach to business and the development of the corporate culture. As noted in the 1991 Annual Report, referring to a recent development program, "We stepped outside our retailing world to examine the best managed companies in the United States in an effort to determine the fundamentals of their success and to 'benchmark' our own performances." The name Total Quality Management (TQM) was used to identify this "vehicle for proliferating the very best things we do while incorporating the new ideas our people have that will assure our future."

THE GROWTH CHALLENGE

David Glass, 53 years old, had assumed the role of president and chief executive officer at Wal-Mart, the position previously held by Sam Walton, founder of the company. Known for his hard-driving managerial style, Glass gained his experience in retailing at a small supermarket chain in Springfield, Missouri. He joined Wal-Mart as executive vice president for finance in 1976. He was named president and chief operating officer in 1984.

And what of Wal-Mart without Mr. Sam? "There's no transition to make," said Glass, "because the principles and the basic values he used in founding this company were so sound and so universally accepted." "As for the future," he suggested, spinning around in his chair at his desk in his relatively spartan office at corporate headquarters in Bentonville, "there's more opportunity ahead of us than behind us. We're good students of retailing and we've studied the mistakes that others have made. We'll make our own mistakes, but we won't repeat theirs. The only thing constant at Wal-Mart is change. We'll be fine as long as we never lose our responsiveness to the customer."

Wal-Mart Stores, Inc. had for over 25 years experienced tremendous growth and, as one analyst suggested, "been consistently on the cutting edge of low-markup mass merchandising." Much of the forward momentum had come from the entrepreneurial spirit of Samuel Moore Walton. Mr. Sam remained chairman of the board of directors and corporate representative for the immediate future. A new management team was in place. As the largest retailer in the country, the firm had positioned itself to meet the challenges of the next decade as an industry leader. The question now was, could the firm maintain its blistering growth pace, outmaneuvering the competition with the innovative retailing concepts that it has continued to develop better than anyone else?

REFERENCES

"A Supercenter Comes to Town." *Chain Store Age Executive*. December 1989, pp. 23–30+.

Abend, Jules. "Wal-Mart's Hypermart: Impetus for U.S. Chains?" *Stores*, March 1988, pp. 59–61.

"Another Record Year at Wal-Mart." *Chain Store Age, General Merchandise Edition*. June 1984, p. 70.

Bard, Ray, and Susan K. Elliott. *The National Directory of Corporate Training Programs*. New York: Doubleday, 1988, pp. 351–352.

Barrier, Michael. "Walton's Mountain." *Nation's Business*. April 1988, pp. 18–20+.

Beamer, Wayne. "Discount King Invades Marketer Territory." *National Petroleum*. April 1988, pp. 15–16.

Bergman, Joan. "Saga of Sam Walton." *Stores*. January 1988, pp. 129–130+.

Blumenthal, Karen. "Marketing with Emotion: Wal-Mart Shows the Way." *The Wall Street Journal*, November 20, 1989, p. B3.

Bradford, Michael. "Receiver Sues to Recoup Comp Payments." *Business Insurance*. September 11, 1989, p. 68.

Bragg, Arthur. "Wal-Mart's War on Reps." *Sales & Marketing Management*. March 1987, pp. 41–43.

Brauer, Molly. "Sam's: Setting a Fast Pace." *Chain Store Age Executive*. August 1983, pp. 20–21.

Brookman, Faye. "Will Patriotic Purchasing Pay Off?" *Chain Store Age, General Merchandise Trends*. June 1985, p. 95.

Caminiti, Susan. "What Ails Retailing." *Fortune*. January 30, 1989, pp. 63–64.

Cochran, Thomas N. "Chain Reaction." *Barron's*. October 16, 1989, p. 46.

Corwin, Pat, Jay L. Johnson, and Renee M. Rouland. "Made in U.S.A." *Discount Merchandiser*. November 1989, pp. 48–52.

"David Glass's Biggest Job Is Filling Sam's Shoes." *Business Month*. December 1988, p. 42.

"Discounters Commit to Bar-code Scanning." *Chain Store Age Executive*. September 1985, pp. 49–50.

Edgerton, Jerry, and Jordon E. Goodman. "Wal-Mart for Hypergrowth." *Money*. March 1988, p. 12.

Endicott, R. Craig. "'86 Ad Spending Soars." *Advertising Age*. November 23, 1987, pp. S-2+.

Endicott, R. Craig. "Leading National Advertisers (Companies Ranked 101–200)." *Advertising Age*. November 21, 1988, pp. S-1+.

"Explosive Decade." *Financial World*. April 4–17, 1984, p. 92.

"Facts about Wal-Mart Stores, Inc." press release, Corporate and Public Affairs, Wal-Mart Stores, Inc.

Fisher, Christy, and Patricia Strand. "Wal-Mart Pulls Back on Hypermart Plans." *Advertising Age*. February 19, 1990, p. 49.

Fisher, Christy, and Judith Graham. "Wal-Mart Throws 'Green' Gauntlet." *Advertising Age*. August 21, 1989, pp. 1+.

Gilliam, Margaret A. "Wal-Mart and the Investment Community." *Discount Merchandiser*. November 1989, pp. 64+.

"Glass Is CEO at Wal-Mart." *Discount Merchandiser*. March 1988, pp. 6+.

"Great News: A Recession." *Forbes*. January 8, 1990, p. 194.

Gruber, Christina. "Will Competition Wilt Rose's." *Chain Store Age, General Merchandise Edition*. May 1984, p. 40.

Hartnett, Michael. "Resurgence in the Sunbelt." *Chain Store Age, General Merchandise Trends*. October 1985, pp. 13–15.

Helliker, Kevin. "Wal-Mart's Store of the Future Blends Discount Prices, Department-Store Feel." *The Wall Street Journal*. May 17, 1991, pp. B1, B8.

Higgins, Kevin T. "Wal-Mart: A Pillar in a Thousand Communities." *Building Supply Home Centers*. February 1988, pp. 100–102.

Huey, John. "America's Most Successful Merchant." *Fortune*. September 23, 1991, pp. 46–48+.

Huey, John. "Wal-Mart, Will It Take Over the World?" *Fortune*. January 30, 1989, pp. 52–56+.

"Hypermart USA Makes a Few Adjustments." *Chain Store Age Executive*. May 1988, p. 278.

"In Retail, Bigger Can Be Better." *Business Week*. March 27, 1989, p. 90.

"Jack Shewmaker, Vice Chairman, Wal-Mart Stores, Inc." *Discount Merchandiser*. November 1987, pp. 26+.

Jacober, Steve. "Wal-Mart: A Boon to U.S. Vendors." *Discount Merchandiser*. November 1989, pp. 41–46.

Jacober, Steve. "Wal-Mart: A Retailing Catalyst." *Discount Merchandiser*. November 1989, pp. 54–58.

Johnson, Jay L. "Are We Ready for Big Changes?" *Discount Merchandiser*. August 1989, pp. 48, 53–54.

Johnson, Jay L. "Hypermarts and Supercenters—Where Are They Heading?" *Discount Merchandiser*. November 1989, pp. 60+.

Johnson, Jay L. "Hypermart USC Does a Repeat Performance." *Discount Merchandiser*. March 1988, pp. 52+.

Johnson, Jay L. "Internal Communication: A Key to Wal-Mart's Success." *Discount Merchandiser*. November 1989, pp. 68+.

Johnson, Jay L. "Supercenters: Wal-Mart's Future?" *Discount Merchandiser*. May 1988, pp. 26+.

Johnson, Jay L. "The Future of Retailing." *Discount Merchandiser*. January 1990, pp. 70+.

Johnson, Jay L. "The Supercenter Challenge." *Discount Merchandiser*. August 1989, pp. 70+.

Johnson, Jay L. "Walton Honored by Harvard Business School Club." *Discount Merchandiser*. June 1990, pp. 30, 34.

Keith, Bill. "Wal-Mart Places Special Emphasis on Pharmacy." *Drug Topics*. July 17, 1989, pp. 16–17.

Kelly, Kevin. "Sam Walton Chooses a Chip off the Old CEO." *Business Week*. February 15, 1988, p. 29.

Kelly, Kevin. "Wal-Mart Gets Lost in the Vegetable Aisle." *Business Week*. May 28, 1990, p. 48.

Kerr, Dick. "Wal-Mart Steps Up 'Buy American.'" *Housewares*. March 7–13, 1986, pp. 1+.

Klapper, Marvin. "Wal-Mart Chairman Says His Buy American Program Working." *Women's Wear Daily*. December 3, 1985, p. 8.

"Leader in New Construction." *Chain Store Age Executive*. November 1985, p. 46.

Levering, Robert. *The 100 Best Companies to Work for in America*. 1984, pp. 351–354.

Lloyd, Bruce A. "Wal-Mart to Build Major Distribution Center in Loveland, Colo." *Site Selection*. June 1989, pp. 634–635.

"Management Style: Sam Moore Walton." *Business Month*. May 1989, p. 38.

Marsch, Barbara. "The Challenge: Merchants Mobilize to Battle Wal-Mart in a Small Community." *The Wall Street Journal*. June 5, 1991, p. A1, A4.

Mason, Todd. "Sam Walton of Wal-Mart: Just Your Basic Homespun Billionaire." *Business Week*. October 14, 1985, pp. 142–143+.

McLeod, Douglas. "Miro Exceeded Authority on Wal-Mart Cover: Judge." *Business Insurance*. July 20, 1987, p. 28.

McLeod, Douglas. "Transit Liquidator Can't Collect from Wal-Mart, Court Rules." *Business Insurance*. October 3, 1988.

"$90 Million Expansion Bill at Wal-Mart." *Chain Store Age Executive*. November 1982, p. 73.

"Number of Units Set to Climb by 62%." *Chain Store Age Executive*. November 1983, p. 34.

"Our People Make the Difference: The History of Wal-Mart." Bentonville, Ark.: Wal-Mart Video Productions, 1991. Videocassette.

Padgett, Tim. "Just Saying No to Wal-Mart." *Newsweek*. November 13, 1989, p. 65.

"Perspectives on Discount Retailing." *Discount Merchandiser*. April 1987, pp. 44+.

Peters, Thomas J., and Nancy Austin. *A Passion for Excellence*. New York: Random House, pp. 266–267.

Rawn, Cynthia Dunn. "Wal-Mart vs. Main Street." *American Demographics*. June 1990, pp. 58–59.

Reed, Susan. "Talk about a Local Boy Making Good! Sam Walton, The King of Wal-Mart, Is America's Second-Richest Man." *People*. December 19, 1983, pp. 133+.

Reier, Sharon. "CEO of the Decade: Sam M. Walton." *Financial World*. April 4, 1989, pp. 56–57+.

"Rex Chase—Pure Wal-Mart Lore." *Chain Store Age, General Merchandise Edition*. March 1983, p. 35.

Rudnitsky, Howard. "How Sam Walton Does It." *Forbes*. August 16, 1982, pp. 42–44.

Rudnitsky, Howard. "Play It Again, Sam." *Forbes*. August 10, 1987, p. 48.

"Sam's Wholesale Club Racks Up $1.6 Billion Sales in 1986." *Discount Merchandiser*. Feburary 1987, p. 26.

"Sam Walton, The Retail Giant: Where Does He Go from Here?" *Drug Topics*. July 17, 1989, p. 6.

"Sam Moore Walton." *Business Month*. May 1989, p. 38.

Saporito, Bill. "The Mad Rush to Join the Warehouse Club." *Fortune*. January 6, 1986, pp. 59+.

Schachner, Michael. "Wal-Mart Chief Fined $11.5 Million for Court Absence." *Business Insurance*. January 9, 1989, p. 1+.

Schwadel, Francine. "Little Touches Spur Wal-Mart's Rise." *The Wall Street Journal*. September 22, 1989, p. B1.

Sheets, Kenneth R. "How Wal-Mart Hits Main St." *U.S. News & World Report*. March 13, 1989, pp. 53–55.

"Small Stores Showcase Big Ideas." *Chain Store Age, General Merchandise Trends*. September 1985, pp. 19–20.

"Small Town Hit." *Time*. May 23, 1983, p. 43.

Smith, Sarah. "America's Most Admired Corporations." *Fortune*. January 29, 1990, pp. 56+.

Sprout, Alison L. "America's Most Admired Corporations." *Fortune*. February 11, 1991, pp. 52+.

Taub, Stephen. "Gold Winner: Sam M. Walton of Wal-Mart Stores Takes the Top Prize." *Financial World*. April 15, 1986, pp. 28+.

Taylor, Marianne. "Wal-Mart Prices Itself in the Market." *Chicago Tribune*. April 28, 1991, Section 7, pp. 1+.

"Tending Wal-Mart's Green Policy." *Advertising Age*. January 29, 1991, pp. 20+.

The Almanac of American Employers. Chicago: Contemporary Books, 1985. p. 280.

"The Early Days: Walton Kept Adding 'a Few More' Stores." *Discount Store News*. December 9, 1985, p. 61.

"The Five Best-Managed Companies." *Dun's Business Month*. December 1982, p. 47.

Thurmond, Shannon. "Sam Speaks Volumes about New Formats." *Advertising Age*. May 9, 1988, p. S–26.

Trimble, Vance H. *Sam Walton: The Inside Story of America's Richest Man*. New York: Dutton, 1990.

"Wal-Mart's 1990 Look." *Discount Merchandiser*. July 1989, p. 12.

"Wal-Mart Associates Generate over $5.5 Million for United Way." Press Release, Wal-Mart Stores, Inc., January 2, 1990.

"Wal-Mart Beats the Devil." *Chain Store Age*. August 1986, p. 9.

"Wal-Mart Expands; Tests New 'Wholesale' Concept." *Chain Store Age, General Merchandise Trends*. June 1983, p. 98.

"Wal-Mart's Glass to Reps: 'That's a Bunch of Baloney!'" *Discount Merchandiser*. September 1987, p. 12.

"Wal-Mart's Goals." *Discount Merchandiser*. January 1988, pp. 48–50.

"Wal-Mart Goes on Its Own." *Progressive Grocer*. June 1987, p. 9.

"Wal-Mart's 'Green' Campaign to Emphasize Recycling Next." *Adweek's Marketing Week*. February 12, 1990, pp. 60–61.

"Wal-Mart Has No Quarrel with 1984." *Chain Store Age, General Merchandise Trends*. June 1985, p. 36.

"Wal-Mart on the Move." *Progressive Grocer*. August 1987, p. 9.

"Wal-Mart Policy Asks for Supplier Commitment." *Textile World*. May 1985, pp. 27–28.

"Wal-Mart Raises over $3 Million for Children's Hospital." Press release, Wal-Mart Stores, Inc., June 1989.

"Wal-Mart Rolls out Its Supercenters." *Chain Store Age Executive*, December 1988. pp. 18–19.

"Wal-Mart Stores Penny Wise." *Business Month*. December 1988, p. 42.

"Wal-Mart: The Model Discounter." *Dun's Business Month*. December 1982, pp. 60–61.

"Wal-Mart to Acquire McLane, Distributor to Retail Industry." *The Wall Street Journal*. October 2, 1990, p. A8.

Weiner, Steve. "Golf Balls, Motor Oil and Tomatoes." *Forbes*. October 30, 1989, pp. 130–131+.

Weiner, Steve. "Psst!' Wanna Buy a Watch? A Suit? How about a Whole Department Store?" *Forbes*. January 8, 1990, pp. 192+.

"Wholesale Clubs." *Discount Merchandiser*. November 1987, pp. 26+.

"Why Wal-Mart Is Recession Proof." *Business Week*. February 22, 1988, p. 146.

"Work, Ambition—Sam Walton," Press release, Wal-Mart Stores, Inc.

Zweig, Jason. "Expand It Again, Sam." *Forbes*. July 9, 1990, p. 106.

APPENDIX A Wal-Mart Stores, Inc. Financial Performance, 1991–1987 ($000 except per-share data)

	1991	1990	1989	1988	1987
Earnings					
Net sales	$32,601,594	$25,810,656	$20,649,001	$15,959,255	$11,909,076
Licensed department rentals and other income, net	261,814	174,644	136,867	104,783	84,623
Cost of sales	25,499,834	20,070,034	16,056,856	12,281,744	9,053,219
Operating, selling, general, and administrative expenses	5,152,178	4,069,695	3,267,864	2,599,367	2,007,645
Interest costs					
Debt	42,716	20,346	36,286	25,262	10,442
Capital leases	125,920	117,725	99,395	88,995	76,367
Taxes on income	751,736	631,600	488,246	441,027	395,940
Net income	1,291,024	1,075,900	837,221	627,643	450,086
Stores in operation at the end of the period					
Wal-Mart Stores	1,573	1,402	1,259	1,114	980
Sam's Wholesale Clubs	148	123	105	84	49
Financial Position					
Current assets	6,414,775	4,712,616	3,630,987	2,905,145	2,353,271
Net property, plant, equipment, and capital leases	4,712,039	3,430,059	2,661,954	2,144,852	1,676,282
Total assets	11,388,915	8,198,484	6,359,668	5,131,809	4,049,092
Current liabilities	3,990,414	2,845,315	2,065,909	1,743,763	1,340,291
Long-term debt	740,254	185,152	184,439	185,672	179,234
Long-term obligations under capital leases	1,158,621	1,087,403	1,009,046	866,972	764,128
Preferred stock with mandatory redemption provisions	—	—	—	—	—
Shareholder's equity	5,365,524	3,965,561	3,007,909	2,257,267	1,690,493

Source: Wal-Mart Annual Report, January 31, 1991.

APPENDIX B Wal-Mart Stores, Inc. Financial Performance, 1986–1982 ($000 except per-share data)

	1986	1985	1984	1983	1982
Earnings					
Net sales	$8,451,489	$6,400,861	$4,666,909	$3,376,252	$2,444,997
Licensed department rentals and other income, net	55,127	52,167	36,031	22,435	17,650
Cost of sales	6,361,271	4,722,440	3,418,025	2,458,235	1,787,496
Operating, selling, general, and administrative expenses	1,485,210	1,181,455	892,887	677,029	495,010
Interest costs					
Debt	1,903	5,207	4,935	20,297	16,053
Capital leases	54,640	42,506	29,946	18,570	15,351
Taxes on income	276,119	230,653	160,903	100,416	65,943
Net income	327,473	270,767	196,244	124,140	82,794
Per share of common stock					
Net income	0.5800	0.4800	0.3500	0.2300	0.1600
Dividends	0.5700	0.0525	0.0350	0.0225	0.0163
Stores in operation at the end of the period					
Wal-Mart Stores	859	745	642	551	491
Sam's Wholesale Clubs	23	11	3	—	—
Financial Position					
Current assets	1,784,275	1,303,254	1,005,567	720,537	589,161
Net property, plant, equipment, and capital leases	1,303,450	870,309	628,151	457,509	333,026
Total assets	3,103,645	2,205,229	1,652,254	1,187,448	937,513
Current liabilities	992,683	688,968	502,763	347,318	339,961
Long-term debt	180,682	41,237	40,866	106,465	104,581
Long-term obligations under capital leases	595,205	449,886	339,930	222,610	154,196
Preferred stock with mandatory redemption provisions	4,902	5,874	6,411	6,861	7,438
Shareholder's equity	1,277,659	984,672	737,503	488,109	323,942

Source: Wal-Mart Annual Report, January 31, 1991.

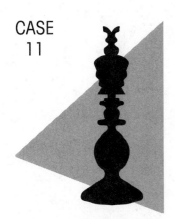

CASE 11

AMERICAN GREETINGS LOOKS TO THE 1990s

DAN KOPP & LOIS SHUFELDT

As CEO Morry Weiss looked at the corporate rose logo of the world's largest publicly owned manufacturer of greeting cards and related social-expression merchandise, American Greetings (AG), he reflected upon the decade of the 1980s. In 1981 he had announced the formulation of a corporate growth objective to achieve $1 billion in annual sales by 1985, which would represent a 60-percent increase over 1982 sales of $623.6 million.

It was 1986 before AG reached that goal with sales of $1.035 billion. The profit margin, however, was 5.75 percent, the lowest in five years and down from its high of 8.09 percent in 1984. In its fiscal year ending February 28, 1990 AG reported sales of $1.286 billion with a profit margin of 5.51 percent. Weiss looked at the 10-year sales, net income, and selling, distribution, and marketing costs summary prepared by his corporate staff (Exhibit 1). He realized its increase in sales had come at a high price with an escalated and intensified battle for market share dominance among the three industry leaders, Hallmark, Gibson, and AG. In the final analysis, market shares had not really changed that much among the big three. Now each was determined to defend their respective market shares.

The nature of the greeting card industry had changed dramatically. Previously, the two leading firms, Hallmark and AG, peacefully coexisted by having mutually exclusive niches. Hallmark offered higher-priced, quality cards in department stores and card shops, and AG offered inexpensive cards in mass-merchandise outlets. However, AG's growth strategy to attack the industry leader and its niche, followed by Gibson's growth strategy and Hallmark's defensive moves, changed the industry. AG was now in the position of defending its competitive position.

THE GREETING CARD INDUSTRY

According to *GM News*, in 1988 Americans exchanged more than 7.1 billion cards—around 29 per person—which is down from the highest per-capita card consumption of 30 in 1985. And with the average retail price per card of $1.10, that

This case was prepared as a basis for class discussion rather than to illustrate either effective or ineffective administrative practices. The authors would like to acknowledge the cooperation and assistance of American Greetings. This case was presented at the 1990 North American Case Research Association's annual conference.

EXHIBIT 1 Sales Trends

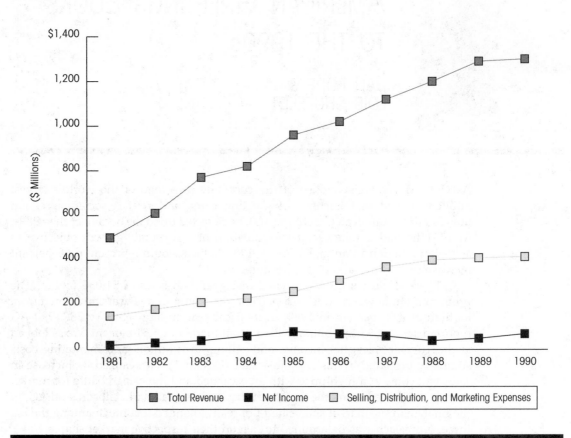

made "social expression" a $4-billion business. According to the Greeting Card Association, card senders sent the following cards:

Holiday	Number	Percentage
Christmas	2.2 Billion	30.99%
Valentine's Day	850 Million	11.97
Easter	180 Million	2.54
Mother's Day	140 Million	1.97
Father's Day	85 Million	1.20
Graduation	80 Million	1.13
Thanksgiving	40 Million	0.56
Halloween	25 Million	0.35
St. Patrick's Day	6 Million	—
Grandparent's Day	10 Million	—
Chanukah	9 Million	—
Other Seasons	5 Million	—

Half of the total greeting cards purchased in 1988 were seasonal cards. The remainder were in the category of everyday cards. Everyday cards, especially nonoccasion cards or alternative cards, are on the increase. According to *Forbes* and *American Demographics,* the alternative card market is the fastest growing segment at 25 percent a year, while general card sales grew at only 0.6 percent a year and the card industry as a whole grew at 5 percent a year. Alternative cards are not geared to any holiday, but can be inspirational, satirical, or ethnic in nature. This segment is directed toward the estimated 76 million baby boomers. Formerly, it was the focus strategy of the many small card makers who had 70 percent of the market. Now, however, the big three have captured 87 percent of the market.

Most industry analysts consider the greeting card industry to be in or near the maturity stage. According to Prudential-Bache, the greeting card industry unit growth rate was 2 to 4 percent from 1946 to 1985. The greeting card industry is comprised of from 500 to 900 firms, which range from three major corporations to many small, family organizations. The industry is dominated by the big three: Hallmark, American Greetings, and Gibson. Their estimated market shares are:

Company	1989	1985	1977
Hallmark	40–42%[a]	42%	50%
AG	32–33	33	24
Gibson	8–10	9	5

[a]Estimates vary according to the source.

During the 1980s the big three engaged in market share battles through intense price, product, promotion, and place competition. The primary price competition (through discounts to retailers) was during the period 1985 through 1987, although it still continues at a lesser rate today. According to Value Line, the end result was the reduction of profits with little change in market shares. In fact, retailer concessions made to gain accounts are difficult to remove; retailers are reluctant to give them up. However, according to Prudential-Bache, price competition may again emerge in the future due to the maturity of the industry, especially in selective target markets, such as large chains, as the card firms try to hold or steal accounts.

Market niches were also attacked. According to the *Insider's Chronicle,* the biggest battlefields were the gift and specialty card shops, which once were the exclusive domain of Hallmark and alternative cards. A 1989 comparison of the three firms reveals the following:

Firm	Sales	Net income	Employees	Products	Outlets
Hallmark	$2.0 billion	N.A.	28,000	20,300	37,000
AG	1.3 billion	$44.2 million	29,000	20,000	90,000
Gibson	0.4 billion	35.0 million	7,900	N.A.	50,000

Source: 10-K forms.

OBJECTIVES

When asked about AG's 1989 performance, Morry Weiss replied,

> Our goal was to improve competitiveness and enhance future earnings prospects in order to maximize shareholder value. AG refocused its worldwide business operating strategies. While we have not reached the upper levels of that goal, substantial progress was made in 1989. We are especially pleased that significant improvement was made in reducing seasonal product returns, accounts receivable, and inventories. These are indicators how well a business is being operated, and the results show that our people have made substantial progress. We are committed to making even further improvement in these areas. (1989 Annual Report.)

Weiss further explained,

> 1989 sales increased despite the loss of revenue caused by the divestiture during the year of the company's AmToy and Plymouth divisions and several foreign subsidiaries.
> . . . [N]et income was affected by restructuring costs which included the cost of relocating Carlton Cards/US to Cleveland, Ohio; consolidating certain manufacturing operations; and selling, consolidating, or downsizing several unprofitable businesses. (1989 Annual Report.)

His assessment of AG's 1990 performance was:

> It was the kind of year you have to feel good about. Our performance demonstrated our ability to produce outstanding earnings, even in a year when the revenue gain was modest. To accomplish this required enormous effort in every department. It required a diligent watch over expenses while increasing productivity. (1990 Annual Report.)

Morry Weiss also commented about AG's growth:

> We are building a more synergistic relationship between our core business and our subsidiary operations in order to increase our value to our retailers.
> Our goal is to be a full-service provider to our retailer accounts. The more we represent a single source for a variety of consumer products, the more important a resource we become. (1990 Annual Report.)
> . . . [G]rowth is expected to continue as we accelerate new product development for the everyday cards. (1989 Annual Report.)

To reach this aim of providing retailers not only greeting cards, but complementary products, AG has made the following acquisitions:

Company	Products
Acme Frame Products	Picture frames
Wilhold Hair Care Products	Hair care products
Plus Mark	Promotional Christmas products
A.G. Industries	Greeting card cabinets/displays

MARKETING STRATEGIES
Product

AG produces a wide product line, including greeting cards, gift wrap, party goods, toys, and gift items. Greeting cards accounted for 65 percent of the company's 1990 fiscal sales. The breakdown of sales by major product categories follows:

Category	1990	1986	1984	1980
Everyday greeting cards	41%	37%	36%	34%
Holiday greeting cards	24	29	27	27
Gift wrap and party goods	17	18	21	21
Consumer products (toys, etc.)	9	7	7	9
Stationery	9	9	9	9

Source: AG Annual Reports.

The essence of AG's product strategy is identifying consumer needs, creating responses that sell, and pretesting to determine the winners. AG believes in identifying consumer needs and responding to them with creative products. Research is a key ingredient. Over 12,000 North American households are surveyed annually to obtain information about every greeting card purchased and received. AG utilizes focus group sessions, simulated shopping surveys, and shopping mall interviews. Especially important is ongoing lifestyle research to identify changing tastes and consumer needs for product development.

Research efforts have resulted in new products. Couples, an everyday card line that answers the trend back to more sincere romantic relationships, and Kid Zone, which responds to the need for more effective communication with children, were introduced during fiscal 1990. Popular 1960s Holly Hobbie designs were reintroduced when research indicated a trend toward more traditional values. Morry Weiss commented on the Couples line:

> We've proven our ability to meet the challenge of the marketplace. Couples takes its place alongside a pantheon of our major greeting card innovations. (1989 Annual Report.)

AG has one of the largest creative staffs in the world with over 550 artists, stylists, writers, designers, photographers, and planners. They create more than 20,000 new greeting card designs each year.

AG also engages in retail pretesting to determine which product ideas have the greatest chance of sales. This is extremely important due to the competitiveness of the market and retailers' need to have fast turnover. A network of retail test stores is used. New cards are rated based upon actual sales performance, and those with the best sales ratings are distributed worldwide.

AG is trying to take advantage of the alternative card segment. Alternative cards now command 20 percent of the everyday greeting card market, and the double-digit annual growth rate is expected to continue. Carlton Cards is AG's specialty card subsidiary, and has been recently moved from Dallas to AG's Cleveland headquarters. Carlton will concentrate on "swiftly developing products unique to the more avant-garde tastes of the specialty store consumer."

AG pioneered licensing and is an industry leader in character licensing. Their strategy has been to maximize the potential of their creative and marketing expertise. The following table identifies some of AG's character licenses.

Character	Year
Holly Hobbie	1968/1989
Ziggy	1971
Strawberry Shortcake	1980
Care Bears	1983
Herself the Elf	1983
Popples	1983

Most of AG's licensed characters have been successful. Strawberry Shortcake has been one of the most popular licensed characters. According to *Forbes*, however, all of AG licensed characters have not been successful. One flop, Herself the Elf, was perceived by retailers as being too much like Strawberry Shortcake; it also missed the Christmas season because of production problems. Another failure was Get Along Gang, which tried to appeal to both little girls and boys. AG's licensing income is shown below:

Year	Income ($millions)
1984	$17.5
1985	20.9
1986	17.6
1988	16.5
1989	13.3
1990	11.8

Source: AG Annual Reports.

Distribution

AG distributes its products through 90,000 retail outlets throughout the world in 50 countries and 12 languages. AG's major channels of distribution, in order of importance, include drugstores, mass merchandisers, supermarkets, stationery and gift shops, combo stores (stores combining food, general merchandise, and drug items), variety stores, military post exchanges, and department stores (AG's 1989 10-K).

AG's primary channels of distribution (which include supermarkets, chain drugstores, and mass retail merchandisers) have experienced growth due to demographic and lifestyle changes. The increase of working women has caused consumers to purchase more cards in convenient locations. Today, 55 percent of all everyday greeting cards are purchased in convenient locations.

AG's five largest customers accounted for about 17.4 percent of net sales. These customers included mass merchandisers, major drugstores, and military post exchanges.

AG has 26 regional and 58 district sales offices in the United States, Canada, United Kingdom, France, and Mexico.

Promotion

Service is a key value to AG's marketing effort, as reflected in the following quote.

> One of our cornerstone values is service to the customer. While we are a leader in marketing innovation, we earned our reputation for superior customer service by clinging to old-fashioned ideas. We get to know our customers—and their customers—and learn how their businesses operate. (1990 Annual Report.)

The services that AG provides its retailers are based upon three key ingredients: knowledgeable sales force, in-store service personnel, and quick response to needs. AG offers:

> The largest full-time sales force in the industry, which is composed of highly trained experts
> A national force of 12,000 part-time in-store merchandising representatives who visit mass retail stores to restock goods, realign products, set up new displays and point-of-purchase materials, generate reorders, and process returns
> A computerized network that allows AG to more quickly and consistently ship complete and accurate orders to retailers (1990 Annual Report.)

According to Weiss:

> AG is focusing on building a strong partnership with retailers and consumers. We will expand distribution of our products in the global marketplace. We will "partner" with retail accounts by making greeting card departments more profitable. And we will improve our response to consumers' needs for appropriate products and attractive, easy to shop departments (1990 Annual Report.)

AG tries to achieve more sales and profits from the space allocated by retailers by making them more productive. This is accomplished by sophisticated merchandising that makes greeting card displays more consumer friendly. Since women purchase approximately 90 percent of all greeting cards, AG has redesigned greeting card cabinets to respond to the fact that women spend less time in stores than previously. Redesigned greeting card cabinets display 40 percent more cards in the same amount of space. Point-of-purchase signs and new caption locators ("Mother," "Stepdaughter," and the like).

Themes are becoming more important in merchandising. These are used for "particular seasons or occasions that project a strong message to consumers and evoke an immediate awareness of the occasion." Related to this is a new concept called "occasion merchandising, which groups various products for everyday occasions such as cards, gift wrap, candles, invitations, party goods, and so on."

AG tries to design its marketing programs to increase customer traffic and profitability of the greeting card department. Realizing the need for retailers to differentiate themselves and their products, AG attempts to work on an individual basis to customize the greeting card department for each retailer. This is accomplished via market research and technology. This is especially important to large chains that must contend with regional differences. Greeting card departments can be customized to reflect a specific area's demographics. If, for example, the demographic profile is comprised of a large number of elderly or "yuppies," specific products would be featured to target that segment.

A summary of AG's selling, distribution, and marketing expenses is displayed below:

Year	Percentage
1981	28.2%
1982	28.7
1983	29.2
1984	29.3
1985	29.0
1986	29.8
1987	31.6
1988	33.4
1989	32.6
1990	32.9

Source: AG Annual Reports.

PRODUCTION STRATEGIES

AG has 34 plants and facilities in the United States, Canada, the United Kingdom, France, and Mexico. This is down from the 49 plants and facilities in 1986. The company owns approximately 4.8 million square feet and leases 11.3 million square feet of plant, warehouse, store, and office space. It meets its space needs in the United States through long-term leases of properties constructed and financed by community development corporations and municipalities.

AG had taken steps in 1987 through 1990 to cut production costs. It has tried to improve its production efficiency by cutting costs and reducing work-in-process inventories. AG also invested heavily in automated production equipment to cut labor costs in 1988. AG has also benefited from lower cost for raw materials and fewer product returns because of better inventory control. AG's material, labor, and other production costs are as follows:

Year	Percentage
1981	44.7%
1982	44.3
1983	41.7
1984	40.5
1985	39.9
1986	40.2
1987	42.3
1988	45.1
1989	42.8
1990	41.5

PERSONNEL STRATEGIES

In 1989 American Greetings employed over 15,000 full-time and 14,000 part-time people in the United States, Canada, Mexico, and Europe. This equates to approximately 20,500 full-time employees.

Hourly plant employees at Cleveland, Ohio; Bardstown and Corbin, Kentucky; Greeneville, Tennessee; Chicago, Illinois; and in the United Kingdom and Canada are union. All other office and manufacturing employees are not union. Labor relations are considered to be satisfactory.

When asked about AG employees, Morry Weiss commented:

> But perhaps our greatest strength is the men and women who create, manufacture, distribute, sell, and support our products. They are committed to knowing our customers, meeting their needs with quality products, and providing service before and after the sale. (1990 Annual Report.)

AG has a noncontributing profit-sharing plan for most of its U.S. employees, as well as a retirement income guarantee plan. It also has several pension plans covering certain employees in foreign countries. (1990 Annual Report.)

FINANCE STRATEGIES

Exhibits 2 through 4 contain relevant financial information of American Greetings. The financial condition of AG has been fluctuating over the years. In the early to mid-1980s, AG profit margins increased from 5.42 percent in 1981 to its high of 8.09 percent in 1984. ROI was 6.14 percent in 1981; its high was 9.94 percent in

EXHIBIT 2 Consolidated Statement of Financial Position, 1981–1990 ($000)

	1990	1989	1988	1987
Assets				
Current Assets				
Cash and equivalents	$ 122,669	$ 94,292	$ 36,534	$ 17,225
Trade accounts receivable, less allowances for sales returns and doubtful accounts	254,285	242,582	278,559	284,135
Inventories				
Raw material	51,075	48,478	56,122	56,057
Work in process	42,139	51,625	61,406	69,668
Finished products	208,918	197,618	245,801	202,412
	302,132	297,721	363,329	328,137
Less LIFO reserve	85,226	83,017	77,274	75,392
	216,906	214,704	286,055	252,745
Display material and factory supplies	25,408	25,192	30,299	29,770
Total inventories	242,314	239,896	316,354	282,515
Deferred income taxes	51,315	49,542	39,935	26,593
Prepaid expenses and other	10,362	11,020	8,672	9,679
Total current assets	680,945	637,332	680,054	620,147
Other assets	107,788	92,285	95,752	89,488
Property, plant, and equipment				
Land	6,229	6,471	7,548	7,956
Buildings	215,458	216,545	223,491	183,481
Equipment and fixtures	354,979	340,233	319,353	269,644
	576,666	563,249	550,392	461,081
Less accumulated depreciation and amortization	224,383	205,246	175,917	148,097
Property, plant, and equipment, net	352,283	358,003	374,475	312,984
Net assets	$1,141,016	$1,087,620	$1,150,281	$1,022,619
Liabilities and Shareholders' Equity				
Current liabilities				
Notes payable to banks	$ 36,524	$ 17,201	$ 13,956	$ 25,092
Accounts payable	75,146	79,591	98,270	69,175
Payrolls and payroll taxes	45,315	38,839	33,759	31,230
Retirement plans	10,878	8,573	4,148	10,966
State and local taxes	—	—	—	3,056
Dividends payable	5,281	5,311	5,338	5,343
Income taxes	6,430	6,693	13,782	—
Sales returns	21,182	24,543	28,273	29,964
Current maturities of long-term debt	—	3,740	54,150	10,894
Total current liabilities	$ 200,756	$ 184,491	$ 251,676	$ 185,720
Long-term debt	235,497	246,732	273,492	235,005
Deferred income taxes	100,159	91,409	86,426	77,451
Shareholders' equity				
Common shares—par value $1				
Class A	29,946	29,692	29,628	29,552
Class B	2,063	2,497	2,528	2,588
Capital in excess of par value	110,234	105,245	104,209	102,718
Shares held in treasury	(26,692)	(14,767)	(14,199)	(15,409)
Cumulative translation adjustment	(8,186)	(4,790)	(7,564)	(11,604)
Retained earnings	497,239	447,111	424,085	416,598
Total shareholders' equity	604,604	564,988	538,687	524,443
Total liabilities and shareholders' equity	$1,141,016	$1,087,620	$1,150,281	$1,022,619

1986	1985	1984	1983	1982	1981
$ 26,853	$ 66,363	$ 62,551	$ 19,950	$ 3,367	$ 2,522
240,471	173,637	146,896	148,018	131,996	114,051
59,343	59,197	48,738	47,636	53,515	39,329
60,179	53,728	43,929	54,756	52,214	37,506
181,237	152,543	139,275	122,167	97,221	88,759
300,759	265,468	231,942	224,559	202,950	165,594
76,552	71,828	63,455	59,345	55,051	46,287
224,207	193,640	168,487	165,214	147,899	119,307
26,826	20,809	11,531	12,245	11,724	14,529
251,033	214,449	180,019	177,459	159,623	133,536
36,669	33,016	26,517	24,847	18,014	17,685
6,228	4,795	4,187	3,524	2,057	1,985
561,254	492,260	420,170	373,798	315,057	270,079
47,085	31,634	34,820	32,866	22,063	17,054
7,523	6,822	6,621	5,427	3,380	2,590
165,241	143,671	133,868	118,598	110,479	101,781
222,718	182,101	158,507	133,731	115,927	108,463
395,482	332,594	298,996	257,756	229,786	212,834
130,519	108,591	95,092	83,745	75,052	66,763
264,963	224,003	203,904	174,011	154,734	146,071
$ 873,302	$747,897	658,894	$580,675	$491,854	$433,204
$ 15,921	$ 4,574	$ 4,647	$ 29,836	$ 4,564	$ 14,087
66,685	56,840	52,302	40,568	39,016	34,479
28,675	26,761	23,160	16,914	17,224	14,191
11,697	12,612	10,362	7,405	5,696	4,990
2,763	2,796	2,811	2,448	3,278	2,920
5,317	4,622	3,304	2,641	1,918	1,776
18,988	27,465	23,672	8,841	12,177	12,079
23,889	21,822	17,795	16,423	9,241	10,752
4,786	4,359	6,432	6,998	6,531	7,033
$ 178,721	$161,851	$144,485	$132,074	$ 99,645	$102,307
147,592	112,876	119,941	111,066	148,895	113,486
64,025	47,422	28,972	21,167	15,530	11,861
29,203	28,835	28,397	27,996	12,293	12,227
2,982	3,046	3,070	3,080	1,413	1,434
94,744	87,545	80,428	76,851	37,690	37,124
(1,689)					
(16,801)	(13,688)	(9,158)	(7,179)	(3,829)	
374,525	320,010	262,759	215,620	180,217	154,765
482,964	425,748	365,496	316,368	227,784	205,550
$ 873,302	$747,897	$658,894	$580,675	$491,854	$423,204

EXHIBIT 3   Consolidated Statement of Income, 1981–1990 ($000)

	1990	1989	1988	1987
Net sales	$1,286,853	$1,252,793	$1,174,817	$1,102,532
Other income	22,131	22,566	24,155	23,463
Total revenue	$1,308,984	$1,275,359	$1,198,972	$1,125,995
Costs and expenses				
Material, labor, and other production costs	543,602	546,214	540,143	476,725
Selling, distribution, and marketing	431,254	415,597	400,033	355,363
Administrative and general	149,771	148,095	135,224	125,407
Depreciation and amortization	40,251	39,527	34,191	29,059
Interest	27,691	33,479	32,787	24,875
Restructuring charge	—	23,591	—	12,371
	$1,192,569	$1,206,503	$1,142,378	$1,023,800
Income before income taxes	116,415	68,856	56,594	102,195
Income taxes	44,238	24,582	23,203	38,834
Net income	$ 72,177	$ 44,274	$ 33,391	$ 63,361
Net income per share	$2.25	$1.38	$1.04	$1.97

1985. However, AG's financial performance in the mid- to late 1980s was disappointing, with the profit margin falling to 2.84 percent in 1988 with an ROI of 2.90 percent. In 1990, AG's profit margin had risen to 5.51 percent with an ROI of 6.33.

Irving Stone commented about AG's 1990 performance:

> Fiscal 1990 revenues were a record $1.31 billion. This marks the 84th consecutive year that revenues have increased since the company's founding in 1906.
>
> And, . . . revenue was driven by higher sales of everyday greeting cards, our low-cost, high-margin core products. Fourth quarter sales were particularly strong. We expect to continue reporting good sales results.
>
> The market value of our common stock rose 47 percent, from $21.25 on February 28, 1989 to $31.25 at the fiscal year close on February 28, 1990. This compares favorably to 27 percent increases for both the Dow Jones Industrial Average and the Standard and Poor's 500 Stock Index. Total return to stockholders—share price appreciation plus dividends—was 50 percent in fiscal 1990. (Source: 1990 Annual Report.)

AG's stock price has ranged from a low of 9½ in 1981 to a high of 37⅛ in 1990.

MANAGEMENT

AG is organized via a divisional profit center basis. Each division has its own budget committee, while an executive management committee comprised of five

1986	1985	1984	1983	1982	1981
$1,012,451	$919,371	$817,329	$722,431	$605,970	$489,213
23,200	26,287	22,585	20,252	17,634	9,059
$1,035,651	$945,658	$839,914	$742,683	$623,604	$498,272
416,322	377,755	339,988	310,022	276,071	222,993
308,745	274,095	246,456	217,022	179,021	140,733
131,928	123,750	112,363	96,012	76,494	61,033
23,471	18,799	15,507	13,890	12,752	10,863
19,125	15,556	16,135	24,086	21,647	13,548
—	—	—	—	—	—
$ 899,591	$809,955	$730,449	$661,032	$565,985	$449,170
136,060	135,703	109,465	81,651	57,619	49,102
61,635	61,338	49,807	37,069	24,776	22,587
$ 74,425	$ 74,365	$ 59,658	$ 44,582	$32,843	$26,515
$2.32	$2.35	$1.91	$1.54	$1.20	$0.97

senior executives approves the strategic plans for all the divisions. Strategic plans are established for 1, 3, 10, and 20 year time frames. Corporate AG maintains strict budgetary and accounting controls.

The basic domestic greeting card business is placed under the U.S. Greeting Card Division. Domestic and International Subsidiary Operations, including the licensing division, are a second unit, with corporate management a third. AG decentralized its structure in 1983.

U.S. Greeting Card Division

This division encompasses the core business of greeting cards and related products, including manufacturing, sales, merchandising, research, and administrative services. It produces and distributes greeting cards and related products domestically. The same products are distributed throughout the world by international subsidiaries and licensees.

Domestic and International Subsidiaries

AG's domestic and international subsidiary operations include the following:

Domestic
Acme Frame Products
A.G. Industries, Inc.

Plus Mark, Inc.
Wilhold Hair Care Products
Summit Corporation/Summit Collection
Those Characters from Cleveland, Inc.

International
Carlton Cards, Ltd.—Canada
Rust Craft Canada
Carlton Cards, Ltd.—England
Carlton Cards France
Felicitaciones Nacionales S.A. de C.V.—Mexico

The number of domestic operations in 1986 included seven versus six in 1990. Firms divested included AmToy, Inc., Drawing Board Greeting Cards, Inc., and Tower Products, Inc.

The number of international operations in 1986 was 13 versus five in 1990. Among the international operations consolidated included one in Canada, four in continental Europe, one in Monaco, and four in the United Kingdom.

Exhibit 5 provides a corporate directory of management personnel and their divisional assignments.

AG's domestic and international sales are listed below:

| | Sales Recap ($000) | | | | Proportions of Total Sales | |
| | | | | | U.S. | Foreign |
Year	Domestic	Gross Profit Margin	Foreign	Gross Profit Margin	Sales	Sales
1990	$1,088,438	11.86%	$220,546	6.79%	83.15%	16.85%
1989	1,039,464	7.75	235,895	9.22	81.50	18.50
1988	996,628	7.79	202,344	5.80	83.12	16.88
1987	940,565	13.28	185,430	1.19	83.53	16.47
1986	874,255	15.38	161,396	12.82	84.42	15.58
1985	799,805	16.51	145,853	13.18	84.58	15.42
1984	717,057	15.18	122,857	13.61	85.37	15.63
1983	631,143	14.29	111,549	13.94	85.00	15.00
1982	523,467	12.54	100,137	13.61	85.40	14.60
1981	440,516	12.27	57,756	14.87	88.41	11.59

Source: AG Annual Reports.

FUTURE OF AG

When asked about the future of AG, Morry Weiss responded,

We are poised for perhaps the most successful period in our history.

We are prepared to strengthen our core business and improve our position in the greeting card industry; to provide a greater return to our shareholders; and to afford our employees even greater opportunities for growth and career advancement.

EXHIBIT 4 Selected Financial Data, Years Ended February 28 or 29, 1990–1986

	1990	**1989**	**1988**	**1987**	**1986**
Summary of Operations					
Total revenue	$1,308,984	$1,275,359	$1,198,972	$1,125,995	$1,035,651
Materials, labor and other production expenses	543,602	546,214	540,143	476,725	420,747
Depreciation and amortization	40,251	39,527	34,191	20,059	23,471
Interest expense	27,691	33,479	32,787	24,875	19,125
Net income	72,177	44,274	33,391	63,361	74,425
Net income per share	2.25	1.38	1.04	1.97	2.32
Cash dividends per share	0.66	0.66	0.66	0.66	0.62
Fiscal year-end market price/share	31.25	21.25	17.63	28.75	35.62
Average number shares outstanding	32,029,533	32,146,971	32,068,752	32,212,556	32,059,851
Financial Position					
Accounts receivable	$ 254,285	$ 242,582	$ 278,559	$ 284,135	$ 240,471
Inventories	243,314	239,896	316,354	282,515	251,033
Working capital	480,189	452,841	428,378	434,427	382,533
Total assets	1,141,016	1,087,620	1,150,281	1,022,619	873,302
Capital additions	42,869	41,938	96,682	68,740	61,799
Long-term debt	235,497	246,732	273,492	235,005	147,592
Shareholders' equity	604,604	564,988	538,687	524,443	482,964
Shareholders' equity/share	18.89	17.55	16.75	16.32	15.01
Net return on average shareholders' equity	12.3%	8.0%	6.3%	12.7%	16.5%
Pretax return on total revenue	8.9%	5.4%	4.7%	9.1%	13.1%

The strategies we will employ to achieve our goals for the new year and beyond are clear. We have well-defined corporate strengths which we will target to build even stronger partnerships with retailers and consumers. (1990 Annual Report.)

Irving Stone's view of the future included:

We are optimistic about the future. We are confident that we can achieve even more exciting results . . . in the future.

We face the future confident that our commitment to help people build and maintain relationships will produce even more innovative products like Couples. (1989 Annual Report.)

According to the *U.S. Industrial Outlook,* industry sales should grow between three to four percent annually through 1992. Moderate growth is predicted due to forecasted moderate growth in the GNP, real disposable personal income, and personal consumption expenditures. For continued growth and profitability, *U.S. Industrial Outlook* recommends diversification into related product lines, institution of more cost-cutting strategies, monitoring of demand for current lines, divesting of unprofitable lines, and better matching of demand with supply to avoid after-holiday returns.

EXHIBIT 5 Corporate Directory

Board of Directors

Irving I. Stone[a]
Chairman

Morry Weiss[a]
President
Chief Executive Officer

Scott S. Cowen[b]
Dean, Weatherhead School
of Management
Case Western Reserve University

Edward Fruchtenbaum[a]
President
U.S. Greeting Card Division

Herbert H. Jacobs
(personal investments and consultant)

Frank E. Joseph[b]
Retired Attorney

Millard B. Opper
Retired Chairman of
Canadian Operations

Albert B. Ratner[a]
President and CEO
Forest City Enterprises, Inc.
(real estate development and operation)

Harry H. Stone[b]
President
The Courtland Group
(personal investments)

Milton A. Wolf[b]
Former United States Ambassador
to Austria
(personal investments)

Morton Wyman[a]
Retired Executive Vice President

Abraham Zaleznik
Professor
Harvard Business School
(consultant to business
and government)

Corporate Officers

Irving I. Stone
Chairman

Morry Weiss
President
Chief Executive Officer

Edward Fruchtenbaum
President
U.S. Greeting Card Division

Ronald E. Clouse
Senior Vice President

Rubin Feldman
Senior Vice President

Henry Lowenthal
Senior Vice President
Chief Financial Officer

Packy Nespeca
Senior Vice President
Corporate Trade Development

James R. Van Arsdale
Senior Vice President

John M. Klipfell
Senior Vice President

Harvey Levin
Senior Vice President
Human Resources

Jon Groetzinger, Jr.
General Counsel and Secretary

William S. Meyer
Controller

Eugene B. Scherry
Treasurer

U.S. Greeting Card Division

Edward Fruchtenbaum
President

Sales and Marketing

Mary Ann Corrigan-Davis
Vice President
Product Management

Gary E. Johnston
Vice President
Creative

Raymond P. Kenny
Vice President
Planning and Research

William R. Mason
Vice President
General Sales Manager

Dan Moraczewski
Vice President, Sales
Zone I

William R. Parsons
Vice President, Sales
Zone II

Donovan R. McKee
Vice President, Sales
Carlton Cards

George Wenz
Vice President, Sales
National Accounts

Operations

James R. Van Arsdale
Senior Vice President

James H. Edler
Vice President,
Materials Management

Dean D. Trilling
Vice President,
Information Services

John T. Fortner
Vice President,
Manufacturing

EXHIBIT 5 Cont'd. Corporate Directory

Operations Cont'd.

Thomas O. Davis
Vice President,
Manufacturing—
Everyday Division

Robert C. Swilik
Vice President,
Manufacturing—
Seasonal Division

Domestic and International Subsidiary Operations

Ronald E. Clouse
Senior Vice President

Acme Frame Products, Inc.
Cleveland, Ohio
Howard Reese, President

A.G. Industries, Inc.
Cleveland, Ohio
Charles H. Nervig, President

Plus Mark, Inc.
Cleveland, Ohio
Erwin Weiss, President

Wilhold Hair Care Products
Cleveland, Ohio
Ronald J. Peer, President

Dale J. Beinker
Vice President, International

Carlton Cards, Ltd.
Dewsbury, England
Alistair Mackay, Chairman

Carlton Cards France
Paris, France
Raphael Barda, Managing Director

Felicitaciones Nacionales S.A. de C.V.
Mexico City, Mexico
Antionio Felix G., President

John M. Klipfell
Senior Vice President

Carlton Cards, Ltd.
Toronto, Ontario
James E. Semon, President

Rust Craft Canada
Brampton, Ontario
Mike Johnson, General Manager

The Summit Corporation
Cleveland, Ohio
Alan Vilensky, Vice President

Summit Collection
Cleveland, Ohio
Joy Sweeney, Vice President

**Those Characters
from Cleveland, Inc.**
Cleveland, Ohio
Jack. S. Chojnacki,
Ralph E. Shaffer,
Co-Presidents

[a]Member of executive committee.
[b]Member of audit committee.
Source: AG 1990 Annual Report.

EXHIBIT 6   Greeting Card Industry Consumption Forecast

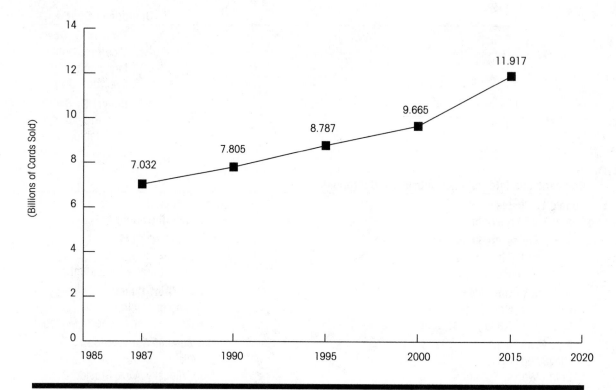

Source: Prudential-Bache Securities, Inc.

The unit growth rate for the greeting card industry between 1987 and 2015 is estimated to be between 1 and 3 percent. Exhibit 6 provides the forecast according to Prudential-Bache Securities. The primary reason for the slowing of unit growth is due to the postwar baby boomers who have already entered their high card-consumption years. With the declining birth rate of the 1970s and 1980s, consumption of cards is expected to decline.

However, greeting card officials optimistically project that the rate of consumption will increase moderately from the current per-capita rate of 29 cards to 44 cards per-capita by 2015. Greeting card sources also report that consumers are upgrading their purchases to higher-priced cards, thus generating more profits per sale. The aging population, those over 55, also tend to send more cards than do younger persons.

Prudential-Bache's expectations for the future of the greeting card industry include:

Price competition will remain a concern because of the maturity of the industry and the limited number of large players.

At least 5–10 percent of the industry's current sales are to retail outlets that the industry leaders will never serve due to the small size of these outlets, which makes [them] too expensive to reach.

The greeting card industry is an area ripe for potential acquisition.

AG is and will continue to experience increased competition in its promotional gift-wrap area.

The big three can be challenged by any small, well-run company.

It is unlikely that the big three with combined market share of 80–85 percent will continue to expand to "own the market." The dynamic competitive nature of the industry prohibits this.

There is not much room for the big three to grow by capturing more of the remaining market they are not reaching. (Prudential-Bache Greeting Cards Industry Update, August 9, 1989.)

As CEO Morry Weiss thought about the future, he wondered what directions he would give his strategic planning committee as they formulated AG's strategies for the 1990s. Looking again at the 10-year summary, he pondered what changes AG should make in its competitive strategies.

REFERENCES

American Greetings Annual Reports, 1981–1990.

American Greetings 10-K Forms, 1988–1989.

"American Greetings." *Insider's Chronicle,* February 8, 1988, p. 3.

"American Greetings Corporation." *Moody's Industrial Manual,* 1989, p. 1,428.

"American Greetings." *Value Line,* April 27, 1990.

"Flounder." *Forbes,* April 25, 1988, p. 352.

"Funny Valentines." *American Demographics,* February 1989, p. 7.

"Greeting Cards Industry Update." Prudential-Bache Securities report, December 30, 1988.

"Greeting Cards Industry Update." Prudential-Bache Securities report, August 9, 1989.

"Greeting Cards Industry Update." Prudential-Bache Securities report, September 27, 1989.

"Greeting Cards Departments . . . Mass Retail Outlets." *GM News,* 1989, pp. 10+.

U.S. Industrial Outlook. Washington, D.C.: U.S. Department of Commerce, 1988, pp. 29–16 to 29–17.

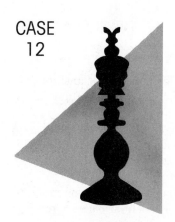

CASE
12

Deere & Company: Into the 1990s

PETER G. GOULET

Worldwide net sales to our dealers increased 30 percent to $5.4 billion in 1988, the highest level since 1981. Net income totaled $315.4 million, a record level of earnings for the company. . . . We view the future, then, with a sense of optimism . . . (Annual Report, Deere & Company, 1988)

Retail Sales Start the Year with a Thud
(Headline in *Implement & Tractor,* March 1989, p. 5)

Deere & Co. Posts Profit Rise of 51% for Its 2nd Period
(Headline in *The Wall Street Journal,* July 1989)

Through most of the 1980s Deere & Company did not experience the success it had in 1988 and 1989. From 1982 to 1987 the firm was battling the impact of the worst recession in the farm belt since the 1930s, suffering six straight years of depressed earnings. Although Deere took a number of steps to diversify, cut costs, and reduce its inventories and breakeven point, its continued heavy reliance on sales to the farm sector produced heavy losses in 1986 and 1987 of $229 million and $99 million, respectively.

The long recession of the 1980s resulted in the financial restructuring of farm assets and the winnowing of the weaker farmers. Those that remained seemed ready to buy new equipment in a search for increased productivity. However, early in 1988 it looked like disaster would strike again as the entire farm belt suffered from the most serious drought since the dust bowl days. In spite of the drought, however, Deere produced record earnings as high farm prices, record government subsidies, and drought payments protected farm income. Further, the drought reduced carryover stocks of feed grains to their lowest levels of the decade, portending higher prices in 1989.

The only cloud on this otherwise sunny horizon is the fact that the drought continued through the winter of 1988 to 1989. This left soil moisture levels critically low and dramatically reduced the winter wheat crop. Spring and early summer rains continued at only half of normal levels through July. In spite of this threat to the otherwise fragile farm recovery, Deere enjoyed record profits in the first half of 1989. Did this mean that the firm's efforts at restructuring had finally begun to pay dividends, or would the next recession in the 1990s again plunge the company into a series of massive losses?

DEERE & COMPANY STRATEGY IN THE 1980s

In the 1970s the management of Deere & Company reacted to growing strength in the farm belt in two ways. First, it made a number of large capital improvements. Manufacturing facilities were reorganized and several new factories were constructed. The firm built an automated engine plant and an automated tractor assembly plant which was widely hailed as one of the most modern manufacturing plants in the world. It also doubled the size of its large research facility. In addition to providing what management felt was a necessary expansion of capacity, these capital projects greatly increased Deere's efficiency. As a result, the sales per employee rose from $56,700 in 1976 to $140,200 in 1988. Through this efficiency Deere sought not only to increase in size, but also to establish itself as the industry's low-cost producer. Moreover, as the 1970s came to a close, Deere's major competitors were struggling, producing much of their output in old, inefficient plants. Case, International Harvester, Massey-Ferguson, and Allis-Chalmers were all in trouble and Deere saw its opportunity to emerge as the clear industry volume leader, as well. What it apparently did not see was the danger that the failure of these other competitors would pose to the whole industry in a severe recession.

The second part of Deere's strategy involved diversification. Two new business lines were given increasing attention in the 1970s: industrial equipment and, later, home and garden tractors and equipment. Both of these product lines were logical extensions of Deere's expertise in manufacturing and its reputation for quality. Industrial equipment shared many design and marketing characteristics with agricultural equipment. Both are based heavily on engine, power train, and hydraulic technology. Quality and reliability, as well as a strong dealer network and the availability of financing, are also important for both types of products. All of these characteristics represent traditional strengths for Deere.

Deere & Company also extended its existing product lines into home and commercial lawn care products, although these lines naturally share less of the firm's expertise than do its other extensions. This lawn and garden product group marked Deere's entrance into consumer markets. Dealer requirements in this market are much different than for agricultural and industrial equipment. More dealers are required and they must be located in suburban rather than rural locations. Although these dealers must also service their customers, repairs and parts represent a smaller part of sales and profits for these dealers than for tractor dealers. Further, consumers are generally less knowledgeable about the product and less willing to engage in necessary maintenance.

As the farm crisis of the 1980s unfolded, both the lawn tractor and industrial equipment product lines were developed with even more urgency to offset steady declines in the agricultural equipment business. This activity was complemented by diversification in Deere's financial subsidiary, including the addition of insurance products and an expansion of the scope of lending activities to include production loans to farmers. In addition, in 1984 and 1985 Deere was operating at such a low level of capacity utilization (less than 25 percent) that it embarked on a number of new manufacturing ventures designed to take advantage of its highly integrated structure by selling up to $100 million of parts annually to original equipment manufacturers (OEMs). The firm began producing engine blocks and diesel engines for various divisions of General Motors and motor home chassis for Winnebago. Further diversification involved the purchase of the world rights to aviation applications for the rotary engine and a major agreement to provide tractor technology to the People's Republic of China. Finally, in its biggest move, Deere signed an agreement to develop a jointly owned diesel engine firm with GM's Detroit-Allison Division. Deere was to provide its engine plant and engineering capability and Allison was to add its plants and products, ultimately producing a firm with expected sales of $1.5 billion to $2 billion a year.

AGRICULTURAL EQUIPMENT INDUSTRY ENVIRONMENT

Although the sales mix of Deere and Company has changed in the last decade, the majority of the firm's revenues are still provided by farm equipment sales (see Exhibit 1). The farm environment is complex and volatile. The 1970s were largely a period of increasing prosperity in the farm economy, based in large part on rising land prices and farm receipts. However, the prosperity did not last. Prolonged inflation in the economy led to higher interest rates and eventually, two recessions. Ultimately, the high interest rates increased the burden on farmers who had borrowed heavily to expand production in the previous decade, forcing many of them into bankruptcy.

An important trend influencing the farm belt of the 1980s was the expansion of farm production in the 1970s. This expansion resulted in a complex chain of events. Government policy had encouraged planting, "from fence row to fence row." Land values increased, causing the book values of farm properties to increase, creating many paper millionaires. However, because the prices received by farmers for their products are determined by supply and demand, they are largely beyond the control of any individual producer. Thus, as Exhibit 2 shows, higher domestic production, coupled with increasing overseas productivity, resulted in increased supplies of farm outputs and reduced growth in the demand for U.S. exports. In addition, the inflation and energy shortages of the 1970s caused the prices of inputs to the farm sector to rise faster than the prices received by farmers, exceeding them for the first time in 1980. This cost–price squeeze further encouraged farmers to increase production to raise revenues and profits through productivity. Exhibits 2 and 3 illustrate how all these trends collectively caused grain stocks to rise to all-time highs by 1986, depressing prices for receipts far below the price levels of inputs. High interest rates, falling farm product prices, and falling values for farm property combined to reduce farm equity and resulted in high numbers of farm bankruptcies in the mid-1980s (see Exhibit 3).

Collectively, all these trends encouraged a dramatic rise in government subsidies and a reduction in the sales of expensive farm equipment (see Exhibit 4).

EXHIBIT 1 Deere & Company Income Statements, Years Ending October 31 ($millions)

Item	1985	Percentage	1986	Percentage	1987	Percentage	1988	Percentage	Average Percentage Growth/Year
Sales									
Farm equipment	$3,118	76.8%	$2,648	75.3%	$3,223	77.9%	$4,203	78.3%	10.5%
Industrial equipment	943	23.2	868	24.7	912	22.1	1,162	21.7	7.2
Net sales	4,061	100.0	3,516	100.0	4,135	100.0	5,365	100.0	9.7
Cost of sales	3,355	82.6	3,271	93.0	3,669	88.7	4,367	81.4	9.2
Gross profit	706	17.4	245	7.0	466	11.3	998	18.6	12.2
Less									
General & admin. expense	508	12.5	317	9.0	304	7.3	315	5.9	−14.7
Other operating expenses	54	1.3	225	6.4	214	5.2	216	4.0	58.7
Depreciation	184	4.5	191	4.7	184	4.4	180	3.4	−.7
Operating profit	(40)	−1.0	(488)	−13.1	(235)	−5.7	287	5.4	N.A.
Other income	206	5.1	188	5.4	213	5.2	225	4.2	3.0
Interest & other	(199)	4.9	(214)	6.1	(189)	4.6	(164)	3.1	−6.3
Income before taxes	(33)	−0.8	(513)	−13.9	(211)	−5.1	349	6.5	N.A.
Income tax	(65)	−1.6	(284)	−8.1	(113)	−2.7	33	.6	N.A.
Net income	32	0.8	(230)	−5.8	(98)	−2.4	316	5.9	114.5
Per share									
Income	0.46		−3.38		−1.46		4.32		
Dividends	1.00		0.75		0.25		0.65		
Capital expenditure	144		173		171		185		
R & D	223		225		214		180		
Employees	40,509		37,793		37,931		38,268		
Sales/Employ ($)	100,249		93,033		109,014		140,195		
Farm equipment									
Sales	3,118		2,648		3,223		4,203		
Operating profit	65		(392)		(136)		284		
Identified assets	3,625		2,960		2,909		3,207		
Industrial equipment									
Sales	943		868		912		1,162		
Operating profit	22		4		9		97		
Identified assets	732		646		742		916		
Corporate and Subsidiaries									
Pretax income	−120		−125		−84		−32		
Identified assets	4,787		5,330		4,657		5,173		
Foreign sales	22.0%		25.1%		24.7%		24.1%		

EXHIBIT 2 Selected Farm Price Indexes, 1977 = 100

	All Farm Receipts	All Farm Inputs	Equipment Expenditures	Agricultural Land and Buildings	Value of Interest Paid	Consumer Prices
1980	134.0	138.0	131.0	145.0	174.0	136.0
1981	139.0	150.0	145.7	158.0	211.0	150.1
1982	133.0	157.0	157.2	157.0	241.0	159.3
1983	134.0	160.0	164.9	148.0	250.0	164.4
1984	142.0	165.0	169.8	146.0	251.0	171.4
1985	128.0	163.0	170.5	134.3	250.0	177.5
1986	123.0	159.0	171.8	112.0[a]	211.0	180.9
1987	127.0	161.0	171.5	105.0[a]	190.0	192.4
1988E	138.0	170.0	187.6	108.0[a]	186.0	195.2

[a]Estimated from graphs produced by the U.S. Department of Agriculture.
Sources: Farm price data from U.S. Department of Agriculture; consumer price data from U.S. Department of Labor.

This decline was even more dramatic when viewed in real terms (exclusive of price increases). As Exhibit 4 illustrates, the real value of customer expenditures on agricultural equipment in 1988 was estimated at only 40 percent of its 1980 level. This means that on a constant-dollar basis, the purchase of farm equipment units has declined 60 percent in the decade of the 1980s. Industry shipments to dealers showed a similar trend, falling 58 percent during the same time period.

This reduction in real equipment sales had a dramatic effect on the industry's dealer network. Dealers failed in record numbers. As a result dealers have adopted

EXHIBIT 3 Selected Farm Financial Data

	Net Farm Income ($billions)	Net Cash Income ($billions)	Farm Assets ($billions)	Farm Debt ($billions)	Average Farm Size (Acres)	Grain and Feed Stocks (millions of metric tons)[a]			
						Supply	Domestic Use	Exports	Ending Stock
1980	$18.8	$34.2	$996.1	$166.8	427	357.7	171.0	114.9	71.8
1981	28.6	32.8	996.7	182.3	425	400.6	178.6	110.8	111.2
1982	23.5	37.8	961.2	189.5	428	442.6	193.1	96.3	153.2
1983	12.2	36.9	945.3	192.7	432	360.1	183.0	97.7	79.4
1984	30.0	38.7	848.5	190.8	438	393.1	197.0	97.3	98.8
1985	28.9	46.6	749.0	175.2	446	444.3	200.8	62.8	180.9
1986	32.8	51.4	691.6	155.3	456	497.0	217.0	76.0	204.0
1987	39.5	57.1	708.9	142.7	461	483.0	215.0	98.0	169.0
1988E	33.0	58.0	743.0	139.0	465[b]	368.0	206.0	94.0	68.0
1989E	38.0	50.0	757.0	143.0	—	—	—	—	—

[a]Supply equals previous year's ending stock plus domestic production.
[b]Estimated from graphs prepared by the U.S. Department of Agriculture.
Source: U.S. Department of Agriculture.

EXHIBIT 4 Agricultural Equipment Sales ($billions)

	Total Customer Expenditures			Industry Shipments to Dealers		
	Total Expenditures	Price Index for Agriculture Equipment Expenditures (1977 = 100)	Real Expenditures (1 ÷ 2)	Value of Shipments	Price Index for Industry Shipments (1977 = 100)	Real Industry Sales
1980	$10.64	131.0	$8.12	$12.84	132.9	$9.66
1981	10.22	145.7	7.01	13.95	148.5	9.39
1982	7.67	157.2	4.88	10.74	160.5	6.69
1983	7.34	164.9	4.45	8.98	164.8	5.45
1984	7.22	169.8	4.25	9.86	169.5	5.82
1985	5.60	170.5	3.28	8.21	169.8	4.84
1986	4.61	171.8	2.68	6.74	171.0	3.94
1987	5.76	171.5	3.36	6.95	171.6	4.05
1988E	6.05	187.6	3.22	7.09	174.8	4.06

Source: Data on expenditures from U.S. Department of Agriculture; data on shipments from U.S. Department of Commerce.

numerous strategies to survive. Parts sales and service have become increasingly important. Price pressures have forced dealers to become more aggressive marketers, focusing more closely on selected customer groups. Dealers will probably seek inventory reductions by encouraging their customers to plan ahead and order equipment in advance of their needs. This action will lower dealer investments and carrying costs, as well as the markdowns which go along with high stock levels.[1] Finally, it is expected many dealers have begun to abandon their traditionally exclusive approach to producers by broadening the number of product lines they carry. To combat this trend, Deere has announced that beginning May 1, 1990 it will amend its dealer agreement to allow it to demand that dealers separate their non-Deere business if, in the company's opinion, they conflict with the dealers' fulfillment of their obligations to the company. This proposal has been met with nearly universal objection.[2]

The behavior of the agricultural environment and the resulting trend in industry sales have caused significant changes in the industry. J. I. Case and International Harvester are now both owned by Tenneco. Tenneco and Deere are the only remaining firms producing tractors in the United States. Massey-Ferguson has been reorganized as Varity Corporation (Canada) and farm equipment accounts for less than half of its sales. Ford, the leading producer of tractors in unit volume, purchased the New Holland equipment division of Sperry Corporation and moved all tractor production overseas. The farm equipment business of Allis-Chalmers is now owned by German producer Deutz. Although exact figures are not available, the market shares of these producers are estimated in Exhibit 5.

At the present time most, if not all, of the tractors below 100 horsepower (hp) are produced outside the United States, largely by subsidiaries of U.S. firms and by the Japanese. These tractors are designed primarily for smaller farms and are

EXHIBIT 5 Estimated Market Shares in Agricultural Equipment Industry

Company	Overall Share, 1984	1988 Farm Tractor Sales, Estimated Market Share			
		<40 hp	40–99 hp	>100 hp	4WD
Deere & Company	32.4%	17%	27%	45%	30%
Case-IH (Tenneco)	19.8	8	18	31	36
Ford-New Holland	15.0	18	22	7	27
Varity	11.1	12	11	4	1
Deutz-Allis	4.0	4	5	5	3
Kubota (Japan)	9.0	33	10	—	—
Others	8.7	8	7	8	3
Unit sales, 1987		30,718		15,911	1,653
Unit sales, 1978		66,836		65,257	8,744

Sources: Wertheim & Co. (1984 shares); *Implement & Tractor*, January 1989, pp. 6–7, 30 (1988 shares); Standard and Poor's (unit sales).

considerably lower in price than the higher-horsepower and large four wheel drive (4WD) models. Deere, especially, has concentrated on the larger models because they feel that for farmers to achieve satisfactory productivity, it is inevitable that they will be forced to work on large farms and utilize powerful equipment.[3]

This trend toward rising farm size is illustrated in Exhibit 3. In 1980, there were more than 2.4 million farms in the United States. By 1987 that number had dropped to less than 2.2 million. In addition, the U.S. Department of Labor estimates that the number of farmers and farm workers will drop by nearly 30 percent by the year 2000.[4] Although these trends point to a rise in the capital intensity of farming, there are reasons why the trend may not continue indefinitely. As farm size increases and heavy equipment must be used, there are some negative consequences. Large tractors use a great deal of energy and there have been few improvements in efficiency in recent years.[5] Heavy equipment also causes soil compaction, which has negative environmental consequences. Heavy equipment may also destroy valuable top soil, which cannot be replaced in any reasonable time frame.

In addition to environmental problems, heavy equipment is very expensive. The typical 4WD tractor costs over $100,000 and purchases have been subject to high interest rates. In 1987 only 14 percent of the farms in the United States even had annual sales exceeding $100,000.[6] Although these high-revenue farms accounted for 76 percent of the total cash receipts and 89 percent of the net income received by all farms, they had less than half the farm assets. Also, a considerable number of the most prosperous farms in the United States, for example, are less than 40 acres in size, too small to need heavy equipment.[7] Finally, a tractor is not enough to run a farm. Plows, cultivating and planting equipment, and some means of harvesting the crop are also needed. Harvesting equipment can also cost in excess of $100,000. The net effect of these factors is illustrated in Exhibit 5, which shows that while unit sales of tractors under 100 hp have declined 54 percent in the last decade, unit sales of over-100 hp tractors and four wheel drive models declined 76 percent and 81 percent, respectively, from 1978 to 1987. Self-propelled combine sales declined 77 percent during the same period.

CONSTRUCTION EQUIPMENT INDUSTRY ENVIRONMENT

Although the market for industrial and construction equipment is not affected by exactly the same factors which influence farming, there are similarities. Users of this equipment require reliable products, high levels of service in the field, and financing for product purchases. There are also many technological similarities between the two types of equipment. The market for industrial equipment is strongly influenced by interest rates for two reasons. High interest rates influence the ability to finance new construction as well as the ability to purchase the equipment. As a result of the influence of interest rates and overall economic activity, the sale of construction equipment tends to be cyclical. This is illustrated in Exhibit 6, which shows industry sales for the decade of the 1980s in current dollars and in real terms. For comparison, the exhibit also presents Deere & Company sales for both its heavy equipment product lines for the same period.

The decade of the 1980s has been characterized by a more or less continuous rise in the general level of construction activity. Although growth in new construction has slowed since 1986, growth has been continuous since 1982. The real sales of construction equipment, however, have not kept pace with the level of activity. Uncertainty over interest rates in 1987 to 1988, the latest two years of a prolonged economic expansion, and the resulting impact on housing starts may be

EXHIBIT 6   Construction Equipment Data and Deere & Company Sales Summary ($billions)

| | Index of Construction Activity (1977 = 100) | Construction Equipment Industry Shipments to Dealers | | | Deere & Company Sales[a] | |
		Value of Shipments	Price Index for Industry Shipments (1977 = 100)	Real Industry Sales	Agricultural and Garden Equipment	Industrial and Construction Equipment
1980	133.9	$15.99	135.2	$11.82	$4.488	$0.981
1981	138.4	16.93	151.1	11.20	4.665	0.782
1982	131.1	11.66	157.0	7.42	4.034	0.575
1983	149.6	10.31	161.8	6.37	3.314	0.654
1984	174.8	12.69	164.5	7.71	3.505	0.894
1985	189.3	12.80	166.4	7.69	3.118	0.942
1986	206.8	12.99	167.8	7.74	2.649	0.868
1987	207.3	13.77	170.2	8.09	3.223	0.911
1988E	210.6	14.45	175.0	8.26	4.203	1.162

[a]Sales for Deere & Company are for fiscal years ended October 31.
Source: Shipment data from U.S. Department of Commerce.

one major reason for declining construction growth. In addition, budget pressure on public works and defense spending may also be a major factor influencing current conditions.

The markets for industrial and construction equipment are distinctive and highly segmented. Industrial equipment includes such product groups as forklift trucks and other types of material handling equipment such as overhead cranes, conveyors, and automated inventory storage and retrieval systems. This market is not included in the sales data in Exhibit 6 because Deere does not participate in it. The product segments in the construction equipment market include earthmoving and excavation equipment, logging equipment, mining machinery, paving machines, and other related products. This industry and its various segments are dominated by a few large firms.

Deere & Company participates in many of these product segments, although its primary emphasis is on earthmoving and smaller types of excavating equipment, markets traditionally dominated by Caterpillar. Deere also produces some specialized logging equipment and, through its OEM product lines, it produces original equipment (OEM) parts for many of the market leaders such as Caterpillar and Dresser Industries.

Because of its fundamental role in the building of an infrastructure and the production of natural resources, construction equipment plays a major role in economic development, especially in less developed nations. For this reason the industry has traditionally been heavily involved in exporting its products. Historically, approximately 20 percent of U.S. production has been exported. Caterpillar has typically exported about half of its output. Although the industry contains over 700 firms, six of these provide over 70 percent of the total value of all worldwide production and two-thirds of U.S. exports.[8] Caterpillar is the clear world leader in the industry, with roughly a 35 percent worldwide market share. Other large broad-line producers include Case (Tenneco), Deere, Ingersoll-Rand, Dresser Industries, Clark Equipment, and Komatsu. The market segments dominated by these major producers include:

1. Earthmovers—Caterpillar, Komatsu, Deere
2. Excavators and cranes—American Hoist and Derrick, FMC, Manitowoc
3. Mining machinery—Joy Manufacturing
4. Paving and road building—Barber-Greene, Ingersoll-Rand, Koehring, Dresser Industries, Rexnord

As was the case in the agricultural equipment industry, the decade of the 1980s has been a period of industry consolidation. Many older plants have been closed and more efficient ones constructed. Breakeven points have been lowered dramatically. Caterpillar, in order to be more competitive internationally, closed nine plants from 1983 to 1987 in an attempt to save $250 million and lower overall costs 15 to 20 percent by 1991. Deere has also proceeded in much the same way, cutting the labor content of its industrial equipment by 50 percent in the mid-1980s. To combat the falling dollar, Komatsu, a leading Japanese producer, built a major plant in Tennessee and entered into a joint venture with Dresser Industries. In spite of all these changes, however, the overall outlook for real growth in the industry is not expected to be greater than 2 to 3 percent per year for the next few years.[9]

OTHER MARKETS SERVED BY DEERE

In addition to its domestic agricultural and industrial equipment markets, Deere and Company serves several other markets with lesser amounts of output.

Lawn Care Products

A significant proportion of Deere's agricultural product sales results from the sales of small garden tractors, lawnmowers, and other lawn care equipment, and snow removal equipment for both the consumer and commercial markets. Although reliable figures are not available, these sales probably range between $700 and $750 million.[10] In the few years since it has been in the commercial lawn care market Deere has become the market leader and has added a new golf course turf care line. Deere's lawn care products are sold through a network of over 5,000 dealers, nearly 100 of which have sales in excess of $1 million annually. Overall, the consumer segment of this market is estimated at $3.75 billion in 1988. The market is tied closely to consumer income growth and new housing construction. Accordingly, annual real growth is expected to average 1.5 to 2 percent through 1993.[11] Sales in this market are also affected by the weather and the level of interest rates.

Deere's lawn care lines have achieved strong market positions for many of the same reasons as its other products. The products in the lawn care line are characterized as well-designed, and among the safest, most reliable, and most reasonably priced. *Consumer Reports* recently rated Deere's line among the safest and most effective.[12] Although riding mowers and lawn tractors can easily cost from $1,000 to $4,000, Deere's equipment also rates well on price compared to some of its lower-quality competitors.

OEM Parts

As part of its industrial sales, Deere sells a variety of parts and products to original equipment manufacturers (OEMs). The OEM product line was originally developed as a way of offsetting low capacity utilization. Although reliable figures are not available, this segment of the firm has grown dramatically in recent years. A major product group in this segment is a line of diesel engines and power trains for off-road vehicles. The proposed joint venture with Detroit-Allison was broken off in 1987 for undisclosed reasons. Allison then formed a joint venture with the Penske Company, a firm managed by famous race team manager Roger Penske. In spite of this setback, however, Deere reported that its own diesel engine group sold in excess of 25,000 units in 1988, an increase of 38 percent over the previous year. The engine group has also been successful in achieving a modest level of diesel sales to the government and plans to expand its rotary engine product to operate in land vehicles such as assault craft.

Financial Services and Health Care

As a result of its need to finance the sales of its products, Deere maintains a number of financially-related subsidiaries. Through these operations (currently not consolidated for financial reporting purposes) Deere provides customer financing, loans, leases, and insurance. On January 1, 1989, the credit and leasing subsidiaries were reorganized to form the John Deere Credit Company which, in turn, became the owner of the other finance subsidiaries. This was ostensibly done to coordinate the activities of the finance group and give it greater emphasis in corporate strategic planning. It may also have been done in anticipation of the rising trend toward consolidation of such activities into the regular financial statements. The primary function of this group is to purchase customer loans from dealers. (These receivables appear only in the nonconsolidated balance sheet shown in Exhibit 7.) Loans to dealers for the purchase of equipment are carried on the regular balance sheet shown in Exhibit 8.

The operation of this group closely resembles other such subsidiaries such as General Motors' GMAC. In addition, this subsidiary also purchases loans on boats and recreational vehicles from various dealers of these products. Further, the group also makes farm production and related loans to customers through the Farm Plan division and provides significant amounts of lease financing for equipment. (Over $355 million was outstanding in 1988.)

The other major part of Deere's financial services business centers on insurance. Initially offered to employees and customers, this subsidiary now produces about $350 million in revenues annually. In an effort to control its health care costs, Deere established its own HMO. Its success in this effort encouraged it to sell health care management expertise to other firms. Established in 1985, the firm's health care services subsidiary now generates $140 million in annual revenues.

International Markets

Although Deere produces most of its output in the United States, it also has significant operational capacity outside the United States. Manufacturing plants for tractors, engines, and other equipment are operated in Canada, Spain, France, Germany, South Africa, Australia, and Argentina. In addition, the firm has industrial affiliates in Brazil and Mexico. Sales branches are operated in all the countries where manufacturing is done, as well as Sweden, Italy, and England. As Exhibit 9 shows, the sales in these overseas markets is approximately 25 percent of the total sales of the firm. Exhibit 9 presents additional detail on the firm's foreign operations. As noted earlier, the production of small tractors is almost entirely outside the United States. However, the world market shares shown in Exhibit 5 also show that this production is dominated by U.S.-based firms. Deutz and Kubota are the only major foreign-based producers. As a side note, however, the

EXHIBIT 7 Deere & Company Financial Results—Finance Subsidiaries, Years Ending October 31 ($millions)

	Finance Subsidiary				Insurance Subsidiary			
	1985	1986	1987	1988	1985	1986	1987	1988
Income Statements								
Net revenues	$ 335	$ 324	$ 306	$ 385	$260	$308	$313	$356
Less: expenses	63	58	68	80	227	259	266	306
Operating profit	272	266	238	305	33	49	47	50
Less: interest	172	176	153	180				
Income before taxes	100	90	85	125	33	49	47	50
Less: income taxes	40	36	33	35	7	12	9	13
Net income[a]	$ 60	$ 54	$ 52	$ 90	$ 26	$ 37	$ 38	$ 37
Balance Sheets								
Cash								
Notes receivable	$2,624	$2,540	$2,374	$2,620	$ 40	$ 42	$ 45	$ 31
Investments	443	740	690	521	410	485	539	652
Other assets	94	72	108	132	71	83	93	95
Total assets	$3,161	$3,352	$3,172	$3,273	521	610	677	778
Notes payable	$1,288	$1,344	$1,628	$1,720				
Due John Deere & Company	76	193	17	37				
Policy reserves					218	254	292	350
Unearned premiums					57	70	74	88
Other	370	362	270	218	32	45	46	50
Long-term debt	818	813	598	590				
Total debt	2,552	2,712	2,513	2,565	307	369	412	488
Owners' equity	609	640	659	708	214	241	265	290
	$3,161	$3,352	$3,172	$3,273	$521	$610	$677	$778

[a]Income from both these subsidiaries is entered on the income statement (Exhibit 1) under Other Income.
Balance sheet items above are not included on the consolidated balance sheet (Exhibit 8).

Russians shipped around 2,500 small tractors to the United States in 1988.[13] Because of its existing presence in Europe, Deere should be in a good position to take advantage of the changes in the common market in 1992.

RECENT EVENTS AND PROSPECTS

Since 1985, the return of Deere & Company to profitability has been marked by a number of critical events. Although small profits were reported in 1985, negative operating profits were offset only by profits in the financial services segment. While operating at extremely low levels of capacity utilization in late 1986 and early 1987, the firm suffered from a costly strike. This reduced operations to less than 10 percent of capacity and created huge operating losses.[14] Although the growth in 1987 and 1988 did raise utilization considerably, Deere's state-of-the-art tractor assembly plant still has the capacity to produce more than twice as many tractors as the whole industry sold in the 100 hp and four wheel drive markets in

EXHIBIT 8 Deere & Company Balance Sheets, Years Ending October 31 ($millions)

Item	1985	Percent	1986	Percent	1987	Percent	1988	Percent	Average Percent Growth/Y
Assets									
Current assets									
Cash and marketable securities	$ 88	1.6%	$ 182	3.7%	$ 116	2.4%	$ 49	0.9%	−17.7
Accounts receivable	2,749	50.3	2,079	41.8	2,111	44.3	2,308	44.0	−5.7
Inventory	447	8.2	483	9.7	465	9.8	708	13.5	16.6
Other	150	2.7	218	4.4	45	1.0	50	1.0	−30.7
Total current assets	3,434	62.9	2,961	59.5	2,737	57.5	3,115	59.4	−3.2
Fixed assets									
Plant and equipment	2,629	48.1	2,767	55.6	2,943	61.8	3,056	58.3	5.1
Less accumulated depreciation	1,613	29.5	1,816	36.5	1,960	41.2	2,063	39.3	8.6
Other fixed assets, net	1,012	18.5	1,062	21.3	1,040	21.9	1,137	21.7	3.9
Total fixed assets	2,028	37.1	2,013	40.5	2,023	42.5	2,130	40.6	1.6
Total assets	$5,462	100.0	$4,974	100.0	$4,760	100.0	$5,245	100.0	−1.3
Liabilities and Owners' Equity									
Current liabilities									
Accounts payable	$1,044	19.1	$1,003	20.2	$1,037	21.8	$1,122	21.4	2.4
Notes payable	521	9.5	383	7.7	342	7.2	455	8.7	−4.4
Current payable long-term debt	16	.3	12	.2	13	.3	21	.4	9.7
Taxes payable	333	6.1	111	2.2	58	1.2	84	1.6	−36.8
Other					79	1.7	46	.9	−41.8
Total current liabilities	1,914	35.0	1,509	30.3	1,529	32.1	1,728	33.0	−3.3
Long-term debt Bonds and notes	1,130	20.7	1,290	25.9	1,062	22.3	817	15.6	−10.2
Deferred taxes and pensions	160	2.9	176	3.5	248	5.2	244	4.6	15.1
Total long-term debt	1,290	23.6	1,466	29.5	1,310	27.5	1,061	20.2	−6.3
Equity									
Common stock	491	9.0	492	9.9	497	10.4	760	14.5	15.7
Retained earnings	1,767	32.4	1,507	30.3	1,424	29.9	1,696	32.3	−1.4
Total equity	2,258	41.3	1,999	40.2	1,920	40.3	2,456	46.8	2.8
Total liabilities and owners' equity	$5,462	100.0	$4,974	100.0	$4,760	100.0	$5,245	100.0	−1.3

EXHIBIT 9 Overseas Activity ($millions)

	1988	1987	1986	1985
Net sales				
United States and Canada	$4,418	$3,308	$2,821	$3,432
Overseas	1,574	1,209	1,077	1,070
Less: interarea sales	(627)	(382)	(382)	(441)
	$5,365	$4,135	$3,516	$4,061
Operating profits[a]				
United States and Canada	325	(114)	(403)	33
Overseas	61	(7)	5	45
	$ 386	$ (121)	$ (398)	$ 78
Assets				
United States and Canada	$3,203	$2,782	$2,838	$3,677
Overseas	920	869	768	680
Corporate	1,122	1,109	1,368	1,105
	$5,245	$4,760	$4,974	$5,462
Employees				
United States and Canada	28,200	27,700	26,700	29,600
Overseas	10,100	10,200	11,100	10,900

[a]Includes equity investments in nonconsolidated subsidiaries and affiliates.
Note: Canadian sales are historically about 11 percent of total U.S. and Canada sales. About 82 percent of these are made in the United States and 79 percent of Canadian production is exported to the United States.

1988. Some of this capacity has been absorbed by new products, increases in market share, and the production of chassis for motor homes. Although Deere may never utilize all of its available capacity, cost cutting and increased productivity have allowed the firm to break even on manufacturing operations at only 35 percent of capacity.[15]

Deere's lawn and garden and industrial lines have been expanded since 1985 and have provided increasing profits to the firm, as has the financial service segment. Some of the prospects for the OEM group were reduced when the GM joint venture was dropped and a major GM engine block contract was lost in 1989. Some chassis production has also been sold to a Wisconsin truck manufacturer. However, engine sales have been improved in spite of these setbacks. Further, the firm acquired Funk Manufacturing, a small ($50 million in sales) producer of off-road transmission equipment. In addition, Deere introduced a broad line of new products in its agricultural equipment group in 1989. This was the largest package of new products in the firm's history.

Deere & Company faces the 1990s having diversified, cut costs, and restructured itself to emphasize new products. However, its sales are still dominated by mature, cyclical product markets. In spite of success in consumer markets, the lawn care market, too, is not expected to achieve much real growth, and major competitors such as Toro are not likely to let Deere increase its market share at will. Although the financial services business is growing, Deere lacks the local office network required to become a large consumer lender. Financial services revenues are still dominated by dealer financing in heavy equipment markets. OEM sales are promising, but do not yet provide material revenues. Further, these sales are competitive, as the loss of the engine block contract illustrates, and many of the firm's largest customers are also its competitors. How long can the firm afford to sell its technology to its competitors? Further, Deere still has considerable excess capacity it must eventually utilize.

Endnotes

1. J. Ecker, "Dealers of the '90s," *Implement & Tractor*, April 1989, pp. 24–26.

2. R. Rose, "Deere, Dealers Cross Swords over Plows," *The Wall Street Journal*, November 7, 1989, p. B2.

3. A. Anderson, Jr., "Future Farming," *Omni*, June 1979, pp. 90–94.

4. J. Rachlin, "Best Jobs in the Future," *U.S. News and World Report*, April 25, 1988, pp. 60–62.

5. F. Buckingham, "Why Doesn't Fuel Efficiency Get Any Better?" *Implement & Tractor*, April 1989, pp. 22–23.

6. U.S. Department of Commerce, *Statistical Abstract of the United States* (Washington, D.C.: U.S. Government Printing Office, 1988), Table 1070, p. 614.

7. D. Kendall, "'Superfarm' Numbers Have Grown Rapidly in the Past Decade," *Waterloo Courier*, February 16, 1986.

8. "Steel and Heavy Machinery," *Standard and Poor's Industry Surveys*, July 7, 1989, pp. S35–37.

9. U.S. Department of Commerce, *1989 U.S. Industrial Outlook*, pp. 21-1–21-2.

10. K. Deveny, "As John Deere Sowed, So Shall It Reap," *Business Week*, June 6, 1988, pp. 84–85.

11. *1989 U.S. Industrial Outlook*, pp. 43-8–43-9.

12. "Lawn Tractors: Can They Cut It?" *Consumer Reports*, June 1989, pp. 368–373.

13. J. Zweig. "'It was a matter of economics,'" *Forbes*, February 22, 1988, pp. 106–107.

14. K. Deveny, "Thinking ahead Got Deere in Big Trouble," *Business Week*, December 8, 1986, p. 69.

15. Deveny, "As Deere Sowed," p. 84.

CASE
13

ORYX ENERGY COMPANY

NABIL AHMED,
DALE CHAMNESS,
S. JILL THOMAS,
CATHERINE TOMPKINS &
CONNIE WILLIAMS

Monday Morning Meeting, 7:30 A.M., Oryx Corporate Headquarters

Robert Hauptfuhrer, chairman and CEO of Oryx Energy Company, entered the meeting room briskly. He sat down in his chair and threw the latest copy of *Fortune* magazine on the conference room table. "Gentlemen," he said, "according to *Fortune*, we rank 303 in the list of 500 and third in our individual industry category.[1] This represents a real milestone for our company. As you all know, the last several years have been hard for our company. In 1986, the bottom fell out of oil prices, causing our company a great many problems and forcing layoffs. Fortunately, it looks like things have finally started to turn around for Oryx. Our costs are now under control, we're developing new technologies for oil and gas exploration, and the price of crude oil is on its way back up." Hauptfuhrer paused and looked around the table. He continued, "Now that the crisis is over with, my question to all of you is, 'How do we position Oryx to survive for long-term growth?'"

William Stokes, vice president in charge of planning and development, commented, "The oil and gas market is extremely volatile and cyclical in nature; I think we're already doing the most we can to ensure Oryx's future."

Hauptfuhrer leaned forward in his chair, "What I want is a creative plan for the future, not just the usual stuff. I want to see something that addresses the intermediate and long range and I want it in one week. Stokes, you're in charge of the overall project, however each vice president is to provide you with a report on their respective areas."

Stokes shook his head in agreement. With Hauptfuhrer there was no arguing. It was his way or no way. He wondered where he should begin. He thought to himself, "I guess in order to plan the future, I must start by examining the past and the present situation."

This case was prepared under the supervision of Professor Sexton Adams, University of North Texas, and Professor Adelaide Griffin, Texas Woman's University. © 1992 Sexton Adams & Adelaide Griffin.

INDUSTRY

Jerry Box pulled out his files of news articles. The oil and gas industry had become so volatile in the recent past. He thumbed through them, noting some of the headlines:

> "Pennzoil Sues Texaco over Breach of Contract"
> "Texaco Files for Chapter 11 Reorganization"
> "Diamond Shamrock Restructures into Maxus Energy"
> "Exxon Spills 11 Million Barrels of Oil into Prince William Sound"
> "FTC Investigates Antitrust Violations of Major Oil Companies"

"Indeed," he thought to himself, "the oil and gas industry is full of changes and controversy, but then it always has been."

Perhaps no other major U.S. industry had experienced as colorful a history as the oil and gas industry. The industry was born in this country when the first commercial oil-drilling rig was put into operation near Titusville, Pennsylvania in 1859. From the late 1800s and through 1915, the great oil barons came into power. By the 1880s, the Standard Oil Company controlled approximately 90 percent of the refining industry. Standard remained in complete control until 1915, when the government passed antitrust legislation and forced Standard to dissolve.[2] Today, the industry is full of small, medium, and large producers that compete on a global basis.

There were three primary countries that produce the majority of the world's oil production. Surprisingly, the Soviet Union was the world's largest producer, accounting for approximately 12 million barrels per day of production.[3] The United States produced approximately 7.7 million barrels per day.[4] Saudi Arabia had the world's largest proven oil reserves, estimated at 252 billion barrels.[5] (For a discussion of OPEC, see the Marketing section later in this case.) Total U.S. proven reserves of oil were estimated to be 27.2 billion barrels.[6]

In the past, the Soviet Union had kept a low profile in the world oil markets; however, with the advent of perestroika, it was striving to bring itself to the forefront. The Soviets let it be known that they were looking for joint venture partners with oil and gas exploration expertise. Both Saudi Arabia and the Soviet Union each exported about 4.4 million barrels per day.[7] Total world production of oil was estimated at 58 million barrels per day.[8]

Though the United States was not number one in producing or exporting oil, it was the top importer of energy. This made the United States the single most important market in the oil and gas industry. Imports had steadily climbed over the past decade, despite the oil shortage scares of the 1970s. Exhibit 1 depicts the increase in imports of oil in the United States over the past 10 years. Despite an upward trend in U.S. demand for oil, U.S. production of crude oil was declining, as shown in Exhibit 2.

The oil and gas industry suffered from cyclical ups and downs. In 1980 under the Reagan administration oil prices were deregulated. Oil prices rose, peaking at $32 per barrel in 1981.[9] Prices remained fairly high until 1986, when Saudi Arabia

EXHIBIT 1   U.S. Crude Oil Imports (000 barrels/day)

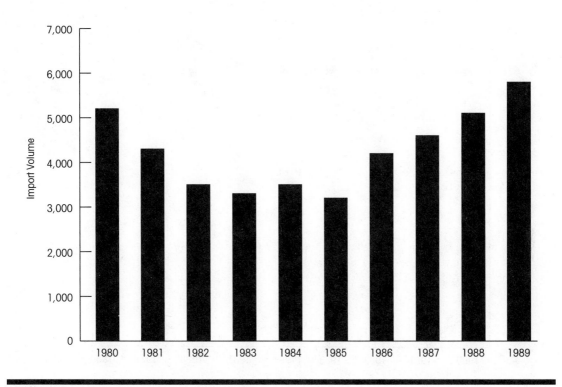

Source: *Oil and Gas Journal,* January 29, 1990.

flooded the market with an extra 2.5 million barrels per day. At that time, prices plummeted to close to $10 per barrel.[10] Since then, prices have risen slowly, and are estimated to reach an average of $18.37 in 1990.[11] Industry experts had predicted that world demand for oil was increasing. Exhibit 3 shows the trends in oil prices over the last 10 years.

Since 1987, independent oil producers had moved to emphasize gas exploration and production. Gas is cheaper to recover and was predicted to increase in price in the future at a faster rate than oil. Like oil, world demand for natural gas was increasing. Exhibit 4 reflects the price trends over the last 10 years for natural gas.

Still gun-shy from the abrupt decline of oil prices in the mid-1980s, producers were reluctant to invest large amounts of capital in oil exploration and discovery. Instead, they tried to acquire much of their oil and gas replacement reserves by purchasing proven reserves owned by other companies.

Recently, acquisitions of oil and gas companies and properties had become especially attractive to U.S. producers. Merger-mania and takeover had become commonplace. In fact, Oryx was rumored to be a takeover target for Pennzoil in mid-1989, however this never materialized.[12]

EXHIBIT 2 U.S. Production of Crude Oil (000 barrels/day)

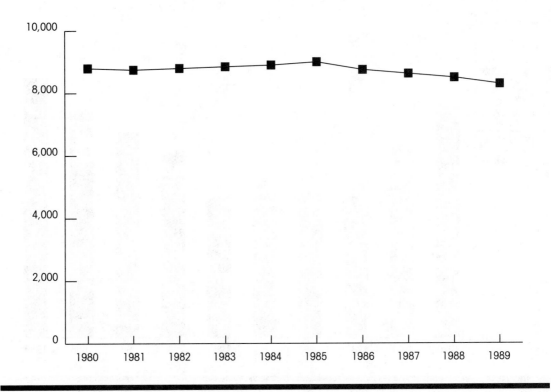

Source: *Oil and Gas Journal,* January 29, 1990.

HISTORY

With the stroke of a pen on November 1, 1988 Oryx Energy Company bounded into the public sector as the largest independent exploration and production company in North America with $3.9 billion in assets and $1.6 billion in equity. For nearly 88 years, Oryx existed as a subsidiary of the Sun Company, Inc., a fully integrated energy company that produced oil and gas and operated refineries, pipelines, and wholesale outlets. To accomplish the spinoff, Sun distributed shares of Oryx's stock to the shareholders of Sun in proportion to their Sun shares owned. The shares quickly began to trade on the New York Stock Exchange.

Sun Company, Inc. decided to spin off Oryx for several reasons. First, as an integrated oil and gas company, Sun was not eligible to take advantage of the several tax deductions and credits that the so-called "independent" producers were allowed. Second, the spinoff allowed the stockholders of the company to realize the equity value that Oryx had accrued over the years. Third, the spinoff allowed the company greater autonomy and flexibility to engage in the competitive and risky business of oil and gas exploration and production. Oryx Energy was in the business of developing, producing, and marketing crude oil, condensate,

EXHIBIT 3   Crude Oil Prices (dollars per barrel)

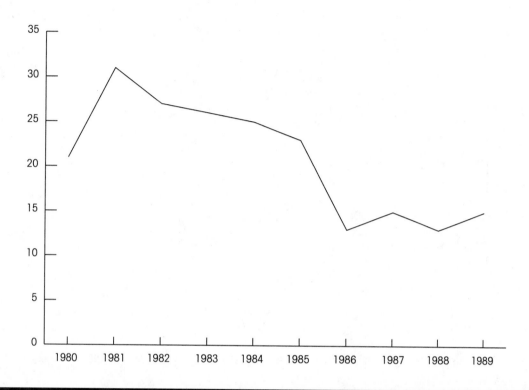

Source: *Oil and Gas Journal,* January 29, 1990.

natural gas, and natural gas liquids.[13] It operated on- and offshore drilling operations in the United States and the United Kingdom.

After the spinoff, the company quickly acted to organize and to streamline its operations. One of management's first actions was to immediately lay off or transfer 800 of its personnel.[14] In July 1989 6 of the 12 field offices were closed.[15] The company had virtually no information systems of its own, so it brought in Price Waterhouse to implement a fully integrated business system. This project was affectionately nicknamed by the staff as "the Blob." The Blob even had a creed of its own, "Thou shalt simplify, simplify, simplify."[16] According to one Oryx manager, Price Waterhouse did not produce an information system that worked, despite the fact they were costing Oryx $1.3 million per month in fees and opportunity costs. Everyone was frustrated with the situation.

Even prior to the spinoff, management was moving to reduce costs. The company had a severe problem with paper overflow and duplication of effort. One executive stated in a meeting with his employees, "We are generating almost one million reports annually; we're not in the oil business—we're in the paper business."[17] A consulting company, United Research Company (URC), was hired to develop a plan to streamline the company and to eliminate the duplication of

EXHIBIT 4 Natural Gas Prices (dollars per MCF)

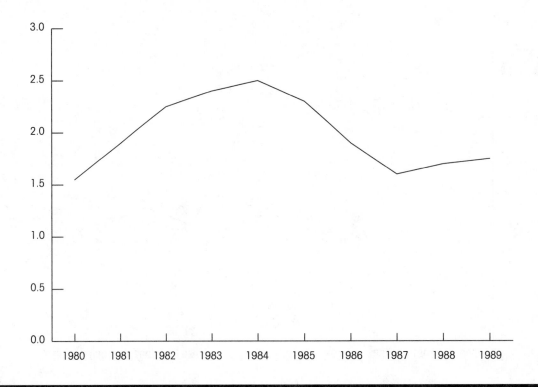

Source: *Oil and Gas Journal*, January 29, 1990.

effort.[18] URC completed its work by the end of 1989 and management was extremely pleased with the results.[19] The effect of the URC plan was to eliminate multiple levels of management and to streamline all approval processes.

In May 1989 the company changed its name to Oryx Energy Company. Prior to that time, it had still been known as the Sun Exploration and Production Company. The company decided on the name change in order to escape being confused with its former parent company and to reflect its new purpose, direction, and "lean and mean image."[20] Employees liked the idea of changing the company's name, as they felt it was important to divest themselves of the conservative image associated with the former parent, Sun Company, Inc.[21]

After consulting with The Richards Group, a local advertising agency, the name Oryx was selected. An oryx is a species of antelope which is native to Africa and the Middle East. According to Robert Hauptfuhrer, "The oryx is sleek, fast-running, aggressive—and one of the few animals that lions avoid. . . . We hope this symbol comes to stand for the kind of company we aspire to be; strong, spirited, and prospering in any environment."[22] One former employee quipped, "It won't be the lion that kills the Oryx, but rather starvation."

Oryx, headquartered in Dallas, Texas, had approximately 3,200 employees. Its regional production offices were in Houston, Oklahoma City, Midland (Texas) and Valencia (California). A state-of-the-art, $36-million Technology Center was located in Dallas, and production platforms exist offshore California and in the Gulf of Mexico. In addition, some 35 natural gas processing facilities and 50 on-shore field offices were located in 11 other states. At the end of 1989, Oryx had net proven reserves of 600 million barrels of crude oil, condensate, and recoverable natural gas liquids, and approximately 2.1 billion cubic feet of natural gas.[23]

PRODUCTS

Experts generally agree that crude oil and natural gas originated from organic matter in sedimentary rocks. Layers of sediment, animal, and plant deposits were buried layer after layer for millions of years. Over time the materials decomposed into the minerals known as oil and gas. The term *crude oil* is used to distinguish the unprocessed oil brought up from the ground from the oil that has been processed in a refinery.[24]

Natural gas found underground consists primarily of the hydrocarbon known as *methane*. Natural gas may be found with crude oil, or it may be found by itself, in separate fields. Natural gas is a clean-burning fuel and is fast becoming a popular source of world energy.

Also found in gas reservoirs is a substance called *condensate*. Condensate is a mixture of liquid hydrocarbons that occur as vapors. Once separated from the gas, they are referred to as Natural Gas Liquids (NGL). Types of natural gas liquids are propane, butane, and heavier hydrocarbons used in making gasoline.[25]

Exploration for crude oil and gas is not an exact science, although several methods have been developed to aid in its discovery.[26] Once it has been determined with reasonable certainty that oil and/or gas exists in a location, the site becomes known as a *proven reserve*. Because of the high capital cost and uncertainty associated with new discoveries, oil exploration and production are a very risky business.

PROCESSES

As Jerry Box, vice president of exploration, returned to his office following the meeting, he pulled open the top drawer of his mahogany desk and opened a bottle of Extra Strength Excedrin. His head was pounding from the tension of the morning's meeting and he needed relief fast. Hauptfuhrer was asking him to perform a monumental task within a very limited period of time. Since the spinoff from Sun Corporation, Oryx had a multitude of projects under way, not to mention the vast reserves of oil and natural gas around the world. He hoped the information that he needed would be available somewhere. To make matters worse, the recent reduction of the work force left many of the company's internal reporting procedures severely lacking. Those employees who remained had been forced to continue with their original responsibilities, not to mention those duties vacated by the cutback in staff. Among the major deficiencies in reporting was the lack of a system for tracking the amount of natural gas in the pipelines. Box knew that his employees were not going to be able to take much more of this. They had already been working weekends and evenings for the last four months. Any additional responsibilities given to them now would surely lower morale even more. He swallowed a capsule and called the vice president of production, Jerry Roberts, into his office. Together the two would have to figure out a plan for compiling the information that Hauptfuhrer needed by the next week. The two sat back in their chairs and reviewed the projects currently under way around the world and the industry in general.

Oryx Energy Company had developed a number of innovative techniques for exploring and producing its products. The most significant of these innovations were two new processes called *cogeneration* and *horizontal drilling*. These two processes had been developed for recovering oil from the land. In addition, the company was pursuing a new technique for recovering coal seam methane. Below is a description of each of these processes.

Cogeneration

Oryx joined together a company named Mission Energy Company to combine technology for the creation of cogeneration. The joint venture was known as the Midway Sunset Oil Field project, and management was extremely enthusiastic about its potential.

The term *cogeneration* refers to a process in which oil is recovered from the ground very efficiently. Most people are unaware that it is very difficult and expensive to retrieve the heavy, thick oil at the very bottom of most reserves. The technique Oryx used in the past to bring this oil to the surface was called *thermal enhanced oil recovery* (TEOR). Under this method, heat was used to melt or thin the oil underground, and then it was brought to the surface. Ironically, the energy used to create the heat or steam in TEOR was oil. Approximately one barrel of oil was used for every five or six barrels recovered. Needless to say, the company was eager to develop a more efficient oil recovery method.

Rather than utilizing oil to create heat and steam, the process of cogeneration used natural gas. In addition, it created a useful byproduct in the form of electrical energy. The advantages of using natural gas to create steam are many. The gas itself is clean burning, and produces less environmental threats than oil. Company officials believed that cogeneration could account for a reduction of as much as 12.2 million pounds of air pollutants over the next 20 years. Second, the natural gas technique was cheaper because it utilized one-third less energy than the TEOR method. It would also help to increase reserves because one barrel of oil would not be lost for every five barrels recovered. Third, cogeneration produced valuable electricity in addition to steam. The electricity could be used by the company to power its plants, and could also be sold to customers throughout the United States. Utilities were heavily regulated by the government, which prevented wild fluctuations in sales prices and provided utility companies a reasonable return on investment.

The Midway Sunset Cogeneration Project proved to be a huge success, according to company officials. They estimated that the new process would save the company approximately 200,000 barrels of oil per day by the year 1995.

Officials also believed that cogeneration was more reliable than the traditional utility plants. Those plants usually produced electricity only 60 percent of the time. Cogeneration, by comparison, would produce electricity 90 percent of the time. Exhibit 5 shows the cogeneration process.

Finally, the cost of building cogeneration facilities was far less than the cost of building nuclear-powered plants. Historically, electricity produced by nuclear-powered plants costs about $1,000 per kilowatt. Compared to the $640 per kilowatt at the Midway Cogeneration Project, the benefits are obvious. Cogeneration would also allow Oryx to expand beyond the traditional business of oil and natural gas recovery to include utilities. It was estimated that by the year 2000 cogeneration will be providing at least 10 percent of the nation's electricity. Clearly, cogeneration had the potential to be the energy source of the future.

Horizontal Drilling

In addition to cogeneration, Oryx researchers had recently developed another technique which could revolutionize the oil industry. Instead of drilling vertically for each pocket of oil and hoping they will find it, experts would now be able to utilize a horizontal drilling procedure which could eliminate the need for multiple oil wells on one piece of property.

EXHIBIT 5   Cogeneration Process

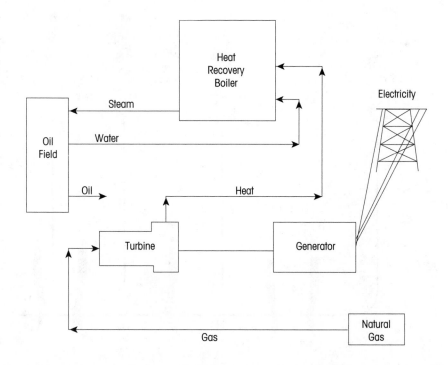

Source: *Oryx company literature.*

The procedure involved two steps. First, a vertical hole was drilled for several thousand feet. Then, special equipment was used to bend the drill, which enabled it to drill horizontally. The advantage to this technique was that with one rig, the company would tap into a number of smaller pockets of oil in the same area, reducing the cost of recovery. Exhibit 6 illustrates the concept of horizontal drilling. Unfortunately, however, the process had only been tested on one patch of land near Austin, Texas known as the Austin Chalk. It might not work in other parts of the country where the soil content is vastly different.

Coal Seam Methane

Natural methane gas is formed inside of coal over many centuries. As coal slowly develops from organic matter, occasionally gas is trapped inside the coal. Such is the case at one of Oryx's older production sites high in the Rocky Mountains of Colorado. Although the gas was discovered in the early 1950s, recovery of the gas was not attempted until the 1980s. Due to the tax laws of the period, and the relative difficulty in retrieving natural gas from the coal seams, the project was shut down.

EXHIBIT 6   Horizontal Drilling

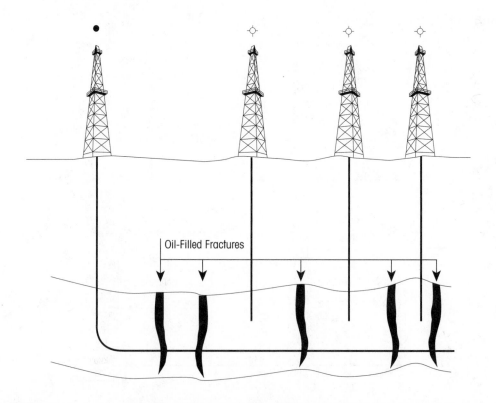

Source: Oryx press release, November 6, 1989.

"Producing coal seam gas poses challenges not found with more convention-al natural gas. Methane is contained in the molecular structure with coal and is held back by water which fills the cleats and fractures. To produce water from the coal, Oryx uses gas for artificial lifting, literally bubbling the water up like a cola drink."[27]

Although conditions were not conducive to coal seam recovery in the past, Oryx had announced efforts to once again begin drilling at Divide Creek in the Colorado mountains in 1990. The new technique mentioned previously would help in recovery, but was likely to remain extremely expensive. Oryx owned 98 percent of the land on which the coal lies, but weather conditions made drilling difficult beyond the month of November. Nonetheless, the company hoped to drill 38 wells in 1990, and another 28 wells in 1991.

COMPETITION

The oil and gas industry was highly competitive. Major oil and gas companies, independent concerns, drilling and production purchase programs, individual producers, and operators were active bidders for desirable oil and gas properties, as well as the equipment and labor required to operate and develop such properties. Although several of these competitors had financial resources substan-tially greater than those of Oryx, Oryx management believed that they were in a position to compete effectively.

According to *Oil and Gas Journal*, Oryx ranked 31st in total revenues and 21st in total assets out of the top 400 oil exploration companies in the United States. Ranked by total assets, the top four companies on the list were Exxon, Mobil, Chevron, and Amoco.[28] Exhibit 7 reflects the total assets for the Oil and Gas 400 companies. Exhibit 8 shows revenues for the top four companies, Oryx, and the rest of the 395 companies on the list ranked by total revenues according to the Oil and Gas 400. While Oryx ranked 31st in total revenues, it ranked 400th in terms of net income. This was due to the $305 million loss posted in 1988.

MANAGEMENT

Harold Ashby, vice president of human resources and administration, left the Monday morning meeting with a deep concern about how this effort had aspects similar to the one involved during the spinoff. He recalled vividly the conversation he had had with Hauptfuhrer when suggesting that Oryx bring in a consulting firm to evaluate and assist in the downsizing of the work force. "Harold, I'm not at all opposed to the idea of bringing in outside consultants to evaluate our human resources situation. I think you should know, however, the implication of such a move." Ashby asked what the implications were. Hauptfuhrer answered, "Basical-ly, if the project is successful, you and I will both retire rich men. However, if it doesn't work, I will retire and you will be fired." Ashby realized that this situation could be politically deadly.[29]

Ashby thought to himself, "In one week I have to go to the Monday morning meeting to describe how we are going to further streamline our operations and

EXHIBIT 7 Total Assets ($billions)

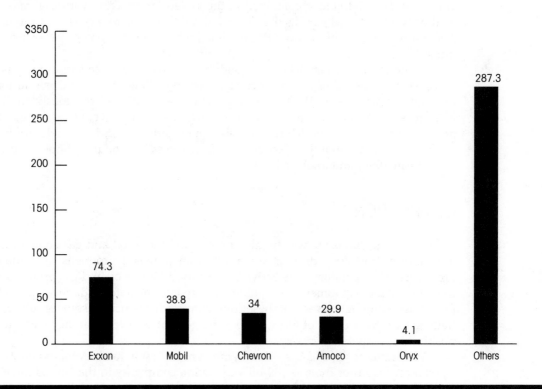

Source: *Oil and Gas Journal,* September 1989.

make them more efficient. It's a momentous task, but at least I won't be alone in my dilemma." Ashby was part of the core management team of Oryx Energy Company. He, along with the other members shown in Exhibit 9, all had their jobs cut out for them, especially for the next week.

Each of the functional heads had as their charter the task of developing the tactical and operational aspects necessary to support the strategic direction set forth in the meeting. They all knew they would not be allowed any excuses, nor given any quarter. They had to produce or else, as Bob was the principal decision maker.

Management consisted of the individuals shown in the organization chart. Each had held that position or similar position prior to the spinoff, with the exception of Bob Keiser, who had been promoted to CEO of Oryx UK Energy. His previous position had been filled by Bill Stokes. This continuance of management from the days of Sun had allowed for an uninterrupted transition of management from Sun to Oryx. Basically, they were all experienced and familiar with the operations. The basic changes resulting form the spinoff occurred not in people, but in the operation of the company.

Oryx could now operate free of any interference from a conservative parent company. Given the instability of the oil industry, Oryx had positioned itself to function with the margin of $2 per barrel. To operate at this level required that all

EXHIBIT 8 Total Revenues ($billions)

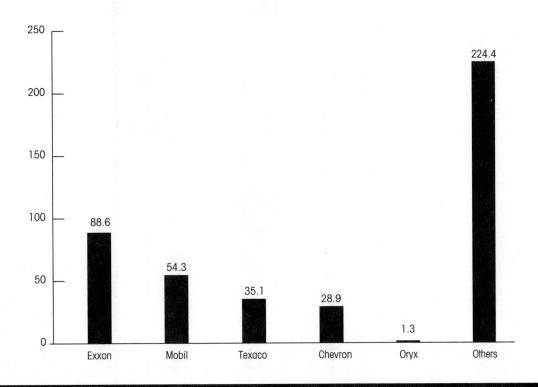

Source: *Oil and Gas Journal,* September 1989.

unnecessary persons and or operations be eliminated, with the exception of top management. The company would have to be aggressive, forward thinking, and able to analyze and forecast trends in the industry with a high degree of accuracy. Hauptfuhrer believed that his team could function in such capacity.

This mean-and-lean attitude, however, did not permeate all levels of the company. With the layoff of 800 people shortly after the spinoff, morale was at a very low level with a significant number of people more concerned with how long they would have their jobs. What the personnel saw at the levels below top management was the philosophy of an elite organization. This elite organization would utilize management-by-objectives in their approach to management. This was further emphasized by the periodic reviews performed throughout the company. Great weight was given to the performance aspects of individuals, the departments, and all operations in general. If you didn't carry your weight, you would not be around.

In the months following the layoffs, management tried to boost morale. It continued to publish its company newsletter, the *Oryx Outlook,* as a vehicle for keeping communication open with the employees. It created two incentive programs to give employees a greater personal financial stake in the company. The first program, called the Impact Award Program, was designed to reward employees on the spot with cash and noncash bonuses for demonstrating outstanding

EXHIBIT 9 Organization Chart

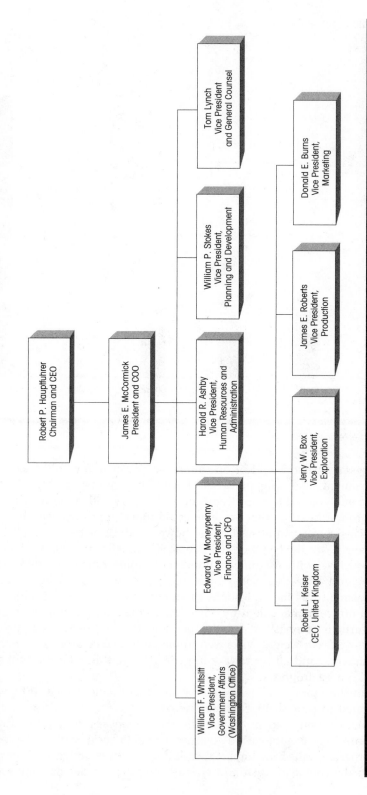

Source: Company records and Annual Report, Oryx Energy, 1988.

ideas and to encourage them to take risks. The second program, called the Employee Incentive Plan, was intended to recognize and reward employees who met or exceeded their goals. Because of these efforts, employee morale did improve; however in April 1990 rumors began to circulate among the employees that another layoff of 800 may be forthcoming.[30]

OPERATIONS

Jerry Box and Jim Roberts found themselves meeting again about the special assignment handed out by Hauptfuhrer. They were beginning to get a little edgy as they fell further and further behind their regular work load. Box was worried about the impending layoffs. He hated the thought of losing valuable employees who could have been transferred to new positions within the company if they had been cross-trained. "Well," said Jerry, "we still need to address our operations. Let's get to it." Box pulled out from his desk the essential tools to accomplish the project: one ballpoint pen and two Havana stogies.

Since its inception as an independent energy producer on November 1, 1988, Oryx operated under a new set of objectives. Its newly developed goals included aggressively pursuing plentiful reserves on an international scope, pursuing natural gas domestically, and cutting costs overall to become North America's largest independent oil and gas producer.

In addition, Oryx aggressively pursued the goal of increasing its reserves. For example, in 1988 alone the company drilled 107 net exploratory and 240 net development wells, making Oryx the number one wildcatter in terms of wells drilled and new field discoveries. Furthermore, in 1988 Oryx announced on-shore discoveries in Texas, Mississippi, and North Dakota, and 12 offshore discoveries in the Gulf of Mexico. Moreover, in the first half of 1989 Oryx had completed seven more discovery wells in the Gulf, from which total gross production was expected to be more than 80 million cubic feet.

As a result of its own progressive innovations, such as horizontal drilling, Oryx reduced its finding costs by 50 percent. Also, by drilling horizontally, the amount of gas and oil produced daily increased from 37 barrels of oil and 22 metric cubic feet (mcf) to 1,300 barrels of oil and 600 mcf.

International Operations

In September 1989 Oryx Energy took a big step in its effort to expand internationally. It acquired British Petroleum (BP) Exploration for $1.3 billion, and increased its reserves by 283 million barrels. According to Kim Costa of Salomon Brothers, "This purchase is a good move for Oryx. The company acquired substantial producing properties and exploratory acreage outside the U.S., one of management's chief goals. Also, this move will position Oryx Energy in some of the most important energy producing areas in the world."[31]

Most of the reserves acquired were in the United Kingdom and the North Sea, but the transaction also included interests in Indonesia, Dubai, Ecuador, Colombia, Gabon, and Italy. Exhibit 10 depicts the locations of Oryx's reserves

EXHIBIT 10   Worldwide Portfolio of Properties

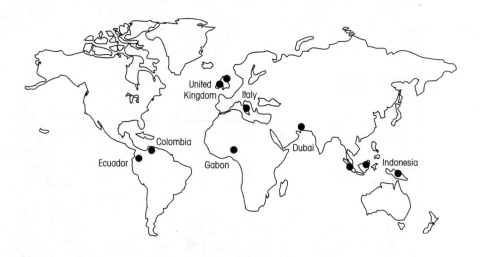

Source: *Oryx Outlook*, October 1988, p. 9.

around the world. All in all, the company estimated total proven and probable reserves from all of its own properties to be 405 million barrels of proven reserves.[32] "We expect these properties to produce about 34 million equivalent barrels in 1990. That's a 40 percent increase over our current level of domestic production," said chairman Bob Hauptfuhrer.[33] Exhibit 11 shows the reserves and initial production levels for Oryx's international operations. Oryx expected to increase the total proven reserves from these properties to about 384 barrels by 1994 at a cost of less than $4.59 per barrel.[34] Production was also expected to remain stable at 34 million barrels for the first three years, and to increase to 36 million by 1994.[35]

As Philip J. Kehl of Dean Witter recently stated, "In addition to 405 million of proved and probable reserves, Oryx has identified 100 million to 200 million of 'possible' reserves in areas where at least one discovery well has been drilled. These properties provide growth opportunity for Oryx over the next several years after the initial development work is completed."[36] It is, in fact, estimated that Oryx will spend more than $850 million overseas in exploration and development over the next five years.

MARKETING

Donald E. Burns, vice president of marketing, pushed the empty Domino's pizza box to the far left corner of his desk. He picked up *The Dallas Morning News* and scanned an article. As of Wednesday, it said oil was $17.78 a barrel. By comparison, oil in January had been running as high as $24.20.[37] "Oil prices have become so volatile in recent times, it's like riding on a roller coaster. I wonder what

EXHIBIT 11   Oryx International Reserves and Initial Productions

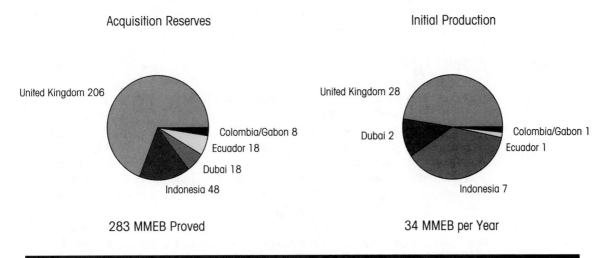

Acquisition Reserves

Initial Production

United Kingdom 206

Colombia/Gabon 8
Ecuador 18
Dubai 18
Indonesia 48

283 MMEB Proved

United Kingdom 28

Dubai 2

Colombia/Gabon 1
Ecuador 1
Indonesia 7

34 MMEB per Year

Source: *Oryx Outlook*, October 1989.

OPEC will do?" he thought to himself. Burns quickly shifted his attention to proofing his report for Hauptfuhrer's project.

Crude Oil and Condensate

The most pervasive influencer of crude oil prices is the Organization of Petroleum Exporting Countries (OPEC). OPEC was created in 1960, with Venezuela acting as the impetus. Current members included Algeria, Ecuador, Gabon, Indonesia, Iran, Kuwait, Libya, Nigeria, Qatar, Saudi Arabia, United Arab Emirates, and Venezuela. The purpose of OPEC was to control crude oil prices by using supply-side economics. In other words, OPEC attempted to limit production, which in turn created shortages and increased the price of crude oil. OPEC was the dominant supplier of world crude oil in 1986, producing 33 percent of the total world supply.[38] In 1986, the OPEC strategy broke down and resulted in an oversupply of crude oil. Correspondingly, prices plummeted.

Though OPEC had attempted to reverse the trend, prices had remained unstable since 1986. For Oryx, the average price per barrel had fluctuated. For 1989 the average price for the year was at a three-year high of $16.83.[39] Bob Hauptfuhrer remained optimistic about the future. He stated, "We believe in the industry. We believe that ultimately the price of oil will go up, for two reasons. First, demand continues to rise. Second, OPEC is showing some signs of controlling production closer to demand levels."[40]

In 1988 52 percent of Oryx's crude oil production was sold to Sun Refining and Marketing, a subsidiary of its former parent company.[41] In 1989 the company reduced sales to Sun Refining and Marketing to 25 percent of total sales.

Additionally, in 1989 Oryx sold 9 percent of its total sales volume to Chevron U.S.A. The 10 largest customers (including Sun Refining and Marketing and Chevron U.S.A.) comprised 71 percent of total sales in 1989.[42]

Natural Gas

Not only had oil suffered from market instability, but so had the natural gas industry. The market influencers, however, were different for gas. In the past, natural gas prices had been heavily regulated by the government. The Natural Gas Decontrol Act of 1989 substantially deregulated natural gas making the pricing now more influenced by market conditions. As a result of this deregulation, there was currently an oversupply of natural gas and too many competitors in the marketplace. Competition tended to be more on a regional basis. Thus, the price for natural gas continued to be depressed.

Oryx increased its prices by 10 percent in 1988 from $1.49 per thousand cubic feet to $1.64 in 1988. There were no real increases in the average price of gas in 1989, however, prices did remain stable. Management believed gas prices would continue to be constrained by competition from competing fuels.[43] In addition, pipelines eased the burden of transporting oil and natural gas across many miles, and improved communications aided in marketing products domestically and overseas.

Oryx did not sell any of its natural gas to its old parent company and there were no large customers for gas that comprise more than 5 percent of the company's total sales. Unlike crude oil, spot sales of gas were significant and were 60 percent of total sales.[44] In 1988 Robert Hauptfuhrer had stated, "In the intermediate term, we think natural gas prices will rise, on a relative basis, more than oil prices."[45] Apparently, he was wrong.

Thus, Oryx was positive about its future in the marketplace. Oryx saw its key marketing strategy to be in pricing. According to Jim McCormick, president and chief operating officer, "Clearly, the near term direction of this company is to remain competitive in the current price environment."[46]

FINANCE

Edward Moneypenney, vice president of finance and CFO, answered his ringing phone. "Hello, may I please speak with Fred Moneypenney?" asked the other voice.

"The name is Ed Moneypenney!" he said as he rolled his eyes up to the ceiling. No doubt it was one of those Price Waterhouse fellows.

"This is Stan Kenton with Price Waterhouse. I'm the new manager on the job."

"You people must have a revolving door at your place! What happened to the old manager?" he inquired.

"Oh, he quit." said Kenton.

"Typical," said Moneypenney. The Price Waterhouse staff was turning over so fast it was impossible to know who was in charge on the systems project anymore.

"Well, I just wanted to inform you that we'll be late in getting the next part of the information systems installation done," said Kenton.

"What? We'll see about this!" snapped Moneypenney. With that he slammed down the phone and muttered, "I ought to sue the bastards!" It was a well-known fact, according to one employee, that Moneypenney had an ongoing battle with the information systems department and that the continued delays on Price Water-house's part were aggravating the situation. Moneypenney finished fuming over the phone call. He then turned his attention to the task at hand. He began to work on his report for the Monday morning meeting.

Since 1987, Oryx has failed to show any consistent profits, as shown in the financial statements in Exhibit 12. In 1987 the company posted a $158 million profit, however $90 million of this was due to a benefit created from a windfall profits tax adjustment.[47] In 1988 the company posted a net loss of $305 million. Included in this loss was a one-time, after-tax charge of $260 million related to the write-down of certain oil and gas assets which the company intended to sell.[48] For 1989 the company reported a net income of $139 million, however $85 million of this was due to a mandatory accounting change related to income taxes.[49] After-tax return on equity in 1989 was 9 percent.

As with most oil and gas companies, Oryx had suffered from the reduction of crude oil prices during the middle and late 1980s, however these prices have continued to rise over the last three years. Unfortunately, total revenues decreased by 5.8 percent from 1988 to 1989. This decrease in revenue was primarily from decreases in crude oil volume.[50] Revenues also decreased by 9.4 percent from 1987 to 1988.[51] The company contends that price declines during 1988 were primarily due to OPEC over-production of crude oil volume.[52] Return on sales increased significantly from 1988 to 1989 due to the write-off of certain assets in 1988. Additionally, volume was down in both 1987 and 1988. (See the Marketing section earlier in this case for a further discussion of OPEC.) Average crude oil prices received by the company in 1987, 1988, and 1989 were $16.48, $13.78, and $16.83 per barrel, respectively.[53] Nevertheless, the company claimed it could turn a profit at $15 per barrel.[54] Average gas prices received by the company for 1987, 1988, and 1989 were $1.49, $1.64, and $1.63 per thousand cubic feet, respectively.[55] Gas volume increased during all three years.[56]

Oryx operations were highly capital intensive. Eighty percent of the capital asset base was in the property, plant, and equipment and consisted of acquisition costs for proved and unproved reserves, exploration costs, and development costs.[57] Capital expenditures for 1987, 1988, and 1989 were $554 million, $580 million, and $428 million, respectively.[58] The company was confident that it had sufficient liquidity and capital funding resources to continue making these large capital expenditures and to fund operations. Oryx's current ratio was only 1.05, indicating that balance sheet liquidity was poor. The company had available to it a $1.375 billion credit facility. At the end of 1989 Oryx had not used any of this credit facility. Additionally, the company had the option of issuing additional shares of common stock, and up to 15 million shares of preferred stock.[59] As of the

EXHIBIT 12 Consolidated Balance Sheet December 31, 1989, 1988, and 1987 ($millions)

	1989	1988	1987
Assets			
Current assets			
Cash and cash equivalents	$ 16	$ 138	$ 533
Accounts and notes receivable	390	225	932
Total current assets	406	363	1,465
Properties, plants, and equipment, net	3,324	3,713	3,934
Cash reserved for acquisitions	407	—	—
Deferred charges and other assets	48	18	65
Total assets	$4,185	$4,094	$5,464
Liabilities and Shareholders' Equity			
Current liabilities			
Accounts payable	$ 220	$ 200	$ 261
Accrued liabilities	159	121	103
Current portion of long-term debt	7	—	122
Total current liabilities	386	321	486
Long-term debt	1,509	1,082	2,388
Deferred income taxes	616	870	950
Other liabilities	189	210	57
Total liabilities	2,700	2,483	3,881
Shareholders' equity	1,485	1,611	1,583
Total liabilities and shareholders' equity	$4,185	$4,094	$5,464

Note: The successful efforts method of accounting is followed.
Source: Annual Report, Oryx Energy, 1989.

end of 1989 the company had no plans to issue additional equity instruments. Additional sources of capital funds were provided by sales of assets. In September 1989 the company announced that it had an agreement to sell 107 oil and gas fields in 12 states for $106 million and expected to record a net after-tax gain from this sale of $13 million.[60]

The company had in excess of $1.5 billion of long-term debt as of December 31, 1989. $600 million of this debt was issued in conjunction with the spinoff of Oryx from Sun. The company had also issued $414 million of commercial paper. The interest rates paid on all of this debt range from 8.25 percent to 9.10 percent.[61] The debt-to-equity ratio increased dramatically for 1988 to 1989 by 52 percent, reflecting a $427,000 increase in debt in 1989.

Even though Oryx had yet to show a consistent upward trend in profitability, investors seem to agree with its contention that the future is bright for the company. When the company was originally spun off, the per-share stock price was $27.75.[62] As of April 13, 1990, the per-share stock price was $44.38.[63]

Oryx had spent a great deal of consulting fees and time trying to figure out how to cut more costs. As a result, several levels of approval had been eliminated,

EXHIBIT 12 Cont'd. Consolidated Statements of Income For the Years Ended December 31, 1989, 1988, 1987 ($millions except per-share amounts)

	1989	**1988**	**1987**
Revenues			
Oil and gas	$1,140	$1,070	$1,161
Other	71	216	258
Total revenues	$1,211	$1,286	$1,419
Costs and expenses			
Production cost	$ 361	$ 397	$ 261
Exploration cost	194	232	190
Depreciation, depletion, and amortization	319	354	334
General and administrative expense	154	143	143
Interest and debt expense	102	231	217
Provision for write-down of assets	—	395	14
Total costs	$1,130	$1,752	$1,159
Income (loss) before taxes	$ 81	$ (466)	$ 260
Provision (benefit) for income taxes	27	(161)	102
Net income (loss) before cumulative effect of accounting change	54	(305)	158
Cumulative effect of accounting change for income taxes	85	—	—
Net income (loss)	$ 139	$ (305)	$ 158
Net income (loss) per share of common stock	$1.32	$(2.89)	$1.49
Cash dividend per share of common stock	$1.20	$0.30	none
Common shares outstanding (in millions)	105.5	105.7	105.7

Source: Annual Report, Oryx Energy, 1989.

impacting the company's internal control system. One current employee felt they had gone too far. She commented, "The other day I figured out a way to embezzle $10 million. The company is lucky that I'm an honest person."

LEGAL/GOVERNMENT/ENVIRONMENTAL

William Whitsitt, vice president of governmental affairs, and Tom Lynch, vice president and general counsel, sat in a conference room in the Oryx corporate headquarters pondering over what the best approach to their report should be. Sometimes the legal, governmental, and environmental issues could be overwhelming. Whitsitt commented, "There are currently 143 different state and federal agencies that regulate and monitor the oil and gas industry. It's quite a chore to keep up with."[64]

Answered Lynch, "I know, but we'll just have to do our best to boil it all down into a concise report."

The legal and governmental environment for oil and gas was becoming very complex and unfavorable for the oil and gas industry. Prior to the Tax Reform Act of 1986, oil exploration and production companies enjoyed numerous and lucrative tax advantages. These tax shelters allowed producers to attract investors and obtain the capital necessary for their business. The new tax law wiped out a lot of these tax benefits, which in turn drove investors away. Congress did, however, leave some tax breaks intact. For instance, a percentage depletion allowance to recover capitalized leasehold costs was still allowed. (Depletion is a similar concept to depreciation, except it is typical for a producer's depletion allowance to exceed his cost basis; therein lies the tax benefit.)

The new tax law did just as much damage to the industry as did the supply glut of the mid-to-late 1980s. A recent study was commissioned by the Wharton Econometric Forecasting Associates and Chase Econometrics to determine the impact of creating new tax benefits for oil and gas producers. The study concluded that although additional tax incentives would help substantially, they may not be able to return the domestic market to its level of activity in the early 1980s.[65]

Although tax incentives would stimulate the industry, the current political environment in Congress was such that most of the producers' pleas for tax relief fell on deaf ears. Congress no longer seemed concerned with relying on foreign imports to bridge the gap in U.S. energy needs. According to Frank Pitts, president of Pitts Energy Group and a longtime lobbyist on energy issues, foreign imports could rise to as high as 65 percent by 1995.[66]

In order for any oil and gas producer to be eligible for the remaining tax incentives, it must be considered to be "independent" by IRS standards (i.e., not a fully integrated energy company). As stated earlier, one of the reasons for the spinoff from Sun Company was so that Oryx could obtain this status. Due to a quirk in the tax laws, however, the IRS determined in November 1989 that Oryx did not qualify as an independent producer.[67]

Not only did the oil and gas companies have to worry about the tax implications to their industry, but they also had to concern themselves with environmental issues. The Exxon Valdez accident in Alaska, which could have been prevented had Exxon used tankers with double hulls, catapulted the environmental concerns regarding oil and gas into the forefront in 1988. Since then, environmental issues continued to plague the industry at an increasing rate. Recently, Oryx Energy was assessed a hazardous waste fine of $2 million by the state of California. This caught Oryx's management by complete surprise, as they were only expecting a $4,000 fine.[68] Since it is becoming clear that local, state, and federal governments will increasingly pursue oil and gas producers for the negative externalities they create, many producers have found natural gas to be increasingly attractive.

Also, the company had problems with its offshore project in California called The Harvest Project. Due to the Long Beach oil spill by British Petroleum, the California Coastal Commission became extremely cautious and restrictive. Because of this, it had prevented the Harvest Project from continuing operations. The platform had a maximum capacity of 50,000 barrels a day. The company had $182 million invested in the project.[69]

Until recent years, natural gas had been heavily regulated by both state and federal governments. For a further discussion of the impact of the deregulation of natural gas, see the Marketing section earlier in this case.

The Meeting

William Stokes looked at all of the reports before him. He rubbed his fatigued eyes as he rose from his chair. He wearily walked to the Monday morning meeting. As he sat down in his chair, Hauptfuhrer walked in and said, "Well, Stokes, how about it? What are your recommendations?"

Stokes rubbed his perspiring palms together as he thought of the impact on his career this report would have. He rose from his chair and began to speak.

Endnotes

1. "The Fortune 500," *Fortune*, April 23, 1990, p. 382.
2. *Audits of Entities with Oil and Gas Producing Activities*, Oil and Gas Committee, AICPA, pp. 1–2.
3. John J. Murphy, "Energy: A Key Factor in Perestroika," *Petroleum Independent*, October 1989, p. 35.
4. "U.S. Oil Demand to Climb in 1990," *Oil and Gas Journal*, January 29, 1990, p. 49.
5. Speech given by His Excellency Hisham Mohadin Nazar, minister of petroleum and mineral resources of the Kingdom of Saudi Arabia, 60th Annual Meeting of the Independent Petroleum Association of America, November 1989, as reprinted in *Petroleum Independent*, December 1989, p. 26.
6. "U.S. & Texas Proved Reserves—1969–1988," *Dallas Business Journal*, as reprinted from a report by the Energy Information Administration, May 29, 1989, p. 20.
7. Murphy, "Energy."
8. *The World Almanac 1990*, p. 154.
9. Robert Beck, "U.S. Oil Demand to Climb in 1990," *Oil and Gas Journal*, January 29, 1990, p. 54.
10. J. Tom Dougherty, "An Exploration Retrospective," *Oil and Gas Investor*, 9, no. 5 (1989), p. 39.
11. "Salomon Survey: Solid E & P Spending Hikes Planned for 1990," *Oil and Gas Investor*, 9, no. 7 (1990) p. 11.
12. Loren Steffy, "Pennzoil Co. Reportedly Has Eye on Oryx," *Dallas Business Journal*, June 26, 1989, p. 26.
13. Annual Report, Oryx Energy, December 31, 1989, p. 8.
14. Annual Report, Oryx Energy, December 31, 1988, p. 3.
15. "New Land Operations to Support Business Strategies," *Oryx Outlook*, August 1989, p. 4.
16. "Blob Takes Shape with New Integrated Business Systems," *Oryx Outlook*, p. 5.
17. Interview with former employee, March 28, 1990.
18. Ibid.
19. James E. McCormick, "Winning in the '90s Must Continue," *Sun E & P News*, January 1989, p. 1.
20. "Company Plans Name Change to Reinforce Independence," *Sun E & P News*, February 1989, p. 1.
21. Ibid., pp. 1–2.
22. "Hauptfuhrer Unveils 'Oryx Energy Company,'" *Sun E & P News*, April 1989, pp. 1–2.
23. Annual Report 1989, p. 29.
24. The terms *crude oil* and *oil* are used interchangeably in this case.
25. *Audits of Entities*, p. 21.
26. Max W. Ball et al., *The Fascinating Business of Oil* (New York: 1965), pp. 49–50.
27. *Oryx Outlook*, December 1989, p. 3.
28. Robert J. Beck and Joan Briggs, "OGJ 400," *Oil and Gas Journal*, September 1989, pp. 6–11.
29. Harold Ashby, speech at the University of North Texas, February 12, 1990.
30. Personal interview with a current employee, March 25, 1990.
31. *Oryx Outlook*, October 1989, p. 9.
32. Ibid, p. 1
33. Ibid.
34. Ibid, p. 6.
35. Ibid.
36. Ibid.
37. "Oil Prices Slide; OPEC May Meet," *The Dallas Morning News*, April 13, 1990, Business section, p. 1.
38. Annual Energy Information Review, 1986.
39. 10-K Report, Oryx Energy, p. 5.
40. Annual Report 1988, p. 4.
41. 10-K Report, Oryx Energy, 1989, p. 9.
42. Ibid.
43. 10-K Report 1989, p. 9.

44. 10-K Report, Oryx Energy, 1988, p. 7.
45. Annual Report 1988, p. 4.
46. Ibid, p. 6.
47. Annual Report 1988, p. 15.
48. Ibid.
49. Annual Report 1989, p. 18
50. Annual Report 1989, p. 18
51. Annual Report 1988, p. 12
52. Ibid, p. 16
53. 10-K Report, p. 5.
54. Annual Report 1988, p. 12.
55. Ibid, p. 16.
56. 10-K Report 1989, p. 5.
57. Annual Report 1989, p. 20.
58. Ibid, p. 12.
59. Annual Report 1989, p. 29
60. 10-K Report 1989, p. 7

61. Ibid., p. 29.
62. Annual Report 1988, p. 13.
63. *Dallas Morning News,* April 15, 1990.
64. *U.S.A. Oil Industry* (New York: PennWell Publishing Company, 1989), pp. 485–486.
65. Deborah Rowell, "Tax Incentive Bill Can Promote Energy Security," *Petroleum Independent,* December 1989, p. 6.
66. Loren Steffy, "Low Prices Seen Hindering Effective Energy Policy," *Dallas Business Journal,* December 26, 1989, p. 9.
67. Loren Steffy, "IRS Disputes Oryx Claim as 'Independent,'" *Dallas Business Journal,* November 11, 1989.
68. "Sun E & P Says Hazardous Waste Procedures Unfair," *The Daily Oil,* December 7, 1988.
69. Annual Report, 10-K Report, p. 17.

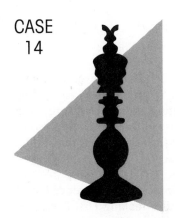

CASE
14

CAROLCO PICTURES, INC.

JAMES BRESNAHAN,
KAREN KENIFF,
MARK MITCHELL &
DAN TWING

PROLOGUE

"Gentlemen, Place your bets."

Mario F. Kassar, chairman of Carolco Pictures, Inc., pushed a stack of thousand-dollar chips forward. He turned toward a nearby waitress and ordered another bottle of Taittinger Compte de Champagne, 1981. Tonight he was in his element, the casino at Monte Carlo, and, as usual, the forthcoming bottle would be gratis. He was a favorite of the casino and would often vacation there to relax after the premiere of a Carolco production. The casino was expecting an active night for, in recreational pursuits, as in business, Mario Kassar spent freely. On this occasion Mario Kassar was celebrating the premiere of the most expensive movie ever made.

Terminator 2: Judgment Day had a production cost of $90 million. Did the movie's foreboding title allude to a coming apocalypse for Carolco? Indeed the auditors had felt compelled to include a statement in the annual report addressing their concerns over the company's viability as an ongoing entity. The production had left Carolco in an ominous financial position. Cash strapped, the company had had a negative cash flow from operations from 1988 through 1991. In addition to reporting a $6.3 million loss, the company had to seek concessions from its debt holders.[1]

None of that mattered to Kassar for he was in the casino to unwind and escape such concerns. Here he could more easily control the outcome and receive instant gratification for his efforts. He motioned toward his evening companion to place all his bet on one number. "Let her roll," he announced as the roulette wheel began to spin. "I need a winner."

HISTORY

Mario F. Kassar first met Andrew Vajna at the Cannes Film Festival in 1975.[2] "Andrew Vajna was born in Hungary, raised in Los Angeles, and made his first fortune in Hong Kong manufacturing wigs and later blue jeans. In the early 1970s Vajna bought two Hong Kong movie theaters, which led him to become a film

This case was prepared under the supervision of Professor Sexton Adams, University of North Texas, and Professor Adelaide Griffin, Texas Woman's University. ©1991 Sexton Adams and Adelaide Griffin.

licensing agent in the Far East. Mario Kassar, born in Beirut and raised in Rome, became a sales agent for movies at age 18, specializing in the Middle East."[3] They formed a movie distribution company soon after meeting and later ventured into film production in the early 1980s.[4] The original purpose of the partnership was to obtain better terms by buying rights to movies for both the Far East and the Middle East.[5]

Kassar and Vajna incorporated Carolco Pictures, Inc. in Delaware in April 1986.[6] They set up desks facing each other and together picked and produced most of Carolco's movies.[7] "They hit the jackpot quickly after making *First Blood* and later *First Blood II*, starring Sylvester Stallone. The two movies took in $420.5 million at the box office domestically and in foreign distribution." Soon after going public, Peter Hoffman, a top entertainment and tax lawyer, was recruited to be president and chief executive.[8] One of his first duties was to establish a tax haven for Carolco in the Netherlands.[9] "Hoffman also acquired operations in video and television distribution and production to help maximize revenues from Carolco movies."[10]

Carolco pursued a strategic agenda dissimilar to other independent movie producers. Rather than limiting risks by making numerous small-budget productions, "Carolco's main strategy has been to make four or five 'event' pictures a year with budgets of $20 million and up while selling distribution rights in advance to help cover costs."[11] "Because of the risk involved, Carolco had not engaged in the domestic theatrical distribution of its films. Instead, they entered into a distribution agreement with Tri-Star Pictures. The company usually reserved all domestic pay and free television, domestic home video and foreign rights to its films."[12]

In 1989 Carolco released three low-budget, nonaction films, all of which scored poorly at the box office. This led to a 61-percent drop in net income for the year. The same year co-chairman Andrew Vajna decided to break up the 13-year partnership. "Colleagues say a clash in the style of the two co-founders contributed to the split, with Mr. Vajna opposing the high spending and rapid growth. At the time, a company official said Mr. Vajna 'would prefer to have a bag of cash instead of the pressure and stress in building a large public company.'"[13] Mr. Vajna indeed received his bag of cash. Mario Kassar bought 11.2 million shares from his partner for $108 million in December 1989.[14] This gave Kassar a controlling 63-percent interest in the company. Mario Kassar had the reputation within the industry of a gambler. Said David Goldman, an agent at International Creative Management, "He's a movie mogul in the style of Samuel Goldwyn."[15]

MANAGEMENT

When he co-founded Carolco Pictures, Mario Kassar stated three basic principles to the stockholders. These guidelines, under which the company would operate, were:

1. To produce and distribute a limited number of "event" motion pictures, i.e. movies with cast and production values which would give them major box office appeal both within and beyond the borders of the United States
2. To finance these often expensive productions through presales of exhibition

rights in various media in countries around the world, with nearly all the marketing costs borne by our subdistributors, not by us

3. To maximize returns from such rapidly growing "ancillary" markets as video and television, both pay and free, via the establishment of a distribution capability for these markets, either within Carolco or in a separate publicly owned subsidiary[16]

These three basic principles upon which Carolco was founded were the same principles upon which they were operating in 1991. Carolco's mission was to develop an "integrated worldwide independent motion picture, television and video company with important strategic relationships. This would create a company equal of any major in the quality, if not quantity, of its film release schedule."[17] As a basis for the creation of Carolco, Kassar and Vajna were to use their proven ability in the film industry.[18]

Carolco's organization structure, shown in Exhibit 1, was derived from limited published sources, and is somewhat vague. Since much of Carolco's operations was performed either through contractual arrangements with outside directors or through Carolco subsidiaries, the parent company's executive structure was difficult to define.

Kassar endeavored to establish relationships with the most talented and sought-after creative individuals in the film industry. Both directors and stars of

EXHIBIT 1 Carolco Organization Structure

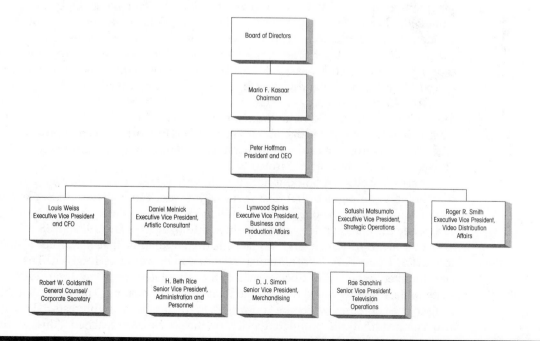

Source: Derived from *Annual Report,* Carolco Pictures, 1990; and *Form 10-K,* Carolco Pictures, 1990.

Carolco's films included the most consistently popular box office attractions. Carolco had produced such box office hits as *Rambo: First Blood Part II*, *Red Heat*, and *Total Recall*. They also produced other major event films such as *Rambo III*, *Basic Instinct*, *Extreme Prejudice*, *Johnny Handsome*, *Air America*, *Narrow Margin*, and *L.A. Story*.[19]

In conjunction with Kassar's style of seeking out the most creative and talented individuals, he spared no expense. Industry analysts cited Kassar's management style as the leading cause of Carolco's soaring overhead. Kassar received a salary of $1.5 million in 1990, as well as a Carolco jet. Carolco paid $410,000 to install security devices in Kassar's Beverly Hills mansion in 1988 and an additional $259,000 in security services in 1990.[20]

Directors, actors, and producers that contracted with Carolco enjoyed Kassar's liberal spending, as well. "'Mario Kassar does everything with a great deal of style, and he does it bigger and better than anyone else,' said David Goldman."[21] In 1990 Carolco flew 70 of Hollywood's most famous to the Cannes Film Festival, transported them via a fleet of limousines, accompanied by a police motorcade, to the Hotel du Cap, where they lodged courtesy of Carolco. In addition, Kassar threw a gala aboard a yacht to promote Carolco's film. The party, complete with fireworks, was reported to be the most expensive party in Cannes.[22]

Carolco was also setting spending precedents at home in Hollywood. In early 1990 Carolco paid script writer Joe Esterhas $3 million, with a $1-million producing fee to Irwin Winkler, for *Basic Instinct*. This was the highest amount ever paid for a spec script. Later that same year, Kassar set a new record by paying what was to be the highest amount ever to a writer on assignment. Kassar paid the Oscar-winning screen writer of *Rain Man* $2 million to script an idea based on a supernatural thriller by T. M. Wright, *Manhattan Ghost Story*. One top agent remarked, "I've never heard of a deal where a writer is guaranteed $2 million for an idea."[23] In negotiations with Kassar people rarely walk away feeling short-changed. When producer Brian Grazer's rights to *The Doors* were within hours of expiring, he contacted Kassar. After a 10-minute phone conversation, Kassar had agreed to do the movie and Grazer had a check within a few hours.[24]

Arnold Schwarzenegger, star of Carolco hit *Terminator 2: Judgment Day*, received approximately $15 million for the movie. According to *Entertainment Weekly*, Schwarzenegger spoke about 700 words. This cost Carolco approximately $21,429 per word. For example, Schwarzenegger's famous line from the move, "Hasta la vista, baby," cost Carolco $85,716.[25]

Kassar's free spending did not sit well with shareholders, however, and the shareholders complained that Kassar stacked the deck in his favor. In September 1990 Carolco agreed to purchase 3.4 million shares from Kassar at a price of $13 each when the market price was $7.25. In addition, in 1988 and 1989 an $8-million loan was made to Kassar and Vajna with the stipulation that if Carolco's stock reached $11 per share before August 1989, the loan would be forgiven. The loan was forgiven when the stock reached the stipulated price in June 1989. A shareholders' suit was filed that charged Kassar of self-dealing. The suit stated that he used the company, which he controlled, to further his own interests.[26] The suit also charged that the stipulated price of the stock was reached "due to the manipulative actions of Kassar and others."[27] A judge froze 2.2 million shares of Carolco stock owned by Kassar and limited his ability to draw funds from the company pending further motions. Carolco has never paid dividends to its shareholders.[28]

OPERATIONS
Major Motion Picture Production

To produce its major event films, Carolco enlisted top producers, directors, writers, and stars. Some of Hollywood's most artistic, exciting, and commercially successful directors and producers worked on Carolco's films. These included Tim Burton, James Cameron, George Cosmatos, John Hughes, Robert Redford, Oliver Stone, and Paul Verhoeven.[29] Big-name stars were also part of Carolco productions, including such names as Arnold Schwarzenegger, Sylvester Stallone, Michael Douglas, Lou Gosset, Jr., Steve Martin, John Candy, Val Kilmer, and Jean-Claude Van Damme.[30]

Carolco did not maintain a substantial staff of creative or technical personnel. Management believed that sufficient motion picture properties and creative and technical personnel (such as screenwriters, directors, and performers) were available in the market at acceptable prices, enabling the company to produce as many motion pictures as it planned or anticipated, at the level of commercial quality the company required.[31] To ensure the availability of such personnel, Carolco had multiple-year production and development agreements with a number of prominent directors. Typically, under such agreements, the director submitted to Carolco on a "first-look" basis any project he wished to direct. In some cases, the director was obligated to direct one or two films for the company within a set period of time. Carolco provided office support and development funding for the director. In many cases, the director rendered services on outside projects controlled by other studios.[32]

As of April 1, 1991, Carolco employed approximately 295 full-time employees. Certain subsidiaries of Carolco were subject to the terms of collective bargaining agreements with the Writers Guild of America, Directors Guild of America, Screen Actors Guild, and International Alliance of Theatrical Stage Employees (concerning certain technical crafts such as director of photography, sound recording, and editing). A strike, job action, or labor disturbance by the members of any of these organizations could have had a tangible adverse effect on the production of a motion picture within the United States. Carolco believed their current relationship with their employees was satisfactory.[33]

Due to the level of talent and the grand scale of Carolco's major event productions, large budgets, usually over $25 million per film, were not uncommon.[34] *Total Recall* cost $59 million to make.[35] *Terminator 2: Judgment Day* was rumored to cost $90 million.[36] While some industry observers questioned the logic of such spending, Carolco continued to produce high-budget, high-tech action thrillers.

Besides making major event films, Carolco had several subsidiaries to perform such functions as production of moderate-budget films, foreign leasing of theatrical productions, domestic and foreign distribution to television, merchandise licensing, operation of production studios, and home-entertainment software distribution. These subsidiaries are shown in Exhibit 2.

EXHIBIT 2 Carolco Major Subsidiary Operations

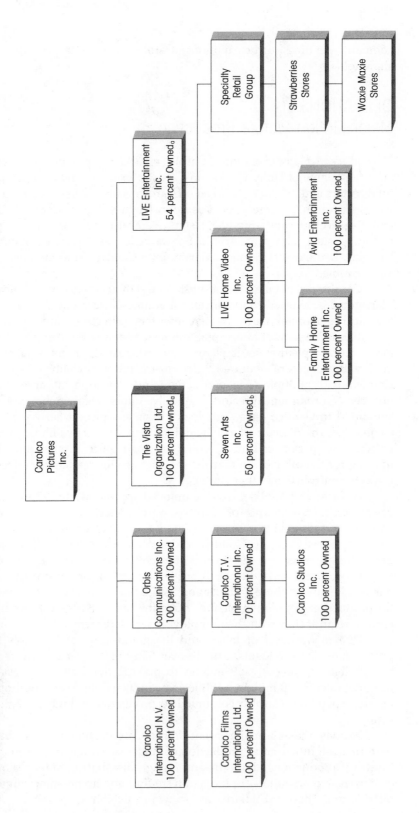

a Ownership based on percentage of revenues recognized by Carolco.

b Estimated–Joint Venture with New Line Cinema.

Source: Derived from *Annual Report*, Carolco Pictures, 1990; and *Form 10-K*, Carolco Pictures, 1990.

Moderate-Budget Film Production

In 1989 Carolco purchased a one-third interest in The Vista Organization Ltd. Vista formed Seven Arts in 1990 as a joint venture with New Line Cinema. This venture was established to supplement the production of major event films.[37] Seven Arts financed, produced, acquired, and distributed moderate-budget motion pictures. This new division was formed to capitalize on Carolco's expertise in motion picture finance, strength in foreign distribution, and relationships with leading talent from around the world.[38]

Seven Arts' films were released theatrically in the United States through a joint venture with New Line Cinema. Seven Arts also made arrangements with LIVE Home Video (a partially owned subsidiary of Carolco) for domestic video release of its pictures, and with Carolco International for the foreign distribution of its pictures.[39]

Foreign Leasing of Theatrical Productions

As the international appetite for American-made movies expanded into new markets, Carolco Pictures, Inc. and its subsidiaries continued to be the leading independent suppliers of major motion pictures throughout the world. At the international film festivals and markets held in Cannes, Milan, and Los Angeles, groups of Carolco's films were successfully sold to leading international distribution firms around the world. Carolco conducted foreign distribution through a wholly owned subsidiary, Carolco International N.V. (CINV), with offices and employees in Curacao, Netherlands Antilles; Zurich, Switzerland; and London, England. While CINV's main activities involved the international leasing of Carolco-produced films, the division also acquired foreign distribution rights for important films produced by other studios and producers.[40]

Television Distribution

While domestic theatrical distribution of Carolco major event films was accomplished through an agreement with Tri-Star Pictures, and Seven Arts films were distributed domestically through an arrangement with New Line Cinema, Carolco retained the rights to television distribution through its wholly owned subsidiary, Orbis Communications Inc.

Orbis Communications operated three main areas of business in 1990: domestic distribution of motion pictures for free and pay television, licensing of Carolco films and other programming in the international television market, and production and acquisition of television programming such as telefilms, mini-series, and game shows.[41] Revenues from Orbis reached $42 million in 1990, almost double those of 1989.[42]

All foreign rights to Orbis's television product and television rights to Carolco's theatrical motion pictures were distributed to worldwide television outlets by Carolco Films International Ltd. (CFIL), a London-based, wholly owned subsidiary of Carolco International N.V. (CINV). During 1990, CFIL's priorities included licensing Carolco feature films in those territories where TV rights were available and marketing Orbis's catalog of television programming.

While Orbis continued to make substantial progress in domestic syndication and international television licensing of Carolco's and others' films, Orbis's production activities consistently failed to reach management profit objectives. Television productions were not staying in syndication; for example, the game show *Joker's Wild* was not picked up for a second season. As a result, on April 11, 1991, Carolco signed an agreement with Multimedia, Inc. to sell Orbis's production and development activities.[43]

Merchandise Licensing

In operation since 1987, Carolco Licensing Division had evolved into a full-service licensing entity. In 1990 Carolco Licensing successfully exploited merchandising rights to *Total Recall* in a variety of categories. The *Total Recall* Nintendo game was a landmark for the video game industry, as the game was marketed in conjunction with the film's release. Carolco Licensing remained extremely active in publishing, and 1990 saw the *Total Recall* novelization become a top seller.[44] Through an expanding network of foreign licensing agents, Carolco Licensing coordinated the licensing of Carolco's properties worldwide, and was also responsible for the placement of products and corporate signage in Carolco films.[45]

Production Studio Operations

In May 1990 a wholly owned subsidiary of Carolco merged with De Laurentiis Entertainment Group Inc. to form Carolco Television Inc. (CTI). CTI included a development library containing over 100 feature film projects and a full-service 32-acre production facility in Wilmington, North Carolina. The studio housed eight fully equipped sound stages with all necessary support facilities and services. The studio backlot had three blocks of city streets, which were transformed to represent specific eras and locations. Carolco, as well as other companies, used these facilities for productions.[46]

Home Entertainment Software Distribution

Carolco distributed home entertainment software through its partially owned subsidiary, LIVE Entertainment Inc. In 1990 Carolco recorded 54 percent of LIVE's net income in its earnings as a result of its ownership of approximately 47 percent of LIVE's outstanding common stock and 100 percent of its Series A common stock.[47] As of July 22, 1991 Carolco's annual stockholders' meeting had been postponed to allow Carolco's board of directors to consider a proposal by LIVE to discuss a possible business combination of the two companies.[48]

LIVE's operations were conducted through the following operating entities: Video distribution through LIVE Home Video Inc. (LHV); rackjobbing through Lieberman Enterprises Incorporated (Lieberman); and entertainment software retailing through the Specialty Retail Group.[49]

LIVE Home Video

LHV provided a broad selection of high-performance programming from Carolco Pictures, as well as such top filmmakers as IndieProd, Miramax Films, New Visions Pictures, Avenue Pictures, Gladden Entertainment, and Working Title Films, among others. Children's films were distributed through a division called Family Home Entertainment and a newly formed division, Avid Entertainment, distributed midline home videos.[50]

Lieberman Enterprises

Lieberman Enterprises was the nation's second largest supplier of prerecorded music, prerecorded videocassettes, and personal computer software to mass merchandisers and specialty retailers in over 3,400 retail locations.[51] Carolco was searching for sources of cash, and, in an effort to allay their cash-poor standing, sold Lieberman Enterprises in 1991 for approximately $100 million.[52]

LIVE Specialty Retail Group

The LIVE Specialty Retail Group operated 144 retail stores in 11 states offering compact discs, audio cassettes, prerecorded videos, and accessories. The stores operated under the name of Strawberries in the Northeast, including New England, New York, Pennsylvania, and New Jersey, and under the name Waxie Maxie in the mid-Atlantic area, including Maryland and Virginia.[53]

MARKETING

Carolco's market niche was to produce big-star, action films that had as much or more success abroad than in the United States. This meant they produced high-action movies starring popular actors with broad-based appeal to insure that these films would perform very well, both domestically and overseas. In fact, their high-action films, such as the Rambo series and *Total Recall*, brought in more revenue abroad than nationally.[54]

Once Carolco completed a motion picture, it would generally be distributed and made available for license in the following steps:

Marketplace	Months after Initial Release	Approximate Period
Domestic theatrical		6 months
Domestic home video	6 months	6 months
Domestic pay television	12–18 months	12–24 months
Domestic network television	30–36 months	30–36 months
Domestic syndication television	30–36 months	30–60 months
Foreign theatrical		4–6 months
Foreign video	6–12 months	6–18 months
Foreign television	18–24 months	18–30 months

Source: *Form 10-K,* Carolco Pictures, 1990 p. 8.

During the late 1980s, revenues from licensing of rights to distribute motion pictures in ancillary (i.e. other than domestic theatrical) markets, particularly pay television and home video, had significantly increased. The company had obtained a substantial part of the advances and guarantees for its pictures from the license of distribution rights in these ancillary markets.[55]

Domestic Markets

Tri-Star handled domestic distribution of Carolco's feature products, which freed Carolco of the significant overhead and marketing costs which accompanied film distribution. Under the arrangement, Tri-Star paid the print and advertising costs, and after recouping those expenses, kept an average of 35 percent of Carolco's net profits.[56] Carolco did not want to distribute its own films domestically since the demise of several other independent filmmakers was attributed to these costs.

Orbis Communications, Inc. conducted Carolco's domestic distribution of motion pictures for free and pay television, production and acquisition of television programming, miniseries, and game shows. Orbis packaged and sold motion pictures to the U.S. broadcast market. In 1989 Carolco marketed its first motion picture package in domestic syndication under the Carolco I banner, containing *First Blood, Angel Heart, The Terminator, Kiss of the Spider Woman*, and other motion pictures. In 1990 it sold Carolco II, which included films such as *Rambo: First Blood Part II, Rambo III* and *Hoosiers* to The USA Network for $25.5 million.[57] In December 1990 Carolco introduced Carolco III, a package of 25 titles including such artistically successful pictures as *Platoon, The Last Emperor,* and *Red Heat*. As of April 15, 1990, this package had been sold to more than 60 percent of the U.S. broadcast markets generating over $21 million in revenue. Carolco continued to receive revenue from the earlier packages, and anticipated that an additional one or two motion picture packages would be marketed domestically in 1992 and 1993.[58]

Also in 1990, under Carolco Television Productions (CTP), Orbis reintroduced the game show *Joker's Wild*, but it met with limited success. Orbis found greater success in the game show business with *The $100,000 Pyramid* before it sold CTP due to its inability to meet management's profit objectives.[59]

Carolco distributed its own, as well as others' moderate-budget motion pictures domestically through its Seven Arts division. Seven Arts' films and videos were released domestically through a joint venture with New Line Cinema and LIVE Home Video, respectively.[60] During 1990 Seven Arts released *Repossessed* and *King of New York*. In February 1991 Seven Arts released *Queens Logic*. Other films planned for a 1991 release included *Rambling Rose, The Dark Wind, Aces: Iron Eagle III*, and *Petleir*.[61]

LIVE Entertainment Inc. (LIVE) was a leading distributor of home videos, which it marketed through LIVE Home Video Inc. (LHV) and LIVE Specialty Retail Group (LSRG). In 1990 LHV was the leading independent home video company and was fifth among all video software suppliers in the country. LHV had the second largest market share, falling just behind Disney in the sell-through video market. This market consisted of videos selling for less than $25, mainly from its Family Home Entertainment division sales. LHV's revenues from newly released rental titles rose by one-third in 1990 and sell-through revenues saw a five-fold increase, boosted in particular by two mega-hits: *Teenage Mutant Ninja Turtles: The Movie* and Carolco's *Total Recall*.[62] LHV expanded in 1990 with Avid Entertainment, which offered titles generally priced under $15. Initial releases included such hits as *Eddie and the Cruisers II, Millennium*, and *Wired*. Strawberries and Waxie Maxie, LSRG's retail outlets, made them the leading music retailer in the greater Boston and Washington D.C. areas and a strong retailer in upstate New York, Philadelphia, and Baltimore.[63]

International Markets

In 1991 the international market for American-made movies had expanded and Carolco was a leading independent supplier of major motion pictures, videos, and related accessories throughout the world. In 1990 *Total Recall* met with great success overseas, bringing in $260 million, as opposed to $118 million domestically. The film's overseas success was mainly attributable to its star, Arnold Schwarzenegger, who was probably the biggest box office attraction of the world at the time.[64]

Carolco's overseas marketing activities were conducted by Carolco International N.V. (CINV) and included international leasing of Carolco-produced action films, Seven Arts films, and foreign distribution rights for important films produced by other studios. In 1990 foreign rights were acquired to three pictures from Universal Studios: *The Wizard, Opportunity Knocks*, and *Career Opportunities*.[65] Carolco also acquired the foreign theatrical distribution rights to the 20th Century Fox production, *Robin Hood*. Peter Hoffman speculated that Fox believed Carolco could generate more revenue through its distribution system than could Fox through its own channels.[66]

During 1990 CINV signed distribution agreements with leading distributors including Guild Entertainment Ltd. in the United Kingdom, Unirecord International S.A. in Spain, Pentafilm S.P.A. in Italy, and others in Europe, Japan, Australia, and Latin America. Foreign leasing amounted to 60 percent of Carolco's feature film revenues in 1990, and with the strong lineup of releases scheduled for 1992, it was expected to continue to be a major profit center for the company.[67]

To distribute Orbis's television products and Carolco's theatrical motion pictures worldwide, the firm used Carolco Films International Ltd. (CFIL). During 1990, CFIL sold $20 million in license fees through 150 licenses for Carolco feature films, telefilms, and miniseries, and Orbis's catalog of television programming.[68]

Foreign sales were headed by Guy East, former international sales director for Goldcrest Film and Television. He commented on the prospects of Carolco in the foreign market: "There is every indication of huge growth in the foreign area that Carolco wants to position itself to be part of."[69] East saw an expansion of the European market with the advent of private television in France, Italy, and Spain, and from heightened construction of new screens. Additionally, the demise of several competitors including PSO, Goldcrest, and Thorn EMI in Europe, gave Carolco opportunities to increase its market share by capturing its competitors' lost distribution agreements.[70] Executive vice president of foreign sales Rocco Viglietta stated, "The TV market overseas continues to grow particularly given the pending single Euro market in 1992 and the privatization of stations worldwide."[71]

As part of Carolco's international thrust, the company considered entering the home video market in the Soviet Union through an arrangement with Sintez International in Moscow. Orbis Executive Vice President Ethan Podell said, "We're very interested in exploiting opportunities in Eastern Europe and the Soviet Union." The Carolco exchange would have initially provided Sintez with television documentaries, specials, and children's programming for the Soviet market. Revenues were to be split between Sintez and Carolco and were required to remain in the Soviet Union where Orbis could use the rubles to finance productions in Russia.[72] A note of caution in this market was expressed by Viglietta: "People there are looking to be fed first . . . it will be some time before the Eastern Bloc becomes capitalized and people get VCRs in their homes."[73]

Licensing

Many of Carolco's popular films created a great worldwide demand for action figures, books, games, and toys. Carolco's licensing division developed into a full-service licensing entity. For example, *Total Recall* was a great success for Nintendo. Carolco also published the novel, which became a top seller.[74] For *Terminator 2: Judgment Day*, Carolco licensing was also involved in heavy licensing activity of toys, Nintendo and computer software games, video and pinball arcade games, publishing, comic books, apparel, and collectible products. Also national promotions were planned during the release of the film, including promotional tie-ins with Pepsi, Subway sandwich chain, and Hero Cologne by Faberge.[75]

Carolco licensing very successfully coordinated the licensing of Carolco's properties worldwide. For example, Rambo remained the number one action figure in Brazil and Argentina years after the series was released, and demand remained high for the toy in Europe and the South Pacific, as well.[76]

The licensing division was also responsible for product and corporate identity signage in Carolco films. The placement of products and logos in movies not only generated revenue for Carolco, but it also served as a base to build consumer promotion relationships with the client companies.[77]

ECONOMIC ENVIRONMENT

In January 1991 reports from Washington regarding the nation's economic recession offered little encouragement. As real incomes were falling, consumer spending subsequently took a downturn. Consumer confidence fell approximately 12 percent in January to reach its lowest level in 10 years.[78] As the nation was at war with Iraq, consumer spending continued to decline. However, consumers were also faced with rising inflation and increasing federal income and payroll taxes. This double whammy affected the typical family, consisting of two full-time earners with two dependent children, by lowering their real after-tax net income.[79]

The movie business has historically fared well in bad, even disastrous, economies. Economist Albert Kapusinki's study of the years 1928 to 1975 showed that approximately 70 percent of the time the film industry thrived in economic troughs. In each of the three major recessions from 1971 to 1991, the strong countercyclical nature of the film industry has triumphed.[80]

The recession of the early 1990s found the film industry competing in a diverse media spectrum. Viewers had the option to choose from a widening range of film entertainment, basic cable television, to pay-per-view movies and events. Also in the arena was a fully matured home video business.[81] "'The case has been made that people are going to go out to the video store and rent a cassette and bring it home rather than going out to the movie theater and having a pizza and getting a babysitter, and I would agree with that,' says analyst Chris Dixon, Kidder, Peabody and Co."[82] Dixon also noted that the film industry was driven by demand and revenues will continue to be at rates above normal in the consumer sector. Strength in the overseas theatrical market and increased penetration of television households in Europe were credited for these revenues.[83]

COMPETITION

Carolco competes in the motion picture production and distribution industry. This industry is divided between two groups of competitors. The first is major film production companies, such as:

Warner Brothers
20th Century Fox
MGM/United Artists

Orion
Paramount
Walt Disney-Buena Vista
Others

The second group of competitors includes independent film companies, such as:

Carolco
Nelson Entertainment
Samuel Goldwyn
Miramax
New Line/Seven Arts
Castle Rock
Cinergi Productions (formed by Carolco co-founder Vajna)
Others

During the 1970s and 1980s the number of films produced by independents increased from 133 in 1970[84] to a peak of 380 in 1987.[85] As shown in the table below, U.S. new film releases by independents increased between 1985 and 1987, while U.S. new film releases by majors decreased. During the period of 1988 through 1990, the majors released more films while independents released less, showing the direct competition for market share between the two groups.

New U.S. Feature Film Releases

	1985	**1986**	**1987**	**1988**	**1989**	**1990**
Majors	150	144	135	161	159	164
Independents	304	333	380	352	287	253

Source: Lawrence Cohn, "Fewer New Pix in '90, but More by Majors," *Variety*, December 24, 1990, p. 8.

Carolco's positioning between the two groups by releasing major event films, distributing videos and television programming, and offering packages of movie titles, all worldwide, helped hedge their position, protecting them from the cyclical swings in market share between the two segments.

Carolco's worldwide distribution network was beneficial as earnings from the domestic film market only covered the costs of making films. For example, the approximate aggregate investment by domestic producers in summer 1991 films, including ad costs, was $2 billion. However, the 1991 summer market size for the films was only approximately $2 billion. The summer season provided 40 percent of the total annual U.S. box-office gross. Therefore, there were many pictures that did not receive a return on their investment from U.S. theatrical distribution, and had to turn to ancillary markets around the world to make a profit. With so many pictures crammed into such a narrow corridor, it became intimidating for even the most stalwart veterans of the distribution wars. As one Hollywood CEO remarked,

"No matter how you rationalize it, this exercise is basically suicidal. . . . By mid-summer you're going to see a succession of pictures yanked from the schedule."[86]

In 1991 industrywide domestic theatrical income accounted for only about 20 percent of the total revenue stream, and rose to 35 percent including all foreign theatrical earnings. The rest of the pie consisted of worldwide video, television syndication, cable, satellites, and other esoteric new markets. This meant that U.S. theatrical openings were helpful, but not necessarily vital to a new film. If a movie did poorly in the United States, it could still be successful in foreign markets and from studio output deals with the Showtimes and the HBOs.

Since domestic markets failed to provide enough return on investment, offshore markets became vital to filmmakers. For many producers, foreign markets accounted for nearly half the gross of a hit film. Carolco claimed between 65 percent and 75 percent of their revenues from overseas. So vital were the foreign markets that independents were caught in a vice between major U.S. studios, which were intensifying their quest for a bigger share of the foreign market, and the changing tastes of foreign viewers. Foreign audiences were becoming more sophisticated, switching from low-budget action, horror, and slam-bang adventures to movies with big budgets, big stars, and big production values. The independents were known for the low-budget films, but these movies were not selling overseas anymore. Sigrid Ann Davidson, a vice president at Skouras pictures, said, "The most important thing is to acquire better-quality star vehicles, not necessarily stars of the quality of Meryl Streep, but actors who have value overseas. The days of selling a film with boobs, bullets, and happy endings are a fading memory."[87]

One problem facing all U.S. film companies was the development of quotas within the European Community. France, for example, set a local quota of 60 percent for all its filmed entertainment, and unless the independents associated with foreign firms in co-productions or had local offices, their opportunities in the expanding European market were limited. One independent, Nelson Entertainment, secured films from Columbia and Orion and was successful in distributing them in the foreign market. These types of arrangements allow an independent to swing some heavy weight behind its name.[88]

Many independents accumulated catalogs of titles to sell to foreign operations. As Herb Fletcher, Crown International vice president for international sales, said, "We have the advantage of being able to sell groups of pictures to television," but even companies with large catalogs are discovering narrower buying patterns. For the independents operating on a shoestring budget, the fear of being put out of business because they failed to keep up-to-date with changing global tastes became their number one concern.[89]

LITIGATION AND CONTINGENCIES

In September 1990 two similar lawsuits were initiated, one in a Delaware Court of Chancery, the other in a California Superior Court, by certain stockholders of Carolco. These suits were aimed at the directors of Carolco and certain lenders with whom the company had loans outstanding.[90] The lawsuits, which sought unspecified compensatory damages, stemmed from alleged self-dealings and breach of various fiduciary duties in connection with an approval of a stock purchase by CINV (the company's wholly owned foreign affiliate) from New CINV (a Netherlands corporation which at that time owned 62 percent of Carolco's common stock).[91] Under the terms of the previously negotiated agreement, CINV purchased 3,461,538 shares of Carolco's common stock from New CINV at a price of $13 per share. At the time the agreement was executed, the shares were trading at about $7.25 on the NYSE.[92] Furthermore, New CINV was deemed to be beneficially owned by Mario Kassar and certain trusts set up for the benefit of his family. CINV paid New CINV a total of $44,999,994 for the stock, which consisted of cash and the assumption of a significant amount of New CINV's liabilities. The breakdown of the $44,999,994 included (1) the assumption of obligations New CINV owed the company totaling $25,050,075, (2) the payment of a loan outstanding to Credit Lyonnais Bank Nederland N.V. of $8 million, and (3) a promissory note payable to New CINV from CINV of $11,949,319.[93]

On December 24, 1990 a Los Angeles Superior Court judge imposed a freeze on 2.2 million shares of Carolco stock owned by Kassar.[94] This freeze was made in lieu of the transaction between CINV and New CINV. Carolco claimed the transaction was approved by its board and that the transaction had received support from large stockholders that represented a majority of the shares not owned by Kassar and his family. The court, however, remained intent on imposing the order stating that, in its view, based on the evidence, there was a high probability that the plaintiffs would prevail in the litigation.[95]

Carolco and its predecessors paid little or no federal or state income taxes, as a significant amount of the company's total revenues were recognized from the foreign releases of its films through CINV, a Netherlands Antilles subsidiary of the company, which, under the United States–Netherlands Antilles Tax Treaty, was not subject to U.S. taxation.[96] (See the explanation of CINV's tax situation in the later financial analysis section.) Although the company anticipated that it would not pay substantial U.S. taxes in 1991, this tax position could have been adversely affected by the following:

1. The allocation of income and deductions between Carolco and CINV may have been subject to challenge by the Internal Revenue Service.
2. Carolco and its subsidiaries could have been deemed personal holding companies and the company's foreign subsidiary could have been deemed a foreign personal holding company due to the substantial stock ownership potentially attributable to Kassar, thus requiring the company to pay dividends or a penalty tax on its income from motion pictures.
3. Even with the tax treaty in place, the Internal Revenue Service could have contended that some of CINV's income was directly subject to U.S. tax.

As of December 31, 1990 management stated that, in its opinion, none of these theories could have applied to Carolco's tax situation.[97]

FINANCIAL ANALYSIS

The financial structure of Carolco included wholly owned and partially owned subsidiaries, as well as wholly owned foreign affiliates. As previously mentioned, Carolco attempted to minimize the risks associated with the production and distribution of its major motion pictures through its distribution agreement with Tri-Star Pictures. Under this agreement, Tri-Star was obligated to make certain advances to the company to cover Carolco's negative costs associated with the production of a motion picture, and to spend significant amounts on printing and advertising expenses associated with the marketing of the theatrical releases.[98] For the year ending December 31, 1990, approximately one-fourth of the company's revenues were derived from the sale of both theatrical and nontheatrical rights of its major motion pictures to Tri-Star.[99] The remaining three-fourths of Carolco's revenues were received through its affiliates and wholly owned subsidiaries.

For the year ending December 31, 1990, approximately 15 percent of the company's revenues were derived from the domestic production and distribution of motion pictures to television through Orbis Communications.[100] LIVE Entertainment was responsible for approximately 13 percent of Carolco's revenues for the year ending December 31, 1990.[101]

Carolco International N.V. (CINV), a wholly owned foreign subsidiary, was responsible for the leasing of motion picture rights in foreign markets. CINV, as distinguished from other subsidiaries responsible for distribution, incurred only minimal distribution expenses and was responsible for only a small portion of general overhead expenses.[102] Due to the nature of the leasing transactions, CINV was responsible for a significant amount of Carolco's revenues (approximately 47 percent in 1990).[103] Furthermore, under the United States–Netherlands Antilles Tax Treaty, none of the foreign source income from CINV was subject to U.S. taxation. Therefore, CINV's tax rates were significantly lower than U.S. statutory rates, resulting in substantial tax savings and deferrals for Carolco. As of December 31, 1990, CINV had accumulated approximately $153 million of earnings not subject to U.S. taxes.[104]

The breakdown of operating revenues by line of business for the year ending December 31, 1990 is included in Exhibit 3. Films released in the United States contributed 23 percent of Carolco's revenue, while films released outside the United States contributed 35 percent. Video releases inside the United States represented 13 percent of revenue and television releases in the United States represented 15 percent. Revenues from distribution of television and video outside the United States represented 10 percent. Other operating revenues from Canadian partnerships and unrelated foreign corporations, including interest from related parties, amounted to 4 percent.

The very nature of Carolco's business required huge amounts of working capital to fund the production of the films. A portion of these costs was borne by Tri-Star. However, in order to meet additional working capital requirements, the company and certain of its subsidiaries had to enter into agreements with two banks (BT/Chemical and CLBN) for revolving credit facilities.[105] The amount of credit that both banks were committed to extend totaled $225 million as of December 31, 1990. This amount was based upon intercreditor agreements and

EXHIBIT 3 Breakdown of 1990 Revenues

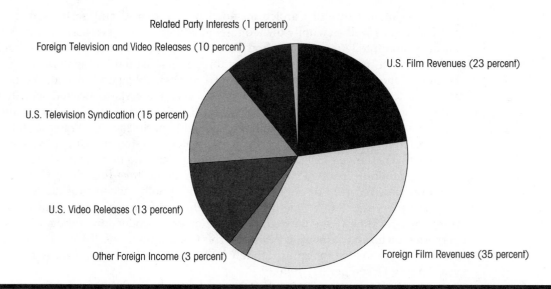

Related Party Interests (1 percent)

Foreign Television and Video Releases (10 percent)

U.S. Film Revenues (23 percent)

U.S. Television Syndication (15 percent)

U.S. Video Releases (13 percent)

Other Foreign Income (3 percent)

Foreign Film Revenues (35 percent)

Source: Derived from *Annual Report,* Carolco Pictures, 1990; and *Form 10-K,* Carolco Pictures, 1990.

contingent upon certain accounts receivable outstanding, as well as additional collateral with sufficient value to collateralize the borrowing.[106] As of December 31, 1990, Carolco had a cumulative outstanding balance of approximately $156 million to BT/Chemical and CLBN.[107] Substantially all of the company's assets were pledged under the credit agreements. Although the company was in compliance with its debt covenants at year end, the disclosures in the 1990 audit report indicated that the company might not be able to continue to conform to these covenants in 1991.[108] Therefore the company submitted a Consent Solicitation Statement to the Securities and Exchange Commission that sought to have the holders of the company's 14 percent senior notes approve a change in the financial covenants. On May 15, 1991 Carolco issued a press release stating that it had indeed received consent from the noteholders.[109] Among other things, the new amendments allowed the company to reduce its required cash flow coverage ratio from 1.5:1 to 1.2:1., and to restructure the restrictions on liens which the company was permitted to incur. In return for these concessions, the company was required to make a one-time cash payment of $15 per $1,000 principal of notes, and to issue approximately 202,000 shares of its common stock to the noteholders.[110]

In addition to the revolving line of credit with BT/Chemical and CLBN, the company had outstanding at December 31, 1990 approximately $76 million of 14 percent senior notes and $16 million in subordinated notes.[111] Proceeds from the issuance of the senior notes were used to repay a large portion of the subordinated notes, as well as to fund additional working capital requirements.

Carolco also had an additional outstanding loan for $25 million from CLBN to finance the cash flow needs of Vista (the company's domestic group responsible for the Seven Arts joint venture).[112] Vista was totally dependent on Carolco to finance its cash flow needs since its purchase September 20, 1989.[113] Although the

EXHIBIT 4 Selected Financial Information for Carolco Pictures, Inc. ($000)

	Year Ended December 31			
	1987	**1988**	**1989**	**1990**
Income Statement Data				
Operating revenues				
Feature films and videocassettes	$ 54,477	$138,461	$115,113	$216,720
Television syndication	42,790	19,597	21,552	42,130
Total operating revenues	$ 97,267	$158,058	$136,665	$258,850
Operating expenses				
Film and television amortization	74,158	116,735	104,892	204,108
Total operating expenses	$ 74,158	$116,735	$104,892	$204,108
Gross operating profit	$ 23,109	$ 41,323	$ 31,773	$ 54,742
Gross profit percentage	24%	26%	23%	21%
Other revenues				
Interest income—related parties	$ 2,452	$ 1,696	$ 858	$ 2,148
Other income—foreign affiliates	4,002	4,147	3,940	8,147
Other expenses				
General and administrative expenses	12,907	14,122	19,879	32,942
Interest expense	4,911	7,906	12,598	24,314
Income before equity income and income taxes	11,745	25,138	4,094	7,781
Equity in income of affiliates	2,682	11,197	10,862	13,340
Provision for income taxes	95	831	920	3,823
Net income attributable to common stock	$ 14,332	$ 35,504	$ 14,036	$ 17,298
Balance Sheet Data				
Cash	$ 11,191	$ 8,094	$ 8,871	$ 12,552
Accounts receivable	41,217	49,566	41,156	84,558
Film costs, net of amortization	113,723	180,776	333,303	387,845
Total assets	229,555	342,410	520,148	631,907
Long-term debt, including related parties	80,582	136,788	274,368	294,934
Stockholders' equity	79,266	118,894	134,243	191,077

Sources: *Form 10-K,* Carolco Pictures, 1990.

company owned only one-third of the outstanding stock of Vista, it accounted for its investment as a purchase since it funded all of Vista's cash needs and guaranteed Vista's loan from CLBN.

As shown in Exhibit 4, Carolco's debt load had increased significantly from 1988 through 1991. The majority of the debt was generated to provide the company with the needed capital to finance its major films as well as acquisitions. All costs associated with the production and filming of motion pictures were initially capitalized and subsequently written off as the films and made for television movies were released, based on management's expectations regarding the life of the films.

Operating revenues increased steadily from 1988 to 1991, but operating and general and administrative expenses associated with these revenues also rose sharply. Management attributed the large increases in general and administrative expenses in 1990 to an increase in the company's personnel in the legal and accounting areas, as well as increased distribution expenses. The company publicly stated that these increases would not continue. However, the first quarter results for the period ending March 31, 1991, showed a 46-percent increase in general and administrative costs over the first quarter results for 1990.[114]

Analysis of the company's cash flows from operations, shown in Exhibit 5, indicated large negative cash flows from 1988 to 1991.[115] The negative cash flows forced the company to incur additional debt and issue equity capital in order to generate the cash needed to fund the company's ongoing operations. Management relied heavily on the success of its major motion picture releases in 1991 to provide the cash flows needed for operations.[116]

Carolco's management stated that it was determined to build the equity base of the company during the 1990s through the formation of a series of strategic alliances with major worldwide entertainment and media companies. In 1990, three such alliances took place with the following companies: Canal+, an entertainment company based in France; Technicolor, a U.S. film products company; and RCS Video, a media and publishing company in Italy. These companies purchased substantial amounts of Carolco stock during 1990, investing heavily in the long-term outlook of Carolco.[117]

Carolco had approximately 4,500 beneficial holders of common stock as of April 17, 1991. The amount of beneficial ownership that was attributable to officers and directors of the company constituted 79.2 percent of the common shares outstanding. Furthermore, Kassar was deemed to beneficially own up to 58.9 percent of the company, either directly or through entities that benefitted Kassar or members of his family.[118]

Carolco's common stock traded on the NYSE under the symbol CRS. Since January 1989 the firm's stock had ranged from a high of $13.875 in the second quarter of 1990 to a low of $5.125 during the fourth quarter of 1990.[119] Carolco's stock traded at $7.75 on July 23, 1991. Carolco never paid cash dividends on its common stock and intended to retain all future earnings to finance the expansion and development of its business. The consolidated balance sheet as of December 31, 1990 and the statement of operations for the year ending December 31, 1990 appear in Exhibit 5.

EPILOGUE

The champagne Mario Kassar ordered arrived perfectly chilled and in the hotel's signature crystal ice bucket. On the tray next to the bottle was an envelope bearing his name. Kassar ignored the envelope for the moment, as the roulette wheel began to slow and the ball began its descent. It bounced several times before settling to rest on BLACK 2.

"Gentlemen, we have a winner."

Squarely positioned on the winning number was Kassar's stack of chips. With a sense of exhilaration, he reached for a flute from the tray at his side and,

EXHIBIT 5 Carolco Pictures, Inc. and Subsidiaries, Consolidated Statement of Cash Flows ($000)

	Years Ended December 31		
	1988	**1989**	**1990**
Net cash flow from operating activities			
Net income	$ 35,504	$ 14,036	$ 17,298
Adjustments to reconcile net income to net cash provided (used) by operating activities			
Amortization of film costs	96,287	80,091	175,601
Depreciation and amortization	5,387	4,797	9,874
Equity in income of affiliates	(11,197)	(10,862)	(13,340)
Conversion of video guarantees to LIVE Series B preferred stock	(15,000)	(4,900)	—
(Increase) decrease in receivables	(8,949)	8,410	(35,753)
Increase (decrease) in payables, accrued liabilities, accrued residuals and participations, income taxes payable and other assets	2,883	(24,418)	11,353
Increase in film costs and rights	(163,340)	(232,618)	(224,540)
Payments on contractual obligations	(3,207)	(2,927)	(18,201)
Increase in contractual obligations	15,494	2,350	24,552
Increase (decrease) in advance collections on contracts	(8,214)	40,641	4,225
Net cash used in operating activities	(54,352)	(125,400)	(48,931)
Cash flow from investing activities			
Purchase of property and equipment	(11,746)	(3,065)	(2,420)
Sale of marketable securities	3,049	—	—
Investment in LIVE Entertainment, Inc.	(6,738)	805	(414)
Purchase of The Vista Organization, Ltd., The Vista Organization Partnership, L.P., and Carolco Television, Inc., net of cash acquired	—	—	(21,003)
Net cash used in investing activities	(15,435)	(2,260)	(23,837)
Cash flow from financing activities			
Proceeds from debt	50,925	—	133,054
Payments on debt	(71,913)	(1,077)	(106,166)
Increase in borrowings from banks	98,200	109,318	—
Borrowings from Vopic	—	30,000	—
Proceeds from building financing	12,900	—	—
Proceeds from property and equipment financing	5,791	—	—
Decrease in notes payable to related parties	(4,000)	(941)	(17,003)
Increase in receivables from related parties	(10,636)	(6,003)	4,905
Repurchase of senior subordinated notes	(20,915)	(500)	(872)
Redemption of warrants	—	—	(5,559)
Net proceeds from issuance of preferred stock—Series B	—	—	29,456
Net proceeds from issuance of preferred stock—Series C	—	—	56,559
Payment of preferred dividends	—	—	(971)
Proceeds from sale of stock	13,133	—	—
Repurchase of common stock	(1,379)	—	(45,385)
Increase in debt acquisition costs	(3,089)	(4,037)	(2,221)
Exercise of stock options/warrants	416	1,677	1,327
Issuance of senior notes and common stock in connection with the purchase of The Vista Organization Ltd., and The Vista Organization Partnership, L.P.	—	—	29,325
Net cash provided by financing activities	69,433	128,437	76,449
Increase (decrease) in cash	$ (354)	$ 777	$ 3,681

EXHIBIT 5 Cont'd. Carolco Pictures, Inc. and Subsidiaries Consolidated Statement of Cash Flows and Consolidated Balance Sheet ($000)

	Years Ended December 31		
	1988	**1989**	**1990**
Supplemental disclosure of cash flow information			
Cash paid during the year for			
Interest (net of amount capitalized)	$ 6,245	$ 23,167	$ 17,145
Income taxes	$ 1,054	$ 637	$ 581

	December 31	
	1989	**1990**
Assets		
Cash	$ 8,871	$ 12,552
Accounts receivable, net of allowances of $2,545 (1989) and $5,821 (1990)	41,156	84,558
Accounts receivable, related parties	10,839	5,933
Film costs, less accumulated amortization	333,303	387,845
Property and equipment, at cost, less accumulated depreciation and amortization	31,123	30,223
Investment in LIVE Entertainment Inc.	76,974	91,044
Other assets	17,882	19,752
Total assets	$520,148	$631,907
Liabilities and Stockholders' Equity		
Accounts payable	$ 11,816	$ 16,775
Accrued liabilities	26,717	26,159
Accrued residuals and participations	21,656	28,528
Income taxes current and deferred	943	4,159
Debt	252,915	289,328
Advance collections on contracts	49,112	53,337
Contractual obligations	1,293	7,644
Notes payable, related parties	21,453	5,606
Total liabilities	385,905	431,536
Commitments and contingencies	—	—
Due to minority shareholders	—	9,294
Shareholders' equity		
Preferred stock—$1 par value, 10,000,000 shares authorized		
Series A convertible preferred stock; 4,000,000 shares authorized, none issued	—	—
Series B convertible preferred stock, 30,000 shares authorized and issued (30,000,000 aggregate liquidation preference)	—	30
Series C convertible exchangeable preferred stock, 60,000 shares authorized and issued ($60,000,000 aggregate liquidation preference)	—	60
Common stock—$.01 par value, 100,000,000 shares authorized, 29,834,681 shares issued and outstanding in 1989 and 30,281,075 shares issued and outstanding, including 3,475,538 shares in treasury in 1990	298	301
Additional paid-in capital	39,347	125,146
Treasury stock	—	(45,385)
Retained earnings	94,598	110,925
Total stockholders' equity	134,243	191,077
Total liabilities and stockholders' equity	$520,148	$631,907

EXHIBIT 5 Cont'd. Carolco Pictures, Inc. and Subsidiaries, Consolidated Statement of Operations ($000, except per-share data)

	Years Ended December 31		
	1988	**1989**	**1990**
Revenues			
Feature films (including $15,000 in 1988, $17,850 in 1989, and $27,625 in 1990 from a related party)	$138,461	$115,113	$216,720
Televsion syndication	19,597	21,552	42,130
Interest income from related parties	1,696	858	2,148
Other	4,147	3,940	8,147
Total revenues	163,901	141,463	269,145
Costs and expenses			
Amortization of film and television costs, residuals and profit participations	116,735	104,892	204,108
Selling, general, and administrative expenses	14,122	19,879	32,942
Interest	7,906	12,598	24,314
Total costs and expenses	138,763	137,369	261,364
Income before equity in income of affiliated companies and provision for income taxes	25,138	4,094	7,781
Equity in income of affiliated companies	11,197	10,862	13,340
Income before provision for income taxes	36,335	14,956	21,121
Provision for income taxes	831	920	3,823
Net income	35,504	14,036	17,298
Preferred dividends	—	—	971
Net income attributable to common stock	$ 35,504	$ 14,036	$ 16,327
Net income per share (based on weighted average shares and common share equivalents outstanding of 30,999,608 shares (1988), 30,296,670 shares (1989), and 30,015,720 shares (1990))	$ 1.15	$ 0.46	$ 0.49

Source: *Annual Report,* Carolco Pictures, 1990.

after inhaling the quintessential effervescence of its contents, emptied the flute in one celebratory flourish. As he set the stem back on the tray, his eyes fell upon the envelope. Kassar immediately knew its contents and ripped open the flap in anticipation. With a quick glance at the single sheet inside, he shouted "Yes, indeed! We do have a winner."

The envelope contained the opening box office report for *Terminator 2.* The movie had opened to massive crowds and the box office take had exceeded even Kassar's expectations. But as the euphoria of the moment subsided, Kassar reflected. Would it be enough to save Carolco? Or, would it be "Hasta la vista, baby"?

Endnotes

1. "Carolco Needs A Hero, and the Terminator May Prove to Be It," *The Wall Street Journal*, Southwest edition, July 9, 1991, p. A1.
2. Ibid.
3. Alex Ben Block, "Is There Life beyond Rambo?" *Forbes*, June 1, 1987, pp. 88–92.
4. *The Wall Street Journal*, July 9, 1991, p. A1.
5. *Forbes*, June 1, 1987, p. 88.
6. *Moody's Industrial Manual 7*, (1990), p. 2,707.
7. *The Wall Street Journal*, July 9, 1991, p. A10.
8. Ibid.
9. *Forbes*, June 1, 1987, p. 92.
10. *The Wall Street Journal*, July 9, 1991, p. A10.
11. Ibid., p. A1.
12. *Standard and Poor's Stock Reports*, February 1991, p. 448.
13. *The Wall Street Journal*, July 9, 1991, p. A10.
14. Ibid.
15. Ibid., p. A1.
16. *Annual Report*, Carolco Pictures, 1990, p. 2.
17. Ibid., p. 4.
18. Ibid., p. 5.
19. Ibid., p. 5.
20. *The Wall Street Journal*, July 9, 1991, p. A1.
21. Ibid.
22. Ibid.
23. Claudia Eller, "Scripter to Get $2 Million to Adapt 'Manhattan.'" *Variety*, October 8, 1990, p. 28.
24. *The Wall Street Journal*, July 9, 1991, p. A1.
25. "News Summary—People," *The Dallas Morning News*, July 15, 1991, Sec. A, p. 2.
26. *The Wall Street Journal*, p. A1.
27. Ibid.
28. Ibid.
29. *Annual Report*, Carolco Pictures, 1990, p. 12.
30. Ibid., pp. 15–22.
31. *Form 10-K*, Carolco Pictures, 1990, p. 1.
32. Ibid., p. 5.
33. Ibid., p. 21.
34. *Annual Report*, Carolco Pictures, 1990, p. 15.
35. Claudia Eller and Don Groves, "Carolco Prexy Defends Its Talent Megadeals," *Variety*, October 29, 1990, p. 10.
36. *The Wall Street Journal*, July 9, 1991, p. A1.
37. *Form 10-K*, Carolco Pictures, 1990, p. 20.
38. *Annual Report*, Carolco Pictures, 1990, p. 29.
39. Ibid.
40. Ibid., p. 25.
41. Ibid., p. 26.
42. Ibid., p. 5.
43. Ibid., p. 5.
44. Ibid., p. 30.
45. Ibid., p. 31.
46. Ibid., p. 28.
47. Ibid., p. 33.
48. News Release, Carolco Pictures Inc., June 10, 1991.
49. *Annual Report*, Carolco Pictures, 1990, p. 33.
50. Ibid., pp. 34–35.
51. Ibid., p. 35.
52. *The Wall Street Journal*, July 9, 1991, p. A1.
53. *Annual Report*, Carolco Pictures, 1990, p. 36.
54. Ibid., p. 25.
55. *Form 10-K*, Carolco Pictures, 1990, p. 8.
56. Geraldine Fabrikant, "Finding Success in Movie Niches," *The New York Times*, April 4, 1990, p. C1.
57. *Form 10-K*, Carolco Pictures, 1990, p. 11.
58. Ibid.
59. Ibid., p. 5.
60. Ibid., p. 29.
61. Ibid., p. 29.
62. Ibid., p. 34.
63. Ibid., p. 36.
64. Ibid., p. 25.
65. Ibid., p. 25.
66. *Variety*, October 29, 1990, p. 10.
67. *Annual Report*, Carolco Pictures, 1990, p. 25.
68. Ibid., p. 27.
69. James Greenberg, "Newly Formed Carolco Intl. Gets O'Seas Rights to Carpenter Pix," *Variety*, August 5, 1987, p. 28.
70. Ibid.
71. "Carolco Presses on without Its Cofounder Vajna: Has 9-Title Package Ready." *Variety*, February 21, 1990, p. 88.
72. "Carolco Says 'Da' to Pact." *Variety*, December 3, 1990, p. 19.
73. *Variety*, February 21, 1990, p. 88.
74. *Annual Report*, Carolco Pictures, 1990, p. 30.
75. Ibid.
76. Ibid., p. 31.
77. Ibid., p. 31.
78. James C. Cooper and Kathleen Madigan, "The Consumer Is Blue, Broke and Burdened with Debt," *Business Week*, February 11, 1991, p. 17.
79. Gene Koretz, "A Double Whammy for Double-Income Families," *Business Week*, December 31, 1990, p. 32.
80. Paul Noglows, "Will B.O. Prove Recession-Proof This Time Out?" *Variety*, December 10, 1990, pp. 1–3.
81. Ibid., p. 1.
82. Ibid., p. 3.
83. Ibid., p. 3.
84. Todd McCarthy, "Whopping Year for U.S. Independents," *Variety*, June 22, 1988, p. 22.
85. Lawrence Cohn, "Fewer New Pix in '90, but More by Majors," *Variety*, December 24, 1990, p. 8.
86. Peter Bart, "View from the War Room," *Variety*, May 27, 1991, p. 3.
87. Elliot Tiegel, "Surviving as an Indie," *California Business*, August 1990, p. 18.

88. Ibid., p. 19.
89. Ibid., p. 67.
90. *Form 10-K*, Carolco Pictures, 1990, p. 22
91. Ibid., p. 23.
92. *The Wall Street Journal*, December 24, 1990, p. 9.
93. *Form 10-K*, Carolco Pictures, 1990, p. 23.
94. *The Wall Street Journal*, December 24, 1990, p. 9.
95. *Form 10-K*, Carolco Pictures, 1990, p. 23.
96. Ibid., pp. 32–33.
97. Ibid., p. 33.
98. *Form 10-K*, Carolco Pictures, 1990, p. 1.
99. Ibid.
100. Ibid., p. 9.
101. Ibid., p. F9.
102. Ibid., p. 32.
103. Ibid., p. F26.
104. Ibid., p. 32.
105. Ibid., p. F14.
106. Ibid.
107. Ibid.
108. Ibid.
109. News Release, Carolco Pictures, June 5, 1991.
110. Ibid.
111. *Form 10-K*, Carolco Pictures, 1990, p. F14.
112. Ibid.
113. Ibid.
114. News Release, Carolco Pictures, May 16, 1991.
115. *The Wall Street Journal*, July 9, 1991, p. 1.
116. *Annual Report*, Carolco Pictures, 1990, p. 2.
117. Ibid., pp. 39–40.
118. *Form 10-K*, Carolco Pictures, 1990, p. 42.
119. Ibid., p. 25.

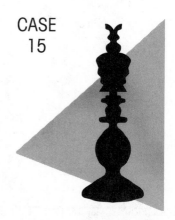

STM Technology, Inc.

Raymond M. Kinnunen, John A. Seeger & James F. Molloy, Jr.

It was May 1990, and Jerry Budinoff, founder, president, and 80 percent owner of STM Technology, Inc., sat in his office, looking at the large framed print on the wall. It showed a C-130 military transport plane, the kind Jerry had navigated for two years in Vietnam. "That's what I want this company to be," he said. "A vehicle, capable of supporting large-scale projects in systems development. A rugged vehicle. The C-130 is exciting to fly and tough to shoot down."

Jerry grinned as he contrasted that vision for the future with the short-run plans facing his nine-person firm. "First, we have to develop the expanded system features demanded by our present customers, then I have to rewrite the business plan in order to attract $900,000 in new capital, then I'll switch back to my salesman role, to bring in the new business." He mused about the change in his thinking about the company's growth:

> Originally, I thought if you developed good software and supported it well, you would be successful. That was all you had to worry about. That got us up to this point, but we really won't go any further until I worry about the business stuff.
>
> We're at $750,000 a year in revenue now, but it isn't going to get any bigger without marketing, distribution, people, money—all of them. Just doing good software doesn't get it any bigger than this.
>
> I just figured that out. It hit me like a club. It's that simple. We never had a business plan. We never had *any* long-range plan. The company just grew.

STM Technology, Inc., located near Boston in Acton, Massachusetts, was founded in 1983 to exploit Jerry Budinoff's skills in systems design and application. The first commercial customer was a small mental health center. STM had gone on to specialize in microcomputer-based management information systems for smaller health care providers and nonprofit human service agencies. The

This case has accompanying videotapes in a question and answer session in front of an Executive MBA class that can be purchased from Northeastern University, College of Business Administration, Boston, MA 02115. This case was prepared as a basis for class discussion. Distributed by the North American Case Research Association. All rights reserved to the authors and the North American Case Research Association. Permission for use should be obtained from the authors and the North American Case Research Association. Copyright © 1990 by Raymond M. Kinnunen and John A. Seeger.

product STM offered was more than just software. The company sold total systems. Its Customer Support Department provided training, software support and consulting services, while its Hardware and Network Department provided hardware, multiuser local area networks, and on-site maintenance services.

Since its founding, STM had installed some 129 systems in a wide variety of outpatient health care facilities. Revenues had grown steadily since 1983 and the company had been consistently profitable. By 1989 the company had developed a hospital management system based on personal computers—the first to run on PCs, according to Budinoff. This new product development prompted him to seek outside financing for STM, which had, until this point, financed its growth internally. Budinoff had concluded that proper exploitation of this new product and other systems required financial backing. (See Exhibits 1, 2, and 3 for financial and sales data.)

MICROCOMPUTER SOFTWARE INDUSTRY

In the early 1980s, following the introduction of IBM's personal computer and wide market acceptance of microcomputers, demand for application software skyrocketed. Hundreds, then thousands of individual entrepreneurs founded businesses as designers, programmers, distributors, or retailers of microcomputer software. By 1988 there were approximately 30,000 microcomputer software manufacturers in the United States producing more than 70,000 products.[1] In the Boston area alone, the Business to Business telephone directory listed 906 computer software and service firms, and 555 computer systems designers and consultants.

This proliferation of entrants in the industry required firms to do more than just produce technologically sound products if they wished to grow. By 1990 success in the industry called for brand development, firm name recognition, marketing, support, and product development and enhancement. Business expertise in marketing, sales, and support became increasingly more significant as prerequisites for success. Jerry Budinoff commented on the importance of providing service:

> Hardware and software require a lot of support. Technology changes quickly and if you're not supporting the changes they just run by you. We're small, but we try to provide all of the services. That's what really sells our products. It's not just the system; it's all of the training and support. A system is not just software. It's the whole human element and you have to concentrate on the people side with your service organization. Without that we'd be out of business.

HEALTH CARE INDUSTRY

For several decades, expenditures on health care had represented the fastest growing sector of the American economy. The adoption of government payment

EXHIBIT 1 STM Technology, Inc. Comparative Balance Sheet, Years Ended December 31 ($000)

	1985	1986	1987	1988	1989
Assets					
Current assets					
Cash	$ 0	$55	$ 89	$ 83	$ 79
Accounts receivable	0	0	73	90	127
Supplies	0	0	1	2	7
Prepaid income taxes		0	0	15	3
Total current assets	0	55	163	190	216
Property and Equipment (at cost)					
Equipment	21	26	35	47	59
Motor vehicles	14	14	14	40	40
Total property and equipment	34	39	48	86	98
Less accumulated depreciation	14	22	32	45	59
Net property and equipment	20	17	16	41	40
Miscellaneous costs	0	0	0	0	0
Organization costs	3	2	2	1	0
Total assets	$23	$74	$180	$232	$256
Liabilities and Stockholders' Equity					
Current liabilities					
Accounts payable	$ 4	$ 5	$ 10	$ 12	$ 25
Accrued taxes	0	27	13	0	0
Deferred taxes	0	0	4	4	7
Deferred revenue	0	0	63	70	76
Total current liabilities	4	33	90	86	108
Notes payable—stockholders	22	24	22	48	48
Total liabilities	26	57	112	134	156
Stockholders' equity					
Common stock, no par value; 1,250 shares issued and outstanding	4	4	4	4	4
Retained earnings	(7)	14	64	94	96
Total stockholders' equity	(3)	18	68	98	100
Total Liabilities and Stockholder Equity	$23	$74	$180	$232	$256

programs (Medicare and Medicaid) in the mid-1960s and growth in private insurance (such as Blue Cross/Blue Shield) encouraged the use of health care, since most people could pass their medical costs on to third-party payers. Estimated total U.S. health care expenditures for 1990 were 2.6 times the level of 1980 at $647 billion (see Exhibit 4).

As medical costs rose, governments and employers who were paying the bills came under increasing budget pressure. Repeated efforts to control costs showed little effect. In October 1983 the federal government changed its Medicare payment policy from full reimbursement for hospital charges to reimbursement at predetermined rates for specific treatments. The government set rates for hospital services

EXHIBIT 2 STM Technology, Inc. Comparative Statement of Income, Years Ended December 31 ($000)

	1985	1986	1987	1988	1989
Sales and service	$93	$331	$555	$680	$700
Cost of sales and service	64	174	404	353	380
Gross profit	28	157	151	327	320
General and administrative costs	N.A.	N.A.	78	144	184
Product development costs	N.A.	N.A.	N.A.	148	133
Total operating expenses	28	133	78	292	317
Income from operations	0	24	73	35	3
Interest income	1	1	4	3	3
Interest expense	0	0	3	5	5
Miscellaneous income	0	0	0	3	1
Miscellaneous expenses	0	1	0	0	0
Income before provision for income taxes	1	25	73	37	3
Provision for income taxes	0	4	23	7	1
Net income	$ 1	$ 21	$ 51	$ 30	$ 2

Cost Breakdown by Category

	Cost of Sales and Service		Product Development Expenses		Selling, General and Administrative Expenses	
	1989	1988	1989	1988	1989	1988
Purchases	$174	$189				
Salaries	141	118	$96	$113	$113	$90
Auto expenses and travel	21	17			14	11
Payroll taxes	12	10	8	10	7	6
Consultants	9	3	2	—	3	
Employee benefits	8	1	7	4	5	4
Telephone	4	5	1	—	7	5
Depreciation	4	3	7	10	3	—
User meetings	2	1				
Insurance	2	3				
Equipment repair	1	1				
Printing	1	1			1	1
Recruiting expenses			13	9	1	
Development supplies			—	1		
Rent					13	2
Accounting and legal fees					5	8
Commissions					3	5
Office expenses					3	1
Sales exhibits					2	3
Sales expense					1	1
Miscellaneous					3	3
Advertising					—	1
Seminar costs					—	2
Bad debt expenses					—	1
	$380[a]	$353	$133	$148	$184	$144

[a]Totals may not add due to rounding.

EXHIBIT 3 STM Sales Restated by Business Line (000)

Item	Actual			Estimated			
	1987	**1988**	**1989**	**1990**	**1991**	**1992**	**1993**
Hospitals and Clinics							
Software sales							
New clients	$412	$248	$350				
Old clients	19	137[a]	20				
Subtotal	431	385	370				
Hardware							
Contracts	61	85	101				
Equipment/labor[b]	66	103	110				
Subtotal	127	188	211				
Total hospitals and clinics	$558	$573	$581	$1,125	$3,160	$5,305	$ 8,030
Software Support							
Contracts[c]	36	70	94				
Training[d]	10	16	22				
Consulting	8	19	21				
Total support	54	105	137	286	760	1,196	1,748
Tracking	—	—	—	45	200	300	400
Total revenues	$612	$678	$718	$1,456	$4,120	$6,081	$10,178

[a]Includes one special contract for $80,000.
[b]Labor for installation.
[c]Extended service contracts.
[d]Special training programs not associated with sales.
Source: Estimates by Jerry Budinoff.

according to Diagnostic Related Groups (DRGs), resulting in standard reimbursements for medical treatments, regardless of how long the patient remained in the hospital. This new fixed-fee payment system provided strong incentives for health care facilities to control costs since payment rates were not negotiable. Hospitals immediately began to send patients home to complete their recuperations.

Employers also responded to the ever-rising costs of employee health benefits. Some companies raised their employees' portion of health insurance premiums; some increased efforts to promote overall healthy living; still others encouraged employees to elect lower-cost plans like health maintenance organizations (HMOs).

These changes in health care payment did not, however, curtail national health care spending. Health care's portion of the gross national product grew steadily from 5.2 percent in 1960 to 11.5 percent in 1988. The increase, due partly to the aging population and partly to costly advances in medical technology, was expected to continue. In 1989 11 percent of the total national population was over 65 years of age and generated 35 percent of 1989's total health care bill.[2] Older patients required more attention, thus increasing the labor costs of most health care facilities. Additionally, the number of diagnostic tests, medical treatments,

EXHIBIT 4 U.S. Health Expenditures, by Type ($millions)

Type of Expenditure	1980	1981	1982	1983	1984	1985R	1986R	1987R	1988	1990E
Health service and supplies	$237,100	$273,500	$308,300	$341,800	$375,400	$407.8	$443.0	$485.4	$535.7	$626,500
Personal health care	219,400	254,600	286,900	314,800	341,900	373.4	406.0	447.0	494.8	573,500
Hospital care	100,400	118,000	135,500	148,800	156,300	168.6	180.4	196.9	216.2	250,400
Physicians' services	46,800	54,800	61,800	68,400	75,400	79.3	89.2	100.1	112.9	132,600
Dentists' services	15,400	17,300	19,500	21,700	24,600	27.5	29.9	33.2	37.0	41,800
Other professional services	5,600	6,400	7,100	9,300	10,900	15.7	18.0	20.8	24.1	22,900
Drugs and medical sundries	19,300	21,300	22,400	24,500	26,500	32.1	34.1	36.5	39.0	42,100
Eyeglasses and appliances	5,100	5,700	5,700	6,200	7,000	7.7	8.5	9.4	10.5	11,200
Nursing home care	20,600	24,200	27,300	29,400	31,700	34.1	36.8	40.0	43.8	54,500
Other health services	6,000	6,900	7,600	8,400	9,400	8.3	9.1	10.1	11.3	18,000
Prepayment and administration	10,700	11,100	12,700	17,100	22,600	22.1	23.5	24.0	25.0	34,600
Government public health activities	7,000	7,700	8,600	10,000	11,000	12.3	13.5	14.4	15.9	18,500
Medical facilities	11,800	13,100	14,100	15,400	15,600	19.1	20.4	21.6	23.0	20,700
Research	5,300	5,700	5,900	6,200	6,800	11.0	12.3	13.4	14.6	11,500
Construction	8,500	7,500	8,200	9,200	8,900	8.1	8.0	8.3	8.4	9,300
Total health expenditures	$249,000	$286,600	$322,400	$357,200	$391,100	$426.9	$463.4	$507.0	$558.7	$647,300

R = Revised, E = Estimated

Source: Health Care Financing Administration; "Health Care," Standard & Poor's Industry Survey, July 13, 1989, p. H15.

and prescribed pharmaceuticals billed by hospitals to their patients increased greatly, even as hospital stays dropped under the pressure of the DRG payment system.

Except for outpatient services, hospital utilization declined steadily after 1983. Hospitals faced tighter margins, due to lower admissions and inadequate reimbursement. DRG rate increases lagged behind actual cost increases for health services, and under the Bush administration this condition was expected to continue: Medicare's fiscal 1990 budget was cut by more than $2 billion. Additionally, hospitals had to contend with the high cost of preventing in-hospital contraction of infectious diseases such as AIDS along with increasing liability insurance.[3]

Declining usage and tightening margins hit small public and rural hospitals (those having fewer than 100 beds) especially hard. Many public and rural hospitals faced the threat of bankruptcy or closure. In addition to inadequate DRG rates, these hospitals were adversely affected by demographic changes and the distribution of federal health care funds. Increasing numbers of young rural residents moved away, reducing the tax base that supported community health care and shifting the balance of patients to an older, more Medicare-dependent base. Rural hospitals generally received 40 percent less in Medicare reimbursement per case than did urban hospitals because government audits showed that rural hospitals had lower operating costs. A study by the University of Illinois Center for Health Services Research found that 161 rural hospitals closed between 1980 and 1987, with 70 percent of those remaining losing money in 1987. And 600 more rural hospitals were expected to close before 1990.[4]

Many hospitals attempted to compensate for declining revenues by shifting the weight of costs to private patients. Private and corporate consumers, however, reacted by seeking alternate means of health care. Outpatient services grew substantially in usage. In 1980 18 percent of all surgical procedures were performed on an outpatient or ambulatory basis. This increased to 28 percent in 1985 and was expected to be at 59 percent by 1990.[5]

Health maintenance organizations first became a key component of health care in 1973 with a law requiring many corporations to include HMO coverage in their health care benefit menus. HMOs operate on fixed cost contracts with health care providers, eliminating any fee for service. Although there was some concern that HMOs' protection might be discontinued, a Duff & Phelps HMO industry analysis expected annual membership growth to continue (see Exhibit 5) and revenue growth to remain near 20 percent.[6]

In summary, health care providers felt intense pressure in 1990 to control costs. A prime area for their attention was administrative systems, where hospitals had automated many of their processes, but smaller institutions had been unable to afford the high costs of modernizing systems to improve their efficiency.

STM'S COMPETITIVE SITUATION

A number of large competitors and a multitude of small ones served the medical market with computer systems, according to Budinoff:

EXHIBIT 5 Growth of HMOs: 1980 to 1988

Date	Prepaid Plans	Enrollment (millions)	Population (percentage)
June 1980	236	9.1	4.0%
June 1981	243	10.2	4.4
June 1982	265	10.8	4.7
June 1983	280	12.5	5.3
June 1984	306	15.1	6.4
December 1984	337	16.7	7.1
December 1985	480	21.0	8.8
December 1986	593	25.0	10.4
December 1987	650	30.0	12.2
June 1988	643	N.A.	N.A.

Source: Adapted from "Health Care," *Standard & Poor's Industry Survey*, July 13, 1989, p. H32.

Meditech, IDX, and Baxter are big in the hospital systems market, for example, but they don't bother with outpatient clinics. Baxter is huge. But their product sells for $250,000 to $300,000 to get the whole system in, including hardware. Baxter and IDX will both lease their systems at $75,000 per year. Clinics can't even look at that kind of money, and even a hospital of 100 to 125 beds can't afford it. They may pay it, but they're real unhappy.

Baxter International, a major supplier to large hospitals, was a manufacturer and distributor of health care products whose 1988 sales reached $6.8 billion. Baxter's products included intravenous solutions, dialysis and blood collection equipment, drugs, urological and diagnostic products, cardiovascular devices, and information systems. Additionally, Baxter operated 120 of its own outpatient health care facilities.

The big guys have had their systems out there for several years, and they're all based on minicomputers. We want to go in with a PC-based system that sells in the neighborhood of $75,000 to $90,000. We're the first ones to do it on PCs, and we have to get the financing so we can develop it properly and grow it before the others copy us. It's not easy to downsize a system from minis to micros, and the big guys have a minicomputer mindset. We have maybe a year's lead.

STM did not offer a lease plan to its customers. "I have no training in business," said Jerry, "and that kind of arrangement requires a lot of expertise."

Small hospitals and clinics, Jerry said, were "an everywhere market." Some 60 percent of hospitals tabulated in the 1989 American Hospital Association's data were below 200 beds in size (see Exhibit 6), and there was evidence that the smaller hospitals were having difficulty finding the systems they wanted. A survey of 3,000 hospitals with more than 100 beds conducted by *Modern Healthcare* (see Exhibit 7)

EXHIBIT 6 Health Facilities in Target Areas, 1989

	Hospitals[a]					Psychological	Substance	Total
	Total	**<50**	**<100**	**<200**	**HMOs**	**Facilities**	**Abuse**	**Facilities[b]**
New England								
Connecticut	65	7	23	34	12	8	32	117
Maine	46	11	29	34	4	0	9	59
Massachusetts	173	12	52	98	26	4	34	237
New Hampshire	41	9	24	34	5	6	14	66
Rhode Island	19	2	11	15	4	1	6	30
Vermont	86	0	18	37	3	0	4	93
Total[c]	450	41	157	252	54	19	99	602
Mid-Atlantic Coast								
New Jersey	125	4	14	37	22	8	43	198
New York	322	25	72	138	30	23	119	494
Pennsylvania	302	19	72	160	26	5	90	423
Total	749	48	158	335	78	36	252	
South Atlantic Coast								
Florida	276	27	82	164	39	25	100	440
District of Columbia	18	0	2	4	8	0	7	33
Georgia	204	39	98	147	11	5	49	269
South Carolina	90	14	41	67	5	1	12	108
North Carolina	159	24	71	115	9	3	25	196
Maryland	85	8	18	40	22	6	51	164
Virginia	136	9	40	87	19	2	43	200
West Virginia	70	19	39	48	4	1	14	89
Delaware	13	1	4	8	7	1	4	25
Total	1,051	141	395	680	124	44	305	1,524
Miscellaneous								
Texas	553	184	313	437	47	31	139	770
California	566	91	233	386	119	21	163	869
Total	1,119	275	546	823	166	52	302	1,639

[a]Hospitals are grouped by number of beds. Each category includes the previous category's number. Total refers to all hospitals with unlimited bed size.
[b]Total facilities equal sum of total hospitals, HMOs, psychological, and substance abuse facilities.
[c]Total refers to sum of geographic groups column.
Source: *1989 AHA Guide to the Health Care Field* (Chicago: American Hospital Association, 1989).

indicated a large number of small shoppers for systems, with many purchase plans cancelled or delayed for years.

The small institutions were served by a few small companies (Practice Management Systems, at about $5 million annual sales, was the largest) and by a legion of independent operators. Many of these, Jerry thought, were amateurs or programmers who had built a system for their own employers and were trying to peddle it to others. As basement operators, they often quoted unrealistically low

EXHIBIT 7 Buying Plans

| | | | Still pending | | | |
| | Implemented | Cancelled | From | From | New Plans | Total |
Bed Size	Plans	Plans	1986	1987	in 1988	Plans
Buying Plans for Patient Care Systems (1987 plans, as of end of 1988)						
100–199	58	19	79	37	117	233
200–299	47	23	46	13	71	130
300–399	24	13	29	18	37	84
400–499	10	5	14	0	13	27
500 and over	21	5	33	10	27	68
Total	160	65	201	78	265	542
Buying Plans for Patient Accounting Systems (1987 plans, as of end of 1988)						
100–199	53	14	32	30	112	174
200–299	58	12	20	16	54	90
300–399	34	2	29	12	29	70
400–499	14	4	13	1	13	27
500 and over	25	2	13	10	28	51
Total	184	34	107	69	236	412

Source: *Modern Healthcare*, July, 1989, p. 58.

prices. Wise buyers in the market had come to demand evidence of a supplier's financial stability.

Every successful installation, Budinoff felt, would generate new sales through word-of-mouth contact from satisfied customers. Already, STM's development work in five hospitals was generating inquiries beyond the firm's capacity to service them. Jerry had just decided against pursuing a California hospital inquiry; the distance made installation and support unfeasible. Still, many hospital and clinic administrators desperately wanted economical systems. Budinoff had first-hand knowledge of their problem:

> I've had directors of facilities get a little annoyed with me because they wanted something like our system but didn't know we existed, so they bought something else. When they found out about us they'd call and say, "Where the hell were you when I needed you?"

STM TECHNOLOGY, INC.: CURRENT PRODUCTS

The success to date of STM was attributed to the sales of its Outpatient Billing and Administration System, with an installed base of 129 systems in fall 1989. Jerry estimated the market to be approximately 2,500 clinics in New England; he was targeting an additional 335 installations over the next four years. This estimate was based on a significant upgrade to the present system, automating nearly the entire billing process. This new "Robotic" version would incorporate automatic scanning of services at the front end and electronic transmission and posting of receipts at the back end. Little or no hand data entry would be required. This new version could be marketable in four months with additional research and development funding, Jerry said.

Two additional products had been developed: a microcomputer In-patient Billing and Administrative System targeted at small hospitals (under 150 beds), clinics, and HMOs, and a Patient Database which provided a Medical Tracking and Analysis System linked with either hospital or clinic systems. These programs formed an interrelated family of products which met the need for affordable, integrated medical systems. STM continued its market research in order to add to this family of products further through the development of new and followup software.

The Medical Tracking and Analysis System was a system to track the health care data of patients throughout their lifetimes. It could be integrated into the Billing and Accounting System, but could also be available as a stand-alone product. The product needed six to nine months to complete after funding came in. Jerry viewed the market as nationwide and potentially worldwide. He had targeted 245 sales within four years to employee-assistance program providers, employers, government agencies, and health care practices.

STM TECHNOLOGY, INC.: HISTORY

Jerry Budinoff was an electrical and astronautical engineer by training (see Exhibit 8). He began working with computer systems shortly after leaving active duty with the Air Force, and joined Proctor & Gamble as a production manager. While working with computer professionals there, Budinoff discovered that he really enjoyed systems design. This would be his new profession.

After P&G, Budinoff worked for DEC and Raytheon to gain management experience. Budinoff says, "I had a friend who thought you couldn't really run your own company unless you could be an executive in a large corporation. So I got to where I worked for a vice president. Then I said, 'Okay, I can do this,' and started this company."

In 1982 Budinoff left Raytheon to develop systems and start STM. He describes his entry into the health care market:

> It was an accident. The first person I found who wanted a system developed happened to own a mental health center. That was it. There was no formal market research. It could have been a gas station. It didn't make a difference to me. I was a techie, and I just wanted to develop software.

After Budinoff incorporated the company in 1983, he brought in Evelyn Mittler, a Raytheon programming consultant, as a 10-percent stockholder, and Richard Kelley, a software development administrator from Honeywell. It was with this limited staff that STM developed software products to enter the health care market, focusing on systems for nonphysician, outpatient facilities. Budinoff saw STM's ability to serve a wide variety of outpatient clinics as his competitive advantage. He commented on this and the derivation of the company's name:

EXHIBIT 8   Resume: Jerold E. Budinoff

Summary of Qualifications
6 years president software development company.
17 years system development experience.
Designed and implemented systems in health-care billing and administration, order processing, production
control, bill of materials, MRP, receivables and general ledger.

Education
Purdue University—M.S. Astronautical Engineering, 1965
U.S. Air Force Academy—B.S. Engineering Science (Distinguished Graduate), 1964

Job History
1983 to present   President, STM Technology, Inc.
1981 to 1983   Senior Analyst, Raytheon Corporation
1975 to 1981   Manufacturing/MIS Manager, Digital Equipment Corporation
1972 to 1975   Systems Analyst, Keydata Corporation
1971 to 1972   Production Manager, Proctor & Gamble
1964 to 1970   Officer, U.S. Air Force

8/83 to present: STM Technology, Inc., Acton, Massachusetts
President

Founded company which develops and installs a wide variety of software for the health-care industry.
STM's health care Office Management Systems are the most advanced patient registration, billing, and
accounts receivable systems available today in Massachusetts.

Serves as STM's primary systems developer. All STM systems have been designed by Mr. Budinoff working
with agency executive directors, business managers, and administrative personnel throughout Massachusetts. Also serves as STM's only salesman. Responsible for all sales and marketing of STM's products.
STM employs eight people.

12/81 to 8/83:   Raytheon Computer Services, Wellesley, Massachusetts
Senior Analyst

Developed systems for Raytheon commercial customers. Responsibilities included client interface, project
management, specification, design, testing, and implementation. Produced systems in medical insurance
and retail sales for IBM mainframes.

10/75 to 7/81:   Digital Equipment Corporation, Maynard, Massachusetts
Group MIS Functional Manager, Headquarters (4/80 to 7/81)

Responsible for program management of all common systems in the areas of manufacturing engineering
and quality. Established strategies, business plans, and staffing. Coordinated system development
between plants.

Systems Development Manager, Westminster Plant (2/78 to 4/80)

Managed 15 analysts and programmers developing systems in materials, BOMs, quality assurance, and
purchasing. Responsibilities included planning, budgeting, staffing, and project management. Successfully
developed and implemented the first common material requirements planning and BOM system in the
systems manufacturing group. DEC hardware.

Manufacturing Planning Manager, Westminster Plant (2/77 to 2/78)

Managed a group that accomplished long-range planning and developed tools for management
analysis.

EXHIBIT 8 Cont'd. Resume: Jerold E. Budinoff

Systems Analysis Manager, Product Line Systems (10/75 to 2/77)

Built and managed a team of analysts working in the product line order processing group. Accomplished feasibility studies and functional specifications for order-processing systems.

6/72 to 10/75:   Keydata Corporation, Watertown, Massachusetts

Manager of Communications, Headquarters (1/75 to 10/75)

Managed 35 people responsible for Keydata's nationwide 1,000-terminal teleprocessing network. Department included communication customer services, line trouble shooting, contracts, and evaluation of new equipment.

Systems Analyst/Customer Rep, National Accounts Region - (6/72 to 1/75)

Developed systems for Keydata's major national accounts. Worked closely with salespeople and customers in the sales phase and assumed full account responsibility after contract was signed. Designed and implemented systems in manufacturing, order processing, accounting, and electronic mail.

9/71 to 5/72:   Plast-Alum Manufacturing Company, North Hollywood, California

Partner

Managed the entire operation of a small (20 people) manufacturing business including manufacturing operations, budgeting, inventory, and inside sales.

6/70 to 9/71:   Proctor & Gamble Corporation, Cape Girardeau, Missouri

Production Manager

Managed a 22-person crew operating four Pampers production lines. Responsibilities included personnel supervision, training, production, maintenance, and packaging.

6/64 to 6/70:   United States Air Force

Officer

Was primarily a flyer with over 3,000 hours flying time. Two years in Vietnam. Was also an instructor at the U.S. Air Force Academy in the Department of Engineering Mechanics.

Mental health facilities, rehabilitation facilities, substance abuse facilities . . . there are no other general-purpose systems out there that are right for all of them. Maybe 50 to 60 percent of them are nonprofit, and systems for them are much more difficult to do than for physicians. So there is much less competition for systems work for these facilities: everyone sees physicians as the big market, and these other things are much smaller.

There is no one who competes in all the different kinds of places we're in. We run into one set of competitors in mental health facilities, and another set in substance abuse companies. We're the only one with a generic product—one that serves all kinds of clinics. That is an advantage because when one of these guys gets aggressive and starts doing very well in some market, we can turn to another market. We're always going one direction or another within health care, while our competition is tied to one market and they go up and down as that market moves.

One thing all our customers have in common: they all want to save time and money. That's what STM stands for—Save Time and Money. When I first went out to the market, I asked what people wanted. They said, "anything that saves me time and money," so I put that right into the name. A panel at Harvard said it was a "harsh and nondescriptive" name for a company, where you want a name that's warm and friendly. But I want to tell you our customers and prospects remember it and identify with it. It always gets a smile. They greet me, "here's the guy who'll save us time and money." Maybe that's why I haven't gone to Harvard.

In its first six years of operation, STM did not have an office facility; all employees operated out of their homes. In July 1989 Jerry leased a 1,400-square-foot, ranch-style building. A classroom for weekly training sessions and tastefully decorated offices for all the staff occupied the first floor. An equal-sized basement, vacant but subject to rental, would provide expansion space when funding permitted the increased staff. STM at the time employed nine people who provided administration, hardware maintenance, customer support, training, and programming. Budinoff did most of the systems design work and was also the company's only salesperson. Evelyn Mittler, whose 24 years of systems and programming experience included extensive service with Raytheon, Varian, and Wang, assisted with design and was in charge of coding. All STM programs were written in COBOL. "It may not be the newest language, but it is much easier to find customer support people who understand COBOL," Mittler said.

STM had no affiliation or official status with the computer manufacturers whose hardware they selected for customer systems. Some years earlier, an IBM value added reseller had offered Jerry a System 36 minicomputer, hoping he would program the Outpatient Management System for their machine. "Even then, we thought the minis were dinosaurs, so we didn't do it," Jerry said. IBM itself was now showing interest, this time with the thought of selling STM's software along with their PCs and the new 6000 series machines. Budinoff was hesitant, however; "I don't understand that kind of intercompany dealing," he said, "and it would take an immense amount of time to learn it."

As it became apparent during 1989 that the year would be profitable—so profitable that substantial taxes would be due—Jerry Budinoff decided to invest in additional marketing. He employed a salesperson for six months. Budinoff described him as "not having an in-depth knowledge of the product and the market. He tried to sell on personality and didn't get anywhere. This isn't like selling a car. And he didn't want to *get* the knowledge. We parted company." In 1990 STM's marketing still relied only on Budinoff's efforts, word-of-mouth between health care organizations, a couple of ads in the Yellow Pages, and past attendance at a few trade shows.

STM BUSINESS PLAN

In January 1990 Jerry had developed a business plan which aimed to take advantage of STM's innovative, PC-based systems for small hospitals. The plan sought $900,000 in new capital, which would support the hiring of ". . . a director of operations, who will relieve Mr. Budinoff's time for concentration on the key skill of systems design . . . immediate expansion of the programming and system analyst staff . . . a director of sales and marketing, who will hire the telemarketing and sales support staff . . . and a Chief Financial Officer." The plan projected growth to 74 employees by the end of 1993, with sales just over $10 million (see Exhibits 9 through 11). Jerry Budinoff commented on the opportunity:

> I never wanted to get financing before. I never understood the business side, or the huge need for capital. But we've been in the health care market for six years now, and I do know what that market needs and how to design for it. We've got a real lock on it. I am positive that if we get the financing this thing is going to go through the roof like a rocket ship. There is just no doubt in my mind. So I'm not worried about the financing; it will be paid back. We just need the $900,000; that's the difference between total expenses and total income in the first year of the plan.
>
> But we have to take the new In-patient Hospital System into the market the right way, not just dribble it in, because as soon as we get visibility and prove to the market that 386s and 286s can do the job, then one of the big companies will come in. When we break the idea barrier, they'll get going with their resources, and go right by us with marketing. We have maybe a year's lead, but if we don't get going we'll lose our real window.

EXHIBIT 9 STM Technology, Inc. Estimated Profit and Loss Statement, Years Ending December 31 ($000)

Item Description	1990	1991	1992	1993
Revenues				
Hospitals	$ 675	$2,425	$4,345	$ 7,100
Clinics	450	735	960	930
Tracking	45	200	300	400
Support	286	760	1,196	1,748
Total	1,456	4,120	6,801	10,178
Less cost of sales/service	562	1,315	2,057	2,906
Gross profit	894	2,805	4,744	7,272
Operating expenses				
Product development	346	659	931	1,377
Marketing sales	665	1,169	1,874	2,455
General and administrative expenses	311	452	768	1,025
Total	1,322	2,280	3,573	4,857
Operating profit	(428)	525	1,171	2,415
Nonoperating expenses	27	63	66	45
Profit before tax	(455)	462	1,105	2,370
Taxes	0	0	400	950
Profit after tax	($ 455)	$ 462	$ 705	$ 1,420

EXHIBIT 10 STM Technology, Inc. Pro Forma Balance Sheet, Years Ending December 31 ($000)

	1990	1991	1992	1993
Assets				
Current assets				
Cash	$140	$ 254	$ 325	$1,114
Accounts receivable–net	260	517	830	1,213
Inventory	11	29	41	53
Prepaid/deposits	3	6	11	21
Total current assets	414	806	1,197	2,401
Fixed assets				
Equipment at cost	199	299	499	699
Reserve for depreciation	89	141	201	261
Net fixed assets	110	158	298	438
Other assets				
Research and development	150	280	390	350
Miscellaneous	10	40	90	160
Total other assets	160	320	480	510
Total assets	$684	$1,284	$1,975	$3,349
Liabilities and Equity				
Current liabilities				
Accounts payable/accruals	$ 58	$ 96	$ 132	$ 186
Deferred taxes	7	7	57	157
Deferred revenues	126	226	326	426
Notes payable–current	0	100	100	—
Total current liabilities	191	429	615	769
Long-term notes				
New	500	400	200	0
Stockholders	48	48	48	48
Total liabilities	739	877	863	817
Equity				
Common stocks	304	304	304	304
Earned surplus	(359)	103	808	2,228
Total equity	(55)	407	1,112	2,532
Total liabilities and equity	$684	$1,284	$1,975	$3,349

Of the five hospitals with installed systems in 1990, two were in Massachusetts; one each were in Connecticut (at Yale University's infirmary), New Hampshire, and Maine. The business plan estimated the market as 3,000 small hospitals nationwide and 450 in New England. It targeted 235 installations in the next four years, representing a 12 percent market share nationwide.

The plan envisioned growth in STM's Outpatient System as well, based on selling the new Robotic integrated system to clinics throughout New England. Nineteen new sales in 1990 to Massachusetts facilities would bring that state's total to 143, representing 13 percent of its potential market. Twenty-six new sales were targeted for the six other New England states. For the first time in its history, a

EXHIBIT 11 STM Technology, Inc. Estimated Cash Flow Years Ending December 31 ($000)

Item Description	1990	1991	1992	1993
Beginning balance	$ 79	$140	$254	$ 325
Cash in:				
Profit (loss)	(455)	462	705	1,420
Depreciation	30	52	60	60
Amortization	0	70	190	340
Accounts receivable decrease (increase)	(133)	(257)	(303)	(393)
Inventory decrease (increase)	(4)	(18)	(12)	(12)
Prepaid decrease (increase)	0	(3)	(5)	(10)
Research and development decrease (increase)	(150)	(200)	(300)	(300)
Loans/Notes	500	100	0	0
Equity	300	0	0	0
Miscellaneous assets decrease (increase)	0	10	10	10
Total in	$ 88	$216	$345	$1,115
Total cash available	$167	$356	$599	$1,440
Cash out				
Accounts payable decrease (increase)	$(33)	$(38)	$(36)	$ (54)
Taxes decrease (increase)	0	0	(50)	(100)
Deferred revenue decrease (increase)	(50)	(100)	(100)	(100)
Equipment purchases	100	100	200	200
Note repayment	0	100	200	300
Miscellaneous purchases	10	40	60	80
Total out	$ 27	$102	$274	$ 326
Ending balance	$140	$254	$325	$1,114

marketing campaign of mailings, trade journal advertising, and telemarketing would supplement the word-of-mouth networking which had so far carried STM.

The proposed marketing program began with direct sales by STM's own staff, expanding to branch offices in New York City and Tampa in 1991. California, Texas, Chicago, Denver, and St. Louis would follow in 1992. These remote sites would cultivate local vendors to provide hardware and maintenance, and eventually distribution of STM software. New products, including some for diagnostics, would be sold through mail order and off-the-shelf through computer stores. By 1993 the plan called for marketing outside the continental United States. To support these efforts, a variety of new promotional tools had to be developed, including new product packaging, advertisements, news releases, brochures, an exhibit booth for trade shows, a sales kit, sales training materials, professional videotapes, and telemarketing scripts. The business plan put the cost of these marketing and sales tools at $260,000.

STM AND THE FUTURE

To Jerry, the new financing was absolutely critical. Without it, he saw little point in continuing development work on the hospital system at all. In May 1990 no new sales of the existing inpatient system were contemplated. The development work had to come first. Jerry commented:

> I deeply believe in the philosophy I learned at DEC: don't try to force a product onto an unwilling market—let the market pull you in. Well, we were pulled into the hospital market, without knowing better. It is a very difficult system, and we might not have done it if we'd analyzed it first. We successfully automated what the hospitals were doing already. In the process, we have learned what the market really wants, and that would be a product that opens up the entire market.
>
> But we ought to do it right. Without financial backing, we can't even begin to cope with that market. We would just make a little dent in it. I know how to go piecemeal into these markets, and that's exactly what I don't want to do.

Budinoff and STM's two other equity holders were willing to relinquish 33 percent of the ownership for the financial backing. STM had already refused a $500,000 offer from one of its customers for 48 percent of the company. Jerry talked of his ideal investor:

> Health care is a very parochial, localized market. And we've got an image problem because we're the little guy in the market and people worry about us going out of business. My criterion for capital is credibility. I want someone who can give us credibility and who can give us second and third rounds. Ideally I would like a large computer-based company such as an insurance company to back us. That way they would have an interest in us. They could turn to us for consulting help. I'd be more comfortable with that.
>
> I suppose one of our options, though, if the financing didn't come through, would be to shift into retirement mode—stay small and make a pile of money.

Evelyn Mittler, who had been quiet through much of the conversation, winced at this last suggestion. "Oh, no," she said. Jerry continued:

> Yeah, we could stay at about $750,000 a year, with a gross profit of maybe $300K. There are lots of other people who need systems work done, outside of the business. It's a never-ending market. I get calls all the time; it's hilarious. I was down in Washington [Jerry served one week per month as Reserve Assistant Division Chief for the Air Force Arms Control and International Negotiations Division, designing computer systems to comply with the Star Wars arms control treaty], and they wanted to know how to automate a whole Pentagon division of operations. I'm no expert in that, but

it doesn't matter to them. I've got the reputation, and that's it. So we could turn away from growth in the medical systems.

"But none of us wants to," said Evelyn Mittler.

We could cut back on the R&D, and reap profits for the business. But we're not interested in just going along at a steady size.

"That would be boring," said Evelyn Mittler.

I view the company as a vehicle, a resource base for the fabulous systems we'll develop next year and the year after that. That's what my core group of people like doing and we're very good at that. Now I have to get the company big enough to support what we come up with. I want to move it out of health care and into other markets, too, eventually. In six years I would like us to be a $20 to $30 million company.

Endnotes

1. Eberstadt Fleming, Inc., "The PC Software Industry," August 3, 1988, p. 5; reprinted in *CIRR Index*, 1989.
2. "Health Care," *Standard & Poor's Industry Survey*, July 13, 1989, p. H15.
3. Ibid. p. H29.
4. Ibid.
5. Keithley, Joyce, et al., "The Cost Effectiveness of Same-Day Admission Surgery," *Nursing Economics*, March-April 1989, vol. 7, no. 2.
6. Fuller, Jerry E., "The HMO Industry", Duff & Phelps, Inc. December, 1987, p. 3.

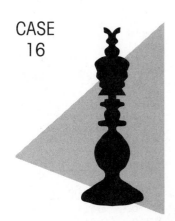

CASE 16

BROOKTROUT TECHNOLOGY, INC.

RAYMOND M. KINNUNEN, WENDY VITTORI & JOHN A. SEEGER

It's violent out there, and people in violent industries sometimes get killed. It's violent because it's changing rapidly. There are bodies all over the place in the voice mail segment. Computerm, for example, had $14 million invested and sold out for a pittance.

There are some very big companies, like AT&T, that are our potential customers—but they can also produce their *own* electronic messaging products. When you go to these big companies it's like walking underneath elephants—you just hope the elephant doesn't step on you. But they don't move real fast, so you can watch out for them.

It was June 1989 and Eric Giler, president of Brooktrout Technology, Inc. knew his company was at a crossroads. What strategy would best bring the high growth he wanted, while minimizing risk? Giler faced tough choices in marketing and finance as he wondered how to capitalize on his firm's technical skills.

Brooktrout designed and built electronic messaging systems—the equipment which automatically answers a business telephone and accepts a message for a specific individual. Some products were full systems in their own cabinets; others were separate electronic cards to be plugged into computers. Brooktrout sold mainly to original equipment manufacturers (OEMs) in the telecommunications industry. Its customers included some of the world's largest builders of telephone equipment.

Brooktrout Technology was founded in 1984 by Eric Giler, David Duehren, and Patrick Hynes; all had worked together previously at Teradyne, Inc. The company lost money in each of its first five years, but expected 1989 to be profitable, with sales approaching $5 million (see Exhibit 1). Eric commented,

> It's high risk, but also high reward. We can build a $100-million company in this business; after all, it's a multibillion dollar industry. The

This case has accompanying videotapes of Eric Giler in a question and answer session in front of an Executive MBA class that can be purchased from Northeastern University, College of Business Administration, Boston, MA 02115. This case was prepared as a basis for class discussion. Financial statements have been disguised. Distributed by the North American Case Research Association. All rights reserved to the authors and the North American Case Research Association. Permission to use the case should be obtained from the authors and the North American Case Research Association. Copyright © 1990 by Raymond M. Kinnunen and John A. Seeger.

EXHIBIT 1 Brooktrout Technology, Inc. Statement of Operations ($000)

	1985	1986	1987	1988	Projected 1989	Projected 1990
Revenues						
Voice					$3,490	$6,396
Facsimile					1,231	3,444
Total revenues	$271	$ 510	$1,378	$2,418	$4,721	$9,840
Cost of sales						
Voice					1,920	3,518
Facsimile					391	1,722
Total cost of sales	114	191	566	1,076	2,311	5,240
Gross profit	$157	$ 319	$ 812	$1,342	$2,410	$4,600
Operating expenses						
Sales and marketing	79	134	425	682	685	1,118
Research and development	214	553	354	568	726	1,332
General and administrative expenses	289	622	474	422	568	925
Total expenses	$582	$1,309	$1,253	$1,672	$1,979	3,375
Net interest expenses	(5)	(175)	(391)	(120)	(110)	(198)
Net income/(loss)	($430)	($1,165)	($ 832)	($ 450)	$ 321	$1,027

Brooktrout Technology, Inc. Balance Sheet ($000)

	1985	1986	1987	1988
Assets				
Current assets				
Cash	$ 96	$ 82	$ 274	$ 122
Accounts receivable	115	74	318	402
Inventory	62	44	124	236
Other current assets	0	26	5	24
Total current assets	273	226	721	784
Property and equipment (net of accumulated depreciation)	86	81	101	119
Other assets	26	16	13	8
Total assets	$385	$ 323	$ 834	$ 912
Liabilities and Shareholders' Equity				
Current liabilities				
Accounts payable	$110	$ 126	$ 254	$ 440
Notes payable	72	160	102	90
Current portion of long-term debt	12	28	85	84
Other liabilities	70	71	86	140
Total current liabilities	264	385	527	754
Notes payable to stockholders	88	416	578	548
Other long-term debt	6	340	300	331
Total liabilities	358	1,141	1,405	1,633
Net stockholders' equity	28	(818)	(571)	(722)
Total liabilities and stockholders' equity	$385	$ 323	$ 834	$ 912

expertise we have is our technology. We understand what makes it possible to do electronic messaging and our goal in life is to sell it on an OEM basis to companies that need it. We will make a product that is cheaper, or faster, or both.

TELECOMMUNICATIONS INDUSTRY: HISTORY

From 1876 when Alexander Graham Bell invented the telephone, until his patents expired in 1894, the American Bell Telephone Company enjoyed a pure monopoly. When competitors became free to enter, however, the market was still largely untapped. Few people had telephones; many wanted them. Independent companies strung their own wires to connect their own subscribers to their own central switchboards. By 1907 the independents had 57 percent of the market.

A shrewd American Bell obtained the patent rights to a new technology, the long-distance coil and refused to connect the independents to Bell's wires. Subscribers wanting to call distant friends or relatives switched to the Bell system. As its subscriber base grew, so did the value of Bell's services, which attracted even more subscribers. American Bell set out to acquire most of the by-then-desperate independent companies.

This spiraling effect outraged the public, and in 1912 the Justice Department threatened to file an antitrust suit. Given the choice of either fighting the case or accommodating the government, American Bell chose the latter. They were required to stop acquiring companies and to allow the remaining independents access to the long-distance service. In the 1934 Communications Act, the company submitted to being a regulated monopoly.

Thus was born the regulated telephone industry. The company—by now American Telephone & Telegraph Company—provided local phone service through its wholly owned geographic subsidiaries (e.g., New England Telephone and Telegraph) to 80 percent of American homes. Through its Western Electric manufacturing arm, it made virtually all of the nation's telephone equipment. Through its Bell Laboratories, renowned as the leading electronics R&D center of the world, it developed new technologies (including, for example, the first transistors). Unfettered by competition, AT&T devoted itself to providing superb quality and service. To preserve the quality of its lines, the company absolutely prohibited any other company's equipment from being attached to its network. By regulation, it was assured a profit based on its investment. AT&T's asset base thus grew phenomenally; by 1984 its total of $150 billion in assets dwarfed the size of most nations' economies. In assets and profits AT&T was the largest company in the world.

By the late 1950s many smaller companies were attempting to infiltrate various market niches in telecommunications, but were greatly impeded by the technical and regulatory barriers to entry. Then a 1956 consent decree restricted Bell to its own regulated business, and forced them to freely license any patents resulting from the technology developed by Bell Labs. Technology was no longer a stumbling block for new entrants.

Now the only barrier was regulatory and firms seeking entry were obligated to pursue their case before the government. Court rulings in 1956, 1959, and 1971 were major breakthroughs, permitting firms to use private microwave systems and opening private lines to anyone. The historic Carterfone decision in 1968 made it legal for non-Bell equipment to be attached to public lines; the first privately owned telephone answering machine, barred by AT&T for years, now had to be admitted to the network and the market for terminal equipment was opened.

AT&T responded to these attacks in a number of ways such as cross-subsidizing its services, denying access to its lines, and making protective arrangements. Many industry participants complained loudly at these tactics. With public sentiment again antimonopolistic, the Justice Department filed an antitrust suit against Bell in 1974. For its part, AT&T wanted to compete in markets beyond its regulated realm, and felt constrained by its narrow domain. (It was widely thought that AT&T saw itself as the major potential competitor to IBM in the computer industry.) On January 8, 1982 the company officially acceded to being dismantled. Its local operating companies, still working as regulated monopolies, were spun off into seven regional holding companies. The divestment, the largest financial transaction in world history, was completed in late 1983. AT&T was now free to compete. (See Exhibits 2 and 3 for comparative sizes of the units.)

TELECOMMUNICATIONS INDUSTRY: STRUCTURE

The telecommunications industry consisted of three major segments—local-exchange operators, long-distance carriers, and telephone equipment manufacturers—and one relatively small segment—information products and services, where Brooktrout Technology competed. (See Exhibit 4 for examples of leading entrants in all four segments.)

EXHIBIT 2 Values and Operating Results of Leading Telephone Companies ($millions)

	Assets	Sales	Market Value	Net Profit
AT&T (1983)	$149,530	$69,403	$59,392	$5,747
AT&T (1988)	35,152	35,210	30,868	−1,669
Bell Operating Companies, 1988				
Ameritech	19,163	9,903	12,888	1,237
Bell Atlantic	24,729	10,880	14,013	1,317
BellSouth	28,472	13,597	18,504	1,666
Nynex	25,378	12,661	12,997	1,315
Pacific Telesis	21,191	9,483	12,934	1,188
Southwestern Bell	20,985	8,453	12,129	1,060
U.S. West	22,416	9,221	10,548	1,132
Other Firms, 1988				
GTE	31,104	16,460	14,520	1,225
MCI Communications	5,843	5,137	5,498	356

Source: "The *Forbes* 500," *Forbes*, April 30, 1984, and May 1, 1989.

EXHIBIT 3   Rankings of Leading Telephone Companies (among the top 500 American businesses, including banks and financial-services firms)

	Assets	Sales	Market Value	Net Profit
AT&T (1983)	1	3	2	1
AT&T (1988)	36	9	4	N/M
Bell Operating Companies, 1988				
Ameritech	85	66	28	19
Bell Atlantic	63	51	22	16
BellSouth	52	38	12	13
Nynex	60	41	26	17
Pacific Telesis	75	72	27	24
Southwestern Bell	79	83	32	30
U.S. West	69	73	38	27
Other Firms, 1988				
GTE	41	32	20	20
MCI Communications	271	154	81	142

N/M = Not meaningful.
Source: "The *Forbes* 500," *Forbes*, April 30, 1984, and May 1, 1989.

The information products and services segment resulted from the combination of computer and telecommunications technologies during the 1980s. These combined technologies made it possible for data to be processed as well as transmitted by communications networks, thus creating intelligent communications. By 1989 this segment of the telecommunications industry was a hotbed of competitive marketing activity, with contenders ranging from heavyweights like AT&T's own Bell Laboratories, to entrepreneurial newcomers such as Brooktrout Technology, Inc.

Local-Exchange Operators

Before deregulation local telephone companies (exchange operators) enjoyed a monopoly over the interface between phone users and the telephone network. They were the only source for all telephone equipment and services. After deregulation the local companies were prohibited from some activities (such as long-distance services) and forced for the first time to compete in most others (such as equipment leasing). They retained their public utility, and hence monopolistic, position in providing local phone service and connecting customers to the long-distance carriers. The local exchange operators included the former Bell operating companies (BOCs), the general telephone operating companies (owned by GTE), and a handful of independents. The BOCs had 80 percent of the existing local lines, but no single BOC controlled more than one-eighth of the nation's local access lines.

EXHIBIT 4 Segments of the Industry and Examples of Active Competitors

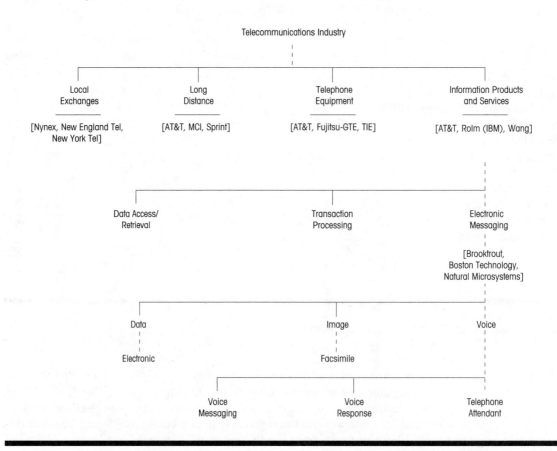

Local telephone companies transmitted the majority of local calls, but alternative forms of local service were increasing. Many businesses were purchasing and installing private branch exchanges (PBXs), which performed all the telephone functions that were internal to a given business. PBXs were sold based on lower costs, more features, and greater control for a business over its phone usage than the telephone company's standard service could offer. Alternatives for local transmission outside the confines of a business were also increasingly available. These included private microwaves and satellite-to-earth stations. Technical advances in these areas were continually improving their quality and decreasing their cost.

With competition increasing, local-exchange operators enhanced the level of service they provided beyond simple transmission. Since local phone rates were regulated, their principal competitive weapons were additional services. Opposing the high-tech PBXs was the venerable Centrex system, a telephone management and switching system first developed by AT&T in the 1960s, which operated on switching equipment of the local exchanges and was sold as a service to their larger business customers. Recent enhancements to Centrex incorporated sophisticated call management and reporting features first introduced on PBXs.

On March 7, 1988 U.S. District Judge Harold Greene (who had presided over the AT&T breakup) ruled that local exchanges could transmit information services. Options such as call forwarding and call waiting could now be offered to even single-line subscribers. In the future lay provision of services such as stock quotations and transactions and merchandise selection and purchase, all through the telephone company. A recent advance allowed multiple phone numbers to be channeled to a single line, a cost-effective solution for home businesses with only one phone line. Publishing and computer/telecommunications integration were major new business thrusts.

Long-Distance Carriers

Long-distance transmission continued to be dominated by AT&T following deregulation, with 87 percent of the long-distance customers handled by AT&T in 1988. The only major competitors to AT&T were MCI and US Sprint, each with 5 to 6 percent of the customer base. In terms of revenues, AT&T had 68 percent of the $50-billion long-distance market, MCI 12 percent, and Sprint 8 percent. Both these new firms were pursuing high-growth strategies in 1989 based on the lower cost and higher quality of fiber optic, microwave, and satellite transmission technologies. Both competitors had grown by 27 percent in revenues in 1986 to 1987, versus 2 percent for AT&T. Dedicated long-distance services, such as private networks, were also attracting a share of the total long-distance transmissions in the United States.

Actions by the local-exchange operators could have a direct impact on the long-distance companies since 80 percent of traffic movement was routed to them through local exchanges. To reduce dependence on the local companies, the long-distance carriers were moving toward vertical integration. The carriers were beginning to install end-to-end transmission services for large customers. This connected long-distance service directly to a PBX, eliminating the need to connect via the local exchange.

Telephone Equipment Manufacturers

Equipment installed at a customer site was referred to as *customer premise equipment* (CPE). Prior to deregulation, the decision of where to install switching equipment for a given customer (at either the customer site or the local exchange) was made by the local telephone company, which leased the required equipment to the customer. After deregulation this choice was made by the customer, who could lease or purchase and install on its own premises as much or as little equipment as desired from a vendor of its choice. The most significant change in the telephone equipment market resulting from this situation was tremendous growth in private branch exchange (PBX) equipment sales.

Twenty years after the Carterfone decision, the CPE market had grown to $8 billion per year, but the growth rate was expected to slow from 8.7 percent in 1988 to 4.8 percent by 1992. Several larger firms (AT&T, Northern Telecom, Siemens) together controlled more than 50 percent of the market. However, smaller manufacturers, like TIE Communications, had made inroads by offering price

EXHIBIT 5 Merger and Acquisition Activity in Consumer Premises Equipment Firms, Representative Activity, 1987–1988

| CPE Manufacturer | CPE Sales ($millions) | | | Acquired by |
	1986	1987	1988[a]	
Contel/Executone	$268	$305	$335[b]	Isotek/Vodavi
Tel Plus Communications, Inc.	255	283[b]	320	Siemens
RCA Telephone Systems	120	130	140[b]	Mitel
Universal Communication Systems	87	106[b]	n/a	BellSouth
Jarvis Corp.	36	38[b]	40	Isotec
All American Businessphones	25	28	30[b]	TIE[c]
Gray Communications	25	22	25[b]	AIM Tel
Henkel & McCoy/Telecom	19	21[b]	25	Star Datacom
Interconnect Communication Corp.	7	22[b]	38	Inter-Tel
	$842	$955	$953	

[a]Estimated sales following acquisition.
[b]Year of acquisition.
[c]Acquisition proposed.
Source: *Telephony*, April 11, 1988.

decreases, enhanced features (least-cost routing, voice messaging, and other advanced exchange and information services), quality of service, testing, and maintenance. Acquisition and merger activity was high (see Exhibit 5). Customer premise equipment sales through the BOCs were also increasing, representing one-fourth of the total in 1988.

A second spur to the growth of the PBX market was the control over telecommunications costs that PBXs provided. While the overall cost of transmission (local and long-distance) had remained relatively static, many businesses saw that significant decreases in equipment costs and tighter control of phone usage might be achieved with a PBX. Furthermore, because PBXs were largely based on computer technology, a customer who *leased* his own PBX experienced incremental reductions as the price of electronic components fell by half every two to three years. In 1989, however, the manufacturers' profit margins on basic PBXs were very small.

Recent enhancements to the Centrex system offered by the BOCs (and similar systems from other local-exchange operators) appeared to be making some inroads into PBX sales. "Centrex has done well in the last few years because it takes away the risk and hassle," according to Charlie Nichols, analyst at Shearson Lehman Hutton Inc.[1]

Information Products and Services

A large and diverse array of information products and services had emerged as a high-growth segment of the telecommunications industry during the late 1980s.

The compound annual growth rate for this segment was forecast to be approximately 25 percent from 1988 to 1992.[2] Some of the major subsegments (see also Exhibit 4) were as follows.

Data Access and Retrieval

Principally comprised of vast, online databases accessed via a personal computer and modem, a few large players included Quotron (financial information services), Dow Jones (news and retrieval), Chilton (credit services), and The Source and CompuServe, both providing a broad range of applications for home use. Small competitors numbered in the thousands.

Transaction Processing

These services provided real-time access via specialized terminals and/or telephone handsets to dynamic databases. Examples of services were ordering products and receiving account information, as with bank withdrawals, student registration, and sales order tracking. Systems often were heavily customized for individual businesses.

Electronic Messaging

These applications allowed users to send and receive messages from other users by voice, data, or image transmission. The messaging product either replaced or augmented a person-to-person phone conversation. Specific examples included electronic mail, electronic conferencing, and facsimile. Also included were voice storage and forward (VSF) products, such as those manufactured by Brooktrout and its 30 to 40 competitors.

Principal VSF products were telephone attendant systems, voice messaging, and voice response systems. Telephone attendant systems replaced a switchboard operator with an automated system—a "silicon Sally" computerized voice which prompted the caller to enter codes in order to route a call to the proper extension. Voice messaging provided for recording, storing, and playing back messages, as with a simple telephone answering machine, but using a much more flexible computer storage and retrieval technology. Voice response systems could carry on a dialogue with the caller in order to perform functions such as order-taking and account inquiry.

Although VSF was a small subsegment within the overall telecommunications industry, in 1989 it was growing very rapidly (see Exhibit 6). From revenues of $200 million in 1986 and $426 million in 1988, the VSF segment was expected to reach $1 billion in 1990.

Voice Store Forward

A VSF system was based on a technology known as digital signal processing, used to capture voice signals and convert them into a string of digital bits which could be computer processed. Only a few VSF manufacturers, such as Brooktrout, had developed in-house expertise in this basic technology.

Traditionally, voice-processing applications had required the processing power of a host minicomputer, and products based on these large systems still

EXHIBIT 6 Market for Telecommunications, 1988 ($millions)

	1988 Revenues	Projected Compound Annual Growth Rate[a]
Public Network Services		
Local services	$ 87,558	
Long-distance services	52,400	
Cellular/public data networks	2,842	
Total network services	$142,800	
Business Communications CPE Market: Voice		
Private branch exchanges (PBXs)	$ 3,182	2.6%
Key systems	2,316	0.9
Facsimile	1,041	17.8
Voice messaging	426	23.6
Automated call distribution	284	7.1
Call accounting	281	4.4
Video teleconferencing	264	26.5
Phones	125	6.9
Integrated voice–data terminals	73	2.9
Total voice CPE market	$ 7,992	
Business Communications CPE Market: Data		
Local area networks	$ 2,400	22.4%
Modems	1,200	−6.2
Front-end processors	625	6.7
Network management systems	457	13.8
Private packet switching	432	17.0
T-1 multiplexors	403	12.9
Statistical multiplexors	299	−5.5
Circuit/data switching units	122	12.7
Data PBXs	85	−4.7
Total data CPE Market	$ 6,023	

[a]Estimated annual growth rates for the period 1988 to 1992.
Source: Dataquest Inc., *Forecast '88*.

represented the vast majority of the market in 1989 (see Exhibit 7). However, the new generation of more powerful personal computers was creating an increasingly strong alternative for low-end VSF host computers. In fact, the market researcher Dataquest had predicted:

> The low-end segment [of VSF] brings to the voice messaging market what PCs brought to the computer industry—cost-effective, flexible, powerful applications processors for small to medium-size businesses or organizations.[3]

EXHIBIT 7 VSF Equipment Market, 1987

System Size	Number of Ports[a]	System Size As Percentage of Total Market	Market Share for Segment Size	
Large systems (mainframes)	32–1,500	52%	Rolm	45%
			AT&T	13
Medium systems (minicomputers)	8–32	47	Centigram	17
			Opcom	17
			Rolm	14
			Wang	13
			Digital Sound	11
			Genesis	11
			AT&T	3
Small systems (personal computers)	1–8	1	Natural Microsystems	30
			Brooktrout	20
			AT&T	15

[a]Ports are the number of telephone lines a system is capable of accommodating simultaneously. System capacities here are estimates by Eric Giler.
Source: Frost and Sullivan, Report Number A1867, 1988 (quoted with permission).

Others had forecast that PC-based systems were not likely to achieve significant market share since telephone answering machines and service bureaus could provide the services needed by a small user at a lower cost (almost no cost with a telephone answering machine). Service bureaus used VSF systems based on minicomputers or mainframe computer hosts, and rented voice-messaging services to companies without their own on-site VSF systems. This could be a cost-effective alternative to PC-based systems for small users who needed the sophisticated capabilities of VSF. Even larger firms were contracting service bureaus for voice services. Probe Research, Inc. forecast VSF service bureau revenues to be $271 million by 1990.

Local exchange operators were also looking at the opportunities that voice messaging might offer. Ameritech, one of the regional Bell companies, had acquired Tigon Corp., the nation's largest voice-messaging service bureau with corporate clients like Ford Motor Company, in late 1988. Bell Atlantic had recently contracted with Boston Technology, a small voice-messaging company founded in 1986, for its newly introduced central-office-based voice-processing system. Although Boston Technology had first developed small, stand-alone systems, "from the beginning, we believed that there was a need for a huge voice-processing system," said Greg Carr, the firm's president. "Their proposal got our attention immediately," commented Kathy Maier, Bell Atlantic's product manager for enhanced voice services. "Its size—1,536 ports, 7,000 hours of voice storage capacity, support of 104,000 voice mailboxes—is a major factor."[4]

Other alternatives existed for electronic messaging. Facsimile machines were the most recent addition to the electronic messaging domain. These machines, which were priced as low as $600, used digital-signal processing technology similar to that used in VSF to transmit images via telephone lines. Sales of facsimile machines in 1988 of $2.2 billion were projected to reach $6.6 billion by 1992.[5] A final alternative, electronic mail, involved computer-to-computer communication of data (rather than voice) messages. Although more expensive and not so easy to use as VSF or facsimile (because it required specialized training for each user), electronic mail had the great advantage of transmitting both messages and data in a format that could be understood and further manipulated by computer programs.

Distribution

The distribution system for information products and services was complex. For example, all of the following were being used to distribute VSF systems.

Telephone Equipment Manufacturers   These firms would purchase and incorporate VSF products into their own devices, such as PBXs. In some cases, they would simply license the VSF technology and manufacture the actual products themselves. Many of these manufacturers would customize their VSF systems in order to differentiate their end products in the minds of end users, even though the VSF components might have a common origin. The identity of the VSF manufacturer was generally not revealed in the end product. Prominent among these original equipment manufacturers (OEMs) were AT&T, Rolm, TIE, and Iwatsu. The largest suppliers of VSF products to OEMs were Brooktrout, Genesis, and AT&T.

Direct Sales   Some firms, most notably Natural Microsystems, had promoted and sold their products directly to end users, using methods such as direct mail.

Computer Stores   Low-end VSF systems could be sold as add-ons to personal computers through computer stores.

Telephone System Dealers   Dealers were either independent or affiliated with an equipment manufacturer. Independent dealers generally carried multiple brands of business telephone systems, PBXs, and other telecommunications equipment. There had been an increasing trend for equipment manufacturers to integrate forward by purchasing independent dealers. As a result, some of the dealers sold only one brand of equipment, for example Rolm and GTE, while others still represented multiple brands. Dealers generally provided complete installation and maintenance service.

Service Bureaus   These firms purchased large VSF systems to be time-shared by both small and large businesses.

Local-Exchange Operators   VSF capabilities could be incorporated in customer services such as Centrex. GTE, for example, offered many services including Telemessager (voice mail) and Telemail (electronic mail). The regional Bell operating companies also sold customer premise equipment.

Historically, PC-based VSF systems had been sold principally on an OEM basis to the telephone equipment manufacturers. Approximately two-thirds of VSF manufacturers' revenues were derived from OEMs. The remaining third was split between direct sales and computer and telephone system dealers.

Industry Trends

Several key trends were apparent in the telecommunications-equipment industry at the end of the 1980s. Competition seemed likely to intensify due to such factors as cost reduction (particularly from Asian manufacturers), new technology, and a continued lessening of regulation of the BOCs.

A second trend had been a push from customers and suppliers alike to use industrywide communications standards, rather than vendor-specific codes. This would eliminate many difficulties that currently existed in transferring information across networks containing hardware from many different makers. Information service providers stood to benefit directly from standardization, as their products could be used on a wider array of equipment.

Finally, the key phrase for the future of the telecommunications industry appeared to be system integration. One industry analyst stated:

> Computers can switch phone calls, and PBXs can do computing. [We can] predict a day, perhaps five or ten years away, when system integration for the business customer will include not only telephone service but word processing, commercial data processing, and facsimile data transmission.[6]

BROOKTROUT TECHNOLOGY, INC.: HISTORY

In 1984 Eric Giler, Dave Duehren, and Pat Hynes, a technical marketer and two design engineers, founded Brooktrout Technology to take advantage of the technical ideas they had begun to think about at their previous jobs. With their expertise in digital-signal processing, they felt, they could integrate voice messaging into office automation systems along with text, graphics, image processing, and data communications.

Armed with a business plan projecting $3 million in sales the first year, they began to seek financing. Eric Giler reflected on the early efforts:

> We thought at first that raising capital would be easy. But when we tried, we found doors closing on us for two reasons. One, we were young. Second, the venture capitalists couldn't believe that people would talk to machines, even if the systems worked perfectly. So for the first 6 months we operated the company out of an apartment.

Eric and his partners decided to seek money privately, and in several private placements in the first two years raised $1.5 million from approximately 50 investors. In 1987 a major telephone equipment manufacturer injected $1 million in cash for a minority equity position. By 1989 Brooktrout had raised a total of $2.5 million to finance its growth, and was anticipating its first profitable year (see Exhibit 1 for financial data and projections). The founders, equal owners from the beginning, still retained a 30 percent ownership stake in Brooktrout.

Eric Giler, Brooktrout's president, had received an undergraduate degree in management science from Carnegie-Mellon and an MBA from Harvard in 1982. Pat Hynes, vice president of engineering, and Dave Duehren, vice president of research and development, were both bachelors graduates in electrical engineering from M.I.T.; Duehren's M.S. was also from M.I.T., while Hynes's was from Columbia. Hynes, an avid trout fisherman, chose the name for the new company.

In 1987 Eric hired Stephen Ide, a 20-year veteran in telecommunications and a former consultant to Brooktrout, as vice president of sales and marketing. Ide had founded and served as president of Computer Telephone Corp., a publicly held company with $14 million in sales. In 1988 Bob Leahy, former controller and treasurer of Cambridge Robotic Systems, was hired as treasurer. Leahy, holder of a B.S. in accounting from Bentley College, brought a diverse background in high-technology finance. Eric was comfortable with the progress they had made building the top management team as well as the technical organization; by mid-1989, six additional engineers hired directly out of local colleges supplemented the efforts of Hynes and Duehren. Five worked in production and seven in marketing. "We have the team in place; now we have to figure out how to grow it," said Eric.

BROOKTROUT STRATEGY

Electronic messaging included three different modes of communication: voice (voice mail), data (electronic mail), and image (facsimile). Traditionally each of these was implemented in different products, and firms specialized in one particular modality. Brooktrout believed these three modes of communication would become integrated in the near future, as the technology of digital signal processing became cheaper and better:

> Nobody does all three. Our goal over the long term is to provide solutions in all three areas, for all the major telecommunications and computer manufacturers. We want to do something different from what other people are doing, based on our expertise in technology and our understanding of what makes it possible to do electronic messaging. In the beginning we decided that the voice area looked the best and constructed a product for that area. Then we moved into the imaging area with a fax product. Finally we will pull them together.

Brooktrout estimated it had 5 to 10 percent of the voice segment market, selling against 30 to 40 competitors. Several of those were achieving success by selling further down the distribution channel, directly to dealers. Brooktrout, on the other hand, sold mainly to OEMs. An advantage to selling to the OEMs was the ready access gained to certain segments of the industry. For instance, TIE Communications had developed a product using Brooktrout's technology that it sold to the Bell operating companies. Occasionally Brooktrout was called upon by their OEMs to assist in developing end user applications for their products. Although this required additional effort, successful applications translated directly into more demand for Brooktrout's products.

Brooktrout had major OEM agreements for its VSF products with TIE, the second-largest customer premise equipment (CPE) supplier of small-business phone systems behind AT&T, and with the American division of Iwatsu, a major Japanese equipment manufacturer. Both TIE and Iwatsu built Brooktrout products into their own offerings; both also labeled the Brooktrout equipment with their own name and sold it separately. TIE's dealers sold only TIE products, where Iwatsu dealers also sold products made by other manufacturers.

Although Eric felt that selling to OEMs was the best bet for the future, his sales department saw things differently. They believed the company could grow more rapidly by promoting and selling through dealers. Eric reported:

> What the salespeople are saying is, "Here we have stuff we can sell now. We can make money. We can sell lots of them." The problem I have is that our organization is not set up to deal directly with dealers.

All the sales department employees had either worked for dealers or owned their own dealerships. Eric felt, however, that the Brooktrout organization was not prepared to meet the needs of dealers or the dealers' customers. For example, operating manuals and instruction books would be required, along with 24-hour telephone and technical support.

> We can sell to dealers to the extent it furthers our OEM goals. To the extent it isn't supporting those goals, I'm not sure it's worth it. Recently a potential investor complained about our selling to OEMs. He said, "Oh, that's the wrong way to do it. What you do is sell to users, then the users like it and they tell the dealers, the dealers like it and they tell the manufacturers, and the manufacturers have to have it." I never thought of it that way. The reason I never thought of it is simple: that's what you do when you have money!

Although distribution was an important consideration, many industry experts felt that market timing was also a critical success factor. The major task was to build a competitive product. Once the product was sold to an OEM and incorporated in its products, it became very difficult for competitors to dislodge it. Eric commented,

> The biggest competitive advantage I've seen in this business is what I call the first-mover advantage. The guy who's first to do something kicks ass.

It doesn't matter what anyone else does. Over the long haul, that's our best bet. And it probably doesn't matter where in the channel you sell as long as you're the first mover.

Anyone can do anything—that's my premise. I have never seen anything in technology that is totally proprietary. You have to be careful, though. There are also the pioneers with arrows in their backs; I've seen a bit of that also.

Sometimes being first was not that easy. A new facsimile board for personal computers had recently been introduced by a small California firm, Gamma Fax, while Brooktrout's similar product, fully designed and ready for production, sat on the shelf. Eric had felt the market wasn't ready: "naw, fax for personal computers? Who understands that stuff?" Now he saw that Brooktrout had to make up for the first-to-market advantage that Gamma Fax had captured.

BROOKTROUT PRODUCTS

The first products to be made by Brooktrout were for voice messaging. At the time this seemed the most logical segment to enter; the technology was just beginning to take off, while the facsimile machine as an image communication device was not that far along. They then moved into the imaging segment with facsimile-messaging systems. These products enabled computer data to be translated electronically into facsimile images. (See Exhibit 8 for a description of Brooktrout's voice and fax products in mid-1989.)

Brooktrout also had several products in the design phase. It was under contract with a major manufacturer to develop data transfer between modems and facsimile machines. Even AT&T had made inquiries about Brooktrout's capabilities. A major advantage of designing under contract was avoiding the need to raise additional capital for the research effort. However, in the end you might not have full rights to the product you developed.

THE FUTURE

Eric and his partners aimed to be the first company to fully integrate voice, data, and image messaging—"tying all these things together; that's the long-term vision." Brooktrout would soon gain access to key technology they needed for the integrated product as a result of one of their current development contracts. To exploit this opportunity, however, would take more capital and other resources that Brooktrout did not presently have.

I have a voice machine right now that will let a company handle requests for literature with no human intervention at all. The customers call in and the machine asks what they want. When it defines what literature they want, the machine faxes the stuff to them instantly. The customer should love it: he doesn't even have to wait for the mail, much less for some clerk to fulfill the request. There isn't any other product like that, anywhere.

EXHIBIT 8 Brooktrout Products as of Mid-1989

Voice Messaging

Operator Plus	Advanced call processing systems for small and medium-sized companies
	Automated attendant, voice messaging, and voice response capabilities
	Digital-signal processing technology to record, store, and play back digitized human voice
	Up to six ports capacity
	Up to 24 hours of stored messages
V-Mail 210/DID	Allows outside callers to leave messages for individuals without dialing extensions, mailbox numbers, etc.
	Each user assigned an individual Direct Inward Dial number
	Ideal for answering services, voice-mail service bureaus, and cellular telephone sites
Phoneware 470	* Development system
	* Speeds creation of telephone-based speech processing applications software
	* Ideal for voice-prompted order entry, voice bulletin boards, and information dissemination

Fax Messaging

Fax-mail systems	Complete hardware/software systems
	Allows personal computers and fax machines to communicate worldwide over standard telephone lines
	Plugs into any IBM PC/XT/AT or compatible computer
	Permits PCs to receive transmissions from fax machines, store files on disk, display them on PC monitors, or print them out
	Compatible with CCITT Group III fax (machines transmitting a letter-sized page in less than one minute)

If I had the money I would pursue the integrated product. I know it's going to hit, but I have to consider the effects of more stock dilution. I'd really prefer not to sell any stock.

But people don't operate strategically on a day-to-day basis. If a venture capitalist called me right now and made the right kind of deal I would take the dilution.

Eric was at a crossroads. He knew that the capital structure of Brooktrout, with 50 shareholders, was not very attractive to venture capitalists. It had actually scared some away. Also, he had products which had not been brought to market because of capital needs.

In the short run he wanted to bet on the fax product where literature could be requested over the phone. That product was very different. It would allow Brooktrout to diversify its customer base and, if successful, could possibly get it to the point of going public or being acquired by a larger company.

He also knew that there was some merit in selling directly to dealers as the salespeople wanted, and that being first was the best possible thing to do.

Say we go out and raise more money and get diluted. Does the stock's value get pumped up? Some of the investors want out now. We have 50 investors and there's not a day that goes by that I don't talk to one of them.

If I had the capital resources right now I would just be the best voice and fax company around. There is nobody there yet. We know it's going to be a big market; it doesn't take a rocket scientist to figure that out. It does take some thinking about how you want to position yourself, because it's a very fragmented set of business opportunities. Do you want a turnkey setup? Do you want to sell to OEMs? Do you want to build a system or do you want to just sell components?

This is a very complex industry. There are people who spend their lives trying to figure this stuff out; they get paid a lot of money for being wrong. I've never seen so many consultants in all my life.

When asked where he thought Brooktrout would be in five years, Eric replied:

Five years is too long to project in a violent industry. I would probably like to see the harvest point before that. If your business is really hot, it's very hard to maintain your independence, because the thing grows and you get assimilated into something whether you want to or not. Ultimately, you go public or you get acquired. We just want to keep playing the game, growing the beast as big as we can.

From a personal perspective, it will be fun at $10 million [in sales]. That's when it starts to get fun. You're not playing around as much, and you have enough mass to expect the bottom line to hit about 15 percent. That's what I'd like to see.

Endnotes

1. *Telephony*, April 11, 1988.
2. *Telephony*, May 16, 1988.
3. "Voice Mail Matures: Sales Boom as Applications Explode," *Teleconnect*, September 1988.
4. *Telephony*, November 14, 1988.
5. *Communications Week*, February 20, 1989.
6. Gerald R. Faulhaber, *Telecommunications in Turmoil: Technology and Public Policy* (Cambridge, Mass.: Ballinger, 1987), pp. 129–130.

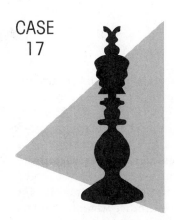

CASE
17

Wall Drug Store: Facing the '90s

Phil Fisher, Robert Johnson & James Taylor

SIZZLING STEAK: WALL DRUG
WESTERN ART: WALL DRUG
BEAUTIFUL WESTERN ART: WALL DRUG
FREE COFFEE AND DO-NUTS FOR VIETNAM VETERANS: WALL DRUG
FREE COFFEE AND DO-NUTS FOR HONEYMOONERS: WALL DRUG
MAKE YOUR DAY: WALL DRUG
W'ALL MAKE YOU HAPPY: WALL DRUG
FREE ICE WATER: WALL DRUG

Travelers driving across the rolling prairie of western South Dakota on Interstate Highway 90 are amused, irritated, and beguiled by scores of roadside signs and billboards advertising the attractions of something called Wall Drug. There are signs promising 5-cent coffee, homemade rolls, and roast beef dinners; signs intended to amuse (HAVE YOU DUG WALL DRUG?; W-A-A-L I'LL BE DRUGGED), signs publicizing publicity (FEATURED ON TODAY SHOW: WALL DRUG; WALL DRUG FEATURED IN PEOPLE; WALL DRUG AS TOLD BY WALL ST. JOURNAL; WALL DRUG AS TOLD BY TIME), and signs advertising Black Hills gold jewelry, cowboy boots, and camping supplies. By the time travelers reach the little town of Wall (population 770), more than half of them are curious enough to exit under the friendly stare of an 80-foot, bright green, concrete brontosaurus which towers over the Wall Auto Livery, a Sinclair station. Two blocks to the left they find Main Street and a block-long business district with a hardware store, a grocery store, a dozen gift shops, restaurants, museums, and Wall Drug, the self-proclaimed "World's Largest Drugstore."

The Wall Drug Store occupies half of the east side of this block. Behind the iron hitching posts lining the curb and the pine board store front are a restaurant and 20-odd small shops selling souvenirs, western clothing, moccasins and boots, Indian pottery, western jewelry, western books, stuffed jackalopes,[1] fudge, posters, oil paintings and, of course, prescription drugs. Life-sized concrete or fiberglass Old West characters lounge on benches in an enclosed mall giving tourists opportunities for photos of themselves sitting on a cowboy's lap or with an arm around a dance hall girl. Two animated, life-sized, mannequin cowboy orchestras

---

This case was presented at the North American Case Research Meeting, 1990. All rights reserved to the authors and the North American Case Research Association.

771

play and sing for the crowds, and nearby a more menacing mannequin shouts out challenges to passers to try and match his quick draw in a gun fight for only a quarter.

In back of the store is an open yard ringed with buildings featuring more animated displays, including a piano playing gorilla and a singing family on a Sunday drive in a restored 1908 Hupmobile. This area, termed the "backyard," includes a six-foot stuffed rabbit, a stuffed buffalo, a stuffed bucking horse, and a large, saddled, fiberglass jackalope, all providing more photo opportunities for visiting tourists. An old-fashioned covered well dispenses free ice water for coolers and thermos bottles from a modern faucet.

A private collection of over 300 original paintings portraying the American West is displayed on the walls of the restaurant dining rooms. Throughout the store, those walls not covered with shelves of merchandise are covered with photographs. There are old photographs of Sioux chiefs, and western characters such as Calamity Jane, General Custer, and Wild Bill Hickock. There are hundreds of photographs of less famous cowboys and homesteaders. There are photographs showing people standing in front of signs giving the mileage to Wall Drug from such places as Paris, Amsterdam, Cairo, London, New Delhi, and Tokyo, and there are pictures of the generations of the Hustead family who created, own, and manage this unique drugstore, which is visited each year by approximately 2 million people.

As the tourist season opened in spring 1990, Bill Hustead, the CEO of Wall Drug, his parents, Ted and Dorothy, his wife, Marjorie, and his sons, Rick and Ted, made last-minute preparations for the flood of expected customers. At the same time they continued to consider the pros and cons of plans for the most ambitious expansion in the company's history.

WALL DRUG HISTORY

Ted Hustead graduated from the University of Nebraska with a degree in pharmacy in 1929. In December 1931 in the depths of the depression, Ted and his wife, Dorothy, bought the drugstore in Wall, South Dakota for $2,500. Dorothy, Ted, and their four-year-old son, Bill, moved into living quarters in the back 20 feet of the store. Business was not good (the first month's receipts were $350) and prospects in Wall did not seem bright. Wall, South Dakota in 1931 is described in the following selection from a book about the Wall Drug Store.

> Wall, then, a huddle of poor wooden buildings, many unpainted, housing some 300 desperate souls; a 19th century depot and wooden water tank; dirt (or mud) streets; few trees; a stop on the railroad, it wasn't even on the highway. U.S. 16 and 14 went right on by, as did the tourists speeding between the Badlands and the Black Hills. There was nothing in Wall to stop for.[2]

Neither the drugstore nor the town of Wall prospered until Dorothy Hustead conceived the idea of placing a sign promising free ice water to anyone who would stop at their store. The first sign was a series of small signs along the highway that read "GET A SODA/GET A BEER/TURN NEXT CORNER/JUST AS NEAR/TO HIGHWAY 16 AND 14/FREE ICE WATER/WALL DRUG." On a blazing hot Sunday afternoon in summer 1936, Ted put the signs up and travelers were turning off the highway to stop at the drugstore before he got back. Located at the western edge of the Badlands National Monument, and near the major highway between the monument and the Black Hills 50 miles further to the west, they began to draw a stream of weary, thirsty tourists into the store.

Ted began putting signs up all along the highways leading to Wall. One series read "SLOW DOWN THE OLD HACK/WALL DRUG CORNER/JUST ACROSS THE RAILROAD TRACK." The attention-catching signs were a boon to Wall Drug and the town of Wall prospered, too. In an article in *Good Housekeeping* in 1951, the Hustead's signs were called "the most ingenious and irresistible system of signs ever devised."

Just after World War II, a friend of the Husteads, traveling across Europe for the Red Cross got the idea of putting up Wall Drug signs overseas. The idea caught on and soon South Dakota servicemen who were familiar with the signs back home began to carry small Wall Drug signs all over the world. Many wrote the store requesting signs. For example, a sign was placed in Paris reading, "WALL DRUG STORE, 4,278 MILES." Wall Drug signs were placed all over the world including areas near the north and south poles, the 38th parallel in Korea, and on jungle trails in Vietnam. The Husteads sent more than 200 signs to servicemen requesting them from Vietnam. These signs led to news stories and publicity which further increased the reputation of the store.

Articles about Ted Hustead and the Wall Drug Store began appearing in newspapers and magazines. In August 1950 *Redbook Magazine* carried a story which was later condensed in *Readers' Digest*. The number of newspapers and magazines carrying feature stories or referring to Wall Drug increased over the years. As of May 1990, Wall Drug files contained over 700 clippings of stories about the store. The store had also been featured on several network and cable television shows.

The store and its sales grew steadily. From 1931 to 1941 the store was in a rented building on the west side of Wall's Main Street. In 1941 the Husteads bought an old lodge hall in Wasta, South Dakota 15 miles west of Wall and moved it to a lot on the east side of the street. This building became the core around which the current store was built.

Tourist travel greatly increased after World War II, and the signs brought increasing numbers of people to the store. Bill Hustead recalls that he was embarrassed because the facilities were not large enough to service the crowds of customers. The store did not even have modern rest rooms, but sales during this period grew to $200,000 annually by 1950.

In 1951 Bill Hustead, now a pharmacy graduate of South Dakota State University, joined his parents in the store. In 1953 they expanded the store into a former store room to the south. This became the Western Clothing Room. In 1954 they built an outside store on the south of the Western Clothing Room. This resulted in a 30 percent increase in sales. In 1956 a self-service cafe was added on the north side of the store. The cafe expansion was built around a large cottonwood tree which remained, its trunk rising out of the center of the dining area up through the roof.

By 1958 the Wall Drug Store had two men in a truck working full-time to maintain 600 signs displayed along highways throughout the Midwest. The store also gave away thousands of small signs each year to people who requested them.

In the early 1960s, Highway 16, the main east–west route across South Dakota to the Black Hills, was replaced by Interstate Highway 90. The new highway was routed near the south edge of Wall. The Husteads, who had been considering building an all new Wall Drug Store along with a gasoline service station near the old highway, did build the station, the Wall Auto Livery, at the new highway interchange.

In 1963 they added a new fire-proof construction coffee shop. A new kitchen, also of fire-proof construction, was added to the back of the coffee shop the following year. Also in 1964 and 1965 new administrative offices and a new pharmacy were opened on a second floor over the kitchen. Another dining room and the backyard area were added in 1968. This was followed in 1971 with the Art Gallery Dining Room. By the early 1970s annual sales volume had reached $1 million.

In 1971 the Husteads bought a theater that bordered their store on the south. The next year they demolished it and constructed a new addition, called the Wall Drug Mall. All previous expansions had been financed from profits of the business or short-term loans. Ted and Bill broke with this by borrowing $250,000 for 10 years to finance the mall.

The mall was designed as a miniature western town within a large enclosure. The strolling mall was designed as a street between shops fashioned like two-story frontier stores. The store fronts and interiors were made of various kinds of American wood: pine, black walnut, gumwood, cedar, hackberry, maple, and oak. The store fronts were recreated from photographs of western towns in the 1880s. These shops stocked products which were more expensive than the souvenir merchandise of the older shops. In 1983 the mall was extended to include a half-dozen more shops, a travelers' chapel modeled after one built by Trappist Monks in Dubuque, Iowa in 1850, and a replica of the original 1931 drugstore called Hustead's Apothecary, which serves as a museum of Hustead family and Wall Drug artifacts.

The store was also expanded on the north end in 1975 and 1976 and on the south of the original mall in 1978. Wall Drug continued to have increased sales every year until 1979. That year, a revolution in Iran started a chain of events which resulted in a doubling of the price of crude oil and temporary shortages of gasoline in the United States. This caused many service stations to experience periods of time that summer when they were out of gasoline. Travel by automobile decreased, and Wall Drug was one of many businesses hit by a decrease in sales. By 1981, however, sales had recovered. Exhibit 1 gives sales and net income after taxes for 1975 through 1989. In 1990 the store and its backyard covered 48,000 square feet and sales were $7.4 million. A map of the Wall Drug Store as it was in 1990 is shown in Exhibit 2.

HIGHWAY BEAUTIFICATION ACT AND WALL DRUG SIGNS

In 1965 Congress passed the Highway Beautification Act, which was designed to reduce the number of roadside signs. Anticipating the removal of many Wall Drug

EXHIBIT 1   Wall Drug Store Sales and Net Income

	Sales ($000)	Net Income ($000)
1975	$2,679	$118
1976	3,464	165
1977	3,777	155
1978	4,125	206
1979	3,552	33
1980	3,970	185
1981	4,821	224
1982	4,733	203
1983	4,851	257
1984	5,055	285
1985	5,273	161
1986	5,611	233
1987	6,142	249
1988	6,504	204
1989	7,419	242

Source: Company records.

signs, the Husteads invested in new signs that were allowed under the initial legislation. Since these signs could be no closer than 660 feet from the highway, they had to be very large and cost around $9,000 each. By the time they were installed, the laws had been amended to exclude them.

In the late 1960s, concerned about the effects of losing their roadside signs, the Husteads began advertising in unusual and unlikely places. They began taking small advertisements in the European *International Herald Tribune* and Greenwich Village's *Village Voice*. They advertised 5-cent coffee, 49-cent breakfasts and veterinary supplies. They put advertisements on double-decker buses in London, on the walls in the Paris Metro (subway), along the canals in Amsterdam, and in rail stations in Kenya. These ads brought letters and telephone calls and then news articles. First, the *Village Voice* carried an article, and in 1971, the Sunday *New York Times*. Bill Hustead appeared on the network television show "To Tell the Truth." In all, 260 articles about the store were printed in the 1970s and approximately the same number during the 1980s.

Passage of the Highway Beautification Act did not mean an end to roadside signs. Compliance with this legislation was slow in many states. Disputes over whether sign owners should be compensated for removed signs and a lack of local support for the law meant that some signs remained.

Bill Hustead served in the South Dakota state legislature during the 1960s and was chairman of the state joint senate–house Committee on Transportation when the Highway Beautification Act was passed. He and his committee wrote South Dakota's compliance law which resulted in the removal of 22,000 of the 28,000 roadside signs in the state. The federal government then fined the state for noncompliance, objecting to the establishment of commercial zones in which signs were permitted. The owners of roadside businesses challenged this federal

EXHIBIT 2 Wall Drug Map, 1990

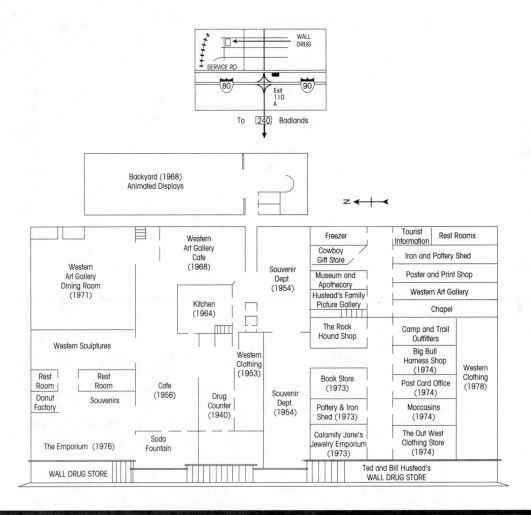

Source: Company document.

enforcement and were successful. The federal government finally accepted a plan which allowed county governments to establish zones where signs were permitted. In South Dakota this zoning resulted in an additional 1,000 signs being erected, bringing the total to 7,000. Bill also testified at federal and state legislative hearings on laws to comply with the federal law. In 1981 Bill Hustead was appointed to the South Dakota Highway Commission, a position he still held in 1990.

By 1990 most remaining Wall Drug roadside signs were located in South Dakota, and there were fewer than 300. Existing signs were being permitted, but no new signs could be erected. Existing signs could be maintained and repainted, but could not be moved or enlarged. Federal legislation proposed in 1989 would have removed these signs without compensation, but the proposed bill was not passed, and the Husteads were more optimistic about the future of roadside advertising than they had been in many years.

Wall Drug sign coverage was still fairly intensive along Interstate 90. In 1990 a count of signs over a 250-mile stretch of I-90 east of Wall identified 86 Wall Drug signs. No two signs were alike, although about half had a characteristic design. These contained a short message, "HAND MADE JEWELRY," for example, in dark green letters on a white background, and the logo "WALL DRUG" below in yellow letters on a dark green background. Other signs had a variety of colors and formats. A crew still serviced the signs twice a year, and all signs observed in 1990 were in excellent condition.

BUSINESS ENVIRONMENT

Wall is located at the northwest edge of the Badlands National Monument (see Exhibit 3), The Badlands Monument is an area of over 120,000 acres of barren ridges and peaks formed by centuries of erosion which exposed colorful layers of different minerals and fossil remains of prehistoric animals. Approximately one million people visit the monument each year.

Rapid City, South Dakota (population 44,000) is 50 miles west of Wall. Rapid City is on the eastern rim of the Black Hills, a forested mountain region and the site of several active gold mines. The Black Hills is also the site of the Mount Rushmore

EXHIBIT 3   Location of Wall Drug Store

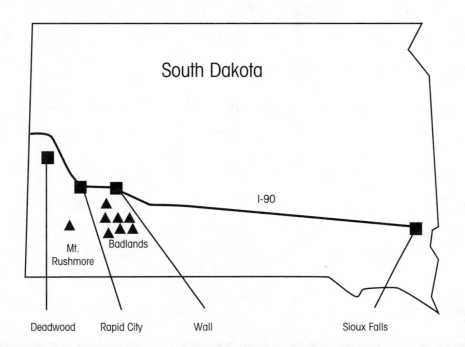

EXHIBIT 4 Annual Visitors

	Badlands National Monument	**Mount Rushmore Memorial**
1971	1,293,011	2,314,522
1973	1,400,000	N.A.
1975	1,165,161	1,994,314
1977	1,303,471	2,271,838
1979	870,000	1,642,757
1981	1,187,970	2,054,567
1983	1,038,981	1,983,710
1985	962,242	2,112,281
1987	1,186,398	1,949,902
1988	1,122,040	2,013,749
1989	1,249,956	2,075,190

Source: U.S. Forest Service.

Memorial which attracts about 2 million visitors each year. Forest Service visitation figures for the Badlands and Mount Rushmore are given in Exhibit 4.

Interstate Highway 90 is the only east–west interstate highway in South Dakota. It passes near the Badlands National Monument and through the Black Hills carrying most of the tourists who visit these areas. Exhibit 5 gives the traffic count on I-90 by month for 1988 and 1989. According to Ted Hustead, counts of traffic in the area of Wall showed that 78 percent of all cars which left Interstate 90 to drive a parallel road through the Badlands also entered Wall. For westbound I-90

EXHIBIT 5 Average Daily Traffic on I-90 near Wall

	1988	**1989**
January	1,674	1,975
February	1,867	1,954
March	2,184	2,353
April	2,567	2,606
May	3,361	3,420
June	4,919	5,160
July	5,615	5,847
August	5,629	6,086
September	3,875	4,233
October	3,401	3,609
November	2,675	3,141
December	2,372	2,374
Annual daily average	3,345	3,563

Source: South Dakota Department of Transportation.

traffic, 55 percent exited at Wall, and 45 percent of eastbound traffic turned off at the Wall exit. These counts were made during the summer months.

There were seven other gift shops in Wall, and an Old West wax museum, a wildlife museum, a taffy shop, and a Cactus Saloon and a Badlands Bar on Wall's Main Street. All depended primarily upon tourist business during the summer months. In spring 1990 the Hustead family was preparing two new gift shops for June 1 openings. These shops were across the street from the main store. They were called Dakota Mercantile and The Tumbleweed.

Voters in South Dakota approved a referendum in 1988 to permit limited-betting ($5) casino gambling to be licensed in the city of Deadwood, South Dakota (population 2,409). Situated in the Black Hills 90 miles west of Wall and 11 miles off Interstate Highway 90, Deadwood was founded by gold miners and is near to several still-active gold mines. During the 1880s it was home to well-known western characters such as Calamity Jane and Wild Bill Hickock. Hickock, in fact, was shot in the back and killed while playing poker in Deadwood. Legal gambling began again in November of 1989. While the full impact of the Deadwood gambling casinos on tourism in South Dakota could not yet be measured in early 1990, it was expected to result in an increase in traffic on Interstate 90, the most direct highway from the East. Exhibit 6 shows sales for all eating establishments and hotels and motels in Wall and Deadwood by two month periods from January 1988 through February 1990.

MANAGEMENT

Bill Hustead, 63, was the president and chief executive officer of the Wall Drug Store. Bill and his wife, Marjorie, owned 60 percent of the stock in the company. Marjorie was the corporation secretary and was active in the business and in charge of merchandise buying. Ted and Dorothy Hustead owned the remaining 40 percent of the stock. Both were in their late 80s and still participated in the store management. Ted was chairman of the board and was involved primarily in public and employee relations. Dorothy was also an officer of the corporation and managed the store's cash receipts, accounting, and banking.

Two of Bill and Marjorie's sons, Rick, 40, and Teddy, 39, were also active in store management. Rick had a master's degree in guidance and counseling and had worked as a high school guidance counselor before joining the store in 1980. His primary responsibility was managing restaurant operations. Teddy had a degree in business and had worked for several years in the Alaskan oil fields before Rick persuaded him to join the store in 1988. He was responsible for day-to-day management of the shops. Both brothers participated in strategic planning and policy making for the overall business.

While neither Rick or Teddy were pharmacists, Rick's wife, Kathy, was a registered pharmacist and worked three days a week managing the store's prescription drug business. In 1990 Teddy married and his wife, Karen, was to become the newest member of the Hustead family management team. Karen was the executive vice president of the Badlands and Black Hills Association. This was an organization of tourism-related businesses in the region. It was expected that she would start as a floating troubleshooter involved in day-to-day store operations

EXHIBIT 6 Sales Receipts for Eating and Lodging Establishments ($000)

	Wall		Deadwood	
	Eating	**Lodging**	**Eating**	**Lodging**
1988				
Jan.–Feb.	$106	$ 16	$275	$172
Mar.–Apr.	118	37	285	145
May–Jun.	358	366	502	318
Jul.–Aug.	550	740	823	613
Sep.–Oct.	270	204	372	434
Nov.–Dec.	115	32	296	158
1989				
Jan.–Feb.	83	13	277	201
Mar.–Apr.	124	45	295	141
May–Jun.	385	414	538	344
Jul.–Aug.	641	911	883	724
Sep.–Oct.	328	300	434	243
Nov.–Dec.	134	54	495	265
1990				
Jan.–Feb.	103	28	715	363

Source: South Dakota Department of Revenue.

to learn the business, and that she would also have a role in public and governmental relations for the store.

Bill spoke about the significant roles of his mother and wife in the success of the Wall Drug Store.

It's known as Ted and Bill Hustead's Wall Drug, but for years Dorothy was the backbone of the store. A few years ago, Dad and I were honored at a banquet and as I sat there and listened to the speeches a voice deep within me cried, "Dorothy, Dorothy." She was the one with the idea to put up the signs. She was the one who worked behind the counter and in the restaurant.

My wife, Marjorie, is the most valuable asset we have. After she took over the buying, we raised our net from the jewelry store by $50,000. She has a wide sphere of influence and is a stabilizing force.

If the Wall Drug Store was a family institution, it was also seen as an institution of great importance to the town of Wall and to the store's full-time employees. Bill Hustead's conversations about the Wall Drug Store frequently emphasized the importance of the business to the economy of the town of Wall, its importance as the only source of income in Wall for most of its full-time employees, and of the need to secure its continued success for the sake of the town and the store's employees. He also spoke of the business in terms of personal and family pride.

The priest here in Wall thought I might have a calling for the priesthood, so my folks sent me to Trinity High School in Sioux City, Iowa. . . . One time I had a date with a girl who took me to her home. Some relatives, a married sister, I think, and her husband were there, and they made some slighting remarks about that "little store with all the signs." I was embarrassed. Gosh, Mom had the idea about the signs, but then did Dad have to put them up all the way from Wisconsin to Montana?

Then, when I worked in the store during the summer, I was embarrassed sometimes at some of the things customers would say about the store. Our facilities were so poor. We didn't even have indoor rest rooms.

There were two key managers who were not family members. Mike Huether worked with Rick in managing restaurant operations. The two were about the same age and had the same level of responsibility, but Bill noted that, "Mike isn't as likely to go to the mat with me." Huether was a long time employee who had worked at the Wall Drug Store since he was 18. Karen Poppe, with 16 years' experience, was the personnel manager. As the store grew and the competition for seasonal employees increased, this function had become critical to the store's ability to grow or even function at the current level of operations.

The Wall Drug Store had no organization chart or written job descriptions, but all the managers believed that they had clear understandings as to their responsibilities and authority. Rick explained, "There is overlap. Ted [Teddy] and I have specific and joint responsibility. Ted's focus is more in retail. My focus is more in the restaurant. There is no organizational chart, but we spend enough time talking to each other so that our roles are defined."

Rick thought the store needed a more complete management staff, but that they had made progress toward that in his 10 years there. "Bill is a builder and a brilliant businessman. What I wanted to do is run the business more efficiently. It's paid off with more profits."

MANAGEMENT SUCCESSION

Asked about the difficulties of having three generations of the family active in the store management, Bill spoke of his own plans. "I went to a religious retreat earlier this month, then attended my cousin's funeral in the East and a funeral of a high school friend and I'm 10 days behind in my work. Sometimes I think this darn job is killing me. I can't work 10- or 12-hour days anymore."

The aspirations of his sons were a factor also. "My 40-year-old sons will have to have independence. The boys in the store (a brother and three sisters were not involved with the store) will get as much of the store as I can give them, but it's not that good a business. There's too much pressure." Asked about the fact that his father at 87 was still active in the business, he said, "I love my father. He's the best P.R. man anybody ever had."

He elaborated more on his past contributions to the business. "My plan was to work for a while and then buy a drugstore in Jackson Hole, Wyoming, but Dad and Mom encouraged me to come here. They needed me desperately. Dad was never a floor man and they really needed someone on the floor."

Rick discussed the issue of management succession from his perspective. "We have a clear understanding with some documentation, but no time table. Teddy came in with the understanding that we'd be partners. I'd like to see my Dad stay on as long as he wants. He is politically influential. He's a tremendous businessman. He's an asset to the business and to us. I hope he'll keep involved to the point he enjoys it. Control is not a major issue. If anyone is concerned about succession it's Bill." Rick also pointed out that the family had life insurance protection to assure that the business would not be crippled by inheritance taxes should anyone in the family die.

Ted Sr. made it clear that he no longer expected to take an active role in making policy decisions. The 1989 South Dakota legislature had approved the licensing of video poker and keno machines which would accept bets up to $2. The Husteads had installed a few in the Western Art Gallery dining room where they had a liquor license and bar. Their intent was to evaluate the results and either remove them or install more depending on their profitability and their perceived contribution or detraction from the atmosphere. Asked about his attitude toward the decision to install video lottery machines, Ted said, "They don't need to ask me, and I don't want them to ask me, but if they had, I'd have said I didn't think much of them" (the video lottery machines).

Speaking of Bill's contribution to the store, Ted Sr. commented, "My son Bill is an idea man. The mall was his. He called in an architect and gave him the plans. Bill has built the art collection. He has a great appreciation for art. I bought the first few paintings, Bill bought the rest."

STORE OPERATIONS

The Wall Drug Store had approximately 30 permanent employees. Peak summer employment would reach 225. About 100 people from the local area were employed to do seasonal work and 120 college students were recruited to complete the work force. Ninety-five percent of the local seasonal employees would be people who had worked at Wall Drug in previous years. Many were housewives and senior citizens who could begin work in May and work during September and October when the college students were not available. About 40 percent of the college students each year were repeat employees from previous years, but Wall Drug had to recruit about 70 new employees each year.

Student recruiting was handled by Karen Poppe. Each year 200 colleges and universities were sent recruitment information just prior to the Christmas break. She also made recruiting trips to about six colleges and attended several job fairs. Recruitment of seasonal employees was becoming increasingly difficult and was seen by the Wall Drug management as a potential limit to their growth.

Mrs. Poppe and the Husteads thought that Wall's remoteness was a major obstacle to recruitment of summer employees from college campuses. The nationwide increase in the tourism industry meant that there were more companies recruiting from the same source. At the job fairs, Mrs. Poppe found herself competing with such major attractions as Disney World and other theme parks and better-known vacation areas such as Yellowstone Park. This made persuading students to choose the little town of Wall on the treeless plains of South Dakota more difficult each year.

Summer employees were housed in small dormitories and houses owned by the store. The store owned a swimming pool for employees and would have social gatherings such as picnics or volleyball games. Summer employees were paid $4 an hour and worked 40 hours plus 8 hours of overtime, for which they were paid time-and-a-half. They paid $25 per week for their rooms. Students who stayed through the Labor Day weekend also got 5-percent bonuses and a rent reduction of $17 per week for the entire summer.

While the gambling casinos in Deadwood, South Dakota, 90 miles to the West, were expected to result in increased traffic on I-90, they also competed for seasonal employees. In 1990 unskilled casino employees in Deadwood were being paid $7 an hour.

Wall Drug had formerly hired one of every five applicants for summer jobs. By 1990, they were having difficulty filling their positions. The labor scarcity had also had an effect on their personnel policies. As Bill explained, "We would exercise discipline. We expected to send a few people home just to let everyone know that we were serious. Now we get them out here and try to make it work. If they can't make change, we try to find a place for them. And it works better. We have a better atmosphere now."

New employees were trained to be courteous and informed about the Badlands, Black Hills, and other sites of interest in the area. Karen Poppe coordinated new employee orientation, but most of the members of the Hustead family participated. Ted Sr. studied the applications and pictures of all summer employees so that he could greet them by name when they arrived and whenever he saw them working in the store.

The Wall Drug Store and restaurant had a total area of 48,000 square feet. By comparison, the average Wal-Mart store covered a little more than 56,000 square feet. In 1989 Wall Drug merchandise sales were $5.6 million. The restaurant was a self-service restaurant with seating for 500; it had sales of $1.8 million. In 1989 the average McDonald's had $1.6 million in sales. The opening of the two new stores, Dakota Mercantile and The Tumbleweed, would add another 6,000 square feet.

Wall Drug visitors frequently asked about purchasing items by mail. For several years the store had about $50,000 in mail-order sales without catalogs or order forms. In 1989 Teddy designed a simple order form with the title, "Order By Mail Year Around From WALL DRUG." It listed a few items under the categories of jewelry, western art, boots and moccasins, western wear, western books, and "Etc., Etc., Etc." Items listed under this last category were "jackalopes, flying jackalopes, steer skulls, rattlesnake ashtrays, horse twitches, and souvenirs galore." This one-page sheet also included a map of the store, but listed no prices. It was available at cash registers for customers to take with them. Mail-order sales increased to over $87,000 in 1989 and sales for the first three months of 1990 were up 47 percent over 1989. Most mail-order sales were for bigger ticket items such as jewelry. The store also sold over 60 jackalopes by mail in 1989.

Commenting on Teddy's success with increasing mail-order sales, Rick said, "A catalog would be the next step. We talk about building a model for this business, but we need to hire the talent to run it."

The Husteads were also trying to expand their tour bus business. Bus tours were an increasingly important factor in tourism. They were especially popular with senior citizens and foreign visitors. The Husteads believed that the ability to provide fast-food service from their 500 seat, self-service restaurant would be a reason for bus tours to include them as a stop. They were also interested in persuading tour operators now running buses from Denver to the Black Hills to include the 100-mile round trip from Rapid City to the Badlands as part of the tour. This would also include a stop at Wall Drug. Attracting more of this business was assigned to Teddy, who had increased the store's promotional efforts at bus tour operator conventions and trade shows. This had resulted in some increase in business, and about 90 buses were expected to include Wall Drug as a stop in 1990.

FINANCE

Exhibits 7 and 8 present income statements and balance sheets from 1983 through 1989. Historically, the store's growth and expansion projects had been financed through retained earnings and loans of up to 10 years' duration. The long-term debt of $151,000 outstanding in 1989 consisted of approximately $82,000 owed on

EXHIBIT 7 Wall Drug Store Income Statement ($000)

	1983	1984	1985	1986	1987	1988	1989
Net sales	$4,851	$5,055	$5,273	$5,611	$6,142	$6,504	$7,419
Cost of goods sold	2,586	2,553	2,793	2,854	3,338	3,579	4,164
Gross profit	$2,265	$2,502	$2,480	$2,757	$2,804	$2,925	$3,255
General and administrative expenses							
Wages and salaries	$1,006	$1,129	$1,233	$1,274	$1,305	$1,443	$1,541
Officers' salaries	143	154	135	151	164	155	178
Depreciation	123	136	148	149	170	168	200
Profit-sharing contribution	100	113	119	135	126	146	157
Advertising	93	82	99	122	107	123	44
Utilities	84	111	106	124	120	129	141
Conventions and conferences	1	1	3	3	16	14	21
Other	356	424	465	501	505	534	655
Total general and administrative expenses	$1,906	$2,150	$2,308	$2,459	$2,513	$2,712	$2,937
Income from operations	$ 359	$ 352	$ 172	$ 298	$ 291	$ 213	$ 318
Dividend and interest income	48	57	52	68	71	69	63
Other income (expenses)	13	18	6	15	2	(6)	(7)
Pretax income	$ 420	$ 427	$ 230	$ 381	$ 364	$ 276	$ 374
Income tax	162	143	69	148	115	72	132
Net income	$ 258	$ 284	$ 161	$ 233	$ 249	$ 204	$ 242
Preferred stock dividend	1	1	0	2	1	1	1
Addition to retained earnings	$ 257	$ 283	$ 161	$ 231	$ 248	$ 203	$ 241

Source: Company records.

EXHIBIT 8   Wall Drug Store Balance Sheet, Years Ended December 31 ($000)

	1983	1984	1985	1986	1987	1988	1989
Assets							
Current assets							
Cash	$ 40	$ 12	$ 18	$ 29	$ 70	$ 59	$ 267
Current marketable securities	205	0	0	1	1	2	0
Accounts receivable	13	25	24	25	36	48	41
Merchandise inventory	405	616	718	968	1,322	1,429	1,330
Prepaid taxes and other	33	32	114	57	68	112	52
Total current assets	$ 696	$ 685	$ 874	$1,080	$1,497	$1,650	$1,690
Investments and other assets							
Noncurrent marketable securities	402	489	600	785	739	646	487
Life insurance and other	7	7	7	8	14	13	79
Total other assets	$ 409	$ 496	$ 607	$ 793	$ 753	$ 659	$ 566
Property and equipment							
Land	$ 174	$ 177	$ 187	$ 186	$ 171	$ 181	$ 181
Building and improvements	1,935	2,057	2,112	2,160	2,434	2,495	2,567
Equipment, furniture, and fixtures	1,065	1,232	1,278	1,372	1,492	1,628	1,795
Construction in progress	0	0	0	55	0	0	148
Total property and equipment	$3,174	$3,466	$3,577	$3,774	$4,097	$4,304	$4,691
Less accumulated depreciation	1,475	1,609	1,732	1,869	2,032	2,182	2,385
Net property and equipment	$1,699	$1,857	$1,845	$1,905	$2,065	$2,122	$2,306
Goodwill at cost less							
accumulated amortization	16	14	12	10	9	7	5
Total assets	$2,820	$3,052	$3,338	$3,788	$4,324	$4,438	$4,567
Liabilities and Equity							
Current liabilities							
Current maturities of long-term debt	$ 40	$ 10	$ 2	$ 2	$ 2	$ 2	$ 2
Notes payable	50	85	175	310	598	500	275
Accounts payable	61	40	41	54	60	44	77
Taxes payable	93	67	75	95	81	75	128
Accrued profit-sharing contribution	100	113	119	135	127	146	157
Accrued pension plan payable	0	0	29	25	31	15	0
Accrued payroll and bonuses	65	50	34	48	56	56	73
Accrued interest payable	4	2	4	1	7	5	2
Total current liabilities	$ 413	$ 367	$ 479	$ 670	$ 962	$ 843	$ 714
Long-term debt	182	173	173	172	156	154	152
Deferred income taxes	10	25	27	56	68	101	121
Stockholders' equity							
Preferred stock	$ 30	$ 30	$ 30	$ 30	$ 30	$ 30	$ 30
Class A common stock	48	48	48	48	48	48	48
Class B common stock (nonvoting)	53	53	53	53	53	53	53
Capital in excess of par	52	52	52	52	52	52	52
Reserve for self-insurance	300	300	300	300	300	300	300
Retained earnings	1,732	2,004	2,176	2,407	2,654	2,857	3,097
Total stockholders' equity	$2,215	$2,487	$2,659	$2,890	$3,137	$3,340	$3,580
Total liabilities and equity	$2,820	$3,052	$3,338	$3,788	$4,322	$4,438	$4,567

Source: Company records.

a stock repurchase agreement and a $69,000 interest-bearing note. These debts were held by Hustead family members not active in the business and were being paid in monthly installments.

Wall Drug had a profit-sharing plan for all employees who worked more than 1,000 hours during any year. At the discretion of the four senior Husteads, who were the corporate officers, the plan paid up to 15 percent of employees' salaries into a retirement trust fund managed by an independent financial institution. Profits had always been sufficient to pay the full 15 percent. The store terminated a smaller, noncontributory defined-benefit plan in 1988. All participating employees were fully vested in their earned benefits in the old plan.

Inventory levels are shown as of December 31. Orders for the coming season began arriving in December, but most would arrive from January through April. Peak inventory levels would reach $2.5 million. Many suppliers would post-date invoices for July and August, which eased the cash flow burden of financing this seasonal inventory.

The art collection was used primarily to attract customers and repeat customers. Prices for the paintings were not established. When paintings were sold the prices were negotiated. The collection was carried in the accounts as merchandise inventory and valued at cost.

A small part of the inventory consisted of gold bullion which would be sold periodically to the store's main jewelry supplier in Rapid City. This practice provided a hedge against rising gold prices. In 1990 because of the need to finance the new stores the stocks of bullion were low.

The $300,000 reserve for self-insurance was established in 1982. The store was a self-insurer for collision and comprehensive coverage of its motor vehicles, of the deductible portion of its employees' medical coverage, and a portion of the casualty coverage of some buildings and their contents. A portion of the store's marketable securities funded this reserve.

EXPANSION PLANS FOR THE 1990s

As he prepared for the 1990 tourist season, Bill Hustead, CEO of Wall Drug, was making plans for the store's most ambitious expansion. This expansion would include a large, open mall ringed with shops to be built to the rear of the existing backyard area. Houses along the street to the rear of the store, already owned by the Husteads, would be moved or razed to make room for this expansion.

New shops with a combined floor space of nearly 15,000 square feet would include a shop selling Indian handicraft items, a poster store, a yogurt shop, a fast-food hamburger shop, and a store for motorcyclists. (Sturgis, South Dakota, in the Black Hills is the site of an annual summer motorcycle rally which attracts thousands of motorcyclists from all over North America.) A major feature of the new addition would be a free gallery displaying a recently acquired collection of over 700 old photographs of cattle drives, rodeos, Indians, cowboys, and other early settlers of South Dakota and Montana. The Husteads estimated that approximately 12 to 14 additional employees would be required to staff this expansion during the peak season.

Bill planned to build this expansion over a period of three to five years. As with previous expansions, he planned to act as his own general contractor and direct the actual construction. When the project was finished, the existing backyard would be removed. This was constructed of metal buildings and had about 3,000 square feet of floor space.

The last project being planned was to build the Wall Drug Western Art Gallery and guest house. This would be a three-story mansion, a replica of an old Southern plantation house, to display the best of the Wall Drug Store's western art collection. It would also display beautiful furnishings, elegant table settings, crystal, and other accoutrements of graceful living. The Hustead art collection included 30 paintings portraying Christmas in the West. Bill planned to have a Christmas room in the mansion to display these paintings and a permanent Christmas tree with antique ornaments. The third floor was planned as a theater which would show films or videotapes about some of the artists and a film or a videotape about the Wall Drug Store. Some rooms in the mansion were to be set aside as guest quarters.

Bill planned to charge a small admission fee to the mansion. This income would be used to purchase new paintings for the art collection. Bill explained:

> There is more to business than just profit. We are aiming at sophisticated people who will get a kick out of this. Forty percent of our business is from repeat customers so we've got to keep moving in such a way as to impress people. We've got to keep forward momentum.

Bill believed that the very survival of the business and the jobs and aspirations of his full-time employees depended on Wall Drug's continued development. "We are not Wal-Mart. We are in the entertainment business. We can't just sit here with what we've got and expect people to keep coming."

Bill Hustead was aware that his two sons had serious reservations about his expansion plans. Commenting on the proposed expansion, Rick said,

> Dad is more oriented to seeing the business as a real attraction—a "must stop" attraction. I'm more concerned with the nuts and bolts. I want to be profitable. I want a better handle on our inventory and labor. My concern is always that we are profitable and don't overextend or build things that won't be profitable. What he plans to do is interesting, but I have real questions about the mansion. Are we going to realize a profit? This could cost $1.5 or $2 million. Fortunately it is the farthest down the road. We should expand the food service first.
>
> I'm conservative. I resisted the new shops (Dakota Mercantile and The Tumbleweed) at first. The building estimates were $210,000. They cost $300,000. They are nice shops, but getting personnel to run them is an issue.

The Husteads did not use a formal system of evaluating return on investment in making decisions about expansion. Rick noted, however, that these decisions were subjected to analysis. "Dad knows his expenses and his volumes. We know that we have to gross $200,000 or better in the new shops to be successful."

Bill estimated that the new stores would have a payback of approximately five years. He reported that their cost had actually been about $240,000. As to the expense of the proposed expansion plans, he said, "There is no way we are going to spend $1.5 to $2 million. The total cost of the backyard expansion and the art gallery will be between $800,000 to $900,000 and $1.5 million."

Teddy felt that he was somewhere in the middle on the expansion plans.

> We have got to replace the backyard and make the store more interesting, but the mansion never has made too much sense to me. I have a lot of respect for my father, but he got this idea from homes in the South. I don't know if it applies to the West. On the other hand, we are getting to have a world-class collection of western art. I don't ever want to underestimate him.

Teddy also pointed out that the existing building needed extensive repairs. "The roof around the tree needs to be replaced. A few years ago the tree was trimmed back, and it died so now it has to go." Teddy estimated that these repairs would cost $200,000. He noted further that the store's administrative offices had been built in 1964 for a much smaller staff and were inadequate for current operations.

Bill commented on the objection his sons had raised to the mansion-style art gallery. "People from the South settled in South Dakota and some houses of this type were built here, but it wouldn't have to be a southern style mansion. It could be another type of building."

In May the 1990 season began on a promising note. The first two weeks of sales in the Dakota Mercantile and Tumbleweed stores were very good. "It's now or never," Bill commented, reflecting on the seasonal character of their business. Sales in the main store were also running ahead of 1989, and bus loads of travelers bound for Deadwood were stopping to eat and shop.

Endnotes

1. Jackalopes are stuffed jackrabbits with antelope or deer antlers. Flying jackalopes have pheasant wings. These creations of taxidermy were priced from $99 to $129.

2. Dana Close Jennings, *Free Ice Water: The Story of Wall Drug* (Aberdeen, S. D.: North Plains Press, 1969), p. 26.

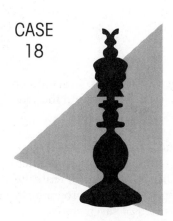

CASE
18

LONGS DRUG STORES

JAMES W. CLINTON

PREFACE

Longs Drug Stores, as of January 1989, operated 236 retail drugstores in six western states: California (200 stores), Hawaii (21), Nevada (6), Colorado (5), Alaska (2), and Arizona (2). Total sales were $1.9 billion for the fiscal year ending January 26, 1989; net profit was $55.9 million; both totals were records for the company.

COMPANY HISTORY

In the mid-1920s, a few years before the Great Depression, brothers Thomas and Joseph Long lived with their parents in Covelo, a very small town in northern California. Their father ran a general merchandise store in a rural, agricultural community, extending credit to customers, most of whom were farmers. In 1928 the arrival of an agricultural depression made it impossible for most farmers to pay their bills, and their father's country store, with no income coming in to pay off creditors, closed its doors.

From this personal experience with a credit operation, the Long brothers, who worked their way through the University of California at Berkeley, believed they could succeed in retailing by operating a self-service drugstore on a cash-and-carry basis. Consequently, on May 12, 1938, Thomas and Joseph Long opened a 7,000-square-foot retail drugstore, Long's Self-Service Drugs, in Oakland, California. The store was a success and the Long brothers opened another store in Alameda, California. Joe Long managed the Alameda store and Tom Long managed the Oakland store. According to retired vice president and former board member Norm Adams, lobby department manager of the Alameda store in 1939:

> The hours were long. . . . The early shift was from 7 a.m. to 6 p.m. and the late shift from 12 noon to 11 p.m. After the late shift you could take your time

---

sweeping up and scrubbing the floor. However, we did take every other Sunday off . . . . The fact that we all worked as a team [Adams and founder Joseph Long] was satisfying.

A third store was opened in San Jose in 1941 and a fourth store in Fresno, California. For several months, until an ad writer was found, Joe Long commuted to Fresno once a week from a newly opened general office in Alameda to write the store's newspaper ads. World War II slowed the Longs' expansion program. In 1950, five years after the war's end, Longs Drugs consisted of seven stores.

In 1949, while vacationing in Hawaii, Joseph Long became upset with the high prices he paid for items at a local drugstore and decided to open a drugstore in Honolulu. It was not until 1953, however, that Long obtained the Hotel and Bishop Street location in downtown Honolulu he wanted. Longs' first Hawaii drugstore opened in 1954; a second was added in 1959 at the Ala Moana shopping center (at that time one of the world's largest shopping malls) near Waikiki. In 1967 Longs created a district office and the company's first distribution center—in Honolulu—to break down shipping containers received from the United States mainland into smaller lot sizes for efficient delivery of merchandise to the two Hawaii stores. By 1960 Longs Drugs consisted of 16 drugstores in California and Hawaii. In 1961 Longs Drugs stock went public. By 1971 Longs operated 54 drugstores.

Longs' headquarters initially was located in Alameda, but later was relocated to Oakland. To allow for future expansion not available at the Oakland location, and to provide employees with a work location closer to their homes, Longs later moved the General Office to its present site—Walnut Creek, California.

When Robert Long, son of cofounder and present board chairman Joseph Long, was appointed president in 1975, Longs Drugs operated approximately 92 drugstores.

Longs entered the Phoenix, Arizona market in 1978, and by 1987 operated 15 stores in metropolitan Phoenix. In 1987, however, Longs sold its Phoenix drugstores to the Osco/Sav-On Drug Store division of American Stores in exchange for 12 Osco drugstores—11 in northern California and 1 in Colorado. At the time of the sale, Longs' major Phoenix competitors consisted of the Walgreen, Thrifty, Revco, Osco, and SupeRx drug chains. Industry analysts evaluated the exchange favorably because Longs withdrew from a market of firmly entrenched competitors in which Longs was relatively weak in terms of number of stores, market penetration, market share, and profitability when compared with Longs' more successful and well-established California stores, in return for stores that added to Longs' already strong position in the San Francisco Bay area.

MANAGEMENT PHILOSOPHY

In September 1988 CEO Robert M. Long, concerned that the size of Longs Drugs made it less likely that all employees would personally meet the company's founders, Thomas and Joseph Long, and benefit directly from their expressed values, put the company's beliefs into writing. According to Long, the company's first principle is the Golden Rule, that is, "treating others, as we ourselves would like to be treated." Long also believed that:

> Our first responsibility is to our customers. . . . Everything we do and sell must be of high quality. . . . We are responsible to our employees, who must be treated as individuals. . . . We care about their growth and success. . . . We must develop competent management, and their actions must be just and ethical. . . . We are responsible to the communities in which we reside. . . . We are responsible to our shareholders. Our business must make a sound profit, and reserves created for adverse times. . . . We believe that when we honor these responsibilities, and operate by these principles and beliefs, all of us will realize a fair return.

Founders Joseph and Thomas Long encouraged informality and open communications among managers, a tradition continued today. "Longs Drugs, 1938–1988, 50th Anniversary Commemorative Album" described the Long brothers' approach to management:

> The first organized management meeting . . . took place in the late 1940s at Joe Long's cabin at Lake Tahoe . . . [and] involved approximately eight to ten managers (drug managers and lobby managers). Everyone stayed in the cabin. . . . You'd wake up in the morning to the smell of breakfast cooking in the kitchen . . . Joe [Long] would be cooking bacon and eggs and sausage . . . After breakfast . . . everyone would sit around that same table for the meetings. There was no agenda . . . in those days. . . . Joe and Tom would talk about everything—about running a store, about merchandising, about one-on-one with our employees. . . . We came back inspired. . . . In later meetings, other speakers were added . . . on operating topics. . . . Many managers refer to the camaraderie that has been a special part of their careers with Longs. . . . No one can really understand what we shared.

Longs' underlying values are reflected in company policies and store practices, some of which are unique to the industry. Each store, for example, is autonomous. The store manager operates his store as if an independent entrepreneur, selecting, buying, and pricing as he chooses. Longs also attempts to provide a merchandise mix desired by customers at prices competitive or lower. Key employees, through stock options, participate in the company's growth and profitability. The Long brothers believed managers who shared in profits would recognize that they literally worked for themselves and work that much harder. Store managers and assistant managers receive a percentage of the profits from their own stores, based on the principle that the more they earn for the company, the more they earn for themselves.

MANAGEMENT AND ORGANIZATION

In a presentation to security analysts in Hawaii given on April 14, 1989, President R. M. Long stated that:

The conventional organizational chart places the president and CEO on top with subordinate layers underneath. Our organization is just the reverse; cashiers and clerks are on the top, because they're closest to the customer. And I'm at the bottom. . . . [C]ompared to other drug chains our corporate headquarters is very small. Our general office's primary function is to serve the stores. We perform those tasks which could take store management away from the customer, such as accounting, legal work, and site selection. At Longs, attention is focused on the stores and their ability to serve customers.

BOARD OF DIRECTORS

Joseph M. Long, cofounder, Chairman of the Board, age 76

Robert M. Long, President and Chief Executive Officer, director since 1968, 50

Thomas J. Long, cofounder, Retired Chairman of the Board, 78

Richard M. Brooks, President and CEO, SF Adams Management Corporation; formerly Vice President, Finance and Treasurer, Lucky Stores, appointed August 1988, 61

William G. Combs, Vice President, Administration and Treasurer, joined Longs in 1943; Treasurer since 1961; director since 1980, 58

E. E. Johnston, Insurance Consultant, Member, Audit Committee; director since 1972, 71

D. E. McHenry, Chancellor Emeritus, University of California-Santa Cruz, Member, Audit Committee, director since 1974, 78

Ronald A. Plomgren, Senior Vice President, Development, joined Longs in 1950, Senior Vice President since 1983, director since 1972, 54

Steven D. Roath, Executive Vice President, hired as staff pharmacist in 1964, Senior Vice President since 1983, director since 1979, currently responsible for store operations and management information systems, 48

I. W. Rowland, Pharmacy Consultant, Dean Emeritus, School of Pharmacy, University of the Pacific, Member, Audit Committee, director since 1971, 79

S. B. Stewart, Attorney at Law, Member, Audit Committee, 80

T. R. Sweeney, Vice President, District Manager, director since 1978, 50

CORPORATE OFFICERS

In addition to the officers identified above (J. M. Long, R. M. Long, W. G. Combs, R. A. Plomgren, S. D. Roath, and T. R. Sweeney), Longs has four senior vice presidents:

William Brandon, Regional Senior Vice President of Southern California stores, began as a clerk in 1959, promoted to district manager in 1974

George A. Duey, Regional Senior Vice President of Northern California, Colorado, Alaska, and Arizona stores, joined Longs in 1958, promoted to district manager in 1972

Orlo D. Jones, Senior Vice President, Properties and Secretary, joined Longs as an attorney in 1971, Vice President since 1979

Daniel R. Wilson, Senior Vice President, Marketing, joined Longs as a pharmacist in 1964, appointed district manager in 1981, Vice President since 1983

Other officers are:

Al A. Arrigoni, Vice President, Construction, joined Longs in 1972 as project coordinator, appointed Vice President in 1988
Lester C. Anderson, Vice President, Personnel, joined Longs as manager in 1972, Vice President since 1979
David J. Fong, Vice President, Pharmacy, joined Longs as pharmacist in 1975, appointed Vice President in 1988
Michael K. Raphel, Vice President, Real Estate, Vice President since 1988, joined in 1978
Kyle J. Westover, Vice President, Training, joined in 1968, Vice President since 1988

The remaining vice presidents are District Managers Jack Daleth, Sal Petrucelli, and Victor H. Howe, D. D. England, R. W. Vienop, R. W. Wilson, and Grover L. White, Controller. At the close of fiscal 1989, Longs had approximately 12,400 employees, of whom approximately 400 were located at corporate headquarters. Longs' area of operations is divided into two regions and 11 districts: (1) Northern, (2) Sacramento, (3) Delta, (4) Coast, (5) East Bay, (6) Santa Clara, (7) Central, (8) East Los Angeles, (9) Los Angeles West, (10) San Diego, and (11) Hawaii.

MERCHANDISING AND OPERATIONS
Store Siting and Store Size

Of Longs' 236 drugstores, Longs owns both the land and buildings of 42 percent of the stores and the buildings on leased land of 16 percent of the stores. The remaining store buildings and store land sites are leased. (See Exhibit 1.)

Before choosing a store site, Longs Drug conducts demographic studies to evaluate: population of the surrounding area, access to the shopping area, the nature of the competition (with regard to pharmacy, cosmetics, photo, liquor, and general sundry products as well as competitive pricing), average family income in the area to be served, etc. Longs also plays a role in selecting cotenants in a new shopping center. According to former board member Norm Adams:

> We attempt to [choose] our competition in the small shopping center [typically consisting of two anchors: a grocery and a drugstore] for the mere fact that a grocery store will be in the shopping center is enough competition. Grocery stores now carry large quantities of over-the-counter drugs as well as many sundries. . . . We, in turn, carry many grocery items, but . . . only buy them when they are good buys and pass them on to the public. . . . by featuring spectacular grocery prices we generate traffic in the shopping center at no cost to [the grocery store] . . . and frequently the grocery stores ask us to let them know when we are coming out with a "hot" ad so they can put on

EXHIBIT 1 Store Data: Total, Openings, Closings, and Square Feet, by Fiscal Year, 1980–1989

Fiscal Year	Year-End Totals	Opened	Sold/Closed (net)	Total Square Feet (000)
1989	236	11	4[a]	6,046
1988	229	10	3[b]	5,877
1987	222	15	1	5,614
1986	208	17	0	5,272
1985	191	13	0	4,845
1984	178	5	0	4,507
1983	173	12	1	4,360
1982	162	14	1	4,089
1981	149	19	0	3,728
1980	130	11	1	3,212

[a]Two stores sold; two stores closed.
[b]Fifteen stores sold; eleven stores acquired.

additional help to take care of the increased business—business on which they can make a profit.

Longs seeks centers with adequate parking. Longs attempts to locate its stores in a center away from fast-food restaurants or theaters because of the latter's high utilization of parking spaces. Longs also prefers aggressive shopping center tenants who generate foot traffic for several of the center's stores. A center that contains a variety of stores, representing a truly one-stop shopping center, is also high on Longs' site priorities.

Local zoning sometimes denies Longs a prime store location. In other cases, leasing costs are so high Longs cannot justify joining the site as a tenant. District managers recommend new store sites to a real estate committee composed of key executives in the general office, who make the final decision. Longs prefers to buy or lease the land and build its own store but will accept a turnkey lease (a site and space ready for fixtures) if the terms are attractive.

Longs' 1989 Annual Report notes:

> Most stores range in size from 15,000 to 40,000 square feet. Stores which opened in the last five years averaged approximately 23,000 square feet, with 66 percent selling space. . . . Sales of merchandise averaged $8.3 million per store for the year ended January 26, 1989.

Longs is becoming increasingly flexible in store siting decisions. CEO Robert Long told a group of Hawaii security analysts on April 14, 1989:

> We are looking at more than just sites which can accommodate Longs' typical 25,000-square-foot store with a supermarket as a cotenant. Today's varied marketplace calls for a diversity of retail applications. . . . Later this year we

will open a 17,000-square-foot store in Davis, California [home to the University of California-Davis agricultural college] which will feature what the architect calls "a contemporary agricultural, college decor." Another store will experiment with new colors and large backlit transparencies, while another will be built in a downtown location. . . . Many have asked why we're only opening 12 to 14 stores this year compared to others. The reason is, we are more selective in choosing our locations. We don't build cookie-cutter stores; we stylize our stores to conform to the particular requirements of a given location.

Store closings, as Exhibit 1 shows, are rare and usually the result of an unusual combination of circumstances. The Bakersfield, California store, for example, was closed down after two earthquakes and low volume. The National City, California store, located between San Diego and the Mexican border, was closed after Mexico devalued the peso. Many customers were Mexican nationals from whom Longs accepted pesos for store purchases. As the value of the peso dropped, however, Longs experienced significant currency exchange losses, and business generated by local residents was insufficient to operate the store profitably.

Store Inventories

CEO Long views Longs' market niche to be "a drug and convenience store." Store pharmacies are considered to be community health centers, and represent the prime focuses of the stores. All stores include cosmetics and photo departments and carry health-oriented merchandise. Longs, in addition to carrying brand name merchandise, also features house brand merchandise including over-the-counter medications and liquors. (Longs' product mix appears in Exhibit 2.)

Longs' market research, according to Vice President Combs, shows that most customers want to shop quickly and conveniently (close to home). Superstores carry most of the items frequently purchased by consumers—groceries, personal care needs, and prescription items. Strip-center stores (a small group of stores not including a superstore) also carry most of these convenience items. To appeal to customers' diverse needs, therefore, Longs carries grocery items and other items customers might wish to purchase at a single shopping stop.

Longs' store managers select and price merchandise in line with the cofounders' belief that decision making should be pushed down to the operating level where employees meet the customer. Store managers purchase most merchandise, therefore, directly from manufacturers and wholesalers.

Forbes, in an October 31, 1988 article titled, "Managers as Entrepreneurs," noted the freedom exercised by Longs' store managers:

One store, [close to] . . . a large retirement community, stocks plenty of aspirin, laxatives, and other products used primarily by senior citizens. . . . The Longs store across town, however, serves a neighborhood dominated by upper-income professionals with young families. Store manager Danny Van Allen does especially well selling videocassette recorders, stereos and

EXHIBIT 2   Longs Drugs' Product Mix, 1988

Prescription drugs	18%
Cosmetics	10
Housewares and appliances	9
Candy	7
Liquor, wine, and beer	7
Over-the-counter drugs	6
Food	6
Household supplies	6
Photofinishing/camera supplies	6
Stationery and greeting cards	5
Related drug items	4
Sporting goods and toys	3
Toiletries	2
Tobacco and magazines	2
Miscellaneous	9
Total	100%

Source: *Chain Drug Review*, November 7, 1988.

cameras. . . . "I like to think of myself as the chairman of an $8 million company," said one Longs manager.

Store managers have an incentive to choose inventories carefully and move them quickly. The store manager and assistant store manager receive quarterly bonuses based on a percentage of net profits for their stores. Hence, they strive to keep their costs of doing business down. The department managers' bonus, on the other hand, is based on gross profit. Hence, they work hard to keep volume up.

Redistribution Centers

In January 1989 Longs was utilizing four redistribution centers. The three located in California—Ontario, San Diego, and Vacaville—were not owned by Longs. According to Vice President Combs, "Longs is not in the warehouse business." By not being tied to a particular mode of distribution, Longs is able to select (in California's very competitive environment) the most effective and economical distribution channel. Longs does, however, own and operate the company's fourth redistribution center, located in Honolulu, Hawaii. The centers range in size from approximately 10,000 square feet (San Diego) to 250,000 square feet (Vacaville). Store managers staff committees that decide which merchandise the centers purchase. In fiscal 1989 over 13 percent of Longs' merchandise, consisting primarily of promotional and seasonal goods, flowed through these four centers to Longs' retail drugstores.

Longs also opened a pharmacy distribution center in Southern California at the close of 1988 which, by the end of 1989, was expected to supply pharmacy items to 90 percent of Longs' drugstores. The center does not stock every pharmacy item, only those high-volume items that offer the advantage of ordering in bulk.

The centers, through economies of scale, enable Longs to reduce distribution costs. According to Executive Vice President Roath, as quoted in the November 7, 1988 issue of *Chain Drug Review*, the distribution center concept:

> has made the ordering of ad merchandise easier for managers . . . without diluting at all the manager's role in ad or seasonal item selection. . . . We will not use distribution centers (however) where using them adversely impacts or reduces the authority of our store managers to select merchandise.

Longs presently is studying whether or not additional merchandise, specifically health and beauty aids items, should be shipped through distribution centers.

Promotion

Longs' general office receives a steady stream of salesmen offering promotional buys. The general office disseminates merchandise information to the stores pertaining to merchandise sources, such as jobbers and manufacturers, and prices available.

Store managers have joined to form what are termed "ad groups," logical store groupings with a common major advertising medium. For example, approximately 20 Longs drugstores have combined to form an ad group in Contra Costa County, California, because each of the 20 stores draws customers from readers of the *Contra Costa Times*, a local newspaper. Store managers meet once a week to develop a single ad for the 20 stores. Store managers are assigned merchandise categories and asked to recommend promotional items and selling prices for inclusion in a common ad. The managers review merchandise data provided by the general office and submit their recommendations to the ad group. The store managers review and then vote on whether to accept or reject these merchandise suggestions. Store managers individually determine quantities ordered for their stores. Their orders, however, are then combined with those of other ad group members to achieve economies of scale.

In addition to the major ad group, store managers may use another, smaller newspaper, either exclusively or with one or several other store managers, to form another ad group. Composition of this secondary ad group is determined by the extent to which the medium's circulation matches the selling area of the stores. Merchandise selection and pricing is determined by the same process outlined above for the larger ad group. Essentially, store managers determine which merchandise will be promoted, at what price merchandise will be sold, and in which medium the merchandise will be advertised.

In 1988, Longs, to differentiate itself from competitors and increase consumer awareness of the company, circulated a newspaper advertising supplement,

"Health News," containing health information on such topics as cholesterol and generic drugs. A companion insert, "Longs Beauty News," discussed questions frequently asked by customers. Still a third supplement, "Today's Lifestyles," promotes products directed at a variety of customer segments. Consumer surveys conducted after distribution of these supplements, accompanied by increased employee contact with customers and a broader line of merchandise, indicated customers had a clearer perception of Longs. The difference that set Longs apart from competitors was Longs employees' closer attention to customer needs. The promotion was considered a success and additional supplements are planned. Longs' stores also conduct senior citizen health fairs and provide free cholesterol and blood pressure screenings.

Longs first used corporate-level advertising in 1982. Prior to 1982 all Longs' advertising was placed at the store or multistore level. Currently, most of Longs' advertising continues to be prepared at the store level or by ad groups. Only a small proportion of Longs' advertising is prepared at the corporate level.

Employee Training

Store managers hire, train, and promote store employees. A library of videotapes is supplied to store managers by the corporate headquarters covering such subjects as operating the cash register, cosmetics, photography, special occasions, the difficult customer, shoplifting, inventory, etc. The corporate telecommunications studio facility at Walnut Creek distributes a video entitled "Merchandising Muscle" to each store every six to eight weeks. According to Executive Vice President Roath:

> "Merchandising Muscle" shares ideas from throughout the chain. . . . [It] is also used to relate hero stories about Longs people who exemplify Longs service ethic. . . . [Longs also conducts] specialty education programs, such as our pharmacy and cosmetic schools and photo seminars. . . . Recently in our East Los Angeles District we have begun testing a training center prototype where we can provide computer training in groups to our stores . . . [through] our pharmacy computer system. . . . A second, more advanced prototype of a Longs training center is currently under construction . . . in Hawaii.

Longs believes their trained employees enable the company to provide superior customer service of a specialized and personalized nature.

Technology

Each store pharmacy has a computer tied into Longs' Pharmacy Information System, maintained at corporate headquarters, that not only provides pharmacy item price and sales data specific to the store, but also enables each store managers to access merchandise purchase information on nonpharmacy items pertaining to their stores. The system also allows store managers to communicate almost instantaneously with all other stores and the Walnut Creek headquarters. Satellite links join Hawaii stores to this management information network. Longs designed its own retail management software.

Longs' stores do not presently use optical scanning devices at checkout stands. Costs of installing such devices in all Longs stores are estimated to exceed $25 million. Currently, however, Longs is testing scanners in two of its stores. Two additional stores are scheduled to test and evaluate the equipment of other scanner manufacturers. If the tests are successful, other stores will adopt the scanners. Longs is trying to determine if scanner technology is compatible with (and economically justified in) Longs' decentralized management structure in which pricing and merchandise decisions are made at the store level.

During 1988 Longs modernized prescription departments at 22 locations, introducing conveyors and specially designed fixtures. These pharmacies, called "Super Pharmacies," reduce the time required to fill prescriptions and reduce customer waiting time.

Longs recently built a new facility to process prescriptions by mail. The facility significantly expanded Longs' mail-order processing capability, and currently represents less than 5 percent of total prescriptions filled.

Longs produces its own video programs, as noted above, in a Longs-owned and -operated studio. Longs' video network, to which all stores are connected, can distribute videos to all stores in one day.

PERSONNEL

Longs, as a general rule, promotes only from within. Fifteen of Longs' 20 corporate officers previously served as store managers. If a particular skill, however, is needed that is not available within the firm, Longs will go outside the company to obtain that needed expertise. Recently, for example, Longs hired a corporate executive skilled in applications of computer technology to very large operations.

Department managers and higher-ranking employees are eligible to purchase low-cost group life insurance up to $200,000 based upon salary. Employees are eligible, after one year's service, or 1,000 hours, to participate in a profit-sharing plan financed by company contributions, but administered by a committee of employees. Employees are vested gradually into the plan until fully vested after seven years. Company contributions to the plan have averaged about 15 percent of the payroll since the plan was adopted in 1956. Longs' 1989 *Annual Report* noted that:

> At the end of our fiscal year 1989, the (ESOP) plan held 11.3 percent of the company's stock. In March of 1989, the company guaranteed a loan to the plan from an outside source of approximately $25 million to purchase 696,864 shares of Longs common stock from the company, increasing the plan holdings to 14.3 percent. The loan will be repaid from future company contributions and dividends on stock held by the plan.

LONGS' COMPETITIVE PERFORMANCE

Longs' competitors include other independent drug chains; drug chains that are subsidiaries of conglomerates; supermarkets that feature pharmacies (combination stores); independent drugstores; deep discount drugstores that feature low-priced prescription medicines; discount retailers such as Kmart and Wal-Mart that include pharmacies; health maintenance organizations (HMOs), such as Kaiser Permanente; hospitals and physicians who dispense prescription medicines directly to patients; department and retail stores that carry health and beauty aids, camera supplies, etc., also carried by Longs; independent mail-order prescription drug services; mail-order prescription drugs available through consumers' health insurance contracts; etc.

Longs Drug ranks 14th in total number of stores in the chain drugstore industry, but 8th in sales and 3rd in net income. Longs is industry leader in sales per square foot ($455 versus $326 for Walgreen Drugs and $275 for Osco, according to *Forbes,* October 31, 1988) and number of inventory turns (7.1 versus an industry average of 4). See Exhibit 3.

Longs' definition of earning power, that is, margin multiplied by inventory turnover, leads the industry. Longs' average store sales, over $8 million, also is the

EXHIBIT 3 Selected Financial Ratios, Drug Chains, 1986–1988

	Industry	Longs	Walgreen	Rite-Aid
Current ratio				
1988	1.9 to 1	1.39	1.99	1.62
1987	2.1	1.51	1.77	1.90
1986	1.9	1.56	1.85	1.70
Quick ratio				
1988	0.5 to 1	0.30	0.65	0.38
1987	0.6	0.27	0.28	0.42
1986	0.5	0.23	0.43	0.37
Inventory turnover				
1988	6.1 turns	9.0	7.5	4.8
1987	5.8	9.2	6.2	4.8
1986	5.8	9.0	6.6	4.1
Net profit margin				
1988	2.6%	2.9	2.6	3.32
1987	2.5	2.8	2.4	3.77
1986	2.7	2.4	2.8	4.44
Return on net worth				
1988	15.5%	16.5	18.1	15.0
1987	14.9	16.4	16.6	16.4
1986	15.6	13.3	18.6	17.2

Source: *Value Line Investment Survey;* and *RMA: Annual Statement Studies, 1988.*

industry leader. *Drug Store News* reported drugstore industry prescriptions increased 1 percent in 1988; drug chains' prescriptions increased by 7 percent; and Longs Drugs' prescriptions increased by 19 percent. Longs, according to *Forbes*, has a 20 percent share of the California market.

FINANCE

The board of directors amended an earlier 1986 Shareholders Rights Plan on November 15, 1988, according to a Longs' press release, "to provide [stockholders] additional protection against abusive takeover tactics." During the past few years Longs has been the subject of takeover rumors. If someone acquires 20 percent or more of Longs' common stock, existing Longs' shareholders will have the right to acquire additional common stock at one-half the stock's market value. Longs believes such rights "will not prevent a takeover, but should encourage anyone seeking to acquire the company to negotiate with the board of directors before making a takeover attempt." Longs insiders, i.e., founders, officers, and employees (through the ESOP), own over 40 percent of the company's outstanding stock.

In fiscal years 1987 to 1989 Longs repurchased approximately three million shares of the company's common stock. Dividends paid by the firm have increased for 25 consecutive years. (Pertinent financial data appear in Exhibits 4 through 7.)

FUTURE PROSPECTS

According to *Value Line* analyst Claire Mencke (January 20, 1989, p. 789):

> With its high sales per store, booming market area, and debt-free balance sheet, Longs has the resources to be a more aggressive market force. Our

EXHIBIT 4 Selected Financial Data, 1980–1989

Fiscal Year	Cash Flow per Share	Earnings per Share	Book Value per Share	Net Profit Margin	Return on Net Worth
1989[a]	$3.60	$2.75	$16.25	2.9%	16.5%
1988	3.09	2.33	14.59	2.8	16.4
1987	2.42	1.78	13.74	2.4	13.3
1986	2.29	1.74	13.33	2.6	13.0
1985	2.31	1.88	12.23	2.9	15.4
1984	2.10	1.72	10.57	3.0	16.2
1983	1.79	1.46	9.38	2.8	15.5
1982	1.72	1.43	8.42	3.0	17.0
1981	1.45	1.23	7.44	2.9	16.5
1980	1.46	1.27	6.62	3.5	19.1

[a]Adapted from *Value Line*, January 20, 1989, p. 789.

EXHIBIT 5   Longs Drugs Consolidated Balance Sheet, 1988–1989 ($millions)

	Fiscal Years Ending	
	1989	**1988**
Assets		
Current assets		
Cash and equivalents	$ 21.8	$ 20.3
Pharmacy/other receivables	23.0	15.7
Merchandise inventories	196.7	192.3
Other	8.3	6.2
Total current assets	$249.8	$234.5
Property		
Land	$ 54.4	$ 49.1
Buildings/leasehold improvements	177.5	165.7
Less depreciation	(94.5)	(81.9)
Equipment/fixtures	114.2	100.4
Beverage licenses	6.5	6.2
Property, net	$257.8	$239.5
Total assets	$507.6	$474.0
Liabilities and Stockholders' Equity		
Current liabilities		
Accounts payable	$105.7	$ 96.7
Compensation	29.0	23.3
Income taxes	5.0	4.3
Other taxes	21.9	18.5
Other	18.0	13.0
Total current liabilities	$179.6	$155.8
Deferred income taxes	18.9	18.4
Stockholders' equity		
Common stock[a]	$ 10.0	$ 10.3
Additional capital	31.5	21.4
Common stock contributions to benefit plans	0.7	4.5
Retained earnings	266.9	263.6
Total stockholders' equity	$309.1	$299.8
Total liabilities and stockholders' equity	$507.6	$474.0

[a]Shares outstanding for fiscal years 1986 to 1989 were 21.7, 21.1, 20.5, and 19.9 million, respectively. The board, in February 1988, authorized repurchase of up to 2 million shares.

projections, however, assume it will continue on a cautious path of expansion over the [next] 3- to 5-year period."

Several years ago, former board member Norm Adams echoed the philosophy of the company's founders:

EXHIBIT 6 Longs Drugs Income and Retained Earnings, 1987–1989 ($millions)

	Fiscal Years		
	1989	1988	1987
Sales	$1,925.5	$1,772.5	$1,635.4
Cost of good sold	1,445.9	1,333.2	1,241.3
Gross margin	$ 479.6	$ 439.3	$ 394.1
Other expenses			
Operating/Administration	315.4	284.1	258.3
Occupancy	71.5	66.8	60.9
Total	$ 386.9	$ 350.9	$ 319.2
Income before taxes	92.7	88.4	74.9
Taxes	36.8	39.1	36.3
Net income	$ 55.9	$ 49.3	$ 38.6
Retained earnings, start of year	$ 263.6	$ 260.9	$ 266.9
Repurchase of common stock	(35.1)	(29.7)	(28.3)
Dividends	(17.5)	(16.8)	(16.3)
Add net income	55.9	49.3	38.6
Retained earnings, end of year	$ 266.9	$ 263.7	$ 260.9
Earnings per share of common stock	$2.75	$2.33	$1.78
Dividends per share of common stock	$0.86	$0.79	$0.75
Stock price range	$31–$38	$25–$41	$27–$35

EXHIBIT 7 Longs Drugs Consolidated Cash Flows, 1987–1989 ($millions)

	Fiscal Years		
	1989	1988	1987
Cash receipts			
Customer sales	$1,918.1	$1,770.1	$1,632.5
Sale of property	3.1	17.4	3.0
Stock options exercised	6.5	3.5	2.3
Total cash receipts	$1,927.7	$1,791.0	$1,637.8
Cash disbursements			
Inventory purchases	$1,441.3	$1,332.0	$1,235.0
Operating, administrative, occupancy expenses	357.1	323.5	294.8
Income tax payments	35.6	38.8	30.7
Investment in property	37.6	41.5	41.9
Repurchase of common stock	37.0	31.2	29.3
Dividend payments	17.5	16.8	16.3
Total cash disbursed	$1,926.1	$1,783.8	$1,648.0
Net additions to cash	$ 1.6	$ 7.2	$ (10.2)

Note: totals may differ due to rounding.

[W]e *have* to be bullish [about the future]. We owe it to our employees and to our stockholders. Without opening new stores we would lessen the chances for advancement for our employees. We would not have an orderly expansion in sales and profits. We could not increase our dividends to our stockholders in an orderly fashion.

THE DRUGSTORE INDUSTRY

JAMES W. CLINTON

INTRODUCTION

The label *drugstore industry* does not accurately describe those stores that today call themselves drugstores. For the first half of this century, small neighborhood drugstores provided customers with prescription medicines, nonprescription over-the-counter (OTC) remedies, and health-related merchandise. Many of these corner drugstores also featured soda fountains.

Today's drugstore consists of a wide variety of retail combinations. A few, amazingly, are images of the past, continuing to focus on prescription and nonprescription medicines. They can properly be described as pharmacies. Even the soda fountain is making a comeback, although on a very small scale. For the most part, however, drugstores now carry a broad line of merchandise, including items commonly available at supermarkets, discount stores, camera shops, jewelry and department stores, gift shops, sporting goods stores, etc.

In 1986 there were 50,900 drug/proprietary stores in the United States, a decline of 1,100 drugstores since 1982. Drug/proprietary sales totaled $56 billion in 1987, an increase of $19.6 billion over 1982 sales of $36.4 billion. Sales by multiunit drugstore chains (11 or more stores) in 1987, $32.9 billion, accounted for 58.7 percent of total sales of $56 billion. (*U.S. Statistical Abstract*, 1989.)

At the same time that drugstores have expanded lines of merchandise, the number and types of retail outlets at which pharmacy services are available have multiplied, blurring the distinction between pharmacy, drugstore, supermarket, etc. Supermarkets and discount stores prominently promote their pharmacy services.

Prescription medicines now are available directly from physicians, hospitals, clinics, and mail-order organizations that compete for the consumer's medical dollar. Just as large shopping centers attempt to provide the mobile shopper with one-stop shopping service, more and more health care providers offer one-stop medical service that includes prescription medicines.

THE COMPETITIVE ENVIRONMENT

The chief players in the drugstore industry consist of: (a) independent single-store druggists, (b) small, independent drugstore chains, (c) large, independent drugstore chains, (d) drugstore chains controlled by parent companies, (e) supermarkets with pharmacies (called combination stores) including single units, independent chains, and subsidiary chains, (f) discount retailers with pharmacies, (g) department stores and retail specialty shops carrying merchandise or selling services that overlap drugstores' lines of products and services, (h) hospital and clinic pharmacies, including health maintenance organizations (HMOs), (i) physicians who sell prescription medicine to patients, (j) independent mail-order services of either health and beauty aids or prescription medicines, (k) mail-order pharmacy services provided as part of an overall health insurance program, and (k) independent health and beauty consultants who visit the consumer at home.

Independent Pharmacists

Thousands of independent drugstores continue to operate in today's complex environment, competing on the basis of personal service to customers and neighborhood convenience. According to Martha Glaser (*Drug Topics,* November 21, 1988), "independents constitute about two-thirds of all community pharmacies; they fill about 80 percent of all Medicaid Rxs [prescriptions]."

Independents, like their larger competitors, are serviced by about 80 national drug wholesalers whose sales have grown from $8.6 billion in 1981 to $19.5 billion in 1987, according to Val Cardinale (*Drug Topics,* November 21, 1988). One of these wholesalers is the product of a merger of Affiliated Drug Stores and Associated Chain Drug Stores representing "more than 100 chains with more than 10,000 stores," according to Iris Rosendahl (*Drug Topics,* September 19, 1988). The wholesaler, because of volume buying, offers members lower prices, particularly for generic drugs.

An alternative for the independent pharmacist is the franchise. Medicine Shoppe, with 750 units, is the largest pharmacy franchise in the country. Prescriptions account for 90 percent of sales for both Medicine Shoppe and Medicap, (another franchisor), according to Marianne Wilson (*American Druggist,* October 1988). In addition to conventional pharmacy franchises, deep-discount drugstore franchise outlets such as Drug Emporium and Drug Castle emphasize low prices for a broad line of products.

Independent Chain Drugstores

Fidelity Prescriptions   Fidelity Prescriptions, a small, independent drug chain located in the midwest United States, operates specialty pharmacies. A ten store chain of 1,500-square-foot drugstores, Fidelity drugstores sell prescription medications and offer limited home health care and services. Fidelity's prime customers are over 45 years old and "pre-teen, teen, and college students looking for dermatological items and young mothers who have pre-schoolers." (*Chain Store Age Executive,* May 1988.)

Walgreen   The largest drugstore chain in the country, independent or otherwise, in terms of total sales and profits is the Walgreen Company. Walgreen operates over 1,400 drugstores in 30 states. Walgreen opened more than 400 new drugstores between 1984 and 1988. During the fiscal year ending August 31, 1988, Walgreen opened 88 new stores, remodeled 60 stores, and expanded pharmacies in 50 stores. Walgreen plans to remodel an additional 165 stores during fiscal 1989. Pharmacy sales represent 27 percent of Walgreen's sales. Walgreen also owns and operates four photoprocessing facilities.

Rite-Aid   Rite-Aid, another independent drugstore chain, is a fast-growing drug chain whose growth has been fueled by acquisition of other drugstore chains. The typical Rite-Aid drugstore has 6,700 square feet of selling space and averages $1.1 million in sales. Rite-Aid, formed in 1962, operated 2,128 drugstores in 22 northeastern, middle and south Atlantic, and midwestern states, and the District of Columbia.

Rite-Aid purchased 533 stores from Kroger (Super RX), Gray Drug, and Drug Fair in 1987 (*Annual Report,* 1988). "Rite-Aid's strength lies in its ability to buy stores cheap that lost money for others and quickly turn them around." (*Forbes,* July 13, 1987.) During 1987, Rite-Aid added 99 stores on its own, enlarged or relocated 47 others, and closed 33 stores. During fiscal 1989, Rite-Aid plans to add 90 new stores and renovate 225 stores acquired in 1987.

In spring 1989 Rite-Aid purchased the Lane Drug Company from Peoples Drug Stores, adding 114 drugstores located primarily in Ohio. Rite-Aid carries more than 1,000 private-label products which account for over 14 percent of sales. Pharmacies account for over 39 percent of sales, and third-party transactions (purchases reimbursed either to the consumer or the drugstore through a medical insurance program—the third party) represent about 40 percent of prescription sales. Rite-Aid emphasizes discount prices instead of frequent sale prices.

Rite-Aid drugstores typically locate in low-rent strip malls and low-income areas. Rite-Aid targets Medicaid patients, ". . . health clinics, group health plans, and any other state, federal, or company-funded insurance programs." (*Forbes,* July 13, 1987.)

Longs Drug   Longs Drug Stores is an independent drugstore chain of 236 outlets concentrated in California (200) and Hawaii (21). Longs began as a single pharmacy in 1939 and, unlike Rite-Aid and Walgreen, emphasizes decision making at the store manager level. Almost 87 percent of store merchandise is shipped directly by vendors to the drugstores, enabling managers to tailor store inventories to local customer tastes. Less than 14 percent of merchandise sold by Longs in 1988 was processed through the company's three redistribution centers (warehouse operations).

Longs drugstores vary in size from 15,000 to 40,000 square feet. During the last five years, newly opened Longs drugstores averaged 23,000 square feet (*Annual Report,* 1989). Longs earned a record $55.9 million on record sales of $1.9 billion in fiscal 1989 versus $49.2 million on $1.7 billion in sales the previous year.

Hook-SupeRx   Hook-SupeRx, Inc. (HSI) of Cincinnati, Ohio was incorporated in October 1986 to acquire, on a leveraged basis, portions of the retail drugstore business owned by the Kroger Company of Cincinnati, Ohio. In November 1987 HSI acquired 19 drugstores from Jack Eckerd Corporation. In June 1988 HSI acquired all of the stock of Brooks Drug, Inc., a drugstore chain of 348 retail stores, for $80 million from the Andrews Group, which previously acquired Brooks from Revlon in September 1986 for $95 million. Brooks drugstores operated under the names of Brooks, Brooks Drugs, Brooks Pharmacy, Brooks Discount Center, Mall Drug, Sav-A-Lot, Nescott, Eckerd Drug, and Whelan Drug Company. The

Andrews group lost $3.7 million on revenues of $385.3 million in 1987 versus a loss of $3.2 million on revenues of $155.7 million in 1986.

HSI operates 357 Hook drugstores, 323 SuperRx drugstores, 348 Brooks drugstores, 30 Hook convalescent aid centers, and 13 SuperRx deep-discount drugstores, a total of 1,071 outlets. Hooks' Indianapolis, Indiana warehouse processed 87 percent of all merchandise sold by Hook drugstores in fiscal 1988. Similarly, 80 percent of all Brooks Drug sales moved through Brooks' Pawtucket, Rhode Island warehouse. For fiscal 1988, HSI lost $402,000 on sales of $1.3 billion.

Dart Drug   Dart Drug was incorporated in 1928 as the United Drug Company. The company's name changed to United Rexall in 1945, to Rexall Drug Company in 1946, Rexall Drug and Chemical in 1959, and in 1969 to Dart Industries. In 1984 the Drug Store Division of Dart Group Corporation was taken private in a leveraged buyout. The company operated 58 drugstores and five deep-discount drugstores in the Washington, D.C. and Richmond, Virginia markets. Most stores were located in suburban shopping centers. All store locations were leased. The merchandising department at company headquarters in Landover, Maryland makes most product selections for the company's stores. Eight district managers oversee store operations.

In 1987 Dart Drug went public. Dart lost $23.6 million on sales of $218.2 million in 1988 versus a loss of $1.8 million on revenues of $265.6 million in 1987. In 1988 the company had a negative net worth of $11.1 million. The company's name recently was changed to Fantle Drug Stores under CEO Sheldon Fantle. As of August 1989, Fantle Drug was unable to pay interest payments on its debt. (Exhibit 1 summarizes selected data for major independent drugstore chains just discussed.)

Drugstore Subsidiaries

Osco/Sav-On   Osco/Sav-On Drug Stores, formerly an independent drug chain, is now a subsidiary of American Stores. (American Stores moved its headquarters

EXHIBIT 1   Independent Drugstore Chains' Sales ($billions), Net Income ($millions), and Number of Stores, 1988

Chain	Sales	Net Income	No. of Stores
Walgreen	$4.9	$129.1	1,421
Rite-Aid	2.9	95.2	2,312
Longs Drug	1.9	55.9	236
Hook-SupeRx	1.3	(0.4)	1,041
Drug Emporium	0.4	7.2	74
Dart Drug	0.2	(23.6)	63

from Salt Lake City, Utah to Irvine, California in 1988, but then returned to Salt Lake in 1989 (*Value Line,* March 15, 1989). At present, Osco's California stores are converting to the Sav-On name to improve economies of scale possible in advertising and distribution; when the conversion is complete, Sav-On will operate 160 drugstores in California.

American Stores' 1987 *Annual Report* noted that "Osco Drug, Inc. . . . did not reach . . . objectives . . . operating profits decreased 24.4 percent to $97 million on a sales increase of 4.2 percent to $3 billion." American Stores, as 1988 began, operated 1,460 retail food and drugstores in 39 states concentrated primarily in the western United States: Acme Markets, Alpha Beta Stores (supermarkets), American Superstores, Jewel Food Stores, Osco Drug, Skaggs Alpha Beta (combination supermarket/drug), and Star Market, Inc. During 1987 Osco Drug remodeled 25 drugstores, opened six stand-alone stores, and closed 10 stores. Ten large drug/food combination stores also were opened. American Stores earned $154.3 million in 1987 on sales of $14.3 billion versus $144.5 million in 1986 on sales of $14 billion.

Thrifty Drug   Thrifty Corporation of Los Angeles, California, a chain of drugstores and sporting good outlets, recently was acquired by Pacific Enterprises, a conglomerate engaged also in natural gas transmission, energy, and financial services. Thrifty operates full-sized Thrifty Drug Discount stores and Thrifty Jr. convenience stores. Thrifty operated a total of 801 stores at the close of 1987, an increase of 89 stores from the previous year, 20 of which were Thrifty Drug Discount stores and 27 Thrifty Jr. stores.

Thrifty's operating income was $66 million in 1988 on sales of $2.4 billion versus net income of $39.5 million in 1987 on $1.84 billion in sales (*Annual Report,* 1988). Parent Pacific Enterprises earned $251.2 million net income on $5.4 billion sales in 1987. In June 1988 Thrifty acquired 110 Pay N'Save drugstores in the Pacific Northwest (*Value Line,* September 15, 1988). Thrifty plans annual growth of 4 to 7 percent in number of drugstores "over the near term." (*Annual Report,* 1987).

Thrift Drug   J. C. Penney, this country's fourth largest retailer (*Standard & Poor's,* Corporation Records), owns and operates as a subsidiary operation 434 Thrift Drug Stores (not to be confused with Thrifty Drug, described above). Penney's operates department stores, catalog stores, supermarkets, and drugstores, and is involved in banking, insurance, real estate, telemarketing, and travel services. Penney's earned $608 million in 1988 on $15.3 billion in revenues versus $530 million net income on $14.7 billion 1987 revenues.

Pay Less Drug   Retailer Kmart acquired Pay Less Drug Stores Northwest in 1986 and planned to upgrade and modernize the 254 newly acquired stores. Pay Less operates drugstores in Oregon, Washington, Idaho, and Nevada. Kmart's net income in 1988 was $802.9 million on sales of $27.3 billion; 1987 income was $692.2 million on sales of $25.6 billion.

Comprehensive financial data (including number of stores) pertaining specifically to subsidiary drugstore chains owned by American Stores, Pacific Enterprises and Kmart, i.e., Osco/Sav-On, Thrifty, and Pay Less, respectively, are not readily available since most operating data for these companies are consolidated and comingled under their larger parent companies.

Peoples Drug   Imasco, Ltd. of Montreal, Quebec, a diversified Canadian company, acquired Peoples Drug Stores in 1985. Peoples, at that time, consisted of a chain of 831 company-owned drugstores, the sixth largest chain in the United States. Peoples drugstores operated under trade names of Peoples, Lane, Reed, Lee, Health Mart, Rea and Derick, and Bud's. Peoples drugstores were located in 150 markets in 14 states and the District of Columbia.

Imasco's Imperial Tobacco subsidiary controls over one-half of the Canadian cigarette market; Imasco owns the Hardees fast-food chain of over 3,000 outlets, and operates Canada's largest drugstore chain, Shoppers Drug Mart—614 outlets (*Value Line,* June 30, 1989). About 40 percent of Imasco's common stock is owned by BAT Industries. Imasco netted $314.3 million in 1988 on $6.0 billion in sales.

As noted above, Rite-Aid purchased 114 drugstores from Imasco's Peoples in spring 1989. Peoples planned in 1989 to sell a total of 300 outlets that fell below management's profit expectations.

Imasco's 1987 annual report noted that Peoples drugstores suffered an operating loss of $32 million on revenues of $1.9 billion and an additional extraordinary charge of $39 million before taxes because of "costs associated with restructuring and disposing of certain assets and unproductive store locations." The previous year Peoples' operating earnings were $46.4 million on $1.8 billion in sales.

Peoples is leader or second best in market share in most of its markets (*Annual Report,* 1987). Because of problems in distribution, operating margins, and excessive inventory, Peoples inaugurated a program called CSP, that is expected to improve store performance. Basic elements of CSP are (a) convenient store locations, (b) pharmacists whom customers perceive as community health professionals, and (c) a wide range of products and services.

Deep-Discount Drug Chains

Deep-discount drugstores are expected to total 650 (including Canada) by 1990, over twice their number of 1985—313. Major retailers operating deep-discount drug chains are Wal-Mart's Dot drugstores, F. W. Woolworth's Rx Place, and Safeway's Drugs for Less.

F&M Distributors operates 52 deep-discount drugstores in the midwestern and middle Atlantic states, averaging sales of $700 per square foot in its 25,000-square-foot stores. F&M "has merchandise . . . shipped directly from manufacturers to stores unless . . . warehousing [is more] . . . profitable." (*Chain Store Age Executive,* March 1988.)

Contract Pharmacies

True Quality Pharmacies (McKinney, Texas) operates 31 contract pharmacy units in Wal-Mart stores. True Quality provides customers with health care information, including delivery of brochures to local nursing homes (*Chain Store Age Executive,* December 1987).

Discount Retailers

Discounters such as Wal-Mart, Kmart, and Target normally feature cut-rate, generic prescription drugs and house brands of nonprescription drugs. Their lines of merchandise overlap and duplicate drugstore product lines.

Supermarkets

Supermarkets' merchandise includes food items, sundries, and pharmaceuticals, etc. These combination stores generally occupy over 30,000 square feet with $12 million in annual sales. Over 3,500 supermarket combination stores operate in the United States, many of them owned by major food chains such as Safeway, Kroger, Albertson's, Giant Foods (Washington, D.C.), and King Soopers. Average sales volume of health and beauty aid (HBA) sections in combination stores ($1.1 million) typically is twice that of the average chain drugstore. HBA combination store sales in 1987 were $3.9 billion.

> Total pharmacy dollars generated in supermarkets in 1987 are estimated at $2.75 billion . . . nearly one-third as much as the $8.47 billion generated by the nation's 19,412 chain drugstores in 1986. (*Progressive Grocer,* February 1988.)

Hypermarkets

Hypermarkets are another dimension beyond supermarkets in size, product line, and product variety. Wal-Mart opened hypermarkets in Topeka, Kansas and Garland, Texas during 1988. Wal-Mart's Hypermart USA Topeka store is 200,000 square feet and features a pharmacy accessible from an adjoining mall for the convenience of older shoppers. Wal-Mart's hypermart is over 100 times the size of the average independent Fidelity Prescription drugstore, cited earlier. (See Exhibit 2.)

Specialty Stores

Specialty stores, such as camera shops, gift shops, and beauty shops carry merchandise lines offered by most drugstores.

Mail-Order Services

Mail-order operations, such as the American Association of Retired People (AARP), offer discounted prices on prescription drugs to members. AARP's membership is in the millions because of the rapid growth in the senior citizen

EXHIBIT 2 Average Store Size in Square Feet, Selected Drugstore Chains, Supermarkets, and Hypermarkets

Retail Outlet	Store Size
Fidelity Prescriptions	1,500
Rite-Aid	6,700
Longs Drugs	23,000
F&M Distributors	25,000
Supermarkets	30,000+
Hypermarkets	200,000+

population. AARP offers prescription, travel, and financial services and health, life, and automobile insurance. AARP's support for the 1988 Catastrophic Health Care Act was considered by many instrumental in passage of the bill.

Medco, another mail-order firm, recently obtained a contract to provide prescription services for 190,000 retired California employees and their dependents. Medco plans to serve customers through the company's mail-order service pharmacies and through the Public Employees Retirement System network of 50,000 member pharmacies (*Drug Topics*, July 17, 1988).

Third-Party Providers

Third-party providers are organizations, such as Blue Cross, that receive policy-holder health insurance premium payments, and in turn reimburse the health professional or agency (doctor, nurse, or hospital) that provided products or services to the insured. They are called third-party providers because they serve as intermediaries between two parties—patient and health care provider—and provide funds to the health care professionals for their services. Some third-party providers contract with either mail-order pharmacies or other pharmacies for prescription medicines at discounted prices. The third-party provider may even, as part of the health insurance policy, require members to have their prescriptions filled at the contract pharmacy.

Health Maintenance Organizations (HMOs)

HMOs receive member insurance payments directly from members and provide services that include discounted prescription medicines. Kaiser operates HMOs, among other locations, at San Francisco, California, Portland, Oregon, and Denver, Colorado.

Hospitals

More than 13 percent of this country's hospitals include pharmacies that furnish prescription medicines to patients and others. An additional 13 percent of all hospitals are considering adding pharmacies to hospital facilities (*Drug Topics*, August 1988).

TECHNOLOGY

The following paragraphs summarize some of the activity related to technology within the industry.

Walgreen is installing checkout scanners and expects to have them in all stores by 1991 (*Value Line*, March 30, 1989). Scanners are part of Walgreen's Information Network (WIN), intended to (a) speed customer checkout, (b) reduce labor costs, (c) improve pricing accuracy, (d) simplify promotional pricing, and (e) keep stock in better condition because of higher inventory turnover. WIN is part of Walgreen's Strategic Inventory Management System (SIMS) expected to improve inventory control and reduce merchandise delivery costs (*Value Line*, March 30, 1989). Walgreen newspaper ads note that all Walgreen stores are linked to one another through in-store computers.

Rite-Aid's 265,000-square-foot distribution center in Winnsboro, South Carolina serves 426 stores in six states and has the capacity, according to management, to serve 650 units. Rite-Aid's 1988 *Annual Report* notes that:

> Store managers place orders through a computerized inventory system with the Harrisburg (PA) warehouse but are allowed no other buying or pricing decisions. Their order arrives prepriced and accompanied by a detailed diagram of how to display it in the store . . . all the stores look exactly alike.

Thrifty Corporation completed computerization of its pharmacy operations during 1987, computerized point-of-sale cash registers in 385 drugstores in 1988, and plans to introduce unit pricing code (UPC) technology in all stores over the next four years (*Annual Report*, 1988).

The Catastrophic Health Act calls for the federal Health Care Financing Administration to provide a free computer terminal and related software to pharmacists who request such equipment to facilitate delivery of prescription medicines to Medicare patients. (Under this act, consumers pay for prescriptions until a deductible cap is reached. Beyond this deductible cap, Medicare pays for the prescriptions.) Doctors who wish to dispense prescription medicine directly to Medicare customers also are eligible to receive both hardware and software free of charge (*Drug Topics*, October 3, 1988).

INDUSTRY ASSESSMENT

Vice President William Combs of Longs Drugs, Walnut Creek, California, noted at an April 14, 1989 presentation to the Hawaii security analysts:

> The 45 to 64 age group will increase by 33 percent in the next 10 years. This group requires more medication. In addition, hospital stays are shorter (as patients attempt to avoid high hospital in-patient charges by leaving the hospital early), more people self-medicate (to keep medical care costs down),

and there is a greater awareness of health. . . . In 1991, conservative estimates indicate the Catastrophic Health Bill will add between a billion and a half to two billion dollars in prescription drug sales, represented by a projected 700 million prescription claims in the mid-90s. Longs expects to be part of the pharmacy provider network which will be used by Medicare (for the over-65 population).

Walgreen Drug identified the following factors as favorable to the drugstore industry: (a) aging of the population, (b) increasing births, (c) shorter hospital stays, and (d) more working women (*Value Line*, March 1989).

Value Line believes:

> Drug stores are, as a group, less vulnerable to the vagaries of the business cycle than most other industries. That's because of the inelasticity of much of their product line—especially pharmacy items.

Value Line's assessment is confirmed by the steady upward movement of health care costs. Medical care, which includes pharmaceuticals, accounted for $360.3 billion of consumers' personal consumption expenditures in 1987, $404.1 billion in 1988, and increased to an annual rate of $439.9 billion for the first quarter of calendar 1989 (*Survey of Current Business*, June 1989). (See Exhibit 3 for recent drugstore chain financial data.)

During the past year drug manufacturers increased prices charged wholesalers 10 percent, according to Richard Koenig (*The Wall Street Journal*, April 6, 1989) while pharmacists raised prices to consumers only 7.6 percent. Since third parties, such as insurance companies or governmental health programs, pay for over one-third of prescription sales, druggists can expect continued pressure on margins.

POSSIBLE CHANGES FACING THE INDUSTRY

Analysis of the drugstore industry has become increasingly complex and difficult as drugstore chains are acquired by larger companies and as store labels, such as *drugstore, supermarket,* and *discount store,* no longer accurately represent either the nature or scope of merchandise offered to customers. These acquisitions, along with increased overlap in merchandise lines indicate that further changes in the industry are likely.

Possible changes include: (a) fewer independent chains due to additional acquisitions by larger corporations; (b) cooperative arrangements between physicians, hospitals, and third-party providers for filling prescriptions that reduce those filled by drugstores and combination stores; (c) development of computerized lifetime prescription drug histories as a marketing tool; (d) computer networks tied to vendors that enable individual chain drugstores (and perhaps even independent drugstores) to reorder merchandise as economically as if centrally ordered; (e) federal health care programs that assure that no one is denied needed medication due to a lack of funds; (f) cooperative arrangements between colleges and universities and drugstore chains that arrange for contract pharmacies on

EXHIBIT 3 Selected Financial Ratios, Drug Chains, 1986–1988

	Industry	Longs	Walgreen	Rite-Aid
Current ratio				
1988	1.9 to 1	1.39	1.99	1.62
1987	2.1	1.51	1.77	1.9
1986	1.9	1.56	1.85	1.7
Quick ratio				
1988	0.5 to 1	0.30	0.65	0.38
1987	0.6	0.27	0.28	0.42
1986	0.5	0.23	0.43	0.37
Inventory turnover				
1988	6.1 turns	9.0	7.5	4.8
1987	5.8	9.2	6.2	4.8
1986	5.8	9.0	6.6	4.1
Net profit margin				
1988	2.6%	2.9	2.6	3.32
1987	2.5	2.8	2.4	3.77
1986	2.7	2.4	2.8	4.44
Return on net worth				
1988	15.5%	16.5	18.1	15.0
1987	14.9	16.4	16.6	16.4
1986	15.6	13.3	18.6	17.2

Source: *Value Line Investment Survey;* and *RMA: Annual Statement Studies, 1988.*

campuses; (g) development of major retirement communities that contract for both pharmacy and nonprescription drug items for residents; and (h) widespread formation of associations of consumers that contract as a group for prescriptions and other drugstore merchandise at discounted prices.

Independent pharmacists, operators of drugstore chains and supermarkets, health care providers, health insurance companies, government agencies, and consumers can expect continued change in the structure of the drugstore industry and how goods and services are made available to consumers. Each industry stakeholder must develop his or her own vision of what the future drugstore environment is going to be and how best to adjust to, and perhaps even profit from, that environment.

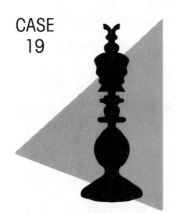

A NUCOR COMMITMENT

F. C. BARNES

INTRODUCTION

Nuclear Corporation of America had been near bankruptcy in 1965 when a fourth reorganization put a 39-year-old division manager, Ken Iverson, into the president's role. Iverson's team built Nucor, a steel mini-mill and joist manufacturer which by 1990 was the seventh-largest steel company in the United States, and set a new standard for all U.S. businesses.

The Wall Street Journal commented, "The ways in which management style combines with technology to benefit the mini-mill industry [are] obvious at Nucor Corp., one of the most successful of the 40 or more mini-mill operators." Ken Iverson was featured in an NBC special, "If Japan Can, Why Can't We?" for his management approach. As *The Wall Street Journal* commented, "You thought steel companies are only a bunch of losers, with stodgy management, outmoded plants, and poor profits?" Well, Nucor and Iverson were different.

As the 1980s began the U.S. steel industry faced a crisis. The big, integrated producers closed hopelessly outdated plants and reduced their market share, smaller companies reorganized or closed for good, new technology mini-mills took over most of sales in the 25 percent of the market they could produce, and foreign competition took a toll on the rest. By the end of the decade competitive forces and the economy had even ruined some mini-mills. Nucor, on the other hand, had moved steadily upward, doubled production, raised dividends every year, and become an example of management excellence for Tom Peters.

With all this success, analysts began to debate what Nucor should do next—how to diversify from a mature, troubled industry. Instead Nucor moved into a new market, structural steel. In a joint venture with the Japanese it opened the first new fastener plant in the United States in 20 years, and then, in 1989, opened the first thin-slab mini-mill in the entire world. This last move gave mini-mills access to another 50 percent of the total steel market and, Iverson believed, nearly guaranteed Nucor 15-percent annual sales increases for years to come.

Sidney, a college senior home for the holidays, was surprised to find thoughts of Nucor intruding upon the enjoyment of a favorite beverage. What has been Nucor's gimmick, its secret to success, in just another dying U.S. industry? Maybe Sidney could set up a consulting firm to package and sell it. When graduation came, maybe the gifts could be put toward the purchase of Nucor's stock, or members of the family should be advised to invest in Nucor. Sidney decided to take a closer look at Nucor; afterall it was time to start getting some payback from all this education.

BACKGROUND

Nucor was the descendant of a company that manufactured the first Oldsmobile in 1897. Before the surviving business, a truck company, could be liquidated, a merger was arranged with Nuclear Consultants, Inc., and the stock of Nuclear Corporation of America was first traded in 1955. Nuclear, following the conglomerate trend, acquired a number of companies in high-tech fields, but continued to lose money into 1960, when an investment banker in New York acquired control. New management continued with a series of acquisitions and dispositions in diverse fields, including Vulcraft Corporation, a South Carolina steel-joist manufacturer. Over the next four years, sales increased five times, but losses increased seven times. In 1965 a New York investor purchased a controlling interest in the nearly insolvent company and installed the fourth management team. The new president was Ken Iverson, who had been in charge of the Vulcraft division.

Ken Iverson had joined the Navy upon graduation from a Chicago-area high school in 1943. The Navy first sent him to Northwestern University for an officer training program, but then decided it needed aeronautical engineers and transferred him to Cornell. After graduation and six months to finish up his service obligation, he found he wasn't too excited about an AE career and so returned to Purdue to get a masters in mechanical engineering metallurgy. At Purdue he had worked with the new electron microscope, so International Harvester hired Iverson as a research assistant. Iverson stayed there five years and felt he was set for life. He had great respect for his boss, who would discuss with him the directions businesses took and their opportunities. One day his boss asked if that job was what he really wanted to do all his life. There was only one job ahead for Iverson at International Harvester and he was too ambitious to end his career in that position. At his boss's urging, he considered smaller companies.

Iverson joined Illium Corporation as chief engineer (metallurgist). Illium was a 60-person division of a major company, but functioned like an independent company. Iverson was close to the young president and was impressed by his good business skill; this man knew how to manage and had the discipline to run a tight ship, to go in the right direction with no excess manpower. The two of them proposed a new foundry which was necessary for them to become competitive. When the parent company insisted they delay 3 to 4 years until they could handle it without going into debt, Iverson began looking at new jobs.

After two years at Illium, Iverson joined Indiana Steel Products as assistant to the vice president of manufacturing for the sole purpose of setting up a spectrographic lab. After completing this job within one year, he could see no other opportunity for himself in the company and left to join Cannon Muskegon as chief metallurgist.

The next seven years were "fascinating." This small ($5 to $6 million in sales and 60 to 70 people) family company made castings from special metals that were used in every aircraft made in the United States. The company was one of the first to get into vacuum melting and Iverson, because of his technical ability, was put in charge of this activity. Iverson then asked for and got responsibility for all company sales. He wasn't dissatisfied, but realized that if he was to be really successful he needed broader managerial experience.

Cannon Muskegon sold materials to Coast Metals, a small, private New Jersey company in the aircraft industry. In 1960 the president of Coast hired Iverson as executive vice president with responsibility for running the whole company. Nuclear Corporation of America wished to buy Coast; however, Coast wasn't interested. Nuclear's president then asked Iverson to act as a consultant to find metal businesses Nuclear could buy. Over the next year, mostly on weekends, he looked at potential acquisitions. He recommended buying a joist business in South Carolina. Nuclear said it would, if he would run it. He joined Nuclear in 1962 as a vice president, Nuclear's usual title, in charge of the 200-person joist division.

By late 1963 he had built a second plant in Nebraska and was running the only division making a profit. The president asked him to become a group vice president, adding the research chemicals (metals) and contracting businesses, and to move to the home office in Phoenix. In mid-1965 the company defaulted on two loans and the president resigned. During that summer Nuclear sought some direction out of its difficulty. Iverson knew what could be done, put together a pro forma statement, and pushed for these actions. It was not a unanimous decision when he was made president in September 1965.

The new management immediately abolished some divisions and went to work building Nucor. According to Iverson, the vice presidents of the divisions designed Nucor in hard-working group meetings. Iverson was only another participant and took charge only when the group couldn't settle an issue. This process identified Nucor's strengths and set the path for Nucor.

By 1966 Nucor consisted of the two joist plants, the Research Chemicals division, and the Nuclear division. During 1967 a plant in Fort Payne, Alabama was purchased for conversion into another joist plant. In 1968 Nucor opened a steel mill in Darlington, South Carolina and a joist plant in Texas. "We got into the steel business because we wanted to make steel as cheaply as we were buying it from foreign importers or from offshore mills." Another joist plant was added in Indiana in 1972. Steel plant openings followed in Nebraska in 1975 and in Texas in 1977. The Nuclear division was divested in 1976. A fourth steel plant was opened in Utah in 1981 and a joist plant was opened in Utah in 1982. By 1984 Nucor consisted of six joist plants, four steel mills, and a Research Chemicals division. Against a background of a crumbling U.S. steel industry, Nucor and Iverson had become a model of success for U.S. industry.

In 1983, in testimony before the Congress, Iverson warned of the hazards of trade barriers, that they would cause steel to cost more and that manufacturers would move overseas to use the cheaper steel and ship back into this country. He commented, "We have seen serious problems in the wire industry and the fastener industry." *Link* magazine reported that in the last four years, 40 domestic fastener plants had closed and that imports held over 90 percent of the market.

In a dramatic move, Nucor began construction in 1986 of a $25-million plant in Indiana to manufacture steel fasteners. Iverson told the *Atlanta Journal*, "We are going to bring that business back." He told *Inc.* magazine, "We've studied for a year now, and we decided that we can make bolts as cheaply as foreign producers and make a profit at it." He explained that in the old operation two people, one simply required by the union, made 100 bolts a minute, "but at Nucor, we'll have an automated machine which will manufacture 400 bolts a minute. The automation will allow an operator to manage four machines." Hans Mueller, a steel industry consultant at East Tennessee State University, told the *Journal,* "I must confess that I was surprised that Iverson would be willing to dive into that snake pit. But he must believe that he can do it because he is not reckless." By 1988 the plant was operating at capacity.

In what the *New York Times* called its "most ambitious project yet," Nucor signed an agreement in January 1987 to form a joint venture with Yamato Kogyo, Ltd., a small Japanese steelmaker, to build a steel mill on the Mississippi River with a 700,000-ton-per-year capacity. The $200-million plant would utilize the Japanese experience to make large structural products with mini-mill technology. Structural steel products are those used in large buildings and bridges. Iverson noted, "These are now only made by the Big Three integrated steel companies."

Nucor's innovation was not limited to manufacturing. In the steel industry it was normal to price an order based on the quantity ordered. In 1984 Nucor broke that pattern. As Iverson stated, "Some time ago we began to realize that with computer order entry and billing, the extra charge for smaller orders was not cost justified. We are confident that the best competitive position is one that has a strong price-to-cost relationship." He noted that this policy would give Nucor another advantage over foreign suppliers in that users could maintain lower inventories and order more often. "If we are going to successfully compete against foreign suppliers, we must use the most economical methods for both manufacturing and distribution."

In August 1986 Iverson told Cable News Network, "We are talking about within the next two years perhaps building a steel mill to make flat-roll products, that would be the first time a mini-mill has been in this area." Flat-rolled steel was the largest market for steel products at 52 percent of the U.S. market. This is the thin, sheet steel used in car bodies, refrigerators, and countless products. Making flat-rolled steel required casting a slab rather than a billit and had not been achieved in the mini-mill. The thin slab would also produce feed stock for Vulcraft's steel deck operation.

In December 1986 Nucor announced its first major acquisition, Genbearco, a steel bearings manufacturer. At a cost of more than $10 million, it would add $25 million in sales and 250 employees. Iverson called it "a good fit with our business, our policies, and our people." It was without a union and tied pay to performance. In October 1988 Nucor agreed to sell its Chemicals Division to a French company for a $38-million gain.

In January 1987 Nucor announced an 800,000-ton, $265-million flat-roll plant would be built in Crawfordsville, Indiana with an April 1988 start up. It was expected that labor hours per ton would be half the integrated manufacturers' 3.0, yielding a savings of $50 to $75 on a $400-a-ton selling price. If the project were completed successfully, Nucor planned to have three plants in operation before others could build. Investment advisors anticipated Nucor's stock could increase to double or triple by the mid-1990s. However, it would not be as easy as earlier ventures. In April 1989 *Forbes* commented, "If any mini-mill can meet the challenge, it's Nucor. But expect the going to be tougher this time around." The flat-rolled market was the last bastion of the integrated manufacturers and they had been seriously modernizing their plants throughout the 1980s. In July 1989 when Nucor announced a 14-percent drop in second quarter earnings due to startup costs, its stock went up $1.62 to $63. The new plant was breaking even in 1990 as Nucor announced plans to build a second plant. Exhibit 1 shows the history of sales for several product lines. Iverson stated, "We hope this will map out the future of the company for the next decade."

THE STEEL INDUSTRY

The steel industry was one of those industries in the United States facing major problems. The early 1980s had been the worst years in decades for the steel industry. The large, integrated steel firms, such as U.S. Steel and Armco, which made up the major part of the industry, were the hardest hit. *The Wall Street Journal* stated, "The decline has resulted from such problems as high labor and energy

EXHIBIT 1 Nucor Product Mix

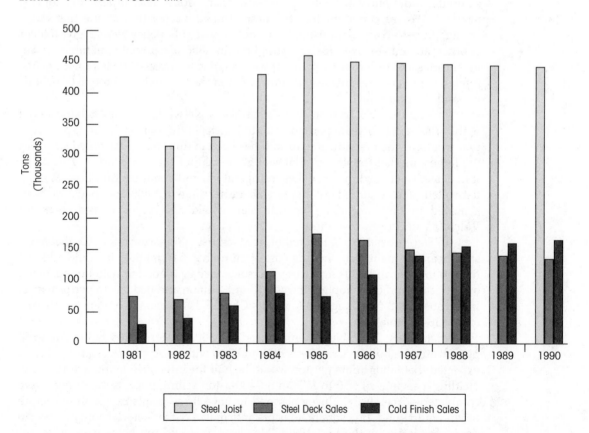

costs in mining and processing iron ore, a lack of profits and capital to modernize plants, and conservative management that has hesitated to take risks."

Data from the American Iron and Steel Institute showed shipments falling from 100 million tons in 1979 to mid-80 levels in 1980 and 1981. (See Exhibit 2.) In 1986 when industry capacity was at 130-million tons, the outlook was for a continued decline in per-capita consumption and movement toward capacity in the 90- to 100-million-ton range. The chairman of Armco saw "millions of tons chasing a market that's not there; excess capacity that must be eliminated."

These companies produced a wide range of steels, primarily from ore processed in blast furnaces. They had found it difficult to compete with imports, usually from Japan, and had given up market share to imports. They sought the protection of import quotas. Imported steel accounted for 20 percent of U.S. steel consumption, up from 12 percent in the early 1970s. The U.S. share of world production of raw steel declined from 19 to 11 percent over the period. The product lines of the steel industry were composed of wire rod, structural, plate, bar, pipe, and sheet. Imports of bar products, Nucor's main product line, accounted for 10 percent of U.S. shipments in 1989 while imports of wire rod totaled 26 percent. "Wire rod is a very competitive product in the world market because it's very easy

EXHIBIT 2   Shipments, Imports, and Production

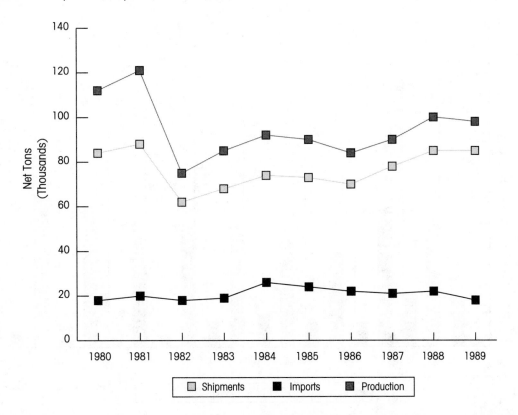

to make," Ralph Thompson, the Commerce Department's steel analyst, told the *Charlotte Observer*. *Iron Age* stated that exports, as a percentage of shipments in 1985, were 34 percent for Nippon, 26 percent for British Steel, 30 percent for Krupp, 49 percent for USINOR of France, and less than 1 percent for every American producer on the list.

Iverson was one of very few in the steel industry to oppose import restrictions. He saw an outdated U.S. steel industry which had to change. In 1987 he testified:

> About 12 percent of the steel in the United States is still produced by the old open hearth furnace. The Japanese shut down their last open hearth furnace about 5 years ago. [See Exhibit 3.] . . . The United States produces about 16 percent of its steel by the continuous casting process. In Japan over 50 percent of the steel is continuously cast. . . . We Americans have been conditioned to believe in our technical superiority. For many generations a continuing stream of new inventions and manufacturing techniques allowed us to far outpace the rest of the world in both volume and efficiency of

EXHIBIT 3   Industry Raw Steel Production by Type of Furnace

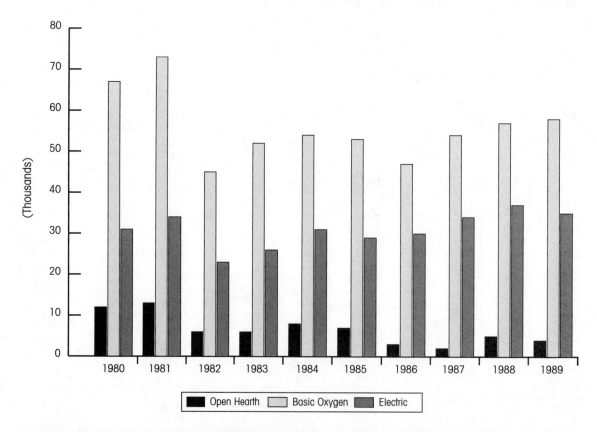

production. In many areas this is no longer true and particularly in the steel industry. In the last three decades, almost all the major developments in steelmaking were made outside the United States. There were 18 continuous casting units in the world before there was one in this country. I would be negligent if I did not recognize the significant contribution that the government has made toward the technological deterioration of the steel industry. Unrealistic depreciation schedules, high corporate taxes, excessive regulation, and jaw-boning for lower steel prices have made it difficult for the steel industry to borrow or generate the huge quantities of capital required for modernization.

By the mid-1980s the integrated mills were moving fast to get back into the game; they were restructuring, cutting capacity, dropping unprofitable lines, focusing products, and trying to become responsive to the market. The president of USX explained: "Steel executives, in trying to act as prudent businessmen, are seeking the lowest-cost solutions to provide what the market wants." Karlis Kirsis, director of World Steel Dynamics at Paine Webber, told *Purchasing Magazine*, "The industry as we knew it five years ago is no more; the industry as we knew it a year ago is gone."

Purchasing believed that buyers would be seeing a pronounced industry segmentation. There would be integrated producers making mostly flat-rolled and structural grades, reorganized steel companies making a limited range of products, mini-mills dominating the bar and light structural product areas, specialty steel firms seeking niches, and foreign producers. There would be accelerated shutdowns of older plants, elimination of products by some firms, and the installation of new product lines with new technologies by others. There would also be corporate facelifts as executives diversified from steel to generate profits and entice investment dollars. They saw the high-tonnage mills restructuring to handle sheets, plates, structurals, high-quality bars, and large pipe and tubular products which would allow for a resurgence of specialized mills: cold-finished bar manufacturers, independent strip mills, and mini-mills.

Wheeling-Pittsburgh illustrated the change under way in the industry. Through Chapter 11 reorganization in the late 1980s, it had cut costs by more than $85 per ton. It divided into profit centers, negotiated the lowest hourly wage rate ($18 per hour) among unionized integrated steel plants, renegotiated supply contracts, closed pipe and tube mills, and shut 1.6 million tons of blast-furnace capacity in favor of an electric furnace with continuous casting.

The American Iron and Steel Institute (AISI) reported steel production in 1989 of 97.9 million tons, down from 99.9 in 1988. As a result of modernization programs, 65 percent of production was from continuous casters. Japan and the ECC achieved 90 percent. Exports of steel were increasing, 2 million tons in 1988 and 4.5 million in 1989, and imports were falling, 18 percent in 1989. Some steel experts believed the United States was now cost-competitive with Japan. Because of strong worldwide demand, several countries did not fill their quotas (19 percent) allowed under the 5-year-old voluntary restraint agreement, which was extended three years to March 1992. [See Exhibit 4.] The increased role of service centers in the distribution of steel continued with its fifth consecutive record year in 1988 of 23.4 million tons.

EXHIBIT 4 Utilization of Industry Capacity

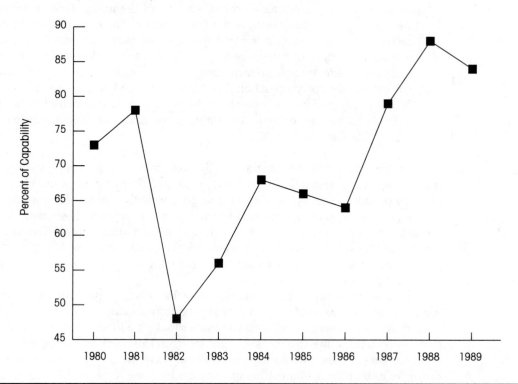

"If 1988 is remembered as the year of steel prosperity despite economic uncertainties, then 1989 is just as likely to go down as the year of 'waiting for the other shoe to drop,'" according to *Metal Center News* in January 1989. The fears and the expectation of a somewhat weaker year arose from concerns of a recession, expirations of the voluntary import restraints, and labor negotiations schedules in several companies. Declines in car production and consumer goods were expected to hit flat-rolled hard. Service centers were also expected to be cutting back on inventories. AUJ Consultants told MCN, "The U.S. steel market has peaked. Steel consumption is tending down. By 1990 we expect total domestic demand to dip under 90 million tons." Nucor had achieved record sales and earnings in 1990. As 1991 opened the slow economy had weakened demand for all its products. It had cut prices and cut the hours of work at several plants, but was continuing its record capital expenditure program.

THE MINI-MILL

A new type of mill, the mini-mill, emerged in the United States during the 1970s to compete with the integrated mill. The mini-mill used electric arc furnaces to manufacture a narrow product line from scrap steel. In 1981 *The New York Times* reported:

The truncated steel mill is to the integrated steel mill what the Volkswagen was to the American auto industry in the 1960s: smaller, cheaper, less complex, and more efficient. Although mini-mills cannot produce such products as sheet [flat-rolled] steel and heavy construction items, some industry analysts say it is only a matter of time before technological breakthroughs make this possible.

Since mini-mills came into being in the 1970s, the integrated mills' market share has fallen from about 90 percent to about 60 percent, with the loss equally divided between mini-mills and foreign imports. While the integrated steel companies averaged a 7-percent return on equity, the mini-mills averaged 14 percent, and some, such as Nucor, achieved about 25 percent.

The leading mini-mills had been Nucor, Florida Steel, Georgetown Steel (Korf Industries), North Star Steel, and Chaparral. Nucor produced light bar products: bars, angles, channels, flats, smooth round, and forging billets. It was beginning to make more alloy steels. Florida Steel made mostly reinforcing bar (rebar) for construction and dominated the Florida market. Korf Industries had two mini-mill subsidiaries which used modern equipment to manufacture wire rod.

The mini-mills were not immune to the economic slump in the early 1980s. Korf Industries, which owned Georgetown Steel, found its interest charges too large a burden and sought reorganization in 1983. In March 1983 Georgetown followed the historic wage-cutting contract between the United Steel Workers of America and the major steel companies and asked its union to accept reductions and to defer automatic wage increases. In 1982 Nucor froze wages and executives took a 5-percent pay cut. Plants went to a four-day schedule.

Florida Steel, with two-thirds of its sales in Florida, also felt the impact. At its headquarters in Tampa, a staff of over 100 handled accounting, payroll, sales entry, and almost all other services for all its facilities. Its division managers did not have sales responsibilities. Florida Steel experienced a sales decline for 1982 of 22 percent and an earnings drop from $3.37 per share to a loss of $1.40. The next year was also a year of losses. Florida Steel employees had faced periodic layoffs during the recession. The firm was nonunion (although the Charlotte plant lost an election in 1973) and pay was based on productivity. A small facility at Indian Town, near West Palm Beach, never became productive, even with personnel changes, and had to be closed. A new mini-mill in Tennessee was completed in late 1983.

Mini-mills had tripled their output in the last decade to capture 17 percent of domestic shipments. Paine Webber predicted at the time the big integrated mills' share of the market would fall to 40 percent, the mini-mills' share would rise to 23 percent, "reconstituted" mills would increase from 11 percent to 28 percent, and specialized mills would increase their share from 1 percent to 7 percent. Iverson stated mini-mills could not go beyond a 35-percent to 40-percent share due to technical limitations; mini-mills could not produce the flat-rolled sheet steel used in cars and appliances.

Iverson told *Metal Center News* in 1983:

We are very interested in the development of a thin slab, which would then allow mini-mills to produce plate and other flat-rolled products . . . . [A]ctually, the thinnest slab that can now be produced is about 6 inches thick . . . . (That results in a plant that is too large.) There are a number of people working to develop the process. There are more efforts by foreign steel companies in that direction than in the United States. . . . I'd say probably a minimum of three to five years, or it could take as much as 10 to achieve this.

In 1983 Iverson described the new generation of mini-mills he foresaw:

If you go way back, mini-mills got started by rolling reinforcing bar. With the advent of continuous casting and improvements in rolling mills, mini-mills gradually got into shapes. Now they have moved in two other directions: one being to larger sizes, and the other being a growing metallurgical expertise for improved product quality and production of special bar quality in alloys. Both of these represent expansion of markets for mini-mills.

In the late 1980s the new competitive environment was apparent. Four mini-mills had closed their doors and Iverson saw that more shutdowns were ahead. The overcapacity of steel bar products and the stagnant market had made it difficult for some companies to generate the cash needed to modernize and expand their product lines.

The mini-mills are going through the same kind of restructuring and rethinking as the integrated mill. They know the problem of overcapacity isn't going to go away quickly. And, for some of the remaining firms to survive, they will have to move into more sophisticated products like special quality and clean-steel bars and heavier structurals and, once the technology is perfected, flat-rolled products. You won't see the market growth by the mini-mills the way it was in the past until the overcapacity issue is resolved and the mills begin entering new product areas.

ORGANIZATION

Nucor, with its 20-person corporate office located in Charlotte, North Carolina, had divisions spread across the United States. The 15 divisions, one for every plant, each had a general manager, who was also a vice president of the corporation, directly responsible to Iverson and Aycock. (See Exhibit 5.) The divisions were of two basic types, joist plants and steel mills. The corporate staff consisted of single specialists in personnel and planning and a six-person financial function under Sam Siegel. Iverson, in the beginning, had chosen Charlotte "as the new home base for what he had envisioned as a small cadre of executives who would guide a decentralized operation with liberal authority delegated to managers in the field," according to *South* magazine.

Iverson gave his views on keeping a lean organization:

Each division is a profit center and the division manager has control over the day-to-day decisions that make that particular division profitable or not profitable. We expect the division to provide contribution, which is earnings before corporate expenses. We do not allocate our corporate expenses, because we do not think there is any way to do this reasonably and fairly. We

EXHIBIT 5 Nucor Organization Chart

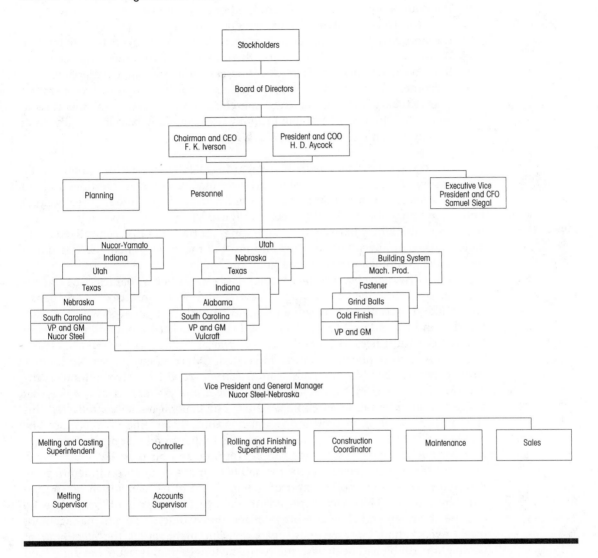

do focus on earnings. And we expect a division to earn 25-percent return on total assets employed, before corporate expenses, taxes, interest, or profit sharing. And we have a saying in the company—if a manager doesn't provide that for a number of years, we are either going to get rid of the division or get rid of the general manager, and it's generally the division manager.

A joist division manager commented on being in an organization with only four levels:

I've been a division manager four years now and at times I'm still awed by it: the opportunity I was given to be a *Fortune* 500 vice president. . . . I think we are successful because it is our style to pay more attention to our business than our competitors. . . . We are kind of a "no nonsense" company.

Mr. Iverson's style of management is to allow the division manager all the latitude in the world. His involvement with the managers is quite limited. As we've grown, he no longer has the time to visit with the managers more than once or twice a year. . . . Whereas in many large companies the corporate office makes the major decisions and the people at the operating level sit back to wait for their marching orders, that's not the case at Nucor. . . . In a way I feel like I run my own company because I really don't get any marching orders from Mr. Iverson.

The divisions did their own manufacturing, selling, accounting, engineering, and personnel management. A steel division manager, when questioned about Florida Steel, which had a large plant 90 miles away, commented, "I really don't know anything about Florida Steel. . . . I expect they do have more of the hierarchy. I think they have central purchasing, centralized sales, centralized credit collections, centralized engineering, and most of the major functions." He didn't feel greater centralization would be good for Nucor.

South Magazine observed that Iverson had established a characteristic organizational style described as "stripped down" and "no nonsense." "Jack Benny would like this company," observed Roland Underhill, an analyst with Crowell, Weedon and Co. of Los Angeles, "so would Peter Drucker." Underhill pointed out that Nucor's thriftiness didn't end with its "spartan" office staff or modest offices. "There are no corporate perquisites," he recited. "No company planes. No country club memberships. No company cars." *Fortune* reported, "Iverson takes the subway when he is in New York, a Wall Street analyst reports in a voice that suggests both admiration and amazement." The general managers reflected this style in the operation of their individual divisions. Their offices were more like plant offices or the offices of private companies built around manufacturing rather than for public appeal. They were simple, routine, and businesslike.

In 1983 one of Iverson's concerns had been that as Nucor continued to grow it would have to add another layer of management to its lean structure. In June 1984 he named Dave Aycock president and chief operating officer, while he became chairman and chief executive officer; they would share one management level. Aycock had most recently been division manager of the steel mill at Darlington, but he had been with the company longer than Iverson, having joined Vulcraft in 1955, and had long been recognized as a particularly valued and close advisor to Iverson. In June 1991 Aycock retired and John Correnti, who was 43, moved to COO from general manager of Nucor-Yamato.

DIVISION MANAGERS

The general managers met three times a year. In late October they presented preliminary budgets and capital requests. In late February they met to finalize budgets and treat miscellaneous matters. At a meeting in May they handled personnel matters, such as wage increases and changes of policies or benefits. The general managers as a group considered the raises for the department heads, the next lower level of management.

The corporate personnel manager described management relations as informal, trusting, and not "bureaucratic." He felt there was a minimum of paperwork, that a phone call was more common, and that no confirming memo was thought to be necessary. A Vulcraft manager commented: "We have what I would call a very friendly spirit of competition from one plant to the next. And of course all of the vice presidents and general managers share the same bonus systems so we are in this together as a team even though we operate our divisions individually."

A Vulcraft general manager in his early 40s who had been promoted to the division manager level nine years earlier said:

> The step from department manager to division manager is a big one. There are five department heads in six joist plants, which means there are 30 people who are considered for division manager slots at a joist plant. Mr. Iverson selects the division managers.
>
> When I came to this plant four years ago, we had too many people, too much overhead. We had 410 people at the plant and I could see, because I knew how many people we had in the Nebraska plant, we had many more than we needed. That was my yardstick and we set about to reduce those numbers by attrition. . . . We have made a few equipment changes that made it easier for the men, giving them an opportunity to make better bonuses. Of course the changes were very subtle in any given case, but overall in four years we have probably helped the men tremendously. With 55 fewer men, perhaps 40 to 45 fewer in the production area, we are still capable of producing the same number of tons as four years ago.

The divisions managed their activities with a minimum of contact with the corporate staff. Each day disbursements were reported to Siegel's office. Payments flowed into regional lockboxes. On a weekly basis, joist divisions reported total quotes, sales cancellations, backlogs, and production. Steel mills reported tons rolled, outside shipments, orders, cancellations, and backlogs. Mr. Iverson graphed the data. He might talk to the division about every two weeks.

Each month the divisions completed a two-page (11-inch × 17-inch) "Operations Analysis" that was sent to all the managers. Its three main purposes were (1) financial consolidation, (2) sharing information among the divisions, and (3) Iverson's examination. The summarized information and the performance statistics for all the divisions were then returned to the managers.

VULCRAFT—THE JOIST DIVISIONS

Half of Nucor's business was the manufacture and sale of open-web steel joists and joist girders at six Vulcraft divisions located in Florence, South Carolina; Norfolk, Nebraska; Ft. Payne, Alabama; Grapeland, Texas; St. Joe, Indiana; and Brigham City, Utah. Open-web joists, in contrast to solid joists, were made of steel angle iron separated by round bars or smaller angle iron. These joists cost less and were of greater strength for many applications; they were used primarily as the roof support systems in larger buildings, such as warehouses and stores.

The joist industry was characterized by high competition among many manufacturers for many small customers. The Vulcraft divisions had over 3,000 customers, none of whom dominated the business. With an estimated 35 percent of the market, Nucor was the largest supplier in the United States. It utilized national advertising campaigns and prepared competitive bids on 80 percent to 90 percent of buildings using joists. Competition was based on price and delivery performance. Nucor had developed computer programs to prepare designs for customers and to compute bids based on current prices and labor standards. In addition, each Vulcraft plant maintained its own engineering department to help customers with design problems or specifications. The Florence manager commented, "Here on the East Coast we have six or seven major competitors; of course none of them are as large as we are. The competition for any order will be heavy, and we will see six or seven different prices." He added, "I think we have a strong selling force in the marketplace. It has been said to us by some of our competitors that in this particular industry we have the finest selling organization in the country."

Nucor aggressively sought to be the lowest-cost producer in the industry. Materials and freight were two important elements of cost. Nucor maintained its own fleet of over 150 trucks to ensure on-time delivery to all of the states, although most business was regional because of transportation costs. Plants were located in rural areas near the markets they served. The Florence manager stated, "I don't feel there's a joist producer in the country that can match our cost. . . . We are sticklers about cutting out unnecessary overhead. Because we put so much responsibility on our people and because we have what I think is an excellent incentive program, our people are willing to work harder to accomplish these profitable goals."

PRODUCTION

On the basic assembly line used at Nucor, three or four of which might make up any one plant, about six tons per hour would be assembled. In the first stage eight people cut the angles to the right lengths or bent the round bars to the desired form. These were moved on a roller conveyer to six-man assembly stations where the component parts would be tacked together for the next stage, welding. Drilling and miscellaneous work was done by three people between the lines. The nine-man welding station completed the welds before passing the joists on roller conveyers to two-man inspection teams. The last step before shipment was the painting. The workers had control over and responsibility for quality. There was an independent quality control inspector who had the authority to reject the run of joists and cause them to be reworked. The quality control people were not under the incentive system and reported to the engineering department.

Daily production might vary widely, since each joist was made for a specific job. The wide range of joists made control of the workload at each station difficult; bottlenecks might arise anywhere along the line. Each work station was responsible for identifying such bottlenecks so that the foreman could reassign people promptly to maintain productivity. Since workers knew most of the jobs on the line, including the more skilled welding jobs, they could be shifted as needed. Work on the line was described by one general manager as "not machine type, but mostly physical labor." He said the important thing was to avoid bottlenecks.

There were four lines of about 28 people each on two shifts at the Florence division. The amount of time required to make a joist had been established as a result of experience; the general manager had seen no time studies in his 15 years with the company. As a job was bid, the cost of each joist was determined through the computer program. The time required depended on the length, number of panels, and depth of the joist. The jobs on the line were rated on responsibility and assigned a base wage, from $6 to $8 per hour. In addition, a weekly bonus was paid on the total output of each line which about doubled the pay. Workers received the same percentage bonus on their base wages.

At the time of production the labor value of production, the standard, was determined in a similar manner. The general manager stated, "In the last nine or ten years we have not changed a standard." The standards list in use was over 10 years old. Previously, they adjusted the standard if the bonus was too high. He said the technological improvements over the last few years had been small. The general manager reported that the bonus had increased from about 60 percent nine years earlier to about 100 percent in 1982 and had stabilized at that point. Exhibits 6 and 7 show data typically computed on performance and used by the manager. He said the difference in performance on the line resulted from the different abilities of the crews.

In discussing his philosophy for dealing with the work force, the Florence manager stated:

> I believe very strongly in the incentive system we have. We are a nonunion shop and we all feel that the way to stay so is to take care of our people and show them we care. I think that's easily done because of our fewer layers of management. . . . I spend a good part of my time in the plant, maybe an hour or so a day. If a man wants to know anything, for example an insurance question, I'm there and they walk right up to me and ask me questions which I'll answer the best I know how. . . .
>
> We don't lay our people off and we make a point of telling our people this. In the economic slump of 1982, we scheduled our line for four days, but the men were allowed to come in the fifth day for maintenance work at base pay. The men in the plant on an average running bonus might make $13 an hour. If their base pay is half that, on Friday they would only get $6 to $7 an hour. Surprisingly, many of the men did not want to come in on Friday. They felt comfortable with just working four days a week. They were happy to have that extra day off.

In April 1982 the executive committee decided, in view of economic conditions, that a pay freeze was necessary. The employees normally received an

EXHIBIT 6 Tons per Man-hour 52-Week Moving Average

1977	0.163	1983	0.215
1978	0.179	1984	0.214
1979	0.192	1985	0.228
1980	0.195	1986	0.225
1981	0.194	1987	0.218
1982	0.208		

EXHIBIT 7 Sample of Percentage Performance, July 1982

	Line			
Shift	**1**	**2**	**3**	**4**
First	117	97	82	89
Second	98	102	94	107

increase in their base pay the first of June. The decision was made at that time to freeze wages. The officers of the company, as a show of good faith, accepted a 5 percent pay cut. The 1991 economic slowdown had put several plants on short workweeks. About 20 percent of the people took the fifth day at base rate, but still no one had been laid off.

STEEL DIVISIONS

Nucor had six steel mills in five locations: Indiana, Nebraska, South Carolina, Texas, and Utah. The first mill was built in 1968 to supply the joist plants. The mills were modern mini-mills, all built within the last 20 years to convert scrap steel into standard angles, flats, rounds, and channels using the latest technology. Sales in 1990 were 2.8 million tons, a 42-percent increase over that of 1989. This figure represented about 80 percent of the mills' output, the remainder (0.6 million) being used by other Nucor divisions. In recent years Nucor had broadened its product line to include a wider range of steel chemistries, sizes, and special shapes. The total capacity of the mills had risen from 120,000 tons in 1990 to about 4 million tons in 1990.

Iverson explained in 1984:

In constructing these mills we have experimented with new processes and new manufacturing techniques. We serve as our own general contractor and design and build much of our own equipment. In one or more of our mills we have built our own continuous casting unit, reheat furnaces, cooling beds, and in Utah even our own mill stands. All of these to date have cost under $125 per ton of annual capacity, compared with projected costs for large integrated mills of $1,200 to $1,500 per ton of annual capacity, ten times our cost. Our mills have high productivity. We currently use less than four man-hours to produce a ton of steel. This includes everyone in the operation: maintenance, clerical, accounting, and sales and management. On the basis of our production workers alone, it is less than three man-hours per ton. Our total employment costs are less than $60 per ton compared with the average employment costs of the seven largest U.S. steel companies of close to $130 per ton. Our total labor costs are less than 20 percent of our sales price.

In contrast to Nucor's less than four man-hours, similar Japanese mills were said to require more than five hours and comparable U.S. mills over six hours.

Nucor's average yield from molten metal to finished products was over 90 percent, compared with an average U.S. steel-industry yield of about 74 percent, giving energy costs of about $39 per ton compared with their $75 a ton. Nucor ranked 46th on *Iron Age*'s annual survey of world steel producers. It was second on the list of top ten producers of steel worldwide based on tons per employee, at 981 tons. The head of the list was Tokyo Steel at 1,485. U.S. Steel was seventh at 479. Some other results were: Nippon Steel, 453; British Steel, 213; Bethlehem Steel, 329; Kruppstahl, 195; Weirton Steel, 317; and North Star Steel, 936. Nucor also ranked seventh on the list ranking growth of raw steel production. U.S. Steel was fifth on the same list. U.S. Steel topped the list based on improvement in tons-per-employee, at 56 percent; Nucor was seventh with a 12-percent improvement.

THE STEELMAKING PROCESS

A steel mill's work is divided into two phases, preparation of steel of the proper chemistry and forming of the steel into the desired products. The typical mini-mill utilized scrap steel, such as junk auto parts, instead of the iron ore which would be used in larger, integrated steel mills. The typical mini-mill had an annual capacity of 200,000 to 600,000 tons, compared with the 7 million tons of Bethlehem Steel's Sparrow's Point, Maryland integrated plant.

A charging bucket fed loads of scrap steel into electric arc furnaces. The melted load, called a *heat*, was poured into a ladle to be carried by overhead crane to the casting machine. In the casting machine the liquid steel was extruded as a continuous, red-hot, solid bar of steel and cut into lengths weighing some 900 pounds called *billets*. In the typical plant the billet, about four inches in cross-section and about 20 feet long, was held temporarily in a pit where it cooled to normal temperatures. Periodically billets were carried to the rolling mill and placed in a reheat oven to bring them up to 2,000°F at which temperature they would be malleable. In the rolling mill, presses and dies progressively converted the billet into the desired round bars, angles, channels, flats, and other products. After cutting to standard lengths, they were moved to the warehouse.

Nucor was also perhaps the only mill in the country which regularly avoided the reheating of billets. This saved $10 to $12 per ton in fuel usage and losses due to oxidation of the steel. The cost of developing this process had been $12 million. All research projects had not been successful. The company spent approximately $2 million in an unsuccessful effort to utilize resistance heating. It lost even more on an effort at induction melting. As Iverson told *Metal Producing*, "That cost us a lot of money. Timewise it was very expensive. But you have got to make mistakes and we've had lots of failures."

The first plant at Darlington became the basis for plants in Nebraska, Texas, and Utah. The Texas plant had cost under $80 per ton of annual capacity. Whereas the typical mini-mill in 1988 cost approximately $250 per ton, the average cost of all four of Nucor's mills was under $135. An integrated mill was expected to cost between $1,200 and $1,500 per ton.

The Darlington plant was organized into 12 natural groups for the purpose of incentive pay: two mills each had two shifts with three groups—melting and casting, rolling mill, and finishing. In melting and casting there were three or four different standards, depending on the material, established by the department manager years ago based on historical performance. The general manager stated, "We don't change the standards." The caster, the key to the operation, was used at a 92-percent level, 1 percent greater than the claims of the manufacturer. For every good ton of billet above the standard hourly rate for the week, workers in the group received a 4-percent bonus. For example, with a common standard of 10 tons per run hour and an actual rate for the week of 28 tons per hour, the workers would receive a bonus of 72 percent of their base rate in the week's paycheck.

In the rolling mill there were more than 100 products, each with a different historical standard. Workers received a 4-percent to 6-percent bonus for every good ton sheared per hour for the week over the computed standard. The Darlington general manager said the standard would be changed only if there was a major machinery change and that a standard had not been changed since the initial development period for the plant. He commented that in exceeding the standard, the worker wouldn't work harder, but would cooperate to avoid problems and move more quickly if a problem developed: "If there is a way to improve output, they will tell us." Another manager added: "Meltshop employees don't ask me how much it costs Chaparral or LTV to make a billet. They want to know what it costs Darlington, Norfolk, or Jewitt to put a billet on the ground. Everybody from Charlotte to Plymouth watches the nickels and dimes."

The Darlington manager, who became COO in 1984, stated:

> The key to making a profit when selling a product with no aesthetic value, or a product that you really can't differentiate from your competitors, is cost. I don't look at us as a fantastic marketing organization, even though I think we are pretty good; but we don't try to overcome unreasonable costs by mass marketing. We maintain low costs by keeping the employee force at the level it should be, not doing things that aren't necessary to achieve our goals, and allowing people to function on their own and by judging them on their results.
>
> To keep a cooperative and productive work force you need, number one, to be completely honest about everything; number two, to allow each employee as much as possible to make decisions about that employee's work, to find easier and more productive ways to perform duties; and number three, to be as fair as possible to all employees. Most of the changes we make in work procedures and in equipment come from the employees. They really know the problems of their jobs better than anyone else.

THE INCENTIVE SYSTEM

Although the most famous aspect of Nucor's personnel system was its incentive plan, a major personnel policy was providing job security. Also, all employees at Nucor received the same fringe benefits; there was only one group insurance plan and holidays and vacations did not differ by job. The company had no executive dining rooms or restrooms, and no fishing lodges, company cars, or reserved parking places.

Absenteeism and tardiness were not problems at Nucor. Each employee had four days of absence before pay was reduced. In addition to these, missing work was allowed for jury duty, military leave, or the death of close relatives. After this, a day's absence cost them bonus pay for that week and lateness of more than one half-hour meant the loss of bonus for that day.

The average hourly worker's pay in 1987 in South Carolina was $31,000, compared with the average earnings in manufacturing in that state of slightly more than $13,000. The personnel manager believed that pay was not the only thing the workers liked about Nucor. He said that an NBC interviewer, working on the documentary "If Japan Can, Why Can't We," often heard, "I enjoy working for Nucor because Nucor is the best, the most productive, and the most profitable company that I know of."

"I honestly feel that if someone performs well, they should share in the company and if they are going to share in the success, they should also share in the failures," Iverson stated. There were four incentive programs at Nucor, one each for production workers; department heads; staff people such as accountants, secretaries, or engineers; and senior management, which included the division managers. All of these programs were on a group basis.

The first program, for the production lines, has been described. The second incentive program was for department heads in the various divisions. The incentive pay here was based on division contribution, defined as the division earnings before corporate expenses and profit sharing are determined. Bonuses were reported to run as high as 82 percent of a person's base salary in the divisions and 59 percent for corporate positions.

There was a third plan for people who were neither production workers nor department managers. Their bonus was based on either the division return on assets or the corporate return on assets.

The fourth program was for the senior officers. The senior officers had no employment contracts, pension or retirement plans, or other normal perquisites. Their base salaries were set at about 80 percent of what an individual doing similar work in other companies would receive. Half the bonus was paid in cash and half was deferred. Once return on equity reached 8 percent, slightly below the average for manufacturing firms, 5 percent of net earnings before taxes went into a pool that was divided among the officers based on their salaries. "Now if return on equity for the company reaches, say 20 percent, which it has, then we can wind up with as much as 190 percent of our base salaries and 115 percent on top of that in stock. We get both." In 1982 the return was 9 percent and the executives received no bonus. His pay in 1981 was approximately $300,000, but dropped the next year to $110,000. "I think that ranked by total compensation, I was the lowest-paid CEO in the *Fortune* 500. I was kind of proud of that, too." In 1986 Iverson's stock was worth over $10 million. The young Vulcraft manager was likewise a millionaire.

The company had no retirement plan at all, income or medical. Instead, the company had a profit-sharing plan with a deferred trust. Each year 10 percent of pretax earnings was put into profit sharing. Fifteen percent of this was set aside to be paid to employees in the following March as a cash bonus and the remainder was put into trust for each employee on the basis of percent of their earnings as a percent of total wages paid within the corporation.

Nucor had no trouble finding people to staff its plants. When the mill in Texas was built in 1975 there were over 5,000 applications for the 400 jobs, many coming from people in Houston and Dallas. Yet everyone did not find work at

Nucor what they wanted. In 1975 a Harvard team found high turnover among new production workers after startup. The cause appeared to be pressure from fellow workers in the group-incentive situation. A survival-of-the-fittest situation was found in which those who didn't like to work seldom stuck around. "Productivity increased and turnover declined dramatically once these people left," the Harvard team concluded. Iverson commented: "A lot of people aren't goal-oriented. A lot of them don't want to work that hard, so initially we have a lot of turnover in a plant, but then it's so low we don't even measure after that."

The Wall Street Journal reported in 1981:

> Harry Pigg, a subdistrict director for the USW in South Carolina, sees a darker side in Nucor's incentive plan. He contends that Nucor unfairly penalizes workers by taking away big bonus payments for absence or tardiness, regardless of the reason. Workers who are ill, he says, try to work because they can't afford to give up the bonus payment. "Nucor whips them into line," he adds. He acknowledges, though, that high salaries are the major barrier to unionizing the company.

Having welcomed a parade of visitors over the years, Iverson had become concerned with the pattern: "They only do one or two of the things we do. It's not just incentives or the scholarship program; its all those things put together that results in a unified philosophy for the company."

AS 1991 BEGAN

Looking ahead in 1984, Iverson had said: "The next decade will be an exciting one for steel producers. It will tax our abilities to keep pace with technological changes we can see now on the horizon." Imports didn't have to dominate the U.S. economy. He believed the steel industry would continue to play a pivotal role in the growth of American industry. He pointed out comparative advantages of the U.S. steel industry: an abundance of resources, relatively low energy costs, lower transportation costs, and a change in the government's attitude toward business.

The excitement he had predicted had occurred. Imports were a challenge for steel, just as for textiles, shoes, machine tools, and computers. The old steel companies were flexing their muscles and getting back into the game. Overcapacity hadn't left the mini-mill immune, there was no safe haven for anyone. Nucor was no longer a small company, a David with free shots at Goliath. The honeymoon appeared over. Wall Street worried about what Nucor should do. Cable News Network posed the position of some on Wall Street:

> They say basically you guys are selling to the construction companies, you are selling to some fairly depressed industries. They also say, Nucor, they were a specialized little niche company. They did what they did very well; but now all of a sudden, they are going out, building these big mills to make huge pieces of steel and they are talking casted cold, all that stuff. They're worried that you may be getting into deals that are a little too complicated from what they perceive you as being able to do well.

Iverson told CNN in 1991:

We've decided that really we want to stay in that niche [steel]. We don't want to buy any banks. . . . All of the growth of the company has been internally generated. We think there are opportunities in the steel industry today. . . . There are ample opportunities, although they are somewhat harder to find than they used to be.

Another of my strengths is the ability to stick to my knitting. The reason executives make a lot of mistakes is that sometimes they get bored. They think the grass is greener on the other side so they go out and buy a bank or an oil company or they go into businesses where they have no expertise. . . . I have never gotten bored with this company. I've done this job so long that I think I have some insight into the needs and the capabilities of the company. I'm not misled into thinking we can do something that we can't.

Nucor had sold the Chemicals Division, gotten into the structural steel components business, into the fastener industry, and was now ready to go head-to-head with the major integrated producers for the lucrative flat-rolled market. Sales and earnings were projected to double in the next few years, as the stock price doubled or tripled. Iverson's position was clear: "We're going to stay in steel and steel products. The way we look at it, this company does only two things well, builds plants economically and runs them efficiently. That is the whole company. We don't have any financial expertise, we're not entrepreneurs, we're not into acquisitions. Steel may not be the best business in the world, but it's what we know how to do and we do it well."

Sidney wanted to draw lessons from Nucor and to decide who in the family to recommend the company to. One more beverage then to work.

APPENDIX A Nucor Corporation Balance Sheet Data, 1981 through 1991

	1981	1982	1983	1984	1985	1986
Assets						
Current assets						
Cash and short-term investments	$ 8,704,859	$ 44,892,546	$ 79,054,410	$112,710,490	$185,144,473	$128,736,584
Accounts receivable	42,983,058	34,685,498	51,110,372	58,408,244	60,390,448	61,268,892
Inventories	78,715,785	52,488,077	63,613,905	82,260,117	89,120,101	105,594,811
Other current assets	978,590	476,527	110,475	74,522	114,125	137,968
Total current assets	131,382,292	132,542,648	193,889,162	253,453,373	334,769,147	295,738,255
Property, plant, and equipment						
Land and improvements	12,142,613	12,215,375	12,577,104	12,918,519	12,818,723	15,041,782
Buildings and improvements	53,037,722	53,668,523	55,971,208	58,909,921	61,709,286	75,217,588
Plant machinery and equipment	245,037,510	244,143,769	258,305,715	277,553,868	279,579,407	331,945,921
Office and transportation equipment	6,868,069	9,565,667	9,736,448	8,643,752	14,883,272	16,358,988
Construction in process and equipment deposits	2,559,867	3,279,232	2,444,220	2,576,972	7,505,692	18,736,585
Total property, plant, and equipment	319,645,781	322,872,566	339,034,695	360,603,032	376,496,380	457,300,864
Less accumulated depreciation	66,245,946	83,782,273	107,356,805	131,867,940	150,954,339	181,431,475
Net property, plant, and equipment	253,399,835	239,090,293	231,677,890	228,735,092	225,542,041	275,869,389
Total assets	$384,782,127	$371,632,941	$425,567,052	$482,188,465	$560,311,188	$571,607,644
Liabilities and Stockholders' Equity						
Current liabilities						
Long-term debt due within 1 year	$ 1,654,784	$ 1,603,462	$ 2,402,462	$ 2,402,462	$ 2,402,462	$ 3,052,462
Accounts payable	32,237,889	22,948,867	37,135,084	32,691,249	35,473,011	53,165,551
Federal income taxes	10,733,627	12,535,096	14,813,909	23,705,195	27,597,464	14,309,565
Salaries, wages, and related accruals	13,599,760	12,278,322	13,610,725	19,968,420	24,342,710	21,267,243
Accrued expenses and other current liabilities	14,806,253	16,736,959	20,524,615	21,766,358	31,440,181	26,646,152
Total current liabilities	73,032,313	66,102,706	88,486,795	100,533,684	121,255,828	118,440,973
Long-term debt due after 1 year	83,754,231	48,229,615	45,731,000	43,232,384	40,233,769	42,147,654
Deferred credits and other liabilities	15,619,563	25,019,563	33,219,563	38,819,563	41,319,563	27,319,563
Minority interest	—	—	—	—	—	—
Stockholders' equity						
Common stock	2,797,948	2,802,796	5,642,727	5,669,757	5,732,382	8,665,397
Additional paid-in capital	16,531,759	17,696,568	17,022,043	18,991,334	24,299,195	25,191,988
Retained earnings	193,355,403	211,921,654	235,569,108	275,035,788	327,816,850	367,575,659
Treasury stock	(309,090)	(139,961)	(104,184)	(94,045)	(346,399)	(17,733,590)
Total stockholders' equity	212,376,020	232,281,057	258,129,694	299,602,834	357,502,028	383,699,454
Total liabilities and stockholders' equity	$384,782,127	$371,632,941	$425,567,052	$482,188,465	$560,311,188	$571,607,644

	1987	1988	1989	1990	1991
Assets					
Current assets					
Cash and short-term investments	$ 72,779,584	$ 26,380,115	$ 32,553,520	$ 51,648,627	$ 38,294,777
Accounts receivable	80,080,553	97,427,217	106,950,620	124,255,998	109,458,440
Inventories	81,497,469	123,215,022	139,449,786	136,643,745	186,074,784
Other current assets	359,631	736,262	1,080,008	89,116	465,243
Total current assets	234,717,237	247,758,616	280,033,934	312,637,486	334,293,244
Property, plant, and equipment					
Land and improvements	23,143,374	30,309,295	29,829,310	30,642,736	31,471,757
Buildings and improvements	87,690,196	113,985,857	118,362,171	125,917,477	133,508,869
Plant machinery and equipment	375,446,242	604,990,695	866,721,302	905,687,289	925,224,504
Office and transportation equipment	15,080,397	14,416,129	13,318,378	14,961,929	15,614,487
Construction in process and equipment deposits	117,174,597	178,569,987	19,781,432	9,154,660	157,712,936
Total property, plant, and equipment	618,534,806	942,271,963	1,048,012,593	1,086,364,091	1,261,532,553
Less accumulated depreciation	199,161,904	240,368,869	294,215,015	363,115,517	414,248,999
Net property, plant, and equipment	419,372,902	701,903,094	753,797,578	723,248,574	847,283,554
Total assets	$654,090,139	$949,661,710	$1,033,831,512	$1,035,886,060	$1,181,576,798
Liabilities and Stockholders' Equity					
Current liabilities					
Long-term debt due within 1 year	$ 2,210,154	$ 2,214,000	$ 2,267,000	$ 2,204,500	$ 1,999,000
Accounts payable	68,459,917	93,171,767	89,746,212	82,221,596	93,761,659
Federal income taxes	24,343,944	35,803,552	13,203,371	10,650,895	11,069,489
Salaries, wages, and related accruals	21,959,086	32,846,065	31,612,176	44,040,574	43,021,229
Accrued expenses and other current liabilities	30,500,169	52,071,918	56,731,786	63,671,729	79,314,871
Total current liabilities	147,473,270	216,107,302	193,560,545	202,789,294	229,166,248
Long-term debt due after 1 year	35,462,500	113,248,500	155,981,500	28,777,000	72,778,000
Deferred credits and other liabilities	19,319,563	15,319,563	18,819,563	46,121,499	43,975,161
Minority interest	23,825,439	72,704,896	81,024,425	105,441,051	124,048,398
Stockholders' equity					
Common stock	8,701,944	8,737,064	8,781,534	8,815,775	8,860,517
Additional paid-in capital	27,379,060	30,542,937	34,226,463	37,669,232	42,814,342
Retained earnings	410,510,347	511,456,991	559,895,248	624,662,995	678,160,942
Treasury stock	(18,581,984)	(18,455,543)	(18,457,766)	(18,390,786)	(18,226,810)
Total stockholders' equity	428,009,367	532,281,449	584,445,479	652,757,216	711,608,991
Total liabilities and stockholders' equity	$654,090,139	$949,661,710	$1,033,831,512	$1,035,886,060	$1,181,576,798

APPENDIX B Nucor Corporation Sales, Earnings, and Statistical Data, 1981 through 1991

	1981	1982	1983	1984	1985	1986
For the Year						
Sales, costs, and earnings						
Net sales	$544,820,621	$486,018,162	$542,531,431	$660,259,922	$758,495,374	$755,228,939
Costs and expenses						
Cost of products sold	456,210,289	408,606,641	461,727,688	539,731,252	600,797,865	610,378,369
Marketing, administrative, and other expenses	33,524,820	31,720,377	33,988,054	45,939,311	59,079,802	65,900,653
Interest expense (income)	10,256,546	7,899,110	(748,619)	(3,959,092)	(7,560,645)	(5,288,971)
Total costs and expenses	499,991,655	448,226,128	494,967,123	581,711,471	652,317,022	670,990,051
Earnings from operations before federal income taxes	44,828,966	37,792,034	47,564,308	78,548,451	106,178,352	84,238,888
Federal income taxes	10,100,000	15,600,000	19,700,000	34,000,000	47,700,000	37,800,000
Earnings from operations	34,728,966	22,192,034	27,864,308	44,548,451	58,478,352	46,438,888
Gain on sale of Research Chemicals	—	—	—	—	—	—
Net earnings	$ 34,728,966	$ 22,192,034	$ 27,864,308	$ 44,548,451	$ 58,478,352	$ 46,438,888
Earnings per share						
Earnings per share from operations	$1.67	$1.06	$1.32	$2.10	2.74	2.17
Gain per share on sale of Research Chemicals	—	—	—	—	—	—
Net earnings per share	1.67	1.06	1.32	2.10	2.74	2.17
Dividends declared per share	0.16	0.17	0.20	0.24	0.27	0.31
Percentage of earnings from operations to sales	6.4%	4.6%	5.1%	6.7%	7.7%	6.1%
Percentage of earnings from operations to average equity	17.8%	10.0%	11.4%	16.0%	17.8%	12.5%
Average shares outstanding	20,756,583	20,912,577	21,066,448	21,169,492	21,345,852	21,405,440
Sales per employee	$155,663	$133,156	$148,639	$176,069	197,011	181,983
At Year End						
Working capital	$ 58,349,979	$ 66,439,942	$105,402,367	$152,919,689	$213,513,319	$177,297,282
Current ratio	1.8	2.0	2.2	2.5	2.8	2.5
Stockholders' equity per per share	10.17	11.07	12.21	14.10	16.65	18.16
Shares outstanding	20,890,521	20,987,823	21,135,272	21,241,618	21,472,508	2,131,298
Stockholders	22,000	22,000	21,000	22,000	22,000	22,000
Employees	3,700	3,600	3,700	3,800	3,900	4,400

	1987	1988	1989	1990	1991
For the Year					
Sales, costs, and earnings					
Net sales	$851,022,039	$1,061,364,009	$1,269,007,472	$1,481,630,011	$1,465,456,566
Costs and expenses					
Cost of products sold	713,346,451	889,140,323	1,105,248,906	1,293,082,950	1,302,744,052
Marketing, administrative, and other expenses	55,405,961	62,083,752	66,990,065	70,461,830	66,986,699
Interest expense (income)	(964,823)	2,558,914	11,132,657	6,869,970	(90,684)
Total costs and expenses	767,787,589	953,782,989	1,183,371,628	1,370,414,750	1,369,640,067
Earnings from operations before federal income taxes	83,234,450	107,581,020	85,635,844	111,215,261	95,816,499
Federal income taxes	32,700,000	36,700,000	27,800,000	36,150,000	31,100,000
Earnings from operations	50,534,450	70,881,020	57,835,844	75,065,261	64,716,499
Gain on sale of Research Chemicals	—	38,558,822	—	—	—
Net earnings	$ 50,534,450	$ 109,439,842	$ 57,835,844	$ 75,065,261	$ 64,716,499
Earnings per share					
Earnings per share from operations	2.39	3.34	2.71	3.50	3.00
Gain per share on sale of Research Chemicals	—	1.82	—	—	—
Net earnings per share	2.39	5.16	2.71	3.50	3.00
Dividends declared per share	0.36	0.40	0.44	0.48	0.52
Percentage of earnings from operations to sales	5.9%	6.7%	4.6%	5.1%	4.4%
Percentage of earnings from operations to average equity	12.5%	15.4%	10.4%	12.1%	9.5%
Average shares outstanding	21,153,584	21,224,217	21,342,888	21,441,079	21,559,933
Sales per employee	189,116	218,838	241,716	271,859	264,046
At Year End					
Working capital	$ 87,243,967	$ 31,651,314	$ 86,473,389	$ 109,848,192	$ 105,126,996
Current ratio	1.6	1.1	1.4	1.5	1.5
Stockholders' equity per share	20.19	25.00	27.31	30.38	32.94
Shares outstanding	21,196,088	21,287,691	21,399,620	21,487,674	21,604,451
Stockholders	27,000	28,000	25,000	27,000	27,000
Employees	4,600	5,100	5,400	5,500	5,600

APPENDIX C Nucor Corporation Cash Flow Data, 1981 through 1991

	1981	1982	1983	1984	1985	1986
Operating activities						
Earnings						
Earnings from operations	$34,728,966	$22,192,034	$27,864,308	$ 44,548,451	$ 58,478,352	$ 46,438,888
Gain on sale of Research Chemicals	—	—	—	—	—	—
Net earnings	34,728,966	22,192,034	27,864,308	44,548,451	58,478,352	46,438,888
Adjustments						
Depreciation of plant and equipment	21,599,951	26,286,671	27,109,582	28,899,421	31,105,788	34,931,520
Gain on sale of Research Chemicals	—	—	—	—	—	—
Deferred federal income taxes	8,100,000	9,400,000	8,200,000	5,600,000	2,500,000	(14,000,000)
Minority interest	—	—	—	—	—	—
Changes in						
Accounts receivable	(7,445,099)	8,297,560	(16,424,874)	(7,297,872)	(1,982,204)	(878,444)
Inventories	(21,130,535)	26,227,708	(11,125,828)	(18,646,212)	(6,859,984)	(16,474,710)
Accounts payable	(4,403,102)	(9,289,022)	14,186,217	(4,443,835)	2,781,762	17,692,540
Federal income taxes	6,371,008	1,801,469	2,278,813	8,891,286	3,892,269	(13,287,899)
Other	4,225,183	1,663,550	5,644,537	7,911,650	14,747,671	(7,518,749)
	$42,046,372	$86,579,970	$57,732,755	$ 65,462,889	$104,663,654	$ 46,903,146
Investing activities						
Capital expenditures	($99,521,176)	($14,023,849)	($19,971,317)	($ 26,333,882)	($ 28,701,463)	($ 86,201,391)
Disposition of plant and equipment	276,200	1,494,501	115,712	101,000	49,565	567,933
Proceeds from sale of Research Chemicals	—	—	—	—	—	—
	($99,244,976)	($12,529,348)	($19,855,605)	($ 26,232,882)	($ 28,651,898)	($ 85,633,458)
Financing activities						
New long-term debt	$46,400,000	$ 7,500,000	—	—	—	$ 6,234,450
Reduction in long-term debt	(2,292,969)	(43,075,938)	($ 1,699,615)	($ 2,498,616)	—	(3,670,565)
Issuance of common stock	3,368,960	1,459,008	2,201,183	2,006,460	5,387,182	3,954,559
Contribution for (distribution to) minority interest	—	—	—	—	—	—
Cash dividends	(3,325,596)	(3,625,783)	(4,216,854)	(5,081,771)	(5,697,290)	(6,680,079)
Acquisition of treasury stock	—	(120,222)	—	—	(269,050)	(17,515,942)
	$44,150,395	($37,862,935)	($ 3,715,286)	($ 5,573,927)	($ 3,577,773)	($ 17,677,577)
Increase (decrease) in cash and short-term investments	($13,048,209)	$36,187,687	$34,161,864	$ 33,656,080	$ 72,433,983	($ 56,407,889)
Cash and short-term investments—beginning of year	21,753,068	8,704,859	44,892,546	79,054,410	112,710,490	185,144,473
Cash and short-term investments—end of year	$ 8,704,859	$44,892,546	$79,054,410	$112,710,490	$185,144,473	$128,736,584

	1987	1988	1989	1990	1991
Operating activities					
Earnings					
Earnings from operations	$ 50,534,450	$ 70,881,020	$ 57,835,844	$ 75,065,261	$ 64,716,499
Gain on sale of Research Chemicals	—	38,558,822	—	—	—
Net earnings	50,534,450	109,439,842	57,835,844	75,065,261	64,716,499
Adjustments					
Depreciation of plant and equipment	41,793,009	56,264,631	76,571,240	84,960,263	93,577,626
Gain on sale of Research Chemicals	—	(38,558,822)	—	—	—
Deferred federal income taxes	(8,000,000)	(4,000,000)	3,500,000	7,000,000	(4,000,000)
Minority interest	(1,007,761)	(16,937,343)	8,319,529	29,708,626	26,114,147
Changes in					
Accounts receivable	(18,811,661)	(18,928,357)	(9,523,403)	(17,305,378)	14,797,558
Inventories	24,097,342	(45,807,837)	(16,234,764)	2,806,041	(48,431,039)
Accounts payable	15,294,366	25,357,059	(3,425,555)	(7,524,616)	11,540,063
Federal income taxes	10,034,379	(8,540,392)	(22,600,181)	(2,552,476)	418,594
Other	6,070,625	23,605,230	3,561,781	42,172,185	15,662,629
	$120,004,749	$ 81,894,011	$ 98,004,491	$214,329,906	$173,396,077
Investing activities					
Capital expenditures	($188,990,476)	($345,632,411)	($130,200,982)	($ 56,753,994)	($217,721,085)
Disposition of plant and equipment	1,947,526	399,137	1,255,711	831,719	547,182
Proceeds from sale of Research Chemicals	—	78,500,908	—	—	—
	($187,042,950)	($266,732,366)	($128,945,271)	$ 55,922,275	($217,173,903)
Financing activities					
New long-term debt	—	$ 80,000,000	$ 45,000,000	—	$ 46,000,000
Reduction in long-term debt	($ 7,527,462)	(2,210,154)	(2,214,000)	($127,267,000)	(2,204,500)
Issuance of common stock	2,337,525	3,325,438	3,861,092	3,587,312	5,353,828
Contribution for (distribution to) minority interest	24,833,200	65,816,800	—	(5,292,000)	(7,506,800)
Cash dividends	(7,599,762)	(8,493,198)	(9,397,587)	(10,297,514)	(11,218,552)
Acquisition of treasury stock	(962,300)	—	(135,320)	(43,322)	—
	$ 11,081,201	$138,438,886	$ 37,114,185	($139,312,524)	$ 30,423,976
Increase (decrease) in cash and short-term investments	($ 55,957,000)	($ 46,399,469)	$ 6,173,405	$ 19,095,107	($ 13,353,850)
Cash and short-term investments—beginning of year	128,736,584	72,779,584	26,380,115	32,553,520	51,648,627
Cash and short-term investments—end of year	$ 72,779,584	$ 26,380,115	$ 32,553,520	$ 51,648,627	$ 38,294,777

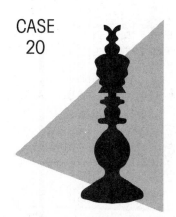

CASE
20

CHAPARRAL STEEL COMPANY—1990

JOHN W. SIMMONS &
MARK J. KROLL

COMPANY HISTORY

In 1973 Texas Industries, Inc. of Dallas, also known as TXI, a construction materials (cement, aggregates, and concrete products) company, and Co-Steel International, Ltd. of Canada decided to build a steel mill as a joint venture. The initial attraction of a small town 25 miles south of Dallas to the constructors of a steel mini-mill was its proximity to a major population center, large power suppliers, highways, and railroads. At the time, Midlothian, Texas seemed an unlikely choice, but, as the story goes, Co-Steel Chairman Gerald Heffernan saw a Midlothian Chamber of Commerce bulletin board notice that read, "Need money? Try working," and he was finally convinced that they had found the sought-after site for the new mill. The farm and ranch lands in the area are peopled with hard-working people deeply imbued with the work ethic that management was seeking. Few of the local residents had ever worked in a steel mill, and as one manager observed, "We didn't want people who had learned bad work habits."

TXI's decision to start its own steel company sprang naturally from its building materials business, since steel reinforcement is required in so much construction. Forecasting a reinforcing bar shortage that never developed, the new TXI venture, called the Chaparral Steel Company, had its initial steel production greeted by a glut in the rebar market. Observed one member of Chaparral's top management: "We had to diversify, and fast." Fortunately for the new manufacturer, flexibility, a trait that has virtually eluded domestic Big Steel firms, is one of the drawing cards in the mini-mill segment of the steel industry. Unlike the bigger, more complex integrated mills, the mini-mills are basically recycling plants, albeit technologically sophisticated ones. Having scaled-down operations and fewer steps in the manufacturing process provides the mini-mill with significantly more margin for error and therefore more flexibility than exists in the typical integrated mill.

The town of Midlothian (population 3,219) has achieved acclaim as the setting for a successful player in the nation's steel industry. Chaparral has proven it possible to be profitable and competitive in an industry facing perhaps the most difficult period in its history (Exhibit 1). Whereas U.S. Steel (now USX) lost $2.5 billion in 1982, Chaparral had a profit of $11 million. In fiscal 1987 Chaparral produced and shipped a company record of over 1.2 million tons of steel, and, for the first time, over half of the sales for TXI, which became the full owner in November 1985, were represented by Chaparral. Pursuing market share amid its efforts to be the primary low-cost producer in the marketplace, Chaparral in fiscal 1987 produced and sold more tonnage in a greater variety and over a wider geographic market than in any previous year. This record production was achieved in the face of what TXI's president and CEO, Robert D. Rogers, referring to Texas

EXHIBIT 1   TXI Business Segment Information ($000)

	1988	1987	1986
Net sales			
Steel	$376,398	$318,807	$297,155
Cement/concrete	258,936	270,254	351,075
	$635,334	$589,061	$648,230
Operating profit			
Steel	$ 60,496	$ 42,171	$ 37,178
Cement/concrete	3,233	14,150	32,431
	63,729	56,321	69,609
Corporate expense (income):			
Administrative and general	14,605	16,912	14,836
Interest expense	38,043	38,740	41,880
Other income	(998)	(2,262)	(14,107)
Income before taxes and other items	$ 12,079	$ 2,931	$ 27,000
Depreciation, depletion and amortization			
Steel	$ 21,566	$ 23,567	$ 22,433
Cement/concrete	29,339	31,347	33,221
Corporate	634	510	790
	$ 51,539	$ 55,424	$ 56,444
Capital expenditures			
Steel	$ 22,265	$ 14,281	$ 7,019
Cement/concrete	17,443	14,422	40,969
Corporate	259	403	573
	$ 39,967	$ 29,106	$ 48,561
Identifiable assets			
Steel	$313,452	$310,063	$298,666
Cement/concrete	281,635	299,874	323,510
Corporate	67,026	68,836	86,607
	$662,113	$678,773	$708,783

and surrounding states, TXI's locus of operations, called, "the most stagnant economic growth since before Texas Industries was founded in 1951." In his letter to shareholders dated July 15, 1987 Rogers announced that initial shipments of steel were made that same month to Western Europe and noted that Chaparral's impressive results were accomplished in "only an average market for structural products and a declining market during the year for bar products." Chaparral is one of the most productive steel firms in the world in terms of labor and the nation's tenth largest steel maker, providing steel products to 44 states, Canada, and now Western Europe. The firm has been the only U.S. mini-mill to lower costs enough to make a profit in foreign markets. Efforts have also been made to crack the bureaucratic Japanese market.

Since its first day of operations, May 5, 1975, Chaparral has used unorthodox managerial methods to achieve and maintain its competitiveness. According to Tom Peters, "If you wrote down the ten most widely believed principles about managing in this century, you would find that Chaparral violates every one of them." Peters, one of the authors of *In Search of Excellence*, writes that some business savants consider Gordon Forward, Chaparral's president and CEO, to be "the most advanced thinker in American management today." Notwithstanding such hyperbole, the Midlothian steel firm is ever-watchful of its competitive environment and looks to the future rather than resting on its impressive early accomplishments. Noting that this U.S. steel producer is "one of the few profitable ones," Peters explains that Forward manages his firm "more as a laboratory than as a factory." Forward, a native of Canada, armed with a Ph.D in metallurgy from MIT and a healthy distaste for the traditional inefficiencies of big steel, has directed his company with managerial acumen, perceptive marketing, and a drive toward technological innovation. Company executives credit Chaparral's success to three major factors: a marketing strategy sympathetic to customers' needs, an insatiable thirst for technological improvement, and, perhaps most significantly, the application of participatory management techniques that encourage employee creativity.

At startup in 1975 Chaparral operated with only the basics of a mini-mill plant: a single electric arc furnace, a continuous billet caster, and a rolling mill, with an annual capacity of just over 400,000 tons. By 1978 the firm was a leader in mini-mill technology. From 1978 to 1981 Chaparral earned a pretax average of $18 million per year. Again, this was at a time when the U.S. steel industry as a whole was in the doldrums. Early in 1982 Chaparral's second phase of expansion brought on line a second electric arc furnace, another continuous billet caster, and a larger rolling mill. This $180-million, largely debt-financed expansion could not have occurred at a worse time, paralleling the start of the most serious steel recession in 50 years. Steel prices tumbled 20 to 50 percent, the industry's operating rate fell below 40 percent of capacity, and much of Chaparral's debt, at floating rates, floated to the outer reaches of the biosphere. Fueled by high interest rates, the dollar climbed to new heights, imported steel flooded domestic markets, and due to merciless economic conditions, Chaparral incurred losses between 1982 and 1984, returning to profitability in mid-1985. Maintaining a long-term vision of its industry, the highly automated mini-mill tripled its annual capacity between 1982 and 1987. With its new product development program, the firm shipped approximately 1.3 million tons of steel to more than 900 customers in fiscal 1988. Furthermore, Chaparral has added an average of 100,000 tons to its annual output during each of the past 13 years.

From the outset, TXI and Co-Steel wanted to build the most modern mini-mill possible. Free of the myopia that has diminished Big Steel, Chaparral has changed and grown constantly, if only incrementally. The attitude at TXI and Chaparral is that it is possible to make money in nongrowth industries if you are good enough. As a result of its vision and diligence, the Midlothian firm currently produces and ships more tonnage than any single U.S. steel mill constructed in the past 30 years. Although future growth in the mini-mill segment is expected to slow somewhat compared to the past decade or so, industry experts still see opportunities for additional growth. The "minis" are expected to retain an advantage because of their lower raw material costs, utilization of new technology, efficient operation, plant location, perceptive marketing, flexible work rules, and consequent higher productivity, but saturated markets and cheap imports are forcing the mini-mills to continue seeking new ways to grow. Prior to 1982 Chaparral was a part of the much publicized mini-mill phenomenon, but the future holds great challenges. In 1985 four Sunbelt mini-mills closed their doors, and global overcapacity portends a continued threat of industry shakeout. Older, less technologically competent minis are particularly vulnerable. Today producers of steel are differentiated mostly by price, product mix, and service. State-of-the-art technology is so accessible throughout the world that quality is no longer optional. The challenge that Chaparral has successfully faced in the past and will continue to face in the foreseeable future is to maintain its responsive managerial style, marketing sensitivity, and technological currency and consequent productivity gains. It appears that Chaparral is not striving to become the new Big Steel, but rather desires to maintain its status as a highly competitive niche player.

CHAPARRAL'S MANAGEMENT
Robert D. Rogers, Chairman of the Board

Robert Rogers, a graduate of Yale and the Harvard Business School, has been with TXI for 25 years. Mr. Rogers, chairman of the board of TXI and a TXI director since 1970, is chairman of the board of the Dallas Chamber of Commerce and the immediate past chairman of the 11th Federal Reserve District, and has numerous additional professional and community associations. Another TXI director, Edward W. Kelley, Jr., joined the Board of Governors of the Federal Reserve System in 1987.

In an interview, Mr. Rogers reflected on the unlikely success of an upstart company in a declining steel industry:

> We went into the carbon steel business when everyone else was going out of it. The biggest advantage we had was that we didn't have any plant, didn't have any customers, didn't have any employees or management, and we didn't really know anything about how to make steel. We're still learning. Once we learn it, we're going to be in big trouble.[1]

Pondering further the benefit of being the new kid on the block, Rogers observed:

> If we had known the steel business, we would have known that the only way you could go forth with a company of any size would be to be unionized. Not knowing the steel business and being the largest nonunion cement company in the United States, we felt it was far better to represent the legitimate interests of employees ourselves rather than turn it over to some outside partner.[2]

Concluding his remarks on Chaparral's unorthodox approach, Rogers said:

> Another thing was to hire employees who, by and large, did not come from industrial backgrounds. They came from rural backgrounds. The steel plant is next door to our largest cement plant, and we have the same type of employees there. We knew they were hard-working and imaginative, so they didn't know you were supposed to spend 3 to 4 manhours per ton of steel. When we got to 1.8 or 1.6 and were working to get down substantially less than that, they didn't know that there's a limit on how many tons of steel you can get per manhour.[3]

Despite recent economic setbacks for TXI as a whole, Chaparral remains strong and is moving forward, and Rogers and the TXI board of directors are still planning for the long term. Fiscal 1988 was the 26th consecutive year of increased cash dividends to TXI shareholders. Notwithstanding the virtual absence of earnings, due largely to the regional construction slump and the dumping in TXI markets of imported cement, the directors maintained cash dividends at the annual rate of $0.80 per year, with a year-end stock dividend of 4 percent (Exhibit 2).

Board of Directors

Chaparral's board of directors provides a wealth of educational, professional, and cultural experience. Past and present directors have served as university trustees and in other capacities of institutional leadership, and most have other corporate affiliations. Co-Steel Chairman Heffernan, who is involved with several Canadian mining and metallurgical professional groups, has been a TXI director since 1986 and is also a director of Chaparral. In October 1987 the board was reduced in number and reorganized to have a non-TXI majority. New board members are John M. Belk, chairman, Belk Stores Services, Inc., Charlotte, North Carolina; Dr. Gerhard Liener, chief financial officer, Daimler-Benz AG, Stuttgart, West Germany; and William J. Shields, president and CEO, Co-Steel International, Ltd., Toronto, Ontario, Canada.

Gordon E. Forward, President and CEO

Gordon Forward is described as the architect of the winning Chaparral formula and has received from various quarters the lion's share of the credit for making the

EXHIBIT 2 TXI and Subsidiaries: Selected Financial Data ($000 except per-share amounts)

	1988	1987	1986	1985	1984	1983	1982	1981
Results of operations								
Net sales	$635,334	$589,061	$648,230	$343,688	$335,381	$321,468	$282,713	$285,003
Net income	13,053	1,253	22,114	17,597	12,300	18,691	18,332	30,411
Return on common equity	6.8%	0.6%	11.9%	9.9%	7.2%	11.4%	11.9%	22.4%
Per-share information								
Net income	1.09	—	2.26	1.93	1.32	2.00	1.96	3.22
Cash dividends	0.80	0.76	0.73	0.70	0.67	0.64	0.62	0.60
Stock dividends, distributions	4%	4%	4%	4%	4%	4%	4%	4%
Other information								
Average common shares outstanding (000)	10,160	10,039	9,574	9,074	9,285	9,299	9,339	9,427
Number of common stockholders	5,632	5,975	5,508	5,811	6,111	6,286	6,605	6,785
Common stock price (high–low)	40–24	31–22	31–23	29–21	38–25	36–15	30–14	31–18

formula a success. After leaving a successful career with Big Steel, Forward has come up through the ranks of the mini-mill industry and has displayed a willingness to undertake managerial experiments. Forward claims that the legendary Captain Bill "Scrap Heap" Jones, a 19th-century steel mill superintendent, is a role model for his approach. Of Jones, Forward says:

> If there was a better machine to do a job, the old one went quickly on the scrap heap. He also fought for his men's welfare and inspired them to set world steel production records. And they loved him for it. I think the industry ought to take a new look at Captain Jones' ideas.[4]

Chaparral's operating philosophy of concentrating on technological movement, as well as on marketing and participatory management, emerged as early as 1974.

Mr. Forward, a native of Vancouver, British Columbia, has been referred to as "a refugee from Big Steel bureaucracy." He was hired as Chaparral's executive vice president in 1974. A vocal critic of the stagnating domestic steel industry, Forward, in an interview, remarked:

> U.S. steel producers had no real competition after [World War II]. Every time the unions demanded more wages or whatever, the managers said, "Fine, we'll simply pass the costs on to the consumer." Well, this went on for more than 20 years and had a real effect on how managers thought about staying on top technologically. . . . Of course, they spent money on improvement. But they went about it the way that bureaucracies are likely to go about something like that: they kept tacking new things on to their established operations.[5]

As steel labor costs rose in the 1970s, the mini-mills, quickly adopting foreign technological improvements, were able to seize new markets, and Chaparral was a leader of the pack. Says Forward: "In our end of the business, we can't afford to act like fat cats."

NATURE OF THE STEEL INDUSTRY
Big Steel

The term *Big Steel* generally refers to the large, traditional, integrated steel mills, so named because they have the capability of processing coke and iron ore into a number of steel products in a wide range of sizes and shapes. Steel mill products are consumed by industries touching virtually every aspect of daily life, principally transportation, construction, machinery, and containers. Prior to 1970, the United States had long been the world's leading steel producer, but by that time the domestic steel industry had been declining for over 20 years. Most U.S. steel mills were of pre–World-War II vintage and, despite periodic renovation, lacked the efficient layouts, the economies of scale, and the more productive technologies utilized in the greenfield mills of Japan and Western Europe.

After World War II, domestic negotiations with the United Steelworkers began an upward spiral of wage rates, disproportionate to the growth of labor productivity, thereby increasing unit labor costs. Wishing to reduce the escalating wage increases, which averaged 6.6 percent annually between 1947 and 1957, a period of relatively low inflation, Big Steel accepted a long strike (July to November 1959). Foreign producers consequently filled the gap, and the United States became a net importer of steel in 1959. Imports grew to an average 15 percent of consumption in the 1970s, 19 percent in 1981, and over 20 percent in 1982.

The world steel industry was becoming much more competitive and internationalized. World exports of finished steel products increased dramatically during the 1960s, prompted by declining raw material and shipping costs and powered by foreign investment in modern facilities. U.S. steel exports tumbled as Japanese and Western European exports skyrocketed. State-of-the-art technology became available to any producer willing to pay for it, and product quality became essentially uniform across geopolitical boundaries. During the 1970s U.S. domestic steel production grew only modestly, profits remained depressed as competition from imports grew, and, as a result, the U.S. industry's ability to add new capacity was severely constrained. Domestic industry employment began a steady decline in 1972, and in 1982 reached the lowest level since data collection began during the Great Depression. In 1982 the U.S. steel industry lost a record $3.2 billion. By mid-1987 the industry's operating losses had reached some $6 billion.

In March 1982, testifying before the U.S. Senate, Dr. Donald F. Barnett, speaking for the American Iron and Steel Institute (AISI) regarding international competitiveness in the domestic steel industry, stated:

> Perhaps the most significant determinant of international competitiveness is labor productivity. . . . However, even if labor productivity is low, a product can still be competitive if there are other compensating advantages, for example lower labor rates, as persist in many developing countries. Alternately, an investment which raises productivity can actually decrease cost competitiveness if the capital cost of the investment outweighs the labor savings. Hence, improved labor productivity cannot be the ultimate goal in and of itself. International competitiveness in the steel industry, therefore, must also look at capital efficiency, for example, capacity use, labor costs, raw material costs, yield rates, and energy efficiency.[6]

Other factors that determine industry competitiveness include regulatory costs and materials availability. Despite recent turmoil, the domestic integrated mills have increased their productivity in the last decade considerably vis-à-vis the Japanese mills (Exhibit 3). By 1986, AISI reports, the U.S. steel industry had become the most efficient in the world. Generally speaking, however, while the domestic steel industry is competitive in energy and materials costs and use, it is less competitive in terms of labor costs and productivity than foreign competitors.

Clearly, the integrated mills were attempting to respond to changing market conditions, as indicated by improved productivity rates. The big mills have gradually improved their marketing techniques by specializing in limited ranges of higher-quality, cost-competitive products. In a word, the Big Steel firms are no longer able to function as steel "supermarkets." The emphasis in recent years has been on restructuring, what one industry executive referred to as a "state of accelerating self-liquidation." Yet, the great shakeout has had a positive side.

EXHIBIT 3 Average Man-hours Required to Produce One Ton of Steel

	1977	**1986**	**1988**
U.S. integrated mills	10.04	6.91	—
Japanese integrated mills	8.94	8.61	—
U.S. mini-mills	—	2.00	1.50
Chaparral	—	1.60	—

Corporate reorganizations, steel unit spin-offs, forced mergers, management or employee buyouts, and Chapter 11 bankruptcies have required firms to pare costs and exit from unprofitable markets. In 1987 the domestic integrated mills began to emerge from this period of price-war activity; prices firmed for the first time in years as the dollar declined in relation to other currencies, earnings improved amid productivity gains, and export activity began to awaken. Unfortunately, the stock market crash of October 19, 1987, occurred just as the moribund steel industry was reviving. Despite the 33-percent drop in steel stock prices, analysts predict sharp increases in earnings, due to a falling dollar and steel import quotas legislated through September 1989. Despite recent difficulties in earning, attracting, and borrowing sufficient investment capital, the domestic integrated firms have retained a large share of the U.S. market.

The growth of U.S. production is projected to remain relatively low due to trends in consumption and output. Projections of world steel production indicate a continuing malaise in the industrialized nations, in contrast to rapid growth in the developing countries. Steel production capacity, by one estimate, is expected to increase by 20 percent in developing countries and to erode by 3 percent in the United States by the year 1990.

The hard times that domestic steel has been facing have many causes, including poor management, labor squabbles, obsolete technology, foreign competition, and product substitutes such as aluminum and fiber-reinforced plastics. Many of Big Steel's problems can be attributed to the industry's sluggishness and complacency in technology and marketing matters, but the problems of integrated mills are proving to be somewhat systemic; the industries in Japan and Europe have begun to face problems similar to those of their American counterparts. As Dr. Barnett foresaw, developing countries are entering the steel industry with relative ease and success, and some experts doubt whether the large, inflexible, integrated mills will survive the 20th century.

Mini-Mills

The steel industry can be divided into three segments with different economic and technical profiles: the integrated mills, the mini-mills, and the specialty mills. Domestically, the minis are the chief competitors of the integrated mills. The specialty mills account for only 5 percent of U.S. output, but they manufacture much more expensive products than do the minis and account for a much higher percentage of total revenues. The minis and specialty steel mills have avoided the worst of the recent industry turmoil, but it is the mini-mills that are expected to make the greater gains in the domestic market in the 1990s, at the expense of the integrated mills.

The mini-mill concept was relatively slow in arriving in the United States. The method had thrived in Japan and Western Europe for over 20 years when Chaparral was founded as one of the first U.S. operations of the kind in 1973. Interestingly, North America's first mini-mill was established in Canada in 1962 by a former manager of Co-Steel, the Canadian holding company that played a seminal role in the creation of Chaparral. Since the 1960s, when 10 to 12 mini-mills shared roughly 2 percent of the domestic steel market, the number of domestic mini-mills is now around 55, with a market share of just over 20 percent.

The mini-mill segment has been able to remain relatively profitable by restricting its product range, and therefore the level of capitalization required, by utilizing locally generated scrap and thereby lowering transportation costs, and by marketing in the vicinity of the mill. Furthermore, the mini-mills have typically concentrated on relatively high-volume, low-cost steels. Unlike Big Steel, the minis, in order to increase productivity, have relied on innovative processing technology, much of which comes from abroad and can be adapted to suit their purposes. In contrast, the specialty steel industry has typically developed its new technologies in-house. Whereas the specialty steel mill invests in its own R&D and the integrated mill is constrained by relatively larger capital investment requirements and must work under restrictive union labor contracts, the mini-mill is more able to invest capital in new technology. By so doing, the mini-mills have recaptured markets that Big Steel had abandoned to imports.

The significance of potential foreign competition in the mini-mill segment is mitigated by the dominant role played by transportation costs. On this topic, Mr. Forward has said of Chaparral:

> We adopt certain goals. In our beams, for instance, the Koreans are the most efficient producers. So we just adapt so that we will have a lower labor content than the shipping costs of beams from Korea to the West Coast. If they have zero labor costs, we'll still have a competitive advantage.[7]

Furthermore, as mentioned earlier, the minis have the advantage of relatively low raw material costs and flexible work rules. In addition, firms such as Chaparral, Nucor, and Birmingham Steel have much lower base wage rates, but provide generous bonus programs for high levels of team productivity.

The *mini-mill* is so-named not because it is small, but because its operations entail only a part of the integrated steel making process (Exhibit 4). The mini-mill avoids almost entirely the integrated mill's energy- and capital-intensive "front-end" of steelmaking, that is, the iron-smelting process, including the mining and preparation of raw materials and the blast-furnace operation. The mini-mill begins with steel scrap, flux, and occasionally directly reduced iron. The scrap is melted in an electric furnace, poured into ladles, and then transferred to a continuous-casting machine. Continuous casting is the casting of billets, blooms, or slabs directly from the molten steel. The success of domestic minis is due in part to the use of continuous billet casting, which has been standard practice in minis since

EXHIBIT 4 Comparison of Integrated Steel Mills and Mini-mills

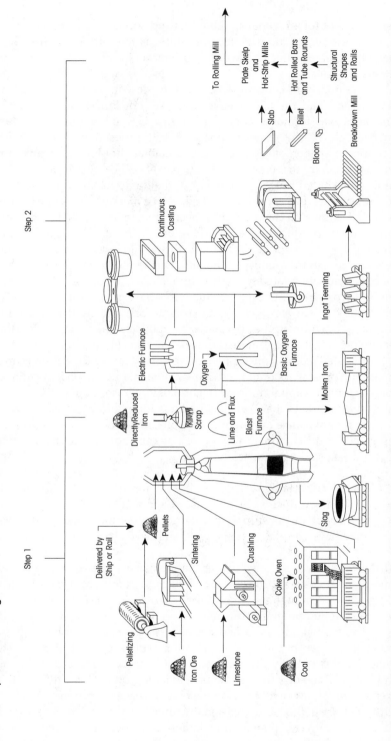

Integrated steel mills produce steel using Steps 1 and 2, beginning with iron ore, coal, and limestone; they go through most of the steps presented here. Mini-mills use scrap as their raw material, and go through Step 2, using either an electric furnace or a basic-oxygen furnace. Most recently built mini-mills use an electric furnace and continuous casting technology.

around 1970 and which increases the yield 18 percent over ingot casting, common to conventional steel mills. Only about one-half of the domestic integrated mills utilize continuous casters. Continuing to emphasize innovation, Chaparral has a recently commissioned horizontal casting machine that came on line in 1988 and should add materially to productivity (Exhibit 5).

Recycling scrap, or the processing of secondary materials, results in less waste and reduces overall raw materials requirements. All three segments of the domestic industry use scrap to some degree, but only the mini-mills are almost wholly dependent on it. The United States was estimated to have had a scrap inventory of 620 billion metric tons in 1982 and, with annual accumulations, the supply is expected to meet the demand for at least several decades. Chaparral processes some 300,000 cars per year, or one every 20 seconds, and this provides roughly 30 percent of the firm's raw material. The use of steel substitutes (plastic, etc.) in automobiles is cause for some concern in the industry, but Mr. Forward maintains a sense of humor:

> There is a possibility that we may have to go back to an iron ore base some day. For the moment, however, we are all right. We keep on importing Toyotas, which have a seven-year life. It takes us seven years to get a new Toyota into our furnace.[8]

In the meantime, there is what some call the "ubiquitous availability" of domestically generated scrap. Another problem is the impurity content of the scrap, which prevents production of certain high-quality grades of steel.

The mini-mill products of the recent past were simple and limited in variety. They included wire rods, reinforcing rods, and various bar products. The bar forms, classified by cross-sectional shape, include flats, rounds, and squares. Mini-mills may also manufacture light *I* beams, *T* beams, angles (with a 90-degree cross section), and channels (with a shallow *U* in cross section). A product is a light section if the longest part of a shape viewed in cross section is 75 mm or less; a heavy section measures more than 75 mm. Merchant bars are bars made of carbon steel and rolled hot. An alloy steel is made when small amounts of manganese,

EXHIBIT 5 Horizontal Continuous Caster, Baltimore Works, Armco

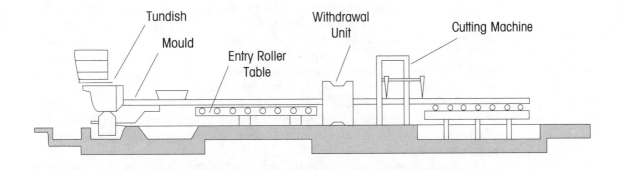

chromium, nickel, and other metals, singly or in combination, are added to the melt. A product made increasingly by mini-mills is termed *special bar quality (SBQ)* grade. Recently, mini-mills have been venturing into lines of higher-grade products. These items are mainly for the construction industry, but Chaparral and other minis also sell such products to the auto makers.

Steel sheet and large structural girders have long been the mainstay of integrated steelmakers and out of the province of the minis. Until now, mini-mills haven't been able to manufacture sheet, but the Nucor Corporation, the most successful of the minis, is building a sheet mill that will use a new technology to make sheet in mini-mill quantities and of mini-mill thicknesses. Furthermore, Nucor, which already owns a number of mini-mills, has announced a joint venture with the Yamato Kogyo Company, a large Japanese steel maker, to build a mill in Arkansas that will manufacture large structural girders. Similarly, Chaparral has indicated an interest in buying or building a plant that can turn out large structural beams. With continued adaptation of new technologies, the mini-mill segment of the industry is expected to continue to increase its market share at the expense of the less efficient, older mills. Estimates for the mini-mill share range as high as 40 percent of domestic output by the end of the century. The locations of many of the larger mini-mills are presented in Exhibit 6.

Clearly, mini-mills have natural cost advantages over integrated mills. Indeed, minis are sometimes referred to as "money mills." The capital cost of building an integrated plant is approximately $1,600 per ton of annual capacity, whereas for a mini-mill it is only $200 to $300. The capital outlay for an integrated steel plant can easily approach several billion dollars. As mentioned, the man-hours per ton are also substantially different (Exhibit 3). Raw materials and energy costs also favor the minis. For a comparison of mini-mill and integrated steel mill cost structures, see Exhibit 7. Chaparral's financial status is described in Exhibits 8 to 11.

THE CHAPARRAL WAY OF RUNNING A PROFITABLE BUSINESS
Market Responsiveness

In 1987 Gordon Forward set forth Chaparral's marketing goal: to become the "easiest steel company to buy from." The strategy for accomplishing that objective is to provide service by developing new products, raising quality, and extending shipping capabilities. Flexibility and responsiveness to changing customer needs are crucial. As a recent example, Forward recalls how the company's quality control department introduced a micro-alloy steel production capability and began marketing the resultant product in an unconventional way, thereby expanding the firm's SBQ customer base. As an additional service, Chaparral customers have full access to the marketing and quality control departments. Furthermore, the Midlothian firm offers flexible rolling schedules and newly developed remote shipping points.

The classic mini-mill concept is grounded in the strategy of locating where the mill can take advantage of locally available markets and sources of labor and

EXHIBIT 6 Mini-mill Sites in the United States

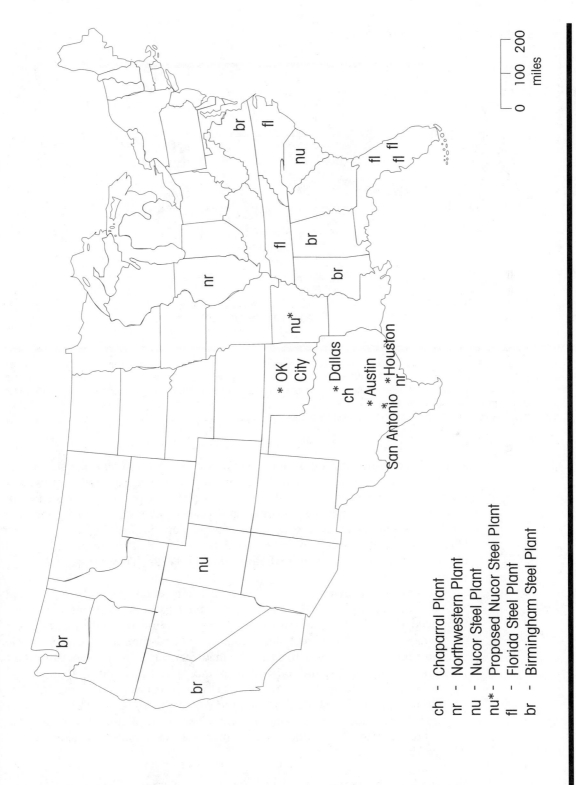

ch – Chaparral Plant
nr – Northwestern Plant
nu – Nucor Steel Plant
nu* – Proposed Nucor Steel Plant
fl – Florida Steel Plant
br – Birmingham Steel Plant

EXHIBIT 7 Comparison of Cost Structures

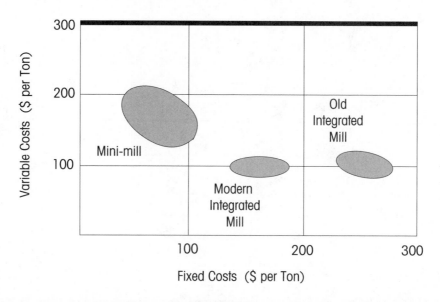

Typical range of costs per ton of annual capacity for an old integrated mill, a modern integrated mill, and a mini-mill can be expressed in terms of fixed and variable costs. Fixed costs are expenditures for such items as capital, manpower, and maintenance, which do not vary significantly once a plant is operating. Variable costs include expenditures for raw materials, other supplies, and energy, which may change from year to year. Since mini-mills do not have to wait as long as integrated mills to recoup the investment in setting up operations, they can consider replacing old equipment with new sooner.

scraps. Subcategories of mini-mills include the *neighborhood mill,* the strategy of which is to locate in an area where the demand for steel is expected to grow, and the *market mill,* which concentrates on one or two specific products to meet a given market. When Chaparral began operating 14 years ago, it was essentially a market mill, producing rebar for the regional construction market. Richard T. Jaffre, Chaparral's vice president of raw materials, noting that domestic and global mini-mill capacity was being overbuilt in the late 1970s, has written:

> It became clear that if Chaparral was to continue to prosper and grow, we had to rethink our place in the market. From the beginning, our focus has always been on steel. We had no interest in diversifying into oil, insurance, or whatever. We believe that steel business can and should be both profitable and fun. So, in 1979, Chaparral decided that our primary opportunity for growth was to expand our product mix and transcend the traditional mini-mill size range (structural shapes up to 6 inches in cross section). The problem with this strategy is that the cost of building a facility for larger shapes can flatten a mini-mill's wallet. The price of steel mill equipment tends to rise exponentially with the cross-sectional dimensions of its products.[9]

Nevertheless, the perception of Chaparral as a market mill persisted at least throughout the mid-1980s, but a recent comment by Forward is revealing:

EXHIBIT 8   Chaparral Steel Company and Subsidiaries
Consolidated Income Statement, Year Ended May 31 ($000 except per-share amounts)

	1989	1988	1987
Net sales	$451,490	$376,398	$318,807
Costs and expenses			
Cost of sales	324,719	278,148	245,099
Selling, general, and administrative expenses	23,774	18,607	13,353
Depreciation expense	17,671	16,452	14,980
Amortization expense	251	5,114	8,587
Interest expense	15,050	17,027	18,463
Other expense	(4,650)	(2,419)	(5,383)
	376,815	332,929	295,099
Income from operations before income taxes	74,675	43,469	23,708
Provision for income taxes	25,569	12,755	10,978
Income from operations	49,106	30,714	12,730
Cumulative effect of change in accounting for income taxes	—	3,895	—
Net income	$ 49,106	$ 34,609	$ 12,730
Income per common share			
Income from operations	$1.57	$0.98	
Cumulative effect of change in accounting for income taxes	—	0.13	
Net income per share	$1.57	$1.11	

Source: Chaparral Steel Company, *Annual Reports*, 1987–1989. Used with permission.

> Although Chaparral is classified as a mini-mill, this year we began producing a range of steels traditionally supplied only by larger, integrated steel mills. And when the recently commissioned horizontal casting machine comes on line in 1988, Chaparral will have even greater opportunities to serve customers more completely.[10]

The horizontal caster is expected to make it easier to get Chaparral down to *micro-mill* size. Rejecting the prospect of making the Midlothian plant bigger or increasing its 950-member employee roster, Forward asserts that his firm is steadfast in its intent to remain relatively flat organizationally, acknowledging that small is better in today's steel industry. After looking hard at microtechnology and studying how McDonald's fast-food chain does what it does, Forward claims, "We figured out how to build something small enough so that you could literally put it on a barge and run it with only 40 people." Says Forward, "We could almost franchise it."

Technological Currency

A scientist by training, Mr. Forward views his mill as a laboratory and encourages experimentation. Saying that research is too often mistakenly isolated as a staff position, Forward explains:

EXHIBIT 9 Chaparral Steel Company and Subsidiaries
Consolidated Balance Sheet, May 31 ($000)

	1989	1988
Assets		
Current assets		
Cash and cash equivalents	$ 45,917	$ 16,242
Trade accounts receivable, net of allowances		
of $3,023,000 and $2,316,000, respectively	37,460	32,317
Inventories	73,001	68,301
Prepaid expenses and other	2,431	2,371
Total current assets	158,809	119,231
Property, plant, and equipment		
Buildings and improvements	29,477	26,732
Machinery and equipment	298,765	272,760
Land	926	926
Total property, plant, and equipment	329,168	300,418
Less allowance for depreciation	123,602	106,105
Net property, plant, and equipment	205,566	194,313
Other assets		
Goodwill and other assets, net of accumulated		
amortization of $1,211,000 and $922,000, respectively	9,563	9,837
Total assets	$373,938	$323,381
Liabilities and Stockholders' Equity		
Current liabilities		
Trade accounts payable	$ 29,519	$622,969
Accrued interest payable	5,308	5,935
Other accrued expenses	15,571	8,376
Current portion of long-term debt	18,683	18,238
Total current liabilities	69,081	55,518
Long-term debt	95,546	119,616
Deferred federal income taxes and other credits	46,609	39,362
Stockholders' equity		
Preferred stock, $0.01 par value, 500,000		
authorized, none outstanding	—	—
Common stock, $0.10 par value, 29,940,000 and		
24,000,000 shares outstanding, respectively	2,994	2,400
Paid-in capital	115,271	33,160
Retained earnings	44,437	73,325
Total stockholders' equity	162,702	108,885
Total liabilities and stockholders' equity	$373,938	$323,381

Source: Chaparral Steel Company, *Annual Reports*, 1988 and 1989. Used with permission.

We've tried to bring research right into the factory and make it a line function. We make the people who are producing the steel responsible for keeping their process on the leading edge of technology worldwide. If they have to

EXHIBIT 10 Chaparral Steel Company and Subsidiaries
Selected Financial Data ($000 except per-share amounts)

	1989	1988	1987	1986	1985
Results of operations					
Net sales	$451,490	$376,398	$318,807	$297,155	$259,130
Gross profit	126,771	98,250	73,708	67,432	39,978
Employee profit sharing	6,935	3,067	1,627	962	—
Interest expense	15,050	17,027	18,463	21,935	25,921
Income (loss) from continuing operations	49,106	30,714	12,730	8,778	(7,481)
Net income (loss)	49,106	34,609	12,730	8,778	(9,558)
Per-share information					
Income from operations	$1.57	$0.98			
Net income	1.57	1.11			
Dividends[a]	0.10	—			
For the year					
Funds from operations	$ 74,275	$ 67,989	$ 48,603	$ 38,148	$ 8,061
Capital expenditures	28,924	22,204	14,279	7,019	4,658
Year-end positions					
Total assets	$373,938	$323,381	$320,579	$309,924	$309,636
Net working capital	89,728	63,713	58,513	42,607	25,135
Long-term debt	95,546	119,616	140,516	158,297	173,229
Stockholders' equity	162,702	108,885	94,276	81,546	61,708

[a]Does not include cash dividends paid to Texas Industries, Inc., previously its sole shareholder, in the amounts of $75 million and $20 million in 1989 and 1988, respectively.
Source: Chaparral Steel Company, *Annual Reports*, 1985–1989. Used with permission.

travel, they travel. If they have to figure out what the next step is, they go out and find the places where people are doing interesting things. They visit other companies. They work with universities.[11]

According to the AISI, the integrated steel industry spends an average of 4 to 7 percent of annual sales on modernizing plant and equipment. Chaparral, by contrast, spends 15 percent of annual gross profits on upgraded equipment and new technologies. As a matter of policy, the Midlothian firm has an annual summer shutdown in order to make the necessary capital improvements. Having labor costs at 9 to 10 percent of sales, compared with an integrated steel industry average of 40 percent, is another factor that makes technology funding an easier task for Chaparral.

Chaparral has fought to maintain a work environment that nourishes people, innovation, and accomplishment. The total involvement of the work force is critical because, as one writer notes:

This is really the heart of the matter, because high tech is something people create, implement, and maintain. You can't just go out and buy it. Bodies and dollar bills aren't enough. Big Steel went out and hired thousands of researchers, industrial engineers, corporate planners, and staff specialists and the world still passed them by.[12]

EXHIBIT 11 Chaparral Steel Company and Subsidiaries
Consolidated Statements of Cash Flows, Year Ended May 31 ($000)

	1989	1988	1987
Operating activities			
Income from operations	$49,106	$30,714	$12,730
Adjustments to reconcile income from operations to net cash provided by operating activities			
Depreciation and amortization	17,922	21,566	23,567
Provision for deferred income taxes	5,188	11,551	10,978
Other deferred credits	2,059	4,158	1,328
Funds from operations	74,275	67,989	48,603
Changes in operating assets and liabilities			
(Increase) decrease in trade accounts receivable, net	(5,143)	(1,601)	(4,868)
(Increase) decrease in inventories	(4,700)	(1,156)	133
(Increase) decrease in prepaid expenses and other	(60)	2,059	(1,686)
Increase (decrease) in trade accounts payable	6,550	(4,392)	(622)
Increase (decrease) in accrued interest payable	(627)	(530)	(359)
Increase (decrease) in other accrued expenses	7,195	2,037	277
	3,215	(3,583)	(7,125)
Net cash provided by operating activities	77,490	64,406	41,478
Investing activities			
Capital expenditures	(28,924)	(22,204)	(14,279)
Acquisition of other assets	22	82	107
Net cash used in investing activities	(28,902)	(22,122)	(14,172)
Financing activities			
Proceeds from sale of common stock	82,705	—	—
Principal payments on long-term debt	(23,624)	(20,798)	(13,975)
Dividends paid	(77,994)	(20,000)	—
Net cash used in financing activities	(18,913)	(40,798)	(13,975)
Increase in cash and cash equivalents	29,675	1,486	13,331
Cash and cash equivalents at beginning of year	16,242	14,756	1,425
Cash and cash equivalents at end of year	$45,917	$16,242	$14,756

Source: Chaparral Steel Company, *Annual Reports*, 1987–1989. Used with permission.

What are typically staff functions at other mills are dovetailed with line functions at Chaparral. For example:

> When there's a need for new production equipment, a line manager is put in charge of the entire project, including conceptual design, budgeting, purchasing, construction, installation, and startup. Maintenance people are also included in the conceptual design stage, with the result that the equipment is easier to maintain. We've found that when forces shaping the design come from our production managers—when their egos get hooked—the odds of success are greatly enhanced. They make it work.[13]

People who are involved in the decision-making process are more likely to be committed to the decision reached.

Naturally, computers are a major technology that any efficient steel mill will utilize. According to Mr. Jaffre, Chaparral uses computers in "planning, forecasting, inventory management, control of receipts, control of purchase orders, issuance of purchase orders, extensions, payables . . . the whole nine yards." Because the Chaparral operation consumers 100 million tons of junk automobiles, refrigerators, stoves, and so on per year, Jaffre notes that computers are most useful as repositories of historical cost-trend information. Like most firms, Chaparral tries to minimize its investment of cash in inventory, but the mini-mill must buy numerous lots of scrap—and frequently. Therefore, "we're bound by the market." In conclusion, Jaffre states, "in the main, the computer is for short-term, medium-, and long-term planning. It's the data base for our formal planning—the corporate financial forecast, done typically once a year with quarterly updates." The firm relies not only on a talented, motivated work force, but also on its investment in sophisticated computerized systems and production facilities.

Participatory Management

During the 1970s, U.S. Steel (USX) had as many as 11 layers of management. This quintessential Big Steel firm subsequently "evolved down" to four layers. A key initial Chaparral decision was to create only four layers. Decision making at Chapparal is forced down to the shop floor, where actual production takes place. It has been said of Gordon Forward that he is "a man of many slogans," including "Participatory management means taking decision making to the lowest competent level—and making the lowest level competent." Says Chaparral's CEO, "We believe that people want to work and do a good job if you give them some responsibility and reward them with more than a paycheck." Chaparral's pioneering participatory management strategies appear to bear fruit for the firm as well as for the employees. A clear indication is the fact that a 1977 attempt by the United Steelworkers of America to unionize the mill was soundly rejected by 73 percent out of the 98 percent of the work force voting. A former worker at U.S. Steel's South Works mill in Chicago was quoted as saying, "At the other mill I was stuck in a craft line. I couldn't help somebody in a different job, and he couldn't help me. That was because of the union. Here we do what we have to do to get the job done."

Chaparral is described by some in the business literature as a "maverick mini-mill." The us-versus-them attitude that haunts so many of the older mills is largely absent from the Midlothian firm. Rather than *steel workers*, some employees prefer to refer to themselves as *Chaparral people*. Chaparral is a people-oriented firm, whether dealing with employees or with customers. The Chaparral work force is governed by an esprit de corps that is hospitable to risk taking and forgiving of setbacks. Although such incidents are not unique to Chaparral or common there, one $15,000 mistake, which at a less dynamic firm might have cost the melt shop superintendent his job, has been stoically dubbed a "$15,000 paperweight." In addition, the company has a no-layoff policy and claims never to have laid off an employee, not even during the difficult 1982 to 1984 period. In fact, during that time, employees with construction skills were used to construct Chaparral's second mill, rather than bringing in outside builders and firing superfluous steel makers.

Numerous other policies and programs distinguish Chaparral as a steelmaker. For instance, the seniority system, common at Big Steel mills, was never adopted at the Midlothian firm, and promotions are based upon job performance. There are no time clocks to punch, and all Chaparral employees have been salaried since 1981. Furthermore, there are no assigned parking spots, no dress codes or color-coded hard hats, and no executive lunchroom. Claims one Chaparral manager, "We've eliminated every barrier to communication, every barrier to identification with management and company goals." Of Chaparral, Peters writes:

> Imagine a $300 million company where the vice president of administration fills in on the switchboard, where there are no formal personnel and purchasing departments and no personal secretaries. There isn't much for secretaries to do because executives are discouraged from writing memos. For that matter, there aren't that many executives.[14]

Moreover, Peters declares, "You won't find a corporate organization chart like that in any business text." Team spirit is further promoted by the companywide practice of communication on a first-name basis, decentralized offices, and the minimization of formalized meetings.

Although Chaparral workers are not paid extravagantly, job security and other benefits take up the slack. Bonuses and profit sharing were introduced from the start and together have run as high as 20 percent of wages. Management further shows its trust in labor by delegating to every member of the firm responsibility for quality control and sales, thus removing what they see as two inessential managerial layers. Says Forward:

> Everyone in the company pays attention to our customers. Everyone in the company is a member of the sales department. Literally. About four years ago, we made everyone in the company a member of the sales department. That means people in security, secretaries, everyone.[15]

At Chaparral there is a conscious effort to "bash barriers between jobs." Security guards, for example, are paramedics, run the company ambulance, administer employee hearing tests, and enter safety and quality-control data into the computer. Foremen remain responsible for hiring, education, training, and benefits. To prevent employee burnout, Chaparral has a compulsory annual sabbatical program that permits people at the front-line supervisor level to visit other mills, customers, and so on for a period ranging from two weeks to six months.

THE FUTURE OUTLOOK FOR CHAPARRAL

Asked if Chaparral would "swallow hard and scrap unamortized equipment and put in new technology—even if [the firm] didn't feel competition nipping at [its] heels," Forward responded:

> Absolutely. We simply can't wait until we've been forced into a corner and have to fight back like alley cats. In our end of the business, we can't afford to act like fat cats. We have a system that's tough by its own definition. If we succeed in making our business less capital intensive, we'd be naive not to expect that a lot of others will want to get into it. If we succeed at what we are trying to do as a mini-mill, we'll also lower the price of entry. So we have to go like hell all the time. If the price of what we sell goes up too high, if we start making too much money on certain parts of our product line, all of a sudden lots of folks will be jumping in. And they can get into business in 18 months or so. They can hire our people away. . . . This makes us our own worst enemy. We constantly chip away the ground we stand on. We have to keep out front all the time. Our advantages are the part of the industry we're in, but also the kind of organization we have. We have built a company that can move fast and that can run full out. We're not the only ones—there are others like us. Nucor does many of the same things, but it has a slightly different personality. And there's Florida Steel. There are a number of quality mini-mills. We are all a bit different, but we all have to run like hell.[16]

Today's steel industry is increasingly dichotomized into two segments: the quick and the dead. Forward likens firms that don't utilize ever-improving technologies with Forest Lawn, "Not because there are no good ideas there, but because the good ideas are dying there all the time."

Observing that mini-mills are no longer very labor intensive, Forward, taking a cue from Dr. Barnett, believes that the next big step for Chaparral is to use new technology to cut energy usage drastically. Technological developments in the forging process are also receiving close scrutiny. Jaffre states that Chaparral maintains a competitive edge,

> by never forgetting the magnitude and strength of international competition; by maintaining our capacity to anticipate and manage change; by continuously developing our skills in the application of new technology and the service of our markets; by providing an environment that taps our greatest natural resource—our people.[17]

Furthermore, Jaffre asserts that Chaparral has aggressively chosen not to be a part of any deindustrialization but rather to be a forceful player in the new industrial renaissance.

The question before Chaparral's management now is "How do we grow in the future?" Should they keep expanding the Texas facility, or expand into a new area and attempt to duplicate their success? With the opening of the Nucor plant in Arkansas, the competition in both structural steel and scrap will heat up. This is especially true given the reopening of a Houston plant by Northwestern Steel. With these additions, the regional market may be reaching saturation. On the other hand, with the dollar declining against other major currencies, both the share of the domestic market and export opportunities will be expanding. For all of these reasons, the possibility of a new mill will have to be addressed. Problems may develop if Chaparral continues expanding the present plant. The firm will have to go further and further for scrap. More important, Chaparral's management believes that the success formula is susceptible to diseconomies of scale. As Forward has pointed out, small is beautiful in terms of the Chaparral formula. The firm cannot continue to grow and stay small indefinitely. By the same token, it may not be able to reproduce its magic everywhere it goes. At this juncture, the real question facing Chaparral is, "Which way to grow?"

REFERENCES

Carey, David. "Forecast: Industry Analysis—Metals." *Financial World,* January 5, 1988, p. 40.

Eichenwald, Kurt. "America's Successful Steel Industry." *Washington Monthly,* February 1985, pp. 40–44.

The Elements of Leadership: Texas Industries Inc. 1987 Annual Report, July 15, 1987.

Flint, Jerry. "Help Wanted: Stakhanovites Only." *Forbes,* September 7, 1987, pp. 82+.

Freeze, Karen. "From a Casewriter's Notebook." *HBS Bulletin,* June 1986, pp. 54–63.

Jaffre, Richard T. "Chaparral Steel Company: A Winner in a Market Decimated by Imports." *Planning Review,* July 1986, pp. 20+.

Keefe, Lisa M. "Forward's March." *Forbes,* April 20, 1986, pp. 20+.

Lee, Robert E. "How They Buy Scrap at Chaparral." *Purchasing,* August 22, 1985, pp. 98A1–98A4.

May, Todd, Jr. "The Economy: Surprising Help from the Crash." *Fortune,* January 18, 1988, pp. 68–87.

McManus, George J. "Horizontal Casting: A New Direction for Steel." *Iron Age,* April 5, 1985, pp. 29+.

McManus, George J. "Mini-Mill Report: The Honeymoon Is Over." *Iron Age,* March 1, 1986, pp. 26+.

Miller, Jack Robert. "Steel Mini-Mills." *Scientific American,* May 1984, pp. 32–39.

"Mini-Mills Up the Heat on the Maxis." *Fortune,* April 13, 1987, pp. 8–9.

Stundza, Tom. "Steel: Making More with Less." *Purchasing,* February 1987, pp. 50–57.

Szekely, Julian. "Can Advanced Technology Save the U.S. Steel Industry?" *Scientific American,* July 1987, pp. 34–41.

Endnotes

1. George Melloun, "Making Money Making Steel in Texas," *The Wall Street Journal*, Southwest ed., January 26, 1988, p. 29.
2. Ibid.
3. Ibid.
4. "Chaparral Steel Company," in *Making America Competitive: Corporate Success Formulas*, special report, Bureau of National Affairs, Washington, D.C., n.d.
5. Gordon G. Forward, "Wide-Open Management at Chaparral Steel," Interview by Alan M. Kantrow, *Harvard Business Review* 64, no. 3 (1986), p. 96.
6. *Critical Materials Requirements of the U.S. Steel Industry.* U.S. Department of Commerce, Washington, D.C., March 1983.
7. Melloun, "Making Money Making Steel."
8. Forward, "Wide-Open Management."
9. Richard T. Jaffre, "Chaparral Steel Company: A Winner in a Market Decimated by Imports," *Planning Review*, July 1986, p. 21.
10. *How We Compete: Texas Industries, Inc., 1988 Annual Report*, July 13, 1988.
11. Forward, "Wide-Open Management," p. 99.
12. Jaffre, "Chaparral Steel Company," p. 22.
13. Ibid., p. 27.
14. Tom Peters, *Achieving Excellence*, monthly newsletter, San Francisco, May 1987, p. 2.
15. Forward, "Wide-Open Management," p. 100.
16. Ibid., p. 96.
17. Jaffre, "Chaparral Steel Company," p. 27.

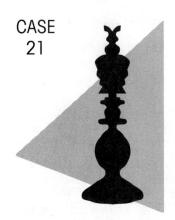

CASE 21

Goodyear: Beyond Goldsmith—an Update from 1988 to 1991

BERNARD A. DEITZER, ALAN G. KRIGLINE & THOMAS C. PETERSON

In fall 1986 Goodyear Tire & Rubber Company, under the leadership of its chairman of the board and chief executive officer, Robert Mercer, had successfully blocked a takeover attempt by the Anglo-French financier Sir James Goldsmith. Goodyear's victory, however, did not come without great cost. Indeed, effects from the struggle are still surfacing in 1991.

The two areas of the company that were immediately impacted and changed the most were financial, in the form of long-term debt, and structural, resulting in a changed product mix. In order to restructure, including buying back 43 percent of its outstanding shares, long-term debt was increased by $2.6 billion. This doubled Goodyear's debt ratio to about 72 percent.

Goodyear's grand strategy had been to reduce its dependence on the uncertain demand for original equipment tires supplied to the cyclical new-car industry by diversification. Only 50 percent of revenues were to come from tire sales. After the restructuring forced upon it, 85 percent of Goodyear's business came from the sales of tires. In this restructuring Goodyear sold all of its oil and natural gas reserves for a total of $685 million; sold the assets of two Arizona subsidiaries involved in agricultural products, real estate development, and a resort hotel for $220 million; sold Goodyear Aerospace Corporation for $588 million; sold Motor Wheel Corporation in a leveraged buyout to its management for $175 million; and also closed a plant in Cumberland, Maryland and a plant in Toronto, Canada. Other casualties were reduced R&D spending, the loss of 6,786 jobs, and placing the ill-fated Celeron All American hot-oil pipeline up for sale at a price of $1.3 billion after its completion.

At this point in 1988 Goodyear was reorganized into two major divisions, tire and nontire products, each operating independently from the other. Formerly separated geographic business segments were combined into global units. Goodyear's management was now flatter with fewer layers of middle management between the top and bottom, thus reducing communication time and speeding up reactions to business situations.

RESTRUCTURING CONTINUES AT GOODYEAR

In the 1988 letter to shareholders, the current changes at Goodyear were characterized by Robert E. Mercer, chairman of the board, who relinquished his duties as chief executive officer to Tom H. Barrett, the president and former chief operating officer, as, "This reorganization represents a continuing process versus a one-time action, and is expected to yield ongoing improvements in the effectiveness and efficiency of our operations."[1] That continual reorganization alluded to was demonstrated by restructuring charges of $66.4 million, $18.4 million, $27.9 million, and $331.5 million for the years 1990, 1989, 1988, and 1986, respectively.[2] The breakdown of the restructuring charges for the most recent year, 1990, were $20.0 million in the United States, $31.0 million in Europe, and $5.0 million in Latin America, with the total amount of $66.4 million being used in the tire products division.[3]

The corporate management structure was changing from the matrix type and was turning toward the flat lines of an authority-and-responsibility type of structure. This was done in order to be "more quickly responsive to competition, the market place, business conditions and the concerns of . . . shareholders."[4]

The restructuring that started in mid-1988 resulted in two worldwide divisions, tire products and general products. Each division had its own manufacturing, sales, distribution, and support responsibilities. Each operated independently of the other. Goodyear Executive Vice President Jacques R. Sardas was also president and COO of the tire division. Similarly, Hoyt M. Wells, another Goodyear executive vice president, was now also president and COO of the general products (nontire) division. Robert Mercer retired, and Tom Barrett was elected chairman of the board. CEO Barrett also retained the title of president since Goodyear, with its independent two-tiered structure, did not have an individual between his level and the divisions to act as president of Goodyear.[5]

The year 1990 was described as "The Year of the Blowout" for Goodyear. It had its first ever back-to-back quarterly losses and its first annual loss since 1932. The market value of Goodyear crumbled to a third of its late-1989 value. It also lost its position as the world's largest tiremaker, a title held since 1916, to Group Michelin of France when Michelin bought Uniroyal-Goodrich Tire Company.[6]

After posting a loss of $38.3 million, or 66 cents per share (see Exhibits 1 through 3) in 1990, cost cutting moves to stem the flow of red ink were intensified. Goodyear cut the pay of its five highest-paid executives in 1990 from 16 to 35 percent, largely by paying only salaries without the usual performance bonuses and other types of benefit payments (profit sharing, stock options, noncash payments, etc.).[7] Just before the announcement of a first-quarter-1991 loss of $90.1 million, an additional cut of 1,100 white-collar jobs over the next 12 to 18 months, including 300 jobs at its headquarters in Akron, was announced. This followed two major cuts in the salaried work force in 1990.

Goodyear actually turned an operating profit of about $20 million in the 1991 first quarter, but a $25.1-million loss by its All American Pipeline, a $60-million loss for restructuring, and the decision to drop plans to build a tire factory in South Korea forced Goodyear into the red ink.[8] Intentions to build the South Korean

EXHIBIT 1 Goodyear Tire & Rubber Company Consolidated Income Statement, Years Ended December 31 ($millions except per-share amounts)

	1990	1989	1986
Net sales	$11,272.5	$10,869.3	$10,810.4
Other income	180.6	216.1	217.6
	11,453.1	11,085.4	11,028.0
Cost and expenses			
Cost of goods sold	8,805.1	8,234.7	8,291.0
Selling, administrative, and general expenses	1,999.6	1,863.7	1,745.1
Interest expenses	328.2	255.3	231.8
Unusual items	103.6	109.7	78.8
Other expenses	74.5	44.6	37.0
Foreign currency exchange	72.1	87.9	87.6
Minority interest in net income of subsidiaries	14.1	18.6	19.2
	11,397.2	10,614.5	10,490.5
Income before income taxes and extraordinary item	55.9	470.9	537.5
United States and foreign taxes on income	94.2	281.5	187.4
Income (loss) before extraordinary item	(38.3)	189.4	350.1
Extraordinary item—tax benefit of loss carryovers	—	17.4	—
Net income (loss)	$ (38.3)	$ 206.8	$ 350.1
Per Share of Common Stock			
Income (loss) before extraordinary item	$(0.66)	$3.28	$6.11
Extraordinary item—tax benefit of loss carryovers	—	0.30	—
Net income (loss)	$(0.66)	$3.58	$6.11
Average shares outstanding	58,215,897	57,727,577	57,322,165

Source: *Annual Report*, Goodyear Tire & Rubber Company, 1990.

plant had been announced at the same time in 1987 as those for a $320-million Canadian tire plant in Napanee, Ontario. The Canadian plant is operational and should deliver tires to auto manufacturers during the second quarter of 1991. Because of complex and cumbersome land acquisition procedures in South Korea, Goodyear was not able to piece together a tract large enough for its 3-million-tires-per-year plant, even though it had received permission from the South Korean government to build the high-technology plant in 1988.[9] The $250-million radial tire plant was to be built near Chongu, South Korea in order to establish a stronger presence in the Pacific Rim. Fear of handing over critical technology led Goodyear to refuse taking on a Korean partner, which would have made land acquisition easier. Without a joint-venture partner, industry sources in Seoul said that financing would be all but impossible due to so many restrictions imposed on Goodyear in the approval granted. A second joint-venture partner to possibly be considered was the Korean petrochemical giant Sunkyong Ltd.[10]

EXHIBIT 2   Goodyear Tire & Rubber Company Consolidated Balance Sheet
as of December 31 ($millions)

	1990	1989	1986
Assets			
Current assets			
Cash and cash equivalents	$ 220.3	$ 122.5	$ 234.1
Short-term securities	56.4	92.1	10.7
Accounts and notes receivable	1,495.2	1,244.6	1,578.4
Inventories	1,346.0	1,642.0	1,635.5
Prepaid expenses	206.3	170.7	99.2
Total current assets	3,324.2	3,271.9	3,557.9
Other assets			
Investments in affiliates, at equity	127.6	125.9	122.3
Long-term accounts and notes receivable	292.5	189.2	313.7
Deferred charges and other miscellaneous assets	410.9	258.0	197.0
	831.0	573.1	633.0
Properties and plants	4,808.4	4,615.3	4,427.4
Total assets	$8,963.6	$8,460.3	$8,618.3
Liabilities and Shareholders' Equity			
Current liabilities			
Accounts payable—trade	$ 986.8	$ 924.0	$ 781.3
Accrued payrolls and other compensation	442.7	395.6	412.2
Other current liabilities	282.5	278.9	347.2
United States and foreign taxes	248.6	219.3	391.0
Notes payable to banks and overdrafts	247.6	316.0	354.2
Long-term debt due within 1 year	85.4	66.4	172.6
Total current liabilities	2,293.6	2,200.2	2,458.5
Long-term debt and capital leases	3,286.4	2,963.4	3,044.8
Other long-term liabilities	550.0	364.7	435.7
Deferred income taxes	622.9	681.8	555.4
Minority equity in subsidiaries	112.8	106.4	96.8
Shareholders' equity			
Preferred stock, no par value			
Authorized, 50,000,000 shares (unissued)	—	—	—
Common stock, no par value			
Authorized, 150,000,000 shares			
Outstanding 58,477,890 shares in 1990	58.5		
57,806,869 shares in 1989		57.8	
57,430,526 shares in 1988			57.4
Capital surplus	65.1	46.5	29.3
Retained earnings	2,135.4	2,278.4	2,175.4
	2,259.0	2,382.7	2,262.1
Foreign currency translation adjustment	(161.1)	(238.9)	(235.0)
Total shareholders' equity	2,097.9	2,143.8	2,027.1
Total liabilities and shareholders' equity	$8,963.6	$8,460.3	$8,618.3

Source: *Annual Report*, Goodyear Tire & Rubber Company, 1990 and 1989.

EXHIBIT 3   Comparison with Prior Years Goodyear Tire & Rubber Company
(\$millions, except per-share amounts)

	1990	1989	1988	1987
Financial results				
Net sales	\$11,272.5	\$10,869.3	\$10,810.4	\$9,905.2
Income (loss) from continuing operations before extraordinary item	(38.3)	189.4	350.1	513.9
Discontinued operations	—	—	—	257.0
Extraordinary item				
Gain on long-term debt retired	—	—	—	—
Tax benefit of loss carryovers	—	17.4	—	—
Net income (loss)	\$ (38.3)	\$ 206.8	\$ 350.1	\$ 770.9
Net income (loss) per dollar of sales	(0.3)¢	1.9¢	3.2¢	7.8¢
Per share of common stock				
Income (loss) from continuing operations before extraordinary item	\$(0.66)	\$ 3.28	\$ 6.11	\$ 8.49
Discontinued operations	—	—	—	4.24
Extraordinary item				
Gain on long-term debt retired	—	—	—	—
Tax benefit of loss carryovers	—	.30	—	—
Net income (loss)	\$ (0.66)	\$ 3.58	\$ 6.11	\$12.73
Dividends	\$ 1.80	\$ 1.80	\$ 1.70	\$ 1.60
Book value at December 31	\$ 35.88	\$37.08	\$35.30	\$32.19
Financial position				
Total assets	\$8,963.6	\$8,460.3	\$8,618.3	\$8,395.9
Properties and plant—net	4,808.4	4,615.3	4,427.4	4,128.3
Depreciation and depletion	415.0	383.5	357.1	349.9
Capital expenditures	574.5	775.7	743.7	665.6
Long-term debt and capital leases	3,286.4	2,963.4	3,044.8	3,282.4
Shareholders' equity	2,097.9	2,143.8	2,027.1	1,834.4
Other information				
Shareholders of record	48,209	43,277	46,435	45,878
Common shares				
Outstanding at December 31	58,477,890	57,806,869	57,430,526	56,986,579
Average outstanding during year	58,215,897	57,727,577	57,322,165	60,564,981
Price range				
High	\$46⅜	\$59¾	\$67⅞	\$76½
Low	12⅞	42⅛	47	35
Employees				
Average during year	107,671	111,469	114,161	114,658
Total compensation for year	\$2,881.4	\$2,775.0	\$2,790.7	\$2,592.8

Source: *Annual Reports*, Goodyear Tire & Rubber Company, 1986 and 1990.

1986	1985	1984	1983	1982
$9,040.0	$8,377.7	$8,494.9	$8,074.4	$8,004.1
216.8	251.5	303.8	189.9	232.4
(92.7)	160.9	107.2	80.5	80.2
—	—	—	35.1	17.2
—	—	—	—	—
$ 124.1	$ 412.4	$ 411.0	$ 305.5	$ 329.8
1.4¢	4.9¢	4.8¢	3.8¢	4.1¢
$ 2.02	$ 2.34	$ 2.86	$ 1.90	$ 2.35
(0.86)	1.50	1.01	0.81	0.81
—	—	—	0.35	0.18
—	—	—	—	—
$ 1.16	$ 3.84	$ 3.87	$ 3.06	$ 3.34
$ 1.60	$ 1.60	$ 1.50	$ 1.40	$ 1.40
$30.93	$32.44	$29.78	$28.61	$28.09
$9.039.3	$6,953.5	$6,194.3	$5,985.5	$5,885.9
4,583.4	4,025.0	3,036.7	2,819.2	2,718.2
349.0	277.7	270.8	260.0	232.0
1,130.8	1,623.3	585.6	455.2	364.7
2,914.9	997.5	656.8	665.2	1,174.5
3,002.6	3,507.4	3,171.3	3,016.2	2,777.2
62,007	72,582	75,619	76,014	83,915
97,080,482	108,110,085	106,492,709	105,425,079	98,866,612
107,092,197	107,369,517	106,138,171	99,907,522	98,794,352
$50	$31¼	$31½	$36⅜	$36⅞
29	25⅛	23	27	17⅞
121,444	123,231	123,104	119,732	123,030
$2,557.4	$2,337.1	$2,272.3	$2,158.1	$2,125.7

In the same announcement of the 1,100 job cuts, a new management structure was released that had eight independent, business-driven company units replacing the former two-headed structure.[11] Barrett relinquished his title of president to Wells, who moved into the office at headquarters that had literally been vacant for nearly three years. The realignment was aimed at streamlining and eliminating management layers in order to shorten reporting lines.[12] One of the positions eliminated in this management realignment was that of Jacques Sardas. Although taking early retirement, Sardas would be paid his current level of compensation through 1992, which will total about $1 million.[13] Commenting on the loss of a key manager, the retired chairman, Robert Mercer, said, "It gets very confining at the top; you run out of positions."[14] The current chairman, Tom Barrett, spoke about the evolving changes to a recent management meeting.

> The time has come to put behind the internal changes that Goodyear has undergone in recent months and capitalize on the benefits for which they were intended.
>
> Our industry has changed, the global economic climate has changed, the financial markets have changed, and we must be prepared psychologically to work and succeed in this different business environment that none of us has dealt with before.
>
> The implementation of a total quality culture (TQC) and the further development of strategic business units (SBU) are the keys to make reality of Goodyear's corporate vision: We offer products and services in the market that customers recognize as so superior in quality and total value that they choose our products and services over all others.

Noting that 14 business units expect zero to negative earnings before interest and taxes in 1991, the chairman said every SBU must understand that its business stands on its own to succeed or fail.

> Good businesses grow sales, and quality and productivity improve continuously and adjust quickly to changes that can affect sales and profits.
>
> Businesses will only survive if they are willing to change the instant a problem is seen.
>
> Through TQC a streamlined work force will not be burdened by menial tasks but will eliminate inefficiencies to more meaningful work, dropping nonvalue added jobs. Performance appraisals of all employees are being changed to include measurements of quality performance.
>
> But traditional Goodyear values of family, security, being number one, and high morale—values that have been under attack in the past few years—can still be our best assets.
>
> It is time to return these traditional values to the stature they enjoyed in previous years. There is no quicker way than to return Goodyear to a position of financial strength.[15]

Because of all the sweeping changes in structure that had recently taken place, the next announcement just a few weeks later was a complete surprise, catching most observers unaware. Chairman and CEO Tom Barrett took an immediate early retirement and was to be replaced by outside board member Stanley C. Gault. Gault, at age 65, five years Barrett's senior, had retired only five weeks earlier as chairman of the board and CEO of Rubbermaid. With 1990 sales of $1.5 billion and 9,300 employees, Rubbermaid is a fraction of the size of Goodyear, which employed 108,000 and had sales of $11.3 billion in 1990. Gault's salary in 1990 while at Rubbermaid was $894,000; Barrett earned $800,000 (down 16 percent from 1989) at Goodyear.[16]

GOODYEAR ELECTS A NEW CEO

On June 4, 1991 in a public relations release, Goodyear announced its board of directors' election of Stanley C. Gault as chairman and chief executive officer to succeed Tom H. Barrett, who retired after 38 years with Goodyear. [See Exhibit 4.]

Gault had retired in May as chairman and chief executive officer of Rubbermaid Incorporated of Wooster, Ohio, which he joined in 1980 after a 31-year career with General Electric. He had been an outside director of Goodyear since 1989.

At its regularly scheduled meeting, Goodyear's board accepted Barrett's resignation and stated its intention to enter into a three year employment agreement with Gault.

Former CEO Tom Barrett, in his concluding remarks to the board, stated:

> Over the past several months, we concluded a three-year labor agreement, we are renewing our bank credit arrangements through June 30, 1994, we reorganized our senior management team, and we launched a total quality culture throughout the company. With these achievements behind us, I thought now would be an opportune time to pass the reins to a new leader. Stan Gault is a personal friend and an outstanding manager and marketer. With Goodyear now facing formidable challenges in changing markets created by industry consolidation, he is the perfect man to lead Goodyear.[17]

The board of directors, in a statement released after the election meeting, commented:

> Goodyear is exceedingly fortunate that Stan Gault has agreed to lead the company for at least the next three years. In addition to being one of America's most able corporate managers, with an outstanding record of accomplishment at Rubbermaid, he brings to Goodyear the unique advantage of having both the perspective of an outsider as well as a thorough knowledge of the company's businesses gained from his service as Goodyear director. The board is very grateful to Tom Barrett for his distinguished 38 years of service and leadership.[18]

Stanley C. Gault headed Rubbermaid from 1980 to 1991 and currently serves as chairman of its executive committee. During his tenure as chairman, Rubbermaid's sales increased nearly five-fold, its net income increased more than six-fold,

EXHIBIT 4   Barrett's Notice to Employees of His Retirement

June 5, 1991

Dear Goodyear Employees:

For the last 38 years, I have lived and breathed The Goodyear Tire & Rubber Company, and, for the last two years, I have had the great honor to serve as your chairman and chief executive officer.

During that tenure, Goodyear has endured one of the most difficult periods in its history. We have made more changes in two years than were made during the past two decades. And they were tough decisions that had to be made to shape Goodyear to compete in our rapidly changing industry and a chaotic market that was created by the massive consolidations.

Today, our manufacturing is probably in the best condition in our history, our products have achieved all-time high performance levels; financing arrangements are being made to carry us well into the future; we have a new three-year contract with the URW; and we've trimmed employment without sacrificing quality, volume, or service. Most important, we have a streamlined, flexible organization that can meet the challenges of the future, and we have started on the road to a total quality culture, which is the only way to success.

Now the challenge facing Goodyear is in how we compete in the new global marketplace, and I believe it is the right time to turn over the reins of this company to a man who has achieved a worldwide reputation as a marketing expert and business leader—a member of our board of directors, Stanley C. Gault.

We have a rock-solid foundation for the future. The elements are there and they are held together by people—Goodyear people. I am deeply grateful to each and every one of you for your support, especially in the recent trying times. It has been your commitment that made possible the changes that have placed this company squarely on the threshold of a bright tomorrow.

I now ask that you show your new chairman the same friendship and loyalty that you have shown me. He has the talent and the drive to lead Goodyear to new heights, but he needs and wants your dedication and support, your talents and your efforts.

As I go from Goodyear, I am proud to leave it in your hands—the hands of the family of Goodyear—and in the hands of such an outstanding leader as Stan Gault.

My best wishes to you all,

Tom H. Barrett

---

and the company consistently was included on several business publications' lists of America's most-admired and best-managed corporations.

Gault, in responding to Barrett's commendation, remarked:

I am very pleased to be joining the team at Goodyear, which is the greatest name in the rubber industry. It has a superior brand franchise, high-quality products, state-of-the-art technology and manufacturing facilities, broad distribution, and very promising new products scheduled to be introduced

EXHIBIT 4 Cont'd.   Gault's Notice to Employees of His New Post

June 5, 1991

Dear Associate:

I am indeed honored to be asked to join you as a full-time associate of Goodyear.

Although I am your newest associate, I feel as if I have been a part of the Goodyear family for decades. In 1949 as a young salesman in Akron, I called on Goodyear. Later on when I was in charge of General Electric's major appliance and television businesses, Goodyear was my largest customer. When I managed GE's Industrial Products sector, Goodyear was again a highly valued customer.

In recent years, I have been privileged to serve on your board of directors and to have learned more about Goodyear's businesses from the inside. Our company has experienced extremely difficult times lately, triggered by industry consolidation and compounded further by the current economic recession. Had I not been convinced that Goodyear has the finest associates, products, and brand name in its industry, I would not have accepted this challenge. Tom Barrett deserves much credit for having made some tough decisions that were required to reposition Goodyear to operate more effectively in the new environment.

As we all know, we still have a tremendous amount of hard work ahead of us. I need to get up to speed and to have the opportunity to know you better. I already know that Goodyear is an outstanding company that has a great heritage and that is capable of producing a great future.

I seek and I need your fullest support and your very best efforts to make that happen. You in turn can count on me to be highly involved, fully committed, and a hands-on CEO. I know that I can count on each and all of you.

Most sincerely,

Stanley C. Gault

---

later this year. Although the rubber business is experiencing industrywide problems, I am confident that Goodyear shareholders can look forward to a bright future. As a strong believer in hands-on management and open communication between corporate managers and the investment community, I intend to keep our lenders and shareholders fully informed about the company's progress.[19,20]

In commenting on his predecessor, Gault complementingly stated:

Tom Barrett deserves an enormous amount of credit for his leadership during a very difficult time in the industry. He has strengthened the company by achieving a more streamlined, flexible organization and by continuing to advance Goodyear's efforts to have the industry's most efficient, technologically advanced plants. Thanks to his efforts, we have a strong foundation to build upon in striving to meet the challenges that face the company.[21]

Gault joined General Electric in 1948 as a sales trainee and held various sales, marketing, and general management positions. In 1977 he was named vice president and sector executive of the consumer products and services sector, of which Goodyear was a major customer. From 1978 to 1980 he served as senior vice president and sector executive of GE's industrial products and components sector.

Gault serves on the boards of directors of Avon Products Inc., International Paper Company, PPG Industries Inc., Rubbermaid, The Timken Company, and the New York Stock Exchange. He also is the chairman of the board of trustees of his alma mater, The College of Wooster in Wooster, Ohio. He was appointed by President Reagan and reappointed by President Bush to the Advisory Committee for Trade Policy and Negotiations. He is a director and former chairman of the board of the National Association of Manufacturers.

Gault, in accepting his biggest managerial challenge, told how he plans to make things better at Goodyear.

> We're going to examine everything. One of the things that's different here from my past experience, even at GE, is the debt. At GE we were very thrifty people, and at Rubbermaid we drove debt down to where it was 5 percent of total capitalization. [Goodyear's is 66 percent.] So I'm not used to spending more than a million dollars a day for interest, every day of the week, even on Saturdays, Sundays, and holidays. That we cannot live with. We will undoubtedly sell some assets that are not directly related to the tire business. And we are going to expand and enhance our marketing, sales, merchandising, and advertising efforts to get a bigger piece of the market. If done well, those things obviously spell improved cash flow, and that means debt reduction.[22]

Stanley Gault arrives at Goodyear with the reputation of having made the wide-ranging changes at Rubbermaid that became the foundation for its decade of spectacular business successes. While at Rubbermaid, Gault was named as one of America's best corporate managers by *Fortune* and other business magazines and trade groups.[23] An Akron councilman summarized the opinion of many when saying, "I don't like the news that Barrett is out, but I commend the board for bringing Stanley Gault in. When a company gets in serious trouble and changes have to be made, it's easier for an outsider to make those changes than it is for someone who has spent his entire career with the company. I have a feeling there will be big changes, but they will be done humanely."[24]

Gault is the second outsider to be hired by Goodyear. The first was E. G. Wilmer, who served from 1921 to 1926 as part of the management team that led Goodyear back from the verge of bankruptcy in the 1921 reorganization mandated by the banks that had financed Goodyear.[25]

TIRE INDUSTRY RESTRUCTURING EXAMINED

Just as Goodyear was structuring and restructuring, the tire industry itself was undergoing restructuring and becoming more concentrated. The tire industry changed from a group of ten leaders in 1985 having about 78 percent of the world's market for auto, truck, and farm tires to a group of six merged firms in 1990 having 80 percent of the world tire market shares.

World Tire Market Shares, 1985

Goodyear	20.0%
Michelin	12.8
Firestone	9.4
Bridgestone	9.2
Sumitomo	6.4
Uniroyal	4.7
Pirelli	4.6
Continental	4.0
General	3.9
Goodrich	3.5
Others	21.5

Source: *Annual Report,* Goodyear Tire and Rubber Company, 1990, p. 4.

All of the major players in the global tire market, except Goodyear, acquired other tire makers or were acquired by them in the decade of the 1980s. And, while Goodyear considered taking on a European partner, any suitable candidates disappeared while Goodyear was engaged in successfully fighting off a takeover attempt.[26]

Several of the smaller-scale acquisitions involving U.S. tire plants were: Yokohama with Mohawk Rubber Company (Mohawk at one time advertised that it was "Next to the largest tire company in the world"—it had a tire plant adjacent to the Goodyear plant in Akron, Ohio); Sumitomo, owner of Dunlop Tire Company; and the Pirelli acquisition of Armstrong Tire Company.[27]

Three large-scale acquisitions were made in the industry in order to gain entrance into the North American original equipment (supplied to auto manufacturers) and replacement tire markets. The first was the purchase of General Tire from GenCorp Inc. in 1987 for $643 million by Continental A.G. of Hannover, West Germany.[28] The second acquisition was the purchase of Firestone Tire & Rubber Company for $2.6 billion in 1988 by Tokyo-based Bridgestone Tire Corp. to form the "stones"—Bridgestone/Firestone Inc. This also gave Bridgestone entrance into the European market through Firestone dealer outlets. The third and most recent combination involved the merger of Uniroyal with Goodrich, and the Uniroyal/Goodrich unit was then purchased for $1.5 billion in 1990 by the French tiremaker Michelin as an avenue into the low end of the 155-million tire North American replacement tire market, with an estimated 50 percent of the market being in the low end.[29] Now Michelin is able to sell lesser-quality tires that do not bear its premium name.

The global tire market as it emerged from concentration is as follows:

World Tire Market Shares, 1990

Michelin/Uniroyal-Goodrich	21.5%
Goodyear	20.0
Bridgestone/Firestone	17.0
Continental/General	7.5
Pirelli/Armstrong	7.0
Sumitomo/Dunlop	7.0
Others	20.0

Source: *Annual Report*, Goodyear Tire & Rubber Company, 1990, p. 5.

From the market share listings above, it can be seen that Goodyear did not gain or lose any market share. But, where just five years ago it dominated the world tire market leading a fragmented market in which ten participants controlled about 78 percent, it now finds itself an equal among giants. The result is that Goodyear now has rivals in its own league. It can no longer dictate prices as the industry leader to followers or count on capturing customers with technological or design changes. Previously, Goodyear dwarfed its competitors, having huge advertising budgets to easily highlight its own products and R&D spending that smothered rivals. Goodyear's products were able to command premium prices.[30]

In a commodity market, it is questionable whether Goodyear's top-of-the-line tires can remain dominant when brand names mean less and less in the marketplace. There is not anything to differentiate one tire from another, and Goodyear may be resisting the idea that it has a commodity product.[31]

The industry, rather than acting like an oligopoly where a small number of companies compete in a way that makes each profitable, is acting as if the companies each face numerous major competitors in pure competition as found in a commodity market where the firm must accept the given market price.[32]

The pricing irrationality in the industry is an all-out war for market share. The industry giants are depicted as "great names bled white by self-consuming battle," and their operations are "strategies that, if taken too far, lead to mutually assured destruction." Actions and reactions are guided by the words *pride, tradition,* and *ego.*[33]

Each of the three giants has the lion's share of the market on its own turf. Bridgestone has more than half of the tire market in Japan.[34] A top priority at Goodyear is to protect its number one position, with an estimated one-third share, in the North American market, which provides about 41 percent of all Goodyear tire sales.[35] Michelin is clearly dominant in European auto, truck, and farm tire sales with a 34-percent market share.[36]

Bridgestone is credited with starting a price war in the European market when it tried to increase its 9-percent market share that it had gained through acquired Firestone outlets. Michelin countered by slashing prices, and Goodyear's profits skidded when it got caught in the cross-fire. It seems that Michelin is willing to sustain large and continuing losses in order to preserve its market share in Europe. Goodyear's 14-percent share of the European market accounts for about 25 percent of its tire sales.[37]

Goodyear finds itself in a cutthroat, highly competitive, commodity-like market with two rivals that are not only willing, but able to sustain large losses in order to gain market share. Like most American corporations, Goodyear is concerned that shareholders see quarterly profits on its balance sheet, whereas foreign firms and their stockholders seem to be less concerned with short-term losses if they can eventually win out. It has been claimed that some Japanese corporations have a strategic planning time horizon that extends 100 to 200 years into the future.

As poor as Goodyear's financial performance appears to be, with its $38 million loss in 1990 on sales of $11.3 billion with $66.4 million in restructuring charges followed by a first-quarter-1991 loss of $90.1 million with a $65-million restructuring writeoff, the worst slump in the auto industry in a decade and the recession that started in mid-1990 have left Goodyear's rivals in much worse positions.[38]

The world's number one tire maker in 1990, Group Michelin, posted a loss of $972 million on sales of $11.6 billion. Michelin's debt of $6 billion requires $517 million each year in interest payments. Restructuring at Michelin will cost 16,000 jobs worldwide, close a Uniroyal-Goodrich plant in Eau Clair, Wisconsin, and may close a plant in Kitchener, Ontario, where Michelin owns a former Uniroyal plant and a former Goodrich plant. Profitability is not expected to return until 1992, and analysts forecast that Michelin will not see the full benefits of the Uniroyal-Goodrich purchase until 1993.[39]

While Tokyo-based Bridgestone Corp. had a 1990 profit of $33 million on sales of $13.2 [sic] billion, its North American operation, Bridgestone/Firestone Inc., had a $350-million loss. Since foreign stock exchanges do not have the stringent reporting requirements that U.S. exchanges have, Bridgestone does not disclose total debt.

Previously, Firestone had been run to maximize earnings. Now, Bridgestone/Firestone is not expected to be in the black until 1992 because of restructuring and modernization costs, according to President and CEO James McCann. He also said, "We didn't buy Firestone because it was a bargain; we bought it because it fit the globalization plan."[40]

The Bridgestone/Firestone contribution to job losses in the industry is about 1,000 layoffs in the United States, including 250 at its Akron headquarters.[41] In addition, another 300 jobs that were projected to be added in 1991 will not be filled.[42] Another 1,800 jobs worldwide are being eliminated by Pirelli, which also announced a loss of $4.9 million for 1990.[43]

The Italian tire maker Pirelli was stymied in its 1991 takeover bid for Continental A.G. of Germany. Pirelli is expected to continue the pursuit of Continental despite the rebuff. If successful, the combination would create another peer for Goodyear, and it would become the fourth global giant in the industry.[44]

The tire industry is not expected to rebound and become profitable again until the current recession, which began in 1990, is over. When the economy and tire industry turn upward again, Goodyear will have an edge because it will not be trying to digest acquisitions or merge corporate cultures, and it already has made many of the adjustments that are now being made at Michelin and Bridgestone/Firestone.[45] Goodyear's Barrett points out, "I think you're going to see some improvements for the industry. I feel that Goodyear is in a position to maybe improve at a better rate than the rest of them."[46]

GOODYEAR CUTS COSTS

With higher labor and raw materials costs squeezing operating profits, Goodyear raised tire prices by about 15 percent in fall 1988. Other manufacturers held the line on prices, and consumers left Goodyear and went elsewhere for their tire purchases. Goodyear's share of the U.S. replacement market dropped by about 4 percentage points. The dual rebellion from their dealers' resistance to price increases and consumers' balking at the higher prices forced Goodyear to cut prices. After matching the competition, market share returned to previous levels.[47]

Goodyear again increased its prices in early 1989. Competitors used the move as an opportunity to gain market share by cutting their prices. Goodyear soon lowered prices as its U.S. market share dipped by 1.5 percentage points.[48] Jacques Sardas, president of Goodyear's tire division, said of the move, "We gave that policy four to five months, then said, that's enough, let's forget about price enhancement and put the emphasis on costs."[49]

Goodyear's chief financial officer, Oren Shaffer, said the company would put cost-containment programs into effect every quarter, even though some would not draw much attention. Efforts will range from streamlining raw material purchases to finding less expensive ways to store inventory.[50] Travel budgets have been cut.[51]

R&D and Marketing

Two functional areas contributing to and possibly being the determinant of future success are not being squeezed by the company for cash. The first, where new products are developed and existing products are improved, is R&D. Spending for R&D increased, from $304.8 million in 1988 and $303.3 million in 1989, to $331.3 million in 1990.[52]

Additional spending can also be found in marketing. Recognizing that an estimated one-half of the replacement tire market is in the lower end of the market, two lines of lower-cost tires were introduced. In addition, Goodyear started test marketing a chain of stores called Just Tires to target price-conscious consumers who shop at tire warehouses.[53]

Airship operations at Goodyear may also join the current emphasis on cost cutting. The next Goodyear blimp may be built from spare blimp parts on hand rather than from new ones, according to the manager of operations: "We're trying to contribute—like all the other divisions at Goodyear—to keeping the costs down."

Goodyear's "aerial ambassadors," as the company calls its blimps, have been pressed into service as marketing tools. The blimps are working in what is called Blimp Tour '91, a sales promotion whereby buyers of Goodyear tires in major cities get a free blimp ride. It is the first time that the company, grappling with a poor economy and increased competition, has used blimp rides to entice customers to dealers' stores.[54]

Inventory

All inventories were reduced from $1.6 billion in 1988 and 1989 to $1.3 billion in 1990. Tire inventories have declined by about $180 million.[55]

Capital Spending

Goodyear cut $100 million out of its $700-million capital spending plans for 1990. In 1991 and 1992 capital spending will be less than $450 million.[56] This lower amount is close to the level of depreciation. But, having spent $4 billion on plant improvements over the last decade[57] and nearly completing the switch to all-radial tire production, this level of capital spending for a few years should do no harm and can give some much needed breathing room. At present, Goodyear is certainly one of the most modernized tire makers if not *the* state-of-the-art producer.

Employee Reduction

The most difficult of all savings to achieve is by reducing employment. The emotional impact on employees and those leaving can be long lasting and can have adverse effects on productivity. Tom Barrett realized this when he said, "We are biting the bullet even harder to improve our competitive and financial position." The company expects to save $165 million annually by 1992 over 1990 operating costs by the reduction of expenses.[58] About $200 million in annual savings will start in 1990's fourth quarter from layoffs affecting about 3,000 employees.[59] One employee aptly summarized Goodyear's troubles when he said, "The bottom line is that there are fewer bottoms on the line."[60]

Efficiency

Significant cost reduction has been achieved through improved efficiency. Worker productivity in Goodyear's North American tire plants has risen 25 percent since 1980.[61]

Former Chairman and CEO Robert Mercer said of Goodyear's competitive efficiency:

> In automated plants, we can produce a passenger tire in under 10 man-minutes, compared to 30 to 50 man-minutes in third world countries that pay $3 per hour.
>
> If we work together, I believe we can compete with tire plants anywhere in the world. But this takes a commitment from the union to make us profitable and competitive on a global basis.

It also takes a commitment from the company to provide the capital and the research and development needed to give U.S. workers the tools they need to be competitive.[62]

A veteran tire-industry analyst made the following observation about Goodyear and the other giants:

> Working on an extremely thin [profit] margin has forced all the tire companies to become leaner and meaner as fast as possible. Goodyear has worked hard to streamline the company and make it more efficient and responsive over the last three years.
> But despite having cut about 15 percent of the employees, it is estimated production will have increased nearly 15 percent, so obviously they are working more efficiently.
> Bridgestone/Firestone also is cutting people, and Michelin is going through significant restructuring, particularly in white-collar jobs. Goodyear has just been more aggressive than other major tire companies.[63]

Receivables

A fly in Goodyear's cost reduction/cash generating ointment is in accounts and notes receivable. While sales increased in 1990 by 3.7 percent over 1989 sales, accounts and notes receivable increased by 20.1 percent in the same period (see Exhibits 1 through 3). Tire dealers and buyers owe Goodyear $250 million more this year than they did last year. The customers may be a little slow paying, reflecting the economy, or the extra millions could be related to marketing programs having eased credit restrictions in order to encourage buyers.

THE ALL AMERICAN PIPELINE

Goodyear's oil pipeline, now valued at $1.7 billion, still hangs like a millstone around the neck of profits, dragging them down. It is estimated that annual pipeline expenses are equivalent to $2 per share. The pipeline's operating loss of $53 million for 1990 is a slight improvement over 1989 when the pipeline lost $57 million.

The pipeline was capitalized until October 1989, at which time the company began recognizing depreciation, interest expense, and net operating expenses. Goodyear's Barrett has said that the pipeline will continue to lose money through 1992. When a reporter at a news conference called his projected duration of red ink optimistic, Barrett replied sharply, "I don't think having it in a negative position for two years is very damn positive."[64]

Originally planned as a 1,750-mile underground, heated pipeline, it would pump viscous, sulfurous, outer continental shelf (OCS) crude oil from the California coast to the Gulf coast where refineries could handle the feedstock. Built with a capacity of 300,000 barrels per day, the line is currently pumping 90,000 barrels of Alaskan and inland Californian crude oil. The financial breakeven point for the pipeline is 120,000 barrels per day.[65]

It costs $1.25 to transport a barrel of oil the 1,255 miles between California and mid-Texas where the pipeline terminates at McCamey.[66] The eastern leg to Houston will be constructed only when it is determined that there will be sufficient demand for OCS at refineries along the Gulf coast and that the oil will be available in substantial quantities for transport through the system. So saying, Goodyear sold about 435 miles of unused 30-inch pipe for $70.0 million in the second quarter of 1989 at a loss of $48.3 million ($43.0 million after tax).[67]

The pipeline could yet turn into a cash spigot. In the wake of the *Exxon Valdez* disaster in Alaska and memories of a 1969 oil spill in the Santa Barbara Channel, the California Coastal Commission refused to force Santa Barbara County into granting oil companies permits to ship by tanker. Santa Barbara residents fear an oil spill from tankers could ruin their beaches. The commission ruled that pipelines are reasonably available to move the oil. The ruling appeared to be the last administrative appeal for the oil companies, which have fought for at least three years to obtain permits for tankers to ship oil from offshore fields. A three-platform project at Point Arguello, completed in 1987 from among more than 20 projects planned for Santa Barbara, was mothballed by the oil companies until the tanker issue was settled.[68]

Goodyear believed it could ship 300,000 barrels of OCS oil daily through its pipeline and make a healthy profit. But many of the oil companies delayed or abandoned their plans, and Goodyear has been left holding the bag. Robert Milk, who manages the pipeline as president and chief executive of Goodyear's Celeron Corp., said, "When we started this, the oil companies were saying, 'Hurry up, we're bringing these platforms on as fast as we can.' So now here we are with it completed and not one barrel of the originally intended oil has gotten into our pipeline yet."[69]

Although it is not actively soliciting bids, if someone wanted to buy the pipeline, Goodyear would listen. Milk likes to joke that, "Some day, this will make a good case study for the Harvard Business School."[70]

GOODYEAR'S STOCK, BONDS, AND NOTES

Most agree that Goodyear's financial problems started with the takeover attempt by James Goldsmith in fall 1986. When Goldsmith began buying Goodyear stock, the price ranged between $31 and $35 a share, which was at or above Goodyear's book value in 1986. The attraction for Goldsmith at the time was that Goodyear's breakup value was well above its market value.

After successfully meeting the Goldsmith challenge, Goodyear stock rose on the market to an all-time high of $76½ in 1987, the year of the big stock market crash. The lowest closing price for Goodyear during the year was $35.

Goodyear's stock started down on a long slide until it again looked like an attractive target for a raider in 1990. This time the attraction was that at $12⅞, the stock was selling at just over one-third of Goodyear's book value (or the stated value of its assets). For a brief period the stock traded (but did not close) in the $11 range.

The mixed performance of Goodyear's stock gives rise to equally mixed recommendations from brokers and analysts. A brokerage executive said he used to make investments in tire companies' stock he said, "until I realized they played the game for market share at the cost of profitability. They have a history of pricing products before having any idea of what their manufacturing costs are. Goodyear gave away its space-saver tires to Detroit."[71] A Detroit securities analyst proclaimed that Goodyear is simply in a leaking boat of automotive-related and capital-goods stocks such as Chrysler, Timken, General Motors, and other rubber companies. "They should have a brighter future." This same analyst downplayed a possible raid, saying that borrowing money to finance a takeover is difficult since "The junk bonds have fallen into disfavor and it's pretty much proven that you can't buy quality with junk." He added, "I don't think anybody can run Goodyear but Goodyear. So it's not an attractive takeover candidate."[72]

But most analysts are skeptical about the company's short-term prospects, and they refuse to give even a lukewarm recommendation to the stock even though it is selling for such a low fraction of its book value. A continuing concern on Wall Street is the company's $3.8-billion total debt. Another analyst opined, "I think the stock is very, very cheap, but the macroeconomics stink. It's like a person with $10,000 on their credit card who is laid off—there's no cushion."[73]

Standard & Poor's Corp., citing Goodyear's "weak operating performance, along with failure to take the necessary steps to restore a very stretched capital structure," downgraded its assessment of Goodyear's credit. The action followed similar moves by credit rating agencies Duff & Phelps and Moody's Investors Service. S&P downgraded Goodyear's senior debt to double-B from triple-B-minus and commercial paper to single-B from A-3. The new rating is the highest speculative, or below-investment grade, level. Wall Street slang for below-investment grade is *junk*, as in junk bonds, the financing vehicle made famous in recent high-profile corporate takeovers.[74]

Goodyear called the S&P action disappointing and said the company has taken steps to reduce its leverage and improve operating results. Goodyear noted that it reduced its quarterly dividend from 45 cents to 10 cents per share, reduced capital expenditures 40 percent from 1990 levels to $350 million for 1991, and had taken other "cost containment measures," including reducing employment.[75]

The downgrade coming after moves to cut spending is probably a case of locking the barn after the horse is stolen. Effects on operations are expected to be minimal.[76] Goodyear, having unused bank lines of credit, $471 million short-term and $2,099 million long-term, is not likely to go to the public to raise money soon.[77]

An interesting speculation that has been made is that if Goldsmith had been successful, Goodyear would have $2.6 billion less indebtedness and would probably have been merged with a European partner, leaving Goodyear much better off than it is today.

SIR JAMES GOLDSMITH'S CONTINUING OPERATIONS

A look at the fortunes of Sir James Goldsmith following the 1986 Goodyear takeover attempt will complete the Goodyear drama.

At the same time Goldsmith was bidding over $5.5 billion to take over Goodyear, his biggest deal up to 1986, he was also acquiring L'Express, the number one newsweekly and second-largest publishing company in France, for $450 million. His grand plan was to build a media empire across the Continent, buying or starting publications in every major country and staffing them with editors who shared his conservative beliefs. Goldsmith, the raider, wanted to make money with the Goodyear campaign. But just as important, Goldsmith, the ideologue, is prepared to spend millions to change peoples' minds.[78]

In the United States Goldsmith unsuccessfully negotiated to buy *Esquire, New York Magazine,* and *The Village Voice*; also, he made a $100-million bid for *U.S. News & World Report*. After a look at *The Washington Times,* he was daunted by the amount of red ink, saying, "It's operating at a loss that is incompatible with my fortune."[79]

Operating through offshore companies, Goldsmith escapes capital gains taxes that domestic raiders such as Carl Icahn and T. Boone Pickens, Jr. must pay. Based in the Cayman Islands, the $2-billion empire Goldsmith controls is far from the prying eyes of tax collectors and government regulators from Europe and the United States. His personal holdings are managed, through several intermediary shell companies in Panama, by the Brunneria Foundation of Liechtenstein. This setup protects him from income taxes and provides a discreet way to finance a wide variety of political causes, from the Heritage Foundation and Committee for the Free World in the United States to conservative British think tanks and French political campaigns.[80]

Jacob Rothschild observes, "What is interesting about Goldsmith is that he's probably the only businessman who is truly global, equally at home on the three main battlefields of the West—London, New York, and Paris. [Goldsmith maintains homes in each of these cities in addition to numerous vacation retreats.] Who else can you think of who could find their way around those three cultures?"[81]

In a surprise move late in July 1987, Goldsmith pulled the plug on his French connection, selling his 51-percent stake in a holding company that controlled Générale Occidentale, netting nearly $300 million. The publishing empire he worked so hard to build was given up. The startling sellout left everyone wondering what Goldsmith would do next. Goldsmith's explanation was that "I've never liked the trappings of imperial commercial power. Générale Occidentale just became very big [$2 billion] and I hate empires. I founded the company, it grew, now it's time to get out." Goldsmith is left with 90 percent or more of General Oriental in the Cayman Islands, through which his main deals have been made. It holds North American timberland, oil, and gas properties, copper contracts, and, according to Goldsmith, "mountains of cash."[82]

Following the 1987 stock market crash, Goldsmith was back on Wall Street looking for stocks he believed to be undervalued. In November he was reportedly buying into Federated Department Stores Inc., whose stock tumbled from $47 to $39 on October 19. Federated, with annual sales of $10.5 billion, operates 640 department stores, supermarkets, and other retail stores in 36 states. The breakup value for Federated has been estimated at $80 to $90 a share.[83]

The next time Goldsmith surfaced in the news was when he launched a $21.3-billion bid for BAT Industries PLC (formerly British-American Tobacco Co.), one of Britain's bluest blue chips. BAT is number four in market value and is the owner of such familiar stateside properties as Saks Fifth Avenue; Marshall Field;

Farmers Group Insurance; Kool, Raleigh, and Viceroy cigarettes. It formerly owned Gimbel's department stores.[84]

The offer was made up of a monster $17-billion slug of debt plus a sprinkling of equity in Goldsmith's new investment vehicle, Anglo Group PLC. The bid gives shareholders in BAT 80 percent in various notes and 20 percent in Anglo Group equity. Investors turned thumbs down on the proposal featuring so much paper and no cash. It is expected that the bid will eventually be sweetened.[85]

The deal is four times the size of the largest previous European takeover, and it ranks just behind the $25.1 billion takeover of RJR Nabisco Inc. by Kohlberg Kravis Roberts & Company.

Goldsmith argues that "BAT is a quintessentially supreme example of a company that needs unbundling." If he succeeds in unbundling BAT, Goldsmith and his partners could gain as much as $7.3 billion, the excess of the estimated breakup value over the bid.

The bid for BAT triggered a run-up in the shares of other asset-rich British companies such as Cadbury Schweppes PLC. It also depressed quotes for BAT bonds as traders worried that the company might become overloaded with new debt. A Euromarket specialist noted that "the U.K. corporate bondholder now may be exposed to the same 'event risk' as U.S. bondholders."[86]

Goldsmith and his backers suffered a setback when BAT announced a sell-off of all assets except for its tobacco and insurance interests. Gains from the Goldsmith group's 2.3 percent holding in BAT would be wiped out by the fees already paid for the megadeal. Goldsmith estimated that both sides paid about $150 million to legions of lawyers, accountants, and bankers. A BAT advisor interpreted the remark as, "If they say it's a wash, that probably means they're under water [in losses]."

Goldsmith did manage to galvanize the debate across Europe on the future of conglomerates. Even well-run organizations were eyeing restructuring plans. But Goldsmith failed to convince European investors that huge bids financed with junk bonds are tolerable. "We've won a number of arguments close to my heart," Goldsmith says, "but one is not in this entirely for the debate."[87]

Endnotes

1. *Annual Report,* Goodyear Tire & Rubber Company, 1988, p. 2.
2. *Annual Report,* Goodyear Tire & Rubber Company, 1988, p. 25. *Annual Report,* Goodyear Tire & Rubber Company, 1990, p. 29.
3. *Annual Report,* Goodyear Tire & Rubber Company, 1990, pp. 40, 41.
4. *Annual Report,* Goodyear Tire & Rubber Company, 1988, p. 2.
5. *Annual Report,* Goodyear Tire & Rubber Company, 1989, pp. 5, 6, 14.
6. Steve Weiner, "Debt Focuses the Mind," *Forbes,* January 7, 1991, p. 40.
7. "Goodyear Pay Down," *Akron Beacon Journal,* March 16, 1991, p. B8.
8. Robert Fernandez, "Goodyear's Loss Tops $90 Million," *Akron Beacon Journal,* April 25, 1991, p. B12.
9. Robert Fernandez, "Goodyear Passes on Land for S. Korea Plant," *Akron Beacon Journal,* January 15, 1991, p. C6.
10. Zachary Schiller with Laxmi Nakarmi, "Can Goodyear Pull out of Its Skid?" *Business Week,* March 20, 1989, p. 41.
11. Katie Byard, "More Cost Cuts May Be in Store at Goodyear," *Akron Beacon Journal,* March 15, 1991, pp. C8, C12.
12. Katie Byard, "New President Guides a Slimmer Goodyear," *Akron Beacon Journal,* March 24, 1991, p. A16.
13. "Sardas Will Get $1 Million," *Akron Beacon Journal,* March 30, 1991, p. A7.
14. Byard, "New President."
15. Goodyear Tire & Rubber Company, Public Relations Release 06084–491.
16. Robert Fernandez, "A New Era at Goodyear," *Akron Beacon Journal,* June 5, 1991, pp. A1, A7.
17. Goodyear Tire & Rubber Company, Public Relations Release 06156–691.
18. Goodyear Tire & Rubber Company, Public Relations Release 06155–691.
19. Ibid.
20. Goodyear Tire & Rubber Company, Public Relations Release 06157–691.
21. Goodyear Tire & Rubber Company, Public Relations Release 06155–691.
22. Excerpted from an interview with William Sheelie and Jung Ah Pak, *Fortune,* July 15, 1991, pp. 104–105.
23. Yalinda Rhoden, "Five Weeks Retirement Is Enough for Go-Getter," *Akron Beacon Journal,* June 5, 1991, pp. A1, A7.
24. "Reaction," *Akron Beacon Journal,* June 5, 1991, p. A6.
25. "Goodyear Leaders," *Akron Beacon Journal,* June 5, 1991, p. A7.
26. Gregory Stricharchuk, "Changing Times Take Toll at Goodyear," *The Wall Street Journal,* October 22, 1990, p. A6.
27. Stuart Drown, "Where Now for World's Tire Makers?" *Akron Beacon Journal,* April 29, 1991, p. D1.
28. Peter Geiger and Katie Byard, "Pirelli Makes Bid to Merge with General Tire's Parent," *Akron Beacon Journal,* September 18, 1990, p. A4.
29. Drown, "Where Now," p. D2.
30. Stricharchuk, "Changing Times."
31. Delinda Karle, "Fighting on Numerous Fronts," *Cleveland Plain Dealer,* December 2, 1990, p. 1E.
32. Delinda Karle, "Surviving Tire Firms Fight for Market Share," *Cleveland Plain Dealer,* December 2, 1990, p. 6E.
33. Drown, "Where Now," p. D1.
34. Ibid., p. D2.
35. Gregory Stricharchuk, "Goodyear Squares Off to Protect Its Turf from Foreign Rivals," *The Wall Street Journal,* February 29, 1989, p. A1.
36. Stricharchuk, "Changing Times."
37. Ibid.
38. Drown, "Where Now," p. D2.
39. Ibid.
40. Ibid.
41. Robert Fernandez, "New Firestone President Confident as He Looks at Company's Future," *Akron Beacon Journal,* April 2, 1991, p. B6.
42. Donald Sabath, "Bridgestone/Firestone to Get New Chief Exec in Akron This Spring," *Cleveland Plain Dealer,* February 27, 1991, p. 1E.
43. Robert Fernandez, "Pirelli Posts Loss for '90," *Akron Beacon Journal,* April 3, 1991, p. D7.
44. Robert Fernandez, "Continental Defeats Pirelli Bid," *Akron Beacon Journal,* March 14, 1991, p. B7.
45. Drown, "Where Now," p. D2.
46. Jonathan Hicks, "Chasing Few Buyers with Too Many Tires," *New York Times,* February 3, 1991, p. F5.
47. "Oil Prices Pose Another Problem," *New York Times,* February 3, 1991, p. F5.
48. Karle, "Fighting on Fronts," p. 1E.
49. Karle, "Surviving Tire Firms," p. 6E.
50. Delinda Karle, "Goodyear," *Cleveland Plain Dealer,* December 2, 1990, p. 6E.
51. Robert Fernandez, "Customer Debt to Goodyear Up $400 million," *Akron Beacon Journal,* October 28, 1990, p. D5.
52. *Annual Report,* Goodyear Tire & Rubber Company, 1990, p. 36.
53. Karle, "Goodyear."
54. Katie Byard, "Blimp," *Akron Beacon Journal,* May 10, 1991, p. A13.
55. Fernandez, "Customer Debt."
56. Ibid.
57. Karle, "Goodyear."
58. Katie Byard, "Goodyear to Cut 1,100 Salary Jobs to Stem Red Ink," *Akron Beacon Journal,* March 14, 1991, p. A4.

59. Stricharchuk, "Changing Times."
60. Byard, "Goodyear to Cut."
61. Zachary Schiller et al., "Goodyear Feels the Heat," *Business Week*, March 7, 1988, p. 26.
62. "Mercer, Goodyear Welcome Competition," *Modern Tire Dealer*, September 1988, p. 22.
63. Marcus Gleisser, "Tire Firms Fight to Survive," *Cleveland Plain Dealer*, March 14, 1991, p. 8A.
64. Robert Fernandez, "Goodyear Awaits a Profit," *Akron Beacon Journal*, April 9, 1991, p. C9.
65. Peter Geiger, "Buy Some Lights, Goodyear Stock Undervalued," *Akron Beacon Journal*, September 9, 1990, p. C6.
66. Robert Fernandez, "Goodyear Reports Loss of $90 Million," *Akron Beacon Journal*, April 25, 1991, p. B12.
67. *Annual Report*, Goodyear Tire & Rubber Company, 1989, pp. 19, 27.
68. Robert Fernandez, "Goodyear's Pipeline Aided by Oil Ruling," *Akron Beacon Journal*, April 13, 1991, pp. C8, C12.
69. "Oil Pipeline Still Big Loser for Goodyear," *Akron Beacon Journal*, July 8, 1990, pp. D1, D7.
70. Ibid.
71. Geiger, "Buy Some Lights."
72. Robert Fernandez, "Goodyear Keeping One Eye Out for Raiders," *Akron Beacon Journal*, January 24, 1990, pp. B7, B11.

73. Karle, "Goodyear."
74. Katie Byard, "Goodyear Rating Lowered," *Akron Beacon Journal*, March 26, 1991, p. D6.
75. Ibid., pp. D6, D10.
76. Ibid., p. D10.
77. *Annual Report*, Goodyear Tire & Rubber Company, 1990, p. 31.
78. John Rossant et al., "The Two Worlds of Jimmy Goldsmith," *Business Week*, December 1, 1986, pp. 98, 99, 102.
79. Ibid.
80. Ibid.
81. Ibid.
82. John Rossant et al., "Sir Jimmy Pulls the Plug on His French Connection," *Business Week*, August 10, 1987, p. 24.
83. "Sir Jimmy Goes Shopping Again," *Business Week*, November 16, 1987, p. 188.
84. Richard Melcher, "Storming a British Blue Chip," *Business Week*, July 24, 1989, pp. 18, 19.
85. Ibid.
86. Ibid.
87. Richard Melcher, "Take That, Jimmy Goldsmith," *Business Week*, October 9, 1989, pp. 60, 61.

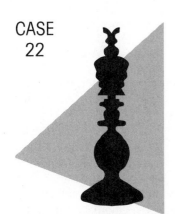

CASE
22

TAURUS HUNGARIAN RUBBER WORKS: IMPLEMENTING A STRATEGY FOR THE 1990s

JOSEPH WOLFE,
GYULA BOSNYAK &
JANOS VECSENYI

Although Taurus had had a three-day top management planning session conducted at its Lake Balaton retreat less than two years ago, many major company decisions had been made since that time. Still the basic implementation of the company's diversification strategy had not been accomplished. As director of the company's Corporate Development Strategic Planning Department, Gyula Bosnyak recognized both the timing and the enormity of the events and issues involved. In early 1988 the Hungarian government had just passed its Corporation Law which put all state-owned firms on notice to reprivatize and recapitalize themselves. Not only did the firm have to deal with the mechanics of going public, it had to obtain the ideal mix of debt and equity capital to insure solid growth for a company which was operating in a stagnant economy and a low-growth industry. Top management was also concerned about the route they should follow in their attempts to invigorate the company. It was an accepted fact that Taurus had to maintain or even improve its international competitiveness, and that it had to diversify away from its traditional dependence on the manufacturing of truck and farm tires.

Rather than viewing this situation as a bothersome threat, Gyula had seen this as an opportunity for Taurus to deal with its working capital problem as well as to begin serious diversification efforts away from its basically noncompetitive and highly threatened commercial tire manufacturing operation. Now, in Spring 1990, he was beginning to sort out his company's options before making his recommendations to both Laszlo Geza, vice president of Taurus's Technical Rubber Products Division, and Laszlo Palotas, the company's newly elected president.

RUBBER AND RUBBER PRODUCTION

Christopher Columbus was probably the first European to handle rubber. Haitian natives had used it for centuries as a football-sized sphere which they threw into a hole in the wall of a playing field. These balls were derived from a dried milky liquid obtained by cutting the bark of a "weeping wood" or cauchuc tree. While

---

This case does not describe either correct or incorrect managerial actions or decisions, but instead is intended to facilitate an understanding of the strategic management issues involved.

the natives also used this substance to make shoes, bottles, and waterproof cloth, the western world's commercial use of the product was limited until two discoveries greatly expanded rubber's usefulness and properties. In 1819 Thomas Hancock discovered latex rubber could be masticated which allowed it to be converted into products of different shapes by the use of pressure and the addition of other materials. Unfortunately mastication deprived rubber of its elastic qualities.

The discovering of vulcanization by Charles Goodyear in 1839 solved this problem and also kept rubber products from becoming tacky. Goodyear found the addition of sulfur to crude rubber at a temperature above its melting point improved its mechanical properties and its resistance to temperature changes. After these twin discoveries, the commercial uses of rubber multiplied greatly with the greatest impetus coming from J. B. Dunlop's rediscovery of the pneumatic tire, which he applied to his son's bicycle in 1888. Shortly thereafter the rise of the automobile industry at the century's turn resulted in a tremendous increase in the demand for rubber and its principle application in the manufacture of automobile and truck tires. The world's long-ton consumption of rubber prior to World War II in approximate 30-year periods was as follows:

1840–1872	150,000
1873–1905	1,000,000
1906–1940	18,850,000

The production of natural rubber entails collecting the juice of the 60- to 80-foot high *Hevea brasiliensis* tree which is now plantation grown in such tropical countries as Brazil, Malaysia, and Indonesia. The trees are tapped by cutting through the tree's bark, which contains latex tubes. A flow of liquid amounting to about five pounds per year can be obtained from each tree. The milky substance is dehydrated for shipment by spraying and drying; by acidification, coagulation, washing, and rolling; or by drying with smoke. Natural rubber is usually transformed into sheet or crepe. Sheet rubber is smoke-dried and obtains a dark brown color while crepe is air-dried, is much lighter in color, and is passed through heavy rollers at the beginning of the drying process.

As shown in Exhibit 1, a wide range of rubber applications can be obtained through the addition of various ingredients to latex rubber during its masticating or compounding manufacturing stages. Carbon black is added for high abrasion resistance, oils for making the material more workable, and paraffin for better light resistance. Other ingredients, such as antioxidants, activators, and various organic and inorganic coloring substances are also employed and various accelerators are used to (1) hasten the vulcanization process, (2) allow it to occur at room temperatures, and (3) improve the product's ultimate quality.

Because of the tremendous increase in the need for natural rubber in the early 1920s and the realization of its strategic importance by both Germany and Russia from their World War I experiences, vigorous research into the creation of a synthetic rubber was conducted in the 1930s. The first butadiene-styrene copolymer from an emulsion system (Buna S) was prepared at the research laboratories of

EXHIBIT 1 Major Nontire Rubber Uses

Mechanical goods
Latex foam products
Shoe products
Athletic goods
Toys
Sponge rubber
Insulated wire and cable
Footwear
Waterproofed fabrics
Hard-rubber products
Flooring
Cements
Drug sundries
Pulley belts
Waterproof insulation
Conveyor belts
Shock absorbers and vibration dampeners

I. G. Farbenindustrie followed shortly thereafter by the analogous butadiene-acrylonitrile copolymer (Buna N). By 1936 Germany was able to produce 100 to 200 tons of synthetic rubber a month while by 1939 the factories at Schkopau and Hüls could produce 50,000 tons per year.

The family of Buna rubbers are produced by polymerizing butadiene with sodium (natrium) acting as a catalyst. This process was originally conducted at a temperature of about 50° centigrade, but the copolymerization of butadiene and styrene is now usually done in aqueous phase.[1] In an emulsion copolymerization process carried out at 5° centigrade, so-called *cold rubber*, the hydrocarbons to be polymerized are in emulsion and contain a constituent of the activator system dissolved in them. The second part of the activator system is present in the watery medium of the emulsion. The combined activator system initiates the process of polymerization and the polymer's molecule size is regulated by adding various substances. The entire process is stopped after about 60 percent of these substances have reacted. The resulting product is very much like latex rubber and from this phase on can be treated like the natural substance. A large variety of other synthetic rubbers can be produced in addition to the Buna rubbers. Exhibit 2 presents a forecast of the demand for these rubbers for the year 1992.

Combining both natural and synthetic rubbers, it has been estimated that world consumption of these substances will be about 15.9 million metric tons in 1992. According to William E. Tessmer, managing director of the International Institute of Synthetic Rubber Producers, this is an 11-percent increase from the 14.4 million tons estimated for 1987. As shown in Exhibit 3 about 70 percent of the world's rubber consumption is in the form of synthetic rubber. Exhibits 4 and 5 show the predicted geographic distribution of rubber demand for the year 1992.

EXHIBIT 2 Predicted Demand for Synthetic Rubbers in 1992
(nonsocialist countries in thousands of metric tons)

Synthetic Rubber	Forecast
Styrene-butadiene[a]	2,819
Carboxylated styrene-butadiene	1,015
Polybutadiene	1,142
Ethylene-propylene diene	556
Polychloroprene	268
Nitrile	238
All others[b]	1,025
Total	7,063

[a]In both liquid and solid forms.
[b]Includes polyisoprene and butyl.
Source: International Institute of Synthetic Rubber Producers, as cited in Bruce F. Greek, "Modest Growth Ahead for Rubber," *Chemical & Engineering News* 66, no. 12 (March 21, 1988), p. 26.

WORLDWIDE RUBBER COMPANY COMPETITION

Rubber firms now compete on the international level because of a number of driving forces. Automobiles and trucks, which are the major users of tire and rubber products, are ubiquitous, the high operating scales required for efficient plant operations compel manufacturers to find markets which can support them, and growth opportunities no longer exist in many of the manufacturers' home countries. As has been the case within its domestic automobile industry, the United States has been invaded by a number of very competitive and efficient foreign tire and rubber manufacturers. Those foreign competitors in turn have acquired firms or have entered into joint ventures on a global scale thereby increasing their penetration into a number of countries. Exhibit 6 displays the financial results which have been obtained by the world's major world rubber manufacturers for 1984 and 1988, while Exhibit 7 reviews the alternative strategies and recent actions taken by the industry's principal actors. As best as can be

EXHIBIT 3 Predicted World Consumption of Rubber (in millions of metric tons)

Type	1986	1987	1988	1989	1990	1991	1992
Synthetic	9.5	9.8	9.8	9.9	9.9	10.0	10.0
Natural	4.5	4.6	4.9	5.1	5.4	5.7	5.9
Total	13.9	14.4	14.6	14.9	15.2	15.5	15.9

Note: One metric ton equals 2,204.6 pounds.
Source: Derived from data in Bruce F. Greek, "Modest Growth Ahead for Rubber," *Chemical & Engineering News* 66, no. 12 (March 21, 1988), pp. 25–26.

EXHIBIT 4   Predicted Changes in Rubber Demand by Geographic Area (in thousands of metric tons)

Geographic Area	1987	1992	Change
North America	3,395	3,432	1.09%
Latin America	788	944	19.80
Western Europe	2,460	2,953	20.04
Africa & Middle East	259	324	25.10
Asia and Oceania	3,060	3,541	15.72
Socialist countries	4,057	4,706	16.00
Total	14,019	15,900	13.42%

Source: Bruce F. Greek, ``Modest Growth Ahead for Rubber,'' *Chemical & Engineering News* 66, no. 12 (March 21, 1988), p. 26.

determined Michelin has recently become the world's largest tire manufacturing firm with a worldwide market share of 21.3 percent with Goodyear and Bridgestone basically tied for second place in world sales. [See Exhibit 8.]

TAURUS HUNGARIAN RUBBER WORKS

Today's Taurus Hungarian Rubber Works has an ancestry dating back more than a century. From its earliest days with the founding of the factory of Erno Schottola, it has been Hungary's most important rubber producer. In growing to its current size Taurus has both grown internally and has acquired several smaller manufacturers.

The first Hungarian rubber factory was established in 1882 and in 1890 it became a public company under the name Magyar Ruggyantaarugyar Rt. Because Hungary lacked a domestic producer of automobiles at the century's turn, the company supported the creation of an automobile plant, which was ultimately

EXHIBIT 5   Predicted Demand for Rubber in Socialist Countries (in millions of metric tons)

Socialist Group	1987	1992
Eastern European		
Synthetic	2.90	3.30
Natural	0.40	0.37
Total	3.30	3.67
Asian socialist		
Synthetic	0.30	0.43
Natural	0.46	0.61
Total	0.76	1.04

Source: Derived from data presented in Bruce F. Greek, ``Modest Growth Ahead for Rubber,'' *Chemical & Engineering News* 66, no. 12 (March 21, 1988), pp. 25–26.

EXHIBIT 6 Selected Company Sales and Profits in U.S. Dollars

Company	1984		1988	
	Sales ($billion)	Profits ($million)	Sales ($billion)	Profits ($million)
B. F. Goodrich (U.S.)	$ 3.40	$ 60.6	n.a.[a]	n.a.
Bridgestone (Japan)	3.38	65.1	$ 9.30	$310.2
Cooper (U.S.)	0.56	23.9	0.73	35.0
Firestone (U.S.)	4.16	102.0	n.a.[b]	n.a.
GenCorp (U.S.)	2.73	7.2	0.50	n.a.[c]
Goodyear (U.S.)	10.24	391.7	10.90	330.0
Michelin (France)	5.08	(256.5)	8.70	397.4
Pirelli (Italy)	3.50	72.0	7.01	172.1
Taurus (Hungary)	0.26	11.5	0.38	9.0
Uniroyal (U.S.)	2.10	77.1	2.19	11.8

[a]Merged with Uniroyal in 1987.
[b]Acquired by Bridgestone in 1988.
[c]Acquired by Continental in 1987.
Sources: *Akron Beacon Journal*, January 13, 1986, p. B8; ''Powerful Profits around the World,'' *Fortune* 120, no. 3 (July 31, 1989), pp. 292, 294; Gary Levin, ''Tire Makers Take Opposite Routes,'' *Advertising Age* 60, no. 6 (February 6, 1989), p. 34.

located in Arad, and the formation of the Autotaxi company in Budapest. During the period before World War I Magyar Ruggyantaarugyar grew rapidly and was soon exporting between 30 and 35 percent of its products outside Hungary. Its rubber balls, toys, asbestos-rubber seals, and Palma heels gained a worldwide reputation for quality.

During the interwar period the Hungarian rubber sector declined dramatically with its export sales dropping to 15 to 18 percent of total production. Its factory equipment deteriorated and only its lines of rubber yarns and latex products could remain internationally competitive. Pre-World War I global market shares of 0.6

EXHIBIT 7 Recent Activities of Various Tire and Rubber Companies

Bridgestone Corporation
Bridgestone's acquisition of the Firestone Tire & Rubber Company in 1988 for $2.6 billion vaulted it into a virtual tie with Goodyear as the world's second-largest tire company. The acquisition has been a troublesome one for Bridgestone with Firestone losing about $100 million in 1989 causing the parent company's 1989 profits to fall to about $250 million on sales of $10.7 billion. Bridgestone has already invested $1.5 billion in upgrading Firestone's deteriorated plants and an additional $2.5 billion will be needed to bring all operations up to Bridgestone's quality standards. Last year's North American sales were $3.5 billion and the firm plans to quadruple the output of its La Vergne, Tennessee plant. Currently Bridgestone is attempting to increase its share of the American tire market while slowly increasing its share of the European market as Japanese cars increase their sales in that area. In mid-1989 nine top executives were forced to resign or accept reassignment over disputes about the wisdom of the company's aggressive growth goals. Bridgestone is a major factor in Asia, the Pacific, and South America where Japanese cars and trucks are heavily marketed.

EXHIBIT 7 Cont'd.   Recent Activities of Various Tire and Rubber Companies

Continental Gummi-Werke AG

Continental is West Germany's largest tire manufacturer and is number two in European sales. It purchased General Tire from GenCorp in June 1987 for $625 million and is basically known as a premium-quality tire manufacturer. Continental entered a $200 million joint radial-tire venture in December 1987 with the Toyo Tire & Rubber Company and Yokohama Rubber Company for the manufacture of tires installed on Japanese cars being shipped to the American market. Another part of the venture entails manufacturing radial truck and bus tires in the United States.

Cooper Tire and Rubber Company

This relatively small American firm has been very successful by specializing in the replacement tire market. This segment accounts for about 80 percent of its sales and nearly half its output is sold as private-labeled merchandise. Cooper has recently expanded its capacity by 12 percent with about 10 percent more capacity scheduled for completion in late 1990. About 60 percent of its sales are for passenger tires while the remainder are for buses and heavy trucks. The company is currently attempting to acquire a medium-truck tire plant in Natchez, Mississippi to enable it to more completely cover the tire spectrum.

Goodyear Tire & Rubber Company

The last of two major rubber companies left in the United States, Goodyear has diversified itself into chemicals and plastics and a California-to-Texas oil pipeline, as well as into the aerospace industry. Automotive products, which include tires, account for 86 percent of sales and 76 percent of operating profits. Its recent sales growth has come from African and Latin American tire sales where the company has a dominant market share. Additional plant expansions have been started in Canada and South Korea (12,000 tires daily per plant) and will be available in 1991 although they should not produce significant revenues until 1992. Goodyear is attempting to sell off its All American pipeline for about $1.4 billion to reduce its $275 million per year interest charges on $3.5 billion worth of debt.

Michelin et Cie.

Although it lost $1.5 billion between 1980 and 1984, Michelin has become profitable again. In late 1988 the company acquired Uniroyal/Goodrich for $690 million which made it the world's largest tire company. Uniroyal had merged in August 1986 with the B. F. Goodrich Company creating a company where 29 percent of output was in private brands. Passenger and light-truck tires were sold in both the United States and overseas and sales grew 44.5 percent although profits fell 11.1 percent. Michelin has entered a joint venture with Okamoto of Japan to double that company's capacity to 24,000 tires a day. While a large company, Michelin is much stronger in the truck-tire segment than it is in the passenger-tire segment.

Pirelli

After having been frustrated in its attempts to acquire Firestone, Pirelli purchased the Armstrong Tire Company for $190 million in 1988 to gain a foothold in the North American market. Armstrong, under the guise of the Armtek Corporation, was attempting to diversify out of the tire and rubber industry by selling off its industrial tire plant in March 1987. Pirelli, which is strong in the premium-tire market, obtained a company whose sales are equally divided between the original equipment and replacement markets and one which has over 500 retail dealers. In the acquisition process Pirelli obtained a headquarters building in Connecticut, three tire plants, one tire textile plant, and one truck-tire factory. Armstrong's 1988 sales were $500 million.

EXHIBIT 8 Top Market Shares in World Tire Market

Company	1985	1990
Goodyear	20.0%	17.2%
Michelin	13.0	21.3
Bridgestone	8.0	17.2

Source: Stuart J. Benway, "Tire & Rubber Industry," *Value Line Investment Survey*, December 22, 1989, p. 127.

percent fell to 0.3 percent and its annual sales growth rates dropped to 1.5 to 2.0 percent per year.

Upon the nationalization of all rubber firms after World War II the Hungarian government pursued a policy of extensive growth for a number of years. From 1950 to 1970 annual production increases of 12.5 percent a year were common while the rubber sector's employment and average gross fixed asset value increased, a respective average of approximately 6.2 percent and 15.7 percent per year. Although growth was rapid, great inefficiencies were incurred. Labor utilization rates were low and productivity ratios lagged by about 1.5 to 3.0 times that obtained by comparable socialist and advanced capitalist countries. Little attention was paid to rationalizing either production or the product line as sales to the Hungarian and CMEA countries appeared to support the sector's activities. At various times the nationalized firm produced condoms, bicycle and automobile tires, rubber toys, boots, and raincoats.

During this period the government also restructured its rubber industry. In 1963 Budapest's five rubber manufacturers, PALMA, Heureka, Tauril, Emerge, and Cordatic, were merged into one company called the National Rubber Company and new locations in Vac, Nyiregyhaza, and Szeged were created. Purchasing, cash management, and investment were centralized and central trade, and research and development apparatus was created. Contrary to the normal way of conducting its affairs, however, the company pioneered the use of strategic planning when the classic type of centralized planning was still the country's ruling mechanism.

In 1973 the company changed its name to the Taurus Hungarian Rubber Works and it currently operates rubber processing plants in Budapest, Nyiregyhaza, Szeged, Vac, and Mugi as well as a machine and mold factory in Budapest. As shown in Exhibits 9 and 10, Taurus operates four separate divisions, while engaging in a number of joint ventures. Sales have increased annually to the 20.7 billion Forint mark with an increasing emphasis on international business.

Tire Division

The Tire Division manufactures tires for commercial, nonpassenger vehicles after having phased out its production of automobile tires in the mid-1970s. Truck tires, as either bias-ply or all-steel radials, account for about 34 percent of the division's sales. Farm tires are its other major product category as either textile radials or bias-ply tires. Farm tires were about 20 percent of the division's sales in 1988. A smaller product category includes tire retreading, inner tubes, and forklift truck tires. About 58 percent of the division's volume is export sales, of which the following countries constituted the greatest amounts (in millions of Forints):

United States	351.7
Algeria	298.2
Czechoslovakia	187.3
West Germany	183.5
Yugoslavia	172.0

EXHIBIT 9 Taurus Hungarian Rubber Works Organization Structure

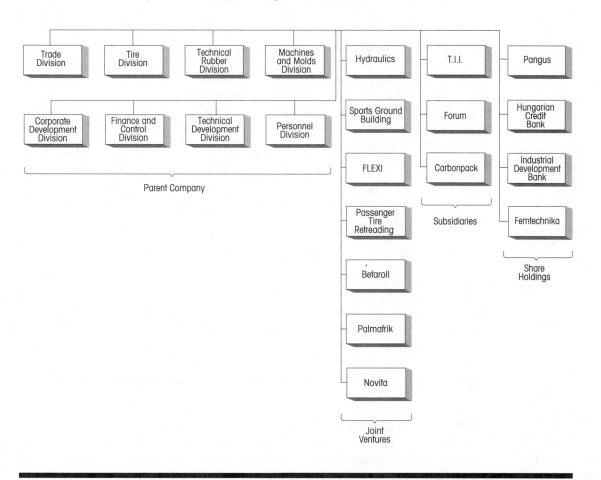

The division has recently finished a World Bank-financed capacity expansion in the all-steel-radial truck-tire operation. This project was begun in December

EXHIBIT 10 Total Company Sales (selected years; in millions of Forints)

Market	1980	1982	1984	1985	1986	1987	1988	1989
Export	2,560	2,588	3,704	4,055	4,517	5,349	6,843	7,950
Domestic	7,890	9,024	9,381	9,979	11,174	12,255	12,056	12,716
Total	10,450	11,612	13,085	14,034	15,691	17,604	18,899	20,666

Source: *Annual Report*, Taurus Hungarian Rubber Works, 1988; and internal company data.

1986. Eleven new tires within the Taurus Top Tire brand have been scheduled for the market, of which two were completed in 1988 and another three in early 1990. The division is also developing a new super-single tire under a licencing agreement with an American tire manufacturer.

Technical Rubber Division

This division manufactures and markets an assortment of rubber hoses, air springs for trucks and buses, conveyor belts, waterproof sheeting, and the PALMA line of camping gear. The PALMA camping gear line has a 15 percent world market share while the company's rotary hose business is a world leader with 40 percent of all international sales. The demand for high-pressure and large-bore hoses is closely related to offshore drilling activity, while the sale of air springs for commercial vehicles is expected to increase as this technology gains increasing acceptance with vehicle manufacturers. The Soviet Union is this division's largest customer with 1988 sales of 380,000 Forints. In recent years sales within the division have been distributed in the following fashion:

Large-bore, high-pressure hoses	6.7%
Rotary hoses	27.1
Hydraulic hoses	14.7
Camping goods	18.0
Waterproof sheeting	13.9
Air springs	5.3
Conveyor belts	14.3

Machines and Molds Division

This division manufactures products which are used in-house as part of Taurus' manufacturing process as well as products used by others. About 70 percent of its sales are for export and its overall sales were distributed as follows in 1988:

Technical rubber molds	24%
Polyurethane molds	17
Machines and components	25
Tire curing molds	34

Trade Division

The Trade Division conducts CMEA purchases and sales for Taurus as well as performing autonomous distribution functions for other firms. Its activities serve both Taurus' other divisions as well as those outside the company. It is expected that this division will continue to function as Taurus's purchasing agent while increasing its outside trading activities; its status regarding CMEA trafficking is in a state of flux.

Exhibits 11 and 12 summarize the sales generated by each division for the years of 1988 and 1989 as well as the assets and personnel dedicated to each operation.

IMPLEMENTING TAURUS' STRATEGY OF STRATEGIC ALLIANCES

Immediately after returning from his company's top management conference, Gyula began collecting materials to confirm the tentative decisions which had been made at Lake Balaton. Based on secondary data collected and assembled into Exhibits 13 and 14, he could see the general rubber industry had fallen from a better-than-average industry growth performance in the 1960 to 1970 period to one that was far inferior to the industrial average during the 1980 to 1987 period. He also saw that other industries, such as data processing, aircraft, medical

EXHIBIT 11   Selected 1988 Division Performance Information (in millions of Forints)

	Division			
Item	**Tires**	**Technical Rubber**	**Machines and Molds**	**Trade**
Revenues	6,591	6,484	212	5,612
Assets				
Gross fixed assets	5,201	2,756	268	—
Net fixed assets	2,934	1,199	123	—
Inventories	1,024	601	100	—
Employees	3,987	3,912	557	208

Note: Machines and molds sales include output used in-house.

EXHIBIT 12 Selected 1989 Division Performance Information (in millions of Forints)

		Division		
Item	Tires	Technical Rubber	Machines and Molds	Trade
Revenues	8,547	7,183	242	4,694
Assets				
Gross fixed assets	5,519	2,787	292	—
Net fixed assets	3,016	1,120	135	—
Inventories	1,126	545	104	—
Employees	4,021	3,851	552	196

Note: Machines and molds sales include output used in-house.

equipment, and telecommunication equipment, had obtained sizeable growth rates from 1977 to 1987. Moreover he was extremely aware of the increasing concentration occurring in the tire industry through the formation of joint ventures, mergers, cooperative arrangements, and acquisitions. It was obvious that at least the rubber industry's tire segment had passed into its mature stage. In response to this, most major rubber companies had obtained diversifications away from the heavy competition within the industry itself as well as attempting to find growth markets for their rubber production capacity. For the year 1987 alone, Gyula listed the various strategic alliances shown in Exhibit 15, while Exhibit 16 reviews the diversification activities of Taurus' major tire competitors in 1989.

Within the domestic market various other Hungarian rubber manufacturers had surpassed Taurus in their growth rates as they jettisoned their low-profit lines and adopted newer ones possessing greater growth rates. Taurus' market share of the Hungarian rubber goods industry had slowly eroded since 1970 and this erosion increased greatly in the decade of the 1980s due to the creation of a number of smaller, startup rubber companies encouraged by Hungary's new privatization laws. While the company's market share stood at about 68 percent in 1986, Gyula estimated Taurus' market share would only fall another 4 percent by 1992. Exhibit 17 displays the figures and estimates he created for his analysis.

With the aid of a major consulting firm, Taurus had recently conducted the in-depth analysis of its business portfolio shown in Exhibit 18. It was concluded

EXHIBIT 13 Comparative Average Annual Growth Rates

Period	Rubber Sector	All Industry
1960–1970	8.3%	6.8%
1970–1980	4.0	4.1
1980–1987	1.7	4.3
Average	5.0%	5.1%

Source: Internal company report.

EXHIBIT 14 Growth Rates for Selected Industries (1977 to 1987)

Sector	Annual Growth Rate
Data processing equipment	21.0%
Transistors	17.0
Aircraft	16.0
Medical equipment	15.0
Measuring and control equipment	13.5
Electronic games	13.2
Telecommunications equipment	12.9
Metal processing equipment	10.4
Synthetic fibers	7.8
Steel	7.4
Building materials	7.3
Fertilizers	7.0
Agricultural equipment	4.5
Coal	3.2
Passenger cars	2.5
Crude oil	0.5

Source: Internal report.

EXHIBIT 15 Strategic Alliances in 1987

Goodrich (USA) and Uniroyal (Great Britain) operated as a joint venture

Pirelli (Italy) acquired Armstrong (USA)

Firestone (USA) acquired by Bridgestone (Japan), which has another type of alliance with Trells Nord (Sweden)

General Tire (USA) acquired by Continental Tire (West Germany) which, in turn, operates in cooperation with Yokohama Tire (Japan); Continental also owns Uniroyal Englebert Tire

Toyo (Japan) operates in cooperation with Continental Tire (West Germany) while also operating a joint venture in Nippon Tire (Japan) with Goodyear (USA)

Michelin (France) operates in cooperation with Michelin Okamoto (Japan)

Sumitomo (Japan) operates in cooperation with Nokia (Finland), Trells Nord (Sweden), and BTR Dunlop (Great Britain)

Source: Corporate annual reports.

EXHIBIT 16   Rubber Company Diversifications[a]

Rubber Company	Nontire Sales	Major Diversification Efforts
Goodyear	27.0%	Packing materials, chemicals
Firestone	30.0	Vehicle service
Cooper	20.0	Laser technology
Armstrong	n.a.	Heat transmission equipment
General Tire	68.0	Electronics, sporting goods
Carlisle	88.0	Computer technology, roofing materials
Bridgestone	30.0	Chemicals, sporting goods
Yokohama	26.0	Sporting goods, aluminum products
Trelleborg	97.0	Mining, ore processing
Aritmos	n.a.	Food processing
Nokia	98.0	Electronics, inorganic chemicals

[a]Major diversifications as of 1988.
Source: Corporate annual reports for citations of diversifications. Source for nontire sales volume: Bruce Davis, ''No Clear-Cut Winner in Tire Crown Fight,'' *Rubber & Plastics News*, August 21, 1989, p. 18.

the company operated in a number of highly attractive markets, but that the firm's competitive position needed to be improved for most product lines. Accordingly the firm's emphasis was to be placed on improving the competitiveness of the company's current product lines and businesses. With 1991 in mind as the target year, Taurus was to implement two types of projects—software projects dealing with quality assurance programs, management development and staff training efforts, and the implementation of a management information system; and hardware projects dealing with upgrading the agricultural-tire compounding process, as well as upgrades in the infrastructures of various plants.

Fundamental to Taurus' desire to be more growth oriented was its newly enunciated strategy shown in Exhibit 19. As formally stated, the company was seeking strategic alliances for certain business lines rather than growth through internal development which had been its previous growth strategy. While it was felt that internal development possessed lower risks as it basically extended the

EXHIBIT 17   Distribution of Rubber Goods Production between Taurus and All Other Hungarian Rubber Manufacturers

Manufacturer	Percentage of Market			
	1970	1980	1986	1992
Taurus	95%	80%	68%	65%
All others	5	20	32	35

Source: Internal company data for years 1970 to 1986, and personal estimate for 1992.

EXHIBIT 18 The Taurus Portfolio

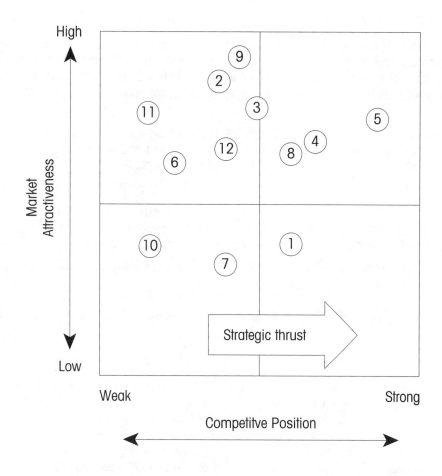

1. Bias Tires
2. Steel Radial Truck Tires
3. Agricultural Tires
4. Rotary Hoses
5. Special Hoses
6. Conveyor Belts
7. Camping Mattresses
8. Rubber Sheets
9. Air Springs
10. V-Belts
11. Precision Technical Rubber
12. Machines and Molds

Source: Company documents and consulting group's final report.

company's current areas of expertise, benefited the various product lines already in existence, and better served its present customer base while simultaneously using the company's store of management knowledge and wisdom, internal development possessed a number of impediments to Taurus' current desires for accelerated growth. Paramount was its belief that management was too preoccupied with its current activities to pay attention to new areas outside its specific areas of expertise.

EXHIBIT 19   Taurus' Strategy for the 1990s

The decade of 1990 is predicted to be a busy stage for the rubber sector worldwide.

There are strong factors of concentration in traditional manufacturing business[es] and particularly in tire operations. The role of substitute products is growing in several areas. On the other hand the fast end-of-century growth of industrial sectors is expected to stimulate the development of sophisticated special rubber products. In the face of these challenges, TAURUS bases its competitive strategy on the following:

A continuous structural development program has been started aimed at *increasing the company's competitive advantage*, with scope to cover a range from manufacturing processes, through quality assurance, to the reinforcement of strengths and elimination of weaknesses.

Efficiency is a prerequisite of any business activity. The company portfolio must be kept in good balance.

Associated with profitability, the company keeps developing its *sphere of operations*, determining the direction of diversification according to the criteria of potential growth and returns.

Our pursuit of competitive advantages and diversification must be supported by a powerfully expanding *system of strategic alliance and cooperation*.

Source: *Annual Report*, Taurus Hungarian Rubber Works, 1988, p. 3.

Now ranked at 30th in size in the rubber industry, Taurus found it was facing newly formed international combinations with enormous financial strength, strong market positions, and diverse managerial assets. Given the high degrees of concentration manifesting themselves in the rubber industry and that even the largest firms have had to accomplish international cooperative relationships, Taurus determined that it too should seek cooperative, strategic alliances. In seeking these affiliations the company would be very open and responsive to any type of reasonable alternative or combination that might be offered. These alliances could include participating with companies currently in operation or the creation of new, jointly held companies whether they are related or unrelated to the rubber industry. The only real criteria for accepting an alliance would be its profitability and growth potential.

In pursuing strategic alliances Gyula noted that Taurus' bargaining position differed greatly between the various business lines in its portfolio. As an aid to understanding its bargaining strategy with potential allies, Taurus's businesses were placed into one of three categories as shown in Exhibit 20. Category I types were those where Taurus' bargaining position was relatively weak as it felt it had little to offer a potential suitor. Category II types were those where Taurus could contribute a sizeable dowry and had much to offer the potential ally, while Category III types were those businesses with mixed or balanced strengths and weaknesses.

The problem now came to the restructuring of the company's current divisions to make them into rational and identifiable business units to outside investors as well as serving Taurus's own needs for internal logic and market focus.

EXHIBIT 20   Cooperation Potentials by Product Line

	Cooperation Category		
Product Lines	**I**	**II**	**III**
Truck tires	*		
Farm tires			*
Rotary hoses		*	
Specialty hoses			*
Hydraulic hoses	*		
Waterproofing sheets		*	
Belting	*		
Camping goods			*
Air springs			*
Machines and molds		*	
Precision goods			*

Source: Internal company report.

Which product lines should be grouped together and what should be the basis for their grouping? Gyula saw several different ways to do this. Products could be grouped based on a common production process or technology, or they could be based on their capital requirements, or they could be grouped by markets served or trade relations which had already been established by Taurus. Depending on how he defined the company's new SBUs he knew he would be making some major decisions about the attractiveness of the company's assets as well as defining the number and the nature of Taurus' potential strategic alliances. As he explained:

> If I create an SBU which manufactures hoses, a good joint-venture partner might be someone who manufactures couplings for hoses—this would be a match that would be good for both of us and it would be a relatively safe investment. If on the other hand I create a business which can use the same hoses in the offshore mining and drilling business, and this is a business that is really risky but one that could really develop in the future, what do I look for in partners? I need to find an engineering company that's creating large mining exploration projects. For every type of combination like this I can create, I have to ask myself each time, "What are the driving questions?"

In reviewing the company's portfolio he immediately saw three new SBUs he could propose to Laszlo Geza, vice president of the Technical Rubber Division. One SBU would serve the automobile industry through the manufacture of rubber profiles (rubber seals and grommets which provide watertight fits for car windows), V-belts for engines and engine components such as their air conditioning, power steering, and electrical units, and special engine seals. Another unit would serve the truck and bus industry by manufacturing the bellows for articulated buses, and air springs for buses, heavy-duty trucks, and long-haul trailers. The last newly created SBU would target the firm's adhesives and rubber sheeting at the construction and building industry where the products could be used to water-proof flat roofs as well as serving as chemical-proof and watertight liners in irrigation projects and hazardous-waste landfill sites.

Although top management knew ''the house wasn't on fire,'' and that a careful and deliberate pace could be taken regarding the company's restructuring, Gyula wanted to make sure the proposals he was about to make to the Technical Rubber Products Division were sound and reasonable. Moreover the success or failure of this restructuring would set the tone for Taurus' future diversification efforts.

REFERENCES

Benway, S. J. ''Tire & Rubber Industry.'' *Value Line Investment Survey*, December 22, 1989, p. 127.
Garvey, B. S., Jr. ''History and Summary of Rubber Technology.'' In *Introduction to Rubber Technology*. Edited by M. Morton. New York: Reinhold, 1959, pp. 1–43.
Greek, B. F. ''Modest Growth Ahead for Rubber.'' *Chemical & Engineering News* 66, no. 12 (March 21, 1988), pp. 25–29.
Thompson, A. A., Jr. ''Competition in the World Tire Industry.'' In A. A. Thompson, Jr., and A. J. Strickland, *Strategic Management: Concepts and Cases*. Homewood, Ill.: Irwin, 1990, pp. 518–548.

Endnote

1. Polymerization is a reaction involving the successive addition of a large number of relatively small molecules (monomers) to form a final compound or polymer. A polymer is a giant molecule formed when thousands of molecules have been linked together end to end. A copolymer is a giant molecule formed when two or more unlike monomers are polymerized together.

APPENDIX A   Taurus Hungarian Rubber Works
Income Statements, Years Ending December 31, 1987–1989 (in millions of Forints)

	1987[a]	**1988**	**1989**
Basic activities	10,637.7	12,193.4	14,918.6
Nonbasic activities	6,270.0	6,705.5	5,747.0
Total revenues	16,907.7	18,898.9	20,665.6
Direct costs	12,022.1	13,095.0	13,819.6
Indirect costs	4,235.6	4,963.3	5,714.8
Production and operating costs	16,257.7	18,058.3	19,534.4
Before-tax profit	650.0	840.6	1,131.2
Taxes	290.0	386.0	491.4
After-tax profit	360.0	454.6	639.8

[a]1987 data adjusted for better comparability to reflect the effects of tax changes initiated in 1988.
Sources: 1987 and 1988 data from *Annual Report*, Taurus Hungarian Rubber Works, 1988; 1989 data from internal reports.

APPENDIX B   Taurus Hungarian Rubber Works
Balance Sheets, Years Ending December 31, 1987–1989 (in millions of Forints)

	1987[a]	**1988**	**1989**
Assets			
Cash, bank deposits, and receivables	2,491.1	3,157.0	3,763.2
Inventories	2,749.6	2,803.8	2,888.3
Other current assets and capital investments	577.4	739.7	938.6
Current assets	5,818.1	6,700.5	7,590.1
Property	2,480.7	2,772.0	3,008.8
Machines and equipment	4,718.2	6,202.6	6,357.9
Fleet	46.3	46.4	48.6
Other	27.9	25.9	25.6
Fixed asset value	7,273.1	9,046.9	9,440.7
Accumulated depreciation	3,977.0	4,303.8	4,687.7
Unaccomplished projects	541.4	272.2	541.6
Total fixed assets	3,837.5	5,015.3	5,294.6
Total assets	9,655.6	11,715.8	12,884.6
Liabilities			
Short-term loans	1,531.7	1,684.3	1,444.0
Accounts payable	922.7	1,378.5	2,072.8
Accrued expenses	95.8	141.4	151.6
Provisions for taxes	(274.1)	195.0	34.7
1989 long-term debt service	267.0	129.9	314.3
Other liabilities due within 12 months	58.0	5.4	242.1
Total current liabilities	2,601.1	3,534.5	4,259.5

APPENDIX B Cont'd.   Taurus Hungarian Rubber Works Balance Sheets,
Years Ending December 31, 1987–1989 (in millions of Forints)

	1987[a]	1988	1989
Liabilities (cont.)			
Provisions and noncurrent liabilities	61.4	335.1	0.4
Long-term loans	725.4	1,453.1	1,815.7
Equities and funds reserves	5,907.7	5,938.5	6,169.2
Current year after-tax profit	360.0	454.6	639.8
Total equity and funds	6,267.7	6,393.1	6,809.0
Total liabilities	9,655.6	11,715.8	12,884.6

[a]1987 data adjusted for better comparability to reflect the effects of tax changes initiated in 1988.
Sources: 1987 and 1988 data from *Annual Report,* Taurus Hungarian Rubber Works, 1988; 1989 data from internal company reports.

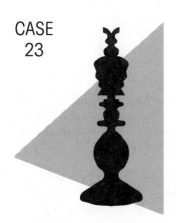

WORDPERFECT
FACES THE 1990s

CHARLES BOYD

In early 1990 WordPerfect Corporation was the market leader in word processing software. Yet signals in the rapidly changing personal computer (PC) software market indicated that no firm can rest on past successes. Computer-savvy customers wanted products with more features for their faster and more powerful machines. At the same time, the advent of laptop computers required that scaled-down versions of popular programs fit on a single floppy disk. It was not enough to have a single successful product, such as a word processing package. Many users had become sophisticated enough to integrate spreadsheet and database files into their documents. This meant providing a family of programs that could be integrated easily.

The combination of these forces caused WordPerfect and their competitors to upgrade their products constantly and provide excellent support service for their customers. Management had to keep particularly close watch on their closest competitor, Microsoft Word (often just called Word). In recent performance tests, Word compared very favorably to WordPerfect.

A BRIEF HISTORY OF WORD PROCESSING[1]

In July 1961 IBM introduced the Selectric typewriter. For the first time, typists could control the typeface with which they printed by changing a print ball. It was another 10 years before the next notable advance in document preparation would occur: Wang Labs' introduction of the Wang 1200. This small-screen typing workstation could retrieve documents stored on cassette tape. Five years later, the Wang WPS (Word Processing System) was introduced. This machine permitted storage of up to 4,000 pages on disk.

The 1975 introduction of the Altair marked the beginning of the era of PCs. Disks became the storage system of choice for PCs when Digital Research Corporation introduced the CP/M (Computer Program Management) System in 1976. Dedicated word processing systems dominated the corporate office market until the introduction of the IBM PC in 1981. By that time, users had become

---

This case was prepared by Professor Charles Boyd of Southwest Missouri State University as a basis for class discussion rather than to illustrate either effective or ineffective handling of an administrative situation.

comfortable with the available word-processing packages they had used on CP/M equipment. These included the IBM Displaywriter System, Wang Labs' Wang-Writer, and the popular WordStar. Users were reluctant to switch from these programs to new ones written for the IBM PC such as EasyWriter and Volkswriter. In fact, many users installed a "Baby Blue" card in their early IBM PCs that permitted the machines to run CP/M programs.

Meanwhile, vendors were busy rewriting their programs so they would run on the PC. By 1982 several word-processing programs were available for the PC: Micropro's WordStar 2.3, Wang's Wordmate (now named Multimate), and Word-Perfect Corporation's program. Micropro was the first to capture the heart of the corporate PC word-processing market with the release of WordStar 3.3 in 1983. About the same time, PFS:Write became the first personal word-processing program to make full use of the PC's capabilities with its *what you see is what you get* (WYSIWYG) screen displaying margins, line spacing, and other attributes. Micro-soft Corporation also entered the arena in 1983 by introducing Microsoft Word. Word further expanded the WYSIWYG concept by enabling the user to see attributes on the screen. Bold and underlined words appeared on screen as they would on the printed page.

Advances in the speed and power of word-processing software and PC hardware continued to occur during the 1980s. IBM's introduction of the Personal System/2 (PS/2) line of computers in 1987 marked a crossroad for word-processing and other software. Existing software would run on PS/2 machines, but more powerful software could be written to run only on PS/2 machines. Software companies had to decide which way to orient new versions of their products. They can write separate versions for PCs and PS/2 equipment or write versions that will run only on PS/2 machines.

HISTORY AND MANAGEMENT OF WORDPERFECT CORPORATION

In 1975 Alan Ashton, then a Brigham Young University professor, met a young music student named Bruce Bastion. Bastion was trying to write software to choreograph the university's marching band. The two men created the first version of WordPerfect in a garage operation in a Salt Lake City suburb in 1979. Initial sales reached $36,000 and have grown rapidly every year since 1980, reaching $178 million in more than 20 countries in 1988.[2]

WordPerfect's 1989 sales reached $281 million. WordPerfect passed Ashton-Tate during the second quarter of 1989 to attain third place in the microcomputer software market on quarterly sales of $67 million. The firm's share of the word-processing software market increased from 35 percent in early 1988 to 60 percent by fall 1989.[3] WordPerfect was a closely held corporation. Management would not release its financial statements.[4] The firm does make available some performance data. Exhibit 1 reports WordPerfect's meteoric growth in sales, number of employees, and user base (the number of its programs in use).

Computer-industry writer Will Fastie remembers that Bruce Bastion was the person who answered the company telephone to field users' questions back in

EXHIBIT 1 WordPerfect's Growth in Sales, Employees, and User Base

	1979	**1980**	**1981**	**1982**	**1983**	**1984**	**1985**	**1986**	**1987**	**1988**	**1989**
Annual sales ($millions)	$0.036	$0.45	$0.85	$1	$3.5	$9	$23	$52	$100	$178	$281
Employees	3	6	11	18	47	84	199	306	554	1,130	1,612
User base (000 omitted after 1982)	5	85	260	605	11	47	175	485	1,159	2,621	3,856

Source: Company outline, WordPerfect Corporation, undated.

1979. He was always friendly, had time to talk, and always asked for suggestions that might improve the product. Mr. Fastie has found that the firm's friendly atmosphere has prevailed through the years. WordPerfect employees staff trade-show booths. Some software companies use attractive young women known as spokesmodels for this purpose. Mr. Fastie has found the employees friendly and excited about their work and their product, both at trade shows and during his many company visits over the years. He believes this attitude trickles down from the two company founders at the top.[5]

WordPerfect's corporate culture is largely a result of the Mormon virtues of hard work and loyalty. Alan Ashton and Bruce Bastion are Mormons, as are most WordPerfect employees. In fact, WordPerfect is but one of several successful firms and recent scientific achievements that have their roots in Utah's Salt Lake Valley. The list is pretty impressive: two other word-processing companies, Software Systems and Electronic Word Corporation; Linguatech and Alpnet, two leaders in language-translation software that is selling well in Europe; the Jarvik-7, the first reliable artificial heart; and the controversial 1989 discovery of a cold fusion process that has the possibility of producing vast amounts of cheap energy. Many of the founders of these innovations come from either Brigham Young University or the University of Utah. While the Mormon Church owns Brigham Young University, the University of Utah is in a state where the governor, the two senators, and 85 percent of the state legislators are Mormons.[6]

Managers at WordPerfect encourage initiative and creativity from employees and reward achievers with incentives and promotions. This work ethic has paid off time and again as the firm has surpassed competitors in this highly competitive—sometimes ruthless—industry. Bruce Bastion has commented, "We treat our programmers with respect and win their loyalty."[7] David Tebbut, consulting editor of Europe's *PC Dealer*, has said of WordPerfect employees, "They are the most dedicated, bubbly bunch of people I have ever met in my life."[8]

WordPerfect Corporation also has been successful in Europe. Aggressive marketing has captured 30 percent of the British and West German markets, 60 percent of the market in Holland, and 70 percent of the Scandinavian market. WordPerfect translates its word-processing packages into the language of a local market. Many competitors don't take the time and effort to do this.[9] "International expansion is essential to the life of this company, and we see Europe as a prime market," Alan Ashton said. "We want to become the standard for word processing in Europe and we are confident we can do it."[10] In mid-1989 management

EXHIBIT 2 WordPerfect's International Expansion

International Versions Released

1982	Finnish	1986	UK English
1983	French, German, Norwegian	1987	Icelandic, Swedish, Canadian French
1984	Spanish	1988	Italian, Portugese
1985	Danish, Dutch		

International Territories Opened
1980   Canada
1981   Finland, France, Switzerland, Sweden
1982   West Germany, United Kingdom
1983   Denmark, Norway, the Netherlands
1984   Australia, Brazil, New Zealand, Belgium/Luxembourg
1985   Mexico, Spain
1986   Hong Kong
1987   Italy, Japan, Austria
1988   Malaysia, Singapore
1989   Argentina, Bolivia, Botswana, Brazil, Chile, Colombia, Ecuador,
       India, Lesotho, Mexico, Mozambique, Namibia, New Caledonia,
       Paraguay, Peru, South Africa, Swaziland, Switzerland, Uruguay,
       Venezuela, Zambia, and Zimbabwe.

WPCorp International Offices

WordPerfect Danmark	WordPerfect Pacific	WordPerfect France
WordPerfect Iberica	WorkPerfect Sweden	WordPerfect Nederland
WordPerfect Europe	WordPerfect Norway	WordPerfect Software
WordPerfect Switzerland	WordPerfect U.K.	GmbH (West Germany)
WordPerfect Japan		

Source: Company outline, WordPerfect Corporation, undated.

projected that the firm will own 80 percent of the European market within five years.[11] Exhibit 2 recounts WordPerfect's international expansion.

WordPerfect's incursion into Europe has not been without problems. The firm created some ill will at first by offering only short-term contracts to small distributors. This approach saved capital investment cost and allowed WordPerfect to switch distributors quickly if sales were disappointing. But it failed to generate much loyalty and enthusiasm from the distributors. Now WordPerfect distributes differently in Europe. Managers have concluded that they will need to spend some money to win the European market. Peter Ferguson, managing director of WordPerfect U.K. says, "Previous distributors failed miserably because they had little incentive to perform. Our approach is very different; we invest in advertising, offer free training to dealers, and we go to 12 computer shows each year."[12]

Pete Peterson, a WordPerfect vice president and the firm's chief financial planner, says, "We treat our people with decency and we reward them for good work. We've only lost one programmer in the last eight years."[13] Peterson started working for the company in 1980, earning $5 an hour to organize the company's accounts. He has resisted offering a public stock issue by exercising the Mormon value of thriftiness. He has said, "Innovative companies should never be answerable to investors, because investors only think of short-term profit while innovation requires time and patience. So we have to be careful: We always budget from the previous quarter's receipts and, above all, we never borrow money."[14] This financial philosophy stands in stark contrast to the huge amounts of venture capital that often fund the startups of many high-tech firms. Such capital dilutes the entrepreneur's ownership. It also places them under pressure to produce returns on investment in the 40 to 50 percent range early in the firm's life. It contrasts also with the heavy doses of debt many more established firms incur to fuel impressive growth rates. WordPerfect has grown the old-fashioned way: by selling a good product and backing it with excellent service after the sale.

THE WORD-PROCESSING SOFTWARE INDUSTRY IN 1990

By 1989 the word-processing software market for PCs was well-developed and competition was keen. The market was divided into three segments: lower-priced, limited-function programs; high-end programs rich with features; and a middle market consisting of programs fitting between the other two segments in price and features. WordPerfect was the market leader at the high end of the market. This segment mostly appeals to corporate users and professional writers.

The dividing lines between these three market segments are not distinctly drawn. For example, while the latest version of WordPerfect lists for $495, an excellent shareware product with a good reputation, PC-Write, sells for $99. Shareware products are made available by their authors at a nominal fee for a trial period, usually 30 days. If users like the product, they pay the asking price and become registered owners. Shareware is one of the few products a customer can try before buying. A customer can buy a trial copy of PC-Write from a mail-order house. PC-Write offers many of the features found in high-end products. These include a manual, tutorial, spelling checker, extensive printer support, and macros (keystroke-saving functions). PC-Write released a new version in 1989 that offered users 500 new features. A condensed version, PC-Write Lite, has been developed and sells for $69. PC-Write has been respected in the market for years. It is site licensed at *The Los Angeles Times*, where all the paper's reporters use it.[15] With 500,000 registered copies in use, PC-Write has 13 percent as much user base as does WordPerfect.[16] This illustrates just how competitive the PC-software industry can get.

Heavy competition was taking place at the high end of the market as the 1980s drew to a close. Organizations and individuals using the latest computers with fast microprocessors and large disk-storage capacity could take best advantage of the many features the latest programs offered. New features are periodically accumulated and incorporated into a new version of a product. For example, WordPerfect 5.0 was released in May 1988, followed by version 5.1 in late 1989. Chief competitor Microsoft Word released Version 5.0 earlier in 1989.[17] Each vendor tries to add more impressive features in each new version than its competitors have in their current versions.

While WordPerfect 5.1 lists for $495 and Microsoft Word 5.0 lists for $450, registered owners of the previous versions can upgrade to WordPerfect 5.1 for $85 and to Word 5.0 for $75. These reduced upgrade prices are typical for most software products. They foster customer loyalty by allowing current users to benefit from new features without paying the full price for an upgraded version, which few probably would do anyway. Still, customers have incentives to stay with their current programs. It takes many hours to become proficient in using a word-processing program. For this reason, it is extremely difficult to entice users to abandon their present programs unless they can see many advantages in doing so. This problem is multiplied for an organization that has purchased a package and trained hundreds of employees to use it effectively. Both increased cost and temporarily lowered productivity would result from changing to a new program. Managers would have to see tremendous benefits before changing programs. This reluctance to change makes it easier for software companies to hold their customers. Still, they must add new features as the state of word-processing software and the computer hardware that runs it improves.

Hard disks for desktop PCs have enabled users to store and use larger programs with more features, but the advent of laptop and notebook computers in the late 1980s created a new need. Some of these smaller computers have hard disks, but prices for these machines start about $2,500. Many users choose a less expensive computer with one or two floppy disk drives and no hard disk. These machines could be purchased for as little as $1,000 in early 1990. Students, traveling executives, and professionals find these smaller, portable computers desirable. Software vendors had to respond to this trend by trimming down their programs to fit on a floppy diskette. WordPerfect responded with WordPerfect Executive. This program retained the most commonly used features from version 4.3. Advanced word-processing features were omitted and the spelling checker dictionary was reduced. The program also included a limited version of WordPerfect's spreadsheet package, PlanPerfect, and some features from WordPerfect Library 1.1, the company's desktop-tools program. The entire package fits on one standard 3½-inch floppy diskette and lists for $249.[18] Failure to offer programs like WordPerfect Executive would leave the growing laptop- and notebook-computer market to the lower and middle segments of the software market.

EVERYONE WANTS A PIECE OF THE ACTION

Another advantage enjoyed by users of best-selling software programs is the availability of third-party, add-in programs. Some of these programs simplify program functions. A disk of macros would do this. Others are utilities, such as menu systems that make it easier to select program functions or that offer functions not available within the program itself. For example, a program called Sideways is packaged with the popular Super-Calc spreadsheet program. As the name implies, this program permits large spreadsheets to be printed sideways on a standard 80-column printer. This permits all the columns to be displayed on one page. Lotus packages the program Allways with the latest version of its popular 1-2-3 spreadsheet program. Allways enables the user to create more eye-appealing spreadsheet printouts.

The popularity of WordPerfect has attracted a host of such third-party software. These include menu programs that can be popped to the screen when the user needs to execute some program functions. Up to 70 WordPerfect macros can be purchased on a single floppy diskette. Shareware diskettes containing WordPerfect utilities and macros are also available.

Software programs typically come packaged with explanatory user manuals and have online help that users can access on-screen from within the programs. Despite this, many explanatory manuals are published by other companies. These third-party manuals go into extensive detail explaining the programs' functions in very accessible language. Many of them are available in local bookstores and are typically priced in the $20 to $30 range. Several such books are available for WordPerfect. WordPerfect 5.1 was first released in mid-November 1989 and books for it were available by April 1990.

Keyboard templates are another popular third-party item. These cardboard or plastic templates fit over a computer keyboard's function keys. The primary functions the program will execute when certain keys are pressed are printed on these templates.

These third-party books, add-in software, and keyboard templates bolster the confidence of potential customers as they consider the purchase of a program. They confirm the popularity of the programs for which they are written; no one would bother to write products to support a program that did not have huge market share. The software add-ins also help WordPerfect and other vendors of popular software in two ways: They increase sales of the current version of their programs, and they help them see what new features users want in the next version. It doesn't hurt to get this free information when competing in such a volatile market. Exhibit 3 provides a partial list of third-party, add-in software and books for WordPerfect.

A FRIEND FOR LIFE

WordPerfect and other quality software vendors compete fiercely in providing customers with toll-free telephone support. Users can call these numbers when

EXHIBIT 3   Selected Third-Party Software and Books for WordPerfect

Commercial Software

Name	Type	Publisher	Price
Perfect Complement	Multipurpose utility	Perfect Complement Corporation	$149.95
Perfect Addition	Pop-up menus	Applause Software	54.95
Winning WordPerfect 5.0	20-lesson tutorial	T.S. MicroTech, Incorporated	29.95
Grammatik IV[a]	Grammar checker	Reference Software	97.00
RightWriter[a]	Grammar checker	RightSoft	95.00

EXHIBIT 3 Cont'd. Selected Third-Party Software and Books for WordPerfect

Shareware

WordPerfect Macros	Available for versions 4.2 and 5.0
WordPerfect 5.0 Tools	Multipurpose utilities
WordPerfect 5.0 Clip Art	Graphic images that can be inserted into documents
WordPerfect 5.0 Business Letters	More than 70 fill-in-the-blanks form letters
HelpPerfect for WordPerfect	Memory-resident pull-down menus, file search utility, calculator, 300-number phone book and dialer, and more (Available for 4.1, 4.2, and 5.0.)
WP Learning System	WordPerfect tutorial
WordPerfect 5.0 Menu/Mice	Menu system and mouse drivers

Books and Manuals

Alfieri, Vincent, revised by Ralph Blodgett. The Best Book of WordPerfect 5.1, second ed. Hayden Books, 1989.

Kelly, Susan Baake. Mastering WordPerfect 5. Sybex, 1988.

Mincberg, Mella. WordPerfect Secrets, Solutions, Shortcuts: Series 5 Edition. Osborne McGraw-Hill, 1988.

Mincberg, Mella. WordPerfect Made Easy: Series 5 Edition. Osborne McGraw-Hill, 1989.

Neibauer, Alan R. WordPerfect 5.1 Tips and Tricks, 4th ed. Sybex, 1990.

Parker, Roger C. Desktop Publishing with WordPerfect. Ventana Press, 1988.

ᵃGrammatik IV and RightWriter work with several other word processors in addition to WordPerfect.

they encounter problems using the software. Microsoft, the largest software firm, uses 2,200 employees to answer such calls. This costs the firm $8 to $10 million per year. Fifteen percent of Ashton-Tate's employees provide user support.

Between the May 1988 release of version 5.0 and November of that year, WordPerfect's support staff increased from 200 to 420, which was 37 percent of total employees.[19] By the end of the first quarter of 1989 450 employees were answering 10,000 calls per day.[20] The state of Utah's entire telephone system was once shut down due to the number of incoming calls to WordPerfect Corporation.[21] The cost of providing this support equals 5 percent of the firm's gross revenues. M. Daniel Lunt, vice president of marketing at WordPerfect, said, "I view the expense of support as a marketing expense, similar to advertising."[22] WordPerfect maintains many toll-free numbers around the nation for user support. The average call lasts seven minutes, longer if it is printer-related. WordPerfect often hires students at nearby Brigham Young University to answer the calls. Beginning salaries start as low as $13,000 and rise to the middle-to-high $20,000s after two or three years' service.[23]

Major hardware and software vendors conducted an informal survey of technical support telephone service. They found that staff at Lotus, Ashton-Tate,

Microsoft, AST, and WordPerfect answered the phone on the first ring. Some vendors took up to five rings. AST ranked first in overall service. AST and WordPerfect tied for first in technical competence, with Lotus and Compaq tying for last. Microsoft and Ashton-Tate took the least amount of time to solve a problem, while WordPerfect and IBM took the longest.[24]

The Europeans must pay higher wages than those paid in Utah, and Europeans do not share the same work ethic as the employees at WordPerfect's headquarters. In addition, WordPerfect's European sales have grown so fast that it has been difficult for the support to keep up. For these reasons, the firm hasn't been as successful with its European telephone support service as it has been in the United States.[25] The manager of one European computer store that sells $2 million of equipment to corporate customers each year said, "Even major corporate customers say they cannot get an answer on the help lines, so they come back to us. People are cut off, messages are not returned, and it can sometimes take two or three months to solve a problem."[26] Quality support will ultimately be important to WordPerfect's efforts to win the continent.[27]

As PC hardware and software become increasingly sophisticated, service is expected to become increasingly important to customers. Jim Manzi, president of Lotus Development Corporation, stated, "Service, rather than raw technology, will drive the next cycle of growth in the PC industry."[28] Lotus has a toll-free line for the releases 2.2 and 3.0 of its 1-2-3 program. Service is free for the first six months, after which customers can renew it for $49 per year. In early 1990 the firm was testing a 900 line that will provide quicker response for a small cost to the customer.[29] WordPerfect's telephone support is free for as long as the customer owns the firm's product(s). WordPerfect is the customer's friend for life.

THE COPY PROTECTION ISSUE

During the early and mid-1980s, many software vendors placed copy-protection code in their programs to prevent customers from making more than one or two copies. A customer is always advised to make a working copy of newly purchased software and to store the original diskettes in a safe place. Often customers would place a working copy on their hard disk and later experience a hard-disk crash (mechanical disk failure) or accidental erasure of the program. The copy protection code prevented them from replacing the lost copy. This created some unhappy customers. Programs that could strip the copy protection code from commercial software were written to address this problem. Software vendors soon gave in to customers' demand for software without copy protection. The vendors knew that this would result in lost revenue resulting from customers making illegal copies to distribute to friends and fellow employees. They also knew it would make software piracy (mass copying for black-market sales) easier. The consensus was that these risks would be less of a problem than the customer ill will they had already experienced. As a result, just about all commercial software was being distributed without copy protection by the late 1980s.

It is impossible to know how much revenue software vendors have lost from unauthorized copies. The Association of Data Processing Service Organization estimates that software piracy cost the industry between $800 million and $1 billion in 1985. Research estimates of the percentage of illegal software in use by 1989 range from 50 percent to 80 percent of all programs in use.[30] Copying commercial software for resale or to give to others is a violation of the copyright laws. But like most copyright violations, it is extremely hard to detect and prosecute.

The issue of copy protection surfaced again early in 1990. A group of companies in Europe proposed a strict law to prevent software companies from reverse engineering other companies' software. Reverse engineering involves examining the coded instructions in a software program. It is a common industry practice. Companies do it to figure out how to write their own programs so they will interact smoothly with a competitor's program. IBM, Digital Equipment, and Apple Computer were leading the effort to ban this practice in Europe. Together they lead the Software Action Group for Europe (SAGE). They are opposed by another group, the European Committee for Interoperable Systems, which wants the relevant laws to remain as they are. Amdahl, Fujitsu, NCR, and Unisys are key members of this group. The European Commission's ruling on this issue is likely to have profound worldwide results for both software companies and consumers. If the law SAGE wants is passed in Europe, experts expect that a similar law will be passed in the United States. Attorney Michael Jacobs said, "Everything everyone thought was legal is now being called into question."[31] If companies are prevented from examining competitors' software, they can't develop similar interfaces (screens which provide users a common look and feel necessary for interacting with those other programs). As Norbert Kuster, manager of the Association of German Corporate Consultants has said, "Whoever controls the interface controls the market."[32]

The proposed European law also seeks tighter control of software piracy and illegal copying of programs, as practically difficult as that would be. Computer magazine writer John Dvorak believes this software-copying issue is surfacing again because of the proliferation of laptop PCs. A customer who buys a software program can legally copy that program for use on only one computer. This means that a person who uses a program on a desktop machine at the office and on a laptop computer used on trips must legally buy two copies of the program, one for each machine. Dvorak considers the laptop as an extension of the person's desktop machine. He thinks that laptops should be given consideration in software licensing agreements. His position is that copy protection is counterproductive to software companies' marketing efforts and that companies that adopt it will suffer lost sales.[33]

SOFTWARE INDUSTRY OUTLOOK

Analysts expect software sales by U.S.-based vendors to increase worldwide at an average rate of 21.25 percent from 1988 to 1991 (see Exhibit 4). Growth rates will be somewhat stronger outside the United States.

New versions of high-end software continue to include additional features to attract new customers and retain old ones. Even as features multiply, users want their programs to be easy to use and to include well-documented instructions through manuals and online help. They also want training, service, and support

EXHIBIT 4   Forecasted Software Sales, 1990–1991

	United States			International		Worldwide	
	Sales ($millions)	Percentage Change (from Previous Year)	Percentage of Total	Sales ($millions)	Percentage Change (from Previous Year)	Sales ($millions)	Percentage Change (from Previous Year)
1990	$23,095	+18%	58%	$16,590	+23%	$39,685	+20%
1991	27,095	+17	57	20,255	+22	47,350	+19

Source: *Standard & Poor's Industry Surveys*, June 15, 1989, p. C93.

from the vendor. Exhibit 5 reports these and other software selection criteria from a survey of 1,900 data processing and other corporate managers responsible for buying and evaluating software. Supplying these customer desires and holding the line on prices poses a big challenge for software vendors in coming years.

WORDPERFECT'S PRODUCT LINE

Several young software companies that have great success with their first product never develop a successful followup product. This soon results in sluggish sales. Continued success in the software industry demands that a vendor continually develop new programs and periodically upgrade existing programs. This need is often best met by developing a family of programs that work together and

EXHIBIT 5   Software Selection Criteria, by System Size
(percentage of responses claiming "very important")

Selection Criteria	Mainframe Software	Minicomputer Software	Microcomputer Software
Ease of use	67%	75%	73%
Features and performance	69	65	66
Documentation	63	63	66
Vendor support	67	51	39
Compatibility with other software	48	49	46
Error handling	39	33	35
Portability to other hardware	25	30	32
Vendor size, reputation	25	18	17
Price	26	22	20
Site licensing	—	—	16
Removal of copy protection	—	—	31
Limited liability for unauthorized copying	—	—	7
Ability to transfer between mainframes, minis, and micros	—	—	22

Source: *Standard & Poor's Industry Surveys*, June 15, 1989, p.C9.

complement one another. Each of these programs typically has a common command structure and familiar screen so users of one program can easily use the others. This enhances the company's sales and develops customer loyalty.

WordPerfect has developed such a family of products. Its flagship word-processing program is supplemented by its PlanPerfect spreadsheet program, DataPerfect database program, WordPerfect Library desktop-utility program, and DrawPerfect graphics program. These programs allow users to integrate spreadsheet data, file data, and graphic images into their word-processing documents. WordPerfect and other quality word-processing programs also will accept these kinds of data from other vendors' popular programs. For example, many word-processing programs will directly import Lotus 1-2-3 spreadsheet files because that program is considered to be the industry standard in spreadsheet software. WordPerfect 5.0 will directly import graphic images from 11 other vendors' graphics programs. In addition, it will capture images directly from the screen from 22 additional graphics programs.[34] Still, having their own spreadsheet and other complementary programs enables WordPerfect and other vendors to offer their users an option many prefer: a familiar interface and command structure in all the types of programs needed to write a professional-looking document. The complementary programs also increase sales and enable vendors to create a presence in additional segments of the software market. This spreads competitive risks.

When it was introduced in 1988 WordPerfect 5.0 had several features that competing packages did not have. The program included the following key features:

1. Screen and keyboard customization
2. A powerful macro editor and macro language
3. Outlining capability
4. The ability to view a full page on-screen
5. The ability to incorporate graphics into a document
6. Modest desktop publishing capabilities[35]

WordPerfect 5.0 received the following awards in 1988:

1. *PC World*'s Class Award for word processing
2. *InfoWorld* Product of the Year Award
3. *InfoWorld* MS/DOS Word Processor of the Year Award
4. *PC Computing*'s Most Important Products of 1988 Award
5. *PC Magazine*'s Best of 1988 Award for word processing
6. *Computer Dealer*'s "Best-to-Sell Product"[36]

PlanPerfect 5.0 is a full-featured spreadsheet program that is easy to learn and has a user interface similar to the word processor's. The program also has Lotus 1-2-3-type commands and will read Lotus files, as will most seriously competitive spreadsheets. PlanPerfect also supports all 450 printers that the word processor supports.[37] One evaluator of the program felt that while it was satisfactory, it had few distinctive features that would attract users who did not use WordPerfect's word-processing program.[38]

DataPerfect is a program for defining and managing many kinds of data—names and addresses, invoices, or whatever can be stored and sorted as the user wishes. Users can print reports in various formats.

WordPerfect Library contains six integrated utility programs: a calculator, calendar, file manager, notebook, program editor, and macro editor. Users can easily switch between Library and WordPerfect's other programs. Users can share data among the programs. Library received the following awards in 1987 and 1988:

1. Finalist in *PC Magazine*'s 1987 Awards for Technical Excellence
2. *PC World*'s World Class Award for utilities package (1988)
3. *Commodore Magazine*'s Best Productivity Software Program Award (WordPerfect Library for the Amiga) (1988)[39]

WordPerfect Executive, described earlier, is a condensed program designed for laptop and notebook computers. It features selected word-processing, spreadsheet, and desktop-utility functions from WordPerfect's other programs. The entire package fits on one standard 3½-inch floppy diskette.

DrawPerfect was designed to give WordPerfect a presence in the growing field of graphics programs and to improve the desktop publishing capabilities of the firm's word-processing package. The package enables users to incorporate charts and graphic images into presentations or word-processing documents. DrawPerfect contains 500 clip-art images that the user can edit.[40]

WordPerfect Office 2.0 is a groupware package, which means that it is to be used simultaneously by many employees in an office setting. Its functions include a scheduler, database program, calculator, file manager, and macro editor.[41] Version 2.1 of WordPerfect Office was scheduled for release in January 1990. This new version will work across several local area networks and will use the popular Novell Message Handling Service. This will give users access to electronic mail systems, including MCI and Telenet.[42]

This family of WordPerfect products will allow many users to do just about any type of work on the PC using products produced by WordPerfect Corporation. They provide users a familiar look and feel from one type of task to another. As users begin to use the computer for more different tasks, they can select a WordPerfect product and have confidence in its quality and reliability. They also know that they have access to quality, lifetime, toll-free technical support. The third-party software add-ins and books on the market add even more value to the products.

THE BATTLE OF THE WORD PROCESSORS

WordPerfect was clearly the market leader in word processing software in 1989. Its leadership was being challenged by three competitive forces:

1. Recent upgraded versions of competing word processors
2. The uncertainty of which operating system for PCs would predominate in the future (The resolution of this issue will affect how many versions of a software product must be written and the look and feel of each version to users.)

3. The mergers and consolidations among software firms (A realignment of power in the industry is likely to result.)

Each of these competitive forces is discussed below.

Recent Upgrades

Software vendors introduced a rash of new versions of popular word-processing packages during the late 1980s. Each of these upgrades packs an array of new features designed to lure first-time purchasers and to attract users of competing products to switch. Persuading a user of another word-processing program to switch is a difficult task due to the time and effort involved in learning a feature-packed, top-quality package.

WordStar was a very popular program during the early 1980s. But the package lost significant market share during the middle and latter part of the decade due to some marketing miscues. Micropro introduced snappy new versions during 1988 and 1989. The latest version is 6.0, which lists for $495. It features more desktop publishing features than previous versions, and it is the first package to support scalable (sizeable) fonts for the new Hewlett-Packard LaserJet III printer.[43]

Ashton-Tate released version 4.0 of its Multimate word processing package in spring 1990. The program contains 150 new features, including an electronic mail service and Reference Software's Grammatik IV grammar checker. Suggested retail price is $565. Owners of the previous version can upgrade for $75.[44]

While there are many excellent word-processing programs on the market, clearly Microsoft Word poses the greatest challenge to WordPerfect. These two programs constantly compete against each other. Perhaps WordPerfect has maintained the market lead because in the past Word seemed always to be a version behind it in features and performance. For example, when WordPerfect 5.0 was introduced in May 1988 it had a clear advantage in features over the then-current Word 4.0, but the introduction of Word 5.0 in 1989 brought the two packages abreast of each other. Word 5.0 featured many improvements in graphics importing and page previewing. The package also offered automatic document saving, automatic pagination, and integrated spell checking. Both programs offer modest desktop-publishing capability, in which WordPerfect has a slight graphics-handling advantage. Word offers superior group document handling, which is important to office use. Overall, Word 5.0 effectively closed the features gap between the two packages. As one writer put it, "Word 5.0 matches WordPerfect feature for feature."[45]

Word 5.0 has a list price of $450, while WordPerfect 5.0 lists for $495. Both packages use 384 kilobytes (KB) of memory. This was a modest amount of computer memory by 1989 standards, especially for the vast array of features that these programs offer. This is competitively significant in that it means owners of PCs dating back to the mid-1980s can use these programs. As features multiply, many programs require more computer memory and faster microprocessors. This often means that only the newer, more expensive PS/2s and compatible computers can run these programs. PS/2s have faster operating speeds, more internal memory, and fixed disk drives with large storage capacities. Version 3.0 of Lotus Development Corporation's popular 1-2-3 spreadsheet program, released in 1989, required PS/2 equipment. When initial sales were disappointing, Lotus released version 2.2. This version contained most of the features of 3.0, would print better, would run on both old and new computers, and cost $100 less than 3.0. Version 2.2 has been Lotus' big 1-2-3 seller since its introduction. Version 3.0 has accounted for only 25 percent of 1-2-3 sales.[46] Like version 2.2 of Lotus 1-2-3, WordPerfect and Word have positioned their products to be available to owners of both newer and older PCs.

The release of Word 5.0 in 1989 put the ball back in WordPerfect's court. The next competitive move was predictable. Later in 1989 WordPerfect released version 5.1. This new version featured pull-down menus that supported the use of a mouse (a convenient device for selecting options from an on-screen menu). Word already had mouse support. WordPerfect 5.1 also contained automated table creation. In addition to many other new features, users could write longer, more-descriptive file names.[47] The package lists for $495, the same as 5.0. Upgrades cost $85. Despite its many new features, 5.1 still occupies only 384 KB of memory, the same as 5.0. This means that it will still run on just about all PCs in use.

The Operating System Wars

Computers must have operating-system software. The operating system functions much as a traffic cop. It directs the flow of application software such as word processors and spreadsheets in and out of the computer's memory and enables their commands to be executed. It also performs routine chores such as file and directory management.

The majority of personal computer software is written for the largest-selling class of PC on the market: the IBM PC and the many compatibles. Many of the top-selling packages also make available versions for other types of computers and for the variety of operating-system software that controls IBM and compatible computers. For example, both WordPerfect and Microsoft Word are available for use on the popular Apple Macintosh computer. Both will run on the majority of existing IBM and compatible machines that use the older MS-DOS (Microsoft Disk Operating System). They will also run on newer PS/2s controlled by Microsoft's OS/2 operating system.

The Macintosh computer upped the ante in the PC market with its easy-to-use operating system. The Macintosh features icons (pictures) to present menu choices that a user can select with a mouse. The user does not need to learn text commands to operate the computer. This is in stark contrast to the almost blank screen with a single command prompt that stares at those who use computers controlled by an older version of MS-DOS. To bridge this difference, Microsoft Corporation developed the new OS/2 operating system when IBM introduced its line of PS/2 computers. Along with OS/2 they introduced a graphical interface called Presentation Manager.

Sales of the OS/2 software have been disappointing. The system just has not caught on well with users. Industry analysts estimate that Microsoft had shipped 200,000 copies of OS/2 by the end of the first quarter of 1990. It is unlikely that

Microsoft's projection of one million copies shipped by the end of 1990 will be met. Paul Maritz, Microsoft's vice president of advanced operating systems, stated, "Our early expectations [for the success of OS/2] were incorrect; we did not do ourselves or the industry a service by setting those expectations. We should have realized that moving from DOS is a multilayered decision that takes five to seven years to do."[48]

To address this problem, Microsoft developed another graphical interface named Windows. Windows will operate with later versions of MS-DOS. These versions are widely used and are still being purchased. To date, users have preferred Windows to OS/2 with Presentation Manager. Microsoft estimates there are about 600 OS/2-based software packages on the market. Only a few of them support Presentation Manager. But there are about 20,000 packages available for MS-DOS, around 700 of which run under Windows.[49] Exhibit 6 shows the projected worldwide shipments of DOS and OS/2 through 1997. With MS-DOS and OS/2, Microsoft provided the operating systems running on 87 percent of the world's PCs at the end of the first quarter of 1990.[50]

As if MS-DOS and OS/2 did not provide enough confusion in the market, there is a third contender: the UNIX operating system developed by AT&T. Like OS/2 and Windows, UNIX sports a graphical interface. And like OS/2, UNIX will enable a user to run several programs at once on a PC. This is called *multitasking.* UNIX's major weakness is that a jumble of versions are available, leading to confusion and postponed purchases. Some analysts cite this as a reason they expect OS/2 to surpass UNIX in sales.[51]

This proliferation of operating systems complicates software decisions for both users and software vendors. WordPerfect has developed different versions of its software for a variety of computers. Recent versions of the company's software are available for the Macintosh, Apple IIGS, Amiga, Atari ST, Data General, VAX (Digital Equipment Corporation's minicomputer), and the large IBM 370 mainframe.[52] WordPerfect also made great strides in releasing new products for various operating systems during 1989. These included PlanPerfect 3.0 for VAX/VMS, WordPerfect 5.0 for OS/2, WordPerfect Office for UNIX systems, PlanPerfect for Data General, and DataPerfect 2.1 for MS-DOS. Versions of WordPerfect for IBM and compatible PCs accounted for 70 percent of the firm's 1989 sales.[53]

WordPerfect and other software can run under Microsoft Windows, but software must be written in a certain way to make full use of this increasingly

EXHIBIT 6   Projected Worldwide Unit Shipments of MS-DOS and OS/2, 1991–1997

	MS-DOS	**OS/2**
1991	13.9	2.2
1993	16.1	6.1
1995	16.1	11.1
1997	16.3	16.6

Source: Patricia Keefe and Charles Von Simson, "Overblown Promises Give Way to Reality," *Computerworld*, April 30, 1990, p. 1.

popular graphical interface. In spring 1990 only three word-processing programs could use all the advantages of Windows: Microsoft's Word for Windows 1.0, Samna Corporation's Ami Professional, and NBI, Inc.'s Legend. All three of these programs were released in 1989. They are all priced at $495, the same as WordPerfect 5.1. While they require more computer memory and PS/2 hardware, they add one important feature not possessed by WordPerfect 5.1, Word 5.0, or other character-based packages: true WYSIWYG. The on-screen display reveals exactly how a document will appear when printed. The ability to see both text and graphic images before printing positions these programs much closer to the higher-priced desktop publishing packages. These programs also provide many layout tools for desktop publishing work. Their main disadvantage is that they run much slower than their character-based counterparts. They will run faster under the new version 3.0 of Windows, which is scheduled to be released by Microsoft in May 1990.[54] Both Word for Windows 1.0 and Ami Professional received *PC Magazine*'s Best Buy Award. Ami Professional also received one of *PC Computing*'s 16 Most Valuable Product awards for 1989. The latter award was for Ami's leadership in Windows word processing and for the overall elegance and design of Ami Professional.[55]

Mergers and Consolidations

On November 13, 1989 Lotus Development Corporation announced that it was working with WordPerfect Corporation to develop a similar command structure for Lotus' new version 1-2-3/G spreadsheet program and the forthcoming WordPerfect 5.1. Both programs will run under OS/2 Presentation Manager. Lotus surprised the executives at WordPerfect a year before this announcement by offering the firm the code to 1-2-3/G. Vice President Pete Peterson said, "It took us six months to believe they were really sincere."[56] Lotus and WordPerfect are clearly aiming at another word-processor–spreadsheet combination: Microsoft Word and Microsoft's Excel spreadsheet package. Excel also runs under Windows and integrates with Word for Windows.

On April 9, 1990 *The Wall Street Journal* reported that Lotus Development Corporation was attempting to acquire Novell Inc. of Provo, Utah for $1.5 billion in stock. Novell produces a best-selling networking software program. Networks link together the computers in an organization so they can share programs and databases. Networking is a rapidly growing business. "The merger rearranges the power structure of the software industry," stated Aaron Goldberg, a market researcher for International Data Corporation.[57] Analysts expect the two companies' sales to exceed $1.2 billion in 1990. This would surpass the $1.1 billion of sales that industry leader Microsoft is predicted to receive.[58] When Lotus announced the merger, it had 65 percent of the $350-million spreadsheet market, even though it still had no product for the Macintosh or for Windows. Novell controlled two-thirds of the PC networks in America's offices at the time. Analysts predicted Novell's sales would reach $500 million during the current fiscal year. Twenty percent of the nation's PCs are networked, and the number is increasing 30 percent each year. Novell's new product, NetWare 386, can link together hundreds of computers. Lotus was expected to help Novell capture some larger corporate accounts by providing better name recognition. The main competition in that market segment was coming from Digital Equipment Corporation's PC Network and IBM's network system. IBM controlled 13 percent of the market.[59]

The Lotus–Novell merger appeared to have great market potential; however, some who are familiar with the two companies expressed concern about the different cultures of New England-based Lotus and Utah-based Novell. A distributor said, "The boys in Cambridge go out drinking every night. That doesn't happen in Provo."[60] Consultant John McCarthy said, "The shortest book of all time is about successful technology mergers."[61]

On April 11, 1990 *The Wall Street Journal* reported that Lotus, Novell, and WordPerfect Corporation would combine their customer service operations. Jim Manzi, Lotus' chief executive officer, said, "Wouldn't it be wonderful if a customer gets to call one place and gets an answer to their [sic] question?"[62] WordPerfect's management team was not interested in merging with the other two companies. Still, Ray Noorda, Novell chief executive, said the three companies "are now in a position where they can help guide the [personal computer] industry."[63]

A few days later Novell shareholders filed a lawsuit claiming the price management accepted from Lotus for the company was inadequate. Lotus and Novell issued a statement saying that they believed the suit to be without merit.[64] Shareholders of both companies will vote on the proposed merger in July 1990.[65]

In May 1990 Lotus announced that it would develop a future version of 1-2-3 that would run under Windows 3.0. Analyst David Readerman of Shearson Lehman Hutton said, "It's a concession by Lotus that the groundswell for Windows is pretty strong."[66]

ENTER THE 1990s

WordPerfect Corporation sits at the top of the word-processing industry after barely a decade of existence. The firm's 1989 sales increased 60 percent over 1988 sales. Marketing Department Director Ross Wolfley said, "Considering that WordPerfect 5.1 wasn't released until the middle of November, I think our 1989 sales of $281 million are exceptional. We also expect healthy increases in 1990."[67] About $48 million, or 17 percent, of those 1989 sales came from abroad as WordPerfect opened offices in Denmark, the Netherlands, and the United Kingdom. The firm's products were sold in 22 new countries during 1989.[68]

This continued growth led the company to add 482 new employees, bringing the total to 1,612. The Customer Support Department was over 500 strong by year-end. These employees responded to 2 million calls during 1989.[69]

It has been said that it is more difficult for World Series and Super Bowl champions to repeat their feat the following year than it is to achieve it the first time. This may be true for WordPerfect in its second decade. Alan Ashton and Bruce Bastion must successfully respond to many uncertainties the firm faces in the 1990s. Their judgment regarding which (if any) of the three major PC operating systems will rise to prominence will help determine how the firm's application programs are written. This is very important because front-end research and development costs are high in the software industry. It is very inexpensive to produce copies of a program after it is developed, so the margins are high as sales volume builds. But volume won't build if the right programs are not written. So each upgrade and each new program must be just right for customers' needs.

Decisions must be made about the future of each program in the family of WordPerfect products. The new ability of WordPerfect's word-processing package to interact with Lotus 1-2-3/G must be considered in this decision.

How will the WordPerfect, Lotus, and Novell handle the increased burden of customer service now that three companies' products must be supported? With all of these domestic issues to consider, how will WordPerfect manage its international operations? WordPerfect Corporation has no shortage of challenges for the 1990s.

Endnotes

1. This section is adapted from Carol Ellison, "The Trek from Typewriters," *PC Magazine*, February 29, 1988, pp. 96–97.
2. Richard Evans, "Mormon Spearhead," *International Management*, July–August, 1989, pp. 30–32.
3. Sandra D. Atchison, "A Perfectly Good Word for WordPerfect: Gutsy," *Business Week*, October 2, 1989, pp. 99–100.
4. Author's telephone conversation with Vice President Pete Peterson, April 10, 1990.
5. Will Fastie, "WordPerfect's Corporate Culture Is a Model," *PC Week*, September 26, 1988, p. 53.
6. "The Mormon Touch," *International Management*, July–August, 1989, p. 31.
7. Evans, "Mormon Spearhead," p. 31.
8. Ibid.
9. Ibid.
10. Ibid., p. 30.
11. Ibid.
12. Ibid., p. 32.
13. Ibid.
14. Ibid.
15. John C. Dvorak, "Tools of the Trade: What PC Writers Use," *PC/Computing* 3, no. 5 (May 1990), p. 15.
16. Deborah Asbrand, "Six Who Share," *PC Computing* 3, no. 2 (February 1990), pp. 102–107.
17. Robert L. Scheier, "Rumors Aside, Vendors Spend a Mint on Support," *PC Week*, November 14, 1988, p. 48.
18. Catherine D. Miller, "WordPerfect on the Fly," *PC Magazine*, December 26, 1989, pp. 170–171.
19. Scheier, "Rumors Aside."
20. WordPerfect Corporation newsletter, April 4, 1989.
21. Amy Bermar, "Rapid Success of WordPerfect 5.0 Causes Support Headaches," *PC Week*, September 19, 1988, p. 120.
22. Scheier, "Rumors Aside."
23. Ibid.
24. Robert L. Scheier, "Tech Support or Russian Roulette?" *PC Week*, November 14, 1988, pp. 45–46.

25. Evans, "Mormon Spearhead."
26. Ibid., p. 32.
27. Ibid.
28. "Computer Industry Finds Profits in Customer Service," *PC Resource*, April 1990, p. 17.
29. Ibid.
30. G. Stephen Taylor and J. P. Shim, "Attitudes of Business Faculty and Business Practitioners toward the Unauthorized Copying of Microcomputer Software," *Proceedings*, Southern Management Association, November 1989, pp. 193–195.
31. John W. Verity, "Defense against Pirates or Death to the Clones?" *Business Week*, May 7, 1990, p. 138.
32. Ibid.
33. John C. Dvorak, column, *PC Magazine*, May 15, 1990, p. 73.
34. *WordPerfect for IBM Personal Computers* (Orem, Utah: WordPerfect Corporation, 1989), pp. 489–491.
35. Christopher O'Malley, software review, *Personal Computing*, August 1988, pp. 165–166.
36. Company outline, WordPerfect Corporation, undated.
37. Janet Lou Darby and Rita Johnson, software review, *Personal Computing*, November 1989, pp. 149–150.
38. "PlanPerfect: A Few Advantages," *Computerworld*, December 11, 1989, pp. 45–46.
39. Company outline, WordPerfect Corporation, undated.
40. Lisa Picarille, "DrawPerfect Wins Early Praise for Text-Handling Capabilities," *PC Week*, October 2, 1989, pp. 41–42.
41. M. Keith Thompson, software review, *PC Magazine*, September 26, 1989, pp. 266–267.
42. Lisa Picarille, "WordPerfect Office Gains Remote Links, *PC Week*, November 13, 1989, p. 4.
43. "A Surprise First," *PC/Computing* 3, no. 5 (May 1990), p. 44.
44. "Upgrades," *PCResource*, May 1990, p. 16.
45. George Campbell, "Word Closes the Gap," *PC World*, September 1989, pp. 98–103.
46. William F. Bulkeley, "Lotus Spreadsheet to Accommo-

date Microsoft Program," *The Wall Street Journal*, May 8, 1990, p. B4.

47. Frank Hayes, "Mouse-Ified and Feature-Laden," *Byte*, December 1989, p. 89.

48. Patricia Keefe and Charles Von Simson, "Overblown Promises Give Way to Reality," *Computerworld* 24, no. 18 (April 30, 1990), p. 119.

49. Patricia Keefe and Charles Von Simson, "OS/2 Fever Is Burning Slowly But Strongly," *Computerworld* 24, no. 18 (April 30, 1990), p. 119.

50. Keith H. Hammonds, Richard Brandt, and Sandra Atchison, "Overnight, Lotus Blossoms into No. 1," *Business Week*, April 23, 1990, pp. 28–29.

51. Charles Von Simson and Patricia Keefe, "And Then There's UNIX," *Computerworld* 24, no. 18, April 30, 1990, p. 118.

52. Company outline, WordPerfect Corporation, undated.

53. WordPerfect Corporation newsletter, January 15, 1990.

54. George Campbell, "Picture-Perfect Word Processing," *PC World*, May 1990, pp. 104–111.

55. Preston Gralla, "Most Valuable Products of the Year," *PC Computing* 3, no. 1 (January 1990), pp. 69–85.

56. "Why Lotus and WordPerfect Are Suddenly So Cozy," *Business Week*, December 4, 1989, p. 114G.

57. William F. Bulkeley, "Lotus to Acquire Novell for $1.5 Billion; Possible Challenge to Microsoft Is Seen," *The Wall Street Journal*, April 9, 1990, p. A3.

58. Ibid., pp. A1, A5.

59. Hammonds et al., "Lotus Blossoms."

60. Ibid., p. 29.

61. Ibid.

62. "WordPerfect, Novell, Lotus to Combine Customer Services," *The Wall Street Journal*, April 11, 1990, p. B4.

63. Ibid.

64. "Novell Holders Sue to Prevent Takeover by Lotus Development," *The Wall Street Journal*, April 17, 1990, p. B7.

65. "WordPerfect, Novell, Lotus."

66. Bulkeley, "Lotus to Accommodate."

67. WordPerfect Corporation newsletter, January 15, 1990.

68. Ibid.

69. Ibid.

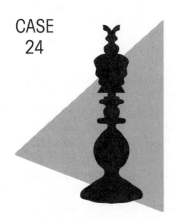

MICROSOFT CORPORATION

GEORGE W. DANFORTH,
ROBERT N. McGRATH &
GARY J. CASTROGIOVANNI

Microsoft began in 1975 in the midst of great excitement and anticipation among American back-room computer hobbyists who began to foresee the advent of microcomputers made possible by the development of the microprocessor. Until then, computers were very large, usually filling an entire room, and thus computer enthusiasts were forced to buy expensive computer time on mainframes. But microprocessor technology was rapidly advancing, and pockets of young computer enthusiasts watched eagerly, waiting for the pivotal breakthrough that would launch a revolution.

Shortly after Intel announced development of the 8080 chip in 1974, the December issue of *Popular Mechanics* featured the Altair, the world's first minicomputer, produced by a small company called MITS (Micro Instrumentation and Telemetry Systems). Finding practical applications for the Altair was extremely difficult, though, because it required the user to be technically proficient with programming in machine language, a skill only the most gifted possessed.

One week after reading the article on the Altair, two 19-year-old computer buffs, Paul Allen and Bill Gates, called MITS and claimed to have written a program that would allow the Altair to be programmed in BASIC, a programming language that had been used on larger computers. Two months later, in February 1975, they successfully demonstrated their program at a MITS laboratory in Albuquerque. In July 1975 Gates and Allen formed a partnership called Microsoft (short for *microcomputer software*) with the intent of developing computer languages for the Altair and other microcomputers that were sure to follow. Microsoft's first contract was to develop BASIC for the Altair.

MS-DOS

In 1980 IBM covertly decided to enter the burgeoning microcomputer industry. At this time IBM contacted Microsoft and asked if it could write a BASIC program to reside in the permanent memory of an 8-bit computer. IBM also asked Microsoft to furnish languages for the machine to include FORTRAN, Pascal, and COBOL. In order to do this, Microsoft had to gain access to operating system software. While BASIC had its own operating system embedded within itself, the other languages worked off of CP/M which was then the dominant operating system in the industry and was produced by Digital Research. Both Gates and IBM representatives approached Digital Research about supplying CP/M as the operating system for the IBM machines, but Digital balked because IBM insisted on extremely restrictive contract provisions. Gates was disappointed. He had hoped to gain access to Digital's CP/M for the 8086 chip which was then in development. Then, Microsoft could have adapted its languages to the emergent operating system.

Until then Digital Research had developed operating systems and Microsoft had focused on programming languages, and both had respected the other's domain. A year earlier Digital Research had violated this implied understanding by adding languages to its catalog. Microsoft's relationship with Digital Research was disintegrating.

Bill Gates decided on a bold move. He told IBM that Microsoft could not only supply the languages for the IBM machine, but also the operating system. IBM, now miffed with the inflexibility of Digital Research, accepted.

Microsoft's contract to supply the IBM operating system started a battle with Digital Research over which company would supply the dominant operating system in the industry. Many proponents of CP/M argued that, as the industry standard, CP/M was best for linking existing languages, applications software, and hardware. Nonetheless, less than a year following the announcement of the IBM PC, numerous microcomputer manufacturers signed contracts with Microsoft to include MS-DOS (the Microsoft operating system) as their hardware's resident operating systems. If a major player like IBM was entering the market, it was highly likely that application software programmers would write programs that were compatible with the IBM system. If a manufacturer's machine could not run popular applications programs, customers would not buy it.

In 1983 Lotus released what was to be the most popular applications software ever produced, an electronic spreadsheet program called Lotus 1-2-3. Lotus 1-2-3 was written for and operated only under MS-DOS. Largely due to the phenomenal demand for 1-2-3, MS-DOS was used by over 80 percent of all users in 1984. By 1986 half of Microsoft's annual revenues of $61 million came from the sale of MS-DOS.

Although Microsoft had made short shrift of Digital Research in the MS-DOS–CP/M battle, there is little doubt that its remarkable success was due to MS-DOS's affiliation with the IBM name. CP/M was by all standards an excellent operating system, and nearly all software and hardware were tuned into it. It was the quick and powerful emergence of the IBM PC that catapulted MS-DOS and Microsoft into success. The IBM PC quickly became the industry standard machine, forcing other manufacturers to make machines that were compatible with the IBM system, and 99 percent of IBM compatibles carried MS-DOS as their operating system.

Digital Research learned a costly lesson. Whether a company produced hardware, operating systems, languages, or applications software, its product had to be positioned so as to be included in the dominant configuration of these products. Customers bought hardware that was capable of running certain programs, and likewise bought software that would run on the particular machine they owned. Understanding this interdependence between microcomputers and various types of software was the key to positioning both hardware and software in the market. Holding a commanding position in operating systems software, Microsoft turned its attention to applications software.

THE ELECTRONIC SPREADSHEET

In the early 1980s many computer companies did not believe that microcomputers held significant potential for business applications. Then, the appearance of the first electronic spreadsheet, called VisiCalc, met a specific and powerful business need. Previously, managers interested in calculating solutions to complex problems were forced to either spend hours using a calculator or to get company computer personnel to write a specific program for the company mainframe. VisiCalc enabled managers to define their model and run countless alternative solutions. Initially, the program could be run only on an Apple II (and this was a primary determinant of the Apple II's success). It was later adapted to run on the IBM PC. Another spreadsheet program, SuperCalc, was developed by Sorcim to run on CP/M systems. There was little doubt that the advent of spreadsheets heralded a boom in hardware and software sales to businesses.

When Gates and Allen decided to enter the applications software market in 1980, the spreadsheet was a logical starting point. Because there was no hardware standard at the time, Microsoft's strategy was to develop a spreadsheet that could be ported to as many different machines as possible. The two dominant spreadsheet programs were limited in this respect. VisiCalc could not run under the CP/M operating system, and SuperCalc could only operate on Apple IIs. Gates decided to develop a spreadsheet that was ported to all the operating systems on the market, including CP/M, Apple DOS, Unix, and of course MS-DOS.

While Microsoft was developing its spreadsheet, dubbed Multiplan, IBM placed great pressure on Microsoft to ensure that the new spreadsheet could run on its limited 64K PC models. Gates acquiesced to the computer giant, sacrificing many design attributes in order to keep in the good graces of Microsoft's primary customer.

When released in late 1982, Multiplan met with some initial success but then was quickly eclipsed by Lotus 1-2-3 in 1983. Unlike Multiplan, 1-2-3 was aimed at 256K machines and reflected the richness of capability that the increased RAM afforded. Sales of Lotus 1-2-3 took off. In 1982 Lotus 1-2-3 settled into the number-one-selling-software spot, a position it held for the following six years. With the extraordinary success of 1-2-3, Lotus became the top maker of software in 1982 having annual sales of $157 million compared to $125 million for Microsoft.

Microsoft had made a costly mistake. By agreeing to IBM's request that Multiplan be operable on 64K machines, Microsoft had been blind to the growing demand for more powerful, high-end machines and their associated software. Interestingly, IBM's sales of 256K PCs skyrocketed that year. IBM felt that 1-2-3 had done for the IBM PC what VisiCalc had done for the Apple II.

However, the Multiplan project was not a complete loss. Although 1-2-3 had taken firm control of the U.S. spreadsheet market, accounting for 80 percent of all sales in 1986, Microsoft had adeptly positioned Multiplan in Europe. In 1982 Microsoft began to adapt Multiplan to each of the European languages. In addition, Gates decided to open up subsidiaries in each of their three major European markets, England, France, and Germany. Multiplan's ability to run on many different systems proved to be a great advantage. Unlike the U.S. market, IBM PCs and compatibles did not dominate in Europe. Apple controlled 50 percent of the market and Commodore 30 percent.

When IBM arrived in Europe in 1984, its PC included Multiplan rather than Lotus 1-2-3. By the time Lotus brought 1-2-3 to Europe in 1985, it was too late. In 1987 while Lotus 1-2-3 held 80 percent of the American spreadsheet market to Multiplan's 6 percent, Multiplan dominated the European market, accounting for 60 percent in Germany and 90 percent in France.

Because Multiplan was so successful overseas, Microsoft continued to distribute it. But Bill Gates would not forget why the package had failed in the United States and 1-2-3 had succeeded instead.

WORD PROCESSING

In 1983 Microsoft launched its offensive on a second front, word processing. At that time WordStar, developed by MicroPro, was the most popular word processing software. The Microsoft designers believed they could best WordStar by including in their program a number of additional characteristics. Microsoft Word would be the first word processing software that displayed bold-type, underlining, italics, subscripts, and superscripts on the screen. In addition, the screen could be divided into windows, allowing the user to work with more than one text at a time. Instead of requiring the user to format each text individually, Word would offer style sheets which stored formats created by the user for repeated use. Last, Word would be capable of printing out in any of the fonts available in the state-of-the-art laser printers.

Word was introduced to the U.S. market in a novel way. Demonstration copies which would do everything but save or print files were sent out at great expense to the 100,000 subscribers of *PC World* in its November 1983 special edition. Although many newspapers lauded the unique and imaginative marketing technique employed by Microsoft, Word was greeted with a marginal response. The word processing program, although extremely powerful, proved to be too complex for the average user. Subsequent improved versions in 1984 and 1985 steadily increased sales, however Microsoft was again beat out, this time by a small software publisher called WordPerfect.

WordPerfect was jointly founded by a computer science professor and his student in 1979. The company's only employees were a group of students that helped with distribution tasks, yet the fledgling enterprise was able to differentiate its program through a heavy emphasis on service. WordPerfect provided free telephone support to customers and followed up every inquiry until the customer was satisfied.

While Microsoft spent millions promoting Word, WordPerfect avoided sophisticated promotional campaigns, building a loyal following by word of mouth. Microsoft was at a loss as to how to respond to WordPerfect's ingenious grassroots campaign. WordPerfect's sales grew steadily and quickly. In 1986 it became the top-selling word processing software. Info Corp listed the top-selling word processing programs for 1986 as follows:

1. WordPerfect   31%
2. WordStar   16
3. IBM Vision   13
4. pfs: Write and Multimate   12
5. Word   11

Word was losing out to WordPerfect and others for a very different reason than Multiplan lost to Lotus 1-2-3. Multiplan failed in the United States because Microsoft was coerced by IBM to gauge the program for IBM's low-end machines. Word was losing because Microsoft, in its zeal to create the most powerful word processing program available, had failed to consider the full array of user needs.

Just as the success of Multiplan was resurrected by turning to the European market, so too would Word fare better there. When Word arrived in France in 1984 with mixed reviews, WordStar and Textor, produced by a French company, were already well-positioned. Gates and his European staff decided on a three-prong penetration strategy. First, to encourage distributors to sell Word, Microsoft France provided distributors with free training and a free copy of Word. Second, Microsoft arranged to have all retailer demonstrations of Hewlett Packard's new LaserJet printer performed using Word. Last, Microsoft France convinced many printer manufacturers to promote Word because of its ability to port to sophisticated, high-end, multifont printers. Michael Lacombe, CEO of Microsoft France, explained:

> When a client would go to a retailer and ask to see how Word worked with a printer, in 95 percent of the cases, the distributor would not be able to answer the question. We visited all the printer manufacturers and sold them on the idea of a Microsoft Word binder with several pages of printing samples.

As a result of this aggressive marketing effort, Word began making inroads into the French market in 1985. After a much-refined Word 3.0 was released in April 1986, sales of Word rose fast. In 1987 it was the highest-selling word processing software in France with sales of 28,700 copies compared to 10,300 for IBM VisiOn, 7,000 for Textor, 3,800 for WordPerfect, and 3,300 for WordStar.

While Microsoft had again created a phenomenal success in Europe with a program that had been unsuccessful in the United States, the great improvements made in the 3.0 version of Word also substantially increased its U.S. market share. In this version the previous problems experienced by users in learning Word were solved by what was then an ingenious solution. Included with all 3.0 versions of Word was a step-by-step, online tutorial that replaced the traditional user's manual. U.S. sales of Word climbed substantially. By 1989 Word's sales had reached 650,000 compared to 937,000 of WordPerfect. Although Word was by many standards a superior product, WordPerfect had firmly established itself as the word processing software of choice for PC users. Once customers learned and grew comfortable with a program, it was often difficult and costly for them to switch.

While Microsoft was having difficulty capturing market share with its earlier versions of Word in 1984 and 1985, it was working feverishly on a Word program for the Apple Macintosh computer which was the only substantial challenger to the IBM standard. When Word for the Mac was released in 1985, there were no other word processing programs available for the Macintosh except Apple's own software called MacWrite which was included with the sale of each machine. Although Word for the Mac had some bugs, it began to gather a following among Macintosh users. When the 3.0 version was released in 1986, it was a tremendous success. By 1988 with annual sales of 250,000 copies, it was second only to the PC versions of WordPerfect and Word. WordPerfect released its own version for the Macintosh in 1988, but it was too late. As WordPerfect had beaten Microsoft to the U.S. PC market, so had Microsoft preempted WordPerfect in the Macintosh market. When Word version 4.0 was released in 1989, 100,000 copies were sold immediately, confirming Word's preeminence with the Macintosh.

GRAPHICAL USER INTERFACES

Although the IBM PC was the best-selling microcomputer in the industry and was copied by a great number of other manufacturers, the Apple Macintosh surpassed all others in user friendliness due to Apple's unique work with graphical user interfaces. While users of IBM PCs and compatibles had to interact with their machines using learned text commands such as *erase*, the Macintosh user employed a mouse to connect icons or simple images on the screen. For instance, instead of typing the command, *erase*, the Mac user could use a mouse to point to a file icon and pull it to an icon of a trash can. Both Gates and Apple co-founder Steve Jobs believed that the future of microcomputing was in graphical interface technology because it made computers extremely user friendly, opening up the world of computers to the most unsophisticated user.

In 1981 Apple asked Microsoft to write applications programs for the Macintosh, realizing that the availability of high-demand software could determine the success of the Macintosh just as the popularity of VisiCalc had launched the Apple II. Microsoft and Apple began a close collaboration aimed at designing an optimum match between the Macintosh configuration and Microsoft's applications programs. The agreement specified that Microsoft versions of Multiplan, Chart, and File would be shipped with each Macintosh machine, and that Microsoft could not publish software with a graphical user interface until one year after the Macintosh was released or December 1983 at the latest.

In the following years Microsoft enjoyed tremendous success with its Macintosh applications programs. In addition to Word for the Mac, Microsoft's new spreadsheet program, Excel, sold at a rapid rate, beating out Lotus's new integrated software called Jazz. In 1986 Microsoft sold 160,000 copies of Excel to Mac users compared to 10,000 copies of Lotus's Jazz. By 1989 Lotus had decided to stay away from the Macintosh market altogether. Microsoft's success with Macintosh users made it the number one developer of applications software for the first time. The key lesson learned from Microsoft's experience in the Macintosh market was that Microsoft's primary competitive advantage was in graphical user interfaces. As it was clear that the PC market would inevitably move toward graphical interface technology, Microsoft appeared to be in a commanding position to expand its influence in the development of software for that market.

WINDOWS

Windows was Microsoft's attempt to change MS-DOS into a graphical user interface. Although IBM had been successful in setting its hardware and operating system (MS-DOS) as industry standards, no such standardization applied to PC applications software. Each applications program written for the PC was unique in the method demanded to modify or print a file. In addition, the popular PC applications programs communicated with printers differently. Different printers demanded different intermediary programs called drivers to enable printers to receive data from applications. Consequently, when a customer bought a copy of a particular applications software, she often received as many as a dozen diskettes, only one of which carried the applications program. The extra diskettes contained drivers to adapt the program to various printers.

To address this problem, Microsoft decided in 1981 to develop a program that would act as a layer between the operating system and applications software, interpreting the particular communications requirements of the printer and monitor being used. The second purpose of this program would be to place a graphical interface over MS-DOS that would standardize the appearance of applications so that they would share common commands for such actions as modifying text or printing files.

While Microsoft was working on its graphical interface, dubbed Windows, other companies began to develop their own versions. VisiCorp, for example, released VisiOn in 1983. More perturbing, however, was that some industry analysts were speculating that IBM was working on its own version of a graphical interface. In the past powerful IBM had largely looked to Microsoft to develop the software for its PC; however Gates suspected that IBM wanted to grab a piece of the highly lucrative software market for itself. Past dealings with Big Blue proved that the computer giant was intent on expanding its control to include standardization of the entire computer configuration to include not only hardware, but also software.

When IBM announced in 1983 that it was releasing TopView, a graphical interface to rest on top of DOS, it was a clear signal that IBM was no longer content to remain in the domain of hardware. This action by IBM, although disturbing to Microsoft, was not at all surprising. The computer industry in general was characterized by Machiavellian moves and countermoves. While companies were often dependent on others to develop and position their products into a dominant or advantageous hardware–software configuration, collaborative efforts and contracts were usually characterized by ulterior motives and covert countervailing thrusts.

Recognizing that IBM was attempting to squeeze Microsoft out of future software sales, Gates acted quickly. He contacted the manufacturers of IBM-compatible computers and tried to persuade them to follow Microsoft's lead with Windows, and thus isolate IBM. A large group of IBM-compatible manufacturers did not want IBM to further monopolize standards and were amenable to waiting for Microsoft's version of Windows rather than following IBM's lead by including TopView with its machines. Although competitors, many software companies also pledged their support to Microsoft Windows. The support of Lotus was particularly appreciated as it was the primary supplier of applications software for the PC and compatibles. It was apparent that they did not relish the thought of a stronger, more influential IBM and were willing to accept Microsoft's lead to prevent it. The software publishers were also confident that Microsoft would create an interface environment into which they could easily port their applications programs. IBM, on the other hand, had released a version of TopView configured in such a way that, if successful, would give Big Blue a significant advantage in the development of future applications.

Gates' success in this effort would prove critical to the success of Windows. He had never hesitated to play hardball in the past with larger, more powerful companies. While some criticized Gates as an opportunist, others saw him as an astute and resolute visionary.

The Windows project was characterized by lengthy and embarrassing delays. Although Gates announced the imminent release of Windows in 1983, it did not hit the market until November of 1985. Over 20 software publishers had to delay their Windows-ported applications software. By 1985 most of these companies had put all Windows associated software projects on hold. Nevertheless, shortly after its introduction, Windows was a great success. After sales exceeded 1 million copies of Windows, the 2.0 version was released in 1987. This version offered a user interface that was very similar to that of the Macintosh. When Microsoft released its PC version of Excel that same year, Windows' credibility increased even more, and PC manufacturers began positioning their machines against Apple's Macintosh.

THE APPLE LAWSUIT

On March 17, 1988 Apple announced that it was suing Microsoft over Windows 2.03 and Hewlett Packard over New Wave, its graphical interface environment. What made the announcement particularly unsavory to Gates was that he had just seen the CEO of Apple, John Sculley, and no mention was made of it. Apple announced the news of the suit to the press before notifying Microsoft.

Apple argued that it had spent millions creating a distinctive visual interface which had become the Macintosh's distinguishing feature and that Microsoft had illegally copied the look and feel of its Macintosh. Microsoft countered that its 1985 contract with Apple granting it license to use the visual interface already included in six Microsoft programs, and that this license implicitly covered the 1987 version, Windows 2.03. In July 1989 Judge Schwarzer dropped 179 of the 189 items that Apple had argued were copyright violations. The ten remaining items were related to the use of certain icons and overlapping windows in Windows 2.03. In February 1990 Judge Walker of the Federal District Court of San Francisco took over the case. He had previously ruled against Xerox in its suit against Apple over the same copyrights. In March 1990 Walker ruled that the portions of 2.03 under debate were not covered by the 1985 agreement between Apple and Microsoft.

As of late 1991 the case is still in litigation. If Apple should lose the case, it would also lose a competitive advantage in terms of distinctive visual interface. If

Microsoft should lose, it might have to take all current versions of Windows off the market and pay royalties on past sales to Apple.

A DISTINCTIVE ORGANIZATION

Computer programming is an activity dominated by the young. It is also an extremely intense activity that demands absolute focused concentration on the part of the programmer for extended periods of time. The software industry can be characterized as competition between groups of minds. It is an utterly innovative industry in which relatively little resources are spent on anything but the support of the imaginative process.

Finding its genesis in the early days of Microsoft when Gates and Allen and a small coterie of programmers literally worked and slept at work for weeks at a time under incredible pressure, the Microsoft culture has gelled into its present and unique form. The working atmosphere at Microsoft counterbalances the intensity of activity with an offbeat emphasis on an unstructured and informal environment. Working hours are extraordinarily flexible. Dress and appearance are extremely casual. Many programmers work in bare feet. It is not unknown for a team of programmers working on an intense project to take a break at 3 a.m. and spend 30 minutes making considerable racket with their electric guitars and synthesizers.

The present Microsoft complex in Redmond, Washington looks more like a college campus than the headquarters of a *Fortune* 500 company. It can be almost surrealistic. Most of the 5,200 employees have offices with windows. The courtyards adjoining the principal structures are often rife with the activity of employees juggling, riding unicycles, or playing various musical instruments.

Microsoft employs many people from foreign countries, giving the company grounds an international flavor. Some of these employees work on the many foreign translations of Microsoft's software. Others are simply many of the best programmers in the world that Microsoft attracts to its fold.

Microsoft hires the very best and hardest-working programmers, and then allows them wide discretion in their work. When hiring, Microsoft cares little about a candidate's formal education or experience. After all, neither Bill Gates nor Paul Allen ever graduated from college. No matter how lofty an applicant's credentials appear to be, she is not hired until she has been thoroughly questioned on programming knowledge and skills. Charles Simonyi, chief architect of the developers' groups for Multiplan, Word, and Excel, insisted for some time on personally interviewing each applicant. He explained:

> There are a lot of formulas for making a good candidate into a good programmer. We hire talented people. I don't know how they got their talent and I don't care. But they are talented. From then on, there is a hell of a lot the environment can do.

Microsoft employees earn relatively modest salaries, compared to the rest of the industry. Bill Gates himself has never earned more than $175,000 in salary per year. (He is, however, a billionaire due to his 35-percent share of Microsoft stock.) Employee turnover is about 8 percent, well below the industry standard.

Microsoft is loosely structured. Programmers are usually assigned to small project teams. Gates explains that "it takes a small team to do it right. When we started Excel, we had five people working on it, including myself. We have seven people working on it today."

Communications at Microsoft are open. Everyone is tied together in a vast electronic network, and anyone can send a message to anyone else via electronic mail regardless of relative status.

One of the keys to Microsoft's success is that it attracts the finest programmers in the industry and creates an environment that not only pleases and retains employees, but is also conducive to high computer programming productivity. No amount of financial might can make a software company successful. There are no apparent economies of scale to be realized. The primary asset that determines success or failure of a software company is the creativity and performance of its people.

POSITIONING FOR THE '90s

In 1987 Microsoft began collaborating with IBM on the development of a new operating system called OS/2 and a new, more powerful graphical interface named Presentation Manager. In late 1989 IBM released OS/2 version 1.2 for IBM PCs. Microsoft released OS/2 version 1.21 for IBM-compatible machines in mid-1990. Sales of OS/2 have been far lower than hoped.

Many industry observers consider OS/2 the inevitable replacement of DOS, however DOS version 5.0 was released in 1991, fueling speculation and confusion as to what direction Microsoft was leading the industry. In fact, IBM appears to believe it was double-crossed. When the introduction of OS/2 went poorly, Microsoft continued to upgrade and push MS-DOS and Windows, at the expense of OS/2 and Presentation Manager. IBM has since taken over the majority of the development on OS/2 and distanced itself from Microsoft.

In June 1991 IBM and Apple began a joint venture to develop an entirely new PC standard in which they will control the rights to the operating system and the microprocessor. This cooperation between the two largest microcomputer manufacturers could have a tremendous impact on the software industry. If IBM and Apple are successful in developing and controlling a new industry standard operating system, Microsoft would lose its preeminent position in the industry. Right now, nearly all applications programs written are ported through Microsoft's MS-DOS/Windows environment, enabling Microsoft to determine the direction and makeup of future computer applications. If the IBM–Apple initiative proves successful, Microsoft could be placed in the unfamiliar position of following another company's lead for the first time in its history.

The IBM–Apple venture is not a sure bet, though. The advanced technology they are working on is extraordinarily complex, and the risks are high for both companies. John Sculley, CEO of Apple, has said, "This is something only Apple and IBM could pull off. Still, it's a big gamble, and we're betting our whole company on it." Another concern is that the radically different cultures of the two manufacturers and their historical disdain for one another may make progress difficult.

In addition, Microsoft still holds significant sway over the applications development efforts of other software companies. Over time, customers have made significant investments in hardware and software that operate in the MS-DOS/Windows environment. It is questionable whether software publishers or customers would make wholesale changes so readily.

Bill Gates comments:

Sure, we're being attacked on all sides, but that's nothing new. Customers will vote on all of this. I think ours will thank us for preserving their current investment in PCs, while improving that technology. That has always been our strategy.

REFERENCES

"How Bill Gates Keeps the Magic Going." *Fortune*, June 18, 1990, pp. 82–89.

"IBM, Apple in Pact to Control Desktop Standard." *Computerworld*, July 8, 1991, pp. 1, 102–103.

Ichbiah, D., and S. Knepper. *The Making of Microsoft*. Rocklin, Calif.: Prima Publishing, 1991.

"It's Grab Your Partner Time for Software Makers." *Business Week*, February 8, 1988, pp. 86–88.

"PCs: What the Future Holds." *Business Week*, August 12, 1991, pp. 58–64.

"Redrawing the Map: Will IBM/Apple Alliance Shift the Balance of Power." *InfoWorld*, July 22, 1991, pp. 44–436.

"Software: The New Driving Force." *Business Week*, February 27, 1984, pp. 74–98.

"The Future of the PC." *Fortune*, August 26, 1991, pp. 40–49.

APPENDIX A Microsoft Corporation Consolidated Statements of Cash Flows ($000)

	Year Ended June 30		
	1990	**1989**	**1988**
Cash flows from operations			
Net Income	$279,186	$170,538	$123,908
Depreciation and amortization	46,318	24,191	16,035
Current liabilities, excluding notes payable	44,107	37,857	54,064
Accounts receivable	(62,223)	(20,004)	(38,864)
Inventories	(15,630)	14,660	(37,169)
Other current assets	(13,474)	(4,766)	(6,232)
Net cash from operations	278,274	222,476	111,472
Cash flows from financing			
Notes payable	(19,636)	5,160	15,087
Common stock issued	72,738	6,282	1,682
Common stock repurchased and retired	(46,665)	—	—
Income tax benefits related to stock options	37,103	14,098	11,554
Net cash from financing	43,540	25,540	28,323
Cash flows from investments			
Additions to property, plant, and equipment	(158,090)	(89,362)	(71,794)
Investments in the Santa Cruz Operation	—	(19,900)	—
Acquisition of intellectual property rights	(16,203)	(12,049)	(12,427)
Short term investments	(95,519)	(15,656)	(23,156)
Other	(1,908)	(8,063)	(4,929)
Net cash used for investments	(270,720)	(145,030)	(112,306)
Net change in cash and equivalents before effect of exchange rate			
changes on cash and equivalents	51,094	102,986	27,759
Effect of exchange rate changes on cash and equivalents	2,834	(1,076)	(174)
Cash and equivalents at beginning of year	192,388	90,478	62,893
Cash and equivalents at end of year	$246,316	$192,388	$ 90,478

Source: Microsoft Corporation, *Annual Report*, 1990, page 27.

APPENDIX B Five-Year Summary of Microsoft's Financial Performance

Date	Sales ($000)	Net income ($000)	EPS
1990	$1,183,446	$279,186	$2.34
1989	803,530	170,538	1.52
1988	590,827	123,908	1.11
1987	345,890	71,878	0.65
1986	197,514	39,254	0.39
Growth rate	56.4%	63.3%	56.5%

Source: *Compact Disclosure* (information database), Disclosure Inc.

APPENDIX C Microsoft Corporation Consolidated Statements of Stockholders' Equity ($000)

Balance, June 30, 1987	105,426	$ 76,864	$161,106	$ 1,135	$239,105
Common stock issued	1,900	1,682	—	—	1,682
Income tax benefit related to stock options	—	11,554	—	—	11,554
Net income	—	—	123,908	—	123,908
Translation adjustment	—	—	—	(751)	(751)
Balance, June 30, 1988	107,326	90,100	285,014	384	239,105
Common stock issued	1,846	6,282	—	—	1,682
Income tax benefit related to stock options	—	14,098	—	—	11,554
Net income	—	—	170,538	—	123,908
Translation adjustment	—	—	—	(4,636)	(4,636)
Balance, June 30, 1989	109,172	110,480	155,552	(4,252)	561,780
Common stock issued	5,321	72,738	—	—	72,738
Common stock repurchased and retired	(794)	(801)	(45,864)		(46,665)
Income tax benefit related to stock options	—	37,103	—	—	37,103
Net income	—	—	279,186	—	279,186
Translation adjustment	—	—	—	14,421	14,421
Balance, June 30, 1990	113,699	$219,520	$688,874	$10,169	$918,563

Source: Microsoft Corporation, *Annual Report*, 1990, p. 26.

APPENDIX D Microsoft Corporation Consolidated Statements of Income
($000, except net income per share)

	Year Ended June 30		
	1990	**1989**	**1988**
Net revenues	$1,183,446	$803,530	$590,827
Cost of revenues	252,668	204,185	148,000
Gross profit	930,778	599,345	442,827
Operating expenses:			
Research and development	180,615	110,220	69,776
Sales and marketing	317,593	218,997	161,614
General and administrative	39,332	27,898	23,990
Total operating expenses	537,540	357,115	255,380
Operating income	393,238	242,230	187,447
Nonoperating income	23,326	16,566	10,750
Stock option program expense	(6,000)	(8,000)	(14,559)
Income before taxes	410,564	250,796	183,738
Provisions for income taxes	(131,378)	(80,258)	(59,830)
Net income	$ 279,186	$170,538	$123,908
Net income per share	$ 2.34	$ 1.52	$ 1.11

Source: Microsoft Corporation, *Annual Report*, 1990, p. 23.

APPENDIX E   Microsoft Corporation Consolidated Balance Sheets ($000)

	Year Ended June 30	
	1990	**1989**
Assets		
Current assets		
Cash and short term investments	$ 449,238	$300,791
Accounts receivable	180,998	111,180
Inventories	55,565	37,755
Other	34,089	19,223
Total current assets	719,890	468,949
Property, plant, and equipment	325,447	198,825
Other assets	60,012	52,824
Total assets	$1,105,349	$720,598
Liabilities and Stockholders' Equity		
Current liabilities:		
Accounts payable	$ 51,012	$ 41,953
Customer deposits	17,172	10,043
Accrued compensation	28,770	25,718
Notes payable	6,500	25,619
Income taxes payable	42,582	30,269
Other	40,750	25,416
Total current liabilities	186,786	158,818
Commitments and contingencies	—	—
Stockholders' equity		
Common stock and paid in capital - shares authorized 160,000; issued and outstanding 113,699 and 109,172	219,520	110,480
Retained earnings	688,874	455,552
Translation adjustment	10,169	(4,252)
Total stockholders' equity	$ 918,563	$561,780
Total liabilities and stockholders' equity	$1,105,349	$720,598

Source: Microsoft Corporation, *Annual Report*, 1990, p. 25.

APPENDIX F   Three-Year Summary of Microsoft's International Revenues ($000)

	1990	**1989**	**1988**
European operations	$363,294	$212,018	$144,825
Other international operations	102,522	72,456	46,874
Export	184,433	153,787	90,537
Total international revenues	$650,249	$438,261	$282,256
Percentage of total revenues	54.9%	54.5%	447.8%

Source: *Compact Disclosure* (information database), Disclosure Inc.

APPENDIX G   Microsoft's Earnings-per-Share Growth (actual and future estimates)

	Microsoft versus Industry EPS Growth Rates				P/E
	Last 5 Years Actual	1991/1992	1992/1993	Next 5 Years	on 1992 EPS
Microsoft	51.8%	35.1%	23.8%	27.7%	26.5%
Industry	9.3	30.6	25.7	20.4	21.3
S&P 500	6.5	1.7	17.5	7.8	17.7
Microsoft/industry	5.6	1.1	0.9	1.4	1.2
Microsoft/S&P 500	8.0	21.1	1.4	3.5	1.5

Source: *Compact Disclosure* (information database), Disclosure Inc.

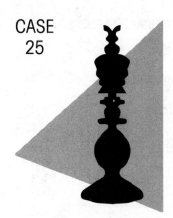

SYSTEMATICS INC.

JOSEPH WOLFE

After experiencing dramatic growth by providing financial services to both American and foreign banks since its formation in Little Rock, Arkansas in 1968, Systematics Incorporated now faces many internally and externally generated problems and opportunities. Since it was acquired by ALLTEL Corporation in May 1990 for $528 million in stock, Systematics has suddenly obtained access to a vast amount of capital that it can use to pursue additional growth avenues. For its part, ALLTEL expects its average annual five-year growth rate of 10.0 percent to be greatly enhanced by Systematics' 21.1-percent rate while simultaneously capturing various operating and technological synergies.

In the face of this pressure for profits and growth, John Steuri, president and chief executive officer of Systematics, must deal with several violent changes occurring in the banking industry. Some describe a general sickliness associated with America's banking institutions. In recent years profit performance has been low or negative, much of the banking public has lost confidence in the system's strength and integrity, and massive consolidations and mergers have been completed in attempts to seek either safety in size or to obtain various operating economies or portfolio diversifications. These problems have affected Systematics, which is a major supplier of software and other financial services to over 800 banks in 45 states and nearly 20 countries.

How Systematics should respond to these pressures has divided its management team. Many feel the company should stick to the banking industry which has been the source of its past successes. Other executives feel they must capitalize on ALLTEL's strengths as a telephone holding company that has diversified into cellular telephone and other communications services.

THE BANK FINANCIAL SERVICES INDUSTRY

In 1980 the *ABA Banking Journal* sensed the development of a new trend in bank operations management. Given an average-sized bank devotes about 8 percent of its expenses to data processing (DP), various economies could be realized by a

---

This case was based on a graduate student research project conducted by Robert Knapp. The situation described does not indicate either correct or incorrect managerial actions, but instead is intended to foster a discussion of the various issues involved.

bank if this work could be farmed out to a more efficient data processor. Five forces seem to be driving this development:

1. The scarcity and high price of technical talent—Many banks find it difficult to attract and hold DP personnel. Rather than creating their own programs, many banks must buy off-the-shelf software or contract outside technical labor.
2. Pressure for more sophisticated applications—As technological capabilities increase, banks, as well as their customers, wish to realize the cost and convenience advantages these technologies can bring to an operation.
3. Greater competition from bank saturation or industry deregulation—Competition is fierce between the savings and loan banks versus commercial banks and credit unions. Small banks are attempting to match the services provided by the larger banks while the larger banks are attempting to prevail by providing the best services available.
4. Pressure for profits—As various markets converge and growth cannot come from increased revenues banks must find profit sources through operating efficiencies.
5. Changes in the capabilities of those offering financial services to the banking industry—Computer service companies have grown in their size and in their financial stability thus they have become dependable suppliers of DP skills and applications. Many service organizations have created software and possess technical talent which can only be duplicated by an individual bank at a very high cost.

It has been estimated that by 1994 this trend will result in the doubling of the industry to one with sales of over $2.6 billion or an annual growth rate of over 17 percent per year. Exhibit 1 suggests this growth has occurred mainly among the smaller institutions although various industry experts feel the trend may spread to the larger banks once they succumb to the natural pressures building within the industry.

A bank's data processing system helps in the delivery of many bank services:

1. Basic operations—This entails keeping track of teller operations, handling demand and time-deposit accounting, and processing installment and mortgage loan applications and payments.

EXHIBIT 1 Source of Bank Data Processing Services

Bank Size (assets in $millions)	In-House		Outside	
	1978	1984	1978	1984
Very large (over $1,000)	95.0%	96.0%	5.0%	4.0%
Large ($500 to $1,000)	92.0	94.0	8.0	6.0
Medium ($100 to $500)	79.0	72.0	20.0	28.0
Small (under $100)	9.0	12.0	56.0	68.0

Source: *Input*, Palo Alto, California.

2. Trust services—Manages the various investments contained in customers' trust portfolios.
3. Financial analysis—Poses "what if" questions to aid in the selection and balancing of investment portfolios owned by either bank customers or the bank itself.
4. Automated customer services—Handles the accounting and electronic operation of the bank's automated teller machines.
5. Specialized services—These services vary from bank to bank based on the clientele it wishes to cultivate and special needs associated with that clientele. Once this audience is identified, the operations associated with this group are automated through computer support.

Banks have historically attempted to solve their data processing needs three ways. Some have done all the work themselves from programming to computer operations with in-house personnel. This has been difficult to do even by the largest banks. Most banks use what is called a *double approach.* They employ outside services for their routine DP work while using in-house personnel to handle their unique or critical needs. A third approach has been to completely rely upon third-party consulting firms to perform all DP work. These firms range from general accounting firms to specialized DP management consulting companies.

Just as competition within the banking industry has increased, competition between those servicing the industry has also increased. More than 640 vendors supply the industry and these vendors differ regarding their product strategies. Some can satisfy all a bank's data processing needs while others offer a more limited variety of products or services. Those products and services are the following:

1. Software packages—These are preprogrammed computer programs purchased by the bank rather than having the bank create its own programs with in-house personnel. The DP servicer's range of participation can vary from merely selling the software off-the-shelf to installing and customizing the product (within its own preprogrammed limitations) to meet the bank's specific needs.
2. Remote computing services—These are mainframe computer timesharing operations in which banks use online computing through an off-site computer via office terminals in a real-time mode.
3. Remote batch processing—This is a slower data processing method which involves the bank entering data on-site and sending it to a central computer that will process the data overnight and redistribute the information the following day.
4. Turnkey purchase—This method does not entail the direct purchase of equipment or software by the bank, but instead has the vendor select the equipment, program it, and get it up and running, while providing ongoing maintenance once the bank itself has taken custody of the operation.
5. Facilities management—This is the most comprehensive set of services a vendor can provide. In this method the vendor assumes full responsibility for hiring and training operators, installing and running the computer, programming all bank computer applications, and delivering results according to the

basic contract in force between the bank and the facilities management supplier.

Exhibit 2 outlines the products and services offered by several firms in the information technology industry while Exhibit 3 outlines the characteristics of some of the industry's major competitors. Among the top ten suppliers, seven sell application software, nine offer data processing services of some kind, and three offer facilities management. In 1990 the aggregate revenues for these firms were $3.7 billion. This was a 32-percent increase over the prior year although this increase was less than the 50-percent increment that occurred between 1987 to 1988.

EXHIBIT 2 Products and Services Offered by Selected Bank Vendors

Vendor	1989 Revenue ($millions)	Products and Services
Electronic Data Systems, Plano, Texas	$900.0	Applications software Turnkey systems Local batch processing Remote, noninteractive processing Interactive processing Facilities management Custom programming Consulting Education/training
First Financial Management, Atlanta, Georgia	741.0	Applications software Turnkey systems Local batch processing Remote, noninteractive processing Interactive processing Custom programming Consulting Education/training
Systematics, Little Rock, Arizona	224.7	Applications software Remote, noninteractive processing Interactive processing Turnkey systems Facilities management Custom programming Consulting
Mellon Information Services, Pittsburgh, Pennsylvania	170.9	Applications software Interactive processing
NCR, Dayton, Ohio	168.1	Applications software Interactive processing Custom programming Consulting Education/training

EXHIBIT 2 Cont'd. Products and Services Offered by Selected Bank Vendors

Vendor	1989 Revenue ($millions)	Products and Services
SunGard Data Systems, Wayne, Pennsylvania	125.0	Applications software Interactive processing
Citicorp Information Resources, Stamford, Connecticut	104.0	Turnkey systems Interactive processing Facilities management Custom programming
Unisys, Detroit, Michigan	99.9	Applications software Consulting
BISYS, Houston, Texas	54.2	Facilities management Custom programming Consulting
The Kirchman Corporation, Orlando, Florida	54.0	Applications software Local batch processing Education/training
National Computer Systems, Eden Prairie, Minnesota	38.4	Turnkey systems
Financial Information Trust, West Des Moines, Iowa	31.1	Interactive processing

Source: Adapted from ''America's Top Fifty Banking Software Products,'' *Banking Software Review,* Autumn 1990, pp. 28–31.

Given the banking industry's rather bleak profit situation, a strong cost-control trend has exerted itself. As observed by Frank Martire, chairman of Citicorp Information Resources, a devilish dilemma exists within the industry.

> What we hear—and we talk regularly to a couple of hundred bankers across the country—is cost control, and it's not different by size of bank or location—it's across the country. If banks can delay investments, they're going to do it, but intelligent banks with real foresight are not going to try to control costs so much that it harms service to the customer. They still want to position the right product or right service for a recovery, which will come in 1993 or '94.

Accordingly banks have begun to look more intensely at the financial service industry's offerings. Extreme concentration has been placed on maximizing short-term efficiency combined with major, long-term technological improvements. Many feel this will lead to an increase in banking's search for alliances and technology partners to aid in sharing the costs and risks of technological advancement during a period of severe cost control.

SYSTEMATICS INC.

Systematics Inc. was founded by Walter Smiley after having been a systems engineer for IBM and an eight-year data processing manager for the First National

EXHIBIT 3 Company Sketches

Electronic Data Systems (EDS) This company has been providing services in general for more than 25 years to all 50 states and 27 countries. They attempt to create solutions through their 2,000 employees that best accomplish the individual financial institution's goals while still maintaining EDS's unique corporate personality. EDS offers an almost complete line of services including such others as systems integration and communication facilities management. Because of its size it can process more than 3 billion instructions per second, 24 hours a day, 365 days a year. It can transmit voice, data, and video around the world using terrestrial, satellite, microwave, and fiber optic technology.

IBM Corporation IBM brings its image of reliability plus its dominance of the mainframe computer to the financial services industry. It is a prime contractor in many banks, but daily operations are subcontracted to a third-party vendor. IBM's marketing strategy involves tailoring each contract to the customer's individual requirements; it refuses to use the term *facilities management* as it implies an off-the-shelf approach that they reject.

Software Alliance Software Alliance markets its UNIX-based Total Banking Solution to small- to medium-sized banks while it markets its Marshall & Isley Integrated Banking System to larger banks. The company's software interfaces with all IBM-compatible computers. Rather than developing their own applications, Software Alliance obtains the marketing rights from successful software developers. After obtaining these rights it targets banks with up to $750 million in assets and a second group of those with assets ranging from $2 to $200 billion.

Newtrend Miser2 Founded in 1977 this company's software consists of over 40 deposit, loan, customer service, financial control, management support, and EFT/ATM applications, all operating on Unisys hardware. Newtrend's components are not sold individually. Customers purchase an integrated core system to which modules are added as needed. The company is well-known for individually customizing its integrated system which is available through in-house use, a service bureau, or facilities management.

The Kirchman Corporation Kirchman claims over 6,000 clients and it allocates approximately 20 percent of its gross revenues to research and development. The company operates solely on IBM machines designed for single or multibank environments. Its newest product is called Dimension Software, which is an integrated system for small- to medium-sized banks.

Bank of Fayetteville, Arkansas. By 1977 its sales had grown to $13.3 million after having begun as an eight-person company just nine years before. In 1980 the company began to market software packages to banks other than the one it was servicing in Fayetteville and by 1981 its sales had reached $36.3 million. Shortly after that Systematics began to service international customers and Smiley began to voluntarily take on a less dominant role within the company.

In August 1988 John Steuri took over Smiley's position as Systematics' CEO. Steuri was himself a 24-year IBM veteran beginning as a sales representative in Topeka, Kansas and ultimately heading an IBM marketing force of 9,000 people doing more than $6 billion worth of business a year. Systematics was an attractive opportunity for him when he left IBM at the age of 49 with an attractive early-out package.

The qualities I admired in IBM were evident in Systematics. It was a well-run, focused, growth-oriented company with a commitment to customer service.

EXHIBIT 4 Actual and Forecasted Revenues ($millions)

	Revenues
1985	$ 95.9
1986	122.6
1987	141.6
1988	179.5
1989	206.8
1990	254.8
1991	305.5
1992	365.0
1993	440.0

Source: Form 10-K, Systematics Inc., various years; and The Yankee Group, 1991. (Revenues after 1991 are Yankee Group estimates.)

Systematics also was still small enough that I felt I had a chance to be a part of a real entrepreneurial enterprise.

Sales have continued to grow and many expect, as shown in Exhibit 4, that its revenue prospects are very bright. Exhibit 5 displays the income from operations obtained by Systematics. Industry experts feel the firm's strengths lie in the integrated, IBM-based COBOL software it possesses as well as in its reputation for quality service. The software addresses a wide range of applications, including deposits, loans, profitability analysis, branch automation, electronic funds transfer, and marketing. Its newest product is Extended Application Architecture (EAA) and it allows banks to migrate to new technologies, such as regional databases, in an orderly manner when it becomes cost effective. Systematics has also begun to offer an Advanced Loan System which was created with the EAA. This is a comprehensive loan servicing system that allows users to introduce new loan products with little programming support. It also offers many debt management features not offered by other systems.

Systematics delivers its products three ways depending on the size of the bank being serviced. First, it provides facilities management and data processing services for 390 American and foreign bank clients. Second, it sells its applications software to financial institutions for their in-house use. Third, they sell turnkey operations consisting of mid-range systems and applications software through an IBM remarketing agreement.

Approximately 75 percent of its revenues are derived from facilities management. In December 1990 Systematics Inc. signed a 10-year service contract valued at between $350 and $500 million with the City National Bank of Beverly Hills, California and another contract to operate First New Hampshire Bank's data processing center was announced in February 1991. As of January 1991 Systematics had over 80 on-site financial management agreements. Exhibit 6 presents a summary of the company's past and forecasted activity in the area of facilities management.

EXHIBIT 5 Operating Income ($millions)

	Operating Income
1985	$15
1986	17
1987	20
1988	28
1989	32
1990	34

Source: Company stockholder reports.

To some degree the banking industry's generally poor financial condition, plus the closing or consolidation of smaller banks, which are an important target group for Systematics Inc., has had an effect on the company's thinking. Steuri, however, saw a silver lining in this cloud.

> Everyone knows there is a general malaise in the financial sector. Granted, that hurts our software sales, which accounted for only 10 to 12 percent of our business last year. There is another side though. If they turn their data processing over to us, we can help them. We can reduce their costs at least 10 to 15 percent and put money on their bottom line real fast.

Despite the industry's doldrums, Systematics met its 12-month goal for facilities management contracts within the first nine months of the 1990 fiscal year. In fact Steuri has said, "There have been occasions when our sales reps have been sent home for a week or two so we would not sign more contracts than we could service."

EXHIBIT 6 Actual and Forecasted Facilities Management Contracts

Activity	1984	1985	1986	1987	1988	1989	1990	1991	1992	1993
New contracts added	4	6	6	12	16	13	12	14	15	16
Contract expirations due to										
Client mergers and consolidations	1	2	4	6	2	4	2	3	4	6
In-house conversions with Systematics software	0	0	0	1	1	0	0	1	1	2
Year-end contracts in effect	39	43	45	50	63	72	82	92	102	110
Contracts renewed	6	8	10	5	5	7	8	6	8	12

Notes: Activities are for fiscal years ending May 31.
Source: Systematics, Inc.; and The Yankee Group, 1991. Data after 1990 are Yankee Group estimates.

ALLTEL ENTERS THE PICTURE

With the acquisition of Systematics Inc. by another Little Rock, Arkansas company, ALLTEL became a $1.57-billion operation with diversified interests in cellular telephone systems, natural gas service, air traffic control voice switching and control systems, signal data converters, encrypted voice communications systems, and high-resolution color graphic display systems. Exhibit 7 shows that Systematics would garner about 16 percent of ALLTEL's total sales, but would contribute more than that percentage to its operating income. Accordingly Joe Ford, ALLTEL's president and CEO, called this acquisition, "one of the most significant of our strategic moves." Various industry observers are more skeptical about the acquisition and its long-term benefits to either company. James Stork, a security analyst for Duff & Phelps Inc., stated:

> There are really no strategic reasons or synergies [here]. We do not view this as a strategic acquisition, although data processing and telecommunications may be converging, it is difficult to see how the combination of these two companies will result in much in the way of synergy over the next five years. We get the impression that ALLTEL acquired Systematics simply because it became available, and ALLTEL felt it could increase its consolidated growth potential for a reasonable price.

Both John Steuri and Joe Ford have begun to rise to the occasion. Steuri says, "we foresee some potential synergies as the communications and computer industries continue to converge." Because there are about 1,300 telephone companies currently competing in the United States, he felt they could be approached by the same sales pitch used to recruit banks and savings and loan institutions. "Let us do your data processing for you. We can do it cheaper and more efficiently than you can do it in-house."

In this quest for synergies between the two companies, Systematics completed a deal in March 1991 to acquire C-TEC Corporation's cellular-telephone billing and information system and ALLTEL turned its cellular data-processing operation over to Systematics. ALLTEL has also begun to sell off various operations not

EXHIBIT 7 ALLTEL 1990 Sales and Operating Income by Business Segment ($000)

Business Segment	Sales	Operating Income
Telephone	$818,150	$290,032
Systematics	254,806	34,159
Product distribution	331,565	22,507
Cellular systems	42,272	2,227
Other	126,992	14,965

Notes: Fiscal year ending December 31, 1990.
Source: Form 10-K, Systematics Inc., 1990.

related to telecommunications and information processing. It sold its natural gas distribution systems in Nevada and California to Southwest Gas Corporation for $16 million in June 1991 and it is attempting to sell off its Ocean Technology, Inc. subsidiary as well as its alternate energy investments.

Although moves are being made to make this a successful acquisition for ALLTEL, and John Steuri feels pressure is being placed on him to help his new parent corporation realize its own growth goals, he thinks numerous, diverse factors need to be considered. Admittedly the banking industry is in a state of turmoil, but Systematics' business strengths lie within that industry. What path or paths should Systematics pursue? Should the company attempt to ride out the banking industry's storm while possibly incurring the wrath of ALLTEL's management for failing to move ahead with applications in the telecommunications industry? Could Systematics attempt to fill other product/service niches in the banking industry despite the awesome size of its major competitors? Does Systematics have any other options?

APPENDIX A Systematics Inc. Income Statements, 1987–1989 ($000)

	1989	1988	1987
Net sales	$206,786	$179,474	$141,577
Cost of goods sold	153,223	133,262	105,053
Gross profit	53,563	46,212	36,524
R&D expenditures	9,476	9,064	7,741
Selling and general administration expenses	15,056	14,070	11,895
Interest expense	517	621	514
Operating income	28,514	22,457	16,374
Nonoperating income	1,702	2,425	3,164
Pretax income	30,216	24,882	19,538
Taxes	11,352	9,458	9,376
Net income	$ 18,864	$ 15,424	$ 10,162

Notes: Fiscal year ends May 31.
Source: Form 10-K, Systematics Inc., various years.

APPENDIX B Systematics Inc. Balance Sheet, 1987–1989 ($000)

	1989	1988	1987
Assets			
Cash	$ 2,858	$ 4,931	$ 879
Marketable securities	32,477	22,013	37,704
Receivables	26,569	20,536	20,083
Other current assets	3,941	1,123	1,156
Total current assets	65,845	48,603	59,822
Property, land, and equipment	108,313	95,855	80,078
Accumulated depreciation	51,788	44,683	34,243
Net property, land, and equipment	56,525	51,172	45,835
Other noncurrent assets	5,635	5,635	0
Deposits and other assets	4,768	1,658	1,848
Total assets	$132,773	$107,068	$107,505
Liabilities and Stockholders' Equity			
Notes payable	$ 1,456	$ 9,366	$ 1,010
Accounts payable	15,272	8,812	4,003
Accrued expenses	12,052	10,237	7,035
Income taxes	1,446	910	2,296
Other current liabilities	12,427	5,407	5,015
Total current liabilities	42,653	34,732	19,359
Deferred charges	7,109	6,443	8,936
Long-term debt	5,626	2,911	3,777
Other long-term liabilities	0	0	5,631
Total liabilities	55,388	44,086	37,703

APPENDIX B Cont'd.   Systematics Inc. Balance Sheet, 1987–1989 ($000)

	1989	**1988**	**1987**
Stockholders' equity			
Net common stock	$ 278	$ 276	$ 272
Capital surplus	28,876	26,655	24,917
Retained earnings	51,860	37,399	45,656
Treasury stock	3,629	1,348	1,043
Shareholders' equity	77,385	62,982	69,802
Total liabilities and shareholders' equity	$132,773	$107,068	$107,505

Note: Fiscal year ends May 31.
Source: Form 10-K, Systematics Inc., various years.

HIPPOPOTAMUS

JACQUES HOROVITZ

INTRODUCTION

What lies behind these restaurants whose emblem is a friendly hippopotamus with a broad smile and a mischievous glint in his eye? In 1988 Hippopotamus represented a turnover of 400 million FF, a total work force of 958 people and 17 restaurants which had served more than 3.5 million meals in the year, that is nearly 10,000 customers per day. The name also evoked the story of a French company belonging to the son of a restaurateur, Christian Guignard, who decided to give up his study of medicine to launch out into the restaurant business.

While staying in California, Christian Guignard had had the opportunity to sample some excellent beef grilled over a wood fire in a steak house, the name of which he remembered: Hippopotamus. Back in Paris he persuaded his father to join him in opening a steak house on the avenue Franklin Roosevelt. This restaurant was opened in June 1968 under the unusual name of Hippopotamus.

Beneath the eye-catching sign, Christian Guignard sought to implement an original formula: good meat, grilled over wood and served with a single vegetable—potatoes—all this in a pleasant setting and with the emphasis on good quality at the right price. With the passing years, the Hippopotamus style developed and took shape in the new restaurants which opened in Paris, in the provinces, and abroad.

For the consumer the Hippopotamus emblem represented not only a product, but also a certain setting, created by a simple, natural decor to which plants, materials (stone/bricks), colors that were in keeping with the mood of the restaurant (red, black, white), and pleasant lighting all contributed. Added to this was a special sort of service: the staff who received the customers and served at the tables were smiling young women. The menu held no surprises and the customers knew the prices before they ordered.

The formula was successful, and so from 1974 to 1986 16 new establishments opened their doors to the public, 11 in Paris and the other 5 abroad and in the provinces at Brussels (1981), St. Etienne (1982), Nice (1984), Toulouse (1985), and Bordeaux (1986). All were situated in excellent locations.

The turnover grew at the same time. In 1975 it was FF 9.5 million and in 1980 FF 83.5 million, rising to FF 400 million in 1988. For some time, Hippopotamus had been starting to diversify. Among the new Parisian establishments, a restaurant had been launched with a new concept, called Stefany.[1] Hippolisson was the first link in a chain of *pâtisserie* and sandwich shops started in 1984.

THEME RESTAURANTS

Hippopotamus belongs to the theme-restaurant sector in which it was a forerunner. Some years ago restaurants tried to shake off their competitors and to acquire fame by making the most of specialities. The adoption of an original theme allied to a product and a setting is a recent development in the restaurant business. The first was Courtepaille, then came Hippopotamus. Others followed: Chantegrill, Amanguier, Cour St. Germain, the Bistro Romain, etc. The basic concept behind this type of restaurant is the offer of a limited menu, the quality and presentation of which remain constant and 100-percent predictable.

The Market

According to a study carried out under the auspices of the EAP,[2]

> The restaurant business has undergone a marked decline since 1982 in at least three European countries: France, Great Britain, and West Germany. In this climate of recession, steak houses, taken as a whole, have performed well and have enjoyed a bigger growth than that of commercial restaurants generally.
>
> In this sector two categories live side by side: the independent restaurants and the chains; the share of chains is growing steadily in relation to that of the independent restaurants.
>
> In Great Britain the chains are very big in size and controlled by the big hotel/restaurant/brewery groups. In Germany the chains are few in number and average in size; in France the chains are average in size and are either independent or controlled by the hotel/distribution groups. The names/logos are numerous. . . . In France a selectivity stage is now being reached: a certain number of ill-fitting concepts are disappearing (e.g., Churrasco), and the chains that have managed to perfect an effective concept are developing at a very rapid rate. (See Exhibit 1.)

HOW HIPPOPOTAMUS FUNCTIONS

The identity of Hippopotamus is colored very much by the personality of its chairman, Christian Guignard, who holds 50 percent of the capital, on an equal basis with the Casino group. He has a very strong determination to succeed and to innovate and has used modern management techniques to develop his business. In his marketing he has practiced for a long time now a policy of institutional

EXHIBIT 1 The Different Categories of Theme Restaurants in France

Category	Type of Location	Chain Names
Top of the range	Center of Paris Starting up in the provinces	Hippopotamus, Cour St. Germain, Amanguier, Bistros
Middle of the road	Edge of main roads and in small- and medium-sized towns	Courte-paille, Chantegrill
Budget	Town centers	Pizza Paï Pizza del Arte

La Restauration—DAFSA n⁰-3è T 1986.
Source: GIRA in Néo Restauration.

communication in which humor is present, and he uses the services of an advertising agency.

In the heart of the company an Integrated Data Processing Center collects and exploits the encoded data coming up daily from the units. The cash registers are connected to microcomputers which are themselves linked up with the central computer. Purchases, investments, advertising, marketing, the expansion of the chain, all these questions are settled at the head office, still called Hippoconseil to show the top management's intention to bring down-to-earth assistance to the individual restaurants and always to remain in contact with them. The structure of the company is shown in Exhibits 2a and 2b.

THE WORK
The Hours

Hippo restaurants are open to the public seven days out of seven, 365 days a year, from 11:30 a.m. to 1:00 a.m. Nevertheless, most of the units, with the exception of the four largest, close after lunch to open again 2½ hours later. The working hours are staggered between 7:00 a.m. to 4:00 a.m. according to the job and the schedule. Everyone has two days off per week. These are rarely Saturday and Sunday.

It has been noted that one-third of the sales are made at lunchtime, two-thirds in the evening. The rotation of staff is five per day; it can rise to six or seven at the weekend.

The Market

In Paris there is a restaurant every 10 meters or almost, which means that competition is fierce and things have to be right first time. The customer is present every day and his sanction is immediate. The consumer judges the quality of a restaurant according to the following criteria:

The setting and atmosphere of the restaurant
The welcome

EXHIBIT 2a   Structure of the Company

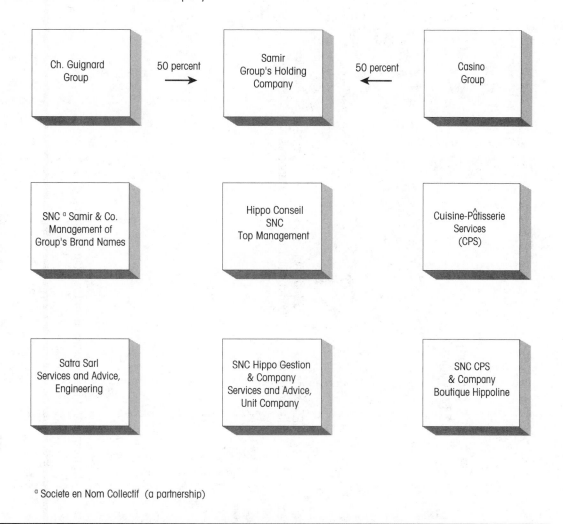

ᵃ Societe en Nom Collectif (a partnership)

The waiting time before a table becomes available
The waiter/waitress service
The quality of the food
The attention given to the customer in the restaurant
The price paid
Consistency in the overall quality of service

At Hippopotamus it is estimated that a satisfied customer will mention the restaurant to, perhaps, three people, while a dissatisfied one, on the other hand, will mention it to at least eleven people. The restaurateur's job is made up of a thousand details. The customer accepts it as normal if none of these is overlooked; if a single one is neglected, the customer is dissatisfied.

EXHIBIT 2b Company Organization Chart

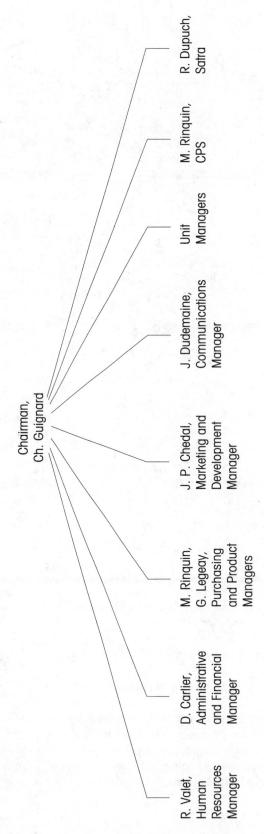

The members of the executive board work in a network

Hippopotamus' Clientele

At Hippopotamus one customer in seven is new every day (14 percent). The average age has remained constant, which means that the clientele has changed. The results of a market study carried out in 1987 provided the following information:

On the whole the age of the customers varies between 25 and 49 years with significant differences for:

Hippo-Citroën, the clientele of which is very young (18 to 24 years, 30 percent)

Les Halles, target 25 to 34 years (46 percent)

The Elysées Roundabout, with the target group 35 to 49 years (49 percent)

Their educational standard is quite high: 59 percent have had some kind of higher education. This is particularly true of

Hippo-Citroën (65 percent)

St. Germain Maubert (70 percent)

As for the sex of the customers, the only significant result concerns Saturday lunchtime when the proportion of men to women is more balanced.

Again as far as age is concerned, the lunchtime customers tend generally to be older (35 to 49 years) and this is the same during the week (42 percent) as it is on Saturdays (41 percent).

In the evening the age of the customers varies. It is rather higher on Mondays (47 percent, 25 to 34 years), and rather younger on Saturdays (33 percent, 18 to 24 years).

With regard to their socioprofessional background, Hippopotamus customers generally come from quite a high socioeconomic category. Professions of householders:

Businessmen, senior managers (38 percent)

Middle managers, staff (43 percent)

The customers interviewed (in particular at the Montparnasse-Maine Hippo and at the Opera Hippo), when in active employment, belong predominantly to the middle class (45 percent).

On Monday evenings there is a larger proportion of middle managers/staff, which is probably a reflection of the fact that cinema seats are cheaper then. There is a greater representation of the upper class in the three Champs-Elysées Hippos.

Students meet in the biggest numbers at Montparnasse (26 percent), with very few at the Champs-Elysées roundabout (8 percent).

The Running of a Restaurant

The Actors   According to the size of the concern, the manpower ranges between 50 to 100 people who serve from 600 to 1,300 meals a day. The chain's restaurants operate, broadly speaking, in the same way. See Exhibit 3. In the small restaurants

EXHIBIT 3 Unit Organization Chart

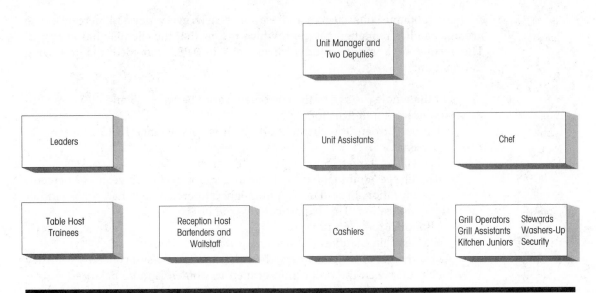

the post of chef does not exist; it is the grill operator who does his job. The existence/number of deputies to the manager is also dependent upon the size of the establishment.

The main duty of the grill operator is to cook the meat. The grill assistant prepares the accompanying vegetables and trimmings. The kitchen junior prepares everything which is not the main course: starters, desserts, coffee. The leader supervises the hostesses. The hostesses play an important role as far as the service is concerned. There are the reception hostesses and the hostesses who wait at table.

The hostess trainee is appointed to become a table hostess. She is learning the job and sees to the cleaning of the premises. The steward keeps the stocks of crockery, table linen, etc., and the food and drink. It is estimated that about 90 percent of the personnel were trained on the job.

In the restaurant business the human factor plays a role of paramount importance. The quality of the service depends upon the professionalism of all the employees, those who see to the cleaning as much as those who prepare the meals, wait at table, greet customers, and work out the bill. The attainment of a constantly high level of quality is dependent upon the actors' being constantly motivated.

The Remuneration of the Restaurants' Personnel

One part of the personnel receives a fixed pay, while the other receives a remuneration which is linked directly to the turnover. The salary of the manager, his deputies, his dining room and reception staff is governed by a calculation based on 15 percent of takings received under the heading of "service." The unit manager can reserve a percentage of the total of the 15 percent for monthly, variable bonuses which are paid to the most deserving. The pay of the kitchen staff and the cashiers is fixed.

From 1989 the "barometer" readings measuring the level of customer satisfaction will be taken into consideration when determining the profit sharing of the restaurant managers. Broadly speaking, salaries at Hippopotamus are higher than average in the restaurant business.

Recruitment

The working conditions in the restaurant business lead to a very high turnover of personnel in the order of 300 percent. At Hippopotamus this figure has been reduced by half, but efforts are being made to reduce it still further.

The unit manager himself carries out the recruitment of personnel for his restaurant. Restaurant managers and deputies are recruited by the human resources manager of the group.

Other Specific Features of the Chain

Each restaurant has the benefit of contributions made by the group's Culinary Research Laboratory.

The purchasing department at head office negotiates prices with the suppliers so as to obtain the best possible terms. It subsequently forwards the list of these suppliers and the prices agreed upon to the restaurants. These then get their stocks directly from the suppliers.

The restaurant puts in its order for the day that is beginning at about 3:00 a.m. Generally it does not get more than one-half day's stock in advance. The meat delivered is checked as soon as it is received and returned to the supplier if it is not up to standard or not what was ordered.

The cakes and pastries served in the chain's Parisian restaurants come from the group's Confectionery Laboratory, Cuisine-Pâtisserie Services (**CPS**).

The chain's restaurants have layouts which are similar in a number of ways. Their three focal points were designed and created by the group's architect and decorator:[3]

The bar—reception—dining room

The kitchen

The cashier's desk—secretarial office

THE SERVICE QUALITY PROGRAM: WHY?

The year 1986 saw the beginning of a turning point for the company. It was a time for reflection in order to prepare better for the future.

Hippopotamus had at that time important advantages: the locations of the restaurants on excellent sites; the architectural designs of the establishments; the welcome and atmosphere to be found there. All this meant that the chain made a name for itself on the market as a point of reference. The price for the quality of service given seemed right, but the number of customers had dropped slightly. Studies showed that the level of customer satisfaction stood at 77 percent and that if this were 100 percent the turnover could be increased by a third.

The personality of the chairman was an asset. He was a young man whose charisma was acknowledged by all. He was dynamic and strong-willed and he intended to lead the company to success. He was determined to examine lucidly the threats which were looming on the horizon. He went through all the possible factors that might be throwing the company off balance.

He was alone and at that time he had not yet formed any real management team. He now needed help in guiding and inspiring all the individuals who made up the company.

There was a shortage of driving forces, or at least they were not always in keeping with the company's philosophy.

Weren't the practical values of Hippopotamus in danger of disappearing from its culture because they had not been formalized or passed on?

The expansion had generated a compartmentalization and lack of communication. The chairman knew that those who had been with the company for some time were sorry not to have direct contact with him any more and that they were perhaps no longer as enthusiastic as they had been. Wasn't there some wastage of human resources?

There was no real personnel policy as far as salaries, recruitment, training, and communication were concerned.

To sum up, Christian Guignard wondered whether his business was going to be in a position to forge ahead with the same dynamism while remaining faithful to its image. Would it be able to keep its customers?

Finally he selected some priorities and decided to take steps that would hopefully answer the following four questions:

1. How to avoid letting the Hippopotamus tradition die as the company grew?
2. How to remain the best when faced with the growing competition?
3. How to pass on the company's culture to new colleagues?
4. How to motivate the scattered teams to work toward the same objective?

The actions destined to answer these questions are contained in the Service Quality Program which Christian Guignard drew up using the services of a consulting firm specializing in quality problems.

DESCRIPTION OF THE SERVICE QUALITY PROGRAM

On June 25, 1987 Christian Guignard invited his executives to a meeting that he had carefully prepared and he put before them the axes on which he was going to ask them to work. The objective was to implement the Service Quality Program as from September 1987.

A few weeks beforehand a market research study had been carried out. A survey covering 1,325 customers in nine establishments had revealed the level of satisfaction of the clientele, their profile, and their expectations. This study had presented the opportunity for the company to define accurately the product and the service it wanted to put on the market.

The plan proposed by the chairman to his executives was as follows:

1. To work out a service agreement
2. To formulate standards of service quality, that is to write down the know-how of Hippopotamus
3. To communicate the standards to everyone
4. To train all the teams
5. To improve the quality of the service
6. To innovate

This is how each of the points of this plan has been implemented.

To Work Out a Service Agreement

A committee composed of members of the top management and unit managers clarified and carefully worked out "The promise to the customer." The following was going to constitute the basic reference text. Each word had been carefully weighed:

The Sources of Success: Hippo's Promise to Its Customers

To always be able to have a good meal centered round a red meat, grilled, always tender, always fresh, always tasty and chosen from a wide range of good quality cuts at the right price.

To always be served generously and to enjoy, at your own speed, a meal—meat and accompanying vegetables of your choice—the preparation and presentation of which are flawless.

To always be welcomed warmly, known and recognized, put at ease, guided and then accompanied to your table with a pleasant manner, good humour, and simplicity.

To relax in an atmosphere which is always cheerful, in a clean, tidy restaurant with a warm decor.

Hippopotamus' promise conveys without any ambiguity the originality of the company's formula, its comparative advantage (why go to Hippopotamus rather than somewhere else), and the principal dimensions of the service. Through this promise, the company states its position to the outside world. It serves as a point of reference for the quality charter and its formalized expression in measurable standards.

To Formulate Standards of Service Quality

On the basis of Hippopotamus' Promise, measurable standards of service quality were defined, and on two levels:

On the level of the restaurant chain taken as a whole, general standards were drafted by a working group made up of individual restaurant managers, who put them to the top management.

On the level of the service of each individual restaurant, once formulated, the general standards were presented to more specialized groups so that they could define the standards applicable to each job: reception, bar, waitress service, kitchen, and general organization.

In total 60 people belonging to all levels of the hierarchy and to all the departments in the company were involved in working out the service quality standards. It took six months for the document to be finalized. In the last analysis it is a lot more than an instruction manual. It is the product of 20 years' experience and it expresses all the know-how and originality of the chain.

The quality standards, as presented in the document, were suggested by the stages through which the customer passes when he comes for a meal at Hippopotamus. He arrives and enters, he is greeted, he waits, he is accompanied to his table, he orders, he is served, he eats/drinks, he pays, he leaves.

At each of these stages the points in the promise were gone through so as to define what this promise meant for the customer (the result expected), what had to be done to give him satisfaction (tasks), and the resources to be used (methods and processes).

To Communicate the Standards to Everyone

The service quality standards were given to each member of staff and have subsequently been given to newcomers. They are put up in the departments of the individual restaurants (out of sight of the customers). Any training undertaken is centered round these standards.

To Train All the Teams

The implementation of the Service Quality Program required wide-ranging training operations. This training was carried out in two phases:

First of all, the training of 250 people by outside training specialists (A training of this kind was also given to the members of the executive board.) Then the training of the rest of the personnel by in-house training specialists in the restaurants and at Hippo-School

First Phase: The Training by Outside Training Specialists
This meant a big investment, which was considered essential for the success of the program. It concerned those with leadership responsibilities.

The 250 people took part, in groups of 30, in a residential Quality Seminar lasting five days. The chairman and the human resources manager attended each of the seven seminars personally, speaking at the beginning and the end.

The teaching method involved, essentially, trainee participation. It used the study of cases (specially devised at Hippopotamus), exercises with Hippopotamus data, and role-plays with video cameras and debriefing. The following is a very brief résumé of the content of the Quality Seminars:

The Hippo promise and quality standards
How to communicate the standards to someone else (training methods in the field)
How to improve current service quality: Presentation of the tools required to "hunt the mistake," How to lead a Quality Group,
The contribution to be made by the satisfaction barometer recently introduced

The objective was that, back at his unit, the course participant would constantly ask himself questions concerning the way to reach the standards, that he would be convinced of his responsibility to pass on the quality message, and that he would be able to lead in-House meetings on this theme.

In February 1988 an appraisal of the Quality Seminars showed that the entire message had been conveyed and that each participant had fully understood that his prime objective was the satisfaction of the customer. Each now knew what was expected of him and what he had to do.

It seemed that the numerous exchanges which took place during the seminars and the mixture of participants gave a new dynamism to the discussions between individuals and improved relations between the different departments such as the kitchen and dining room.

Thanks to the contacts made between the different hierarchical levels and the communication between the provincial restaurants and the Parisian ones, everyone acquired a much better understanding of the company's organization and the spirit of Hippopotamus as a group.

Second Phase: The Training by In-House Training Specialists

In-house training specialists took over from the Quality Seminars and were given the responsibility of providing training for the people who had not attended one. Hippo-School was created as a means of continuously communicating the service quality standards to colleagues at all levels. The training specialists were line executives who, after participating in the Quality Seminars, were given a specific training in teaching skills.

Hippo-School has training rooms equipped with audiovisual material at its center in Paris. Seminars of one or two days are organized there, for example:

Two-day seminars for table hostesses
One-day seminars for the kitchen juniors and the washers-up

Three subjects figure prominently in the program: the presentation of Hippo's Promise to its clientele, the quality standards, and role-plays intended to convey unequivocally the importance of the customer. Hippo-School has an extension in each unit where managers participate in the training of the teams using the teaching aids specially devised for this purpose.

Improve the Quality of the Service

Improve the Quality of the Service through In-House Communication In Hippopotamus's line of work it is necessary to win over not only the customer, but also the personnel. The Service Quality Program inevitably has to be diffused through in-house communication. This is being done in several ways.

A Quality Campaign The communication of the standards is reinforced by humorous posters put up in the restaurants. . . . Every month the human resources manager sends to all the personnel a copy of the *Quality Letter,* the purpose of which is to inspire and communicate total quality to all levels within the company. See Exhibit 4.

Quality Group Activity Since September 1988 working groups have been set up in every unit. Their aim is to "hunt the mistake" in order to reach a "zero-fault" level. The groups operate under the responsibility of the unit's manager, with management personnel, and on a voluntary basis.

The Hippo-Quality Contest This is a means of spurring on the units. It revitalizes and rewards the individuals and units reaching excellence. The Quality cup is awarded ceremoniously to the most deserving. In 1988 this was the occasion for a dinner at Maxim's for the winners.

The Quality Committee This authority includes certain members of the chain's top management including the chairman. It is expected to meet to help solve the problems coming from the units in the hunt-the-mistake process. Up to now the Quality Committee has not yet had the opportunity to meet. The implementation of the Quality Program is a long process and the problems likely to be settled at the Quality Committee level have not yet percolated through to it.

The "Promise of Human Resources to Our Customers" The quality of the service is transmitted through the quality of the personnel and their motivation. In 1987 the chairman had decided that human resources would also be a priority and that a recruitment and training policy was to be worked out. A new human resources manager had been taken on at that time.

To obtain the maximum level of support for the company project, the human resources manager in his turn made promises to the in-house customers: the personnel. This pledge is drawn up in five points:

The promise of Human Resources to Its Customers

To be available to welcome them in a kindly manner with good humor and without reserve

EXHIBIT 4   Example of a Quality Letter

HIPPOQUALITY

INAUGURATION OF HIPPOSCHOOL

---

18 APRIL, 16.30 : OUR TRAINING SCHOOL
has brought together in its premises at the Bastille 135
people representing all the colleagues of the Hippo Group

IT IS A GREAT NEW STAGE

ITS GOAL: TO ALLOW US TO REACH, TOGETHER, THE 95 PERCENT LEVEL OF CUSTOMER
SATISFACTION!!!

HIPPOSCHOOL, IT WORKS.

From 19th May, groups of 15 colleagues are going to attend the school, following on
from one another at the rhythm of one group for 1 to 2 days per week in order to
LEARN WITH THE HELP OF 15 IN-HOUSE TRAINING SPECIALISTS why and how we
must SATISFY OUR CUSTOMERS EVERY HOUR OF EVERY DAY.

To assist them in legal and social matters, in questions of insurance and other
administrative formalities

To give them every support in order to have quality personnel (promotion,
training, and recruitment)

To inform them about the life of the group and the human potential at Hippo

To give them precise and rapid answers (24 hours)

In line with this promise, important training and recruitment activities are forecast
in 1989 for unit managers and their deputies.

Improve the Quality of Service by Regularly Assessing It   To improve service quality one has to be able to measure it. Hippopotamus therefore uses measuring tools.

The Satisfaction Barometer   This has enabled the level of customer satisfaction to be assessed. Every three months a survey is carried out on 400 customers in each of the 15 restaurants, in the course of a week. Forty questions, concerned with concrete and precise points, such as the dress and behaviour of the receptionists and waitresses, the cleanliness of the establishment, the quality of the food and drink, etc., are thus put to the customers.

Careful study of the 5,000 completed questionnaires has led to the setting up of the Hippo barometer, which helps the company to:

Evaluate the cost of inadequate quality

Focus improvement efforts on the most sensitive points as far as customer satisfaction is concerned

Reward those giving the best performances

The Quality Audit   This was launched in October 1987 and its aim is to help a unit improve its service quality. It works on the principle that the manager of one restaurant audits another. It represents in a way the help given by one manager to his colleague.

Two managers never audit one another. The results are communicated only to the manager whose restaurant has been audited. It is in no way an inspection.

To carry out his audit a manager has a checklist specially designed for the purpose. He fills this in after making one or several visits to the restaurant and after having a meal there. The checklist can be used by restaurant managers for their own unit.

The Hippo-Suggestions Table   In the course of a month, a manager systematically and punctually invites eight customers to dine at his restaurant. This allows him to make a qualitative assessment of customer satisfaction between each quarterly barometer reading.

To Innovate

To succeed Hippopotamus has to be constantly seeking new ways to improve its service. Here is an example of innovation: In the course of the surveys carried out on the clientele, it became apparent that the customer was occasionally dissatisfied with the time he had to wait before a table became available. Action was therefore taken:

Hippo-Truth: the reception hostesses have been asked to tell the customer truthfully how long he will have to wait. If the actual waiting time proves longer than anticipated, he is to be offered a free drink.

Ideas regarding possible ways of livening up the waiting time are currently being studied.

By putting this sixth point in the Service Quality Program, the chairman of the Hippopotamus chain wanted to emphasize that stringency, that is the strict application of exact standards, must be combined with flexibility and creativity in order to reach the desired objective: excellence.

APPLICATION OF THE SERVICE QUALITY PROGRAM IN THE UNITS

The description of the program has shown the means put at the disposal of leaders and management, but what happens next in the field? Each unit manager is quite free to work out his own strategy and each does so in his own way.

The Experience of the Restaurant Hippo-Citroën

It has been the most spectacular. This case is special in as far as the restaurant has recently been taken over by a new manager, who has been given the task of boosting an establishment the results of which were falling. In October 1988 50 percent of the unit's personnel (about 100 people) underwent quality training: 40 percent attended the Quality Seminar; 10 percent went on a course at Hippo-School. The Hippo-Citroën manager explains what happened:

> Returning from the Quality Seminar a manager has his head full of ideas. There was a great deal of thought about a profession which is concerned with doing things and wanting to do things. There were some very strong messages. We were shown tremendous tools. . . . On getting back, I wondered how we were going to use all this, if we were ready to digest everything, if it wasn't too much.

But the manager of Hippo-Citroën is convinced that the program is good and fully justified, for at the seminar he rediscovered things that he was trying to do or that he was already doing to a certain extent.

The first decision was to have a meeting room converted into what he baptized the Quality Sanctuary. This was equipped with the teaching material and audiovisual aids necessary for personnel training. Messages were stuck up on the walls: Hippopotamus's promise to the customer, and Hippo-Citroën's plan of action for the implementation of the Quality Program.

However, such a plan of action could not be worked out immediately. First of all, the manager devoted a lot of time to meetings with his management personnel. It was then that he became aware of the following phenomena:

> There is now a common language: each person can see where he stands in his particular job. The posts which have been described and commented upon have gained in depth; they have been identified and developed; their standing has been increased. Everyone is now able to describe his duties. He

knows the vocabulary and concepts to be able to explain what he does (which was not the case before for a lot of the personnel). He feels that he can get on, that the company is offering him more than just a salary.

Communicating took a lot of the Hippopotamus manager's time. He became aware that he had to delegate a certain number of tasks to his colleagues if he was to cope. The following action was taken:

Communication of "the Standards"

In the Quality Sanctuary the standards were communicated to all the personnel with the visual tools worked out by the group.

Coaching

Coaching was started in the field. This step, in conjunction with the theoretical training and the Quality Group meetings, seemed both natural and indispensable for the attainment of the appointed goal. The coaching is carried out by the hierarchy (indeed, colleagues) who fulfil their management role in a more educational way than previously. In the kitchen, in the dining room, at the bar, at reception, the manager shows how something is to be done by doing it himself. He gets others to do it, and explains what can be improved. "When a remark is made during the service, a few minutes are taken afterwards to discuss the matter." The Hippopotamus manager has noticed, "The staff are more receptive to instructions and they really understand them."

The Quality Group Meetings

As a complement to theoretical and on-the-job training activities, service quality problems are dealt with in the Quality Groups. Four groups have been created, with about 10 people in each group:

> Bar/reception group
> Product group
> Dining room service group
> Citroën information bank

The Quality Groups' objective is to hunt the mistake. For the manager of Hippo-Citroën, the terms used are important: they highlight the fact that it is not a question of man-hunting or fault finding, but a common search for solutions in order to improve the running of the company.

What happens at a Quality Group meeting?

The agenda has been given to the participants a few days in advance.
There are about 10 participants. They have volunteered to be members of the Quality Group.
At every meeting there is a chairman, who must have attended the Quality Seminar, an observer, and a reporter, who takes the minutes. The unit manager is almost always present at the meetings. The Hippopotamus manager points out, "At the beginning nobody wanted to take the minutes;

people were afraid of not knowing, of making spelling mistakes. Now they all volunteer.'' The minutes play an important role. Through them the entire personnel can be kept informed of the decisions taken to remedy the problems under discussion, and the actions decided upon can subsequently be followed up and monitored.

Number and length of the meetings: an hour once a fortnight in the restaurant's slack period, that is the afternoon

Subjects tackled: A few examples from Hippo-Citroën:

   With the Dining Room Service Quality Group:

      Food served lukewarm to the customer

      Orders taken down badly worded

      Crockery breakages

   With the Bar/Reception Group: the problem of the discrepancy between the number of bottles of champagne charged to the customer and the number charged by the supplier

The method for conducting the meeting is simple. It is the method of Ichikawa and that of Pareto. It has been explained during the Quality Seminar and it allows solutions to be found relatively quickly, with the consensus of a group where several levels of hierarchy are represented. The chairman goes around the table and asks each member of the group what, in his opinion, are the possible causes of error, and he lists the causes on a board. When he goes around the table a second time, the participants indicate the importance they attribute to each of the causes listed. This means that they can then concentrate on the two or three causes judged by the group to be essential. For example, to resolve the problem of the champagne discrepancy the group agrees that the principal sources of error are:

1. Too large a goblet for the capacity indicated
2. A lack of precision in pouring out the appropriate measure of champagne

Going round the table for the third time, the chairman draws together the solutions put forward by each participant. In the final phase, two decisions to be taken are noted (in this case: 1. The replacement of glasses that are too big by smaller glasses which they will be able to serve well-filled to the customer's satisfaction; 2. staff training; how soon and by whom).

The Hippo-Citroën Manager stresses the following points:

To make the meeting as effective as possible figures need to be given so that one can put one's finger on the financial consequences of the mistake; for the badly measured-out champagne it's a turnover loss of so much per month and so much per year. You also have to think about the customer and the impact that the solutions considered will have on the quality of the service.

   It is important too that the group members get the feeling that they have taken the decisions themselves. The hunt-the-mistake process also serves to show the personnel that there is a permanent check on what is happening in the company.

For their part, the employees have expressed the following opinions:

It's good that time's taken to talk about our problems. We have a better idea of what we've got to do. We think more about the customer's opinion. Here you don't get the impression that you're just a number. I've been learning more about the job, and yet I've been in the restaurant business for a long time.

General meetings: For the implementation of the Quality Program and the relaunching of his restaurant, the manager of Hippo-Citroën felt the need to organize meetings to which the unit's entire personnel would be invited. In 1988 he held one in February and another in November. Those meetings provided him with the opportunity to remind everyone of the company's objectives, to point out the good work done by the Quality Groups and to sustain enthusiasm. The participation of the chairman of the company and the human resources manager in these meetings was a reminder that the unit is part of a group and that the latter helps and advises.

The manager of Hippo-Citroën believes that his restaurant benefits substantially from these general meetings. (The last one was filmed and a lot of people expressed their views in it.) They contribute to the creation of a good atmosphere, a common language, an internal cohesion and a feeling of belonging.

The results of the implementation of the Service Quality Program at Hippo-Citroën:

Growth in the level of customer satisfaction

October 1987: 75 percent

February 1988: 85 percent

May 1988: 98.5 percent, the best score in the group

Growth in the turnover (+5 percent) and therefore corresponding increases in pay

The unit no longer needs to have recourse to advertisements for personnel recruitment. The salaries are on display in the restaurant.

The achievement of Hippo-Citroën has had repercussions within the group and at the request of the human resources manager, the unit's manager has given a presentation of his plan of action to the managers of the other restaurants and the chairman of the company. It goes without saying that such a step has had its own impact on the state of mind of Hippo-Citroën's personnel: the restaurant was becoming a point of reference.

The Point of View of Hippo-Wagram's Manager

Before 1987, this unit's results, unlike those of Hippo-Citroën, were already very satisfactory. They were the best in the chain. For several years the restaurant's personnel had been the most stable in the group and the manager was anxious to maintain this situation by taking precautionary measures. In this unit, small group and general meetings were already taking place.

Here is the opinion of Hippo-Wagram's Manager:

As far as motivation is concerned, the positive benefits of the Quality Seminar have been extraordinary. A seminar of this type organized outside the company increases the participants' potential. Meeting people from different units is enriching and encourages a group spirit and consequently the sense of belonging, . . . but personnel motivation is not something to be done for a few days each year.

The Quality Program has allowed us to develop an attitude which was already present; we have subsequently changed certain things in the field. We think more in customer terms. . . . We've done things in a more standardized —and at the same time, more rational—way. Before it was more intuitive.

The actions associated with the quality program have been like those at Hippo-Citroën:

The communication of the standards to the restaurant's personnel and to newcomers
Hunting the mistake, through the organization of three Quality Groups meeting once a month

The mistakes dealt with have been, for example, meat sent back, errors in the bill, running out of an item on the menu, problems concerning the changeover of staff, the clearing of tables, etc. Some very important work has been done at reception level to make the waiting time given to the customer by the hostesses exact.

The Service Quality Program suggests a comparison between units with reference to the satisfaction barometer, for this gives the results of all the units of the chain and leads to a grading process and rewards.

This comparison is not always possible, for the clienteles are not the same and their expectations differ. . . . The important thing is that a unit should be able to measure itself against its own achievements.

The Hippo-Wagram manager considers that the Service Quality Program is one of the tools of Human Resources Management. "Others, like the annual individual interview, are equally necessary. The program is not an end in itself, but it has built up a state of mind."

A Few Opinions Collected within the Company

A year after the launching of the Service Quality Program the consulting firm specializing in quality problems, whose services the chairman of Hippopotamus used, audited the program and its implementation in the company. Discussions held with about 30 people belonging to the different units brought to the fore the positive repercussions and the difficulties.

Positive Repercussions of the Quality Program that Have Been Cited
The unit managers consider that Hippo-School, the prime function of which is to diffuse the standards, contributes a lot more in other ways:

"The personnel who go through Hippo-School understand the general organization of Hippopotamus."

"They become aware of the importance of each person's role."

"They can stand back from the unit in which they live and be enriched by the experience of others; they come back with something in their heads."

"Hippo-School gives them an extra motivation to reach a better level of quality. For the grill assistants/operators it's a plus."

"The definition of quality standards and precise objectives binds the teams together. Everyone is in agreement over the essentials. It's the basis of the profession; it's logical. Anyone who doesn't believe in logic isn't with it."

"There are exceptions, but by and large, everyone's focusing more on the customer."

"Everyone knows what he has to do and tries to come as close as possible to the service quality standard. There is a determination in people, a better team spirit."

"Now there are railings and landmarks. . . . Anyone straying from the quality standard gets brought back into line by the team. The girls know what to say when the food comes out of the serving hatch, and a hostess told *me*, the manager, that I was below standard."

Difficulties Mentioned by the Personnel Consulted   Certain unit managers took quite a while to consider service quality as a priority and to believe in it.

"I didn't have enough time; there was the problem of management being understaffed."

"It isn't always easy to get standard communication groups meeting together because you first have to find a slot in the schedule that everyone can make."

"The team turnover means that you're forever having to start all over again." When they talk about hunting the mistake, certain unit managers say, "We don't always have the time to meet."

The results of the Hippo barometer, especially the first, came as a shock to a few units: "Some people wept at the results."

"The results aren't precise enough; for example, when people talk about the quality of the starters, we don't always understand exactly what is wrong."

"We'd rather use the Hippo barometer to measure our own restaurant over a period of time than compare ourselves to other units, for we are not in the same districts. The different clienteles don't have the same expectations."

The automatic control quality audit has its supporters and its opponents: "It's dangerous." "I have learnt something." "I'm not going to stab a pal in the back." "The person who was to do it for me never came."

"We realize that it takes several months (three to four) for certain habits to be formed, like the introduction of the hostesses by their first name, the indication of the exact waiting time, speed in producing the bill. We also realize that, if these three points are satisfactory in a restaurant, all the rest will be, for they are the most difficult to achieve."

EXHIBIT 5

October 1987	February 1988	May 1988

Objective ━━━━━━━━━━━━━━━━━━━━━━━━━━━━━━ 95 Percent

77 Percent	82 Percent	87 Percent

CONCLUSION

The Service Quality Program was worked out in the course of 1987; it was first implemented in September of the same year and is to continue in the future.

It was wanted by the Chairman who has followed its progress very closely. Practically every individual in the company has been approached. It has involved a very big financial investment: FF 4.5 million for the period from November 1987 to December 1988, and it has been similarly expensive in terms of human effort, but it has produced results.

As Far as the Commercial Situation Is Concerned

The customer satisfaction level went up by 10 points between October 1987 and May 1988. See Exhibit 5.

As Far as the In-House Situation Is Concerned

Although these results are more difficult to measure in concrete terms, there is no doubt that the company has grown in dynamism and has improved the performances and the potential of its human resources. By giving precise objectives, by making everyone understand the importance of his role, by reinforcing the feeling of belonging to a company that's different, by providing training, the Service Quality Program has brought back enthusiasm and given a noticeable boost to the culture of the company.

The staff turnover has not come down sufficiently yet. (It stands at the rate of 1.26 for 1988 as compared with 1.50 in 1986, but the figure 1.00 is being aimed at for 1989 to 1990.) However, it is easier to manage thanks to the existence of training tools.

Finally the formalization of the Hippopotamus quality standards is making it easier for the company to get franchisees. It seems that the program must be coming up to the expectations of the chairman, Christian Guignard, who wanted the group to refocus its efforts and have better assets at its disposal prior to launching into a new phase of expansion. Nevertheless, it is recognized that the process is cumbersome and takes a long time to set up and that its practical application needs to be very closely supervised.

It must be pointed out in particular that, if all the restaurants have indeed formed Quality Groups, the frequency of meetings varies considerably. It is thought that the Service Quality Program has been put into practice at a rate which fluctuates from 20 to 80 percent depending on the restaurants, and the results of the satisfaction barometer seem to mirror in the same way the extent to which the program is being implemented in the units.

Endnotes

1. This is not a steak house and has a feminine decor.
2. Ecole Européenne des Affaires (European School of Business), Paris Chamber of Commerce and Industry.
3. The architect and decorator belong to the architecture and works company, SATRA, which the group created in 1985 and of which it is the chief customer. SATRA has the job of making the necessary studies and creating the new restaurants, while, at the same time, improving and maintaining the existing ones.

APPENDIX A Evaluation of the Price

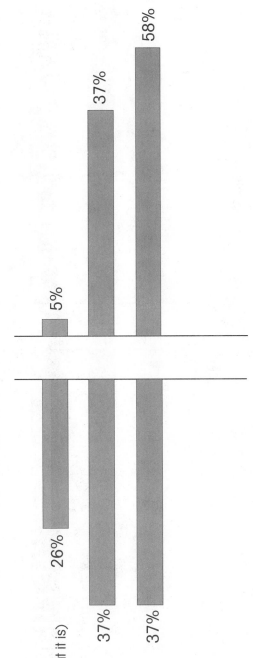

Unsatisfied

Satisfied

It is too expensive (for what it is)   26%   5%

It is somewhat expensive   37%   37%

It is just the right price   37%   58%

APPENDIX B By Word of Mouth

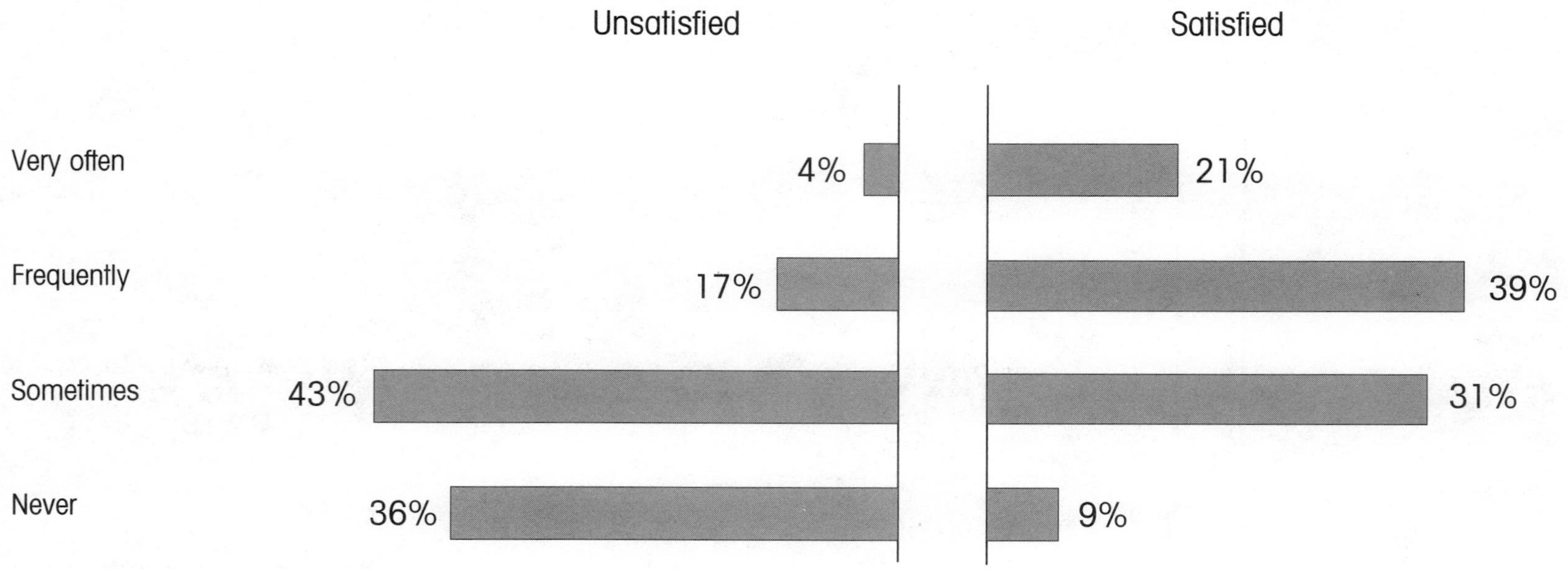

Unsatisfied   Satisfied

Very often   4%   21%

Frequently   17%   39%

Sometimes   43%   31%

Never   36%   9%

APPENDIX C   Visiting Hippopotamus Is Related to Satisfaction

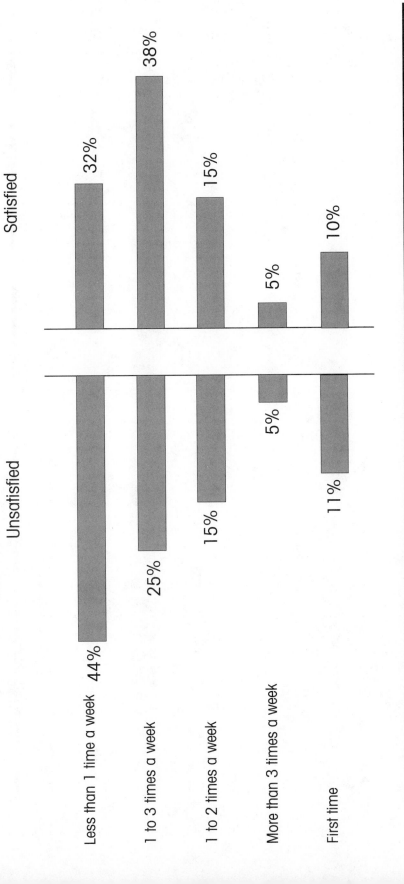

APPENDIX D The Success of the Hippo Formula

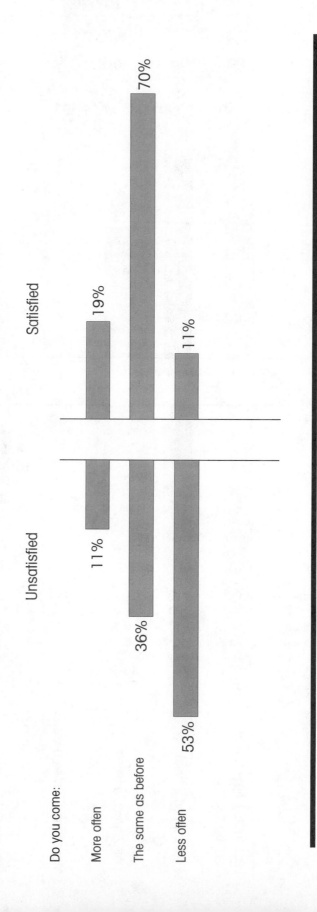

Do you come:

More often

The same as before

Less often

Unsatisfied

Satisfied

11%

36%

53%

19%

70%

11%

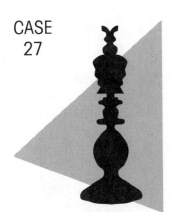

CINEPLEX ODEON CORPORATION

JOSEPH WOLFE

In mid-February 1989 Jack Valenti, head of the Motion Picture Association, reaffirmed the film industry's basic health by citing 1988 movie theater attendance figures surpassing 1.0 billion people for the seventh year in a row. While this magnitude translated into box office revenues of over $4.4 billion, there are indications the industry is in a state of both absolute and relative decline. It is also undergoing a restructuring that is fundamentally changing the nature of competitive practices for those in the film exhibition business. In the first instance a lower proportion of America's aging population attends the movies each year, partially due to the use of VCRs for film viewing, the presence of television in both its broadcast and cable versions, and other uses of the consumer's leisure-time dollar. In the second instance a great degree of owner-concentration is occurring due to separate actions by both the Hollywood producers of films and their exhibitors.

Despite the apparent decline of the motion picture theater as the major supplier of America's needs for mass entertainment, the Toronto-based firm of Cineplex Odeon has quickly become North America's second-largest and most profitable theater chain through a series of shrewd and adventuresome acquisitions while creating a large number of upscale, multiscreen theaters in key cities and market areas. With 482 theaters and 1,809 screens in 20 states, the Washington, D.C. area, six Canadian provinces, and the United Kingdom, the firm posted record sales of $695.8 million and profits of $40.4 million in 1988 while standing on the verge of developing and operating more than 110 screens in the United Kingdom by 1991. Central to Cineplex Odeon's success is the firm's driven and often abrasive chairman, president, and CEO, Garth Drabinsky. It is against the backdrop of the industry's fundamental changes and basic decline that Drabinsky must chart his firm's future actions to insure its continued growth and prosperity.

THE MOTION PICTURE THEATER INDUSTRY

The motion picture theater industry (SIC 783) has undergone a number of radical transformations since its turn-of-the-century beginnings. The first movies were

This case was prepared from primary and secondary materials by Joseph Wolfe of the University of Tulsa as the basis for class discussion rather than to illustrate either effective of ineffective handling of a managerial situation. Distributed by the North American Case Research Association. All rights reserved to the author and the North American Case Research Association. Permission to use the case should be obtained from the author and the North American Case Research Association.

shown in cramped and hastily converted storefront locations called nickelodeons, so-named for their 5-cent admission charges. Their numbers grew rapidly because the costs of entering this industry were relatively low and a plentiful supply of films was available in both their legal and pirated versions. By 1907 it was estimated the United States had about 3,000 movie theaters mainly concentrated in the larger cities. Rural areas were serviced by traveling film shows which made their presentations in local town meeting halls.

The typical show lasted only 15 to 20 minutes, augmented by song slides or lectures. As the film medium's novelty declined, audiences began to clamor for more lavish and ambitious productions using recognizable actors and actresses. Feature-length movies replaced one-reel short subjects and comedies in the middle to late 1910s and the theater industry's greatest building period began. Opulent, specially built structures soon became the focal point of every major city's downtown area. Often possessing more than 5,000 seats they came complete with a pit orchestra with vocalists and chorus, baby-sitting facilities, elevators, grand staircases to a heaven-like balcony, numerous doormen, and a watchful and attentive fleet of uniformed ushers.

By the mid-1920s over 19,000 theaters were in operation and Hollywood's film producers began what was a continuing attempt to control via acquisitions the first-run exhibitors of their films. The battle was initially waged between Paramount and First National, but soon Loew's (MGM), Fox, and Warner Brothers joined in, with First National being the major loser. By 1935 the twin realities of the Great Depression and the advent of sound films caused the number of theaters to plummet to about 15,000. Because of the nation's bleak economic outlook, many theaters had become too run down or too costly to convert to the greater demands of sound films. Many Americans also substituted radio's free entertainment for their weekly, lemming-like trek to the movies. Surviving theaters introduced the double feature to create more value for the entertainment dollar while obtaining the major source of their profits from candy, soft-drinks, and popcorn sales.

During World War II motion picture attendance and Hollywood's profits reached their all-time highs with about 82 million people a week going to the nation's 20,400 theaters. This pinnacle did not last long, however, as postwar incomes were spent on new cars, television sets, and homes built in the newly emerging suburbs. Motion picture attendance began its precipitous fall in 1947, with attendance reaching its all-time low of 16 million per week in 1971. The number of theaters followed the same downward trend, although a steady increase in the number of drive-in theaters temporarily took up some of the slack. [See Exhibit 1.]

The postwar period also saw the effects of the government's 1948 consent decree. By the early 1940s Hollywood's five major studios had obtained control or interests in 17 percent of the nation's theaters. This amounted to 70 percent of the important large-city, first-run theaters. Although certain studios were stronger in different parts of the country—Paramount dominated New England and the South, Warner Brothers the mid-Atlantic region, Loew's and RKO the New York–New Jersey area, and 20th Century-Fox the western states—each controlled all stages of the distribution chain from its studios (manufacturing), its film exchanges (wholesaling), and its movie theaters (retailing). Under the consent decree the studios could either divest their studios and film exchanges or get rid of

EXHIBIT 1 Number of U.S. Movie Theaters (in thousands, selected years, 1923–1989)

	Theaters	Drive-Ins	Total	Screens
1923	15.0		15.0	
1926	19.5		19.5	
1929	23.3		23.3	
1935	15.3		15.3	
1942	20.3	0.1	20.4	
1946	18.7	0.3	19.0	
1950	16.9	2.2	19.1	
1955	14.1	4.6	18.7	
1965	9.2	4.2	13.4	
1974	9.6	3.5	13.2	14.4
1980	9.7	3.6	13.3	17.6
1981	11.4	3.3	14.7	18.0
1984	14.6	2.8	17.4	20.2
1985	15.1	2.8	17.9	20.7
1986	16.8	2.8	19.6	22.8
1987[a]	17.9	2.8	20.7	23.6
1988[a]	18.1	2.7	20.8	24.3

[a]Estimated

Sources: Joel W. Finler, *The Hollywood Story* (New York: Crown, 1988), p. 288; "The Motion Picture Rides into Town, 1903," *The Wall Street Journal*, February 7, 1989, p. B1; *1989 U.S. Industrial Outlook* (Washington, D.C.: U.S. Department of Commerce/International Trade Administration, 1989), p. 57–1.

their movie theaters. Hollywood chose to sell their cinemas thereby opting to control the supply side of the film distribution system.

In an effort to arrest the decline in attendance and to counter the relatively inexpensive and convenient medium of black-and-white television in the 1950s, the film studios retaliated by offering movies that dealt with subject matter considered too dangerous for home viewing shown in formats and hues beyond television's technical capabilities. Moviegoers heard the word *virgin* uttered for the first time, women with child actually looked pregnant rather than merely full-skirted, and couples were shown in bed together without having to put one foot on the floor. From 1953 to 1968 about 28 percent of Hollywood's films were photographed and projected in a bewildering array of widescreen processes such as Cinerama, CinemaScope, RegalScope, SuperScope, Technirama, VistaVision, Panavision, Techniscope, and even three-dimensional color.

As movie attendance has stabilized in the mid-1980s to a little more than 20 million patrons per week, two new trends have established themselves in the movie-theater business. The first has been the creation of multiple-screened theater sites while the second trend has been Hollywood's reacquisition of theaters and theater chains as part of a general consolidation within the industry. Many theater chains have rediscovered the glitz and glamour of old Hollywood by either subdividing and rejuvenating old theaters or by constructing multiplexes from scratch in suburban malls and shopping districts.

The economies of multiple-screened operations are compelling at the local level. Rather than needing a separate manager and projectionist for each theater, a number of variously sized auditoriums can be combined and centrally serviced. Box-office operations and concession stands can also be centrally managed and operated. The availability of a number of screens at one location also yields programming flexibility for the theater operator. A small film without mass appeal can often turn a profit in a room seating only 300 people while it would be unprofitable and would be lost in a larger auditorium. Having a number of screens in operation also increases the likelihood the complex will be showing a hit film, thereby generating traffic for the other films being shown at the site. Having multiple screens also allows the operator to outfit various rooms with different sound systems (the THX System by Lucasfilm versus the standard four-track optical stereo system) and projection equipment (at least one 70mm, six-track, magnetic sound projector in addition to the usual 35mm projector) thereby offering the very finest possible viewing.

The second trend toward consolidation is occurring at all levels of the film distribution chain. A number of studios have recently purchased major theater chains after sensing a relaxation of the enforcement of the consent decree (in 1984 the Justice Department offered advance support to any studio financing a lawsuit to re-enter the movie theater business) plus their promise to limit their ownership to less than 50 percent of any acquired chain. MCA, owner of Universal Studios, has purchased 49.7 percent of Cineplex Odeon; the Cannon Group has purchased the Commonwealth chain; United Artists Communications purchased the Georgia Theatre Company, the Gulf States and Litchfield chains, and in 1988 alone the Blair, Sameric, Commonwealth (from the Cannon Group), and Moss theater chains. Gulf & Western's Paramount Studios purchased the Mann Theaters and Festival Enterprises while Columbia and Tri-Star (owned by Coca-Cola) bought the Loews chain. On the retailing side, Cineplex Odeon has purchased the Walter Reade, Plitt, RKO, Septum, Essaness, and Sterling chains; Carmike Cinemas has purchased Stewart & Everett while AMC Entertainment purchased the Budco Theatres. Through these actions and others the top six chains now own nearly 40 percent of America's screens. This is a 67 percent increase in just three years.

Wholesaling operations have been drastically reduced over the years on a scale unnoticeable to the public, but very significant to those in the business. When film going was in its heyday, each studio operated as many as 20 or so film exchanges in key cities across the country. Hollywood's studios have since closed many exchanges until they are now operating only five to eight branch offices each. Paramount recently merged its Charlotte and Jacksonville branches into its Atlanta office while Chicago now handles the business once serviced by its Detroit, Kansas City, Des Moines, and Minneapolis branches. As observed by Michael Patrick, president of Carmike Cinemas, "as the geographical regions serviced by these offices increase, the ability of smaller exhibitors to negotiate bookings is diluted relative to the buying power of the larger circuits."[1]

COMPETITIVE CONDITIONS

Despite the glamor associated with Hollywood, its stars, its televised Academy Award show, and such megahits as *Who Framed Roger Rabbit?*, *Rain Man*, and

Batman, theater operators are basically in the business of running commercial enterprises dealing with a very perishable commodity. A movie is a merchandisable product made available by Hollywood and various independent producers to commercial store-front theaters at local retail locations. Given the large degree of concentration in the industry, corporate-level actions entail the financing of both acquisitions and new construction, while local operations deal with the booking of films that match the movie-going tastes of the communities being served.

To the degree a movie house merely retails someone else's product, the theater owner's success lies in the quality and not the quantity of products produced by Hollywood. Accordingly the 1987 to 1988 Christmas season did not produce any blockbusters, while 1987's two big hits were *Beverly Hills Cop II* and *Fatal Attraction*, and 1986's hits were *Top Gun, Crocodile Dundee,* and *The Karate Kid, Part II*. Under these conditions of relatively few real money-makers, the bargaining power shifts to the studios, leaving the exhibitors with more screens than they can fill with high-drawing films. Although the independent producers (the "indies") such as the De Laurentiis Entertainment Group, New World, Atlantic, Concorde, and Cannon are producing proportionally more films every year and the majors are producing fewer, their product is more variable in quality and less bankable. Additionally, theaters often pay a premium for the rights to exclusively show first-run movies in a given area or film zone such as the May 1989 release of *Indiana Jones and the Last Crusade*. This condition hurts the smaller chains especially hard as they do not have the resources to outbid the giant circuits.

Marketing research conducted by the industry has consistently found young adults are the prime consumers of motion picture theater entertainment. This group is rather concentrated, but not organized. A study by the Opinion Research Corporation in July 1986 found those under the age of 40 accounted for 86 percent of all theater admissions. Frequent moviegoers constitute only 21 percent of the eligible filmgoers, but they account for 83 percent of all admissions. A general downward attendance trend has been occurring, as shown in Exhibit 2, where 43 percent of the population never attended a film in 1986. The long-term demographics also appear to be unfavorable as America's population is moving toward those age categories least likely to attend a movie. Those 40 and over make up only 14 percent of a typical theater's admissions while they account for 44 percent of the

EXHIBIT 2   Frequency of Attendance by Total Public, Ages 12 and Over

Attendance	1986	1985	1984
Frequently	21.0%	22.0%	23.0%
Occasionally	25.0	29.0	28.0
Infrequently	11.0	9.0	8.0
Never	43.0	39.0	39.0
Not reported	0.0	1.0	2.0

Frequently: At least once a month.
Occasionally: Once in two to six months.
Infrequently: Less than once in six months.
Source: *1988 International Motion Picture Almanac* (New York: Quigley, 1988), p. 29A.

EXHIBIT 3 U.S. Population by Age Group for 1980, with Projections for 1990 and 2000

Age Range	Year	Number (in millions)	Percentage of Total	Percentage Change
5–17	1980	47.22	20.7%	—
	1990	45.14	18.1	− 4.4%
	2000	49.76	18.6	10.2
18–24	1980	30.35	13.2	—
	1990	25.79	10.3	−15.0
	2000	24.60	9.2	− 4.6
25–44	1980	63.48	27.9	—
	1990	81.38	32.6	28.2
	2000	80.16	29.9	− 1.5
45–64	1980	44.49	19.5	—
	1990	46.53	18.6	4.4
	2000	60.88	22.7	31.1
65 and over	1980	25.71	11.3	—
	1990	31.70	12.8	23.3
	2000	34.92	13.0	10.2

1980 total: 227,705,000.
1990 total: 249,675,000.
2000 total: 267,955,000.
Adapted from U.S. Bureau of the Census, *Statistical Abstract of the United States, 1985* (Washington, D.C.: Government Printing Office, 1985), pp. 26–27.

nation's population. [See Exhibit 3.] Those from 12 to 29 years of age make up 66 percent of admissions while accounting for only 36 percent of the population.[2]

It appears that certain barriers to entry into the motion picture theater industry exist. Economies of scale are present with the advantage given to operations concentrated in metropolitan areas where one omnibus newspaper advertisement covers all the chain's theaters. As shown in Exhibit 4, the largest chains in the United States lost the least during the period July 1984 to June 1985. Based on these results scale economies appear to exist in the areas of operating costs, executive compensation, advertising, and rental expenses. Those choosing to enter the industry in recent years have done so through the use of massive, conglomerate-backed capital. The possibility that an independent can open a profitable movie theater is very remote. [Exhibit 5 lists the largest theater circuits.] "There's no way the small, independent operator can compete against the large screen owners these days," says John Duffy, cofounder of Cinema 'N' Drafthouse International of Atlanta, Georgia.[3] As a way of carving a niche for himself, Duffy's chain charges $2 for an "intermediate-run" film, but serves dinner and drinks during the movie thereby garnering more than $5 in food revenue compared to a theater's average $1.25 per admission.

Despite attempts by various theater owners to make the theater-going experience unique, customers tend to go to the most convenient theater showing the film they want to see at the time which is best for them. Accordingly a

EXHIBIT 4 Average Operating Results for Selected Motion Picture Theater Corporations by Asset Size, July 1984 to June 1985

Operating Results	Smaller-Sized		Middle-Sized		Larger-Sized	
Revenues	$224,171	100.0%	$4,476,042	100.0%	$151,545,455	100.0%
Cost of operations	93,917	41.9	1,780,066	39.8	54,707,909	36.1
Operating income	130,254	58.1	2,695,976	60.2	96,837,546	63.9
Expenses						
Compensation of officers	6,788	3.0	150,647	3.4	2,121,636	1.4
Repairs	5,497	2.5	74,134	1.7	2,438,504	1.6
Bad debts	170	0.1	4,196	0.1	82,661	0.1
Rent	32,195	14.4	315,841	7.1	11,489,901	7.6
Taxes (excluding federal tax)	12,904	5.8	179,881	4.0	5,689,843	3.8
Interest	8,045	3.6	117,216	2.6	8,031,909	5.3
Depreciation	8,866	4.0	269,122	6.0	8,954,959	5.9
Advertising	16,004	7.1	152,745	3.4	5,689,843	3.8
Pensions and other benefit plans	—	—	42,662	1.0	771,504	0.5
Other expenses	70,971	31.7	1,682,992	37.6	55,245,207	36.5
Net profit before taxes	$(31,186)	(13.9)	$(293,460)	(6.6)	$(3,678,421)	(2.4)
Current ratio	1.0		1.3		0.7	
Quick ratio	0.6		1.0		0.5	
Debt ratio	140.6		52.9		74.2	
Asset turnover	3.0		1.3		1.0	

Source: L. Troy, *Almanac of Business and Industrial Financial Ratios* (Englewood Cliffs, N.J.: Prentice-Hall, 1988), p. 332.

particular theater chain enjoys proprietary product differentiation to the degree it occupies the best locations in any particular market area. Additionally the cost of building new facilities in the most desirable areas has increased dramatically. Harold L. Vogel, of Merrill Lynch, Pierce, Fenner, and Smith, has observed the average construction cost comes to over $1 million per screen in areas such as New York or Los Angeles.[4]

EXHIBIT 5 North America's Largest Theater Circuits

Circuit	Headquarters	Screens
United Artists Communications	Denver, Colorado	2,677
Cineplex Odeon	Toronto, Canada	1,825
American Multi-Cinema	Kansas City, Missouri	1,531
General Cinema	Chestnut Hill, Massachusetts	1,359
Carmike Cinemas	Columbus, Georgia	742

Source: Form 10-K, Cineplex Odeon Corporation, various years; and various stockholder's reports for 1988.

Just as the motion picture was a substitute for vaudeville shows and minstrels at the turn of the century, radio, and now television, have been the major, somewhat interchangeable, substitutes for mass entertainment in America. Most recently cable television, pay-per-view TV, and videocassettes have eaten into the precious leisure-time dollar. It has been estimated that 49.2 million homes now subscribe to cable television, 19 million homes have pay-per-view capability, and 56 million homes have VCRs with 20 percent of those homes having more than one unit. The greatest damage to theater attendance has been accomplished by videocassettes which deliver over 5,000 titles to viewers at a relatively low cost in the comfort of their own living rooms. As Sumner Redstone, owner of the very profitable National Amusements theater chain says, "Anyone who doesn't believe videocassettes are devastating competition to theaters is a fool."[5]

Although the motion picture medium has been characterized as one that provides visual mass entertainment, those going to movies must ultimately choose between alternative forms of recreation. In that regard, skiing, boating, baseball and football games, books, newspapers, and even silent contemplation vie for the consumer's precious time. Exhibit 6 shows the movie-theater industry has declined in its ability to capture both America's total recreation dollars or its thirst for passive spectator entertainment. During the period from 1984 to 1987 the greatest increases in consumer recreation expenditures were for bicycles, sports equipment, boats and pleasure aircraft, and television and radio equipment and their repair.

Different marketing strategies are being employed in an attempt to remain viable in this very competitive industry. Some chains, such as Cinemark Theaters

EXHIBIT 6   Motion Picture Exhibitors' Share of Entertainment Expenditures: Receipts as a Percentage of Total for Selected Years, 1929–1989

	Consumer Expenditures	Recreation Expenditures	Spectator Expenditures
1929	0.94%	16.6%	78.9%
1937	1.01	20.0	82.6
1943	1.29	25.7	87.6
1951	0.64	11.3	76.3
1959	0.31	5.6	61.0
1965	0.21	3.5	51.2
1971	0.18	2.7	47.7
1977	0.56	5.8	34.8
1983	0.16	2.4	41.9
1986	0.14	1.9	37.3
1987	0.14	1.8	36.9
1988	0.13	1.8	36.5
1989[a]	0.13	1.7	36.1

[a]Estimated by the casewriter.
Sources: Joel W. Finler, *The Hollywood Story* (New York: Crown, 1988), p. 288; U.S. Bureau of Economic Analysis, *Survey of Current Business,* July issues; and U.S. Bureau of the Census, *Statistical Abstract of the United States, 1989,* 109th ed. (Washington, D.C.: U.S. Government Printing Office, 1988).

and Carmike Cinemas, specialize in $1 or low-price, second-run multiplexed theaters in smaller towns and selected markets. In a sense, they are applying Wal-Mart's original market strategy of dominating smaller, less competitive rural towns. Others, such as General Cinema, United Artists Communications, and AMC Entertainment, favor multiplexed, first-run theaters in major markets. Within this group AMC Entertainment has been a pioneer as a multiscreen operator. It opened its first twin theater in 1963 and its first quadplex in 1969. As of mid-1988 AMC was operating 269 complexes with 1,531 screens with most of its expansion in the Sunbelt. General Cinema has been diversifying out of the movie theater business through its nearly 60 percent interest in the Neiman Marcus Group (Neiman Marcus, Contempo Casuals, and Bergdorf Goodman) and 18.4 percent interest in Cadbury Schweppes. Most recently General Cinema sold off its soft-drink bottling business to PepsiCo for $1.5 billion to obtain cash for investments in additional nontheater operations.

A great amount of building has occurred in the theater industry in the past few years. Since 1981 the number of screens has increased about 35 percent, but the population proportion attending movies has actually fallen. Additionally the relatively inexpensive days of "twinning" or quadplexing existing theaters appear to be over and the construction of totally new multiplexes is much more expensive. Exhibit 7 shows that operating profit margins peeked in 1983 at 11.7 percent and they have fallen dramatically since then as the industry has taken on large amounts of debt to finance the construction of more and more screens now generating 24.6 percent fewer admissions per screen. Many operations are losing money, although certain economies of scale exist and labor-saving devices have allowed industry employment to fall slightly while the number of screens has increased substantially. The Plitt theaters were money losers before being acquired by Cineplex Odeon, and AMC Entertainment lost $6 million in 1987 and $13.8 million in 1988 on theater operations. Carmike was barely profitable in 1988 and General Cinema's earnings from its theater operations have fallen for the past three years, although the operation's assets and sales have been increasing. Generally speaking about half of the nation's motion picture theaters and chains have been unprofitable in the 1980s while numerous chains have engaged in the illegal practice of splitting, wherein theater owners in certain markets decide which one will negotiate or bid for which films offered by the various distributors available to them.

EXHIBIT 7 Per-Screen Admissions, Capital Expenditures, and Operating Profit Margins (selected years, 1979–1987)

Item	1979	1981	1983	1985	1987
Tickets sold (000,000)	1,121	1,067	1,197	1,056	1,086
Average admission per screen	65,575	58,422	63,387	49,936	47,797
Capital expenditures ($000,000)	$19.0	$57.4	$77.6	$164.0	$515.7
Profit margin	9.3%	9.1%	11.7%	11.6%	8.8%

Source: Peter Waldman, "Silver Screens Lose Some of Their Luster," *The Wall Street Journal*, February 9, 1989, p. B1.

A LOOK AT CINEPLEX ODEON CORPORATION

Today's exhibition giant began in 1978 with an 18-screen complex below the parking garage of a Toronto shopping center. Garth Drabinsky, a successful entertainment lawyer and real estate investor, joined with the Canadian theater veteran, Nathan Aaron (Nat) Taylor, in this enterprise. After three years and dozens of new theaters, Cineplex entered the American theater market by opening a 14-screen multiplex in the very competitive and highly visible Los Angeles Beverly Center. Despite the chain's growth, however, it was only marginally profitable. When the fledgling chain went public on the Toronto Stock Exchange in 1982 it lost $12 million on sales of $14.4 million.

Cineplex nearly went bankrupt, but not through poor management by Drabinsky or Taylor. Canada's two major theater circuits, Famous Players (Paramount Studios) and the independent Odeon chain, had pressured Hollywood's major distributors into keeping their first-run films from Cineplex. But in 1983 Drabinsky, who as a lawyer had written a standard reference on Canadian motion picture law, convinced Canada's version of the U.S. Justice Department's antitrust division that Famous Players and Odeon were operating in restraint of trade. Armed with data gathered by Drabinsky, the Combines Investigative Branch forced the distributors to sign a consent decree thus opening all films to competitive bidding. Ironically, without the protection provided by its collusive actions, the 297-screen Odeon circuit soon began to lose money whereupon Cineplex purchased its former adversary for $22 million. The company subsequently changed its name to Cineplex Odeon.

In its development as an exhibition giant, the chain has always been able to attract a number of smart, deep-pocketed backers. Early investors were the since-departed Odyssey Partners, and, with a 30.2 percent stake, the Montreal-based Claridge Investments & Company, which is the main holding company of Montreal financier Charles Bronfman. The next major investor was the entertainment conglomerate MCA Incorporated of Universal City, California. MCA purchased 49.7 percent of Cineplex's stock (but is limited to a 33 percent voting stake because of Canadian foreign-ownership rules) in January 1986 for $106.7 million. This capital infusion gave Cineplex the funds to further pursue its aggressive expansion plans. As Drabinsky said at the time, "There's only so much you can do within the Canadian marketplace. It was only a question of when, not where, we were going to expand."[6] In short order the company became a major American exhibitor by acquiring six additional chains. [See Exhibit 8.] Some rival and fearful exhibitors, because of Drabinsky's quest for growth via the acquisition route, have been tempted to call him Darth Grabinsky.

Despite these rumblings, Cineplex Odeon has reshaped the movie-going experience for numerous North Americans. Many previous theater owners had either let their urban theaters fall into decay and disrepair or they had sliced their larger theaters into unattractive and sterile multiplexes. Others had built new, but spartan and utilitarian facilities in suburban malls and shopping centers. When building their own theaters from the ground up or when refurbishing an acquired theater, Cineplex pays great attention to making the patron's visit to the theater a pleasurable one.

When the Olympia I & II Cinemas in New York City were acquired a typical major renovation was undertaken. As originally built in 1913, the theater seated

EXHIBIT 8 Cineplex Odeon Theater Acquisitions

Odeon
Plitt Theatres
RKO Century Warner Theaters
Walter Reade Organization
Circle Theatres
Septum
Essaness
Sterling Recreation Organization
Maybox Movie Centre Limited

1,320 and was billed as having the world's largest screen. New owners subsequently remodeled it in 1939 in an art deco style and in 1980 it was renovated as a triplex with a fourth screen added in 1981. As part of Cineplex's renovation, the four smaller auditoriums were collapsed into two larger, 850-seat, state-of-the-art, wide-screen theaters featuring Dolby stereo sound systems and 70mm projection equipment. Its art deco design was augmented by post-modern features such as marble floors, pastel colors, and neon accents.

Whether through new construction or the renovation of acquired theaters, many Cineplex cinemas feature entrance ways made of terrazzo tile, marble, or glass. The newly built Cinema Egyptien in Montreal has three auditoriums and a total seating capacity of 900. It is replete with mirrored ceilings and hand-painted murals rendered in the traditional Egyptian colors of Nile green, turquoise, gold, lapis lazuli blue, and amber red. Historically accurate murals measuring 300 feet in length depict the daily life and typical activities of the ancient Egyptians. Toronto's Canada Square office complex features a spacious, circular, art deco lobby with a polished granite floor and recessed lighting highlighted by a thin band of neon encircling the high, domed ceiling. On the lobby's left side, moviegoers can snack in a small cafe outfitted with marble tables, bright red chairs, and thick carpeting. In New York City the chain restored the splendor and elegance of Carnegie Hall's Recital Hall as it was originally conceived in 1891. The plaster ceilings and the original seats were completely rebuilt and refinished in the gold and red velvet colors of the great and historic Carnegie Hall.

Just to make the evening complete, and to capture the high profits realized from concession operations, patrons of a Cineplex theater can typically sip cappucino or taste 14 different blends of tea served in Rosenthal china. Those wanting heavier fare can nibble on croissant sandwiches, fudge brownies, carrot cake, or *latte macchiato* while freshly popped popcorn is always served with real butter. In-theater boutiques selling movie memorabilia to add to the dollar volume obtained from the moviegoer were created, but discontinued due to unnecessarily high operating costs.

This glamor does not come cheaply as the chain usually charges the highest prices in town. For those in a financial bind, the American Express credit card is now honored at many of the chain's box offices. Cineplex broke New York City's $6 ticket barrier by raising its prices to $7, thus incurring the wrath of Mayor Ed Koch who marched on picket lines with other angry New Yorkers. Cineplex's action also caused some to suggest that the New York state legislature pass a measure requiring all exhibitors to print admission prices in their newspaper advertisements. When justifying the increased ticket price, Drabinsky said the alternative was "to continue to expose New Yorkers to filthy, rat-infested environments. We don't intend to do that."[7] Instead of keeping prices low, $30 million was spent refurbishing Cineplex Odeon's 30 Manhattan theaters to attract better-paying customers. Another unpopular and somewhat incongruous action, given the upscale image engendered by each theater's trappings, is the running of advertisements for Club Med and the California raisins before its films. Regardless of the anger and unpopularity created among potential patrons, Cineplex is not interested in catering to the average theater patron. Rather than trying to attract the mass market, the theater chain aims its massive and luxurious theaters at the aging baby-boomers who are becoming a greater portion of America's population.

Over the years Cineplex Odeon and Garth Drabinsky have received high marks for their creative, show business flair. As observed by theater industry analyst Paul Kagan, "Garth Drabinsky is both a showman and a visionary. There were theater magnates before him, but none who radiated his charisma or generated such controversy."[8] These sentiments are reiterated by Roy L. Furman, president of Furman Selz Mager Dietz & Birney Inc., one of Drabinsky's intermediaries in the Plitt acquisition. "Too many people see the [theater] business as just bricks and mortar. Garth has a real love for the business, a knowledge of what will work and what won't."[9] When a new Cineplex Odeon theater opens, it begins with a splashy, by-invitation-only party, usually with a few movie stars on hand. Besides his ability to attract smart investors, Drabinsky believes moviegoers want to be entertained by the theater's ambience as well as by the movies it shows. Accordingly about $2.8 million (about $450,000 per screen) is spent when building one of the chain's larger theaters as opposed to the usual $1.8 million for a simple, no-frills sixplex. "People don't just like coming to our theaters," says Drabinsky. "They linger afterward. They have another cup of cappuccino in the cafe or sit and read the paper. We've created a more complete experience, and it makes them return to that location."[10] This company has attempted to change the basic thinking. "We've introduced the majesty back to picture going."[11]

Drabinsky dates his fascination with the silver screen to his childhood bout with polio which left him bedridden much of the time from the ages of 3 to 12. His illness also imbued him with a strong sense of determination and this resolution has helped to drive Cineplex Odeon forward. No one speaks for the company except for Drabinsky and he logs half a million miles a year visiting his theaters and otherwise encouraging his employees. The energetic CEO likes to drop by his theaters unannounced to talk with ushers and cashiers, and he telephones or sees 20 to 25 theater managers a week. His standards are meticulously enforced, often in a very personal and confrontational manner. He has been known to exemplify his penchant for detail by stooping in front of one of his ushers to pick up a single piece of spilled popcorn.

The combative nature that helped Drabinsky break the Famous Players and Odeon cartel in the early 1980s still resides in him. When Columbia Pictures temporarily pulled its production of *The Last Emperor* out of distribution, he retaliated by canceling 140 play dates of the studio's monumental bomb, *Leonard Part 6* starring Bill Cosby. "Some people are burned by his brashness," says Al

Waxman, formerly of the television series *Cagney & Lacey.* "There's no self-denial. He stands up and says, 'Here's what I'm doing.' Then he does it."[12] As his long time mentor Nat Taylor has observed, "He's very forceful, and sometimes he's abrasive. I think he's so far ahead of the others that he loses patience if they can't keep up with him."[13] This nature may have long-term negative consequences for Cineplex, however, as Drabinsky has recently had heated arguments with Sidney Jay Sheinberg, president of MCA Incorporated, the head of the circuit's largest shareholder group.

In addition to its motion picture theater operations, Cineplex Odeon has been engaged in other entertainment-related ventures such as television and film production, film distribution, and live theater. In the latter area the company is restoring the Pantages Theatre in downtown Toronto into a legitimate theater for the housing of its $5.5 million production of Andrew Lloyd Webber's *The Phantom of the Opera* scheduled for fall 1989.

Cineplex also began a 414-acre motion picture entertainment and studio complex in Orlando, Florida as a joint venture with MCA Incorporated, but sold its stake to an American unit of the Rank Organization PLC for about $150 million in April 1989 after having invested some $92 million in the project. Various industry observers felt Cineplex withdrew from the potentially profitable venture to help reduce its bank debt which had grown to $640 million.

The firm also created New Visions Pictures as a joint venture with a unit of Lieberman Enterprises Inc. in August 1988 to deliver 10 films over a two-year period. Cineplex Odeon also owns Toronto International Studios, Canada's largest film center. This operation licenses its facilities to moviemakers and others for film and television production. In a related motion picture production move, Cineplex acquired The Film House Group Inc. in 1986 to process 16mm and 35mm release prints for Cineplex Odeon Films, another one of the company's divisions, and other distributors. After doubling and upgrading its capacity in 1987 it sold 49 percent of its interest to the Rank Organization in December 1988 for $73.5 million. Rank has a one year option to buy the remaining portion of The Film House Group by December 1989.

The company has also engaged in various motion picture distribution deals and television productions, none of which have been commercially successful. Cineplex has distributed such films as Prince's *Sign o' the Times*, Paul Newman's *The Glass Menagerie, The Changeling* with George C. Scott, and *Madame Sousatzka* starring Shirley Maclaine, while its television unit contracted 41 new episodes of the revived *Alfred Hitchcock Presents* series for the 1988 to 1989 television season. The series, however, was cancelled. For future release Cineplex is financing five low-budget ($4 to $5 million each) films joint-ventured with Robert Redford's Wildwood Enterprises through Northfork Productions Inc. The five movies will be distributed through Cineplex Odeon Films.

Garth Drabinsky's financial dealings and his ability to attract capital to his firm have always been very important to its success. Serious questions have been raised, however, into the propriety of some of Cineplex's financial reporting methods. Charles Paul, a vice president of MCA Incorporated and Cineplex board member, says various members are very concerned about the company's financial reporting practices and procedures. In a highly critical report distributed by Kellogg Associates, a Los Angeles accounting and consulting firm, a number of questionable practices were noted. Most frequently cited is Cineplex's treatment of the gains and losses associated with asset sales with the overall effect being an overstatement of operating revenues. As an example, Cineplex treated its gain of $40.4 million from the sale of The Film House Group as revenue rather than as extraordinary income. The report also criticized (1) Cineplex's $18.7 write-off on the value of its film library, thereby postponing losses on the sale of American theaters, and (2) its inclusion of the proceeds from the sale of theaters as nonoperating income in its cash flow statement, but calling it operating revenue in its profit and loss statement. In 1988 alone Cineplex reported a profit of $49.3 million from the sale of certain theater properties.

Also of concern is the role asset sales play in the company's revenue and cash flow picture. Jeffrey Logsdon, a Crowell Weedon analyst, believes Cineplex has been selling its assets just to keep operating, citing as evidence the sale of both The Film House Group and its 50 percent stake in MCA's Universal Studios tour project to the Rank Organization. Exhibit 9 demonstrates how Cineplex's revenue sources have changed since 1985 with box-office receipts constantly falling and property sales constantly rising. Over the period shown, the sale of theater assets has increased 98 percent as a source of corporate revenues. Additionally, the return on those sales, based on selling price over acquisition costs, has fallen every year from a high of 139.1 percent in 1985 to their low of 13.3 percent in 1988.

There is also a question as to whether Cineplex can continue its current growth rate via acquisitions and debt financing. The cost of acquisitive growth may become more expensive as many of the bargains have already been obtained by Cineplex or other chains. The early purchase of the Plitt Theater chain in November 1985 cost about $125,000 per screen, although the bargain price for Plitt may have been a one-time opportunity as it had just lost $5 million on revenues of $111 million during the nine months ending June 30, 1985. To get into the New York City RKO Century Warner Theaters chain in 1986, Cineplex had to pay $1.9 million per screen while it paid almost $3 million a screen in 1987 for the New York City-based Walter Reade Organization. Overall, Cineplex Odeon paid about $276,000 each for the screens it acquired in 1986 and some are questioning the prices being paid for old screens as well as the wisdom of expanding operations in what many see is a declining and saturated industry. A past rule of thumb has been that a screen should cost 11 times its cash flow, but some experts feel a more reasonable rule should be 6 to 7 times cash flow given the glut of screens on the market. The changing effects of Cineplex's acquisition and debt structure since 1984 have been summarized in Exhibit 10.

Given the nature of the North American market and Cineplex Odeon's penchant for growth, it is currently implementing a planned expansion into Europe. Cineplex is scheduled to build 100 screens in 20 movie houses throughout the United Kingdom by 1990 and it has further plans in Europe and Israel for the early 1990s. Exhibit 11 lists the comparative per-capita motion picture attendance rates found in various European countries. Other exhibitors are also interested in bringing multiscreen theaters to Europe. In addition to Cineplex's plans, Warner Brothers, American Multi-Cinema, and National Amusements have announced their intentions of opening a total of more than 450 screens in the United Kingdom with further theaters scheduled for later dates.

EXHIBIT 9   Cineplex Odeon's Revenue Sources, 1985–1988

Revenue Source	1988	1987	1986	1985
Admissions	51.1%	62.5%	64.5%	68.0%
Concessions	16.5	18.2	20.0	20.0
Distribution and other	22.5	11.1	8.6	7.0
Property sales	9.9	8.0	6.8	5.0

Source: Form 10-K, Cineplex Odeon Corporation, various years; and *Annual Report*, Cineplex Odeon Corporation, 1988.

EXHIBIT 10   Selected Summary Financial Data ($millions, except percentages)

	1989[a]	1988	1987	1986	1985	1984
Revenue	$710.0	$695.8	$520.2	$357.0	$124.3	$67.1
Net profit	43.0	40.4	34.6	22.5	9.1	3.5
Net profit percentage	6.1%	5.8%	6.6%	6.3%	7.3%	5.3%
Long-term debt	$720.0	$600.0	$464.3	$333.5	$ 40.7	$36.1
Interest	52.6[b]	40.2[b]	33.8	16.4	3.9	2.1
ROE	10.2%[b]	10.3%	11.0%	18.1%	40.7%	30.5%

[a]Estimated by Value Line.
[b]Estimated by the case writer.
Source: Value Line Report 1756, December 9, 1988; and *Standard NYSE Stock Reports* 55, no. 176, sec. 6 (September 12, 1988), p. 536F.

EXHIBIT 11   1988 Per-Capita Attendance Rates

United States	4.4
Great Britain	1.4
Canada	2.8
France	1.9
West Germany	1.9
Italy	1.6

Source: "Movies 'Held Firm' Last Year," *Tulsa Tribune*, February 16, 1989, p. 9C.

While few deny the attractiveness of the theaters owned and operated by Cineplex, the firm may have overextended itself both financially and operationally. Is Cineplex Odeon on the crest of a new wave of creative growth in North America and Europe, or does it stand at the edge of an abyss? [See Exhibits 12 through 15.] Is consolidation or a thorough review of past actions in order? What next moves should Garth Drabinsky and Cineplex make to continue their firm's phenomenal success story?

EXHIBIT 12   Cineplex Odeon Corporation Unaudited First Quarter Consolidated Statement of Income (U.S. $000)

	1989	1988
Revenue		
Admissions	$ 85,819	$ 80,389
Concessions	26,657	24,082
Distribution, post production, and other	70,033	28,782
Sale of theater properties	5,731	1,600
Total revenue	188,240	134,853
Expenses		
Theater operations and other expenses	133,158	97,733
Cost of concessions	5,085	4,466
Cost of theater properties sold	5,837	550
General and administrative expenses	8,035	6,310
Depreciation and amortization	11,207	7,923
Total expenses	163,322	116,982
Income before the undernoted	24,918	17,871
Interest on long-term debt and bank indebtedness	12,257	9,138
Income before taxes	12,661	8,733
Minority interest	978	—
Income taxes	968	727
Net income	$ 10,715	$ 8,006

Source: *First Quarter Report*, Cineplex Odeon Corporation, 1989, pp. 12–13.

EXHIBIT 13   Cineplex Odeon Corporation Consolidated Statement of Income (U.S. $000)

	1988	1987	1986	1985
Revenue				
Admissions	$355,645	$322,385	$230,300	$ 84,977
Concessions	114,601	101,568	71,443	24,949
Distribution, post production, and other	156,372	61,216	30,846	7,825
Sale of theater properties	69,197	34,984	24,400	6,549
Total Revenue	695,815	520,153	356,989	124,300

EXHIBIT 13 Cont'd. Cineplex Odeon Corporation Consolidated Statement of Income (U.S. $000)

	1988	1987	1986	1985
Expenses				
Theater operations and other expenses	$464,324	$371,909	$258,313	$ 89,467
Cost of concessions	21,537	18,799	13,742	5,980
Cost of theater properties sold	61,793	21,618	11,690	2,736
General and administrative expenses	26,617	17,965	15,335	5,701
Depreciation and amortization	38,087	23,998	14,266	3,678
	612,358	454,289	313,346	107,562
Income before the undernoted	85,457	65,864	43,643	16,738
Other income	3,599	—	—	(330)
Interest on long-term debt and bank indebtedness	42,932	27,026	16,195	3,961
Income before taxes, equity earnings, pre-acquisition losses, and extraordinary item	44,124	38,838	27,448	13,107
Income taxes	3,728	4,280	6,310	5,032
Income before equity earnings, preacquisition losses, and extraordinary item	40,396	34,558	21,138	8,075
Add back: Preacquisition losses, attributable to 50 percent interest Plitt not owned by the corporation	—	—	1,381	—
Equity in earnings of 50-percent owned companies	—	—	—	1,021
Income before extraordinary item	40,396	34,558	22,519	10,374
Extraordinary item	—	—	—	9,096
Net income	$ 40,396	$ 34,558	$ 22,519	$ 10,374

Source: *Annual Reports*, Cineplex Odeon Corporation, 1987 and 1988.

EXHIBIT 14 Cineplex Odeon Corporation Unaudited First Quarter Consolidated Balance Sheet (U.S. $000)

	1989	1988
Assets		
Current assets		
Accounts receivable	$ 229,961	$ 151,510
Advances to distributors and producers	18,334	26,224
Distribution costs	9,695	10,720
Inventories	7,781	7,450
Prepaid expenses and deposits	6,756	5,505
Properties held for disposition	23,833	25,557
Total current assets	296,360	226,966
Property, equipment, and leaseholds	844,107	824,836
Other assets		
Long-term investments and receivables	35,169	130,303
Goodwill (less amortization of $3,545; 1988–$2,758)	53,589	53,966
Deferred charges (less amortization of $8,456; 1988–$7,724)	30,222	27,100
	118,980	211,369
Total assets	$1,259,447	$1,263,171

EXHIBIT 14 Cont'd. Cineplex Odeon Corporation Unaudited First Quarter Consolidated Balance Sheet (U.S. $000)

	1989	1988
Liabilities and Shareholders' Equity		
Current liabilities		
Bank indebtedness	$ 37,185	$ 21,715
Accounts payable and accruals	98,876	107,532
Deferred income	38,167	21,967
Income taxes payable	3,726	5,651
Current portion of long-term debt and other obligations	12,174	10,764
Total current liabilities	190,128	167,629
Long-term debt	625,640	663,844
Capitalized lease obligations	14,213	14,849
Deferred income taxes	10,920	10,436
Pension obligations	6,847	6,326
Shareholders' equity		
Capital stock	284,533	283,739
Translation adjustment	12,473	13,348
Retained earnings	88,571	77,856
Total shareholders' equity	385,577	374,943
Total liabilities and shareholders' equity	$1,259,447	$1,263,171

Source: *First Quarter Report*, Cineplex Odeon Corporation, 1989, pp. 14–15.

EXHIBIT 15 Cineplex Odeon Corporation Consolidated Balance Sheet (U.S. $000)

	1988	1987	1986
Assets			
Current assets			
Accounts receivable	$151,510	$ 42,342	$ 20,130
Advances to distributors and producers	26,224	10,704	4,671
Distribution costs	10,720	10,593	4,318
Inventories	7,450	8,562	6,978
Prepaid expenses and deposits	5,505	4,683	4,027
Properties held for disposition	25,557	22,704	16,620
Total current assets	226,966	99,588	56,744
Property, equipment, and leaseholds	824,836	711,523	513,411
Other assets			
Long-term investments and receivables	130,303	49,954	14,292
Goodwill (less amortization of $2,758; 1987–$1,878)	53,966	52,596	40,838

EXHIBIT 15   Cineplex Odeon Corporation Consolidated Balance Sheet (U.S. $000)

	1988	1987	1986
Deferred charges (less amortization of $7,724; 1987–$1,771)	27,100	12,015	6,591
	211,369	114,565	61,721
Total assets	$1,263,171	$925,676	$631,876
Liabilities and Shareholders' Equity			
Current liabilities			
Bank indebtedness	$ 21,715	$ 20,672	$ 30
Accounts payable and accruals	107,532	74,929	47,752
Deferred income	21,967	755	—
Income taxes payable	5,651	4,607	1,926
Current portion of long-term debt and other obligations	10,764	5,965	6,337
Total current liabilities	167,629	106,173	55,945
Long-term debt	663,844	449,707	317,550
Capitalized lease obligations	14,849	14,565	15,928
Deferred income taxes	10,436	13,318	11,142
Pension obligations	6,326	4,026	3,668
Minority interest	25,144	—	—
Shareholders' equity			
Capital stock	283,739	289,181	212,121
Translation adjustment	13,348	1,915	(3,591)
Retained earnings	77,856	46,791	19,113
Total shareholders' equity	374,943	337,887	227,643
Total liabilities and shareholders' equity	$1,263,171	$925,676	$631,876

Source: *Annual Reports*, Cineplex Odeon Corporation, 1987 and 1988.

REFERENCES

Finler, Joel W. *The Hollywood Story*. New York: Crown, 1988.

Gertner, Richard, ed. *1988 International Motion Picture Almanac*. New York: Quigley, 1988.

Green, Wayne R., ed. *Encyclopedia of Exhibition*. New York: National Association of Theatre Owners, 1988.

Hall, Ben M. *The Best Remaining Seats: The Story of the Golden Age of the Movie Palace*. New York: Bramhall House, 1961.

Harrigan, Kathryn Rudie. *Managing Mature Businesses*. Lexington, Mass.: Lexington, 1988.

Harrigan, Kathryn Rudie. "Strategies for Declining Industries," *The Journal of Business Strategy* 1, no. 2 (Fall 1980), pp. 20–34.

Musun, Chris. *The Marketing of Motion Pictures*. Los Angeles: Chris Musun Company, 1969.

1989 U.S. Industrial Outlook. Washington, D.C.: U.S. Department of Commerce/International Trade Administration, 1989.

Tromberg, Sheldon. *Making Money, Making Movies*. New York: New Viewpoints/Vision Books, 1980.

Troy, L. *Almanac of Business and Industrial Financial Ratios*. Englewood Cliffs, N.J.: Prentice-Hall, 1988.

U.S. Bureau of the Census. *Statistical Abstract of the United States, 1989*, 109th ed. Washington, D.C.: U.S. Government Printing Office, 1989.

U.S. Bureau of the Census. *Statistical Abstract of the United States, 1985*. Washington, D.C.: U.S. Government Printing Office, 1985.

Waldman, Peter. "Silver Screens Lose Some of Their Luster." *The Wall Street Journal*, February 9, 1989, p. B1.

Endnotes

1. Michael W. Patrick, "Trends in Exhibition," in *The 1987 Encyclopedia of Exhibition*, edited by Wayne R. Green (New York: National Association of Theatre Owners, 1988), p. 109.

2. Presented in *1988 International Motion Picture Almanac*. (New York: Quigley, 1988), pp. 29A–30A.

3. Quoted in Peter Waldman, "Silver Screens Lose Some of Their Luster," *The Wall Street Journal*, February 9, 1989, p. B1.

4. Harold L. Vogel, "Theatrical Exhibition: Consolidation Continues," in *1987 Encyclopedia*, p. 62.

5. Quoted in Stratford P. Sherman, "Movie Theaters Head Back to the Future," *Fortune*, January 20, 1986, p. 91.

6. Quoted in David Aston, "A New Hollywood Legend Called—Garth Drabinsky?" *Business Week*, September 23, 1985, p. 61.

7. Quoted in Richard Corliss, "Master of the Movies' Taj Mahals," *Time*, January 25, 1988, pp. 60–61.

8. Ibid., p. 60.

9. Aston, "New Legend," p. 62.

10. Quoted in Alex Ben Block, "Garth Drabinsky's Pleasure Domes," *Forbes*, June 2, 1986, p. 93.

11. Mary A. Fischer, "They're Putting Glitz Back into Movie Houses," *U.S. News & World Report*, January 25, 1988, p. 58.

12. Block, "Pleasure Domes," p. 92.

13. Aston, "New Legend," p. 63.

NCNB

FRANK C. BARNES

While most states restricted banks to one county, North Carolina had allowed statewide banking since 1804. This had important implications of size and operating style for the banks. In 1960 Commercial National Bank was a medium-sized state bank with assets of $480 million in a southern state, hardly known to the major money-center banks of New York or Chicago. CNB had its hands full competing with its two state rivals, rock-solid Wachovia Bank & Trust and third-place First Union National Bank. In 1960 Hugh McColl was a C-student college kid from Bennettsville, South Carolina who was just free from his hitch in the military. He was ready with his new bride to move into the big city, Charlotte, North Carolina, to see if he could hold onto a job with CNB.

By 1990 CNB was NCNB and the seventh-largest bank in the nation with $64 billion in assets. Wachovia was in third place in the state with $24 billion, behind First Union, with $39 billion. NCNB had a worldwide reputation for initiative, ambition, and aggressiveness stemming from such achievements as beating every other bank in the nation into the lucrative Florida market by two years and outwitting the largest U.S. bank, Citicorp of New York, in acquiring failing RepublicBank of Texas in what some called the deal of the century. The rapid growth of all three North Carolina banks increased the chances they would be among the survivors from the revolution of banking in the deregulated environment.

By 1990 Hugh McColl was at the top of NCNB and the most famous of a new breed of bankers. His 1989 compensation was $1.5 million and his stock was worth $8 million. His reputation for aggressiveness and frankness of speech made him a prime target for newspaper controversy and was reported to make him feared by the managers in acquisition targets. The military jargon he used to describe strategic moves was emphasized by the press and upset the traditional country-club banker. Numerous writers played up the idea of merger targets taking the attitude of "anyone but NCNB." They reported that in 1985 First Atlanta took a $30-per-share offer from Wachovia instead of $33 from NCNB in rejection of McColl. But people in NCNB disagreed and were solidly behind McColl.

NCNB reportedly had a corporate culture which emphasized competitiveness and aggressiveness. They were among the most active in recruiting talent on

---

This case was prepared by Frank C. Barnes, Professor of Operations Management at The University of North Carolina at Charlotte. It was presented at the North American Case Research Association. All rights are reserved to the author.

college campuses and were innovators in employee policies such as employee child care, and valued entrepreneurial behavior. Acquisitions were firmly integrated into the NCNB culture.

By 1990 the first great wave of regional bank mergers across state lines was subsiding. The survivors, like NCNB, were working to strengthen their financial position and integrate all the new banks and people into their organizations. It wasn't exactly clear who had actually won, though states like Florida and South Carolina, whose banks had been acquired by others, might have lost. In a few years a larger wave of mergers was expected as the United States would go to full interstate banking and the super-regional NCNBs and First Unions would have to go head-to-head with the money-center CitiCorps. Interstate mergers might eliminate 80 percent of existing banks and many wondered who would survive.

A January 1989 article in *Business—North Carolina* suggested NCNB had the answer:

> You make things happen. You don't sit and wait. You lead by example. You go out, you compete, and you do your damnedest to win. This is more than Hugh McColl's approach to banking; it is his approach to life. This is why NCNB is one of the most aggressive, feared competitors in banking today. This is why NCNB succeeds when others don't even try.

Some analysts predicted the entire 1990s would be bearish for banking. Stock prices were off in September 1990, NCNB down 43 percent, First Union down 23 percent, and Wachovia down 14 percent. The savings and loan crisis, the slowing economy with its continuing budget deficit, the increased competition from banks and nonbank financial companies, all created a challenging situation. McColl was concerned about the path NCNB must take to succeed.

BACKGROUND

The predecessor to NCNB, Commercial National Bank, was formed in 1874 in Charlotte, North Carolina. In 1901 American Trust Company opened in Charlotte. In 1957 American Trust, which had become the largest unit bank in the Carolinas and primarily a wholesale (commercial) bank, merged with Commercial National, which had become primarily a retail bank. American Commercial added First National of Raleigh in 1959.

In 1933 Security National Bank had been formed in Greensboro, later adding offices in six cities from Burlington to Wilmington. Security merged with a Durham bank in 1959. Then on July 1, 1960 American Commercial merged with Security to form North Carolina National Bank, NCNB. This created the second-largest bank in the state with assets of $480 million and 1,300 employees in 40 offices in 20 North Carolina cities.

During the 1960s, NCNB, headquartered in Charlotte, acquired or opened 51 more offices and doubled deposits as it completed a statewide expansion strategy. The holding company, NCNB Corp., was formed in 1969. In the 1970s they added 82 more offices, increased assets to $6 billion, and achieved a 20 percent market share. First Union National Bank (FUNB) and Wachovia Bank had similar market shares.

It was generally agreed that this merger activity by NCNB, and also FUNB, was in response to the competitive dominance of Wachovia. In the 1930s under the presidency of Robert Hanes of the hosiery family, Wachovia became the largest bank in the state with a reputation for quality. They were slow to jump on fads, instead seeking growth through conservative management, soundness, and profitability. They were considered the corporate bankers in the state. Tom Storrs, chairman of NCNB through the 1970s, said this history explained the competitiveness of the North Carolina banks.

GOVERNMENT REGULATION AND DEREGULATION: 1982

Banking had always been an industry which was closely regulated by government. For many years the government set the interest rates that all banks could pay or charge customers. At the same time they controlled the price and quantity of money. In this way banks and savings and loans were shielded from most competition and pretty much guaranteed a profit. The activities that banks could undertake were narrowly defined, but also were protected from nonbank competitors.

Historically, bank regulations were concerned with the impact of bank failures on the economy. In recent years in addition to the safety issue regulation has been concerned with the size and distribution of banks (structure issues) and consumer protection issues. Congress periodically enacts new legislation. The process was a political one of treating differences in viewpoints between rich and poor states, large and small banks, North versus South, East versus Midwest and West, etc. Since 1970 banking had undergone dramatic change. Information technology was speeding and simplifying financial activities and eroding the separation between commercial banks and investment banks. The entire system was becoming international. The financial system was subject to greater volitility and the risk it involved.

Interest rates had been the subject of much regulation. The 1933 Banking Act prohibited banks paying interest on demand deposits and placed ceilings on rates on other accounts. This part of the law, Regulation Q, did not apply to S&Ls, which gave them a small edge in this area until 1984. In the 1970s inflation caused the market rate for money to increase beyond bank ceiling rates. Other nonbank financial institutions, such as brokerage houses, who were not subject to Federal regulations, raised rates and took deposits from banks. Congressional acts of 1980 and 1982 responded to this situation by phasing out interest rate ceilings, lessening the regulatory difference between banks and nonbanks, and reducing regulatory burdens.

The activities permitted to banks had also changed. In 1960 only banks provided checking accounts and provided installment and business loans. Banks and S&Ls provided savings accounts. Banks and retailers had credit cards. Insurance companies provided insurance, and stockbrokers bought and sold stocks. In September 1990 J. P. Morgan became the first bank since the Depression to receive government permission to underwrite corporate stock. Today all of these activities could be provided by some nonbank institutions. Banks, or bank holding companies, were providing all these services except insurance, which was expected in the near future.

The bank holding companies increased significantly after the Bank Holding Company Act of 1956. This act, designed to restrict holding companies, actually encouraged their growth. One-bank holding companies, as opposed to multibank ones, were excluded from the act, which gave them the right to engage in most nonbanking activities. This loophole was closed by a 1975 act.

Holding companies had three potential advantages: avoiding restrictive state laws on interstate banking, diversifying into nonbank activities, and lowering tax burdens. An acquisition by a holding company could leave the acquired bank with a president instead of a branch manager. It was possible for a holding company to delete some of the usual bank activities from a bank and create a bank which was not subject to the bank holding company acts. This nonbank bank could engage in a much wider range of activities, such as insurance activities, providing data processing services, underwriting, consulting, gold and silver futures trading, and securities brokerage. After the rapid growth in bank holding companies, a 1987 act put a moratorium on the creation of new holding companies and slowed their growth.

In 1982 Congress enacted major deregulation which left banks substantially free to pay what they wanted on interest-bearing accounts and charge what they wished for their services. A profit was no longer guaranteed, instead it had to be achieved, as in any business, by good management. In this environment, fees charged for services were expected to be a major source of income. There would be movement toward charging for traditionally free services, such as check writing, in addition to the creation of new services, such as credit and financial services. In succeeding years laws would also less sharply separate between the banks and nonbank financial institutions. Banks would move into discount brokerage while stockbrokers would move into checking accounts. All of these changes were expected to have a major impact on the financial landscape of the United States.

HUGH McCOLL AND NCNB

Hugh McColl was closely associated with the development and style of NCNB. His tenure covered the last 30 years of strategic development. McColl came from a competitive family. He told the story of proudly coming home from school one day to tell his grandmother of coming in second in something. She responded, "You'll do better next time." He was expected to win. His father, Hugh McColl, Sr., told *Business—North Carolina,* "I think he got his fighting spirit from his mother; I give her credit for a lot of Hugh's ability and success." Hugh McColl spoke of her as a talented and "very, very competitive," woman born in the wrong era. All of the men in the family had been small-town bankers—his grandfather, father, and his two brothers. He is the oldest.

In high school in Bennettsville, South Carolina he was active in everything from the Latin Club and Radio Club to almost every sport, though only 5 feet, 7 inches, and was voted Best All-Round. In the graduation yearbook, he is nicknamed "Happy" and recognized with "He who's talented in leadership/ Holds the world's dreams in his grip."

In 1953 he went off to UNC–Chapel Hill, like most of the family had, without much thought. He was cut from the basketball and baseball teams and lost his bid for freshman class president. He worked hard at intramural sports since he was "more interested in athletics than anything else." He wasn't very interested in his business major or in the required ROTC, using "minimum maintenance" to make mostly Cs. "It just didn't matter;" he figured after graduation he would go home and run the family business.

He went into the military because it was practically required, but chose the Marines for his two years. He thoroughly enjoyed the "maturing" experience and had his eyes opened by living with people from all over the country. It was an important lesson for the young southerner from a well-off family. "It was a great graduate school, a great management training program, to be an officer and to be responsible for other people." Leadership, he learned, required that he be out with his people all the time.

When he returned home in 1959 from the Marines to join the family business, his father surprised him by telling him to look elsewhere. McColl says, "He did me the greatest favor in the world, sending me off." His father sent him to the bank with which he did his business, American Commercial Bank in Charlotte. He was interviewed by President Addison Reese, but not hired. Hugh, Sr. called another contact in the bank and Hugh had the job. He didn't report until September because, first, he and a friend were headed to Europe for the summer. As the trip started, he met a girl from South Carolina he would end up marrying that fall. In Belgium he bought her a whole cart of flowers.

His first job was scouring South Carolina for corporate accounts. He left Charlotte in his VW by 6 a.m. and returned at night to the office to look for new leads. Long hours away from home was the pattern for many years. "It cost me a lot of my family time, my wife had to be both father and mother." But success wasn't guaranteed. In 1983 he remembered for the *Charlotte Observer*, "What drove me was feeling inadequate. I remember telling Jane not to get too comfortable in Charlotte, that I might not make it here."

When Addison Reese became chairman of CNB in 1957, it was still a small wholesale and commercial bank. His aim was to make the bank large enough to compete with Wachovia. Reese hired Tom Storrs in 1960 as an executive vice president to lead the expansion across North Carolina with acquisitions and mergers. Storrs' 25-year career had been split between the Federal Reserve Board in Richmond and wartime Navy duty as an executive officer on a destroyer. He was a professional economist with a masters and doctorate in economics from Harvard. In 1960 Storrs was working with a merger partner in Greensboro and having trouble with bickering between Greensboro and Charlotte. He called McColl with a task and got immediate cooperation: "He stood out, he responded." Storrs became his mentor as McColl took on more responsibilities.

In 1968 NCNB was the third bank in the country to form a one-bank holding company. They were the first to use commercial paper to finance the activities of its nonbank subsidiaries and the first to go to the long-term debenture market to raise money for the holding company, setting a pattern which others followed. In 1969 Storrs became president.

In 1973 Storrs succeeded Reese as chairman and named McColl and two other rising stars, Luther Hodges, Jr. and Bill Dougherty, to run the bank. Each expected to succeed Storrs. Hodges, son of a former governor, was seen as an outside P.R. man, while Dougherty, a CPA, was more of a back-office expert. During the 1974 to 1975 recession, a company with a $28-million loan got into trouble and McColl helped them reorganize without bankruptcy. McColl said, "Losing that $28 million would have taken us out, we only made $16 million the year before." This was one example of McColl's performance which Storrs said the Executive Committee viewed as the "best track record of the three."

1979 was a pivotal year. NCNB's 1979 Annual Report proposed, "An Orderly Approach to Interstate Banking" in recognition of the fact that continued rapid growth could only be achieved by crossing state lines, though interstate branching was still not permitted. NCNB began to build equity for out-of-state expansion and looked for opportunities. In December 1980 as Chairman Storrs had completed a stock sale in anticipation of eventual opportunities to go into interstate banking, he stated:

> Two things are going to be very important to financial institutions in the 1980s as regulations change and opportunities for expansion arise: the quality of their people and the adequacy of their capital. NCNB has done a good job of attracting and developing competent people. And we are committed to continuing that effort. With the stock sale . . . we have strengthened the capital base that will also be required for future asset expansion.

McColl was president of NCNB bank, the retail operation, and active in carrying out Storrs' statewide acquisitions. In 1981 McColl was named vice chairman, which indicated he would be the one to succeed Storrs. In 1981 Hodges left the chairmanship of the bank to run, unsuccessfully, for governor. Dougherty left his presidency of the holding company in 1982. On September 1, 1973 McColl became chairman and CEO of the corporation.

Bill Weiant, who followed NCNB for First Boston, noted that McColl had spent his entire career with the bank in the headquarters city and predicted he would be a hands-on chief executive: "He is the kind of guy who gets involved in every detail." McColl believed in being in touch with all parts of the organization. He noted that too many executives forgot that information is filtered as it comes up through the organization. He said, "I try to remove some of the filters. I'm an in-the-field manager. There's never a day I'm not out in someone's area. I go and look; it keeps people honest. If I've seen it myself no one's going to say it isn't so."

People in the bank describe him as demanding and impatient to get on with decisions. He wanted consensus and was impatient with people who didn't contribute. "He's quick to have an opinion, and he's very perturbed if others involved don't participate," one executive told *Business—North Carolina*. Another added, "He always says what he has to say. He's open, honest, and forthright. You always know where he stands. It's gotten him into trouble outside the bank, but that's how it is." For example, in discussing expansion with reporters, he said he didn't need to be in "every pig path," in Georgia. When this was reported, a big flap developed.

People inside and outside the bank credited him with creating the entrepreneurial, can-do culture. His style had no critics inside the bank. He was described as being very accessible and valuing his associations with employees at all levels. He jogged and entered fun-runs with others from the bank, played racquetball with young employees at lunch, and visited sick employees in the hospital. He was energetic and inquisitive. Employees commented it was hard to mention a book he hadn't read. If a trip to a foreign country was ahead, he would be studying the maps and reading several books about it. The bank had been a leader in providing for its employees. For example, in 1990 *Good Housekeeping* magazine praised NCNB as among the best companies for working mothers. Their policies addressing family needs included parental leave, day care at or near work, flextime, and counseling support.

McColl had his style. He told *Business—North Carolina* about being at the beach recently (summer 1988) and going by a newly opened office. He didn't see a sign on the building and the manager said it was being made. It irritated McColl so much that he went to a hardware store and got some letters, board and paint. Then he returned, where he made and installed a sign.

> It's a graphic lesson. You don't wait until things happen. It's part of what leading by example is all about. It would never occur to me to have an office without a sign. I want my managers to feel they can do what it takes to get the job done and not be impeded by bureaucracy and I'll back them up. You are responsible. Be responsible.

EXPANSION INTO FLORIDA: 1981–1984

Interstate banking would not be allowed until 1985, but NCNB was able to expand into Florida in 1981. In 1972 Florida had enacted statutes to prevent acquisition of their banks by out-of-state banks. Just prior to this, NCNB had bought small Orlando Trust Company. In July 1981 NCNB took the position it was a Florida bank because of the Orlando company and offered to buy First National Bank of Lake City. Banks in Florida and across the country opposed NCNB getting this early start at interstate branching. But by December the Federal Reserve Board had ruled in their favor and NCNB became the first bank to expand into the lucrative Florida market.

NCNB moved quickly in 1982 to buy three banks with 67 branches and over $2 billion in assets. In 1984 they added Ellis Banking Corporation with 75 offices and $1.8 billion in assets and in 1985 purchased a $2-billion Miami bank with 51 offices. By 1987 NCNB National Bank of Florida was the fourth-largest in the state with $9.9 billion and over 200 offices.

In June 1982 McColl had stated "our purpose is to build a banking company of a size that can compete more effectively with the money-center banks in providing a range of services to customers here in the Southeast, across the nation and in the world markets." Chairman Storrs warned of the dangers of overemphasizing short-run earnings and ignoring long-term needs: "You would leave your successor with the problem of doing the building that you should have been doing. . . . What we are doing is what Addison Reese did 20 years ago—always building on the foundation for the next decade." McColl forecasted, "By 1984 we will have this ship running hot and heavy. Between now and then we will not divert ourselves with casual mergers. We will pay back our debt, and get in good shape to start over when they drop the barriers on interstate banking." Dick Stillinger, a New York banking specialist, told the *Charlotte Observer*, "I think they will have a tough row to hoe for the next couple of years. I am skeptical if NCNB can make it pay off fast enough to offset the dilution of earnings."

But some people saw a problem with McColl. A former NCNB executive reported to *Business—North Carolina*, "a deal in which a Florida banker was ready to sell, only to pull out after listening to McColl over dinner dictate what changes NCNB would make after the acquisition." In acquisitions the NCNB name would go on the bank, many services would be centralized, and the policies would be those set by Charlotte. After NCNB's Florida expansion, it was reported that 41 of 45 top executives left Gulfstream Bank after the 1982 acquisition and that over 150 of Exchange Bancorporation's 300 managers left after their 1983 takeover. Gulfstream's ex-CEO was quoted as saying NCNB's corporate culture was "a snotty-nosed kid aching for a fight." Exchange's ex-CEO complained of their military style. "Many of our people didn't stay because they didn't like the NCNB culture. There was one way to do things—the NCNB way."

In 1983 as he became CEO, McColl told the *Charlotte Observer* he was working at toning down his image, softening his statements, trying to adopt a posture more appropriate for a CEO. "I have been working on that," McColl said, "But part of our images get to be caricatures. I think people think I'm aggressive. I don't think of myself that way." Yet he was energetic and competitive and admitted to being "downright hostile in competition." "I would probably hurt fewer people's feelings. I might modify my behavior by being less aggressive. But if I tried to be somebody else, I wouldn't do very well at that."

As 1984 began, NCNB showed plans to target services for middle-market firms, $5 million to $250 million, under the direction of 37-year-old Ken Lewis. They already did business with 70 percent of North Carolina companies with $50 million and had the largest market share of business with southeastern firms that size. Lewis said, "The banks that survive are the ones that pick those market segments they can best compete in."

In summer 1984 NCNB stated that they planned to concentrate on increasing shareholder wealth and planned no major acquisitions through 1985. Year-end earnings were projected at $3.85 per share, representing about a 4 percent dilution due to acquisitions. Loan offices had been opened in Washington and Memphis. NCNB told the *American Banker*: "We would think we have to have a presence in Atlanta, but don't think it's necessary to have a big branch system in Georgia."

GOVERNMENT REGULATION AND INTERSTATE BANKING

Interstate banking had long been banned by the federal government. However many experts saw the need for nationwide banks like those common outside the United States and some bankers wanted the growth opportunity. By 1980 it was clear interstate banking was coming. In early 1981 the Southern Growth Policies Board, an important regional study group, recommended that southeastern states let other southeastern banks cross their borders. It was expected that Congress would approve full interstate banking by the end of the decade. This regional expansion was expected to strengthen the regional banks before full competition came. In 1982 Massachusetts and Connecticut approved regional interstate banking. When the Supreme Court upheld the legality of regional compacts in 1985, Justice Rehnquist wrote, "One predictable effect of the regionally restrictive statutes will apparently be to allow the growth of regional multistate bank holding companies which can compete with the established banking giants of New York, California, Illinois, and Texas." In a 1984 meeting Hugh McColl stated, "Our industry is simply not ready for all-out national interstate banking."

Other advantages were put forth for mergers. In 1985 Chairman Storrs cited the "obvious" advantages of creating bigger banks. But the *Charlotte Observer* reported that a senior economist for the Federal Reserve Board had yet to discover any advantages. He pointed out studies had indicated supposed economies of scale were achieved at the $100- to $200-million size and not beyond. Surprisingly the data showed smaller banks tended to be the more profitable; there was an inverse correlation between size and profitability. Some felt the mergers would concentrate political power and stifle competition. A community banker asked, "Why would bigger be better? Banking is a people business." But others spoke of the access to larger amounts of capital for big projects, participation in the total economy and the ability to have a role in the direction of change in the banking industry.

REGIONAL BANKING BEGINS

In February 1984, Georgia was about to become the first southeastern state to approve a regional, reciprocal, interstate banking law. Under these laws, southeastern banks could expand into another southeastern state if the reciprocal was allowed. The entry of other states' banks, primarily major money-center banks like the nation's largest, $150-billion Citicorp of New York, was carefully excluded. Some large northern banks were expected to oppose the move in federal courts if provision were not made for eventual full interstate banking. Two of Atlanta's major banks, Citizens and Southern and First Atlanta, expressed support for the legislation and took steps to prepare for it. *The Wall Street Journal* reported that NCNB was opposing the legislation. They feared that since North Carolina wasn't expected to consider a reciprocal law until 1985, NCNB would not have a chance at the best merger opportunities in Georgia. NCNB was considering using its Florida operation, where there would soon be a reciprocal agreement, to get around this problem. This idea met resistance from Georgians. One executive told *The WSJ*, "the way for NCNB to come into Georgia is through its home state of North Carolina. If NCNB managed to get into Georgia through Florida, you can be sure they'll fight claw and nail to defeat regional banking in North Carolina."

In June 1985 the U.S. Supreme Court ruled that state legislatures could set up reciprocal regional agreements allowing banks from states in their region to merge across their borders, but excluding out-of-region banks. In July six southeastern states enacted such laws and there was immediate action by the region's largest banks: NCNB, SunTrust, Wachovia, First Union, and Citizens and Southern. (See

EXHIBIT 1 The South's Top 10—"New" Banks and Old, 1985

Rank	Bank	Assets[a]	Mergers	Assets[a]	Total
1	NCNB Corp., Charlotte, N.C.	$16,900	Bankers Trust (S.C.)	$2,081	
			Pan American (Fla.)	1,658	
			Southern National Bankshares (Ga.)	93	$20,732
2	SunTrust Banks Inc., Atlanta, Ga.	16,293	SunBanks Inc. (Fla.)		
			Trust Co. of Ga.		16,293
3	First Wachovia Corp., Winston-Salem, N.C., Atlanta, Ga.		Wachovia Corp. (N.C.)	8,932	
			First Atlanta Corp. (Ga.)	7,106	16,038
4	First Union Corp., Charlotte, N.C.	8,250	Northwestern Financial Corp. (N.C.)	2,983	
			Atlantic Bancorp (Fla.)	3,777	15,010
5	Barnett Banks of Florida Inc., Jacksonville, Fla.	13,190			13,190
6	Citizens & Southern Georgia Corp., Atlanta, Ga.	8,480	Landmark Banking Corp. (Fla.)	3,944	12,324
7	Southeast Banking Corp., Miami, Fla.	10,204			10,204
8	Sovran Financial Corp., Norfolk, Va.	8,700	D.C. National Bancorp (D.C.)	400	
			Virginia Southern Bank (Va.)	50	9,100
9	United Virginia Bankshares, Richmond, Va.	6,600	NS&T Bank of Washington, D.C.	900	7,500
10	Florida National Banks, Jacksonville, Fla.	5,367			5,367

[a]Figures in millions as of 6/30/85.
Source: Jenks Southeastern Business Letter and other sources.

Market Capitalization

Rank	Bank	Market Capitalization
1	SunTrust	$1.74
2	First Wachovia	1.71
3	First Union	1.60
4	NCNB	1.40
5	Barnett Banks	1.20
6	Citizens and Southern	1.10
7	Sovran	0.74
8	Southeast	0.52
9	United Virginia	0.51
10	Florida National	0.46

[a]$ billions.

EXHIBIT 1 Cont'd.   The South's Top 10—"New" Banks and Old, 1985

Market Capitalization Leaders

Bank	Assets[a] ($billions)	Market Capitalization[b] ($billions)	Stock Price/ Book Value
Citicorp	$159.9	$5.7	89%
J. P. Morgan	64.3	4.4	115
First Interstate	46.8	2.3	95
BankAmerica	120.6	2.2	55
Chase Manhattan	86.4	2.2	59
Bankers Trust	48.0	2.1	100
Chemical	57.3	2.0	80
Security Pacific	47.9	1.9	93
First Wachovia	16.0	1.8	170
SunTrust	16.1	1.7	185
First Union	18.8	1.6	164
Manufacturers	75.9	1.5	55
NCNB	19.1	1.5	144
FNC Financial	16.7	1.5	132
Mellon	30.5	1.3	82
Banc One	9.6	1.3	174
Barnett	12.8	1.3	168
Sovran	11.9	1.2	129
First Bank System	24.4	1.2	100
Wells Fargo	29.2	1.2	93
First Chicago	39.9	1.1	69
C&S Georgia	13.8	1.1	120

Notes: Figures assume all announced mergers were completed.
[a]As of June 30, 1985.
[b]As of Oct. 18, 1985.
Source: Keofe, Bruyette and Woods Inc.

Exhibit 1.) The race for mergers began immediately. By July C&S of Atlanta had acquired a Florida bank and Wachovia had announced a merger with First Atlanta. The CFO of C&S of South Carolina told *The WSJ*, after agreeing to be acquired by C&S of Atlanta, "Being part of a large institution gives us the marketing and capital resources to continue being a broad based bank." NCNB and FUNB appeared not to have succeeded in moving into Atlanta. NCNB commented, "It would be advantageous to have a bank in Atlanta, but we don't think a major presence is required. We do an awful lot of business there without a loan production office." But rumors were active that NCNB had made a bid for First Atlanta and lost out to Wachovia. While all the banks remained quiet, a New York analyst said, "NCNB was caught off guard a little [by Wachovia]. They are disappointed that they are not going to have as big a presence in Atlanta."

Many reporters alluded to McColl's aggressive, military-jargoned style as a real turnoff. On October 3, *The Wall Street Journal* commented on NCNB as the most aggressive bank in the Southeast:

> But Hugh McColl, Jr., the combative ex-Marine who heads NCNB, often rubs more genteel bankers the wrong way. "He's a little bit more aggressive than the rest of us," says Mr. Poelker [John Poelker, president of Citizens and Southern Georgia Corp.]. The executive has tended to shake up management and insist on the NCNB name on acquired banks. As a result, some banks have taken an anyone-else-but-NCNB stance. First Atlanta rejected a $33.50 a share bid from NCNB in favor of a $30 bid from Wachovia Corp. "Some of NCNB's attitudes came back to haunt it," says a First Atlanta executive.

In response, NCNB's communication chief, Rusty Page, stated the policies on using one name and on centralizing were those of the scholarly, soft-spoken Tom Storrs, not McColl. He believed the approach was sound and that the opportunity to become a part of the South's largest and strongest bank would continue to attract merger partners.

By mid-July *American Banker* reported, "Wachovia and First Atlanta bent over backwards to try to demonstrate that the transaction is a merger of equals in which there is no clear buyer or seller." It had been assumed that First Atlanta would dominate in any merger it pursued. However, the stock prices behaved to indicate Wachovia was the buyer, according to *American Banker*. Earlier FUNB's Crutchfield and McColl had indicated they had no interest in any merger of equals. McColl commented, "I have to say it's like getting married and promising not to sleep with each other."

First Atlanta, with assets of $7 billion, and Wachovia, with assets of $8.7 billion, would be merged into a holding company called First Wachovia. There would be legal addresses in both states and corporate functions would be located wherever they could be performed best. John Medlin, 51, of Wachovia would be president and CEO, while Tom Williams, 56, of First Atlanta would be chairman. Wachovia, with 60 percent of the shares, would name 60 percent of the directors, and First Atlanta would name 40 percent. Board meetings would alternate between the two states.

The *Atlanta Journal* reported on June 23, 1985 that First Atlanta had been eyeing Wachovia for some time. Williams had been educating the directors for months about criteria for merger partners; management compatibility being one of three. "The studies we went through showed us the best combination was unquestionably Wachovia." Earlier in the year the two banks had discussed a combination, but decided to wait for the court's decision. On the day of the decision, Medlin called Williams and two days later they met in Greensboro. The *Charlotte Observer* noted that analysts, such as John Maseir in New York, gave the leadership high marks: "I think Tom Williams is one of the most intelligent, statesmanlike individuals I've come across. Medlin is one of the great heroes of the South. It's a combination of two very intelligent men."

In October 1985 *The Wall Street Journal* noted the South was the most active region in mergers because of fear and opportunity:

The Southeast long has had the smallest banks in the poorest area of the nation. The region's largest bank, NCNB, was only the nation's 25th largest. However, the region now had some of the most attractive retail banking markets in the nation, Atlanta, Nashville, all of Florida. The big, money-center banks, already very active in lending activity in the region, wanted into the retail part of the market. The Executive Director of the Southern Growth Policies Board told the WSJ: "We don't want our capital resources dominated by money-center banks. The South has a long history of being exploited by corporate interests outside the region.

McColl believed the entry of money-center banks and nationwide banking was inevitable, some said as soon as the early 1990s. He felt his state's big three banks had ensured their long-term survival by these mergers. Twenty billion dollars in assets was often mentioned as the minimum size to assure continued competitiveness against the large banks and avoid being takeover targets.

The race to acquire the most attractive merger candidates had stretched resources. McColl said, "There's a limit to what anyone can do in a reasonable time frame." Some dilution of earnings was expected and there were questions of adequate depth of management to run the operations.

In July 1985 NCNB announced plans to acquire Bankers Trust of South Carolina, the state's third-largest with assets of $1.9 billion and 110 branches. NCNB paid 12 to 13 times earnings, which was expected to result in a 2 percent dilution in their earnings. Bankers Trust was a leader in the industry in profitability, unlike the Florida banks. It was the first in the state to install automatic teller machines and the third in the nation to provide personal cash management accounts. The South Carolina papers stressed the friendly nature of the merger. Bankers Trust Chairman "Hootie" Johnson told *The State* of Columbia that he and McColl had been the closest of friends for many years. McColl praised Bankers Trust's leadership in marketing, especially the aggressive marketing of its credit cards. He added, "They are way ahead of a lot of people, including us" in financial services. The bank would operate as an independent subsidiary, NCNB Bankers Trust of South Carolina. He told *The Columbia Record*, "We will be separate banks with the basic same philosophy. All of us will actually be doing business the same way." Johnson, in addition to being chairman of the South Carolina bank, would become chairman of the executive committee of NCNB Corporation, a position held by Tom Storrs. His CFO would move to Charlotte to become an executive vice president of NCNB Corporation. Two of their directors would become directors of NCNB Corporation.

In November 1985 shareholders overwhelmingly (96 percent) approved the merger. The merger would take place after January 1, 1986 when South Carolina's reciprocal banking laws went into effect. NCNB was awaiting approval by regulators of its plan to acquire Southern National Bankshares of Atlanta and Pan American Bank of Miami.

On September 8, 1985 *The Miami Herald*, in an article, "North Carolina Banks Take the Lead," noted that while Florida had none of the region's top four banks, North Carolina had three. "Who's going to be around in 5, 10 years?" asked Hugh McColl. "It's quite clear the North Carolina banks, because they're stronger and better managed, with more capital." *The Herald* noted NCNB tried to be a bank for everyone, while Wachovia was regarded as one of the nation's finest corporate banks. FUNB positioned itself between the two, with a strength in its mortgage operations. FUNB's Ed Crutchfield explained the source of the three banks' strength: "We're at each other's throats on a lot of street corners and that intense competition breeds strength." The rich Florida market bred a group of banks with less drive.

Observers tended to see a race between the three North Carolina banks to see who could be biggest. By 1985 NCNB and FUNB had jumped ahead of Wachovia, the traditional leader. In December FUNB claimed to be the second-biggest behind NCNB. A Wachovia executive referred to "bragging rights," but all disclaimed growth for growth's sake. The pace of expansion in 1985 brought some concern as FUNB faced a 15 percent dilution in earnings, Wachovia 6 percent, and NCNB 4 percent. McColl told analysts, "Instead of concentrating on making money, many banks seem to be concentrating on acquisitions activity. This is certainly not the case at NCNB." He noted the high prices FUNB had paid lately for acquisitions, 2.8 times book compared to NCNB's 1.8. *The Observer* reported Crutchfield's quick response, "If he [McColl] isn't making acquisitions in 1985, I must be reading the wrong papers."

In October 1985 McColl gave up the job of president of NCNB Corporation to 45-year-old Francis "Buddy" Kemp, a Davidson College graduate with a Harvard MBA. McColl planned no major acquisition in the coming 18 months, but spoke of an interest in the northern Virginia market. Ken Lewis moved to Tampa as executive vice president of the Florida banking group. As 1985 ended, NCNB reported earnings up 23 percent to $4.60 per share, in line with expectations. Assets reached $19.8 billion and would be $22 billion with the January 2 Bankers Trust acquisition. McColl was "very pleased . . . with another year of improved profitability and well-planned growth."

THE TEXAS COUP

During planning meetings in December 1987, NCNB, then the 18th-largest U.S. bank with $29 billion in assets, found itself short of opportunities for further acquisitions. Targets above $10 billion were considered too large and those below $1 billion were felt to be too small to have any impact. Their chief strategic planner, Frank Gentry, considered there to be a pool of only 20 southeastern banks, some not in good markets. The idea of considering wider options, such as savings and loans or insolvent banks, was discussed.

First RepublicBank, a Texas bank which was the 13th-largest in the nation with 171 offices, was on the FDIC's list of troubled banks because of the depressed Texas economy and other problems. In March 1988 the FDIC put $1 billion into First Republic as it sought a solution. A number of large banks became interested, including Citicorp, the nation's largest, and Wells Fargo. Gentry and John Mack, NCNB Treasurer, had McColl's support in examining some role for NCNB, though McColl considered the odds slim. As the smallest bank bidding, they knew their plan must be innovative and kept secret to win. The other potential buyers planned to divide First Republic into a good bank and bad bank, and buy only the good one.

This would leave the FDIC the expensive task of liquidating the bad one. NCNB offered to acquire the whole bank, 20 percent at once and the rest over five years. A key feature would be NCNB getting tax credits for First Republic's operating losses. This was considered impossible in the legal opinion of the trade journals and New York lawyers. A private Charlotte tax lawyer thought it was possible.

In April 1988 Gentry, accompanied by McColl, went on an early negotiating trip to the FDIC in Washington. Gentry noted, "the staff guy was shocked when Hugh walked in." A question which would require a decision arose and the staff man said only the FDIC chairman, Siedman, could decide the point. McColl replied, "Well, is he here?" Soon they met face to face discussing their positions. An FDIC official told *Business—North Carolina* in January 1989, "McColl's presence made a difference. I don't think John Reed [Citicorp's chairman] or Wells Fargo's guy ever came by and said, 'We're interested,' at least at that stage of negotiation."

Examination of feasibility went forward in absolute secrecy. Earlier Ross Perot, the Texas billionaire, had been approached by First Republic and briefly considered buying the bank. Lacking banking expertise, he thought of the man he would want for the task, Hugh McColl. He had met and befriended McColl earlier in the year at a dinner in Charlotte. Perot soon dropped the idea, but later played an important role by guaranteeing NCNB's $210 million offer.

In June the IRS ruled in favor of NCNB on the tax credit issue and then only the FDIC's decision remained. One of the three directors of the FDIC who would decide which offer to take was C. C. Hope, retired head of FUNB. He could help or hurt. Ultimately he would vouch for the depth of NCNB's management.

As the time for a decision approached, NCNB prepared to move fast. They wanted to have an NCNB person at all 171 Texas offices on the first day to reassure everyone that they did not plan to make any major changes. After three false starts, on Thursday, July 28 McColl briefed 200 employees in Charlotte for 2 hours and sent them off to Texas to wait. On Friday McColl waited nervously at his command center in the Dallas Sheraton. By noon he began to worry that NCNB had lost. At 12:00 the call came: "Your bank has been selected." By 1:30 all but seven NCNB people were at the branches and all were in place by 3:30. Within a few days, Buddy Kemp, the NCNB executive chosen to head the Texas operation, had sent a yellow rose to each First Republic employee.

William Dougherty, who left NCNB in 1982 when McColl won out in the competition to head NCNB, told *Business—North Carolina* in June 1989, "He has put his job on the line, if he pulls if off, he could be the banker of the century, not just the decade." A year later on May 15, 1989 *U.S. News and World Report* summed it up:

> NCNB's biggest banking coup came last year in acquiring insolvent First RepublicBank of Dallas with the aid of the Federal Deposit Insurance Corporation. Frank Gentry, NCNB's director of corporate planning, calls it the "banking deal of the century." For $210 million, NCNB bought 20 percent of the biggest bank in Texas and received options to buy the rest for another $840 million. For a relative pittance, NCNB has acquired effective control of the bank, all the assets unclouded by bad loans, nearly $2 billion in tax credits and generous incentives to help the FDIC recoup some of the $10

EXHIBIT 2 Top 25 Bank Holding Companies   Based on Total Assets as of March 31, 1990
(assets in $billions and net income in $millions)

Asset Rank 3/31/90	Asset Rank 12/31/89		Total Assets 3/31/90	Total Assets 12/31/89
1	1	Citicorp, New York	$ 233.1	$ 230.6
2	2	Chase Manhattan Corp., New York	106.5	107.4
3	3	BankAmerica Corp., San Francisco	101.1	98.8
4	4	J. P. Morgan & Co., New York	90.8	89.0
5	5	Security Pacific Corp., Los Angeles	86.5	83.9
6	6	Chemical Bank Corp., New York	74.2	71.5
7	7	NCNB Corp., Charlotte, N.C.	63.7	66.2
8	8	Manufacturers Hanover Corp., New York	59.7	60.5
9	10	Bankers Trust New York Corp.	59.3	55.7
10	9	First Interstate Bancorp., Los Angeles	57.4	59.1
11	12	Wells Fargo & Co., San Francisco	50.2	48.7
12	13	First Chicago Corp.	50.0	47.9
13	11	Bank of New York Co., Inc.	47.8	48.9
14	14	PNC Financial Corp., Pittsburgh	46.6	45.7
15	17	First Union Corp., Charlotte, N.C.	39.1	32.1
16	15	Bank of Boston Corp.	37.3	39.2
17	16	Fleet/Norstar Financial Group Inc., Providence, R.I.	36.5	33.4
18	19	SunTrust Banks Inc., Atlanta	30.9	31.0
19	18	Mellon Bank Corp., Pittsburgh	30.8	31.5
20	20	First Fidelity Bancorp., Newark, N.J.	30.2	30.7
21	23	Barnett Banks Inc., Jacksonville, Fla.	29.3	29.0
22	22	Continental Bank Corp., Chicago	29.0	29.5
23	26	Banc One Corp., Columbus, Ohio	27.2	26.6
24	28	Republic New York Corp.	26.2	25.5
25	27	NBD Bancorp., Inc., Detroit	25.7	25.8
		Totals for the top 25	$1,469.1	$1,448.2
Dropping Out of the Top 25				
26	25	Marine Midland Banks Inc., Buffalo, N.Y.	25.7	27.1
29	24	Shawmut National Corp., Hartford, Conn.	24.9	27.9
30	21	Bank of New England Corp., Boston	24.9	29.8
Pro Forma Ranking—Merger in Progress				
12	13	Avantor Financial Corp.[2]	49.5	44.7

Source: Earnings releases from the companies. Net income is income after taxes and minority interest but before preferred dividends and extraordinary items. Income from discontinued operations is excluded. First-quarter net income for 1989 is as reported in 1989. Total assets for Dec. 31, 1989, are as originally reported and have not been restated for mergers, changes in accounting practices,

billion in loans that went sour. NCNB's giant foothold in Texas has given it tremendous advantages at just the right time. The state's economy is beginning to recover from its energy-based depression; branch banking, long prohibited in the state, is now allowed, and NCNB Texas has been able to lend aggressively, becoming the biggest lender in the state at a time when other Texas banks have been financially hobbled. If NCNB buys the rest of

Percentage Change	Net Income First Quarter 1990	Net Income First Quarter 1989	Percentage Change
+1.1%	$ 231.0	$ 529.0	−56.3%
−0.8	44.0	132.0	−66.7
+2.3	218.0	208.0	+4.8
+2.0	399.0	179.6	+122.2
+3.1	188.4	179.3	+5.1
+3.8	151.7	117.9	+28.7
−3.8	140.1	75.8	84.8
−1.3	96.0	103.0	−6.8
+6.5	198.0	164.3	20.5
−2.9	97.1	94.3	+3.0
+3.1	159.8	141.5	+12.9
+4.4	68.6	124.7	−45.0
−2.2	102.3	101.1	+1.2
+2.0	74.5	123.6	−39.7
21.8	77.6	72.2	7.5
−4.8	43.6	89.1	−51.1
+9.3	(98.1)	92.4	−206.2
−0.3	87.9	84.0	+4.6
−2.2	65.0	53.0	+22.6
−1.6	21.1	61.9	−65.9
+1.0	15.5	62.4	−75.2
−1.7	56.7	75.6	−25.0
+2.3	101.8	87.2	+16.7
+2.7	44.5	41.8	+6.5
−0.4	66.6	63.5	+4.9
+1.4	$2,650.7	$3,057.2	−13.3
−5.2	6.0	31.7	−81.1
−10.8	32.1[1]	64.7	−50.4
−16.4	(46.6)	42.3	−210.2
10.7	128.2	119.7	7.1

etc. [1]—Excludes an $8.5 million extraordinary credit arising from the utilization of a net operating loss carryforward. [2]—On 9/26/89, Citizens and Southern Corp., Atlanta, and Sovran Financial Corp., Norfolk, Va., announced a definitive agreement to merge. The deal, expected to be completed at the end of the third quarter, will create Avantor Financial Corp. ( )—Indicates a net loss. Compiled by American Banker, Copyright 1990.

First Republic, it will become the 10th-largest bank holding company in the country. Its Texas earnings will account for 60 percent of its profits by 1992, estimates Bear Stearns banking analyst Mark Alpert. The deal has already fattened NCNB's bottom line in 1989 and has drive its stock price up by 50 percent to nearly $40 a share.

EXHIBIT 3 Principal Officers

NCNB Corporation	NCNB Southeast	NCNB Texas
Hugh L. McColl, Jr. Chairman of the Board and Chief Executive Officer	James W. Thompson Chairman, Southeastern Banking	Francis B. Kemp Chairman
Francis B. Kemp President, NCNB Corporation Chairman, NCNB Texas	William P. Middlemas President, Southeastern Banking	Timothy P. Hartman Vice Chairman and Chief Financial Officer
James W. Thompson Vice Chairman NCNB Corporation Chairman, Southeastern Banking	John G. P. Boatwright President, NCNB Carolinas	Kenneth D. Lewis President
Timothy P. Hartman Vice Chairman, NCNB Corporation Vice Chairman and Chief Financial Officer, NCNB Texas	Edward J. Brown III President, Corporate Bank	James M. Berry Vice Chairman, Houston
	Robert L. Kirby President, NCNB Florida	Ralph M. Carestio Corporate Executive Vice President Specialized Banking
James M. Berry Corporate Executive Vice President NCNB Corporation Vice Chairman, NCNB Texas	G. Patrick Phillips President, NCNB Services, Inc.	John D. Dienes Corporate Executive Vice President Corporate Banking
Fredric J. Figge II Chairman, Credit Policy	Joel A. Smith III President, NCNB South Carolina	James R. Erwin President, Special Asset Bank
James H. Hance Jr. Executive Vice President and Chief Financial Officer NCNB Corporation	F. William Vandiver President, Investment Bank	Raleigh Hortenstine III Corporate Executive Vice President Funds Management
	William L. Maxwell Executive Vice President Funds Management	William G. Kelley Corporate Executive Vice President Credit Policy
Kenneth D. Lewis President, NCNB Texas	James B. Sommers Executive Vice President Trust, Private Banking, Securities	Robert B. Lane Corporate Executive Vice President General Banking
William P. Middlemas President, Southeastern Banking	Craig M. Wardlaw Executive Vice President Corporate Investments	Joseph R. Musolino Vice Chairman, Dallas
Charles J. Cooley Executive Vice President Corporate Personnel		O. Darwin Smith Corporate Executive Vice President Support
James W. Kiser Executive Vice President Corporate Counsel and Secretary		Samuel J. Atkins Executive Vice President Energy
Joseph B. Martin III Executive Vice President Corporate Affairs		David W. Fisher Executive Vice President Trust
		Harry J. Grim Executive Vice President General Counsel
		Calvin C. Hunkele Executive Vice President Control
		Harris A. Rainey, Jr. Executive Vice President Administration

EXHIBIT 3 Cont'd. Boards of Directors

NCNB Corporation

William M. Barnhardt
President, Southern Webbing
Mills Inc. (textiles)

Thomas M. Belk
President, Belk Stores Services Inc.
(retailing)

Wilbur L. Carter, Jr.
Retired President, Southern Life
Insurance Company (insurance)

Charles W. Coker
President, Sonoco Products
Company (manufacturer of paper
and plastic products)

H. L. Culbreath
Chairman, TECO Energy Inc.
(electric utility holding company)

Alan T. Dickson
President, Ruddick Corporation
(diversified holding company)

W. Frank Dowd, Jr.
Chairman of the Executive
Committee, Charlotte Pipe &
Foundry Company (manufacturer
of cast iron and plastic pipe and
fittings)

A. L. Ellis
Senior Chairman, NCNB
National Bank of Florida

Timothy P. Hartman
Vice Chairman
NCNB Corporation
Vice Chairman and Chief
Financial Officer, NCNB Texas

Edward A. Horrigan, Jr.
Former Vice Chairman of the
Board, RJR Nabisco Inc.
(consumer products)

W. W. Johnson
Chairman of the Executive
Committee, NCNB Corporation

Francis B. Kemp
President, NCNB Corporation
Chairman, NCNB Texas

William A. Klopman
Retired Chairman and Chief
Executive Officer, Burlington
Industries Inc. (textiles)

Hugh L. McColl, Jr.
Chairman of the Board and
Chief Executive Officer
NCNB Corporation

Robert E. McNair
Chairman of the Board
McNair Law Firm P.A.

John. C. Slane
President, Slane Hosiery Mills Inc.
(textiles)

Albert F. Sloan
Chairman and Chief Executive
Officer, Lance Inc.
(snack food production)

W. Roger Soles
Chairman and President, Jefferson-
Pilot Corporation (insurance)

Meredith R. Spangler
Trustee and Volunteer

Robert H. Spilman
Chairman and Chief
Executive Officer, Bassett
Furniture Industries Inc.
(furniture manufacturer)

Thomas I. Storrs
Retired Chairman
NCNB Corporation

James W. Thompson
Vice Chairman
NCNB Corporation
Chairman, Southeastern Banking

Wilson C. Wearn
Retired Chairman of the Board
Multimedia Inc. (diversified
communications company)

Michael Weintraub
(private investor)

NCNB National Bank of Florida

Jack M. Berry, Sr.
Chairman, The Berry Companies

Tully F. Dunlap
Corporate Trustee
Representative, Alfred I. du Pont
Testamentary Trust

R. M. Elliott
Chairman and Chief Executive
Officer, Levitz Furniture
Corporation (nationwide chain
of retail furniture stores)

A. L. Ellis
Senior Chairman

Edward L. Flom
Chairman and Chief Executive
Officer, Florida Steel
Corporation (steel manufacturers
and reinforcing steel fabricators)

Timothy L. Guzzle
President and Chief Executive
Officer, TECO Energy Inc.
(electric utility holding company)

James H. Hance, Jr.
Managing Director

Frank W. Harvey
(private investor)

John J. Hudiburg
Former Chairman and Chief
Executive Officer, Florida Power
& Light Company (electric utility)

George W. Jenkins
Founder and Chairman of the
Board, Publix Super Markets Inc.
(chain of supermarkets)

Robert L. Kirby
President

Hugh L. McColl, Jr.
Chairman

William P. Middlemas
Managing Director

Richard L. Schmidt
Certified Public Accountant

1023

EXHIBIT 3 Cont'd.   Boards of Directors

NCNB National Bank of Florida	NCNB National Bank of North Carolina	
John W. Temple President and Chief Executive Officer, VMS/TEMPLE Development Company (real estate development and land acquisition)	Dr. Robert L. Albright President, Johnson C. Smith University	Harold M. Messmer, Jr. Chairman and Chief Executive Officer, Robert Half International Inc. (financial personnel services)
James W. Thompson Managing Director	E. James Becher, Jr. President and Chief Executive Officer, Geneva Corporation (financial holding company)	William P. Middlemas Managing Director
Dr. Israel Tribble, Jr. President, Florida Endowment Fund for Higher Education	John G. P. Boatwright President	Jerome J. Richardson President and Chief Executive Officer, TW Services, Inc. and Spartan Food Systems (food service)
	Dr. G. John Coli Chairman and Chief Executive Officer, Armira Inc. (producer of fashion leather products)	A. Pope Shuford President, Shuford Mills Inc. (textiles and pressure sensitive tapes)
	James H. Hance, Jr. Managing Director	
	John W. Harris President, The Bissell Companies Inc. (real estate development)	Robin W. Sternbergh Vice President and Area General Manager, IBM Corporation (information-handling systems, equipment and services)
	J. R. Hendrick III President, Hendrick Management Corporation (automobile mega-dealer management company)	James W. Thompson Managing Director
	Charles W. Howard, Jr. Retired Tobacco Executive	John T. Warmath, Jr. Executive Vice President-Investments, Jefferson-Pilot Life Insurance Company (life insurance)
	Robert L. Jones President, Davidson and Jones Corporation (general contractors and developers)	
	Hugh L. McColl, Jr. Chairman	

INTO A NEW DECADE

In April 1989 NCNB made a try for C&S of Atlanta. McColl reportedly told C&S Chairman Bennett Brown, "you have three hours to answer, or I will launch my missiles." A few hours later couriers delivered letters from NCNB across the Southeast to C&S's 15 directors. McColl insisted the offer was friendly, but C&S resisted and refused to negotiate. NCNB's planner, Gentry, said, "We felt it was time to move ahead; if something is worth doing, sooner is better than later." A merger "would be bad for our shareholders, bad for our bank, bad for our community, and bad for the banking industry," C&S's chairman declared. C&S was expected to resist with Georgia's antitakeover provisions, including staggered director's terms, arguing that NCNB shouldn't be able to use its Texas tax breaks to finance the offer and that NCNB's stock was overpriced. However, NCNB's offer represented a 36 percent premium over C&S's current stock value and the

NCNB National Bank of South Carolina

Bill L. Amick
Chief Executive Officer, Amick Farms, Inc. (poultry processing)

John G. P. Boatwright
Managing Director

W. Melvin Brown, Jr.
President, American Development Corporation (defense manufacturing)

Madge Chase DeFosset
(personal investments)

James H. Hance, Jr.
Managing Director

Richardson M. Hanckel
Planters Three (farming)

Dwight A. Holder
Chairman of the Board and President, Carolina Financial Corporation (diversified investors)

D. Wellsman Johnson
Vice Chairman, The Abney Foundation

George Dean Johnson, Jr.
President, Johnson Development Associates, Inc. (property development)

W. W. Johnson
Chairman, NCNB South Carolina Chairman of the Executive Committee, NCNB Corporation

R. M. Laffitte
Chairman of the Board, The Exchange Bank, Estill, South Carolina

Edgar H. Lawton, Jr.
President, Hartsville Oil Mill (manufacturers of cottonseed and peanut products)

Hugh L. McColl, Jr.
Chief Executive Officer

Robert E. McNair
Chairman of the Board McNair Law Firm P.A.

William P. Middlemas
Managing Director

Dr. M. Maceo Nance, Jr.
President Emeritus, South Carolina State College

Donald S. Russell, Jr.
Attorney

James C. Self, Jr.
Chairman of the Board Greenwood Mills Inc. (textiles)

Henry R. Sims II
Attorney

Joel A. Smith III
President

James W. Thompson
Managing Director

NCNB Texas Corporation

Robert H. Dedman
Chairman and Chief Executive Officer, ClubCorp International (owns and manages private clubs)

Timothy P. Hartman
President, NCNB Texas Corporation

Ray L. Hunt
Chairman and Chief Executive Officer, Hunt Consolidated, Inc. (oil and gas, real estate, agriculture and ranching)

Francis B. Kemp
Chairman of the Board NCNB Texas Corporation

Kerney Laday, Sr.
Vice President and Regional General Manager, USMG Xerox Corporation (multinational business products and services)

Irvin L. Levy
President, NCH Corporation (international manufacturer of chemical specialties)

Kenneth D. Lewis
President NCNB Texas National Bank

Hugh L. McColl, Jr.
Chairman NCNB Corporation

---

institutions which held 47 percent of their stock might force C&S to accept the offer. NCNB's stock fell about 10 percent during the first two weeks of the battle. A C&S employee pointed out that the cultures of the organizations were entirely opposite. Within a few days NCNB gave up trying to overcome C&S's opposition. In McColl's view, "We offered them an exciting and unique opportunity. We are going to make a lot of money here in the Southeast. We're going to make a lot of money in Texas, and we're going to keep it for ourselves."

Business Week saw the pursuit of C&S as evidence of pressure for NCNB to keep up its earnings momentum with whatever acquisitions remained in the Southeast. *United States Banker* reported NCNB had captured the imagination of investors worldwide with its aggressive interstate expansion, resulting in their stock's price having one of the highest multiples of any banks, 12 against 9.6 for the seven largest southeastern banks. They noted employees and directors held 20 percent of their shares. During 1989 they increased their capitalization by $1.65 billion by adding some subordinated debt and selling 15 million new shares of

EXHIBIT 3 Cont'd. Boards of Directors

NCNB Texas Corporation	NCNB Texas National Bank	NCNB Bank National Georgia
Allen T. McInnes Executive Vice President Tenneco, Inc. (diversified industrial corporation)	James M. Berry Vice Chairman, Houston NCNB Texas National Bank	Edward J. Brown III Chairman
John J. (Jack) Murphy Chairman, President and Chief Executive Officer, Dresser Industries, Inc. (energy-related products and services)	Timothy P. Hartman Vice Chairman and Chief Financial Officer, NCNB Texas National Bank	Graham W. Denton, Jr. Executive Vice President NCNB National Bank of Florida
William T. Solomon Chairman, President and Chief Executive Officer Austin Industries, Inc. (general contractor)	W. W. Johnson Chairman of the Executive Committee, NCNB Corporation	William B. Heberton (private investor)
	Francis B. Kemp Chairman of the Board NCNB Texas National Bank	Blaine Kelley, Jr. Chairman of the Board and Chief Executive Officer, The Landmarks Group (real estate development and management)
V. H. (Pete) Van Horn President and Chief Executive Officer, National Convenience Stores, Inc. (retail convenience stores)	Kenneth D. Lewis President, NCNB Texas National Bank	Jerry R. Satrum President and Chief Operating Officer, Georgia Gulf Corporation (commodity and specialty chemical manufacturer)
John F. Woodhouse Chairman and Chief Executive Officer, SYSCO Corporation (wholesale food service marketing and distribution)	Hugh L. McColl, Jr. Chairman NCNB Corporation	R. Edwin Spears President
	Joseph R. Musolino Vice Chairman, Dallas NCNB Texas National Bank	

common stock for $700 million. Approximately $1 billion was used to complete the purchase of the remaining 80 percent of the Texas banks, giving them $3 billion in tax-loss carryovers. [See Exhibits 2 and 3.]

In the 1989 *Annual Report* [see Exhibits 4 through 7], McColl said, "the 1980s will be remembered as the decade the company built the foundation for a national financial service company," and pointed out with pride that during the decade shareholders had received a yearly compound growth rate of 21.1 percent in stock price and 13.5 percent in dividends. But the 1990s promised rigorous challenges in banking. NCNB's Rusty Page predicted the 14,000 U.S. banks would be reduced to 1,500. Kenneth Guenther of the Independent Bankers Association described 1990 to the *Charlotte Observer* as a lull before the storm, "a transitional year looking to cataclysmic banking legislation in 1991." Deregulation had removed the guarantees of profit which banking had enjoyed and bank managers took increasing risks to hold onto profits, sometimes unwisely. Over 1,000 banks had failed in the last 10 years costing the government over $20 billion. In that time the top 10 U.S. banks wrote off $40 billion in bad loans, while earning less than $30 billion. The cost of the savings and loan debacle was raising questions about the government's role in insuring deposits. Regulators were reviewing banks' portfolios to see that reserves were truly in line with the amount of risk. Most banks were already moving to increase reserves to handle nonperforming assets, or bad loans. Some analysts saw banking at the start of a multiyear decline.

As 1990 unfolded NCNB continued to round out acquisitions. The prior October they acquired a $3.5-billion savings and loan in Houston and Austin from the government's Resolution Trust Corporation. In June they won a bidding battle for nine insolvent banks in the San Antonio area, making NCNB Texas the largest bank in Texas. There was talk that NCNB was preparing to make a private placement of $150 million in preferred stock in anticipation of buying Florida's largest S&L. They completed a realignment of senior management in which there would be an executive in charge of each line of business, such as real estate or trust, instead of a geographical region. Thus Ken Lewis, president of NCNB Texas in Dallas, was responsible for real estate lending wherever it occurred. McColl saw the opportunities for the 1990s to be in fee-income business and nontraditional lines, such as investment banking and trust activity. Against the challenges, McColl saw opportunities. He told stockholders, "Now is not the time to rest. The thing we must guard against is complacency—believing we have arrived. Actually, we still have a long way to go."

EXHIBIT 4 NCNB Corporation and Subsidiaries Consolidated Statement of Cash Flows ($000)

	Year Ended December 31		
	1989	**1988**	**1987**
Operating activities			
Net income	$ 447,069	$ 252,471	$ 166,852
Reconciliation of net income to net cash provided by operating activities			
FDIC interest in earnings of NCNB Texas	116,164		
Provision for loan and lease losses	239,123	121,538	194,632
Depreciation	91,416	43,657	39,419
Amortization of intangibles	39,358	37,575	37,260
Deferred income tax expense (benefit)	14,568	(3,582)	(9,277)
Net (increase) decrease in trading securities	(163,048)	(10,348)	258,573
Net increase (decrease) in interest receivable	(237,690)	(23,351)	(12,288)
Net increase (decrease) in interest payable	(111,255)	45,590	42,157
Other operating activities	(164,924)	(54,253)	(15,456)
Net cash provided by operating activities	270,781	409,297	701,872
Investing activities			
Proceeds from maturities of investment securities	1,836,644	394,977	549,726
Proceeds from sales of investment securities	14,921,349	8,936,643	7,744,388
Purchases of investment securities	(24,523,399)	(6,986,789)	(9,197,560)
Net (increase) decrease in federal funds sold and securities purchased under agreements to resell	1,503,498	(769,719)	34,298
Net (increase) decrease in other short-term investments	(1,269,017)	(209,805)	799,111
Net increase (decrease) in bank card receivables	(449,637)	(203,894)	(68,261)
Net collections (originations) of longer-term loans	107	(1,904,191)	(1,502,360)
Proceeds from sale of factored receivables		82,308	
Net sales (purchases) of premises and equipment	(247,940)	79,624	(132,630)
Purchase of NCNB Texas	(790,000)	(210,000)	
Purchase of banking and financial organizations	(173,088)	(591)	101,566
Other investing activities	3,443	(859)	6,926
Net cash used by investing activities	(9,188,040)	(792,296)	(1,664,796)
Financing Activities			
Net increase in deposits	7,431,461	1,074,811	635,657
Net increase (decrease) in federal funds purchased and securities sold under agreements to repurchase	2,386,409	(941,558)	(134,007)
Net increase in other borrowed funds	52,045	298,812	76,889
Proceeds from issuance of long-term debt	1,003,318		
Repayment of long-term debt	(122,486)	(72,593)	(23,591)
Proceeds from issuance of common stock	690,051	22,423	116,041
Proceeds from issuance of preferred stock		250,000	
Cash dividends paid	(122,308)	(85,238)	(70,569)
Assistance refunded to FDIC	(262,607)		
Other financing activities	1,912	(3,962)	7,173
Net cash provided by financing activities	11,057,795	542,695	607,593
Effect of exchange rate changes on cash and cash equivalents	(592)	(548)	1,780
Net increase (decrease) in cash and cash equivalents	2,139,944	159,148	(353,551)
Cash and cash equivalents at beginning of year	1,971,324	1,812,176	2,165,727
Cash and cash equivalents at end of year	$4,111,268	$1,971,324	$1,812,176

EXHIBIT 5 NCNB Corporation and Subsidiaries Consolidated Statement of Income
($000 except per-share information)

	Year Ended December 31		
	1989	**1988**	**1987**
Income from earning assets			
Interest and fees on loans	$3,776,266	$1,851,394	$1,592,580
Lease financing income	31,379	23,750	21,275
Interest and dividends on taxable investment securities	987,623	352,266	293,605
Interest on investment securities exempt from federal income taxes	71,088	78,493	66,817
Time deposits placed	200,285	60,374	77,862
Federal funds sold	123,031	50,784	35,274
Securities purchased under agreements to resell	55,808	31,321	20,578
Trading account securities	46,449	16,069	20,580
Total income from earning assets	5,291,929	2,464,451	2,128,571
Interest expense			
Deposits	2,830,638	1,039,758	875,399
Borrowed funds	1,074,699	472,844	375,549
Capital leases and long-term debt	107,265	54,165	56,301
Special Asset Division net funding allocation	(423,553)		
Total interest expense	3,589,049	1,566,767	1,307,249
Net interest income	1,702,880	897,684	821,322
Provision for loan and lease losses			
Bank provision	239,123	121,538	194,632
Loans transferred to Special Asset Division	216,699		
Assistance from FDIC	(216,699)		
Total provision for loan and lease losses	239,123	121,538	194,632
Net credit income	1,463,757	776,146	626,690
Noninterest income	860,517	369,055	332,372
Noninterest expense	1,692,042	814,806	758,085
Income before taxes and FDIC interest in earnings of NCNB Texas	632,232	330,395	200,977
Special Asset Division			
Net adjustment for asset valuation allowance	(332,390)		
Other net costs	(616,445)		
Assistance from FDIC	948,835		
Net costs associated with Special Asset Division	—	—	—
Earnings			
Income before taxes and FDIC interest in earnings of NCNB Texas	632,232	330,395	200,977
Income tax expense	68,999	77,924	34,125
Income before FDIC interest in earnings of NCNB Texas	563,233	252,471	166,852
FDIC interest in earnings of NCNB Texas	(116,164)	—	—
Net income	$ 447,069	$ 252,471	$ 166,852
Earnings per common share			
Primary	$4.62	$2.90	$2.03
Fully diluted	4.44	2.87	2.01
Dividends per common share	1.10	0.94	0.86
Average common shares outstanding			
Primary	92,491,551	85,210,165	82,073,254
Fully diluted	100,791,654	88,269,581	83,096,742

EXHIBIT 6 Taxable-Equivalent 12-Month Data (income and expense amounts in $000; balance sheet amounts in $millions)

	1989		
	Balance Sheet Amounts	Income or Expense	Yields/ Rates
Earning assets			
Loans and leases, net of unearned income			
Commercial	$16,703	$1,979,025	11.85%
Real estate–construction	2,144	254,609	11.88
Real estate–commercial mortgage^a	3,099	334,804	10.80
Real estate–residential mortgage	2,506	268,206	10.70
Consumer	5,654	660,557	11.68
Bank card	1,311	217,442	16.59
Lease financing	404	31,944	7.92
Foreign loans	787	90,729	11.53
Total loans and leases, net	32,608	3,837,316	11.77
Investment securities			
Taxable	11,232	1,007,828	8.97
Tax-exempt	895	95,937	10.72
Total investment securities	12,127	1,103,765	9.10
Federal funds sold and securities purchased under agreements to resell	1,957	178,839	9.14
Time deposits placed	2,037	200,285	9.83
Trading account securities	517	47,873	9.26
Total earning assets	49,246	5,368,078	10.90
Cash and cash equivalents	3,597		
Other assets, less allowance for loan and lease losses and excluding Special Asset Division	2,673		
Total assets, net of Special Asset Division	$55,516		
Interest-bearing liabilities			
Consumer savings and other time deposits	$ 3,165	190,260	6.01
Negotiable order of withdrawal and money market deposit accounts	10,087	635,414	6.30
Consumer certificates	10,260	882,211	8.60
Negotiable CDs, public funds and other time deposits	10,259	911,749	8.89
Foreign time deposits	2,157	211,004	9.78
Borrowed funds	11,870	1,074,699	9.05
Capital leases and long-term debt	1,035	107,265	10.36
Special Asset Division net funding allocation	(5,164)	(423,553)	(8.20)
Total interest-bearing liabilities	43,669	3,589,049	8.22
Noninterest-bearing sources			
Noninterest-bearing deposits	7,246		
Other liabilities	1,851		
FDIC interest	412		
Shareholder's equity	2,338		
Total liabilities and shareholders' equity	$55,516		
Net interest spread			2.68
Impact of noninterest-bearing sources			0.93
Net interest income/yield on earning assets		$1,779,029	3.61

^aInformation on real estate–commercial mortgage loans is included with commercial loans for 1988 and previous years.

	1988			1987			1986	
Balance Sheet Amounts	Income or Expense	Yields/ Rates	Balance Sheet Amounts	Income or Expense	Yields/ Rates	Balance Sheet Amounts	Income or Expense	Yields/ Rates
$10,107	$1,012,939	10.02%	$ 9,464	$ 889,397	9.40%	$ 7,856	$ 757,898	9.65%
1,537	157,073	10.22	1,425	131,221	9.21	1,307	123,200	9.43
1,172	120,114	10.25	953	101,380	10.63	954	110,249	11.56
3,469	388,091	11.19	3,037	342,902	11.29	2,448	307,802	12.57
968	171,070	17.67	762	134,215	17.61	717	136,388	19.02
288	24,567	8.53	279	23,254	8.33	254	25,155	9.90
249	30,609	12.27	470	36,388	7.74	541	52,152	9.64
17,790	1,904,463	10.71	16,390	1,658,757	10.12	14,077	1,512,844	10.75
4,702	369,676	7.86	3,936	298,316	7.57	3,450	301,857	8.75
1,014	112,524	11.10	857	110,030	12.84	960	129,973	13.54
5,716	482,200	8.44	4,793	408,346	8.52	4,410	431,830	9.79
1,093	82,105	7.51	839	55,852	6.65	1,020	67,636	6.63
735	60,374	8.22	1,094	77,862	7.12	963	71,235	7.39
206	16,844	8.16	310	22,228	7.16	426	33,326	7.83
25,540	2,545,986	9.97	23,426	2,223,045	9.49	20,896	2,116,871	10.13
1,723			1,706			1,547		
1,587			1,598			1,307		
$28,850			$26,730			$23,750		
$ 2,499	149,007	5.96	$ 2,269	140,342	6.19	$ 1,744	115,456	6.62
4,715	241,106	5.11	4,833	236,625	4.90	4,392	241,379	5.50
3,849	278,723	7.24	3,173	209,685	6.61	3,104	240,549	7.75
3,768	283,834	7.53	2,943	196,162	6.66	2,182	150,428	6.89
1,092	87,088	7.98	1,271	92,585	7.28	975	75,350	7.73
6,533	472,844	7.24	5,847	375,549	6.42	5,703	367,061	6.44
548	54,165	9.89	568	56,301	9.91	504	55,719	11.06
23,004	1,566,767	6.81	20,904	1,307,249	6.25	18,604	1,245,942	6.70
3,415			3,551			3,357		
776			849			570		
1,655			1,426			1,219		
$28,850			$26,730			$23,750		
		3.16			3.24			3.43
		0.67			0.67			0.74
	$ 979,219	3.83		$ 915,796	3.91		$ 870,929	4.17

EXHIBIT 6 Cont'd. Taxable-Equivalent 12-Month Data (income and expense amounts in $000; balance sheet amounts in $millions)

	1985 Balance Sheet Amounts	1985 Income or Expense	1985 Yields/ Rates
Earning assets			
Loans and leases, net of unearned income			
Commercial	$ 5,945	$ 666,009	11.20%
Real estate–construction	868	100,621	11.59
Real estate–commercial mortgage[a]			
Real estate–residential mortgage	840	99,877	11.89
Consumer	1,985	274,162	13.81
Bank card	365	58,305	15.97
Lease financing	225	32,756	14.56
Foreign loans	568	56,472	9.94
Total loans and leases, net	10,796	1,288,202	11.93
Investment securities			
Taxable	2,299	244,413	10.63
Tax-exempt	540	69,978	12.96
Total investment securities	2,839	314,391	11.07
Federal funds sold and securities purchased under agreements to resell	820	66,784	8.14
Time deposits placed	821	74,008	9.02
Trading account securities	188	17,588	9.36
Total earning assets	15,464	1,760,973	11.39
Cash and cash equivalents	1,232		
Other assets, less allowance for loan and lease losses and excluding Special Asset Division	1,192		
Total assets, net of Special Asset Division	$17,888		
Interest-bearing liabilities			
Consumer savings and other time deposits	$ 1,305	92,787	7.11
Negotiable order of withdrawal and money market deposit accounts	3,303	216,100	6.54
Consumer certificates	2,468	226,180	9.16
Negotiable CDs, public funds and other time deposits	1,631	136,927	8.39
Foreign time deposits	1,080	98,299	9.10
Borrowed funds	3,324	261,986	7.88
Capital leases and long-term debt	368	42,872	11.65
Special Asset Division net funding allocation			
Total interest-bearing liabilities	13,479	1,075,151	7.98
Noninterest-bearing sources			
Noninterest-bearing deposits	2,742		
Other liabilities	712		
FDIC interest			
Shareholder's equity	955		
Total liabilities and shareholders' equity	$17,888		
Net interest spread			3.41
Impact of noninterest-bearing sources			1.02
Net interest income/yield on earning assets		$ 685,822	4.43

[a]Information on real estate–commercial mortgage loans is included with commercial loans for 1988 and previous years.

	1984			5-Year Compound Growth Rate 1984/1989	
	Balance Sheet Amounts	Income or Expense	Yields/ Rates	Average Balances	Income or Expense
Earning assets					
Loans and leases, net of unearned income					
Commercial	$ 4,713	$ 620,567	13.17%	33.3%	30.1%
Real estate-construction	509	69,888	13.73	33.3	29.5
Real estate-commercial mortgage[a]					
Real estate-residential mortgage	791	99,707	12.61	25.9	21.9
Consumer	1,785	275,691	15.44	25.9	19.1
Bank card	267	41,657	15.60	37.5	39.2
Lease financing	211	31,461	14.91	13.9	0.3
Foreign loans	672	87,454	13.01	3.2	0.7
Total loans and leases, net	8,948	1,226,425	13.71	29.5	25.6
Investment securities					
Taxable	2,152	237,604	11.03	39.2	33.5
Tax-exempt	472	56,494	11.98	13.7	11.2
Total investment securities	2,624	294,098	11.21	35.8	30.3
Federal funds sold and securities purchased under agreements to resell	813	85,725	10.55	19.2	15.8
Time deposits placed	829	89,050	10.75	19.7	17.6
Trading account securities	110	13,327	12.07	36.3	29.1
Total earning assets	13,324	1,708,625	12.82	29.9	25.7
Cash and cash equivalents	1,152			25.6	
Other assets, less allowance for loan and lease losses and excluding Special Asset Division	1,415			13.6	
Total assets, net of Special Asset Division	$15,891			28.4	
Interest-bearing liabilities					
Consumer savings and other time deposits	$1,261	87,349	6.93	20.2	16.8
Negotiable order of withdrawal and money market deposit accounts	2,542	204,847	8.06	31.7	25.4
Consumer certificates	2,136	214,791	10.06	36.9	32.7
Negotiable CDs, public funds and other time deposits	1,431	147,560	10.31	48.3	43.9
Foreign time deposits	1,192	125,805	10.55	12.6	10.9
Borrowed funds	2,700	277,941	10.29	34.5	31.1
Capital leases and long-term debt	348	41,030	11.79	24.4	21.2
Special Asset Division net funding allocation					
Total interest-bearing liabilities	11,610	1,099,323	9.47	30.3	26.7
Noninterest-bearing sources					
Noninterest-bearing deposits	2,578			23.0	
Other liabilities	885			15.9	
FDIC interest					
Shareholder's equity	818			23.4	
Total liabilities and shareholders' equity	$15,891			28.4	
Net interest spread					
Impact of noninterest-bearing sources			3.35		
			1.22		
Net interest income/yield on earning assets		$ 609,302	4.57		23.9

EXHIBIT 7 NCNB Corporation and Subsidiaries Six-Year Consolidated Statistical Summary

	1989	1988	1987	1986	1985	1984
Taxable-Equivalent Yields Earned						
Loans and leases, net of unearned income:						
Commercial	11.85%	10.02%	9.40%	9.65%	11.20%	13.17%
Real estate–construction	11.88	10.22	9.21	9.43	11.59	13.73
Real estate–commercial mortgage[a]	10.80					
Real estate–residential mortgage	10.70	10.25	10.63	11.56	11.89	12.61
Consumer	11.68	11.19	11.29	12.57	13.81	15.44
Bank card	16.59	17.67	17.61	19.02	15.97	15.60
Lease financing	7.92	8.53	8.33	9.90	14.56	14.91
Foreign loans	11.53	12.27	7.74	9.64	9.94	13.01
Total loans and leases, net	11.77	10.71	10.12	10.75	11.93	13.71
Taxable investment securities	8.97	7.86	7.57	8.75	10.63	11.03
Tax-exempt investment securities	10.72	11.10	12.84	13.54	12.96	11.98
Total investment securities	9.10	8.44	8.52	9.79	11.07	11.21
Federal funds sold and securities purchased under agreements to resell	9.14	7.51	6.65	6.63	8.14	10.55
Time deposits placed	9.83	8.22	7.12	7.39	9.02	10.75
Trading account securities	9.26	8.16	7.16	7.83	9.36	12.07
Total earning assets	10.90	9.97	9.49	10.13	11.39	12.82
Rates Paid						
Savings and interest-bearing demand deposits	6.08	5.09	4.92	5.45	6.32	7.38
Time deposits	8.71	7.43	6.83	7.56	9.00	10.23
Total domestic savings and time deposits	7.76	6.42	5.92	6.55	7.72	8.88
Foreign time deposits	9.78	7.98	7.28	7.73	9.10	10.55
Total savings and time deposits	7.88	6.53	6.04	6.64	7.87	9.11
Federal funds purchased and securities sold under agreements to repurchase	9.03	7.25	6.40	6.42	7.84	10.15
Commercial paper	9.21	7.49	6.55	6.71	8.43	10.60
Other notes payable	9.17	6.95	6.56	6.56	7.89	11.12
Total borrowed funds	9.05	7.24	6.42	6.44	7.88	10.29
Capital leases	11.63	12.34	11.71	11.85	11.32	11.04
Long-term debt	10.31	9.73	9.80	10.99	11.68	11.86
Total interest-bearing liabilities	8.22	6.81	6.25	6.70	7.98	9.47

Profit Margins

Domestic spread	2.83	3.20	3.45	3.64	3.62	3.63
Foreign spread	.01	2.08	.02	.70	1.37	1.15
Consolidated spread	2.68	3.16	3.24	3.43	3.41	3.35
Domestic net interest yield	3.79	3.88	4.15	4.42	4.71	4.95
Foreign net interest yield	.50	2.49	.21	.83	1.47	1.35
Consolidated net interest yield	3.61	3.83	3.91	4.17	4.43	4.57

Year-End Data ($millions)

Loans and leases, net of unearned income	$34,409	$18,908	$17,087	$15,765	$12,134	$10,362
Investment securities	16,170	4,727	6,826	5,653	3,336	2,386
Time deposits placed	2,966	963	855	1,630	979	988
Total earning assets	54,159	26,101	25,491	24,065	17,255	14,559
Total assets, excluding Special Asset Division	61,491	29,848	28,915	27,472	19,754	17,354
Demand deposits	8,439	3,913	3,862	4,510	3,354	3,137
Domestic savings and time deposits	37,988	15,900	14,383	12,542	9,396	8,200
Foreign time deposits	2,149	857	1,305	1,467	1,200	1,361
Total savings and time deposits	40,137	16,757	15,688	14,009	10,596	9,561
Total deposits	48,576	20,670	19,550	18,519	13,950	12,698
Borrowed funds	11,735	5,899	6,542	6,596	3,767	2,583
Obligations under capital leases	35	36	35	36	33	31
Long-term debt	1,430	457	533	537	401	319
Total shareholders' equity	2,962	1,942	1,510	1,309	1,039	902

Earnings Ratios

Return on average						
Total assets[b]	1.01%	.88%	.62%	.84%	.92%	.84%
Earning assets[b]	1.14	.99	.71	.95	1.06	1.00
Common shareholders' equity	20.45	15.55	11.70	16.31	17.23	16.30

Earnings Analysis (taxable-equivalent)

Noninterest income as a percentage of net interest income	48.37	37.31	36.29	35.29	38.24	28.62
Noninterest expense as a percentage of net interest income	95.11	83.21	82.78	80.30	78.40	78.71
Overhead ratio: noninterest expense less noninterest income divided by net interest income	46.74	45.90	46.49	45.01	40.16	50.09
Net income as a percentage of net interest income	25.13	25.78	18.22	22.82	23.98	21.88

Asset Quality

For the year:

Net charge-offs as a percentage of average loans and leases	.45	.83	1.08	.66	.45	.36
Net charge-offs as a percentage of the provision for loan and lease losses	61.52	121.38	90.83	89.49	43.34	55.92

[a]Commercial mortgage loans were included with commercial loans for 1988 and previous years.
[b]Includes FDIC's interest in earnings of NCNB Texas for 1989; excludes special Asset Division assets.

EXHIBIT 7 Cont'd. NCNB Corporation and Subsidiaries Six-Year Consolidated Statistical Summary

	1989	1988	1987	1986	1985	1984
At year-end:						
Allowance as a percentage of total loans and leases	1.35	1.22	1.50	1.50	1.53	1.22
Allowance as a percentage of nonperforming loans	117.67	131.19	96.88	146.23	141.06	93.37
Nonperforming assets as a percentage of loans and leases, net of un-earned income	1.30	1.14	1.67	1.10	1.21	1.44
Nonperforming assets as a percentage of total assets[c]	.73	.72	.99	.63	.74	.86
Nonperforming assets ($ millions)	$ 446	$ 215	$ 286	$ 173	$ 146	$ 149
Capital Ratios						
Primary	5.69%	7.82%	6.56%	6.47%	7.17%	6.44%
Total	7.74	8.98	7.69	7.77	8.55	8.11
Common shareholders' equity as a percentage of total assets at year-end[c]	4.41	5.67	5.22	4.76	5.26	5.20
Dividend payout ratio per common share	23.81	32.41	42.36	30.83	29.78	29.85
Shareholder's equity per common share:						
Average	$22.58	$18.67	$17.38	$15.50	$13.35	$11.99
At year-end	26.79	19.60	17.87	16.42	14.23	12.74
Other Statistics						
Number of full-time employees (not restated for acquisitions)	27,002	12,979	12,334	12,107	9,981	9,329
Rate of increase in average						
Total loans and leases, net of unearned income	83.29%	8.54%	16.43%	30.39%	20.65%	32.79%
Earning assets	92.82	9.03	12.10	35.13	16.06	22.87
Total assets[c]	92.43	7.93	12.55	32.77	12.57	22.94
Total deposits	123.27	7.19	14.51	25.75	12.46	22.60
Total shareholders' equity	41.27	16.07	17.00	27.67	16.70	26.76
Average foreign assets as a percentage of average total assets[c]	5.70	4.37	6.92	6.78	9.13	12.25
Average foreign liabilities as a percentage of average total liabilities	6.05	6.09	7.50	6.70	9.92	12.83
Common Stock Information						
Market price of common stock						
High for the year	$ 55	$ $29\tfrac{1}{8}$	$ $29\tfrac{1}{8}$	$ $27\tfrac{3}{4}$	$ $23\tfrac{5}{8}$	$ $18\tfrac{1}{4}$
Low for the year	27	$17\tfrac{1}{2}$	$15\tfrac{1}{2}$	20	17	$11\tfrac{1}{2}$
Close at the end of the year	$46\tfrac{1}{4}$	$27\tfrac{1}{4}$	$17\tfrac{1}{4}$	$21\tfrac{1}{2}$	$22\tfrac{5}{8}$	18
Daily average trading volume	303,599	189,043	210,644	209,938	132,402	80,834
Number of shareholders of record	29,064	29,344	29,789	28,732	21,004	19,896

[c]Excludes Special Asset Division assets.

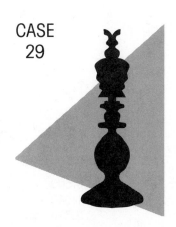

According to Honda, an American Legend Faces the '90s

LYNDA L. GOULET

Events have a way of breaking in favor of the Japanese. When the second oil crunch and double-digit inflation hit in the late 1970s, they had cheap, economical cars to sell. When the yen burst through the roof, they had U.S. factories ready to go. But success, as we all know, goes to those who make their own luck.[1]

Honda has been a success story. In the 40 years since Honda Motor Company was incorporated under the laws of Japan to manufacture engines for motorized bicycles, Honda has grown to become the third-largest auto manufacturer in Japan, the fourth-largest in the United States, and the tenth-largest in the world. In the 1960s Japan's Ministry of International Trade and Industry (MITI) tried to discourage Honda's founder from expanding beyond its original business of motorcycles to restrict competition for Japan's existing automakers.[2] Nevertheless, the firm forged ahead. The trigger for Honda's later success in automobiles came in 1972 when its president, Mr. Tadashi Kume, developed the low-pollution, fuel-efficient CVCC (compound vortex controlled combustion) engine. Honda simultaneously introduced the Civic automobile using this engine. Since then the firm's automobile sales, in both units and yen, have increased every year.

WORLD AUTO INDUSTRY

By 1990 approximately 175 manufacturers will be producing nearly 50 million automobiles, trucks, and buses worldwide, generating sales of about $450 billion.[3] The 12 largest of these producers are listed in Exhibit 1. Although two U.S.-based firms, General Motors and Ford, lead the industry with a combined world share of about 30 percent, the list also includes Chrysler, the four largest European firms, and five Japanese companies. Although the United States is currently the largest market for automotive vehicles, western Europe will shortly take over this number one spot. Western Europe already leads in vehicle production, followed by Japan

This case was prepared by Lynda L. Goulet of the University of Northern Iowa as the basis for class discussion rather than to illustrate the effective or ineffective handling of a managerial situation. Submitted to and accepted by the refereed Midwest Society for Case Research. All rights reserved to the author and the MSCR. © by Lynda L. Goulet, 1990.

EXHIBIT 1 1988 World Automotive Vehicle Production and Sales (millions of units)

	Production		Sales	
	Cars	Trucks/ Buses	Cars	Trucks/ Buses
United States	7.137	4.080	10.545	5.244
Canada	1.027	0.950	1.053	0.509
Western Europe	13.032	1.662	12.682	1.849
Japan	8.198	4.501	3.717	2.715 (est.)
All others	5.803	2.247	3.755	2.049
	35.197	13.440	31.752	12.366

Firms Producing More Than 1 Million Vehicles

Firm	Home Country	Production, All Vehicles, 1988
General Motors	United States	7.8
Ford	United States	6.4
Toyota	Japan	4.0
Volkswagen	West Germany	2.9
Fiat	Italy	2.4
Chrysler	United States	2.4
Nissan	Japan	2.2
Peugeot	France	2.1
Renault	France	1.9
Honda	Japan	1.7
Mitsubishi	Japan	1.3
Mazda	Japan	1.2
Totals		36.3

Sources: "Autos-Auto Parts," *Standard & Poor's Industry Reports*, November 30, 1989, p. A88; *Annual Report*, Ford Motor Company, 1989; *Automotive News*, November 29, 1989, p. 128.

(which exports 50 percent of its production). In contrast, the United States is the only major market in the world which is a net importer of vehicles. As more automakers begin to establish facilities in Europe in the 1990s, worldwide overcapacity and overproduction can be expected to increase beyond the 4.5-million level of the late 1980s. As competition intensifies, the consumer may become the big winner of the auto wars.

European Market

Western Europe is the largest car market in the world. This market is growing as a result of increasing income levels and relatively low existing levels of car ownership (380 cars per 1,000 people, versus 580/1,000 in the United States).

Europe's six major automakers and their share of the European market are summarized below.[4]

Auto Firm	Share	Auto Firm	Share
Fiat	14.9%	Ford	11.9%
Volkswagen	14.8	General Motors	11.0
Peugeot	12.9	Renault	10.4

Japan's automakers have only an 11-percent combined market share in Europe, primarily as a result of restrictions on imports. France restricts Japanese cars to 3 percent of sales; Italy and Spain both limit Japan's share to below 1 percent; Great Britain has a limit of 11 percent. Only Germany permits free access to Japanese automakers. Even though the European Community (EC) is committed to removing all auto quotas eventually, such a free-entry market is unlikely to happen before the turn of the century. In addition to restrictive import barriers, resolving other regulatory differences among the 12 member nations of the EC will require time. Relevant regulatory barriers include price and margin controls, differences in exhaust emission standards and safety feature requirements, and value-added taxes ranging from 12 percent in Luxembourg to 200 percent in Denmark and Greece.[5]

Detroit and the Japanese are turning more of their attention to Europe's lucrative market. Europe already produces the majority of GM's and Ford's profits. Ford has the strongest dealer network in Europe with 8,000 dealers. Their strength is in small cars and their lack of a luxury nameplate was remedied with their $2.5 billion purchase of Jaguar (Britain). GM owns Lotus and recently acquired a 50-percent interest in Saab-Scania's automotive operations. Chrysler has Lamborghini and a small interest in Maserati. Chrysler, however, lacks overseas operations, although it ranks as the number one exporter of vehicles to Europe (mostly minivans and Jeeps). Chrysler will begin making minivans in Europe with Renault in the early 1990s. In 1986 Nissan opened an assembly plant in England and plans to triple capacity to 200,000 by 1993. Toyota expects to manufacture 200,000 cars in England by 1997, while Honda will make 100,000 there by 1994. Meanwhile, Toyota will begin exporting its Lexus to Europe and Honda will export its U.S.-made Accords by 1991. Honda also owns 20 percent of the Rover Group with whom the firm now produces the Sterling and already sells about 150,000 cars in Europe, imported from Japan. Toyota is planning to build light trucks with VW in West Germany. Mitsubishi and Daimler-Benz are working on an agreement to jointly produce small trucks, giving Mitsubishi its first vehicle facility in Europe.[6]

The European automakers will have to work a lot harder to prepare themselves for the Japanese invasion. European car manufacturers are the least efficient in the world and have much to fear if Nissan's plant is any indication that Japanese methods can be successfully transplanted to Europe. Volkswagen's main weakness is the high cost of labor. To partially overcome this problem it plans to move its small-car production to Spain where labor is cheaper. VW, however, ranks first in sales in West Germany, Belgium, Austria, and Switzerland. Peugeot is the only European manufacturer with two full lines of cars—Peugeot and Citroen. However, neither line has a broad European appeal; over 40 percent of all Peugeot's sales are in France. Fiat similarly has a narrow appeal with two-thirds of its sales in Italy. Renault is the weakest of the major European producers, lacks a luxury nameplate, sells 90 percent of its cars in France, and is heavily subsidized by the French government. Renault and Volvo are discussing an alliance to develop new cars jointly as 1992 approaches. Volvo is attempting to increase its efficiency by experimenting with the abandonment of the traditional assembly line concept. Teams of 7 to 10 workers will assemble four cars per shift. Workers will be trained to do all assembly jobs and the teams will largely manage themselves. Volvo hopes to substantially reduce its 20-percent absenteeism rate and its 30-percent annual turnover rate by improving morale and personal satisfaction.[7]

Japanese Market

The Japanese auto market is dominated by five home producers: Toyota, Nissan, Honda, Mazda, and Mitsubishi. Per-capita car ownership in Japan is about half the level experienced in the United States. Imports currently enjoy less than a 5-percent share of the Japanese home market, though this proportion is expected to increase to about 15 percent by the end of the century.[8] In general, the Japanese feel that most imports lack the quality required to penetrate their market. The best-selling imports in Japan currently are produced by BMW, Volkswagen, and Mercedes-Benz. Luxury cars are currently increasing in popularity in Japan, helping to increase import penetration.

There are 11 automotive vehicle firms in Japan. Toyota leads in the car market with about a 40-percent share, followed by Nissan with slightly less than a 25-percent share, and Honda with slightly above a 10-percent share. Mazda and Mitsubishi together account for slightly above a 10-percent share, as well. Toyota also leads in truck sales, followed by Mitsubishi, Suzuki, Daihatsu, Nissan, Honda, Fuji, and Mazda. Mitsubishi sells more trucks than cars, as do all the other smaller Japanese firms except Mazda. Many of Japan's smaller automakers are struggling and cutting their budgets for capital spending. Daihatsu, 14 percent owned by Toyota, wants Toyota to increase its ownership to 20 percent and to assist in product development. This is partially the result of the Japanese government's reduced taxation on large cars, which hurts sales of smaller cars, the main auto products of these small firms. Cooperative arrangements between these smaller companies, or consolidations, may be necessary if they are to survive.[9]

Honda suffers from several disadvantages in Japan. The firm is still regarded by many consumers as a manufacturer of motorcycles and smaller cars, though the younger Japanese consumers seem to be attracted to Honda's styling and engineering. Honda's dealerships number only half as many as Toyota's. The luxury-car market, defined in Japan as cars having engine capacities of over 2,000 ccs, is the fastest growing segment, but Honda is weakest in this segment. In fact until the introduction of the Acura Legend in 1985, the firm had no entry in this car category. In spite of these weaknesses, Honda is planning to add a third assembly line to one of its Japanese plants.

U.S. Market

The automobile market is affected by a variety of factors. These include:

General economic prospects
Consumer preferences toward auto size, styling, and fuel economy
Availability and prices of raw materials, parts, and components
Exchange rates
Import restrictions and trade protection attitudes
Health, environment, and safety regulations
The trend toward increased local participation in the ownership of enterprises (such as encountered in various countries such as France)[10]

In spite of inroads by the Japanese, automotive vehicle sales in the United States are dominated by the Big Three domestic manufacturers. Financial and sales data for these firms are presented in Exhibits 2a and 2b. Overall automobile sales trends in the market are illustrated in Exhibit 3. Although the Big Three's share of the U.S. market has been declining since the early 1980s, their share of the truck market is rising. Light trucks (10,000 pounds and under) have been the strongest segment for these firms and sales are expected to grow into the 1990s. Sales of compact pickup trucks and vans will come at the expense of car sales and full-size trucks and vans. The highest margins for the Big Three are on light trucks and sporty utility vehicles because these vehicles cost less to make and a 25 percent import duty on these trucks limits foreign competition.[11]

Although light trucks provide U.S. producers with the prospect of growth, the picture for traditional cars is not nearly as bright. Exhibit 4 illustrates recent growth patterns in each of the major auto market segments. In addition to changes in the growth patterns of the various segments, there have also been corresponding changes in the leading car brands. At the beginning of 1990 Honda's car sales surpassed those of Chrysler, making Honda number three in U.S. car sales. Further, Honda's Accord became the largest-selling nameplate in the United States and four of the top ten car models sold in 1989 were Japanese.[12]

1. Honda Accord (compact)
2. Ford Taurus (intermediate)
3. Ford Escort (subcompact)
4. Chevrolet Corsica (compact)
5. Chevrolet Cavalier (compact)
6. Toyota Camry (compact)
7. Ford Tempo (compact)
8. Nissan Sentra (subcompact)
9. Pontiac Grand Am (compact)
10. Toyota Corolla (subcompact)

Only two groups of automakers experienced growth in unit sales in the subcompact category: North American-based Japanese firms and other imports, from South Korea especially. Korean entry Hyundai is the fourth-largest import seller in the U.S. market. In 1991 Hyundai will open a 100,000-unit assembly plant in Ontario, its first in North America. This firm has appealed especially well to the under-24 age group which traditionally purchases a significant number of used cars for economic reasons. The steady rise in the yen–dollar exchange rate in the

EXHIBIT 2a Big Three Performance Summary ($millions)

	1986	1987	1988	1989
General Motors				
Auto sales	$ 90,863.6	$ 89,890.6	$ 97,777.1	$ 99,440.9
Auto operating income	2,014.3	3,379.9	5,614.5	5,131.1
Total auto assets	46,708.0	60,159.5	60,420.4	64,598.0
Auto capital expenditures	10,257.3	6,127.9	4,524.6	6,287.6
Total corporate sales	115,609.9	114,870.4	123,641.6	126,931.9
Total net income	2,944.7	3,550.9	4,856.3	4,224.3
Total assets	150,157.1	162,343.2	164,063.1	173,297.1
Total equity	30,678.0	33,225.1	35,671.7	34,982.5
Ford Motor Company				
Total auto sales	62,868.3	71,797.2	82,193.0	82,879.4
U.S. auto sales	50,135.0	55,412.0	61,814.0	61,452.0
Auto operating income	4,142.2	6,255.9	6,611.9	4,251.6
Total auto assets	34,020.6	39,734.4	43,127.7	45,819.2
Auto capital expenditures	3,409.4	3,674.0	4,711.5	6,695.4
Total corporate sales	69,694.6	79,893.0	92,445.6	97,145.9
Total net income	3,285.1	4,625.2	5,300.2	3,835.0
Total assets	93,231.9	115,994.4	143,366.5	160,893.3
Total equity	14,859.5	18,492.7	21,529.0	22,727.8
Chrysler				
Auto sales	22,269.5	25,489.0	30,804.0	30,987.0
Auto operating income	2,006.0	2,092.0	1,662.0	594.0
Total auto assets	11,885.7	17,472.0	19,718.0	21,670.0
Auto capital expenditures	2,031.7	1,915.0	1,622.0	1,550.0
Total corporate sales	25,220.2	28,308.0	34,148.0	34,922.0
Total net income	1,389.2	1,289.7	1,050.2	359.0
Total assets	33,090.4	42,478.0	48,210.0	51,038.0
Total equity	5,281.2	6,502.9	7,582.3	7,233.0

Note: Total sales and assets figures include assets and results from financial subsidiaries.
Source: *Annual Reports.*

mid-1980s coupled with quotas which encouraged the Japanese to concentrate on well-equipped, expensive models in the U.S. market have helped support the Korean entry. The Korean automakers face no quota restrictions in the United States and are not hurt by the decline of the dollar because the value of their currency is tied to the dollar.[13]

As the U.S. moves into the 1990s intermediate cars are expected to be the only car category with increased sales. This is not unexpected as the population is aging and becoming more affluent, gasoline price increases have moderated, and technological advances have made larger cars cheaper to operate. Further, an older population typically desires larger cars with more interior room. Evidence of this trend can be seen in the fact that seven of the ten top-selling cars were compacts or intermediates in 1989. This trend does not greatly disturb the Big Three because

EXHIBIT 2b Worldwide and U.S. Vehicle Factory Sales (000 units)

	1986	**1987**	**1988**	**1989**
Total worldwide sales				
Cars	30,342	29,862	31,752	32,281
Trucks	11,029	11,457	12,366	12,310
Total, all firms	41,371	41,319	44,118	44,591
Worldwide sales, cars and trucks, U.S. firms				
General Motors	8,576	7,765	8,108	7,946
Ford Motor Company	5,916	6,051	6,441	6,336
Chrysler	2,198	2,260	2,567	2,382
Total worldwide sales, Big Three	16,690	16,076	17,116	16,664
U.S. sales, cars				
General Motors	4,302	3,592	3,516	3,238
Ford Motor Company	2,094	2,171	2,377	2,186
Chrysler	1,298	1,129	1,128	977
	7,694	6,892	7,021	6,401
Total U.S. car sales	11,405	10,192	10,845	9,779
U.S. sales, trucks				
General Motors	1,520	1,520	1,661	1,599
Ford Motor Company	1,404	1,481	1,541	1,523
Chrysler	614	829	1,006	991
	3,538	3,830	4,208	4,113
Total U.S. truck sales	4,921	5,001	5,244	5,067
Total U.S. vehicle sales				
Big Three	11,232	10,722	11,229	10,514
All firms	16,326	15,193	15,789	14,846

Source: *Annual Reports.*

Detroit sells almost one-half of its cars at a loss, the subcompact models especially. Ford expects to lose money on every one of its redesigned Escorts for 1990. However, even as the larger cars become more popular, the Big Three cannot abandon its small cars because their high fuel efficiency is needed to satisfy federal regulations for fleet mileage and the firms need to have entry-level cars for first-time buyers.[14] The trend toward larger cars is more of a threat to the Japanese who have only recently begun to enter the upscale segments.

These factors above, coupled with increasing competition, have encouraged American carmakers not only to increase car size, but also to make them more luxurious as luxury cars have margins of up to 20 percent. Luxury cars have traditionally been considered to be those priced above $20,000. However this is no longer true. A Range Rover four-wheel drive vehicle now costs over $35,000, compared to a Lincoln Town Car or Cadillac which are priced at $25,000 to $30,000. Most European luxury models are now well above $40,000 as a result of the weak U.S. dollar. The gap in the $30,000 to $40,000 price range is now being filled by the Japanese: Toyota's Lexus, Nissan's Infiniti, and Honda's Acura. The top-selling Cadillac and Lincoln models have been and will continue to target the

EXHIBIT 3   U.S. Retail Auto Sales

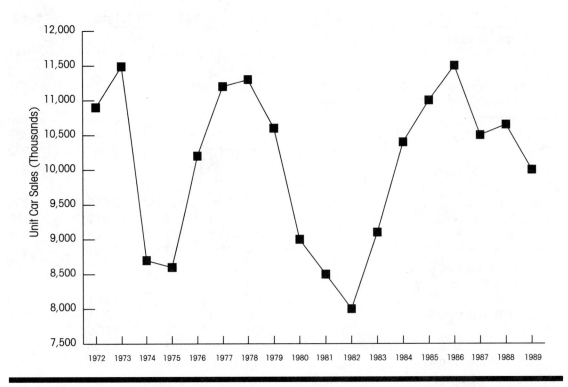

Source: U.S. Department of Commerce.

over-60 age group. The Japanese and Europeans are seeking younger, affluent professionals. Honda's Acura is appealing to the 45-year-old with an average income of $88,000. The Japanese luxury models are intended not only to improve profits, but to broaden product lines and appeal to their own customers who wish to trade up.[15]

To combat shrinking margins from increased competition, U.S. carmakers have also raised prices. In response to pressure on the Japanese firms caused by the strengthening yen, the Japanese carmakers have been forced to raise prices and the Big Three have followed their lead. As a result, the average new car price has increased faster than the Consumer Price Index (CPI). In addition, the 1986 Tax Reform Act phased out deductions on auto loans. The result is that buyers don't trade as often and seek greater value when they do buy.

	1980	1988
Average car age	6.6 years	7.6 years
Average maturity new car loans	45 months	56 months
Average new car price	$7,590	$14,570
Consumer Price Index (1982–1983=100)	82.4	118.3
Average autoworker wage	$10.80/hr.	$16.10/hr.

EXHIBIT 4   U.S. Automotive Vehicle Retail Sales by Category (000 units)

	1986	1987	1988	1994 est.
Subcompact cars				
North America	1,325	1,066	960	1,100
Captives	254	280	388	355
Japanese imports	1,142	961	922	600
European imports	66	73	50	25
Other imports	169	325	343	300
Total	2,956	2,705	2,663	2,380
Compact cars				
North America	2,436	2,433	2,799	2,935
Japanese imports	754	741	716	575
European imports	125	93	79	55
Other imports				50
Total	3,315	3,267	3,594	3,615
Intermediate cars				
North America	2,615	2,215	2,169	2,245
Japanese imports	113	100	74	300
European imports	106	139	119	65
Total	2,834	2,454	2,362	2,610
Luxury cars				
North America	1,866	1,554	1,556	1,345
Japanese imports	67	84	111	300
European imports	382	301	254	195
Total	2,315	1,939	1,921	1,840
Grand total cars	11,420	10,365	10,540	10,445
Light trucks	4,603	4,631	4,824	4,880
U.S. Market Shares[a]				
General Motors	40.9%	36.3%	35.9%	
Ford	18.2	20.1	21.5	
Chrysler	12.0	10.7	11.2	
Honda	6.1	7.2	7.2	
Toyota	5.6	6.1	6.5	
Nissan	4.8	5.6	4.8	
Others	12.4	14.0	12.9	

[a]Based on dealer sales, new auto units.
Sources: *U.S. Industrial Outlook, 1988, 1989, 1990* (Washington, D.C.: U.S. Department of Commerce, various years); "Autos-Auto Parts," *Standard & Poor's Industry Reports*, November 30, 1989, p. A77.

A critical element of the auto distribution channel is the dealer network. This network is under increasing stress. Increased competition and the need to control the rising prices of entry-level vehicles, especially, have resulted in lower margins. Aggressive marketing to fill unused capacity resulting from increased competition and rising productivity has led to costly incentive programs that put additional stress on dealers. Such incentives include accessory packages, improved warranties, rebates, and subsidized interest rates. These promotions have become so common that car sales slow significantly between the periodic incentive programs. These trends, in turn, have resulted in a shrinkage in the number of dealerships and a rise in the ownership of multiple dealerships. Between 1979 and 1989 the number of U.S. Big-Three dealers declined from 23,000 to 20,000. In 1989 GM had 9,450 dealers, Ford had 5,430, and Chrysler had 5,300. In contrast, all other manufacturers with sales in the United States had a combined total of only 4,900 dealers.[16] Dealers have also attempted to combat their lower margins and slowing sales by increasing the sales of used cars, which now account for 20 percent of the dealers' total sales.

Although the number of Big-Three dealers has declined, the three major Japanese producers are expanding their dealer networks. All have established separate dealerships to sell their upscale luxury models. When Honda's Acura was introduced in 1986, there were only 60 U.S. dealers, each selling only two basic models, the $11,000 Integra and the $20,000 Legend. By the end of 1988, Honda had almost 300 Acura dealers who together sold 128,000 cars during the year. Half of these upscale Japanese dealerships in the United States are unprofitable as a result of high dealer startup costs and a lack of service business.[17]

AUTO PRODUCTION IN THE UNITED STATES

Although auto production in the United States is still dominated by the Big Three, the Japanese are expected to have the capacity to produce 2 million units annually in North America by the early 1990s (see Exhibit 5). Further, in addition to the outright ownership of a plant by a single company there are a number of production strategies which have begun to blur the distinctions among firms. Captives, transplants, and imports have all clogged the market and have possibly set the stage for the world car.

The Big Three

Ford's Escort, which had held the number one spot in the United States in both 1987 and 1988, and has been the largest-selling car in the world in much of the late 1980s, has lost its market appeal because of an aging design. Ford will be introducing a redesigned Escort in early 1990 at a cost of more than $2 billion. However, Ford's limited production capacity will make it difficult for the firm to increase its overall market share. Beginning in 1984 Ford put its workers on overtime rather than increasing plant capacity to meet the rising demand for the Escort. As a result of this approach Ford leads its competition in plant utilization and has the highest productivity and profit per car among the Big Three. Ford's share of the U.S. truck market of just under 30 percent exceeds its auto market share.

Although Chrysler has steadily recovered from its near bankruptcy in the late 1970s and raised its market share from a low of 7 percent in 1980, the company still faces numerous difficulties. It lacks the diversification into nonauto businesses and

EXHIBIT 5 North American Automotive Assembly Facilities of Foreign Firms

Company	Location	Date Open	Unit Capacity	Comments
Mitsubishi	Illinois	1988	120,000[a]	Diamond-Star Motors is a joint venture with Chrysler (which owns 12 percent of Mitsubishi)
		1991	240,000[a]	Planned expansion of Diamond-Star
Mazda	Michigan	1987	200,000[a]	Joint venture with Ford (which owns 24 percent of Mazda)
		1992	360,000[a]	Planned expansion of joint venture
Toyota	California	1984	200,000[a]	NUMMI plant is a joint venture with General Motors
		1991	300,000[a]	Planned expansion of joint venture
	Kentucky	1988	200,000	
	Ontario	1988	50,000	
Nissan	Tennessee	1983	220,000	
		1992	440,000	Planned expansion of above
	Mexico	1966	120,000	
		1993	200,000	Planned expansion of above
	Ohio	1992	100,000[a]	Joint venture with Ford to build minivans
Honda	Ohio	1982	360,000	
	Ontario	1986	50,000	
		1990	80,000	Planned expansion of above
	Ohio	1989	150,000	
Suzuki	Ontario	1989	200,000[a]	Joint venture with GM (which owns 5 percent of Suzuki)
Fuji-Isuzu	Indiana	1989	120,000[a]	Joint venture of Fuji and Isuzu
		1993	240,000[a]	Planned expansion of joint venture
Hyundai	Quebec	1991	100,000	

[a]All joint venture facilities split 50-50 with partners noted.

Note: Planned expansion capacity figures represent *total* capacity after expansion.

Sources: L. Chappell, ``Big 3, Transplant 7,'' *Automotive News*, November 29, 1989, pp. 190–192; ``Autos-Auto Parts,'' *Standard & Poor's Industry Surveys*, May 12, 1988, p. A62, and November 30, 1989, pp. A87–89; J. Treece and J. Hoerr, ``Shaking Up Detroit,'' *Business Week*, August 14, 1989, pp. 74–80.

penetration into European markets needed to counter the U.S. auto cycle. Chrysler's acquisition of American Motors in 1987 removed the last remaining domestic firm, gave Chrysler added strength in the utility vehicle market with the Jeep line, and increased the firm's dealer network. However, although Chrysler has six different lines of cars, only one fewer than GM, it still lacks a strong mid-sized entry and a full-sized pickup truck. Further, many of its cars lack a distinct image and the cost of differentiating and updating them puts a good deal of strain on Chrysler's limited resources. Chrysler's strength is in its highly profitable Jeep vehicles and minivans. Although the firm now commands over 50 percent of the minivan market, which has grown to 800,000 units per year, competition is intensifying. This rising competition, coupled with aging capacity and the need to support its broad product line, has dramatically reduced Chrysler's profit per unit in recent years.[18]

General Motors' market share continues to decline, although truck sales are relatively stable at about 30 percent. By the end of the 1980s GM's auto share was 10 points below that in 1980. In a 1989 survey by J. D. Power and Associates, GM owners were the least likely to recommend their cars to others.[19] Criticisms include a lack of competitive designs and features, such as sophisticated engines and transmissions, a tendency to load many of its models with too many options, raising prices above those of rivals, and a lack of distinctive styling. GM's performance difficulties may have their source in a number of differences between the firm and its rivals. GM has the broadest product line and is the most integrated of the Big Three, making 70 percent of its own parts. This gives the firm an enormous investment in parts production facilities which is difficult to reduce. Once a source of competitive advantage, this high level of integration has limited GM's flexibility in the increasingly dynamic auto environment. It has also reduced profits by exposing the firm to higher labor costs than those experienced by Ford, Chrysler, and the Japanese who can more easily control costs though outside purchase agreements. GM's huge bureaucracy may also contribute to its difficulties; the firm has 22 layers of management between the CEO and the production worker, compared to 7 for Toyota.[20]

However, GM has set major goals to overcome its difficulties. Its primary goals are to raise its market share and profitability, to become the low-cost domestic producer, and to increase factory utilization to 100 percent by 1992 (now at 75 to 80 percent). During the 1980s GM has spent $70 billion worldwide to improve its facilities. Nine new assembly plants have been built and 31 other plants modernized. During the last two model years of the 1980s GM introduced more new or restyled products than in any other two-year period in the firm's history (17 new and 14 redesigned vehicles). In the 1990 model year GM introduced as many new model cars as Ford, Chrysler, Toyota, and Honda combined.[21]

GM's Saturn project is expected to begin production in mid-1990, eight years after conception. At that time Saturn was envisioned as the future model for automotive vehicle production and sales using the most modern robotic technology available to produce 500,000 subcompact cars per year. It has since been scaled down to produce 240,000 compact cars and will incorporate a blend of new technology and a team approach to production. The cars will compete with the Honda Civic and the Toyota Corolla models in both size and price.[22]

To improve their competitive positions, insulate themselves from the U.S. auto cycle, create synergies to improve auto productivity, and to provide growth opportunities, all of the Big Three firms have made numerous acquisitions. Chrysler purchased Electrospace Systems in 1987 to add to its existing Gulfstream Aerospace Division, but then reconsidered and sold the entire aerospace division in 1989 to concentrate on its auto and related financial-services businesses. Ford's nonauto businesses include Ford Aerospace and tractors and implements. GM has made several significant acquisitions in recent years including Hughes Aircraft, Electronic Data Systems, significant interests in the home-mortgage market to augment its financial-services division, and a joint venture to become the largest manufacturer of industrial robots in the United States.

Japanese Firms

Perhaps the two most critical factors affecting all Japanese auto producers wishing to supply the U.S. market are the voluntary import restrictions and the strength of the yen relative to the U.S. dollar. In 1981 the Japanese government voluntarily imposed quotas on the export of Japanese-made cars to the United States in an effort to avoid potentially more restrictive trade barriers being established by the U.S. government. These voluntary quotas, now set at 2.3 million units annually, have been responsible for several changes in strategy by Japanese firms.

Imports of light trucks are not subject to the quota, although they are subject to a duty of 25 percent, and this has been responsible for the development of the minitruck market. Japanese firms have also entered joint ventures and built plants in the United States to avoid the quotas and deal with the changing value of the yen. The primary factors which led to the establishment of the import quota were the rising trade deficit with Japan because of the strong dollar in 1980, and the increasing market share of the imports. The trend toward a rise in onshore production in the United States has been increasingly supported, however, by other economic factors including weakness in the dollar and the rising cost of labor in Japan. By 1988 the average manufacturing wage in Japan was the equivalent of $12.06 per hour, compared to $10 in the United States.[23]

Perhaps the single most important factor affecting the behavior of Japanese auto firms since 1985 has been the changing relationship between the yen and the dollar. (See Exhibit 6 for the trend in the dollar–yen exchange rate.) At the beginning of fiscal 1986 (March) one dollar would buy 250 yen. By the end of Honda's fiscal 1988, one dollar would by only 125 yen. Thus, a car costing the equivalent of $5,000 to manufacture in Japan in 1985, would have had an equivalent cost of ¥1,250,000 ($5,000 × 250). By 1988, assuming the yen cost of

EXHIBIT 6   Dollar–Yen Exchange Rates

	Number of Yen Purchased by $1	
	Fiscal Year End	**Average**
1989	132.7	129.1
1988	124.7	137.7
1987	153.3	161.3
1986	180.6	223.5
1985	259.5	242.7
1984	233.5	237.1
1983	237.5	250.7

Source: *Annual Reports*, Honda Motor Company, various years.

the car in Japan did not change, the U.S. equivalent cost would have risen to $10,000 (¥1,250,000 ÷ 125). It may be noted that at 125 yen to the dollar, it is estimated that it is now less costly to manufacture a typical car in the United States than it is to build a similar car in Japan.[24] Thus, to cover their equivalent costs, the Japanese manufacturers should have raised prices on their exports as much as 100 percent. Instead, they only raised their prices about 30 percent. This should have caused U.S. cars to be more competitive. However, Detroit used this opportunity to raise its own prices about 12 percent during the 1985 to 1987 period, thus reducing their potential gain in relative prices.[25]

Because competitive pressure did not permit Japanese exporters to raise prices as much as they would have liked, their profits eroded. However, the Japanese have employed several strategies to improve the situation. First, they have found ways to further reduce production costs. The U.S. dealers of these exporters have absorbed some of the price differences through reduced margins. In addition, by building U.S. facilities and reducing dependence on imported parts (Honda cars built in the United States will have 75 percent domestic parts in 1991) Japanese producers have reduced effective cost increases to the domestic inflation rate. Further, by convention, plastics and oil imported by Japan are priced in U.S. dollars, thus lowering the yen equivalent cost of these inputs.

Captives, Transplants, and Imports

The definitions of an American car and an American carmaker are not as clear as they once were. Japanese car companies operate in the United States, building cars with U.S. parts and labor. U.S. companies have cars with their nameplates built for them in foreign plants, with foreign parts and labor. These latter cars are called *captives*. Examples of some of these captives are listed in the table below.[26]

Car Model	Manufacturer
Geo Metro (formerly Chevy Sprint)	Suzuki (Japan)
Geo Spectrum (formerly Chevy Spectrum)	Isuzu (Japan)
Geo Tracker	Suzuki
Pontiac LeMans	Daewoo (Korea)
Ford Festiva	Kia (Korea)
Dodge/Plymouth Colt and Vista	Mitsubishi (Japan)
Chrysler Conquest/Eagle Summit	Mitsubishi
Eagle Medallion	Renault (France)

In contrast, *captive transplants* are Big-Three cars made in the United States through joint venture arrangements. Examples include Geo Prizm (formerly Chevy Nova) made in the NUMMI plant, a joint venture with GM and Toyota; Ford Probe, produced in the Mazda–Ford joint venture plant in Michigan; and the Plymouth Laser made in Illinois in Chrysler's joint venture plant with Mitsubishi.

By the end of the 1980s, the Big Three had slightly less than 300,000 units of captive transplant capacity. This will grow to 500,000 in the early 1990s. However, when the GM/Toyota joint venture ends in 1996, GM may lose its NUMMI capacity as Toyota has an option on the plant.[27]

Agreements between the Big Three and other firms are not limited to manufacturing, however. Design and engineering is more frequently a joint arrangement as well, as are the development and production of parts. Ford's hope of the 1990s, the redesigned Escort, was largely designed by Mazda, for example. Corvette's transmission is built by ZF, a West German firm; the engine of the Taurus SHO was designed and is produced by Yamaha. Nor are all joint ventures of the Big Three aimed at U.S. cars. Chrysler will make minivans in France with Renault, for example. Ford will expand one of its U.S. plants to make Jeep-type utility vehicles for Mazda and minivans for Nissan. Chrysler markets the Mitsubishi Eclipse and Fiat's Alfa Romeo through its dealers. Mazda dealers in Japan are marketing Ford's Taurus and Probe models. As of 1990 there were 300 joint relationships among automotive firms throughout the world.[28]

Transplants also include vehicles manufactured by foreign firms for their own nameplates in the United States. In 1989 the Japanese had 1.3 million units of capacity in the United States. By the early 1990s this is expected to rise to nearly 2 million units as shown in Exhibit 5. While the Japanese opened five new plants in the United States from 1987 to 1989, the Big Three closed five plants. Three more assembly plants are expected to be closed by the Big Three in 1990. Altogether, Japanese transplants and imports accounted for about 25 percent of all U.S. auto sales in the late 1980s.

Quality and Productivity

A critical factor which enabled the Japanese to penetrate the U.S. auto market in the late 1970s and 1980s was the quality gap between U.S. and Japanese manufacturers. As may be seen below, this gap has narrowed significantly in the last decade.[29]

Defects per Car Produced:

	1980	**1989**
Chrysler	8.1	1.8
General Motors	7.4	1.7
Ford	6.7	1.5
Japanese	2.0	1.2

In spite of tremendous quality improvements, however, the gap between the Big Three and the Japanese big three remains significant. Of the 31 best-rated 1989 car models according to *Consumer Reports* (April 1990), 28 were Japanese cars; of the 33 worst-rated, 32 were U.S. Big-Three models. *The Wall Street Journal* converted the *Consumer Reports* ratings into a grade point average with the report card shown below.[30]

	Grade for Each Model					
	A	B	C	D	F	Gradepoint
Honda	5	1	0	0	0	3.83
Toyota	6	4	2	0	0	3.33
Nissan	1	2	2	0	0	2.80
Chrysler	0	2	13	7	8	1.30
Ford	0	1	10	7	8	1.15
General Motors	0	1	9	9	21	0.75

The trend in productivity is much the same as the quality trend. The Japanese are the most productive automakers in the world, although the Big Three are improving. The Japanese require an average of 19 man-hours to assemble a car, compared to 36 man-hours for the average European carmaker. Of the Big Three, Ford is the most efficient. To build a car, GM requires 5 workers, per day, per car; Chrysler requires 4.4; Ford, 3.4; and the Japanese, 3.0. The table below compares productivity levels for 12 major car producers.[31]

Manufacturer	1988 Cars/Worker	Manufacturer	1988 Cars/Worker
Suzuki	70.4	Ford	20.0
Toyota	61.0	Chrysler	18.0
Honda	56.2	Peugeot	13.3
Mitsubishi	50.4	General Motors	12.5
Mazda	42.0	VW	11.2
Nissan	39.5	Fiat	10.1

Parts Production

The output of auto parts and accessories manufacturers peaked in 1978 and was 15 percent below that level in constant dollars in 1988. This drop in output is explained largely by the drop in U.S. production and the fact most imports do not contain many U.S. parts. Even the Japanese transplants still import a large proportion of their parts from Japan. Future prospects for the parts industry are not bright even though the percentage of U.S. parts in Japanese cars is increasing. The average domestic (U.S.) content for transplants is 38 percent, versus 88 percent for the Big Three. Many Japanese firms claim a higher percentage content, but this is

EXHIBIT 7 Honda Production Capacity Utilization in Japan (rated capacity, 000 units)

	1985	**1987**	**1988**	**1989**
Motorcycles				
Capacity	3,559	2,909	2,269	1,176
Utilization	70%	80%	70%	114%
Power products				
Capacity	2,304	1,952	1,964	1,968
Utilization	93%	72%	70%	74%
Automobiles				
Capacity	1,079	1,123	1,240	1,308
Utilization	88%	96%	106%	104%

Source: *Annual Reports.*

the result of a content formula which includes advertising and overhead, not just parts.[32] Nevertheless Japanese firms are increasing the plant capacity of their own parts firms in the United States. Honda, for example, intends to produce 500,000 engines in the United States by 1990. [See Exhibit 7.] It is also estimated that by 1990, the Japanese will operate 300 parts firms in the United States, up from less than 100 in 1987.

One factor that may further hurt the U.S. auto parts industry is the enforcement of the CAFE (Corporate Average Fuel Economy) requirements. Separate CAFE calculations must be made for each of two car categories and both must meet the 27.5 miles-per-gallon requirement in 1990. The distinction between categories is whether a car has above or below 75 percent U.S. parts content. The problem facing both GM and Ford is that many of their fuel efficient small cars fall into the below-75-percent category. Ford has announced it will import a greater percentage of the parts for many of its large cars to reclassify them as below 75 percent. GM's response is more pro-U.S. content as it will increase the percentage of U.S. parts in its small-car production in its NUMMI plant.[33]

HONDA IN THE UNITED STATES

Honda is far more at home abroad.[34] Honda was the first Japanese firm to open an auto manufacturing facility in the United States and at the end of the 1980s had the largest U.S. auto capacity of any foreign firm. Before opening its Ohio facility, Honda flew 200 U.S. workers to its Sayana factory in Japan for up to three months where the American workers joined the Japanese assembly lines. Upon their return the workers were then able to instruct co-workers on Japanese assembly methods.[35] Honda's employees, who must go through three interviews before being hired, are called *associates.* The Ohio workers are given the responsibility for such tasks as inspecting their own work. The plant is essentially democratic, as managers wear the same uniforms as the workers, are on a first-name basis, and share parking and lunchroom facilities. There are no enclosed offices. Honda encourages its workers to form ad hoc groups of five to ten workers (called *New Honda Circles*) who voluntarily work together on an area of common concern such as safety, quality, or production efficiency improvements. Such efforts can earn the workers free cars or trips to Japan for their ideas. Approximately 25 percent of the Ohio workers belong to such groups.

As Honda's methods have met with success in Ohio, the company has increased wages and the number of paid holidays. Attendance bonuses and profit sharing have also been added. The environment encourages management and labor to work together, pursuing a common goal of making quality products economically. Throughout the world, Honda employs more than 71,000 employees, including 19,000 Japanese working abroad. About 90 percent of all nonmanagement employees are members of the Federation of All Honda Workers Union (AHWA), affiliated with the Japanese Council of the International Metalworkers Federation. Basic wages are negotiated annually with the union. Wage increases in fiscal years 1985 to 1989 were 5.9 percent, 5.1 percent, 3.6 percent, 4.6 percent, and 5.4 percent, respectively. Each employee is paid a semiannual bonus, a Japanese custom, which is negotiated separately from wages. Every two years the firm negotiates working conditions with the union.

Only three of the seven Japanese assembly plants in the United States are unionized (United Auto Workers), those which are joint ventures with the Big Three: Toyota's NUMMI plant, Mazda's Michigan plant, and Mitsubishi's Illinois plant. Nissan workers in its solely owned Tennessee facility defeated the union (70 percent against) in mid-1989 and Toyota's new Kentucky plant is also nonunion. However, the nonunion plants pay almost the same wages and benefits as UAW-organized facilities in the United States. While the UAW seems to be establishing wage standards, the Japanese transplants which are unionized have negotiated less restrictive work rules and greater employee involvement in decision making. Many of the Japanese labor practices have been transplanted to the United States: no layoff policies, continual training programs for workers, participation in decision making, team-based production, and profit sharing. As a result of the desire to apply similar work methods in the United States, the Japanese have utilized different hiring criteria. They have mostly hired young, inexperienced workers who have expressed a willingness to work in a team-oriented environment. Their choice of plant locations, in most cases, has also resulted in their hiring a lower percentage of racial minorities than their Big-Three counterparts have. Such practices have provided the transplants with lower health care costs and lower pension liabilities.[36]

Honda Operations

Honda's business consists of four operating segments, as shown in Exhibit 8: automotive vehicles, motorcycles, power products, and parts/other. In addition to its four major sources of revenue-generating activities, Honda manufactures many of the main components and parts used in its products, including engines, frames, and transmissions. Raw materials and other components are purchased from numerous suppliers. Steel plate accounts for about 50 percent of Honda's raw material purchases; other materials include aluminum, glass, plastic, zinc, paint,

EXHIBIT 8   Honda Sales by Business Segment (000 units, revenue in ¥ billions)

	For Fiscal Years Ended[a]				
	1985	**1986**	**1987**	**1988**	**1989**
Automotive Segment					
Total unit sales	1,252	1,368	1,585	1,871	1,903
Japanese unit sales	387	474	518	617	628
Total sales revenue	1,620	1,842	2,011	2,394	2,459
Japanese sales revenue	N/A	500	557	736	780
Motorcycle Segment					
Total unit sales	2,954	3,078	2,615	3,043	3,032
Japanese unit sales	1,006	987	803	943	924
Total sales revenue	423	413	330	379	353
Japanese sales revenue	N/A	129	131	160	157
Power Products Segment					
Total unit sales	1,722	1,815	1,625	1,708	1,543
Japanese unit sales	163	172	207	156	116
Total sales revenue	235	250	164	154	103
Japanese sales revenue	N/A	12	14	12	11
Parts and Other					
Total sales revenue	374	405	454	572	571
Japanese sales revenue	N/A	204	258	346	346
Total company revenue by region:					
Japan	704	845	960	1,254	1,294
North America	1,485	1,604	1,522	1,646	1,585
Europe	247	263	310	403	372
Other	216	198	169	196	238
Total	2,652	2,910	2,961	3,499	3,489
Operating income	299	306	170	177	177
Net income	129	147	84	108	97

[a]Fiscal years 1985 to 1987 ended on February 28, and 1988 to 1989 ended on March 31; 1988 results include 13 months of activity.
Source: *Annual Reports,* Honda Motor Company, various years.

and special steels. No single source accounts for more than 5 percent of these outside purchases. Neither is Honda dependent on any one source for an essential component with the exception of ignition switches and clutches.

Honda has two wholly owned, consolidated subsidiaries specializing in R&D and in the design and manufacture of production machinery. Honda R&D employs approximately 7,600 people and is provided with funds amounting to about 5 percent of annual sales targets. Honda Engineering Company employs 2,400 people. Overall, Honda employs 50 percent more engineers per car produced than does GM.[37] The firm is increasing the amount of product design and factory engineering done in its U.S. plants and has restructured its R&D unit to incorporate both its U.S. and European R&D operations.

Though Honda's cars are not always perfect when introduced, the firm is very quick to respond to dealer and customer feedback. For example, in 1982 the first Prelude model had so little power that many consumers referred to it as the "Quaalude."[38] However, by 1983 the car had been redesigned. Honda continually makes technical improvements in its cars, whether or not consumers can actually notice the difference. The Japanese firms, on average, require about 3 years to develop, design, engineer, and manufacture a new model vehicle. In comparison, the Big Three require 5 years and the Europeans over 5 years. Honda, the fastest of all automakers, is attempting to reduce this time to two years.[39] Honda has recently developed a small, 4-cylinder engine that produces 10 to 15 percent more power than the 6-cylinder engines made by the Big Three. Now in cars sold in Japan, the engine will soon be available in the United States and should help boost Honda's average fuel economy in the future.[40]

Automotive Segment   Honda produces a fairly broad range of auto models for both its domestic and overseas markets. Honda's current automobile models are described in Exhibit 9. These products are produced in two locations in Japan; the United States; the United Kingdom (with Rover by 1989); Ontario, Canada; and New Zealand. Their vehicles are distributed in Japan through three dealer networks consisting of 2,400 total dealerships. In Europe wholly owned subsidiaries distribute autos through Honda's 1,500 dealers (down from 2,200 in 1985). The United States has 1,200 Honda dealers (up from 850 in 1985). A separate network of nearly 300 dealerships distributes the Acura in the United States. Some Honda Civic and Accord models are shipped unassembled to various parts of southern Asia and the Pacific Rim for assembly and sale in various smaller markets.

In 1989 the Accord was the top-selling U.S. car. It accounts for nearly half of Honda's sales in the United States and has had a record of seven straight years of sales growth since its introduction in 1982. Scott Whitlock, executive vice

EXHIBIT 9   1989 Honda Vehicle Models

Model Name	Type of Car	Engine Size (cc)
Civic	Subcompact	1300, 1500, 1600
Accord (Vigor)	Compact	1800, 2000
Prelude	Subcompact sports car	2000
City (Japan only)	Subcompact	1300
Acura Legend	Intermediate	2000, 2700
Acura Integra (Quint)	Subcompact	1600, 1800
Concerto (Japan only)	Subcompact	1500, 1600
Acty (Japan only)	Minitruck	N/A
	Minivan	N/A
Today (Japan only)	Minicar	550

Note: Names in parentheses are comparable Japanese models.
Source: *Annual Reports.*

president of Honda of America Mfg., Inc. believes "This is the car that's going to support us and satisfy our customers for the next four years."[41] What Mr. Whitlock was referring to was the *new* Accord. With the 1990 model year, Accord entered the mid-sized market to compete with such entries as Ford's Taurus and Sable, Toyota's Camry, and Nissan's Stanza. The new Accord will also be available in a station wagon by fall 1990. Although Honda is developing an NSX model for its Acura line, with a planned price range of $50,000 plus, Honda's product line lacks trucks, minivans, and a 4-wheel drive sport vehicle.[42]

Motorcycles   Based on unit production, Honda is the world's largest manufacturer of motorcycles. Honda currently manufactures over 100 different models for the Japanese market and over 140 models for markets outside Japan. These range from 50 cc motorbikes and scooters to 1,500 cc, 4-cylinder motorcycles. The Ohio facility produces the Gold Wing motorcycle, a luxury model selling for around $10,000, which is exported to 15 countries, including Japan. Honda's motorcycles are also produced in three different locations in Japan, as well as in Belgium, Italy, Brazil, and Mexico. In the United States, the largest market for the firm's motorcycles, Honda has 1,400 independent dealers (down from 1,750 in 1985). In Europe the sales network includes 3,200 dealers (down from 4,300 in 1985). Many Honda dealers in the United States also carry Honda's power products, while in Europe many motorcycle dealers also carry both the power products and the firm's automobiles.

Demand for motorcycles in Japan plummeted in 1986 to 1987 when a new law requiring helmets to be worn resulted in negative consumer response. Sales have since rebounded somewhat. The number of motorcycles registered in the United States has dropped steadily since 1981, though sales of new motorcycles peaked in 1984 at 1.3 million units (all manufacturers). Several factors have contributed to this decline. Gasoline prices declined in the early 1980s after the 1979 oil crisis; the health and fitness trend favors walking or bicycling for short-distance travel needs; motorcycle insurance rates have increased as a result of safety concerns (several insurance firms will no longer insure "superbikes"); and almost all states now require helmets. Honda, Kawasaki, and Harley-Davidson are the major U.S. motorcycle manufacturers. Of these three, Harley-Davidson, a U.S.-owned firm, is the only one to have increased sales since 1984. Honda's share in the U.S. market is now around 30 percent, well below its one-time high of 58 percent.[43]

Power Products and Other   Honda produces a variety of power products including portable generators, small agricultural machines, general-purpose engines, outdoor motors, water pumps, snow throwers, lawn and riding mowers, and all-terrain vehicles (ATVs). Production facilities for these products are located in Japan, the United States (North Carolina), the United Kingdom, and France. These products are distributed through 4,000 dealers in Japan, 2,600 in the United States (down from 2,800 in 1985), and 3,000 in Europe (down from 4,300 in 1985). ATV sales plummeted in the late 1980s as a result of major safety concerns. Three-wheel vehicles have been demonstrated to be unstable when making rapid turns.

Young riders (under 16 years of age), often users of these ATVs, are by-and-large untrained in their safe use. These concerns have resulted in litigation, legislation, and mutual agreements with manufacturers to provide free training courses and to cease production of the three-wheel vehicles. Manufacturers may also be required to refund the purchase price to all such vehicle owners.

Parts sales are derived primarily from sales of Honda Motor Parts Service Company and Honda International Sales Corporation which trades in used automobiles acquired from Honda dealers. Parts sales have been increasing recently due mainly to a favorable used car market in Japan.

Honda Strategy

In 1985 Honda's stated direction for its motorcycle and auto segments was to move toward the development of unique products that are of high quality, have high performance, and are fuel efficient. In addition Honda stated a desire to improve the design and operation of its factories and reduce costs to improve their competitiveness. Honda's automotive vehicle strategy has historically been to offer products with more and better features than those of competitors with similar models. The firm now desires to redirect its automotive product emphasis to more expensive product lines where price is less important to the consumer; to move away from the low-price, entry-level, subcompact car segment; and to expand overseas (outside Japan) production facilities.

In a speech on September 17, 1987, Mr. Tetsuo Chino, Head of North American Operations for Honda, announced a five-part strategy for Honda in America.[44]

> One: Expansion of U.S. parts sourcing
> Two: Expansion of research and development in the United States
> Three: Expansion of production engineering in the United States
> Four: A major commitment to export U.S.-made Honda products
> Five: Further expansion of U.S. manufacturing facilities

On the same day, Mr. Kume announced that by December 1987, a new model of the Accord, to be produced only in the United States, would be exported to Japan. The first shipment of 540 cars arrived in Japan in March 1988. By 1991 Honda intends to export 70,000 of the new, redesigned Accord all over the world. Honda also plans to export U.S.-made cars to South Korea to circumvent South Korean import barriers with the Japanese. The expected exports of 2,000 Accord sedans by 1991 will be sold through South Korea's largest motorcycle manufacturer.[45]

Honda's joint venture with another automaker, Rover, may also help ease their entry into Europe. The car produced by this venture, the Sterling, is also exported to the United States where it competes in the low-end luxury category. In late 1989 Honda announced its sales goals for the first half of the next decade. The firm intends to increase car sales in the United States to 1 million units a year and worldwide sales to 2.5 million units annually.[46] Honda also intends to expand its dealer networks in the United States and has also established experimental

EXHIBIT 10   Honda Capital Expenditures (for fiscal years, ¥ billions)[a]

	1985	1986	1987	1988	1989
Total capital expenditures	137.0	267.0	224.0	187.0	279.0
Percentage allocation					
Automotive	44.9%	56.4%	61.0%	56.5%	67.9%
Motorcycle	11.4	9.5	6.1	5.3	5.5
Power products	3.9	1.0	0.9	1.5	0.9
Sales, other	39.8	32.9	32.0	36.7	25.7
Resources supplied by operations	223.0	268.0	219.0	244.0	195.0

[a]Fiscal years 1985 to 1987 ended on February 28, and 1988 to 1989 ended on March 31.
Source: *Annual Reports,* Honda Motor Company, various years.

EXHIBIT 11   Consolidated Income Statements Honda Motor Company (for fiscal years, ¥ billions except per-share amounts)

	1985	1986	1987	1988	1989
Net sales	2,652.2	2,909.6	2,961.0	3,498.5	3,489.3
Cost of sales	1,736.3	1,917.4	2,110.6	2,547.4	2,544.2
Gross profit	915.9	992.2	850.4	951.1	945.1
Operating expenses					
R&D	109.9	131.8	149.6	177.9	183.7
Advertising	73.0	84.2	86.3	85.7	81.8
Depreciation	94.3	121.5	120.7	142.7	130.9
Other, selling, general, and administrative expenses	339.9	349.2	316.4	368.2	371.6
Operating income	298.8	305.5	177.4	176.6	177.1
Interest expenses, net	22.0	9.2	15.6	10.9	11.7
Other expenses/(income), net	4.1	(5.8)	(8.4)	(28.9)	(6.7)
Earnings before tax	272.7	302.1	170.2	194.6	172.1
Income tax	142.9	158.9	89.1	91.0	80.6
Income before EINSA[b]	129.8	143.2	81.1	103.6	91.5
Plus: EINSA	(1.3)	3.3	2.6	3.9	5.8
Net income	128.5	146.5	83.7	107.5	97.3
Dividends	9.7	10.7	10.8	12.0	11.3
EPS	138.71	149.14	85.47	106.75	98.48

[a]Fiscal years 1985 to 1987 ended on February 28, and 1988 to 1989 ended on March 31; 1988 includes 13 months of activity.
[b]EINSA is equity in income of nonconsolidated subsidiaries and affiliates.
It should be noted that Honda is the only Japanese automaker whose stock is listed on the NYSE. Each American share, as evidenced by American Depository Receipts (ADRs), represents 10 shares of the actual Japanese-issued stock. As of March 31, 1989, total issued common shares were 947,994,295, of which 14,318,082 were in the form of ADRs.
Source: *Annual Reports,* Honda Motor Company, various years.

EXHIBIT 12 Consolidated Balance Sheets Honda Motor Company (for fiscal years, ¥ billions)

	1985	1986	1987	1988	1989
Assets					
Cash and equivalents	140.0	118.9	214.5	246.4	247.3
Accounts receivable	132.1	126.5	255.5	330.2	402.1
Inventory	412.4	441.0	428.0	416.9	475.2
Other current assets	133.9	155.3	117.5	138.3	144.6
Total current assets	818.4	841.7	1,015.5	1,131.8	1,269.2
Investments and other assets	211.0	194.0	126.6	114.4	149.1
Fixed assets					
Land	147.4	158.4	169.5	181.4	198.0
Buildings	227.6	298.3	342.7	358.9	411.9
Equipment	515.9	619.4	768.8	816.7	935.6
Construction	51.6	45.4	28.2	44.5	91.9
Less accumulated depreciation	(422.0)	(481.8)	(585.7)	(671.1)	(771.3)
Net fixed assets	520.5	639.7	723.5	730.4	866.1
Total assets	1,549.9	1,675.4	1,865.6	1,976.6	2,284.4
Liabilities and Equity					
Notes payable	122.4	92.4	246.1	265.1	356.1
Accounts payable	324.4	406.9	386.1	436.9	389.1
Accrued expenses	148.4	155.2	172.7	222.8	272.2
Taxes payable	23.6	15.1	39.0	37.4	30.0
Total current liabilities	618.8	669.6	843.9	962.2	1,047.4
Long-term debt	181.9	213.1	240.0	205.3	301.6
Other long-term liabilities	21.1	31.2	28.7	29.4	34.0
Total liabilities	821.8	913.9	1,112.6	1,196.9	1,383.0
Equity					
Common stock	54.6	55.8	57.8	63.3	68.9
Capital surplus	110.8	116.8	127.7	132.7	155.8
Retained earnings	545.1	679.8	751.7	851.8	936.5
Legal reserve[b]	11.6	12.7	13.7	15.2	16.5
Adjustments[b]	6.0	(103.6)	(197.9)	(283.3)	(276.3)
Total equity	728.1	761.5	753.0	779.7	901.4
Total liabilities and equity	1,549.9	1,675.4	1,865.6	1,976.6	2,284.4

[a]Fiscal years 1985 to 1987 ended on February 28, and 1988 to 1989 ended on March 31.
[b]Japanese legal reserve is related to dividend payments. Currency translation adjustments for the balance sheet are accumulated in shareholders' equity.
Source: *Annual Reports*, Honda Motor Company, various years.

consumer finance operations in California and Florida so that it can compete with other U.S. manufacturers offering financial incentives.

Minor Stress at Honda

With the rapid growth and success that Honda has enjoyed during the 1980s comes the inevitable strain on human and financial resources. In support of its objectives and strategic directions Honda expended nearly 1 trillion yen in new capital expenditures from fiscal 1986 through fiscal 1989. A breakdown of these expenditures appears in Exhibit 10. As a result of heavy capital expenditures and reduced net income, Honda's 1989 fiscal year internal cash flow fell short of capital expenditures by a substantial margin and the firm's long-term debt increased to the highest levels ever. The firm's net income has declined dramatically since fiscal 1986, when the dollar began weakening, in spite of increased sales revenue (refer to Exhibit 11). With continued growth in its asset base and equity, the lower net income results in considerably lower return measures for the firm's financial investors (see Exhibit 12).

Growth has also slowed down the speed of decision making. Honda has been working to solve this difficulty by decentralizing its traditional Japan-based R&D unit to increase flexibility. The firm may have made a few errors in marketing, as well. Honda's strategy of emphasizing numerous features and high-margin cars may have resulted in a 1989 model Prelude that included many expensive features that customers didn't particularly want, features that the lower-priced Accord also had, but at thousands of dollars less! In April 1989 Honda was forced to offer dealer incentives on Accords for the first time ever. As a result, their advertising budget has been increased by 25 percent for 1990.

Though Honda installed brand new machinery in the Marysville plant for the redesigned Accord without shutting down for a single day, not everything has gone smoothly. The manager of the new East Liberty, Ohio assembly plant had to borrow workers from the Marysville plant to meet the deadline for its Civic production. Some Civic transmission production had to be transferred to the North Carolina lawnmower plant. Finally, when the Marysville plant began getting ready for the introduction of the redesigned Accord, the workers at East Liberty had to return to Marysville.[47]

As Honda attempts to broaden their product offerings, increase their dealer networks, and expand capacity on three continents, they will be competing head-to-head with larger automakers. Will their strengths, which were the basis for its phenomenal success in the 1980s, be able to carry them forward to even greater heights of achievement in the 1990s?

Endnotes

1. A. Taylor III, "Japan's Carmakers Take on the World," *Fortune*, June 20, 1988, p. 76.
2. S. Toy, N. Gross, and J. Treece, "The Americanization of Honda," *Business Week*, April 25, 1988, p. 91.
3. Based on data presented in A. Taylor III, "Who's Ahead in the World Auto War?" *Fortune*, November 9, 1987, p. 74.
4. S. Tully, "Now Japan's Autos Push into Europe," *Fortune*, January 29, 1990, p. 96.
5. M. Keller, "Facing a United European Automotive Front," *Automotive Industries*, August 1988, p. 8.
6. Tully, "Japan's Autos," p. 97; and J. Lublin, "Honda Rules Out Full Acquisition of U.K. Car Maker," *The Wall Street Journal*, October 5, 1989.
7. Tully, "Japan's Autos," p. 100; and J. Kapstein and J. Hoerr, "Volvo's Radical New Plant," *Business Week*, August 28, 1989, pp. 92–93.
8. Taylor, "Japan's Carmakers," pp. 72–73.
9. A. Borrus, J. Treece, and L. Armstrong, "Not All Japanese Carmakers Are Powerhouses," *Business Week*, February 19, 1990, pp. 46–47; and P. Ingrassia and K. Graven, "Squeeze Ahead," *The Wall Street Journal*, April 24, 1990, pp. A1, A11.
10. *Annual Report*, Honda Motor Company Ltd., 1987.
11. A. Taylor III, "Can American Cars Come Back?" *Fortune*, February 26, 1990, p. 64.
12. "The Top Ten: Now and Then." *Newsweek*, January 22, 1990, p. 42.
13. S. Weiner, "The Road Most Traveled," *Forbes*, October 19, 1987, pp. 60–64.
14. Taylor, "Can American Cars," p. 62.
15. A. Taylor III, "Luxury Cars," *Fortune*, April 10, 1989, pp. 66–74.
16. "Autos-Auto Parts," *Standard & Poor's Industry Surveys*, November 30, 1989, p. A80.
17. Taylor, "Luxury Cars," pp. 66–74; and J. White, "Honda, Trying to Outpace Its Rivals, Unveils New Acura Luxury Cars Today," *The Wall Street Journal*, May 4, 1989, p. B5.
18. M. Guiles, "Bumpy Road," *The Wall Street Journal*, November 29, 1989, pp. A1, A6.
19. P. Ingrassia and J. White, "Losing the Race," *The Wall Street Journal*, December 14, 1989, p. A10.
20. J. Treece, "Will GM Learn from Its Own Role Models?" *Business Week*, April 9, 1990, p. 62.
21. *Annual Reports*, General Motors Corporation, 1988, 1989.
22. J. Treece, "Here Comes GM's Saturn," *Business Week*, April 9, 1990, pp. 56–62.
23. B. Buell, "Why Japanese Workers Got Underwhelming Raises," *Business Week*, April 25, 1988, p. 82.
24. *1989 U.S. Industrial Outlook* (Washington, D.C.: U.S. Dept. of Commerce, 1989), p. 34-1.
25. Taylor, "Japan's Carmakers," p. 67.
26. M. Guiles, "GM Puts Captive Imports to New Test," *The Wall Street Journal*, September 16, 1988, p. B1.
27. R. Hof and J. Treece, "This Team Has It All—Except Sales," *Business Week*, August 14, 1989, p. 79.
28. F. Washington and D. Pauly, "Driving toward a World Car?" *Newsweek*, May 1, 1989, pp. 48–49.
29. "Japanese Cars: Born in the U.S.A.," *Newsweek*, April 9, 1990, p. 37.
30. B. Stertz, "Big Three Boost Car Quality but Still Lag," *The Wall Street Journal*, March 27, 1990, p. B1.
31. Tully, "Japan's Autos," p. 97; P. Ingrassia, "Losing Control," *The Wall Street Journal*, February 16, 1990, p. A6; and J. McElroy, "Worldwide Productivity Comparison," *Automotive Industries*, April 1989, p. 62.
32. J. Treece and J. Hoerr, "Shaking Up Detroit," *Business Week*, August 14, 1989, p. 78.
33. "Autos-Auto Parts," p. A85.
34. Toy et al., "Americanization of Honda," p. 93.
35. F. Rice, "America's New No. 4 Automaker—Honda," *Fortune*, October 28, 1985, p. 32.
36. Treece and Hoerr, "Shaking Up," pp. 74–80.
37. Taylor, "Japan's Carmakers," p. 88.
38. Rice, "New No. 4," p. 32.
39. Taylor, "Luxury Cars," p. 63; and "Autos-Auto Parts," p. A84.
40. Ingrassia, "Losing Control," p. A6.
41. J. White, "Honda Takes Aim at Detroit's Heart," *The Wall Street Journal*, September 18, 1989, p. B1.
42. Taylor, "Luxury Cars," p. 74.
43. *U.S. Industrial Outlook* (Washington, D.C.: U.S. Department of Commerce, various years).
44. Speeches by Mr. Tetsuo Chino and Mr. Tadashi Kume given in Columbus, Ohio, September 17, 1987; Text supplied by management.
45. M. Kanabayashi, "Honda's U.S. Unit to Export Cars to South Korea," *The Wall Street Journal*, June 15, 1988.
46. J. White and K. Graven, "Driving Ambition," *The Wall Street Journal*, October 9, 1989, p. A8.
47. Ibid., pp. A1, A8.

DCM-Toyota Ltd. of India

Madhav S. Shriram, Alan G. Robinson & Dean M. Schroeder

INTRODUCTION

In the five years since the start of the joint venture between DCM Limited of India and the Toyota Motor Company of Japan to produce light commercial vehicles (LCVs), a great deal of progress has been made. The DCM-Toyota Ltd. (DTL) plant in Surajpur is now building a world-class vehicle, one that Mr. Awasthi, the company's executive director, believes is by far the best of its kind manufactured in India. The DTL LCV, called the "Dyna," is equipped with an engine that is more powerful, rugged, and fuel-efficient than its competitors. It has a sturdy construction, and its plush interior and exterior finish are superior to those of most Indian-built cars. The Dyna embodies the latest in LCV technology from Japan; in fact, certain components have even been strengthened for the harsh Indian driving conditions. The DTL plant is modern, well-engineered and managed, and operates under the Toyota Production System. The employees are highly motivated, well-educated, and thoroughly trained. Even Toyota is impressed with the plant and with the high productivity of its Indian workers. And yet the company has been slow to make a profit. In fiscal 1988 DTL lost Rs57,133,420 on Rs904,902,313 in total sales.[1] The company's performance continues to improve, however; it reported a modest profit of Rs3 million in the first quarter of 1989. The strong yen and stiff competition have made things difficult for DTL. In 1984, when DTL was in the planning phase, the exchange rate was 21 yen to the rupee. In February 1989 the rupee bought only 8.25 yen. Critical LCV components imported from Japan now cost two and a half times more than planned. Three of DTL's competitors, which are also Indo-Japanese joint ventures, are suffering from the rapid rise in the yen, as well. Eicher-Mitsubishi, for example, experienced a production cost increase, attributable entirely to the stronger yen, of Rs24,000 per vehicle from May to November 1988.

BACKGROUND
DCM Ltd.

DCM Ltd. is the 14th-largest multiproduct manufacturing company in India. Its product line includes textiles, sugar, both industrial and potable alcohol, fertilizers, edible oils, business machines, cement, polyvinylchloride (PVC), and foundry products. In 1988 its sales were approximately 6.5 billion rupees and it employed 25,000 people.

DCM was founded in 1889 as Delhi Cloth Mills Ltd., largely through the efforts of Gopal Rai, the company's first secretary (i.e., top manager). The venture, which produced textiles, was so successful that it paid its first dividend to investors only six months later. When Gopal Rai's health failed in 1906, his younger brother, Madan Mohan Lal, took over as secretary. Shortly thereafter, the company began to falter, primarily because of the high prices it had to pay for raw cotton. The poor performance persisted until Shri Ram, son of Madan Mohan Lal, became actively involved in the company. It is Shri Ram who was the dominant figure in the growth of DCM into a successful conglomerate.

When he was in high school, Shri Ram got a job selling cloth as a shop assistant. Although it was then standard practice to stretch the cloth on the measuring table and shortchange customers by 2 inches per yard, Shri Ram gave his customers not only the full yard, but an extra 2 inches, as well. The owner of the shop was furious when he found out, but soon realized that customers kept coming back, and that his volume of business was growing quite rapidly. Shri Ram would later bring to DCM this philosophy of treating people fairly.

When Shri Ram first came to work at DCM, the firm was losing money. Shri Ram convinced his father to appoint him head of ginning, which had the worst record of all the departments. By introducing a system of worker incentives (a radical idea at that time in India), Shri Ram turned the department around in short order. The sudden increase in production and profits persuaded an initially reluctant board of directors to approve the companywide implementation of these incentives. After this success, Shri Ram was able to talk the board into giving him control of the other departments, as well. Within three years of his joining the company, Shri Ram became the de facto secretary of DCM and his father a mere figurehead.

World War I brought the company an important break. The British, who had previously repressed the Indian textile industry in order to protect their domestic manufacturers, now encouraged it to produce as much as possible. Through the manufacture of canvas tents for troops DCM grew rapidly and was able to lay down a financial base from which to continue its growth. In World War II DCM started to manufacture hurricane lamps and to diversify into agricultural products such as sugar and fertilizers. These moves were very natural for two reasons. First, the economy of India was largely based on agriculture (which, even in 1987, accounted for 80 percent of GNP). Second, the government, which wished to increase domestic production in order to reduce imports, was encouraging all companies to diversify as much as possible.

By the time India became independent from Great Britain in 1947, DCM had grown into one of the five largest business houses in India. Since Shri Ram's death in 1965, the firm has remained under the control of the Shriram family. In 1985 Bansi Dhar, a grandson of Shri Ram, was appointed chairman and managing director. Throughout all of DCM's divisions, the company still strives to deliver the high quality and extra value implicit in Shri Ram's 2 extra inches. For example, the company's two sugar plants adhere to the rigid international quality standards for crystal size, purity, opacity, evenness of grain, and speed of dissolution in water, rather than the much-less-stringent Indian standards.

The Business Climate

India, a nation of over 800 million people, is the largest democracy in the world. It is an emerging nation with a wide gap between rich and poor. While the average Indian worker earns less than Rs15 ($1) per day, India boasts a world-class scientific community, excellent academic institutions (including five institutes of technology and the world-famous Tata Institute), as well as the ability to produce nuclear weapons and loft satellites into geosynchronous orbit. India has a tightly regulated and mixed economy. Although the private sector is very active, most of the core industries—such as mining and extraction (of coal, iron ore, and gold), steel, banking, electric power, airlines, shipping, railways, communications, and the postal service—are nationalized. Some industries were taken over by the state owing to fears of exploitation by foreigners or monopolies, others because of their immense capital requirements or the desire to subsidize their products and services for the general public. By and large, these state-run industries are inefficient and poorly managed. For example, in 1989 the world price of steel was half of what it cost to produce it in India.

India's infrastructure can make industrial business operations quite challenging. The unreliability of electric power provides a good example. Because it is subject to frequent outages and disruptions, most medium-to-large firms have captive power generation plants to avoid the problems that an interruption in the power supply of even a fraction of a second can cause to equipment and instrumentation. An infrastructural issue of special concern to DTL is the quality of the Indian road system. Many of the roads were built shortly after independence from Britain and were designed to last for only five years. *India Today* recently called attention to the poor condition of these roads, and to the poor management which compounds the problem:

> Though India ranks fourth in the world, after the U.S., Brazil, and the Soviet Union in road length, the quality of the road network would embarrass many small African countries. And the World Bank has categorized India as a country where both the road network and road building technology are obsolete . . .
>
> The fact that many officials connected with the road sector have been busy feathering their own nest has further added to the collapse of the system. The states' Public Works Departments (PWD's) which are responsible for both okaying road-building contracts and approving the work are notorious for corruption. . . . Senior officials estimate that often as much as half the money allocated for the construction of roads may disappear into the pockets of corrupt officials and private contractors. There have been instances of roads being built only on paper in remote areas—all the money having been creamed off.
>
> It has not helped matters that other officials connected with the road sector are equally corrupt. Overloaded trucks are a major cause of road deterioration, yet truckers defy the law with impunity by bribing the highway police. All-India Motor Transport Congress Secretary-General Chitaranjan Das points out that bribing the police is now such an established practice that even trucks which are not overloaded have to fork over money. The Income

Department even accepts these payments as legitimate expenses incurred by truck operations. [See Reference 4.]

Poor road conditions, in their turn, inflict heavy damage on the nation's vehicles—an estimated Rs20 billion annually in excess wear and tear.

In 1947 India inherited a comprehensive system of licensing from the departing British. The system had been set up during World War II to ensure the efficient and equitable allocation of scarce resources such as power, coal, steel, cement, foreign exchange, petroleum products, and rail capacity. Although the system worked well initially, it gradually became more bureaucratic and complex. Nothing could be done until all the appropriate officials had approved and granted licenses. Typical business operations required clearances from the government for foreign exchange, power usage, raw materials, imports, and loans.

In 1980, however, Indira Gandhi was elected prime minister and began liberalizing the private sector. She also encouraged joint ventures with foreign companies, not only for technology transfer, but to open export markets, as well. Licenses for joint ventures with foreign companies could now be obtained with greater speed and ease, and hundreds of foreign joint ventures were formed. In the motor vehicle industry they were begun with such companies as Toyota, Mitsubishi, Mazda, Nissan, Honda, and Suzuki.

In 1984 Mrs. Gandhi was assassinated, and her son, Rajiv Gandhi, became the new prime minister. He continued to improve the Indian business climate: marginal income tax rates were reduced from as high as 97.75 percent down to 50 percent, quotas on imports of many capital goods and raw materials were abolished, and tariffs were lowered. These moves resulted in the rapid growth of exports and foreign investment in India. Industrial investment jumped 50 percent in the first year of the new policies [see Reference 2]. The stock market rose to over 250 percent above its 1980 level and hit new highs throughout fiscal 1986, and interest rates declined dramatically. New capital raised in the market by the private sector rose from almost none in 1980 to Rs10.6 billion in fiscal 1985, and again to Rs24.3 billion in fiscal 1987. Capital raised in the 1990 market is expected to set a new record. Other signs of increasing sophistication in the private financial markets include a rapidly growing number of institutional investors, and new opportunities for foreign investors through mutual fund portfolios of Indian stocks [see Reference 1].

Although the business climate has improved considerably since 1980, many problems remain. Business leaders are calling for increased privatization of government-controlled firms in order to increase the quality and efficiency of the country's infrastructure as well as to help lower the national debt. Nevertheless, moves in these directions continue to meet with considerable resistance, since privatization is heresy to many powerful special interest groups in India [see Reference 1]. Another factor that may slow India's future growth is a projected shortage of electric power brought on by the increase in economic activity. Scheduled hydroelectric projects, which require long lead times under the best conditions, are being slowed by environmental concerns, as are new coal-burning power plants. Current government policy is shifting toward generating electric power with natural gas, to make use of some recent major natural gas discoveries in India, and because the plants are cleaner and can be brought online quickly.

Unfortunately, since there may not be enough capital available to make the needed improvements in the electric power infrastructure, continuing power shortages may slow industrial development.

THE LCV MARKET

The road system has absorbed most of the extra transportation capacity required by India's rapidly growing economy. In 1951 only 11 percent of Indian goods were transported by road; the rest were moved by rail or water. By 1986 this figure had grown to 50 percent; it is projected to reach 62 percent by the year 2001. Consequently, the demand for commercial vehicles has also been rising. Yet until 1980 there was a large gap in the product range of trucks available. The only trucks on the market were either small pickup trucks of capacity less than 1 tonne, or full-sized trucks with a capacity of 7-tonnes or greater.[2] Very few LCVs—trucks with capacity ranging from 2 to 6 tonnes—were manufactured in India. The government projected a national market of 24,000 LCVs annually in 1985, which it expected to grow to 47,000 by 1991. Exhibit 1 gives the annual sales of LCVs since 1984 and the projections through 1991 made by DTL's marketing staff.

Over the last decade, eight companies, four of them joint ventures with Japanese firms, have begun producing LCVs in India. The Indo-Japanese joint ventures include those of DCM and Toyota, Eicher Motors and Mitsubishi, Swaraj and Mazda, and Allwyn and Nissan. Exhibit 2 gives product volume and market share information for all eight firms. Five of them manufacture LCVs rated at 2 tonnes, the others produce 3.5-tonne LCVs. The market for 2-tonne trucks is dominated by two domestic companies, Bajaj and TELCO. Bajaj is known in India for its relatively small, three-wheeled delivery vehicles, while TELCO holds a hefty 75 percent of the full-size truck market. Mahindra, Standard, and Allwyn-Nissan (the only Indo-Japanese joint venture producing a 2-tonne vehicle) all have relatively small market shares in the 2-tonne market. All three of the 3.5-tonne LCV manufacturers are Indo-Japanese joint ventures and produce very similar vehicles. DTL was the first of these companies to begin production; the other two were less than a year behind.

TELCO, the Tata Engineering and Locomotive Company, has been manufacturing large trucks in India since 1964; the LCV is the smallest vehicle it has ever produced. Most of TELCO's truck manufacturing technology is derived from commercial ties with Daimler-Benz of West Germany in the 1960s. Today TELCO is an entirely Indian company that relies exclusively on Indian design and engineering technology. TELCO produces two kinds of LCV: Models 407 and 608.

EXHIBIT 1 LCV Sales and Demand Forecast, Past Trends and Projections on April–March Basis

Class	1984/ 1985	1985/ 1986	1986/ 1987	1987/ 1988	1988/ 1989	1989/ 1990	1990/ 1991
LCV (2T)	23,409	22,881	23,918	30,569	30,651	32,000	34,000
LCV (3.5T)		2,653	5,287	8,375	10,997	12,000	13,000

EXHIBIT 2 Sales and Market Share for Light Commercial Vehicles, 1987–1988 and 1988–1989

Manufacturers	July–June/1987–88	Market Share	July–June/1988–89	Market Share
LCVs (2-Tonne Class)				
Bajaj	12,663	42%	9,513	40%
Mahindra	5,276	17	3,567	15
Standard	1,689	6	857	4
TELCO 407 / 608	8,680	28	8,013	34
Allwyn-Nissan	2,132	7	1,632	7
Total	30,440	100%	23,582	100%
LCVs (3.5-Tonne Class)				
DCM-Toyota	3,417	37%	2,439	29%
Eicher-Mitsubishi	3,373	36	3,496	41
Swaraj-Mazda	2,498	27	2,529	30
Total	9,288	100%	8,464	100%

The Model 608, a 3-tonner, has yet to be successfully launched into the market. It has been introduced several times, but has been pulled back because of technical problems with the gearbox and other components. The Model 407, priced at Rs174,000, is much less expensive than the Indo-Japanese joint-venture LCVs, all of which are priced around Rs230,000. In addition, the 407 is simple and rugged in design. Although rated for loads of up to only 1.5 tonnes, it is in fact capable of carrying up to 4 tonnes. Its technology is older and commonplace. When a 407 breaks down, which happens quite frequently, it can be fixed in almost any village shop. The 407 gets relatively poor gas mileage of 8 to 10 km/liter, whereas all of the Indo-Japanese joint venture vehicles deliver approximately 12 km/liter. Its dominance of the LCV market is credited to its low cost, rugged construction, ease of repair, and to TELCO's name recognition—the company's full-sized trucks are the most common on India's highways.

Bajaj manufactures two-wheeled scooters and three-wheeled delivery vehicles. The market for scooters is very large, because they are a primary mode of transportation for a large percentage of the population of India. Bajaj entered the 2-tonne LCV market by purchasing the Matador line from the Firodia family. The Bajaj LCV comes in two standard configurations: a small bus or delivery van and a fixed-sided truck. The company's strategy is to pursue market share by maintaining the very low price of Rs100,000. Although the Matador has front-wheel drive and a fairly fuel efficient engine, DTL executives do not regard it as state-of-the-art and report that the vehicles often develop maintenance problems after about three years.

Mahindra manufactures four-wheel drive vehicles, including jeeps, which it supplies to the Indian armed forces. The military has also been a primary market for Mahindra's LCV. However, the company has been doing poorly in the civilian LCV market. It recently entered into a technical collaboration with Peugeot to produce an efficient diesel engine. It also purchased Allwyn-Nissan.

Allwyn-Nissan's vehicle is rated at two tonnes, which puts it in more direct competition with the TELCO 407 than with the products of the other Indo-Japanese joint ventures. Allwyn is a state-owned company; the joint venture was also run by the government, which provided most of its business. Sales have been reported to be very low. Rumor has it that workers are called in to manufacture trucks only after the company receives orders. To date, Allwyn-Nissan has not been much of a factor in the LCV market.

Standard is an automobile manufacturer based in Madras in southern India. It sells primarily in the south, and is not a major player in the LCV market. In fact, its LCV operation is now virtually shut down.

Eicher-Mitsubishi was the last to enter the field, beginning production in July 1986, and is so far the most successful of the four Indo-Japanese joint ventures. Eicher is one of the finest tractor manufacturers in India. By avoiding such expensive capital purchases as air-conditioning, conveyor belts, automation, and a modern new plant, great short-term savings and a much lower break-even point were made possible. Its 3.5-tonne vehicle is almost identical to the DTL Dyna, and until recently sold for the same price. (Unlike the Dyna, however, its trucks are not undercoated or painted electrostatically.) Much of the credit for Eicher-Mitsubishi's success is given to its chairman and managing director, Mr. Vikram Lal, who has been described as a human dynamo. Another factor is the company's dealership network; its trucks are sold through its tractor dealerships which are well-established throughout India. Not surprisingly, the company makes many individual sales of trucks to farmers and independent truckers.

Swaraj-Mazda is a government-owned tractor manufacturer in the state of Punjab, a rich agricultural region of northern India. The company, which dominates the Punjab tractor market, intends to anchor its LCV market there, as well. It began producing LCVs in October 1985. Although its truck is almost identical to the Dyna, DTL has nevertheless managed to be quite successful in Punjab, primarily because of an aggressive local DTL dealer.

THE DCM-TOYOTA JOINT VENTURE
History

In 1980 DCM Ltd. proposed to Toyota a joint venture to manufacture LCVs in India. The two companies were well-matched in several respects. Both had similar backgrounds in textiles from which each had diversified, and each had a long tradition of high-quality manufacturing and providing excellent value to the customer.

Established in 1937, Toyota Motor Corporation is the largest automobile manufacturer in Japan and the second-largest in the world. Interestingly, its parent company, Toyoda Automatic Loom Works, once sold textile manufacturing machinery to Delhi Cloth Mills in 1930. In addition to 11 plants in Japan, the company has 30 plants in 15 other countries. It employs over 86,000 people and sells its vehicles in 140 countries. Non-Japanese sales account for almost half of its total production.

After the partners verified the high market potential with their own extensive surveys, DCM-Toyota Ltd. (DTL) was incorporated on August 1, 1983 with its registered offices at the DCM building in New Delhi. Toyota took 26 percent of the equity and DCM 33 percent; the remaining 41 percent was raised in the Indian stock market, where it was oversubscribed seven-fold. The new company planned a plant to manufacture 15,000 LCVs per year, with a maximum annual capacity, with overtime, of 18,000 trucks. It was sited in Surajpur, a town of approximately 20,000 people, located about 35 kilometers southeast of New Delhi.[3] Because it was in an area targeted for economic development by the government, DTL benefited from some considerable tax breaks. All research and development costs are 100-percent deductible in perpetuity, 25 percent of DTL's profits are tax exempt for 7 years after plant startup, and 20 percent of the profits derived from the LCV business are exempt from taxes for 10 years after the first LCV is sold.

The new plant operates under the Toyota Production System (TPS). To learn it, foremen and managers from all levels in DTL were sent to Toyota City in Japan for training. During their absence the personnel department was carefully selecting workers from the local area who fitted desired profiles. TPS selection guidelines require all workers to have a high-school education, or an ITT (technical school) diploma. They must be under 23 years of age, since older applicants are considered too inflexible and fixed in their thinking. Local villagers are preferred; at present they constitute some 120 of the total of 143 production workers. In addition to undergoing tests of intelligence, aptitude, and dexterity, applicants must also have a complete medical examination, including psychological screening to assess whether each applicant is a "good person in heart and mind."

The workers are trained in the Toyota style, beginning with talks and video shows about Toyota. They are taught the aims and values of the TPS, which are rooted in the motto "good thinking, good product." They learn about Quality Circles, *kaizen* (continuous improvement), *muda* (waste), *poka-yoke* (mistake-proof devices), *kanban* (control cards), and all the other tools of the TPS, and also receive training on truck assembly and the DTL plant. The goal of this training is to instill a strong sense of responsibility for high quality in the workers, who are taught to stop the assembly line if any quality problems arise. Not only will no penalties be incurred for interrupting production, but stopping the line is encouraged, since it exposes problems which can be solved once and for all. Because the TPS makes all workers responsible for quality control (QC), DTL keeps only a skeleton QC department of six people. Great care is taken to demonstrate to the workers their vital importance to the organization. To emphasize this, all personnel and guests eat together in DTL's one cafeteria.

The meticulous training has paid off. In the planning stage it was expected that the productivity of DTL's Indian workers would be only 20 to 35 percent of that of the workers in Toyota City. It soon became clear that this had been a gross underestimate; the Indian workers are 65 percent as productive as their Japanese counterparts and continue to improve. This figure is quite impressive since the Japanese plants are more highly automated than DTL's. Interestingly, DTL's target of zero defects before shipment is actually achieved on some days. As in Japan, the line and office workers are all strongly committed to the company; they frequently stay after hours (without pay) for quality circles or when additional production is needed. If the company needs extra workers on the line in peak periods, instead of the normal Indian practice of hiring temporaries, clerical staff are assigned there to help. Even Toyota executives are impressed by the productivity and high-quality output of the Surajpur plant.

The Dyna Truck

The DTL vehicle, the Dyna, comes in two basic models—the Dyna-1 and the Dyna-3. The Dyna-3 is a complete truck with a standard cab and deck. The Dyna-1, a mechanically complete truck without the cab or deck, is for customers who want to finish it for their own special purposes. Approximately 35 percent of the vehicles manufactured by DTL are Dyna-1 models. The Dyna-1 customer can either have DTL custom-finish the vehicle or can take it to a private body builder to be finished inexpensively with wood or other materials. The Dyna-1 trucks finished by DTL are sold mainly to government agencies or institutional buyers with special requirements. The cabs and decks are built in-house by DTL, and conform to Toyota's quality standards. These Special Purpose Vehicles (SPVs) can be delivery vehicles for soft-drink distributors, armored vehicles for the police and security forces, ambulances for emergency services, buses, or anything else a customer may want. Exhibit 3 gives Dyna production information for the last 21 months. SPV sales can be very seasonal for certain markets, such as soft-drink manufacturers who have high summer demand, and for whom it is very hard to build inventories because of planning uncertainty. For example, the factory of Campa Cola, the largest soft-drink manufacturer in northern India, was burned to the ground during demonstrations following Mrs. Gandhi's assassination. This led to a slump in demand for Dyna bottle carriers.

The capacity of the Dyna is 3.5 tonnes, but the truck is actually designed for up to 6 tonnes, and has been operated with loads as high as 10.5 tonnes. It is built for low-fuel-cost transport of goods, possibly perishable, which need to travel quickly. One advantage of a medium-size truck like the Dyna is that it can ply city streets 24 hours a day, whereas bigger trucks cannot because of laws against their daytime use in certain populated areas.

EXHIBIT 3 DCM-Toyota Limited Sales by Model during 1988–1989 (including exports)

Models	July–June/1987–1988	July–June/1988–1989
Dyna-1 Models		
Cowl and chassis	297	191
Bus	193	141
SPV (Special Purpose Vehicle)	32	13
Total	522	345
Dyna-3 Models		
Cabin and chassis	397	205
Highside deck	1,069	710
Drop-side deck	415	359
Fixed-side deck	917	772
SPV	230	164
Total	2,943	2,210
Grand total	3,550	2,555

Experience quickly showed that the Dynas take a lot more punishment than was originally anticipated. They are often overloaded by 100 to 150 percent and driven at great speed over bad roads. The resulting burst tires, broken axles or leaf springs, bent frames, and completely stripped gears meant that, early in the venture, a lot of the parts needed to be upgraded. Also, the vehicles are frequently involved in high-speed accidents and are often dented owing to aggressive driving, since many drivers are unaccustomed to the speeds and acceleration the Dyna can attain. The upgraded Dyna is a far more rugged vehicle than its Japanese counterpart. In fact, when riding with Indian drivers testing it under normal Indian road conditions, Japanese engineers never fail to express amazement at the punishment the Dyna can take.

The Plant

Of all the LCV producers, DTL has the most modern plant. Component parts feeding into the plant are either domestically produced or arrive from Japan in a completely knocked down (CKD) state. The Japanese parts arrive by sea and are brought to the plant by road where they are held in a bonded area in the main plant building. No duties, levies, taxes, or payment for the parts are due until they are withdrawn from the bonded area.

As was mentioned earlier, the plant operates on the TPS, a pull system that was the original just-in-time (JIT) system. All operations are pulled on, ultimately, by the final assembly line; the other lines have only to keep small buffers of their finished products full. Instruction sheets fed in at the beginning of each of the trim, deck, and chassis and final assembly lines assure that they are all synchronized. All work-in-process movement is on dollies custom-designed for each specific operation. The plant has nine production lines: chassis and final assembly, frame assembly, hub and drum machining, axle assembly, engine assembly, and the welding, painting, trim, and deck lines. A diagram of the plant illustrating the process flow is given in Exhibit 4.

Chassis and final assembly is the leading line in the pull system; all the other lines eventually feed into it. After the frame is started on the line, the axles and suspension system are attached and the engine and gearbox are installed. Next come the cooling system and gear levers, the electrical harnesses, the fuel tank, and the wheels. Then the cab is mounted, the vehicle is trimmed, all fluids are poured in, the brakes and clutch are bled, and the engine is started. After this, the vehicle is thoroughly inspected and final adjustments are made to wheels, brakes, and headlights.

Although frame assembly is the smallest line in the plant, it has the most powerful tools. Here the main members of the frame are hydraulically riveted and welded together.

The hub and drum machining line, along with the axle and engine assembly lines, is located in a building adjacent to the main assembly building (see Exhibit 4). Hubs and drums were manufactured in Japan until the end of 1988. Now, the raw castings are made in India and machined by DTL with two advanced, five-axis, computer numerically controlled (CNC) machines. Their controlling computers

EXHIBIT 4 DTL's Surajpur Plant

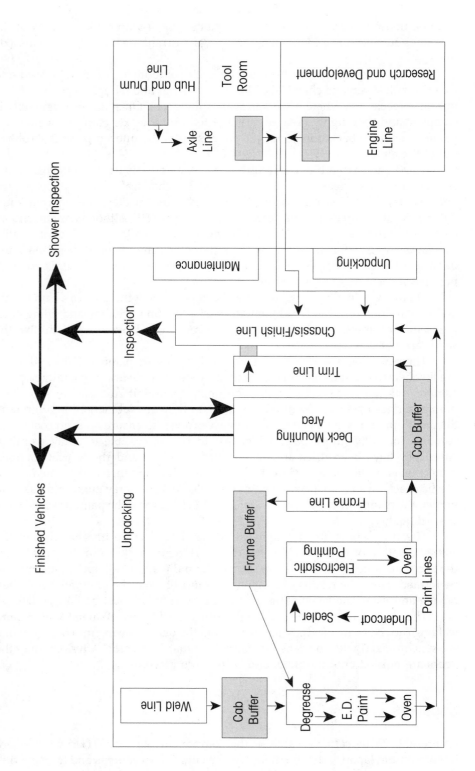

must be housed in an enclosed, air-conditioned room with cables leading to the machines outside. Once completed, the hubs and drums are transported to the axle line.

The axle assembly line begins with each component being degreased and cleaned with steam and chemicals. The axle housings and reduction gears are then put on a special jig, where a worker installs the gears. Once the axle assembly is complete and thoroughly greased, it is hoisted into the axle painting station and painted against a backdrop curtain of water so that the unused paint is scrubbed out of the air.

The engine assembly line receives CKD engine parts from Japan coated in a special protective grease, which is removed by chemical treatment before the engine is assembled in a clean room. It is expected that the block, pistons, and rings will be manufactured in India before the end of 1989. Although many Indian companies produce these parts, at the moment few can attain the exacting quality standards required for the Dyna. LCVs in India have always been diesel-powered because of fuel costs; diesel sells at only Rs3.5 per liter as compared with petroleum gasoline at Rs10 per liter.

On the welding line, the sheet-metal components of the cab are set up in a jig and spot-welded together for alignment prior to the final welding and filling of all joints and crevasses. QC checks that no vital spots have been missed, and that the welds are not defective.

The paint line is where cabs, decks, and frames are painted. Cabs and decks are first degreased and thoroughly cleaned by steam and various chemicals. Next, components are undercoated with phosphate to inhibit rust and to provide a porous surface for better paint adhesion. Then they are submerged in a dip tank filled with primer, which is deposited by electrolysis to ensure an even coat on all surfaces, including those parts which would be inaccessible to spray painting. After they have been dried in a paint oven, a heavy underbody coat for road protection is applied to both the cabs and decks, which are then leakproofed with a plastic paste, given a final coat of paint with electrostatic spray guns, and baked to harden the paint and plastic sealer. Finally, QC checks that the paint finish is of the desired quality.

The trim line is also jokingly known as the make-up line, because of the cosmetic nature of much of its work. This work requires skill and dexterity, since the parts are quite fragile as well as expensive, and many small operations must be performed. Since the results of this line are most of what the customer sees when buying and using the vehicle, the appearance and finish must be immaculate.

The deck line uses the basic fabricating operations of metal cutting and welding (no rivets are used). After fabrication, the decks flowing into the paint line are synchronized with the cabs to ensure they match in color. After painting, the decks are hoisted onto the truck and bolted into place.

Suppliers

At present, 25 percent by value of the component parts of DTL's vehicles are imported from Japan, either because, like the engine components and transmission gears, they require precision and high quality, or because, like the large frame and cab members, they must be stamped using dies and presses larger than those commonly available in India. DTL began with 42-percent local content, reached 75-percent local content by the end of 1988, and must attain 90-percent by the end of 1991, or face severe penalties. One of the problems DTL has encountered in its indigenization efforts is the need for more QC inspection personnel to monitor and control the quality of domestically produced components. Indigenization presents a major challenge for the following reasons:

> Large, high-quality metal stampings and plastic-molded components are not readily available in India, because of a shortage of presses and molding machines capable of handling the sizes of dies required.
> The technology to bond rubber to metal, which is necessary for engine mounts, alternator mounts, and other critical components, is in its infancy in India.
> The precision required for some parts to meet Japanese standards is not achievable in India, where much of the technology in use is very old.

DTL has one advantage over the other Indo-Japanese joint ventures: the company's Indian parent, DCM Ltd., operates a world-class foundry. Plans are in the works to have the engine blocks manufactured there. Pistons may be supplied by Shriram Pistons and Rings Ltd., another firm controlled by the Shriram family. DTL is also considering redesigning the dashboard to be manufactured in six parts instead of one. This would allow it to be produced domestically with smaller machines, but raises concerns of increased assembly costs and lower quality.

Domestic suppliers can be divided into three classes: the large well-established suppliers, the Indo-Japanese joint venture suppliers, and the small, local, independent suppliers. The big manufacturers typically produce high-quality products, have excellent delivery, and are very responsive. Some of these companies, such as the tire suppliers, have affiliations with large international companies and operate in competitive markets. Others, such as Automotive Axles Ltd., which manufactures axle housings and gears, are near-monopolies because no other Indian companies can match their technology. The Indo-Japanese joint-venture suppliers fall into two categories: (a) those established to serve DTL and (b) those established to serve the Indian government's joint venture with Suzuki to produce automobiles. The former deliver to DTL on a JIT basis and have excellent quality, though they tend to be high-priced. DCM and Toyota have established a collaboration, independent of DTL, and located two kilometers from the Surajpur plant to supply wiper motors, starters, and alternators. The joint ventures set up to serve Suzuki do not always deliver reliably, largely because DTL is such a small customer relative to Suzuki. The small, local manufacturers supply various special nuts, bolts, and small metal and plastic components. Delivery is usually not problematic, but quality can be. These suppliers make extensive use of DTL's Ancillary Development Department (ADD) to improve their quality.

Parts supplied by vendors are handled initially by the ADD, whose major tasks are to help indigenize the DTL vehicle, to integrate suppliers into the firm as JIT partners, and to provide suppliers with advice on techniques to improve their quality. Sometimes suppliers genuinely do not understand why higher quality is needed. For example, DTL had to work hard to persuade its bus-body builders that the vehicle needed to be watertight, should have no sharp edges, and should not rattle. One of them is quoted as saying, "This is a bus, not a car."

DTL Marketing

The DTL sales department has a staff of 20 in the head office, and 5 salespeople stationed in regional offices around the country. It is divided into two groups: international/institutional and domestic. Institutional customers include large companies and state and local governments. DTL is waiting for clearance to sell to the national government and armed forces, potentially a very large market. Helped by financial incentives from the government, DTL exports to Bangladesh, Nepal, Sri Lanka, Bhutan, Mauritius, and Pakistan, and is trying to gain business in countries in the Middle East.

Trucks are sold domestically through DTL's network of 53 main dealerships and 57 subdealers or branches. These are also supported by an additional 33 authorized service centers. The locations of all dealers, subdealers, branches, and service centers are marked on the map in Exhibit 5. Dealership status is granted only to those who can meet Toyota's rigorous standards, which require that facilities be staffed with factory-trained technicians with the knowledge and tools to do all required service and repairs to LCVs. Dealers also must maintain large inventories of spare parts. (Subdealers are those who are not yet fully qualified dealers.) The entire dealership network, established from scratch starting in 1985, includes some dealers who sell exclusively DTL products and some who sell other complementary products as well. DTL provides free training to service technicians and helps dealers import service equipment. The dealer's profit on a typical LCV sale is about Rs5,000. The normal procedure is for a dealer to get a customer order and forward it to the factory; delivery usually takes place within a month.

Until mid-1988 DTL competed on the basis of price with Eicher-Mitsubishi and Swaraj-Mazda, its two major rivals in the 3.5-tonne LCV market. All three companies produce vehicles of similar sizes and capacities. Even though DTL executives viewed their vehicle as superior to the others in quality, engineering, and engine size, price was still used as the basis for competition. As a result, DTL held a slightly larger market share than either of the other two companies. In mid-1988 the marketing manager was transferred to another post in DCM and the marketing staff was restructured. A new strategy was adopted which called for disengagement from the price wars and the marketing of the Dyna based on its superior quality. The Dyna is now priced about Rs10,000 higher than its competitors, and eight points of market share have been lost since last year. The strategy shift has resulted in one significant benefit: unlike its rivals, DTL is now profitable for the first time in its history. Vikram Lal, chairman of Eicher-Mitsubishi, now the market leader in the 3.5-tonne LCV class, is quoted as stating that his company would lose, "about Rs3 Crore [30 million] this year." [See Reference 5.]

THE FUTURE

Of the three Indo-Japanese joint ventures, DTL alone uses a JIT manufacturing system and conveyorized assembly lines. In addition, DTL has more modern

EXHIBIT 5 DTL Dealer Network

Toyota Quality Service: Largest Dealer Network

* Quality service network all over India, in over 100 towns and cities
* Complete infrastructure at each dealer point
* Toyota-trained engineers
* Emergency facilities for airlifting spares
* Special training programs for fleet owners
* Free service camps
* Five free services
* 12-month warranty, irrespective of distance clocked

painting facilities, with electrodeposition of primer and electrolytically deposited paint. While this gives DTL a competitive advantage in manufacturing technology and product quality, it is uncertain whether the added expense will be justified, for three reasons. First, consumers are wary of the new technology in the Dyna trucks, particularly with the unfamiliar Toyota name on them. The new truck comes with a higher price tag than people expect, and is built to much higher standards than consumers are accustomed to. The Dyna does not break down every few days, and problems common to older designs of LCVs—like ruptured fuel lines and broken fan belts—have, by and large, been eliminated. Tire wear is one of the major costs of truck ownership, because tires are very expensive in India. Unlike the older truck designs, including TELCO's, the Dyna is designed to have its wheels aligned and tires balanced on computerized equipment, which greatly reduces tire wear. Quite apart from the generally high standards to which the entire vehicle is manufactured, this reduced tire wear alone makes the Dyna a less expensive vehicle to operate in the long term than the other LCVs. The second reason for concern is that service for the Dyna is not available in many parts of the country. India is vast, and the number of dealers capable of providing full service for the vehicle is relatively limited. The DTL dealership network is new, having been established from scratch only in the last four years, whereas competitors have been able to take advantage of long-standing truck or tractor dealership networks spread throughout India. Consequently, DTL has been less successful than the other LCV manufacturers in selling to individual buyers. The third concern for DTL is that its high standards make indigenization of components quite difficult. There are only a handful of suppliers in India capable of manufacturing certain necessary components to DTL's quality standards.

Despite these challenges, Mr. S. G. Awasthi, DTL's executive director, remains a steadfast supporter of his company's current strategy:

> The management policy adopted by DTL so far has paid rich dividends and this policy is likely to yield even richer dividends in the future. I am confident that the corporate strategy adopted by DTL would be a model for other automobile manufacturers in the years to come.

Mr. Vivek Bharat Ram, grandson of Shri Ram and the current managing director of DTL, shares his view of the company's future:

> The basic principle on which DTL has always operated is that of following the customer-first philosophy. This is the policy I intend to firmly adhere to in the future also.

DTL is committed to developing and implementing strategies which will offer the equivalent of Shri Ram's 2 extra inches to the LCV market.

REFERENCES

1. "Country Report No. 1, India." *The Economist* Intelligence Unit, 1989.
2. *The Economist*, February 25, 1989, pp. 75–76.

3. *The Economist*, March 4, 1989, p. 34.
4. *India Today*, March 18, 1989, pp. 78–79.
5. *India Today*, March 31, 1989, p. 80.
6. Singh, K., and A. Joshi. *Shri Ram: a Biography*. London: Asia Publishing House, 1968.

Endnotes

1. The February 1989 exchange rate for Rupees (Rs) was approximately 15 rupees per U.S. dollar.
2. A tonne, or metric ton, is equal to approximately 1.13 tons.
3. A kilometer is approximately six-tenths of a mile.

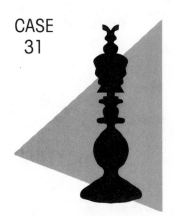

CLUB MED INC.

ROBERT P. VICHAS

INTRODUCTION

Forbes magazine labeled it, "Trouble in Paradise." Richard Phalon wrote in 1988, "Club Med, that once lusty purveyor of packaged sea, sand and sun vacations, is slipping into middle age bearing all the signs of an identity crisis. There are times when an income statement can be more unforgiving than a mirror."[1] Earnings per share had declined 6 percent despite a nearly 10-percent rise in sales; the equity market had become disenchanted with the stock; political and labor problems had caused temporary closings in Haiti and the Turks and Caicos Islands at the same time the popular Paradise Island (The Bahamas) resort was closed for renovations.

A year later in *Forbes*, Club Med responded, "I Am Sorry, We Have Changed."[2] Joshua Levine wrote in 1989, "With a new $12-million advertising campaign, Club Med Inc. is shedding its old image as an endlessly partying, global singles bar. The playboy–playgirl image that Club Med has projected for the last 21 years is being rejected by much of the crucial U.S. market. An aging, more family-oriented U.S. has outgrown the Club Med of the 1970s."[3]

Does peace prevail anew in paradise? Club Med was restructured organizationally. It initiated a strategic shift from an international to a global concept. It refocused its North American marketing strategies. It developed a worldwide growth strategy for the 1990s. Revenues for Club Med, Inc., in 1989 rose 12 percent over 1988, while operating profits increased 128 percent during the same period.

Will Club Med's strategy for the 1990s steer the multinational corporation (MNC) through the straits of adversity or did management build a castle of sand? Serge Trigano, chief executive officer (CEO) of Club Med, Inc., understood the challenge well. He said, "We are beginning 1990, the 40th year of the Club Med concept, with an aggressive strategy for growth. The challenge will be to execute this strategy effectively while rapidly adapting to changes in our markets."

This case was prepared as a basis for classroom discussion to illustrate the challenges of decision making in a changing international environment. It is not intended to illustrate either effective or ineffective management. The author acknowledges the contributions of R. Carl Moor and assistance of researchers Phil Breakwell, David Spencer, Mark Deary, and Luis Figuereido.

HISTORY

A manager's life was not always filled with so many challenges at Club Med. One might have characterized it as idyllic, albeit primitive—a tranquil life on a Mediterranean island. Gerard Blitz, a Belgian, dreamed of providing war-weary continentals a vacation ambience, away from the afflictions and adversities found in a post-World War II Europe, which emphasized sports and love. Gilbert Trigano's family business sold army-surplus tents, the ideal guest accommodations for communal bliss.

On the Spanish island Majorca in Alcudia, Blitz established the first Club Mediterranee village in 1950 where guests helped cook meals and wash dishes and, during balmy evenings, under the blue savannah of Mediterranean skies speckled with white stars of universal love, discussed the harsh realities of capitalism before snuggling down into sleeping bags. Despite its escape-from-civilization concept, Club Mediterranee was predestined for cascading changes and gushing growth from the day Blitz first approached Trigano, the tent seller, for his ideas.

A French communist whose parents were Moroccan Jews, Gilbert Trigano fought in the communist resistance during World War II, became a reporter with the communist daily, *L'Humanite*, after France was liberated, and then drifted into the family tent business.[4] After joining Club Med in 1954 as managing director (MD), Trigano became its gale-level force.

Nevertheless, not everything sailed smoothly for the newly embarked venture. Although the firm nearly ran aground by the end of the decade, the threatening clouds of financial distress dissipated at the start of a new decade in 1961. A rescue ship, in the name of Groupe Edmond de Rothschild, took controlling interest in the sinking Club Med in exchange for a £1.0 million towline. Rothschild subsequently reduced its interest to 2.8 percent.

Transforming the back-to-nature dream of primitive paradise and eternal bliss (for a week or two) into a concept of uninhibited play in the sun, a romp in the sand, and discarding the cares, and clothes, of civilization, Trigano forged a highly profitable chain of resort-villages in France, Italy, Greece, and Africa. Polynesian-styled huts and bungalows replaced tents and sleeping bags, and, today, pampered guests in luxurious accommodations nestled on hilltops along the French Riviera no longer need cook and wash dishes.

Chronologically, the firm opened its first straw-hut village in 1954, its first ski resort in Leysin, Switzerland in 1965, and in the American Zone its first village in 1968 and the first family Mini-Club in 1974. In 1976 the MNC acquired a 45-percent interest in Valtur, an Italian company which had holiday villages in Italy, Greece, and Tunisia, mainly for an Italian market. (Club Med either leased or operated many of its villages under management contract.) As an additional corporate activity, the MNC maintained time-sharing apartments and hotels. Although most members were French in the 1950s, by 1980 the proportion of French visitors had dropped to 45 percent of the total. From global headquarters in Paris (France), Club Mediterranee marketed its products worldwide.

In late 1981 when the firm again attempted decentralization, Serge Trigano, Gilbert's son, assumed leadership of the American Zone. It also began marketing its Rent-a-Village program that year to large corporations for meetings and market incentives.

Then, on May 17, 1984 the firm incorporated its American Zone in the Cayman Islands (B.W.I.) as Club Med Inc. (CMI), a wholly owned subsidiary of Club Mediterranee S.A., and hoisted its new slogan: "The perfect climate for body and soul." To help Serge Trigano relocate from Paris to New York in 1984, the corporation loaned him $1.4 million interest free, a sufficient sum, even at Big Apple prices, for a capacious tent.[5]

With Serge Trigano as its CEO, CMI was chartered to develop markets and operate in the United States and Canada, Mexico, the Bahamas and rest of the Caribbean, Southeast Asia, South Pacific, and parts of the Indian Ocean Basin; while Club Mediterranee, retaining responsibilities for marketing and operations in the rest of the world (Europe, Africa, and South America), mainly focused toward its European market. Worldwide, the organization maintained operations in 35 countries on 5 continents. CMI went public in September 1984. Its initial public offering in the United States of 3.4 million shares of common stock was oversubscribed at $17 per share. (Club Mediterranee shares traded on French, Luxembourg, and Belgian exchanges.) In the same month CMI signed an agreement with the Seibu Saison Group, a Japanese retail and real estate firm, to develop resorts in Japan. A summer mountain resort and winter ski village, Club Med-Sahoro opened on the island of Hokkaido in December 1987.

PRODUCT

The original Trigano formula was to construct villages in exotic places and operate the business as a membership organization. What was Club Med's business? Some say it was the pleasure business. Club Med recently answered the question this way:

> What is Club Med? Quite simply, an inimitable style of vacation, based on some very simple ideas:
> The first is to select the most beautiful locations in the world, and there build our leisurely vacation villages.
> The next is to offer every activity imaginable to make your vacation ideal.
> Then we carefully select a multinational, multilingual team of Gentils Organisateurs (G.O.s, or congenial hosts).
> Finally, we give our villages a sense of complete freedom.[6]

In 1989 the New York office of Club Med circulated a Club Med Fact Sheet which stated that the world's largest vacation village organization (actually the 11th-largest hotel chain) offered, "vacationers unique, all-inclusive escapes from the stresses of daily life in some of the world's most exotic and scenic locations." Although the original concept remained intact throughout its 40 years of operations, product variations abounded.

For instance, Club Med entered the corporate meeting and incentive market with its Rent-a-Village. More than two dozen corporations by the end of 1989 had rented parts of or an entire village. The MNC hosted several vacations for Sober Vacations International, a travel firm which specialized in vacations for recovering alcoholics and their families. Some villages added NAUI and PADI certification scuba diving programs as well as an English-style riding instructional workshop and lectures. In later years the organization cast off strictly sun and sand vacations and added ski, mountain, and other scenic settings to appeal to a diversity of tastes.

The American Way

"The pleasure of leisure is control," said Ron Paul, president of marketing consultant Technomic Inc. of Chicago. "Consumers have lost control in recent years, not just over their careers but even over things like how long it takes to get somewhere by car or airplane."

People ages 18 to 29 prefer to spend leisure time away from home, unlike older baby boomers. Conservatives are more likely to prefer staying at home than liberals. Southerners are the biggest homebodies of all.

The Wall Street Journal, through the Roper Organization, asked more than 2,000 American adults to choose from a list of purchased entertainment experiences. Some results are summarized below.

Best Buys

Percentage of consumers who rate these forms of entertainment as the best values for the money.[1]

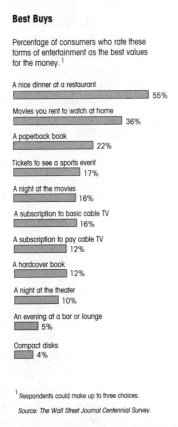

A nice dinner at a restaurant — 55%
Movies you rent to watch at home — 36%
A paperback book — 22%
Tickets to see a sports event — 17%
A night at the movies — 16%
A subscription to basic cable TV — 16%
A subscription to pay cable TV — 12%
A hardcover book — 12%
A night at the theater — 10%
An evening at a bar or lounge — 5%
Compact disks — 4%

[1] Respondents could make up to three choices.

Source: The Wall Street Journal Centennial Survey.

Source: Meg Cox, "Staying at Home for Entertainment," *The American Way of Buying* (New York: Dow Jones & Company, 1990), pp. 37–38.

June 1989 marked the opening of Club Med Opio, a 1,000-bed, 125-acre luxury village nestled in the hills behind Cannes on the French Riviera with a 360-degree view of the sea coast and mountains. The model for future Club Med villages, Opio offered luxury rooms, turkish baths, full convention and seminar facilities, plus an 18-hole golf course and a 9-hole executive course designed by Cabell Robinson.

Brought online in 1989, the firm promoted a new Mini-Club at St. Lucia for children, which offered horseback riding for children ages 8 to 12, and flexi-vacations to encourage visitors to take long weekends at Club Med or combine a village stay with visits to nearby tourist attractions. An example of the new-style village, Huatulco (Mexico), boasted five restaurants, larger rooms, and private terraces. Paradise Island (the Bahamas) and The Sandpiper (Florida) were repositioned as prime short-stay villages. Also, during the year special honeymooners' packages were launched at Moorea, Bora Bora, Caravelle, Huatulco, and Paradise Island, with an additional one planned for *Club Med I*.

In 1990 Club Med spread sail on luxury packages aboard the s/v *Club Med I*, the world's largest automated sailing vessel. The 617-foot ship, with five masts and seven passenger decks, would cruise the Mediterranean Sea during spring and summer months and the Caribbean in winter.

Besides the honeymoon specials and Mediterranean cruise package, Club Med introduced a professional golf academy at The Sandpiper, Culinary Week where renowned French chefs might even share culinary secrets with guests, flexi-vacations, and expanded sports programs.

With its broader line of products, added amenities in many villages to include locks on doors, ice machines, even occasional telephones and televisions, and someday even telefax, plus 110 vacation villages located in 35 countries, Club Med expected to appeal to a wider range of clientele: singles and couples, retired persons and children, organizations and businesses, professionals and the wealthy, the adventurer and the timid. CMI in 1990 owned, operated, or managed 26 vacation villages throughout its geographical area, five archeological villas in Mexico, two in Beijing (PRC), and retained the exclusive rights to sell vacation packages at resorts operated by Club Mediterranee.

MARKETING

Typically, the firm marketed to its GMs (*gentils membres* or gentle members) an all-inclusive prepaid vacation package, which included transportation, lodging, three meals daily, wine and beer with meals, most sports and leisure activities, and evening entertainment. Additional fees were charged for liquor, golfing, and horseback riding. Worldwide there were about 1.2 million GMs. The number of GMs visiting CMI villages rose from 383,600 in 1988 to 425,600 in 1989.

The key to success in the 1980s lay in a carefully orchestrated marketing and ongoing ad campaign begun in 1980 to convey the message that Club Med was for everyone. The ad budget was raised from $8 million in 1983 to $10 million by 1985 to $12 million by 1989 and $25 million for 1990. Management said that expanding penetration in the upscale vacation market was the goal of the firm's five new 30-second television ads. These ads presented vignettes of vacation possibilities

One Family's Perspective

Kevin and Karin fit the U.S. member profile in terms of age, income, and professional status. They enjoyed year-round sports: skiing, diving, horseback riding, sailing, swimming. They had frequently visited Club Med villages in Europe, the Caribbean and the United States. They liked the activities, security of no surprises, and of knowing what to expect from each visit. Besides being a vacationer, Kevin was also a potential investor. Therefore, he carefully observed the care and management of the properties with an eye on potential future growth and competition.

After several visits to the Martinique village in the Caribbean, they witnessed significant deterioration. Kevin said, "When we first started going to Club Martinique, most of the guests were professionals like ourselves. Then Club Med started running vacation specials from New York City. For an $18 an hour New Yorker who might be a street sweeper, the vacation special was cheap. They were noisy, partying all night. They got off the plane drunk. They were rowdy people who didn't fit with the traditional Club Martinique visitor. We didn't need that kind of environment, so we stopped going there. We now go to Copper Mountain, Colorado (a Club Med ski village)." Kevin interpreted the changing character of Club Martinique as a signal of increasing competitive pressures.

Although Kevin and Karin had visited Copper Mountain twice and planned a return trip in Winter 1991, they were unimpressed with management of that village. "Every village has its local clown," explained Kevin, "but after a day on the slopes, we like to sip our drinks quietly in front of the fireplace and meet new people. This clown is loud, doing nothing anyone really thinks is funny, and it's not the before-dinner environment we prefer. Besides, in American villages, they turn the children loose around six, before dinner, so the kids can eat with their parents. We don't care for the noise or children activity while enjoying a gourmet feast. By contrast, in Europe," Kevin continued, "the villages offer more hours of baby sitting. Children eat together and join parents after dinner at 9 o'clock. It's a more sophisticated atmosphere."

Kevin did not like Club Med as an investment in 1990 any more than he did in 1985. "They seem to be growing for the sake of expansion. There's no quality growth, and I think village managers need more training and experience. Club Med is trying to be all things to all people, and I believe the increased competition, especially in the United States, has created some corporate panic."

Will Kevin and Karin return to a Club Med village? "We'll probably return to Copper Mountain. And I'm interested in the new sailing ship. We'll go back to Europe; we like it better," he added.

available to singles, couples, and families. About three-fourths of the ad budget was assigned for television ads, the remainder for newspapers, primarily, and magazines, secondarily. Hard-copy ads in newspapers and magazines featured testimonials from a variety of vacationers; this represented a new thrust for Club Med. Radio spots were aired during summer 1990. Nevertheless, the promotion budget for the American Zone exceeded that of its European counterpart about four-fold.

Paris had its own decisions to make. Serge Trigano said, "We decided that we had three options: to remain a French company and lose markets elsewhere; to compete in each market; or to become European." The first option was inconsistent with the firm's global perspective. The second option would have led to catastrophic results. Trigano said, "If we had built a village just for, say, the German market, we would have had huge occupancy problems. The German market is at its peak in May and June and falls off in July and August." The third option meant acceptance of Europeanization. "In 1992, 1993, or whenever, we will all be Europe. So why not try to be European before Europe?" asked Trigano.[7]

The new brochure would market five levels of products. Level One would market a half-board holiday at a low basic price to overcome price resistance. Level Two would be the classical Club Med product. Level Three would appeal to those who travel business class, want a single room with telephone, and eat breakfast anytime before midday. Level Four consisted of a new product, packaged tours for people who wanted to explore a country. Serge Trigano said, "In the 1991 brochure we will introduce our own tour operator. The margins won't be high, but these tours will bring new customers, more traffic to airlines, and better occupancy in our hotels and villas." Level Five represented a combination of new products and new marketing. Gilbert Trigano envisioned a future, "maybe 50 years from now," when communications would be such that companies would not need working places, only meeting places.

CMI identified families as a fast-growing market segment. About 40 percent of members were married, 40 percent had children, and 8 percent of its members were children. (See Exhibit 1 for a profile of the North American membership.) By late 1989 CMI had opened eight Mini-Clubs and two Baby Clubs, which offered child care and activities up to 12 hours a day and one or two nurses 24 hours each day. The Baby Club, debuted in April 1985 at Club Med Fort Royal in Guadaloupe, was for infants and toddlers ages 4 to 23 months. Some units provided adjoining rooms for parents and their children. Management estimated that more than 100,000 children worldwide shared vacations with parents each year.

To develop a marketing style appropriate for the 1990s, management decided to be European rather than compete in each separate market. Seventeen villages were selected for an international flavor where the MNC would guarantee to customers a welcome in their own language. Instead of a single package, several options surfaced during the 1980s to appeal to different customer segments. Forty new villages were planned for 1990 to 1995.

EXHIBIT 1 1989 Survey of North American Membership

Married	40%
Single, divorced, or widowed	60
Members with children	40
Members who are children	8
Members between ages 25 and 44	71
Members who are college graduates	72
Percentage holding post-graduate degrees	28
Professionals, executives, managers	68
Proportion of repeat visitors	51
Percentage reporting incomes exceeding $75,000	36
Percentage reporting incomes exceeding $100,000	21
Median age	35
Median household income (annual)	$60,000

Source: "Club Med Facts," April 1989.

In Asia the marketing slogan was "Absolutely Paradise." Occupancy in the Asian Zone was less subject to seasonal fluctuations: Australian and New Zealand markets have seasons reversed from Japan and the United States. However, to improve occupancy in Asian Zone villages subject to seasonal fluctuations, Club Med maintained a constant, reduced off-season rate while raising in-season prices during 1989. It also opened a sales office in Taiwan.

The fastest-growing Asian segment, the Japanese market, between 1984 and 1988 grew 200 percent. Links with Seibu Saison gave Club Med crucial distribution outlets through its stores. New destinations in Florida and the Bahamas, were promoted to the Japanese during 1989. The firm advertised its Mexican villages to them in 1990.

Travel agents accounted for about 85 percent of vacation packages of CMI; typically they earned 10-percent commission on each package sold. By contrast, at Club Mediterranee in Paris, about 70 percent of its business was direct-booked. The U.S. travel-agent program included a 4- to 5-day training session at clubs to acquaint agents with services. Following the on-site visit, agents would then receive a barrage of promotional materials, direct-mail flyers, storefront decorations, mailing lists, newsletters, sales manuals, and a priority clearance for the next season. Despite this program, some travel agents claimed that Club Med's marketing efforts tended to neglect, even offend, travel agents. Club Med responded by increasing its sales force from seven regional managers and a six-person "flying team" of troubleshooters to 23 regional and district sales managers with plans to double its sales force by the end of 1991.[8]

Two Florida travel agents interviewed in 1990 said that in the past Club Med had been reluctant to pay commissions. Now, they said, the MNC was increasing commissions (which could reach 18 percent on selected packages), and had improved communications by keeping travel agents informed of new tour offerings. A New Jersey travel agent, who sold many Club Med vacation packages, in 1988 believed that the firm had difficulty selling itself to older clientele in an increasingly competitive market. The agent said, "The idea of free sex and a lot of drinking really turns off the older, more sophisticated people Club Med is trying to reach."[9]

PRICING

Club Med offered a variety of vacation packages: custom-tailored vacations; honeymoon specials; length-of-stay and transportation flexibility; sailing-ship cruises; family villages; singles vacations; luxury packages; as well as standard ones. Most sales required prepayment. Advance payments were collected for air fare, housing, meals, and entertainment. Additional expenditures for beverages, sports equipment, and rentals were settled when the guest checked out. For guests, no one needed worry having enough money after the fact; for Club Med, the MNC earned additional income on the float. Children ages 2 to 5 could stay free at selected locations and dates.

Advance booking, when confirmed, required a 25-percent prepayment per person plus membership fees; an initiation fee of $30 plus annual membership fee of $50 per family. Final payment was required 30 days prior to departure. Not all villages accepted all credit cards for personal expenses, and none accepted personal checks. Membership fees included illness and medical insurance coverage through a policy issued by Union des Assurances de Paris.

However, the inclusive price did not cover costs of entry and exit visas or airport taxes, transfers, beverages after meal periods, snacks, beach towels, optional excursions, equipment rentals, horseback riding, and deep-sea fishing. The strict 44-pound per person luggage allowance necessitated careful packing, because Club Med policy specifically excluded such carry-on items as garment bags and backpacks; extra charges were made for scuba gear and surfboards. Flight times, not guaranteed, were subject to change; other exceptions and caveats required careful perusal of the contract. Nevertheless, more than one-half of the firm's business derived from repeat customers, some of whom were frequent visitors. The following samples of prices represent published off-season rates for summer and fall 1990.

The Honeymoon Package at Caravelle (Guadaloupe) between May 5 and June 23, for two, was $1,998 from New York City and $1,898 from Miami. Double rooms were basic with shower and 220 voltage (adapters not furnished). The facility featured water sports, golf, tennis, archery, and a fitness center plus nightly entertainment and dancing, and even a video room with large-screen TV (no television in rooms). The special honeymoon gift for newlyweds included "a bottle of imported champagne on ice, two exclusive Club Med souvenir T-shirts, a basket of fruit, two complimentary packages of bar beads [i.e., Club Med money, prepaid with hard currency, used to settle the bar bill; unused beads were nonrefundable], a private cocktail party for honeymooners only hosted by the Village Manager. Please ask for the honeymoon gift package at time of booking."[10]

Other off-season rates (usually May 5 to December 15), per week, per person, double occupancy, payable only in U.S. dollars, from major U.S. cities—Chicago, Washington, D.C., Atlanta, New York City—follow (rates for children ages 6 to 11, if available, are in parentheses): Bora Bora, Tahiti, $2,100 ($1,315); Opio, French Riviera, $1,625; St. Lucia, Caribbean, $1,200 ($1,100); Eleuthera, the Bahamas, $1,100 ($650); Huatulco ($1,000) or Ixtapa, Mexico, $1,200 ($700). (Prices are approximate since figures were rounded to simplify presentation.)

To compete with popular cruise-ship and airline offers, independent tour operators, i.e., any person who could put together an affinity group of 20 or more persons, could earn discounts up to 15 percent. Those resorts which offered short-term stays charged an average $165 per day.

For more luxurious accommodations, Club Opio, 12 miles from Cannes (France), supplied air-conditioned rooms with telephones, satellite television, baths with tubs, and hair dryers. (Guests still provided their own adaptors to convert the 220 volts to user-friendly currents.) "Fashioned after a typical Provincial hamlet, [Club Opio] . . . unfolds on 125 acres of undulating countryside, in the midst of olive trees, pine forests, and flowering gardens, at an altitude of 990 feet. There are five restaurants, an outdoor and a heated indoor pool, piano bar, theatre, bridge room, movie and meeting room, and boutique. Opio welcomes ages 12 and over." All of this, for a week of fun, at summer rates, was offered for $1,850 from Los Angeles or $1,725 from Miami, double occupancy, of course.

After a week at Club Opio, one could depart from Pointe-a-Pitre (Cannes) aboard the 14,000-ton *Club Med I,* the fully automated five-sail ship, on a 19-day,

"The Big Blue" tour. Single rates varied from $3,420 on the Bali (lower) Deck to $6,150 for a suite on the Foca Deck. More modest weekly rates for the Mediterranean Cruise depended on the week chosen. In late June weekly rates ranged between $775 and $1,620 for singles. By contrast mid-August rates extended from $2,490 to $4,620. Nevertheless, those on a budget, with three persons to an outside cabin, could sail a week on the blue Mediterranean for as little as $415 per person in late June or as much as $1,330 each in mid-August.

However, a Caribbean Cruise aboard the same ship between late September and mid-December cost a little more. For three in an outside cabin, (Bali Deck) the rates for the low season were $1,075, and the week of November 17, $1,330. On the other hand, singles on the Bali Deck paid $2,010 and $2,490, respectively, for the two fall rates, or they could stay in a Foca Deck suite for $3,780 or $4,620. All *Club Med I* prices above excluded air fare.

The ship boasted eight decks of Burmese teak and the very latest in maritime technology. Created by world-famous designer Alberto Pinto, the ship's interior included 197 guest quarters, "two posh restaurants; four cocktail lounges; a nightclub; a large boutique with a duty-free shop; a casino; a health center with massage, sauna, and U.V. tanning machines; a beauty salon; and a multi-purpose hall for conferences, movies, shows, and special events."[11] Rooms measured about 188 square feet and suites 321 square feet, each with local and closed-circuit television, radio, telephone, minibar, and private bathroom with hair dryer and bathrobe and 24-hour-a-day room service.

ORGANIZATION

Club Mediterranee began with a very simple and informal organization structure. Gilbert Trigano appointed some friends, and original vacationers, to manage different vacation spots in Europe. Gradually, a more complex, functional structure evolved and remained in place until 1971. Between 1971 and 1976 the organization structure was modified. Area managers were named and had 10 to 15 village managers reporting to each. Because operationally it seemed as though several Club Meds had been created, management reverted to the pre-1971 structure.[12] The pre-1971 structure prevailed until the early 1980s, at which time management considered reorganization.

Five key goals dominated the organization:

1. Trigano wanted to double capacity every five years either by adding new villages or increasing the size of existing ones.
2. Innovation drove decisions to make Club Med different from other hotel chains and to respond to changing customer needs.
3. The firm sought to internationalize personnel and its strategy because the proportion of French customers was diminishing.
4. To remain price competitive, management sought ways to improve productivity and control rising costs by standardization of procedures.
5. Trigano insisted on retaining the original concept: protect the villages from the outside world and yet identify with each local environment as closely as possible.[13]

However, as markets changed, new products introduced, and geographical diversification occurred, Serge Trigano, MD of operations, discovered that reporting to him were corporate managing directors, 16 country managers, 100 chiefs of village, plus 8 product managers. Trigano decided that the structure was too centralized, that he faced information overload, that there was too much detail, and that it was difficult to adapt to the international character of customers. Moreover, bottlenecks developed both in assignments and in supervision of personnel.

The corporation was still recruiting its GOs[14] from France, despite that Americans accounted for 20 percent of business which created a potential language and cultural barrier. Additionally, there was poor communications between marketing and operations.[15]

Consequently, the MNC was reorganized along the lines illustrated in Exhibits 2. Some aspects of the old structure remained the same, viz., the chief executive officer (CEO) and his managing directors (MDs) of financial affairs and new development. At the next level, titles of functional MDs were changed to joint MDs to suggest unity among various functional activities.

Another major change in the structure at the corporate level was to combine the MDs of marketing and operations (M&O). The new MD participated both in operations and promotions of vacation programs, according to Jean-Manre Darbouze, a CMI manager in New York City. Instead of assigning responsibilities for managing all product directors and country and village managers directly, a new level of managers, closer to actual areas of operation, now reported to the JMD of M&O.

Two regional JMDs of M&O were appointed to internationalize these activities. The JMD for the American Zone controlled activities in North and South America, the Caribbean, and Tahiti. The JMD of the European Zone controlled activities in Europe, Australia, and the Far East. Geographical regions were subdivisionalized by country, for each of which a country manager was appointed.

To avoid duplication, the MNC developed a layer of product directors between the corporate JMD of M&O and the regional JMDs to allow for global coordination of products through product directors at an upper management level, who could examine challenges worldwide instead of the more narrow country focus.

The villages, at the lowest level of the organizational chart in Exhibit 2, are illustrated in greater detail in Exhibit 3. The *chef de village* (chief of village), at the heart of implementing Club Med's M&O strategies, dealt with daily operations, managed the many GOs, coordinated GO activities with the various programs, and was the direct link between customers and upper management. Through regionalization, problems that surfaced at the village level were dealt with at a lower level in the new organizational hierarchy. Further, the *chefs de village* were now selected from many countries to make this element of operations truly multinational.

At the top of the organization, the Triganos remained firmly in charge. Gilbert Trigano, aged 69, long ago had left the communist party, although his sympathies lay with the political left. "The communists saved my life," he said to a reporter in 1985. He was a long-time friend of socialist French president François Mitterand. In 1985 Mitterand named Trigano to head a project to train thousands of jobless persons to use computers.[16] Gilbert Trigano remained chairman of the

EXHIBIT 2 Organization Charts

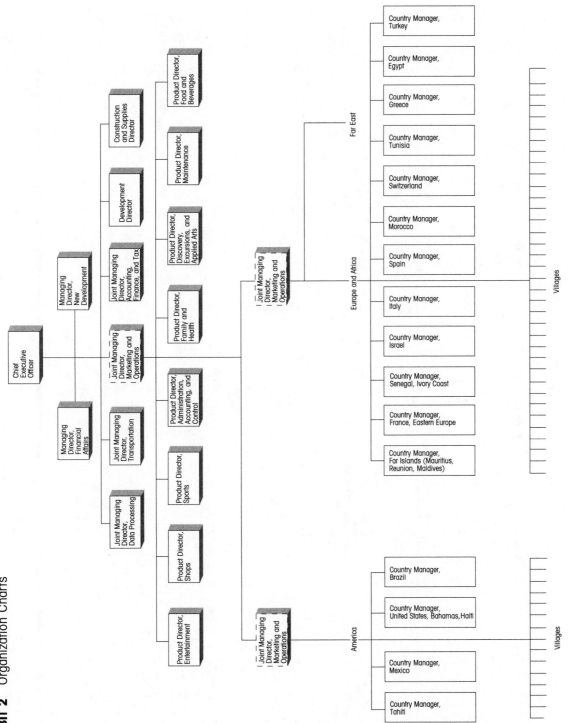

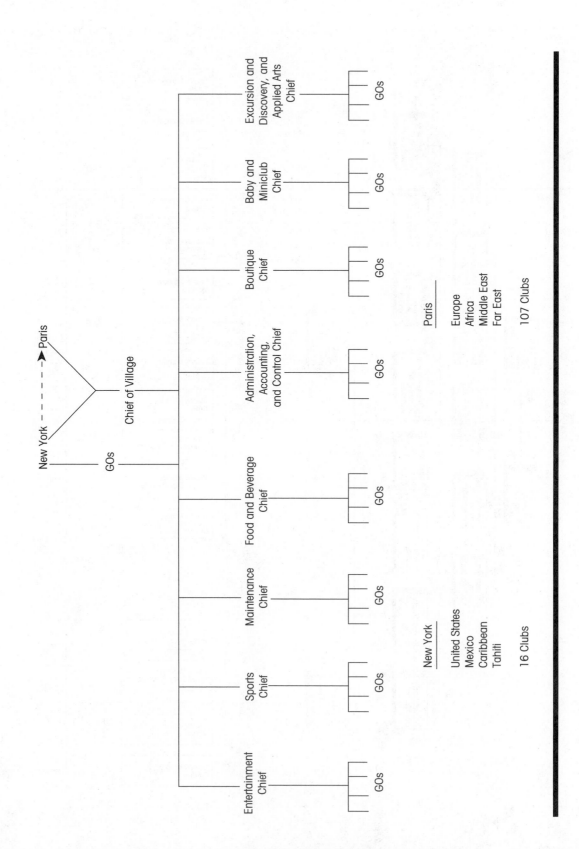

New York - - - - -▶ Paris

GOs

Chief of Village

Entertainment Chief

Sports Chief

Maintenance Chief

Food and Beverage Chief

Administration, Accounting, and Control Chief

Boutique Chief

Baby and Miniclub Chief

Excursion and Discovery, and Applied Arts Chief

GOs

New York
_____
United States
Mexico
Caribbean
Tahiti

16 Clubs

Paris
_____
Europe
Africa
Middle East
Far East

107 Clubs

board of CMI, and chairman of the board, CEO, and MD of Club Mediterranee S.A.

His son, Serge Trigano, born in Paris, May 24, 1946, headed CMI as vice chairman of the board and CEO. Serge worked as a GO during college breaks from the Faculte de Droit et Science (Paris), where he earned a degree in economics. After serving as *chef de village* in six villages, he was considered executive material. In 1981 following some decentralization, Serge assumed leadership of the American Zone and became CEO in 1984 of the newly incorporated CMI. Between 1985 and 1987 he was also Club Mediterranee S.A.'s MD for development and operations of Europe and Africa. In 1987 he became its chief operating officer (COO), dividing time between world headquarters in Paris and offices and villages around the world. Serge concentrated mostly on operational matters, his father on strategic issues.

The president, COO, and chief financial officer (CFO) of CMI, Jean-Luc Oizan-Chapon, who had begun as a GO and sports instructor with Club Mediterranee in its early years, later followed Serge Trigano to the American Zone. Other CMI corporate officers included Alexis Agnello, executive vice president; Jacques Ganin, secretary; and Joseph J. Townsend, treasurer.

The CMI board of directors included Gilbert Trigano, chairman; Serge Trigano, vice chairman; Jacques Giraud, vice chairman; Alexis Agnello; Evan G. Galbraith, former U.S. ambassador to France, director international and senior advisor, Morgan Stanley & Co.; Harvey M. Krueger, MD, Shearson Lehman Hutton Inc.; Stanley Komaroff, partner, Proskauer Rose Goetz & Mendelsohn; Richard A. Voell, president, CEO, The Rockefeller Group.

Stephen Wood described the global organization as too small and too French, with a management system characterized by worship of a 69-year-old guru and a product that was 40 years old.[17] President Jean-Luc Oizan-Chapon admitted that the Americans and the French did not always get along well. Wood continued with his analysis quoting from *Le Figaro*:

> Part of the uncertainty about Club Med's future is due to Trigano's dominant position within it. *Le Figaro* described as a "delightful euphemism" the comment by a senior Club Med manager that "the decision-making here is relatively centralized." Yet, despite his age, to pose the question of Trigano's succession is, the newspaper noted, "considered as sacrilegious inside the club."[18]

OPERATIONS

The basic operating unit, village or villa or comparable unit, was headed by a *chef de village*, who linked customers and JMDs. The life of a *chef de village* might be described in the name of Janyck Daudet, the youngest appointed *chef* at age 26 in 1983. A native of Nimes, France, he began as a ski instructor in Yugoslavia and worked in clubs from Morocco to Thailand as a GO. (Staff members were reassigned every six months, not only to keep them motivated, but also because some seasonal villages were closed part of each year.) Typically a GO earned less than minimum wages paid in most industrialized countries, plus room and board, was under age 30 and unmarried. A U.S. GO earned less than $500 a month in 1990. *Chefs* could earn salaries equivalent to a plant manager or possibly middle management. Daudet worked 18 hours a day, but was on call 24 hours, seven days a week, mingled with guests, performed in after-dinner shows, called midnight staff meetings, and maintained a high level of enthusiasm and energy. "It's impossible to do this too long," said Daudet. "It's fun, but you can't keep up this much energy forever."

There was approximately one GO for every five GMs: a GO for sports, dancing instruction, applied arts, excursions, food, bar, accounting, baby sitting, etc. After every season, or every six months, GOs would be moved from one village to another, with the exception of the chief of maintenance and local people hired as service personnel. The GO concept had remained firmly intact since inception. Worldwide there were more than 8,000 GOs, from 32 countries; in 1990, 25-percent of them were employed by CMI. About 3,000 new GOs were selected each year from an applicants' pool of 100,000. About one-half of the GOs were former GMs.

Toward the end of the 1980s, hiring of French GOs was virtually halted as international teams were employed from the United Kingdom, West Germany, and Italy plus cheaper talent discovered in some less developed countries. In early 1990 Club Mediterranee employed around 250 British GOs to service 17,000 British GMs in popular villages such as Marbella, Kos, Turkey, and Sardinia. Management was also considering the possibility of opening a London Club Med.

The American Zone suffered its share of setbacks during fiscal year 1987 to 1988. Construction delays at Huatulco (1,000 beds) and Playa Blanca (580 beds) in Mexico resulted in lost revenue; openings delayed by a season or two gave competition an edge in these markets. Construction delays in the Bahamas postponed reopening of Paradise Island (670 beds) until February 1988. An adverse political environment resulted in the closing of Magic Isle (704 beds) in Haiti. Occupancy rates declined. (See Exhibit 3 for data on occupancy rates by geographical areas.)

The following fiscal year witnessed more problems. Hurricane Gilbert closed Cancun in September 1988; it was reopened in April 1989. In September 1989 Hurricane Hugo caused temporary closings of Caravelle on Guadeloupe and Turkoise in the Turks and Caicos Islands. Eleuthera was closed in May 1989 for renovations, but it reopened in December 1989. St. George's Cove in Bermuda was also closed while a sale was negotiated.

On the upside, occupancy rates in the American Zone reached a new high at 66.3 percent; hotel days rose from 2,000,000 in 1988 to 2,099,000 in 1989. The number of GMs from France and other European countries rose by nearly 50 percent, and the number of GMs from Mexico, the Caribbean, and South America showed a modest rise. The newest 700-bed CMI village was under construction on San Salvador (the Bahamas); opening was anticipated in 1992, in time for the 500th anniversary of Columbus' landing on that island.

Likewise, the Asian Zone in 1989 achieved new records. Occupancy rates rose to 73.2 percent, and hotel days increased by 24.4 percent to 857,000. Exhibit 4 breaks down hotel days by zone and origin of business. Japan's market represented the jewel of the Pacific. The Japanese not only visited Sahoro, a winter ski resort and summer mountain resort, in record numbers (70.9 percent occupancy), but traveled in large numbers to locations through the Asian and American Zones. The Tahitian villages of Moorea and Bora Bora became more accessible via direct Air France flights between Tokyo and Papeete. (Bora Bora had been closed for several months during 1989 for renovation, but reopened in September.)

EXHIBIT 3   Club Med Inc. Occupancy and Capacity, 1986–1989

	1989	**1988**	**1987**	**1986**
American Zone				
Number of beds				
North America	1,032	1,032	1,030	470
Mexico–Caribbean	8,890	8,956	9,068	9,364
Occupancy (%)				
North America	74.6%	68.5%	56.5%	65.4%
Mexico–Caribbean	65.6	65.4	65.7	64.4
Asian Zone				
Number of beds	3,330	3,330	3,250	2,550
Occupancy (%)	73.2%	61.5%	58.2%	47.3%
Total American and Asian Zones				
Number of beds	13,252	13,318	13,348	12,384
Occupancy (%)	68.7%	65.2%	59.6%	60.5%

Note: Club Med employs a method significantly different than the lodging or hospitality industry, using beds rather than number of rooms. Therefore data are not comparable with the industry. It reports occupancy in terms of beds, based on two beds per room available for guests. It determines capacity on the basis of the average number of bed days available each year, i.e., the number of beds in each village multiplied by the number of days the village was open annually.
Source: *Annual Report*, Club Med Inc., 1988–1989, p. 22.

EXHIBIT 4   Club Med Inc. Hotel Days by Zone, 1986–1989

	1989	**1988**	**1987**	**1986**
American Zone				
American and Canadian	1,480,000	1,510,000	1,495,000	1,574,000
Mexican and Caribbean	113,000	107,000	70,000	130,000
Asian/Pacific/Indian	78,000	71,000	69,000	48,000
French/other European	394,000	280,000	229,000	211,000
South American	34,000	32,000	28,000	32,000
Total	2,099,000	2,000,000	1,891,000	1,995,000
Asian Zone				
American and Canadian	8,000	4,000	4,000	2,000
Asian/Pacific/Indian	607,000	500,000	429,000	306,000
French/other European	242,000	185,000	183,000	94,000
Total	857,000	689,000	616,000	402,000

Note: The above table shows the number of hotel days occupied by national groups from major world regions.
Source: *Annual Report*, Club Med Inc., 1988–1989, p. 23.

During 1990 CMI would increase bed capacity by nearly 500 at Sahoro (400 beds), Bali in Indonesia (800 beds), Phuket in Thailand (700 beds), and La Pointe aux Canonniers (440 beds). A new village in Vietnam was planned for the early part of the decade. On the other hand, the number of European visitors to the Asian Zone actually decreased from 1987 levels. The table in Exhibit 5 summarizes GMs by nationality groups from all regions of the world who visited villages owned or managed by the company.

COMPETITION

Club Med had fashioned its worldwide profile during the 1950s. Because its style and 40-year old product might not carry it through the century, management unfurled a strategy of market segmentation for implementation during the late 1980s and the 1990s. Consequently, the more diverse its products, the more number of new competitors it confronted. By the same token, aggressive competitors, as well as many imitators, also pursued strategies of product and market development, which eroded Club Med's dominant share of its specialty market. Accordingly, occupancy rates suffered.

Despite its global coverage, Club Med was still a small company, based on number of clients, compared with such European rivals as Thompson Travel and the German group TUI. As a tour operator, Club Med fell from third to seventh place between 1984 and 1988. With growth in its home market of less than three percent annually, some 391,000 French clients in 1987 to 1988, the MNC faced rather limited potential in France.[19] Club Mediterranee was both innovator and imitator. When it launched its Europeanization program, the MNC selected 17 villages for conversion to an international flavor because its biggest competitor, Robinson, had 16 of them.

EXHIBIT 5 Club Med Inc. Number of GMs by National Origin, 1986–1989

	1989	1988	1987	1986
American Zone				
American and Canadian	215,100	218,100	210,800	220,000
Mexican and Caribbean	18,000	10,500	8,400	20,000
Asian/Pacific/Indian	13,200	12,700	12,500	6,100
French/other European	38,200	25,500	18,900	17,200
South American	5,000	4,500	3,900	4,400
Total	289,500	271,300	254,500	267,700
Asian Zone				
American and Canadian	1,200	600	600	300
Asian/Pacific/Indian	113,500	94,300	71,100	55,000
French/other European	21,400	17,400	24,200	9,500
Total	136,100	112,300	95,900	64,800

Source: *Annual Report*, Club Med Inc., 1988–1989, p. 23.

Trigano waxed philosophically on the changing markets:

> When we started, 99 percent of the people in the Paris region had never seen the Mediterranean. I hadn't. Just to see the sea was a considerable emotional event. And in my first year we had a water-ski boat . . . and you could walk on the water. When the Club offered wonders like that, you didn't worry about the accommodation—in U.S. Army surplus tents. We were all together, sharing these wonderful experiences, so we became friends; and that friendship was a sort of powerful cement.
>
> But the sense of discovery has gone now. People just want the best. Club Med can't be the same because life is not the same.

By the end of the 1980s, CMI encountered customer price resistance, especially apparent in the winter 1988 season when it raised prices 13 percent. Political unrest and labor problems, coupled with temporary closings, gave competitors an edge during 1988 to 1989.

Additionally, for many, Florida, with its own attractions, represented the gateway to the Caribbean. Because CMI was also in the vacation business, the term, *vacation*, which conjured up different images for vacationers, resulted in yet a broader definition of competition for CMI.

The Walt Disney Corporation, for example, attracted to Florida families and foreigners. With operations in California as well as France and Japan, it generated revenues approaching $5 billion and net income exceeding $700 million. It opened Disney/MGM Studios at Lake Buena Vista, Florida to attract adults. Global revenues rose 150 percent from 1985 to 1989. Its image might best be summarized in an article from *Restaurants and Institutions*:

> You don't have to be a kid to love Disney's new image. You can be a business executive, for instance, booked into one of three new convention hotels opening next year at Disney World. Or you can be a teenager, catching the curl on a boogie board at the new water park. Or a "thirtysomething" baby boomer sitting in a TV kitchen eating a pot roast that would have done Donna Reed proud.[20]

Although Universal Studios' (some said disastrous) inauguration in June 1990 threatened direct competition to Disney's MGM, many competing attractions made central Florida even more interesting to vacationing families. With two working studios, the area was expected to become the East Coast movie capital. Additionally, long-term plans to make Orlando a giant international airline hub, with bullet train service to other Florida cities, could make it a destination city for Asians and Europeans alike. Bargain-basement airfares and tour packages, and a somewhat weaker U.S. dollar, enticed a flood of English and continental travelers to Florida during winter 1989.

Additionally, resorts catering to an upscale business clientele represented a lucrative segment of the lodging industry. Firms such as the Marriott Corporation, Holiday Inn, and Hyatt Regency, competing on a level with Club Med, created luxurious upscale resorts in different environmental settings. Conference centers,

Travel Industry Out of Touch

A special *Wall Street Journal* survey, conducted by Peter D. Hart Research Associates, revealed that many believe travel companies often become fixated on services people do not care about, and ignore many services that people consider important. A survey of 403 of America's most frequent travelers (those who take 12 or more trips annually) found that many care little about in-room bars, computerized travel directions, or new gimmicks. What they do want are simple pleasures: quiet hotel rooms, clean rental cars, comfortable airplane seats.

Travelers like frequent flyer programs, good flight information, nonsmoking hotel rooms, and thick hotel room walls. They also see little real product differentiation among hotels, airlines, or car rentals.

"That's frightening," said John Nicolls, senior V.P. at Hyatt Hotels Corp. "We beat our heads against the wall trying to be different."

The chart below summarizes survey results.

How Travel Services Stack Up

Frequent travelers were asked to rank the services that are most important to them in deciding which hotels, airlines, and rental car companies to use. With five being the top possible score, here are highest and lowest rated services:

■ Highest rated   ▨ Lowest rated

Airlines (Mean score)

Frequent-flier programs	4.0
Special check-in lines for frequent fliers	3.8
Bed recliner on overseas flights	3.5
Movies and stereo entertainment	2.6
Self-ticketing	2.6
Airplane phones	1.9

Rental Cars

Service numbers to call if cars break down	4.4
Express check-in	4.0
Special discounts	3.9

Hotels

Direct-dial phones	4.0
Bathroom amenities	3.7
Nonsmoking rooms	3.5
In-room movies	2.2
In-room bar or refrigerators with snacks	1.9
Telephones in bathrooms	1.7
Accessories like power windows	2.6
Computerized directions	2.5
Car phones	1.6

Source: Wall Street Journal Centennial Survey.

Source: Jonathan Dahl, "Giving People What They Don't Want," in *The American Way of Buying* (New York City: Dow Jones & Company, 1990), pp. 39–40.

meeting rooms, quarters for executives, and getaway packages surfaced among American competitors.

For instance, the Marriott Corporation, the world's seventh-largest hotel chain with approximate 1988 revenues of $7.4 billion and net income of $2.4 million, established resorts in the same locations as Club Med; but these chains had a diversified customer base. For instance, Marriott entered new geographical markets, such as Warsaw, Poland, where it managed a 1,000-bed hotel. Similarly, Holiday Inn created a new line of luxury hotels for executives and vacationers. Although the resort segment of the U.S. lodging industry had been growing steadily, larger national organizations had already set course for markets abroad.[21] Also, as the larger U.S. firms became more family oriented, they developed children's programs in their resorts.[22] (See Exhibit 6.)

Other competitors, such as Hedonism II, Club Paradise, and Jack Tar Village, in imitation of Club Med, packaged lower-priced vacations. Club Med judged these numerous copy-cat villages to be inconsequential competitors, struggling, and second best. Nevertheless, Thomas J. Garzelli, vice president of Fly Fare Vacations said, "There's no question that the people who are filling up these resorts are the right demographics to go to Club Med."[23] Most copy cats, usually located in the Caribbean, were not global players, but they competed effectively in limited markets.

Nevertheless, the newest and fastest-growing wave of competitors, the cruise-ship industry, which hoisted flags of many countries, generated all-inclusive trips and tours, not unlike Club Med's, and frequently traveled to the same exotic destinations. Multinational companies such as Carnival Cruise Lines, Royal Viking, and Norwegian Caribbean packaged multiprice-level programs that

EXHIBIT 6   Resorts with Programs for Children

Year-round
Marriott Mountain Shadows Resort, Scottsdale, Arizona
Marriott Tan Tar-a, Lake of the Ozarks, Osage Beach, Missouri
South Seas Plantation Resort and Yacht Harbor, Captiva Island, Florida
Sonesta Beach Hotel, Key Biscayne, Florida
Summer
Amelia Island Plantation, Amelia Island, Florida
Casa de Campo, La Romana, Dominican Republic
Dunfey Hyannis Resort, Hyannis, Massachusetts
Hyatt Hotel, Hilton Head Island, South Carolina
Hyatt Regency Cerromar Beach, Dorado, Puerto Rico
Mariner's Inn, Hilton Head, South Carolina
Marriott Grand Hotel, Point Clear, Alabama
Marriott Hilton Head Resort, South Carolina
Sagamore Hotel, Lake George, New York

Source: Iris Sanderson Jones, "Traveling with Kids," *Working Woman*, November 1986, p. 232.

appealed to young singles and marrieds, families, as well as leisure trips for retirees. By the end of 1987 it had grown to a $4-billion market in North America alone, and the lines made deep inroads into Club Med's Caribbean domain.

Robert H. Dickenson, vice president of sales and marketing for Carnival Cruise Lines said, "Cruising was once the domain of the rich. Now cruising is open to everyone."[24]

FINANCES

Club Mediterranee, founded as a nonprofit sports organization in 1950, was incorporated as a *societe anonyme* (S.A.) in 1957 in France and went public in 1965. Effective November 1, 1983, via a formation agreement, most of Club Mediterranee villages, sales activities, related operations, investments, contracts, and commitments in the American Zone were transferred at book value. Incorporated in the Cayman Islands in 1984, CMI, a majority-owned (74 percent at October 31, 1989) subsidiary of Club Mediterranee S.A., sold 3,400,000 common shares through a public offering in the United States and 300,000 common shares in a private offering to certain club officers, directors, and employees. CMI maintained financial records in U.S. dollars prepared in conformity with generally accepted U.S. accounting principles.

With profits and dividends stagnating during 1987 to 1988, ownership of Club Mediterranee changed. For example, the Groupe Depots holding company increased its 2.1-percent interest in 1988 to about 9.0 percent by early 1990. The Japanese conglomerate Seibu Saison, with its 3.0-percent stake, was joined in 1989 by Nippon Life and its 4.9-percent interest. Other players included Warburg Mercury with 4.5 percent and the Agnelli family with 2.9 percent. To make a takeover bid more difficult, Club Mediterranee unsuccessfully negotiated inter-locking shareholdings with Nouvelles Frontieres, a tour operator and air-charter company. The joint venture would have boosted the MNC to third place in the tour operators' league table.[25]

Summary financial data appear in Exhibit 7; for 1988 and 1989 detailed balance sheets, refer to the appendix. Of property and equipment shown in the balance sheets, on the basis of cost, less than 5 percent represented land value of the villages. Buildings, plus building and leasehold improvements, accounted for the bulk of the value of villages. Most properties were leased with an average lease of 15 years, ranging from 1 to 27 years. Lease payments could be suspended in case of *force majeure*. Seven leases required rentals based upon occupancy levels. Data in Exhibit 8 summarize per-share highlights for stock issued on CMI.

Because of its international transactions in several currencies, CMI had suffered exchange-rate losses. For several years it endured the negative impact from net French franc-based costs and expenses. Despite a 10-percent worsening of the dollar in international markets, these losses stabilized in 1988 partly due to a 35-percent increase in GMs from European countries who paid for visits to American Zone villages with strong currencies. The firm also experienced the adverse effects of the Mexican decision to maintain a fixed (below-market) exchange rate of pesos for dollars.

EXHIBIT 7   Club Med Inc. Financial Highlights, 1984–1989 ($millions)

	1989	1988	1987	1986	1985	1984
Income Statement Data						
Revenues	$468.8	$412.4	$370.4	$337.0	$279.7	$235.3
Gross profits	159.4	133.2	125.1	115.3	92.4	81.5
Depreciation	17.9	16.4	13.5	11.5	7.8	6.1
Operating income	25.4	11.2	20.0	19.8	16.0	15.1
Income before extraordinary items	20.4	8.7	16.8	17.4	14.2	11.5
Extraordinary items[a]	0.7	0.1	0.6	0.7	1.4	0.6
Net income	21.1	8.8	17.4	18.1	15.6	12.0
Balance Sheet Data						
Working capital	27.5	42.5	4.6	30.9	31.9	34.6
Long-term debt	100.1	131.1	89.4	91.2	76.1	39.3
Shareholders' equity	207.6	189.4	184.2	159.0	142.5	129.5
Total assets	415.5	403.2	353.4	313.8	269.1	212.1

[a]The firm is taxed under many jurisdictions, some of which do not impose an income tax. Resulting from negotiated tax reductions for periods ranging from 1991 to 2005, the firm received incentive concessions from the Dominican Republic, Turks and Caicos Islands, Haiti, Saint Lucia, Mauritius, Thailand, and Indonesia. Also, the firm had net operating losses and various tax-credit carryforwards, as well as tax-loss carryforwards expiring mostly 1990 through 1994.
Source: *Annual Report*, Club Med Inc., 1988–1989.

EXHIBIT 8   Club Med Inc. Per-Share Data, 1984–1989

	1989	1988	1987	1986	1985	1984
Net income share	$1.50	$0.62	$1.23	$1.32	$1.14	$1.14
Weighted average shares outstanding (millions)	14.1	14.1	14.1	13.7	13.7	10.6
Dividends per share[a]	$0.20	$0.20	$0.20	$0.20	n/a	n/a

Range of Stock Prices by Quarter, 1987–1989

Quarter Ended	1989		1988		1987	
	High	Low	High	Low	High	Low
January 31	16.875	12.625	15.000	9.000	29.250	21.500
April 30	19.875	15.750	16.250	11.750	29.000	25.000
July 31	21.875	18.250	16.625	12.250	27.000	22.625
October 31	20.625	17.375	15.750	13.250	24.750	12.250

[a]A semiannual dividend of $0.10 per share was paid in February 1990.
Source: *Annual Report*, Club Med Inc., 1988–1989.

STRATEGY

Typically a firm begins as a domestic organization servicing its home market, then initiates international activities, first with exports, and later opens sales offices abroad and licenses foreign companies to manufacture its products. Subsequently, the multinational company establishes its own manufacturing and services subsidiaries. A few firms globalize operations.

Club Mediterranee began as an international firm with headquarters in Paris, operations in the Balearic Islands (about 120 miles southeast of Barcelona, Spain), and customers predominately, but not exclusively, French. As the firm's operations spread across the globe, management largely maintained the original strategies of Trigano with reactive modifications to those strategies as current conditions dictated.

President Oizan-Chapon said, "In business you take the risk; you cannot control everything." He mentioned two major factors that hurt Club Med in 1988: (1) political unrest, which led to closing its Magic Isle village in Haiti and negatively impacted occupancy rates in New Caledonia; (2) construction problems, which delayed opening of a big new village in Huatulco, Mexico. Richard Phalon estimated that the Mexican misadventure cost Club Med around U.S. $7 million in reimbursements and debits.[26]

EXHIBIT 9 Club Med Inc. Operating Data by Market Segment, 1987–1989 (U.S. $millions)

Regions by Years	Consolidated Regional Revenues	Operating Income (Loss)	Identifiable Assets
1989			
North America	$103.4	$(8.4)	$ 48.1
Mexico–Caribbean	175.4	10.8	264.5
Asia–Pacific	157.9	22.9	102.9
Consolidated	468.8	25.4	415.5
1988			
North America	133.1	(11.7)	55.5
Mexico–Caribbean	151.6	8.2	241.6
Asia–Pacific	127.7	14.7	106.2
Consolidated	412.4	11.2	403.2
1987			
North America	124.6	(1.6)	48.1
Mexico–Caribbean	143.6	12.0	223.3
Asia–Pacific	102.2	9.7	82.0
Consolidated	370.4	20.0	353.4

Note: Consolidated revenues eliminate revenues between geographic areas and revenues originating in another area. Therefore, although the North American area generated nearly twice the revenues shown above, these were spent in another region. By the same token, about 75 percent of revenues attributed to the Mexico–Caribbean region were generated elsewhere. In the Asia–Pacific area, most revenues generated there were spent in the region.
Source: *Annual Report*, Club Med Inc., 1989, p. 41.

Changing demographics and customer tastes could not be denied, although Oizan-Chapon insisted, "Only part of the market is maturing. Part of it is growing." He pointed out, "We are following a life cycle plan."

Product diversification efforts met with limited success. The North American market had encountered problems: West Coast customers were less attuned to French culture than East Coast ones. *Chef de village* Jean-Luc Olivero thought that the problem was even more basic: Americans were puritanical. For instance, when Club Med bought The Sandpiper property in Florida from Hilton Hotels, management ordered removal of TVs and telephones from rooms. Americans preferred them. They were replaced in 1989. (See Exhibit 9 for data on operating results by market segment.)

CMI developed a three-part growth strategy for the 1990s:

1. Broaden the appeal: Increase market penetration of the core product, the Club Med village vacation.
2. Expand the reach: Introduce the Club Med concept to countries with growing economies and desires for new vacation opportunities.
3. Widen the concept: Develop new vacation products, particularly in the rapidly growing cruise market.[27]

Of course, results for the 1990s depended upon how effectively Club Med implemented its strategies.

Endnotes

1. Richard Phalon, "Trouble in Paradise," *Forbes*, September 19, 1988, p. 56.
2. Joshua Levine, "I Am Sorry, We Have Changed," *Forbes*, September 4, 1989, pp. 136–137.
3. Ibid., p. 136.
4. Milton Moskowitz, *The Global Marketplace* (Chicago: 1988), p. 146.
5. Ibid., p. 148.
6. Sales brochure, Club Med, Summer/Fall 1990.
7. Stephen Wood, "Club Med's Global Villages," *Business* (U.K.), January 1990, pp. 68–69.
8. Levine, "I Am Sorry."
9. Phalon, "Trouble in Paradise," p. 61.
10. Sales brochure.
11. Ibid.
12. Jacques Horovitz, "Club Mediterranee [A]," in Leslie Rue and Phyllis Holland, *Strategic Management: Concepts and Experiences* (New York: McGraw-Hill, 1986), pp. 645–646.
13. Ibid., pp. 648–649.
14. GOs, or *gentils organisateurs*, specialized by function, had the task of helping people make this vacation the best. They both organized and participated in events. Typically there were 80 to 100 GOs per village.
15. Horovitz, "Club Mediterranee."
16. Moskowitz, *Global Marketplace*, p. 147.
17. Wood, "Club Med's," p. 67.
18. Ibid.
19. Ibid., p. 66.
20. Brian Quintan, "Disney's World Grows Up," *Restaurant and Institutions*, December 11, 1989, pp. 45–68.
21. "Now Club Med Wants an Antidote for Competition," *Business Week*, November 2, 1987, p. 120.
22. Iris Sanderson Jones, "Traveling with Kids," *Working Woman*, November 1988, pp. 231–232.
23. "Antidote for Competition," p. 120.
24. Ibid.
25. Wood, "Club Med's," pp. 66–67.
26. Phalon, "Trouble in Paradise," p. 61.
27. *Annual Report*, Club Med Inc., 1989.

APPENDIX A Club Med Inc.
Balance Sheet, Years Ended October 31 ($000)

	1989	1988
Assets		
Current assets		
Cash and cash equivalents	$ 56,881	$ 33,697
Marketable securities	15,506	35,000
Accounts receivable	24,488	19,568
Due from affiliates	6,108	4,846
Inventories	14,074	14,276
Prepaid advertising and marketing	8,259	9,571
Other prepaid expenses	6,564	4,668
Total current assets	131,880	121,626
Property and equipment		
Villages	307,633	291,222
Other	10,287	9,367
Construction in progress	6,289	12,588
Total property and equipment	324,209	313,177
Less accumulated depreciation and amortization	(85,426)	(69,970)
Net property and equipment	238,783	243,207
Other assets		
Investments in and advances to affiliates	9,767	6,778
Deposit on equity interest	4,778	4,778
Long-term investments	17,189	17,520
Other	13,115	9,326
Total other assets	44,849	38,402
Total assets	$415,512	$403,235
Liabilities and Shareholders' Equity		
Current liabilities		
Due to banks	$ 418	$ 8,180
Accounts payable	13,133	10,249
Due to Club Mediterranee	6,393	4,107
Due to affiliates	—	220
Accrued expenses	42,120	27,373
Amounts received for future vacations	30,992	25,066
Current maturities of long-term debt		
Club Mediterranee	1,591	—
Other	9,716	3,956
Total current maturities of long-term debt	11,307	3,956
Total current liabilities	104,363	79,151
Long-term debt		
Club Mediterranee	—	1,501
Other	100,103	129,606
Total long-term debt	100,103	131,107

APPENDIX A Cont'd. Club Med Inc.
Balance Sheet, Years Ended October 31 ($000)

	1989	1988
Liabilities and Shareholders' Equity		
Minority interest and other	$ 3,412	$ 3,575
Commitments and contingencies		
Shareholders' equity		
Common shares, par value $1.00 per share, 20,000,000 shares authorized, 14,156,000 shares issued (14,146,000 in 1988), and 14,096,000 shares outstanding (14,087,000 in 1988)	14,096	14,087
Additional paid-in capital	115,036	114,921
Retained earnings	79,061	60,782
Foreign currency translation adjustment	(559)	(388)
Total shareholders' equity	207,634	189,402
Total liabilities and shareholders' equity	$415,512	$403,235

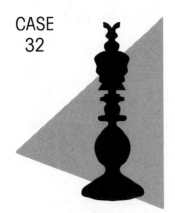

CASE
32

McDonald's Corporation

DAVID GENTRY,
GREGORY MARCHWINSKI &
JIM McSORLEY

INTRODUCTION

When Michael Quinlan, CEO of McDonald's Corporation, returned to work Monday morning, he felt drained and agitated. He had just experienced the 1990 annual shareholders' meeting on Friday, and the experience was not a pleasant one. Mr. Quinlan misses the days when past shareholder's meetings were pleasant and shareholders were content to hear about the continuing growth in restaurants and earnings of the company. Now, shareholder meetings are becoming grill sessions with institutional shareholders putting on the pressure for improved earnings every quarter. Environmentalists attended and asked the company to do more about the environment regardless of impacts to profit, and with threats of boycotts, these people have to be taken seriously.

This particular meeting was the worst the CEO remembers. McDonald's stock has tumbled 4½ points in the last two days. The stock is now down 20 percent from last year. Analysts have been beating the stock down because of slowing domestic sales growth. International prospects will not take up for the domestic slack for several years. U.S. sales are still growing, but are a far cry from the last three decades' growth. The main problem is that customers are changing their tastes to more sophisticated food, and increased competition is taking away customers with more fast-food options than ever imagined. Even worse is the fast food price wars that have started up. This threatens to hurt profitability even more so in the next few quarters.

Mr. Quinlan got even angrier thinking about all these problems. In this state of mind, he called Ron, his secretary. "Ron, get Mr. Rensi and Mr. Walsh in here, right now." As soon as the two of them arrived, Mr. Quinlan told them, "Ed, you are in charge of all the products we sell, and Michael, you are responsible for the marketing of all these great products. The two of you have got to come up with some strategies to increase our sales and profitability. I'm tired of explanations to our shareholders, and you know how important domestic sales are to our international expansion. You boys have two weeks to present some great ideas to me. Now get to it." Mr. Rensi and Mr. Walsh left the office knowing they had a lot to do in the next two weeks.

DESCRIPTION OF BUSINESS

McDonald's Corporation licenses and operates a chain of 11,205 fast-food restaurants throughout the United States, Canada, and overseas under the name of McDonald's. Outlets serve standardized menus built around hamburgers.

HISTORY

Ray Kroc is well-known as the mastermind behind McDonald's. Most people believe he invented fast food, and few people even know how the name *McDonald* fits into the birth of the fast-food giant. The real invention of fast food belongs to the brothers McDonald, known as Dick and Mac. When the McDonald brothers first opened a car hop drive-in in 1937, they stumbled onto the cutting edge of the fast-food service business. They acquired some wealth in 1940 with a drive-in in San Bernadino. This restaurant had a unique design for 1940 in that it exposed the kitchen to the public and had no inside seating except a few stools along the side counter. This restaurant became the town's number one teenage hangout and offered over 25 menu items.

By 1948 they achieved greater wealth when they built a tiny hamburger stand. At this time competitors started entering the car hop business, and the troubles of dealing with leather-jacketed teenage customers and the high-cost, labor-intensive format had the brothers about to quit the car hop restaurant and get into a hamburger restaurant in a strip shopping mall. Just before they were going to execute these plans, they studied their car hop operations for the last three years. They discovered that hamburgers accounted for 80 percent of their business. The attention devoted to the barbecue pit could not be justified.

With this discovery, the brothers decided to try a complete overhaul of the McDonald's drive-in, and this was the beginning of a revolution in food service. The whole concept was now speed, lower prices, and volume. The restaurant was closed for three months in fall 1948 for the changeover. The 20 carhops were fired and two service windows were installed for the customer to place his own order. The kitchen was rearranged for speed and volume. Paper bags, wrappers, and cups replaced the china and flatware which also eliminated the need for the dishwasher. The menu was slashed from 25 items to just 9. The hamburger became smaller, but the price became the cheapest ever heard of at 15 cents. All orders were standardized. All hamburgers were prepared with ketchup, mustard, onions, and two pickles. Any deviation from the standard and the customer was forced to wait. This allowed a major change in restaurant business in that the food was prepared in advance of the order.

The reopening of the drive-in was a disaster. The business level fell to one-fifth the preconversion level. The fired car hops would come in and tease the brothers about getting their uniforms ready. The brothers decided to stick it out and after six months their drive-in business started picking up. The difference was that the teenage appeal was gone and working class families became the new clientele. This worked out for the best since this was a much larger market segment, anyway. The parents could afford to take their kids to a restaurant and the kids were fascinated by seeing a commercial kitchen for the first time. The McDonald brothers did not miss out on the kid connection and advertised the family appeal and had promotions with giveaways to children. The brothers after a year regained all the business they lost following the conversion.

Still the brothers were not satisfied with the present volume. They envisioned a volume of business never seen before. The brothers started experimenting with new techniques to speed up the kitchen operations. They started an assembly-line procedure and started inventing new tools for the kitchen. Since no kitchen equipment at this time was designed for assembly-line production, they designed their own kitchen instruments. One of their advantages was their reliance on a local handyman with no restaurant experience. He had a tiny machine shop and invented many fast food dispensers and kitchen equipment still in use today. His lack of experience in traditional restaurants was helpful in creating many of his new designs.

Customized equipment was just one of the tricks the McDonalds used for speeding up food service. Rigid operating procedures were adopted to eliminate the human factor in slowing down the food process. Food preparation was broken down into simple, repetitive tasks. This also allowed hiring of untrained cooks at lower wages and minimal training with better quality control over the product. These key features of self-service, paper service, and quick service created a unique restaurant and there was nothing in the food-service industry that remotely resembled it.

At this time a postwar America was becoming faster paced, more mobile, and more oriented to convenience and instant gratification. The brothers were hitting the trend perfectly. In fact, their restaurant in San Bernardino was doing such a phenomenal business that the McDonald brothers were getting attention nation-wide. *American Restaurant* magazine ran a cover story in 1952, and that started inquiries from drive-in operators who wanted to copy their operations.

While the McDonald brothers were a success in their San Bernardino operations, their knack as franchisers was the opposite. After two years of licensing other operators, they had sold only 15 franchises with only a one-time fee of $1,000. They did not have the skill or desire to sell franchises. The McDonald brothers were content with the money from their existing local restaurants and were not consumed with the idea of franchising. By 1954, copycat restaurants were starting up and the McDonald brothers were basically giving away their unique concepts.

In summer 1954 the franchise opportunity that escaped the McDonald brothers was seized by a food-service equipment salesman by the name of Ray A. Kroc. Ray Kroc was introduced to the food industry at age 25 through a sales job for Lily Cup Company. He was no ordinary salesman. Kroc could see trends in the market and put himself in the place of the customer. His sales practice was based on analyzing the customers' operations and suggesting changes to enhance them and in the process increase his sales of cups. He proposed to Walgreen a carryout food service to increase sales. Kroc persisted over several months to convince the purchasing manager of the idea. By offering free paper cups for one month, Kroc finally persuaded the manager to try carryout service for one month. After sales nearly doubled, Walgreen added carryout service to its entire chain. Walgreen became one of the largest accounts for Lily, and Kroc became a top salesman.

After 14 years with Lily, Kroc found an opportunity to start his own business. He found a product that would allow the soda fountain chains to add new products. This product, called the multimixer, was more efficient at making ice milk products that tasted like malts and milk shakes. Ray started Prince Castle Sales and started selling the multimixer to soda fountain operations. The company did well at first, but the food industry was changing and the old soda fountain concept was being replaced by Dairy Queens and Tastee Freeze operators that had no use for his machine. With his company's market shrinking, Kroc was looking for a new market for his multimixer. At this time the McDonald brothers' restaurant in San Bernardino had ordered its tenth multimixer. Ray decided to see how one restaurant could have a need for so many.

When Kroc saw his first McDonald's, he knew it could fill a huge void in the food-service market. Ray Kroc was just what the McDonald brothers needed to expand nationally. The McDonald brothers only looked at a local market and rarely traveled. Ray traveled extensively and knew the food-service industry and its operations. The McDonald brothers were looking for a replacement for their current franchising agent and told Kroc to work the multimixer sales contract with the replacement after they found one. After Ray flew home to Chicago, he called Dick McDonald and asked, "What about me?" Kroc soon negotiated a contract that gave him exclusive rights to franchise McDonald's nationally.

With this contract, Ray Kroc formed a new franchising company in 1955 called McDonald's System, Inc. (The name was changed to McDonald's Corporation in 1960.) He set up initial strategies based on his experience as a food-service salesman. Chief among those was to keep the same basic format as the McDonald brothers had developed. His company did make operational changes to improve efficiency and encourage systemwide consistency, but these changes were only refinements of what the McDonald brothers started. Ray Kroc had a totally new approach to franchising for the times. In that day most franchisers were concerned about how much they would get at the expense of the franchisee. Ray believed in a more balanced franchise partnership. His success with franchising was based on encouraging the success of the franchisee first and McDonald's Corporation would benefit later. The product Ray sold had an extremely attractive franchising plan and a better-than-average fast-food format. But the real success in McDonald's growth was based on Ray Kroc's salesmanship. Kroc was a master salesman. He had a gift for communication and used this to inspire his audience about the McDonald's system and the potential McDonald's could offer to the right owner.

In his first year of operation in 1955 18 franchises were started. In 1962 over 400 stores were in operation. Today over 11,200 McDonald's are in full operation.

FINANCE—CURRENT

Capital expenditures and total assets rose 12 percent in 1989. These include new restaurants, relocations, remodelings, and purchase of previously leased properties. Forty-five percent of this occurred in foreign markets compared to 29 percent five years ago. Land costs have increased because of the stringent site standards.

McDonald's has also increased expenditures in other areas such as offices, sites, related equipment, and training facilities in the United States, England, Australia, and other markets.

Ownership of the restaurant real estate continues to be a major focus. Real estate ownership yields long-term benefits, including assured property rights and the ability to fix occupancy costs. In addition to purchasing new properties, previously leased properties are acquired. Restaurant property ownership has increased 5 percent in the last 10 years.

In recent years, property and equipment expenditures exceeded cash provided by operations as expansion and reinvestment were accelerated. Total debt rose $768 million in 1989 to fund accelerated expansion, reinvestment, and treasury stock purchases, and reflected the inclusion of the $200 million of ESOP notes which the company has guaranteed. Total debt as a percentage of total capitalization, defined as total debt and total shareholders' equity, was 53 percent in 1989 and 49 percent in 1988, compared to 40 percent five years ago. Foreign currency financings have been used to lessen impacts of changing foreign currencies on net income and total shareholders' equity by reducing exposure to such fluctuations.

Though relatively steady compared to 1988, return on average assets has been impacted in recent years by growth in operations outside of the United States; reinvestments; acquisitions of previously leased properties; and a greater number of higher-cost, higher-volume locations as McDonald's continues to invest for the future. See Appendixes A through D for financial statements.

FINANCIAL STRATEGIES

McDonald's financial strategy is to maintain its large consistent growth by investing in new restaurants. These restaurants are to be funded mostly by cash from operations. This is going to be increasingly difficult because of the saturation of the U.S. market and its slowing sales growth. Domestic sales growth has declined from 11 percent in 1987 to 5 percent in 1990 (estimated).

STRUCTURE

Franchising at McDonald's is unique. It begins by recruiting and training individuals with motivation and entrepreneurial talent to become active, on-premise owners, not just investors. The franchising relationship stresses personal commitment, involvement, and a sharing of common goals, principles, and ideals. McDonald's looks for franchisees who are involved full-time in the business, applying their entrepreneurial talents and management skills to building sales.

McDonald's cultivates a management environment which places a premium on quality operations; accordingly, the company franchises one restaurant at a time. New restaurants are licensed to existing operators who have proven track records, to new franchisees, and to the company. In 1989 more than 200 new franchisees joined the system, including second and third generations who bring additional vigor and enthusiasm to existing businesses. In virtually all cases, the company does not supply food, paper, or equipment, but approves suppliers from which franchised and company-operated restaurants can purchase these items. The conventional franchise arrangement is generally for a term of 20 years and requires an investment of approximately $610,000, 60 percent of which may be financed.

In addition to the conventional franchise, McDonald's offers the business facilities lease program to enable outstanding individuals who do not have sufficient capital, but who meet all other criteria, to become franchisees.

Candidates for this program generally must have liquid assets of approximately $66,000. Over the past 10 years, approximately 50 percent of new franchisees have joined McDonald's through this program.

McDonald's emphasis on franchising also creates financial leverage. Franchisees provide capital initially by purchasing the equipment, signs, seating, and decor, and over the long term by reinvesting in their businesses. The company shares the investment in the site by owning or leasing the land and building, and leases them to franchisees through franchise arrangements.

Revenues from franchised restaurants consist of fees based upon a percentage of sales with specified minimum payments. These fees, together with occupancy and operating rights, are stipulated in franchise arrangements, which generally have 20-year terms. In 1987 minimum U.S. fees were increased from 11.5 percent to 12.0 percent of sales for new franchise arrangements. In recent years, as more higher-cost, higher-volume locations have been developed, the fee structure has been altered to reflect these higher costs. In 1989 arrangements for 87 percent of U.S. franchised openings had fees in excess of 12 percent, with average fees at 15 percent of sales. Fees paid by franchisees outside of the United States vary according to local business conditions.

FOREIGN MARKETS

McDonald's has recognized the importance of foreign markets early on. These markets provide the customer base necessary to sustain the historical corporate growth. Consequently, the company has taken an aggressive approach to foreign markets. This is evidenced by the fact that over one-third of all corporate restaurants are located outside the United States. McDonald's currently has restaurants in Japan, England, Spain, West Germany, France, Hong Kong, Australia, Brazil, and the Soviet Union.

EXPANSION INTO OTHER AREAS

After nearly three decades of double-digit growth, McDonald's sales growth has slowed in the last few years. U.S. sales are still growing, but have lost their sizzle. Increased competition and more sophisticated consumer tastes are taking its toll on the traditional McDonald's fare. McDonald's is trying several strategies to deal with these problems associated with the changes in the marketplace. Addition of new menu items, new types of restaurants, and expansion into new markets are all being tested or considered to maintain growth.

Today's American consumer is growing more concerned about nutrition. McDonald's has made several changes to deal with this. It has switched to 100 percent vegetable oil for cooking fries and hash browns. This spring McDonald's replaced ice cream with low-fat yogurt, introduced low-fat shakes, and added cereal and bran muffins for breakfast. Also a new technology that allows most of the fat to be taken out of hamburger without changing the taste is being tested by McDonald's. The new product, the Lean Deluxe, was introduced in McDonald's Harrisburg, Pennsylvania restaurants in November 1990. This sandwich is 91 percent fat free versus the typical hamburger, which is 20 percent fat. A McDonald's spokesman said, "This product offers a low-fat ground beef sandwich for those customers who love the taste of beef, but want to cut down on the fat in their diet."

In an attempt to ward off competition and spur evening sales, McDonald's has introduced pizza in about 200 outlets. The company is also experimenting with pasta dishes such as spaghetti and fettucini, plus fish and chips in a few stores. The corporation believes the pizza strategy has the best potential to increase evening sales. There are drawbacks with adding these new dishes. Sustaining a heavier menu on an ongoing basis will slow service and boost costs. There are still kinks in preparing pizza in McDonald's style before going beyond the 200 test stores.

In recognition of the maturing of the fast-food industry and the slower growth in this stage, McDonald's has been looking into nontraditional areas for growth. One of these is the Golden Arch Cafe. This is a diner in Hartsville, Tennessee with a 1950s atmosphere. The decor is counter stools and cozy booths. The jukebox plays hits from the 1950s. The town itself has a population less than 3,000. This store is a one-store test and basically explores the possibilities of small-town America. A traditional McDonald's usually is not built in a town with fewer than 10,000 people, and this strategy will allow growth in new markets without cannibalizing sales of existing McDonald's.

Another new idea is the McDonald's in New York near Wall Street. In an attempt to attract the adult crowd to Big Macs, the Wall Street McDonald's has Italian marble tables and dark wood paneling. On one afternoon, a tuxedoed gentleman played a grand piano and guests were ushered in by a white-gloved doorman. Guests sipped cappuccino during the reception by Cary Leibowitz. All this is part of the experimentation to find the right combination to attract the growing older population into McDonald's of the future. For instance, this McDonald's has espresso as well as cappuccino on the menu at all times. The settings are being altered to entice adults to bring their kids in at dinner time. Analysts doubt that this strategy will work. General Mills' Red Lobster and PepsiCo's Olive Garden are better at attracting the family dinner customer. Even with improving the trappings around the McDonald's, people still view McDonald's for its convenience and consistency and not as a major family dinner place.

INDUSTRY—COMPETITION

The fast-food industry is becoming more competitive in the United States. Major rivals include Wendy's, Taco Bell, Burger King, and many others. McDonald's does not have the unique fast-food concept to itself anymore and intensified competition is slowing McDonald's domestic growth.

Recently, McDonald's, under increasing pressure from its franchisees, responded to competitors' price cutting. PepsiCo Inc., parent of Taco Bell, Pizza Hut, and Kentucky Fried Chicken, started the price war. Impressive sales gains resulted from this strategy. Then Wendy's International created a minimenu of items costing less than $1 and made more in the first nine months of 1990 than in all of 1989.

The price discounting from McDonald's competitors has clearly affected McDonald's sales, and McDonald's has decided to enter the price war to meet its competitors strategy. McDonald's will mark down several of its menu items below $1. This move will intensify the brutal price wars in the industry, but the strategy is deemed necessary due to slipping profit margins and lower customer counts. Many franchisees independently adopted discounting months ago in desperation to retain market share. In recession-hurt areas such as Boston, local McDonald's have already featured 59-cent hamburgers and 99-cent Big Macs to entice an increasing price-conscious lunch crowd. These independent operators are willing to give up margin, hoping to make it up on volume. McDonald's now has adopted this strategy officially.

Such high-margin items as french fries, soft drinks, salads, and entree sandwiches wouldn't be discounted much if at all. The selections tapped for long-term reductions will most likely be the plain hamburger, regular sized coffee, dessert pies, and perhaps one of the breakfast sandwiches. The corporate office said that price cuts are being considered and "There is nothing we are doing that will hurt our profitability." McDonald's stock dropped $1.125 after the price discount information came out. McDonald's franchisees spoke enthusiastically about the plan, saying, "Permanent value pricing is right. We're in a recession. The consumer needs value, but we operators need to make money." Value pricing implementation may vary from market to market due to the independence of some franchisees. McDonald's usually only suggests strategies to independent operators, but this time it will provide free promotional store signs that work in the franchisees' local markets.

McDonald's has long stated that it wouldn't employ discounting as a strategy, and that it would avoid the word in promotions. Analysts say that by using price discounting as a strategy, McDonald's is acknowledging that competition has made significant inroads. McDonald's same-store sales have slid for nine straight quarters on an inflation-adjusted basis. Some analysts see this as a desperate effort to reverse a two-year slide in customer counts.

Competition is intense over more things than just pricing. Burger King Corporation gave a back-handed salute to McDonald's on its decision to abandon polystyrene packaging. Full-page advertisements in seven newspapers said Burger King "applauds McDonald's for its new environmental consciousness. Welcome to the club." Then went on to say, "We wonder what the planet would be like if you joined us in 1955." McDonald's opened its first outlet in 1955, a year after the initial Burger King opened. Burger King used paperboard hamburger containers since the start. McDonald's responded by saying the hundreds of thousands of dollars spent on the ads could have been spent on doing something positive about the environment. Burger King has attacked McDonald's in past advertisements comparing flame-broiled hamburgers with frying and have it your way versus standard hamburger complements.

OPERATIONS STRATEGIES

McDonald's goal since 1955 has never wavered nor changed: it is to serve high-quality menu products to more customers faster and friendlier, while building sales volumes and dollar profits. Achieving this goal requires the identification of new sites with long-term potential, as well as ongoing enhancement to existing facilities to assure that they are contemporary, inviting, and operationally efficient.

McDonald's serves customers a substantially uniform menu consisting of high-quality menu products. The products are the same, nutritious food most people eat at home—bread, meat, eggs, fish, potatoes, and dairy products. McDonald's establishes specifications for each product that is served, and independent, local suppliers are recruited around the world to ensure that strict quality standards are met.

McDonald's believes you deserve straight answers to questions customers have about menu products. It has taken the lead to voluntarily list and explain the ingredients and nutritional values of all menu products in a publication titled, "McDonald's Food . . . The Facts." This booklet is available from any U.S. restaurant or from the Nutrition Information Center.

McDonald's is committed to establishing and enforcing responsible and appropriate practices in all aspects of the business. As part of this commitment, and in accordance with McDonald's Food Product Specifications, which prohibit the use of misbranded and adulterated foods, McDonald's does not use irradiated food products in the preparation of food sold in its restaurants.

McDonald's menu will continue to evolve to remain responsive to customer preferences, and the commitment to high-quality ingredients will remain unchanged. Ingredients such as 100 percent pure lean beef, Russet Burbank potatoes, and real dairy products will always have a place on the McDonald's menu and as part of a well-balanced diet.

In any retail business the most important attribute is location. McDonald's has always been, and will be, committed to finding and obtaining high-quality locations. Site selection techniques have become more sophisticated—analyzing traffic patterns, walking patterns, and population movements. McDonald's also analyzes access and egress to specific sites to assess volume potential.

An interesting trend in site selection and development in the United States is the utilization of locations that are considered nontraditional—shopping malls, hospitals, toll ways, urban areas, military bases, and airports—which create new markets and increase market share and penetration. Today, these sites account for 9.6 percent of total U.S. restaurants, compared to 8.5 percent five years ago. However, the majority of restaurants continue to be free-standing, suburban facilities because of the sales opportunities in those markets. The higher investment required for today's sites creates increased risk and reward, demanding a flexible fee structure for franchised restaurants. Fees are now based on the company's investment in the site, rather than limited to a standard fixed percentage of sales.

In many markets outside of the United States development began in urban areas, where the majority of the population was concentrated, in order to build awareness and traffic. Since then additional site opportunities have been developed, such as airports, highways, and military bases, as well as free-standing restaurants in suburban areas with drive-through facilities.

The evolution of a McDonald's restaurant, from a red-and-white-tile building with no seating to a contemporary building design with extended drive-through booths, a comfortable dining room, and a state-of-the-art kitchen, has been noteworthy, and in response to changing customer needs.

In the U.S. restaurants that have them, drive-throughs on average account for more than half of sales and reflect customers' preference for convenience and speed of service. In addition to extended drive-through booths, tandem menu boards nearly double capacity. There are more than 5,000 extended drive-through booths and 500 tandem menu boards in operation in the United States today.

McDonald's believes that reinvestment strengthens its leadership position in the food-service industry. Reinvestment is an ongoing process which maintains a competitive edge in the marketplace and ensures future growth. There is one fundamental reason for reinvestment, and that is to build sales. During the past five years, nearly one-third of capital expenditures have been devoted to reinvestment, exclusive of the dollars spent by franchisees and affiliates. Reinvestment creates an ambience consistent with the times and the environment in which the restaurant is located. Dining room remodelings have included contemporary design and decor; flexible seating; natural, brighter lighting; and refreshing colors. Kitchen remodelings have improved operating efficiencies as the menu was expanded.

The focus on equipment development is important to improving productivity and enhancing crew experience, while investing in more efficient and cost-effective equipment. Equipment development has been a major focus over the past several years. Nearly 5,000 restaurants around the world have patented two-side grills, which cook both sides of a hamburger patty at the same time. This method shortens preparation time, reduces labor required, and results in a tastier hamburger.

The in-store computer processor, now in all U.S. company-operated restaurants, allows managers to spend more time managing the business and less time sitting at a desk doing paperwork. This computer-based system accounts for cash and inventory, computes yields and food costs, schedules labor, and analyzes sales by product and hour.

HUMAN RESOURCES

McDonald's Corporation is an operations-based company whose focus is serving customers high-quality menu products in a fast and friendly manner. Attention to detail and a single-minded focus on the basics of the business are the key reasons for McDonald's success. Customers expect consistent, high-quality food; fast, friendly service; and a clean, pleasant environment at every McDonald's store. Training the McDonald's crew is the major factor in meeting these customer expectations.

Training the managers, franchisees, suppliers, and store workers has been a top priority at McDonald's since day one. The first formal training center opened in 1961 in the basement of a McDonald's restaurant. Today, training occurs at every one of the 11,200+ restaurants, at offices around the world, and at the Hamburger Universities located in Oak Brook, Illinois; Munich, West Germany; Tokyo, Japan; and London, England.

The professors at the Hamburger Universities have extensive operational experience. Most have been restaurant managers or field consultants who consult with franchisees on improving daily operations. The professors' hands-on experience allows them to relate to the real-life challenges and concerns of managers and franchisees.

Crew people train in restaurants with videotapes, one-on-one instruction, and on-the-job coaching. Assistant managers participate in a management development program and attend basic and intermediate operations and applied equipment classes at regional offices, complementing restaurant training. Managers and franchisees are required to graduate from Hamburger University before operating their own McDonald's restaurants. All levels of management spend a significant amount of time in the restaurants, evaluating procedures and operations. This hands-on management style assures that the business is operated in the best interests of crew and managers, franchisees, suppliers, and most importantly, customers.

MARKETING

In 1989 McDonald's maintained its position as the most-advertised single brand in the world. The corporate advertising budget was $424,789,900, an increase of 6.1 percent over 1988. McDonald's Corporation, franchisees, and affiliates spent an estimated $1.1 billion, 6.3 percent of systemwide sales, on advertising and promotion in 1989.

The Operators National Advertising Fund provides funds to purchase national television advertising time via voluntary contributions by U.S. restaurants. McDonald's Corporation pays for commercial production costs. In addition, restaurants around the world make voluntary contributions to local advertising cooperatives.

Contributing to U.S. sales in 1989 were successful marketing and promotional programs, including Happy Birthday Big Mac, the McRib sandwich for a limited time, Scrabble, and Blast Back with Mac. More recent promotions have included the McMillions contest. This was a joint marketing venture with NBC. Numbered game pieces were distributed at McDonald's. Cash prizes were given to those who could match these numbers with numbers revealed during certain NBC television shows.

McDonald's has changed its main advertising jingle. The new jingle is, "Food, Folks, and Fun." This has replaced, "Good times, Great Tastes." These new advertisements are a simple version of the McDonald's marketing message. McDonald's tries to communicate that message to the broadest group of customers. That message focuses on tasty and nutritious food, friendly folks, and fun.

The 1989 marketing calendar in the United States contained food focuses and strong reputation advertising, interwoven with promotions. The new McChicken sandwich debuted in May, breakfast was advertised throughout the year, and various Big Mac-related and Happy Meal promotions appeared throughout 1989.

The goals of foreign marketing plans are different from the domestic goals. The marketing plans for markets outside of the United States included a wide range of programs designed to build sales and generate customer awareness. McDonald's tests items and offers items for a limited time in order to generate customer interest and to evaluate the product.

The United States has seen an environment in which there has been significant discounting by the competition and a slowing of U.S. sales growth. Burger King has executed two advertising coups recently. It has signed up the year's two hottest licensed properties, The Simpsons and the Teenage Mutant Ninja Turtles.

McDonald's enjoys a great advantage over its competition because of its numerous restaurants that are in great locations. Domestically McDonald's faces saturation, because available prime locations will cannibalize the sales at present stores. McDonald's prices are at the high end of the fast-food market. The average ticket at McDonald's is about $5.

FUTURE DIRECTION

McDonald's has always enjoyed rapid growth in the past. The combination of fast food, consistency, and low price has always been the key to its growth success. Now the market for fast food is saturated with competitors offering many different options to the customers. Demand for franchises in America has declined as the adult customer is becoming more sophisticated in his dining tastes. McDonald's faces a crossroads in its product life. Should it proceed into new areas to sustain growth? Can McDonald's be successful in other restaurant endeavors beyond fast food? Mr. Rensi and Mr. Walsh had these and many other questions to answer before their meeting with their CEO.

APPENDIX A McDonald's Corporation Balance Sheet (annual)

	Assets Fiscal Years Ending		
	12/31/89	12/31/88	12/31/87
Assets			
Cash	$ 137,000	$ 184,000	$ 183,206
Receivables	207,000	179,000	156,632
Inventories	46,000	49,000	48,453
Notes receivable	27,000	25,000	27,323
Other current assets	78,000	80,000	67,942
Total current assets	495,000	517,000	483,556
Property, plant and equipment	9,874,000	8,647,000	7,392,955
Accumulated depreciation	2,116,000	1,847,000	1,573,379
Net property, plant and equipment	7,758,000	6,800,000	5,819,576
Invest and adv to subs	291,000	226,000	N.A.
Other non current assets	76,000	60,000	N.A.
Intangibles	326,000	315,000	261,725
Deposits and other assets	229,000	241,000	416,752
Total assets	$9,175,000	$8,159,000	$6,981,609
Liabilities and Shareholders' Equity			
Notes payable	$ 76,000	$ 115,000	$ 61,975
Accounts payable	413,000	453,000	322,463
Current long-term debt	59,000	43,000	37,321
Accured expenses	398,000	359,000	126,909
Income taxes	71,000	34,000	84,688
Other current liabilities	N.A.	N.A.	222,808
Total current liabilities	1,017,000	1,004,000	856,164
Deferred charges/income	613,000	543,000	440,200
Long-term debt	3,901,000	3,111,000	2,685,095
Other long-term liabilities	94,000	88,000	83,435
Total liabilities	5,625,000	4,746,000	4,064,894
Preferred stock	200,000	N.A.	N.A.
Common stock, net	46,000	46,000	23,081
Capital surplus	159,000	145,000	150,787
Retained earnings	4,546,000	3,935,000	3,396,046
Treasury stock	1,172,000	717,000	621,412
Other liabilities	(228,999)	4,000	(31,786)
Shareholders' equity	3,550,000	3,413,000	2,916,715
Total liabilities and shareholders' equity	$9,175,000	$8,159,000	$6,981,609

APPENDIX B McDonald's Corporation Income Statement (annual, $000)

	Fiscal Years Ending		
	12/31/89	**12/31/88**	**12/31/87**
Net sales	$6,142,000	$5,566,000	$4,894,000
Cost of goods sold	2,581,000	2,378,000	2,098,000
Gross profit	3,561,000	3,188,000	2,796,000
R&D expenditures	N.A.	N.A.	N.A.
Selling, general, and administrative expenses	1,873,000	1,581,000	1,355,000
Income before depreciation and amortization	1,688,000	1,607,000	1,441,000
Depreciation and amortization	229,000	324,000	279,000
Interest expense	302,000	237,000	203,000
Income before taxes	1,157,000	1,046,000	959,000
Provision for income taxes	430,000	400,000	410,000
Net income before extraordinary items	727,000	646,000	549,000
Extraordinary items and discontinued operations	N.A.	N.A.	47,000
Net income	$ 727,000	$ 646,000	$ 596,000
Outstanding shares	362,000,000	375,000,000	207,567,390

Cash Flow Statement ($000)

	Fiscal Years Ending		
	12/31/89	**12/31/88**	**12/31/87**
Cash Flow Provided by Operating Activity			
Net income (loss)	727,000	646,000	549,000
Depreciation/amortization	438,000	383,000	338,000
Net increase (decrease) in assets/liabilities	30,000	94,000	79,000
Other adjustments, net	51,000	54,000	85,000
Net cash provided (used) by operations	1,246,000	1,177,000	1,051,000
Cash Flow Provided by Investing Activity			
(Increase) Decrease in property, plant, and equipment	(1,555,000)	(1,321,000)	(1,027,000)
(Acquisition) disposal of subsidiaries, business	120,000	37,000	48,000
(Increase) decrease in securities investments	(5,000)	20,000	40,000
Other cash inflow (outflow)	(73,000)	(43,000)	33,000
Net cash privided (used) by investing	(1,513,000)	(1,307,000)	(906,000)
Cash Flow Provided by Financing Activity			
Issue (purchase) of equity	(279,000)	(126,000)	(195,000)
Increase (decrease) in borrowing	601,000	345,000	105,000
Dividends, other distributions	(115,000)	(103,000)	(93,000)
Other cash inflows (outflows)	13,000	15,000	16,000
Net cash provided (used) by financing	220,000	131,000	(167,000)
Net change in cash or equivalents	(47,000)	1,000	(22,000)
Cash or equivalents at year start	184,000	183,000	205,000
Cash or equivalents at year end	137,000	184,000	183,000

APPENDIX C McDonald's Corporation Balance Sheet (quarterly $000)

	Fiscal Quarter Ending			
	6/30/90	**3/31/90**	**9/30/89**	**6/30/89**
Assets				
Cash	$ 119,500	$ 105,600	$ 353,601	$ 125,676
Receivables	191,200	182,300	177,971	165,011
Inventories	39,900	41,300	42,926	45,448
Notes receivable	30,700	28,800	26,113	26,296
Other current assets	88,900	72,700	77,646	81,293
Total current assets	470,200	430,700	678,257	443,724
Property, plant, and equipment	10,514,900	10,105,000	9,301,850	8,854,415
Accumulated depreciation	2,289,500	2,195,900	2,030,370	1,938,216
Net property, plant, and equipment	8,225,400	7,909,100	7,271,480	6,916,199
Deferred charges	N.A.	572,200	N.A.	N.A.
Intangibles	359,500	338,600	324,239	317,925
Deposits and other assets	600,000	N.A.	564,793	539,297
Total assets	$ 9,655,100	$ 9,250,600	$ 8,838,769	$ 8,217,145
Liabilities and Shareholders' Equity				
Notes payable	$ 158,700	$ 212,200	$ 279,449	$ 239,015
Accounts payable	310,700	317,700	305,822	295,021
Current long-term debt	61,000	56,100	31,812	55,826
Accrued expenses	343,200	315,200	342,379	283,099
Income taxes	31,600	65,300	60,083	45,150
Total current liabilities	905,200	966,500	1,019,545	918,111
Deferred charges/income	666,400	636,700	602,500	575,600
Long-term debt	4,221,800	3,996,500	3,467,996	3,117,810
Other long-term liabilities	102,800	100,500	90,203	88,554
Total liabilities	5,896,200	5,700,200	5,180,244	4,700,075
Preferred stock	199,900	200,000	200,000	N.A.
Common stock, net	46,200	46,200	46,166	46,166
Capital surplus	166,600	164,700	155,451	151,946
Retained earnings	4,854,100	4,672,300	4,406,156	4,217,817
Treasury stock	1,303,600	1,295,400	907,369	834,922
Other liabilities	(204,300)	(237,400)	(241,879)	(63,937)
Shareholders' equity	3,758,900	3,550,400	3,658,525	3,517,070
Total liabilities and shareholders' equity	$ 9,655,100	$ 9,250,600	$ 8,838,769	$ 8,217,145

Income Statement (quarterly $000)

Net sales	$ 1,701,300	$ 1,533,100	$ 1,631,750	$ 1,548,089
Cost of goods sold	1,087,700	956,800	1,045,005	995,495
Gross profit	613,600	576,300	586,745	552,594
R&D expenditures	N.A.	N.A.	N.A.	N.A.
Selling, general, and administrative expenses	186,300	237,000	164,562	166,005
Income before depreciation and amortization	427,300	339,300	422,183	386,589
Interest expense	92,700	89,500	76,779	73,197
Income before taxes	334,600	249,800	345,404	313,392
Provision for income taxes	118,800	91,700	127,500	117,400
Net income before extraordinary items	215,800	158,100	217,904	195,992
Net income	$ 215,800	$ 158,100	$ 217,904	$ 195,992
Outstanding shares	358,502,043	358,500,000	369,993,906	371,965,706

APPENDIX D McDonald's Corporation Number of Restaurants in Operation

	1989	1988	1987	1986
Operated by franchisees	7,135	6,732	6,383	6,058
Operated under business facilities lease arrangements	438	378	377	348
Operated by the company	2,691	2,600	2,399	2,301
Operated by 50 percent or less owned affiliates	898	803	752	703
Systemwide restaurants	11,162	10,513	9,911	9,410

International Operations ($millions)

	1989	1988	1987
Revenues			
United States	$3,923	$3,716	$3,438
Europe	1,168	1,015	767
Canada	621	540	468
Other	430	295	221
Total revenues	$6,142	$5,566	$4,894
Operating Income			
United States	$ 995	$ 908	$ 883
Europe	203	163	109
Canada	118	109	91
Other	143	103	79
Total operating income	1,459	1,283	1,162
Interest expense	(302)	(237)	(203)
Income before provision for income taxes	$1,157	$1,046	$ 959
Total Assets			
United States	$5,646	$5,148	$4,509
Europe	2,063	1,703	1,460
Canada	562	510	422
Other	904	798	591
Total assets	$9,175	$8,159	$6,982

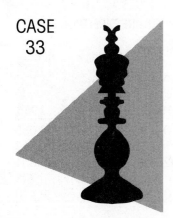

CASE
33

THE ZEEBRUGGE CAR FERRY DISASTER

COLIN BOYD

It is with profound sadness that I must introduce this report with the tragic loss of the "Herald of Free Enterprise" off the Belgian coast. The Herald is a Townsend Thoresen ship and, as you know, Townsend Thoresen became part of P&O in January. At the time of writing the precise cause of the disaster is unknown. We have instituted an immediate investigation and of course both the British and Belgian governments are conducting enquiries. Whatever the outcome of these, you may be assured that the safety of our ships and those who man them and travel in them is our overriding priority.

So began the somber letter by Chairman Jeffrey Sterling introducing the 1986 P&O *Annual Report*. The roll-on/roll-off passenger car ferry *Herald of Free Enterprise* capsized in the approaches to the Belgian port of Zeebrugge en route to Dover in England at 7:05 p.m. local time on March 6, 1987. There was a light easterly breeze and the sea was calm. The ship had a crew of 80, and carried 459 passengers, 81 cars, 3 buses, and 47 trucks. She capsized in about 90 seconds soon after leaving the harbor, ending up on her side half-submerged in shallow water. Only a fortuitous turn to starboard in her last moments prevented her from sinking completely in deeper water.

Following the capsize, a heroic search and rescue operation was mounted. At least 150 passengers and 38 members of the crew lost their lives, most inside the ship from hypothermia in the frigid water. Many others were injured. It soon became apparent to the rescuers that the *Herald of Free Enterprise* had left the port of Zeebrugge with her bow doors open. The death toll was the worst for a British vessel in peacetime since the sinking of the Titanic in 1912.

THE CROSS-CHANNEL TRANSPORT MARKET

The English Channel between England and the continent of Europe is one of the most heavily traveled waterways in the world. In 1985 a total of 20,056,000 passengers and 3,387,200 cars, buses, trucks, and unaccompanied trailers were

EXHIBIT 1 Selected U.K Air and Sea Passenger Travel Data, 1975–1985 (by country of embarkation or disembarkation, arrivals plus departures, 000)

	1975	1976	1977	1978	1979	1980	1981	1982	1983	1984	1985
By Sea[a]											
Belgium	3,641	3,975	4,391	4,428	4,421	5,192	4,714	4,678	4,415	4,608	4,411
France	7,739	7,861	8,602	9,805	11,112	12,621	14,734	15,747	16,140	15,353	15,645
Holland	1,496	1,841	1,977	2,056	2,044	1,940	1,958	1,968	2,210	2,191	2,207
Totals	12,876	13,677	14,970	16,289	17,577	19,753	21,406	22,393	22,765	22,152	22,263
By Air											
Belgium	788	850	854	874	867	809	757	748	824	942	988
France	2,740	2,901	2,904	3,026	3,102	3,070	3,105	3,193	3,275	3,537	3,746
Holland	1,634	1,835	1,934	1,994	1,959	1,903	1,813	1,843	1,808	2,014	2,227
Sub totals	5,162	5,586	5,692	5,894	5,928	5,782	5,675	5,784	5,907	6,493	6,961
FR of Germany	2,277	2,470	2,619	2,882	3,081	3,136	2,948	2,998	3,006	3,384	3,644
Switzerland	1,093	1,181	1,289	1,372	1,413	1,444	1,469	1,576	1,711	1,875	2,016
Italy	1,860	1,941	2,037	2,279	2,550	2,692	2,335	2,378	2,494	2,582	2,583
Greece	691	882	884	1,162	1,562	1,839	2,095	2,123	2,006	2,301	2,875
Portugal	309	296	399	474	591	701	849	963	1,068	1,248	1,547
Spain	5,298	4,667	4,617	5,553	5,654	5,592	6,332	7,624	8,293	9,543	7,751
All air	16,690	17,023	17,537	19,616	20,779	21,186	21,703	23,446	24,485	27,426	27,377

[a]Some traffic through these three countries is in transit to or from adjacent European countries.
Source: U.K. Department of Transport Statistics Digest, 1975–1985.

ferried across the channel. The most popular crossing is the shortest one, between Dover and Calais in France, a 22 mile trip that takes 90 minutes. Exhibit 1 shows selected data on sea and air travel to and from the United Kingdom.

Fares for cross-channel travel had historically been high in comparison to other intensive ferry routes in the world, and drew criticism from British consumer groups. In the 1980s, however, prices began to decline, as shown in Exhibit 2.

The mixture of demand for channel ferry services was changing. Passenger travel had remained stable since 1982, but freight traffic was increasing. Part of this increase was due to increased trade (particularly since Britain became a member of the European Economic Community), and part was due to the technological advance represented by the introduction of roll-on/roll-off (ro-ro) ships. These ships, essentially flat pontoons covered by superstructures, have bow and stern doors which enable vehicles to be driven on and off via adjustable ramps at the dock. The speed of ferry loading and unloading is vastly improved for a ro-ro ship, which reduces the unproductive time a ship spends in port.

For the freight shipper, ro-ro ferries also improve productivity. A tractor-trailer (or just the trailer unit) can be driven straight on and off the ferry's deck as if it were part of the road to the freight's destination. Costly intermediate transfers of cargo are eliminated, and the quantity of inventory in the distribution pipeline is reduced by speedier transportation. Exhibits 3 and 4 show data on cross-channel ro-ro freight growth.

EXHIBIT 2   Ferry Fares at 1985 Prices for Short Sea Routes across the Channel (4.5 metre car, Ford Cortina, 2 adults plus 2 children, one-way; £1.00 = US$1.80)

	1975	1980	1985
Peak (most expensive single fare)	£78.21	£72.72	£81.00
Standard (cheapest published no-discount single fare)	69.83	55.61	38.00

Source: Flexilink.

Competition on cross-channel ferry services was influenced by the British government's July 1984 privatization of Sealink UK Ltd., previously a subsidiary of government-owned British Rail. At that time Sealink UK, its European state-owned counterparts, and Townsend Thoresen dominated the industry. Historically, channel ferry services had functioned mainly as the sea link between rail terminus points at channel ports.

Other recent developments in the industry had included the introduction of high-capacity, mixed freight, and passenger "jumbo" ferries; reductions in crew levels, despite the strong opposition of the maritime unions; the modernization of dock-side facilities to help speed ferry turn-round time; the introduction of special freight-only ro-ro ferries; and the promotion of a wider range of fares, especially for day trippers and off-peak travel.

The Channel Tunnel poses an extreme threat to the ferry industry. After 100 years of aborted attempts to initiate a tunnel project, the French and British governments finally allowed the project to go ahead in 1986. This was bitterly opposed by the ferry operators. Eurotunnel, the Anglo–French company that will finance and manage the tunnel, plans to have the 30-mile long, dual railway tunnels underneath the channel in operation by 1993. Eurotunnel's finances of £1

EXHIBIT 3   Roll-on/Roll-off Road Goods Vehicles to Mainland Europe, by Country of Disembarkation, 1975–1985 (departures from U.K. only)

	1975	1976	1977	1978	1979	1980	1981	1982	1983	1984	1985
Powered Vehicles											**thousands**
Belgium	75.1	72.7	103.9	110.3	123.0	122.1	119.6	136.3	146.1	163.7	163.3
France	94.4	107.8	128.7	131.1	150.6	140.4	152.9	168.0	187.3	215.8	230.6
Holland	31.7	32.4	32.9	31.9	39.8	36.8	41.3	41.5	40.3	40.8	48.0
Totals	201.2	212.9	265.5	273.3	313.4	299.3	313.8	345.8	373.7	420.3	441.9
Unaccompanied Trailers											**thousands**
Belgium	33.6	37.1	45.8	44.6	57.5	48.2	63.5	99.1	104.4	103.6	129.9
France	25.3	28.8	35.8	43.0	56.4	53.7	63.1	58.2	61.5	59.9	65.8
Holland	72.2	81.7	69.8	94.0	103.3	97.6	110.4	128.1	140.8	147.6	145.0
Totals	131.1	147.6	151.4	181.6	217.2	199.5	237.0	285.4	306.7	310.2	340.7
Grand totals	332.3	360.5	416.9	454.9	530.6	498.8	550.8	631.2	680.4	730.5	782.6

Source: U.K. Department of Transport Statistics Digest, 1975–1985.

EXHIBIT 4 Port of Dover Ferry Traffic, 1981–1985 (arrivals and departures)

	1981	1982	1983	1984	1985
Passengers (millions)	12.46	13.82	13.95	13.86	13.78
Percentage change from prior year	+12.96	+10.94	+0.94	−0.67	−0.56
Passenger vehicles (millions)	1.65	1.78	1.74	1.73	1.72
Percentage change from prior year	+11.41	+7.42	−1.99	−0.69	−0.06
Freight vehicles (millions)	0.51	0.61	0.69	0.74	0.80
Percentage change from prior year	+5.88	+19.48	+13.36	+14.73	+7.96

Source: Port of Dover Authority.

billion in share capital and £5 billion in loan facilities compare with planned spending on the project of £4.9 billion.

TOWNSEND THORESEN

The following description is from the 1985 *Annual Report:*

European Ferries Group plc[1] is a U.K. public company, with three separate classes of shares listed on the London Stock Exchange, giving a current market capitalization approaching £500 million.

The origins of the group can be traced back nearly 60 years to the time when Captain Stuart Townsend pioneered the first specialist car ferry service between Dover and Calais. Through a mixture of skillful management and acquisition the group's Shipping Division, under the marketing name Townsend Thoresen, is now the major ferry operator in Europe, with services from Dover, Portsmouth, Felixstowe, and Cairnryan to destinations in France, Belgium, Holland, and Northern Ireland.

In the 1970s the group began diversifying, initially into harbor operations with the acquisition of Larne Harbour in Northern Ireland and the Felixstowe Dock & Railway Company, and then by the formation of a U.K. Property Division. The major asset within this U.K. Property Division is a 34.7 percent holding in Stockley plc, a listed property company operating in London and the southeast of England.

The group became involved in U.S. property (real estate) in 1979, and this particular area has seen significant expansion in the intervening period, such that the group now has an interest, both directly and through joint ventures, in substantial holdings of land in Denver, Atlanta, and Houston. The 1980s have seen further property acquisitions at La Manga Club in Spain, and, in a smaller way, in Germany.

Significant development projects have been in progress since the beginning of 1985 in our shipping and harbour divisions. Six vessels are being substantially extended ("jumboisation") and two new vessels have been ordered for delivery next year. We are also developing a major new

EXHIBIT 5 European Ferries Group plc Directors

Kenneth Siddle	Chairman and Group Managing Director (Succeeded by Geoffrey Parker in July 1986)
W. James Ayers	Group Technical Director
Roger G. Braidwood	Group Finance Director, Director of Stockley plc, Controller of Group Property interests
John J. Briggs	Managing Director of Townsend Thoresen's Dover operations, Group Freight Director
John W. Dick	Chairman of E F International Inc., Director of Stockley plc
Geoffrey J. Parker	Chairman and Managing Director of Harbor Operations Division, Managing Director of Townsend Thoresen's Felixstowe and Larne operations
John R. Parsons	Deputy Managing Director of Townsend Thoresen's Dover operations
William B. Pauls	Vice Chairman and Chief Executive Officer of E F International Inc.

Non Executive Directors
Roald P. Aukner
David J. Bradford
Knut Dybwad
Colin H. Fenn
Sir Jeffrey Sterling
Alternate—Bruce D. MacPhail

Townsend Thoresen Management

Dover	J. J. Briggs	Managing
	J. R. Parsons	Deputy Managing
	A. P. Young	Operations
Portsmouth	D. S. Donhue	Managing
	R. N. Kirton	Operations
Felixstowe and Larne	G. J. Parker	Managing
	S. Livingstone	Operations
Technical Services	W. J. Ayers	
Tourist Marketing	B. H. Thompson	

Source: *Annual Report*, European Ferries Group plc, 1985.

terminal, the Trinity Container Terminal, at the Port of Felixstowe which will be completed later this year.

Exhibit 5 lists the Directors of European Ferries Group plc and the managers of Townsend Thoresen, as detailed in the 1985 *Report*. Background financial data is given in Exhibits 6 and 7.

In 1982 the Townsend Thoresen ferry *European Gateway* capsized with the loss of six lives after a collision with a Sealink ship in the approaches to the port of Harwich. The speed of the capsize drew speculation on the lack of stability of ro-ro ferries when water enters the main vehicle deck.[2] Like the *Herald* after her, the *European Gateway* came to rest on her side half-submerged in shallow water, narrowly avoiding a deep water sinking with heavy loss of life.

EXHIBIT 6   European Ferries Group plc 5-Year Financial Record

	1985	1984	1983	1982	1981
Sales revenue (£millions)	403.5	309.4	322.9	292.9	277.7
Profit before taxation (£millions)	48.4	44.4	45.0	30.4	26.8
Earnings per share	13.7p	14.9p	12.3p	10.5p	9.4p
Net dividend per ordinary share	4.75p	4.3p	3.8p	3.35p	3.1p
Dividend cover	2.9x	3.5x	3.2x	3.1x	3.0x
Year-end share price	139.5p	128.0p	88.5p	57.0p	74.0p
Year-end FT Industrials index	1130.0	945.2	775.7	593.6	528.8
Assets (£millions)					
Capital expenditures	82.6	45.3	16.2	14.4	18.2
Depreciation	17.7	15.0	13.3	12.3	12.0
Tangible fixed assets	267.7	206.9	176.6	183.1	180.5
Investments in associates	118.5	73.4	79.2	62.1	30.2
Stocks	163.3	302.7	121.1	110.3	75.3
Borrowings net of cash and deposits	159.7	164.6	113.4	121.0	88.6
Shareholders' funds at December 31	327.1	302.4	254.9	225.2	207.8

£1.00 = 100p = US$1.80
Source: *Annual Report*, European Ferries Group plc, 1985.

In January 1984 European Ferries purchased from The Peninsular and Oriental Steam Navigation Company (P&O) its loss-making Normandy Ferries subsidiary for £12.5 million. In January 1986 P&O acquired a 50-percent interest in a firm that held shares equivalent to 16.1 percent of the voting share capital of European Ferries. Sir Jeffrey Sterling, the chairman of P&O, was invited to join the board on January 21, 1986.

On December 4, 1986 the boards of European Ferries and P&O jointly announced a recommended £340 million takeover offer for the shares of European Ferries by P&O. Geoffrey Parker, executive chairman of European Ferries, gave reasons for his firm's recent poor performance in a letter to shareholders:

EXHIBIT 7   European Ferries Group plc Division Sales and Profitability (£millions)

	Sales Revenue					Profit before Taxation				
	1985	1984	1983	1982	1981	1985	1984	1983	1982	1981
Shipping	280.1	236.4	226.7	207.7	183.0	19.0	17.5	16.6	12.8	1.9
Harbor operations	46.3	42.1	38.4	34.4	29.4	10.9	9.6	9.5	8.5	6.2
U.K. property	14.6	14.0	13.7	33.9	33.3	2.0	3.0	2.3	2.4	9.2
U.S. property	48.8	13.9	43.0	16.5	31.4	17.4	14.6	12.7	(0.9)	7.7
Spain property	13.7	3.0	1.1	—	—	(0.5)	(4.3)	(3.4)	—	—

Table ignores some interest charges, other income, and exceptional items and excludes the small Banking Division, disposed of in April 1984.
Source: *Annual Reports*, European Ferries Group plc, various years.

In the early part of the year our property activities in Houston were affected by the severe fall in the price of oil, upon which the economy of Houston is critically dependent. In the late spring our shipping activities were seriously affected by strike action which was not resolved for 10 weeks. Your board estimates that the strikes will be responsible for some £10 million in lost profits in 1986 . . . and that our US activities will now make a negative contribution compared with profits before taxation of £17 million in 1985.

The majority of European Ferries shareholders accepted the P&O offer by the deadline of 3:00 p.m., January 16, 1987. Exhibit 8 outlines P&O's recent business history.

THE CAPSIZE OF *MV HERALD OF FREE ENTERPRISE*

The *mv Herald of Free Enterprise*,[3] like her sister ships *Pride of Free Enterprise* and *Spirit of Free Enterprise,* was a modern ro-ro passenger/vehicle ferry designed for use on the high-volume, short Dover–Calais ferry route. She could accelerate rapidly to her service speed of 22 knots. She was certificated to carry a maximum total of 1,400 persons.

At 433 feet long and 7,950 gross tons, the *Herald* was of record size at her launching in 1980 and was one of the prides of the 22 ship Townsend Thoresen fleet. She had two main vehicle decks, and at Dover and Calais double-deck ramps connected to the ferry, allowing simultaneous vehicle access to both decks. At Zeebrugge there was only a single level access ramp which did not allow simultaneous deck loading, and thus ferry turn-round time was longer at this port. Also, this ramp could not quite reach the upper vehicle deck, and water ballast was pumped into tanks in the bow of the *Herald* to facilitate loading.

When the *Herald* left Zeebrugge on March 6, 1987 not all the water had been pumped out of the bow ballast tanks, causing her to be some three feet down at the bow. Mr. Stanley, the assistant bosun, was responsible for closing the bow doors. He had opened the doors on arrival at Zeebrugge, and then supervised some maintenance and cleaning activities. He was released from this work by Mr. Ayling, the bosun, and went to his cabin.[4] He fell asleep and was not awakened by the harbour stations public address call alerting crew to take their assigned positions for departure from the dock.

The bosun left the car deck at the harbour stations call to go to his assigned station. He later said, "It has never been part of my duties to close the doors or make sure that anyone is there to close the doors." The chief officer, Mr. Leslie Sabel, stated that he remained on the car deck until he saw—or thought he saw—Mr. Stanley threading his way through the parked cars toward the door control panel. He then went to the bridge, his assigned position.

The *Herald* backed out of the berth stern first. By the time the *Herald* had swung around the bow was in darkness and the open bow doors were not obvious to the ship's master, Captain David Lewry. As the ship increased speed, a bow wave began to build up under her prow. At 15 knots, with the bow down 2 to 3 feet lower than normal, water began to break over the main car deck through the open doors at the rate of 200 tons per minute.

EXHIBIT 8   The Peninsular and Oriental Steam Navigation Company (P&O)

P&O was incorporated in England on December 31, 1840 in order to establish a shipping service between the United Kingdom and the Far East and to take over shipping services, established in August 1837, to Spain, Portugal, and Mediterranean ports.

Shipping routes were established throughout the Near and Far East and to Australia and the business expanded both organically and by acquisition over the ensuing century. However, in the 1960s radical changes began to affect P&O's cargo and passenger shipping activities as a result of the introduction of cargo containerization and the growth of intercontinental passenger air transport.

In view of the high level of capital expenditure which containerization required, P&O and three other United Kingdom shipping companies formed OCL (Overseas Containers Limited) to take over their cargo liner trades as they were converted to container shipping. By the early 1970s P&O had phased out its scheduled passenger liner services to the Far East and Australia, while during the same period the concept of ocean cruising was being developed as a leisure market.

As a result of the economic recession and the rapidly changing environment for both cargo and passenger shipping, P&O began to diversify its activities in the 1970s. This led to the acquisition of the house building and property construction group Bovis, with its banking subsidiary TCB Limited, and to the continued development of P&O's integrated road and sea through-transport freight haulage operators, Ferrymasters Limited and Pandoro Limited, as well as the growth of its integrated subsidiary, P&O Australia, largely in materials handling, off-shore supply services, and cold storage and distribution.

Investments were also made by P&O in this period in oil- and gas-related activities mainly in the United States and in the North Sea, in ferry services (to Orkney and Shetland, Northern Ireland, and the Republic of Ireland, Sweden, Holland, Belgium, and France), and in liquefied petroleum gas (LPG) carriers and other bulk ships. The oil- and gas-related activities were subsequently sold. In January 1985 P&O sold its cross-channel ferry activity and in May 1985 P&O sold a 50 percent interest in its LPG carriers operation.

In February 1985 P&O merged with SGT, thereby bringing into the P&O Group the ownership and management of a substantial portfolio of offices, shops, and commercial properties located largely in the United Kingdom (owned by Town and Country Properties) and in the United States.

In the financial year ended December 31, 1985, profits before tax of the P&O Group were £125.6 million on sales of £1,629.3 million. At December 31, 1985, stockholders' funds amounted to £746.8 million. In May 1986 P&O acquired that proportion of OCL that it did not previously own, and in June 1986, P&O acquired Stock Conversion, a United Kingdom property company.

Reasons for the Offer

The directors of P&O believe that there is a clear commercial logic for the acquisition of European Ferries by P&O, which will undoubtedly result in improved profit potential for both companies. European Ferries will bring to P&O a range of businesses, including Townsend Thoresen, the principal European car ferry operator, and the Port of Felixstowe, the United Kingdom's leading container port. P&O's management is familiar with these businesses, which are allied to those in which P&O is already engaged both in the United Kingdom and overseas. The combination of the two groups will be a further logical step in P&O's strategy of developing its existing businesses and will increase the scope for maximizing returns to stockholders.

European Ferries' ferry services and port interests complement P&O's shipping interests and will increase P&O's participation in the continuing growth of trade within Europe. European Ferries will benefit from the addition of P&O's skills and resources in property management and development and P&O's size and financial strength will enable the problems currently being experienced in European Ferries' United States property portfolio to be dealt with effectively over an appropriate timescale.

Source: Various circulars sent to shareholders by P&O.

In common with other ro-ro vessels, the *Herald*'s main vehicle deck had no subdividing bulkheads. If water entered the deck it could flow from end to end or from side to side with ease. The flood of water through the bow doors quickly caused the vessel to become unstable. The *Herald* listed 30° to port almost instantaneously. Large quantities of water continued to pour in and fill the port wing of the vehicle deck, eventually causing a capsize to port. The *Herald* settled on the sea bed at slightly more than 90°, with the starboard half of her hull above water.

Under the 1894 Merchant Shipping Act, a Court of Formal Investigation of the capsize of the *Herald of Free Enterprise* was held in London between April 27 and June 12, 1987 before the Wreck Commissioner, the Hon. Mr. Justice Sheen, a respected judge. The proceedings of the Court were subject to intense public scrutiny, with the tabloid press in particular concentrating on the more sensational aspects of the tragedy.

To encourage full disclosure at this Court of Investigation, the U.K. Department of Transport, which is responsible for enforcement of the various shipping acts, indicated that it did not intend to prosecute anyone responsible for the fact that the *Herald* went to sea with her bow doors open. This was a common practice for such courts of enquiry. The Court had investigative powers, the power to suspend or remove a Merchant Officer's Certificate of Competency, and the power to determine who should contribute to payment of the investigation's costs. The Court had no other powers.

EXTRACTS FROM THE REPORT OF THE COURT OF FORMAL INVESTIGATION: *MV HERALD OF FREE ENTERPRISE*

The remainder of this case study consists of verbatim extracts from the report of the Court of Formal Investigation written by the Hon. Mr. Justice Sheen, and released on July 25, 1987. Statements of opinion and interpretation of facts are his, and not the casewriter's. [Any comments or elaborations by the casewriter are shown in square brackets.]

The Manning of the *Herald* on the Zeebrugge Route

On the Dover–Calais run these ships are manned by a complement of a master, two chief officers, and a second officer. The officers are required to work 12 hours on and not less than 24 hours off. In contrast, each crew was on board for 24 hours and then had 48 hours ashore. . . . The sea passage to Zeebrugge takes 4.5 hours . . . which gives the officers more time to relax. For this reason the company employed a master and two deck officers [instead of three] on this run. . . .

Captain Kirby was one of five masters who took it in turn to command the *Herald.* He was the senior master . . . a coordinator between all the masters and officers in order to ensure uniformity in the practices operated by different crews. As three different crews served with five different sets of officers, it was essential that there should be uniformity of practice. Furthermore there were frequent changes among the officers. Captain Kirby drew attention to this in an internal memo dated November 22, 1986 addressed to Mr. M. Ridley, chief superintendent.

> The existing system of deck officer manning . . . is unsatisfactory. When *Herald* took up the Zeebrugge service our deck officers were reduced from 15 to 10. The surplus 5 were distributed around the fleet. On *Herald's* return to the Calais service, instead of our officers returning, we were and are being manned by officers from whatever ship is at refit. Due to this system, together with trainee master moves, *Herald* will have had a total of 30 different deck officers on the books during the period September 29, 1986 to January 5, 1987. . . .

Captain Kirby returned to this theme with a further memorandum dated January 28, 1987 which was also addressed to Mr. Ridley:

> I wish to stress again that *Herald* badly needs a *permanent* complement of good deck officers. Our problem was outlined in my memo of November 22. Since then the throughput of officers has increased even further, partly because of sickness. During the period from September 1 to January 28, 1987 a total of 36 deck officers have been attached to the ship. We have also lost two masters and gained one. To make matters worse the vessel has had an unprecedented seven changes in sailing schedule. The result has been a serious loss of continuity. Shipboard maintenance, safety gear checks, crew training and the overall smooth running of the vessel have all suffered. . . .

Pressure to Leave the Berth

Why could not the loading officer remain on deck until the doors were closed before going to his harbor station on the bridge? The operation could be completed in three minutes, but the officers always felt under pressure to leave after loading. The *Bridge and Navigation Procedures* guide which was issued by the company included the following:

> Departure from Port
>
> a)   OOW/Master should be on the Bridge approximately 15 minutes before the ship's sailing time; . . .

That order does not make it clear whether it was the duty of the OOW or the master to be on the bridge 15 minutes before sailing, or whether the officer was to remain on the bridge thereafter.[5] If the OOW was the loading officer, this order created a conflict in his duties. The conflict was brought to the attention of Mr. Develin[6] by a memorandum dated August 21, 1982 from Captain Hackett, Senior Master of *Free Enterprise VIII* in which he said:

> It is impractical for the OOW (either the chief or the second officer) to be on the Bridge 15 minutes before sailing time. Both are fully committed to

loading the ship. At sailing time, the chief officer stands by the bow or the stern door to see the ramp out and assure papers are on board, etc. The second officer proceeds to his after mooring station to assure that the propellers are clear and report to the bridge.

The order illustrates the lack of thought given by management to the organization of officers' duties. [On the Zeebrugge run there was a reduced number of officers, and the loading officer's task was more complex because of the single-level loading ramp.] The sense of urgency to sail at the earliest possible moment was exemplified by an internal memorandum dated August 18, 1986 sent to assistant managers by Mr. D. Shipley, who was the operations manager at Zeebrugge:

> . . . put pressure on the first officer if you don't think he is moving fast enough. . . . Let's put the record straight, sailing late out of Zeebrugge isn't on. It's 15 minutes early for us.

Mr. A. P. Young sought to explain away that memorandum on the basis that the language was used merely for the purpose of what he called "motivation," but it was entirely in keeping with his own thoughts at the time. . . . The Court was left in no doubt that deck officers felt that there was no time to be wasted. The company sought to say that the disaster could have been avoided if the chief officer had waited on deck another 3 minutes. That is true, but the company took no proper steps to ensure that the chief officer remained on deck until the bow doors were closed.

The Negative Reporting System

The company has issued a set of standing orders which include the following:

> *01.09 Ready for Sea*
> Heads of departments are to report to the master immediately they are aware of any deficiency which is likely to cause their departments to be unready for sea in any respect at the due sailing time. In the absence of any such report the master will assume, at the due sailing time, that the vessel is ready for sea in all respects.

That order was unsatisfactory in many respects. . . . Masters came to rely upon the absence of any report at the time of sailing as satisfying them that their ship was ready for sea in all respects. That was, of course, a very dangerous assumption.

On March 6, Captain Lewry saw the chief officer come to the bridge. Captain Lewry did not ask him if the ship was all secure and the chief officer did not make any report. Captain Lewry was entitled to assume that the assistant bosun and the chief officer were qualified to perform their respective duties, but he should not have assumed they had done so. He should have insisted on a report to that effect.

In mitigation of Captain Lewry's failure to ensure that his ship was in all respects ready for sea a number of points were made on his behalf, of which the three principal ones were as follows:

1. Captain Lewry merely followed a system which was operated by all the masters of the *Herald* and approved by the senior master, Captain Kirby.
2. The court was reminded that the orders entitled "Ship's standing orders," issued by the company make no reference, as they should have done, to opening and closing the bow and stern doors.
3. Before this disaster there had been no less than five occasions when one of the company's ships had proceeded to sea with bow or stern doors open. Some of these incidents were known to management, who had not drawn them to the attention of other Masters. . . .

The system . . . was defective. The fact that other masters operated the same defective system does not relieve Captain Lewry of his personal responsibility for taking his ship to sea in an unsafe condition. In so doing he was seriously negligent in the discharge of his duties. That negligence was one of the causes contributing to the disaster. The court is aware of the mental and emotional burden resulting from this disaster which has been and will be borne by Captain Lewry, but the Court would be failing in its duty if it did not suspend his Certificate of Competency.

The Management of Townsend Thoresen

[A] full investigation into the circumstances of the disaster leads inexorably to the conclusion that the underlying or cardinal faults lay higher up in the company. The board of directors did not appreciate their responsibility for the safe management of their ships. They did not apply their minds to the question: What orders should be given for the safety of our ships?

The directors did not have any proper comprehension of what their duties were. There appears to have been a lack of thought about the way in which the *Herald* ought to have been organized for the Dover–Zeebrugge run. All concerned in management, from the members of the board of directors down to the junior superintendents, were guilty of fault in that all must be regarded as sharing responsibility for the failure of management. From top to bottom the body corporate was infected with the disease of sloppiness. . . . It is only necessary to quote one example of how the standard of management fell short. . . . It reveals a staggering complacency.

On March 18, 1986 there was a meeting of senior masters with management, at which Mr. Develin was in the chair. One of the topics raised for discussion concerned the recognition of the chief officer as head of department and the roles of the maintenance master and chief officer. Mr. Develin said, although he was still considering writing definitions of these different roles, he felt "it was more preferable not to define the roles but to allow them to evolve." That attitude was described by Mr. Owen, with justification, as an abject abdication of responsibility.[7] It demonstrates an inability or unwillingness to give clear orders. **Clear instructions are the foundation of a safe system of operation** [original emphasis].

It was the failure to give clear instructions about the duties of the officers on the Zeebrugge run which contributed so greatly to the cause of this disaster. Mr. Clarke, [counsel] on behalf of the company, said that it was not the responsibility of Mr. Develin to see that company orders were properly drafted. In answer to the question, "Who was responsible?" Mr. Clarke said, "Well in truth, nobody, though there ought to have been." The board of directors must accept a heavy responsibility for their lamentable lack of directions. Individually and collectively they lacked a sense of responsibility. This left, what Mr. Owen so aptly described as, "a vacuum at the center."

. . . Mr. Develin [director and chief superintendent] was prepared to accept that he was responsible for the safe operation of the company's ships. Another director, Mr. Ayers, told the court that no director was solely responsible for safety. Mr. Develin thought that before he joined the board, the safety of ships was a collective board responsibility.

[A]s this investigation progressed, it became clear that shore management took very little notice of what they were told by their masters. The masters met only intermittently. There was one period of two-and-a-half years during which there was no formal meeting between management and senior masters. Latterly there was an improvement. But the real complaint, which appears to the Court to be fully justified, was that the Marine Department did not listen to the complaints or suggestions or wishes of their masters. The Court heard of four specific areas in which the voice of the masters fell on deaf ears ashore [each detailed in separate sections below].

Carriage of Excess Numbers of Passengers

During the course of the evidence it became apparent from the documents that there were no less than seven different masters, each of whom found that from time to time his ship was carrying substantially in excess of the permitted number [1,400].

[The report then details a series of memoranda between various masters and Mr. A. P. Young, the operations manager, on the topic of excess passengers. These were exchanged in 1982, 1983, and 1984.] . . . But the matter became really serious in 1986. The Court heard evidence from Captain de St. Croix, who was master of the *Pride of Free Enterprise*. On August 1, 1986 he sent a memorandum to Mr. Young:

Passenger Numbers on 15.00 D/C, 1.8.86

On the above sailing from Dover, the first passenger total given to the RO [radio operator] by the Purser was 1,228. A call from the manifest office then informed the RO to add on another 214. The RO queried this as the total then had been way over the top. After a short delay the manifest office came back with a figure of 1,014 plus an add-on of 214 making a total of 1,228.

As seeds of doubt had by then been sown in my mind I decided to have a head count as they went off at Calais. The following figures were revealed . . . [detail of count omitted]

Total passengers	1,587
Crew	95
Total on board	1,682

This total is way over the life saving capacity of the vessel. The fine on the master for this offense is £50,000 and probably confiscation of certificate. May I please know what steps the company intend to take to protect my career from mistakes of this nature.

[The report details 6 more memos sent to Mr. Young between August and October 1986 by various masters complaining about overloading. In a memo sent on October 31, 1986, Mr. Develin attempted to arrange a meeting with Mr. Young to discuss the problem with a representative of the senior masters. Mr. Young did not invite Mr. Develin to meet him to discuss the subject. Mr. Young took the view that this was not a marine matter and deliberately excluded Mr. Develin from further investigation of the problem.

. . . **The court reluctantly concluded that Mr. Young made no proper or sincere effort to solve the problem** [original emphasis]. The court takes a most serious view of the fact that so many of the company's ferries were carrying an excessive number of passengers on so many occasions. . . .

After it became apparent that this court was greatly interested in the system for checking the number of passengers carried on each ship further thought was given to the matter by the company. On May 29, 1987 Mr. Young produced a memorandum containing some ideas for improving the system of counting the number of passengers.

Door Status Warning Lights for the Bridge

On October 29, 1983 the assistant bosun of the *Pride* neglected to close both the bow and the stern doors on sailing from No. 5 berth Dover. It appears he had fallen asleep. . . . On June 28, 1985 Captain Blowers of the *Pride* wrote a sensible memorandum to Mr. Develin:

In the hope that there might be one or two ideas worthy of consideration I am forwarding some points that have been suggested on this ship and with reference to any future new-building program. Many of the items are mentioned because of the excessive amounts of maintenance, time and money spent on them.

4. Mimic Panel   There is no indication on the bridge as to whether the most important watertight doors are closed or not. That is the bow and stern doors. With the very short distance between the berth and the open sea on both sides of the channel this can be a problem if the operator is delayed or having problems in closing the doors. Indicator lights on the very excellent mimic panel could enable the bridge team to monitor the situation in such circumstances.

Mr. Develin circulated that memorandum amongst managers for comment. It was a serious memorandum that merited serious thought and attention, and called for a serious reply. The answers which Mr. Develin received will be set out verbatim. From Mr. Alcindor, a deputy chief superintendent: "Do they need an indicator to tell them whether the deck store-keeper is awake and sober? My goodness!!" From Mr. Reynolds: "Nice but don't we already pay someone!" From Mr. Ellison: "Assume the guy who shuts the doors tells the bridge if there is a problem." From Mr. Hamilton: "Nice!" It is hardly necessary for the court to comment that these replies display an absence of any proper sense of responsibility. Moreover the comment of Mr. Alcindor on the deck store-keeper was either ominously prescient or showed an awareness of this type of incident in the past.

If the sensible suggestion that indicator lights be installed had received, in 1985, the serious consideration which it deserved, it is at least possible that they would have been fitted in the early months of 1986 and this disaster might well have been prevented [original emphasis]. [The report details further requests for indicator lights made by two masters in 1986, and also records their written rejection by Mr. King:]

> I cannot see the purpose or the need for the stern door to be monitored on the bridge, as the seaman in charge of closing the doors is standing by the control panel watching them close.

[The report notes] that within a matter of days after the disaster indicator lights were installed in the remaining Spirit class ships and other ships of the fleet.

Ascertaining Draughts

[Following the loss of the passenger ferry *European Gateway* in 1982, Townsend Thoresen instituted an investigation into passenger safety.] As a result of that investigation, on February 10, 1983, Captain Martin sent a report to Mr. Develin. That report was seen by Mr. Ayers. It begins with the words:

> The company and ships' masters could be considered negligent on the following points, particularly when some are the result of "commercial interests:"

a. the ship's draught is not read before sailing, and the draught entered into the Official Log Book is completely erroneous.[8]
b. It is not standard practice to inform the master of his passenger figure before sailing.
c. The tonnage of cargo is not declared to the Master before sailing.
d. Full speed is maintained in dense fog.

. . . For the moment we are only concerned with the draught reading. Later in the report under the heading "recommendations" there is the statement "company to investigate installing draught recorders on new tonnage."[9] Mr. Ayers was asked if he did investigate. His answer was, "somewhere in this period the answer was yes." In the light of later answers given by Mr. Ayers, that answer is not accepted by the court.

. . . Mr. Ayers may be a competent naval architect, but the court formed the view that he did not carry out his managerial duties, whatever they may have been. Mr. Ayers was asked whether each director of Townsend Car Ferries was given a specific area of responsibility. His [verbatim] answer was, "No; there were not written guidelines for any director." When he was asked how each director knew what his responsibilities were his [verbatim] answer was, "It was more a question of duplication as a result of not knowing than missing gaps. We were a team who had grown together." The amorphous phrasing of that answer is typical of much of the evidence of Mr. Ayers. He appeared to be incapable of expressing his thoughts with clarity.

[Mr. Ayers had previously not answered another master's request for the installation of draught recorders. The draught of the *Herald* turned out to be a critical question. Research undertaken for the court revealed that the *Pride* and the *Spirit* each weighed about 300 tons more than previously thought. The origin of most of this excess weight was a mystery. The *Herald* was probably 300 tons overweight also. Further loading miscalculations arose from the estimates of the tonnage of freight vehicles on the ship. No weigh scales were used, as the tonnage was calculated by using drivers' declarations of vehicle weights. Experiments revealed that these were frequently false. An average ferry-load of trucks was found to weigh 13 percent more than the sum of drivers' declarations.]

Captain Lewry told the court quite frankly that no attempt had been made to read the draughts of his ship on a regular basis or indeed at all in regular service. Fictitious figures were entered in the Official Log which took no account of the trimming water ballast. . . .

The difficulties faced by the masters are exemplified by the attitude of Mr. Develin to a memorandum dated October 24, 1983 and sent to him by Captain Martin:

For good order I feel I should acquaint you with some problems associated with one of the Spirit class ships operating to Zeebrugge using the single deck berths. . . .

4. At full speed, or even reduced speed, the bow wave . . . comes three quarters of the way up the bow door. . . .

6. Ship does not respond so well when trimmed so much by the head [i.e., with water ballast in the bow], and problems have been found when maneuvering. . . .

8. As you probably appreciate we never know how much cargo we are carrying, so that a situation could arise where not only are we overloaded by 400 tons, but also trimmed by the head by 4.5 feet. I have not been able to work out how that would affect our damage stability.

Mr. Develin was asked what he thought of that memorandum. His answer was: "Initially I was not happy. When I studied it further, I decided that it was an operational difficulty report and Captain Martin was acquainting me of it." Later he said: "I think if he had been unhappy with the problem he would have come in and banged my desk." When Mr. Develin was asked what he thought about the information concerning the effect of full speed he said: "I believe he was exaggerating." In subsequent answers he made it clear that he thought every complaint was an exaggeration. In reply to a further question Mr. Develin said: "If he was concerned he would not have sailed. I do not believe there is anything wrong sailing with the vessel trimmed by the head."

The Need for a High-Capacity Ballast Pump

On February 28, 1984 Mr. R. C. Crone, who was a chief engineer, sent a memorandum to Mr. Develin. . .

Ballasting Spirit Class Ships on Zeebrugge Service

Normal ballasting requirements are for Nos. 1 and 14 tanks . . . to be filled for arrival at Zeebrugge and emptied on completion of loading. . . . Using one pump the time to fill or empty the two tanks is 1 hr. 55 mins. With two pumps the time can be reduced to 1 hr. 30 mins. . . . Problems associated with the operation. . .

a. Pumping time amounts to approximately half the normal passage time.
b. Ship well down by the head for prolonged periods causing bad steerage and high fuel consumption.
c. Continuous pressurizing of tanks to overflow/vent level.
d. Time consuming for staff.
e. Bow doors subjected to stress not normally to be expected, certainly having its effect on door locking gear equipment.
f. Dangerous complete blind operation that should not be carried out as normal service practice, i.e. no knowledge of tank capacity during operation, the tanks are pumped up until the overflow is noticed from the bridge, thereafter emptied until the pump amperage/pressure is noted to drop!

Purely as a consideration realizing the expense compared with possible future double ramp berths [he recommends fitting a high-capacity ballast pump].

Mr. Develin . . . said that he did not agree with some of the contents. He appeared to think that the chief engineer was grossly exaggerating the problem. . . . Mr. Develin said that Mr. Crone came to his department on several occasions to press for the implementation of his recommendations, but that after discussion he must have been satisfied. . . . In due course an estimate was obtained for the installation of a pump at a cost of £25,000.[10] This cost was regarded by the company as prohibitive.

The Court's Conclusion

The court . . . finds . . . that the capsizing of the *Herald of Free Enterprise* was partly caused or contributed to by serious negligence in the discharge of their duties by Captain David Lewry (master), Mr. Leslie Sabel (chief officer), and Mr. Mark Victor Stanley (assistant bosun), and partly caused or contributed to by the fault of Townsend Car Ferries (the owners). The court suspends the certificate of the said Captain David Lewry for a period of one year . . . [and] suspends the certificate of the said Mr. Leslie Sabel for a period of two years.

[The court had no power to sanction the assistant bosun, who was not a certificated officer. The final section of the report addresses the issue of payment of costs of the enquiry. The last paragraph deals with Townsend Thoresen.]

There being no other way in which this court can mark its feelings about the conduct of Townsend Car Ferries Limited other than by an order that they should pay a substantial part of the costs of this investigation, I have ordered them to pay the sum of £350,000. That seems to me to meet the justice of the case.[11]

Endnotes

1. *Plc* is an abbreviation of *public limited company.*
2. According to Lloyd's Register in London, over 30 accidents to ro-ro ferries had involved loss of life. The worst previous British accident was in 1953, when the *Princess Victoria* sank in the Irish Sea killing 134. The world's worst disaster was in 1981, when 431 died on an Indonesian ferry which caught fire and sank in the Java Sea. In roughly two-thirds of the cases, the capsize took less than 5 minutes.
3. *Mv* is an abbreviation of *motor vessel.*
4. The bosun (a variant spelling of the word *boatswain*) is responsible for ship maintenance. The rank is equivalent to sergeant; assistant bosun is equivalent to corporal.
5. OOW stands for officer of the watch, who is one of the deck officers and not the master.
6. Mr. Develin joined the company in May 1975. In 1978 he became the chief marine superintendent, and in 1986 he became a director of the company.
7. Counsel for the National Union of Seamen, certain surviving crew, and the next-of-kin of deceased crew.
8. The depth of a loaded vessel in the water, taken from the level of the water-line to the lowest point of the hull. Section 68(2) of the Merchant Shipping Act 1970 makes it a legal requirement for a master to know the draught of his ship and to enter this in the official log book each time the ship puts to sea.
9. Such recorders enable anyone on the bridge to determine how low in the water the ship is. Without such devices the draught markings can only be read from outside the ship.
10. Equivalent to $45,000 at an exchange rate of US$1.80 = £1.00.
11. Townsend Thoresen had previously made some payments to the injured and to the relatives of the deceased. Note that the total level of payments received by relatives in a case of wrongful death in the United States of America is extremely high compared to the sums paid in the rest of the world. It would be a serious miscalculation to apply U.S. values, often up in the millions of dollars per victim, to this case. The actual sum that will be paid per victim of the Zeebrugge disaster is not known exactly, but would probably average £80,000 or US$144,000.

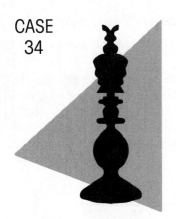

CASE
34

FIRST INTERSTATE BANK
OF CALIFORNIA

SUE GREENFELD

CORPORATE BACKGROUND

First Interstate Bank of California is one affiliate of First Interstate Bancorp. The latter is a bank holding company comprised of banks and franchised banks in 19 states plus Washington, D.C. First Interstate Bancorp focuses mainly in the western United States. In 1982 First Interstate Bancorp established a franchise program where its name and logo are licensed to other banking companies. The Bancorp makes available to the franchisees a basic package of First Interstate products and services. According to a management's discussion as reported in a 1989 *Annual Report*, "franchising enables the corporation to expand its service area without incurring the costs associated with outright acquisitions." By 1990 First Interstate Bancorp also had foreign locations in Abu Dhabi, Bangkok, Beijing, Hong Kong, Jakarta, Lima, London, Madrid, Mexico City, Nassau, Rio de Janeiro, Seoul, Singapore, Sydney, Taipei, Toronto, and Vancouver.

As shown in Exhibit 1, First Interstate Bancorp has affiliates from Alaska to Wyoming. As the largest affiliate of First Interstate Bancorp, First Interstate Bank of California has 335 company-owned branches.

Basically, First Interstate Bank of California engages in general commercial banking and other related nonbanking business. This includes international banking, real estate, mortgage banking, information processing and communication services, investment management, and other related services. According to the 1989 *Annual Report* of First Interstate Bancorp, First Interstate Bank of California has a real estate portfolio reflecting "common sense diversity." Real estate construction credit is divided between residential and commercial activities. However 1989 has not been a good year for the banking industry. Banks, including First Interstate of California, had been hit with fluctuating interest rates and competition intensified by deregulation. Diversification within areas of risk appears to be a main objective of management.

Support for the case was provided by a grant from The Minerva Education Institute. This case is presented as the basis for education discussion rather than to illustrate either effective or ineffective handling of an administrative situation. Material in this case has not been approved by First Interstate Bank of California.

EXHIBIT 1   First Interstate Bancorp Affiliates

Banking Affiliates

Alaska
First Interstate Bank of Alaska

Arizona
First Interstate Bank of Arizona, N.A.

California
First Interstate Bank of California
First Interstate Bank, Limited

Colorado
First Interstate Banks of Denver, N.A.; Englewood,
N.A.; and Fort Collins, N.A.

Idaho
First Interstate Bank of Idaho, N.A.

Montana
First Interstate Banks of Glacier County, Great
Falls, and Kalispell, N.A.

New Mexico
First Interstate Banks of Albuquerque, Lea County,
Roswell, and Santa Fe, N.A.

Oklahoma
First Interstate Bank of Oklahoma, N.A.

Oregon
First Interstate Bank of Oregon, N.A.

Texas
First Interstate Bank of Texas, N.A.

Washington
First Interstate Bank of Washington, N.A.

Wyoming
First Interstate Banks of Casper, N.A.; Laramie,
N.A.; and Riverton, N.A.

Bank Licensees

Colorado
First Interstate Banks of Arvada, N.A.; Centennial,
N.A.; Golden, N.A.; and Westminster, N.A.
First Interstate Bank of South Fort Collins

Hawaii
First Interstate Bank of Hawaii, N.A.

Iowa
First Interstate Bank of Iowa

Louisiana
First Interstate Bank of Southern Louisiana

Montana
First Interstate Banks of Billings, N.A.; Billings
Heights, N.A.; Colstrip; Hardin; Miles City;
Missouri, N.A.; Missoula, N.A.; and West
Billings

New Mexico
First Interstate Bank of Farmington, N.A.

North Dakota
First Interstate Bank of Fargo, N.A.

South Dakota
First Interstate Bank of South Dakota, N.A.

Wyoming
First Interstate Banks of Buffalo; Gillette; Greybull,
N.A.; Sheridan; and Sugarland

Source: First Interstate Bancorp, *Update: Forecast 1990/1991*, 1990.

HISTORY OF FIRST INTERSTATE BANK OF CALIFORNIA

According to the book *Their Bank, Our Bank, the Quality Bank,* the history of First Interstate Bank of California starts with Andrew McCord Chaffey (born 1874) who founded the California Bank in 1920. This bank system is the antecedent system of both the United California Bank and later the First Interstate Bank of California. The California Bank, however, was the 17-year culmination of Andrew Chaffey's banking efforts in Los Angeles. His venture dates back to 1903 when, at the age of 28, Andrew Chaffey purchased the American Savings Bank. In 1913 he acquired the Home Saving Bank system and in 1919 the Hibernian Savings Bank. These mergers meant more branches.

In 1920 the California Bank began business with deposits of $31 million. By 1929 California Bank had 46 branches and over $100 million in deposits. The future looked rosy, but the stock market crash changed all that. Like other banks, the California Bank struggled to remain solvent, and appreciated surviving the bank holiday of 1933. The collapse of the Richfield Oil Company hurt the California Bank tremendously.

One bright spot, though, was Andrew Chaffey's leadership in building the L.A. Colosseum for the 1932 Olympics. This allowed the California Bank to handle all the financing for the Olympics. Yet despite the success of the Olympics, the decade of the '30s were years of struggle for the bank. Finally, in June 1940, the bank paid its first dividend in years.

The war years (1941 to 1945) saw California Bank prosper. A major expansion began under the Frank King administration with its stronger emphasis in commercial banking. The bank lessened its dependency on real estate mortgages, and it consolidated its branches from 57 to 39. More industries located in Southern California.

Deposits reached $440 million in 1950 and $570 million in 1952. King began a strong bank acquisition program. From 1949 to 1966 California Bank acquired 25 banks with 39 offices.

ENTER TRANSAMERICA

In the meantime, two forces occurred in the 1950s which greatly affected the destiny of California Bank. One was the Transamerica Corporation and the other, the Bank Holding Company Act of 1956.

The Bank Holding Act of 1956 was a significant factor. Once passed the bill would prohibit organizations such as Transamerica from holding banks if they also held nonbanking assets. Ultimately Transamerica decided to sell off their bank holdings rather than their other assets.

Hence, the merger of the bank portion of Transamerica, known as First-America, and California Bank involved 24 banks and nearly 350 branches with offices in 11 states, but the negotiations were not always calm. The government intervened, charging the new bank system would eliminate competition in the smaller communities of California. A northern California Bank claimed too much similarity with their own name.

Finally, a compromise was reached with the government; two new banking systems would be carved out from the combined merger. One system would be part of California Bank and the other system would become Western Bancorporation. In addition, the name of California Bank would change to the United California Bank (UCB). This merger was accomplished on February 24, 1961. Clifford Tweter became the first president of United California Bank. Later in 1981 these two systems would both assume a new name.

THE UNITED CALIFORNIA BANK

After the merger, the United California Bank prospered as the state of California grew in population. By December 1965 UCB had 6,652 staff members around the state and across the country. The 1960s also saw the first women managers in UCB. Previously management had only selected men as branch managers or department heads. UCB established a branch bank in London, and later opened offices in Madrid, Mexico City, New York, and Tokyo. Norman Baker, Jr. became UCB's second president in May 1968.

Unfortunately one scandal occurred in 1969 when UCB purchased 58 percent of the Salik Bank in Basel, Switzerland. Unknown to the management of UCB, the books of the Salik Bank had been doctored. The reputation of UCB was at stake. The net result: seven bank associates in Basel were arrested and served time in jail. Management closed the UCB office in Basil with a total loss over $40 million. The entire morale of the international division slumped and it took about 10 years for UCB to put the incident behind them.

THE 1970s

The 1970s observed further expansion for UCB including a new 62-story head-quarters. At the time of its construction, it was the tallest building west of Chicago. UCB and Equitable Life Assurance Society created a joint venture to finance the $84-million building. The huge building housed 31 elevators and it was this building that would suffer a devastating fire on May 4, 1988, more than a decade later. Built prior to 1974, this building did not have a sprinkler system. In 1974 the L.A. City Council required all new high-rises to install sprinklers, but did not make the law retroactive.

THE DECADE OF THE 1980s

The arrival of the 1980s saw UCB changing its name. In a series of very rapid decisions, the boards of directors for both UCB and Western Bancorp decided to adopt a new name for all the banks and branches within these entire two systems. UCB would become First Interstate Bank of California while the banks in Western Bancorp would become First Interstate for their state or city. This occurred on June 1, 1981 after management had reviewed more than 45,000 names. This meant updating over 6,000 UCB signs, forms, memos, and stationery. The job was enormous, but management wanted a name which would fit the organization, was legally obtainable and was the most descriptive of the territorial franchise.

This decade was also marked by the leadership of Joseph J. Pinola, UCB's fourth president, who later became its chairman of the board of First Interstate Bancorp. Pinola previously worked in Bank of America for 23 years before being approached by the management of UCB.

Pinola's plan included bringing in discipline and definition to the organization. The bank had trouble with its real estate development area. Pinola felt the bank lacked some sophistication in its operations. Pinola moved people overseas to get needed foreign experience.

The decade of the 1980s witnessed the growth of automated teller machines (ATMs) with more emphasis on electronic transfers of funds. In addition, when the 23rd Olympiad held their games in Los Angeles, the Olympic Committee named First Interstate Bank as the official bank.

The late 1980s also observed a strange maneuver as First Interstate Bancorp in a hostile move attempted to take over BankAmerica when the latter faced bankruptcy. According to one First Interstate branch manager, "Yes it is true. First Interstate tried to buy BankAmerica. That's like the fish trying to swallow the whale." Exhibits 2 and 3 show the consolidated balance sheet and income statements for First Interstate Bank of California. Exhibit 4 shows the accounting Note O, which states the bank's Commitments and Contingent Liabilities.

MAJOR CHANGES IN THE INDUSTRY FOR THE 1990s

The past decade of the 1980s holds major implications for the future of First Interstate Bank of California and for banking in general. Specifically, Congress passed the Depository Institutions Deregulation and Monetary Control Act of 1980. The consequence of deregulation has been the ability of financial institutions to engage in a wider range of financial activities than previously allowed.

Deregulation has also blurred the distinction between banks and nonbanks. The industry has become very competitive. The idea of the banker sitting behind a desk reading a *Wall Street Journal* is outmoded. Today's bankers are likely to go out to service their accounts. The industry has evolved tremendously since the 1980s. Both Sears and Kmart, nonbank institutions, provide financial services. Stock brokerage firms such as Merrill Lynch have checking accounts for their customers. Savings and loans provide customers with checking accounts when before they did not. According to one First Interstate manager, the piece of the banking pie has shrunk. It is harder and harder for First Interstate of California to maintain market share.

Interestingly, federal legislation of 1991 allows banks to have branches in more than one state. Many East Coast banks are expected to move west. However, by 1990 the U.S. Congress had not abolished or amended the Glass-Steagall Act, which places restrictions on bank entry into the securities business.

Richard M. Rosenberg, vice chairman of BankAmerica in 1990, predicted more *versateller* ATMs in bank branches in 1999. Long lines will be gone as the routine transactions are done at the versateller. More banking will be performed at off-peak hours. Rosenberg expects customers will be able to place orders for stocks, bonds, mutual funds, and insurances at their local branch bank. Automation is the byword of 1990s in banking. The high-technology product is the smart card, a plastic card embedded with an integrated circuit. An individual's entire financial record would be placed on this card. Major consolidation of branch banks is expected in the 1990s.

EXHIBIT 2 First Interstate Bank of California Consolidated Balance Sheet ($000)

	December 31,	
	1989	**1990**
Assets		
Cash and due from banks	$ 2,515,563	$ 2,619,856
Time deposits, due from banks	1,403,926	1,866,414
Investment securities		
U.S. Treasury/agencies	387,193	305,936
State/political subdivisions	309,888	338,107
Other securities	386,936	423,289
Total investment securities	1,084,017	1,067,332
Trading account securities	55,841	96,078
Federal funds sold	1,148,415	828,594
Loans	14,577,641	13,918,306
Less: unearned income	320,919	446,228
Less: allowance for losses	337,710	493,067
Net loans	13,919,012	12,979,011
Bank premises and equipment	288,443	259,320
Customers' liability	369,880	335,494
Other assets	443,410	437,446
Total assets	$21,228,507	$20,489,545
Liabilities and Equity		
Deposits		
Domestic offices		
Noninterest-bearing	$ 6,120,413	$ 6,188,638
Interest-bearing	10,525,593	9,486,439
Foreign offices		
Noninterest-bearing	134,426	107,245
Interest-bearing	1,066,569	831,301
Total deposits	17,847,001	16,613,623
Short-term borrowing	1,070,866	1,854,312
Acceptances outstanding	369,880	335,494
Accounts payable/accrued liabilities	487,904	412,835
Notes and long-term debt	415,071	416,861
Total liabilities	20,190,722	19,624,125
Commitments and contingent liabilities (Note O)		
Equity		
Contributed capital	439,428	428,181
Retained earnings	581,996	422,951
Equity adjustment from foreign currency	16,361	14,288
Total equity	1,037,785	865,420
Total liabilities and equity	$21,228,507	$20,489,545

EXHIBIT 3 First Interstate Bank of California Consolidated Statement of Income ($000)

	December 31,	
	1989	**1990**
Interest income		
Loans, including fees	$1,583,242	$1,442,993
Investment securities		
Taxable	68,399	42,726
Exempt from federal income tax	18,362	21,459
Trading account securities	9,881	20,785
Federal funds sold	85,683	59,231
Time deposits, due from banks	135,231	109,603
Total interest income	1,900,798	1,696,797
Interest expense		
Deposits	722,701	595,873
Short-term borrowing	105,144	89,204
Notes and long-term debt	41,273	39,330
Total interest expense	869,118	724,407
Net interest income	1,031,680	972,390
Provision for loan losses	82,800	67,000
Net interest income after provision for loan losses	948,880	905,390
Noninterest income		
Trust fees	47,806	44,822
Service charges on deposit accounts	146,428	153,602
Other service charges	100,276	80,321
Other trading account	51,208	30,689
Investment securities gains (losses)	813	(153)
Gain on settlement of pension	16,574	—
Other income	43,194	47,249
Total noninterest income	406,299	356,530
Noninterest expense		
Salaries and employee benefits	462,513	431,257
Net occupancy of bank premises	98,040	94,905
Other expense	355,578	391,975
Total noninterest expense	916,131	918,137
Income before income taxes and extraordinary item	439,048	343,783
Income taxes	167,303	105,484
Income before extraordinary item	271,745	238,299
Extraordinary item	—	35,000
Net income	$ 271,745	$ 273,299

According to *Update: Forecast 1990 of First Interstate Bancorp,* the thrift crisis that occurred in the saving and loan industry will negatively affect the entire U.S. economy and financial markets. "Dumping" of savings and loan assets is expected to affect real estate and prices will take longer to recover. "Ultimately, deposit insurance reform will need to be addressed—to remove the moral hazard

EXHIBIT 4   Balance Sheet Note O: Commitments and Contingent Liabilities

Standby letters of credit totaled $1,400 million, net of $122 million of participations sold at December 31, 1989. In the normal course of business, the bank enters into various other contingent liabilities and commitments, such as guarantees, commitments to extend credit, future contracts, interest rate swaps, etc. which are not required to be reflected in the accompanying consolidated financial statements. Management does not anticipate any material losses as a result of these transactions.

The bank is required to maintain balances with the Federal Reserve Bank based on percentage of deposit liabilities. Such balances averaged approximately $497 million in 1989 and $510 million in 1988.

There are presently pending against the bank a number of legal proceedings. It is the opinion of management after consulting with counsel that the resulting liability, if any, from these actions and other pending claims will not materially affect the consolidated financial statements.

[encouraging high risk-taking without penalties] and to reduce taxpayer exposure." In addition, the update reports the problem areas of loan portfolios involve debt of less developed countries, leveraged buyouts of banks, and low reserves.

Some of these concerns can be summarized as follows: How will First Interstate Bank of California adjust to deregulation in the banking industry? As competition increases in the banking industry, how will First Interstate of California maintain its market share?

DISASTER STRIKES FIRST INTERSTATE BANK OF CALIFORNIA

On May 4, 1988 the history of First Interstate Bank of California added a new page when a devastating fire struck four floors of the firm's tallest building in Los Angeles. The fire started at 10:30 p.m. One person died and 40 others were injured. The blaze reminded some of the film *The Towering Inferno.* Ironically, a $3.5-million sprinkler system was 85 percent finished, but the evening of the blaze, workers had turned off the system in order to continue the installation.

According to the *L.A. Times,* the fire developed on the 12th floor of a 62-story building which also housed trader operations for First Interstate Bank. During the blaze, temperatures reached 2,000° F. Tragically, Alexander John Handy, 24, died after being ordered to take a freight elevator to check out a persistent fire alarm. The elevator car became stuck on the 12th floor.

The *Times* also reported another near fatality occurred when a cleaning crew member became stranded on the 40th floor. He took refuge in an office and waved curtains at the helicopters circling outside. Two hours after being spotted, the unconscious man was rescued by two firefighters. They had made their way down through the smoke.

Two other cleaning crew members appeared trapped on the 13th floor, but miraculously managed to get to the smoke-filled stairwell. They scrambled down to safety. A financial analyst and a bank vice president found themselves cornered on the 37th floor. Right before their phone went dead, they signaled their location.

They rationed their air. Five hours later firefighters rescued them, the last people known to leave the building alive. Both had collapsed on the floor, overcome by smoke. When all was said and done, more than 300 firefighters were needed to control the blaze. Four floors were completely destroyed by the flames. Water and smoke significantly ruined ten others.

According to the newspaper reports, numerous problems were cited: lack of a sprinkler system, low water pressure, and malfunctioning valves. Worse though, officials in the building turned off the fire alarms thinking the warnings false. In the fire's aftermath other questions arose around protecting sensitive computer data and other systems. After four days of intensive investigation, L.A. and federal fire officials could not identify the exact cause of the blaze. According to the *L.A. Times,* some feared arson. It took over 1,100 individuals to help in the cleanup.

Normally, 2,500 First Interstate employees would be at work during regular business hours, and possibly a greater tragedy could have occurred. Officials at First Interstate Bank of California wondered what happened: what could they have done differently to prevent such a tragic fire from occurring in the first place, and how would this incident affect the future of First Interstate Bank of California? The worst U.S. high-rise office fires are shown in Exhibit 5.

EXHIBIT 5   Worst High-Rise Office Fires

The most catastrophic high-rise office fire was on February 1 when 179 people were killed in the 25-story Joelma Building in Sao Paulo, Brazil. The worst in the United States occurred in July 28, 1945 when 11 died in the resulting fire when a plane crashed into an upper floor of the Empire State Building. Fatal fires in high-rise apartments and hotels are more prevalent, including the 1980 MGM Grand Hotel fire in Las Vegas that killed 85 and the 1986 fire in Puerto Rico that killed 96.

Worst U.S. High-Rise Office Fires Since 1970

	Building	City	Stories	Fatalities
Aug. 21, 1986	580 Building	Cincinnati	14	1
Sept. 5, 1986	In construction	San Diego	24	2
Aug. 12, 1984	Gibraltar	Newark, N.J.	14	1
Sept. 22, 1981	Wiloughby	Chicago	38	2
May 10, 1977	U.S. Fidelity	Baltimore	40	1
Nov. 29, 1972	Rault Center	New Orleans	16	6
Apr. 8, 1971	John Hancock	Chicago	100	1
Dec. 4, 1970	919 3d Ave.	New York	47	3
Aug. 5, 1970	One New York Plaza	New York	50	2

Deadliest U.S. High-Rise Office Fires

	Building	City	Stories	Fatalities
Jul. 28, 1945	Empire State	New York	102	11
Jan. 9, 1912	Equitable	New York	10	6
Dec. 5, 1968	Atlanta Gaslight	Atlanta	24	4
Nov. 22, 1961	The Times Tower	New York	25	3
Feb. 7, 1968	Borax Building	Los Angeles	9	1

Source: National Fire Protection Association, as reported by Ted Vollmer, "Resistance to Sprinkler Retrofitting Predicted," *L.A. Times,* May 7, 1988, Part I, p. 1.

EMERGENCY PLANNING AND RECOVERY

First Interstate Bank's business resumption planning process began in 1985 when senior management perceived that an unacceptable level of risk existed. In 1986 senior management authorized and funded a project which identified potential losses in a large-scale corporate disaster. Later that same year this unit was staffed with a vice president in charge. This individual also serves as the director of the emergency operation center.

In its emergency plan First Interstate has three levels of organization. At the top is the policy group consisting of senior management. At the second level are the operational groups which represent key departments affected by a crisis and which would most likely serve in the emergency operations center. The third level is the response group, or emergency response teams.

In addition, First Interstate Bank has a staff unit directly responsible for emergency planning. This function had been well-established within the corporation, but prior to 1987, the program was not centralized. Each high-rise building had its own separate plan. In 1987 First Interstate Bank hired a new manager (a female) for emergency planning. She instituted more generic plans which could be usable at any of the branches.

Her office is located in Los Angeles, but not in the building which experienced the May 4, 1988 fire. She handles emergency planning for 335 branches of First Interstate Bank of California. This includes 14 high-rise buildings in the state. California law defines a high-rise as any building 75 feet or higher. Each high-rise must provide life-safety training at least once a year.

She reports support for emergency planning as very high at the bank. She has four people who work with her on emergency planning. This means planning for approximately 12,000 employees throughout the state. To date, all branch managers have received an emergency plan and are expected to train their employees in the elements of that plan.

All managers must be aware of emergency supplies and what the emergency response team is expected to do. When she arrived, no command and control structure existed for First Interstate Bank. In rewriting the corporate disaster plan, she stated the five objectives of the corporate disaster plan are as follows:

1. Protect life, safety, and health of staff and customers
2. Establish priorities for utilization of internal resources which consist of personnel, talent, and materials
3. Protect property and assets
4. Be as self-sufficient as possible for at least 72 hours after an event
5. Resume business as soon as possible to minimize risk exposure and financial loss

The department of business resumption is located in the same Los Angeles building as emergency planning, but is a different department. The manager of this department is also female. She has seven employees each with a defined job function: business consultants, testing coordinators, or project analysis. Their focus is on how to get the business going once a major disaster has occurred, and they work with 79 individuals throughout the state designated as point-people. These key people are required to develop their own emergency recovery plan for their special business area. Even minor problems may need the services of the business resumption department. Power outages, for example, require backup systems to be in place. When the disaster struck on May 4, 1988, this manager took charge of the command center for restoring the building back to operation.

The business resumption unit is responsible for the California region including the California Bank (all 335 branches with 420 locations), the Limited Bank (a wholesale bank), and the holding company. The mission of this unit is to facilitate the process of business resumption, to be the consultant to help the people go through the process, and to establish the process of business recovery. They inform senior management who in turn reports to the board of directors. They act to insure the plan's consistency throughout the state.

The primary focus of resumption is backing up the business such as checking process or loans. For example, does the business need to make loans during an emergency situation such as an earthquake? For First Interstate, the answer is yes. After this crisis time, it may be very important to make loans to people. Other questions the plan covers: where should the phones be located? How will they let people know the bank will make loans?

People are going to want to send large sums of money after a disaster, either to or from relatives. These are the services the bank plans to supply after a major earthquake.

In 1986 the strategy used to develop its business resumption plan was nontraditional. The bank engaged a business-driven rather than data-processing-planning approach. By 1988 the bank had in place a plan for the worst-case scenario, a 8.3-Richter-scale earthquake. The unit set up an infrastructure to guide the plan. The emphasis was on each critical unit taking ownership for their own plan development. The ultimate authority for the business resumption plan is the managing committee of the bank which reviews the progress of the plan on a regular basis. Division managers who set policy serve on a business resumption plan steering committee.

Each critical unit is charged with gathering the minimum requirements for a recovery. This information resides in a disaster recovery software program which is centrally administered by the business resumption plan, but stored on PCs in the individual units. An offsite facility stores this data to facilitate recovery in the case of a regional disaster. One policy: in case of a disaster, First Interstate endeavors for each branch or unit to be self-sufficient for at least 72 hours. This means that following a major earthquake, each unit would have emergency supplies to last three days.

Testing the plan must be done to see if the recovery scripts work, to check the emergency voice communication system, and to coordinate the emergency operations center.

Evidence of the need for such planning occurred in October 1987 when a 6.5-Richter-scale earthquake hit in Whittier, California. The shake happened very early in the morning. Luckily, no one was hurt, but the chaotic situation highlighted the need for centralizing emergency planning throughout the State.

The manager of emergency planning wrote an internal grant to supply all the 300 plus branches with emergency supplies, food, and water for a two-day period. This would service 15,000 employees. After five months of research, she developed a program which cost $260,000. The shelf life of the emergency food is five years.

Food supplies include high-energy food bars which require no cooking; a three-day supply for each person on a floor. Each supply kit contains essential first aid bandages and supplies. Other survival items are AM/FM radio, light sticks, emergency blankets, rope, tools, pry-bar, heavy work gloves, and goggles. Supplies are managed by the emergency response team who are responsible for their storage and security. In April 1988 the bank had a first-time exercise using the emergency operations center and life safety systems. The three objectives of the drill were: (1) to teach employees to react instinctively, (2) to get emergency response teams together, and (3) to test the emergency operations center.

Two weeks after testing the corporate disaster plan, the May 4, 1988 fire occurred. The emergency supplies were in place, but a significant number were destroyed or contaminated in the fire.

ADDITIONAL FACTORS SURROUNDING THE FIRST INTERSTATE BANK FIRE

According to the *L.A. Times* in a preliminary report issued right after the fire, officials disclosed security workers turned off fire alarms originating on the 12th floor. They did this in the belief the alarms were false. False alarms were common occurrences in the weeks prior to the fire. Attempting to investigate one alarm had directly led to the death of Alexander Handy. On June 30, 1988 his wife and his daughter filed a lawsuit seeking an undisclosed amount against the tower's owners.

Also from news reports, the lack of a sprinkler system meant a fire which quickly went out of control. Also problematic was the lack of water pressure due to the building's pumping system being nonoperational. Malfunctioning valves allowed the pressure to soar out of control once the pumps were started. Even though 85 percent of the sprinkler was operational, the system had been turned off because the crew was working on it when the fire started. At one point when the fire officials thought the fire was out of control, they had considered turning on the sprinkler system.

Severe soot damage occurred above the fire, and severe water damage occurred below the fire. The blaze had gutted the middle of the building. As humidity of the building rose in days following the fire due to no air conditioning, rivers of water ran down the walls. With the humidity rising, it mixed with the soot causing hydrochloric acid to develop. This acid caused everything to corrode within the building. Every piece of equipment, drapes, furniture, etc. suffered primary damage as well as secondary damage. This meant everything on every floor would have to be thoroughly cleaned.

As the executives of First Interstate met to review the fire's consequences, several questions arose. They had a business resumption plan, but primarily the plan had been developed for the case of a catastrophic earthquake. Only the top tier of priorities had been established. Not all areas had been fully addressed. They wondered: how soon could they get the building ready to reopen? How fast should they move? How long should they ask the reassigned personnel to help with the crisis? How should they establish their priorities for the others? Would the other tenants be patient as they waited for the building to reopen?

EXHIBIT 6   What to Do in a High-Rise Fire

Know your building. Know the locations of the stairwells and where they lead.

Do not panic. Assess where you are and where the fire is.

Do not get into an elevator.

If the staircase is clear of smoke, walk down the stairs. If there are flames or heavy smoke, proceed upward to the roof.

Do not break any windows. Breaking a window aggravates a fire. Place a cloth near the window so firefighters know someone is inside.

Wait in a bathroom because it is mostly tile and porcelain. Seal vents and cracks with clothing or paper towels to prevent breathing the smoke.

If smoke seeps in, drop to the floor and crawl.

Adapted from comments by County Fire Inspector Tim Stomer, as reported by Robert Welkos, "Tower May Have Escaped Serious Structural Damage," *L.A. Times*, May 6, 1988, Part I, p. 4.

Within the building, they had parts of all three bank entities: the California Bank, the Limited Bank (a wholesale bank), and the First Interstate Bancorp (the holding company). They had to decide which group would get their equipment cleaned first. Who should get phones restored first? Should it be the traders or some other group? What other lessons could be learned about handling the media? What should they know about their insurance policies? They wondered how this would affect them in the future. Exhibit 6 shows what people should do in case of a fire.

REFERENCES

Becklund, Laurie. "Stress of Survival Lingers Months after Tower Fire." *L.A. Times*, October 2, 1988, Section I, pp. 1, 3, 40, and 51.

———. "Two Trapped on 37th Floor Improvise to Survive Fire." *L.A. Times*, May 6, 1988, Part I, pp. 1, 2.

First Interstate Bancorp. *Update: Forecast 1990/1991*, First Interstate Territory Edition.

First Interstate Bank of California, *Financial Report*. 1989.

Frantz, Douglas. "First Interstate Staff Struggles to Cope after Fire." *L.A. Times*, May 23, 1988, Section CC/Part IV, pp. 1 and 10.

Greenfeld, Sue. "Management's Safety and Health Imperative: Eight Essential Steps to Improving the Work Environment." The Minerva Education Institute Occasional Paper Series, Ref. 9.02, July 1989.

Kendall, John. "Main Lesson of High-Rise Fire: Sprinklers Are Vital." *L.A. Times*, May 16, 1988, Part II, pp. 1 and 2.

Keppel, Bruce. "1st Interstate's Insurers Face a Complex and Costly Task." *L.A. Times*, May 7, 1988, Part IV, p. 1.

Kibbie, Daniel C. *Their Bank, Our Bank, The Quality Bank: A History of the First Interstate Bank of California*. Costa Mesa, Calif.: Professional Publications, 1982.

Kissel, Elaine. "On the Line: Developing a Corporate Disaster Preparedness Program." First Interstate Bank handout, n.d.

Malnic, Eric. "Blaze Spurs Call for Sprinkler Laws." *L.A. Times*, May 6, 1988, Part I, p. 1.

Muir, Frederick M. "D.A. Probing Death in Bank Tower Fire." *L.A. Times,* July 8, 1988, Part II, pp. 1 and 8.

Rosenberg, Richard. "Banking: Charting New Courses in the 1990s," Speech to Economic Forecast Breakfast, California State University, San Bernardino, January 19, 1990.

Soble, Ronald L. "Fire Death in Elevator Laid to Human Error." *L.A. Times,* May 10, 1988, Part I, p. 1.

CASE
35

TEKTRONIX, INC.

STEVEN N. BRENNER,
PATRICIA BISHOP &
COLLEEN MULLERY

ETHICS PROGRAM (A)

Earl Wantland, president and CEO of Tektronix, Inc. (Tek), a Beaverton, Oregon-based electronic instrument manufacturing company, sat at his desk looking at the September 14, 1987 *Wall Street Journal* article reporting improprieties and possible fraud in the company's West German subsidiary, Tektronix GmbH. This was just the latest problem facing the company, which had grown from an eight-person operation to a world leader in oscilloscope manufacturing in just over 30 years. In the 1980s Tek faced a recession in high-technology industries, intensified global competition, and shortened product life cycles, all of which put severe profit pressures on the company (see Exhibit 1).

The company's financial difficulties resulted in several expense reduction decisions which tended to change the atmosphere within the company. Tek's management tried to avoid work force size reduction by implementing shortened work schedules, unpaid shutdowns, mandatory vacation usage, voluntary leaves of absence, hiring and pay freezes, upper management pay cuts, and the combining of redundant functions. Unfortunately, revenue growth slowed and the company undertook three major layoffs which trimmed its size from 24,000 to 17,000 employees.

Employees at all levels questioned the cutback decision, believing that management had violated the values and morality inherent in the Tek culture. Tek's corporate strategist felt so strongly that the personnel level reductions should have been avoided that he resigned from his position noting, "I'm not sure that because business conditions change, the ethics on which you operate a business has to change."

Historically, ethical issues had not been a concern for Tektronix. The company's founders, Jack Murdock and Howard Vollum, had a strong belief in the honesty and integrity of the individual employee. When the company was small there were open cash drawers, free coffee, and a tacit no-layoff policy. As the company grew larger and more divisionalized, it became more difficult to continue these policies. With growth there also came a diminution of commitment to the

This case was prepared by Professor Steven N. Brenner and Research Assistants Patricia Bishop and Colleen Mullery as a basis for class discussion rather than to illustrate either effective or ineffective handling of an administrative decision. The help of present and former Tektronix employees is acknowledged. This research was supported in part through a grant from the Chiles Foundation, Portland, Oregon. Copyright 1988 by Steven N. Brenner.

EXHIBIT 1 Tektronix Consolidated Financial Performance ($000 except per-share amounts)

	1979	1980	1981	1982	1983	1984	1985	1986	1987
Net sales	$786,936	$971,306	$1,061,834	$1,195,748	$1,191,485	$1,332,958	$1,438,082	$1,352,212	$1,395,885
Earnings	77,151	85,072	80,167	79,290	46,807	112,054	90,181	39,327	51,188
Gross margin	54.3%	52.8%	51.7%	49.6%	47.6%	48.8%	50.9%	50.9%	54.2%
Operating margin	15.4%	15.2%	13.0%	12.2%	9.4%	9.8%	8.9%	5.1%	7.3%
Return on equity	21.3%	19.4%	15.5%	13.4%	7.2%	16.1%	11.1%	4.7%	5.9%
Return on capital	18.7%	15.8%	12.3%	11.0%	6.4%	13.5%	10.2%	4.7%	5.7%
EPS	2.14	2.33	2.17	2.12	1.22	2.87	2.20	0.98	1.33
Total assets	$642,907	$841,693	$ 953,753	$1,044,188	$1,092,446	$1,222,168	$1,224,372	$1,196,947	$1,159,413
Inventory turns	4.19×	4.02×	3.66×	4.04×	3.91×	4.60×	5.97×	6.94×	8.68×
Asset turns	1.44×	1.34×	1.19×	1.20×	1.12×	1.18×	1.22×	1.15×	1.16×
Debt/total assets	18.5%	27.4%	26.1%	23.9%	21.9%	20.3%	11.5%	10.3%	6.0%
Employees	21,291	23,890	24,028	23,241	21,121	20,816	20,525	19,251	17,099
Share price (year-end)	$24.63	$24.88	$30.38	$26.32	$37.00	$28.25	$29.00	$30.75	$34.88

Returns, ratios, and turnover are based on average assets and capital.

company. Examples of a change in atmosphere were numerous, including employees working for their divisions at the expense of the entire company, defections to competitors or to new startup companies, and moonlighting ventures (some of which were carried out on Tek premises).

In partial response to these issues, the electronic industry's ethical standards, and the overall climate at Tektronix in 1987, Earl Wantland decided to hold a business ethics seminar for upper-level managers. The intent of the seminar was to identify corporate values and the pressures which make it hard to live up to those values and to develop an action plan for managing ethical issues. The German subsidiary fraud disclosure coming only a few weeks after the initial ethics seminar made Wantland wonder if his decision to initiate an ethics program had come too late or had been too limited in scope. Was this the best method of reinforcing the Tek culture and values given the problems and pressures of the past decade? Should Tek pursue further ethics-related steps and if so, what should be the actions' focus?

TEK HISTORY

The principal founders, Jack Murdock and Howard Vollum, started Tektronix in 1946. Their goal was to manufacture the finest oscilloscope in the world. (The function of an oscilloscope is to visually display the electrical signals of electronic devices.)

The 1950s were a time of dramatic innovation in the electronics industry. Tek introduced numerous innovations in its products and began to develop a reputation for producing the highest-quality, most technologically advanced oscilloscopes in the world. To assure that its customers were well-served, Tek established its own sales force of technically knowledgeable "field engineers" rather than depending on independent electronics distributors (which was the normal industry marketing approach). This sales technique was consistent with the founders' view of Tek's responsibility to its customers. Tek continued to grow and in 1956 purchased 313 acres in Beaverton, Oregon for a new Tektronix "campus" (a term purposefully used to denote the collegiality and intellectual rigor of the work environment).

A new executive vice president was appointed in 1959 to deal with the management problems which followed the company's rapid growth. At the same time both Murdock and Vollum sought to reduce their responsibilities for day-to-day operations. The early years of the 1960s were among the most technologically challenging yet faced and Tek funded virtually any research and development project which might meet the new marketplace demands. While such scientific freedom was important at Tek, it was a relatively expensive, duplicative approach to product development. Concerns about lack of direction and unsatisfactory financial results caused Vollum to resume direct leadership of Tek in 1962. In the next 9 years Tek increased international sales, restructured into a functional organization, had its first public stock offering, and formed a joint venture with Sony Corporation.

Tektronix suffered its first downturn in 1971. Net sales dropped 11.6 percent to $146 million from the 1970 high of $162 million, while earnings fell from $14.3

million to $9.3 million in the same period. Tek's problems at this time were not just caused by the general economic climate. Explosive expansion, high profits, and inattention to management processes during the initial growth years had resulted in a poorly coordinated, complex organization. Informal communications channels that were effective in the old days were no longer adequate. As a result of the downturn Tek was forced to have its first layoff (350 manufacturing employees). A significant proportion of these workers were rehired within 90 days, but for many old timers the level of trust in management never returned.

While Tek had expanded its product line during its early years, it still concentrated on oscilloscope manufacturing. In an effort to increase revenue, R&D efforts were expanded and by the end of 1971 Tek had introduced over 100 new products. In December 1971 sales, orders, and earnings were at a record rate. Real diversification came as Tek moved into the information display business which became 20 percent of company sales by 1987.

In 1972 Howard Vollum stepped down as president. The new president, Earl Wantland, retained the Boston Consulting Group and Stanford Research Institute to help Tek deal with its organizational problems. An insider described the company at that time as "a strong vertical organization centered around the oscilloscope." The informal leadership styles of both Jack Murdock and Howard Vollum had fostered an intensely competitive atmosphere within Tek. Efforts to diversify suffered from this situation. Ideas which were brought up within one part of Tek would not get support from the others. The organizational challenge was to improve efficiency and control without stifling creativity and innovation while preserving major managers' influence and status. The proposed solution was a divisionalized structure composed of two business groups and eight divisions.

The 1980s were marked by a recession in high-technology industries and increased competition. By 1984 Tek's core business (oscilloscopes) was under pressure from competitors both at home and abroad. Tek missed the emerging market for color display terminals (even though it was a leader in all aspects of the technology required to produce the devices) and it was slow to move into the new generation of digital test equipment known as computer-aided workstations. As a result, Tek experienced flat sales and declining profits and responded with a series of layoffs which reduced the work force from 24,000 to 17,000 (see Exhibit 1). The layoffs further reduced the morale and loyalty of many long-term employees, who still believed in the unwritten no-layoff policy.

Between 1985 and 1987 Tek repurchased over 10 million shares of its stock at a cost of over $400 million. The company indicated that the goal of this use of funds was to increase shareholder return and to reduce the company's cost of capital. Observers questioned whether share repurchase was the best use of these resources given the competitive trends and conditions existing in the industry during these years.

Despite its recent economic problems Tektronix finished the 1987 fiscal year as Oregon's largest private employer and was ranked 249th on the *Fortune* 500. Within the United States there were six manufacturing facilities, eight manufacturing subsidiaries, and 44 field offices. International operations included manufacturing in Japan (joint venture with Sony), the Channel Islands, the Netherlands, and the United Kingdom and 62 field offices in 23 countries. (For a more complete chronology, see Exhibit 2.)

EXHIBIT 2 Tektronix Chronological History

Date	Operations	Technology
1946	Tektronix, Inc, an Oregon corporation, certified 2/2/46	
1947	Move to new location on Hawthorne Blvd., Portland, Oregon	511 series: first triggered scope
1948	Production sharing bonus instituted	
1949	Profit-sharing introduced (25 percent of pretax income)	Transformers and inductors produced in-house
1950	Tek's own sales force created	
1951	Move to Sunset Hwy. location, Beaverton, Oregon	Cathode ray tubes (CRTs) produced in-house
1952	Tektronix Foundation established	
1953	Profit Sharing Retirement Trust established	530 series: first plug-in scope
1954	Stock split (2,000 for 1) creating 266,000 shares with $1.00 par value	315D series: first portable scope
1955	10th Anniversary Bonus (15 percent of pretax income)	540 series: fast-rising, plug-in scope with vertical amplifier
1956	Purchase of 313 acres in Beaverton for Tek campus	
1957	Completion of first building on Beaverton campus	First transistor curve tracer
1958	Foreign operation established on island of Guernsey; First TEKEM shares issued in June; TEKEY program instituted for rewarding employees	
1959	Davis replaced Murdock as EVP	525 series: first vectorscope
1960	Profit share revised to 35 percent of pretax income; expansion into the Common Market	321 series: first solid scope
1961		Ceramic CRT envelope developed; 661 series: first sampling scope
1962	Vollum replaces Davis; retains presidency and assumes EVP duties	
1963	First public stock offering (54,000 shares)	
1964	Listed on New York Stock Exchange; acquires Pentrix Corp. (manufacturer of spectrum analyzers)	547 series: first all-transistorized scope
1965	Sony/Tektronix established	
1966	Employee Share Purchase Plan instituted	
1968		Decision to produce information display products (IDP)
1969	Corporate Group created	7000 series
1970	Began reorganization into functional groups	Development of Gilbert gain cell
1971	Death of Jack Murdock, May 16, 1971; first employee layoff; 110 new products announced or introduced	

EXHIBIT 2 Cont'd. Tektronix Chronological History

Date	Operations	Technology
1972	Wantland replaces Vollum as president; Stanford Research Institute and Boston Consulting Group create formal planning system for Tek	326 series: dual-trace miniaturized scope
1973	Operational planning leads to formation of business units; first dividend paid—$0.20/share	
1974	Statement of Corporate Intent developed; pension plan established; Grass Valley Group, Inc. acquired	200 series: ultraminiaturized scope
1975	Formation of business units leads to divisionalization	
1976	Formal corporate objectives published	
1977	Walker Road plant opened; 100 percent stock dividend paid	
1978	First executive incentive plan begun	
1979		7104 series: first gigahertz scope (fastest-writing scope in world)
1981	Functional division structure in place: Instruments Division Communications Division Design Automation Division Information Display Division	
1983	Downsizing begins (early retirement package offered)	2400 series: state-of-the-art, small, portable scope
1984	Employee layoffs (severance pay provided)	Entered computer-aided engineering market
1986	Death of Howard Vollum	
1987	Fraud discovered in West German subsidiary	

THE TEK CULTURE

The Tek culture is, in many ways, a direct reflection of the personalities, motivations, and values of Tek's two founders: Jack Murdock and Howard Vollum. The corporate motto, "Tektronix: Committed to Excellence," expressed their belief that customer service and quality products were the key ingredients to a successful enterprise. Success was not defined as acquiring great wealth, but rather as occupying honorably a financially secure market niche. An equally important guiding principle was the founders' innate respect for, and belief in, the dignity of the individual. They believed that the goals of the enterprise and of the employee should be complementary, not contradictory.

In the early days of the company there was no organization chart and no specific personnel policies. The founders wanted a small, friendly, family atmosphere. Early management practices and values such as open cash drawers, free coffee, use of first names, company-sponsored Friday afternoon birthday parties, and no reserved parking evolved out of the founders' personal views about the integrity of people and the climate in which they felt creativity and excellence could be fostered.

A Tektronix *Annual Report* put into words the elements which seemed to make up this culture:

Respect for the individual human being
Profit sharing as part of the pay system
Open communications
Trust as evidenced by the honor system
Informal atmosphere
Little built-in awe of management
High tolerance of criticism
Absence of formal organization charts
Preference for nonauthoritarian behavior
Promotion from within the company
Respect for technical expertise
Absence of labor unions
Passion for quality

While actual practices and procedures did not always follow the ideal (e.g., organization charts did exist and open communications were not always present), there were many examples of these values in action. An early expression of Tek's commitment to quality and service was its policy of providing replacement parts virtually at cost. Management assumed that the need to replace a component was caused by a design error and therefore the resulting costs should not be borne by the customer.

The founders believed that a successful enterprise could only be built through the close cooperation of all employees. Sharing a substantial portion (targeted at 35 percent) of the company's pretax earnings with employees was instituted as a method of instilling pride, creating a sense of ownership, and providing above-average compensation. This profit-sharing system was an enlightened management concept at its inception in 1949.

The egalitarian attitude of the Tek founders led to other innovative management and employee relations programs, including:

A retirement trust fund was established in 1953 and two employee stock plans, TEKEM and TEKEY, were set up to enable employee ownership in the company prior to the stock being issued to the public.
Workers were regarded as individuals with lifelong tenure; consequently, extreme care was taken in hiring.
Some employees were kept on the payroll even when their performance was not up to Tek's standards.
Direct effort was exerted, long before it became fashionable, to hire minorities and handicapped persons.

Employees had access to an in-house counseling staff of psychologists and the company retained the Menningers, nationally known industrial psychologists.

Employee participation in management was encouraged and formalized through the Advisory Group in the 1950s.

The plant was designed to be bright and airy with the physical surroundings as natural as possible. Corporate signs were understated.

THE FOUNDERS' MANAGEMENT STYLE AND LEADERSHIP

Howard Vollum's and Jack Murdock's talents complemented one another as if they had been preordained to start a company together. Murdock, general manager and personnel director until 1958, represented the company in the business community and was influential in the development of many of Tek's innovative personnel policies and practices. In the early years at Tek he personally knew every employee and assumed the role of corporate father figure. As the company grew he was intimately involved in instituting humanistic policies aimed at imparting self-worth to every employee. He was particularly identified with maintaining the informal atmosphere throughout the company, encouraging participative management, and promoting company-sponsored social and recreational activities. These practices are credited by many in the company with creating high morale and increasing productivity.

Under Murdock's leadership Tek implemented a carefully designed profit-share program. Recognizing the cyclical nature of the electronics industry, Murdock sought a way to provide a soft landing to profits when volume declined and to share profits with employees when times were good. The program ultimately combined a salary (which averaged about 90 percent of the industry norm) and a profit-share payment (which generally ranged from 10 to 15 percent of the individual's salary). In most years the total of salary and profit share resulted in a rate of pay above industry average. When demand diminished, the profit-share percentage was reduced, thus trimming expenses.

Vollum, the engineer, pioneered the development of the oscilloscope and guided product development until 1971 when he resigned as president of Tek. His first love was the engineering lab and technical world. His leadership was marked by an "active interest in many aspects of the company: The design of the buildings, the landscaping, the tone and wording of ads . . . and the annual report to shareholders. Howard," someone said, "added value to everything."

The 1986 Tektronix *Annual Report* quoted Vollum as saying that he "disagreed with the concept of 'managing' and believed that a company should develop leaders rather than managers." To encourage creativity in product development he promoted an unstructured work environment. Neither Murdock nor Vollum were comfortable with confrontation. Their management style, and thus the style of the company, was one of consensus and careful decision making.

Generosity was the hallmark of both founders and this was mirrored in the large-scale philanthropic actions of the company. The Tektronix Foundation was established in 1952 with 5 percent of the company's net profits. Since Tek was a closely held company at that time, a substantial share of these monies came directly out of Vollum's and Murdock's pockets, as did the profit share, which routinely exceeded 50 percent of pretax profits in the 1950s. Social responsibility and corporate generosity were values practiced by Tektronix as it became one of Oregon's major philanthropic donors.

Both founders believed in leadership by example and the provision of unconditional support to their employees. A Tek executive described Murdock and Vollum as having an "impeccable personal code of conduct." Honesty, humility, egalitarianism, and straight-forward dealings with people characterized their management style. Their belief that human nature was basically good was expressed in Vollum's words, "Every individual wants to do the best job he or she can." This attitude permeated the company. One former employee indicated that for many years there were no strong controls to ensure honesty—it was expected.

ETHICAL PROBLEMS, THE GERMAN SUBSIDIARY, AND TEK'S ETHICS PROGRAM

Ethical values have a special place at Tektronix. The founders' basic beliefs about the inherent integrity of the individual employee and the importance of an open and trusting environment set a clear behavioral tone for the organization.

Conversations with current and former employees indicate that Tektronix management believed its policies and controls were sufficient to eliminate significant unethical behavior. While this may have been true during the early years when the organization was small and top management knew each worker by name, some observers have questioned the ethical correctness of a number of employee actions, including:

> Going to work for a competitor
> Conducting an outside small business on Tek premises
> Killing a project proposed by another division even though it would be good for the company as a whole
> Circumventing the resource allocation approval system by acquiring capital equipment in component parts
> Laying off workers during downturns (even though the benefits provided were considered generous) without seeking to take other possible steps, including living with reduced profits

Beyond these activities, the most significant ethical problem in Tektronix history came to light on September 14, 1987. On that day *The Wall Street Journal* reported that:

> Tektronix, Inc. said "improprieties and possible fraud" in its West German unit forced it to take a charge of $3.4 million, or 10 cents a share for its fiscal quarter . . . .
>
> For the quarter, ended Aug. 22, the maker of scientific instruments posted an 88 percent drop in net income to $1.8 million, or 5 cents a share, from $14.6 million or 38 cents a share, in the year earlier period. . . . Sales fell 1.8 percent to $299.5 million from $304.9 million . . . .
>
> A Tektronix spokesman said the company's finance manager in West Germany and his assistant loaned money, without the company's knowledge, to Rhein Neckar, a West German leasing concern. The leasing concern

went into bankruptcy-law proceedings in August, he said. . . . The finance manager and his assistant have been fired . . . no legal action had been taken against the pair so far, but [the spokesman] declined to say whether any would be pursued.

A few days later at Tek's annual stockholders' meeting Larry Choruby, senior vice president and chief financial officer, reported that the fraud was not just a singular type of action, but instead involved a number of different "scams." While Tektronix indicated, in public documents, that its review of the matter showed that all prudent precautions had been taken to prevent criminal conduct, some observers felt that pressures for results and lack of attention to the accuracy of reports may have contributed to the problem.

The announcement of the German subsidiary problem came more than six months after Tek took the first steps toward implementing a more formal ethics program. Larry Choruby directed a memo on January 13, 1987 to Earl Wantland indicating that more than 5 years had passed since the senior management group had reviewed the company's written statements of business ethics. The memo further proposed that Tek's policy council meet to review existing ethics policies, discuss and document proposed changes, and verify the process of communicating these policies throughout the company.

The idea of reviewing Tektronix ethics-related policies and taking steps to refine and renew them seemed very appropriate to Earl Wantland, especially at a time when the entire corporation was looking to him for direction and leadership. After some thought he recalled that Kirk Hanson of Stanford Graduate School of Business had presented some interesting ethics materials to Tek's Manager of Managers internal management education program. He contacted Professor Hanson to explore the development of an ethics-focused corporate values workshop for Tek's senior management. At the conclusion of the discussions Earl was convinced that Hanson's approach would result in greater ethical awareness at Tek.

After some initial discussion between Tektronix and Professor Hanson it was decided to modify and use a one day business ethics seminar which Kirk Hanson had previously developed. After senior managers had gone through the seminar a decision would be made about extending it to lower levels of management. The seminar was aimed at an "examination of the operating principles and values of the firm, the strains on those values, and techniques for managing the risks when those values are under pressure." The initial seminar was held for the policy council on June 9, 1987 and it was repeated for one Tek divisional management team on September 16, 1987.

The workshop's morning session explained the importance of the role that values and ethics play in an organization and used two case studies to involve participants and to communicate concepts. The afternoon session focused on identifying Tektronix stakeholders; the organization's values; pressures on these values; and an action plan to deal with these pressures.

Earl Wantland decided to initiate a more active ethical program at this time because he perceived a need to raise consciousness on ethical issues and bring ethics discussions to the table. He explained, "it's important that ethics is a legitimate thing to talk about with your subordinates, especially due to the number of unresolvable dilemmas present in the business world today."

Responses to the ethics workshop were mixed. Some people were quite positive indicating that it was taken very seriously and was found to be useful. One participant said that "it raised a lot of issues which is good . . . it made it an OK thing to talk about." Another attendee said that some participants were disappointed with the lack of concrete guidelines, "we were hoping to have some very clear-cut guidelines that you could pull out of your pocket and use to know what to do in any circumstance. . . . I'm not sure what we really got out of it . . . but it made people aware that there were shades of grey and there were behaviors that some thought acceptable and others unacceptable." Some insiders expressed frustration over the timing of the seminars and felt it was a "diversion from working on the things that we really needed to make decisions on. . . . [T]here were too many other pressing, critical business priorities and tremendous business pressures at that time."

At the same time the ethics workshops were being developed and presented, two other components of Tek's ethics program were moving forward. Alan Leedy, vice president, secretary, and general counsel of Tektronix, was given the task of updating the company's code of conduct. During summer 1987 a number of meetings were held and redrafts of the code of conduct written. The version, current at the time of the case, is shown in Exhibit 3. Tek's corporate controller and director of internal auditing were working on an internal controls seminar which was tentatively scheduled for early November 1987.

EARL WANTLAND'S DILEMMA

Earl Wantland realized that he was expected to improve Tektronix' profitability and to deal with the German subsidiary situation. Wantland was concerned whether recent external competitive and internal organizational pressures had simply overwhelmed both the company's traditional ethical values and its newly implemented ethics program.

Earl realized that his personal situation was a factor which had to be taken into consideration. It was common knowledge that Tek's board of directors was in the process of searching for a new president for the company. In fact, Earl, himself, had been quietly encouraging the board to find a successor so that he could move out of direct, day-to-day responsibility for operations.

As he sat and considered his alternatives, he was aware that there was a certain tension between increasing company profitability and improving the ethical behavior of its employees. By putting more emphasis on an ethics program, time and money which might be devoted to improved results would be allocated instead to assuring more proper behavior. For example, steps taken to assure product quality would be consistent with the Tek values, but such actions were likely to increase operating expenses and unlikely to increase revenues in the near term.

Some Tek employees and stockholders were urging Earl Wantland to expand its ethical programs. Suggestions for additional steps came from many differing sources. Earl hoped that he could gather information about the ethics programs of other firms and thereby not have to reinvent the wheel. (In February 1988 the Business Roundtable, a Washington, D.C.-based group of major United States

EXHIBIT 3   Tektronix Code of Conduct

Business conduct that meets the highest ethical standards is fundamental to our success as a company. These standards were not acquired by accident at Tektronix. They grew out of the basic beliefs and values on which our company was founded and has operated since 1946. Today, Tektronix is a large and complex organization, operating in an increasingly complex world. Our traditional management and communication practices, based on individual initiative, judgment, and responsibility, are the ''active ingredients.'' Preserving the advantages of this traditional Tek environment requires that we periodically revisit and reacquaint ourselves with the values on which it is based. That is what this brief statement is designed to do.

The basic standards of ethics and conduct that apply to Tektronix are simply stated. They are:

1. *Respect for the Individual*
   To base our business actions on a fundamental respect for the dignity and rights of each individual—including both those within our company and those outside it.
   Examples include the way we deal with our fellow employees and with our suppliers', customers', and competitors' representatives, and what we say about people, wherever they may work.

2. *Loyalty to Tektronix*
   To bring to Tektronix our undivided business loyalty.
   Examples include avoiding both actual and apparent conflicts of interest. (A conflict of interest exists when someone at Tektronix has an advantage from a position, or has a duty to take a position, that is opposed to the position of Tektronix.) Further examples include avoiding situations involving favors offered, given, or received, or any appearance of favoritism.

3. *Compliance with the Law*
   To know, and conform our action to, the requirements of all applicable laws.

4. *Observance of Other Ethical Standards*
   To conduct the company's business in accordance with the highest standards of ethics and integrity.
   Examples of those ethical standards, in addition to those listed above, include honesty, candor, and integrity, which are the essential bases for our relationships with customers, suppliers, fellow employees, shareholders, and the communities of which we are a part.

There is one further guidepost that belongs on this list: our primary, fundamental, and continuing commitment to give unmatched value to our customer. Customers keep us in business. They pay for our facilities and raw materials, our labor, our research and development efforts, our taxes, and the profits that go to our employees as profit share and to our shareholders as dividends and capital appreciation.

Much of what is included here is also reflected in our Statement of Corporate Intent, which underscores the importance to us as a company of these basic values. Whenever we depart from the basic standards set out in this brief list, we only diminish our ability to keep this central promise to our customers.

October 11, 1988

companies, published a study of the corporate ethics programs of 10 major United States firms.[1] See Exhibit 4 for a selected look at corporate ethics program components.) As he thought about his situation his eyes glanced across the room at the plaque containing Tektronix's Statement of Corporate Intent which served as a reminder of what Tek stood for:

EXHIBIT 4 Corporate Ethics Program Components

In February 1988 the Business Roundtable of Washington, D.C. published *Corporate Ethics: A Prime Business Asset*. It contains descriptions of the ethics programs in 10 major international corporations: The Boeing Company, Champion International Corporation, Chemical Bank, General Mills, GTE Corporation, Hewlett-Packard Company, Johnson & Johnson, The McDonnell Douglas Corporation, The Norton Company, and Xerox. Six of these companies' ethics programs are summarized below.

The Boeing Company

1. All Boeing ethics policies are printed in one booklet entitled, *Business Conduct Guidelines*.
2. Operating divisions conduct ethics training programs which are presented by divisional top management and roll down to lower levels in each division.
3. An Ethics Advisor is designated for the entire company. The advisor's role is to interpret ethics policies and provide advice and clarification.
4. Some of Boeing's subsidiary companies organize Ethics Focal Points which serve as ethics advisors.
5. An Office of Business Practices handles employee calls relating to misuse of funds.
6. The Ethics and Business Conduct Committee, composed of Boeing's vice chairman and the senior corporate executives from the legal, controller, and human resources functions, oversees all company ethics programs.

Chemical Bank

1. The Code of Ethics is the keystone of the bank's standards of conduct. It is revised approximately every 18 months.
2. Specific functional areas have drafted behavioral guidelines and standards of conduct (e.g., the purchasing department has its Standards and Ethics of Buying).
3. The chairman reinforces the code and guidelines in speeches, meetings, articles, and letters to employees.
4. Employee ethics education begins with new-employee orientation. A video features the bank's chairman discussing corporate values and employees agree in writing to abide by the Code of Ethics.
5. Outside consultants conduct a two-day, off-site management seminar (Decision Making and Corporate Values). This seminar uses 12 case studies of actual ethical dilemmas faced by Chemical Bank managers.
6. A variety of special programs and procedures are used to head off unethical conduct (e.g., the reporting and compliance department and a hot line for employees with personal financial problems).
7. Various committees and units monitor enforcement of bank standards (e.g., the board of directors audit committee does ethics reviews).
8. Chemical Bank maintains a long-standing reputation for corporate responsibility through a variety of community outreach programs.

General Mills

1. A strong, continuous, clearly communicated ethics leadership stance is taken by the company's CEO.
2. The company tradition of ethical behavior is based on actual management action.

EXHIBIT 4 Cont'd.   Corporate Ethics Program Components

3. Explicit statements of belief and policy were developed, including a Statement of Corporate Values and Business Ethics and Conduct.
4. Compensation and performance evaluation is closely linked to individual social responsibility objectives.
5. High value is placed on open decision making and honesty.
6. A strong internal control network is maintained to supplement trust with awareness of actual behavior.
7. Violations of law or policy are punished.
8. The General Mills Foundation's gifts show support for community needs.

Hewlett-Packard Company

1. Three documents summarize HP values and ethics: "The HP Way" describes how employees are expected to act; "The Corporate Objectives" outlines the objectives and principles which govern behavior of managers and employees at HP; and "Standards of Business Conduct" spells out an employee's ethical obligations to HP, to customers, to competitors and to suppliers.
2. The core HP values include: confidence in and respect for people, open communications, honesty, integrity, concern for the individual and the sharing of benefits and responsibilities.
3. The Internal Audit Department reviews compliance with the standards (e.g., the auditing team interviews the top managers of each entity asking a series of detailed questions related to ethical behavior and training of subordinates).
4. HP educational programs dedicate a major portion of their time to ethics.
5. A bimonthly magazine and video tape featuring company news items communicate HP values directly to all employees.

Johnson & Johnson

1. Our Credo is the ethical framework for all business decisions of the 150 J&J companies. It describes J&J's relationships with customers, employees, communities, and stockholders. The credo is revised every 3 years.
2. The Credo Survey provides employee feedback on company performance in relation to credo principles.
3. Management willingness to take stands on ethical matters reflects its commitment to the credo.
4. Compliance procedures include:
   a. The executive committee meets twice a year and goes over consumer complaints, surveys, audits, and safety records.
   b. Internal audits include safety, quality, and financial areas.
   c. Manager performance assessments cover credo-related factors.

Xerox

1. An Understanding states the basic code of ethics in straightforward, informal, understandable language.
2. The Xerox Policy on Business Ethics outlines how managers should deal with customers, government officials, political contributions, and conflicts of interest.

EXHIBIT 4 Cont'd. Corporate Ethics Program Components

3. The manager's handbook, Managing in Xerox, discusses traditions, beliefs, values, policies, and practices in employee relations.
4. A large number of policy statements focus on specific issues or functional areas (e.g., Statements of Corporate Policy deals with antitrust laws, ethics of selling, and the ethics of buying).
5. An annual letter from the chairman and periodic letters from the president emphasize ethics and compliance.
6. Articles about ethics often appear in corporate publications like the *Agenda* or *Xerox World*.
7. Numerous training, development, and education programs focus on values and standards of conduct.
8. Strong internal control systems and an active audit committee of the board of directors monitor and enforce ethics.
9. Corporate responsibility is manifested in a number of company actions (e.g., the Xerox Foundation disburses over $10 million annually).

To provide unmatched value in the product and service we offer customers

To recognize the one limitless resource: the individual and collective potential of the human being

To provide employees with maximum opportunity to exceed their own expectations

To achieve continued improvement in the use of company resources

To grow as a means of maintaining and renewing vitality

To insure that corporate objectives, wherever possible, enhance the goals of the immediate and larger communities of which we are a part

Earl wondered whether this document, which he had helped develop in the early 1970s, would help him sort out just what to do about Tek's ethics program.

ETHICS PROGRAM (B)

The Oregonian newspaper reported on October 24, 1987:

Tektronix, Inc. announced Friday that Earl Wantland will step down as president and chief executive officer of the Beaverton based electronics company on November 1. He will be succeeded by David P. Friedley, vice president and general manager of Tektronix communications group, one of the company's four operating divisions.

Although it was no secret at Tek that the board of directors had been interviewing possible successors for Earl Wantland, Friedley was not in the rumor mill as a possible choice and he experienced the same surprise expressed by other Tek insiders, "We're all sort of reeling over here . . . . This really came out of left field."[2] In their unanimous choice of Dave Friedley, the board had bypassed three senior vice presidents and an executive vice president.

The board's choice drew support from a number of Tek insiders. One manager explained, "Of all the dark horses, Dave's the best in my mind, partly because it is such a shock and partly because he does come with such a fresh attitude." Another manager described him as "very independent, strong minded, self-confident and a bit of a maverick." Friedley describes his own leadership style as "relatively informal and direct." He does not like meetings or memos. Instead he prefers to talk with people as soon as a problem or issue surfaces. He wants a simple, lean organization where communication is fast and actions are taken rapidly.

Friedley, a marketing-oriented engineer, joined Tektronix in 1974 and spent his first four years in various marketing, engineering, and general management jobs. He then served a five-year stint as executive vice president and general manager of Tek's wholly owned subsidiary, The Grass Valley Group Inc. in Grass Valley, California. Friedley moved to the Beaverton campus when he was promoted to vice president in charge of Tek's communications group and proceeded to distinguish himself as the leader of the most successful and fastest-growing of Tek's primary business groups. Friedley explained, "I haven't been assimilated into the Tektronix culture for that long, and even when I was, I think I was somewhat of a rebel."

Friedley was well-aware of the problems he faced as the new president and CEO of Tektronix. The 1980s had challenged the high-tech industry with a sluggish world economy, intensified competition, and a rapidly changing market-place. This was a crucial time for the company given the past few years of flat sales and declining earnings. Analysts claimed that Tektronix must become faster on its feet and more customer driven. Increased competition had eroded some of Tek's markets and human resource problems provided additional complications. In recent years Tektronix had suffered from the loss of a large pool of talent as a number of key middle managers, engineers, and marketers departed. Employee morale was battered by several rounds of layoffs in the past six years.

Friedley knew that Tektronix' board of directors expected him to turn the company around and to regain the profitability and market position it enjoyed in previous years. He knew that among the key decisions he would make were the leadership style he would assume and the actions he would take to reach the board's goals. He was concerned about how the qualities which had earned him the job as president (a hard-driving, bottom-line, market orientation) would fit with Tek's traditional values and culture. He asked himself whether it would be more desirable to maintain the old culture or to forge a new culture which would be more compatible with today's competitive world? Along with these issues was the question of whether he should continue the ethics seminars initiated by Earl Wantland or make a clean break with past leadership? As Friedley mulled over these questions he realized that soon he would be called upon to announce his strategic plan to Tek's employees, management, and board of directors.

ETHICS PROGRAM (C)

In a memo dated June 6, 1988, Dave Friedley made it perfectly clear that the business ethics seminars conducted by Kirk Hanson were being put on the back burner: ". . . Because of the urgent profitability issues on our plate today, I do not plan to conduct follow-up sessions at this time." (See Exhibit 5.) While not

EXHIBIT 5 Tek Interoffice Communication and Subsequent Ethics Summary Report

---

TO: DISTRIBUTION   DATE: June 6, 1988
FROM: Dave Friedley
SUBJECT: Ethics Sessions

At the time the Business Ethics sessions with Kirk Hanson were conducted, feedback was promised regarding the issues that surfaced and recommendations for next steps. Attached is a brief description of participant reaction to the sessions and a summary of the lists generated regarding guiding principles and pressures to violate those principles. Please make this available to the appropriate people in your organization, especially those who attended a session.

One of the things that attracted me to Tektronix originally was the high sense of ethics of its people. I continue to believe in that today and indeed to expect it of us all. Because of the urgent profitability issues on our plate today, I do not plan to conduct followup sessions at this time. However, I'm counting on you to continue communicating to your organizations the importance of maintaining high ethical standards in all facets of our operations.

If you would like additional information regarding the sessions or the resulting roll downs that have been designed and delivered in various parts of Tek, call Pat Willard.

DISTRIBUTION

Larry Choruby
Fred Hanson
Larry Kaplan
Dick Knight
Stan Kouba
Pat Kunkle
John Landis
Allan Leedy
Tom Long
Phil Robinson
Wim Velsink
Dan Wright

Evaluation Summary

In fall 1987 ten sessions on business ethics were conducted with vice presidents and their direct reports. One additional session was held for corporate staff. Kirk Hanson, from Stanford University, facilitated these sessions.

    Overall, the sessions were well-received. A number of people attending said the sessions brought out important and needed conversation about Tek's values and ethical standards. Some participants said the sessions reaffirmed their values as Tek employees. Participants' most frequently mentioned concern

EXHIBIT 5 Cont'd.   Tek Interoffice Communication and Subsequent Ethics Summary Report

was the desire for greater clarity on Tek's values and ethical guidelines—they would have liked more guidance on specific tough calls and more dialogue about how Tek's historical values (as espoused by Jack and Howard) apply in today's competitive environment. Participants also commented that the purpose and outcomes of the ethics sessions should have been better defined.

**Summary of Principles and
Pressures Identified**

During the sessions, participants identified the principles which should guide their behavior in working with various stakeholder groups. They also identified the pressures that push on managers to violate those guidelines.

The seven stakeholder groups considered were:

Customers
Vendors/suppliers
Employees
Divisions
Shareholders/the corporation
Government
Community

The following is a summary of the principles and pressures identified in each stakeholder group, listed by major categories in order of frequency mentioned. You may obtain a complete list from each session by calling Pat Willard.

1. **Customers (8 groups responding)**
    Principles

Serve customers with honesty and integrity. This principle included the need to be fair, honest, provide equitable treatment, respect, and confidentiality; take no kickbacks; comply with legal requirements; and advertise what can be provided in fact.
Provide quality, value-added products and services that meet customer needs
Work in partnership with the customer
Meet commitments; deliver what you promise when you promise it

Pressures

Although the pressures identified vary depending on the group, they fall into three major categories:

Pressures to meet budget objectives
Pressures to make the sale/keep the order
Competitive pressures

Also mentioned were pressures created by pay/incentive plans, pressure from bosses to act in ways that violate principles, and pressures resulting from limited resources.

EXHIBIT 5 Cont'd.   Tek Interoffice Communication and Subsequent Ethics Summary Report

2. **Vendors/Suppliers (6 groups)**
   Principles

> Establish long-term partnerships based on mutual commitments and goals
> Provide fair, equitable qualifying criteria
> Pay vendors within agreed upon times and not accept favors or gifts
> Vendor/supplier relationships should value confidentiality, teamwork, and competitive performance

Pressures

> Personal relationships that foster decisions based on friendship
> Personal gain
> Pressures from timelines

3. **Employees (8 groups)**
   Principles

> Respect the individual and his/her contribution; treat individuals with honesty and dignity
> Provide an opportunity for employees to grow and develop to their full potential
> Maintain open communication channels with employees: employees need to be provided with information about business, corporate values, and feedback on their performance; the corporation must be willing to listen to their ideas
> Provide a fair, clearly communicated reward system for employee contributions
> Provide equal opportunity
> Maintain long-term relationships

Pressures

> Budget and profitability issues (e.g., lack of adequate resources, tradeoffs between profitability and commitment to employees)
> Unclear standards for evaluating performance and current pay practices (Some mention was made of discomfort and biases in dealing with employee performance.)

4. **Divisions (4 groups)**
   Principles

> Build partnerships characterized by trust, openness, cooperation, shared strategies
> Share accurate, relevant information

Pressures

> Budget and financial performance issues
> Timelines
> Conflicts between meeting division needs and meeting customer needs, personal needs, business goals

EXHIBIT 5 Cont'd.   Tek Interoffice Communication and Subsequent Ethics Summary Report

5.   Shareholders/Corporate Management (4 groups)
Principles

> Manage assets and resources for the growth and success of the company
> Open and honest disclosure of information
> Implement corporate goals and values and letting management know when you disagree with
> them

Pressures

> Meeting fiancial plans, including APIP, as a pressure related to a number of violations
> Demands for short-term results
> Little reward for ``wearing the corporate hat''
> The desire to look good

6.   Government (2 groups)
Principles

> Compliance with the spirit and letter of local laws
> Challenge and/or participate in the formation of legislation
> Cooperate with law enforcement

Pressures

> Financial targets
> Lack of information and resources
> Misguided loyalty
> Desire to maintain face

7.   Community (4 groups)
Principles

> Be environmentally responsible
> Support education efforts
> Support employee involvement in community activities
> Maintain a company image based on stability, consistency, honesty, and openness

commented on directly in the memo, work on a code of conduct and the internal controls seminar continued.

Friedley explained his decision this way,

> The reason is that Tek has such a strong culture related to ethics. Ethics is one of the things we're noted for in the industry. Our reputation on the outside world is based upon quality, honesty in business practices, and conservatism . . . .

The electronics industry is not fraught with unsavory practices . . . both the internal and external environment we're operating in is just not that tempting . . . I don't think our business lends itself that much to unethical behavior as a way of improving performance. The nature of the business, the controls we have, and the historical values and culture, are strong enough to limit unethical behavior.[3]

Friedley further indicated that his primary goals for his first year as CEO were increased profitability and a revised corporate mission statement.

Friedley moved rapidly and aggressively in pursuit of his increased profitability goal. He implemented dramatic management and strategic changes including the replacement of three of Tek's top four executives and the reassignment of its chief marketing officer. The work force was reduced by 1,000 (which impacted largely middle management); a $24-million third-quarter write-off was taken to restructure or close unprofitable businesses; a CAE (computer-aided engineering) business was sold to rival Mentor Graphics Corporation for $5 million after Tek had invested some $150 million in it.[4] "I think Friedley is doing exactly what people thought he would do and that's shake up the troops," remarked a Tek marketing director.[5]

Increased pressures for profitability and the direction taken by Friedley called into question the viability of the traditional Tek culture and value system. A Tek executive remarked, "we have an old, reasonably defined culture that is in transition." Another manager stated, "in some ways we've gotten away from our values and we're just not living them like we have in the past."

In his first interview after being named CEO, Friedley affirmed his intention to have Tek become a faster-moving, more responsive, more competitive company. He commented, "a 41-year old culture can get in the way. It can turn into a form of inertia which makes it difficult to change and be responsive."[6]

Friedley felt that certain cultural changes were necessary. These included increased expectations of accountability and productivity for employees. "We will not provide on-the-job retirement," and, "we will be tougher in terminating nonperforming employees," Friedley asserted. Tek would move away from being technology/engineering-driven toward being more market/customer-driven. He believed that "in striving for elegance in engineering we have taken too long to get products to market and the competition has outperformed us."

Friedley's refocusing of the Tek culture and delayed followup on the business ethics seminars drew mixed support from Tek insiders. One executive commented, "I wouldn't encourage him to do more ethics seminars right now because they come across as airy, fairy, and fuzzy and we've got to make money." Former CEO, Earl Wantland, saw a need to have ethics discussions "at reasonable intervals" because "unless there is a pretty strong code of ethics driving what you're doing you can get into some pretty wrong behavior."[7]

While Friedley acknowledged that ethics are important, he indicated that he was not sure if a seminar or some other mechanism was the best way to remind employees of the necessity for ethical behavior. Friedley, true to his action-oriented management style, fired three employees who violated company policy even though their behavior did not result in personal gain.

A number of questions linger in the minds of Tek employees and observers: Is Dave Friedley making a wise management decision in putting Tek's ethics seminar on the back burner? Does increased emphasis on profitability necessitate or abrogate the need for focus on ethical issues? What will be the immediate and long-range effects of this decision?

Endnotes

1. *Corporate Ethics: A Prime Business Asset* (New York: Business Roundtable, 1988).
2. *The Business Journal*, November 2, 1987, P. 1.
3. Interview with David Friedley, August 3, 1988.
4. *The Business Journal*, April 18, 1988. (Note: the company would not confirm these numbers.)
5. *The Business Journal*, February 25, 1988.
6. *The Business Journal*, November 2, 1987.
7. Interview with Earl Wantland, July 28, 1988.

CREDITS

The author is indebted to the following for permission to reprint from copyrighted material:

INDEX